An Introduction to
Biblical Hebrew Syntax

An Introduction to Biblical Hebrew Syntax

Bruce K. Waltke

and

M. O'Connor

Eisenbrauns
Winona Lake, Indiana
1990

Library of Congress Cataloging-in-Publication Data

Waltke, Bruce K.
    An introduction to biblical Hebrew syntax.

    Includes bibliographical references.

    1. Hebrew language—Syntax. 2. Hebrew language—
Grammar—1950–   . 3. Bible. O.T.—Language,
style. I. O'Connor, Michael Patrick. II. Title.
PJ4707.W35   1989   492.4′82421   89-17006
ISBN 0-931464-31-5

97 98 99

10 9 8 7

in memory of

W. J. Martin

25 May 1904 ~ *21 March 1980*
Broughshane, Co. Antrim   *Cambridge*

Contents

Abbreviations and Sigla

Grammatical Terms

abs.	absolute
bis	twice
C	consonant
C	construct term
c.	common
coll.	collective
cstr.	construct
ENWS	Early Northwest Semitic
f(em).	feminine
Foc	focus marker
G	genitive term
impfv.	imperfective
inf. abs.	infinitive absolute
inf. cstr.	infinitive construct
m(asc).	masculine
non-pfv.	non-perfective
pf.	perfect
pfv.	perfective
pl.	plural
pleo	pleonastic pronoun
Pred	predicate
S	subject
s(ing).	singular
V	vowel
V	verb
*	unattested form
**	impossible form
~/≅	approximately equal to

Versions and Translations

AV	Authorized Version (1611)
LXX	Septuagint
MT	Masoretic Text
NAB	New American Bible (1970)
NIV	New International Version (1973)
NJPS	New Jewish Publication Society Version (1982)
RSV	Revised Standard Version (1952)
Sam	Samaritan Pentateuch

Bibliography

BL	Hans Bauer and Pontus Leander. 1922. *Historische Grammatik der hebräischen Sprache des Alten Testamentes.*
GAHG	Wolfgang Richter. 1978–80. *Grundlagen einer althebräischen Grammatik.*
GB	[Wilhelm Gesenius-]Gotthelf Bergsträsser. 1918–29. *Hebräische Grammatik.*
GKC	[Wilhelm Gesenius-]Emil Kautzsch, trans. A. E. Cowley. 1910. *Gesenius' Hebrew Grammar.*
Joüon	Paul Joüon. 1923. *Grammaire de l'hébreu biblique.*
LHS	Ernst Jenni. 1981. *Lehrbuch der hebräischen Sprache des Alten Testaments.*
MPD	P. Swiggers and W. Van Hoecke. 1986. *Mots et Parties du Discours.*
SA/THAT	Statistischer Anhang to Ernst Jenni and Claus Westermann. 1971–76. *Theologisches Handwörterbuch zum Alten Testament.*
UT	Cyrus H. Gordon. 1965. *Ugaritic Textbook.*

Preface

The Scope and Purpose of This Book

An Introduction to Biblical Hebrew Syntax is in two senses an intermediary grammar of the language of the Hebrew Bible. It is, first of all, a grammar designed for study by those who have mastered the fundamentals of the language and possess a good grasp of its phonology and morphology as well as a working vocabulary. Second, it is an intermediary between basic study and the vast array of research literature, a tool to prepare readers to take up that body of writing as they take up the great and difficult corpus of ancient Hebrew scriptures. This volume is presented both as a textbook and as a work of reference and study. There exists in English no up-to-date intermediate or advanced grammar of Biblical Hebrew and the lack has long been recognized. We have attempted to present both a body of knowledge (providing, as it were, the "right answers") and a sample of analytical and descriptive approaches (suggesting the "right questions"). Introductory Hebrew grammar is largely a matter of morphology, and the word-class or part-of-speech approach we have taken up should follow from such an introductory program. Word-class theory has a respectable antiquity and, as a result of recent research on the organization of the lexicon, a brightening future. The framework is, we hope, conservative enough to be broadly accessible but serious enough to allow us to escape some of the confusions of earlier grammars of Hebrew. New terminology has been introduced cautiously.

Reference grammars are available; every advanced student of the Hebrew text needs to have at hand the grammar of Gesenius, Kautzsch, and Cowley to check a variety of details in an ample and well-informed framework. This volume does not seek to replace GKC or comparable works available in other languages. We do not take account of every exception and anomaly. The book rather seeks to be used both before and alongside such works, pointing to the explorations of more recent generations of scholars, both in detail and in the structure of the overall framework and reconsidering the views of the older works in light of those explorations.

As a teaching grammar, this volume seeks not merely to describe the syntax of Biblical Hebrew, but to provide some explanatory depth to the description. Students emerge from an introductory course in Hebrew ready to begin to confront the text, and this volume stands among the books that can help them. Among these books, it will have, we hope, a distinctive place. Reference grammars and advanced lexicons, if consulted on the fly, tend to fragment a reader's view of problems, while commentaries tend to narrow the focus too closely. Specialized grammatical studies are sometimes forced to argue a thesis too closely or to cover all the data too briskly.

As a tool in reading and exegesis, this volume seeks to encourage attention to the difficulties of a text in a written language from the ancient world of a different culture. Too brief a program of study in Hebrew can be misleading or even dangerous; facile mastery can make students believe that they grasp a text when all they hold is a memory of a received translation. The distortions of using the Hebrew language as the key to an alien mindset are not part of our program; current scholarship has outgrown such views. But Hebrew remains a foreign language to native speakers of English and other European languages. This grammar seeks to help them realize the character of that foreignness, primarily with regard to the interaction of syntax and semantics. We are concerned with what the forms of Hebrew mean, how those meanings can be appropriated, and, incidentally, and chiefly by example, how those meanings can be rendered in English.

The great native-speaker tradition of Hebrew grammar associated with medieval Jewry is the first basis of this study. This tradition has been passed on for centuries, and it fed into the modern European tradition canonized by Wilhelm Gesenius in the first quarter of the nineteenth century. The second basis is modern linguistic study, its roots contemporary with Gesenius and its first flowers contemporary with the edition of Gesenius's grammar currently in print in English (1910). On these two bases this grammar stands, leaning now more on one, now more on the other. The aim of this volume is not novelty; indeed, too much novelty would not be appropriate. Yet the enormous body of scholars concerned with the Hebrew Bible has produced much that is new, and each new view or concept repositions and reshapes all other facets of the grammar, however slightly. It is safe to say, then, that any reader will find something new here, and safer to say that each reader will find something to disagree with.

Although this is not a comprehensive syntax of the Hebrew Bible, it provides a full overview of the topic and draws on a rich and diverse body of scholarship. Important studies by, for example, F. I. Andersen, Ernst Jenni, and Dennis Pardee, are here for the first time brought into a survey of Hebrew grammar; other studies are evaluated, still others cited only in passing. Like David Qimḥi, we are often gleaners following reapers. Some of the distortions to be found in the literature are criticized. The bibliography will direct students not only to the works we have used here, but also to reference works and to studies on Hebrew phonology and morphology, topics not treated here. We have provided a basic bibliography of Biblical Hebrew studies because no such tool is currently available.

Though we aim to help students in evaluating and appraising the secondary literature, we are not directly concerned with such appraisals. We have not been able to use and cite as wide a range of materials as we would like, but the range is considerable. Much new literature has appeared during the years we have been at work. In cases where only details of our exposition were affected, we were better able to incorporate new findings and views. On larger issues we were often unable to revise and reshape as much as we would have liked, in response to a variety of recent introductory grammars as well as major scholarly contributions, for example, Shelomo Morag's paper on Qumran Hebrew,

Jaakov Levi's essay on *Die Inkongruenz im biblischen Hebräisch*, and John Huehner-gard's monograph on Ugaritic. Issues of Hans-Peter Müller's new journal *Zeitschrift für Althebraistik* only reached us in the last stages of our work.

Some other bases of the volume need notice. Comparative Semitic data has been drawn on to illuminate and provide perspectives, though we presuppose no knowledge of the other languages. Given our two primary bases, this use is inevitable. The earliest Hebrew grammarians spoke Arabic as well as Hebrew, so the tradition begins with a comparative bias. The decipherment of cuneiform and the development of modern grammars of Akkadian has affected the interpretation of every facet of the Hebrew verb. Alongside Arabic and Akkadian, the great languages originally spoken south and east of Hebrew, are the other languages of the ancient Levant, Hebrew's closest relatives— Moabite, Ammonite, and Phoenician-Punic as well as the older language of Ugarit and the more distantly related Aramaic languages. Citation of comparative Semitic data is re-strained, but is always in our judgment crucial to the argument at hand. Similarly crucial is comparative data from English and other European languages. Contrastive analysis of languages is now commonplace in modern language teaching. Such information serves to remind students how their own and related languages work. Not all students have a broad and firm grounding in linguistics—this book presupposes no acquaintance with that subject—and English may be taken as a fixed and engaging point of reference. The use of English-language data serves, at least in part, to expose the preunderstandings of English readers. Indeed, in the light of an "exotic" language like Hebrew, English turns out to be an "exotic" language, too. In the labor of reading or translation, the target language is no more "natural" or "correct" than the source language.

The shape of the book is irregular—we have not sought to balance exactly the various aspects of Hebrew or to divide up the materials into equal portions. A proper grasp of the *Piel* stem or the prefix conjugation requires the use of concepts and notions that may seem overly theoretical. The chapter on the preposition, in contrast, may seem too largely lexical. Certain topics are not treated fully: the adverbs, especially the negative particles, do not receive the focused attention they might, though there are relevant references throughout. The labor of the writing of each book must be limited or at least called to a halt.

The Use of This Book

The structure of this volume is largely topical and logical rather than pedagogical. Teachers and students are free to approach the material as they like and make adapta-tions appropriate to their own program and circumstances. After the opening section, any of the four remaining sections can be taken up; the various tables of contents and the topical index should facilitate cross-checking. In each of those sections, certain chapters require conceptual exposition, while others demand review and consideration of the examples in context. We have provided many, many examples in full or extended citation, with glosses (*not* translations). The examples are all from the Bible, with three or four exceptions, where it is clear that a modern imitation of Biblical Hebrew is being given. Students are urged to read the examples quoted here and eventually to check them (and the other examples cited in the notes) in the biblical context. Because examples are sometimes excerpted and abridged, they do not necessarily reflect the actual text. The renderings given here tend to present a dynamic equivalent, sometimes complemented by a more literal gloss reflecting the grammatical point at issue—though the term *lit.* is sometimes used loosely. A few Hebrew words are left unglossed, and renderings of a biblical excerpt may vary from section to section of the book. The English versions are not strictly a help or a trot—readers should try to explain (or improve on) our suggestions, often drawn from modern versions, and should consider possible alternatives. Interpretive additions are given in brackets, while other additions, including grammatical information, appear in parentheses. Final ellipses are generally not used in Hebrew text. Verse is set off in lines where such an arrangement would require no extra space. Single quotation marks (' / ') are used for glosses and renderings, double marks (" / ") for quotations and technical terms.

A one-year-long approach to teaching the work would involve devoting approximately one week to each of twenty-eight chapters or pairs of chapters, leaving for cursory review or study outside classes Chapters 1–3, 5, 15–19 and combining 11 and 12, 24 and 25, and 27 and 28. Some teachers may prefer to skip individual sections and reshape the material in other ways. We anticipate preparing a shorter version of this grammar, perhaps equipped with exercises and key and more suitable for a brief course, and invite comments from users of this volume. Experienced teachers know that grammar becomes significant to students only as they are led to use it. In any format, intermediate or advanced grammatical study should accompany the reading of the masterpieces of biblical prose, such as the Joseph and Ruth stories, as well as some of the major biblical poems such as Psalm 100 and the Song of Hannah. During such reading students should apply the principles outlined here and begin to use the grammar both for reference and for extended study. The brief glossary covers chiefly grammatical terms, chiefly those liable to confusion and those unlikely to be found in other reference works; in no sense is it intended to compete with the text of the book.

The indexes cover four fields: topics, modern authorities cited, Hebrew words, and biblical passages. Used with the chapter tables of contents the topical index should direct students to any relevant discussion here.

The biblical text is generally quoted from *Biblia Hebraica Stuttgartensia* (1977), though in some cases we have preferred the evidence of the Masoretic margins (*Qere*) or other Masoretic manuscripts, or the Samaritan Pentateuch, or we have cited a text reflected in the ancient versions or an emendation. For the perpetual *Qere* readings, we use the long form of Jerusalem and the feminine third-singular pronoun where appropriate; we leave the Tetragrammaton unpointed. Cases in which we vary from *BHS* are rare: this volume is no substitute for an introduction to text-critical problems. In quoting the Hebrew text some of the more anomalous readings of the Leningrad Codex are retained (e.g., 1 Sam 9:21 and Ruth 3:9, with *BHS* against the text of the earlier *Biblia Hebraica* of 1937 [*BH3*]; Gen 32:18, with *BHS* and *BH3* against other editions), though some are silently replaced by a standard text (e.g., a *sop pasuq* missing from Leningrad but reported for other texts by *BHS*, as in Exod 20:3). (On the basis of his autopsy of the 1971 Makor facsimile edition of Leningrad, J. Alan Groves, of Westminster Theological Seminary, informs us that the Gen 32:18 variant is probably a typographical error in both *BH3* and *BHS*.) The Masoretic accents are given in some cases, and the stress, where it is not final, is marked. *Athnach* and *sop pasuq* (but not *silluq*), major verse dividers, are given from the text, and stress is shown with the mark ˹. The verse dividers give a sense of a verse's overall shape and are given even where the stress mark is also found; this redundancy reflects the mixed phonological and syntactic bases of Masoretic accentuation. Stress is shown only as a feature of the word; only main stress is shown; and stress groups covering several words are thus not set off. In citing single items attested forms are usually given, rather than dictionary forms; in a few cases in lists *athnach* instead of *sop pasuq* is used to show that a form is pausal. Once or twice the verse divider of the MT is retained even though the gloss shows that we believe a transposition is necessary. *Methegh* is given either from *BHS* or as needed, though not all possible cases are supplied. Transliterations follow the now widely accepted systems of the major scholarly journals, except in two features: turned *e* (ǝ) is used for *shewa* and *e* with breve (ĕ) for *hateph seghol*; and the *matres lectionis* of plene short vowels are not written with parentheses. This standard system, based as it is on a dubious reconstruction of Hebrew phonology, is not perfect but it is workable and should be familiar to every student. In general, Hebrew is given in characters in the text and in transliteration in the notes, but some variation is to be found in both directions. We have been spare in using the single asterisk (to mark unattested or primitive linguistic forms; **yaqtul*) and the double asterisk (to mark forms that would be impossible in Hebrew; ***yaqtal*). Diacritics are, as often as possible while still preserving clarity, omitted from pattern words (*Piel*, not *Piᶜēl*).

Acknowledgments

Both authors wish to take this opportunity to thank their teachers: Waltke was trained by T. O. Lambdin, F. M. Cross, and the late G. Ernest Wright of Harvard; and O'Connor by C. R. Krahmalkov, D. N. Freedman, and G. E. Mendenhall of Michigan. All graduate study is a collaborative endeavor, and we want to take this opportunity to thank our fellow students, often now colleagues and advisers. Our publishers have been involved closely with the project for over eight years, and James E. Eisenbraun has worked on every aspect of the book, in the great tradition of scholar-publishers. Both authors take full responsibility for the work.

PHILADELPHIA
ANN ARBOR

Note to the Third, Corrected Printing

Typographical errors have been corrected and some garbled or badly written passages rectified as a result of the vigilance of reviewers and other colleagues, including David W. Baker (Ashland, Ohio), Adele Berlin (College Park, Maryland), Walter R. Bodine (Dallas), C. John Collins (Spokane), Edward L. Greenstein (New York City), Frederic C. Putnam (Hatfield, Pennsylvania), Leona Glidden Running (Berrien Springs, Michigan), and Mark F. Willson (Juàzeiro do Norte, Ceará, Brazil). Our thanks to them.

1 DECEMBER 1990

Note to the Fourth, Corrected Printing

We continue to be gratified by the generous reception accorded this book. Once again, we are happy to correct errors and amend infelicities pointed out by students at Westminster Theological Seminary (Philadelphia) and Regent College (Vancouver), by reviewers, and by other colleagues and friends, including Ralph L. Bogle (Ann Arbor), James H. Charlesworth (Princeton), Terence Collins (Manchester), Peter T. Daniels (Chicago), John Huehnergard (Cambridge, Massachusetts), and W. G. E. Watson (Edinburgh).

Vancouver
St. Paul
7 APRIL 1993

Introductory

1

Language and Text

Introduction

The Hebrew language has been in use from the time of Moses (the archeological era   a
known as the Late Bronze Age II, 1400–1200 B.C.E.) to the present. The topic of this
grammar, Biblical Hebrew—we use the term for the Hebrew used in the composition of
scripture as well as in the Masoretic Text (abbreviated MT)—was in use from that time
through the exilic, post-exilic, and Second Temple periods, a span corresponding in
large part to the Imperial Age (Neo-Babylonian Empire, 625–540; Persian Empire,
540–330; Hellenistic, 330–60; Roman, 60 B.C.E.–330 C.E.). Over the course of more than
three millennia the Hebrew language has experienced many changes; indeed, even over
a period of several generations a language undergoes modification. The English we
speak is not the language of Shakespeare or even Thomas Jefferson. The Middle English
language of Chaucer and, even more so, the Old English of King Alfred the Great

9th century C.E.) are to us virtually foreign languages. The interval between the earliest biblical literature, such as the Song of Moses (Exodus 15) or the Song of Deborah (Judges 5), and the latest books of the Bible, such as Esther or Chronicles, is as long as the interval between Alfred the Great and us. In contrast to the history of most languages, the Hebrew language has exhibited a remarkable uniformity over time. A well-educated Hebrew speaker can read and understand Hebrew literature from all stages, from the oldest portions of the Hebrew Scriptures to Modern Hebrew.[1]

b   To understand the nature of Biblical Hebrew one needs to know both the family background and history of Hebrew in general (1.2–3) and the history of the biblical text in which it was recorded through the time of the Masoretes, who standardized all aspects of its transmission (1.5).[2] So fundamental is their work to the writing of a Hebrew grammar that it deserves separate treatment (1.6). An understanding of the text's history and the work of the Masoretes provides insight into some of the problems confronting a linguist attempting to write a grammar of the Masoretic Text. It also helps to explain why variations are not as marked as we would expect in view of the geographical, political, and cultural diversity of the tribes in Israel's early history, its bifurcation into two kingdoms in its later history, and its later existence in dispersion and exile. Fundamental to the study of Biblical Hebrew is the tension between synchrony and diachrony (see also 3.4). A synchronic view considers a language at a single point in time. A synchronic view of present-day English would be based on the way the language is used by a variety of speakers, speakers from all those areas of the world where English is natively spoken or used as a common language of officials (cf. the role of Aramaic in 2 Kgs 18:26 and Ezra 4:7) or scholars or merchants. Such a study might also consider written uses of the language, newspapers, magazines (both popular and literary), and genre and serious fiction, as well as reports and documents. A diachronic study of English would necessarily rely on written sources more than speakers. As the sources grew less familiar, the study would need to devote more attention to characterizing them as well as their language. Ideally a linguistic analysis of Biblical Hebrew would represent the language diachronically by describing its various stages synchronically; we can only broadly analyze the Hebrew language in this way. In a separate section (1.4) we show the limitations of such an approach when applied to the Masoretic Text.

---

1. For a good survey, see Chaim Rabin, "Hebrew," *Current Trends in Linguistics. 6. Linguistics in South West Asia and North Africa*, ed. T. A. Sebeok et al. (The Hague: Mouton, 1970) 304–46; or William Chomsky's *Hebrew: The Eternal Language* (Philadelphia: Jewish Publication Society, 1957). E. Y. Kutscher's *History of the Hebrew Language* (Jerusalem: Magnes, 1982) was unfortunately unfinished at the time of the author's death; his editor R. Kutscher has supplemented the manuscript, but the result is unbalanced though it remains valuable in parts; note the major review by P. Wexler, *Language* 62 (1986)

687–90. Still notable older studies include R. Meyer, "Probleme der hebräischen Grammatik," *Zeitschrift für die Alttestamentliche Wissenschaft* 63 (1951) 221–35; and Z. Ben-Hayyim, *Studies in the Traditions of the Hebrew Language* (Madrid: Instituto "Arias Montano," 1954).

2. In addition to materials cited below, see in general J. Barr, "The Nature of Linguistic Evidence in the Text of the Bible," *Languages and Texts: The Nature of Linguistic Evidence*, ed. H. H. Paper (Ann Arbor: Center for Coördination of Ancient and Modern Studies, University of Michigan, 1975) 35–57.

Hebrew as a Semitic Language   **1.2**

Hebrew belongs to the Semitic language family, the historically predominant lan-   a
guage group of southwestern Asia, the region usually known as the Near East or Middle
East. The Semitic family is itself part of the Afroasiatic language phylum, the major
language group that spans the continents of Africa and Asia.[3]

The Semitic family is attested primarily in the relatively compact area of the Near   b
East; accounting for the family members is a complex task chiefly because of the enor-
mous time span over which they are used and the multiplicity of influences on the region.
The languages form a cohesive group linguistically, comparable to the Romance languages of Europe, the modern relatives of Latin: French, Spanish, Catalan, Portuguese,
Italian, Roumanian, and others. There are two major branches of the family, East and
West Semitic. Only one language belongs to the East Semitic subgroup, Akkadian, the
language of the Babylonians and Assyrians of Mesopotamia; Akkadian records, in the
cuneiform writing system, have historical and literary as well as linguistic relevance to
biblical studies. The West Semitic group includes Northwest Semitic, Arabic, and South
Semitic.[4] (North) Arabic is the language of the Qurʾān and the Islamic religion; the
South Semitic group includes the various South Arabian languages and the Ethiopian
languages. Classical Ethiopic or Geez is no longer spoken; the major Semitic languages
of the land of Ethiopia are Amharic and Tigrinya. Northwest Semitic languages include
the Canaanite languages, Biblical Hebrew and its immediate congeners, and the Aramaic languages, important in the biblical world.[5] About two percent of the Hebrew Bible
is written in Aramaic.[6] The term "classical Semitic languages" is used to refer to the
great, pre-modern literary languages, Hebrew, Syriac (an Aramaic tongue), Geez, Arabic,

3. See G. Bergsträsser, *Introduction to the Semitic Languages*, trans. and sup. P. T. Daniels (Winona Lake, Indiana: Eisenbrauns, 1983); M. L. Bender, ed., *The Non-Semitic Languages of Ethiopia* (East Lansing: African Studies Center, Michigan State University, 1976; esp. the paper by C. Hodge); M. Ruhlen, *A Guide to the World's Languages. 1. Classification* (Stanford, California: Stanford University, 1987); and the references in 2.5.

4. The controversies about subgroupings are consider-able and relevant; see, e.g., J. Blau, "Hebrew and North West Semitic: Reflections on the Classification of the Semitic Languages," *Hebrew Annual Review* 2 (1978) 21–44, as well as the materials cited in 1.3.2, for an approach different from the one taken here.

5. The bulk and diversity of materials in the Aramaic languages are considerable. The earliest materials, from the tenth through the eighth or seventh centuries, are called Old Aramaic. During this phase of the language and the following period, dialect divergences are difficult to detect. The great age of Official or Imperial Aramaic is the Persian Empire, when Aramaic was a quasi-official or even official language, but the term is applied to materials from the eighth through the third centuries; the largest corpus of material is derived from Egypt (notably the Jew-

ish military colony at Elephantine), and the term Egyptian Aramaic is sometimes used. In succeeding ages, there are (*a*) archeologically recovered bodies of materials, both epigraphic (from the Nabatean realm, Palmyra, and Hatra) and manuscript (from Qumran); (*b*) literary languages preserved in religious communities, Jewish (Jewish Pales-tinian Aramaic; Jewish Babylonian Aramaic), Christian (Syriac), and Mandaic; and (*c*) the modern languages, spoken in several small pockets in Syria and Iraq (as well as the American Midwest). See, e.g., J. C. L. Gibson, *Textbook of Syrian Semitic Inscriptions. 2. Aramaic Inscrip-tions* (Oxford: Clarendon, 1975); Bezalel Porten, *Archives from Elephantine* (Berkeley: University of California, 1968); J. A. Fitzmyer, *A Wandering Aramean* (Missoula: Scholars Press, 1979).

6. Of 305,441 words (graphic words, divided by spacing or *maqqeph*), the Aramaic portions make up 4,828, chiefly in the Book of Daniel; a small portion of Ezra is in Ara-maic, and by custom the Aramaic verse of Jeremiah (10:11) and two words of Genesis (in 31:47) are also counted. See SA/THAT. Biblical Aramaic is a variety of Imperial Aramaic, but is often treated independently. See, e.g., F. Rosenthal, *A Grammar of Biblical Aramaic* (Wies-baden: Harrassowitz, 1961).

and sometimes also Akkadian; all these are well attested over significant periods of time.[7] The major modern languages are Arabic (spoken in a variety of dialects as well as a commonly used standard form), Amharic, Tigrinya, and Modern Hebrew.

c   Texts from the third-millennium site of Tell Mardikh in Syria (ancient Ebla) are written in both Sumerian and a Semitic language. The affiliation of this language is unclear: some scholars claim that it is close to the earliest forms of Akkadian, while others view it as a primordial Northwest Semitic language. Still other scholars claim that Eblaic (or Eblaite) antedates the East–West split in Semitic. Because of the complexity of the ways in which the cuneiform writing system was used at Ebla, only prolonged study will resolve the debate.[8]

d   The similarities of the Semitic languages and various tongues of Africa have long been noted. The larger family or phylum was once called Hamito-Semitic, based on the idea that the phylum had two distinct parts; in fact, it has five (or six). The term Afro-asiatic is now standard; also found are Afrasian, Lisramic, and Erythrean. Two Afro-asiatic families are North African in location: Egyptian, the now extinct language of ancient Egypt (known in its later stages as Coptic), and Berber, a group of languages used chiefly in Algeria and Morocco. Still disputed is the view that, within Afroasiatic, Egyptian and Semitic have a close relationship.[9] In sub-Saharan Africa are found the Chadic family (in Nigeria, Chad, and neighboring countries; major language Hausa) and the Cushitic-Omotic family (in the Horn of Africa, i.e., Ethiopia and Somalia; major Cushitic languages are Oromo and Somali). Numerous aspects of the development of the Semitic languages can be illuminated by reference to the larger Afroasiatic context.

1.3   History of Hebrew

1.3.1   Prehistory

a   It is one of the great ironies of Syro-Palestinian archeology that vastly more documentation for what may be called the prehistory of Biblical Hebrew has been found than for the history of the language at the time the Scriptures were being recorded. Use of this documentation is difficult, both because the sources are of various types and because they are scattered over the whole range of the ancient Near East. These materials are recorded in a variety of scripts; in some cases a single personal name contributes evidence of importance comparable to that of an entire literary text. A survey of these materials, best called Early Northwest Semitic (ENWS), is beyond the scope of this

---

7. These are the languages treated in Bergsträsser's *Introduction* (along with a few modern forms).

8. The scholarly literature on Ebla is voluminous. After an introduction to the site (e.g., G. Pettinato, *The Archives of Ebla* [Garden City, New York: Doubleday, 1981]; P. Matthiae, *Ebla: An Empire Rediscovered* [Garden City, New York: Doubleday, 1981]), the student may turn to a variety of text publications and discoveries; both genres

are represented in C. H. Gordon, G. A. Rendsburg, and N. H. Winter, eds., *Eblaitica: Essays on the Ebla Archives and Eblaite Language 1* (Winona Lake, Indiana: Eisenbrauns, 1987).

9. A leading proponent of this view has been C. H. Gordon; though his discussions are widely scattered, his *Ugaritic Textbook* (*UT*) provides a good sample of his suggestions.

grammar, but a chronological review of major sources may be useful.[10] Such a review makes it possible to sidestep the questions of exactly how many languages (or dialects) are involved and exactly how they are interrelated.

Late Third Millennium (2350-2000). Traces of ENWS are found in cuneiform **b** Sumerian and Akkadian texts from a variety of sites, perhaps including Ebla.[11]

Old Babylonian Period (2000-1600). Personal names in the Amorite language are **c** found in texts from the Babylonian heartland, from the kingdom of Mari (in the Middle Euphrates valley), and from other Syrian sites. The texts from Mari, written in Akkadian, also show common vocabulary of Amorite origin. Amorite names also occur in a series of Execration Texts from Twelfth Dynasty Egypt (ca. 2000-1750).[12]

Late Middle Bronze-Early Late Bronze (1600-1400). The documentary evidence **d** from this period is slender, confined to the so-called Proto-Sinaitic texts, written in the earliest form of the linear alphabet. These inscriptions, found on the walls of Serābît el-Khādem, a turquoise-mining area of the Sinai, are usually dated around 1475, although some scholars have proposed a higher date. Alphabetic signs are found on jars from Gezer dated to the same period, and a few short texts have been found in Palestine.[13]

Late Bronze II (1400-1200). There are a small number of alphabetic inscriptions **e** from Syria-Palestine in the Late Bronze II period, but pride of place for ENWS studies belongs to materials from Amarna and Ugarit. The Egyptian city of Amarna yielded correspondence sent to the pharaohs Amunhotpe III and his son Akhenaten between 1400 and 1350, largely from the latter half of the period. These letters are written in a form of Akkadian strongly influenced by the native Canaanite or ENWS languages of the scribes, employees of the minor kings of Syro-Palestinian city-states; the letters also contain Canaanite glosses.[14] Among the larger of the petty kingdoms of the region was Ugarit. It has preserved not only texts written in Akkadian but also texts written in the native language, Ugaritic. The script for these is alphabetic in type but, unlike the writing of the Proto-Sinaitic texts and related texts ancestral to the European alphabets, the Ugaritic script is wedge-based. Texts written in an Ugaritic-type alphabet script have been found at Ras Ibn Hani, a site near Ugarit, and at other sites in Syria-Palestine.[15]

---

10. There is unfortunately no up-to-date survey, but the range of illumination available from Amorite, Ugaritic, and the Amarna texts is well exemplified in the classic essay of W. L. Moran, "The Hebrew Language in Its Northwest Semitic Background," *The Bible and the Ancient Near East: Essays in Honor of William Foxwell Albright*, ed. G. E. Wright (Garden City, New York: Doubleday, 1961; rpt. Winona Lake, Indiana: Eisenbrauns, 1979) 54-72. No reliable popular introduction is available for the other materials treated here.

11. Syllabically written texts from the city of Byblos in the late third millennium may also witness an ENWS language; see G. E. Mendenhall, *The Syllabic Inscriptions from Byblos* (Beirut: American University of Beirut, 1985).

12. See, e.g., D. Pardee and J. T. Glass, "The Mari Archives," *Biblical Archaeologist* 47 (1984) 88-100; A.

Lemaire, "Mari, the Bible, and the Northwest Semitic World," *Biblical Archaeologist* 47 (1984) 101-9.

13. For a recent survey, see E. Puech, "Origine de l'alphabet: Documents en alphabet linéaire et cunéiforme du IIe millénaire," *Revue biblique* 93 (1986) 161-213.

14. The character of the Canaanite materials in Amarna Akkadian is unclear. Most scholars believe that linguistic interference is involved: the scribes sought to write Akkadian but failed for lack of expertise in the language. This explanation does not, however, cover all the facts. On the matter of the linguistic diversity within the Amarna corpus (and in relation to Ugaritic), see J. Huehnergard, "Northwest Semitic Vocabulary in Akkadian Texts," *Journal of the American Oriental Society* 107 (1987) 713-25.

15. Though outdated in details, C. H. Gordon's *Ugaritic Textbook* remains standard.

1.3.2   Biblical Hebrew and Congeners

a   Biblical Hebrew is the language of the Hebrew Scriptures.[16] The history of that language is bound together in part with the history of textual transmission (1.5). Other factors skewing a diachronic analysis of the language deserve a separate treatment (1.4). A variety of related languages and dialects, more or less closely related to Hebrew, were recorded at the time the Hebrew Scriptures were being written. The Iron Age (1200–540 B.C.E.) forms a convenient watershed in the history of Syro-Palestinian languages, though the significance of the year 1200 should not be exaggerated: the earliest Biblical Hebrew had a great deal in common with Ugaritic and Amarna Canaanite.

b   The extrabiblical linguistic material from the Iron Age is primarily epigraphic, that is, texts written on hard materials (pottery, stones, walls, etc.). The epigraphic texts from Israelite territory are written in Hebrew, in a form of the language which may be called Inscriptional Hebrew; this "dialect" is not strikingly different from the Hebrew preserved in the Masoretic text. Unfortunately, it is meagerly attested. Similarly limited are the epigraphic materials in the other South Canaanite dialects, Moabite and Ammonite; Edomite is so poorly attested that we are not sure that it is a South Canaanite dialect, though that seems likely.[17] Of greater interest and bulk is the body of Central Canaanite inscriptions, those written in the Phoenician language of Tyre, Sidon, and Byblos, and in the offshoot Punic and Neo-Punic tongues of the Phoenician colonies in North Africa.[18] An especially problematic body of material is the Deir Alla wall inscriptions referring to a prophet Balaam (ca. 700 B.C.E.); these texts have both Canaanite and Aramaic features.[19] W. R. Garr has recently proposed that all the Iron Age Canaanite dialects be regarded as forming a chain that actually includes the oldest forms of Aramaic as well.

> At one linguistic extreme of the dialect chain is standard Phoenician, and at the other end is Old Aramaic. Of the dialects known, Ammonite was most closely related to standard Phoenician. Edomite was related to Phoenician as well as to Hebrew. On this dialectical continuum, Hebrew lies closer to standard Phoenician than it does to Old Aramaic. Moabite was most closely related to Hebrew; it also possessed distinctive Aramaic features. The Deir Alla dialect shared some features with Hebrew (and Canaanite), but most of its phonological and morphological inventory was derived from Old Aramaic. Finally, Old Aramaic lies at the end of the continuum.[20]

16. The name of the language (or forms of it) is given as *yəhûdît* 'Judean' (2 Kgs 18:26) and *śəpat kənáʿan* 'Canaanite' (Isa 19:18); the term *ʿibrît* 'Hebrew' is earliest attested by the Greek adverb *Hebraïsti* (Ben Sira Prologue 22; cf. John 19:20). For a useful review of biblical allusions to Hebrew as a language, see W. Weinberg, "Language Consciousness in the Old Testament," *Zeitschrift für die Alttestamentliche Wissenschaft* 92 (1980) 185–204.

17. See, for an introduction, Gibson, *Textbook of Syrian Semitic Inscriptions. 1. Hebrew and Moabite Inscriptions* (Oxford: Clarendon, 1971); D. Pardee et al., *Handbook of Ancient Hebrew Letters* (Chico: Scholars Press, 1982).

18. See, e.g., Gibson, *Textbook of Syrian Semitic Inscriptions. 3. Phoenician Inscriptions* (Oxford: Clarendon, 1982); Z. S. Harris, *A Grammar of the Phoenician Language* (American Oriental Series 8; New Haven: American Oriental Society, 1936); Y. Avishur, "Studies of Stylistic Features Common to the Phoenician Inscriptions and the Bible," *Ugarit-Forschungen* 8 (1976) 1–22.

19. J. Hoftijzer and G. van der Kooij et al., *Aramaic Texts from Deir ʿAlla* (Leiden: Brill, 1976); J. Hackett, *The Balaam Text from Deir Alla* (Harvard Semitic Monographs 31; Chico: Scholars Press, 1984).

20. W. R. Garr, *Dialect Geography of Syria-Palestine, 1000–586 B.C.E.* (Philadelphia: University of Pennsylvania, 1985) 229. Note that Hackett treats the Deir Alla language

Linguistic affiliation is a comparatively minor issue in relation to the Iron Age epigraphic remains. They are a rich source of information about Canaanite morphology, syntax, and literary usage whatever model of dialect structure is accepted.

Later History of Hebrew   1.3.3

The Hebrew Scriptures are profoundly united in themselves, and because of their   a
focal role in the Jewish community they have served to unify that community. This use of scripture has preserved the language against forces encouraging diversity and drastic change. The entire range of the sources for the Hebrew language—extending from scripture through Mishnah, Midrashim, and medieval poetry—retains a degree of linguistic uniformity. The greatest influence has been the biblical text. Here is a sample of a relatively free use of biblical pastiche in a public letter written by the Renaissance rabbi, physician, and teacher Judah Messer Leon (in the translation the biblical references have been supplied):

> I have heard that *the cry is gone round about the borders* [Isa 15:8] of Bologna, has *broadened and wound about higher and higher* [Ezek 41:7] *in the full assemblies* [Ps 68:27]. In your *house of prayer* [Isa 56:7] *my glory* has been *put to shame* [Ps 4:3] by *men of blood and deceit* that *shall not live out half their* days [Ps 55:24]. It is *an enemy that taunts me* [Ps 55:13], and all the *people perceive the thunderings* [Exod 20:15].

The author claims here that "an enemy's slanderous vilification . . . has been spread throughout the whole of the Jewish community of Bologna. He has been held up to public obloquy even in the house of divine worship by destructive and deceitful persons, who accordingly are under the curse of a shortened life."[21] This passage is one example of the style of *melisa* 'adornment'; there are other ways in which Hebrew authors of all ages have infused their writings with the language of scripture and the other sources.[22]

The first stage in the post-biblical history of Hebrew is one unknown to the tradi-   b
tion. The scrolls and fragments of manuscripts found in the vicinity of the Dead Sea, mostly at the site of Qumran, include, in addition to biblical texts and anthologies, a great number of contemporary texts in Hebrew; the texts date from around 200 B.C.E. through 135 C.E., some of them antedating the founding of Qumran. Since the Qumran texts are often close in subject matter to the biblical text, dealing with cultic behavior, for example, and divine praise, the Hebrew of these texts is of special interest.[23]

---

as South Canaanite (*Balaam Text*, 8). Another approach to the dialectology, profiting from Garr's wave-theory or continuum model, would take Hebrew as central (on an east–west axis) with Phoenician as a western extreme and Ammonite as an eastern extreme.

21. Translation and summary from I. Rabinowitz, *The Book of the Honeycomb's Flow . . . by Judah Messer Leon* (Ithaca, New York: Cornell University, 1983) xxxii–xxxiii.

22. The enormous role of the Luther Bible in German and the Authorized Version in English is not comparable, since there is no real Hebrew (real in the sense of contributing to the rhythm and lexis of the language) before, behind, or around Biblical Hebrew.

23. On the distinctive Hebrew of Qumran, see E. Qimron, *The Hebrew of the Dead Sea Scrolls* (Atlanta: Scholars Press, 1986); S. A. Kaufman, "The Temple Scroll and

c   The first major work in the post-biblical Jewish tradition, the Mishnah, deals with the discussion and resolution of problems involving the application of the religious law; it was compiled in the mid-second century C.E. Mishnaic Hebrew is the language of the Mishnah and various related contemporary documents. The two Talmuds, the Babylonian (בַּבְלִי) and the Palestinian (יְרוּשַׁלְמִי), supplement the Mishnah and contain Mishnaic Hebrew materials, as do the Tosefta and halakhic (legal) Midrashim.[24] Some of this material was recorded during or reflects the age when Mishnaic Hebrew was a language spoken in Palestine (up to 200 C.E.?), and some is later. Mishnaic Hebrew is not an offspring of Biblical Hebrew, but a distinct dialect, with its own, largely unknown prehistory.[25]

d   During the period from the early third century C.E. to the late nineteenth century, Hebrew was in continuous use as a religious language, that is, as a language of prayer and worship as well as religious-legal and scientific discussion.[26] All educated Jews (viz., Jewish males) were familiar with it to some degree. The language was used only in limited speech situations but extensively in writing; its vocabulary was enlarged over earlier forms of the language, but its other resources tended to be stable.

e   This form of Medieval–Early Modern Hebrew was the basis for the modern language, the spoken tongue of the emigrant Jewish community in late nineteenth-century Palestine.[27] This language has grown steadily since and is the official language of the State of Israel. It is of interest to scholars of Biblical Hebrew as a research language and as a source of information about change in phonology and morphology. Many aspects of the syntax of the modern language show non-Semitic influence.[28] The complexity of the interaction of various phases of Hebrew in the modern tongue makes it attractive to students of historical linguistics in general.

Higher Criticism," *Hebrew Union College Annual* 53 (1982) 29–43. On the texts generally, see, e.g., T. H. Gaster, *The Dead Sea Scriptures* (3d ed.; Garden City, New York: Anchor/Doubleday, 1976); many scrolls remain to be published.

24. It may be possible to distinguish a midrashic form of the language which together with Mishnaic Hebrew proper would compose Tannaitic or Rabbinic Hebrew. A certain amount of traditional Jewish prayer is in Mishnaic (or Tannaitic) Hebrew.

25. See M. H. Segal, *Grammar of Mishnaic Hebrew* (Oxford: Clarendon, 1927), on the language. Some of the differences between Biblical and Mishnaic Hebrew may reflect the differences in the genres that the languages are used for. On Mishnaic Hebrew and Late Biblical Hebrew, see R. Polzin, *Late Biblical Hebrew: Toward an Historical Typology of Biblical Hebrew Prose* (Harvard Semitic Monographs 12; Missoula: Scholars Press, 1976) 167–73; on Mishnaic features in the Song, see M. V. Fox, *The Song of Songs and the Ancient Egyptian Love Songs* (Madison: University of Wisconsin, 1985) 187–90.

26. Some of the most interesting material is the poetry, well represented in T. Carmi's *The Penguin Book of Hebrew Verse* (New York: Penguin, 1981).

27. Hebrew was spoken in Palestine with Sephardic pronunciation prior to the rise of Zionism; see T. V. Parfitt, "The Use of Hebrew in Palestine, 1800–1882," *Journal of Semitic Studies* 17 (1972) 237–52.

28. Modern Hebrew "syntax is no longer Semitic, but is closer to the syntax of Indo-German[ic] languages"; so N. Stern, "The Infinitive as a Complement of a Predicate of Incomplete Predication," *Hebrew Annual Review* 10 (1986) 337–49, at 347, based on a review of infinitival use, much more frequent in Modern Hebrew than in any earlier form of the language. For discussion of a variety of facets of Modern (and not only Modern) Hebrew, see the papers in H. B. Rosén, *East and West: Selected Writings in Linguistics. 2. Hebrew and Semitic Linguistics* (Munich: Fink, 1984). On morphology, various papers by Ruth A. Berman are valuable; see, e.g., Eve V. Clark and Ruth A. Berman, "Structure and Use in the Acquisition of Word Formation," *Language* 60 (1984) 542–90.

Synchronic/Diachronic   **1.4**

Literary Studies and Grammar   **1.4.1**

The study of Biblical Hebrew is neither synchronic, focused clearly on the language   a
at one point in time, nor diachronic, directed to the language as it changes over time.[29] A
number of factors impinge on the question of how to view the biblical corpus in relation
to the time span during which it was written. Most broadly, two major factors concern
us: uncertainty about the time of composition, and complicating factors in the production and transmission of the text. (A variety of other factors deserve study; there are
signs that the speech of men differs from that of women; speech addressed to young or
old may vary from a standard. Speech itself often differs from narrative prose, and there
are traces of dialect variation based on region in both.)

If we consider the dating of only the prose sections of the Hebrew Scriptures, we   b
can see the problems clearly. Much of the prose is anonymous and undated, and the
extent of various alleged units within the mass of prose is unclear. To what extent should
the three core books of the Pentateuch be taken together? And to what extent should
they be taken with Genesis and Deuteronomy? The stories of Elijah and Elisha differ in
important ways from the archival material that precedes and follows them—how do we
account for those ways? These are matters for introductory courses in scripture; what is
important here is that we note that biblical critics regularly disagree about the dating,
authorship, unity, and extent of biblical prose works.[30] These problems also obtain in
the study of the verse, dated and undated, of the Psalter, the sapiential books, and in the
prophetic corpus.

Judgments regarding these literary matters are precisely judgments, considered deci-   c
sions based on assumptions and investigations. In relatively few matters are the judgments well enough grounded to carry conviction for the grammarian, especially in light
of factors to be mentioned below. Most of the unquestionable judgments involve relative
dating; for example, all scholars grant that Chronicles is later than (and in some sense
based on) the Pentateuch and the Former Prophets.

There are three related skewing processes which are involved in text production and   d
preservation: archaizing, modernizing, and smoothing. *Archaizing* involves writing a text
or adjusting a text being copied or edited in such a way that it looks or sounds old-
fashioned. Often archaizing betrays itself by using older forms or constructions in the
wrong way. It is important to distinguish archaic usage from archaizing usage. The
Authorized Version of the English Bible is full of archaisms, that is, words and structures
no longer in use in English in the early seventeenth century, when it was written, but

---

29. The tension between a written (or dead) language as
a synchronic or frozen record and as a record of variation
over time (and region and social class and genre) takes on
a different form for each written language. Canonicity is a
far more important factor for Hebrew than for Classical
Greek, Akkadian, or Egyptian; the Hebrew record is also

shorter than for any of these.

30. See, e.g., R. N. Whybray, *The Making of the Pentateuch* (Sheffield: JSOT Press, 1987); B. S. Childs, *Introduction to the Old Testament as Scripture* (Philadelphia:
Fortress, 1979); N. K. Gottwald, *The Hebrew Bible—A
Socio-Literary Introduction* (Philadelphia: Fortress, 1985).

rather carried over from the first three quarters of the sixteenth century, when the AV's antecedents were written. There is an immense gap between Early Modern English, as the English of the AV and Shakespeare is called, and our own; a modern writer or preacher who wishes to sound like the AV is engaging in archaizing—such a modern will sometimes err in using the wrong form, for example, or in only using a few stylistic tics of AV English.

e   It is often difficult to distinguish archaisms and archaizings. The major recent study of archaizing in biblical prose is based in part on the kinds of literary judgments referred to earlier. Robert Polzin distinguishes Classical Biblical Hebrew (CBH), described on the basis of a corpus including parts of the Pentateuch and Former Prophets, from Late Biblical Hebrew (LBH), the corpus of which includes Ezra–Nehemiah, Esther, and the nonsynoptic parts of Chronicles. Esther, Polzin argues, is written in an archaizing form of LBH, and the nonbiblical Dead Sea Scrolls carry the archaizing process even further. Esther and the Dead Sea Scrolls are revealed as archaizing rather than archaic by the presence of LBH features, Aramaisms (Aramaic was more widely used than Hebrew after the Exile), and even proto-Mishnaic features.[31]

f   *Modernizing* is the opposite of archaizing, the tendency to replace older forms and constructions with those used in current speech. This tendency, too, was at work among the transmitters of scripture. Gillis Gerleman turned to Chronicles, as Polzin did, but Gerleman examined the synoptic sections of Chronicles. He found that the author/compiler used a modernized text type of the Pentateuch, one in which the outmoded constructions of the original were replaced by constructions current in the Chronicler's time.[32] The textual tradition represented by the Samaritan Pentateuch reflects a further modernizing of the text.[33]

g   The linguistic problems of archaizing and modernizing are complementary. An archaizing text records the work of author/compilers trying to use forms of speech not their own; the results of these efforts may confuse the linguist investigating those forms of speech. A modernizing text records the work of compiler/copyists trying to make an old-fashioned text look or sound current. If the linguist describes the updated text as if it were in pristine form, the description will err in not allowing for the very changes in the language that the compiler/copyists were most conscious of.

h   In addition to archaizing and modernizing, the process of *smoothing* may overtake a text, leveling out unusual features and patterns. The transmitters of the received text of scripture tended to level the text to a more or less common standard. This operation

31. Polzin, *Late Biblical Hebrew*; A. Hurvitz, "The Chronological Significance of Aramaisms in Biblical Hebrew," *Israel Exploration Journal* 18 (1968) 234–40; cf. Rabin, "Hebrew," 316.

32. G. Gerleman, *Synoptic Studies in the Old Testament* (Lunds Universitets Årsskrift 1/44; Lund: Gleerup, 1948). Kenneth A. Kitchen has shown that modernizing can also be demonstrated in extrabiblical ancient Near Eastern sources. See his *Ancient Orient and the Old Testament* (Chicago: InterVarsity, 1966) 142–43; "Egypt," *The*

New Bible Dictionary, ed. J. D. Douglas (Grand Rapids: Eerdmans, 1962) 337–53, at 349–51.

33. B. K. Waltke, *Prolegomena to the Samaritan Pentateuch* (Harvard Dissertation, 1965) 285–94; summarized as "The Samaritan Pentateuch and the Text of the Old Testament," *New Perspectives on the Old Testament*, ed. J. B. Payne (Waco, Texas: Word, 1970) 212–39, on modernizing, 213–17; cf. J. E. Sanderson, *An Exodus Scroll from Qumran* (Atlanta: Scholars Press, 1986).

skews the evidence regarding the grammar of the literature as it was first written down. Some smoothing, especially of a phonological sort, would have been entirely unconscious; we shall discuss the reliability of the Masoretic Text below (1.6). Other aspects of smoothing are entirely conscious, for example, those involving word choice. Morphological smoothing falls between conscious and unconscious extremes. An example from American English may clarify this matter: linguistically untrained students will record spoken participles and gerunds as ending in -*ing* (ɪŋ), whether or not the nasal is pronounced as velar (*ŋ*) or dental (*n*). They write the -*ing* because they know the spelling conventions of the written language and because they know that "dropping the *g*" is an "improper" thing to do, even though the *g* is frequently dropped in the spoken language. Morphological leveling may have been similarly stimulated in the transmission of the text of the Hebrew Bible. The transmitters of the text type represented by the Samaritan Pentateuch smoothed the text to a greater extent than that represented by the MT.[34]

The linguistic analysis of Hebrew is, as Chaim Rabin puts it, "rather a cross-section   i
than a synchronic analysis." He goes on to write,

> It is another problem whether . . . a grammar distinguishing the different *états de langue* [states/stages of the language] could be written in practice. At present too many Biblical books still are of disputed date, quite apart from the debates as to which portions of datable books are later additions. . . . The undisputed corpus for each period is rather small for an effective structural analysis.[35]

The processes of archaizing, modernizing, and smoothing have as much bearing on grammatical problems as do the more traditional literary questions.

If we consider poetry, the problem of dating becomes further complicated. Poetic   j
traditions may transcend chronological, national, and dialect barriers. For that reason late Hebrew poetry may contain parallels with the Ugaritic texts not found in earlier Hebrew poetry. Cyrus Gordon put it this way: "The poetic tradition of Canaan cut across time and space in Canaan much as Homeric epic tradition cut across time and space among the Greeks, regardless of whether they were Ionian or Attic, early or late."[36]

Recent Research   1.4.2

Despite the difficulties we have discussed, various scholars have sought to consider   a
the problem of dating the biblical text on linguistic grounds. We shall briefly discuss as examples of such study three recent projects, one based on external sources compared to the biblical text and two dependent largely on inner-biblical comparisons. Such serious historical studies have been less common than more anecdotal reflections.[37]

---

34. Waltke, *Prolegomena*, 294–99; "Samaritan," 217–20.

35. Rabin, "Hebrew," 310 n. 30.

36. C. H. Gordon, "North Israelite Influence on Postexilic Hebrew," *Israel Exploration Journal* 5 (1955) 85–88, at 86. In the same article Gordon argues that the lan-

guage of (northern) Israel influenced the Hebrew of postexilic books such as Esther, Chronicles, and, in his view, Qoheleth.

37. Note, e.g., W. F. Albright, *The Proto-Sinaitic Inscriptions and Their Decipherment* (Harvard Theological

b   W. J. Adams Jr. and L. LaMar Adams base their work on a limited number of grammatical elements and seek to determine how those elements changed over a period. They use as their control 470 lines drawn from twenty-seven nonbiblical texts in Hebrew and closely related documents, ranging from the Mesha Stone in Moabite (ca. 850 B.C.E.) to the Qumran Community Rule (1QS; ca. 200 B.C.E.). On the basis of the control sample the Adamses suggest that both Ruth and Obadiah should be assigned a pre-exilic date.[38]

c   The work of Robert Polzin on Hebrew prose has already been mentioned (1.4.1). Polzin's two givens, as it were, are (a) Classical or Early Biblical Hebrew (CBH), based on the Yahwist and Elohist portions of the Pentateuch, the Court History of David (2 Samuel 13–1 Kings 1), and the framework of Deuteronomy, all of which show a "remarkable grammatical/syntactical homogeneity,"[39] and (b) Late Biblical Hebrew (LBH), best shown in the nonsynoptic parts of Chronicles. Polzin's project in hand is the dating of the so-called Priestly Document of the Pentateuch, including four major strands, P^g (the base text), P^s (the supplement), P^t (the principal law code), and P^h (the earlier law code known as the Holiness Code). Polzin focuses on the largest bodies of material, P^g and P^s. He finds that P^g exhibits some features of LBH but retains more features of CBH, while P^s shows more features of LBH. He therefore proposes that typologically the major P sources are intermediate in date between CBH and LBH and that P^g is earlier than P^s.[40] The relationship between typological dating, which is necessarily relative dating ("A and B were written before C and D"), and absolute dating is a matter distinct from Polzin's major line of argumentation.

d   The third project we shall mention, that of David Robertson, concerns Hebrew poetry and is similar in design to the work of the Adamses.[41] Robertson focuses on archaic versus archaizing verse and considers the so-called early poetry, the poetry of the Pentateuch and the Former Prophets, as well as Habakkuk 3 and the Book of Job. The body of characteristics to be expected in early poetry is established on the basis of Ugaritic poetry and the ENWS material in the Amarna correspondence (see 1.3.1e). Standard poetic Hebrew is described on the basis of prophetic material dated to the eighth century and later. On the basis of morphological and syntactic features a variety of poems resemble the early material: Exodus 15, Deuteronomy 32, Judges 5, 2 Samuel 22 (= Psalm 18), Habakkuk 3, and Job. All except the first show standard poetic forms

Studies 22; Cambridge: Harvard University, 1966; 2d ed. in 1969) 12, 13. The overview of A. R. Guenter, *A Diachronic Study of Biblical Hebrew Prose Syntax* (Toronto Dissertation, 1977), remains unpublished.

38. W. J. Adams Jr. and L. LaMar Adams, "Language Drift and the Dating of Biblical Passages," *Hebrew Studies* 18 (1977) 160–64.

39. Polzin, *Late Biblical Hebrew*, 20.

40. Polzin, *Late Biblical Hebrew*, 112. See, for an extension of Polzin's method, A. E. Hill, "Dating the Book of Malachi: A Linguistic Reexamination," *The Word of the Lord Shall Go Forth: Essays in Honor of David Noel Freedman*, ed. C. L. Meyers and M. O'Connor (Winona Lake, Indiana: Eisenbrauns, 1983) 77–89. Other scholars using similar data argue for an earlier relative dating of putative P; see A. Hurvitz, *A Linguistic Study of the Relationship between the Priestly Source and the Book of Ezekiel* (Paris: Gabalda, 1982) 157–71; G. Rendsburg, "Late Biblical Hebrew and the Date of 'P,'" *Journal of the Ancient Near Eastern Society* 12 (1980) 65–80.

41. D. A. Robertson, *Linguistic Evidence in Dating Early Hebrew Poetry* (Missoula: Scholars Press, 1972).

and patterns, and each may therefore be the result of archaizing in the use of older forms or of composition during a transitional period of linguistic history.[42]

Several points emerge from these studies. The first is that relative and absolute   e
dating studies are different endeavors. Relative dating is logically prior to absolute dating; virtually any absolute date entails a relative date, while the converse is not true. In general, absolute dates cannot be derived from linguistic evidence. The second important point is that abundant material for dating studies exists, both within the biblical corpus and outside it.

The most important aspect of these studies is their statistical character. The Hebrew   f
of the Bible is sufficiently homogeneous that differences must be tracked on a statistical basis. The sophistication of such study is not in the statistics; advanced statistical methodologies are generally designed to deal with bodies of evidence quite different from what the Bible presents. The sophistication is rather in the linguistic discrimination of what is counted and in the formulation of ensuing arguments.

The Hebrew of scripture, though far from uniform, is essentially a single language.   g
In the oldest poetry, archaic forms, known from Ugarit, endure. Certain post-exilic materials differ from earlier texts. The bulk of the Hebrew Bible, later than Exodus 15 and earlier than Esther, presents a single if changing grammar. The final, edited corpus of Hebrew scripture was prepared for and understood by a common audience.

History of the Biblical Text   1.5

Introduction   1.5.1

The amount of time that elapsed between the composition and editing of the Hebrew   a
Scriptures and the medieval Masoretic manuscripts, the foundations of Biblical Hebrew grammar, has always attracted attention. Early in the modern period some scholars tended to dismiss the MT wholesale, sometimes on the unfortunate grounds that it was the work of Jews. Such scurrilous anti-Semitic attacks have long since disappeared, but suspicion of the MT has remained. Serious consideration of the text's history should help to dispel any deep distrust and lead to a cautious conservatism in using it.[43]

The history of the text can be divided, on the bases of the kinds of evidence avail-   b
able and the text's fortunes, into four periods: from the time of composition to ca. 400 B.C.E., from 400 B.C.E. to ca. 100 C.E., from 100 C.E. to 1000, and from 1000 to the present. Since the text, and hence the basis for the grammar of Biblical Hebrew, was standardized during the third period, and the fourth pertains mostly to minor modifications within the Masoretic tradition and to the printing of the text, we limit our survey to the first three.[44]

---

42. Robertson, *Linguistic Evidence*, 153–56.

43. On the subject of this section, see, in general, P. R. Ackroyd and C. F. Evans, eds., *The Cambridge History of the Bible. 1. From the Beginnings to Jerome* (Cambridge: Cambridge University, 1970); and F. M. Cross and S. Talmon, eds., *Qumran and the History of the Biblical Text* (Cambridge: Harvard University, 1975).

44. The story of the printing of the Hebrew Bible is summarized by N. M. Sarna, "Bible Text," *Encyclopedia Judaica* (Jerusalem: Keter, 1971), 4. 816–36. The discussion that follows is based on B. K. Waltke, "Textual Criticism of the Old Testament," *Expositor's Bible Commentary*, ed. F. E. Gaebelein (Grand Rapids: Zondervan, 1979), 1. 211–28, at 211–13; used by permission.

1.5.2   Earliest Period (to 400 B.C.E.)

a   No extant manuscript of the Hebrew Bible can be dated before 400 B.C.E. by the disciplines of paleography or archeology (even with the help of nuclear physics).[45] Scribal practices before this time must be inferred from evidence within the Bible itself and from known scribal practices in the ancient Near East at the time the books were recorded. These two sources suggest that scribes variously sought both to preserve and to revise the text.

b   *Tendency to preserve the text.*   The very fact that the Scripture persistently survived the most deleterious conditions throughout its long history demonstrates that indefatigable scribes insisted on its preservation. The books were copied by hand for generations on highly perishable papyrus and animal skins in the relatively damp, hostile climate of Palestine; the dry climate of Egypt, so favorable to the preservation of such materials, provides a vivid contrast. Moreover, the prospects for the survival of texts were uncertain in a land that served as a bridge for armies in unceasing contention between the continents of Africa and Asia—a land whose people were the object of plunderers in their early history and of captors in their later history. That no other Israelite writings, such as the Book of Yashar (e.g., 2 Sam 1:18) or the Diaries of the Kings (e.g., 2 Chr 16:11), survive from this period indirectly suggests the determination of the scribes to preserve the books that became canonical. The foes of Hebrew Scripture sometimes included audiences who sought to kill its authors and destroy their works (cf. Jeremiah 36). From the time of their composition, however, they captured the hearts, minds, and loyalties of the faithful in Israel who kept them safe often at risk to themselves. Such people must have insisted on the accurate transmission of the text.

c   In addition, both the Bible itself (cf. Deut 31:9ff.; Josh 24:25, 26; 1 Sam 10:25; etc.) and the literature of the ancient Near East show that at the time of the earliest biblical compositions a mindset favoring canonicity existed. This mindset must have fostered a concern for care and accuracy in transmitting the sacred writings. For example, a Hittite treaty (of the Late Bronze Age), closely resembling parts of the Torah, contains this explicit threat: "Whoever . . . breaks [this tablet] or causes anyone to change the wording of the tablet— . . . may the gods, the lords of the oath, blot you out." Likewise, one of the Sefire Steles (ca. 750 B.C.E.) reads, "Whoever . . . says: 'I shall efface some of [the treaty's words]' . . . that man and his house and all that is in it shall be upset by the Gods, and he . . . [shall] be turned upside down, and that (man) shall not acquire a name." Again, at the conclusion of the famous Code of Hammurabi (ca. 1750 B.C.E.) imprecations are hurled against those who would try to alter the Code.[46] Undoubtedly this psychology was a factor in inhibiting Israelite scribes from multiplying variants of the texts.

---

45. The oldest manuscripts from Qumran are dated by F. M. Cross on paleographic grounds broadly to between the late fourth century and the first half of the second century B.C.E.; Cross, "The Oldest Manuscripts from Qumran," *Journal of Biblical Literature* 74 (1955) 147–72; more narrowly he would date the oldest manuscripts between 275 and 225.

46. See J. Pritchard, *Ancient Near Eastern Texts Relating to the Old Testament* (Princeton: Princeton University, 1969) 205–6, 660, 178–80.

Moreover, scribal practices through the ancient Near East reflect a conservative   d
attitude. W. F. Albright noted, "The prolonged and intimate study of the many scores of
thousands of pertinent documents from the ancient Near East proves that sacred and
profane documents were copied with greater care than is true of scribal copying in
Graeco-Roman times."[47] To verify this statement one need only consider the care with
which the Pyramid texts, the Coffin Texts, and the Book of the Dead were copied, even
though they were never intended to be seen by other human eyes. K. A. Kitchen called
attention to an Egyptian scribe's boast in a colophon of a text dated ca. 1400 B.C.E.:
"[The book] is completed from its beginning to its end, having been copied, revised,
compared and verified sign by sign."[48]

Tendency to revise the text.   On the other hand, scribes, aiming to teach the people   e
by disseminating an understandable text, felt free to revise the script, orthography (i.e.,
spelling), and grammar, according to the conventions of their own times. Albright said,
"A principle which must never be lost sight of in dealing with documents of the ancient
Near East is that instead of leaving obvious archaisms in spelling and grammar, the
scribes generally revised ancient literary and other documents periodically. This practice
was followed with particular regularity by cuneiform scribes."[49] The many differences
between synoptic portions of the Hebrew Bible strongly suggest that those entrusted with
the responsibility of teaching felt free to revise texts (cf. 2 Sam 22 = Ps 18; 2 Kgs 18:13–
20:19 = Isa 36–39; 2 Kgs 24:18–25:30 = Jer 52; Isa 2:2–4 = Mic 4:1–3; Pss 14 = 53;
40:14–18 = 70; 57:8–12 = 108:2–6; 60:7–14 = 108:7–14; Ps 96 = 1 Chr 16:23–33; Ps
106:1, 47–48 = 1 Chr 16:34–36; and the parallels between Samuel–Kings and Chronicles).
These variant forms are best taken as mutually dependent final texts, sometimes involving primary literary variants, as well as secondary, transmissional variants.

Language and script development.   From the Amarna correspondence, Ugaritic   f
texts, and other evidence, we can infer with reasonable confidence that before the
Amarna period (ca. 1350 B.C.E.) Hebrew possessed final short vowels, which would have
differentiated cases with nouns (see 8.1) and distinguished various prefix conjugations
(see 29.4). The grammar preserved by the Masoretes, however, represents a later period,
after these vowels had been dropped.

From the epigraphic evidence it appears that in its earliest stages the text was writ-   g
ten in the Proto-Canaanite alphabet, such as is found at Serābît el-Khādem. At a later
stage it would have been recorded in the Hebrew script (a descendant of the Proto-
Canaanite script) and still later in the form of the Aramaic script (another descendant of
the Proto-Canaanite script, sometimes called the "square script") known as the Jewish
script.

Epigraphy also enables us to reconstruct the history of the text's orthography.[50]   h
Before 1000 B.C.E. the Phoenician practice of phonetic consonantism (that is, the

---

47. W. F. Albright, *From the Stone Age to Christianity*
(Garden City, New York: Doubleday/Anchor, 1957) 78–79.
48. Kitchen, *Ancient Orient and Old Testament*, 140.
49. Albright, *Stone Age*, 79.
50. For the basic statement of the orthographic devel-

opment, see F. M. Cross and D. N. Freedman, *Early
Hebrew Orthography: A Study of the Epigraphic Evidence*
(American Oriental Series 36; New Haven: American
Oriental Society, 1952); on the linguistic background, see
M. O'Connor, "Writing Systems, Native Speaker Analyses,

representation of only consonants) was observed. Shortly after the Arameans borrowed the alphabet from the Phoenicians (ca. 11th–10th centuries B.C.E.), they began to indicate final vowels by using consonants which were homogeneous to them, namely, *yod* for final *ī*, *waw* for final *ū*, and *he* for the remaining signs. (In the MT *he* is sometimes used for *ō* as well as for *ā*; this archaic spelling has largely been replaced by *waw* for *ō*.) Consonants used for indicating vowels are known as *matres lectiones* ('mothers of reading'). The same system for the representation of final vowels was used in Moabite and Hebrew from the ninth century on. In Aramaic texts the system of vowel representation was extended sporadically to medial vowels after the ninth century. It was begun in Hebrew thereafter. The process coincided with diphthongal contractions in both Aramaic and Hebrew (e.g., **aw > ô* as **yawm > yôm*), and as a result *yod* and *waw* acquired new values: *yod* for *ê < ay*, and *waw* for *ô < aw*; *he* later came to represent only the *â* vowel. Eventually other medial long vowels came to be notated, with *yod* used for *-ī/ē-* and *waw* for *-ū/ō-* (the last from historical long *-ā-*).

1.5.3   From 400 B.C.E. to 100 C.E.

a   The same tendencies to preserve and revise the text, labeled by S. Talmon as centrifugal and centripetal,[51] manifest themselves in the manuscripts and versions extant from the time of the formation of the canon and the final standardization of the consonantal text.[52]

b   *Tendency to preserve the text.* The presence of a text type among the Qumran biblical texts (ca. 100 B.C.E. to 130 C.E.) similar to the one preserved by the Masoretes, whose earliest extant manuscript dates to ca. 1000 C.E., gives testimony to the achievement of the later scribes in faithfully preserving the text. This text type must have been in existence before the time of Qumran, and its many archaic forms give strong reason to believe that it was transmitted in a circle of scribes dedicated to the preservation of the text. M. Martin's studies show that the Dead Sea Scrolls reveal a conservative scribal tendency to follow the exemplar both in text and form.[53]

c   According to rabbinic tradition, the scribes attempted to keep the text "correct."[54] The MT itself preserves some remnants of earlier scribal concern with preserving the text: (1) the fifteen extraordinary marks that either condemn the Hebrew letters so marked as spurious or else simply draw attention to some peculiar text feature, (2) the four suspended letters that may indicate intentional scribal change or scribal error due to a faulty distinction of gutturals, and (3) perhaps the nine inverted *nuns* apparently marking verses thought to have been transposed.

and the Earliest Stages of Northwest Semitic Orthography," *The Word of the Lord Shall Go Forth: Essays in Honor of David Noel Freedman*, ed. C. L. Meyers and M. O'Connor (Winona Lake, Indiana: Eisenbrauns, 1983) 439–65.

51. See S. Talmon, "Aspects of the Textual Transmission of the Bible in Light of Qumran Manuscripts," *Textus* 4 (1964) 95–132, reprinted in Cross and Talmon, *Qumran and the History of the Biblical Text*, 226–63.

52. Again, the discussion follows Waltke, "Textual Criticism," 213–16.

53. M. Martin, *The Scribal Character of the Dead Sea Scrolls* (Louvain: Publications Universitaires, 1958).

54. Babylonian Talmud, *Nedarim* 37b–38a.

Tendency to revise the text. Some scribes, "authorized revisers of the text," some time after the return from the Babylonian captivity, altered the *script*.[55] The earlier Hebrew script was replaced by the Aramaic script, which aided the division of words by distinguishing five final letter forms; eventually a distinctively Jewish form of the Aramaic script evolved. It is often called the "square script." The process of inserting *matres lectionis* also continued. A few Qumran manuscripts are in an archaistic form of the Hebrew script known as Paleo-Hebrew, but the majority of biblical texts from Qumran and later are in the Jewish script.[56] There are three classes of script problems: (*a*) those arising from letters that resemble each other in the Hebrew script but not in the Jewish script, (*b*) those arising from the transition between the scripts, and (*c*) those arising from letters that resemble each other in the Jewish script. Problems of the *b* class are the direct result of script change, while those of the *a* class are a hidden by-product of it. We must add that the scripts have certain constant similarities (ר and ד are liable to confusion in both scripts) and the scripts themselves assume different forms over time and in various media (e.g., stone, papyrus, clay).

More significantly, scribes altered the text for both *philological and theological reasons*. They modernized it by replacing archaic Hebrew forms and constructions with forms and constructions of a later age. They also smoothed out the text by replacing rare constructions with more frequently occurring constructions, and they supplemented and clarified the text by the insertion of additions and the interpolation of glosses from parallel passages. In addition, they substituted euphemisms for vulgarities, altered the names of false gods, removed the phrases that refer to cursing God, and safeguarded the sacred divine name or tetragrammaton (Yʜwʜ), occasionally by substituting forms in the consonantal text.

Conclusions. As a result of these intentional changes, along with unintentional changes (errors in the strict sense), varying recensions emerged. These are evidenced by the Samaritan Pentateuch and a similar text type at Qumran without its sectarian readings, by other varying text types among the Dead Sea Scrolls, and by the ancient versions—the Greek Septuagint (LXX) and recensions and surrecensions (R,[57] Aquila, Symmachus, Theodotion, and Origen) based on it, the Peshitta in Syriac, the Vulgate in Latin, and others. The relationship of text types to actual texts is rarely simple: some

---

55. On the scribes' work, see C. D. Ginsburg, *Introduction to the Massoretico-Critical Edition of the Hebrew Bible*, proleg. H. M. Orlinsky (New York: Ktav, 1966) 307; and M. Fishbane, *Biblical Interpretation in Ancient Israel* (Oxford: Clarendon, 1985) 23–43. On Semitic alphabetic scripts, see Joseph Naveh, *Early History of the Alphabet* (Jerusalem: Magnes, 1982), for abundant illustrations, and the still basic work of I. J. Gelb, *A Study of Writing* (Chicago: University of Chicago, 1963), for theoretical and historical background.

56. See K. A. Mathews, "The Background of the Paleo-Hebrew Texts at Qumran," *The Word of the Lord Shall Go Forth: Essays in Honor of David Noel Freedman*, ed. C. L. Meyers and M. O'Connor (Winona Lake, Indiana:

Eisenbrauns, 1983) 549–68. Medieval and modern Hebrew scripts (e.g., the Rashi script, the modern cursive) are derived from the square script. The Samaritan script is derived from the paleo-Hebrew script.

57. R is also known as the *kaige* recension. The fundamental studies are those of D. Barthélemy, "Redécouverte d'un chaînon manquant de l'histoire de la Septante," *Revue biblique* 60 (1953) 18–29; and *Les Devanciers d'Aquila* (Supplements to Vetus Testamentum 10; Leiden: Brill, 1963). The first is fully reprinted and the second partially reprinted in Barthélemy's *Etudes d'histoire du texte d'Ancien Testament* (Fribourg: Editions Universitaires/Göttingen: Vandenhoeck und Ruprecht, 1978).

books had more than one final form and recensions were followed by surrecensions. Tracking the types in translated texts can be especially tricky; the rendering of particles is often a basic diagnostic tool. The study of these materials is textual criticism.[58]

1.5.4   From 100 to 1000 C.E.

a   *Standardization of the text.*   Rabbinic testimony reflects a movement away from a plurality of recensions toward a stabilization of the text at about the beginning of the Common Era.[59] The seven rules of biblical hermeneutics, compiled by Hillel the Elder (fl. 1st century C.E.) at the time of Herod, demanded an inviolable, sacrosanct, and authoritative text. The exegetical comments and hermeneutical principles of tannaim (teachers of the first two centuries C.E.), notably Zechariah ben ha-Kazzav, Nahum Gimzo, Rabbi Akiva, and Rabbi Ishmael, presuppose that in this period a single stabilized text had attained unimpeachable authority over all others.[60] Justin Martyr (fl. early 2d century) complained that the rabbis had altered the venerable LXX to remove an essential arm from the Christian propaganda, which also demonstrates that the rabbis desired an authoritative text. A recension of the Greek Old Testament (R) found at Naḥal Ḥever in the Dead Sea region and dated by its editor, D. Barthélemy, to 70–100 C.E. confirms Justin's complaint in one sense. Barthélemy has demonstrated that this recension witnesses to the text Justin used for debate. The recensional character of the text (also known as the *kaige* text) is evident from the fact that all the modifications of the traditional Greek text can be explained by a concern to model it more exactly after the Hebrew text that ultimately crystallized as Masoretic. (Justin's belief that the changes were made merely for the sake of controversy is to be dismissed.) Barthélemy also noted that, alongside hundreds of variants of this type, there are also readings in which the recension departs from both the LXX and the MT, suggesting that in these instances the Hebrew text on which the recension is based differed from the received Hebrew text.

b   Rabbinic testimony combined with the evidence of manuscripts bears witness to the existence of an official Hebrew text with binding authority at a time shortly after the destruction of the Temple (70 C.E.), in the days of Rabbi Akiva. The dominance of a text like that used by the Masoretes is amply attested by the Hebrew biblical scrolls discovered at Masada (occupied 66–73 C.E.) and at Wadi Murabbaʿat, as well as by the text from Naḥal Ḥever (occupied 132–35 C.E.). These scrolls largely lack even the minor variants found in the great recensions of the Greek Old Testament attributed by

---

58. See B. K. Waltke, "Aims of OT Textual Criticism," *Westminster Theological Journal* 51 (1989) 93–108. The range of textual criticism described here is much larger than that encompassed by H. F. D. Sparks's remark: "If it were not for the carelessness and waywardness of scribes there would be no need for text-critics at all" ("Jerome as Biblical Scholar," in Ackroyd and Evans, *Cambridge History of the Bible*, 1. 510–41, at 526. An important alternative approach to the categorization of ancient exemplars has been suggested by S. Talmon and E. Tov, who propose

that at least in some cases texts were known from the beginning in a variety of forms, not easily or usefully classified as types. The texts are related "to each other . . . in an intricate web of agreements, differences, and exclusive readings," Tov notes; see *The Text-Critical Use of the Septuagint in Biblical Research* (Jerusalem: Simor, 1981) 274.

59. Again, following Waltke, "Textual Criticism," 216–17.

60. Sarna, "Bible Text," 835.

tradition to Aquila (based on R; ca. 120 C.E.), Symmachus (ca. 180 C.E.), and Theodotion (ca. 180 C.E.); these minor Greek versions were further attempts to bring the Greek translation of the Bible closer to the accepted Hebrew text during the second century C.E. Their variants, as well as most of those found in later rabbinic literature, in the Targums (Aramaic translations), and in Jerome (the Latin Vulgate), do not represent a living tradition but are either survivals predating the official recension or secondary corruptions after its acceptance. In effect, the combined evidence essentially supports Paul de Lagarde's nineteenth-century view that all Hebrew medieval manuscripts of the Bible were descended from a single master scroll dated no earlier than the first century of the Common Era.[61]

Thus in the course of the first century C.E. the scribal mentality had changed from   c
one of preserving and clarifying the text to one of preserving and standardizing the text. By at least 100 C.E. the rabbis had settled on one recension, which, in the case of the Pentateuch, is conservative and disciplined.[62] Its adoption as the official text in effect destroyed all variant lines of tradition in established Judaism. Possibly the need to stabilize Judaism by strong adherence to the Law after the fall of Jerusalem spurred these efforts. This text was not, as Paul Kahle theorized early in this century, the beginning of an attempt to standardize a canon that finally became fixed only in the time of Maimonides (12th century C.E.), after a long and bitter struggle among the rabbinical schools.

The activity of the Masoretes (ca. 600 to 1000 C.E.).[63]   Between 600 and 1000 C.E.   d
schools consisting of families of Jewish scholars arose in Babylon, in Palestine, and notably at Tiberias on the Sea of Galilee to safeguard the consonantal text and to record—through diacritical notations added to the consonantal text—the vowels,[64] liturgical cantillations, and other features of the text. Until these efforts such features had orally accompanied the text. These scholars are known as Masoretes or Massoretes, possibly from the (post-biblical) root *msr* 'to hand down.'[65] In their endeavor to conserve the text, they hedged it in by placing observations regarding its external form in the margins. In the side margins they used abbreviations (*Masorah parvum*), in the top and

61. Paul de Lagarde, *Anmerkungen zur griechischen Übersetzung der Proverbien* (Leipzig: Brockhaus, 1863). E. F. C. Rosenmueller's similar, late eighteenth-century formulation, that they all represent one recension, may be more correct.

62. F. M. Cross, *The Ancient Library of Qumran and Modern Biblical Studies* (2d ed.; Garden City, New York: Doubleday, 1961) 188–94. B. Albrektson has rejected the notion that the rabbis consciously produced a standard text, arguing that the MT emerged as a standard in the context of religious growth; see "Reflections on the Emergence of a Standard Text of the Hebrew Bible," *Congress Volume: Göttingen 1977* (Supplements to Vetus Testamentum 29; Leiden: Brill, 1978) 79–85.

63. Again, following Waltke, "Textual Criticism," 217–18.

64. See S. Morag, *The Vocalization Systems of Arabic, Hebrew and Aramaic* (The Hague: Mouton, 1962), for a comparative study of three related systems; E. J. Revell has written a number of papers on the development of the

system—"Aristotle and the Accents," *Journal of Semitic Studies* 19 (1974) 19–35; "The Hebrew Accents and the Greek Ekphonetic Neumes," *Studies in Eastern Chant* 4 (1974) 140–70; "The Diacritical Dots and the Development of the Arabic Alphabet," *Journal of Semitic Studies* 20 (1975) 178–90.

65. The reasons why the Masoretes undertook their work are not clear: recognition of the unavoidable decay in an oral tradition was partially responsible, but external stimuli, including models (from Syriac or Arabic; see n. 64) and theological controversies (notably the Qaraites; see 2.1d), were also involved. A critical point in the evaluation of their work may be the one thousand or so *Qere-Kethiv* variants; these have been associated with theories involving types of manuscript correction and manuscript collation. J. Barr has argued that the variants involved antedate the Masoretes; see "A New Look at *Kethibh-Qere*," *Oudtestamentische Studiën* 21 (1981) 19–37, esp. 23–25.

bottom margins they gave more detailed and continuous explanations (*Masorah magnum*), and at the end (*Masorah finalis*) provided alphabetical classification of the whole Masoretic material. In addition to these annotations made directly in the text, they compiled separate manuals. When the traditions they inherited differed, they preserved the relatively few variants within the consonantal tradition by inserting one reading in the text, called *Kethiv*, and the other in the margin, called *Qere*. Other alternative readings are indicated in the margin by *Səbir*, an Aramaic word meaning 'supposed.'

e   Sometimes the Masoretes may have used *daghesh* in unexpected places to call attention to unusual readings. With the help of hints supplied by the ancient versions, the Masorah, and other codices, E. A. Knauf explained the Leningrad Codex's use of the daghesh in קָצִיר (Gen 45:6) as a way to call attention to the apparent contradiction with Gen 8:22, in אֲבִימֶלֶךְ (Gen 26:1) as a device to insinuate the idea, in view of the previous text, that we have to do here with another Abimelech, and in תֵּאתֶה (Mic 4:8) as a mark to signal that the punctuation was uncertain.[66]

f   Of the three competing Masoretic schools, one in the East and two in the West, each with its own system of diacritical notations, the Tiberian school prevailed. The school's most important work is a model codex prepared by Aaron ben Asher around 1000 C.E.; this codex was preserved in the old synagogue of Aleppo until shortly after the Second World War, when it was removed to Jerusalem.[67] Contemporary study of the MT is based on a variety of texts slightly later than and similar to the Aleppo Codex, notably the Leningrad Codex.[68] Earlier modern study was based on late medieval manuscripts and early printed Bibles. A photographic reprint of the Aleppo Codex is available, and an edition of the Bible based on it is in preparation in Jerusalem. The commonly available editions of the MT differ from it only in certain minor phonological materials, involving some accents and some reduced vowels, and in the pointing of a few eccentric forms.

1.6   Masoretic Text

1.6.1   Character

a   The history presented above places in bold relief two fundamental characteristics of the MT. First, it preserves one of several recensions that emerged in the post-exilic era. Second, it is a composite text consisting of (*a*) an original consonantal text, often

66. E. A. Knauf, "Dagesh agrammaticum im Codex Leningradensis," *Biblische Notizen* 10 (1979) 23–35.

67. M. H. Goshen-Gottstein, "The Aleppo Codex and the Rise of the Massoretic Bible Text," *Biblical Archaeologist* 42 (1979) 145–63. Technically, the Aleppo Codex is "the oldest codex containing the *entire* Tiberian massoretic Bible" i.e., text and a full set of correct notes, except for the places where it is damaged (p. 148); due to the complexity of the Masoretic annotations, it stands out as "the only manuscript of the *entire* massoretic Bible in which the correspondence between text and massoretic

notation is practically perfect" (p. 149).

68. The Leningrad Codex is the basis for both *Biblia Hebraica*[3], ed. R. Kittel (originally 1937; New York: American Bible Society, 1972 and other reprints; abbreviated *BH3* or *BHK*), and *Biblia Hebraica Stuttgartensia*, ed. K. Elliger and W. Rudolph (Stuttgart: Deutsche Bibelstiftung, 1977; abbreviated *BHS*). More and more scholars are turning to the computer to assist them in their research; E. Tov provides a succinct introduction to such methods in "Computers and the Bible," *Bible Review* 4 (1988) 38–43.

originally written without *matres lectiones*, (*b*) the vowel letters, (*c*) the Masoretic additions of the vowel points, and (*d*) the accentual or cantillation marks. Let us look at each of these more closely.

Consonants

It cannot be overemphasized that, although the script preserving the consonants was a evolving during the first two periods described above (1.5.2–3), the Masoretic consonantal record is archaic. The evidence of epigraphy, especially touching inscriptional Hebrew and the Iron Age congeners of Biblical Hebrew, puts the issue beyond doubt. Unless the text had been faithfully transmitted, the work of both comparative Semitic philologists and biblical scholars attempting to date the text (see 1.4.2) would be impossible.

Nevertheless, scribes changed not only the script (essentially, the shape of the con- b sonants), but occasionally the consonants themselves. They did so both intentionally, by smoothing and modernizing it (1.4.1), and unintentionally. The unintended changes are of two kinds: errors in the strictest sense of the term and misunderstandings. We can classify the former as problems with the MT as recorded and the latter as problems with the MT as a record.

Problems with the MT as recorded. All text critics agree that the MT contains c errors in all its composite layers.[69] True textual variants rarely involve matters of direct concern to the grammarian, and discriminating among such variants is a critical rather than a purely linguistic task. Errors of this sort are either visual or auricular. They are well known to anyone who has done much handcopying. A scribe may omit a word or group of words, sometimes for no reason and sometimes for visual reasons. A repeated sequence of letters (identical or nearly identical) may prompt the eye to jump from the first occurrence to the second (haplography); often in Hebrew the triggering repetitions involve words with similar final letters (homoioteleuton), though similar initial letters may have the same effect (homoioarkhton). Similarly, a scribe may repeat a word or group of words (dittography), another sort of visual error. Auricular errors are also of linguistic interest because they may reveal phonological changes, leading to, for example, the formation of homonyms within the language. Such lapses of the ear are, however, difficult to study.

Problems with the MT as a record. We have already called attention to the ten- d dency to modernize and smooth the text. Certain problems arise because the tradition did not keep pace with linguistic change. An example from English may clarify this group of problems. In late medieval English manuscripts, the letter *y* and the now obsolete letter *þ* ("thorn," for *th*) became similar, and the word 'the' was written in such a way that it might be mistaken for *ye* or *yᵉ*. This short form was retained in early printing faces, but readers of the manuscripts and early books knew that the article was 'the,' not 'ye.' Modern misunderstanding of this short form has led to the pseudo-archaic word 'ye'

69. The statement of James Barr, *Comparative Philology and the Text of the Old Testament* (Oxford: Clarendon, 1968; rpt. Winona Lake, Indiana: Eisenbrauns, 1987) 34–37, is representative.

found in shop signs, for example, 'Ye Olde Junke Shoppe.' Thus hundreds of years after the letter *þ* disappeared from English orthography, many well-educated people believe that English once had an article pronounced 'ye.'

e   Such morphological complexities affect Hebrew also. The archaic grammatical formant called the enclitic *mem*, of uncertain function (see 9.8), was generally reinterpreted by later scribes as a plural marker; the orthography was revised to match, so מ- became (among other things) ים-, and the oral tradition was reshaped.

f   *Vowel letters of the MT.*   We noted above that vowel letters were only later introduced into the oldest texts, at first only for final long vowels, and later for medial long vowels. These letters were added sporadically and inconsistently. The MT reflects all stages of this practice. F. M. Cross and D. N. Freedman put it this way:

> Although persistent efforts were made to standardize the orthography of the Bible, they were never completely successful, and clear evidence of the earlier stages of the development of Hebrew spelling has been preserved in the text. Thus the Hebrew Bible which tradition has delivered to us is in reality a palimpsest; underlying the visible text, the varied spelling customs of older ages have been recorded.[70]

The lack of vowel letters, especially in the very early period of the text, was an undoubted source of ambiguity and may have contributed to textual error. For example, the sequence of letters in the MT of Exod 15:3

יהוה איש מלחמה
יהוה שמו

would originally have appeared as

יהואשמלחמיהושמ

It is easy to appreciate that a scribe whose grasp of the oral tradition was weak might, for example, read שֵׁם for שְׁמוֹ or misdivide the sequence יהוא, writing הוּא and assigning the י to the previous word. (Word spacing or, more commonly, word dividers were not regularly used in early alphabetic writing.) In Exod 15:1 the MT has the sequence גָּאֹה גָּאָה, while the Samaritan Pentateuch reads גוי גאה; erroneous orthographic revision accounts in part for the Samaritan reading.

1.6.3   Vocalization

a   The relative uniformity of Biblical Hebrew results primarily from two factors: the largely consonantal presentation of the language throughout its pre-Masoretic history and the unified representation of it by the Tiberian Masoretes. The consonantal representation, both with and without *matres lectiones*, effectively "covers up" vocal variations both on the synchronic and diachronic levels. The consonantal phonemes, those

70. Cross and Freedman, *Early Hebrew Orthography*, 1. See also the fuller and more nuanced discussion of F. I.   Andersen and A. Dean Forbes, *Spelling in the Hebrew Bible* (Rome: Biblical Institute, 1986).

represented by most of the letters, are precisely those that are most stable and not given to change, whereas the vocalic phonemes, those most given to change, are not graphically represented apart from the limited use of vowel letters. Even more significantly the Tiberian tradition aimed to squelch variation in order to produce a normative text. Our expectation that the vowels changed within both the phonological and morphological systems can be verified. Nevertheless, the MT's vocalization essentially represents an ancient and reliable tradition. Here too we must exhibit the tension, which once again leads to the posture of cautious conservatism before the MT.

Evidence of change.   The type of phonological changes that occurred in Biblical   b
Hebrew before it was standardized in the MT may be illustrated from English. On historical grounds, the word 'wind' should be pronounced *waɪnd*, to rhyme with 'find' and 'bind,' but since the eighteenth century 'wind' has been pronounced *wɪnd*, to rhyme with 'thinned' and 'sinned.' Because the older form occurs in poetry (and is in fact preserved in poetic usage long after it has disappeared from speech), readers can easily reconstruct its shape, even if they are ignorant of the historical development of the word.

Hebrew phonology shows two changes for which the MT provides late evidence.   c
One affects original short *a* in word-initial closed syllables; in the MT *a* in such a position has shifted to *i* but at the time of the LXX the shift had not occurred. Thus we have in the LXX (and elsewhere) *Sampsōn* but in the MT שִׁמְשׁוֹן; in the LXX, Moses' sister is *Mariam* (whence Maria), but the MT calls her מִרְיָם. A second change involves anaptyxis, the insertion of a vowel to break up a consonant cluster; the vowel used in Hebrew is usually a *seghol*, and nouns that show this change are called segholates. The process took place after Aquila and Origen, who record the segholates in the shape CVCC, and before Jerome and the MT, who use the shape CVCVC. Thus Origen has *sethr* (σεθρ) for MT סֵתֶר, while Jerome has *aben* and *qedem*, more or less matching MT אֶבֶן and קֶדֶם.

The *a > i* shift in word-initial closed syllables and the segholate anaptyxis are fairly   d
straightforward developments. Other evidence which indicates that the MT reflects postbiblical developments is complex. Some issues involve (*a*) the differentiation of *wə* and *wa* (Origen differs from the MT),[71] (*b*) the double pronunciation of the "begadkephat" letters (external evidence is confused), and (*c*) the value or values of *qāmeṣ*. In these cases and other lesser matters, the treatment in the MT is open to scrutiny.

In addition to accidental changes in the transmission of the oral tradition, textual   e
corruption of the consonantal text may prompt the accompanying oral tradition to adjust to the new reading. In Ps 73:7, the MT reads יָצָא מֵחֵלֶב עֵינֵמוֹ, which seems to mean 'Their eye goes out (*or* bulges?) from (i.e., because of?) fat'; this is sometimes taken as 'Fat shuts out their eyes' (so NJPS). The versions suggest, however, that the reading originally was עונמו, that is, עֲוֺנָמוֹ, 'Their iniquity goes out of fatness,' namely, 'Their iniquity proceeds from fat(tened hearts).'[72] The confusion of ו and י is commonplace;

---

71. See C. Brockelmann, "Die 'Tempora' des Semitischen," *Zeitschrift für Phonetik und allgemeine Sprachwissenschaft* 5 (1951) 133–54, at 147; Alexander Sperber,

A Historical Grammar of Biblical Hebrew (Leiden: Brill, 1966) 192.
72. Cf. Ps 17:10, 119:70.

after such an error was made here, the oral tradition adjusted to it, yielding the MT reading with 'eye' as a subject with the verb יצא 'to come out.'[73]

f   During the more fluid stages of the text we might also expect confusion between forms such as I-*yod* verbs where the initial *yod* on the purely graphic level is ambiguous between the prefix and suffix conjugations. MT pairs like יָשַׁב and יֵשֵׁב or יָדַע and יֵדַע require careful attention. The "hidden" definite article with the inseparable preposition also illustrates the problem (cf. לָאָדָם in Gen 2:20).

g   *The validity of the MT.* The Masoretic tradition, including the vowel points, represents the overall grammatical *systems* current during the period when biblical literature was being created. We may say this, despite the problems we have reviewed, because of a considerable body of evidence indicating that the traditioning function was taken seriously and that the linguistic data of the MT could not be faked.[74]

h   On the labors that culminated in the Tiberian manuscripts, consider a talmudic passage that evinces the concern for accuracy:

> It is written: "For Joab and all Israel remained there until he had cut off every male in Edom [1 Kings 11:16]." When Joab came before David, David said to him, "Why have you acted thus?" He replied, "Because it is written, 'Thou shalt blot out the males [זְכַר] of Amalek [Deut 25:19].'" David said, "But *we* read, 'the remembrance [זֵכֶר, with MT] of Amalek.'" He replied, "I was taught to say זְכַר." He [Joab] then went to his teacher and asked, "How did you teach me to read?" He replied, "זְכַר." Thereupon Joab drew his sword and threatened to kill him. "Why are you doing that?," asked the teacher. He replied, "Because it is written, 'Cursed be he that does the work of the Law negligently.'"[75]

This anecdote suggests that teachers in Israel were expected to pass on faithfully the received vocalization.

i   A complex body of evidence indicates that the MT could not, in any serious or systematic way, represent a reconstruction or faking of the data. The first clue that the Masoretes and their predecessors were preservers and not innovators lies in the history of Hebrew. By the time of the Qumran community, Biblical Hebrew was no longer a spoken language; Mishnaic Hebrew and Aramaic were the vernaculars of Palestine. The

---

73. A number of widespread emendations have recently been questioned. Prov 26:23 reports that 'Burning lips and an evil mind (*leb*) are *ksp sygym* poured over earthenware,' where the MT has *kesep sîgîm* 'silver (of?) dross.' Some decades ago H. L. Ginsberg proposed reading *kspsg(y)m* 'like glaze,' citing Ugaritic *spsg*, a word not attested in Hebrew. The tradition that eventuated in the MT was influenced by the close association of *ksp* and *sygym* in several other passages (Isa 1:22, Ezek 22:18, and above all Prov 25:4) and so redivided and revocalized the phrase. This proposal is accepted by, e.g., Barr, *Comparative Philology*, 219–20, 331; Kitchen, *Ancient Orient and Old Testament*, 163; and, more recently, B. Margalit, "Lexicographi-cal Notes on the *Aqht* Epic (Part I)," *Ugarit-Forschungen* 15 (1983) 65–103; but it has been questioned on the basis of the external evidence by M. Dietrich, O. Loretz, and J. Sanmartín, "Die angebliche ug.-he. Parallele *spsg*// *sps(j)g(jm)*," *Ugarit-Forschungen* 8 (1976) 37–40. For a similar case involving 2 Sam 1:21, see M. O'Connor, *Hebrew Verse Structure* (Winona Lake, Indiana: Eisenbrauns, 1980) 231.

74. We lean heavily in what follows on Barr, *Comparative Philology*, 207–22.

75. Babylonian Talmud, *Baba Bathra* 21a–b; cf. Barr, *Comparative Philology*, 213–14.

scribes were dealing with linguistic material they understood well but could use with no more spontaneity than we can speak English of the Tudor–Stuart period.

Some of the later ancient students of scripture are careful enough with the biblical   j
text to preserve signs that they were dealing with a text close to the MT. Aquila's bar-baric Greek reflects the Hebrew as closely as possible; in his farrago he often supplies Hebrew words and forms in a vocalization close to that of the MT (except for the segholates; see 1.6.3c); even rare words are given in forms close to those of the MT.

Jerome (346–420) is another careful student of the Hebrew text of his own time, not   k
out of the pious textual conservatism of Aquila but rather out of philological zeal: "Almost from the very cradle," he tells us, "I have spent my time among grammarians and rhetoricians and philosophers."[76] Jerome's work, most of it carried out after he learned Hebrew, supports the MT. Most impressive here is the contrast between Jerome's earlier version of the Psalter, based on the LXX, and the later one, based on the Hebrew. Often the LXX represents the same consonantal text as the MT but not the same vocali-zation. Consider Ps 102:24–25a.[77] The consonants of the MT are:

ענה בדרך כחו [Qere] כחי
קצר ימי: אמר אלי

At Ps 101:24, the LXX reads:

> ἀπεκρίθη αὐτῷ ἐν ὁδῷ ἰσχύος αὐτοῦ
> τὴν ὀλιγότητα τῶν ἡμερῶν μου ἀνάγγειλόν μοι.

> He replied to him in the way of his force:
> The fewness of my days report to me.

which is rendered in the Gallican psalter,[78]

> Respondit ei in via virtutis suae:
> Paucitatem dierum meorum nuntia mihi.

These two versions reflect a Hebrew text like this one, taking the last two words of the first line as a construct chain:

עָנָ֣ה[וּ] בְּדֶ֣רֶךְ כֹּחוֹ
קֹצֶר יָמַי אֱמֹר אֵלָֽי

In his later psalter, "Juxta Hebraeos," Jerome renders

> [24] Adflixit in via fortitudinem meam
> adbreviavit dies meos
> [25] Dicam, Deus meus. . . .

---

76. Quoted in Sparks, "Jerome," 510.
77. After Barr, *Comparative Philology*, 213.
78. The Gallican Psalter (ca. 385), based on the Vetus La-tina and Origen's Hexapla, is the standard psalter of the Vulgate, but not Jerome's final effort; the "Juxta Hebraeos" (ca. 395), based on the MT, never received full acceptance.

> He broke my strength on the way,
> he cut short my days.
> I said, My God. . . .

This version corresponds to the MT,

$$^{24}\text{עִנָּה בַדֶּרֶךְ כֹּחִי}$$
$$\text{קִצַּר יָמָי}:$$
$$^{25}\text{אֹמַר אֵלִי.} . . . .$$

The LXX text differs from the MT in (*a*) reading *ʿnh* (*Qal*) 'to answer,' rather than *ʿnh* (*Piel*) 'to humble,' (*b*) taking *bdrk kḥy/w* as a construct, (*c*) the vocalization of *qṣr*, *ʾmr*, and *ʾly*, as well as in (*d*) the division of the poetic lines. Our point here is not that the MT and Jerome are correct, though they probably are, but that they agree. The erratic and often improbable LXX vocalization of the MT suggests that it was the Alexandrian Jews who did not possess an entirely fixed or reliable tradition of vocalization.

l   In addition to ancient evidence for the general validity of the MT, there is modern evidence, both systematic and incidental. On the whole the grammar of the MT admirably fits the framework of Semitic philology, and this fact certifies the work of the Masoretes. When in the 1930s Paul Kahle announced his theory that the Masoretes made massive innovations, Gotthelf Bergsträsser sarcastically observed that they must have read Carl Brockelmann's comparative Semitic grammar to have come up with forms so thoroughly in line with historical reconstructions.[79] Further, there are numerous individual patterns of deviation within the MT which reflect ancient phonological and morphological features of Hebrew known from other sources;[80] yet again, numerous isolated oddities in the MT have been confirmed by materials unearthed only in this century.

m   The evidence shows that the language of the MT represents the grammar of the Hebrew used during the biblical period. Our stance toward the MT is based on cautious confidence. It must be shown rather than assumed to be in error; the burden of proof rests on the critic.

1.6.4   Accentuation

a   Drawing on the oral tradition, the Masoretes added to the text accent signs giving directions for its performance. The chant, that is, the intoning of the text with appropriate pauses, adds dignity, solemnity, beauty, and clarity to the reading. Each sign represents groups of notes to which the words of the verse are chanted.[81] The manner of

79. Barr, *Comparative Philology*, 217; cf. Rabin, "Hebrew," 306. The apparent preservation of much apparently unrecoverable information must be handled with caution. Note, for example, the case of Chemosh. The MT nearly always has the form *kəmoš*, in agreement with the bulk of extrabiblical (mostly onomastic) evidence from the Iron Age, but the *Kethiv* of Jer 48:7 has *kmyš* for *kəmiš*, apparently agreeing with the Ebla texts, which know this god as Kamish (*^dka₃-mi-iš*); see Pettinato, *Archives of Ebla*, 245, 291–92.

80. Compare the views of Bo Johnson, *Hebräisches Perfekt und Imperfekt mit vorangehendem wᵉ* (Lund: Gleerup, 1979) 23.

81. I. Yeivin, *Introduction to the Tiberian Masorah*, ed. E. J. Revell (Masoretic Studies 5; Missoula: Scholars Press, 1980) 157–60.

reading the text can still be heard in the Jewish communities of our days; the ancient chant traditions of the Roman Catholic, Greek Orthodox, and Syrian churches are related. All of them use a basic "recitation note" (and related motifs or tropes) that carries the bulk of each clause. The accent system punctuates the text and is therefore a very important feature in its syntactic analysis; despite the term accent, the system does not primarily refer to the pitch or duration of the words. This feature of Hebrew grammar is so important for understanding that medieval Jewish sources paid more attention to it than to establishing the correct pronunciation of words.[82]

Accents in the MT are of two kinds: disjunctives and conjunctives. Disjunctive b accents, euphemistically dubbed "lords" by earlier scholars, mark the length of pauses from full stop to various shades of shorter pauses; conjunctives, dubbed "servants," control the text up to the disjunctive. According to W. Wickes's comprehensive study of the accents, the disjunctives mark a continuous "dichotomy" of the verse, that is, they divide larger units, beginning with the verse itself (marked off by *silluq* closing the verse), into successively smaller half-units on a syntactic (or logico-syntactic) basis. A unit ending with a disjunctive of one grade is divided into halves, and its halves in turn are divided into smaller units by other disjunctive signs until the whole verse is divided into single words, or groups of words joined by conjunctives.[83] Israel Yeivin groups the major disjunctive accents as follows: "Generally *atnaḥ* divides the verse, *zaqef* the verse halves, *pashṭa* or *revia* the unit ending with *zaqef*, and so on."[84]

The accent signs in the MT also preserve a tradition. The Talmud mentions פסקי c טעמים 'the stops of the *ṭaʿamîm*' which were learned as a normal part of learning the text.[85] According to S. Morag some punctuation signs were added to the text before vowel signs,[86] and E. J. Revell suggests that the punctuation was the first feature after the consonantal text to become stabilized in the Jewish biblical tradition.[87] Revell has found the oldest evidence for the Hebrew accent system in the spacing of an early Septuagint text (2d century B.C.E.), which corresponds almost exactly with the accents in the Hebrew Bible.[88] He postulates the existence of an early "Syro-Palestinian" accent system that marked the syntax of a text in a simplified way that mostly agrees with the more complex system of the MT; pausal forms of the MT represent one manifestation of the simpler system.[89] Morag's striking study of the reading traditions of the Yemenite Jewish

---

82. E. J. Revell, "Biblical Punctuation and Chant in the Second Temple Period," *Journal for the Study of Judaism* 7 (1976) 181–98, at 181.

83. W. Wickes, *Two Treatises on the Accentuation of the Old Testament: On Psalms, Proverbs, and Job; On the Twenty-one Prose Books*, proleg. A. Dotan (New York: Ktav, 1970), originally 1881, 1887.

84. Yeivin, *Tiberian Masorah*, 172.

85. Yeivin, *Tiberian Masorah*, 163–64, reviews the talmudic references. Note the mention of the use "of the right hand to indicate the *tʿmy twrh*, presumably referring to the practise known as 'cheironomy', still in use in some Jewish communities," the most antique practices probably being those of the great synagogue at Rome.

86. Morag cited by Revell, "Punctuation and Chant," 181.

87. Revell, "Punctuation and Chant," 181.

88. There are also important data from Qumran; see E. J. Revell, "The Oldest Evidence for the Hebrew Accent System," *Bulletin of the John Rylands Library* 54 (1971–72) 214–22.

89. Revell, "Punctuation and Chant." Revell describes manifestations of the Syro-Palestinian system in (a) Syriac biblical texts, (b) Samaritan Hebrew biblical texts, (c) Jewish texts of the Mishnah, (d) a few early Greek manuscripts of the Bible, both of the Septuagint (a second-century-B.C.E. text usually considered the oldest LXX manuscript) and of the R or *kaige* recension (the text

community also reopens the question of the validity of the Masoretic system in intoning the text.[90] The variety of pronunciations among various Jewish communities signals that caution must be used in absolutizing any one accentual system, though the extreme neglect of traditional philology is not justified. At present it is best to consider the accents as an early and relatively reliable witness to a correct interpretation of the text.

---

published by Barthélemy and described in 1.5.4), and (e) most importantly for us, the pausal forms of the MT, which match the final disjunctive accents irregularly enough that they must reflect an early, independent system with its own significance.

90. S. Morag, "Pronunciations of Hebrew," *Encyclopedia Judaica* (Jerusalem: Keter, 1971), 13. 1120–45; cf. Barr, *Comparative Philology*, 217.

2

History of the Study of Hebrew Grammar

Beginnings (10th century C.E.)   2.1

Near the middle of the tenth century of the Common Era, Saadia ben Joseph   a
(882–942) launched the linguistic study of Hebrew with two books written in Arabic.[1]
This versatile Jewish scholar, usually known as Saadia Gaon, after his service as dean or
gaon of the Jewish academy at Sura in Babylonia, is most famous for his translation of
the Hebrew Bible into Arabic. His *Agron* (*Vocabulary*) deals with lexicography, and
Kutub al-Lugha (*Books on the* [*Hebrew*] *Language*) treats grammar.[2] Saadia's works

1. In this chapter we follow closely the survey of "Hebrew Linguistic Literature" in the *Encyclopedia Judaica* (Jerusalem: Keter, 1971), 16. 1352–1401; the first part, on pre-sixteenth-century literature, is by David Tene, and the second by James Barr. (The attributions are, unfortunately, somewhat garbled.) On the intellectual context of medieval grammatical study, see the essays in B. W. Holtz, ed., *Back to the Sources: Reading the Classic Jewish Texts* (New York: Summit, 1984), especially those of E. L. Greenstein, "Medieval Bible Commentaries" (pp. 213–59), and N. M. Samuelson, "Medieval Jewish Philosophy" (pp. 261–303). For an orientation to the earlier stages of medieval grammatical study, the long introduction to William Chomsky, *David Ḳimḥi's Hebrew Grammar (Mikhlol)* (New York: Bloch, 1952), is useful, although the work is not suitable for study because the parts of Qimḥi's grammar are rearranged and the terminology misleadingly (if carefully) modernized (see pp. xxix–xxxii); the material in

the introduction is summarized in Chomsky, *Hebrew: The Eternal Language* (Philadelphia: Jewish Publication Society, 1957) 117–38. Note also the survey of early grammatical work by Leslie McFall in *The Enigma of the Hebrew Verbal System* (Sheffield: Almond, 1982) 1–16. C. H. J. van der Merwe presents a helpful study of the recent history of the discipline in "A Short History of Major Contributions to the Grammatical Description of Old Hebrew since 1800 A.D.," *Journal of Northwest Semitic Languages* 13 (1987) 161–90. On both medieval comparative Semitic studies and early modern work (where textual criticism provided a model for comparative linguistics), see P. Swiggers, "Comparison des langues et grammaire comparée," *Linguistica* 27 (1987) 3–10.

2. On Saadia's work, see S. L. Skoss, *Saadia Gaon, the Earliest Hebrew Grammarian* (Philadelphia: Dropsie College, 1955); Tene, "Literature," 1367–69; Chomsky, *Mikhlol*, xii.

were largely lost many centuries ago, but knowledge of them has come down through his successors, especially through the writings of Abraham ibn Ezra, who revered Saadia as the first grammarian of Hebrew and "chief spokesman everywhere" for such study. Profiat Duran tells us that Saadia wrote three grammatical works which did not survive in his own time. Saadia's works were read and studied during the brilliant creative period of Hebrew grammar and served to shift the attention of Jewish intellectuals from talmudic to linguistic studies. Modern scholars still regard him as the father of our discipline. Saadia's grammatical work presented various elements basic to any modern grammar, for example, paradigms for the *Qal* and *Hiphil* verbal stems and careful distinctions among various classes of sounds. What motivated Saadia to give birth to our discipline?

b   The prehistory of Hebrew grammatical study is meager. It is true that in talmudic and midrashic materials the rabbis make occasional grammatical observations, for example, that the ending הָ- in such forms as מִצְרַ֫יְמָה and חוּצָה indicates direction and stands in place of a prefixed ל, as in שָׁלְמִצְרַיִם and לְחוּץ, and that כִּי has four different meanings: 'if,' 'lest,' 'indeed,' and 'because.'[3] Further, considerable grammatical material is to be found in the *Sepher Yeṣirah*, an early medieval qabbalistic work. But these sporadic comments provided neither basis nor motivation for the work of Saadia and his successors. Rather, the impetus for describing the rules of the Hebrew language came from the following factors: (1) the argument that grammar is basic to understanding scriptural literature, (2) the threat of the Qaraite sect, (3) the foundational work of the Masoretes, (4) the example of Arabic grammars, and (5) the ongoing literary use of Hebrew, especially in devotional poetry. Let us consider each of these factors in detail.

c   The first Jewish grammarians defended their activity with the philosophical and theological argument that proper knowledge of the Hebrew Scriptures depends on grammar; it is the basic exegetical tool. David Tene has observed:

> Around the end of the first millennium C.E. writing about linguistic issues was a new phenomenon in Jewish literature, considered by many important people as a vain, senseless activity. Therefore, in their introductions, the authors [of grammatical works] discuss the motivating factors which stimulated them to write their linguistic works. They seek to prove to their readers that it is incumbent upon Jews to take up the investigation of their language and their arguments include the following points: (1) language is the means for all discernment and linguistics is the means for all investigation and wisdom; (2) the fulfillment of the commandments depends upon the understanding of the written word, and in turn, the proper knowledge of the language is impossible without the aid of linguistics.[4]

Such arguments are still cogent and inescapable for any community that builds its faith on scripture.[5]

---

3. Babylonian Talmud, *Yebamoth* 13b; *Giṭṭin* 90a. Cf. S. Rosenblatt, "Materials toward a Biblical Grammar in the Bible Exegesis of the Tosefta," *Biblical and Related Studies Presented to Samuel Iwry*, ed. A. Kort and S. Morschauser (Winona Lake, Indiana: Eisenbrauns, 1985) 219–26.

4. Tene, "Literature," 1360–61. Hebrew was also regarded as the primordial language.

5. The medieval Jewish grammarians, like most grammarians of Hebrew since, concentrated on the language of the Bible and neglected later developments; cf. Tene, "Literature," 1361–62.

The Qaraite sect, which appeared toward the end of the eighth century, rejected   d
rabbinic traditions and insisted on the diligent study of the Scriptures themselves as the
only basis for Judaism. This movement, which made serious inroads into the academies
of Babylonian Jewry, spurred both friends and foes to a more searching study of the
biblical text and its language. Saadia, as head of one of those academies, was directly
involved and led the rabbinite counterattack. More specifically, Qaraism prompted him
to write *Kitāb al-Sabʿīn Lafẓa al-Mufrada* (*The Book of the Seventy Isolated Words*), a
brief lexicographical essay in Arabic which treats some of the *hapax legomena* of the
Bible.[6]

The Masoretes, whose work had culminated in the tenth century with the school of   e
Ben Asher in Tiberias, were concerned not with describing the language but with record-
ing the text. Nevertheless their activity in vocalizing the text and in commenting on it in
the Masorah, both activities aimed at preserving an essentially oral body of tradition,
formed the basis for early grammatical descriptions. Concerning the relevance of the
pointed text, Tene writes:

> It is rather astonishing that the initial emergence of the linguistic literature of the Jews
> had to be so late in time. There is, however, general agreement that in Semitic this
> kind of metalinguistic discourse could not have begun before the invention of the
> vowel points.[7]

Concerning the more specific contributions of the Masoretes to Hebrew grammar, Israel
Yeivin notes:

> Some of the terminology used in the Masorah was taken over by the grammarians.
> Terms such as masculine, feminine, singular, plural, the names of the letters, the vowel
> and accent signs, and other features of the pointing . . . were all used by the Masoretes
> and taken over by the grammarians. . . . Since the Masoretes compared all the occur-
> rences of particular words, their lists formed the basis for grammatical observations on
> changes in vowel patterns: either conditioned changes, such as changes in forms in
> contextual or pausal situations, changes in words with or without *maqqef*, with or
> without the definite article, or *waw* simple and *waw* consecutive, etc., or uncondi-
> tioned variation in the vowelling of the word.[8]

The Masoretes had a sophisticated linguistic theory with an underdeveloped expression;
the grammarians, in taking the step of making the theory explicit, were able to advance
it because they could appreciate gaps and inconsistencies in it.[9]

---

6. On the role of the Qaraites, see Chomsky, *Mikhlol*,
xiii. On the *Book of the Seventy*, see Tene, "Literature,"
1356, 1362. The Qaraite (Karaite) sect has an uncertain
early history. Some scholars link the canonization of Masoretic study to the earliest stages of the movement, suggesting that the Masoretes were either arch-anti-Qaraites or
Qaraites themselves. The Qaraite sect survives in modern
times as a tiny remnant located in both the Soviet Union
and Israel. In late medieval and Renaissance times, Jewish
controversy with Christians played a role in the development of linguistic science.

7. Tene, "Literature," 1353.

8. Israel Yeivin, *Introduction to the Tiberian Masorah*,
ed. E. J. Revell (Masoretic Studies 5; Missoula: Scholars
Press, 1980) 153.

9. Cf. Tene, "Literature," 1354.

f   The Arabic grammars of Muslim scholars provided an immediate impetus and model for similar work on the Hebrew language. The influence of the Arab grammarians on Saadia Gaon, who wrote in Arabic, is plain. Like them, for example, he classifies the words of the language into three divisions, nouns, verbs, and particles. Although Hebrew was the focus of his study, Arabic was the language of science throughout the tenth century in the Near East, North Africa, and Spain. In the second half of this fruitful century, some Hebrew lexical studies produced in Spain were written in Hebrew, but most grammatical works over the next two centuries were in Arabic.

g   Finally, in the introduction to his *Agron*, Saadia informs his readers that, disturbed by the style of various contemporary religious poets, authors of *piyyûṭîm*, and by the confusion of grammatical categories in their poems, he designed his work to guide the Hebrew writers of his day in the correct use of the language.[10]

h   Another pioneer in Hebrew linguistics is Menaḥem ibn Saruq (ca. 910–ca. 970), who read Saadia's commentaries. He wrote the *Maḥberet*, the first complete Hebrew dictionary and the first linguistic work to be written in Hebrew.[11] It was severely criticized in linguistic matters by Saadia's pupil, Dunash ben Labraṭ (ca. 920–990), whose family came from Baghdad, although he himself was born in Fez; he settled in Cordova. Dunash and Menaḥem mediated Saadia's learning, and other features of Babylonian Jewry, to Spain.[12] Leslie McFall cogently observes: "Jewish scholarship in Spain owed not only its pronunciation (Sephardic) but its beginnings to Babylonian Jewry."[13]

2.2   Medieval Jewish Studies (11th to 16th centuries)

2.2.1   Creative Period (1000–1150)

a   The period from the end of the tenth century to the middle of the twelfth century is designated by David Tene as "the creative period." Yehuda Ḥayyuj (ca. 940–ca. 1010), a disciple of Menaḥem, scientifically and systematically expounded the theory that all Hebrew words have a triradical root, a notion he adapted from the Arab grammarians. Grammarians were now in the heuristic position to understand phenomena such as the assimilated *nun* and the compensatory *daghesh*, as well as various features of the weak verbs, those with one or more of the letters א ה ו י as a radical. It was Ḥayyuj who adopted from the Arabic grammars the burdensome פעל as the paradigmatic verb and introduced the designation of the three radicals of the root by *Pe* (first radical), *Ayin* (second radical), and *Lamedh* (third radical).[14]

b   The successors of Saadia pursued their studies with zeal and profundity, as illustrated by the famous literature of "objections" and "replies" between the brilliant gram-

---

10. See Chomsky, *Mikhlol*, xix. The history of payṭanic verse can be conveniently traced in T. Carmi's *Penguin Book of Hebrew Verse* (New York: Penguin, 1981); he includes works (not all devotional) of Saadia Gaon, Menaḥem ibn Saruq, Dunash ben Labraṭ, Samuel ha-Nagid, Moses ibn Ezra, and Abraham ibn Ezra. On Saadia as grammarian and writer, see Y. Tobi, "Saadia's Biblical Exegesis and His Poetic Practice," *Hebrew Annual Review* 8 (1984) 241–57.

11. Tene, "Literature," 1356.

12. Chomsky, *Mikhlol*, xiii.

13. McFall, *Hebrew Verbal System*, 4.

14. Tene, "Literature," 1356, 1369–70; Chomsky, *Mikhlol*, xiv, xxiv.

marian Jonah ibn Janāḥ (Abū al-Walīd Marwān ibn Janāḥ, ca. 990–1050), and the statesman, soldier, and poet Samuel ha-Nagid (993–1056). William Chomsky recapitulates the controversy:

> Samuel ha-Nagid apparently aroused by Ibn Janāḥ's criticism of some of the views of his teacher, Yehudah Ḥayyuj, sent a messenger from Granada to Saragossa, the place of Ibn Janāḥ's residence, charged with the task of challenging Ibn Janāḥ to a verbal duel on certain grammatical issues and of exposing publicly the "fallacy" of his theories. On his arrival in Saragossa, the messenger stayed at the home of . . . a friend of Ibn Janāḥ. A public reception was arranged in honor of the visitor, to which Ibn Janāḥ was invited. The latter, without suspecting the chief purpose of the gathering, accepted the invitation. During the reception, the visitor began to inveigle Ibn Janāḥ gradually and subtly into a discussion. Some of the questions raised by him were readily disposed of and adequately answered by Ibn Janāḥ. But others followed, and Ibn Janāḥ, unprepared for this barrage of questions, was befuddled, and he promised to reply at some future time.
>
> He did so and sent his reply to the visitor. The latter, however, superciliously remarked that it would be wiser for Ibn Janāḥ to withhold his reply until the Nagid's book was published, where he would find even more serious criticism leveled against him. This Ibn Janāḥ refused to do. He issued his reply in book form and called it *Kitab at-Taswiya* [*The Book of Rebuke*]. After the publication of the Nagid's attack on him, Ibn Janāḥ retorted with a violent counter-attack in a book, which he called *Kitab at-Tashwir* [*The Book of Shaming*].[15]

The sophistication of Hebrew grammar at this time can be seen in the issues being argued over: the *Qal* passive, a subject independently examined in modern times by Böttcher and Barth (see 22.6), the use of the term *Inphial* for transitive *Niphal* forms, etc. Of this literature Tene writes: "The study of the language never attained such fine and sharp distinctions as those in the controversy which developed around the works of Ḥayyuj in the generation of Ibn Janāḥ and Samuel ha-Nagid."[16] Of Ibn Janāḥ's later works, written in Arabic as all his books were, the most important is *Kitāb al-Tanqīḥ* (Hebrew *Sepher ha-Diqduq*, *The Book of Detailed Investigation*). This consists of two parts, *Kitāb al-Lumaᶜ* (grammar) and *Kitāb al-Uṣūl* (a dictionary). Tene rhapsodizes on the great *Kitāb*:

> This two-part work, with the writings of Ḥayyuj and the shorter works of Ibn Janāḥ . . . , form[s] the first complete description of biblical Hebrew, and no similar work—comparable in scope, depth, and precision—was written until modern times.

---

15. Chomsky, *Mikhlol*, xvi–xvii, cf. xix; see also Tene, "Literature," 1356–57, 1370–71. On Ibn Janāḥ, see E. A. Coffin, *Ibn Janāḥ's Kitāb al-Lumaᶜ: A Critique of Medieval Grammatical Tradition* (University of Michigan Dissertation, 1968), and her summary, "Ibn Janāḥ's *Kitāb al-Lumaᶜ*: An Integration of Medieval Grammatical Approaches," *Michigan Oriental Studies in Honor of George*

G. Cameron, ed. L. L. Orlin et al. (Ann Arbor: Department of Near Eastern Studies, University of Michigan, 1976) 65–79. On Samuel's varied career, see S. Stroumsa, "From Muslim Heresy to Jewish-Muslim Polemics," *Journal of the American Oriental Society* 107 (1987) 767–72, and references.

16. Tene, "Literature," 1357; cf. Chomsky, *Mikhlol*, xix.

This description constitutes the high point of linguistic thought in all [medieval grammatical] literature.[17]

He comments in summary, "The authors of this period are the great creators of Hebrew linguistics."[18]

2.2.2   Period of Dissemination (1150–1250)

a   The century following the middle of the twelfth century was a period of dissemination, directly stimulated by the political tribulations of 1148, brought on by the Almohade conquest of southern Spain. Jewish intellectuals, exiled to Italy and to southern France, brought with them the works of Ḥayyuj, Ibn Janāḥ, Samuel ha-Nagid, and others. These works were both adapted and translated. The traveling scholar Abraham ibn Ezra (1089–1164), through his copious writings, notably commentaries and grammatical works, popularized the ideas of the Spanish grammarians and in general brought the benefits of Arab science to European Jewish communities cut off from Spanish Jewry. In Rome around 1140 he produced his grammar in Hebrew, a first, based on Arabic sources.[19]

b   The labors of adaptation culminated in the works of the Qimḥi family: Joseph, the father (ca. 1105–1170), and his sons Moses and David (1160–1235).[20] In the introduction to the section of his *Sepher Mikhlol* (*Compendium*) dealing with Hebrew grammar, David likened himself to a "gleaner after the reaper," whose task it has been to compile and present succinctly and simply the voluminous findings of his predecessors. He selected his material so judiciously and presented it so effectively that his work eclipsed and eventually displaced the more original and profound work of Ibn Janāḥ and served as an authoritative standard until the nineteenth century. Posterity held his works in such high regard that a mishnaic dictum was adapted to them: אם אין קמחי אין תורה, 'If there were no Qimḥi, there would be no Torah.' We are indebted to Joseph and David Qimḥi for the now-standard formulation of the patterning of long and short vowels in closed and open syllables and of the relationship of these to silent and vocal *shewas*; the system of verbal stems (*binyanim*) as it is understood today was first elaborated by them.[21]

---

17. Tene, "Literature," 1357.
18. Tene, "Literature," 1358.
19. According to C. Rabin, *The Evolution of the Syntax of Post-Biblical Hebrew* (Oxford Dissertation, 1943) 91, his Hebrew is more mishnaic than Rashi's; see more generally F. Greenspahn, "Abraham Ibn Ezra and the Origin of Some Medieval Grammatical Terms," *Jewish Quarterly Review* 76 (1985–86) 217–27. Joseph Qimḥi (see below in text) fled to Provence during the persecutions in southern Spain and probably met Abraham ibn Ezra in 1160. Abraham ibn Ezra, best known as a biblical commentator (and the speaker of Browning's "Rabbi Ben Ezra"), should not be confused with his contemporary, the poet Moses ibn Ezra (1055–1135), also a distinguished

reader of Biblical Hebrew—see N. Roth, "'Seeing the Bible through a Poet's Eyes': Some Difficult Biblical Words Interpreted by Moses ibn Ezra," *Hebrew Studies* 23 (1982) 111–14.
20. Tene, "Literature," 1372–73; David Qimḥi is also known as RaDaQ (*R*abbi *Da*vid *Q*imḥi).
21. See Chomsky, *Mikhlol*, xx–xxi. The ten-vowel, quantitative/qualitative system of Joseph Qimḥi is a radical reconceptualization of the seven-vowel qualitative Tiberian or Masoretic system. Its accuracy and usefulness have been questioned; also open to question is whether the Qimḥis meant vowel length as (what we now call) phonemic. (Vowel quantity refers to shortness/length; quality refers to the character of the sound.)

David Tene appraised this period of dissemination as follows: c

> Although the works of adaptation and translation obviously made but a slight original
> contribution to linguistic thought, it would be difficult to exaggerate the importance of
> this literary activity. It was the translators and adaptors who saved Hebrew linguistics
> from oblivion and made it a permanent branch in the history of Jewish literature.
> They also translated into Hebrew the Arabic grammatical terms . . . , and they fixed a
> mode of exposition for grammatical and lexicographical issues . . . that has existed
> until today in the study and teaching of the Hebrew language and in Hebrew biblical
> exegesis.[22]

Waning Period (1250–1550)   2.2.3

In the late Middle Ages, as the intellectual and demographic center of Jewry shifted   a
away from the Near East, so too the study of Hebrew grammar took on a European
cast.[23] Latin models replaced Arabic models. Though the grammatical works of this
period are generally inferior,[24] they are not without interest. Arab grammarians treated
the domain of language as dominant, including not only linguistics but also rhetoric (the
science of persuasion) and poetics as part of grammar. The European schools, in contrast, grouped grammar, rhetoric, and logic as three co-equal language sciences (the
trivia, as opposed to the natural and technical sciences, the *quadrivia*).[25]

In the *Maᶜaseh Ephod* (1403) of Profiat Duran (1360–1412), the philosophical shift   b
is evident: Duran calls for a more theoretical basis for grammar, opposing the mechanical character of the *Mikhlol*.[26] The immediate model of the Latin language is important
for Abraham de Balmes (ca. 1440–ca. 1523). His *Miqneh Abram* seeks to bridge the
Arab and Latin grammatical traditions. It is the first work to divide Hebrew grammar
into phonology, morphology, and syntax. It gathers together previous research regarding
the pronoun's agreement in gender and number, and government of the verb, and introduces new topics such as the combination of nouns with verbs, the combination of nouns
with other nouns, the agreement of noun (subject) and verb (predicate), and the combinations possible with the aid of particles. Of all the medieval works after Ibn Janāḥ,
Balmes's may be considered the most original.[27] The medieval Jewish grammatical tradition died with Elijah Levita, who, as we shall see, passed this heritage to Christian hands.

---

22. Tene, "Literature," 1359.

23. A general decrease in interest in grammatical studies
is sometimes said to be a by-product of the work of
Maimonides (1135–1204), the greatest of medieval Jewish
intellectuals. This supposed relationship should not be
exaggerated: "Tension and antipathy between grammarians
and Talmudists [such as Maimonides] seem to have been
rather common, a particular embodiment of a general
rivalry between protagonists of various disciplines who
viewed other disciplines as competing and diversionary
rather than complementary and supportive." So I. Twersky,
Introduction to the Code of Maimonides (New Haven:
Yale University, 1980) 204.

24. Thus Tene evaluates this period as one of stasis,
showing "almost a complete lack of progress"; "Literature," 1359.

25. Tene, "Literature," 1374. Judah Messer Leon (1.3.3a)
wrote a grammar (1454) and a rhetoric (1475) based on
the Bible, the latter among the earliest printed Hebrew
books (Tene, "Literature," 1375, 1389), translated by
I. Rabinowitz, *The Book of the Honeycomb's Flow* (Ithaca,
New York: Cornell University, 1983); on the *trivia*, see
pp. 1–liv, lxi. Messer Leon claims that his "rules of grammar . . . are sweeter than honey [Ps. 19:11]" (p. xli).

26. Tene, "Literature," 1373–74.

27. Tene, "Literature," 1374–75.

2.3   Christian Hebrew Studies (16th to mid-18th centuries)

2.3.1   Earliest Stages (1500–1550)

a   Linguistic literature on Hebrew from the tenth to the fifteenth centuries was an exclusively Jewish province.[28] With the shifts in European culture associated with the revival of classical learning and the reform of the Christian church, Hebrew grammar shifted to Christian scholars. The church's new interest in what it referred to as the Old Testament was one of the reasons Jews lost interest. Alleging that the *Mikhlol* marks the closing of the "Golden Era" of Hebrew medieval philology, William Chomsky writes:

> Most of the Jewish scholars of the subsequent generations regarded the study of grammar as a waste of time, and some even considered such study heresy. Even the study of the Bible began to be regarded as of secondary importance and was gradually dwindling to such an extent that a German rabbi of the 17th century complained that there were certain rabbis in his generation "who had never in their lifetime seen a text of the Bible."[29]

When Jews reentered the field of grammatical study, the context had changed vastly. The philosopher Baruch Spinoza (1632–1677), "the greatest thinker ever to write a treatise on the Hebrew language,"[30] wrote his *Compendium grammatices linguae hebraeae* in Latin and with an awareness of biblical writing that would have been incomprehensible to his forebears.

b   Interest in Hebrew grammar developed among Christian scholars in the early part of the sixteenth century.[31] The humanist Johann Reuchlin established the study of Hebrew grammar in the Christian European world through his book *Rudimenta linguae hebraicae* (1506), as well as through his immense personal reputation.[32] The interest in scripture that mandated the study of Hebrew was new with Reuchlin's age and its concern for returning to ancient sources and reforming the church.

c   Although the Schoolmen of the High and Late Middle Ages did not believe that scripture had one single simple meaning, as the Reformers did, some of them did hold

---

28. Tene, "Literature," 1355. On the phenomenon of the Bible as achieving its existence only or chiefly in Hebrew, see E. L. Greenstein, "Theories of Modern Bible Translation," *Prooftexts* 3 (1983) 9–41. On Christian Hebraic studies, see M. H. Goshen-Gottstein, "Humanism and the Rise of Hebraic Studies: From Christian to Jewish Renaissance," *The Word of the Lord Shall Go Forth: Essays in Honor of David Noel Freedman*, ed. C. L. Meyers and M. O'Connor (Winona Lake, Indiana: Eisenbrauns, 1983) 691–96; G. L. Jones, *The Discovery of Hebrew in Tudor England* (Manchester: Manchester University, 1983); J. Friedman, *The Most Ancient Testimony: Sixteenth-Century Christian-Hebraica in the Age of Renaissance Nostalgia* (Athens: Ohio University, 1983); P. Lapide, *Hebrew in the Church* (Grand Rapids: Eerdmans, 1984); P. Swiggers,

"L'Histoire de la grammaire hébraïque jusqu'au xvie siècle," *Orientalia Lovaniensa Periodica* 10 (1979) 183–93.

29. Chomsky, *Mikhlol*, xxviii.

30. Barr, "Literature," 1393; cf. J. Gruntfest, "Spinoza as a Linguist," *Israel Oriental Studies* 9 (1979) 103–28.

31. For general background, see S. L. Greenslade, ed., *The Cambridge History of the Bible. 3. The West from the Reformation to the Present Day* (Cambridge: Cambridge University, 1963), especially B. Hall, "Biblical Scholarship" (pp. 38–93). On Reuchlin's grammar, see Tene, "Literature," 1389.

32. The title is given in various forms: *Rudimenta linguae hebraicae* (so, e.g., Tene, "Literature," 1360) and *De Rudimentis Linguae Hebraicae* (so Hall, "Biblical Scholarship," 44).

that its fundamental sense must be everywhere ascertained in accordance with the principles of grammar and human discourse; only then could other senses be considered. Nicholas of Lyra (d. 1349) took special pains to insist that all the senses presuppose the historical, grammatical sense as their fundamentum and norm. Following Hugh of St. Victor (d. 1141) and other scholars of the Victorine school, Nicholas complained that the historical sense had become much obscured because of the all too common practice of ignoring it in favor of mystical exegesis. These Scholastics recaptured the thought of Augustine and especially Jerome—who almost a thousand years earlier had studied Hebrew with the rabbis in Israel—through the influence of the Jewish scholars, especially Rashi.[33] Although the study of Hebrew was often neglected, it is an unwarranted distortion to make Nicholas of Lyra a complete eccentric, out of place in the Middle Ages. Beryl Smalley has criticized the view that Lyra was the first to come under Jewish influence and was thus a proto-Reformer:

> The Christian knowledge of rabbinics in the middle ages used to be underestimated. Rashi was thought to have made his first appearance in Latin commentaries with Nicholas of Lyre in the early fourteenth century. His influence on Lyre was classed not as typically medieval, as indeed it was, but as a factor in the Reformation:
>
> Si Lyra non lyrasset   ["If Lyra had not played.
> Lutherus non saltasset.   Luther would not have danced."]
>
> This *dicton absurde* ["silly ditty"] . . . has been . . . disproved.[34]

In spite of various contacts between Jewish and Christian scholars during the medieval period, no single name stands out in the history of "Christian Hebrew studies between Jerome and Johann Reuchlin."[35] Reuchlin is a thoroughly humanistic figure. His brief *Rudimenta* is not so much based on David Qimḥi's *Mikhlol* as on Moses Qimḥi's elementary *Mahalakh Shebile ha-Daʿat* (*The Journey on the Paths of Knowledge*), the first printed Hebrew grammar (Soncino, 1489).[36] Reuchlin's significance does not rest on the content of his simple grammar but rather on his pioneering efforts and tactical activity. Luther learned Hebrew using either Qimḥi's *Mikhlol* or Reuchlin's *Rudimenta*. Conrad Pellicanus (1478–1556), a Dominican monk who taught himself Hebrew under the most arduous circumstances, actually wrote the first Hebrew grammatical work in Latin (1503 or 1504).[37] Pellicanus taught the Swiss reformer Wolfgang Capito (1478–1541), who in turn instructed John Calvin.

d

---

33. See the superb study of Herman Hailperin, *Rashi and the Christian Scholars* (Pittsburgh: University of Pittsburgh, 1963).

34. Beryl Smalley, *Study of the Bible in the Middle Ages* (Oxford: Basil Blackwell, 1952; rpt. Notre Dame: University of Notre Dame, 1964) xvi.

35. Barr, "Literature," 1391.

36. Hermann Greive, "Die hebräische Grammatik Johannes Reuchlins *De rudimentis hebraicis*," *Zeitschrift für die Alttestamentliche Wissenschaft* 90 (1978) 395–409. On early Hebrew printing, associated with Italy and with the Soncino family, see Hall, "Biblical Scholarship," 48–50; Goshen-Gottstein, "Hebraic Studies," 692–93; and n. 25 above.

37. On Pellicanus's preliminary work, *De modo legendi et intelligendi Hebraeum*, little more than a squib on reading, see Barr, "Literature," 1391; Hall, "Biblical Scholarship," 45.

2.3.2   Development (1550–1750)

a   Among the factors that spurred on the work effectively begun by Reuchlin were the spread of printing and the controversies in the church. The itinerant Jewish scholar Elijah Levita (1468–1549) played a special role. His books include a commentary on the grammar of Moses Qimḥi (1504), his own grammar (1517), and his studies on the Masorah (1538). His personal contact with Christian scholars was also important; among his pupils was Sebastian Münster (1489–1552), professor at Basle from 1529 on, who translated his works into Latin. Levita transported the great fund of medieval Jewish philology with the Qimḥian stamp into the Christian universities.[38]

b   The sixteenth century was the first great age of modern grammatical study. Near the end of the century John Udall produced the first Hebrew grammar in English (1593), a translation of Pierre Martinez's grammar written in Latin (1567). In time the humanistic pursuit of Hebrew gave way to theological interests; chairs came to be occupied by men with theological training.[39]

c   In Chapter 29, discussing in more detail developments in the understanding of the Hebrew verbal system, we will again have occasion to look at the history of Hebrew grammatical studies. We need only note here that during the first two centuries of Christian Hebrew studies, from Reuchlin to the epoch-making *Institutiones* (1737) of Albert Schultens, the vast majority of Hebrew grammars did little to advance the scientific study of the language.

2.4   Comparative Method (mid-18th to mid-19th centuries)

a   At the brilliant beginning of Hebrew grammatical studies, creative lexicographers and grammarians compared Biblical Hebrew with the cognate languages with which they were familiar, as well as with later forms of Hebrew. For example, Yehuda ibn Quraysh (fl. 10th century), a contemporary of Saadia, attempted in his *Risāla* (*Report*) a systematic comparison of Biblical Hebrew words to Aramaic words, to Hebrew words used in the Mishnah, and to Arabic words; Dunash ibn Tamim (ca. 900–960) dealt with the close connections between Hebrew and Arabic vocabulary. With the shift of the centers of learning from the Arab world to Europe, where scholars communicated in Latin, these studies were largely lost.[40]

b   Between the sixteenth and eighteenth centuries Christian scholars independently resumed the study of "Oriental" languages other than Hebrew, languages we now call Semitic. To Arabic and Aramaic these scholars added Syriac and Classical Ethiopic. As Barr noted, "Material was being assembled for a comparative philological approach more comprehensive and wide-ranging than that which had been possible for the medieval Jewish philologists."[41] These studies paved the way for the Dutch scholar Albert

---

38. On Levita and Münster, see Tene, "Literature," 1360, 1390; Barr, "Literature," 1392; Hall, "Biblical Scholarship," 45–46.

39. Barr, "Literature," 1391.

40. Tene, "Literature," 1356, 1362–64.

41. Barr, "Literature," 1394; note also Barr's comments on the contrasting roles of textual and "higher" criticism, p. 1393.

Schultens (1685–1750), who in his *Institutiones* (1737) laid Hebrew grammar on the new foundation of comparative Semitic philology. In this perspective Hebrew is no longer regarded as the first language, from which the other Oriental languages diverged, but as one Semitic language among the others. Barr evaluates Schultens's work thus:

> Schultens emphasized with revolutionary exaggeration the extent of the change brought about by the new knowledge. Far from accepting the traditional view that Arabic (like other languages) was a degenerate form of Hebrew, Schultens maintained that Hebrew was only one Semitic dialect, while the purest and clearest such dialect was Arabic. . . . But in spite of the high value accorded to Arabic by Schultens, his use of it was infelicitous and far from commendable even from the point of view of an Arabist. He nevertheless marked the beginning of an epoch which continued into the mid-20th century, in which one of the main forms of learned linguistic study was the use of cognate languages for the elucidation of difficulties in Hebrew.[42]

c This new approach found further expression in N. W. Schröder (1721–1798) and more substantially in Johann David Michaelis, professor of Oriental languages and theology at Göttingen. The new approach also produced a new type of Hebraist. Barr comments:

> The academic Hebraist was now expected to be an Orientalist; this meant not only knowledge of Arabic, but also an awareness of the new information brought by travelers from the East about customs, the physical surroundings of life, and now—in its first rudimentary form—archaeology.[43]

d The grammarian whose work enjoyed the widest currency and influence both in his own time and ever since is (Heinrich Friedrich) Wilhelm Gesenius (1786–1842), professor at Halle.[44] His lexicon, *Thesaurus linguae hebraicae* (published from 1829 to 1858), was successively revised and reached classic proportions in the seventeenth edition, edited by Frants Buhl (1921); an earlier edition was used as the basis for the English dictionary of Francis Brown, Samuel Rolles Driver, and Charles A. Briggs (1907). Gesenius's grammar, *Hebräische Grammatik* (1813), went through many profound transformations. He produced thirteen editions, his pupil E. Rödiger did the fourteenth through the twenty-first editions, and Emil Kautzsch did the next seven. The latest English edition, by Arthur Ernest Cowley (Oxford, 1910), is based on Kautzsch's last edition. Later editors of Gesenius's work had to take into account the vast knowledge of ancient Near Eastern languages and literatures being uncovered by the spade of indefatigable archeologists and their decipherment and publication by brilliant linguists. None of them, however, attempted to write a truly comparative-historical grammar. Gesenius's grammar, with numerous amendments and revisions and in various editions, still remains a standard reference work today.

42. Barr, "Literature," 1394–95.
43. Barr, "Literature," 1395.

44. Barr, "Literature," 1395–96. He was also the decipherer of Phoenician.

2.5   Comparative-Historical Method (mid-19th to 20th centuries)

a   The impetus for a comparative-historical approach to Hebrew grammar came from the study of the Indo-European family of languages, which includes most of the languages of Europe and many languages of Asia. The discovery of regular correspondences between Greek, Latin and its Romance relatives (French, Spanish, Italian, and others), and the Germanic tongues, including English, was followed by work on Sanskrit. The tracking of correspondences by scholars was one of the principal factors in the development of comparative-historical philology. It became clear that two related languages may develop from a single earlier language and that the historical development from the earlier stage through its evolutionary changes into later stages could sometimes be stated. In sum, comparative philology was replaced by historical-comparative philology. This most significant achievement of nineteenth-century linguistic scholarship was applied to the Semitic family.[45] The comparative-historical study of the Semitic languages reached monumental proportions in Carl Brockelmann's two-volume work, *Grundriss der vergleichenden Grammatik der semitischen Sprachen* (1908; *Guide to the Comparative Grammar of the Semitic Languages*) and in Gotthelf Bergsträsser's *Einführung in die semitischen Sprache* (1928; translation, *Introduction to the Semitic Languages*, 1983).[46]

b   By comparing Hebrew with the other Semitic languages and by working with the internal evidence of Hebrew itself it became possible to penetrate back to earlier stages of the language and to trace various later developments—Mishnaic, Medieval, and eventually Modern Hebrew. This revolutionary approach to Hebrew first appeared in the grammars of Justus Olshausen (1861),[47] and Bernhard Stade (1879).[48] It reached classic proportions in Eduard König's syntax (1897)[49] and in the grammar of Hans Bauer and Pontus Leander (1922),[50] the twenty-ninth revision of Gesenius's grammar by Gotthelf Bergsträsser (1918),[51] and the grammar of Rudolf Meyer (1966).[52] Astonishingly, no complete comparative-historical grammar of Hebrew has ever appeared in English, be it an original or a translation!

45. On the development of historical philology and linguistics and applications to Semitic, see Merritt Ruhlen, *A Guide to the World's Languages. 1. Classification* (Stanford, California: Stanford University, 1987) 4–22 (method), 25–35, 38–56 (Indo-European), 87–89 (Semitic and Afroasiatic). See also Barr, "Literature," 1396–97.

46. Carl Brockelmann, *Grundriss der vergleichenden Grammatik der semitischen Sprachen* (Berlin: Reuther und Reichard, 1908–13; rpt. Hildesheim: Georg Olms, 1961); Gotthelf Bergsträsser, *Einführung in die semitischen Sprachen* (Munich: Hueber, 1928); *Introduction to the Semitic Languages*, trans. and sup. P. T. Daniels (Winona Lake, Indiana: Eisenbrauns, 1983); cf. S. Moscati et al., *An Introduction to the Comparative Grammar of the Semitic Languages* (Wiesbaden: Harrassowitz, 1964).

47. Justus Olshausen, *Lehrbuch der hebräischen Sprache*, 2 vols. (Braunschweig: Vieweg, 1861). For the list of grammarians given here, see Barr, "Literature," 1397, and note also the valuable surveys in C. Rabin, "Hebrew," *Current Trends in Linguistics. 6. Linguistics in South West Asia and North Africa*, ed. T. A. Sebeok et al. (The Hague: Mouton, 1970) 304–46; and N. M. Waldman, "The Hebrew Tradition," *Current Trends . . . 13. Historiography of Linguistics* (1975) 1285–1330.

48. B. Stade, *Lehrbuch der hebräischen Grammatik* (Leipzig: Vogel, 1879).

49. Fr. Eduard König, *Historisch-Comparative Syntax der hebräischen Sprache* (Leipzig: J. C. Hinrichs, 1897).

50. Hans Bauer and Pontus Leander, *Historische Grammatik der hebräischen Sprache des alten Testamentes* (Halle: Niemeyer, 1918–22; rpt. Hildesheim: Georg Olms, 1962).

51. G. Bergsträsser, *Hebräische Grammatik* (Leipzig: Vogel, 1918–29; rpt. Hildesheim: Georg Olms, 1986).

52. Rudolf Meyer, *Hebräische Grammatik*, 4 vols. (Berlin: de Gruyter, 1966–72), the first grammar to take account of Ugarit and Qumran.

During the nineteenth century Jewish scholars rejoined the mainstream of Hebrew   c
linguistic work, a reentry "facilitated by the fact that non-Jewish [Hebrew] studies
became once again more humanistic and less definitely attached to theology."[53] A signal
figure in this reentry was S. D. Luzzato (1800–1865), a scholar and (like Saadia Gaon
and other medieval grammarians) a poet.[54] As our discipline has grown in the last
hundred years it has brought together, albeit in a small way, Jews and all variety of
Christians.[55]

More recently, especially since the 1940s, the comparative-historical approach to   d
Hebrew has been giving ground to the contribution of modern linguistics, which looks to
the great Swiss scholar, Ferdinand de Saussure, as its father.[56] Descriptive and structural
linguists have in this century clarified the methods by which language is studied and the
ways in which its component parts interact. Biblical scholars have also had to reckon
with ever-expanding horizons in comparative philology and with an ever-increasing
number of ancient sources for Hebrew.

53. Barr, "Literature," 1399. Cf. Goshen-Gottstein, "Hebraic Studies," on the parallels between Renaissance Humanism and the nineteenth-century *Wissenschaft des Judentums* ("Science of Jewry").

54. On Luzzato's role, see Barr, "Literature," 1399. For a recent reconsideration of Luzzato's views on Isa 6:3, see B. A. Levine, "The Language of Holiness," *Backgrounds for the Bible*, ed. M. O'Connor and D. N. Freedman (Winona Lake, Indiana: Eisenbrauns, 1987) 241–55, at 253.

55. Barr, "Literature," 1399.

56. His lectures (reconstructed from the notes of his students after his death) were published in 1915 as *Cours de linguistique générale*. See the edition of Rudolf Engler (Wiesbaden: Harrassowitz, 1967); English translation, *Course in General Linguistics* (New York: McGraw-Hill, 1966).

3

Basic Concepts

3.1   Introduction

a   Just as Schultens's *Institutiones* (1737) set the grammatical study of Hebrew on the foundation of comparative Semitic philology, so the Swiss scholar Ferdinand de Saussure (1857–1913) set the study of language in general on the foundation of linguistics, which takes all language as its object of study. The character of any one Semitic language stands out more clearly when it is studied in the light of all the Semitic languages, and the character of any language becomes more apparent in the light of languages in general. A linguist scientifically observes patterns and proposes theories pertaining to language in general, enabling the specialist in any given language to interpret the data better. Nowadays the scholarly Hebraist must be both a Semitist and a linguist. In this chapter we attempt to set forth some fundamental linguistic notions. In the chapters that follow we occasionally relate linguistic theories to the various points of Hebrew grammar being discussed.

b   Linguistics is a discipline in itself, and, as in any dynamic and developing science, scholars often do not agree about the best way to systematize the data. Our aim here is practical, and we restrict ourselves to points of theory that enjoy a broad consensus among linguists and that are most pertinent to our study. Three great themes of linguistic study are touched on. The first involves language in relation to the world; language has certain properties that enable it to describe and refer to the real world. The second theme is the structure of language in itself and the various levels used in analyzing it; the levels and units relevant to syntactic study in particular are treated further in Chapter 4. The third theme is variation, difference and change within a single language or a group of related dialects; variation can be tied to many different facets of language and may reflect many different aspects of language use. In conclusion we return to the question of the language and the world and reflect on the process of understanding.

Signification   3.2

Semiotics and Semantics   3.2.1

Language is a medium whereby a speaker communicates something in the world of   a
experience or thought to a listener.[1] Saussure referred to that which is to be communicated as the *signified* (French *signifié*) and the part of the communication system that relates it as the *signifier* (French *signifiant*). Similarly, the French linguist Emile Benveniste suggests that language relies on two kinds of entities: the semiotic entities (that is, the signs) and the semantic entities (the bearers of meaning).[2] Signs are distinctive and combinative units within a specific system: sounds (phonemes) within the phonological system, words and parts of words (morphemes) within the lexical systems, and grammatical patterns (syntagms) within the syntactical system. The signs become semantic entities when they are attached to meaning. In fact, signs and meanings are two aspects of language like two sides of one coin: they cannot be separated in the exercise of language, for language is meaningful sound. The elements of language make up a code consisting of signs that point to meaning: using psychological terms, we may say that language involves images and concepts, so long as we bear in mind that the images and concepts are mediated by words.

Linguists use other terms to describe this dual character or double articulation of   b
language besides *signifiant/signifié* and semiotic entities/semantic entities. Louis Hjelmslev formulated the difference as involving expression and content.[3] Other relevant paired correlates include sense *versus* reference and (intra-linguistic) system *versus* (extra-linguistic) referent. No matter how the two aspects of language are viewed, Saussure's

---

1. Eugene Nida addressed himself to the relationship between linguistics and biblical studies in "Implications of Contemporary Linguistics for Biblical Scholarship," *Journal of Biblical Literature* 91 (1972) 73–89. In preparing this chapter, we have relied heavily on Charles E. Reagan and David Stewart, eds., *The Philosophy of Paul Ricoeur: An Anthology of His Works* (Boston: Beacon, 1978); and J. H. Greenberg, *A New Invitation to Linguistics* (Garden City, New York: Doubleday, 1977). For a survey of contemporary linguistics in relation to the study of Biblical Hebrew, see Richter, *GAHG* 1. 8–39. References here to speech as a medium for language are used for convenience; other media are possible, and much sign language

reflects a fully developed system. For a complete glossary of linguistic terminology, see Mario A. Pei, *Glossary of Linguistic Terminology* (New York: Columbia University, 1966); Mario A. Pei and Frank Gaynor, *A Dictionary of Linguistics* (Totowa, New Jersey: Littlefield, Adams, 1969); or, with more detail, David Crystal, *A Dictionary of Linguistics and Phonetics* (Oxford: Blackwell, 1985).
2. See Emile Benveniste, *Essays on General Linguistics* (Coral Gables, Florida: University of Miami, 1971).
3. Louis Hjelmslev, *Language: An Introduction*, trans. F. J. Whitfield (Madison: University of Wisconsin, 1970) 32–35. Hjelmslev was a major influence on the French structuralist Roland Barthes.

insight that there are two aspects is basic. Similarly basic is his observation that the relationship of the two aspects is largely arbitrary:[4] there is nothing about the substance honey which leads to its being called דבש or *honey* or (in French) *miel* or (in Chinese) *mi-t'ang*. In fact, Saussure believed that the tie between signifier and signified was *entirely* arbitrary, but this view is probably too extreme.[5]

3.2.2   Grammar and Words

a   Language can be analyzed into the broad categories of words (lexis) and their relations (grammar). Grammar involves the closed set of determined systems realized by intra-linguistic signs, the code; words are often signs pointing to extra-linguistic reality. A language's code, or grammar, consists of at least three systems: sounds, forms, and syntagms (i.e., relationships of words to one another in the flow of utterance). The set of words, in contrast, is not "closed" but "open," though not infinite. New words may be coined, and new meanings emerge, according to more or less established patterns. In general, speakers are not free to reconstruct the grammar, but they are free to choose the words representing their experience. M. A. K. Halliday refers to grammar as deterministic, in contrast to vocabulary, which is probabilistic.[6]

b   One way to view the grammar/lexis opposition is based on word types. On this view, there are two classes of words, the large, open class of words with extra-linguistic reference *versus* the small, closed class of "grammatical words"; these are sometimes called "full words" *versus* "form words."[7] Full words include nouns, such as 'trees,' 'uncles,' 'teeth,' 'animals'; verbs, such as 'grow,' 'run,' 'bite,' 'roam'; qualifiers, such as 'large,' 'good,' 'healthy,' 'dangerous'; and relators, such as 'up,' 'down,' 'over,' 'through.' So, for example, the sentences 'The cow jumped over the moon' and 'The sow stomped through the room' share the same grammar: the same meaningful forms (e.g., the definite article, the *-ed* for past tense) and the same meaningful syntax (subject + predicate + adverbial phrase), but the words point to altogether different experiences. Intra-linguistic code words or form words may be illustrated by 'to' in the sentence 'He wanted to run,' and 'did' in 'I did not go.' The speaker does not freely choose such words; they belong to the code. The distinction between form words and full words is not absolute; for some purposes 'not' in the last sentence may be considered a form word, while for others it

---

4. The view that words are arbitrarily associated with their referents derives in the Western tradition from Aristotle; one formulation of the contrary view is found in Plato's *Cratylus*.

5. See the discussion in Roman Jakobson and Linda R. Waugh, *The Sound Shape of Language* (Bloomington: Indiana University, 1979) 177–215, for example; defenses of Saussure's position are given in the anthology of Robert Godel, *A Geneva School Reader in Linguistics* (Bloomington: Indiana University, 1969).

6. See G. R. Kress, ed., *Halliday: System and Function in Language* (London: Oxford University, 1976) 85. The

term grammar is sometimes used to cover all linguistic phenomena, sometimes (as here) all except for the lexicon, and sometimes simply morphology and syntax (and sometimes needlessly avoided as old-fashioned).

7. See Eugene A. Nida, *Componential Analysis of Meaning: An Introduction to Semantic Structures* (Paris: Mouton, 1976) 25. The *closed:open* contrast can be applied elsewhere in language. For example, we can say that English verbs comprise a closed class of modals ('will, would, shall, should, can, could,' etc.) and much larger open class of main verbs ('walk, talk, weep, sleep, budge, nudge,' etc.).

may better be viewed as a full word.[8] In Hebrew, words such as הַ, אֲשֶׁר, and אֶת belong to the system and are better treated in a grammar than in a lexicon.

Linguists disagree as to the extent to which grammar and lexis are truly distinct.   c The argument that they are distinct can be encapsulated in an example from Noam Chomsky, 'Colorless green ideas sleep furiously.' The intra-linguistic *sense* or grammar is impeccable (nominal subject 'ideas,' with qualifying adjectives 'colorless' and 'green,' plural predicate 'sleep,' adverb 'furiously'), but its *reference* to the extra-linguistic world is nonexistent, so the sentence is gibberish.[9] Chomsky argues that if a sentence can be grammatical and still be semantically deviant, then semantical and syntactical components of a language are separate. The terms sense and reference aid in explaining what is wrong with Chomsky's example. Reference involves the relationship between linguistic elements and the non-linguistic sphere. Sense involves the relationships that hold between linguistic elements; it is concerned only with the linguistic sphere.[10] In these terms, the Chomsky sentence makes sense but is non-referential. Whether or not this argument is accepted, it remains the case that the grammatical system of a language can profitably be studied on its own terms.

Polysemy and Context   3.2.3

"Language is an infinite use of finite means," said the German thinker Wilhelm von   a Humboldt.[11] The material that can be "put into" language is unending—it is impossible to name a finite number that cannot be topped—but the code used to communicate that material is finite. The code of language is by no means simple; it is much more sophisticated than most other semiotic systems, for example, facial gestures or clothing. Despite this sophistication language uses a small number of resources.

Since the code of language is finite, the elements of the code must be used in a   b variety of ways. Often one sign has more than one meaning; such a sign is called *polysemous*. In spoken English /tu/ is polysemous; three major meanings are distinguished

8. The study of "semantics," in the sense of the study of individual words and groups of words as a key to modes of thought, requires a brief note. The exaggeration and wrongheadedness of such study have often been criticized, most cogently and frequently by James Barr; see his *Semantics of Biblical Language* (Oxford: Oxford University, 1961) and, for the ensuing debate, M. Silva, *Biblical Words and Their Meaning* (Grand Rapids: Zondervan, 1983; most of the examples are from Christian Scriptures); J. F. A. Sawyer, "Root Meanings in Hebrew," *Journal of Semitic Studies* 12 (1967) 37–50; Barr, "Semantics and Biblical Theology—A Contribution to the Discussion," *Congress Volume: Uppsala 1971* (Supplements to Vetus Testamentum 22; Leiden: Brill: 1972) 11–19; E. A. Nida, "Problems of Cultural Differences in Translating the Old Testament," *Mélanges Dominique Barthélemy*, ed. P. Casetti, O. Keel, and A. Schenker (Göttingen: Vandenhoeck

und Ruprecht, 1981) 297–307. This restricted sense of semantics needs to be replaced by a model distinguishing four levels: (1) extra-linguistic reality, (2) non-language-particular concepts, (3) language-particular meanings, and (4) expression. The idea of family-particular concepts, i.e., Semitic or ancient Semitic, also deserves rigorous review. See B. Kedar, *Biblische Semantik: Eine Einführung* (Stuttgart: Kohlhammer, 1981).
9. See F. R. Palmer, *Semantics: A New Outline* (London: Cambridge University, 1976) 30.
10. Cf. John Lyons, *Introduction to Theoretical Linguistics* (Cambridge: Cambridge University, 1968) 404–5, 424–28. The term "signification" is also used for reference or situational meaning.
11. Quoted in Reagan and Stewart, *Philosophy of Paul Ricoeur*, 127. On this topic, see A. Martinet, "Que faire du 'mot'?," *MPD* 75–84.

in spelling—*to*, *two*, and *too*. Consider the following sentences, each using the word 'with.'[12]

> 1. I ate ice cream with my friend.
> 2. I ate ice cream with my pie.
> 3. I ate ice cream with my spoon.

In the first two sentences the preposition means 'together with,' in one case meaning 'in the company of' and in the other 'in association with'; in the third case it signifies 'by means of.' The same phenomenon occurs with other kinds of grammatical entities. For example, Beekman and Callow have analyzed over thirty meanings for the Greek genitive.[13]

c   A lexicon attempts to uncover a word's polysemy by pointing out its possible meanings in a language, while a grammar aims to reveal the polysemy of the grammatical forms and patterns by citing their potential meanings. There is no absolute separation between lexicon and grammar, and readers need to learn where most efficiently to locate the kinds of information they need. Our grammar focuses on the Hebrew Scriptures, and the following chapters offer a paradigm by which the reader can test the possible meanings of a grammatical form in the same way a lexicon enables the reader to survey various meanings of a word.

d   While polysemy satisfies an elementary requirement of language, namely economy, it exacts a price. Language may be ambiguous (i.e., an utterance may be open to several interpretations), or equivocal (i.e., the listener may be forced to hesitate over intended meanings), or even misunderstood (i.e., the listener may come to a wrong conclusion about the speaker's intended meaning). Even utterances that the speaker regards as perfectly clear can be problematic, as each of us knows from daily experience. Such utterances demand interpretation, the process whereby the listener comes to know the speaker's meaning. In everyday life, interpretation often involves simply looking around at the environment, but as the distance between speaker/writer and listener/reader increases, so does the complexity of the interpretive process. At base, however, the interpretive process always involves what Paul Ricoeur has called "sensitivity to context."[14] Context includes not only the linguistic environment of the actual words, but also the speaker's and the hearer's behavior, the situation common to both, and finally the horizon of reality surrounding the speech situation. Since we are writing a grammar of literary texts, we are restricted in our knowledge of these broader facets of context; our primary resort is to the formal features of language, though we are obliged to bear in mind as much of the rest of the context as we can reconstruct.

---

12. Examples after D. G. Frantz, "Translation and Underlying Structure. I. Relations," *Notes on Translation* (Santa Ana, California: Summer Institute of Linguistics, 1968) 22–23. The example involves the simplest kind of polyseme, the homonym; actual homonyms are rare in Hebrew.

13. John Beekman and John Callow, *Translating the Word of God* (Grand Rapids: Zondervan, 1974) 266.

14. See Reagan and Stewart, *Philosophy of Paul Ricoeur*, 125. The term "co-text" can be used to indicate the literary environment in distinction from "context," which refers to the world environment; see C. Butler, *Interpretation, Deconstruction, and Ideology* (Oxford: Clarendon, 1984) 4.

The need to determine the meaning of linguistic forms through contextual consider-   e
ations is an essential by-product of a polysemous semiotic system. Language itself does
much of the work of interpretation for us, in that language use presupposes a "law of
semantic pertinence," which requires that semantic entities harmonize in such a way as to
make sense together. As the elements of an utterance follow one another in a temporal
string, they screen out unintended meanings; only by their harmonious meanings do the
elements "make sense." For example, the word 'before' may have temporal or spatial
value in the sentence 'I sang before Queen Elizabeth.' In the sentence, 'I sang before
Queen Elizabeth in Buckingham Palace,' 'before' refers to space; in the sentence, 'I sang
before Queen Elizabeth addressed parliament,' 'before' refers to time, as it does in the
sentence, 'I sang before Queen Elizabeth, and after we both had sung we sat down
together for tea.' Since polysemy and context are essential constituents of language we
assume that contextual determinants are normally available. In the paradigmatic presentation of a form's possible meanings, we assume that the meaning in a given case is clear
from other semantic entities in the context.[15]

Levels of Analysis   3.3

Language is made up of a hierarchy of levels. Sounds, words and word elements,   a
and phrases and clauses are successively more complex levels. The interactions and structures within each level are different in kind and extent from those on the other levels. A
vowel reduction, for example, is distinct in character from the formation of a construct
phrase. The three levels mentioned are those traditionally recognized in Western grammar and its successor, modern linguistics. Sounds are studied under the headings of
phonetics and phonology. Morphology treats word elements and words as grammatical
units, in formation ('ride' *versus* 'rode'), derivation ('rider' < *ride* + *er*), and inflection
('riders' < *rider* + *s*). Syntax is the study of higher levels, those of phrases, clauses, sentences, and beyond. The elements or units are larger on each successive level.[16]

This tripartite division, though traditional, is not ideal either from a linguist's point   b
of view or a Semitist's. The general linguist has two objections. First, the building blocks
or units of phonology are arbitrary: sounds in themselves have no meaning, and this fact
separates the study of sound systems from the study of other linguistic realities. Second,
the analysis of the syntactic domain is difficult: should primary attention be given to
phrases or to clauses and sentences or to larger chunks of material (i.e., discourses or
texts)? Only study of larger chunks allows us to explain, for example, aspects of time
reference and narration or rhetorical functions (e.g., linguistic expressions of subser-
vience or sarcasm).

The Semitist's objections point to the same problem areas as the general linguist's   c
do, but for different reasons. First, the traditional understanding of morphology is based

---

15. See further R. Meyer, "Gegensinn und Mehrdeutigkeit in der althebräischen Wort- und Begriffsbildung,"
Ugarit-Forschungen 11 (1979) 601–12.

16. The grammarian and linguist tend to follow an ascending order; a schema based on notional conceptions of
language, based on thoughts and ideas rather than per-
ceptible material, would tend to go in a descending order.

on combining sequences of word elements, as in English 'bridesmaids' < [[[*bride* + POSSESSIVE] + *maid*] + PLURAL]. Hebrew, like the other Semitic languages, uses vowel patterns as much as sequential combinations, and therefore its morphology is more diverse. In particular, its morphology is often closely intertwined with the phonology, in ways that the traditional account does not allow for. Second, the Semitist notes, the domain of language above the phrase level is much harder to subdivide in Hebrew and the other Semitic languages than the traditional formula recognizes. The sentence, for example, is difficult to isolate and define, and thus Semitic grammars tend to treat clauses at great length, with some reference to a few clear types of complex sentences.

d   Despite these two sets of objections, the tripartite division is a useful scheme, still recognized by all grammarians as a convenient and sometimes revealing framework. We discuss the three basic levels mentioned and then turn briefly to work done on a discourse or text level. At the end of this review we take up some approaches that cut across linguistic levels and reveal their commonality.

3.3.1   Sounds

a   The most basic system of the linguistic code involves the sounds themselves. A sound produced by the vocal tract may be called a *phone*, and the sounds are studied in themselves in the science of phonetics. Of greater interest to the linguist is the set of sounds actually used in a given language, the set of *phonemes*, and the ways in which they are used; the set of these usage patterns is called the *phonology* of a language, as is the study of the patterns.

b   A phoneme is a sound or speech unit that makes a difference, that is, it can distinguish one word from another. The English words 'pit' and 'pin' differ only in the final sounds, the *t* and *n*; thus, we say *t* and *n* are phonemes in English. The word pair 'bit' and 'pit' shows that *b* and *p* are phonemes of English; such a pair is called a minimal pair. For many speakers of American English 'pen' and 'pin' are distinct, and for those speakers the two vowels *ɛ* and *ɪ* are phonemic. For many others, however, 'pen' and 'pin' sound alike, and only the *ɪ* vowel is used. Note that these speakers use the *ɪ* vowel in words such as 'rent,' 'sent,' and 'went,' where the first group of speakers uses the vowel of 'pen'; there is no problem with these words, as there sometimes is with the 'pen'/'pin' pair, because there are no words minimally contrasting to 'rent,' 'sent,' and 'went.'

c   The phoneme is not a sound as it is produced in the throats and mouths of a speaker, but rather an abstraction based on how speakers use the sound in the words of a language. Phonemes, the minimal meaningful sounds in a language, do not exist as such; they are the set of sounds we make and hear in our language, irrespective of such obstacles as background noise or personal idiosyncrasy. Speakers of a language may vary tremendously and yet manage to understand each other, because each intuitively knows the sound system of the language and interprets the stream of speech in terms of that system.

d   We have mentioned some sources of sound variations, such as personal speech variations and dialect variations (the *pen/pin* dialect of American English, and the *pen* ≅

pin/pin dialect). There is another source of variation, the linguistic environment of the sound; such variation is said to be conditioned, and the variants are called *allophones*. For example, most speakers of English think of their language as having a single *k* sound. But in fact the *k* in 'key' and 'kin' differs from the *k* in 'ski,' 'skin,' 'sick,' and 'sock.' (Put your finger in front of your mouth to feel the difference in aspiration, which your ear is not trained to detect, and note that only the first set is followed by a small puff of air, the result of aspiration.) Though the two kinds of *k* are phonetically different, English speakers consider them to be "the same sound," because in the system of the English language *k* initiating a syllable is always aspirated whereas *k* after *s* or at the end of a syllable is always unaspirated; this phonetic difference is never associated with a contrast in meaning, that is, it is never phonemic.[17] In contrast, for example, Turkish does distinguish aspirated *k* (written *k'*) and unaspirated *k*, and thus *k'alb* 'dog' is distinguished from *kalb* 'heart.'

Similarly, the variation of the "*begadkepat* letters" of Hebrew (so-called "hard" and   e "soft" sounds) may be analyzed as allophones, on the view that the form that occurs in a given context is predictable from the phonetic environment, specifically whether a vowel or consonant precedes. On this view, the begadkepat letters never lead to a contrast in meaning; note that b/v (~ Hebrew בּ/ב), d/ð (דּ/ד), p/f (פּ/פ), and t/th (תּ/ת) are all contrasting pairs of phonemes in English.

The greatest complexities of Hebrew phonology involve the vowels of the language.   f A complex set of rules reduces vowels in some environments and lengthens them in others; some rules insert vowels (anaptyxis) and others delete vowels (syncope). The fullest form of this set of rules belongs to the Tiberian Masoretic form of Biblical Hebrew, but many of the rules reflect processes much older. The phonology of Hebrew is not dealt with at any length in this grammar; it is a subject of largely secondary importance to the exegete, who should not, however, neglect the proper reading aloud of the text.[18]

Morphemes   3.3.2

A phoneme is a sound that serves to contrast meanings, and the phonemic level of   a analysis is the most basic; the next highest level is the morphemic. A *morpheme* is a minimal unit of speech that is recurrent and meaningful. It may be a word ('ant,' 'rhinoceros') or an affix to a word (e.g., the negative prefix *un-*, as in '*un*friendly,' '*un*available,' or the plural suffix *-s*, as in 'hat*s*,' 'cap*s*'). A free morpheme can stand alone, for example, 'friend,' 'hat'; a bound morpheme cannot be used by itself, as in the case of

---

17. Actually English has a further contrast: the *k* in 'skin' is unaspirated and released, while the *k* in 'sock' is unaspirated and nonreleased.

18. C.-A. Keller, in "Probleme des hebräischen Sprachunterrichte," *Vetus Testamentum* 20 (1970) 278–86, argues that the teaching of Classical Hebrew has been too lopsided in favor of the text and that one should start from the principle that the language is a phonetic system, not a graphic one, and should therefore be learned orally. J. H.

Hospers rightly countered, however, by observing that the practical problem is severe: "We are dealing with a fairly limited linguistic corpus, concerning which it is no longer possible to obtain any direct phonetic information"; "Some Observations about the Teaching of Old Testament Hebrew," *Symbolae biblicae et Mesopotamicae Francisco Mario Theodoro de Liagre Böhl dedicatae*, ed. M. A. Beek et al. (Leiden: Brill, 1973) 188–98, at 190.

affixes. Some morphemes have various forms, and these are called *allomorphs* or, less often, simply *morphs*. When a word can be segmented into parts, these segments may also be referred to as *morphs*. For example, the word 'bigger' contains two morphs, *big* and the comparative suffix *-er*.

b   Allomorphs of a single morpheme may be quite distinct phonetically, for example, the regular English plural suffix consists of *-s* (as in 'hats'), *-z* (as in 'lids'), *-ɪz* (as in 'forces'). The allomorphs may be conditioned by a specific environment: the plural suffix is unvoiced *-s* after unvoiced phonemes, as in 'caps,' 'bits,' 'wicks,' etc.; voiced *-z* after voiced phonemes, as in 'scabs,' 'bids,' 'wags,' etc.; and *-ɪz* after a sibilant or *s*-sound, as in 'senses,' 'censuses,' 'lances,' etc. (There are also a few *historical allomorphs*, such as *-en* in 'oxen,' 'brethren,' and *-e-* in 'men,' 'women.') The prefixal morpheme *in-* meaning 'not' appears as *in-* in 'innumerable,' *il-* in 'illiterate,' *im-* in 'improper,' and *ir-* in 'irrelevant.' Similarly, in Hebrew the allomorphs of the plural morpheme are *-îm, -ê, -ôt*, etc.; the morpheme of the *Qal* perfective consists of several allomorphs with vocalic infix patterns: CāCaC, CāCəC + vocalic suffix, CəCaC + consonantal suffix, as in קָטַל, קָטְלָה, קְטַלְתֶּם.

c   Just as sounds are the reality and phonemes the linguistically functional units, forming an inseparable complex, so are allomorphs and morphemes inseparable. Saussure expressed the distinction between morphemes and allomorphs in terms of *form* and *substance*. Like all grammatical units, the morpheme is an element of "form," necessarily related to its "substantial" realization.

d   The morphemes signifying the grammatical code are bound forms more often in Hebrew than in English. For example, the morphemes signifying definiteness, the infinitive, the genitive relation, etc., are all bound forms in Hebrew, whereas in English the article is the separate word 'the,' and the infinitive and the possessive relation are shown by the prepositions 'to' and 'of.'

3.3.3   Syntagms

a   A *syntagm* is an ordered and unified arrangement of words or word elements in the linear flow of speech. When two or more elements in word, phrase, or idiomatic construction co-occur in a distinctive way, as in the verb + particle phrase 'run away' or in the adjective + noun combination 'poor Nathan,' they may be called a syntagm. Phrasal syntagms may be used in building up clauses, sentences, and higher units. Higher syntagm structures may be seen as involving *slots*, the positions occupied by a word, phrase, or clause in a structure. The slots which elements occupy with respect to each other in syntagms may be significant.[19] Contrast, for example, the English sentences 'The dog bit

---

19. The concept of the tagmeme, developed by Kenneth L. Pike, is another approach to this complex area of study. A tagmeme is "the correlation of a grammatical function or slot with a class of mutually substitutable items occurring in that slot"; B. Elson and V. B. Pickett, *An Introduction to Morphology and Syntax* (Santa Ana, California: Summer Institute of Linguistics, 1964) 57. For example, a noun and a noun clause can both fill the first slot in '_____ is good,' e.g., 'Water is good,' 'Drinking water is good,' 'To wash one's face is good,' etc. In tagmemic theory, a syntagm is a grammatical relationship between tagmemes; see F. I. Andersen, *The Hebrew Verbless Clause in the Pentateuch* (Nashville: Abingdon, 1970) 25–27.

the man' and 'The man bit the dog.' In Hebrew the predicate and attributive adjectives are distinguished by whether they precede or follow the modified noun. The word order of English tends to be more fixed than that of Hebrew. The key to Hebrew word order involves one basic relation, requiring that the governing element (*regens*) generally precede the governed (*rectum*). Thus, in Hebrew generally the relational particle precedes (and is thus called a *pre*position) the object (בִּשְׂדֵי מוֹאָב), the possessed precedes the possessor (שֵׁם הָאִישׁ), the noun precedes the attributive adjectives (נָשִׁים מֹאֲבִיּוֹת), and the verb precedes the subject (וַיָּמָת אֱלִימֶלֶךְ).

Discourse and Text

a

Most linguists take as the upper boundary of their field of study the sentence, consigning consideration of larger units to folklorists or literary critics. Semitists, as noted earlier, have tended to focus on the clause. Thus the study of syntax is taken as the study of the use of individual words, phrases, and clauses. Relatively recently, however, a number of theorists have expressed dissatisfaction with this limitation. In part they have been prompted by a desire to study systematically certain facets of language use that philosophers, anthropologists, and literary critics have observed. These scholars have seen that contextual or enunciative determination of a clause's meaning follows certain patterns. Politeness, for example, has distinct linguistic consequences and, it is argued, linguistics should be able to describe them. In part, those who would reject the standard limits on linguistics are motivated by a desire to clarify problems of reference: the system of pronouns, for example, cannot be examined properly in isolated sentences, but only over a series of sentences.

b

Discourse analysis or text linguistics is a relatively new field of study based on these efforts to go beyond the sentence. Robert Longacre states the case for discourse grammar forcefully:

> In earlier work, discourse analysis was regarded as an option open to the student of a language provided that he was interested, and provided that he had a good start on the structure of lower levels (word, phrase, clause). But ... all work ... on lower levels is lacking in perspective and meets inevitable frustration when the higher levels—especially discourse and paragraph—have not been analyzed. One can describe the verb morphology of a language but where does one *use* a given verb form? ... One can describe linear permutations of predicate, subject, and object, but what factors control alternative word orderings? One can call the roster of sentence-initial conjunctions, but where does one use which? ... To answer these and other problems one needs discourse perspective.
>
> In view of these considerations, discourse analysis emerges not as an option or as a luxury for the serious student of a language but as a necessity.[20]

20. Quoted in Wilbur Pickering, *A Framework for Discourse Analysis* (SIL Publications in Linguistics 64; Dallas: Summer Institute of Linguistics and the University of Texas at Arlington, 1980) 4. See also R. E. Longacre, ed., *Theory and Application in Processing Texts in Non-Indoeuropean Languages* (Papiere zur Textlinguistik 43; Hamburg: Buske, 1984); and Longacre's own analysis of Hebrew, *Joseph, A Story of Divine Providence: A Text Theoretical and Textlinguistic Analysis of Genesis 37 and 39–48* (Winona Lake, Indiana: Eisenbrauns, 1989).

In light of these claims, we must cautiously defend the more traditional path followed in this grammar. Unquestionably a phrase or sentence is but a part of a larger discourse, bound together by grammatical elements giving it unity and cohesiveness and determining the grammatical shape of its phrases and its sentences. A comprehensive grammar would lay out the systems whereby the whole discourse makes sense. Nevertheless, we have contented ourselves here with writing a more modest grammar for both logical and practical reasons. The principal reason is that phrases and clauses comprehend within themselves most of the elements of a language's grammatical systems.

c   If we took discourse analysis to its final conclusion, we could "accurately" write a grammar of only an entire literary text; in the biblical context, that would mean an entire book. The hierarchical constituent elements of the grammar would be, in descending order of rank: book, pericope or section, paragraph, sentence, clause, phrase, word, morpheme.[21] For our purposes a grammar of this magnitude is not prudent.

d   The clause or sentence is a logical breaking place in the rank of hierarchies because the elements involved in systems that relate semantic entities above that level are qualitatively different from those involved in writing a more traditional grammar. For example, Wilbur Pickering in his discourse analysis investigates hierarchy (outline perspective), cohesion (linear perspective), prominence (thematic perspective), style (social perspective), and strategy (pragmatic perspective). These elements of discourse deserve separate treatment, but it is not yet clear that a strictly linguistic account would be an improvement over a more prosaic and less formal treatment, such as might be found in an advanced commentary on a biblical text.[22] In one of the most engaging text-grammatical studies of Biblical Hebrew, Wolfgang Schneider aims to describe the language not on the basis of the sentence, but on the basis of texts (which he takes to be coherent structures of sentences).[23] He emphasizes those linguistic phenomena that embody textual relations, analyzing them into three different groups: (1) forms that refer to other words (e.g., pronominal suffixes), (2) forms that refer to a relationship between clauses (conjunctions), and (3) forms that refer to relations between segments of text (he calls these macro-syntactic signs; e.g., discourse-initial וַיְהִי).[24] As E. Talstra notes, Schneider's

21. A variety of higher units (clauses, verses, paragraphs, chapters, etc.) have a place in the Masoretic system and in earlier manuscripts; see E. J. Revell, "Biblical Punctuation and Chant in the Second Temple Period," *Journal for the Study of Judaism* 7 (1976) 181–98.

22. For an example of the convergence of genre study and discourse grammar, see D. W. Baker, "Leviticus 1–7 and the Punic Tariffs," *Zeitschrift für die Alttestamentliche Wissenschaft* 99 (1987) 188–97.

23. See Wolfgang Schneider, *Grammatik des biblischen Hebräisch* (Munich: Claudius, 1974); note the major review by E. Talstra, "Text Grammar and Hebrew Bible. I. Elements of a Theory," *Bibliotheca Orientalis* 35 (1978) 169–74. Earlier, D. Vetter and J. Walter, in "Sprachtheorie und Sprachvermittlung: Erwägungen zur Situation des hebräischen Sprachstudiums," *Zeitschrift für die Alttestamentliche Wissenschaft* 83 (1971) 73–96, had advocated

the level of discourse as the starting point for the teaching of Hebrew. J. H. Hospers comments, in a practical response, "Although I am ready to agree to much, yet I wonder if all this is so easily applicable to the teaching of Classical Hebrew" ("Teaching of Old Testament Hebrew," 195). A related problem, as Hospers notes, involves the difficulty of Hebrew. Henri Fleisch has said that Hebrew is not a difficult language but one where one finds some difficulties; *Introduction à l'étude des langues sémitiques* (Paris: Adrien-Maisonneuve, 1947) 55. James Barr has also said that it is not an extremely difficult language; "The Ancient Semitic Languages—The Conflict between Philology and Linguistics," *Transactions of the Philological Society* 1968: 37–55, at 52.

24. For another treatment of macro-syntactic signs, see Richter, *GAHG* 3. 205–6; they are there called text-deictics (e.g., ʿattâ, wayhî, wəhāyâ).

observations are not in themselves new; what is new is the way the phenomena are organized, according to function in the text. Schneider distinguishes anaphoric signs (those that refer backwards, e.g., most personal pronouns in Hebrew), cataphoric signs (those that refer forwards, e.g., interrogative pronouns), and deictic signs (those that refer to the situation of communication, pointing outside the discourse, e.g., demonstrative pronouns). All these signs are treated in the present grammar in a more traditional framework; it is the merit of Schneider's work to bring them together in their common pointing function and distinguish among them on the basis of orientation (pointing back, pointing forward, pointing out), in ways not possible in traditional grammar.

We have resisted the strong claims of discourse grammarians in part for the theoretical and practical reasons mentioned earlier: most syntax can be and has been described on the basis of the phrase, clause, and sentence. Further, it is evident that the grammatical analysis of Hebrew discourse is in its infancy. As an infant, it offers little help for the many problems of grammar which have not been well understood. Most translators, we think it fair to say, fly by the seat of their pants in interpreting the Hebrew conjugations. Hebrew grammarians have only recently come to appreciate morphemes as diverse as the "object marker" את and the enclitic *mem*. No modern grammar, further, has begun to gather together the wealth of individual studies that have been carried out in a more traditional framework; thus it is not surprising that some students know little about the case functions and some commentators make egregious errors in their interpretations of prepositions. For our purposes, therefore, we are content to stay with more traditional bases than those of discourse grammar.

Analytical Approaches   3.3.5

Each of the linguistic levels involves units or elements. To analyze how a given level works, the type of units must be isolated. In phonology, sounds are recognized and major features that go with them—tone, pitch, or stress—are described. Morphology studies word classes and the formative processes associated with them. Syntax takes up phrase, clause, and sentence types.

Once the type of units on a given level is established in a preliminary way, the next stage of analysis can be undertaken. In the work of grammarians and linguists before the nineteenth century, this stage tended to be comparative, at least implicitly. One language (in Europe, most often Latin) served as a model and other languages were described as deviations from that model. By the end of the nineteenth century the inadequacies of such an approach were obvious, as a result of work on a variety of languages. In the work of Saussure, an alternative to earlier comparative and historical study emerged. Linguistic *structuralism* is based on the idea that a language can be described on its own terms: without its history and apart from comparisons to languages, related or unrelated. In a structuralist view the units on a given grammatical level are considered as a system, in relation to each other.

The years after Saussure's death were great years for linguistics, and structuralist methodologies were elaborated in various settings and with different emphases. The

Geneva school of Saussure's students thus takes up a set of problems distinct from the literarily oriented Prague school or the anthropologically dominated American school.[25] The diversification of linguistic structuralism led to structuralist methodologies in other fields, and for a time in the sixties and early seventies structuralism seemed a likely model for the master "human science," capable of unifying anthropology, psychology, and criticism. Claude Lévi-Strauss, a French anthropologist, studied myths and systems of myths from a linguistically informed base; various mythic characters and actions are seen as units making up a "language of myth."

d   The role of structuralism has altered in recent years. In the "human sciences" structuralism is seen, somewhat unfairly, as outmoded, and newer approaches are called "post-structuralist." Linguists, in contrast, have come to see structuralist methods as tools that may enable us to return to an earlier approach with a vastly increased fund of data. It is now possible to use a comparative base in evaluating a given language, where the base is not merely Latin or a few languages but a broadly representative sample of all language. Not all languages have been studied, to be sure, but enough have been described in detail that few surprises are expected. Studies in language universals and language typologies, pioneered by Joseph H. Greenberg, have recently assumed a major role in linguistics.[26]

e   The essence of structuralist method is, as noted earlier, a systematic approach to a level or other domain. Thus we ask questions such as: how do the units differ?, how do contrasts operate?, and how are oppositions used? The ways in which answers are elaborated are the ways the various structuralisms are differentiated. One major concept is *markedness*: in a paired opposition, one member of the pair is considered unmarked (i.e., simpler, shorter, more "obvious," more "natural"), while the other member is considered marked. In the sound system of English, there is a *voiceless:voiced* contrast for consonants, and each of the pairs *p:b*, *t:d*, *k:g* has an unmarked, voiceless member (*p*, *t*, *k*) and a marked, voiced member (*b*, *d*, *g*). The voicing (vibration of the vocal cords) is the "mark" of the marked members.[27] English morphology contrasts singular and plural, and each of the pairs *door:doors*, *book:books*, *fiche:fiches* has an unmarked, singular member (*door*, etc.) and a marked, plural member (*doors*, etc.); the plural ending is the "mark" of the marked members. In cases in which the usual meaning of that mark is irrelevant, the mark can take on other meanings. The plural form 'waters' does not have an ordinary plural sense; rather, it usually has the sense of referring to great quantity of water in a natural setting ('the waters of the Nile,' 'the waters of Baden-Baden'). The marked plural forms are longer in physical terms and more complex in semantic terms,

---

25. One element of American structuralist methodology that retains a special allure is the "discovery procedure," a series of well-described steps that begins with a body of language material and yields a precise and determinate description of it. In reality, a discovery procedure is usually an inductive extension of a definition. Any linguistic analysis results from much more than mechanical application of fully specifiable technique; discovery-procedure lin-

guistics tends to be a form of empiricist extremism.

26. J. H. Greenberg, ed., *Universals of Language* (Cambridge: MIT, 1966) is the still engaging preliminary survey; cf. B. Comrie, *Language Universals and Language Typology* (Chicago: University of Chicago, 1981).

27. For the psychological correlates of this distinction, see Greenberg, *New Invitation to Linguistics*, 109–14.

usually (though not always) with the meaning "plural." Hebrew has a double set of markedness contrasts for number. Singular is unmarked in opposition to plural, and singular and plural together are unmarked in opposition to dual. This double scheme can have a straightforward representation: singular יוֹם is one syllable, plural יָמִים is two syllables, dual יֹמָ֫יִם is three syllables. Markedness is not always so simple, and the mark is not always so clearly an added feature or element.[28] In terms of higher linguistic units, the structure of a marked opposition is often difficult to work out. The medieval Hebrew grammarians saw the stem system as divided between *Qal* 'light' and the derived or 'heavy' stems. This is a markedness opposition, since all the derived stems have some additional mark. It is not, however, obvious what linguistic conclusions follow from this conception.[29]

One of the bases of markedness theory is found in the lexicon. The unmarked form   f
of a word that can be inflected is the *dictionary* or *citation form*. In a lexicon of English one turns to 'day' to investigate the forms *days* and *day's*, and to 'daze' for *dazed* and *dazes*. In word-based lexicons of Hebrew (those in the Koehler-Baumgartner mold), the citation form of the word is basic, while in traditional Semitic lexicons (including the Gesenius dictionaries of Hebrew) the words are further categorized by the citation forms of the roots. It is important not to mistake the forms used in lexicons for actual un-marked forms, since lexicons must make a variety of compromises between the most economical representation of the words and the practical needs of users. Rather, we can say that the idea of the unmarked form of a word grew out of the idea of the citation form; spelling conventions also played a role in shaping the concept of markedness.[30]

Variation   3.4

Language varies along the same parameters as other aspects of human culture, that   a
is, it varies through time, according to geographical, social, and political context, and in

---

28. Multiple-markedness systems can take various forms, often involving a notion of *neutralization*. For example, we might oppose English 'man' and 'woman' as unmarked: marked, with 'human' as neutral (i.e., for the 'mark' of gender). On the relation between unmarked forms and the zero (German *Null*) morpheme, see Richter, *GAHG* 1. 104–30.

29. A related and still more difficult matter is the fact that languages differ in the extent to which they mark phenomena: "The practical workings of language also re-quire such minimal grammatical meanings as the past tense. And they require a minimal logical symbolism that has to include, for instance, negation, class inclusion, con-junction, and various kinds of levels of non-contradiction within discourse. The logical and syntactic operations . . . differ greatly from one language to the next in their status and frequency. For example, Homeric Greek has more overt logical operators and they are more frequent than is

the case in Classical Hebrew. Similarly, we find enormous differences between speakers of the same language when it comes to the frequency and status of minimal grammatical and logical meanings"; Paul Friedrich, *The Language Parallax* (Austin: University of Texas, 1986) 125.

30. The application of markedness within the lexicon is most successful in dealing with well-bounded semantic fields, e.g., kinship terms (Greenberg, *New Invitation to Linguistics*, 79–80) and color terms (pp. 82–83). On color terms in Hebrew (in all phases of the language, despite the title), see A. Brenner, *Colour Terms in the Old Testament* (Journal for the Study of the Old Testament Supplement 21; Sheffield: JSOT Press, 1982). For a model study in precision, again related to *realia* (readily identified ele-ments of the ordinary world) of meat, fish, and bread, see P. Swiggers, "The Meaning of the Root *LḤM* 'Food' in the Semitic Languages," *Ugarit-Forschungen* 13 (1981) 307–8.

conjunction with the age, gender, and relationship of the users.[31] Historical variation is the most obvious sort: our English is not Shakespeare's, and Modern Hebrew is not the language of Ezekiel. We have discussed some features of the history of Hebrew in Chapter 1, and there we alluded to the opposition *synchronic:diachronic*. In Saussure's view, the study of a given state of a language at a given time (synchronic study) is an endeavor different from the study of the relationship of various states of a language (diachronic study). As we argued earlier, a variety of problems makes a strictly synchronic or diachronic study of Biblical Hebrew difficult.[32] Despite the standardization and homogeneity reflected in the biblical text, it is possible to appreciate aspects of historical change within it. Since the Second World War, linguists have come to appreciate many other kinds of variation in language use, and these, too, may be relevant to the study of Hebrew.

b   Change over time and variation due to other circumstances reflect diversities in a community of speakers. Some changes, called "free variations," reflect spontaneous or nonsystematic variations that arise as speakers utter a language. All other forms of change ultimately reflect either linguistically or culturally conditioned variation. Some changes reflect analogies within the system: if the plural of 'rat' is 'rats,' a child might pluralize 'mouse' as 'mouses.' The form 'rooves,' on analogy to 'loaves,' has acquired some currency in American English, and 'have went' sometimes replaces 'have gone.'[33] In cultural terms, words disappear from use as the things they name become unimportant; English 'jesses' is usually seen in Shakespeare rather than heard in reference to hawks and falcons. Contrariwise, new things bring new words: a German institution led to the borrowing of 'kindergarten,' and the musical vocabulary of English is largely Italian in origin ('soprano, piano, pianissimo'). Social change is reflected in new uses such as 'gay' and coinages such as 'house husband' and 'latchkey child.' Technology is ever changing: the old vocabulary of hydrology ('milldam, millstream, waterwheel') has disappeared; a new vocabulary of fabrics ('nylon, cotton-poly blend, permanent press') has appeared. Commerce is also a factor: 'muslin' (cf. Mosul) and 'scallion' (cf. Ashqelon) came to Europe from the Near East.[34]

c   Poetic traditions (and to a lesser extent all literary traditions) preserve older vocabulary and grammatical forms that have been lost from ordinary speech and plain prose. The lexical and morphological resources thus tend to be larger. These linguistic facts

---

31. See Greenberg, *New Invitation to Linguistics*, 61–96, and some of the essays in E. Haugen and M. Bloomfield, eds., *Language as a Human Problem* (New York: Norton, 1974), esp. Dell Hymes, "Speech and Language" (pp. 45–71). On the work of Antoine Meillet, a major theorist of language as a social fact, see P. Swiggers, "La Conception du changement linguistique chez Antoine Meillet," *Folia Linguistica Historica* 7 (1986) 21–30. Meillet distinguishes three types of variation: dialectal, stylistic (reflecting special contexts and uses), and externally conditioned (reflecting language contact and borrowing; here bilingualism plays a major role).

32. See further Hospers, "Teaching of Old Testament Hebrew," 192–93. The problem cited here is of a pragmatic order; there is also the problem of where language change comes from. It must, in some sense, be built into the language as an object of synchronic study.

33. Greenberg, *New Invitation to Linguistics*, 64.

34. There is no up-to-date study of loanwords in Biblical Hebrew. M. Ellenbogen, *Foreign Words in the Old Testament* (London: Luzac, 1962), is badly outdated. A model treatment of loans and their context is S. A. Kaufman, *The Akkadian Influences on Aramaic* (Assyriological Studies 19; Chicago: The Oriental Institute, 1974); cf. M. O'Connor, "The Arabic Loanwords in Nabatean Aramaic," *Journal of Near Eastern Studies* 45 (1986) 213–29.

interact in complex ways with other structural features of Hebrew verse. It is important
to see the grammar *in poetry* in the context of Hebrew grammar. Loose notions of a
special vocabulary and grammar *of poetry* are linguistically uninformed.[35]

A major source of variation is geography, although geographical variation is fre-   d
quently also determined by other factors as well. It is customary to call geographically
distinct language systems *dialects*, and to speak of a language as a group of mutually
intelligible dialects. This terminological distinction should not be taken too seriously:
languages and dialects overlap and interlock in various ways. Some types of English are
not intelligible to one another, but a common tradition of writing and culture binds them
together. A priori we would expect that the geographical area of southern Palestine
would have been linguistically diverse in ancient times, particularly since social instruments of standardization were not well developed. Some of the inscriptional evidence
supports this expectation, as does the biblical text to a slight degree. Most of Biblical
Hebrew is, in fact, in the dialect of Jerusalem, and little material remains to fill in the
dialect geography of the surrounding areas.

The Bible does itself bear witness to regional linguistic differences among the Israel-   e
ites, in Judges 12. The Ephraimites in Cisjordan could not pronounce *šibbolet* in the
same way as the Gileadites in Transjordan. The Ephraimite variant, *sibbolet*, was used as
a linguistic marker: a Gileadite, suspecting someone of being Ephraimite, would test that
person by pointing to an ear of corn (or perhaps a stream; *šibbolet* means both) and
asking what he called it. Using the Ephraimite *s* would cost the speaker's life.[36] There is
evidence of a north–south split as well (cf. 1.4.1). Traces of non-Jerusalemite Hebrew
can be found in biblical passages associated with the northern kingdom; such passages
may refer to northerners (the Elijah stories) or even Phoenicians (Psalm 45), they may
quote northerners (Amos), or they may be attributed to northerners (Hosea). Linguistic
study of such passages is aided by epigraphic remains from both Israel and Phoenicia.

Other sources of linguistic variation seem to have left even fewer traces in the Bible,   f
but further study may be fruitful. Some factors may be mentioned. First, urban *versus*
rural: non-urban speech is often more conservative than that of city dwellers, especially
elite or educated groups. Second, male *versus* female and subordinate *versus* master: the
different social situations of the genders and classes may affect their speech. Third, young
versus old: the historical development of language is enacted bit by bit in the speech of
all speakers as they master a language and mature in it. The study of these and other
linguistic types of variations in the Bible is complicated by questions of genre and literary usage.

---

35. See D. A. Robertson, *Linguistic Evidence in Dating Early Hebrew Poetry* (Society of Biblical Literature Dissertation Series 3; Missoula: Scholars Press, 1972); M. O'Connor, *Hebrew Verse Structure* (Winona Lake, Indiana: Eisenbrauns, 1980); A. Berlin, *The Dynamics of Biblical Parallelism* (Bloomington: Indiana University, 1985); E. L. Greenstein, "Aspects of Biblical Poetry," *Jewish Book Annual* 44 (1986–87) 33–42.

36. The point about how the test was carried out was made by W. J. Martin in discussions with us. On the linguistic change involved, see the views of E. A. Speiser summarized in R. G. Boling, *Judges* (Anchor Bible 6A; Garden City, New York: Doubleday, 1975) 212–13.

g   We speak of Biblical Hebrew grammar as a single system because variations and dialects seem to exist within a single language, and no feature of the diversity of that language is surprising in light of our knowledge of modern languages. Speakers of the American English dialects that distinguish the vowels of 'pin' and 'pen' have little trouble understanding speakers who do not, those from the Appalachians, the Ozarks, and much of the Deep South. The lines dividing variation, dialect, and language are fuzzy, because accumulated variations lead to dialects, and divergent dialects lead to languages. Other cultural factors play a role in the real-world situation. Ephraimites and Gileadites, in spite of their different pronunciations, communicated with one another in a common language. Speakers of American English display rich variations in their linguistic utterances and in their literary expression; nevertheless they communicate their thoughts and experiences through a common language. So also the speakers encountered in the Hebrew Scriptures communicated their messages to a common audience in spite of variations. Those who share a common culture and politic tend to keep a common linguistic structure. We aim in this grammar to focus not on variations within Biblical Hebrew but on the common systems; we do not doubt that the grammar of any given body of material or author would be revealing.

3.5   Understanding

a   In the course of this chapter we have reviewed a number of the basic concepts of modern linguists. Here we consider two pairs of concepts and briefly touch on a question behind grammar and exegesis, the question of how people understand one another across the "barrier" of different languages. This question is at the juncture of all the human sciences.

b   A Saussurian pairing developed for linguistic analysis is *syntagm* and *paradigm*. The term syntagm is introduced above. The word paradigm is familiar in its ordinary sense of an ordered list of inflectional forms; the Saussurian usage is slightly different. In his terms, relations between the linguistic elements in the linear flow of speech (i.e., the ordered arrangement of phonemes and morphemes as they occur in the speech act) are *syntagmatic*; relations between linguistic items not present in this ordered arrangement in the act of speaking are *paradigmatic*. The two categories represent two basically different modes of organizing linguistic material. For example, we can distinguish a linear sequence or syntagmatic relation such as "noun + attributive adjective" in Hebrew. The paradigmatic categories involved here are the class of nouns and the class of attributive adjectives. Consider these groups:

nouns	attributive adjectives
אִישׁ	עִבְרִי
בַּת	טוֹב
גָּמָל	נָבָל
דָּבָר	רִאשׁוֹן

Each group is a sample of the paradigmatic classes, and since the classes are those specified in the syntagmatic relation "noun + attributive adjective," all sixteen possible combinations would be syntagmatically available. The phrases with בַּת would require that the adjective be in the feminine gender. We cannot be sure that phrases not actually attested would be good Hebrew; גָּמָל נָבָל might have seemed redundant—are not all camels foolish? Such a judgment would be a matter of semantics.

Scholars have long suspected that a sentence may have structural features which,   c
though not apparent in the surface form, are basic to it. Noam Chomsky distinguished between "surface structure" and "deep structure." He defined the surface structure of a sentence as the linear sequence of elements; the deep structure, which need not be identical with the surface structure, is seen as a more abstract representation of grammatical relations. The distinction between these two levels of language has been responsible for the enormous amount of linguistic thinking carried out under the heading of generative-transformational grammar and various more recent developments.

M. A. K. Halliday has observed that the two sets of distinctions we have just   d
reviewed are similar. The syntagmatic side of language use is revealed in the surface structure, what Halliday calls "chain"; in fact, Halliday has proposed that all structure is surface, and all "choice," systematic consideration of the paradigmatic, is deep. Language structure, then, would be the device for realizing in physical, sequential representation the choices made in nonsequential, abstract deep grammar.[37]

These oppositions—syntagmatic/paradigmatic, surface structure/deep structure,   e
chain/choice—are parts of larger and more sophisticated theories of how language works. They allow us to sketch a view of the transcultural problem, the problem of how communication gets across the language divide. Let us take one formulation of the problem.[38] The British anthropologist Bronislaw Malinowski's fieldwork in Polynesia led him to think that the "translating" of terms and texts from the language of one culture to the language of another is impossible. Speaking absolutely this is true, because both extra-linguistic reality and the intra-linguistic expression of it are socio-culturally conditioned. Nevertheless, on the deeper level of language there seems to be a common bond among people enabling them to communicate adequately with one another and to objectify their socio-cultural differences. This bond is based in part on the commonalities of deep structural grammar. Malinowski himself was not anti-universalistic. He wrote: "It would be both preposterous and intellectually pusillanimous to give up at the outset any search for deeper forces which must have produced [the] common, universally human features of language."[39] More recently, Chomsky has been even more pointed in his advocacy of the study of universal grammar. John Lyons explains:

---

37. On Halliday's association of surface structure with chain (or syntagmatic relations) and deep structure with choice (or paradigmatic relations), see Kress, *Halliday*, 84–87.

38. Another formulation of linguistic determinism is associated with the Americans Benjamin Lee Whorf and Edward Sapir (who was acquainted with Hebrew); see the discussion of Greenberg, *New Invitation to Linguistics*, 80–83.

39. Quoted in Kress, *Halliday*, xx.

A few years ago the majority of linguists would have rejected the possibility of constructing a universal theory of grammatical categories. This is no longer so. As Chomsky has pointed out: "modern work . . . has shown a great diversity in the surface structures of languages", but "the deep structures for which universality is claimed may be quite distinct from the surface structures of sentences as they actually appear". It follows that "the findings of modern linguistics . . . are not inconsistent with the hypotheses of universal grammarians". Once again Roger Bacon's famous statement about universal grammar is being quoted with approval by linguists: "Grammar is substantially the same in all languages, even though it may vary accidentally."[40]

Since there are many things and experiences in the extra-linguistic realm that people share universally, Bacon's medieval view is perhaps not surprising.[41] Thus in part because of the universal properties of language in its deeper, abstract, non-physical dimension, we, as speakers and readers of English, are able to understand Hebrew.

---

40. Lyons, *Theoretical Linguistics*, 333. The exact history of the idea of general grammar as distinct from particular grammar is much disputed. The respective roles of the Port Royal grammarians (17th century) and the French Encyclopedists (18th century) are discussed by S. F. D. Hughes, "Salutary Lessons from the History of Linguistics," *The Real-World Linguist*, ed. P. C. Bjarkman and V. Raskin (Norwood, New Jersey: Ablex, 1986) 306–22; and P. Swiggers, "L'Encyclopédie et la grammaire," *Acta Linguistica Hafniensa* 20 (1987) 119–56, esp. 127–31.

41. Since languages are codes for a message, there is *in theory* (but only in theory) no reason why sentences in different languages cannot be semantic equivalents: "For two sentences of different languages to be exact translations of each other they must be semantically related to other sentences of their respective languages in exactly the same way"; E. L. Keenan, "Logic and Language," *Language as a Human Problem*, ed. E. Haugen and M. Bloomfield (New York: Norton, 1974) 187–96, at 193.

4

Grammatical Units

Introduction   4.1

Traditional grammatical theory operates with two fundamental units: the *word* and   a
the *sentence*. Linguists associate the word with minimal units of meaning called *morphemes* (see 3.3.2). Intermediate between the word and the sentence, grammarians commonly recognize *phrases* and *clauses*. These five units are related by way of composition. A unit has a "higher rank" if it is composed of other units; the units stand in order of descending rank: sentence, clause, phrase, word, morpheme. A particular linguistic form may stand in several ranks: frequently a morpheme is a word, that is, words are often monomorphemic. A word may even be a clause or sentence. In 2 Kings 4, Elisha instructs Gehazi to approach the Shunammite and say,

הֲשָׁלוֹם לָךְ הֲשָׁלוֹם לְאִישֵׁךְ   Are you well? Is your husband well? Is the boy well?
הֲשָׁלוֹם לַיָּלֶד   2 Kgs 4:26

The woman replies with the single word,

שָׁלוֹם   (We are all) well.
    2 Kgs 4:26

This reply may be considered a word, a clause (of a reduced type treated below), and a simple sentence. This element of overlap among the units is often useful in analysis. Since higher units depend on lower units, we shall present them in ascending order. Having already clarified the notion of morpheme, we begin in this chapter with the *word*.

4.2   Word

4.2.1   Definition

a   The word is a unit of language consisting of one or more spoken sounds (or their written representation) that can stand as a complete utterance or can be separated from the elements that accompany it in an utterance by other such units; words are composed of one morpheme or several morphemes.[1] In the latter case the morphemes are often combined into a word by linking conditions, for example, in English the loss of primary accent that distinguishes *bláckbird* from *bláck bírd*. Some morphemes are always linked or bound and never occur in isolation: this is true of affixes in Hebrew—for example, in שָׁבְרָה 'she broke' the suffix ה‍ָ- 'she' is bound to a form of a verbal root. In other cases the morpheme may occur in isolation. Some morphemes are joined by the loss of accentuation or *proclisis* (leaning forward, viz., of one word on another); the word that loses its accent is said to be proclitic. Proclisis is marked in the MT by *maqqeph*, as in עַל־פְּנֵי 'upon the face of' (Gen 1:2). Proclisis is common with the monosyllabic prepositions and particles, for example, אֶל, עַל, עַד, עִם, מִן, פֶּן, and the negative אַל. Words are distinguished in speaking by stress, accent, or tone and in writing by spaces. Words are typically thought of as representing an indivisible concept, action, or feeling; such a notional definition is too imprecise to be useful.

b   Words can be defined phonologically or grammatically. For example, *down* is phonologically the same word in the sentences 'He ran *down* the hill' and 'She stroked the soft *down* on his cheek'; grammatically the occurrences involve two words which have different meanings (i.e., representing a spatial relationship and an entity, respectively) and enter into different contrastive and combinatorial functions in the language; the two *downs* cannot be syntactically interchanged with each other. The homophony of the two words is largely incidental to basic grammatical study. Grammatically, words function by referring to an extra-linguistic reality or by serving as part of the intra-linguistic code (3.2.2).

4.2.2   Parts of Speech

a   Words can be classified according to the way they function (i.e., according to their distribution) in the higher units, phrase, clause, and sentence. This classification refers to

---

1. On the problem of defining "word," see P. Swiggers, "Le Mot: Unité d'intégration," *Études de linguistique générale et de linguistique latine . . . Guy Serbat* (Paris: Société pour l'Information Grammaticale, 1987) 57–66. The definition must refer to morphology (one or more morphemes), syntax (a syntactic function), and phonology (cannot be broken down). There is no workable basis for strictly notional or semantic definitions. Notwithstanding the definitions given, there are linguists who seek to drop the term "word" completely (notably André Martinet) and many others avoid it (Swiggers, "Le Mot," 57–58); the terms "syllable" and "sentence" are similarly difficult.

the syntagmatic relations among the various types of words and the various word orders possible in higher units. In English, 'black dog' is an acceptable phrase, 'dog black' is not. Similarly, the combining of words in the following English sentences is acceptable:

> The black dog bites cruelly.
> The brown chimpanzee eats heartily.
> The strong wind blew furiously.

On the other hand one never finds the sentences,

> Dog the bites black.
> The heartily chimpanzee eats brown.
> The strong blew wind furiously.
> Bit ate opened.

'The' occurs with some words and not with others, and the same sort of restrictions are found for the other words. By noting words that can occur in comparable environments we can group words into classes. On formal grounds we can group the words in these sentences as

> T class: *the*
> W class: *black, brown, strong*
> X class: *dog, chimpanzee, wind*
> Y class: *bites, eats, blew*
> Z class: *cruelly, heartily, furiously*

b   Traditionally, grammarians call the *T class* "the article," the *W class* "the adjective," the *X class* "the noun," the *Y class* "the verb," the *Z class* "the adverb." Such a formal system of categorization yields parts-of-speech groups. Words belonging to a part-of-speech class can be analyzed into semantic subclasses. For example, 'dog' and 'chimpanzee' can occur with the verbs 'bite' and 'eat' but not with 'blew,' whereas 'wind' can occur with 'blew' and not with 'bite' and 'eat' (except metaphorically). On the basis of distribution we can analyze *Noun class* into *Noun (a) class* and *Noun (b) class*. We aim here not to exhaust the possible classes into which words can be categorized but to explain how such categorization is done on both formal and semantic grounds.

c   Grammarians have abstracted notional values for these classes; for example, the noun class, it is said, typically signifies persons, places, and things; the adjective class attributes a quality to the noun; etc. Semantic subclasses are also described according to notional values. Members of the *Noun (a) class* cited above belong to the class of "animate nouns," while the example of the *Noun (b) class* is an "inanimate noun." The way in which word classes are notionally labeled is a matter distinct from the linguistic procedures used to isolate the classes; the labels may be in themselves misleading. By "parts of speech" we mean both the classes to which words belong on formal distributional grounds and the abstract, common notion belonging to the class. In Hebrew, the principal parts of speech are noun and verb; adjectives belong to the class of nouns, along with substantives; adverbs are a small class. The categories of preposition and conjunction overlap; these two, along with some adverbs, are often simply called particles. The class of exclamations and interjections, for example, הוֹי 'woe,' חָלִ֫ילָה 'far be it!,' נָא 'I pray,' is of lesser importance.[2]

d   The parts of speech have mixed definitions, in part based on semantic or referential factors and in part based on various formal features. There is no single universal scheme of the parts of speech, and no universal set of matchings between the parts of speech and syntagms more complicated than phrases. Since syntax, as we are presenting it here, is the systematic study of how words are used, some aspects of the history of word classification are worth mentioning. The word-class system goes back to Hellenistic times (its continuity with earlier, Near Eastern models remains unexplored), and, although grammatical papyri from Egypt show that the system assumed many different forms, tradition assigns it to Dionysius Thrax (ca. 100 B.C.E.). The whole scheme reflects both classical and later Stoic philosophical thought, but Dionysius and the papyri authors are properly grammarians rather than philosophers.[3] There is a threefold base: Greek *onoma* 'the naming,' *rhēma* 'the speaking,' and *syndesmos* 'the binding'; under these three headings we can arrange the eight categories of Dionysius:

class	*part of speech*
the naming	1. name (i.e., noun)
	2. interjection
	3. adverb[4]
the speaking	4. speaking (i.e., verb)
	5. participle
the binding[5]	6. preposition
	7. conjunction
	8. pronoun

The first category includes both nouns and adjectives, while # 8 covers articles as well as pronouns. If noun and adjective are separated, and verb and participle combined, this scheme, of the Hellenistic age, comes close to those still in use in many teaching grammars of the European languages.[6]

e   The medieval grammarians of Arabic and Hebrew used only three parts of speech, corresponding to the three general headings above: Arabic *ism* 'name; noun'; *fiᶜl* 'act;

---

2. If we distinguish "content" and "function" words (3.2.2), nouns and verbs are roughly equivalent to "content" words and particles are "function" words. H. Irsigler takes nouns and verbs as *Hauptwörter* ('principal words') and conjunctions, prepositions, pronouns, adverbs, and interjections as *Funktionswörter* ('function words'); see *Einführung in das biblische Hebräisch* (St. Ottilien: EOS, 1978), 1. 49. For further preliminaries to Hebrew word classification, see Richter, *GAHG* 1, esp. 43–45, 64–65; for a technical survey (notably good on particles and pronouns), pp. 80–91; see further below on Richter's word-class scheme.

3. See *MPD* 9–12 (R. H. Robins).

4. The term "adverb" here refers to content-full adverbs; see, on the various possible definitions of the category, *MPD* 44, 54, 67 (P. Swiggers); 80 (A. Martinet); 93, 96 (W. P. Schmid).

5. Dionysius listed these and only these as closed categories; see *MPD* 29–30 (Robins).

6. See Robins in *MPD* 9–37; and P. Swiggers, "L'Encyclopédie et la grammaire," *Acta Linguistica Hafniensa* 20 (1987) 119–56, esp. 134–36; "Le mot comme unité linguistique dans la théorie grammaticale au dix-huitième siècle," *Indogermanische Forschungen* 91 (1986) 1–26.

verb'; and *ḥarf* (plural *ḥurūf*) 'motion; particle.'[7] This simpler scheme should not be taken to indicate that the Semitic languages lack the problem areas of the European classical languages, but simply that their grammarians erected a foundation lower to the ground. Some of the problem areas as they are reflected in Hebrew can be mentioned. First, proper nouns (names) seem different in character from other nouns (Latin *nomina*), and, among these, substantives are different from adjectives (though less different than in most European languages); numbers, further, seem a special sort of adjective. Second, some verb forms are used as nouns (verbal nouns, i.e., the two infinitives and participles). In some respects adjectives are more like verbs than nouns: nouns (and pronouns) are determined in themselves while verbs and adjectives are only determined in relation to nouns or noun equivalents; they refer to accidents (in the philosophical sense). Third, most of the particles are unchanging in form, but some vary, and a few nomina and verbs are unvarying. Some particles refer to the immediate context (e.g., adverbs), while others refer to a larger, discourse context (e.g., conjunctions). If we bear these considerations in mind, it is easy to see how the traditional European list developed and easy, too, to appreciate Wolfgang Richter's classification for Hebrew:[8]

> verb
> verbal noun (infinitive; participle)
> nomen (substantive; adjective; numeral)
> proper name
> pronoun
> particle (adverb; preposition; conjunction; modal
>   word, e.g., negative; article; interjection)

f It is not our purpose to defend a particular list, however, but rather to point to the usefulness of a word-class approach, despite its mixed origins. These origins could be covered up or transcended, if strictly formal indicators were found to replace the referential factors. We have not done so because the weight of the traditional witness is part of our assurance that the word classes facilitate the mapping and understanding of syntax. Because the referential background of terms like "nouns" and "verbs" remains, the difficulty of moving from word class to syntagm arises again and again. The alternative, we believe, is a grammar in which the elements combine smoothly into syntagms, but the elements are themselves not recognizable to readers without special preparation in a narrow and (usually) new theoretical framework. A strictly syntagmatic (or strictly paradigmatic) framework would be less accessible and, we suspect, less amenable to "working with no data" (in T. O. Lambdin's phrase).

g One drawback of a conservative, part-of-speech approach to syntax is that it may lead to fragmentation of organization (we have tried to avoid this as much as possible)

---

7. See the references in Chapter 1 as well as M. O'Connor, *Hebrew Verse Structure* (Winona Lake, Indiana: Eisenbrauns, 1980) 68. The three-way division is also found in the Latin grammatical tradition.

8. From Richter, *GAHG* 1. 156–94. For a modern scheme based on a broad base of languages and a vigorous defense of the approach, see W. P. Schmid in *MPD* 85–99.

and to the loss of overarching generalizations and regularities. The approach tends to separate and isolate syntactic phenomena, in some ways the opposite of a discourse grammar. Certain phenomena that cut across the various categories are not given their due. Congruence or agreement is the feature that holds phrases and clauses together, the basis of all syntagmatic patterns. Inflection is the feature that creates the diversity of verbal and (to a lesser extent) nominal forms, the basis of paradigmatic patterns. A grammar of Hebrew that began with congruence and inflection would be a quite different grammar than we have written.

4.3   Phrase and Clause

a   A *phrase* is, in one sense, a group of words used as an equivalent of a single word class.[9] Consider the earlier example sentence, 'The brown chimpanzee eats heartily,' alongside the sentence, 'The brown chimpanzee eats with zeal'; 'with zeal,' a group of words, follows the same distribution pattern and has the same grammatical value as 'heartily,' in the sense that both modify a verb. Thus, just as 'heartily' is an adverb, 'with zeal' is an "adverbial phrase." In the sentence, 'The dog with shaggy hair bites cruelly,' the group of words 'with shaggy hair' functions like the adjective 'black' in the sentence, 'The black dog bites cruelly.' We call a group of words that function like an adjective an "adjectival phrase." There are similarly nominal phrases, verbal phrases, etc.

b   Another, distinct sense of *phrase* is also useful. In this sense a phrase includes a governing word and all it governs. A prepositional phrase is a preposition and its object; a participial phrase is a participle and the words it governs, whether in construct or through a preposition; and a construct phrase includes all the nouns in a construct chain.

c   We noted in Chapter 3 that language serves as a medium or code by which a speaker communicates thoughts or experiences to an audience. A *clause* designates an utterance in which the speaker makes a comment on a topic. The topic is called "the subject" and the comment "the predicate."[10] The subject is expressed by a noun or an equivalent; the predicate of a verbal clause is a verb or an equivalent, while that of a verbless clause is a complementing noun.

d   A clause is the syntactic combination of a subject and predicate. The subject or predicate may be compound, as in, 'The dog and the chimpanzee bit cruelly' (compound subject) or 'The dog bit and ate its victim cruelly' (compound predicate) or 'The dog and the chimpanzee bit and ate their victims cruelly' (compound subject, compound predicate). Each of these utterances consists of a single topic and a single comment about it. In contrast, the sentence, 'The dog was eating its victim when the chimpanzee arrived,'

---

9. On word combinations and phrases (*Wortgruppe*), see Richter, *GAHG* 2. 3–4; on phrase types and agreement with them, *GAHG* 2. 9–69, 3. 14–34.

10. The distinction of subject/predicate ~ onoma/rhēma ~ topic/comment goes back to Plato's *Sophist*. The various sets of terms are not always mutually equivalent. Some authors take *subject/predicate* as properly terms of logic. Some take *topic/comment* as properly referring to a larger discourse structure (cf. 4.8). The functions involved in this set of oppositions can, if taken from an extra-linguistic perspective, be seen as variously distributed in the parts of a given utterance. It is sometimes argued that the *subject/predicate* relation can involve predication or determination (or even coordination); see 8.4 on verbless clauses. Cf. on this topic Swiggers, "L'Encyclopédie," 133–34, 138–43.

consists of two clauses; the utterance contains two separate topics (subjects), each with its own comment (predicates). The two clauses together constitute a sentence, a term we discuss below. When a sentence consists of only one clause it is called a "simple sentence"; when it consists of more than one clause it is called a "compound" or "complex" sentence, depending on how the clauses within the sentence are joined (38.1).

In addition to subject and predicate the clause may include modifiers of either of   e
these elements, and conjunctions may show a clause's relationship to other clauses or sentences. Modifiers or complements may be either necessary (nuclear) or omissible (peripheral); they may be *adjectival* or *adverbial*.

Subject   4.4

Expressions of the Subject   4.4.1

A noun, noun equivalent, or complex nominal construction may express the topic.   a
A part of speech other than a noun that functions in a clause as a noun is called a *noun equivalent*. Here are examples of a substantive or noun equivalent functioning as a grammatical subject.

(1) *Substantive* (8.3)

       1.   וְהַנָּחָשׁ הָיָה עָרוּם   Now *the serpent* was crafty.
                                               Gen 3:1

(2) *Pronoun* (16.3.2)

       2.   וְהוּא יִמְשָׁל־בָּךְ   *He* will rule over you.
                                                 Gen 3:16

(3) *Adjective* (14.3.3)

       3.   חָכָם יָרֵא וְסָר מֵרָע   (*The*) *wise* (*one*) fears and turns from evil.
                                                 Prov 14:16

(4) *Participle* (37.2)

       4.   הַמֵּתָה תָמוּת   *The dying* (*one*) will die.
                                                 Zech 11:9

(5) *Infinitive absolute* (35.3.3)

       5.   אָכֹל דְּבַשׁ הַרְבּוֹת לֹא־טוֹב   *To eat* too much honey is not good.
                                                 Prov 25:27

(6) *Infinitive construct* (36.2)

       6.   הַמְעַט קַחְתֵּךְ אֶת־אִישִׁי   Was it a small matter that *you stole* my husband?
                                                 (lit., Was *your stealing* of my husband. . . ?)
                                                 Gen 30:15

       7.   וְאִם רַע בְּעֵינֵיכֶם לַעֲבֹד   If *serving* YHWH seems bad to you. . . .
                                        אֶת־יהוה   Josh 24:15

(7) *Adverb*

8. הַרְבֵּה נָפַל מִן־הָעָם   *Many* fell from the troops.
                              2 Sam 1:4

b   Complex nominal constructions—noun phrase, prepositional phrase, clause—may also express the subject. (1) In *noun phrases* two or more nouns are bound together in one of the following ways:

(a) *apposition*, the asyndetic juxtaposition of two or more nouns with a single extra-linguistic referent

9. וַיְהִי אִישׁ לֵוִי גָּר בְּיַרְכְּתֵי   There was *a man, a Levite, a sojourning* (one) in the
    הַר־אֶפְרַיִם   flanks of the Ephraimite hill country.
                                          Judg 19:1

(b) *hendiadys*, the juxtaposition of two nouns with a single referent, with or without the conjunction; compare with # 10 English 'assault and battery.'

10. חָמָס וָשֹׁד יִשָּׁמַע בָּהּ   *Violence and destruction* resound in her.
                                   Jer 6:7

(c) *coordination* (a compound subject), the coordination of several nouns with different referents

11. וַיִּתְחַבֵּא הָאָדָם וְאִשְׁתּוֹ   *The man and his wife* hid themselves.
                                        Gen 3:8

(d) *construct relationship*

12. וַתִּפָּקַחְנָה עֵינֵי שְׁנֵיהֶם   *The eyes of both of them* were opened.
                                        Gen 3:7

(2) A *prepositional phrase* used as a subject is usually a *partitive phrase*, introduced by מִן 'from,' either in such phrases as '(some) from' or, after a negative, '(not even one) from.'[11]

13. וַיִּז מִדָּמָהּ אֶל־הַקִּיר   And *some of her blood* spattered on the wall.
                                    2 Kgs 9:33

(3) A *clause* often occurs as a subject of a verb of telling, knowing, or other mental activity.

14. וּלְשָׁאוּל הֻגַּד כִּי־נִמְלַט דָּוִד   *That David had escaped* was told to Saul.
                                              1 Sam 23:13

4.4.2   Indefinite Subject

a   Sometimes no particular person(s) is (are) in view as the topic of the sentence. In such cases of *indefinite subject*, English idiom, demanding in its surface structure that a

---

11. Cf. Exod 16:27; 2 Sam 11:17; negative, 2 Kgs 10:10.

noun or its equivalent express the subject, supplies a "dummy" subject, be it a noun (e.g., 'men,' 'people'), a pronoun ('they,' 'your'), or an adjective ('one'); none of these has a distinct extra-linguistic referent in view.

> *Men* fight and die for freedom.
> *They* told me you had an accident.
> *You* can only hope and wait.
> *One* looks for rain.

In Hebrew, indefinite subjects can be expressed by the bound form of the third-person pronoun with a finite verb; if a participle is used in such a construction, it is usually plural. The finite verb may be singular or plural, active (cf. 22.7) or passive; the plural active construction is the most common.

(1) *Third-person singular pronoun, active verbal form*

1. עַל־כֵּן קָרָא שְׁמָהּ בָּבֶל — Therefore *one* calls its name Babel (or, *men* or *people* call it Babel). Gen 11:9

(2) *Third-person singular pronoun, passive verbal form*

2. וְלֹא יוּכַל לִרְאֹת אֶת־הָאָרֶץ — *One* is unable to see the land. Exod 10:5

3. אָז הוּחַל לִקְרֹא בְּשֵׁם יהוה — At that time *people* began to call on the name of YHWH. Gen 4:26

(3) *Third-person plural pronoun, active verbal form*

4. כִּי מִן־הַבְּאֵר הַהִיא יַשְׁקוּ הָעֲדָרִים — because *they* watered the flocks from that well Gen 29:2

(4) *Plural participle*

5. וְאֶת־כָּל־נָשֶׁיךָ וְאֶת־בָּנֶיךָ מוֹצִאִים אֶל־הַכַּשְׂדִּים — *They* are bringing all your wives and children out to the Babylonians. Jer 38:23

The impersonal construction (in which the condition expressed by the predicate is the topic) is treated in 22.7a.

Predicate

4.5

The predicate is that part of the utterance making a comment about the subject. The term may be used broadly for the entire comment, including both the verb or equivalent, or alternatively the copula 'to be' (expressed or unexpressed) with a complement (a noun or adjective) *plus* modifying words; or it may be used more narrowly to exclude modifying words. Let us consider the possible types of predication without reference to modifying words.

a

b   In a *verbal clause* the predicate is a verb.

(1) *Finite verb*

1.   וַיֹּאמֶר אֱלֹהִים   And God *said*. . . .
Gen 1:3

(2) *Infinitive absolute* (35.5.2)

2.   זְרַעְתֶּם הַרְבֵּה וְהָבֵא מְעָט   You have sown much and *brought in* little.
Hag 1:6

(3) *Infinitive construct* (36.3.2)

3.   . . . יַעַן הַכְאוֹת לֵב־צַדִּיק   because you have *disheartened* (lit., struck the heart
וּלְחַזֵּק יְדֵי רָשָׁע   of) the righteous . . . and *encouraged* (lit.,
strengthened the hands of) the wicked
Ezek 13:22

Quasi-verbal indicators are particles denoting existence.

4.   יֵשׁ גֹּאֵל קָרוֹב מִמֶּנִּי   *There is* a kinsman-redeemer nearer than I.
Ruth 3:12

c   In a *verbless* (or nominal) *clause* there is no verbal marker of predication. Hebrew,
like many other languages, including Latin and Classical Greek, may predicate an adjective or noun directly, without a *copula* (i.e., some form of היה, which corresponds to
English 'to be'). In languages where the copula may be optional, it is usually required if
the comment is set in past or future time in contrast to present time (or in some mood
other than indicative), or if the situation is highlighted. The principal function of the
copula is thus to mark in the surface structure tense, mood, or aspect. John Lyons notes:

> [Any verb equivalent to] "*to be*" is not itself a constituent of deep structure, but a
> semantically-empty "dummy verb" generated by the grammatical rules of [certain lan-
> guages] for the specification of certain distinctions (usually "carried" by the verb) when
> there is no other verbal element to carry these distinctions. Sentences that are tem-
> porally, modally and aspectually "unmarked" . . . do not need the "dummy" carrier.[12]

The verbless clause is common in Hebrew. The following grammatical units may serve as
predicates in the deep structure of a sentence; they are said to "complement the subject"
of a verbless clause.

(1) *Noun* ("predicate nominative"; 8.4)

5.   עֵד הַגַּל הַזֶּה   This heap is a *witness*.
Gen 31:52

6.   מְרַגְּלִים אַתֶּם   You are *spies*.
Gen 42:9

---

12. John Lyons, *Introduction to Theoretical Linguistics* (Cambridge: Cambridge University, 1968) 322–23.

(2) *Indefinite adjective* ("predicate adjective"; 14.3.2)

7.	צַדִּיק אַתָּה	You are *righteous*. Jer 12:1

(3) *Pronoun* (16.3.3, 17.4.1)

8.	וְנַ֫חְנוּ מָה	Who are *we*? Exod 16:7

(4) *Adverb*

9.	כִּי זֶ֫בַח הַיָּמִים שָׁם	The annual sacrifice is *there*. 1 Sam 20:6

(5) *Adverbial prepositional phrase*

10.	לָ֫נוּ הַמַּ֫יִם	The water is *ours* (lit., the water is *to us*). Gen 26:20
11.	לֹא בָרַ֫עַשׁ יהוה	Yhwh was not *in the earthquake*. 1 Kgs 19:11

Modifiers   4.6

Adjectival Modifiers   4.6.1

An *adjectival modifier* is a construction that qualifies a noun or its equivalent. Such   a
a construction is "adnominal" ("to the noun"), in contrast to a construction that modifies
a verb (*ad-verbial*, "to the verb"). There are many ways in which nominal forms may be
qualified in the surface structure. Consider, for example, these phrases, all with shapes
attested in Hebrew (though not all the equivalents are attested).

adjective:	*foreign* gods
construct:	gods *of foreignness*
adjectival apposition:	gods, *the foreigners*
hendiadys:	gods *and foreigners*
prepositional phrase:	gods *in foreignness*
adverbial apposition:	gods (with reference to) *foreignness*
relative clause:	gods *that are foreign*
relative clause:	gods *belonging to foreigners*

The favored expression among these in Hebrew is a construct, אֱלֹהֵי הַנֵּכָר (Gen 35:2,
etc.). One of these shapes or constructions may be chosen either for reasons of style
or emphasis, or because of linguistic factors. Here are some examples of adjectival
constructions:

(1) *Adjective*

1.	וְהָלַכְתָּ אַחֲרֵי אֱלֹהִים אֲחֵרִים	. . . and (if) you follow *other* gods Deut 8:19

(2) *Participle*

2.   יהוה אֱלֹהֶיךָ אֵשׁ אֹכְלָה   YHWH your God is a *consuming* fire.
Deut 4:24

(3) *Pronominal suffix*

3.   וּבָנֶיךָ וְאִשְׁתְּךָ וּנְשֵׁי־בָנֶיךָ   *your* sons and *your* wife and the wives of *your* sons
Gen 6:18

(4) *Construct state*

4.   בִּנְאוֹת דֶּשֶׁא יַרְבִּיצֵנִי   He makes me lie down in pastures *of grass.*
Ps 23:2

(5) *Adverbial apposition* ("accusative of limitation"; 10.2.2)

5.   הַכְּרֻבִים זָהָב   the *golden* cherubim (lit., the cherubim *with reference to gold*)
1 Chr 28:18

(6) *Apposition*

6.   וַיֹּאמֶר קַיִן אֶל־הֶבֶל אָחִיו   Cain said to Abel *his brother.* . . .
Gen 4:8

(7) *Hendiadys*

7.   בְּאֹהֶל וּבְמִשְׁכָּן   with a *tent as my dwelling* (lit., a *tent and dwelling*)
2 Sam 7:6

(8) *Relative Clause* (with or without relative pronoun)

8.   וְכָל־אֲשֶׁר בָּאֹהֶל יִטְמָא   And everyone *who is in the tent* is unclean.
Num 19:14

9.   וַתִּתֵּן גַּם־לְאִישָׁהּ עִמָּהּ   And she also gave (some) to her husband (who was) *with her.*
Gen 3:6

10.   וְאִישׁ לֹא־אַכְרִית לְךָ   every one *of you* that I do not cut off (lit., a man [that] I do not cut off *belonging to you*)
1 Sam 2:33

4.6.2   Adverbial Modifiers

a   An adverbial modifier is a construction that modifies a verb or its equivalent. There are various kinds of adverbial constructions.

b   When *a noun* modifies a verb, it is said to be in "the accusative function," a construction treated in Chapter 10. Suffice it here to note that there are two principal types of accusative: direct object and adverbial.

1.   וַיִּבְרָא אֱלֹהִים אֶת־הָאָדָם   God created *hāʾādām* (direct object).
Gen 1:27

2.   רַק הַכִּסֵּא אֶגְדַּל מִמֶּךָ   *Only with respect to the throne* (adverbial) will I be greater than you. Gen 41:40

An *infinitive construct* (36.2.1) may be used as a direct object, as a verbal complement, or in a prepositional phrase.

3.   לֹא אֵדַע צֵאת וָבֹא   I do not know (how) *to go out* and *come in* (objects). 1 Kgs 3:7

4.   אוּלַי אוּכַל נַכֶּה־בּוֹ   Perhaps I will be able *to defeat them* (complement). Num 22:6

5.   בְּפִגְעוֹ־בוֹ הוּא יְמִיתֶנּוּ   *When he meets him* (prepositional phrase), he shall be put to death. Num 35:19

An *infinitive absolute* (35.3.3) may be used as a direct object or as an adverb.

6.   לִמְדוּ הֵיטֵב   Learn *to do well* (object). Isa 1:17

7.   קְבוּרַת חֲמוֹר יִקָּבֵר סָחוֹב וְהַשְׁלֵךְ   He will have the burial of a donkey—*dragged away* and *cast off* (adverbs). Jer 22:19

Other types of adverbial modifiers are these.   c

(1) *Adverbs* (Chap. 39)

8.   לֹא תֹאכַל מִמֶּנּוּ   You must *not* eat from it. Gen 2:17

(2) *Particles* (Chap. 40)

9.   גַּם־בָּרוּךְ יִהְיֶה   *Indeed* he will be blessed. Gen 27:33

(3) *Prepositional phrases* (Chap. 11)

10.   עַל־גְּחֹנְךָ תֵלֵךְ   You will crawl *on your belly*. Gen 3:14

(4) *Subordinate clauses* (Chap. 38)

11.   אֲשֶׁר אִם־צָדַקְתִּי לֹא אֶעֱנֶה   *Though I were innocent*, I could not answer (him). Job 9:15

In some cases a verb may modify another verb without being in a subordinate clause; the verb שוב is often used in this quasi-auxiliary function (39.3.1).

12.   וַיָּשָׁב יִצְחָק וַיַּחְפֹּר אֶת־בְּאֵרֹת

And Isaac *reopened* the wells (lit., Isaac *returned and opened* . . .).
Gen 26:18

4.7   Nominative Absolute and Vocative

a   In the clauses we have considered so far, the subject and the predicate have divided the clause between them. Some simple clauses contain other elements, the nominative absolute, which has no regular English equivalent, or the vocative.

b   The *nominative absolute* construction serves to highlight or focus one element of the main clause; it may serve in context to contrast this element to a comparable item in another clause. This construction (or family of constructions) has many names; it is called the *casus pendens* construction, the focus construction, and the topic-comment construction (the terms "topic" and "comment" are used here in a way slightly different than we have been using them).[13] Consider the clause תָּמִים דֶּרֶךְ הָאֵל, 'The way of God is perfect'; here the subject is דֶּרֶךְ הָאֵל and the predicate תָּמִים, in a verbless clause. The role of הָאֵל in the clause is not as prominent as it is in the similar clause with a nominative absolute, הָאֵל תָּמִים דַּרְכּוֹ, 'As for God, his way is perfect' (Ps 18:31).[14] Here the subject is דַּרְכּוֹ, and the predicate תָּמִים; the nominative absolute, הָאֵל, stands outside the clause, as an absolute entity. The relationship between the absolute and the clause is signaled by the initial position of the absolute and by the pronoun in the clause which refers back to it (in this example the וֹ of דַּרְכּוֹ); this pronoun, called *the resumptive pronoun*, is optional.

c   The absolute may be associated as possessor with the subject of the clause, as in Ps 18:31, where הָאֵל is the "possessor" of דַּרְכּוֹ, or in the following case:

1.   שְׁכֶם בְּנִי חָשְׁקָה נַפְשׁוֹ בְּבִתְּכֶם

As for *my son Shechem, his* soul clings to your daughter.
Gen 34:8

The absolute may also be associated as possessor with the direct object of the clause.

2.   שָׂרַי אִשְׁתְּךָ לֹא־תִקְרָא אֶת־שְׁמָהּ שָׂרָי

As for *Sarai your wife*, you shall not call *her* name Sarai.
Gen 17:15

The absolute may refer to the direct object of the clause or the object of a prepositional phrase in the clause.

---

13. *Casus pendens* is a term from Latin grammar; topic-comment is the term favored by European Arabists for a comparable construction in Arabic. The term nominative absolute corresponds to the genitive absolute of Greek and the ablative absolute of Latin; all three constructions are distinct. For the term focus, and on the grammar of vocatives and focus-marked clauses, as well as displacements, see O'Connor, *Hebrew Verse Structure*, 78–86. A full study is W. Gross, *Die Pendenskonstruction im biblischen Hebräisch* (St. Ottilien: EOS, 1987); reviewed by F. I. Andersen, *Biblica* 69 (1988) 436–39.

14. Linguists use the term *copying* to refer to the displacement of a nominal constituent from its basic position in the clause, accompanied by the replacement of it by a pronominal constituent; see P. M. Postal, *Cross-Over Phenomena* (New York: Harcourt, Brace, 1971) 135–37.

3.	אָנֹכִי בַּדֶּרֶךְ נָחַנִי יהוה	As for *me*, Yнwн led *me* (object) in the way. Gen 24:27
4.	שֹׁרֶשׁ יִשַׁי אֲשֶׁר עֹמֵד לְנֵס עַמִּים אֵלָיו גּוֹיִם יִדְרֹשׁוּ	As for *the root of Jesse* which stands as a banner for the people—the nations will rally to *it* (prepositional object). Isa 11:10
5.	הַמִּטָּה אֲשֶׁר־עָלִיתָ שָּׁם לֹא־תֵרֵד מִמֶּנָּה	As for *the bed* into which you climbed up, you shall not come down from *it* (prepositional object). 2 Kgs 1:4

In # 5 the אשר clause includes a resumptive adverb, שם. One reason other than emphasis for the use of the absolute construction is suggested by ## 4–5: it allows a grammatically complex part of the clause to stand on its own, thus increasing clarity. For similar reasons a complex subject may be shifted or displaced to precede the clause, sometimes being separated from it by a conjunction, as in # 6.

6.	כִּי מְעַט אֲשֶׁר־הָיָה לְךָ לְפָנַי וַיִּפְרֹץ לָרֹב	With respect to the little you had before I came, (*it*) has increased greatly. Gen 30:30

d   The *vocative* construction, familiar from English, is similar to the nominative absolute in being an element of the clause other than subject and predicate. Vocatives stand in apposition to the second-person pronoun, expressed or unexpressed, and may occur with either verbless or verbal clauses.

7.	צַדִּיק אַתָּה יהוה	You are righteous, *Yнwн*. Jer 12:1
8.	אֲדֹנִי אַתָּה נִשְׁבַּעְתָּ	*My lord*, you swore. . . . 1 Kgs 1:17
9.	הוֹשִׁעָה הַמֶּלֶךְ	Save (me), *O king*. 2 Sam 14:4

After a vocative, a modifying phrase or clause regularly uses the third-person pronoun (as also in Classical Arabic) and not the second-person pronoun as in English and other languages.[15]

10.	שִׁמְעוּ עַמִּים כֻּלָּם	Hear, O peoples, all of *you* (lit., all of *them*)! Mic 1:2

Sentence   4.8

a   The sentence has traditionally been defined as "a complete thought expressed in words." Such a definition fails in two ways. First, it defines the sentence only in notional

---

15. D. R. Hillers, *Micah* (Hermeneia; Philadelphia: Fortress, 1984) 16. He cites also Isa 44:23, 54:1; Ezek 21:30.

terms and not in descriptive terms, that is, one is not able to decide from the surface
structure when a thought has been completed. Second, it does not distinguish a sentence
from the extended discourse of which it is a part; one could say that an entire discourse
is a "complete thought expressed in words." Linguists have experienced as much difficulty as traditional grammarians in approaching this problem: "It must be admitted,"
writes F. I. Andersen, "that, in spite of constant discussion, no foolproof definition of
sentence has been achieved in theoretical linguistics."[16]

b   One way of developing descriptive criteria for defining the sentence relies on the
melodies and tonal stresses that accompany its words. A declarative sentence in English
is marked by dropping the tone at the end; the tone is raised at the end of an interrogative sentence. Melodic signals are expressed in writing by punctuation marks (periods,
question marks, exclamation points, etc.). Such an approach is of limited use in Biblical
Hebrew because the Masoretic accentuation system—though intended to mark off relationships of words in a chant—does not coincide precisely with the grammatical units.[17]

c   In his work on Hebrew, Andersen settled on the definition, "A sentence is a grammatically self-contained construction," that is, "The grammatical functions of all constituents in a sentence may be described in terms of relationships to other constituents in the
same sentence."[18] This definition is similar to our notion of the sentence as the unit
having the "highest rank" in compositional analysis. It is not clear that Andersen's definition is theoretically adequate; he himself later acknowledged: "Grammatical completeness . . . may prove as hard to establish as completeness of thought."[19]

d   The American linguist Leonard Bloomfield offered a similar definition with some
arresting illustrations. He defined a sentence as "an independent linguistic form, not
included by virtue of any grammatical construction in any larger linguistic form." He
exemplified this definition with the following utterance: 'How are you? It's a fine day.
Are you going to play tennis this afternoon?,' commenting "Whatever practical connection there may be between these three forms, there is no grammatical arrangement unit-
ing them into one larger form: the utterance consists of three sentences."[20] However,
defining the sentence as the largest unit of grammatical description fails because in fact
the sentence is a grammatical constituent of the discourse, a larger grammatical form.[21]

e   Such definitions as these do have the advantage of defining the sentence as a linguistic unit composed of identifiable, lesser linguistic units. More particularly, we can define
a sentence as a linguistic form composed of one or more clauses. If there are multiple
clauses, they are bound together by conjunctions signifying that together they compose

16. F. I. Andersen, *The Hebrew Verbless Clause in the Pentateuch* (Journal of Biblical Literature Monograph 14; Nashville: Abingdon, 1970) 20. Some linguists drop the term altogether. M. A. K. Halliday, for example, treats a sentence as a unit of writing (and of information); a *clause complex*, in contrast, is a unit of grammar (and of syntax); see *Introduction to Functional Grammar* (London: Edward Arnold, 1985). Cf. n. 1 above on the definition of "word."

17. Cf. M. B. Cohen, "Masoretic Accents as a Biblical Commentary," *Journal of the Ancient Near Eastern Society* 4 (1972) 2–11.

18. Andersen, *Hebrew Verbless Clause*, 20.

19. Andersen, *The Sentence in Biblical Hebrew* (The Hague: Mouton, 1974) 22.

20. Leonard Bloomfield, *Language* (New York: Holt, 1933) 170.

21. Lyons, *Theoretical Linguistics*, 172.

one grammatical unit, although we must allow that the discourse is bound together by patterns of "macrosyntactic conjunctions," just as patterns of "microsyntactic conjunctions" bind clauses within a sentence (Chap. 38). A full definition of the sentence, which we shall not undertake to offer, would include a statement of how it differs from the macrosyntactic utterance of discourse.

We define a sentence as a linguistic unit not as large as a discourse but larger than those grammatical elements that cannot exist independently but are syntactically dependent on one another within this larger linguistic unit; namely, the clause, the phrase, the word, the morpheme.   f

Sentences may be incomplete. Some of the smaller units comprising a larger one are left to be inferred from context; in the surface structure of an utterance, words that need "to be supplied" to make it into a typical construction are said to be elided. The words are readily supplied from the surrounding context (in the utterance or in the situation) and from the grammatical systems known to characterize the language. Sometimes the conjunction binding either clauses or sentences together is elided; at other times one of the other elements of a clause is elided, such as the subject or the predicate.   g

A sentence may be coextensive with a single clause, in which case it is a simple sentence, or it may consist of two or more clauses, in which case it is either compound or complex.[22] Consider, for example, the utterance,   h

1.　　　　וַיַּעֲבִדוּ מִצְרַיִם אֶת־בְּנֵי   Egypt made the Israelites serve with harshness.
　　　　יִשְׂרָאֵל בְּפָרֶךְ׃   Exod 1:13

This is a *simple sentence* consisting of grammatical elements that cannot exist apart from their syntactical connection with each other and that together constitute a unified utterance. Its smaller dependent constituents are (leaving aside the initial *waw*):

מצרים	the noun expressing the subject
ויעבדו	the verb expressing the predicate
את־בני ישראל	the noun phrase modifying the verb (direct object)
בפרך	an adverbial prepositional phrase

The last of these is a prepositional phrase, the third a noun phrase; the other two are single words.

The following is a *compound sentence*.   i

2.　　וּבְנֵי יִשְׂרָאֵל פָּרוּ וַיִּשְׁרְצוּ וַיִּרְבּוּ   The Israelites were powerfully fruitful and prolific and
　　וַיַּעַצְמוּ בִּמְאֹד מְאֹד   grew numerous and became strong.
　　　　　　　　　　　　　Exod 1:7

In this sentence the four verbs, with the single subject and the single adverbial modifier, follow each other with only the conjunctions to join them. The following sentence is *complex*.

---

22. For a full typology, see Richter, *GAHG* 3. 50–64.

3.   וַיָּקָם מֶלֶךְ־חָדָשׁ עַל־מִצְרָיִם   A new king arose over Egypt, who did not know
        אֲשֶׁר לֹא־יָדַע אֶת־יוֹסֵף   Joseph.
                                              Exod 1:8

The second clause, אֲשֶׁר לֹא־יָדַע אֶת־יוֹסֵף, is subordinate to the first; it is a relative clause modifying the subject of the main clause, מֶלֶךְ־חָדָשׁ.

Nouns

5

Noun Patterns

Root, Affix, Pattern   5.1

Most words in Hebrew include a *root*, a sequence of consonants associated with a   a
meaning or group of meanings. Most roots are triconsonantal (or triradical); middle-
weak roots (and sometimes other weak roots) are considered biconsonantal.[1] The root is
an abstraction, based on the forms and words that actually occur, and its meaning is also
an abstraction, based on the semantic field of the words as they are used. The system of
roots is part of the speaker's knowledge of the language, but the resulting abstractions
should not be pressed too hard, especially on semantic grounds. Words that actually
occur always have priority over such abstractions. Only the pronouns and some particles
fall entirely outside the root system.

The root may be modified to form a word with an *affix*; it may be a *prefix* (before   b
the root), a *suffix* (after the root), an *infix* (within the root), or some combination of
these. The affixes form various verbal and nominal patterns, and each word is a representative of a formative pattern. The term *stem* is sometimes used to describe a form of
the consonantal root with an affix, from which other words can be derived.

---

1. At various levels of abstraction, some classes of verbs can be considered biconsonantal. In addition to middle-weak roots, final-weak and geminate roots are often so treated. Some words (sometimes called "primitive" nouns) may be said to have monoconsonantal roots, e.g., *peh* 'mouth' (compare Ugaritic *p* and Akkadian *pû*); "primitive" biconsonantals include *bēn* 'son' and *šēm* 'name.' Longer, quadriconsonantal and quinqiconsonantal, roots are rare in Biblical Hebrew (though not in later forms of the language). In a triradical root, only the second and third consonants can have the same point of articulation, and if they do, they must be identical; see J. H. Greenberg, "The Patterning of Root Morphemes in Semitic," *Word* 6 (1950) 162–81. There are a few exceptions, notably the numbers 'three' (Hebrew *šālôš*) and 'six' (Hebrew *šēš*, *šiššîm*; Arabic *sādisa*).

c   The root חבר 'to unite, join' can be used in illustrating these points. Here are a dozen words.

1.	חָבְרוּ	they (were) joined	7.	חֶבְרָה	association
2.	חָבֵר	associate	8.	חֹבֶרֶת	joined thing
3.	חֶבֶר	company	9.	מַחְבֶּרֶת	joining
4.	חִבַּר	he joined (something	10.	מְחַבְּרָה	clamp
		to something else)	11.	חֶבְרוֹן	Hebron
5.	חַבָּר	partner	12.	חֶבְרוֹנִי	Hebronite
6.	חַבֶּרֶת	consort			

In the first three forms, the root is complemented by infixed (and in # 1 suffixed) vowels; in the next two, the medial consonant of the root is also lengthened (or doubled). Forms ## 6–10 bear a feminine suffix; ## 9–10 have in addition a prefixed *mem*. Forms ## 11–12 have an -*ôn* suffix, and the last form has a further -*î* suffix. There are other forms that derive from the root *ḥbr*. The root never occurs in isolation from an affix pattern; the meaning 'to unite, join' is derived from the attested vocabulary.

d   Some of the patterns used in these dozen words are *verb patterns*; such patterns tend to be consistent and regular to a much greater degree than those used to form nouns (substantives and adjectives). The verbal pattern CāCaC (or $C_1\bar{a}C_2aC_3$ or קָטַל) denotes a complete or perfective situation, for example, שָׁבַר 'he broke,' שָׁמַר 'he guarded,' גָּנַב 'he stole,' אָזַל 'it is gone'; thus חָבְרוּ 'they (were) joined.' The verbal pattern C_1iC_2-$C_2\bar{e}C_3$ works in a similar way, for example, כִּבֵּד 'he honored,' סִפֵּר 'he recounted,' גִּדֵּל 'he caused to grow'; thus חִבַּר 'he joined (something).' (The relationship between the first, *Qal*, pattern and the second, *Piel*, pattern is discussed below, 24.1.)

e   Individual nouns are composed of vowels and consonants in a less divisible unity, and so *noun patterns* are less predictable in meaning. Nouns are created afresh much less often than are verbs, and the meanings of such patterns are thus a less active part of a speaker's knowledge of the language. In some cases, one pattern in Biblical Hebrew may be the result of several patterns from earlier stages of the language, which have assumed the same shape because of phonological changes. Some noun patterns can be correlated with specific meanings or ranges of meanings on a regular basis; these patterns are the subject of this chapter.[2]

f   The root and affix system is the heart of Hebrew morphology. The root morpheme is a constant in that system; the verbal affix morphemes are also consistent elements. The morphemes or patterns used to form nouns are much more variable, but they are none-theless an important part of the grammar. Combined with a knowledge of the four hundred or so roots used frequently in the Hebrew Bible, these patterns can contribute to vocabulary building. "If we know the meaning of a root and the rules of inflexion and morphology," writes G. B. Caird, "it is usually possible to work out for ourselves the

---

2. For a complete list of patterns, see BL § 61 / pp. 448–506. See also K. Beyer, *Althebräische Grammatik: Laut-und Formenlehre* (Göttingen: Vandenhoeck und Ruprecht, 1969) 42–51; Richter, *GAHG* 1. 66–69. On the pattern (CVCC >) CVCeC, see W. R. Garr, "The *Seghol* and Segholation in Hebrew," *Journal of Near Eastern Studies* 48 (1989) 109–16.

meaning of cognate forms [that is, forms from the same root]."[3] Geographical and personal names, like # 11 above, and derived forms, like # 12, constitute a special area of the lexicon.

The nominal morphemes are subject to all the laws of Hebrew phonology. Thus the   g
pattern CôCēC, usually associated with the *Qal* active participle, has the form CôCēC if no suffix follows, but the form CôCəC before a vocalic suffix, for example, קוֹטֵל masculine singular, קוֹטְלָה feminine singular, קוֹטְלִים masculine plural. In a few cases, the masculine and feminine forms of what appears to be one pattern are best taken separately.

Pattern Diversity   5.2

The richness and complexity of the semantic associations of Hebrew noun patterns   a
can be illustrated by considering the important CôCēC pattern in its manifestations other than the simple participial use. Benjamin Kedar-Kopfstein proposed an elaborate schema to classify the senses of this pattern; we consider only a portion of his findings.[4]

There is a class of substantives in which, Kedar-Kopfstein alleges, the *ô-ē* pattern   b
"lacks any morphemic value" (# 1) or "denotes objects" (## 2–4).[5]

1.	עֹרֵב	raven		3.	יוֹבֵל	ram's horn
2.	חוֹמָה	wall (fem.; root: *ḥmy*)		4.	שֹׂרֵק	vine

Several groups of nouns using this pattern have no link to a verbal root in the *Qal*.   c
Indeed, in some nouns, where the pattern "indicates the holder of an office or profession," no cognate verb root is used (## 5–6).[6]

5.	כֹּהֵן	priest		6.	נֹקֵד	sheep-raiser

In another group of nouns, also largely professional, each noun is denominative in origin, that is, it is derived from another noun; in this case, the *qôṭēl* form "denotes a person who occupies himself with the object indicated by" the base noun (## 7–8).[7]

7.	בּוֹקֵר	herder	<	בָּקָר	cattle	8.	חֹבֵל	sailor	<	חֶבֶל	rope

Another class of CôCēC forms, also including some profession terms, is derived from roots attested as verbs but not used in the *Qal* (## 9–10).

9.	נוֹקֵשׁ	fowler	<	נקשׁ	*Niphal, Piel, Hithpael*
10.	סֹכֵן	steward	<	סכן	*Hiphil*

3. G. B. Caird, *The Language and Imagery of the Bible* (Philadelphia: Westminster, 1980) 86.

4. Benjamin Kedar-Kopfstein, "Semantic Aspects of the Pattern *Qôṭēl*," *Hebrew Annual Review* 1 (1977) 155–76. Cf. Kedar-Kopfstein, "Die Stammbildung *qôṭel* als Übersetzungsproblem," *Zeitschrift für die Alttestamentliche Wissenschaft* 93 (1981) 254–79.

5. Kedar-Kopfstein, "Semantic Aspects," 161. For another treatment of ʿrb 'raven' from ʿrb 'to be dark,' see A. Brenner, *Colour Terms in the Old Testament* (Journal for the Study of the Old Testament Supplement Series 21; Sheffield: JSOT Press, 1982) 97, 158, 168, 172–74.

6. Kedar-Kopfstein, "Semantic Aspects," 161.

7. Kedar-Kopfstein, "Semantic Aspects," 162.

d   Another major category of *qôtēl* nouns includes those which can be associated with verbs used in the *Qal*. These nouns are not, however, simply *Qal* participles, for "they no longer describe the actual exercise of an activity but have become fixed denotations labeling a subject on the basis of one distinctive feature which is durable and objectively observable."[8] Some of these are, as above, the names of occupations (## 11–16), while others describe an individual's social role (## 17–20). One related subgroup is used for abstractions (## 21–22).

11.	אֹרֵג	weaver	<	אָרַג	to weave
12.	בֹּנֶה	builder, stonecutter	<	בָּנָה	to build
13.	גֹּדֵר	mason	<	גָּדַר	to wall up
14.	זוֹנָה	prostitute (fem.)	<	זָנָה	to whore
15.	חוֹבֵר	diviner (joiner of spells)	<	חָבַר	to join, be joined
16.	חֹזֶה	seer	<	חָזָה	to see
17.	גֹּאֵל	redeemer, family protector	<	גָּאַל	to redeem
18.	יֹלֵד	father, begetter	<	יָלַד	to (bear,) beget
19.	יוֹנֵק	suckling	<	יָנַק	to suck
20.	יוֹשֵׁב	inhabitant, ruler	<	יָשַׁב	to dwell
21.	אֹבֵד	destruction	<	אָבַד	to perish
22.	רֹאֶה	vision[9]	<	רָאָה	to see

e   Kedar-Kopfstein notes two other groups related to this major category. The nouns of one group "denote a permanent feature of the subject in character or behavior"[10] (## 23–26), while those of the other denote a clearly temporary feature, for example, a seasonal occupation (## 27–30).

23.	אוֹיֵב	enemy	<	אָיַב	to be hostile
24.	בֹּטֵחַ	(over)confident	<	בָּטַח	to trust
25.	בֹּעֵר	brutish[11]	<	בָּעַר	to be brutish
26.	בֹּוצֵעַ	covetous	<	בָּצַע	to rob
27.	בֹּוצֵר	gatherer (of grapes)	<	בָּצַר	to cut off
28.	זֹרֵעַ	sower	<	זָרַע	to sow
29.	חֹרֵשׁ	plower	<	חָרַשׁ	to plow
30.	קֹטֵף	plucker	<	קָטַף	to pluck

f   This summary of one effort to describe one major pattern (and the forms could be considered in other perspectives) should make it clear how intricate the nominal system of Hebrew can be. Yet, it is also plain that most of these non-participial uses of the *qôtēl* form are close to the basic participial sense: only six of the thirty examples cited (## 1–4, 21–22) depart drastically from the 'doer' sense. At the same time, the agentive sense is often semantically inappropriate—a *yôšēb* 'inhabitant' is not simply one who performs

---

8. Kedar-Kopfstein, "Semantic Aspects," 164.
9. The same noun occurs with the meaning 'seer.'
10. Kedar-Kopfstein, "Semantic Aspects," 166.

11. It may be that this should be derived from the noun *baʿîr* 'cattle' (cf. examples ## 7–8), from which *bāʿar* is a denominative verb.

the act of dwelling (*yāšab*)—or morphologically impossible—there is no verb **ḥābal* 'to handle ropes,' to yield *ḥōbēl* '(rope-handler,) sailor.'

In this chapter, the goal is more modest than in Kedar-Kopfstein's survey and others like it. The *qôtēl* pattern can be said to form nouns referring to professions, whether or not the root exists (cf. # 5) or occurs as a verb (cf. # 7) or in the *Qal* (cf. # 9). The distinction between permanent and temporary occupations can similarly be passed over. Eccentric uses (## 1–4) can also be omitted. The presentation here is thus at a high level of abstraction. The general shapes and meanings of noun patterns is the focus, rather than a taxonomy of all attested patterns.   g

The nominal patterns listed in this chapter are categorized as substantival or adjectival; the noun class in Hebrew does not rigidly distinguish adjectives from substantives.[12] The term substantive is used to refer to an approximate semantic class of nouns, namely, words referring to persons, places, or things; the term nominal is unfortunately ambiguous.[13] Adjectival words are roughly those that describe a state or condition; Hebrew more often than English uses verbs to describe conditions. On syntactic grounds, substantives and adjectives function comparably (see 4.4.1).[14] Not all the patterns are equally common. The reduplicating patterns, for example, are rare, but they may be usefully studied because of their distinctiveness. Major patterns are semantically more diverse as well as more common.   h

Simple Patterns   5.3

The *qātēl* pattern is generally adjectival (## 1–3; see also 22.3–4); it also occurs with substantives, especially body parts (## 4–5).   a

1.	יָבֵשׁ	dry		4.	יָרֵךְ	(upper) thigh
2.	עָיֵף	exhausted		5.	כָּתֵף	upper arm
3.	שָׁלֵו	unconcerned				

The *qôtēl/qōtēl* pattern is used for substantives referring to professions or occupations (for examples see 5.2). An English counterpart is the *-er/-or* suffix, for example, 'fisher, overseer, actor, counselor.' Other active participles than the *Qal* can designate a profession. This is most common with the participles of the *Piel* (## 6–7; cf. 24.5c) and *Poel* (# 8).   b

---

12. In the counts of SA/THAT, about half the Biblical Hebrew vocabulary is made up of nomina, ca. 4,050 words, of which there are 3,640 substantives, 360 adjectives, 20 pronouns, and 30 numbers. For a different, more restricted used of "substantive," see G. Bergsträsser, *Introduction to the Semitic Languages*, trans. and sup. P. T. Daniels (Winona Lake, Indiana: Eisenbrauns, 1983) 10.

13. In a strictly syntactic framework, nouns would be defined as nominals (or noun equivalents or the like) that can take the definite article or pronominal suffixes. It is possible for prepositional phrases and various types of clauses to be used as nouns. Such use as clausal subjects has been mentioned (4.4.1). These *nominalizations* are found in slots other than subject. Thus, for example, we find a prepositional phrase as the object of a verb (1 Sam 9:24, 2 Sam 2:23) or as the second term (*rectum*) of a construct phrase (Judg 8:11, Isa 32:20). A verbless clause may occur as a prepositional object (2 Chr 16:9). For a discussion and examples, see Daniel Grossberg, "Nominalizations in Biblical Hebrew," *Hebrew Studies* 20–21 (1979–80) 29–33.

14. The patterns are described in more or less their actual shape, rather than in an underlying or historical form, as in many grammars.

6. מְלַמֵּד   teacher
7. מְרַגֵּל   spy
8. מְחֹקֵק   commander

c   The *qātîl* pattern[15] shapes adjectives (## 9–11) as well as substantives. The pattern is used for professional terms, some passive in sense (## 12–14), some stative or active (## 15–17),[16] although the distinctions should not be pressed. The words for certain agricultural activities also employ this pattern (## 18–22).

9.	צָעִיר	little	16.	נָגִיד	leader
10.	נָקִי	pure[17]	17.	נָבִיא	prophet
11.	עָנִי	poor	18.	אָסִיף	ingathering
12.	אָסִיר	prisoner (= one bound)	19.	בָּצִיר	vintage
13.	מָשִׁיחַ	anointed	20.	זָמִיר	vine pruning
14.	פָּלִיט	refugee	21.	חָרִישׁ	plowing
15.	פָּקִיד	overseer	22.	קָצִיר	grain harvest

d   The *qātûl/qātūl* pattern is, like the *qôtēl*, a participial form, designating the object of the verbal action, for example, כָּתוּב 'what is written'; like the *qôtēl*, the *qātûl* has many other uses, many lacking a passive sense. The pattern is used for both adjectives (## 23–25) and substantives (## 26–28). The feminine may show doubling in the final radical (# 26; cf. 5.5b). Abstract nouns with this pattern are frequently plural (7.4.2).

23.	בָּצוּר	inaccessible	26.	אֲחֻזָּה	possession (fem.)
24.	עָצוּם	strong	27.	חָרוּץ	decision
25.	עָרוּם	crafty	28.	יָקוּשׁ	fowler

e   The *qātôl/qātōl* form is used for adjectives (## 29–35).

29.	אָיֹם	terrible	33.	עָמֹק	deep
30.	מָתוֹק	sweet	34.	עָקֹב	hilly; deceitful
31.	נָקֹד	speckled	35.	צָהֹב	golden
32.	עָגוֹל	round			

f   The feminine pattern *qətālâ* commonly designates sounds and noises (## 36–41).

36.	אֲנָחָה	sigh	39.	נְאָקָה	groan
37.	אֲנָקָה	moan	40.	צְעָקָה	cry
38.	יְלָלָה	howl	41.	שְׁאָגָה	roar

---

15. This pattern is similar to that of various passive participles in Aramaic dialects.

16. See K. D. Sakenfeld, *The Meaning of Ḥesed in the*

Hebrew Bible (Missoula: Scholars Press, 1977) 241–45.

17. The root of ## 10–11 is a final-*he* or -*yod* root, and the last radical shows up in these forms as a *yod*.

Patterns with Medial Lengthening   **5.4**

The *qattāl* form, with medial lengthening or doubling, is another that often signifies   a
occupation, profession, or even repeated action (## 1–6).[18]

1.	גַּנָּב	thief		4.	חָרָשׁ	artificer
2.	דַּיָּן	judge		5.	פָּרָשׁ	equestrian
3.	חַטָּא	sinner		6.	צַיָּד	hunter

Adjectives referring to defects, physical or mental, use the *qittēl* pattern (## 7–14).   b

7.	אִטֵּר	disabled		11.	עִוֵּר	blind
8.	אִלֵּם	mute		12.	עִקֵּשׁ	perverse
9.	גִּבֵּן	hump-backed		13.	פִּסֵּחַ	lame
10.	חֵרֵשׁ	deaf		14.	קֵרֵחַ	bald

Three of these terms occur together in Exod 4:11 (## 8, 10, 11).

Qattîl words (like those in other patterns with medial lengthening and a long second   c
vowel) are often said to indicate possession of a quality in an "intensive" way.[19] This is
unlikely because it is based on the dubious notion that the doubling "sharpens" the root
in a semantically straightforward way (24.1). Suffice it to say that *qattîl* is both adjectival
(## 15–17) and a byform of substantival *qātîl* (## 18–19; for # 18, cf. 5.3 # 12).

15.	אַבִּיר	strong		18.	אַסִּיר	prisoner
16.	עָרִיץ	terrifying		19.	סָרִיס	eunuch
17.	צַדִּיק	righteous				

Patterns with Reduplication   **5.5**

Both of the common reduplicating patterns are used for adjectives. The reduplica-   a
tion may involve only C$_3$, as in *qatlāl* (## 1–2). Both second and third radicals are
reduplicated in the *qətaltal* form, used for various adjectives (## 3–5), but especially
common with color words (## 6–8).[20]

1.	רַעֲנָן	luxuriant, green		5.	פְּתַלְתֹּל	tortuous
2.	שַׁאֲנָן	secure		6.	אֲדַמְדָּם	reddish
3.	הֲפַכְפַּךְ	crooked		7.	יְרַקְרַק	greenish
4.	חֲלַקְלַקּוֹת	slipperiness (fem. pl.)		8.	שְׁחַרְחֹרֶת	blackish (fem.)

---

18. This pattern is called the *nomen occupationis*. The *r*,
which cannot be doubled, is said to be "virtually doubled"
in such forms as ## 4, 5, 10, 14, 16, 19. The term *lengthening* "is preferred to 'doubling' and 'gemination' because
a long consonant does not last twice the duration of a

short one"; Daniels apud Bergsträsser, *Introduction*, 5.

19. S. Moscati et al., *An Introduction to the Comparative Grammar of the Semitic Languages* (Wiesbaden:
Harrassowitz, 1964) 78–79.

20. On color words, see Brenner, *Colour Terms*.

b   According to T. N. D. Mettinger, thirty-six nouns display the feminine reduplicated C₃ pattern *qətūllâ*.[21] He analyzes the group as showing three subgroups. The concrete nouns denote the result or product of an act (## 9–11). The abstracts include legal terms (## 12–14; cf. 5.3 # 2b) and terms for "values" in a broad sense (## 15–17). Finally, the collectives are terms for corporations of persons (## 18–20).

9.	אֲלֻמָּה	sheaf	15.	סְגֻלָּה	private purse
10.	אֲסֻפָּה	collection	16.	עֲרֻבָּה	security, pledge
11.	קְוֻצּוֹת	curls, locks	17.	פְּעֻלָּה	wages, reward
12.	בְּכֹרָה	right of the first-born	18.	אֲגֻדָּה	band, troop
13.	גְּאֻלָּה	right of redemption	19.	עֲבֻדָּה	(a body of) slaves
14.	יְרֻשָּׁה	possession	20.	פְּקֻדָּה	governing authorities

5.6   Patterns with Prefixing

a   Biblical Hebrew employs a variety of prefixes that serve to modify the meaning of the roots. Most of the prefixes are elements used in both nominal and verbal patterns, including *ʾ, h, y, m, t,* and *ʿ.* Stanley Gevirtz has argued that "what these appear to have in common with each other is a deictic, demonstrative, defining or specifying force."[22] Not all the prefixes are equally common or important.

b   The most common prefix is *m,* used in substantives of location (## 1–3), instrument terms (## 4–5), and abstractions (## 6–9).

1.	מִדְבָּר	range, steppe	6.	מִשְׁפָּט	judgment
2.	מָקוֹם	place	7.	מַרְאֶה	appearance
3.	מוֹשָׁב	assembly (< *yšb*)	8.	מַרְאָה	vision (fem.)
4.	מַפְתֵּחַ	key	9.	מַמְלָכָה	kingdom, reign (fem.)
5.	מַאֲכֶלֶת	knife (fem.)			

In most of these examples the vowel of the first, prefixed syllable is *a* (## 2–5, 7–9); in the others it is *i.* The first syllable of # 3, *mô-,* is contracted from *maw-;* the *ô* is also seen in *Niphal, Hiphil,* and *Hophal* forms of *yšb* and various other initial-*waw* verbs. In the feminine examples cited, the corresponding masculine form either does not occur (## 5, 9) or has a different sense (# 8, cf. # 7).

c   A *t*-prefix noun usually designates the action of the verb it is derived from (## 10–12). Many such nouns, including the examples, are derived from initial-*waw* roots.

---

21. T. N. D. Mettinger, "The Nominal Pattern 'qətulla' in Biblical Hebrew," *Journal of Semitic Studies* 16 (1972) 2–14.

22. S. Gevirtz, "Formative ע in Biblical Hebrew," *Eretz-Israel* 16 (1982) 57*–66*, at 62*. This group of elements may be called the affixional subset of the sounds of the language; see M. O'Connor, "The Rhetoric of the Kilamuwa Inscription," *Bulletin of the American Schools of Oriental Research* 226 (1977) 15–29, at 16–17, in a discussion of alliteration. For a treatment of this class of sounds in Classical Greek, see E. D. Floyd, "Levels of Phonological Restriction in Greek Affixes," *Bono Homini Donum: Essays in Historical Linguistics in Memory of J. Alexander Kerns,* ed. Y. L. Arbeitman and A. R. Bomhard (Amsterdam: John Benjamins, 1981), 1. 87–106; a comparable study for Hebrew is needed.

10.   תּוֹחֶלֶת   expectation (fem.; < *yḥl*)
11.   תּוֹכַחַת   argument (fem.; < *ykḥ*)
12.   תּוֹדָה   thanksgiving (fem.; < *ydy*)

Nouns with prefix *m*, *t*, and *y* often seem closely related in meaning. Jacob Barth   d
argued, in his classic study of noun formation,[23] that certain *m* and *t* pairs of nouns
(## 13–15) and even a *y* and *t* pair (# 16) and an *m* and *y* pair (# 17) had no significantly
different senses.

13.   מַרְבִּית   תַּרְבִּית   interest, increase (< *rby*)
14.   מִקְוֶה   תִּקְוָה   hope (< *qwy*)
15.   מַחֲלָיִים תַּחֲלֻאִים   illness (< *ḥly/ʾ*)
16.   יְשׁוּעָה   תְּשׁוּעָה   salvation (< * yšʿ*)
17.   מַעַן   יַעַן   on account of, because

Gevirtz cautions against this kind of semantic blurring, both on the sound general
grounds that where there is difference in form, there is a difference in meaning, and on
the grounds of his study of the words.

The terms יַעַן and (לְ)מַעַן both mean 'purpose, intention', . . . ; but the former most
often conveys a sense of causation, whereas the latter does not. The terms מַחֲלָיִים and
תַּחֲלֻאִים, deriving from ḤLʾ/Y, mean 'illness(es), disease(s)', but the *mqtl* form has
reference to illness resulting from the effects of wounds (2 Ch. 24:25), whereas the *tqtl*
form refers to illness resulting from the ravages of hunger (Jer. 14:18; 2 Ch. 21:19).
תַּאֲוָה and [מאוה] both mean 'desire', but the *tqtl* form often signifies 'physical appetite'
(Num. 11:4; Ps. 78:29–30; 106:14; Job 33:20), whereas the *mqtl* form, in the expression, מַאֲוַיֵּי רָשָׁע 'the desires of (the) wicked man', in parallel with זְמָמוֹ 'his plan,
device', would appear to signify 'schemes, plots, machinations', having reference to
'mental appetite'.[24]

A prefixed glottal stop is used in various adjectives (## 18–20),[25] as well as in certain   e
substantival forms (## 21–22).

18.   אַכְזָב   deceptive   21.   אֶזְרוֹעַ   arm
19.   אַכְזָר   cruel   22.   אֶצְבַּע   finger
20.   אֵיתָן   perennial (< *ytn*?)

The א used in nouns such as ## 21 and 22 seems to reflect an effort to reshape the stem,
perhaps in part because of the initial sibilant; the word 'arm,' for example, also occurs in
the more common form זְרוֹעַ. This א prefix is therefore called either prothetic (i.e., prefixed) or prosthetic (i.e., giving additional power).[26]

---

23. Jacob Barth, *Die Nominalbildung in den semitischen
Sprachen* (2d ed.; Leipzig: Hinrichs, 1894) 228.
24. Gevirtz, "Formative ע," 60*–61*, and references.
25. The comparable Arabic form is called the elative,
but the resemblance may be superficial.
26. In some nouns, the ʾ is part of the root, e.g.,
ʾarnébet 'hare' (the *r* is sometimes judged an intrusive or
secondary element in this word).

f   Gevirtz has suggested that ע indicates specification or forcefulness as a root element.[27] He compares similar roots with and without ʿ: *gnn* 'to cover' and *ʿgn* 'to shut
oneself off,' *qwr* 'to dig' and *ʿqr* 'to dig up,' *rwy* 'to be saturated' and *ʿry* 'to pour out' (≠
ʿry 'to be naked'). Particularly striking are roots that occur with both א and ע, *ʾgm* 'to
be sad' and *ʿgm* 'to grieve,' and *ʾṭr* 'to close' and *ʿṭr* 'to surround.' Relevant noun pairs
include

23.	אֱוֶלֶת	fool	עָוֶל	injustice
24.	אֵזוֹר	waistcloth	עֲזָרָה	enclosure, outer court
25.	אַרְבֶּה	locust	עֹרֹב	fly-swarm

The ʾaleph/ʿayin element in these cases is part of the root as it exists in Biblical Hebrew.
The ʿayin element is also found in some quadriliterals designating animals, in which it
may function as a prefix like the others treated here (## 26–30).

26.	עֲטַלֵּף	bat	29.	עַכְשׁוּב	viper
27.	עַכְבָּר	mouse	30.	עַקְרָב	scorpion
28.	עַכָּבִישׁ	spider			

5.7   Patterns with Suffixing

a   The suffixing patterns to be presented here are usually denominatives, that is, they
form nouns from other nouns, rather than from verbal roots.

b   The most common suffix is *-ôn* ~ *-ān*. It may be used for adjectives (## 1–3),
abstract substantives (## 4–6), and diminutives (## 7–8).

1.	קַדְמוֹן	eastern	<	קֶדֶם	east
2.	חִיצוֹן	exterior	<	חוּץ	outside
3.	רִאשׁוֹן	first	<	רֹאשׁ	head
4.	פִּתְרוֹן	solution			
5.	זִכָּרוֹן	memorial			
6.	קָרְבָּן	offering			
7.	אִישׁוֹן	pupil (of the eye)	<	אִישׁ	person
8.	צַוָּרוֹן	necklace	<	צַוָּאר	neck

The 'pupil' or 'apple' of the eye is named for the little person seen reflected in it, both in
Hebrew and in Latin (*pupillus*, whence the English term 'pupil'). The *-ôn* ending is
common in place names (e.g., חֶבְרוֹן), and the *-ûn* ending of Yeshurun (יְשֻׁרוּן), a poetic
term for Israel (cf. יָשָׁר 'upright'), and Zebulun (זְבֻלוּן) is related.

c   The *-î* suffix has established itself in English usage in forms like 'Israeli,' 'Saudi,' and
'Farsi.' In Hebrew, it serves to make adjectives from substantives (## 9–11), including
names (## 12–14). Names with the *-î* suffix are called gentilics or ethnica.[28]

---

27. Gevirtz, "Formative ע."
28. The ending *î* is cognate to Arabic *-īy-* and Akkadian
-ayy- (Arabic *Yahudīyun* 'Jew'; Akkadian *Yaʾudayyu*

'Judahite'); this ending is used most often for forming
place-of-origin names and is called the *nisbe*-ending (Arabic
nisbatun 'affinity, relationship').

9.	רַגְלִי	foot(-soldier)	<	רֶגֶל	foot
10.	נָכְרִי	strange	<	נֵכֶר	strangeness
11.	תַּחְתִּי	lower	<	תַּחַת	below
12.	עִבְרִי	Hebrew	<	עֵבֶר	Eber
13.	מוֹאָבִי	Moabite	<	מוֹאָב	Moab
14.	גִּילוֹנִי	Gilonite	<	גִּלֹה	Giloh

Denominative abstract nouns are formed with the suffix -ût and, less often, -ît. **d**

15.	יַלְדוּת	childhood	<	יֶלֶד	child
16.	מַלְכוּת	royalty, kingdom	<	מֶלֶךְ	king
17.	שְׁאֵרִית	remnant	<	שְׁאָר	residue

The suffix -ām is used to form adverbials (## 18–20; 39.3.1h).[29] **e**

18.	יוֹמָם	by day	<	יוֹם	day
19.	חִנָּם	gratuitously	<	חֵן	grace
20.	רֵיקָם	in vain	<	רֵיק	empty

Excursus: Interchange of Consonants **5.8**

The phonological structure of Biblical Hebrew is outside our purview, but one facet **a**
of it deserves mention in connection with the study of patterns. Consonants occasionally
interchange in Hebrew word formation, and so closely related forms may actually take
on slightly different shapes. There are three groups of interchanges important for Biblical
Hebrew: the gutturals, the liquids (*l* and *r*) and nasals (*m* and *n*), and other consonants.

The interchange of initial ʾaleph and yod is attested in ʾš for standard yš (2 Sam **b**
14:19) and ʾśrʾl for standard yśrʾl (1 Chr 25:2, cf. v 14). Note also the alternate form of
the divine name אֶהְיֶה (Hos 1:9; cf. Exod 3:12, 14).[30] Other interchanges of gutturals,
though common in later forms of the language, are rare in Biblical Hebrew.[31]

The liquid-nasal commutations are best known through the two forms of the name **c**
Nebuchadnezzar (e.g., Jer 29:1) and Nebuchadrezzar (e.g., Jer 21:2). The three sounds *l*,
n, and *r* occasionally show up in closely related forms, for example, *liškâ* and *niškâ*,
'room'; *mazzālôt* and *mazzārôt*, 'constellations'; *lḥṣ* and *nḥṣ*, 'to press, urge.' Aloysius
Fitzgerald has collected examples of other such variants in poetic texts; he alleges that in
such cases the poet "is using a dialectal form that fits better the sound-patterning of his
line" than the standard would.[32]

---

29. The evidence of the El-Amarna letters suggests that this suffix is etymologically composed of an accusative ending -a- followed by an enclitic m (9.8).

30. See C. D. Isbell, "Initial ʾalef-yod Interchange and Selected Biblical Passages," *Journal of Near Eastern Studies* 37 (1978) 227–36; D. N. Freedman and M. O'Connor, "YHWH," *Theological Dictionary of the Old Testament*, ed. G. J. Botterweck and H. Ringgren (Grand Rapids: Eerdmans, 1986), 5. 500–21; cf. E. L. Greenstein, "Another

Attestation of Initial h > ʾ in West Semitic," *Journal of the Ancient Near Eastern Society* 5 (1973) 157–64.

31. See, e.g., E. Qimron, *The Hebrew of the Dead Sea Scrolls* (Atlanta: Scholars Press, 1986) 24–26; M. H. Segal, *A Grammar of Mishnaic Hebrew* (Oxford: Clarendon, 1927) 26–28.

32. A. Fitzgerald, "The Interchange of *L*, *N*, and *R* in Biblical Hebrew," *Journal of Biblical Literature* 97 (1978) 481–88, at 481.

d   Other interchanges are attested for sibilants (ʿlṣ, ʿls, ʿlz, 'to exult'; ṣḥq and śḥq, 'to laugh'), velars (sgr and skr, 'to close'), and bilabials (plṭ and mlṭ, 'to escape').

e   *Metathesis*, that is, the transposition of elements of a word, is part of the regular morphology of the *Hithpael* (see 26.1.1b). It also affects a few roots, which show up in two forms: the common שַׂלְמָה 'mantle,' and the etymologically correct שִׂמְלָה, with the same meaning; the common (and etymologically correct) כֶּבֶשׂ 'young ram' and כִּבְשָׂה 'ewe-lamb,' alongside כֶּשֶׂב 'young ram' and כִּשְׂבָה 'lamb.'

6

Gender

Introduction

6.1

a   Gender is a feature of many languages and plays an important role in the structure of Hebrew.[1] As an aspect of morphology, gender affects both syntax and the lexicon; through the lexicon, gender is a facet of semantics, that is, of the way the world around us is represented in words. Like the other Semitic languages, Hebrew formally distinguishes two genders, *masculine* and *feminine*; the distinction is used for nouns (both substantives and adjectives), pronouns, and verbs. The formal system in nouns involves an unmarked class of masculine forms and a largely marked class of feminine forms.

---

1. For a basic introduction and an extensive and comprehensive bibliography on gender, see Muhammad Hasan Ibrahim, *Grammatical Gender: Its Origin and Development* (The Hague: Mouton, 1973) 105–9. In this chapter we follow Ibrahim's study closely. The most significant older works on Hebrew are Heimann Rosenberg, "Zum Geschlecht der hebräischen Hauptwörter," *Zeitschrift für* *die Alttestamentliche Wissenschaft* 25 (1905) 325–39; and Karl Albrecht, "Das Geschlecht der hebräischen Hauptwörter," *Zeitschrift für die Alttestamentliche Wissenschaft* 15 (1895) 313–25; 16 (1896) 41–121. Among recent studies, note D. Michel, *Grundlegung einer hebräischen Syntax* (Neukirchen-Vluyn: Neukirchener Verlag, 1977), 1. 25–81.

b   In linguistic theory an opposition involves *marking* if one member has something extra or unusual about it to distinguish it from the other (3.3.5e). For example, in the opposition מַלְכָּה : מֶלֶךְ, the gender of מֶלֶךְ is not shown by any evident device, while the gender of מַלְכָּה is shown by the ending ה‑ָ; מֶלֶךְ is the unmarked or zero($\emptyset$)-marked member of the pair, while מַלְכָּה is the marked member. In general in Hebrew the masculine gender is unmarked, while the feminine is marked. The unmarked member *may* have the same value as its opposite, and thus unmarked masculine nouns may refer to females. The marked member of a linguistic pair attracts more attention than the unmarked, and so in studying gender it may seem we are dealing with the "problem" of the feminine, but in reality we are concerned with the grammatical system of *masculine : feminine.*

c   Feminine singular nouns in Hebrew can have a variety of endings: -*â* (# 1) is most common, with -*at* (# 2) its construct, and -*t* (# 3) and -*et* (# 4) are also used. Some nouns with female referents are zero-marked (# 5).

1.	מַלְכָּה	queen (abs.)		4.	גְּדֶרֶת	wall (abs., cstr.)
2.	מַלְכַּת	queen (cstr.)		5.	אֵם	mother (abs., cstr.)
3.	בְּרִית	covenant (abs., cstr.)				

The -*â* ending (the *he* is a *mater lectionis*) and the endings with *t* are all at base related.[2] The -*â* arose as a pausal variant of -*at*;[3] -*t* and -*et* are morphological variants of -*at*. We refer to all these endings as the -*at* suffix, contrasting it to the $\emptyset$ suffix or marker of אָב, אֵם, and similar nouns.

d   Gender-marking has long attracted the interest of students of language. We survey the views of some ancient, medieval, and modern commentators before turning to a comparative study of gender as a linguistic phenomenon. Having established that gender and sex are distinct phenomena and that the -*â*/ -*at* form originally signaled modification of an opposed $\emptyset$-form, we will be better able to look at the actual workings of the Hebrew gender system.

6.2   Study of Gender

6.2.1   Ancient and Medieval Views

a   The Western grammatical tradition, beginning with the Greeks, has speculated on gender.[4] Protagoras, an influential Sophist of the fifth century B.C.E., is credited with

---

2. C. Brockelmann, *Die Femininendung t im Semitischen* (Breslau: G. P. Aderholz, 1903); cf. G. Janssens, "The Feminine Ending -(a)t in Semitic," *Orientalia Lovaniensia Periodica* 6–7 (1975–76) 277–84.

3. As in Classical Arabic. Some Semitic languages exhibit the tendency to drop the historical -*at* of the feminine in the absolute state leading to the morphological alternation: -*â* in the absolute state and -*at* in the construct. Although, as a rule, exceptional morphological facts like this one most strongly attest to inherited features, this alternation in the various Semitic languages has to be interpreted as the result of parallel development because it arose at different times in different places and because of

many differences in detail. See Joshua Blau, "The Parallel Development of the Feminine Ending -*at* in Semitic Languages," *Hebrew Union College Annual* 51 (1980) 17–28. In contrast, M. Palmaitis has attempted to demonstrate that "the real Semitic marker of feminine, i.e., -*ā* (and not -[*a*]*t*!), is in fact the fossilized ending of the inertive case." The widespread ending -*at* was derived secondarily from the bare stem inertive in -*ā*, and both forms became fossilized in the course of the development of the ending for the morphologically marked "weak" gender class. See Palmaitis, "On the Origin of the Semitic Marker of the Feminine," *Archiv Orientální* 49 (1981) 263–69. Cf. n. 29.

4. See Ibrahim, *Grammatical Gender*, 14–15.

being the first to classify the three Greek genders: masculine, feminine, and neuter.[5] Aristotle (384–322 B.C.E.) went on to list the typical endings for each gender, thus classifying nouns according to their inflection or accidence.[6] The innovative and creative grammarians of the Sophist school anticipated the findings of modern linguistics by noting two principles in the field of gender: (1) gender formally marks the *agreement* between words in some kinds of phrases and other syntactic groups, and (2) the correspondence between (linguistic) gender and (natural) sex is only partial.[7] After the early Sophists, Greek grammarians concerned themselves largely with taxonomies. The Roman additions to Greek linguistics were slight; it is of some interest that Sextus Empiricus (late 2d century C.E.) observed that the gender of some nouns differed from one dialect to another.[8]

The true heirs of the Greek grammarians were the Arabs.[9] The earliest Arab gram-   b
marians, in the eighth and ninth centuries C.E., were strictly descriptive and taxonomic. They demarcated gender into masculine and feminine forms, recognizing that the feminine is the marked member of the pair. They essentially classified feminine nouns into the following groups:

(1) the true feminine: animate nouns that denote females, with or without the feminine ending (e.g., *baqarat-*[10] 'cow' and *ʾum* 'mother')
(2) the metaphorical feminine: inanimate nouns, with or without the feminine ending (e.g., *dawlat-* 'state, government' and *yad* 'hand')
(3) the morphological feminine: nouns used exclusively to refer to males and treated as masculine but possessing a feminine ending (e.g., *khalifat-* 'caliph')

Similar categories can be established for Biblical Hebrew.

Modern Views   6.2.2

In contrast to the strictly descriptive approaches of the early Greek and Arab   a
grammarians, eighteenth- and nineteenth-century linguists were long on speculation and short on descriptive analysis.[11] The Germans Herder and Adelung sought to explain the origin and function of gender, focusing on the genders assigned inanimate objects.[12] These scholars thought that so-called primitive peoples individualized objects, sorting them into one of two sex-based genders according to the characteristics of the object. Objects perceived to be strong, large, active, etc., were made masculine, and objects felt

5. John Lyons, *Introduction to Theoretical Linguistics* (Cambridge: Cambridge University, 1968) 10. Things neither "masculine" nor "feminine" were called "neither"; the Latin term for this yielded "neuter" (p. 11).

6. R. H. Robins, *Ancient and Mediaeval Grammatical Theory in Europe* (London: Bell, 1951) 23–24, and *A Short History of Linguistics* (Bloomington: Indiana University, 1967) 27.

7. Robins, *Ancient and Mediaeval Grammatical Theory*, 15.

8. Robins, *A Short History of Linguistics*, 21.

9. See Ibrahim, *Grammatical Gender*, 46–48, 22–23.

10. A hyphen is placed after *-at*, the feminine marker in Classical Arabic, because a case marker must follow.

11. Ibrahim, *Grammatical Gender*, 16–22.

12. See Karl Brugmann, *The Nature and Origin of the Noun Genders in the Indo-European Languages* (New York: Scribner, 1897) 7–8. Johann Gottfried von Herder (1744–1803) was one of the great Romantic students of myth and an early appreciator of Hebrew verse. His contemporary Johann Christoph Adelung (1732–1806) was a grammarian.

to be susceptible, delicate, passive, etc., became feminine. This groundless approach was commonly accepted among successive generations of linguists,[13] passing from late eighteenth-century tomes into many scholarly books of the nineteenth century. One scholar thus wrote of "primitive" people as children and remarks:

> From this source [i.e., imagination] is derived the whole system of genders for inanimate things, which was perhaps inevitable at that early childish stage of the human intelligence. . . .[14]

b   An outstanding authority on Arabic grammar, W. Wright, similarly remarked:

> The vivid imagination of the Semite conceived all objects, even those that are apparently lifeless, as endowed with life and personality. Hence for him there are but *two genders*, as there exist in nature but two sexes.[15]

Such notions lay behind the presentation of gender in most of the great Hebrew grammars, those of Gesenius, Gesenius-Kautzsch-Cowley, Joüon, and others. Paul Joüon, for example, remarks:

> Apart from living beings gender is metaphorical: certain nouns are masculine, by analogy with male beings; others are feminine, by analogy with female beings.[16]

So inadequate is this view that he adds directly:

> It is necessary to confess, for the rest, that the reason which determined the gender often escapes us.[17]

The issue of the gender of inanimates was not the only stimulus for bad theorizing among these scholars. Carl Brockelmann, for instance, having shown, he believed, that there was no overt feminine ending in early Semitic, went on to conclude that females were highly regarded in that culture, which may indeed have had a matriarchal organization.[18]

c   M. H. Ibrahim, deploring the heavy dependence of these scholars on fanciful extra-linguistic speculation, concludes:

> Those grammarians who have written about primitive peoples and their primitive languages were like the "armchair" anthropologists of the nineteenth-century, who wrote about these peoples without any contacts with them or their culture.[19]

---

13. Ibrahim, *Grammatical Gender*, 16.

14. Frederic W. Farrar, *Chapters on Language* (London: Longmans, Green, 1865) 212; quoted by Ibrahim, *Grammatical Gender*, 16.

15. William Wright, *Lectures on the Comparative Grammar of the Semitic Languages* (Cambridge: Cambridge University, 1890) 131; quoted by Ibrahim, *Grammatical Gender*, 20 (incorrectly attributed to Wright's *A Grammar of the Arabic Language* [3d ed.; Cambridge: Cambridge University, 1896], 1. 131).

16. Joüon § 134e / p. 410.

17. Joüon § 134e / p. 410.

18. C. Brockelmann, *Grundriss der vergleichenden Grammatik der semitischen Sprachen* (Berlin: Reuter und Reichard, 1908), 1. 417.

19. Ibrahim, *Grammatical Gender*, 21.

Anthropologists helped to reform the European ideas of pre-industrial ("primitive" or "savage") peoples and to remove them from easy stereotyping. At the same time modern linguistics has returned to its proper starting point, language, in considering gender phenomena.[20]

Modern linguists agree that grammatical gender serves only in part to denote sexual   d
differences among animate beings.[21] The primary function of various systems of gender is syntactic; gender is one of the *concord systems* that connect related words within a sentence. It is of secondary importance that the so-called "feminine" formatives designate natural gender in living beings.

Comparative Perspectives   6.3

Gender in Language   6.3.1

A description of gender as it is used across a variety of languages suggests that   a
grammatical gender does not primarily denote sex in animate beings and "analogous" features of inanimates. Rather, gender is primarily a matter of syntax. The relevant linguistic arguments are diverse; taken together, they point toward a properly linguistic notion of gender.

Typologically, languages may be divided into those having *noun classes* and those   b
that lack them. The most common noun classes are the genders, which may number three (masculine, feminine, neuter) or two (masculine or feminine). Other noun-class systems distinguish animates from inanimates, or count nouns (like 'book,' 'woman,' 'tree') from mass nouns (like 'people,' 'water,' 'salt'). The languages that use gender include most of the Indo-European and Semitic languages; among those that do not are Turkish, Chinese, and Basque. Thus, Turkish nowhere—not even in its pronouns— grammatically distinguishes genders, whereas French, like Hebrew, presses all nouns into either the masculine or feminine genders. Noting this contrast, James Barr points out that it would be nonsensical to suppose that the Turks were unaware of sexual differences or that grammar proves the "legendary erotic interests" of the French![22] It is not true that speakers of a language with a two-gender system think of all objects as male or female; rather, as F. R. Palmer argues, "it is simply that the grammar of their language divides all nouns into two classes."[23]

The error of the idea that gender is attached to an object according to certain per-   c
ceived qualities is further illustrated by comparing the genders of words in one language with those in another. For example, in the Romance languages 'sun' is masculine and 'moon' feminine, but in German the situation is reversed. Indeed, even for animate nouns the referential feature can be weakened or absent. Thus there are nouns in French that, though feminine in form, refer to men, for example, *la sentinelle* 'the sentinel,' *la vigi* 'the night watchman.' In French, most occupational terms are feminine, even if the person

---

20. Ibrahim, *Grammatical Gender*, 22.
21. See especially Ibrahim, *Grammatical Gender*, 25–29.
22. James Barr, *The Semantics of Biblical Language*

(Oxford: Oxford University, 1961) 39.
23. F. R. Palmer, *Grammar* (Harmondsworth: Penguin, 1971) 35.

referred to by the terms is generally a male. On the other hand, some nouns designating professions are masculine (*le professeur, le médicin*) even when referring to a female; thus, the following sentence is possible in French: *Le professeur est enceinte*, 'The professor is pregnant.'

d   In German similar clashes of sex and gender are found. Amused that *Rübe* 'turnip' is feminine, while *Mädchen* 'girl' is neuter, Mark Twain concocted this dialogue in *A Tramp Abroad*:

> Gretchen: Wilhelm, where is the turnip?
> Wilhelm: She has gone to the kitchen.
> Gretchen: Where is the accomplished and beautiful English maiden?
> Wilhelm: It has gone to the opera.[24]

In truth the neuter gender of *Mädchen* is determined by the suffix -*chen*; the base noun is feminine, *die Magd*. Another sort of sex-gender clash arises when adjectives indicating sex occur with nouns of the "opposite" gender. In French, 'the mouse' is *la souris*, and 'the he-mouse' is *la souris mâle*, that is, 'the male (feminine) mouse'!

e   It was Karl Brugmann, at the end of the last century, who most drastically revised his predecessors' views on gender. In fact he completely reversed the priority of grammatical gender and sex from that of earlier linguists. He argued that the grammatical gender, which originally had nothing to do with sex, guided the poetic imagination in mythic personifications.

> In all cases that come into consideration here [the historical period of the Indo-European languages] the grammatical gender of the word, so far as we can judge, is the earlier [i.e., earlier than personifications]. The imagination used this gender and allowed itself to be led by it. . . . When either [primitive people or poets] personified a lifeless concept into a living being, it was the grammatical form of the noun that, through the psychological impulse of analogy, . . . decided the definite direction of the gender—whether it should be masculine or feminine. . . .[25]

His studies find limited confirmation in some areas. For example, the Russians personify the days of the week as male or female on the basis of the day's grammatical gender.[26] Likewise, Hebrew poets sometimes personified non-animates according to gender, for example, חָכְמָה is Lady Wisdom, hostess (Prov 9:1–6), sister (7:4), mediatrix (1:20–33). On balance, however, it is best to see grammatical gender and the natural sex of animate beings as coordinate systems, neither controlling the other.

f   A larger view of gender systems derives from the study of languages with other noun-class systems; these include the Bantu languages, some Sudanic languages, and

---

24. The French example is from Ibrahim, *Grammatical Gender*, 100, citing D. T. Langendoen, *The Study of Syntax* (New York: Holt, Rinehart & Winston, 1969) 40; the German example from Mark Twain, *A Tramp Abroad*, vol. 2, appendix D: "The Awful German Language."

25. Brugmann, *Noun Genders*, 17; cited by Ibrahim, *Grammatical Gender*, 93.

26. Roman Jakobson, "On Linguistic Aspects of Translation," *On Translation*, ed. R. A. Brower (Cambridge: Harvard University, 1959) 232–39, at 237.

some languages of the Caucasus and Australia. The noun classes in these languages have no simple connection to natural sex. For example, in Swahili, there are classes of animates, of small, round things, of long, thin things, and so on; each class is formally indicated by a prefix and stands in concord with its modifying adjectives and verbs. Since there is only a limited correspondence between the formal classes and their "meanings," linguists classify them merely by their accidence.[27] Gender in the Indo-European and Semitic languages appears to be a special case of noun classification; as C. F. Hockett says, "Genders are classes of nouns reflected in the behavior of associated words."[28] From these comparative remarks we can see that grammatical gender does not "attribute" sex to inanimate objects and only imperfectly designates it in animate objects; it is chiefly a syntactic feature, whether the noun be animate or inanimate, not a strictly referential-semantic one.

Gender in Semitic and Hebrew   6.3.2

The basic facts of Hebrew gender may be reviewed before we try to discuss the   a
workings of the system. The grammatical genders are part of the system of Hebrew accidence, that is, gender-markings show that certain parts of speech agree with other parts of speech.

A feminine being can be grammatically marked only in the area of animate objects   b
(e.g., פַּר 'bull' and פָּרָה 'cow'). Lexically opposed "gender nouns" may be used to designate each member of a male-female dyad (e.g., אָב 'father' and אֵם 'mother'). Feminine plural formatives are found with nouns denoting male beings (e.g., אָבוֹת 'forebears, fathers'). On the other hand, masculine plural formatives appear with nouns denoting female beings (e.g., נָשִׁים 'women').[29]

There is no "reason" why inanimate nouns are in a particular grammatical gender.   c
Contrast הַר 'hill' and גִּבְעָה 'hill.' Some inanimate nouns show two genders (e.g., דֶּרֶךְ 'way,' אֲרוֹן 'chest').[30] The same meaning may be associated with two non-animate nouns that differ only in gender (e.g., נָקָם and נְקָמָה, 'dominion, vengeance'). Non-animate feminine nouns may designate a collective (e.g., גּוֹלָה 'exile'), or a single component of a collective (e.g., אֲנִיָּה 'ship,' contrast אֳנִי 'fleet,' both masculine and feminine).

The feminine formative is used to form numbers used with masculine nouns (e.g.,   d
שְׁלֹשָׁה בָּנִים 'three sons').

---

27. E. A. Gregersen, *Prefix and Pronoun in Bantu* (International Journal of American Linguistics, Memoir 21; Bloomington: Indiana University, 1967) 1, 15–16.

28. C. F. Hockett, *A Course in Modern Linguistics* (New York: Macmillan, 1958) 231. See Ibrahim, *Grammatical Gender*, 63–76, on the rationale behind the definition.

29. The use of feminine plural forms of nouns referring to males is found more commonly in other Semitic languages than in Hebrew. The feminine-singular absolute ending in Hebrew is not uniformly -â; there are cases of -āt as an absolute singular form (presumably lengthened from

-at; see, e.g., Gen 49:22, Exod 15:2, Ps 16:6) and some cases of -ôt should probably be taken as singular (e.g., Judg 5:29, Ps 78:15).

30. A survey of the use of *dérek* yields an unusual pattern: "The substantive *derek* governs either masculine or feminine agreements in independent clauses and in some dependent clauses, but only feminine agreements in relative clauses." See R. Ratner, "*Derek*: Morpho-Syntactical Considerations," *Journal of the American Oriental Society* 107 (1987) 471–73, at 473.

e   Comparative study reveals certain patterns of gender. Hebrew (like the Semitic languages generally) conforms to these patterns. If gender primarily serves the syntactic function of concord, how did it acquire any semantic value in the Semitic languages? Did it have an "original meaning"? C. Brockelmann, because of some of the data about noun-class systems presented above, thought that grammatical genders in the Semitic languages originally had nothing to do with natural sex.[31] He associated Semitic gender systems with class systems in other languages and suggested that the feminine ending, along with other minor terminations, reflects a trace of an older noun-class system in Semitic. A number of scholars have theorized that the noun classes represented by the genders were simply classes of *basic* (now masculine) and *derived* (now feminine) *forms*.

f   E. A. Speiser thought that what is now the feminine formative in Semitic began as an accusative element in the larger Semito-Hamitic or Afroasiatic language family.[32] This idea has been dismissed; the abiding value of his study of the problem remains in his contention that the "feminine" originally signified derivative words with some special modifications of the base stem. He observes that in all the Semitic languages -(a)t had not one but at least four semantic values: (1) to form an abstract from an adjective, numeral, or verb (e.g., רָעָה 'evil' from רַע 'bad'); (2) to make a collective out of a participle (e.g., אֹרְחָה 'caravan' from אֹרֵחַ 'traveler'); (3) to build a singulative (*nomen unitatis*) from a collective (e.g., שַׂעֲרָה '[a single] hair' from שֵׂעָר 'hair'); (4) to construct a diminutive or the like (e.g., יוֹנֶקֶת 'shoot' from יוֹנֵק 'young plant'; cf. 6.4.2f). The "remarkable versatility" of a formative that could mark either a collective noun or a *nomen unitatis* led Speiser to conclude:

> It is this seeming inconsistency that furnishes the necessary clue for the appreciation of the principal function of -(a)t. This was not to mark inferior classification, or to form abstracts, collectives, diminutives, or the like, but plainly to construct derivative stems with some special modification of the original meaning.[33]

In time -at came to have the ultimate specialization of the feminine with animate objects. Other features, such as form, tradition, and associations with other words, contributed to the assignment of a noun's gender.[34]

6.4   Gender of Inanimates and Non-Animates

a   There is no "natural" gender for inanimates (objects) and non-animates (abstracts). The earlier grammarians who sought to explain grammatical gender on such a basis were

---

31. C. Brockelmann, *Précis de linguistique sémitique* (Paris: Geuthner, 1910) 126; cf. n. 18 above.

32. E. A. Speiser, "Studies in Semitic Formatives," *Journal of the American Oriental Society* 56 (1936) 22–46; reprinted in J. J. Finkelstein and Moshe Greenberg, eds., *Oriental and Biblical Studies: Collected Writings of E. A. Speiser* (Philadelphia: University of Pennsylvania, 1967) 403–32; on the "feminine" ending see pp. 33–46,

esp. pp. 37–46 (rpt. pp. 416–32, 422–32). Speiser favored the simple -t as the original form of the formative (p. 45 / rpt. p. 430).

33. Speiser, "Studies in Semitic Formatives," 39 (rpt. pp. 424–25).

34. Ibrahim, *Grammatical Gender*, 77–90. The terms "autonomous" and "non-autonomous" are sometimes used for the "masculine" and "feminine" genders.

misled in their correlation of linguistic and non-linguistic phenomena. We analyze these nouns according to whether they have a ∅ or -*at* formative.

Zero-marked Gender Nouns   **6.4.1**

Nouns with a ∅-gender formative may be treated in Hebrew as either masculine or   **a** feminine, though most are masculine. With few exceptions no semantically homogeneous value can be attached to the gender assignment. There are, however, three semantic fields where the gender pattern deserves study: nouns referring to body parts, place names, and figurative terms.

Nouns referring to *parts of the body* tend to be feminine (## 1–17).   **b**

1.	אֹזֶן	ear	10.	לְחִי	jaw
2.	אֶצְבַּע	finger	11.	לָשׁוֹן	tongue
3.	בֶּטֶן	belly	12.	עַיִן	eye
4.	בֶּרֶךְ	knee	13.	צֵלָע	side
5.	זְרוֹעַ	arm	14.	קֶרֶן	horn
6.	יָד	hand	15.	רֶגֶל	foot
7.	יָרֵךְ	thigh	16.	שׁוֹק	leg
8.	כָּנָף	wing	17.	שֵׁן	tooth
9.	כַּף	palm			

A notable exception is שַׁד (masc.) 'breast' (see Hos 9:14).

The gender of *place names* is complicated by the fact that place-name terms fre-   **c** quently lose their head nouns (the grammatical process of "beheading"), while the head noun continues to control the gender of the phrase. Beheading is common in English— we say 'California' for 'the state of California,' 'Mexico' for 'the United States of Mexico.' In languages with grammatical gender-systems, beheading almost invariably affects those systems. The early Arab grammarians noted that a generic term (such as 'city of . . . ,' 'kingdom of . . . ,' 'river of . . . ,' 'mountain . . .') in construct with a place name deter- mines the gender of the phrase and that even if the generic was not expressed, its gender still controls the term, for example, *dijlat* 'Tigris' is feminine in form but is treated as masculine, since the full expression is *nahr dijlat* 'river of Tigris' and *nahr* is masculine.[35] The omission of the noun in the construct (the beheading) is common in Arabic. Thus, most city names are feminine because *madinatu* 'city' is feminine.

The Hebrew situation is similar. Like Arabic *nahr*, Hebrew נָהָר is masculine, as can   **d** be seen in # 18; although פְּרָת seems to be feminine, the pronoun in # 19 is masculine, following נְהַר(-פְּרָת).

18.	הַנָּהָר הַגָּדֹל נְהַר־פְּרָת׃	the great river, the River Euphrates
		Gen 15:18
19.	וְהַנָּהָר הָרְבִיעִי הוּא פְרָת׃	the fourth river was the Euphrates
		Gen 2:14

---

35. Ibrahim, *Grammatical Gender*, 59–60.

Again, אֲמָנָה, though feminine in form, stands in agreement with masculine modifiers because the omitted נָהָר is masculine.

20.   הֲלֹא טוֹב אֲמָנָה   Is not Amana better?
                                                           2 Kgs 5:12 *Qere*

Another masculine head noun is בַּיִת; thus בֵּית־לֶחֶם in Mic 5:1 and בֵּית־אֵל in Amos 5:5 are both masculine. Feminine heads include מַמְלֶכֶת and אֶרֶץ, and either could explain the treatment of בָּבֶל as feminine in Gen 11:9 and Isa 21:9, since בָּבֶל is called both a מַמְלָכָה (Gen 10:10) and an אֶרֶץ (Jer 50:28). Similarly, אַשּׁוּר is feminine in Ezek 32:22 (cf. Isa 7:18). Note the feminines in Exod 12:33; 1 Sam 17:21; 2 Sam 8:2, 24:9. In some cases a place name seems to vary in gender; this is probably a sign that the underlying head varies. Thus יְהוּדָה is masculine in Isa 3:8, perhaps due to the head בַּיִת, but feminine in Isa 7:6, due to the head אֶרֶץ. Similarly, אֱדוֹם is masculine in Num 20:20 (due to בַּיִת), but feminine in Jer 49:17 (due to אֶרֶץ). In some cases the usage is not entirely clear: יְהוּדָה is probably feminine in Lam 1:3 because of עִיר rather than אֶרֶץ, or the place name there may refer by metonymy to the inhabitants of the place. Since עִיר is feminine and therefore names of cities are regarded as feminine, Israel's poets were led to personify cities as women, for example, בַּת־בָּבֶל 'Daughter Babylon' (Isa 47:1) and בַּת יְרוּשָׁלַיִם 'Daughter Jerusalem' (Isa 37:22; see 6.3.1, 9.5.3h). Concerning this method of gender assignment, Ibrahim comments: "It explains in a simple way why thousands of names of countries, rivers, cities, mountains, etc. are assigned one gender or another."[36] There are exceptions to this pattern, in which the place name determines the gender of the phrase; for example, גַּן is usually masculine, but the phrase גַּן־עֵדֶן is feminine (Gen 2:15); גֶּפֶן is probably masculine in Hos 10:1 because of the reference there to יִשְׂרָאֵל.[37]

e   A third semantic area where there is a clear pattern for Ø-marked nouns involves *figurative usage*, an area also important for feminine nouns in *-at*. Where the literal sense of a term is feminine, the figurative may be masculine: עַיִן, feminine 'eye' but masculine 'engraving surface, facet' (Zech 3:9, 4:10); שֵׁן, feminine 'tooth' but masculine 'prong (of a fork)' (1 Sam 2:13), 'point (of a rock)' (1 Sam 14:4, 5).

6.4.2   Feminine Gender-marked Nouns

a   Several important groups of non-animate and inanimate nouns are morphologically feminine. These include abstracts, collectives, and singulatives, as well as infinitives and certain figurative nouns. (On the feminine "dummy" pronoun, see 6.6d.)

b   *Abstract nouns* may be feminine singular (## 1–8) or plural (## 9–11). Singular and more often plural abstracts may be used adverbially (10.2.2e), for example, וַיְדַבֵּר קָשׁוֹת, 'he spoke harsh things (i.e., he spoke harshly)' (Gen 42:7; cf. Isa 32:4 for # 10; cf. 39.3.1).

---

36. Ibrahim, *Grammatical Gender*, 60.
37. Similarly, רוּחַ is usually feminine but רוּחַ יהוה in 2 Kgs 2:16 is masculine in gender, as יהוה is. There are a few other analogous gender exceptions (גֶּפֶן as masculine in 2 Kgs 4:39; כֶּרֶם as feminine in Isa 27:2; cf. פָּנִים as

feminine in Ezek 21:21). It is on the basis of these cases that Brockelmann notes that "the gender of the *regens* is sometimes determined by that of the *rectum*"; *Hebräische Syntax* (Neukirchen: Neukirchener Verlag, 1956) 14.

1.	אֱמוּנָה	firmness		7.	תְּכוּנָה	arrangement
2.	נֶאֱמָנָה	a sure thing		8.	רָעָה	evil
3.	גְּבוּרָה	strength		9.	נְדִיבוֹת	noble things
4.	טוֹבָה	goodness		10.	צָחוֹת	clear things
5.	יְשָׁרָה	uprightness		11.	קָשׁוֹת	harsh things
6.	נְכוֹנָה	steadfastness				

Not all abstract nouns are feminine (e.g., חַיִל 'power,' כָּבוֹד 'glory,' טוֹב וָרָע 'good and evil' [Gen 2:9]).

Collectives, comprehensive designations of a number of things or persons, often   c display the *-at* suffix (## 12–14).[38] Sometimes it is uncertain whether a form is personification or a collective (## 15–16).

12.	אֹרְחָה	caravan		15.	אֹיֶבֶת	enemy
13.	גּוֹלָה	exile		16.	יוֹשֶׁבֶת	inhabitant
14.	דַּלָּה	poor people				

Single components of a collective unit often appear with *-at* suffix; such a form is   d called a *nomen unitatis* or singulative.

17.	אֳנִיָּה	vessel	אֳנִי	fleet
18.	צִיצָה, נִצָּה	flower	צִיץ, נֵץ	blossoms
19.	שַׂעֲרָה	(a) hair	שֵׂעָר	hair
20.	שִׁירָה	(a) song	שִׁיר	song, singing

On the other hand, one finds דָּגָה 'fish (coll.)' but דָּג '(a) fish.' Some forms, for example, שׁוֹשַׁנָּה 'lily,' לְבֵנָה 'brick,' etc., are singulatives for which the collective is not attested. (The masculine שׁוּשָׁן is a metaphorical 'lily,' an architectural decoration.)

The *infinitive* may be treated as feminine.   e

21.	הַנְקַלָּה בְעֵינֵיכֶם הִתְחַתֵּן בַּמֶּלֶךְ	Do you think it a small matter to become the king's son-in-law? 1 Sam 18:23

In some cases it is treated as masculine.

22.	כִּי־רַע וָמָר עָזְבֵךְ . . . אֱלֹהָיִךְ	How evil and bitter it is that you abandoned . . . your God. Jer 2:19

A *figurative sense* may also be denoted by *-at*.   f

23.	יוֹנֵק	suckling/child (masc.)	יוֹנֶקֶת	sucker, shoot
24.	יָרֵךְ	hip (fem.)	יַרְכָתַיִם	sides (of a building, etc.)
25.	מֵצַח	forehead	מִצְחָה	legging, greave

---

38. In Greek, collective neuter plurals, like Hebrew collective feminine singulars, take a singular verb. See 6.6c.

6.4.3   **Gender Doublets**

a   Some non-animate nouns have both masculine and feminine forms. Although these so-called *doublets* may have different connotations, it is best not to rely too heavily on their gender distinctions; both forms mean essentially the same thing. Mordechai Ben-Asher has surveyed 117 non-animate nouns having both masculine and feminine forms, including five collective/*nomen unitatis* pairs (6.4.2d). (He excludes cases where there is no connection between similar forms, e.g., *tôrâ*/*tôr*, or where a connection is dubious, e.g., *ʾadāmâ*/*ʾādām*.) Of these, 61 are abstract nouns and 56 are concrete. These pairs include all kinds of meanings: abstract nouns (## 1–2), parts of body (## 3–4), agricultural terms (## 5–6), words connected with clothing (## 7–8), and pairs of words with initial *ma-*/*mi-* (## 9–12; see 5.6), seven of which are from medial-*waw* roots (## 11–12). He finds no positive difference in meaning between the pairs, apart from the few cases of collectives/*nomina unitatis* (# 6 and perhaps # 3).

1.	אַשְׁמָה / אָשָׁם	guilt	7.	אֵפֻדָּה / אֵפוֹד	ephod
2.	נְקָמָה / נָקָם	dominion, vengeance	8.	חֲגוֹרָה / חֲגוֹר	loin-covering
3.	אֶבְרָה / אֵבֶר	pinion	9.	מַתָּנָה / מַתָּן	gift
4.	גֵּוָה / גֵּו	back	10.	מִמְכֶּרֶת / מִמְכָּר	ware
5.	חֶלְקָה / חֵלֶק	territory	11.	מָגוֹרָה / מָגוֹר	terror
6.	צִיצָה / צִיץ	blossom	12.	מְחוֹלָה / מָחוֹל	dance

In five cases he found that one of the forms occurs in a poetic or elevated style, and the other mainly in an ordinary prosaic style (## 13–17).[39]

	prosaic	*elevated*	
13.	אֲפֵלָה	אֹפֶל	gloom
14.	גַּן	גַּנָּה	garden
15.	חֹשֶׁךְ	חֲשֵׁכָה / חֲשֵׁכָה	darkness
16.	צְדָקָה	צֶדֶק	righteousness
17.	שֹׂבַע / שָׂבָע	שָׂבְעָה / שִׂבְעָה	satiety

The doublet מַשְׁעֵן וּמַשְׁעֵנָה is used as a hendiadys for 'every kind of support' (Isa 3:1).

6.5   **Gender of Animates**

6.5.1   **Natural Dyads**

a   Some natural male-female dyads are designated by unrelated words, neither of which is marked for gender.

---

39. M. Ben-Asher, "The Gender of Nouns in Biblical Hebrew," *Semitics* 6 (1978) 1–14. For differences in connotation between *ṣedeq* and *ṣədāqâ*, e.g., see J. J. Scullion, "*Ṣedeq-ṣedaqah* in Isaiah cc. 40–66," *Ugarit-Forschungen* 3 (1971) 335–48. Related to the style contrast is the interesting material discussed by W. G. E. Watson, "Gender-Matched Synonymous Parallelism in the Old Testament," *Journal of Biblical Literature* 99 (1980) 321–41. Watson notes that in groups (usually pairs) of associated lines, nouns may be arranged by gender *like* with *like* to suggest

1.	אִישׁ	man	אִשָּׁה	woman[40]	
2.	אָב	father	אֵם	mother[41]	
3.	תַּיִשׁ	he-goat	עֵז	she-goat	
4.	חֲמוֹר	he-ass	אָתוֹן	she-ass	
5.	אֲרִי, אַרְיֵה	he-lion	לָבִיא	she-lion	

The nouns in other dyads are designated by word pairs marked ∅ : -at.

6.	אַיָּל	hart	אַיֶּלֶת, אַיָּלָה	hind	
7.	עֵגֶל	calf	עֶגְלָה	heifer	
8.	עֶלֶם	young man	עַלְמָה	young woman	
9.	פַּר	bull, ox	פָּרָה	cow	

Epicene Nouns

6.5.2

Nouns used for a male or female animate, or for a mixed group, are called *epicene*.[42] **a** For example, in the phrase דֹּב שַׁכּוּל 'a bear robbed of her whelps' (Hos 13:8), though both noun and adjective are masculine in form, a she-bear is in view (cf. also Isa 49:15). Epicene nouns in English include 'sheep' (in contrast to 'ewe/ram'), 'secretary' (in contrast to 'male secretary/female secretary'), 'dog' (in contrast to 'bitch, female dog/male dog'). In Hebrew an epicene may be of either gender; an epicene feminine singular may form an epicene masculine plural.

	masculine			*feminine*	
1.	אֶלֶף	cattle (coll.)	5.	אַרְנֶבֶת	hare
2.	דֹּב	bear	6.	חֲסִידָה	stork
3.	זְאֵב	wolf	7.	יוֹנָה	dove
4.	כֶּלֶב	dog	8.	נְמָלָה	ant

Sometimes grammatically masculine epicene nouns are modified according to sense with feminine forms, for example, גְּמַלִּים מֵינִיקוֹת 'nursing camels' (Gen 32:16), in contrast to גְּמַלִּים בָּאִים 'camels were approaching' (Gen 24:63). Similarly וְהַצֹּאן וְהַבָּקָר עָלוֹת 'the small cattle [i.e., sheep and goats] and the cattle which are nursing' (Gen 33:13; cf. 1 Kgs 5:3 for בָּקָר, Gen 30:39 for צֹאן). The most remarkable epicene noun is אֱלֹהִים—Hebrew (like some other Canaanite dialects) has no distinct word for 'goddess.'

---

a global picture (e.g., masc. + masc., gwym + qlwn; fem. + fem., ṣwḥh + ᵓrṣ, in Jer 42:12; cf. Isa 19:2). Nouns may also be paired *like* and *unlike* to suggest contrast (e.g., masc. + fem., zbḥ + twᶜbh; fem. + masc., tplh + rṣwn, in Prov 15:8) or inversion (e.g., fem. + masc., ḥrph + šknym; masc. + fem., lᶜg wqls + sbybwt, in Ps 44:14).

40. Despite similarities, ᵓîš, pl. ᵓănāšîm (rarely ᵓîšîm), and the related word ᵓĕnôš 'humanity,' are from a root different from that of ᵓiššâ, pl. nāšîm (ᵓiššōt occurs once).

41. The 'mother : father' pair is associated in many lan-

guages with an m : b/p/f contrast; English *mama : papa*, Greek *mētēr : patēr*, Latin *mater : pater*, English *mother : father*, Chinese *mu : fu*, etc.

42. The term refers to 'common' gender, cf. Greek *koine dialektos* 'the common tongue.' The interaction of gender and names is complex. Hebrew certainly had epicene names; Gomer is a female name in Hosea, but a male name in a Samaria Ostracon; see N. Avigad, "A Hebrew Seal Depicting a Sailing Ship," *Bulletin of the American Schools of Oriental Research* 246 (1982) 59–62, at 60.

9.   וַיֵּ֣לֶךְ שְׁלֹמֹ֔ה אַחֲרֵ֖י עַשְׁתֹּ֥רֶת   And Solomon followed Ashtoreth, the *godhead*
      אֱלֹהֵ֣י צִדֹנִ֑ים   of the Sidonians.
                                              1 Kgs 11:5

6.5.3   Priority of the Masculine

a   Grammarians speak of the masculine gender as "*the prior gender*" because its form
sometimes refers to female beings.

1.   זָכָ֥ר וּנְקֵבָ֖ה בָּרָ֣א אֹתָ֑ם׃   Male and female he created *them* (masc.).
                                              Gen 1:27

2.   וַיְנַשֵּׁ֥ק לְבָנָ֖יו וְלִבְנוֹתָ֑יו וַיְבָ֣רֶךְ   He kissed his sons and daughters and blessed
      אֶתְהֶ֑ם   *them* (masc.).
                                              Gen 32:1

3.   וְאִישׁ֙ אוֹ אִשָּׁ֔ה כִּֽי־יִהְיֶ֥ה ב֖וֹ נָ֑גַע   As for a man or a woman, when a sore be on
                                              him. . . .
                                              Lev 13:29

4.   לֹֽא־תַעֲשֶׂ֣ה כָל־מְלָאכָ֡ה אַתָּ֣ה   *You* (masc.) will do no work, neither *you* (masc.)
      וּבִנְךָֽ־וּבִתֶּ֡ךָ   nor your son or daughter.
                                              Exod 20:10

This priority of the masculine gender is due in part to the intensely androcentric character of the world of the Hebrew Bible. As Clarence Vos shows, this milieu must be called
a "man's world."[43] The priority of the masculine gender in these examples is due not
only to the linguistic precedence of the unmarked (masculine) over the marked (feminine); it is also due in part to Israel's religion, which, though it allows or recognizes both
nābî and *nəbî*â, has place only for a priest, not a priestess, in contrast to other religions
of the region.

b   The grammatical forms for God are masculine and the representations of God are
mostly masculine. Although God does use a comparison to a woman in childbirth (Isa
42:14), nonetheless there is a strong scholarly consensus that God is regarded as non-
sexual. "If sex must be applied to Israel's deity, it would be monosex, and this is either
an incompleteness or a contradiction in terms."[44] This consensus finds explicit support in
Deut 4:15–16:

> You saw no form of any kind the day YHWH spoke to you at Horeb . . . so that you
> do not . . . make for yourselves an idol, an image in any shape, whether formed like a
> man or a woman.

---

43. Clarence Vos, *Woman in Old Testament Worship*
(Delft: Judels en Brinkman, 1968) 32–50. The classification of animate *versus* inanimate may originally have
enjoyed some priority, as Speiser argues from the isolated
character of the *mî* 'who' : *mâ* 'what' opposition.

44. Vos, *Woman in Old Testament Worship*, 39. Cf.
also Phyllis Trible, *God and the Rhetoric of Sexuality*
(Philadelphia: Fortress, 1978); Peter T. Daniels, "Virtuous

Housewife or Woman of Valor? On Sexist Language in
the Hebrew Bible," *Proceedings* [*of the*] *Eastern Great
Lakes and Midwest Biblical Societies* 4 (1984) 99–106;
Elizabeth Achtemeier, "The Impossible Possibility: Evaluat-
ing the Feminist Approach to Bible and Theology," *In-
terpretation* 42 (1988) 45–57; R. M. Frye, "Language for
God and Feminist Language: A Literary and Rhetorical
Analysis," *Interpretation* 43 (1989) 45–57.

One fact providing inferential support is the use of both sexes of a sacrificial victim as offerings to God. In the ancient Near East it was customary to sacrifice male animals to (male) gods and females to goddesses.[45] In Israel's cultus both males and females of a species were sacrificed to God (cf. Lev 3:1; 4:23, 28). One cannot change or remove the masculine figurative representations of God without distorting the text of the Bible.

Concord   6.6

Grammatical gender involves three distinct systems: morphology, meaning with   a
reference to an extra-linguistic reality, and syntax.[46] In Hebrew the basic morphology opposes ∅-marked masculine to the feminine in -at, though there are many ∅-marked nouns with female reference. In semantic terms, the -at suffix essentially marks derivative words, words with some special modification of the unmarked alternative, though the suffix also serves as the designation of the natural female of animates. The primary function of gender marking is to bind parts of speech together by concord in the same sentence or discourse.

Sometimes the grammatical form of a noun differs from its semantic significance,   b
for example, a collective noun such as מוֹלֶ֫דֶת 'descendants' (fem.) or an abstract noun such as קֹהֶ֫לֶת 'teacher' (fem.) may have a male referent. When such clashes arise in a language, concord can follow grammatical gender (as it does, e.g., in Italian or French), or it can follow the semantic orientation of the noun; Hebrew prefers the latter course, sometimes called the *constructio ad sensum* ("construction according to the sense").[47] Thus we find הָיָה קֹהֶ֫לֶת חָכָם, 'The Teacher was wise' (Qoh 12:9). Moreover, a feminine singular collective noun may be construed with a plural verb because the noun's referent is plural; in the second example 'land' is used for 'inhabitants' by metonymy.[48]

1.	וְאָבְדוּ שְׁאֵרִית פְּלִשְׁתִּים	And the *remnant* of the Philistines *will perish*. Amos 1:8
2.	וְכָל־הָאָ֫רֶץ בָּ֫אוּ מִצְרַ֫יְמָה	And all the *land came* to Egypt. Gen 41:57
3.	וּמוֹלַדְתְּךָ אֲשֶׁר־הוֹלַ֫דְתָּ אַחֲרֵיהֶם לְךָ יִהְיוּ	And your *descendants* whom you begot after them *will be* yours. Gen 48:6

Gender agreement may also lapse when (as is often the case) the verb precedes the   c
subject; the subject may be feminine singular or plural, and the verb may be masculine singular.[49]

---

45. Watson, "Gender-Matched Synonymous Parallelism," 338. Note Watson's discussion of Isa 24:21. We need to keep in mind, however, Speiser's remark, "Too much mystery seems to be made of our feminine ending" ("Studies in Semitic Formatives," 37 [rpt. p. 422]).

46. Ibrahim, *Grammatical Gender*, 97.
47. Ibrahim, *Grammatical Gender*, 34.
48. Cf. GKC § 145e / p. 463.
49. Cf. GKC § 145o / p. 465.

4.	נִעְתַּם אָרֶץ	The *land is scorched.* Isa 9:18
5.	תַּחְתֶּיךָ יֻצַּע רִמָּה	Beneath you *worms* (fem., coll.) *are laid.* Isa 14:11
6.	וַיַּעֲבֹר הָרִנָּה בַּמַּחֲנֶה	A *cry spread* through the army. 1 Kgs 22:36
7.	וְחָשׁ עֲתִדֹת לָמוֹ׃	And *doom* (lit., *prepared things*) *rushes* on them. Deut 32:35
8.	יִתְנַגְּפוּ רַגְלֵיכֶם	Your *feet stumble.* Jer 13:16

The preceding verb may also be a masculine plural, as in # 9; since there are cases of a masculine plural verb *following* a feminine plural noun, as in # 10, it has been suggested that both types of discord reflect an avoidance of feminine plural verbs.[50]

9.	אִם־יֵצְאוּ בְנוֹת־שִׁילוֹ	If the *daughters* of Shiloh *come forth.* . . . Judg 21:21
10.	וְעָרֵיכֶם יִהְיוּ חָרְבָּה׃	Your *cities will become* a desolation. Lev 26:33

Examples like # 10 are far less common than cases of grammatical discord where the verb precedes the subject.

d   Finally we may mention cases in which there is no true antecedent for a pronoun— what, so to speak, is the gender of a situation or an action? Such a dummy or impersonal pronoun is usually feminine (cf. 4.4.2).

11.	כִּי עָשִׂיתָ זֹּאת	Because you have done *this.* . . . Gen 3:14; cf. 3:13, 2:23
12.	וּבָהּ אֵדַע	By *this* I shall know. Gen 24:14

For other examples, see Exod 10:11, Num 14:41, and Isa 43:13; cf. 1 Chr 21:10. Such a vague pronoun can be masculine, as in the stock phrase כָּזֹה וְכָזֶה 'such and such' (1 Kgs 14:5 and often) and in the following example.

13.	וְזֶה־לְּךָ הָאוֹת	And *this* will be the sign to you. Exod 3:12

---

50. Cf. GKC § 145p / p. 465.

7

Number

Introduction

7.1

The patterns of number use seem to reflect so closely the real world that discrepancies among various languages may seem bewildering. In English we refer to the aggregate of flying creatures with a plural, 'birds,' but Hebrew uses the singular עוֹף; contrariwise, English uses a singular to refer to the human 'face,' but Hebrew uses a plural, פָּנִים. Such discrepancies exist because no facet of language mirrors the world directly. Number is a grammatical category, as gender is, and is thus part of the greater system of a given language's grammatical and lexical structure. Further, number usage reveals even more plainly than gender the fact that a language is part of a culture and is thus shaped by that culture. Let us consider this second point further, for it is crucial to the process of understanding a language.

Cultures express collective perceptions of reality differently and therefore represent the world in diverse ways. Hebrew, for example, represents the body part variously labeled in English 'hand' or 'arm' by יָד, a term that denotes that stretch of the appendage from the elbow to the tips of the fingers; further, it subdivides that portion and refers to the lower subdivision as כַּף, the portion from the wrist to the fingertips. English has no word corresponding *precisely* to Hebrew יָד; Hebrew has no word corresponding to English 'forearm.' Words in one language rarely coincide precisely in scope and in content with "corresponding" words in another. The cultural heritage of speakers causes them to perceive reality in a way somewhat different from that of speakers in another

a

b

culture. Linguistic studies cannot be divorced from anthropology and sociology. It is a cultural and linguistic fact that the English speaker, conceiving of 'face' as a countable noun, manifests that perception by the singular, while the speaker of Classical Hebrew probably perceived it as a mass and represented it by a plural.

c   Languages may also differ in their use of grammatical number because of differing perceptions of what counts as "one object" and what counts as "more than one object" (i.e., a *countable*), what counts as a coherent "group of objects" (i.e., a *collective*), or as an undifferentiated "mass of material" (i.e., a *mass*, e.g., 'butter'); these perceptions help to shape a language's lexical structure. For example, English treats 'grape' as a countable ('Will you have some grapes?'), but 'fruit' as a collective ('Will you have some fruit?'); Russian treats them in exactly the opposite way.[1] So also English treats 'birds' as countable but Hebrew refers to them with a collective.

d   Furthermore, a noun's grammatical number is determined by the language's lexical structure, and thus it does not represent the speaker's thought or experience directly. For example, English lexical structure demands that 'oats' be represented as a plural ('The oats are in the field') but 'wheat' as a singular ('The wheat is in the barn'). We cannot argue that speakers of English think of 'oats' as plural and 'wheat' as singular; this is simply false. An old joke plays on this lack of correspondence:

> Teacher: Is 'trousers' singular or plural?
> Johnny: Please, sir, singular at the top and plural at the bottom.

'Trousers' is in fact a plural-invariable noun, like other garment terms ('pants, pajamas') as well as tool names ('pliers, scissors, glasses') in English. Hebrew also has plural-invariable nouns.[2]

e   The most striking culturally determined difference between Hebrew and English number usage involves *honorifics*. Many European languages (e.g., French, Italian, Russian, German) systematically use plural forms with singular referents to express honor to the referent. For example, in the second-person singular, German uses both *Sie*, grammatical plural to express respect, and *du*, grammatical singular for intimacy. English, lacking this linguistic and cultural pattern, uses the singular.[3]

f   Grammatical number thus does not directly and necessarily represent "thought." It is rather a language- and cultural-specific system. It should be no surprise that Hebrew grammatical number cannot always be represented straightforwardly in English. Since number may be used in many different ways within a language and since it is determined

---

1. John Lyons, *Introduction to Theoretical Linguistics* (Cambridge: Cambridge University, 1968) 282.

2. They are sometimes called by the Latin term *plurale tantum* (pl. *pluralia tantum*).

3. English used to distinguish second-person singular pronouns (*thou, thee, thy, thine*) and plural (*ye, you, your, yours*), but the plural forms have taken over completely now. In Early Modern English translations of the Bible God was addressed in the singular ("Heare thou then in heaven, in thy dwelling place," 1 Kgs 8:39, Geneva Bible, 1560); in some modern translations the archaic singular is preserved only in addresses to God ("Then hear thou in heaven thy dwelling place," RSV, 1952). In most European languages with honorifics it is the intimate form that is used for addresses to God ("Toi, écoute au ciel, où tu résides," Bible de Jérusalem).

in part by the meaning of the word, our discussion will touch on many facets of syntax and lexicon.

Hebrew, like other Semitic languages, uses three numbers: singular, dual, and plural.   g
In the following sections we analyze and display the uses of these numbers.[4]

Singular   7.2

Hebrew uses the grammatical singular for countables, for collectives, and for class   a
nouns. Singular nouns may be repeated in various constructions.

Countables and Collectives   7.2.1

With *countables* the singular serves to enumerate one object. With entities that   a
Hebrew counts as "one object" or "more than one object," the singular usually enumerates the referent as an individual. Countable nouns are the most common.

1.	הָבָה אֶת־אִשְׁתִּי	Give (me) my *wife*. Gen 29:21
2.	וְהָאָרֶץ הָיְתָה תֹהוּ וָבֹהוּ	And the *earth* was waste-and-void. Gen 1:2
3.	וַיִּמְצָאֵהוּ אִישׁ	A *man* found him. Gen 37:15

With *collectives* the singular designates a group. Some words in Hebrew, like 'fish,'   b
'sheep,' and 'fruit' in English, are treated as *collectives* and represented by the singular. As noted above, English and Hebrew differ in their distribution of countables and collectives. Collectives occur in both grammatical genders. A collective singular may not agree in number with other words in the sentence syntactically related to it (cf. English 'the sheep are in the field' *versus* 'the wheat is . . .'; 6.6); thus a singular collective noun can govern a plural verb. We distinguish between words in Hebrew that are conventionally collective (i.e., words almost always represented in the singular) and those that are non-conventionally collective (i.e., words that are often represented by the plural but for contextual reasons may be represented by a collective).

Conventional collectives are frequently natural; note the three collectives in this   c
example.

4.	תַּדְשֵׁא הָאָרֶץ דֶּשֶׁא עֵשֶׂב מַזְרִיעַ זֶרַע	Let the earth bring forth *vegetation*, *plants* yielding *seed*. Gen 1:11

Another vegetable collective is פְּרִי 'fruit.' Animal collectives include עוֹף 'birds, the winged kind,' רֶמֶשׂ 'creepy-crawlies, the running-with-the-little-steps kind,' שֶׁרֶץ 'swarmers, the

---

4. On number in Hebrew generally, see, e.g., D. Michel, *Grundlegung einer hebräischen Syntax* (Neukirchen-Vluyn: Neukirchener, 1977), I. 83–89.

wriggling kind,' בְּהֵמָה 'livestock,' רִמָּה 'worms.' A human collectivity is טַף 'children.'
Inanimate collectives include רֶכֶב 'chariotry,' דִּמְעָה 'tears,' צִיצָת 'tassels, fringes.'

d   *Non-conventional collectives* are often human, for example, נֶפֶשׁ in Gen 12:5.

5.	וַיִּשַּׁח אָדָם וַיִּשְׁפַּל־אִישׁ וְאַל־תִּשָּׂא לָהֶם׃	So *mankind* will be brought low and *men* humbled— but do not forgive *them*. Isa 2:9
6.	מַה־נַּעֲשֶׂה לַנּוֹתָרִים לְנָשִׁים כִּי־נִשְׁמְדָה מִבִּנְיָמִן אִשָּׁה׃	How shall we provide wives for the men who are left? for *womankind* have been annihilated from Benjamin. Judg 21:16
7.	טַפְּכֶם נְשֵׁיכֶם וְגֵרְךָ	your little children, your wives, and your *aliens* Deut 29:10
8.	וַיְהִי־לִי שׁוֹר וַחֲמוֹר צֹאן וְעֶבֶד וְשִׁפְחָה	I have cattle and donkeys, sheep and goats, *menservants* and *maidservants*. Gen 32:6

Non-human cases include אֶבֶן (in Job 28:3) and עֵץ (in Gen 3:8).

7.2.2   Class Nouns

a   Like English, Hebrew may use the article with a singular noun to indicate a particular class or group; cf. '*The lion* is king of the beasts.' Such a singular noun has a broad referent, each member of the group. Hebrew may use the singular with this meaning even without the article, especially in poetry. This use of the singular is found in enumerations, after כֹּל and other terms of quantity, with gentilics, and in various expressions.[5]

b   In *enumerations* singular nouns follow the numeral.

1.	וּשְׁלֹשִׁים וּשְׁנַיִם מֶלֶךְ	32 *kings* 1 Kgs 20:1
2.	אֶלֶף גֶּפֶן	1,000 *vines* Isa 7:23
3.	שְׁלֹשֶׁת אֲלָפִים מָשָׁל	3,000 *proverbs* 1 Kgs 5:12
4.	וּשְׁתֵּים עֶשְׂרֵה מַצֵּבָה	12 *pillars* Exod 24:4
5.	אַרְבַּע מֵאוֹת נַעֲרָה בְתוּלָה	400 young *women* Judg 21:12
6.	שְׁמֹנֶה מֵאוֹת חָלָל	800 *wounded* 2 Sam 23:8

---

5. Such uses of the singular exist also in some European languages, but they are not as common as in Hebrew; note that the Latin phrase 'homo est mortalis' is equivalent to 'homines sunt mortales.'

The noun of kind is also frequent with כֹּל 'all, every.'

7.	כָּל־זְכוּרְךָ	all your *males* Exod 34:23
8.	אַתֶּם נִצָּבִים הַיּוֹם כֻּלְּכֶם לִפְנֵי יהוה אֱלֹהֵיכֶם רָאשֵׁיכֶם שִׁבְטֵיכֶם זִקְנֵיכֶם וְשֹׁטְרֵיכֶם כֹּל אִישׁ יִשְׂרָאֵל׃	All of you are standing today in the presence of Yнwн your God—your leaders and chief men, your elders and officials, and *every* (other) *person* of Israel. Deut 29:9
9.	וַיְצַו פַּרְעֹה לְכָל־עַמּוֹ לֵאמֹר כָּל־הַבֵּן הַיִּלּוֹד הַיְאֹרָה תַּשְׁלִיכֻהוּ וְכָל־הַבַּת תְּחַיּוּן׃	Then Pharaoh gave orders to all his people: "*All the sons* that are born you must throw into the river, but let *all the daughters* live." Exod 1:22

Other *terms of quantity* may govern a singular.

10.	רֹב יוֹעֵץ	an abundance of *counselors* Prov 11:14

Gentilic nouns (see 5.7c) are conventionally represented in the singular (see Gen 15:19–21 for nine examples).

11.	וְלָראוּבֵנִי וְלַגָּדִי וְלַחֲצִי שֵׁבֶט הַמְנַשֶּׁה אָמַר יְהוֹשֻׁעַ	But to the *Reubenites*, the *Gadites*, and the half-tribe of Manasseh Joshua said. . . . Josh 1:12

The singular noun of class is also found in a variety of *other expressions*.

12.	רֹעֵה צֹאן עֲבָדֶיךָ	Your servants are *shepherds*. Gen 47:3
13.	כָּשַׁל כֹּחַ הַסַּבָּל וְהֶעָפָר הַרְבֵּה	The strength of the *burden bearers* fails, the *rubbish* is much. Neh 4:4
14.	כִּי־גָמַר חָסִיד	The *godly* fail. Ps 12:2

These sentences are analogous to English generic statements.

Repetition   7.2.3

Singular nouns may be repeated within a short span for a variety of purposes, to   a
express distribution, diversity, or emphasis. The general reference of such expressions is plural, though English does not always use the plural for comparable phrases.

A singular may be repeated for a *distributive sense*, whether asyndetically (## 1–2)   b
or syndetically with ו (## 3–5) or a preposition (## 6–8); in such a phrase the members composing the aggregate are singled out. Such constructions may be represented in

English with 'each' or 'every.'[6] With temporal words a distributive repetition singles out the members diachronically (cf. 15.6).

1.	שָׁנָה שָׁנָה:	*year by year* Deut 14:22
2.	וַיְהִי כְּדַבְּרָהּ אֶל־יוֹסֵף יוֹם יוֹם	She spoke to Joseph *day after day* (or, *every day*). Gen 39:10
3.	דּוֹר־וָדוֹר	*all generations* Deut 32:7
4.	לַעֲשׂוֹת כִּרְצוֹן אִישׁ־וָאִישׁ:	to do according to the desire of *each man* Esth 1:8
5.	יוֹם וָיוֹם	*day after day* Esth 3:4
6.	שָׁנָה בְשָׁנָה	*year by year* Deut 15:20
7.	בַּבֹּקֶר בַּבֹּקֶר	*every morning* Exod 16:21
8.	וְלַבֹּקֶר לַבֹּקֶר:	*every morning* 1 Chr 9:27

c   A singular noun may be repeated syndetically to form a phrase indicating *diversity*.[7]

9.	לֹא־יִהְיֶה לְךָ בְּכִיסְךָ אֶבֶן וָאָבֶן גְּדוֹלָה וּקְטַנָּה:	Do not have *two differing weights* in your bag— one heavy and one light.[8] Deut 25:13
10.	בְּלֵב וָלֵב יְדַבֵּרוּ:	They speak with *a double heart* (i.e., with deception). Ps 12:3
11.	וְלַעֲדֹר בְּלֹא־לֵב וָלֵב:	to help without a *double-dealing heart* 1 Chr 12:34

Similar expressions can be used for *emphasis* (cf. 7.4.1).

12.	זָהָב זָהָב . . . כֶּסֶף כָּסֶף	*pure* gold . . . *pure* silver. 2 Kgs 25:15
13.	בַּדֶּרֶךְ בַּדֶּרֶךְ אֵלֵךְ	I will stay *constantly* on the main road. Deut 2:27

The stock expression מְעַט מְעַט 'little by little' is similar (see Exod 23:30, Deut 7:22).

---

6. For the distributive use of number words, see Gen 7:2, Josh 3:12; for the distributive use of the self-imprecation *ḥālîlâ*, see 2 Sam 21:20.

7. Note also the use in Ps 87:5 and a variety of late prose

texts (Esth 1:22; Ezra 10:14; Neh 13:24; 1 Chr 26:13, 28:14–15; 2 Chr 8:14, 11:12, 19:5).

8. Cf. Prov 20:10 for the same expression in a similar context.

Dual   **7.3**

Hebrew like other languages (e.g., Classical Greek, Sanskrit, and certain Slavic lan-   a
guages) has a morphological dual, used chiefly to refer to two paired objects.[9] Not all
dual forms have only dual reference; some serve as plural forms. The nearest English
equivalent to the Hebrew dual is provided by expressions like 'a pair of' (e.g., 'a pair of
socks') or 'both' (e.g., 'both hands'). As with these English equivalents, the Hebrew dual
is used to refer to certain objects that occur in pairs (e.g., 'a pair of clubs,' 'a pair of
earrings') and even to refer to objects that are in fact singular (e.g., 'a pair of trousers,' 'a
pair of scissors,' etc.). Hebrew also uses its dual to refer to phenomena distinct from
those comparably marked in other languages. The uses of dual can be analyzed according to the referents of the terms: natural pairs and set expressions of time and measurement. A few words, morphologically dual, show no semantic or syntactic features of the
dual.

Natural pairs in the dual usually involve paired human or animal body parts,   b
although not all such occur in the dual.[10]

1.	אָזְנַ֫יִם	2 ears	6.	מָתְנַ֫יִם	loins
2.	יָדַ֫יִם	2 hands	7.	עֵינַ֫יִם	2 eyes
3.	כְּנָפַ֫יִם	2 wings	8.	קַרְנַ֫יִם, קְרָנַ֫יִם	2 horns
4.	כַּפַּ֫יִם	2 palms	9.	רַגְלַ֫יִם	2 feet
5.	לְחָיַ֫יִם	2 cheeks	10.	שְׂפָתַ֫יִם	2 lips

Objects that occur in pairs associated with paired body parts may be referred to with a
dual, for example, נַעֲלַ֫יִם '(a pair of) sandals.' The plural of a word that forms a natural-pair
dual is often the morphological dual.

11.	וְכָל־בִּרְכַּ֫יִם	every knee Ezek 7:17, 21:12
12.	כָּל־יָדַ֫יִם	every hand Isa 13:7, Ezek 21:12
13.	שֵׁשׁ כְּנָפַ֫יִם	six wings Isa 6:2
14.	שִׁבְעָה עֵינָ֫יִם	seven eyes (viz., carving facets) Zech 3:9

As the last example shows, the metaphorical sense of a natural-pair term can be plural-
ized with a dual. Often, however, such a *metaphorical use* will show a regular morphological plural.

---

9. Dual forms are confined to substantives; adjectives, pronouns, and verbs are inflected for singular and plural forms only. More productive systems of the dual are found in Arabic, Akkadian, and Ugaritic.

10. The noun זְרֹעַ has both a masculine plural, זְרֹעִים, and a feminine plural, זְרֹעוֹת, but no dual.

15.	יָדַ֫יִם	2 hands	יָדוֹת	handles
16.	כַּפַּ֫יִם	2 palms	כַּפּוֹת	soles; pans
17.	עֵינַ֫יִם	2 eyes	עֲיָנֹת	fountains
18.	קַרְנַ֫יִם	2 horns (of	קְרָנוֹת	horns (of
		an animal)		an altar)
19.	רַגְלַ֫יִם	2 feet	רְגָלִים	times

c   The dual form of certain countable *units of measurement and time* occurs; the relevant nouns present in most cases a full singular-dual-plural paradigm.

20.	אַמָּה	אַמָּתַ֫יִם	2 cubits	אַמּוֹת
21.	יוֹם	יוֹמַ֫יִם	2 days	יָמִים
22.	מֵאָה	מָאתַ֫יִם	200	מֵאוֹת
23.	פַּ֫עַם	פַּעֲמַ֫יִם	twice	פְּעָמִים
24.	שָׁנָה	שְׁנָתַ֫יִם	2 years	שָׁנִים

d   For complex historical reasons, a few nouns have dual morphology, but behave in no way as duals. The two most common are plurals: מַ֫יִם 'water' and שָׁמַ֫יִם 'heavens'; both words have final-weak roots (מי, שמי), and their plural shapes fall together with the usual dual. Some other terms have been given fanciful "dual" etymologies: נְחֻשְׁתַּ֫יִם '(double?) fetters of bronze,' צָהֳרַ֫יִם 'noon (time of the double shadow?),' עַרְבַּ֫יִם 'evening (time between day and night?),' and מִצְרַ֫יִם 'Egypt (composed of Upper and Lower Egypt).' A handful of toponyms have dual forms of no obvious significance: אֶפְרַ֫יִם 'Ephraim,' קִרְיָתַ֫יִם 'Kiryathaim,' and the *Qere* of 'Jerusalem,' יְרוּשָׁלַ֫יִם (the *Kethiv* is apparently יְרוּשָׁלֵם).

7.4   Plural

a   Whereas English largely restricts its use of the plural to enumerate countables, the Hebrew plural is used with many different significations. It has a variety of basic uses, chiefly with countable and collective nouns, and a special set of senses with abstract nouns. The honorific plurals are important for theological and literary reasons.

b   Some points of morphology are worth noting. The standard plural ending -*îm* has overtaken many of the occurrences of the enclitic *mem* (see 9.8); thus some cases in which a plural form seems difficult may, in fact, be in error. The Hebrew plural ending -*îm* (also found in Phoenician) is rarely replaced by -*în* (standard in Aramaic and Moabite). This occurs in several poetic passages as well as in later books, for example, אַחֲרִין 'other' (Job 31:10), אִיִּן 'islands' (Ezek 26:18), חִטִּין 'wheat' (Ezek 4:9), חַיִּין 'life' (Job 24:22), יָמִין 'days' (Dan 12:13), מִדִּין 'garments' (Judg 5:10), מִלִּין 'words' (Job 4:2), מְלָכִין 'kings' (Prov 31:3), עִיִּין 'rubble' (Mic 3:12), צִדֹנִין 'Sidonians' (1 Kgs 11:33), רָצִין 'runners' (2 Kgs 11:13), שׁוֹמֵמִין 'desolate' (Lam 1:4). The Hebrew plural endings are almost always external to the singular form, but there are some signs of the use of changes in the base to form plurals, as in other Semitic languages. These include (1) the base-stretching -*ōh*- syllable found in the plural of biradical nouns (sing. אֵל 'god,' pl. אֱלֹהִים; the rare, alternative singular, אֱלֹהַּ, is probably a secondary formation; sing. אָמָה 'maid,' pl. אֲמָהֹת); (2) perhaps a variant base in the plurals of segholate nouns (sing. מֶלֶךְ 'king,' pl. מְלָכִים); and (3) the geminating plurals of nouns from geminate roots (הַר 'hill,' regular pl. הָרִים, הָרֵי, geminating pl. הַרֲרֵי, only in poetry; חֵץ 'arrow,' pl. חִצִּים but חַצָּיִךְ; חֹק 'decree,' pl. חֻקִּים but חִקְקֵי; עַם 'people,' pl. עַמִּים, עַמֵּי but also עֲמָמִים, עַמְמֵי; two rare nouns show only geminating plurals: צֵל 'shadow' yields צְלָלִים and תֹּךְ 'injury' yields תְּכָכִים).[11]

Countables, Collectives, and Extensions   7.4.1

The most common use of the plural is to refer to more than one or two of a   a
countable noun.

1.   כְּדָרְלָעֹמֶר וְהַמְּלָכִים אֲשֶׁר אִתּוֹ   Chedorlaomer and the *kings* allied with him
                                         Gen 14:5

2.   הָיוּ שָׂרֶיהָ כְּאַיָּלִים   Her *princes* are like *harts*.
                                         Lam 1:6

3.   וְאֵת כָּל־קִירוֹת הַבַּיִת מֵסַב   All the *walls* of the house round about he carved with
       קָלַע פִּתּוּחֵי מִקְלְעוֹת כְּרוּבִים   *engravings* of *carvings* of *cherubs* and *palms* and
              וְתִמֹרֹת וּפְטוּרֵי צִצִּים   *openings* of *blossoms*.
                                           1 Kgs 6:29

Such plurals may be repeated for *emphasis* (cf. 7.2.3c).[12]

4.   וַיִּצְבְּרוּ אֹתָם חֳמָרִם חֳמָרִם   They piled them into *heaps*.
                                           Exod 8:10

5.   עָשֹׂה הַנַּחַל הַזֶּה גֵּבִים גֵּבִים׃   I will make this (dry) wadi into *pools*.
                                           2 Kgs 3:16

6.   הֲמוֹנִים הֲמוֹנִים בְּעֵמֶק הֶחָרוּץ   *Multitudes, multitudes* in the Valley of Decision!
                                           Joel 4:14

The plural of a singular *collective* noun can indicate *composition*, that is, that the   b
collectivity has been broken apart (cf. 6.3.2f). Thus for the following vegetable nouns the singular refers to the product in its natural state, while the plural refers to the gathered, measured, cooked or sewn material. (On the theory that vegetables are for eating, etc., this is sometimes called the *plural of result*.)

| 7. | חִטָּה | חִטִּים | wheat | 9. | פֵּשֶׁת | פִּשְׁתִּים | flax |
| 8. | כֻּסֶּמֶת | כֻּסְּמִים | spelt | 10. | שְׂעֹרָה | שְׂעֹרִים | barley |

---

11. The chief base-changing plural pattern in Semitic is the Arabic broken plural. On pattern-replacement plurals in Semitic generally and in Akkadian in particular, see J. Huehnergard, "Three Notes on Akkadian Morphology," *"Working with No Data": Semitic and Egyptian Studies* *Presented to Thomas O. Lambdin*, ed. D. M. Golomb and S. T. Hollis (Winona Lake, Indiana: Eisenbrauns, 1987) 181–93. He also discusses the first two points about Hebrew plurals.

12. Note also Num 3:9 = 8:16; Gen 32:17; Isa 6:2.

11. בִּימֵי קְצִיר־חִטִּים   during *wheat* harvest
     Gen 30:14

Generally human blood in its natural state in the body is called דָּם; after it has been spilled, the plural form is used.

12. קוֹל דְּמֵי אָחִיךָ צֹעֲקִים אֵלַי   Your brother's *blood* cries out to me.
     Gen 4:10

Animal blood is always referred to in the singular.

c   Plurals of *extension* indicate that the referent of the noun is inherently large or complex; the plural quality is the result not of a countable multiplicity, but of a multiplicity that is nonetheless perceived as real. The plural may be variable; English 'water' designates most quantities from the smallest up to the very great, but truly enormous quantities take the plural: 'the waters of the Great Lakes.' Many plurals of extension are invariable; some English examples refer to body parts, literal ('guts') or metaphorical ('brains, wits, looks,'), while others refer to complex non-animate entities ('ashes, contents, dregs, stairs'), some abstract ('thanks, amends, auspices'). In Hebrew, some *body parts* are always plural, for example, פָּנִים 'face' and אֲחוֹרִים 'back'; צַוָּארִים 'neck' is much more common than the singular. Also *pluralia tantum* are two words referring to areas around a person while reclining, מְרַאֲשׁוֹת 'area around the head,' and מַרְגְּלוֹת 'area around the feet.'

13. וְרָאִיתָ אֶת־אֲחֹרָי וּפָנַי לֹא   You will see my *back*, but my *face* must not be seen.
     יֵרָאוּ׃   Exod 33:23

d   Just as English contrasts 'water : waters,' so Hebrew contrasts יָם '(a) sea' and יַמִּים 'sea(s), surface of the sea, etc.'; the related term מַעֲמַקִּים 'depths' is always plural. A region across a nearby boundary or body of water is עֵבֶר, while עֶבְרֵי נָהָר (Isa 7:20) is the 'region across the (Great) River,' Trans-Euphratia. This pattern should not be looked for everywhere; both מֶרְחָק and מַרְחַקִּים refer to 'distance.'

e   *Complex inanimate nouns* are referred to sometimes with plural forms, for example, אֹהָלִים means 'dwelling, encampment' (as well as 'tents'), as do both מִשְׁכָּנִים and מִשְׁכָּנוֹת; the singulars of both tend to be reserved for a special religious sense, namely, אֹהֶל for the Tent (of Meeting) and מִשְׁכָּן for the Tabernacle. Compare also מִשְׁכָּבִים for 'bed,' alongside מִשְׁכָּב 'bed' (but also 'the act of lying down').

7.4.2   Abstracts and the Like

a   An *abstract noun* is frequently expressed by a plural, which may have originally signified the diverse concrete manifestations of a quality or state. These plurals are frequently built on the adjectival *qātūl* and *qittûl* patterns (see 5.3d, 5.4). The singular of abstract plurals is rarely attested. Such plurals may refer to *qualities*.

1. אִישׁ מְדַבֵּר תַּהְפֻּכוֹת׃ men whose speaking is *perverse* (lit., men speaking *perverse things*)
    Prov 2:12

2. אִישׁ אֱמוּנוֹת רַב־בְּרָכוֹת A *faithful* man will be richly *blessed*.[13]
    Prov 28:20

3. כִּי לֹא עַם־בִּינוֹת הוּא For this is a people without *understanding*.
    Isa 27:11

Other abstract nouns specifying qualities include אוֹנִים 'strength' (Isa 40:26), בַּטֻּחוֹת 'security' (Job 12:6), מִבְטַחִים 'security' (Isa 32:18, Jer 2:37; sing. frequent), הַוּוֹת 'evil, destruction' (Ps 5:10), חֲמוּדוֹת 'excellence' (Dan 9:23), מַחֲמַדִּים 'charm' (Cant 5:16), חֲרָפוֹת 'shame' (Dan 12:2), דֵּעוֹת 'knowledge' (1 Sam 2:3, Job 36:4; sing. דֵּעָה four times), יְשׁוּעֹת 'salvation' (Isa 26:18; Ps 18:51, 28:8, 42:6, 44:5; sing. frequent), מֵישָׁרִים 'uprightness' (Isa 33:15), מַמְרֹרִים 'bitterness' (Job 9:18), מַמְתַקִּים 'sweetness' (Cant 5:16), שַׁעֲשֻׁעִים 'delight' (Prov 8:30).

Abstract nouns may also refer to *states or conditions*.   b

4. יְהוֹשֻׁעַ בִּן־נוּן מְשָׁרֵת מֹשֶׁה מִבְּחֻרָיו Joshua son of Nun, who had been Moses' aide since his *youth*
    Num 11:28

5. וְהוּא אִשָּׁה בִבְתוּלֶיהָ יִקָּח׃ The woman he marries must be a *virgin*.
    Lev 21:13

6. בֶּן־זְקֻנִים הוּא לוֹ a son born to him in his *old age*
    Gen 37:3

Other nouns of state include כְּלוּלֹת 'engagement' (Jer 2:2), נְעוּרִים 'youth' (Isa 54:6), סַנְוֵרִים 'dimsightedness' (Gen 19:11), עֲלוּמִים 'youth' (Ps 89:46), שְׁכֻּלִים 'childlessness' (Isa 49:20).

A *repeated series of actions or a habitual behavior* can be designated by a plural, and that term can have an abstract sense: the כּוֹס תַּנְחוּמִים (Jer 16:7) is 'a cup' not of repeated acts of comfort, but 'a cup of consolation,' a cup that itself gives 'consolation' by the drinking of it.   c

7. קַח־לְךָ אֵשֶׁת זְנוּנִים Take to yourself an *adulterous wife*.
    Hos 1:2

8. כִּי יוֹם נָקָם לַיהוָה שְׁנַת שִׁלּוּמִים לְרִיב צִיּוֹן׃ For Yнwн has a day of vengeance, a year of *retribution* to uphold Zion's cause.
    Isa 34:8

Other abstracts based on actions include אֲהָבִים 'fornication,' חֲנָטִים 'embalming,' כִּפֻּרִים 'atonement,' מִלֻּאִים 'installation,' פִּתּוּחִים 'engraving.'

---

13. The singular אֱמוּנָה is used frequently; the masculine אֵמֻן occurs once in the singular and five times in the plural.

7.4.3   Honorifics and the Like

a   Related to the plurals of extension and of abstract reference is a group of *intensive* plurals. In this usage (sometimes called the *pluralis majestatis*) the referent is a singular individual, which is, however, so thoroughly characterized by the qualities of the noun that a plural is used. Two of the great monsters in the Bible are designated with intensive plurals.[14]

1. שִׁבַּ֫רְתָּ רָאשֵׁי תַנִּינִים עַל־הַמָּ֫יִם׃
   אַתָּה רִצַּ֫צְתָּ רָאשֵׁי לִוְיָתָ֑ן
   תִּתְּנֶ֫נּוּ מַאֲכָל לְעָם לְצִיִּים׃

   You broke the heads of the *monster* in the water.
   You crushed the heads of *Leviathan*.
   You gave *it* as food for people, for(?) beasts.
   Ps 74:13–14

2. הִנֵּה־נָא בְהֵמוֹת . . .
   הִנֵּה־נָא כֹחוֹ בְמָתְנָ֑יו . . .
   הוּא רֵאשִׁית דַּרְכֵי־אֵל

   Behold *Behemoth*. . . .
   Behold *his* strength in *his* loins. . . .
   He is the *first* of God's ways(?).
   Job 40:15, 16, 19

Related to this intensification is a kind of generalization whereby a whole *species of animal* is designated by a plural form.[15]

3. וְעַל־עַ֫יִר בֶּן־אֲתֹנוֹת׃

   on a colt, the foal of a *donkey*
   Zech 9:9

4. דּוֹמֶה דוֹדִי לִצְבִי אוֹ לְעֹ֫פֶר
   הָאַיָּלִים

   My lover is like a gazelle or *a young stag*.
   Cant 2:9

b   These animal uses are overshadowed by similar plurals used in reference or address to humans or to God, the *honorific* uses. Most honorific plurals in the Bible involve the God of Israel, and the most common of these is אֱלֹהִים, used about twenty-five hundred times. When used of the God of Israel, this term usually takes singular agreement (אֱלֹהִים צַדִּיק 'a just God,' Ps 7:10);[16] when used of various gods, it takes plural agreement (אֱלֹהִים אֲחֵרִים 'other gods,' Exod 20:3; cf. Exod 12:12).

5. וַיֹּ֫אמֶר אֵלָיו הָאֱלֹהִים בַּחֲלֹם גַּם
   אָנֹכִי יָדַ֫עְתִּי

   God said to him in a dream, 'Yes, *I* know. . . .'
   Gen 20:6

Other honorific plurals used for the God of Israel include קְדֹשִׁים 'Holy One' and אֲדֹנִים 'Lord.'

---

14. For תַּנִּינִם as a true plural see Gen 1:21; for בְּהֵמוֹת as a true plural see Ps 8:8 (note כֻּלָּם with the preceding combination of collective and plural). It may be that תְּרָפִים is a plural of this sort, though in 1 Sam 19:13 one object seems to be referred to with that term.

15. A related pattern may be the use of the plural form to indicate that any one of several choices is acceptable. Thus in Deut 17:5 a person is to be sent out אֶל־שְׁעָרֶיךָ, where the sense suggests the gloss 'to (any one of) your (various city) gates.'

16. There are a few exceptions, concentrated curiously in the Pentateuch. The agreement is mixed in, e.g., Josh 24:19, which has plural predicate adjectives and a singular verb.

6. וְדַ֫עַת קְדֹשִׁים בִּינָה׃   Knowledge of *the Holy One* is understanding.
Prov 9:10

7. יהוה . . . הוּא אֱלֹהֵי הָאֱלֹהִים   Yhwh . . . is God of gods and *Lord* of lords.
וַאֲדֹנֵי הָאֲדֹנִים   Deut 10:17

8. יהוה אֲדֹנֵ֫ינוּ   Yhwh is our *Lord*.
Ps 8:2, 10

9. הוֹדוּ לַאֲדֹנֵי הָאֲדֹנִים   Give praise to the *Lord* of lords.
Ps 136:3

The singular אָדוֹן is used of God only in the phrase אֲדוֹן כָּל־הָאָ֫רֶץ (Josh 3:11, 13, etc.).

Humans may be referred to with honorific plurals, chiefly בְּעָלִים 'master' (not 'hus-   **c**
band') and אֲדֹנִים 'lord.' Both these plurals occur generally with suffixes, the first only
with third-singular suffixes.

10. יָדַע שׁוֹר קֹנֵ֫הוּ וַחֲמוֹר אֵבוּס   The ox knows its owner, the donkey its *master's*
בְּעָלָיו   manger.
Isa 1:3

11. הַחָכְמָה תְּחַיֶּה בְעָלֶ֫יהָ׃   Wisdom preserves the life of its *possessor*.
Qoh 7:12

12. אֲדֹנֵ֫ינוּ הַמֶּ֫לֶךְ־דָּוִד הִמְלִיךְ   Our *lord*, King David, has made Solomon king.
אֶת־שְׁלֹמֹה׃   1 Kgs 1:43

A related use of the honorific plural involves participles used to refer to God (## 13–   **d**
15) or humans (## 16–17). The divine references favor the verb עשׂה (see # 13 below and
Isa 22:11, 54:5; Ps 149:2).

13. אַיֵּה אֱלוֹהַּ עֹשָׂי   Where is God my *Maker*?
Job 35:10

14. יהוה לִי בְּעֹזְרָי   Yhwh is with me as my *Helper*.
Ps 118:7

15. בּוֹרֵא הַשָּׁמַ֫יִם וְנוֹטֵיהֶם   he who created the heavens and stretched them out
Isa 42:5

16. כְּהָנִיף שֵׁ֫בֶט וְאֶת־מְרִימָיו   as if a rod were to wield him *who lifts it up*
Isa 10:15

17. וְאַתְּ הָיִיתְ בְּעֹכְרָי   You are my *troubler*.
Judg 11:35

The word אָדוֹן 'lord' may be used in the singular or the plural to refer to a divine or   **e**
human lord; like other honorific terms, אָדוֹן can be used with a first-person pronominal
suffix, אֲדֹנִי, plural אֲדֹנַי. How is this last form related to the similar form אֲדֹנָי, used over
four hundred times of the God of Israel? What is the -*āy* ending? The debate has been

considerable.[17] Some scholars think that the title is a first-person singular suffixed form of the plural noun אֲדֹנִים; as such the form is an honorific plural, a plural of majesty meaning 'my Lord.' This interpretation makes excellent sense in passages where Yhwh's servants and worshipers address him. It also finds support in the fact that the first-person suffixed forms, both singular and plural (אֲדֹנִי, אֲדֹנַי), are used only with reference to people (cf. Gen 23:6, 19:2). Others contend that the -āy is a substantival afformative denoting emphasis by reinforcing the root and the term means 'Lord par excellence, Lord of all.' A number of arguments support this view. אֲדֹנָי occurs in passages where God speaks of himself and where accordingly the reference to 'my Lord' is unlikely (e.g., Ezek 13:9, 23:49; Job 28:28). It also occurs in passages in which the human speaker is plural, making a singular suffix seem incongruous (Ps 44:24).

f   The sense 'Lord of all' fits all texts. There is Ugaritic data to support the existence of a -y (= ăy?) afformative, with an emphatic or intensifying sense. The earliest biblical translators did not render the term with a pronoun; the Septuagint, for example, has *kyrios* 'lord,' not *kyrios mou* 'my lord.' אֲדֹנָי appears to be a divine epithet when used in conjunction with Yhwh or as a parallel to it.

18.   מָכוֹן לְשִׁבְתְּךָ פָּעַלְתָּ יהוה   Yhwh, you made a place for your dwelling,
    מִקְּדָשׁ אֲדֹנָי כּוֹנְנוּ יָדֶיךָ:   a sanctuary, O Lord, your hands established.
    Exod 15:17

We conclude therefore that although אֲדֹנָי may mean 'my Lord' in some passages where God is being addressed (e.g., Gen 15:2), it more probably means 'O Lord of all' everywhere.

---

17. For a review, see O. Eissfeldt, "ʾādhôn," *Theological Dictionary of the Old Testament*, ed. G. J. Botterweck and H. Ringgren (Grand Rapids: Eerdmans, 1977), 1. 59–72; we follow Eissfeldt for the most part.

8

Nominative Function and Verbless Clauses

Case/Function   8.1

The systems of inflection or accidence in a language serve to indicate the ways in   a
which words in phrases, clauses, and sentences are related to each other. Nominal inflection in many languages includes the categories of number and gender, and we have seen some of the ways these categories work in the lexicon and syntax of Biblical Hebrew. Another system of nominal inflection, *case*, is found in related languages and was used in earlier forms of Hebrew; although Biblical Hebrew does not use case, this system provides a convenient framework for studying the use of nouns in Hebrew.[1]

A system of cases is a system of nominal *functions*; words in the same case have the   b
same nominal function. Moderately elaborate case systems distinguish five or six functions; such systems are found in Greek, Latin, and Turkish. Some languages, notably Finnish, have vastly more complex systems.[2] English has a simple case system, differentiating for the noun a common case ('tiger') and a genitive or possessive case ('tiger's'). Some English pronouns have two cases, but a number have three.[3]

---

1. The traditional use of the case system as a component of advanced Hebrew grammatical study has come in for some justified criticism lately, but its usefulness as a tool of pedagogy and comparative study cannot be denied. For examples of the criticism, see J. Hoftijzer, "Remarks Concerning the Use of the Particle *ʾt* in Classical Hebrew," *Oudtestamentische Studiën* 14 (1965) 1–99, at 2–9; Harald Schweizer, "Was ist ein Akkusativ?—Ein Beitrag zur Grammatiktheorie," *Zeitschrift für die Alttestamentliche Wissenschaft* 87 (1975) 133–45; J. Barr, "The Ancient Semitic Languages," *Transactions of the Philological Society* 1968: 37–55, at 39–40; Richter, *GAHG* 1. 38; cf. A. Ungnad,

Hebräische Grammatik (Tübingen: Mohr, 1912) 52–54.

2. On case systems in general, see John Lyons, *Introduction to Theoretical Linguistics* (Cambridge: Cambridge University, 1968) 289–302.

3. The Latinate case names are commonly used in Semitic studies: 'nominative' comes from *nominare* 'to name'; accusative from *accusare* 'to call to account'; genitive from *genere* 'to bear.' Some of the functions of the other Latin cases are usually handled in Hebrew with prepositions (dative, from *dare* 'to give'; ablative from *auferre* 'to remove') or other syntactic devices (vocative, from *vocare* 'to call').

subjective (*nominative*)	I	he	she	we	they	who
objective (*accusative*)	me	him	her	us	them	who(m)
possessive (*genitive*)	my	his	her	our	their	whose

The Classical Semitic case system is like English in distinguishing sometimes two and sometimes three cases. This system is found in Akkadian and Classical Arabic; it has largely died out in modern Arabic dialects. There is abundant evidence for the case system in Early Northwest Semitic (1.3.1), in Ugaritic and the Canaanite glosses in the Amarna letters.

c   In the Classical Semitic system there are usually three case endings in the singular (thus called triptote) and two in the plural and dual (thus called diptote).[4]

	singular	*plural*	*dual*
nominative	-u	-ū	-ā
genitive	-i	-ī	
accusative	-a		-ay

Thus Early Hebrew *malk- 'king' (later *mélek*) would be inflected in approximately this way:

	singular	*plural*	*dual*
nominative	malku	mal(a)kū	malkā
genitive	malki	mal(a)kī	
accusative	malka		malkay

During the last centuries of the second millennium, the case system disappeared. The final short vowels of the singular case inflection were lost, and the ending of the dual and plural genitive-accusative (or oblique) became associated with a final -*m*, yielding the Classical Hebrew endings, dual -*aym* > -*áyim* and plural -*īm*. There are various remnants of the case system to be found in the Bible, largely in names (8.2).

d   Biblical Hebrew is a language without a case system, though it is often helpful to look at various aspects of its nominal use in a case framework. In a formal descriptive analysis of Biblical Hebrew we cannot properly speak of cases. Nevertheless, from a historical, comparative, and syntactic viewpoint we can differentiate three distinct "cases," that is, sets of syntactic functions, of the noun: nominative, genitive, and accusative. It is in this latter sense that we employ the terms "case" and "function."

---

4. Some singular nouns, belonging to well-defined groups, show diptotic inflection. On the system in general, see Gotthelf Bergsträsser, *Introduction to the Semitic Languages*, trans. and sup. Peter T. Daniels (Winona Lake, Indiana: Eisenbrauns, 1983) 16–17, 168–70. Cf. C. Rabin, "The Structure of the Semitic System of Case Endings," *Proceedings of the International Conference on Semitic Studies Held in Jerusalem, 19–23 July 1965* (Jerusalem: Israel Academy of Sciences and Humanities, 1969) 190–204.

Remnants of the Case System   8.2

A few remnants of early case endings still survive in the Hebrew Bible.   a

The old *nominative plural* ending -ū can be seen in the place name פְּנוּאֵל 'face of   b
God' (Gen 32:32); the byform פְּנִיאֵל (Gen 32:31) may contain the old ending of the
genitive-accusative plural. The meanings of the similarly shaped names בְּתוּאֵל (Gen
22:22), לְמוּאֵל (Prov 31:1), and נְמוּאֵל (Num 26:9) are unknown, as is that of חֲמוּטַל
(2 Kgs 23:31) ~ חֲמִיטַל (2 Kgs 24:18 *Kethiv*).

The old *genitive singular* ending is preserved and lengthened in the suffixed forms of   c
some monosyllabic words for family members: אָב 'father,' but אָבִיךָ 'your father'; אָח
'brother,' but אָחִיךָ 'your brother'; חָם 'father-in-law,' but חָמִיהָ 'her father-in-law.'[5] אֲבִי
and אֲחִי also serve as the first element in a great many compound personal names; there
the î may be a case vowel or the first-person singular pronoun: אֲבִימֶלֶךְ 'the/my father is
king' and so also אֲחִימֶלֶךְ, אֲחִימַעַץ, אֲבִינָדָב; cf. מַלְכִּי־צֶדֶק 'my king is righteous' and
גַּבְרִיאֵל 'the/my man is God'.[6]

It is possible that the old *accusative* ending may still be seen in a few forms, for   d
example, לַיְלָה 'night' and אַרְצָה 'land.' These are probably rather faded survivors of the
directional *he* suffix (10.5). Grammarians used to derive that suffix from the old accusative ending, but evidence from Ugarit now rules out this explanation.[7]

An obscure phenomenon often associated with the case system is presented by the   e
suffixes of connection (*litteræ compaginis*), otherwise debated and unexplained -î and -ô
endings usually found on a noun in construct (see 9.2).[8] The second of these is rather
rare, but the *ḥireq compaginis* occurs in a variety of passages, almost all poetic. If these
endings were to be treated as case endings, the -î would be genitive and the -ô either
accusative (< *a*) or nominative (< *u*). No such patterns emerge from the data; if anything,
the *ḥireq compaginis* is most common on nouns serving a nominative function, and
similar forms in Amarna suggest that the î is not a genitive ending.[9] The *ḥireq* occurs on
both masculine (## 1–3) and feminine (## 4–6) forms in construct.

1.   בְּנִי אֲתֹנוֹ   his ass's *colt*
                                    Gen 49:11

---

5. Note also the linking vowels on forms of *kōl* in which
"the case-endings [have] the same vowel as that of the
suffix," e.g., *kullāk* (Mic 2:12) and *kullāh* (he with *mappiq*;
Isa 48:6), with an accusative source for the *ā* vowels; *kullēk*
(Isa 14:29), with a genitive source (-*i*-) for *ē*; and *kullōh*
(Isa 15:3), with a nominative source (-*u*-) for *ō*; T. O.
Lambdin apud J. Huehnergard, "Three Notes on Akkadian
Morphology," *"Working with No Data": Semitic and Egyp-
tian Studies Presented to Thomas O. Lambdin*, ed. D. M.
Golomb and S. T. Hollis (Winona Lake, Indiana: Eisen-
brauns, 1987) 181–93, at 189 n. 47.

6. On the debate, see BL § 65g/ p. 524, who believe that
the vowel is a pronominal suffix. The name of Melchisedeq is spelled on both occasions it is used (Gen 14:18,
Ps 110:4) with the elements of the name separated by a

maqqep, an unusual usage for Hebrew compound names.

7. For the outmoded view, see GKC § 90a / p. 249; for
the Ugaritic evidence, see UT § 8.56. Note also *ʾabî-milkâ*
in Gen 11:29, probably not another name for Haran, but
an epithet, 'father of Milcah.'

8. This construction is not to be confused with the construction where the pronominal suffix anticipates the noun,
for example, *babōʾām hakkōhănîm* 'at their entrance, the
priests(')' (Ezek 42:14) and perhaps *banô ṣippōr* 'his son,
Zippor('s)' (Num 23:18).

9. W. L. Moran, "The Hebrew Language in Its Northwest
Semitic Background," *The Bible and the Ancient Near East:
Essays in Honor of William Foxwell Albright*, ed. G. E.
Wright (Garden City, New York: Doubleday, 1961; rpt.
Winona Lake, Indiana: Eisenbrauns, 1979) 54–72, at 60.

2.	עֹזְבִי הַצֹּאן	*that leaves* the flock Zech 11:17
3.	שֹׁכְנִי סְנֶה	*the dweller* in the bush Deut 33:16
4.	גְּנֻבְתִי יוֹם וּגְנֻבְתִי לָיְלָה:	*that which was stolen* by day or *stolen* by night Gen 31:39
5.	עַל־דִּבְרָתִי מַלְכִּי־צֶדֶק:	after *the order of* Melchizedek Ps 110:4
6.	מְלֵאֲתִי מִשְׁפָּט	*she that was full* of justice Isa 1:21

The ending also occurs before closely bound phrases, prepositional (## 7–10) and adverbial (# 11).

7.	נֶאְדָּרִי בַּכֹּחַ	*glorious* in power Exod 15:6
8.	רַבָּתִי בַגּוֹיִם	*she that was great* among the nations[10] Lam 1:1
9.	שָׂרָתִי בַּמְּדִינוֹת	*a princess* among the provinces Lam 1:1
10.	אֹסְרִי לַגֶּפֶן עִירֹה	*binding* his foal to a vine Gen 49:11
11.	חֹצְבִי מָרוֹם קִבְרוֹ	*who hews* his tomb on the height Isa 22:16

Even in poetic texts, these forms are erratically distributed; note the two instances in Gen 49:11 and three instances in the opening verse of Lamentations.

8.3   Nominative Function

a   The nominative function comprehends four roles: the subject (of both verbal and verbless clauses; see 4.4), the predicate nominative (of verbless clauses), the nominative absolute, and the vocative (in any sort of clause; see 4.7).[11] A noun or noun equivalent may fill these roles.

1.	הַנָּחָשׁ הִשִּׁיאַנִי	*The serpent* (SUBJECT) deceived me. Gen 3:13
2.	יהוה הַצַּדִּיק	*YHWH* (SUBJECT) is *the one in the right* (PREDICATE NOMINATIVE). Exod 9:27

---

10. This form may reflect the preceding *rabbătî ʿām*.
11. Note in particular that a vocative is not a (clausal) subject.

3.   הוֹשִׁ֖יעָה הַמֶּֽלֶךְ׃   Save (me), *O king* (VOCATIVE).
2 Sam 14:4

4.   הָאִשָּׁה אֲשֶׁר נָתַ֫תָּה עִמָּדִי הִיא   *The woman* (NOMINATIVE ABSOLUTE) whom you put
נָֽתְנָה־לִּי מִן־הָעֵץ   with me—*she* (SUBJECT) gave me from the tree.
Gen 3:12

For verbal clauses the basic Hebrew word order is *verb + subject* (VS). This verb-first word order usually obtains where a clause has no introductory material (# 5), where a clause begins with a *waw*-relative (traditionally "*waw*-consecutive") construction (# 6), or where a clause begins with adverbial materials (# 7). b

5.   דָּבְקָה נַפְשִׁי אַחֲרֶ֑יךָ   *My soul* clings to you.
Ps 63:9

6.   וַיֹּ֥אמֶר אֱלֹהִים   And *God* said. . . .
Gen 1:3

7.   אַחַר הַדְּבָרִים הָאֵ֫לֶּה הָיָה דְבַר־   After these things, *the word of* Y<small>HWH</small> came to Abram.
יְהוָה אֶל־אַבְרָם   Gen 15:1

After a *waw*-disjunctive (39.2.3) the word order is normally *waw* + noun (or its equivalent) + verb.

8.   (בָּרָא אֱלֹהִים אֵת הַשָּׁמַ֫יִם וְאֵת   (God created the heavens and the earth.) Now *the*
הָאָ֑רֶץ) וְהָאָ֫רֶץ הָיְתָה תֹ֫הוּ וָבֹ֫הוּ   *earth* was without form and devoid of life.
Gen 1:1–2

9.   וְהָאָדָם יָדַע אֶת־חַוָּה אִשְׁתּ֑וֹ   Now *hāʾādām* knew Eve, his wife.
Gen 4:1

When two clauses in contrast are joined by a *waw*-adversative, a species of *waw*-disjunctive, the subject often comes first in both.

10.   הוּא יְשׁוּפְךָ רֹאשׁ וְאַתָּה תְּשׁוּפֶ֫נּוּ   *He* will crush your head, and *you* will strike his heel.
עָקֵֽב׃   Gen 3:15

11.   אַבְרָם יָשַׁב בְּאֶֽרֶץ־כְּנָ֑עַן וְלוֹט   *Abram* dwelt in the land of Canaan, but *Lot* dwelt in
יָשַׁב בְּעָרֵי הַכִּכָּ֑ר   the cities of the valley.
Gen 13:12

In *verbless (or nominal) clauses* a noun or its equivalent is juxtaposed with the subject to indicate a predication. c

12.   שְׁלֹשָׁה אֵ֫לֶּה בְּנֵי־נֹ֑חַ   These *three* (SUBJECT) are *the sons of Noah*
(PREDICATE).
Gen 9:19

The rules governing the sequence of the subject and predicate deserve separate treatment (8.4).

d   The *vocative* (or nominative of address) designates the one to whom the speaker is addressing a statement. It is most clearly identifiable where the speaker places a definite noun in apposition to a second-person pronoun (# 13) or an imperative (# 14).

13.   בֶּן־מִי אַתָּה הַנָּ֫עַר   Whose son are you, *young man*?
1 Sam 17:58

14.   הַחֵרְשִׁים שְׁמָ֫עוּ וְהַעִוְרִים   Hear, *you deaf*; look, *you blind*.
הַבִּ֫יטוּ   Isa 42:18

8.4   Word Order in Verbless Clauses

a   The order of subject (S) and predicate (Pred) in verbless clauses varies tremendously. In investigating the major patterns, we follow the study of Francis I. Andersen.[12] An understanding of the various clausal patterns depends on a variety of factors. The first is the *definiteness* of predicate and subject. If the predicate is definite, it *identifies* a definite subject (total overlap of S and Pred); if it is indefinite, it *classifies* a definite subject (partial overlap). Roughly speaking, an identifying clause has the order S–Pred and a classifying clause the reverse, although if the predicate is a noun with a suffix, the order is less predictable. The other factors relate to the grammatical context: first, *is the clause independent* (and if so, is it in contrast to what precedes, i.e., disjunctive, or not) *or subordinate* to another clause; and second, *is the clause declarative* (making a statement), *interrogative* (asking a question), *or precative* (expressing a wish). The word order in subordinate clauses is much less predictable than in independent clauses, as is the word order in precative clauses. Interrogatives tend, on the whole, to follow the same patterns as declaratives. Most of the syntactic structures treated here are those of independent declarative clauses.[13]

8.4.1   Clauses of Identification

a   In a verbless clause of identification ("Who or what is the subject?"), the two parts of the clause usually occur in the order *subject-predicate*.

1.   הִיא־צֹ֫עַר: It is Zoar.
Gen 14:2

---

12. Andersen, *The Hebrew Verbless Clause in the Pentateuch* (Journal of Biblical Literature Monograph Series 14; Nashville: Abingdon, 1970). Most of the examples treated here are independent verbless clauses, and thus our treatment avoids some of the more complex areas touched on by Andersen. For a rigorous review of Andersen's book, see J. Hoftijzer, "The Nominal Clause Reconsidered," *Vetus Testamentum* 23 (1973) 446–510; the comments of both Andersen and Hoftijzer are discussed in T. Muraoka, *Emphatic Words and Structures in Biblical Hebrew* (Leiden: Brill, 1985) 1–28, and in Richter, *GAHG* 3. 70–89. Other schemes for verbless clauses have been proposed, involving, in addition to identifying clauses, existential clauses, and in addition to classifying clauses, attributive, qualificational, and situational clauses. The older treatment of K. Oberhuber is still engaging: "Zur Syntax des Richterbuches: Der einfache Nominalsatz und die sog. Nominale Apposition," *Vetus Testamentum* 3 (1953) 2–45. Earlier stages of the Semitic languages probably did not use verbal morphemes for the predicative copula; see A. F. L. Beeston, "Reflections on Verbs 'To Be'," *Journal of Semitic Studies* 29 (1984) 7–13.

13. The predicate may be discontinuous, i.e., part of it may precede the subject and part of it (often a prepositional phrase) may follow; the patterns created by such discontinuity are not treated here.

2.	אֲנִי יהוה:	I am YHWH. Exod 6:2
3.	הוּא מֹשֶׁה וְאַהֲרֹן:	That is Moses and Aaron. Exod 6:27
4.	אֵלֶּה שְׁמוֹת הָאֲנָשִׁים אֲשֶׁר	These are the names of the men who. . . . Num 13:16
5.	שֵׁם הָאֶחָד פִּישׁוֹן	The name of the first (river) is Pishon. Gen 2:11

Although suffixed nouns occasionally present exceptions to this order, they often show it. (Example # 7 is an interrogative, also with the order S–Pred.)

| 6. | הוּא אֲדֹנִי | He is *my master*.
Gen 24:65 |
| 7. | הֲזֶה אֲחִיכֶם הַקָּטֹן | Is this *your youngest brother*?
Gen 43:29 |

As the examples suggest, a pronoun is often the subject of such clauses.[14]

It is possible for a verbless clause to contain three rather than two parts; the relationship between subject and predicate may be effected through what is often called a *pleonastic* or *dummy* pronoun (pleo), personal or demonstrative.

| 8. | עֵשָׂו הוּא אֱדוֹם: | Esau(, he) is Edom.
Gen 36:8 |

The pronoun is here called pleonastic (i.e., redundant) since the clause עֵשָׂו אֱדוֹם is grammatical. On this view, the clause is structured S–pleo–Pred. On another view, the predication can be associated with הוּא אֱדוֹם, as S–Pred, while עֵשָׂו is taken as a nominative absolute (sentential topic or focus marker; Foc; cf. 4.7 and 16.3.3).[15] This analysis would suggest the gloss 'As for Esau, he is Edom'; the structure would then be Foc–S–Pred.[16]

---

14. For some of the complexities associated with the use of specific words in the predicate, notably *kōl* and *šēm*, see Andersen, *Hebrew Verbless Clause*, 41.

15. This general class of constructions is discussed extensively by Muraoka, *Emphatic Words*, 67–77 (in verbless clauses, esp. 72–73), 93–99 (in general); cf. M. O'Connor, *Hebrew Verse Structure* (Winona Lake, Indiana: Eisenbrauns, 1980) 78–86; and W. Gross, *Die Pendenskonstruktion im biblischen Hebräisch* (St. Ottilien: EOS, 1987) 105–46, esp. 128, 132–44. In verbless clauses the linking pronoun (*hûʾ*, *hēm*, *zōʾt*, etc.) is often called a *copula* or *binder*; this sense of copula should not be confused with the more regular description of *hāyâ* as a copula(r verb).

16. For a similar sentence with *hyy* see Num 16:7. The order Pred–pleo–S is virtually nonexistent in identifying clauses in Biblical Hebrew, suggesting that the Foc–S–Pred analysis is correct for that form of the language. The only examples of identifying Pred–pleo–S are found in Isa 9:14, *zāqēn ûnəśû-pānîm hûʾ hārōʾš. wənābîʾ môreh-ššéqer hûʾ hazzānāb*, 'The elder and honored one—that one is the "head" [described in Isa 9:13]. The prophet-falsehood teacher—that one is the "tail" [described in Isa 9:13].' The grammar, as well as the *pesher*-type interpretation involved, are discussed by M. H. Goshen-Gottstein, "Hebrew Syntax and the History of the Bible Text," *Textus* 8 (1973) 100–106; on the role of *hûʾ/hîʾ* as the sign of a gloss, Goshen-Gottstein's treatment may be contrasted with that proposed by M. Fishbane, *Biblical Interpretation in Ancient Israel* (Oxford: Clarendon, 1985) 44–48, 461.

9. יְהוָה אֱלֹהֶיךָ הוּא עֹבֵר לְפָנֶיךָ — YHWH your God(, he) is the one passing before you.
Deut 31:3

10. בְּנֵנוּ זֶה סוֹרֵר וּמֹרֶה — As for our son, he is stubborn and rebellious.
Deut 21:20

11. אַתָּה זֶה בְּנִי עֵשָׂו — You are my son Esau.
Gen 27:24

8.4.2 Clauses of Classification

a   In a verbless clause of classification in which the predicate refers to a general class of which the subject is a member, the two parts of the clause generally occur in the order *predicate-subject*.[17] Clauses of classification answer the question, "What is the subject like?" (Example # 6 contains a partitive phrase, *min* + a plural, meaning 'one of' the object or individuals named; cf. 4.4.1b.)

1. כֵּנִים אֲנַחְנוּ — We are *honest*.
Gen 42:11

2. טָמֵא הוּא׃ — He is *unclean*.
Lev 13:36

3. טוֹב־הַדָּבָר אֲשֶׁר־דִּבַּרְתָּ לַעֲשׂוֹת׃ — What you propose to do is *good* (lit., *Good* is the thing which . . .).
Deut 1:14

4. מְעֹנָה אֱלֹהֵי קֶדֶם — The eternal God is *a dwelling place*.
Deut 33:27

5. גּוּר אַרְיֵה יְהוּדָה — Judah is *a lion cub*.[18]
Gen 49:9

6. מִיַּלְדֵי הָעִבְרִים זֶה׃ — This is *one of the Hebrew children*.
Exod 2:6

If the predicate contains a suffixed form, this order may also be used.

7. אָחִי הוּא — He is *a brother of mine*.
Gen 20:5

8. אֵשֶׁת בִּנְךָ הִיא — She is *a wife of your son*.
Lev 18:15

The predicate-subject order is also favored if the subject is an infinitive.

---

17. In addition to the groups of exceptions noted below, there are other exceptions; see, e.g., Num 28:14 and Ezek 27:3 (the subject in each case is pronoun), Deut 3:5 (the predicate contains *kol*), Gen 18:20 (subject and predicate are separated by *kî*).

18. The similar clause in Deut 33:22 with different word order is probably a precative. Both clauses occur in archaic poems.

9.	לֹא־טוֹב הֱיוֹת הָאָדָם לְבַדּוֹ	It is not *good* for the man to be alone (lit., The man's being by himself is not good). Gen 2:18
10.	הֲלוֹא טוֹב לָנוּ שׁוּב מִצְרָיְמָה:	Wouldn't it be *better* for us to go back to Egypt? Num 14:3
11.	רַב־לָכֶם שֶׁבֶת בָּהָר הַזֶּה:	You have *stayed* at this mountain long enough. Deut 1:6

If a so-called pleonastic pronoun is used in a classifying clause, the subject precedes **b** the predicate and the pronoun follows it (i.e., S–Pred–pleo). On this analysis it seems that the pleonastic pronoun reverses the usual clause structure. If, however, we take the apparent "subject" as a nominative absolute or focus marker and the so-called pleonastic pronoun as the true subject, the basic order of classifying clauses is preserved: Foc–Pred–S.

12.	אִישׁ רֹאשׁ לְבֵית־אֲבֹתָיו הוּא:	As for each man (FOCUS), he (SUBJECT) is *head of his ancestral family* (PREDICATE) *or* Each man is head of his ancestral family. Num 1:4
13.	וְכָל־הַשֶּׁרֶץ הַשֹּׁרֵץ עַל־הָאָרֶץ שֶׁקֶץ הוּא	And as for every swarming thing that swarms on the earth (FOCUS), it (SUBJECT) is an *abomination* (PREDICATE) *or* Every swarming thing that swarms on the earth is an abomination. Lev 11:41

The nominative absolute construction serves here, as often, to clarify potentially complex constructions (see 4.7).

The basic order of classifying verbless clauses is, then, Pred–S. A variety of factors **c** can reverse this pattern, notably contrast with preceding material and the use of a participle in the predicate.

If a clause of classification stands in contrast to (# 14) or in disjunction with (# 15) **d** what precedes, then the order is S–Pred.

14.	הוֹאַלְתִּי לְדַבֵּר אֶל־אֲדֹנָי וְאָנֹכִי עָפָר וָאֵפֶר:	I presume to speak to the Lord, *but* I am *dust and ashes*! Gen 18:27
15.	וְהָיָה כַּאֲשֶׁר יָרִים מֹשֶׁה יָדוֹ וְגָבַר יִשְׂרָאֵל וְכַאֲשֶׁר יָנִיחַ יָדוֹ וְגָבַר עֲמָלֵק: וִידֵי מֹשֶׁה כְּבֵדִים	It was the case that when Moses raised his hand Israel grew strong, while when he rested his hand Amaleq grew strong. *Now* Moses' hands were *heavy*! Exod 17:11–12

The word order S–Pred is also found if the clause is declarative and the predicate **e** contains a participle that, though it modifies the subject, is used in an essentially verbal way (37.6).

16. קוֹל דְּמֵי אָחִיךָ צֹעֲקִים אֵלַי מִן־ הָאֲדָמָה: Your brother's blood *is crying* to me from the ground.
Gen 4:10

17. עֲמָלֵק יוֹשֵׁב בְּאֶרֶץ הַנֶּגֶב   Amaleq *lives* in the Negev land.
Num 13:29

This rule does not apply if the clause is precative (the passive participle is common, ## 18–20) or if the participle is agentive (# 21, cf. 5.2; cf. Num 35:16).

18. אָרוּר כְּנָעַן   *Cursed* be Canaan.
Gen 9:25

19. אָרוּר הָאִישׁ אֲשֶׁר יַעֲשֶׂה פֶסֶל וּמַסֵּכָה   *Cursed* be the man who makes a carved or cast image.
Deut 27:15

20. בָּרוּךְ טַנְאֲךָ וּמִשְׁאַרְתֶּךָ:   May your basket and your kneading trough be *blessed*.
Deut 28:5

21. מְרַגְּלִים אַתֶּם   You are *spies*.
Gen 42:9

In the following example, the pattern of S–Pred is used for both the contrasting clauses; this exception probably reflects the need to point up the contrast.

22. אֹרְרֶיךָ אָרוּר וּמְבָרֲכֶיךָ בָּרוּךְ:   May those who curse you be *cursed*, and may those who bless you be *blessed*.
Gen 27:29

f   In addition to these exceptions to the Pred–S pattern for classifying clauses, there are some kinds of predicates that seem to neutralize the word-order patterns.[19] Either order may be expected if the predicate is a numeral (## 23–25), an adverb (## 26–27), or a prepositional phrase (## 28–33).[20]

23. עַמֻּדֵיהֶם עֲשָׂרָה   Their posts are *ten*.
Exod 27:12; cf. Exod 27:14, 15, 16; 38:10, 11, 12

24. עֶשְׂרִים גֵּרָה הוּא: It is *twenty gerahs*.
Num 18:16

25. תֵּשַׁע אַמּוֹת אָרְכָּהּ   Its length is *nine* cubits.
Deut 3:11; cf. Gen 6:15, 24:22; Exod 25:10

26. וּפְנֵיהֶם אֲחֹרַנִּית   And their faces were *backward* (i.e., they were facing backward).
Gen 9:23

19. For examples of the order S–Pred in dependent clauses, see Gen 13:14, 21:17; Exod 12:13; 1 Sam 19:3 (all with *šām*).
20. For examples of the order S–Pred, see Gen 36:30,

Deut 33:8. For the opposite order, see Lev 23:5, Deut 32:35. In two neighboring dependent clauses, identical except for word order, both orders are used; see Lev 13:45–46 (ʾăšer-bô hannégaʿ, ʾăšer hannégaʿ bô).

27.   וְשָׁם אֲחִימַן שֵׁשַׁי וְתַלְמַי   And Ahiman, Sheshai, and Talmai were *there*.
Num 13:22

28.   וְאַרְבַּע־מֵאוֹת אִישׁ עִמּוֹ:   And there are four hundred men *with him*.
Gen 32:7

29.   וַיהוה אִתָּ֫נוּ   And Yнwн is *with us*.
Num 14:9

30.   הַנִּסְתָּרֹת לַיהוה   The secrets *belong to Yнwн*.
Deut 29:28

31.   וְעִמּוֹ אַרְבַּע מֵאוֹת אִישׁ   And there were four hundred men *with him*.
Gen 33:1

32.   וְאִתּוֹ אָהֳלִיאָב   And Oholiab is *with him*.
Exod 38:23

33.   בַּיּוֹם הָרִאשׁוֹן שַׁבָּתוֹן וּבַיּוֹם הַשְּׁמִינִי שַׁבָּתוֹן: *On the first day* there shall be a rest, and *on the eighth day* there shall be a rest.
Lev 23:39

g   The problems posed by the Shema (Deut 6:4) are numerous.[21] After the initial imperative and vocative, שְׁמַע יִשְׂרָאֵל 'Hear, O Israel,' there follow four words. However they are construed, it is agreed that no closely comparable passage occurs. The simplest solution is to recognize two juxtaposed verbless clauses: (*a*) יהוה אֱלֹהֵינוּ 'Yнwн is our God' (identifying clause, S–Pred); (*b*) יהוה אֶחָד 'Yнwн is one' (classifying clause, S–Pred, with a numeral; cf. # 23). Few scholars favor such a parsing. Andersen takes . . . יהוה יהוה as a discontinuous predicate, with the other two words as a discontinuous subject, 'Our one God is Yнwн, Yнwн.'[22] Other proposed parsings take the first two words as subject (viz., 'Yнwн our God is one Yнwн')[23] or the first three words (viz., 'Yнwн, our God, Yнwн is one') or even the first word alone. It is hard to say if אחד can serve as an adjective modifying יהוה. It is even less clear what the predicate אלהינו יהוה אחד would mean, though some scholars take it adverbially ('Yнwн is our God, Yнwн alone'). As Gerald Janzen observes, "the Shema does not conform exactly to any standard nominal sentence pattern," and further discussion falls outside the sphere of grammar.[24]

---

21. See the discussion of J. G. Janzen, "On the Most Important Word in the Shema (Deuteronomy VI 4–5)," *Vetus Testamentum* 37 (1987) 280–300.

22. Andersen, *Hebrew Verbless Clause*, 47.

23. So, e.g., A. Niccacci and G. Begrich in reviews of this grammar on its first publication, *Liber Annuus* 39 (1989) 310–27, at 316, and *Theologische Literaturzeitung* 115 (1990) 734; Niccacci takes the predicate as *yhwh*, to which *ʾḥd* is an apposition, roughly 'Yнwн our God is Yнwн, who is unique' or, 'Only Yнwн our God is Yнwн'; Begrich renders roughly 'Yнwн is our God, Yнwн alone.'

24. Though not beyond it. Cf. Janzen, "Shema," 296.

9

Genitive Function

9.1   Modification Functions of the Noun

a   A noun in the *nominative* in a verbal clause may be a subject (related to the verb) or a vocative (related to the clause as a whole); all major roles in a verbless clause are nominative. It is possible to form a complete clause using nouns only in the nominative.

1.	יְהוָה דִּבֵּר	Yhwh (SUBJECT) has spoken.
		Isa 1:2
2.	שִׁמְעוּ שָׁמַיִם	Hear, O heavens (VOCATIVE).
		Isa 1:2

Many phrasal and clausal structures require nouns (or pronouns) to stand in other functions. One group of these functions involves nouns that have a direct relation to the verb; this ad-verbial group is called the *accusative*.

3.	בָּנִים גִּדַּלְתִּי	I (SUBJECT) have raised children (ACCUSATIVE).
		Isa 1:2

In English grammar the accusative role shown in Isa 1:2 is called the direct object, that is, the accusative is the object of the verb's action, and its status is not mediated (by, e.g., a preposition).

The other group of modifications covers other nouns, those which are neither the   b
subject nor the modifiers of the verb; this (largely) ad-nominal group is called the *geni-*
tive.[1] This is most often the case of a noun related to another noun.

4.   נָאֲצוּ אֶת־קְדוֹשׁ יִשְׂרָאֵל   They (SUBJECT) spurn the Holy One (OBJECT) of Israel
                                              (GENITIVE).
                                              Isa 1:4

5.   שָׂבַעְתִּי עֹלוֹת אֵילִים   I (SUBJECT) am fed up with ʿōlôt (OBJECT) of
                                              rams (GENITIVE).
                                              Isa 1:11

A pronoun may also fill the genitive slot in a clause.

6.   יָדַע שׁוֹר קֹנֵהוּ   An ox (SUBJECT) knows its (GENITIVE) owner (OBJECT).
                                              Isa 1:3

The object of a preposition is also in the genitive; it is the preposition(al phrase) that is
directly related to the verb.

7.   וְהֵם פָּשְׁעוּ בִי׃   And they (SUBJECT) rebel against (PREPOSITION) me
                                              (GENITIVE).
                                              Isa 1:2

Thus beyond the nominative role, a noun may fit one of two roles (or groups of   c
roles): it may modify the verb (accusative) or another noun (genitive). There is an important similarity these and other relations share: the modified element (or head) usually
precedes the modifier (or dependent).[2] Thus in ידע . . . קנהו, the verb precedes the object
modifying it; in קדוש ישראל, 'the Holy One' is qualified by 'of Israel.' This relation
affects other areas of Hebrew syntax as well, for example, a noun (the modified) usually
precedes an attributive adjective (the modifier): עִיר נְצוּרָה 'a city, a besieged one' > 'a
besieged city' (Isa 1:8). The modified-modifier (or defined-defining) relation is sometimes
described with the Latin terms *regens* ('governor, ruler, head') for the modified element
and *rectum* ('ruled thing') for the modifier.[3] English often uses *regens-rectum* order (verb
before object; the possessed-possessor genitive, e.g., 'the Holy One of Israel'); it may also
use a modifier-modified sequence (e.g., 'besieged city,' 'Gabriel's horn'). Other languages
display a syntax similar to Hebrew (cf. French 'une ville assiégée,' LXX Greek '*pólis
poliorkoúmenē*,' Arabic '*madīnatin muḥāsaratin*').

1. The term adnominal is also used by, e.g., F. Blass
and A. Debrunner, *A Greek Grammar of the New Testament*, trans. R. W. Funk (Chicago: University of Chicago,
1961) 89.

2. For this set of relations, see 3.3.3; M. O'Connor,
Hebrew Verse Structure (Winona Lake, Indiana: Eisenbrauns, 1980) 116–17, 123–26.

3. For the terms, see, e.g., GKC § 89a / p. 247. This
terminology is open to question; as A. Sperber remarks,

"According to the Hebrew way of thinking it is exactly
vice versa: the second noun [in a construct chain] remains
unchanged and even gets the article if determined, and
causes the first noun to undergo certain changes"; see *A
Historical Grammar of Biblical Hebrew* (Leiden: Brill,
1966) 16. In Hebrew the construct is *nismak* 'bound,' the
genitive is *somek* 'unbound,' and the relation is *səmikût*;
in Arabic the construct is *al-muḍāf*, the genitive *al-muḍāf
ʾilayhi*, and the relation is *al-iḍāfa*.

9.2   Construct State

a   In the language antecedent to Biblical Hebrew, the genitive relation was indicated by a final vowel marker, *-i* in the singular and *-ī* in the plural. After the loss of the case system (8.1), the noun in the genitive was left unmarked. If a noun preceded a noun in the genitive, however, that noun often came to be marked; such a "pregenitive" noun stands in the *construct state*. Formation of the construct is a matter of sound and rhythm: in order to bind the pregenitive to the genitive, the pregenitive may be shortened.

b   The construct state is a form of the noun or a nominal equivalent that may serve any syntactic function or case.

1.   וּזֲהַב הָאָרֶץ הַהִיא טֹוב   And *the gold* (CONSTRUCT:NOMINATIVE) of that land is good.
Gen 2:12

2.   בְּתוֹךְ הַגָּן   in *the middle* (CONSTRUCT:GENITIVE) of the garden
Gen 2:9

3.   לִשְׁמֹר אֶת־דֶּרֶךְ עֵץ הַחַיִּים׃   to guard *the way* (CONSTRUCT:ACCUSATIVE) of [i.e., leading to] *the tree* (CONSTRUCT:GENITIVE) of life
Gen 3:24

c   The construct state is often indicated by a weakening of the accent on the word. This may lead to vocalic changes (e.g., דָּבָר 'word,' but דְּבַר־אֱלֹהִים 'word of God'). The construct may be marked by a conjunctive accent (e.g., וְרוּחַ אֱלֹהִים 'the spirit of God,' Gen 1:2) or more rarely by a *methegh*[4] + *maqqeph* (e.g., מֶלֶךְ־צֹר 'king of Tyre,' 2 Sam 5:11). In some instances a distinctive ending marks the form (cf. 8.2e).

		singular	dual	plural
masculine	absolute	∅	*-áyim*	*-îm*
	construct	∅	*-ê*	*-ê*
feminine	absolute	*-â, -t,* or ∅	*-ātáyim, -táyim*	*-ôt*
	construct	*-at, -t*	*-(ət)ê, -tê*	*-ôt*

9.3   Syntax of the Construct-Genitive Relation

a   The genitive function comprehends two roles: the object of a preposition and a noun governed by another noun; pronominal suffixes can fill both roles. The workings of the prepositional system of Hebrew are considered in Chapter 11. The class of noun-noun relations is the major subject of this chapter (9.5). We also discuss several related constructions, in which prepositional phrases (## 1–2) and whole clauses (## 3–4) stand in the genitive role and are thus preceded by construct forms (9.6).[5]

---

4. Or *mayela*.
5. For an example of a relative clause in *š* see Ps 137:8.

1.   חֹסֵי בֽוֹ׃   those seek refuge *in him*
                                Nah 1:7

2.   כְּאַחַד מִמֶּ֫נּוּ   like one *of us*
                                Gen 3:22

3.   מְקוֹם אֲשֶׁר יוֹסֵף אָסוּר שָׁם׃   the place *where Joseph was imprisoned*
                                Gen 40:3

4.   קִרְיַת חָנָה דָוִד   the city *where David encamped*
                                Isa 29:1

Most of the construct chains in Biblical Hebrew involve two items, construct or   b
head (C), and genitive or absolute (G). If the head involves two or more nouns rather
than one, all but the first come after the genitive, often linked to the head with a
pronominal suffix.

5.   וּפָנִ֫יתָ אֶל־תְּפִלַּת עַבְדְּךָ וְאֶל־   And turn to the prayer and supplication *of your*
      תְּחִנָּתוֹ   *servant* (lit., the prayer *of your servant* and *his*
                                supplication).
                                1 Kgs 8:28

There are exceptions to this rule; such *construct overrides* usually occur in verse or
elevated prose.[6]

6.   מִבְחַר וְטוֹב־לְבָנוֹן   the choice and best *of Lebanon*
                                Ezek 31:16

If the *rectum* or modifier involves two or more nouns, the construct is often repeated
with each genitive.

7.   יהוה אֱלֹהֵי הַשָּׁמַ֫יִם וֵאלֹהֵי   YHWH, God *of heaven* and *earth* (lit., God *of heaven*
      הָאָ֫רֶץ   and God *of earth*)
                                Gen 24:3

However, the construct may govern a coordinate noun phrase. The more closely related
the genitives are, the more likely they are to form such a phrase.

8.   בְּהֹנוֹת יָדָיו וְרַגְלָיו׃   his thumbs and big toes (lit., the major digits *of his*
                                hands and his feet)
                                Judg 1:6, cf. 1:7

9.   קֹנֵה שָׁמַ֫יִם וָאָ֫רֶץ׃   creator *of heaven and earth*
                                Gen 14:19

10.   נֶ֫פֶשׁ בָּנֶ֫יךָ וּבְנֹתֶ֫יךָ וְנֶ֫פֶשׁ נָשֶׁ֫יךָ   the lives *of your sons-and-daughters*, and the lives *of*
      וְנֶ֫פֶשׁ פִּלַגְשֶׁ֫יךָ׃   *your wives* and the lives *of your secondary wives*
                                2 Sam 19:6

---

6. For other construct overrides see Prov 16:11 (verse), Dan 1:4 (prose); see, generally, O'Connor, *Hebrew Verse Structure*, 308–11.

c   It is possible for the dependency to extend beyond two (sets of) entities; the genitive of one construct may be the construct of another noun, etc.

11.   לֵב רָאשֵׁי עַם־הָאָרֶץ   the heart of the heads of the people of the land
                                                                          Job 12:24

In this example there are three construct-genitive relations, רָאשֵׁי עַם, לֵב רָאשֵׁי, and עַם־הָארֶץ, fused in a single chain. Such chains are not common, and periphrastic constructions are preferred (9.7). The relation between construct and accompanying absolute is strong, and ordinarily nothing intervenes.

d   When a grammatical element such as a preposition (9.6b), an enclitic *mem* (9.8), or a directional *he* (10.5) intrudes between the construct and the genitive, the result is called a *broken construct chain*.[7] Other intrusive elements found in Hebrew poetry include construct -k[8] (# 12), את (# 13), pronominal suffixes (# 14), and verbal forms (# 15).

12.   בְּעֵינֶיךָ אֲדֹנָי   in your eyes, lord (so MT; better: in the *lord's* eyes)[9]
                                                                          Exod 34:9

13.   לְיֵשַׁע אֶת־מְשִׁיחֶךָ   for the salvation *of your anointed*
                                                                          Hab 3:13

14.   כִּי תִרְכַּב עַל־סוּסֶיךָ מַרְכְּבֹתֶיךָ   When you rode upon your horses, *your* chariots *of*
             יְשׁוּעָה: *victory*. . . .
                                                                          Hab 3:8

15.   דֶּרֶךְ יְרַצְּחוּ־שֶׁכְמָה   They commit murder on the road *to Shechem* (lit., On the road, they commit murder, to Shechem).[10]
                                                                          Hos 6:9

F. I. Andersen rejects the MT of # 12, which parses אדני as a vocative, because "this is not the way Moses usually addresses Yahweh," and "the following sentence shows that speech proceeds in the respectful third person, not the second."[11] D. N. Freedman suggests that the basis of the phrase in # 14 is "probably to be found in the association of *mrkbtyk* and the preceding *swsyk*, as coordinate elements in the compound phrase introduced by ʿl and controlled by *yšwʿh*."[12]

---

7. GKC § 130 / pp. 421–23; D. N. Freedman, "The Broken Construct Chain," *Biblica* 53 (1972) 534–36, reprinted in *Pottery, Poetry, and Prophecy* (Winona Lake, Indiana: Eisenbrauns, 1980) 339–41.

8. On construct -*k*, see F. I. Andersen, "A Short Note on Construct *k* in Hebrew," *Biblica* 50 (1969) 68–69; cf. M. Dahood, *Psalms I: 1–50* (Anchor Bible 16; Garden City, New York: Doubleday, 1966) 152; *Psalms II: 51–100* (Anchor Bible 17; Garden City, New York: Doubleday, 1968) xx, 147, 164.

9. For ʿyny ʾdny see, e.g., Gen 31:35; 33:8, 15; 47:25.

10. Contrast the usual word order in, e.g., *wattiqqābēr bədérek ʾeprātâ*, 'and he was buried on the Ephratah road,' Gen 35:19; *watḗšeb . . . ʿal-dérek timnắtâ*, 'and she sat . . . by the Timnah road,' Gen 38:14.

11. Andersen, "Construct *k*," 68–69.

12. Freedman, "Broken Construct Chain," 535 (rpt. p. 340); cf. O'Connor, *Hebrew Verse Structure*, 234 (on this text), 371–90 (on this type of phrase).

Uses of the Construct-Genitive Relation   **9.4**

Two nouns juxtaposed can form a construct phrase in Hebrew. In the structure   a
construct + genitive, the genitive modifies the construct, just as in *substantive + attributive adjective*, the adjective modifies the substantive. There are three English constructions, apparently similar to the Hebrew construct phrase, that it may be useful to review: (a) noun-noun compounds ('windmill, ashtray, figtree, pigpen'), (b) *'s*-genitives ('Moses' brother, Isaiah's sign'), (c) periphrastic genitives ('word of God, length of years'). In the first case, the similarity is superficial: the relationship in Hebrew of *construct + genitive* is a major inflectional link, while the English process is much less productive. The two English genitives are the proper analogues, and of the two the periphrastic genitive is more similar, for in it the head word comes first; in the *'s*-genitive (as in noun-noun compounds) the head word comes second. English periphrastic genitives, in fact, show some of the same complexity of meaning characteristic of Hebrew construct chains. The phrase 'love of God' (אַהֲבַת אֱלֹהִים) is ambiguous in both languages; it may mean either 'God's love (for someone)' or '(someone's) love for God.' This example illustrates the importance of establishing the possible meanings of the genitive case, sometimes called the "species of the genitive."[13]

In the next several sections we set forth a traditional classification of the species, by   b
which we mean the various notions signified by this polysemic construction (see 3.2.3). By what procedure do grammarians come up with these classes of meanings? And how can a reader identify the workings of a genitive in a specific text? Our analysis of the procedure for identifying and classifying the genitive (and other grammatical constructions) falls into three parts.

To explain the procedure, we turn first to the distinction between surface structure   c
and underlying structure (see 3.5). Possible deep structures are grammatical options aligning elements of a situation. In certain circumstances, one might speak of the idea that God loves people with the prosaic sentence 'God loves people'; in others one might use a genitival phrase, 'the love of God for people' or even 'the love of God.' The three surface structures are quite distinct, but they share a common alignment. It is possible to relieve ambiguity in the surface structure by analysis; ambiguous surface constructions, that is, can be associated with deep structures, which are more explicit. In the case of the genitive, this can be done by rephrasing the genitival construction into a sentence or an adjectival construction. So, for example, the 'love of God' can be rephrased by sentences with God as the subject ('God loves [someone or something]') or as the object ('[Someone or something] loves God') or by an adjectival phrase ('God[-like] love'). Similarly, 'the word of Yhwh' can be rephrased as either 'the word spoken by Yhwh or 'Yhwh spoke the word'; in either case Yhwh is the agent. 'Your vows' (cf. Ps 56:13) is equivalent to 'vows made to you,' a construction that makes it clear that 'you' qualifies the

---

13. Paul Friedrich mentions a total of seventy-eight subtypes of the genitive in Homeric Greek; see *Proto-Indo-European Syntax: The Order of Meaningful Elements*   (Journal of Indo-European Studies Monograph 1; Butte: Montana College of Mineral Science and Technology, 1975) 13.

implicit 'made.' Thus can the ambiguous genitive of the surface structure be transformed into unambiguous grammatical analogues. Often, once the structure of a Hebrew phrase has been found by analysis, the ambiguous genitive can be better rendered in English by a construction that does not rely on the frequently wooden and ambiguous 'of'; such renderings are well used in the NIV, which is therefore quoted in what follows.

d   Such analysis presupposes that the analyst knows both the grammatical options available to replace the ambiguous surface structure and their uses. The options are learned in essentially the same way one learns the meaning(s) of a word, namely, by inference from usage. In the case of a written language with a long tradition of study, the grammarian can make critical use of a venerable heritage. Readers of a written language must constantly be on guard against inadvertently applying categories of usage known from their own language to the language they are studying.

e   We continue the process of analysis by assigning an abstract (and somewhat arbitrary) semantic label to the various types of genitive, for example, "genitive of authorship," "objective genitive," "attributive genitive." We also assign them a grammatical label. A genitive can be analyzed as either a subject (or agent), or as a modifier, either adverbial or adjectival.

f   Let us illustrate the procedure for identifying a genitive phrase's use by contrasting the uses of the English phrase 'love of God' in these sentences: 'As the love of Romeo won Juliet, so the love of God woos sinners' and 'As the love of money inspires some, so the love of God inspires others.' As speakers of English, we know that 'love of someone' can signify either 'someone loved [somebody]' or '[somebody] loved someone.' Here the 'love of Romeo' is a genitive of agent (or a subjective genitive), while in the second sentence 'love of money' must be an objective (or adverbial) genitive. The comparative conjunctions 'as . . . so' show that 'love of' is being used in the same way in both halves of each sentence; therefore, in the first sentence 'love of God' is a genitive of agent (or subjective genitive) and in the second an objective (or adverbial) genitive.

g   Let us now consider the same phrase in another sentence: 'Romeo loved Juliet with the coals of burning, with the love of God, with the grave of grasping.' Here semantic pertinence suggests that 'love of God' means 'God-like love,' an attributive (or adjectival) genitive. As this sentence suggests, creativity plays a role in introducing new uses and meanings of forms. Creativity is not absolute, however, since all speakers are controlled by what Otto Jespersen has called a "latitude of correctness." To communicate, that is, a speaker must be governed by the established and public meanings of lexemes, morphemes, and grammatical structures. Lewis Carroll imaginatively depicted the tension between the public meaning of words and morphemes versus the private use of them.

"There's glory for you!" "I don't know what you mean by 'glory,'" Alice said. Humpty Dumpty smiled contemptuously. "Of course you don't—till I tell you. I meant 'there's a nice knock-down argument for you!'" "But 'glory' doesn't mean 'a nice knock-down argument,'" Alice objected. "When *I* use a word," Humpty Dumpty said, in rather a scornful tone, "it means just what I choose it to mean—neither more nor less." "The

question is," said Alice, "whether you *can* make words mean so many different things."
"The question is," said Humpty Dumpty, "which is to be master—that's all."

The grammarian and lexicographer are on Alice's side.[14]

Species of the Genitive   9.5

The noun-noun genitive phrase or construct chain is "immensely versatile and hard-   a
worked."[15] Three major kinds of construct chain can be distinguished: subjective,
ad-verbial, and adjectival.[16] In what follows, C designates the construct, head, or first
term of the chain and G the genitive, absolute, or second term.[17]

Subjective Genitive   9.5.1

In the various types of *subjective genitive* phrases, the genitive term has an under-   a
lying subject role, as in English 'the boy's leaving,' implying 'The boy left.' In Hebrew a
subjective genitive can have a basically verbal or possessive/qualitative structure.

In a *genitive of agency* G does the action described by C (active, ## 1–3; passive, # 4).   b

1.	לָתֵת נִקְמַת־יהוה בְּמִדְיָן:	to carry out *Yhwh's niqmâ* against Midian Num 31:3
2.	בְּשִׂנְאַת יהוה אֹתָנוּ	because *Yhwh* hates us Deut 1:27
3.	בְּאַהֲבַת יהוה אֶת־יִשְׂרָאֵל	because of *Yhwh's* love for Israel 1 Kgs 10:9
4.	מֻכֵּה אֱלֹהִים	stricken *by God* Isa 53:4

A particular form of agency is involved in speaking and writing, and the *genitive of*   c
authorship denotes that G wrote, spoke, or otherwise originated C.

5.	דִּבַּרְתִּי דְּבָרָי	I have told *my* words. Gen 24:33
6.	הָיָה דְבַר־יהוה אֵלָיו	The word *of Yhwh* came to him. Jer 1:2
7.	דִּבְרֵי לְמוּאֵל	the words *by Lemuel* Prov 31:1
8.	מַשְׂאַת מֹשֶׁה	the tax *imposed by Moses* 2 Chr 24:6

14. For both Jespersen and Carroll, see G. B. Caird, *The Language and Imagery of the Bible* (Philadelphia: Westminster, 1980) 38, 40.

15. To borrow C. F. D. Moule's phrase for the Greek genitive; *An Idiom Book of New Testament Greek* (2d ed.; Cambridge: Cambridge University, 1959) 37.

16. That is, roughly, nominative, accusative, and genitive.

17. We have drawn on a variety of resources for the tradition, and we have also profited from John Beekman and John Callow, *Translating the Word of God* (Grand Rapids: Zondervan, 1974) 249–66. Note also the discussion of a variety of both syntactic and semantic points in Sperber, *Historical Grammar*, 600–622; and Richter, *GAHG* 2. 16–21.

d   An agent or author is animate; the inanimate analogue to the agent role is that of instrument. A *genitive of instrument* involves the relationship G is the instrument of C. (See 9.5.2d.)

9.	לֹא חַלְלֵי־חֶרֶב וְלֹא מֵתֵי מִלְחָמָה:	not slain *by the sword* nor dead *through war* Isa 22:2
10.	מַחֲלִיק פַּטִּישׁ	he who polishes *with a hammer* Isa 41:7
11.	עָרֵיכֶם שְׂרֻפוֹת אֵשׁ	your cities are burned *with fire* Isa 1:7
12.	טְמֵא־נֶפֶשׁ	impure *by* (reason of contact with) *a corpse* Lev 22:4

e   A subjective genitive may involve neither agent nor instrument, but rather a motivation or intention. In an *abstract subjective genitive* G denotes a verbal action affecting C. (The phrase מֵתֵי מִלְחָמָה in # 9 may belong here.)

13.	שִׁלַּחְתָּ אֶת־אִישׁ־חֶרְמִי מִיָּד	You have set free the man *I had determined should die* (lit., man *of my devoting to a consecrated death*). 1 Kgs 20:42
14.	וְעַל־עַם עֶבְרָתִי אֲצַוֶּנּוּ	I dispatch them against a people *who incur my wrath* (lit., a people *of my wrath*). Isa 10:6
15.	נֶחְשַׁבְנוּ כְּצֹאן טִבְחָה:	We are considered as sheep *to be slaughtered* (lit., as sheep *of slaughtering*). Ps 44:23
16.	וַיַּנְחֵם אֶל־מְחוֹז חֶפְצָם:	And he guided them to their *desired* haven (lit., to the port *of their desiring*). Ps 107:30

The sense of the abstract may be passive, in which case G is affected by C.

17.	מְכֹרֹתַיִךְ וּמֹלְדֹתַיִךְ מֵאֶרֶץ הַכְּנַעֲנִי	*Your* ancestry and *your* birth were from the land of Canaan. Ezek 16:3

f   A *temporal genitive* involves a verbal action G associated with a time C (often יוֹם).

18.	יוֹם מְהוּמָה וּמְבוּסָה וּמְבוּכָה לַאדֹנָי יהוה צְבָאוֹת	The Lord YHWH Ṣb°wt has a day *of tumult and trampling and terror* (i.e., The Lord . . . will bring tumult, etc., on a given day).[18] Isa 22:5

---

18. On a single construct governing a coordinate noun phrase see 9.3b; for other examples see Isa 11:2 and 9.5.3 # 39.

| 19. | :וְהַקְדִּשֵׁם לְיוֹם הֲרֵגָה | Set them apart for a day *of slaughter* (i.e., they will be slaughtered on a given day).
Jer 12:3 |

In contrast to the basically verbal character of the types of genitive just outlined is the nonverbal quality of other subjective genitives. In a *possessive genitive*, G owns or has C; the relationships involved may be quite various. g

20.	:בֵּית יהוה וְ . . . בֵּית הַמֶּלֶךְ	the temple *of YHWH* and the *king's* house 1 Kgs 9:10
21.	וּזֲהַב הָאָרֶץ הַהִיא טוֹב	The gold *of that land* is good. Gen 2:12
22.	חָכְמַת שְׁלֹמֹה	the wisdom *of Solomon* 1 Kgs 5:10

A *genitive of inalienable possession* refers to something intrinsically proper to its possessor, chiefly body parts. (Example # 22 may belong here.) h

| 23. | דְּמֵי אָחִיךָ | the blood *of* your *brother*
Gen 4:10 |
| 24. | לִרְחֹץ . . . רַגְלֵי הָאֲנָשִׁים | to wash . . . the feet *of the men*
Gen 24:32 |

If human relationships are involved, the *genitive* is one *of relation* proper; such links could involve either kinship or other social structures.[19] i

25.	יַעֲזָב־אִישׁ אֶת־אָבִיו וְאֶת־אִמּוֹ וְדָבַק בְּאִשְׁתּוֹ	A man shall leave *his* father and *his* mother and be united to *his* wife. Gen 2:24
26.	בְּנִי אַתָּה	You are *my* son. Ps 2:7
27.	מֹשֶׁה עֶבֶד־יהוה	Moses, the servant *of YHWH* Josh 12:6
28.	יַשְׂכִּיל עַבְדִּי	*My* servant will act wisely. Isa 52:13
29.	נִאֲצוּ אֶת־קְדוֹשׁ יִשְׂרָאֵל	They have spurned the Holy One *of Israel.* Isa 1:4

The *genitive of quality* denotes that G has the quality of C; such phrases usually involve people. j

---

19. For the naming formulas (e.g., 'Abner son of Ner' is more common than 'Abner'), see D. J. A. Clines, "X, X *ben* Y, *ben* Y: Personal Names in Hebrew Narrative Style," *Vetus Testamentum* 22 (1972) 266–87.

30.   וִיהִי כַנָּהָר שְׁלוֹמֶךָ וְצִדְקָתְךָ כְּגַלֵּי הַיָּם׃   *Your* peace would have been like a river, *your* righteousness like the waves of the sea.
Isa 48:18

k   The usually inanimate reference of a *partitive genitive* is a substance that can be divided up: G is divided into (parts, including) C.

31.   וַיִּקַּח מֹשֶׁה חֲצִי הַדָּם   Moses took half *of the blood.*
Exod 24:6

9.5.2   Adverbial Genitive

a   The various types of adverbial genitive involve the object, direct or mediated, of the underlying verbal action, as in English 'the king's capture,' implying 'Someone captured the king.' In Hebrew, adverbial genitives can be classified according to the relationship of the verb to the basic object.

b   In the *objective genitive*, the genitive is the (direct) object of the essential verbal action, that is, roughly, C does G.[20]

1.   מֹשְׁכֵי הֶעָוֹן   those who draw *iniquity*
Isa 5:18

2.   מַצְדִּיקֵי רָשָׁע   those who acquit *the guilty*
Isa 5:23

c   In a *genitive of effect* the relationship of C and G is a directly causational one, that is, roughly, C causes G.[21]

3.   רוּחַ חָכְמָה וּבִינָה   the spirit *of wisdom and understanding* (i.e., the spirit *that causes wisdom . . .*)
Isa 11:2

4.   קֻבַּעַת . . . הַתַּרְעֵלָה   the bowl *that causes staggering*
Isa 51:17

5.   מוּסַר שְׁלוֹמֵנוּ   the punishment *that brought us peace*
Isa 53:5

d   The relationship of the genitive and implicit verb may be of the sort usually mediated by a preposition; the *genitive of a mediated object* involves the relation C does to/by/ with G.[22]

20. The classic ambiguity between subjective and objective genitives is illustrated by the phrase in Job 8:8, *ḥēqer ʾăbôtām* 'the investigation of their fathers'—is this 'an investigation undertaken by their fathers' (subjective) or 'an investigation about their fathers' (objective)? The underlying passive sense included under 9.5.1 (e.g., # 17) may belong under 9.5.2.

21. The term "causational" as used here is not to be confused with the "causativity" attributed to the *Hiphil*; see 27.1.

22. It could be argued that the instrumental genitives included under 9.5.1 actually belong here, because Hebrew usually does not allow an inanimate to serve as a clausal subject; an instrument in Hebrew is thus virtually always the object of a preposition or an accusative of means (10.2.3d).

6.	שְׁבֻעַת יְהֹוָה	the oath *to* Y<small>HWH</small> 1 Kgs 2:43
7.	עָלַי אֱלֹהִים נְדָרֶיךָ	I am under vows *to you*, O God. Ps 56:13
8.	חֲמָסִי עָלֶיךָ	May the wrong *done me* be upon you. Gen 16:5
9.	לֹא תִהְיֶה תִּפְאַרְתְּךָ	Glory will not be *yours* (i.e., given you). Judg 4:9
10.	עַד־מֶה כְבוֹדִי לִכְלִמָּה	How long will the glory [bestowed] *on me* serve as a reproach? Ps 4:3
11.	אֶרֶץ זָבַת חָלָב וּדְבָשׁ׃	a land flowing *with milk and honey* Deut 6:3

A special genitive of this sort is the *genitive of advantage* (or disadvantage), in   e
which G is the recipient or beneficiary of a favorable (or unfavorable) action denoted
by C.[23]

12.	נִקְמַת הֵיכָלוֹ׃	*niqmâ for* his *temple* Jer 50:28
13.	אֵבֶל יָחִיד	mourning *for an only son* Amos 8:10
14.	חֲמַס אָחִיךָ	violence *against* your *brother* Obad 10
15.	אֵימַת מֶלֶךְ	fear *due a king* Prov 20:2
16.	לֶחֶם הַפֶּחָה	the bread *due the governor* Neh 5:14
17.	כִּי־אִישׁ מִלְחָמוֹת תֹּעִי הָיָה הֲדַדְעָזֶר	Hadadezer was experienced in battles *against Toi* (i.e., A man of wars that had been fought against Toi was Hadadezer). 2 Sam 8:10

The *genitive of location* designates that G is the location or goal of C; such genitives   f
are alternatives to various prepositional constructions. If the phrase refers to a location,
the basic prepositional construction is usually that of בְּ and there is no implicit verb of
motion.

---

23. This usage is comparable to the Greek dative of advantage, e.g., *erchomai soi* 'I am coming on your behalf,' Rev 2:16; see 23.2.1. On some related Hebrew construc-

tions with *l*, see T. Muraoka, "On the So-called *Dativus Ethicus* in Hebrew," *Journal of Theological Studies* 29 (1978) 495–98.

18.	יֹשְׁבֵי גִבְעוֹן	those living *in Gibeon* Josh 9:3
19.	גִּבְעַת בִּנְיָמִין	Gibeah *in Benjamin* 1 Sam 13:2
20.	אֹכְלֵי שֻׁלְחַן אִיזָבֶל:	eating *at the table* of Jezebel 1 Kgs 18:19
21.	כָּל־עֹשֵׂי שֶׂכֶר אַגְמֵי־נָפֶשׁ:	All the wage earners will be sick *in spirit.* Isa 19:10

If the phrase refers to a goal, there is a verb of motion, either explicit or implicit.[24]

22.	בָּאֵי שַׁעַר־עִירוֹ	who go in *at the gate* of his city Gen 23:10
23.	קְרֹבַי	those who come near *to me* Lev 10:3
24.	בָּאֵי מוֹעֵד	who come *to the feast* Lam 1:4
25.	שֹׁכְבֵי קֶבֶר	lain *in the tomb* Ps 88:6
26.	לְשָׁבֵי פֶּשַׁע	those returning *from sin* Isa 59:20
27.	דֶּרֶךְ עֵץ הַחַיִּים:	the way *to the tree* of life Gen 3:24
28.	יוֹרְדֵי־בוֹר	those who go down *to the pit*[25] Isa 38:18

It is difficult to insist on a rigid distinction between goal and location.[26]

9.5.3   Adjectival Genitive

a   In adjectival genitive phrases, the construct and genitive modify each other, one specifying features of the other. In English, comparable semantic structures often involve adjectives or, less often, noun compounds; genitives are not usually used. Examples are not rare, however: 'a man of many talents,' cf. a 'a multi-talented woman'; 'a coat of wool,' cf. 'a cotton shirt'; 'the city of Lachish,' cf. 'the Beth-Shean area.' Hebrew expressions of attribution, substance, and class-membership often use constructs.

---

24. Compare *maqômî* in Judg 11:19, where the sense is 'the place I am going to.'

25. The same phrase is used often in Ezekiel 26 and 32; cf. the phrase *ywrdy ʾl-ʾbny-bwr* in Isa 14:19.

26. In Job 3:10 the expression *biṭnî* 'my belly' refers to the womb in which the speaker was gestating at the time he is describing, from which he eventually and to his regret emerged.

The largest group of adjectival genitives refers to a feature or quality of something. The most common type of these is the *attributive genitive*, in which C is characterized by G; in English such phrases are often rendered with G as an adjective of C.

1.   וּבִגְדֵי הַקֹּדֶשׁ   *holy* garments
   Exod 29:29

2.   גִּבּוֹר חַיִל   *valiant* warrior
   Judg 11:1

3.   מַלְכֵי חֶסֶד   *merciful* kings
   1 Kgs 20:31

4.   אַיֶּלֶת אֲהָבִים   *beloved* hind
   Prov 5:19

5.   וְנָתַתִּי לְךָ . . . אֶת כָּל־אֶרֶץ כְּנַעַן לַאֲחֻזַּת עוֹלָם   I will give to you . . . all the land of Canaan as a possession *of perpetuity* (i.e., as an *perpetual* possession).
   Gen 17:8

6.   מֹאזְנֵי צֶדֶק אַבְנֵי־צֶדֶק . . . יִהְיֶה לָכֶם   Balances *of righteousness*, stones *of righteousness* . . . you will have (i.e., use *honest* scales).
   Lev 19:36

7.   בְּעִיר אֱלֹהֵינוּ הַר־קָדְשׁוֹ׃   in the city of our God, his *holy* mountain
   Ps 48:2

Closely related to this attributive genitive is the use of the genitive in conventional idioms consisting of construct forms of אִישׁ 'man' (## 8–9), בַּעַל 'master, possessor' (## 10–12), בֶּן 'son of' (## 13–14), or their feminine or plural equivalents, with some noun in the genitive case to represent the nature, quality, character, or condition of (a) person(s). These locutions supplement the meager stock of adjectives in Hebrew. English idiom prefers these constructions be rendered by an adjective.[27]

8.   אִישׁ הַדָּמִים וְאִישׁ הַבְּלִיָּעַל׃   blood-spattered man, you scoundrel (lit., man *of blood*, man *of Belial*)
   2 Sam 16:7

9.   לֹא אִישׁ דְּבָרִים אָנֹכִי   I have never been an eloquent man (lit., a man *of words*).[28]
   Exod 4:10

10.   הִנֵּה בַּעַל הַחֲלֹמוֹת הַלָּזֶה בָּא׃   Here comes that dreamer (lit., possessor *of dreams*).
   Gen 37:19

27. For other phrases with *ʾyš* see Gen 9:20, 2 Sam 18:20; with *bᶜl* see Isa 41:15, 50:8; Jer 37:13; Nah 1:2; with *bn* see Num 17:25, 2 Sam 3:34, 2 Kgs 14:14. For the feminine *bt blyᶜl* see 1 Sam 1:16. Note that *bn* is, after *yhwh*, the most common noun in the Hebrew Bible; SA/THAT mentions 4,929 occurrences.

28. For similar phrases involving mastery over speech and talkativeness in *ʾyš* see Job 11:2, Ps 140:12; in *ʾšt* see Prov 25:24; in *bᶜl* see Exod 24:14.

11.   בַּקְשׁוּ־לִי אֵשֶׁת בַּעֲלַת־אוֹב   Find me a woman, a *possessor of a spirit* (or, a woman *who is a medium*).
1 Sam 28:7

12.   וְהֵם בַּעֲלֵי בְרִית־אַבְרָם: They were allies with Abram (lit., possessors *of a covenant of Abram*).
Gen 14:13

13.   כִּי בֶן־מָוֶת הוּא: He is a *son of death* (i.e., He *must die*).
1 Sam 20:31, cf. 1 Kgs 2:26

14.   אִם יִהְיֶה לְבֶן־חַיִל   If he will be a *son of virtue* (i.e., If he shows himself *a worthy man*). . . .
1 Kgs 1:52

More specifically בֶּן is used in expressions of age.

15.   וְאַבְרָהָם בֶּן־מְאַת שָׁנָה   Now Abraham was a hundred years old.
Gen 21:5

16.   שֶׂה . . . זָכָר בֶּן־שָׁנָה יִהְיֶה לָכֶם   The animal you choose must be a . . . year-old male.
Exod 12:5

Similar expressions indicate the relationship of an individual to a class of beings.

17.   בֶּן־אָדָם   O, Son of man (i.e., O, Human)[29]
Ezek 2:1, etc.

18.   בְּנֵי־הָאֱלֹהִים   sons of God (i.e., divine beings)
Job 1:6

19.   וְקָרַבְתָּ מוּל בְּנֵי עַמּוֹן   When you come opposite the sons of Ammon (i.e., the Ammonites). . . .
Deut 2:19

In an attributive genitive, a pronominal suffix is attached to the genitive but usually modifies the whole chain.[30]

20.   הַר־קָדְשִׁי   *my* holy hill
Ps 2:6

21.   אֱלֹהֵי צִדְקִי   *my* righteous God
Ps 4:2

22.   וַתִּתֶּן־לִי מָגֵן יִשְׁעֶךָ   You have given me *your* shield of victory (*not* the shield of thy salvation, AV).
Ps 18:36

---

29. The phrase indicates the mere humanness and insignificance of Ezekiel in contrast to God; see Clines, "X, X ben Y," 287.

30. See the discussion in J. Weingreen, "The Construct-Genitive Relation in Hebrew Syntax," *Vetus Testamentum* 4 (1954) 50–59.

| 23. | תְּפִלָּה לְאֵל חַיָּי | a prayer to *my* living God (*not* the God of my life) Ps 42:9 |

In an attributive genitive, C is characterized by G; the opposite relation is also   c
found, in the *epexegetical genitive*, wherein G is characterized by C.[31] Many epexegetical
phrases can be rendered by English *of*-genitives; note the phrase 'hard of heart,' cf.
'hard-hearted.' The sense can also be conveyed by the gloss 'as to' or 'with regard to,' for
example, 'stiff with regard to their necks'; this is the meaning of the term "epexegetical."

24.	עַם־קְשֵׁה־עֹרֶף	a stiff-*necked* (lit., stiff-*of-neck*) people Exod 32:9
25.	וְהַנַּעֲרָה טֹבַת מַרְאֶה מְאֹד	The girl was very *pretty* (lit., good *of appearance*). Gen 24:16 Qere
26.	וַיְהִי יוֹסֵף יְפֵה־תֹאַר	Joseph was fair *of form* (or, well built). Gen 39:6
27.	הַפָּרוֹת רָעוֹת הַמַּרְאֶה	the cows that were ugly (lit., bad *as to appearance*) Gen 41:4
28.	וְהָאִשָּׁה טוֹבַת־שֶׂכֶל וִיפַת תֹּאַר וְהָאִישׁ . . . רַע מַעֲלָלִים	The woman was great *as to discretion* and beautiful *as to form*, but the man was . . . evil *as to his doings*. 1 Sam 25:3
29.	טְמֵא־שְׂפָתַיִם	unclean *of lips* Isa 6:5
30.	אֶרֶךְ אַפַּיִם	*patient* (lit., long *as to the nostrils*, the source of anger) Exod 34:6

This symmetrical representation of attributive and epexegetical genitives should not obscure the fact that attributives are much more common.

The remaining types of adjectival genitive involve a wide variety of relationships.   d
Three of them may be called *genitives of substance*, namely, of material, topic, and
measure. The *genitive of material* indicates material of which something is made or with
which it is filled, namely, C is made of G.

31.	מִזְבַּח אֲדָמָה	an *earthen* altar Exod 20:24
32.	כְּלִי־חֶרֶשׂ	a *clay* jar Num 5:17
33.	שֵׁבֶט בַּרְזֶל	an *iron* sceptre Ps 2:9
34.	כְּלֵי כֶסֶף	*silver* vessels 1 Kgs 10:25

---

31. Also called the improper annexation; it is grammatically proper, but it is a minority pattern. M. Greenberg
calls it a "common enough phenomenon" and cites Isa

2:11 and Ps 65:5*bis*; *Ezekiel, 1–20* (Anchor Bible 22; Garden
City, New York: Doubleday, 1983) 375.

| 35. | לְשׁוֹן זָהָב | a *golden* tongue
Josh 7:21 |
| 36. | וַיִּקַּח יִשַׁי חֲמוֹר לֶחֶם וְנֹאד יַיִן | So Jesse took a donkey *loaded with food* and a skin *of wine*.
1 Sam 16:20 |

e   The similar *topical genitive* specifies the topic of a discourse or the like, namely, C is about G.

37.	מַשָּׂא בָּבֶל	oracle *about Babylon* Isa 13:1
38.	שֵׁמַע צֹר	the report *about Tyre* Isa 23:5
39.	זַעֲקַת סְדֹם וַעֲמֹרָה	the outcry *against Sodom and Gomorrah* Gen 18:20

f   In a *genitive of measure*, a counting is specified along with the counted term, namely, G is measured in C. In addition to numbers, general quantifiers such as כֹּל 'all' and רֹב 'multitude' are frequent in such genitives, as are actual measures.

40.	שְׁלֹשֶׁת יָמִים	three *days* Gen 40:18
41.	מַיִם עַל־פְּנֵי כָל־הָאָרֶץ	There was water upon all (the surface) *of the earth*. Gen 8:9
42.	אֵל ... רַב־חֶסֶד וֶאֱמֶת׃	a God ... abounding *in unfailing love and truth* Exod 34:6
43.	לֹג הַשֶּׁמֶן	the (single) log *of oil* Lev 14:12

g   Four further types of genitives involve classes and the interrelationship of either a class and an individual or a class (the superordinate) and a subclass (the subordinate). In the *genitive of species*, the class designated by the construct (C) is narrowed down to a subclass (i.e., "species") indicated by G. Thus, in # 45 the construct includes all workers and the genitive serves to mark out an individual group of workers, 'those who work in wood.'

44.	עֲצֵי־גֹפֶר	*gopher*-wood Gen 6:14
45.	חָרָשֵׁי עֵץ	workers *in wood* 2 Sam 5:11
46.	תְּאֵנֵי הַבַּכֻּרוֹת	figs *of the first fruits* (i.e., early figs) Jer 24:2

47.	עֻגַת רְצָפִים	cakes *baked on hot stones* 1 Kgs 19:6
48.	אֲחֻזַּת־קֶבֶר	*burial* site Gen 23:4
49.	זֶרַע מְרֵעִים	a brood *of evildoers* Isa 1:4

In the *genitive of association*, the individual G belongs to the class of C; though 'of' h
is well established in translations of such phrases, it is not needed in English.[32]

50.	נְהַר־פְּרָת	River Euphrates Gen 15:18
51.	אֶרֶץ מִצְרַיִם	the land [of] Egypt Exod 7:19
52.	גַּן־עֵדֶן	the Garden [of] Eden Gen 2:15
53.	בְּתוּלַת יִשְׂרָאֵל	the virgin [of] Israel Amos 5:2
54.	מְקוֹם פְּלֹנִי אַלְמוֹנִי:	such-and-such a place 1 Sam 21:3

In other genitives of class, the subordinate element (C) precedes the superordinate   i
element (G). In the genitive of genus and the superlative genitive, the individual is in the
construct and the broader class to which it belongs is the genitive. In the *genitive of
genus*, C belongs to the class of G.

55.	כַּף־רַגְלָהּ	the sole *of its foot* Gen 8:9
56.	צֹאן אָדָם	flocks *of men* Ezek 36:38
57.	אֹהֶל בֵּיתִי	*my* tent *house* Ps 132:3
58.	וּכְסִיל אָדָם בּוֹזֶה אִמּוֹ:	A fool *of a man* (i.e., a foolish man) despises his mother. Prov 15:20
59.	עֲלִילֹת דְּבָרִים	plot *involving words* (i.e., any slander) Deut 22:14

---

32. Compare English 'no earthly good,' 'every mother's son.' On *bt yrwšlm* and the like see A. Fitzgerald, "*BTWLT* and *BT* as Titles for Capital Cities," *Catholic Biblical Quarterly* 37 (1975) 167–83; and the spirited polemic of W. F. Stinespring, "Daughter of Zion," *Interpreter's Dictionary of the Bible: Supplementary Volume*, ed. K. R. Crim et al. (Nashville: Abingdon, 1976) 985.

60.   וְלֹא־יִרְאֶה בְךָ עֶרְוַת דָּבָר   . . . so that he not see among you the indecency *of something* (i.e., anything indecent)
Deut 23:15

j   Similar is the construction used for the *superlative genitive*.[33] A superlative may involve two instances of a single noun, the first a singular construct and the second a plural genitive; or two different nouns may be used.

61.   קֹדֶשׁ קָדָשִׁים   most holy
Exod 29:37

62.   עֶבֶד עֲבָדִים   a slave of slaves (i.e., an abject slave)
Gen 9:25

63.   שִׁיר הַשִּׁירִים   the Song of Songs (i.e., the Choicest Song)
Cant 1:1

64.   אֱלֹהֵי הָאֱלֹהִים וַאֲדֹנֵי הָאֲדֹנִים   the Highest God and the Supreme Lord
Deut 10:17

65.   מִבְחַר קְבָרֵינוּ   the choicest of our sepulchers
Gen 23:6

66.   קְטֹן בָּנָיו   the youngest of his sons
2 Chr 21:17

k   This discussion may be summarized by dividing adjectival genitives into two classes. In the first group the construct is the modified element and the genitive the modifier:

attributive	C is characterized by G	הַר־קָדְשׁוֹ	## 7, 20
material	C is made of G	שֵׁבֶט בַּרְזֶל	# 33
topical	C is about G	מַשָּׂא בָּבֶל	# 37
species	C is specified by G	חָרָשֵׁי עֵץ	# 45
association	C is associated with G	אֶרֶץ מִצְרַיִם	# 51

The construct is the modifier and the genitive the modified element in the second group:

epexegetical	G is characterized by C	קְשֵׁה־עֹרֶף	# 24
measure	G is measured in C	שְׁלֹשֶׁת יָמִים	# 40
genus	G is specified by C	כְּסִיל אָדָם	# 58
superlative	G is specified by the best (or most) of C	קְטֹן בָּנָיו	# 66

33. Cf. 14.5. There are other ways of expressing the superlative in Hebrew, notably the use of terms such as ʾēl, ʾĕlōhîm, māwet, šǝʾôl, nēṣaḥ as genitive (compare English 'god-awful,' 'scared to death,' 'like to died,' 'no end of trouble'). See D. Winton Thomas, "A Considera-tion of Some Unusual Ways of Expressing the Superlative in Hebrew," *Vetus Testamentum* 3 (1953) 209–24; P. P. Saydon, "Some Unusual Ways of Expressing the Superlative in Hebrew and Maltese," *Vetus Testamentum* 4 (1954) 432–33.

Construct State before Phrases and Clauses   9.6

The genitive case is ordinarily a property of a single noun or pronoun, but, as   a
mentioned earlier, two nouns can stand for one in the genitive slot, after a construct
(9.3b). It is also possible for prepositional phrases and even entire clauses to stand after a
construct; these constituents are thus treated as a single noun (cf. 4.4.1).

A prepositional phrase most often stands after a construct participle, a usage similar   b
to the genitive of a mediated object; in the usual phrase the preposition is omitted (9.5.2),
while in these constructions it is retained.[34]

1.	כָּל־חֹוסֵי בֹו:	all who take refuge *in him* Ps 2:12
2.	יֹשְׁבֵי בְּאֶרֶץ צַלְמָוֶת	those living *in the land* of the shadow of death Isa 9:1
3.	גְּמוּלֵי מֵחָלָב עַתִּיקֵי מִשָּׁדָיִם:	those weaned *from milk*, those removed *from the breast* Isa 28:9

Other nouns can stand in construct before a prepositional phrase; אַחַד regularly governs
a partitive phrase in מִן.[35]

4.	שִׂמְחַת בַּקָּצִיר	rejoicing *at harvest-time* Isa 9:2
5.	הַאֱלֹהֵי מִקָּרֹב אָנִי . . . וְלֹא אֱלֹהֵי מֵרָחֹק:	Am I a god *from nearby* . . . and not a god *from far-off*? Jer 23:23
6.	קַח־נָא אִתְּךָ אֶת־אַחַד מֵהַנְּעָרִים	Take with you *one of the servants*. 1 Sam 9:3

A clause may also stand after a construct noun.[36] Sometimes the construct has some   c
prepositional force. For example, אַחַר is a noun meaning 'hinder part' but occurs most
often in the plural construct, as a preposition alone (אַחֲרֵי 'after'; 11.2.1), or with other
prepositions (מֵאַחֲרֵי 'after, from behind'; 11.3.3), or as a conjunction (אַחֲרֵי אֲשֶׁר, see,
e.g., Deut 24:4; cf. Chap. 38.7); thus, אַחֲרֵי is well established as a preposition. Similarly,
יָד in the phrase בְּיַד, though a construct noun, may be considered part of a complex
preposition. In clausal cases in which the construct noun cannot be considered a preposition or part of a preposition, relative clauses are most common, though other types of
subordinate clauses do occur.

---

34. Examples similar to Ps 2:12 are Isa 30:18, 64:3. Other cases of the phenomenon include Judg 5:10; Isa 5:11, 9:1, 56:10; Ezek 38:11; Ps 84:7; Job 24:5; cf. Jer 33:22.

35. For ʾḥd see also Gen 3:22, Judg 17:11; cf. Hos 7:5.

36. On similar clause types elsewhere in Semitic see M. O'Connor, "The Arabic Loanwords in Nabatean Aramaic," *Journal of Near Eastern Studies* 45 (1986) 213–29, at 223–24.

d   Relative clauses after prepositionally used constructs are found; in these three examples the relative clause is asyndetic (or headless, i.e., lacks a relative pronoun).

7.	וְאַחֲרֵי לֹא־יוֹעִלוּ הָלָכוּ׃	They followed after (*those who*) *cannot act.* Jer 2:8	
8.	שְׁלַח־נָא בְּיַד־תִּשְׁלָח׃	Send (your message) in the hand of (*him whom*) *you will send.* Exod 4:13	

The relative clause may be used after a construct noun with no prepositional force; # 10 uses a relative pronoun.

9.	קִרְיַת חָנָה דָוִד	the city (*where*) *David settled* Isa 29:1
10.	וַיִּתְּנֵהוּ אֶל־בֵּית הַסֹּהַר מְקוֹם אֲשֶׁר־אֲסִירֵי הַמֶּלֶךְ אֲסוּרִים	And he placed him in the roundhouse, the place *in which the prisoners of the king were imprisoned.* Gen 39:20 *Qere*

e   The construct may also be used before non-relative clauses, if it is prepositional (אחרי) or quasi-prepositional (כל־ימי).[37]

11.	אַחֲרֵי נִמְכַּר	After *he is sold.* . . . Lev 25:48
12.	וְלֹא־פָקַדְנוּ מְאוּמָה כָּל־יְמֵי הִתְהַלַּכְנוּ אִתָּם בִּהְיוֹתֵנוּ בַּשָּׂדֶה׃	We found no fault all the-days-*of-we-went-about* with them during our being in the fields. 1 Sam 25:15

It is also possible for a construct of no prepositional force to stand before a non-relative clause. This construction is extremely rare.[38]

13.	תְּחִלַּת דִּבֶּר־יהוה בְּהוֹשֵׁעַ	The beginning *of YHWH-spoke* through Hosea Hos 1:2

9.7   Determination and Periphrasis

a   The subject of *determination* (*definiteness/indefiniteness*) will be treated in detail in Chapter 13, but one aspect of it must be mentioned here. In Hebrew the definiteness of a noun and that of its modifiers are in agreement. With attributive and demonstrative adjectives this is shown by using the article on both substantive and adjective: הַיּוֹם הַשְּׁמִינִי 'eighth day,' הַיּוֹם הַזֶּה 'this day.' In a construct chain, the construct can never be

---

37. Cf. Jer 50:46*bis*!

38. On the example from Hosea, see F. I. Andersen and D. N. Freedman, *Hosea* (Anchor Bible 24; Garden City, New York: Doubleday, 1980) 153–54. This construction is sometimes associated with Gen 1:1; see, e.g., the discussion in B. K. Waltke, "The Creation Account in Genesis 1:1–3," *Bibliotheca Sacra* 132 (1975) 216–28.

prefixed with the article. The definiteness of the genitive specifies the definiteness of the phrase.[39] If the genitive is indefinite, the phrase is indefinite.

1.	אִישׁ מִלְחָמָה	a soldier (lit., a man *of war*[*fare*]) Josh 17:1
2.	דְּבַר־שֶׁקֶר	a lie (lit., a word *of falsehood*) Prov 29:12

If the genitive is definite, the phrase is definite; the genitive may be definite because it bears the article or a suffix or because it is a name.[40]

3.	בְּנֵי הַמֶּלֶךְ	sons *of the king* (or, the sons of the king or *roughly*, the king's sons) 2 Sam 9:11
4.	אֵשֶׁת־אָבִיךָ	wife *of your father* (or roughly, your father's wife) Lev 18:8
5.	גִּבְעַת בִּנְיָמִין	Gibeah *in Benjamin* 1 Sam 13:2
6.	אֱלֹהֵי יִשְׂרָאֵל	God *of Israel* (or roughly, the God of Israel) 1 Kgs 8:15

The ambiguity of English 'the son of the king' could also theoretically obtain for the comparable Hebrew phrase: is the referent unique or one among others? If the referent is non-unique (i.e., if the king has other sons) and this must be made clear, English uses a phrase like 'a son of the king.' Hebrew cannot use a construct with a definite article in such circumstances but rather resorts to a *periphrastic genitive* with *lamed* (for the construction in verbless clauses, see 8.4.2).

7.	רָאִיתִי בֵּן לְיִשַׁי	I have seen *a son of Jesse*. 1 Sam 16:18
8.	מִזְמוֹר לְדָוִד	*a* psalm of David Ps 3:1

Periphrasis may be used in genitive expressions under other circumstances. It may   b be used where a construct phrase would also be acceptable.

9.	הַצֹּפִים לְשָׁאוּל	*Saul's* watchmen 1 Sam 14:16

---

39. The situation in verse is more complicated.
40. On the required definiteness of the epexegetical genitive in Arabic, a difficult passage in Phoenician, and re-

lated matters, see M. O'Connor, "The Grammar of Getting Blessed in Tyrian-Sidonian Phoenician," *Rivista di Studi Fenici* 5 (1977) 5–11, at 6–11.

Periphrastic *l* is also used in cases in which a construct chain needs to be qualified (notably because of the need for clarity about definiteness, as in # 7 above and # 10 below) or kept brief.

10. חֶלְקַת הַשָּׂדֶה לְבֹעַז the portion of a field *belonging to Boaz*
Ruth 2:3

11. עַל־סֵפֶר דִּבְרֵי הַיָּמִים לְמַלְכֵי in the Book of the Annals *of the Israelite kings*[41]
יִשְׂרָאֵל: 1 Kgs 14:19

In counting expressions the construct chain includes the unit and the thing counted; if the latter is qualified, this must be done by a periphrastic genitive in *l*. Most such expressions involve dates.

12. בַּחֲמִשָּׁה עָשָׂר יוֹם לַחֹדֶשׁ on the fifteenth day *of the month*
Lev 23:6

The periphrastic genitive is used in dates even if the word יוֹם is omitted.

13. בְּאַרְבָּעָה עָשָׂר לַחֹדֶשׁ on the fourteenth day *of the month*
Lev 23:5

c Another form of the periphrastic genitive involves אֲשֶׁר לְ־ 'which/that belongs to.'

14. אֵין מִרְעֶה לַצֹּאן אֲשֶׁר לַעֲבָדֶיךָ There is no pasturage for the small livestock *which belong to your servants* (i.e., our small livestock).
Gen 47:4

A comparable construction involves the rare relative pronoun שֶׁ and yields the combination שֶׁל, the genitive particle of post-biblical Hebrew.[42] A form of the particle is used twice in the Bible.

15. הִנֵּה מִטָּתוֹ שֶׁלִּשְׁלֹמֹה behold, Solomon's couch (lit., his couch which belongs to Solomon)
Cant 3:7

16. כַּרְמִי שֶׁלִּי לֹא נָטָרְתִּי: I did not guard my vineyard (lit., my vineyard which belongs to me).
Cant 1:6

9.8 Enclitic *Mem*

a A variety of external evidence has led scholars to recognize in the biblical text a particle *m*, often associated with the genitive.[43] Whatever shape the particle took (perhaps

---

41. It may be that terms like *dbry hymym* were "fixed," as suggested in GKC § 129d / p. 420, on this passage.

42. The Aramaic relative pronoun *də / dî* serves as genitive particle. On the later Hebrew usage, see M. H. Segal, *A*

Grammar of Mishnaic Hebrew (Oxford: Clarendon, 1927) 43–44, 199–200.

43. There is evidence from ENWS (Ugaritic, El-Amarna), as well as other areas of Semitic. Enclitic *mem* differs from

-*m* after a vowel; or -*mi* or -*ma* in all cases), it seems to have been used at the end of a word, and so it is assumed to have been enclitic on (i.e., to have leaned on) that word.[44] Only the consonantal *mem* is preserved; since its meaning was lost in the course of the text's long transmission, the *mem* became confounded with other common morphemes formed with *mem* such as the masculine plural suffix -*îm*, the pronominal suffix -*ām*, the inseparable preposition *min*, etc. As a result it must be detected behind the Masoretic Text by irregularities and anomalies associated with final or initial *mem*.

Enclitic *mem* is used in sufficiently varied ways in cognate languages to make it certain that the earliest forms of Semitic must have known more than one form of this construction. In Hebrew it sometimes has an emphatic force, while at other times it serves as a morpheme for indetermination. It is seen in connection with almost every part of speech, including verbs, nouns, pronominal suffixes, adverbs, etc. Most common are its uses in the middle of the construct chain.[45] The enclitic *mem* is common in poetry.

The examples most easily seen are those involving external evidence. Here are two forms of one line of verse from Psalm 18 and 2 Samuel 22, parallel texts.

| 1a. | 2 Sam 22:16 | וַיֵּרָאוּ אֲפִקֵי יָם |
| 1b. | Ps 18:16 | וַיֵּרָאוּ אֲפִיקֵי מַיִם |

The first text has lost the enclitic *mem*, while the second has attached it to יָם, yielding a different (and not implausible) reading. The line is best read:

| 1c. | וַיֵּרָאוּ אֲפִיקֵי־ם יָם | The depths of the sea were seen.[46] |

The Pentateuch is preserved not only in various ancient translations but also in a Samaritan text; let us examine a phrase from a prose narrative.[47]

| 2a. | Gen 14:6/MT | וְאֶת־הַחֹרִי בְּהַרְרָם שֵׂעִיר |
| 2b. | Gen 14:6/Sam | ואת־החרי בהררי שעיר |

The proper reading is neither the MT, with the odd suffix -*ām* 'their,' nor the Samaritan, with the simplified reading omitting the *m* (a reading also found in the LXX, Vulgate, and Peshitta). Rather, we should read:

| 2c. | וְאֶת־הַחֹרִי בְּהַרְרֵי־ם שֵׂעִיר | and the Horite, in the hills of Seir |

Akkadian mimation in both form and function. Mimation is almost never found on nouns in construct (the exception furnished by such cases as *damqam inim* 'good of eyes, clear-sighted').

44. Compare the Latin ending *que* 'and,' as in *arma virumque* 'arms and the man.'

45. The classic study is Horace D. Hummel, "Enclitic *Mem* in Early Northwest Semitic," *Journal of Biblical Literature* 76 (1957) 85–107; see also D. N. Freedman, *Pottery, Poetry, and Prophecy: Studies in Early Hebrew Poetry* (Winona Lake, Indiana: Eisenbrauns, 1980); M. Dahood, *Psalms III: 101–150* (Anchor Bible 17A; Garden

City, New York: Doubleday, 1970); and O'Connor, *Hebrew Verse Structure*. On enclitic *mem* with *waw* see the essays in C. H. Gordon, G. A. Rendsburg, and N. H. Winter, eds., *Eblaitica* (Winona Lake, Indiana: Eisenbrauns, 1987), 1. 29–41.

46. F. M. Cross and D. N. Freedman, "A Royal Song of Thanksgiving: II Samuel 22 = Psalm 18," *Journal of Biblical Literature* 72 (1953) 15–34, at 26.

47. See Bruce K. Waltke, "The Samaritan Pentateuch and the Text of the Old Testament," *New Perspectives on the Old Testament*, ed. J. Barton Payne (Waco, Texas: Word, 1970) 212–39; on enclitic *mem*, p. 217.

In the MT of Deut 33:11, one line of the poem contains an absolute noun followed by what looks like it should be its genitive. The Samaritan indeed reads a construct. The better reading is rather

3.   מְחַץ מָתְנַי־ם קָמָיו   Smite the loins of his enemies (lit., those who rise against him).[48]
                                         Deut 33:11 *emended*

In other cases, Hebrew usage in general provides a reliable guide in detecting the enclitic *mem*.[49]

4.   יהוה־אֱלֹהִים (> אֱלֹהֵי־ם)   YHWH God of Hosts
            צְבָאוֹת   Ps 59:6 *emended*

5.   וֵאלֹהִים מַלְכֵּי מִקֶּדֶם   [You,] O God, are the Ancient King.
            (> מַלְכֵּי־ם קֶדֶם)   Ps 74:12 *emended*

6.   זְכֹר אֲדֹנָי חֶרְפַּת עֲבָדֶיךָ   Remember, O Lord of all, how your servants have
        שְׂאֵתִי בְחֵיקִי כָּל־רַבִּים עַמִּים   been mocked, how I bear in my heart all the quarrels
            (> רַבֵּי־ם עַמִּים):   of the nations.
                                         Ps 89:51 *emended*

7.   כִּי־אֲרֻבּוֹת מִמָּרוֹם (> אֲרֻבּוֹת־ם   The windows of heaven are opened.
        מָרוֹם) נִפְתָּחוּ   Isa 24:18 *emended*

---

48. O'Connor, *Hebrew Verse Structure*, 212, and references.

49. On the Psalms passages, see Mitchell Dahood, *Psalms II: 51–100*, 68–69, 204, 320, and references.

10

Accusative Function and Related Matters

Accusative Function   10.1

Like the genitive, the accusative is a function of modification or dependency: nouns   a
used with other nouns or with prepositions are in the genitive, while nouns modifying
verbs are in the accusative. This ad-verbial function can involve recipients or objects of
verbal action, sometimes where definite marked with the particle אֶת.

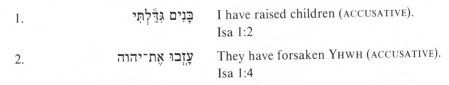

1.	בָּנִים גִּדַּלְתִּי	I have raised children (ACCUSATIVE). Isa 1:2
2.	עָזְבוּ אֶת־יהוה	They have forsaken YHWH (ACCUSATIVE). Isa 1:4

The function can also involve other specifications of verbal action.

3.	נָזֹרוּ אָחוֹר׃	They have turned-away backward (ACCUSATIVE). Isa 1:4

Whereas the genitive case can be identified by its bracketing with a preposition or a   b
noun in the construct state, the accusative case cannot regularly be distinguished by
form. Even the distinction between transitive verbs (which may be qualified by a direct
object accusative) and intransitive verbs (which usually are not) is not particularly helpful; adverbial accusatives may be bracketed with both kinds of verbs. The particle אֵת is

often used with the definite accusative; even this helpful particle is of limited value in identifying the accusative for three reasons: it is used only with substantives that are definite, it can be used with the nominative, and it is rarely used in poetry.[1]

c   Further difficulties are created by Hebrew's relatively free word order, especially in verse. Whereas English distinguishes the subject of a verb from its object by fixed word order (contrast 'John hit Bill' with 'Bill hit John'), the Hebrew accusative is not consistently ordered with regard to the verb. For example, אִישׁ־דָּמִים וּמִרְמָה יְתָעֵב יהוה (Ps 5:7) may mean either 'a bloodthirsty and treacherous man abhors YHWH' or 'YHWH abhors a bloodthirsty and treacherous man.' Exegetes cannot decide on the sense using any strictly grammatical signs within the clause.[2] In this example the preceding line of the poem points decisively toward the second meaning.

d   In spite of this essential lack of formal indicators, the accusative's presence, meaning, and uses can still be identified by considering Hebrew in the context of the other Semitic languages that mark the accusative case with the ending -a (8.1c), and by considering the patterns of Hebrew itself. The Semitic accusative is both historically and descriptively the *ad-verbial* (*to the verb*) case; it brackets a noun or its equivalent with a verb in order to modify it according to the substantive's sense.[3] It is, as always, problematic to abstract "the meaning" of a construction from its many particular uses. Nevertheless, abstractions are helpful and even necessary in making sense of language phenomena. In the light of its many uses displayed in the next section, we can make better sense of the Hebrew accusative by framing the generalization that it is the ad-verbial function.

10.2   Species of the Accusative

a   In the preceding chapter we described some aspects of the process by which the uses of a grammatical form are classified (9.4). Essentially, grammarians attempt to classify the uses most broadly by syntactic considerations and more particularly by semantic considerations. No strict delimitation between syntax and semantics can be set up; for example, the use of a direct-object accusative reflects a verb's transitive meaning, whereas the distinction between adverbial accusatives of place and time is largely but not

---

1. On the use in poetry see, for example, D. N. Freedman, *Pottery, Poetry, and Prophecy* (Winona Lake, Indiana: Eisenbrauns, 1980) 2, 310; for data on the occurrences see Francis I. Andersen and A. Dean Forbes, "'Prose Particle' Counts of the Hebrew Bible," *The Word of the Lord Shall Go Forth: Essays in Honor of David Noel Freedman*, ed. Carol L. Meyers and M. O'Connor (Winona Lake, Indiana: Eisenbrauns, 1983) 165–83. On the use of ʾt in non-accusative functions see 10.3.2. On the supposed accusative use of independent pronouns in Hebrew (as in Ugaritic, cf. *UT* § 6.4), see Mitchell Dahood, "The Independent Personal Pronoun in the Oblique Case in Hebrew," *Catholic Biblical Quarterly* 32 (1970) 86–90; "Northwest Semitic Notes on Dt. 32,20," *Biblica* 54 (1973) 405–6; "Jeremiah 5,31 and *UT* 127:32," *Biblica* 57 (1976) 106–8.

2. There are large-scale patterns of word order in Hebrew verse; see M. O'Connor, *Hebrew Verse Structure* (Winona Lake, Indiana: Eisenbrauns, 1980).

3. The Semitic case/function system does not line up in a straightforward way with other case systems. Consider the example of Koine Greek. In contrast to early Semitic, which had three cases, early Indo-European had at least eight cases. In Koine Greek, only four of these survive: the genitive case serves for earlier genitive and ablative; the dative case for earlier dative, locative, and instrumental; the nominative and accusative continue older patterns. Thus, Semitic accusatives, which would variously correspond to some Greek genitives, some accusatives, and some datives, cannot be understood in terms of oblique cases of Koine Greek.

entirely lexical.[4] Grammarians sometimes distinguish between adjuncts and complements, the former signifying an optional constituent of a sentence, the latter an obligatory constituent.[5] The direct-object accusative is called a complement, and the adverbial accusative an adjunct. For example, in the sentence 'God planted a garden,' 'garden' is an obligatory constituent because 'God planted' is incomplete. By contrast, 'for Adam' in the sentence 'Did you come for Adam?' is an adjunct, an optional constituent. Again, a strict delimitation is not possible.[6]

b In the following sections the uses of the accusative as a verbal object or recipient of action (10.2.1) are distinguished from the adverbial accusatives (10.2.2). The double-accusative constructions are treated last (10.2.3).

Objective Accusative   10.2.1

a Verbs can govern a variety of kinds of objects, and the range of objects associated with a particular verb is at base a feature of the verb. Classification of objective accusatives is therefore based on various categorizations of verbs. Most verbs that govern an objective accusative are both (a) fientive (i.e., they describe actions rather than states) and (b) transitive (i.e., the effect of the verb *passes over* to something). The objects of such verbs may be acted on (direct objects; cf. 'He planted tomatoes') or created (effected objects; cf. 'He raised tomatoes'). Some objects are virtually implied in the verb used (cf. 'He cried tears')—these are internal objects—while some objects are complementary to the verb (cf. 'He wore clothes').

b The proper categorization of Hebrew verbs is a more complex task than hinted at here, for two reasons. First, transitivity is only one aspect of a verb's governing scheme; modifiers other than objective accusatives are relevant. Second, transitivity is variably expressed; direct and prepositional objects may be similarly used in different clause types. Consider, in connection with these points, the following English sentences.

1. She gave at home.
2. She gave up.
3. She gave some pages.
4. She gave the book to them.
5. She gave him the books.
6. She gave away the books.

---

4. Harald Schweizer criticizes traditional grammars for alternating the principles of classification between expression and content; see "Was ist ein Akkusativ?—Ein Beitrag zur Grammatiktheorie," *Zeitschrift für die Alttestamentliche Wissenschaft* 87 (1975) 133–45. It is worth noting that the structural sense of the accusative category plays a conceptual role even in studies where the term itself is eschewed, e.g., W. Gross, *Die Pendenskonstruktion im biblischen Hebräisch* (St. Ottilien: EOS, 1987); the study begins with direct objects and proceeds directly to time and place expressions and then other adverbial accusatives (under the awkward designation, "Phrases that function in the accompanying sentence as obligatory syntagms or as free circumstantial indications," p. 88). Perhaps such carry-over is unavoidable.

5. See John Lyons, *Introduction to Theoretical Linguistics* (Cambridge: Cambridge University, 1968) 343–50.

6. On this hotly debated issue see T. Muraoka, "On Verb Complementation in Biblical Hebrew," *Vetus Testamentum* 29 (1979) 425–35.

The verb 'to give' can be simply transitive, alone (# 3), with a particle (# 6), or with a prepositional ("indirect") object (# 4). But it can also be used with no expressed object (# 1) or with two (# 5) or with a particle (# 2). Such complexities as these, combined with Biblical Hebrew's status as a written language, make it difficult to draft a full scheme of Hebrew accusative types. Both similarities and differences in verbal government between Biblical Hebrew and English also complicate our task, and we will devote attention to insisting on some of the distinctions between the two languages.

c   The *direct-object accusative* is the recipient of a transitive verb's action.

7.	וַיִּקַּח יְהוָה אֱלֹהִים אֶת־הָאָדָם	And Yhwh God took *Adam*. Gen 2:15
8.	הֱבִיאַׄנִי	It brought *me*. Ezek 40:2

Both Hebrew לקח and הביא are transitive, as are both English 'to take' and 'to bring.' In prose, the direct object, if definite, may be governed by את. Contrast # 9 and # 10.

9.	וַיַּסֵּךְ אֶת־נִסְכּוֹ	And he poured out his *libation*. 2 Kgs 16:13
10.	בַּל־אַסִּיךְ נִסְכֵּיהֶם	I will not pour out their *libations*. Ps 16:4

Often a Hebrew transitive verb does not correspond to an English transitive that can appropriately be used in glossing or translating it.[7]

11.	וַתֵּלֶד אֶת־קַׄיִן	She gave birth *to Cain*.[8] Gen 4:1
12.	וּפִי־מִרְמָה עָלַי פָּתָֽחוּ	They have spoken against me *with lying tongues* (lit., opened . . . *a mouth of lying*). Ps 109:2

Contrariwise, many English transitive verbs have no corresponding Hebrew transitives.

13.	נָגַע בְּכַף־יֶׄרֶךְ יַעֲקֹב	He touched *the socket* of Jacob's hip. Gen 32:33
14.	וַיִּבְחַר בְּזַרְעוֹ אַחֲרָיו	And he chose his *offspring* after him. Deut 4:37

---

7. This fact should be borne in mind in evaluating the frequently made claims that it is somehow "better" to translate a Hebrew transitive with an English, and so on; such claims are hogwash and are frequently used to distort the work of translation.

8. This clause illustrates clearly that there is no rigid barrier between transitive verbs and verbs that govern a prepositional object. The gloss given corresponds to the translation of the NIV; AV renders, 'She . . . bare Cain.' The difference between the translations is a function of the difference between sixteenth- and seventeenth-century English and twentieth-century English; it is not a matter of Hebrew at all. It must be admitted, however, that the verb *yld*, with its several quite distinct referents, presents special difficulties of its own; see 10.3.2, ## 6–7.

Within the Hebrew syntactic system, a single verb may vary. Some verbs may d
govern either direct-object accusatives (nouns, # 15; or pronouns, # 16) or prepositional
objects (# 17), with no appreciable difference in meaning.[9]

15.	כַּאֲשֶׁר צִוָּה אֱלֹהִים אֶת־נֹחַ׃	as God commanded *Noah* Gen 7:9
16.	כְּכֹל אֲשֶׁר צִוָּהוּ יהוה׃	all that Yʜᴡʜ commanded *him* Gen 7:5
17.	וַיְצַו יהוה אֱלֹהִים עַל־הָאָדָם	And Yʜᴡʜ God commanded *Adam*. . . . Gen 2:16

Thus *ṣwy Piel* can govern (1) a direct object whether (*a*) a noun (# 15) or (*b*) a pronoun
(# 16), or (2) an object through the preposition עַל (# 17). The verb *ydᶜ* 'to know' can
govern a direct object (# 18) or an object with *l* (# 19), as can *hrg* 'to kill' (## 20–21) and
ʾrk Hiphil 'to lengthen' (## 22–23).[10]

18.	יָדַע שׁוֹר קֹנֵהוּ	An ox knows its *owner*. Isa 1:3
19.	אַתָּה יָדַעְתָּ לְאִוַּלְתִּי	You know my *folly*. Ps 69:6
20.	כִּי בְאַפָּם הָרְגוּ אִישׁ	In their anger they slew *a man*. Gen 49:6
21.	לֶאֱוִיל יַהֲרָג־כָּעַשׂ	Resentment kills *a fool*. Job 5:2
22.	עַל־מִי . . . תַּאֲרִיכוּ לָשׁוֹן	At whom . . . do you stick out (lit., lengthen) (your) *tongue*? Isa 57:4
23.	עַל־גַּבִּי . . . הֶאֱרִיכוּ לְמַעֲנִיתָם׃	On my back . . . they lengthen their *furrows*. Ps 129:3 *Qere*

Niphal forms sometimes govern a direct object (cf. 23.2, 4).

24.	בְּנֵי־בְלִיַּעַל נָסַבּוּ אֶת־הַבַּיִת	The wicked men surrounded *the house*. Judg 19:22
25.	וַיִּלָּחֲמוּנִי חִנָּם׃	They attack *me* without cause. Ps 109:3

---

9. For more examples see Muraoka, "Verb Complementation," 429. He notes that "as opposed to *qinnēʾēt* 'to be jealous (of sombody), to resent (humiliation brought about by somebody),' *qinnēʾ bə* and *qinnēʾ lə* signify 'to envy (somebody's success)' and 'to be zealous for (somebody or some cause),' respectively."

10. Aramaic and the Ethiopic languages often use *l* to mark a "direct object"; see 10.4 for more on the phenomenon in Hebrew as well as the treatment in Khan's paper cited in n. 26.

e   For some verbs, for example, *ng^c* 'to touch,' *ykl* 'to overcome,' a pronoun may stand as a prepositional object (## 26, 28), or as a suffixed (i.e., direct) object (## 27, 29), with no appreciable difference in meaning.[11]

26.   לָגַ֫עַת בָּ֑ךְ   to harm you
                                        2 Sam 14:10

27.   לֹא נְגַעֲנ֫וּךְ   We did not harm *you*.
                                        Gen 26:29

28.   לֹא יָכֹל לוֹ   He could not overpower *him*.
                                        Gen 32:26

29.   יְכָלְתִּ֑יו   I have overcome *him*.
                                        Ps 13:5

When a verb has different meanings or nuances according to the attached prepositional phrase, use of a suffixed pronoun can result in ambiguity. For example, אחז את 'to lay hold of, to grasp' (# 30) contrasts with אחז ב 'to hold firmly' (# 31); # 32 is ambiguous.

30.   וַיֹּאחֲזוּ אֹתוֹ   They *seized him*.
                                        Judg 1:6

31.   וְיָדוֹ אֹחֶ֫זֶת בַּעֲקֵב עֵשָׂו   his hand *holding on to* Esau's *heel*
                                        Gen 25:26

32.   וַיֹּאחֲז֫וּהוּ פְלִשְׁתִּים וַיְנַקְּרוּ אֶת־עֵינָיו   Then the Philistines *seized him*(?)/*held on to him*(?) and gouged out his eyes.
                                        Judg 16:21

f   The *effected-object accusative* is the result or effect of a transitive verb's action.

33.   תַּדְשֵׁא הָאָ֫רֶץ דֶּ֫שֶׁא   Let the earth produce *vegetation*.
                                        Gen 1:11

The 'vegetation' is not acted on by the verb's action (contrast תִּזְרַע אֶת־זַרְעֶ֫ךָ, 'You sow your seed,' Deut 11:10); it rather results from the actions the verb describes. The verb and the effected object are often derived from the same root; such an object is called a *cognate effected accusative*. (As the example from Deut 11:10 makes clear, not all cognate accusatives describe an effected object.)

34.   וְהָיָה בְּעַנְנִי עָנָן עַל־הָאָ֫רֶץ   Whenever I form *clouds* over the earth. . . .
                                        Gen 9:14

---

11. Muraoka, "Verb Complementation," 426–27, lists the following as the more important verbs to which a pronominal complement may be attached either directly (as an unmodified object) or "analytically" (that is, by means of a particle other than *ʾt*, that is, a preposition): *bāqa^c b* 'to break into (a city and conquer it),' *gāmal l* 'to requite, deal out to,' *dābaq b* 'to cling to,' *dālaq ʾaḥărê* 'to chase hotly,' *yākôl l* 'to prevail,' *hôʿîl l* 'to avail,' *nilḥam b/ʿim* 'to fight,' *nāga^c b* 'to touch,' *hēʿîd b* 'to testify concerning,' *pāga^c b* 'to meet (with hostile intent),' *hēṣîq l* 'to harass,' *rāb ʾel/ʾēt* 'to contend,' *hirpâ min* 'to let go.'

| 35. | חֲלֹמוֹת יַחֲלֹמוּן | They will have *dreams*.
 Joel 3:1 |
| 36. | בְּרוֹק בָּרָק | [O God,] flash forth *lightning*.
 Ps 144:6 |

An *internal accusative* is an expression of the verb's action; it is usually anarthrous **g**
(i.e., without the article) and may follow or precede the verb. It resembles in sense both
the infinitive absolute (35.3.1) and various adverbial accusatives (10.2.2). An internal
accusative may be a *cognate accusative*.

37.	הִתְאַוּוּ תַּאֲוָה	They craved *with a craving* (or, *greedily*).[12] Num 11:4
38.	פָּרֹחַ תִּפְרַח וְתָגֵל אַף גִּילַת	It will sprout *sprouts* and rejoice *with rejoicing* (i.e., bloom *luxuriantly* and rejoice *greatly*). Isa 35:2
39.	פָּחֲדוּ פָחַד	They dreaded *with dread* (i.e., were overwhelmed with *dread*). Ps 14:5

A cognate internal accusative may be used in a comparison.

| 40. | קְבוּרַת חֲמוֹר יִקָּבֵר | He will be buried as an ass (lit., *with the burial* of <br> an ass).
 Jer 22:19 |
| 41. | אִם־כְּמוֹת כָּל־הָאָדָם יְמֻתוּן
 אֵלֶּה וּפְקֻדַּת כָּל־הָאָדָם יִפָּקֵד
 עֲלֵיהֶם | If these people die a natural *death* (lit., like the *death*
 of all people) or if they experience a natural *punish-*
 ment (lit., there is punished upon them *a punishment*
 of all people). . . .
 Num 16:29 |

A *non-cognate internal accusative* carries with it a qualifier (cf. English 'She writes a
good hand'). Such an accusative frequently involves a verb of expression where the
organ of expression is mentioned.

| 42. | וְקָרְאוּ . . . קוֹל גָּדוֹל | And they cry out . . . *with a loud voice*.
 Ezek 8:18 |
| 43. | וְכָל־הָאָרֶץ בּוֹכִים קוֹל גָּדוֹל | The whole countryside was weeping *aloud*.
 2 Sam 15:23 |

---

12. Nearly the same expression is used in Prov 21:26.

h   A *complement accusative* specifies the noun associated with an intransitive verb under certain conditions. Several classes of verbs take a complement accusative. Verbs of fullness and want can be transitive as well as intransitive, for example, מָלֵא can mean 'to fill (transitive)' in the *Qal* as well as 'to be full (intransitive)' in both the *Qal* and *Niphal*.

44. יְדֵיכֶם דָּמִים מָלֵאוּ׃   Your hands are full of *blood*.
Isa 1:15

45. וַתִּמָּלֵא הָאָרֶץ אֹתָם׃   And the earth was full of *them*.
Exod 1:7

46. אוּלַי יַחְסְרוּן חֲמִשִּׁים הַצַּדִּיקִם חֲמִשָּׁה   Perhaps the fifty righteous are lacking *five*.
Gen 18:28

47. וְשָׁרַץ הַיְאֹר צְפַרְדְּעִים   The Nile will teem with *frogs*.
Exod 7:28

48. שָׂבַעְתִּי עֹלוֹת   I have more than enough ʿōlôt.
Isa 1:11

Verbs of wearing, donning, or doffing clothes can take a complement.

49. לָבְשׁוּ כָרִים הַצֹּאן   The meadows are covered with *flocks*.
Ps 65:14

50. לְבַשׁ בְּגָדֶיךָ   Put on your *robes*.
1 Kgs 22:30

51. וְנִכְשָׁלִים אָזְרוּ חָיִל׃   Those who stumbled are armed with *strength*.
1 Sam 2:4

52. וְהוּא עֹטֶה מְעִיל   And he is wearing *a robe*.
1 Sam 28:14

53. וַיַּעַט כַּמְעִיל קִנְאָה׃   And he wrapped himself in *zeal* as in a cloak.
Isa 59:17

54. וַיִּפְשַׁט גַּם־הוּא בְּגָדָיו   And he, too, stripped off his *robes*.
1 Sam 19:24

55. פָּשַׁטְתִּי אֶת־כֻּתָּנְתִּי   I have stripped off my *robe*.
Cant 5:3

i   The so-called *"datival accusative"* involves a pronominal direct object where a prepositional object (viz., a "dative") would be expected.[13] Several instances are mentioned above in the treatment of direct-object accusatives; the pattern cited there for *ykl* and

---

13. Since the West Semitic languages do not regularly use a dative function, the term "dative" (derived from Latin grammar) is more objectionable than other case vocabulary; it has nonetheless become established among grammarians. On this class of suffixes see M. Bogaert, "Les suffixes verbaux non accusatifs dans le sémitique nord-occidental et particulièrement en hébreu," *Biblica* 45 (1964) 220–47.

ng^c (## 26–29) also obtains for other verbs. The verb *ntn* takes the preposition *l* for nouns indicating the donnee (the person to whom the object is given; # 56) and some-times pronouns (# 57), but a pronoun indicating the donnee can be suffixed directly to the verb (# 58).

56.	וְנָתַתָּה אֶת־הַלְוִיִּם לְאַהֲרֹן וּלְבָנָיו	And you shall give the Levites *to Aaron and to his offspring.* Num 3:9
57.	וְנָתַתִּי לְךָ אֶת־נַפְשְׁךָ לְשָׁלָל	I'll give *to you* your life as booty. Jer 45:5
58.	מִי־יִתְּנֵנִי שָׁמִיר שַׁיִת בַּמִּלְחָמָה	Oh, that he (indefinite) would give *me* (i.e., Oh that I had) thorns and briers to battle! Isa 27:4

The verb *z^cq* normally takes the preposition *ʾel* before the noun or pronoun indicating the addressee (## 59–60), but a pronoun indicating the addressee can be expressed with a suffixed pronoun (# 61).

59.	וַיִּזְעַק שְׁמוּאֵל אֶל־יהוה	And Samuel cried *to YHWH.* 1 Sam 7:9
60.	וְנִזְעַק אֵלֶיךָ מִצָּרָתֵנוּ	And we will cry *to you* from our troubles. 2 Chr 20:9
61.	וַיִּזְעָקוּךָ	They cried *to you.* Neh 9:28

Other "datival accusatives" occur with less well documented verbs.

62.	לֹא תִנָּשֵׁנִי׃	You will not be forgotten *by me.* Isa 44:21
63.	הֲצוֹם צַמְתֻּנִי אָנִי׃	Did you fast *for me*!? Zech 7:5
64.	בִּעוּתֵי אֱלוֹהַּ יַעַרְכוּנִי׃	The horrors of God are ranged *against me.* Job 6:4

Adverbial Accusative   **10.2.2**

In addition to the objective accusatives, verbs may govern various adverbial accusa-   a
tives; these detail features of the verbal action (and the like), including time, place, condition, manner, and specification. Broadly speaking, these accusatives are adjuncts rather
than complements to the verb (10.2).

The *accusative of place* specifies a location. Ordinarily location without movement   b
is specified by a prepositional phrase with *b* or *l*, but an accusative may be used. The
verbs *yšb* 'to dwell' (## 1–2), *gwr* 'to reside' (## 3–4), and *škb* 'to live' (# 5) are found with
accusatives of place, as are verbs without specifically locational reference (## 6–7).

1.   וְהוּא יֹשֵׁב פֶּתַח־הָאֹהֶל   while he was sitting *at the entrance* to his tent[14]
Gen 18:1

2.   לָשֶׁבֶת בָּיִת: that it may dwell *in a shrine*[15]
Isa 44:13

3.   מִי יָגוּר לָנוּ אֵשׁ אוֹכֵלָה   Who of us can dwell *in the consuming fire*?
Isa 33:14

4.   לֹא יְגֻרְךָ רָע: Evil cannot dwell *with you*.
Ps 5:5

5.   וְהִנֵּה אִשָּׁה שֹׁכֶבֶת מַרְגְּלֹתָיו: And behold, a woman lying *at his feet*!
Ruth 3:8

6.   וְאַתָּה תִּשְׁמַע הַשָּׁמַיִם   Then hear [O God] *from* (i.e., *in*) heaven.[16]
1 Kgs 8:32

7.   הֲיֵשׁ בֵּית־אָבִיךְ מָקוֹם   Is there room *in* your father's *house*?
Gen 24:23

The goal of movement (or directed activity) toward is usually marked with a preposition but may stand as an accusative of place.

8.   וְצֵא הַשָּׂדֶה   Go out *to the open country*.
Gen 27:3

9.   וַיָּבֹאוּ אֶרֶץ כְּנַעַן   And they came *to the land* of Canaan.
Gen 45:25

10.   אוֹצַר יהוה יָבוֹא: It must come *into* YHWH's *treasury*.
Josh 6:19

By analogy, the accusative is also used for the place from which one departs.[17]

11.   הֵם יָצְאוּ אֶת־הָעִיר   They having left *the city*. . . .
Gen 44:4

The constructions with local accusative (## 12, 14) and directive -*āh* (## 12, 13) are sometimes interchangeable.

---

14. Cf. *lpth* ᵓ*hlw* in Num 11:10. It is frequently suggested that the preposition *b* is omitted before the words *pth* 'entrance' and *byt* 'house' by haplology, i.e., the tendency to avoid two similar sounds (here, bilabial stops) or syllables next to one another; see, e.g., Joüon § 126h / p. 380. (Haplology, a phonological process, should not be confused with haplography, a scribal process, though they may have the same effect in a written text. Haplology is best exemplified in English by the avoidance of '-lily' words, e.g., there is no adverb from 'friendly' of the form 'friendlily.') S. R. Driver explains the phenomenon syntactically: "by custom the use of the accus[ative] to express rest in a place is restricted to cases in which *a noun in the genitive follows*"; see *Notes on the Hebrew Text and the Topography of the Books of Samuel* (Oxford: Clarendon, 1913) 37 n. 2; cf., however, ## 2–3.

15. Cf. *bbyt* ᵓ*byh* in Num 30:4; the *b* is omitted before *byt lhm* in Ruth 1:22; cf. n. 14 above.

16. So also in 1 Kgs 8:34, 36, 39, 43, 45, 49; in the parallel text in 2 Chronicles 6, *mn* is supplied (vv 23, 25, 30, 33, 35, 39; v 27 lacks *mn* and thus agrees with Kings). See 11.2.11b.

17. For other examples, see Exod 9:29, 33; Deut 14:22; cf. Jer 10:20.

12.	וַיֵּ֫לֶךְ גַּ֫תָה . . . וַיֻּגַּד לִשְׁלֹמֹה כִּי־הָלַךְ שִׁמְעִי . . . גַּת	And he (Shimei) went *to Gath* . . . and it was told to Solomon that Shimei had gone . . . *to Gath.* 1 Kgs 2:40–41
13.	וְהוֹרַדְתֶּם אֶת־שֵׂיבָתִי בְּיָגוֹן שְׁאֹֽלָה:	You will bring my gray head down *to Sheol* in sorrow. Gen 42:38
14.	וְהוֹרַדְתָּ אֶת־שֵׂיבָתוֹ בְּדָם שְׁאֽוֹל:	You will bring his gray head down *to Sheol* in blood. 1 Kgs 2:9

The local extent of a verbal action can also stand as an accusative of place.

15.	חֲמֵשׁ עֶשְׂרֵה אַמָּה מִלְמַ֫עְלָה גָּבְרוּ הַמָּ֫יִם	And the waters rose to a depth *of fifteen cubits.* Gen 7:20
16.	וַיִּפֹּל מְלֹא־קוֹמָתוֹ אַ֫רְצָה	He fell *full* length on the ground. 1 Sam 28:20
17.	וְהֽוּא־הָלַךְ בַּמִּדְבָּר דֶּ֫רֶךְ יוֹם	He went into the desert a day's *journey.* 1 Kgs 19:4

The *accusative of time* specifies a time. It may refer to the time at which an action   c
takes place.

18.	עַתָּה אֶסָּפֶה יוֹם־אֶחָד בְּיַד־ שָׁאוּל	Now, *one day* I will perish at Saul's hands. 1 Sam 27:1
19.	הַשָּׁנָה אַתָּה מֵת	*This year* you are going to die. Jer 28:16
20.	עֶ֫רֶב וָבֹ֫קֶר וְצָהֳרַ֫יִם אָשִׂ֫יחָה	*Evening, morning, and noon* I cry out in distress. Ps 55:18

It may also refer to the duration of an action.

21.	וְעָפָר תֹּאכַל כָּל־יְמֵי חַיֶּֽיךָ:	You will eat dust *all the days* of your life. Gen 3:14
22.	שֵׁ֫שֶׁת יָמִים תַּעֲבֹד	*During six days* you shall labor. Exod 20:9
23.	יָמִים רַבִּים יֵשְׁבוּ	They will live many *days.* Hos 3:4

The *accusative of state* specifies a feature of the verb's subject or object at the time   d
of the verbal action or in relation to that action. Such an accusative, be it substantive, adjective, or participle, is indefinite. It may refer to the subject of the clause.[18]

---

18. For the grammatical argument showing that such accusatives are not in fact appositional, see GKC § 118o / p. 375. For other adjectival examples see Gen 25:8 ('old and full'), 37:35 ('mourning'); Deut 3:18 ('armed'); Josh 1:14 ('organized for battle'). For participial examples see Num 10:25 ('serving as rearguard'); 1 Sam 19:20 ('presiding'); 1 Kgs 14:15 ('provoking to anger and anxiety'), 22:10 ('dressed'); Ezra 9:3 ('appalled').

24.	וַיֵּצֵא הָרִאשׁוֹן אַדְמוֹנִי	And the first one came out *red*. Gen 25:25
25.	בָּאתִי הַיּוֹם רִאשׁוֹן	I have come today as *the first one*. 2 Sam 19:21
26.	הָלַךְ עַבְדִּי יְשַׁעְיָהוּ עָרוֹם וְיָחֵף	My servant Isaiah went about *nude and barefoot*. Isa 20:3
27.	וּבֶן־שְׁמֹנַת יָמִים יִמּוֹל לָכֶם כָּל־ זָכָר	Every male among you, *when he is eight days old*, will be circumcised. Gen 17:12

It may refer to the object of the clause.[19]

28.	וְלָקַח הַכֹּהֵן אֶת־הַזְּרֹעַ בְּשֵׁלָה	And the priest shall take the shoulder *when it is boiled*. Num 6:19
29.	חָם הִצְטַיַּדְנוּ אֹתוֹ	We packed it *while it was still hot*. Josh 9:12
30.	הוּא יְשׁוּפְךָ רֹאשׁ	He will crush you *on the head*. Gen 3:15
31.	הִרְאַנִי יהוה אֹתְךָ מֶלֶךְ עַל־ אֲרָם:	YHWH has pointed you out to me *as king* over Aram. 2 Kgs 8:13
32.	וַיִּשְׁמַע מֹשֶׁה אֶת־הָעָם בֹּכֶה	Moses heard the people *wailing*. Num 11:10

The accusative of state may disagree with its referent in gender or number.

| 33. | הִכִּיתָ אֶת־כָּל־אֹיְבַי לֶחִי | Strike all my enemies *on the jaw*. Ps 3:8 |

e   The *accusative of manner* describes the way in which an action is performed; it, too, is anarthrous.

34.	וְלֹא תֵלְכוּ רוֹמָה	You will no longer walk *proudly*. Mic 2:3
35.	לְעָבְדוֹ שְׁכֶם אֶחָד:	to serve him *with one accord* Zeph 3:9
36.	מֵישָׁרִים תִּשְׁפְּטוּ בְּנֵי אָדָם:	Do you judge *uprightly* among people? Ps 58:2

---

19. For other examples with objects see Gen 21:9 (participle, 'laughing'), 27:6 (participle, 'talking'); 1 Kgs 11:8 (participles, 'burning incense and sacrificing'); Isa 20:4 (ad- jectives, 'naked and barefoot'); Ps 124:3 (adjective, 'alive'). For an example with the genitive of a construct chain that is the object of a verb, see Gen 3:8 (participle, 'walking').

37.   נוֹרָאוֹת נִפְלֵיתִי   I am made wonderful *fearfully*.
                                                    Ps 139:14

The *accusative of limitation* specifies the extent to which an action is performed.

38.   עֹרֶף יִפְנוּ לִפְנֵי אֹיְבֵיהֶם   They turn *as far as the neck* (i.e., turn their backs)
                                                    before their enemies.
                                                    Josh 7:12

The *accusative of specification* describes a feature of a noun in the absolute state; the accusative is indefinite. This accusative usage is similar to certain genitive patterns.

39. וּמִשְׁקָל לִמְנֹרוֹת הַזָּהָב וְנֵרֹתֵיהֶם   and the weight of the lampstands of gold (GENITIVE)
              זָהָב   and their lamps *of gold* (ACCUSATIVE)
                                                    1 Chr 28:15

40.   וְאַתָּה מַחֲסִי־עֹז: You are my refuge *as to strength*.
                                                    Ps 71:7

The accusative of specification may be used in a comparison.

41.   כַּבִּיר מֵאָבִיךָ יָמִים: more powerful than your father *with regard to days*
                                                    (i.e., men even older than your father)
                                                    Job 15:10

Frequently the Hebrew does not permit one to decide whether the specifying substantive is an accusative, a genitive, or an appositive.

42.   אִטֵּר יַד־יְמִינוֹ   hindered *of*/*in* his *right hand* (ACCUSATIVE or
                                                    GENITIVE) (i.e., left handed)
                                                    Judg 3:15

43.   שְׁלֹשׁ סְאִים קֶמַח   three measures *of flour* (ACCUSATIVE or APPOSITION)[20]
                                                    Gen 18:6

Double Accusative   **10.2.3**

Some verbs are doubly or complexly transitive and may have more than one object   a
associated with them. Such verbs are much more common in Hebrew than in English,
but consider these sentences:

> 1. They made him (OBJECT₁) king (OBJECT₂).
> 2. They thought her (OBJECT₁) a prophet (OBJECT₂).
> 3. They proved him (OBJECT₁) a fool (OBJECT₂).

---

20. Carl Brockelmann at one point identifies this example
as an apposition and at another as an accusative; see

*Grundriss der vergleichenden Grammatik der semitischen
Sprachen* (Berlin: Reuter und Reichard, 1913), 2. 214, 267.

As these examples suggest, complex transitivity is often associated with notions of causation and judgment, notions tied in Hebrew to the *Piel* and *Hiphil* stems. Many of the examples here use verbs in those stems, while others reflect other differences between the Hebrew and English lexica.

b   Let us begin with double accusatives not associated with *Piel-Hiphil* forms. A double accusative of *direct object + "datival" object* is found with verbs of speaking (*šʾl*, *ʿny*, *ṣwy*, ## 4–8) as well as with verbs of giving (*ntn*, *zbd*, ## 9–10). The "datival" object is usually a pronoun. (In the examples below, | is used to separate the two accusatives when they are adjacent in the English gloss.)

4.	יִשְׁאָלוּנִי מִשְׁפְּטֵי־צֶדֶק	They ask *me* | *for* just *decisions.* Isa 58:2
5.	כִּי שָׁם שְׁאֵלוּנוּ שׁוֹבֵינוּ דִּבְרֵי־שִׁיר	For there our captors required *of us* | *songs.* Ps 137:3
6.	וַיַּעַן הַמֶּלֶךְ אֶת־הָעָם קָשָׁה	And the king answered *the people* | *harshly* (lit., *a harsh thing*). 1 Kgs 12:13
7.	וַיְצַוֵּם אֵת כָּל־אֲשֶׁר דִּבֶּר יהוה אִתּוֹ	And he commanded *them* | *all* that Yʜᴡʜ spoke to him.[21] Exod 34:32
8.	מִצְוֹתָיו אֲשֶׁר אָנֹכִי מְצַוֶּךָ	his commandments *which* I have commanded *you* Deut 6:2
9.	אֶרֶץ הַנֶּגֶב נְתַתָּנִי	You gave *me* | *the land* of the Negev. Josh 15:19
10.	זְבָדַנִי אֱלֹהִים אֹתִי זֵבֶד טוֹב	God has presented *me* | *with a* precious *gift.* Gen 30:20

c   Verbs of creation and appointment often govern two accusatives.[22] These may be *thing made + materials.*

11.	וַיִּיצֶר יהוה אֱלֹהִים אֶת־הָאָדָם עָפָר מִן־הָאֲדָמָה	And Yʜᴡʜ God formed *the man* | *from the dust* of the ground. Gen 2:7
12.	כָּל־כֵּלָיו עָשָׂה נְחֹשֶׁת׃	All its *vessels* he made *of brass.* Exod 38:3
13.	עַמּוּדָיו עָשָׂה כֶסֶף	He made its *posts* | *of silver.* Cant 3:10
14.	אֲבָנִים שְׁלֵמוֹת תִּבְנֶה אֶת־מִזְבַּח יהוה	Build *the altar* of Yʜᴡʜ *with fieldstones.* Deut 27:6

---

21. Cf. 10.2.1d on *ṣwy*.

22. With these verbs, the role of the second accusative may be played by the object of a prepositional phrase with *l*; note the two cases in Amos 5:8; see further 11.2.10d.

The accusatives may also be *thing made + thing remade.*

15.	וְעָשׂוּ אֹתוֹ עֻגוֹת	They made *it* (manna) │ *into cakes.* Num 11:8
16.	וַיַּעֲשֵׂהוּ פֶּסֶל	And he made *it* (the stolen silver) │ *into an image.* Judg 17:4
17.	וַיִּבְנֶה אֶת־הָאֲבָנִים מִזְבֵּחַ	He built *the stones* │ *into an altar.* 1 Kgs 18:32

This pair may involve abstract terms.

| 18. | וַיַּחְשְׁבֶהָ לּוֹ צְדָקָה׃ | He credited *it* (Abraham's belief) to him *as righteousness.*
Gen 15:6 |

Verbs of appointment govern as accusatives *person appointed + rank.*

19.	וַיָּשֶׂם אֶת־בָּנָיו שֹׁפְטִים	He made his *sons* │ *judges.* 1 Sam 8:1
20.	לֹא תְשִׂימֵנִי קְצִין עָם׃	Do not make *me* │ *the leader* of the people. Isa 3:7
21.	וָאֶתֵּן אֹתָם רָאשִׁים	And I appointed *them* │ *heads.* Deut 1:15

Similarly, verbs of naming govern *person named + name.*

| 22. | וַיִּקְרְאוּ שְׁמוֹ עֵשָׂו׃ | And they called his *name* │ *Esau.*
Gen 25:25 |

Some verbs govern a double accusative of *direct object + means,* be it instrument (## 23–25) or medium (# 26).

23.	אִישׁ אֶת־אָחִיהוּ יָצוּדוּ חֵרֶם׃	Each hunts his *brother* │ *with a net.* Mic 7:2
24.	וְהִכֵּיתִי אֶת־הָאָרֶץ חֵרֶם׃	I smite *the earth* │ *with a curse.* Mal 3:24
25.	וַיֹּרֵם אֱלֹהִים חֵץ	God shoots *at them* │ *with arrows.* Ps 64:8
26.	מְשָׁחֲךָ אֱלֹהִים . . . שֶׁמֶן	God anointed *you* . . . │ *with oil.* Ps 45:8

With verbs of planting, the direct object is the area planted and the means is the crop.

| 27. | וַיִּטָּעֵהוּ שֹׂרֵק | He planted *it* │ *with choice vines.*
Isa 5:2 |

28.   וַיִּזְרָעֶ֖הָ מֶֽלַח׃   He sowed *it* | *with salt*.
Judg 9:45

e   The double accusatives used with *Piel-Hiphil* verbs follow similar patterns (24.1, 27.1). In a number of cases, the accusatives involve the object of the causation predicate, *the person acted on* (by the primary subject) + the object of the other verbal predicate, *the object acted on* (by the undersubject, the person acted on).

29.   וַיַּאֲכִֽלְךָ֥ אֶת־הַמָּן֙   He fed *you* | *manna* (lit., he caused *you* to eat *manna*).
Deut 8:3

30.   הַשְׁקִינִי־נָ֥א מְעַט־מַ֖יִם   Give *me* | *a little* water to drink.[23]
Judg 4:19

31.   הֶרְאָ֖נוּ . . . אֶת־כְּבֹדוֹ֙   He showed *us* . . . his *glory*.
Deut 5:21

32.   וְאַרְאֶ֖ךָ אֶת־הָאִ֑ישׁ   I will show *you* | *the man*.
Judg 4:22

33.   וְנוֹדִ֥יעָה אֶתְכֶ֖ם דָּבָ֑ר   And we'll teach *you* | *a lesson*.
1 Sam 14:12

34.   וְהוּא יַנְחִ֥יל אוֹתָ֖ם אֶת־הָאָֽרֶץ   He will cause *them* to inherit *the land*.[24]
Deut 3:28

The double accusatives can refer to the *object* of the causation predicate (person or thing) + the *means* or *complement* of the other verbal predicate.

35.   וַיְמַלְא֣וּ אֶת־כְּלֵיהֶם֮ בָּר֒   They filled their *bags* | *with grain*.
Gen 42:25

36.   וָאֲכַלְכְּלֵ֖ם לֶ֥חֶם וָמָֽיִם׃   I supplied *them* | *with food and water*.
1 Kgs 18:13

37.   אֶבְיוֹנֶ֥יהָ אַשְׂבִּ֥יעַ לָֽחֶם׃   Her *poor* I will satisfy *with food*.
Ps 132:15

38.   וְכָב֖וֹד וְהָדָ֣ר תְּעַטְּרֵֽהוּ׃   You crowned *him* | *with glory and honor*.
Ps 8:6

39.   אֲרַיָּ֣וֶךְ דִּמְעָתִ֑י   I drench *you* | *with* my *tears*.
Isa 16:9

Verbs of clothing (or stripping) can govern a personal *direct object* + *complement object*.[25]

---

23. The English verbs 'to feed' and 'to water' have interesting distributional differences from the corresponding Hebrew verbs; in English, the latter is used only of animals, while the former can be used of humans, but only with an intimation of condescension.

24. Cf. *nḥl Hophal* in Job 7:3.

25. For other acts of dressing see Gen 41:42; Isa 22:21; Ps 132:16, 18; for both dressing and stripping see Num 20:26, 28. The reflexive *Hithpael* of these verbs governs only one object (e.g., *ytpšṭ* in 1 Sam 18:4).

40.   וַיַּלְבֵּשׁ שָׁאוּל אֶת־דָּוִד מַדָּיו   Saul clothed *David* | *with* his *garments*.
                                             1 Sam 17:38

41.   וַיַּפְשִׁיטוּ אֶת־יוֹסֵף אֶת־כֻּתָּנְתּוֹ   They stripped *Joseph* | *of* his *coat*.
                                             Gen 37:23

Particle את   10.3

The particle אֵת is one of the most difficult grammatical morphemes in Biblical   a
Hebrew. One set of difficulties is morphological: the particle אֶת/אֶת־ is homonymous
with אֶת/אֶת־, the preposition 'with,' except with pronominal suffixes.[26] With these the
particle base is ʾōt-/ʾet- (אֹתִי, אֹתְךָ, אֹתוֹ, אֶתְכֶם, אֹתָם/אֹתָם, once אוֹתְהֶם/rarely אֶתְהֶם, etc.),
while the prepositional base is ʾitt- (אִתִּי, אִתְּכֶם, etc.).[27] As a result of this similarity, the
two words are sometimes confused.

The other set of difficulties is syntactic. There are two approaches to descriptions of   b
the particle's function. (1) The tradition calls it the *nota accusativi* or "sign of the
accusative" and essentially explains away the occurrences that do not fit this rubric.[28]
(2) More recent grammarians regard it as a marker of emphasis used most often with
definite nouns in the accusative role. The apparent occurrences with the nominative are
most problematic—are they to be denied, emended away or the like,[29] or are they to be
explained? The last course seems best, though the difficulty of the problem cannot be
denied: "No single particle has given rise to more widespread and also mutually more
contradictory discussion than this so-called nota accusativi."[30] A. M. Wilson late in the
nineteenth century concluded from his exhaustive study of all the occurrences of this

---

26. The particle occurs ca. 10,900 times (SA/THAT). The preposition and particle are also homographic. For a review of object markers across the Semitic family see G. A. Khan, "Object Markers and Agreement Pronouns in Semitic Languages," *Bulletin of the School of Oriental and African Studies* 47 (1984) 468–500.

27. For a list of some passages involving supposed "confusions" between the two bases, see A. Sperber, *A Historical Grammar of Biblical Hebrew* (Leiden: Brill, 1966) 63–65.

28. The Samaritan Pentateuch tends to add the particle along the lines of the traditional understanding; see Bruce K. Waltke, "The Samaritan Pentateuch and the Text of the Old Testament," *New Perspectives on the Old Testament*, ed. J. Barton Payne (Waco, Texas: Word, 1970) 212–39, esp. 221. On the other hand, Paul E. Dion notes that the use of ʾt varies in the sectarian documents of the Second Temple period (it is much more common in the Damascus Document than in the Rule of the Community); the semantic range of ʾt in the Damascus Document seems to have been simplified over against Biblical Hebrew; "The Hebrew Particle את in the Paraenetic Part of the 'Damascus Document,'" *Revue de Qumran* 9 (1977)

197–212. In Qumranic Hebrew, ʾt with suffixed pronouns is infrequent, continuing a trend apparent in Chronicles; see E. Qimron, *The Hebrew of the Dead Sea Scrolls* (Atlanta: Scholars Press, 1986) 75–77.

29. This is more or less the position of K. Albrecht, "את vor dem Nominativ und beim Passiv," *Zeitschrift für die Alttestamentliche Wissenschaft* 47 (1929) 274–83; J. Blau, "Zum angeblichen Gebrauch von את vor dem Nominativ," *Vetus Testamentum* 4 (1954) 7–19; Blau, "Gibt es ein emphatisches ʾēt im Bibelhebräisch?" *Vetus Testamentum* 6 (1956) 211–12; T. Muraoka, *Emphatic Words and Structures in Biblical Hebrew* (Jerusalem: Magnes/Leiden: Brill, 1985) 146–58; cf. GKC § 117i / p. 365. Muraoka comments: "After having exhausted all the possibilities imaginable, there remain a considerable number of passages for which we have no alternative but to suggest emendation" (p. 157); but systematic emendation is never acceptable.

30. Muraoka, *Emphatic Words*, 146. It is occasionally proposed that ʾt serves as a gloss-marker, for example, in Hag 2:5 (where the opening clause as a whole would then be taken as a gloss on the preceding verse); see M. Fishbane, *Biblical Interpretation in Ancient Israel* (Oxford: Clarendon, 1985) 48–51, cf. 193.

debated particle that it had an intensive or reflective force in some of its occurrences.[31] Many grammarians have followed his lead.[32] On such a view, את is a weakened emphatic particle, corresponding to the English pronoun 'self' in locutions such as 'He, himself (NOMINATIVE), kept the law' and 'He kept the law itself (ACCUSATIVE).' It resembles Greek *autos* and Latin *ipse*, both sometimes used for emphasis, and like them it can be omitted from the text without obscuring the grammar. This explanation of the particle's meaning harmonizes well with the facts that the particle is used in Mishnaic Hebrew as a demonstrative[33] and is found almost exclusively with determinate nouns.

c   One could argue that את was originally a sign of the accusative with active verbs and that in the historical development of the language it was reinterpreted as the subject of an equivalent passive construction. So, for example, יָלַד חֲנוֹךְ אֶת־עִירָד, 'Enoch begat Irad,' is equivalent to וַיִּוָּלֵד לַחֲנוֹךְ אֶת־עִירָד, 'To Enoch was born Irad' (Gen 4:18). This gave rise, the argument would continue, to the kind of construction known as *ergative*, in which the morphological marking of the subject of an intransitive verb is the same as the direct object of a transitive verb. Thus a hypothetical ergative English paraphrase of 'John moved her' would be 'her moved by John.' The final step, one could conclude the argument, is that even this trace of the original passive construction became lost. Such a development is attested in the movement from early Indo-Iranian to Hindi and Modern Persian.[34] The reconstruction would also find support in the cognate Semitic languages,

---

31. A. M. Wilson, "The Particle את in Hebrew," *Hebraica* 6 (1889–90) 139–50, 212–24. There is an enclitic *t* (*ta* or *ti*) attested in Amorite and possibly in Hebrew; see C. R. Krahmalkov, "The Amorite Enclitic Particle *TA/I*," *Journal of Semitic Studies* 14 (1969) 201–4; Krahmalkov, "The Enclitic Particle *TA/I* in Hebrew," *Journal of Biblical Literature* 89 (1970) 218–19; cf. O'Connor, *Hebrew Verse Structure*, 213.

32. This is more or less the position of Joüon § 125j / p. 370; N. Walker, "Concerning the Function of *ʾt*," *Vetus Testamentum* 5 (1955) 314–15; P. P. Saydon, "Meanings and Uses of the Particle את," *Vetus Testamentum* 14 (1964) 192–210; John Macdonald, "The Particle את in Classical Hebrew," *Vetus Testamentum* 14 (1964) 263–75; R. Meyer, "Bemerkungen zur syntaktischen Funktion der sogenannten Nota accusativi," *Wort und Geschichte: Festschrift für Kurt Elliger*, ed. H. Gese and H.-P. Rüger (Kevelaer: Butzon und Bercker/Neukirchen-Vluyn: Neukirchener, 1973) 137–42; J. Hoftijzer, "Remarks Concerning the Use of the Particle *ʾt* in Classical Hebrew," *Oudtestamentische Studiën* 14 (1965) 1–99 (though Hoftijzer is dubious about notions of emphasis and prefers a historical explanation, he does recognize *ʾt* with the nominative and allows it a special role). Studies of the syntax of late Biblical Hebrew (especially Chronicles) recognize the emphatic use and its importance in later texts; see Arno Kropat, *Die Syntax des Autors der Chronik verglichen mit der seiner Quellen: Ein Beitrag zur historischen Syntax des Hebräischen* (Beiheft zur Zeitschrift für die Alttestamentliche Wissenschaft

16; Giessen: Töpelmann, 1909) 2–3, cf. 33–36; Robert Polzin, *Late Biblical Hebrew: Toward an Historical Typology of Biblical Hebrew Prose* (Missoula: Scholars Press, 1976) 32–37, cf. 28–31 on the decreased use of suffixed forms of *ʾt* in late texts.

John Macdonald observes that *ʾt* is used with the nominative in the Classical Hebrew text known as the *Samaritan Chronicle II*, a historical account intended to follow the (Samaritan) Pentateuch. Note, for example, in this text's version of Josh 7:9: *wšmᶜw ʾt yšby ʾrṣ knᶜn wsbw bnw lhšmydnw mn hʾrṣ*, 'The inhabitants of the land of Canaan will hear and will surround us in order to eradicate us from the land.' Macdonald remarks, "We now have absolute proof that, in the later form of Northern Israelite (Classical) Hebrew at least, את did come in for a much wider range of usages than has hitherto been allowed by the great majority of commentators" (p. 275). The text Macdonald cites is now published by him as *The Samaritan Chronicle No. II (or: Sepher Ha-Yamin) From Joshua to Nebuchadnezzar* (Beiheft zur Zeitschrift für die Alttestamentliche Wissenschaft 107; Berlin: de Gruyter, 1969).

33. On the extensive Mishnaic usage, see M. H. Segal, *A Grammar of Mishnaic Hebrew* (Oxford: Clarendon, 1927) 42, 202.

34. See Bernard Comrie, *Aspect: An Introduction to the Study of Verbal Aspect and Related Problems* (Cambridge: Cambridge University, 1976) 84–86. For related arguments for Hebrew see Francis I. Andersen, "Passive and Ergative in Hebrew," *Near Eastern Studies in Honor of William*

where the accusative case ending is sometimes found with the subject of passive verbs, and from the lack of grammatical agreement between the plural subject and the singular verb. The ergative theory should be rejected because it does not account for the wide use of את in other constructions in Biblical Hebrew.

With the Accusative   10.3.1

The emphatic particle is used most often to mark the *definite direct object* of a transitive verb.   **a**

1.	וַיִּטַּע יהוה אֱלֹהִים גַּן . . . וַיָּ֫שֶׂם שָׁם אֶת־הָאָדָם	And Yʜᴡʜ God planted a garden . . . and placed *Adam* there. Gen 2:8
2.	וְלֹא־יָכֹל עוֹד לְהָשִׁיב אֶת־אַבְנֵר דָּבָר	He was not able to answer *Abner*. 2 Sam 3:11
3.	וַיַּעַשׂ אֱלֹהִים אֶת־חַיַּת הָאָ֫רֶץ	God made *the wild animals*. Gen 1:25

In a series of definite direct objects, if the particle is used on one member of the series it is ordinarily used on each (# 4); occasionally the initial *ʾt* in a series overrides the later objects (# 5).

4.	וַיַּכּוּ אֶת־הַכְּנַעֲנִי וְאֶת־הַפְּרִזִּי׃	They smote *the Canaanites* and *the Perizzites*. Judg 1:5
5.	וַיִּתֵּן יהוה אֶת־הַכְּנַעֲנִי וְהַפְּרִזִּי בְּיָדָם	Yʜᴡʜ gave *the Canaanites* and *the Perizzites* into their power. Judg 1:4

Pronouns with *ʾt* are definite.

6.	גַּם־אֹתְכָה הָרַ֫גְתִּי וְאוֹתָהּ הֶחֱיֵֽיתִי׃	I would certainly have killed *you* by now, but I would have spared *her*. Num 22:33
7.	וּלְקַחְתֶּם גַּם־אֶת־זֶה מֵעִם פָּנַי	And if you also take *this one* from me. . . . Gen 44:29
8.	אֶת־מִי אֶשְׁלַח	*Whom* shall I send? Isa 6:8

Foxwell Albright, ed. H. Goedicke (Baltimore: Johns Hopkins University, 1971) 1–15; and Khan, "Object Markers," 496–97. On comparable developments in the preterite of Eastern Neo-Aramaic dialects spoken in the same region as Persian and related languages, see G. Krotkoff, *A Neo-Aramaic Dialect of Kurdistan* (American Oriental Series 64; New Haven, Connecticut: American Oriental Society, 1982) 30–39, 52–55, 63; R. D. Hoberman, *The Syntax and Semantics of Verb Morphology in Modern Aramaic: A Jewish Dialect of Iraqi Kurdistan* (American Oriental Series 69; New Haven: American Oriental Society, 1989) 95–105; cf. Daniel Boyarin's comments in his review of Yona Sabar's *Pəšaṭ Wayəhi Bəšallah* in *Maarav* 3 (1982) 99–114, esp. 103–6.

Constructions with 'all' and numbers also involve a logical determination.

9.	וַיִּבְרָא אֱלֹהִים אֶת־הַתַּנִּינִם הַגְּדֹלִים וְאֵת כָּל־נֶפֶשׁ הַחַיָּה הָרֹמֶשֶׂת	And God created the great creatures of the sea and *every* living and moving thing. Gen 1:21
10.	קַח־נָא אִתְּךָ אֶת־אַחַד מֵהַנְּעָרִים	Take *one* of the servants with you. 1 Sam 9:3
11.	אֶת־שֶׁבַע כְּבָשֹׂת תִּקַּח מִיָּדִי	Accept these *seven lambs* from my hand. Gen 21:30

The relative marker אֲשֶׁר is governed by את both when it is used as a pronoun (## 12–13) and when it is used to introduce a 'that' clause (## 14–15).

12.	וּמָשַׁחְתָּ לִי אֵת אֲשֶׁר־אֹמַר אֵלֶיךָ:	And you shall on my behalf anoint *the one of whom* I will speak to you. 1 Sam 16:3
13.	וַיֵּדַע אֵת אֲשֶׁר־עָשָׂה־לוֹ בְּנוֹ הַקָּטָן:	And he knew *that which* his youngest son had done to him. Gen 9:24
14.	אַל־תִּשְׁכַּח אֵת אֲשֶׁר־הִקְצַפְתָּ אֶת־יהוה	Do not forget *that* you angered YHWH. Deut 9:7
15.	שָׁמַעְנוּ אֵת אֲשֶׁר־הוֹבִישׁ יהוה אֶת־מֵי יַם־סוּף	We have heard *that* YHWH dried up the water of the Yam Suf. Josh 2:10

T. Muraoka has noted that there is a statistically higher use of את in 1 Samuel 1–8 (only 8 of 116 occurrences of the definite direct object lack it) than in Genesis 12–20 (22 out of 86 instances lack it).[35] He could often find no reason for its omission; compare these examples.

16.	וְהַדֶּלֶת סָגַר אַחֲרָיו:	He shut *the door* behind him. Gen 19:6
17.	וְאֶת־הַדֶּלֶת סָגָרוּ:	They shut *the door*. Gen 19:10

b   The particle את is rarely prefixed to an *indefinite direct-object accusative*. This anomalous use may be explained as due to an attempt to set off accusative function.

18.	וְהִשִּׂיג לָכֶם דַּיִשׁ אֶת־בָּצִיר וּבָצִיר יַשִּׂיג אֶת־זָרַע	Your threshing will overtake (i.e., last until *or* overlap) *grape harvest*, and grape harvest will overtake *planting*. Lev 26:5

---

35. Muraoka does refer to a "historical development" that is "manifest" between the two sections; *Emphatic Words*, 150–51.

19. וְהָיָה אִם־נָשַׁךְ הַנָּחָשׁ אֶת־אִישׁ   And if the snake (i.e., a snake) bit *anyone*. . . .
Num 21:9

20. וְאֶת־קַשׁ יָבֵשׁ תִּרְדֹּף: Do you pursue dry *chaff*?
Job 13:25

The particle is used far less often with other accusative nouns. Of the other objective   c
accusatives, את tends not to occur with internal accusatives but is found with *comple-*
ment accusatives (## 21–22) and "*datival accusatives*" (## 23–26).

21. וּמָלְאוּ בָּתֵּי מִצְרַיִם אֶת־הֶעָרֹב   And the houses of the Egyptians shall be filled *with*
flies.
Exod 8:17

22. וַיִּמָּלֵא אֶת־הַחָכְמָה   And he was filled *with wisdom*.
1 Kgs 7:14

23. וְאָיַבְתִּי אֶת־אֹיְבֶיךָ   I shall be an enemy *to your enemies*.
Exod 23:22

24. הֲדָבָר דִּבַּרְתִּי אֶת־אַחַד שִׁבְטֵי   Have I spoken *to any* of the tribes of Israel?
יִשְׂרָאֵל   2 Sam 7:7

25. וְדִבַּרְתִּי מִשְׁפָּטַי אוֹתָם   I will speak my judgments *to them*.
Jer 1:16

26. אֲדַבֵּר אוֹתָךְ:   I will speak *to you*.
Ezek 3:22

The particle is used sporadically with adverbial accusatives, of *place* (## 27–28), of *time*
(## 29–30), and of *limitation* (## 31–33).

27. יָדַע לֶכְתְּךָ אֶת־הַמִּדְבָּר הַגָּדֹל   He has watched over your journey *through* this vast
הַזֶּה   *steppe*.
Deut 2:7

28. הֵם יָצְאוּ אֶת־הָעִיר   They having left *the city*. . . .
Gen 44:4

29. מַצּוֹת יֵאָכֵל אֵת שִׁבְעַת הַיָּמִים   Unleavened bread must be eaten *for seven days*.
Exod 13:7

30. וָאֶתְנַפַּל לִפְנֵי יהוה אֵת   I lay prostrate before Yнwн *forty days*.
אַרְבָּעִים הַיּוֹם   Deut 9:25

31. וּנְמַלְתֶּם אֵת בְּשַׂר עָרְלַתְכֶם   You will circumcise yourselves *with regard to the flesh*
of your foreskin.
Gen 17:11

32. וְהוּא שֹׁכֵב אֶת מִשְׁכַּב הַצָּהֳרָיִם: And he was lying down *for the midday rest*.
2 Sam 4:5

33. חָלָה אֶת־רַגְלָיו: He became sick *in his feet*.
1 Kgs 15:23

10.3.2 Elsewhere

a   The particle את is prefixed to nouns in the nominative function in both verbal and verbless clauses, usually in cases involving enumerations or appositions (12.1). It is also rarely used in a few other constructions.

b   In verbal clauses את can mark the subject of transitive (# 1) and intransitive active (## 2–5) verbs and passive verbs (## 6–8). The use with transitives is extremely rare; the other two usages are more common.

1. וְאֶת־מְלָכֵינוּ . . . לֹא עָשׂוּ תוֹרָתֶךָ

Our *kings* . . . did not follow (TRANSITIVE) your laws.
Neh 9:34

2. וּבָא הָאֲרִי וְאֶת־הַדּוֹב וְנָשָׂא שֶׂה

When a lion came (INTRANSITIVE) or *a bear* and carried off a sheep. . . .
1 Sam 17:34

3. וַיִּפְּלוּ מִבִּנְיָמִן שְׁמֹנָה־עָשָׂר אֶלֶף אִישׁ אֶת־כָּל־אֵלֶּה אַנְשֵׁי־חָיִל׃

And there fell (INTRANSITIVE) from Benjamin eighteen thousand men, *all* of them men of war.[36]
Judg 20:44

4. וְאֶת־הַבַּרְזֶל נָפַל אֶל־הַמָּיִם

The iron (axhead) fell (INTRANSITIVE) into the water.
2 Kgs 6:5

5. אֶת־עַמּוּד הֶעָנָן לֹא־סָר

The column of cloud did not depart (INTRANSITIVE).
Neh 9:19

6. וַיִּוָּלֵד לַחֲנוֹךְ אֶת־עִירָד

And *Irad* was born (PASSIVE) to Henoch.
Gen 4:18

7. בְּהִוָּלֶד לוֹ אֵת יִצְחָק בְּנוֹ׃

When his son *Isaac* was born (PASSIVE) to him. . . .
Gen 21:5

8. וַיֻּגַּד לְרִבְקָה אֶת־דִּבְרֵי עֵשָׂו

The words of Esau were told (PASSIVE) to Rebekah.
Gen 27:42

The existential verb הָיָה 'to be' and the two existential particles יֵשׁ 'there is' and אֵין 'there is not' take ordinary verbal government, with a nominative subject. The verb היה (with ל 'to belong to'; ## 9–10) and both particles (## 11–12) have subjects, or nouns in apposition to subjects, marked with את.

9. וְאִישׁ אֶת־קֳדָשָׁיו לוֹ יִהְיוּ

As for every person, his *offerings* belong to him.
Num 5:10

10. אֶת־שְׁנֵי הַגּוֹיִם וְאֶת־שְׁתֵּי הָאֲרָצוֹת לִי תִהְיֶינָה

The two nations and *the two lands* will be mine.
Ezek 35:10

11. הֲיֵשׁ אֶת־לְבָבְךָ יָשָׁר

Is your *heart* right?
2 Kgs 10:15

---

36. Technically, the phrase with *ʾt* is in apposition to the genitive *ʾyš*.

12.   וְאֵין־אֶתְכֶם אֵלָי   *You, yourselves,* did not turn to me.
Hag 2:17

With verbless clauses את can be used to mark the subject (# 13) or the predicate   c
(# 15) or both (# 17), or a noun in apposition to them (## 14, 16).

13.   הַמְעַט־לָנוּ אֶת־עֲוֹן פְּעוֹר   Is *the crime* of Peor (SUBJECT) a little thing to us?
Josh 22:17

14.   . . . וְזֶה אֲשֶׁר לֹא־תֹאכְלוּ מֵהֶם   But these are those [birds] you may not eat of . . . *any*
אֵת כָּל־עֹרֵב לְמִינוֹ:   kind *of raven* (SUBJECT APPOSITION).
Deut 14:12, 14

15.   כָּל־הֶעָרִים אֲשֶׁר תִּתְּנוּ לַלְוִיִּם   All the cities you give to the Levites shall be forty-
אַרְבָּעִים וּשְׁמֹנֶה עִיר אֶתְהֶן   eight cities, them and their *pasturelands* (PREDICATE).
וְאֶת־מִגְרְשֵׁיהֶן: Num 35:7

16.   הֵמָּה הַפָּנִים אֲשֶׁר רָאִיתִי   They were the faces which I had seen near the river
עַל־נְהַר־כְּבָר מַרְאֵיהֶם וְאוֹתָם   Chebar, their appearances and *they themselves*
(PREDICATE APPOSITION).
Ezek 10:22

17.   וְאֵת הֶעָרִים אֲשֶׁר תִּתְּנוּ לַלְוִיִּם   *The towns* (SUBJECT) you give the Levites will be the
אֵת שֵׁשׁ־עָרֵי הַמִּקְלָט   *six cities of refuge* (PREDICATE).
Num 35:6

The two remaining uses of את are rare. It may be used to mark a nominative abso-   d
lute (sentential topic or focus marker; see 4.7, 8.3).

18.   אֵת־כָּל־הָאָרֶץ אֲשֶׁר־אַתָּה רֹאֶה   *As for all the land* which you see, I will give it to you.
לְךָ אֶתְּנֶנָּה   Gen 13:15

19.   וְגַם אֶת־מַעֲכָה אִמּוֹ וַיְסִרֶהָ   *And as for his mother Maacah,* he even deposed her
מִגְּבִירָה   as queen mother.
1 Kgs 15:13

20.   וְאֶת־חֻקּוֹתַי לֹא־הָלְכוּ בָהֶם   *And as for my decrees,* they did not follow them.
Ezek 20:16

As several examples have shown, את can mark a noun in apposition (12.1) to a nominative; it is used at least once before a noun in apposition to a prepositional object.

21.   וַיְמָרֲרוּ אֶת־חַיֵּיהֶם בַּעֲבֹדָה   They made their lives bitter in hard labor . . . *in all*
קָשָׁה . . . אֵת כָּל־עֲבֹדָתָם   their labors.
Exod 1:14

Aspects of the Use of ל   10.4

The preposition *l*, like the other monographic prepositions *b* and *k*, serves a wide   a
variety of functions (cf. 11.2.10). It marks location 'to, toward,' and 'at, near,' as well as

analogous time references; it is the preposition of transformation 'into' and belonging 'to,' and it marks purpose clauses ('in order to'). It can also be used in ways analogous to את, prefixed to nouns that do not fall within its usual prepositional range, often nouns in enumerations or in apposition.[37]

b   Like את, ל is used to mark the definite direct object of a transitive verb (cf. 11.2.10, ## 58–60).

1. זְכֹר לְאַבְרָהָם לְיִצְחָק וּלְיִשְׂרָאֵל עֲבָדֶיךָ

Remember *Abraham, Isaac, and Israel*, your servants.[38]
Exod 32:13

2. רְפָא נָא לָהּ׃

Heal *her*, I pray.[39]
Num 12:13

3. לְשַׁחֵת לָעִיר

to destroy *the town*[40]
1 Sam 23:10

4. כַּמַּיִם לַיָּם מְכַסִּים׃

as the waters cover *the sea*[41]
Isa 11:9

It is rarely used to mark an indefinite direct object.

5. לֶאֱוִיל יַהֲרָג־כָּעַשׂ

Resentment kills *a fool*.
Job 5:2

c   The subject of a verb can be marked with *l*; the verb may be intransitive or passive.

6. לְכָל־עֹבֵר עָלָיו יִשֹּׁם

All who pass by it will be appalled (INTRANSITIVE).[42]
2 Chr 7:21

7. פֶּן יְבֻלַּע לַמֶּלֶךְ וּלְכָל־הָעָם אֲשֶׁר אִתּוֹ׃

lest *the king and all* the people with him be swallowed up (PASSIVE)[43]
2 Sam 17:16

A related use of *l* is on the last phrase in a complex noun. In # 8 the noun phrase with *l* is the last part of the subject, while in # 9 the *l* phrase is in apposition to a prepositional object (cf. 11.2.10, ## 62–64).

---

37. This usage is more common in later books (where Aramaic influence may be suspected); see Kropat, *Syntax des Autors der Chronik*, 4–7, cf. 53–57; Polzin, *Late Biblical Hebrew*, 64–69; contrast in part Muraoka, *Emphatic Words*, 120–21.

38. For *zkr* with an accusative direct object of person see, e.g., Ps 9:13.

39. For *rpᵓ* with an accusative direct object of person see, e.g., Gen 20:17.

40. For *šḥt* Piel with an accusative direct object of a building see Lam 2:5.

41. For *ksy* Piel with an accusative direct object of water (*thwm*) see Ps 104:6.

42. Note that the usage is indefinite. There is no *l* in the parallel in 1 Kgs 9:8, suggesting that the Chronicles use is a "late" addition.

43. The construction is difficult; for a different analysis and some relevant examples, see Driver, *Notes on the Hebrew Text and Topography of the Books of Samuel*, 323–24.

8. וַיִּתְנַדְּבוּ שָׂרֵי הָאָבוֹת וְשָׂרֵי
שִׁבְטֵי יִשְׂרָאֵל וְשָׂרֵי הָאֲלָפִים
וְהַמֵּאוֹת וּלְשָׂרֵי מְלֶאכֶת הַמֶּלֶךְ:

And there gave freely the heads of households and the heads of the tribes of Israel and the heads of the thousands and hundreds and *the heads* of the royal labor force.
1 Chr 29:6

9. וַיִּוָּעַץ דָּוִיד עִם־שָׂרֵי הָאֲלָפִים
וְהַמֵּאוֹת לְכָל־נָגִיד:

And David conferred with the heads of thousands and hundreds, with *each leader*.
1 Chr 13:1

Directional ה   **10.5**

Before the decipherment of the Ugaritic texts (1.3.1) grammarians supposed that the   a
unaccented Hebrew suffix -*āh*, signifying "direction," represented a survival of the original accusative case ending -*a*. Ugaritic, however, was found to have both an accusative
case ending -*a* and an adverbial suffix -*h* like the Hebrew so-called "*he*-locale" or "direc-
tional-*he*" suffix.[44] From this evidence it is certain that Hebrew directional *he* is not a
survival of the old accusative,[45] but a distinct adverbial suffix. Roughly equivalent to the
English adverbial suffix '-ward,' this suffix denotes some meanings similar to those designated by the accusative case; it differs from that case in that it may occur with nouns
governed by a preposition and it distinctively emphasizes the notion of direction.[46]

The directional *he* may indicate the *direction toward* which an action is aimed. The   b
simplest such case of directional *he* is the word הֵנָּה.

1.   הָבֵא אֶת־הָאֲנָשִׁים הַבָּיְתָה   Take these men *to* (my) *house*.
Gen 43:16

2.   הַבֶּט־נָא הַשָּׁמַיְמָה   Look *at the heavens*.
Gen 15:5

Directional *he* may break up a construct chain (9.3d).

3. וַיָּבֵא הָאִישׁ אֶת־הָאֲנָשִׁים בֵּיתָה   The man took the men *to* Joseph's *house*.
יוֹסֵף: Gen 43:17

Less often, *he* occurs on a prepositional phrase indicating the *direction away from* which
an action is directed.

---

44. *UT* § 8.56.

45. There are other, phonological arguments against this
explanation.

46. The Samaritan Pentateuch tends to drop the suffix,
as if modernizing; see Waltke, "Samaritan Pentateuch,"
217. For a thorough statement on the biblical use of the
he suffix and the implications of its distribution, see J.
Hoftijzer et al., *A Search for Method: A Study in the*

Syntactic Use of the H-Locale in Classical Hebrew (Studies
in Semitic Languages and Linguistics 12; Leiden: Brill,
1981). The contribution of Hoftijzer's study depends on
his careful discriminations among the blocks, strata, and
genres of material investigated, allowing him to suggest,
for example, that *he*-locale before a *rectum* is a later (more
advanced) construction than a free-standing noun with
he-locale.

4.   כְּלֵי בֵית־יהוה מוּשָׁבִים מִבָּבֶ֫לָה   The vessels of Yhwh's house are about to be brought back *from Babylon.*
Jer 27:16

The *he* suffix is also used on prepositional phrases referring to a *locale.*

5.   וְדָוִד בְּמִדְבַּר־זִיף בַּחֹ֫רְשָׁה׃   And David was in the Steppe of Zif, *at Horesh.*
1 Sam 23:15

6.   וְכָל־בֵּית שְׁאָן אֲשֶׁר אֵ֫צֶל צָרְתַ֫נָה   and all of Beth-Shean which is *near Zarethan*
1 Kgs 4:12

c   Finally, the particle can mark forward progression through *time.*[47]

7.   וְשָׁמַרְתָּ אֶת־הַחֻקָּה הַזֹּאת לְמוֹעֲדָהּ מִיָּמִים יָמִ֫ימָה׃   You must keep this ordinance at the appointed time from year *to year.*
Exod 13:10

---

47. For another example see Judg 11:40.

11

Prepositions

Introduction   11.1

Prepositions are relational terms that stand before nouns and noun equivalents   a
(including certain verb forms) and thereby form phrases (4.3b); prepositional phrases are
used in a variety of ways. The class of prepositions is a closed class, that is, a more or

less small and well-defined group of words, unlike, for example, the open class of verbs, which is both large and (in a living language) readily expanded.

11.1.1 "Nominal" Perspective

a   Hebrew prepositions can be considered in a variety of perspectives. Some prepositions are derived from *nouns*, and the behavior of prepositions can be seen in terms of nominal roles or functions. In this perspective prepositions are taken as nouns in the adverbial accusative, governing nouns in the genitive. At least some Hebrew prepositions in their archaic forms ended with *a*, the historical case ending of the acccusative, and were used in the construct state; the noun governed by them took the genitive case (see 9.3). Traces of such history can still be seen in construct forms like אַחֲרֵי and the complex preposition לִפְנֵי 'to the face of' > 'before' (see 11.3.1); the cognate languages also support this view.[1] The shortening of nominal construct forms is related to the unstressed status of many prepositions, written as prefixes or as proclitics (with *maqqeph*, e.g., עַל־). On this "nominal" view of prepositions, the close relationship of prepositional phrases and the verbs governing them is emphasized; like other accusative roles, the preposition is at base ad-verbial. Prepositions, nominal (and quasi-nominal) expressions of various origins, supplement the accusative case to make more precise the relationship between the verb and nouns it modifies (see 10.2, 11.4.1).[2] The "nominal" perspective on prepositions provides a limited view; a number of prepositions have no evident nominal base, and, more importantly, the prepositions as relational terms work differently than nouns (or any subclass of nouns).[3]

11.1.2 "Particle" Perspective

a   On another perspective, Hebrew prepositions belong to the large class of *particles*. Some prepositions also do duty as adverbs or conjunctions, two other groups of particles. Like many particles, some Hebrew prepositions fall outside the root system. In

1. In Classical Arabic, for example, the genitive case is used after prepositions. See also Wolfram von Soden, *Grundriss der akkadischen Grammatik* (Analecta Orientalia 33/47; Rome: Pontifical Biblical Institute, 1969) § 114a / p. 164.

2. Important information about the prepositional system is furnished by the stages of Northwest Semitic antecedent to Hebrew which retain the case system. The major source for the Ugaritic prepositional system is Dennis G. Pardee, "The Preposition in Ugaritic," *Ugarit-Forschungen* 7 (1975) 329–78; 8 (1976) 215–322; and the supplement, "Attestations of Ugaritic Verb/Preposition Combinations in Later Dialects," *Ugarit-Forschungen* 9 (1977) 205–31; cited as Pardee, *UF* 7, 8, or 9, with page number; see also K. Aartun, *Die Partikeln des Ugaritischen. 2. Präpositionen, Konjunktionen* (Kevelaer: Butzon und Bercker/Neukirchen-Vluyn: Neukirchener, 1978). On the dynamics of the Ugaritic system see Pardee, *UF* 8: 218, 243, 286–91; on the virtual lack of *mn* in Ugaritic see Pardee, *UF* 7: 332; 8: 270, 279, 284, 315–16; K. Aartun, "Präpositional Ausdrücke im Ugaritischen als Ersatz für semitisch *min*," *Ugarit-Forschungen* 14 (1982) 1–14; M. Dietrich and O. Loretz, "Zweifelhafte Belege für ug. *m(n)* 'von'," *Ugarit-Forschungen* 12 (1980) 183–87. Mishnaic Hebrew has a more complicated prepositional system than Biblical Hebrew. See M. H. Segal, *A Grammar of Mishnaic Hebrew* (Oxford: Clarendon, 1927) 141–45. On Phoenician see *UT* § 10.11 n. 1.

3. On the inadequacies of this view see L. H. Glinert, "The Preposition in Biblical and Modern Hebrew," *Hebrew Studies* 23 (1982) 115–25, a model study in syntactic argumentation that yet does not allow for certain complexities in Biblical Hebrew.

fact, the *morphological complexity* of prepositions deserves a separate review. It has three features.

The first of these involves the opposition of the *simple prepositions* (e.g., מִן and עַל), the *compound prepositions*, which are composed of two (or more) simple prepositions (e.g., מֵעַל; 11.3.3), and the *complex prepositions*, made up of a preposition + a noun (e.g., בְּיַד 'by, through' and בְּתוֹךְ 'in the midst of'; 11.3.1).[4]

The second feature of this word class's complexity is the *diversity* of structures associated with simple prepositions:

1. Cə, the prefixed (or monographic) prepositions בְּ, כְּ, לְ; these are written as prefixes to nouns they modify.
2. CVC, the proclitic prepositions מִן־, אֶל־, עַל־, עַד־; these are often joined to nouns they modify with a *maqqeph*.
3. CVC < CVyC, בֵּין.
4. CVCVC < CVCC, e.g., תַּחַת, אֵצֶל.
5. Other, e.g., אַחֲרֵי.

The third feature of complexity is the use of *variant forms*, especially with suffixed pronouns. Prepositions that are derived from geminates show the expected doubling with a suffix (עִם but עִמִּי, אֵת but אִתִּי), and those which are in some way related to plural nouns take plural endings (אֶל־ but אֵלַי; cf. masculine עַד, עַל, תַּחַת, אַחֲרֵי; masculine בֵּינֵי or feminine בֵּינוֹת with plural suffixes). There is a further class of variant forms, an unpredictable group. The variants may be associated with enclitic *mem* (9.8), but the pattern of *use* of variants remains unexplained aside from the fact that the variants are mostly used in poetry, which is often archaic.[5]

regular form	variant form	variant used alone	variant used with suffix	variant with suffix	regular form with suffix
בְּ	בְּמוֹ	yes	no	—	בָּנוּ, etc.
כְּ	כְּמוֹ	yes	yes	כָּמֹוהוּ 'like him'	כָּהֶם, etc.
לְ	לְמוֹ	yes	yes	לָמוֹ 'to him, them'	לוֹ, לָהֶם, etc.
מִן	(מִמֵּי?)	no	yes	מִמֶּנּוּ 'from him, us'	מֵהֶם, etc.
	מִנִּי	yes	no	—	

Even the regularities in this table are misleading: long variants of כ and מִן are regularly used with suffixes, but the long form of ל is found only in לָמוֹ, which is, however, used in

4. There are few compound prepositions in Ugaritic (cf. Pardee, *UF* 8: 293, 306), and few complex prepositions (e.g., *bd/byd* 'through'; Pardee, *UF* 8: 293, 300–301, 306).

5. Ugaritic also has the long variant forms *bm*, *km*, and *lm*; see *UT* § 10.2; Pardee, *UF* 8: 288, 306.

two distinct senses, 'to him' (as if *ləmô* + pronoun *-ô*) and 'to them' (as if *lə* + pronoun *-hem/-am*). The variant long form is used independently only in Job (four times).

11.1.3   "Semantic" Perspective

a   In the two perspectives on prepositions we have described, the words are seen, on the one hand, as essentially nouns in adverbial accusative roles and, on the other hand, as morphologically diverse particles. On a third perspective it is the *semantics* of prepositions that is emphasized. What is the *meaning* of the relation between the noun that the preposition governs and the clause in which the prepositional phrase occurs?[6] The relation proceeds in two directions; consider this clause:

סָמַךְ מֶלֶךְ־בָּבֶל אֶל־יְרוּשָׁלִַם
בְּעֶצֶם הַיּוֹם הַזֶּה:

The king of Babylon leans on Jerusalem on that day.
Ezek 24:2

To describe the prepositions' meanings, two subordinate sets of relations must be noted: (1a) *ʾl* + its object (a place) and (1b) *b* + its object (a time), as well as (2a) *smk ʾl*[7] and (2b) *smk b*. Unfortunately, greater attention has sometimes been paid to the first set of relations than to the second. For some prepositions the first set of relations may be more important, but that is hardly the case for all. The tendency to focus on the preposition only in relation to its object has been exacerbated by recent misuse of comparative data, especially from Ugaritic. Despite the fact that patterns of *verb + preposition + object* are not as fully attested in Hebrew as we might like, prepositions are not to be dealt with as philological "wild cards."[8] It is "the task of a dictionary to set out their often very complex usage patterns, above all in connection with certain verbs,"[9] but it remains the work of a grammar to provide a framework within which a dictionary can properly be used.

b   The bulk of this chapter is concerned with such a framework for the most important simple prepositions (11.2). After a discussion of compound and complex prepositions (11.3), some syntactic features of prepositions are presented (11.4).

11.2   Semantics of Simple Prepositions

a   Prepositions are terms of *relation*, and their great interest is the remarkable economy with which they signify many different *relations*. The number of *types* of relation is

---

6. A related question is the degree to which the preposition is necessary; see 11.4.1. There are certainly cases where the variation between use and non-use of a preposition is stylistic; the addition of a preposition may serve, for example, to smooth out an otherwise harsh and lapidary style.

7. The idiom may be *smk yādô ʾl*.

8. In the phrase of Jared J. Jackson, quoted by Pardee, *UF* 7: 334. Notably misleading in this respect are *UT* § 10.1 and various works by Mitchell Dahood and some of his students; see rather Pardee (particularly on perspective, *UF* 7: 334, 335, 337, 338; 8: 275–85) and Peter Craigie, *Psalms 1–50* (Word Biblical Commentary; Waco, Texas: Word, 1983); R. Meyer, "Gegensinn und Mehrdeutigkeit in der althebräischen Wort- und Begriffsbildung," *Ugarit-Forschungen* 11 (1979) 601–12; Y. Thorion, "The Use of Prepositions in 1 Q Serek," *Revue de Qumran* 10 (1981) 405–33.

9. So von Soden, *Grundriss der akkadischen Grammatik*, § 114b / p. 164.

quite large, though relations of *place* and *time* are of greatest importance, and the schemes of locational and temporal relations are the best developed. Other important relation types frequently signaled by prepositions include *origin, instrument, agent, interest, cause,* and *goal.*

Even an examination of the interrelations of only the spatial uses of Hebrew prepo- b
sitions reveals the complexity of the system, the gaps and overlaps in the lexicon, and the various ways the relational terms are mapped onto the world. The spatial senses of the prepositions can refer either to position or movement. If we mark with arrows prepositions that chiefly describe movement and leave the others unmarked, we can map many of the spatial prepositions onto a simple diagram.[10]

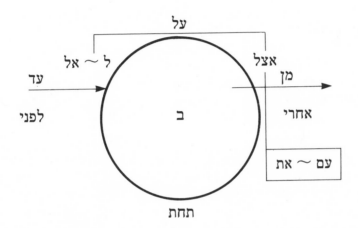

The spatial sense or reference of a given preposition is not an absolute value, how- c
ever; it is always governed by the verb (or predicate) of the clause and, more broadly, by the perspective from which an action is viewed.[11] Dennis G. Pardee illustrates the point:

'He took it from the table' = [in French] *il l'a pris sur la table.* . . . Are we to assume that *sur* in French is ambiguous, meaning both 'on' and 'from'? Such a claim is hardly viable, and no native speaker would accept the general interchangeability of *sur* with *de* [as in *de Paris* 'from Paris'] or *depuis* [as in *depuis le matin* 'from morning on, since morning']. The explanation lies in the perspective of the speaker: English expresses the separation caused by the act through the use of the preposition 'from', while French looks at the position of the object before the action took place.[12]

Similarly in Akkadian the preposition *ina* usually has the sense 'in,' but in the clause *ina našpakim ilteqe* 'he took (it) *from* the granary,' it has an ablative sense.[13]

---

10. Cf. Pardee, *UF* 8: 319, cf. 275–79.

11. On this point generally, originally made in the context of contemporary study by (among others) Edmund Sutcliffe and L. F. Hartman (Pardee, *UF* 7: 334–35), see Pardee, *UF* 8: 280–85.

12. Pardee, *UF* 8: 282, cf. 7: 335. The same point is made with regard to a cognate language by P. Swiggers, "Phoenician *b* 'from'?" *Aula Orientalis* 5 (1987) 152–54.

13. See von Soden, *Grundriss der akkadischen Grammatik,* § 114c / p. 164, cf. § 114g / p. 166.

d   Most prepositions have a spatial sense, which it is convenient to take as basic. From this notion other senses, referring to temporal and logical relations, can be seen as having developed. The role of the spatial sense should be qualified: usage, not etymology, decides meaning. The prepositions have distinctive meanings; although their semantic fields overlap, no two exhibit complete interchangeability.[14] Nonetheless, because of the overlapping meanings, it is possible that sometimes the choice among essentially similar verb-preposition combinations was chiefly stylistic.

e   Ideally, the meanings of prepositions should be classified according to their idiomatic combinations with specific verbs in order to safeguard against unwarranted extensions of a preposition's meaning.[15] One must not assume that a Hebrew speaker would have categorized its meanings according to English equivalents. However, to a large degree the meaning of the preposition is consistent and capturable, even with the variations due to the meanings of the verbs used with it. A precise and exhaustive study of Hebrew verb-prepositions pairings belongs in a dictionary or advanced word book, as noted earlier; for the purposes of this grammar we give a basic overview of most of the simple prepositions and their meanings, without inventorying the verbs associated with each. The student should look on the glosses used in the following examples as guides and remain open to other possible interpretations of the verb-preposition combinations.

f   Of the fifteen simple prepositions discussed here, all but two (כְּ, יַ֫עַן) have a spatial sense. The spatial and temporal senses are usually noted first, and the other relevant relations thereafter.[16]

11.2.1   אַחַר ~ אַחֲרֵי

a   This preposition is used in two forms, one apparently singular, the other, with the ending -ê, apparently plural. The singular form is also used as an adverb, the plural as a substantive. The preposition has the locational sense 'after, behind' (# 1) and a metaphorical locational sense '(to walk) after' > '(to behave) like, after the manner of, according to the norm of' (# 2). The temporal sense is 'after, afterward' (## 3–4),[17] and the major logical sense refers to interest, advantage, or disadvantage ('after, for, against'; ## 5–6). There is a derived sense, arising from the basic geography of the body in

---

14. On overlap see Pardee, *UF* 7: 336; 8: 285–86.

15. A. F. Rainey notes that the superficial resemblance between *lmlk* on standard measures and weights and on private stamp-seals "can be most deceptive when their respective semantic contexts are ignored"; "Private Seal-Impressions: A Note on Semantics," *Israel Exploration Journal* 16 (1966) 187–90, at 187.

16. The prepositions treated here may be listed in order of frequency; the counts (from SA/THAT and the dictionaries, cf. *LHS* 376) include the non-prepositional uses where relevant.

(1) *l*   ca. 20,700   (2) *b*   ca. 15,500
(3) *mn*   ca. 7,430   (10) *ʾhry/ʾhr*   617
(4) *ʿl*   ca. 5,700   (11) *tht*   505
(5) *ʾl*   ca. 5,500   (12) *byn*   408
(6) *k*   ca. 3,030   (13) *bʿd*   101
(7) *ʿd*   1,263   (14) *yʿn*   96
(8) *ʿm*   1,093   (15) *ʾṣl*   61
(9) *ʾt*   ca. 900

Other important elements related to the prepositional system include *tāwek* 418, *sābîb* 336, *qéreb* 227, *néged* 151, and *lipnê* ca. 1,000 (the last statistic is from *LHS*).

17. Pardee argues that the sense is 'immediately after'; *UF* 8: 252.

Hebrew: just as the 'right' side (יָמִין) of the body is 'south' (יָמִין), so the 'behind' side (אַחַר) is the far side or 'west' (# 7).[18]

1.	הִנֵּה־זֶה עוֹמֵד אַחַר כָּתְלֵנוּ	There he stands *behind* our wall. Cant 2:9
2.	וַיֵּלֶךְ אַחַר חַטֹּאת יָרָבְעָם	He went *after* (or, walked *in the manner of*) the sins of Jeroboam. 2 Kgs 13:2
3.	אַחַר הַדְּבָרִים הָאֵלֶּה	*after* these things Gen 15:1
4.	אַחֲרֵי הִפָּרֶד־לוֹט מֵעִמּוֹ	*after* Lot's departing from him Gen 13:14
5.	וְאַחַר כָּל־יָרוֹק יִדְרוֹשׁ׃	And *after* every green thing he searches. Job 39:8
6.	אַחֲרֶיךָ רֹאשׁ הֵנִיעָה	She (Daughter Jerusalem) wags (her) head *at* you. 2 Kgs 19:21
7.	וַיִּנְהַג אֶת־הַצֹּאן אַחַר הַמִּדְבָּר	He drove the flock to the *west* (or, *far*) *side* of the steppe. Exod 3:1

אֶל   11.2.2

The *maqqeph* is almost invariably present with this preposition. There is a long   a
form אֱלֵי־, and it is from this that suffixed forms appear to derive: אֵלַי, אֵלֵינוּ, etc. The contingent locative sense ('at, by, near'; # 1) is less important than the senses involving movement; ᵓl marks a direction ('toward'; ## 2–3),[19] a goal or termination ('into'; # 4), or a limit or degree ('as far as, up to'; # 5, metaphorical). One group of logical senses is "datival" (cf. 11.2.10d): ᵓl marks a simple dative ('to' the recipient of a gift or an address; ## 6–7), an ethical dative of interest, advantage, or disadvantage ('for, against'; ## 8–11), and a normative dative ('in accord with'; # 12). Another group is comitative, the senses of accompaniment ('with'; # 13) and addition ('in addition to'; # 14); the personal comitative prepositions ('with someone') are אֵת and עִם. The preposition ᵓl can also be used with a specification ('concerning'; # 15).

1.	וַיִּמְצְאוּ אֹתוֹ אֶל־מַיִם רַבִּים	They found him *by* the great waters. Jer 41:12

---

18. See also Judg 18:12.

19. Note the complexity of this clause: *wkl-hᵓrṣ bᵓw mṣrymh lšbr ᵓl-ywsp*, 'The whole land came to Joseph, to (*or* in *or* at) Egypt, to buy (grain)' (Gen 41:57; cf. Pardee,

UF 7: 334 n. 24). In Gen 42:28 the clause *wyḥrdw ᵓyš ᵓl-ᵓḥyw* means not 'Each trembled in relation to his brother,' but rather 'Each went trembling to his brother'; the verb of motion is implicit or elided (cf. 11.4.3d).

2. וַתָּשָׁב אֵלָיו אֶל־הַתֵּבָה

And it returned *to* him, *to* the ark.
Gen 8:9

3. לִהְיוֹת עֵינֶךָ פְתֻחוֹת אֶל־הַבַּיִת הַזֶּה

that your eyes may be open *toward* this temple
1 Kgs 8:29

4. בֹּא . . . אֶל־הַתֵּבָה

Go . . . *into* the ark.
Gen 7:1

5. כִּי־נָגַע אֶל־הַשָּׁמַיִם מִשְׁפָּטָהּ

Its judgment reaches *up to* the skies.
Jer 51:9

6. וְנָתַן אֵלֶיךָ אוֹת אוֹ מוֹפֵת:

And he gives (*to*) you a sign or a wonder.
Deut 13:2

7. וַיִּקְרָא אֶל־עֲבָדָיו וַיֹּאמֶר אֲלֵיהֶם

And he called (*to*) his servants and he said *to* them. . . .
2 Kgs 6:11

8. וַיֵּלֶךְ אֶל־נַפְשׁוֹ

And he fled *for* his life.
1 Kgs 19:3

9. כִּי הִנְנִי אֲלֵיכֶם וּפָנִיתִי אֲלֵיכֶם

I am *concerned for* you and will turn *to* you [with favor].
Ezek 36:9

10. אֵין נַפְשִׁי אֶל־הָעָם הַזֶּה

I have no heart *for* this people.
Jer 15:1

11. לִסְפּוֹת עוֹד עַל חֲרוֹן אַף־יהוה אֶל־יִשְׂרָאֵל:

further adding to Yʜwʜ's anger *against* Israel
Num 32:14

12. אֶל־פִּי יהוה לִיהוֹשֻׁעַ

according to the word of Yʜwʜ to Joshua
Josh 15:13

13. וְלֹא־תֶחֶטְאוּ לַיהוה לֶאֱכֹל אֶל־הַדָּם

Do not sin against Yʜwʜ by eating [meat] *with* the blood.
1 Sam 14:34

14. הוֹסַפְתָּ חָכְמָה וָטוֹב אֶל־הַשְּׁמוּעָה אֲשֶׁר שָׁמָעְתִּי:

You added wisdom-and-wealth *in addition to* the report I had heard (i.e., You are wiser and wealthier *than* I had heard).
1 Kgs 10:7

15. וַיִּנָּחֶם יהוה אֶל־הָרָעָה

Yʜwʜ was grieved *concerning* the calamity.
2 Sam 24:16

11.2.3   אֵצֶל

a   This preposition has the locational sense 'beside, next to' (## 1–2).[20]

1. וְהַתּוֹקֵעַ בַּשּׁוֹפָר אֶצְלִי:

And the person who blew the trumpet is *beside* me.
Neh 4:12

---

20. In Mishnaic Hebrew, *ʾṣl* partly replaces *ʾl*; see Segal, *Mishnaic Hebrew*, 142.

| 2. | וְלֹא־שָׁמַע אֵלֶיהָ לִשְׁכַּב אֶצְלָה | And he refused to lie (lit., he did not listen to her about lying) *beside* her.
Gen 39:10 |

אֵת   **11.2.4**

The base of this preposition in suffixed forms is *ʾitt-* (e.g., אִתִּי, אִתָּנוּ), and thus it **a**
contrasts with the base of the particle אֵת, which has the forms *ʾōt-* (e.g., אֹתִי, אֹתָנוּ) and *ʾet-* (e.g., אֶתְכֶם; see 10.3). The basic sense is comitative ('with'); it may mark accompaniment (companionship, fellowship; # 1), interest (accompaniment, literal or metaphorical, for the purpose of helping; ## 2–4), or the complement of verbs of dealing, speaking, and making (## 5–7).[21] The object of *ʾt* may also be an addition ('beside, alongside of, in addition to'; # 8). The preposition has a spatial sense closely related to this last ('near'; # 9); compare English 'alongside of,' as in 'There is a temple alongside of the palace' and 'There is a priesthood alongside of the monarchy.' The possessive can be marked with *ʾt* ('have'; # 10).

1.	וְאַתָּה וּבָנֶיךָ אִתָּךְ	you and your children *with* you Num 18:2
2.	מִי אִתִּי מִי	Who is *on my side*? Who? 2 Kgs 9:32
3.	וַיהוה אִתָּנוּ	Yʜwʜ is *on our side*. Num 14:9
4.	קָנִיתִי אִישׁ אֶת־יְהוָה׃	I have gotten a man *with the help of* Yʜwʜ. Gen 4:1
5.	וַאֲנִי הִנְנִי מֵקִים אֶת־בְּרִיתִי אִתְּכֶם	I am confirming my covenant *with* you. Gen 9:9
6.	דִּבֶּר . . . אִתָּנוּ קָשׁוֹת	He . . . spoke harshly *with* us. Gen 42:30
7.	יָאֵר פָּנָיו אִתָּנוּ	May he make his face shine *toward* us. Ps 67:2
8.	לֹא תַעֲשׂוּן אִתִּי	Do not make [any gods to set] *alongside of* me. Exod 20:23
9.	בְּצַעֲנַנִּים אֲשֶׁר אֶת־קֶדֶשׁ׃	in Zaanaim, which is *near* Qadesh[22] Judg 4:11
10.	מָה אִתָּנוּ׃	What *have* we (at hand)?[23] 1 Sam 9:7

21. Cf. also Deut 1:30 and Judg 11:27 for *ʿśy ʾt*. The accompaniment senses of *ʾt* and *ʿm* are extremely close; in Judg 7:4, we have *yēlēk ʾittāk* (twice) and *lōʾ-yēlēk ʿimmāk*.
22. Cf. 1 Kgs 9:26.
23. Cf. Gen 27:15.

11.2.5   בְּ

a   This preposition, the second most common in Hebrew, occurs both in the simple form בְּ and in the extended form בְּמוֹ; the latter does not take suffixes. The diversity of the senses of ב is remarkable.

b   *Spatial* senses are basic. The preposition *b* marks location *in* or *at* a point (# 1), *on* a surface (# 2), *within* an area (# 3), and *amid* a domain (# 4). It marks, with verbs of movement, both goals ('in, into'; # 5) and areas moved *through* (# 6).

1.	וַיֶּאֱהַב אִשָּׁה בְּנַחַל שֹׂרֵק	He loved a woman *in* Nahal Soreq. Judg 16:4
2.	וַיִּזְבַּח יַעֲקֹב זֶבַח בָּהָר	Jacob made a sacrifice *on* the mountain. Gen 31:54
3.	וְאָכַלְתָּ בָשָׂר . . . בְּכָל־שְׁעָרֶיךָ	You shall eat the meat . . . *within* all your gates.[24] Deut 12:15
4.	אוֹדְךָ בָעַמִּים	I will chant you *among* the nations. Ps 57:10
5.	הַבָּאִים אַחֲרֵיהֶם בַּיָּם	those who went after them *into* the sea Exod 14:28
6.	מִי־הָאִישׁ הַלָּזֶה הַהֹלֵךְ בַּשָּׂדֶה לִקְרָאתֵנוּ	Who is that man coming *through* the field to meet us?[25] Gen 24:65

c   Used *temporally*, *b* may mark an actual time *in*, *at*, or *when* (## 7–9). It may also mark an action simultaneous to that of the main verb; the simultaneous action is shown by an infinitive (36.2.2b) in a circumstantial clause.[26]

7.	בְּכָל־עֵת אֹהֵב הָרֵעַ	A friend is one who loves *at* all times. Prov 17:17
8.	בְּדוֹר אַחֵר יִמַּח שְׁמָם:	*In* (the time of) a future generation may their name be effaced. Ps 109:13
9.	עֶזְרָה בְצָרוֹת נִמְצָא מְאֹד:	What a help he has been *in* (time of) trouble! Ps 46:2

d   A variety of *circumstances* may be marked with *b*, both physical (*beth comitantiæ*; ## 10–12) and mental (## 13–14); such phrases are often to be rendered in English with

---

24. The sense involves the "ideas" of moving to a place and acting in it; see GKC § 119g / p. 379 and cf. German *Ich bin zu Hause*, 'I am at home,' or dialectal American English 'She's not to home.' See further 11.4.3. On *byt* for *bbyt* see 10.2.2 n. 14, and Pardee, *UF* 8: 238, 294.

25. See Pardee, *UF* 9: 210.

26. For the rendering of temporal expressions using *beth* in the LXX, see the review of Ilmari Soisalon-Soininen, "Die Wiedergabe einigen hebräischer, mit der Präpositionen *be* ausgedruckter Zeitangaben in der Septuaginta," *Annual of the Swedish Theological Institute* 11 (1977/78) 138–46.

an adverb. Both instruments (non-animates; ## 15–16)[27] and agents (animates), simple (# 17; note the *Niphal*) and adversative (# 18), take *b*. The preposition can govern the material with which an act is performed (# 19) and the price (*beth pretii*) paid (# 20) or exchanged (# 21).[28] This last use may reflect the idiom *ntn b* 'to effect an exchange by means of.'[29]

10.	וַתָּבֹא יְרוּשָׁלַיְמָה בְּחַיִל כָּבֵד מְאֹד	She entered Jerusalem *with* a very great caravan. 1 Kgs 10:2
11.	נָתַן בְּקוֹלוֹ	He thundered (lit., he gave [out] *with* his voice). Ps 46:7
12.	בֹּכִים בְּקוֹל גָּדוֹל	weeping aloud (lit., weeping *in* a loud voice) Ezra 3:12
13.	וּשְׁאַבְתֶּם־מַיִם בְּשָׂשׂוֹן	You shall draw water joyfully (lit., *in* joy). Isa 12:3
14.	בִּבְכִי יָבֹאוּ וּבְתַחֲנוּנִים אוֹבִילֵם	*With* weeping will they come, and *in* prayer I will bring them back. Jer 31:9
15.	בַּשֵּׁבֶט יַכּוּ	They smite *with* the rod. Mic 4:14
16.	וַתִּבָּקַע הָאָרֶץ בְּקוֹלָם:	The earth was shaken *by* the sound of them. 1 Kgs 1:40
17.	שֹׁפֵךְ דַּם הָאָדָם בָּאָדָם דָּמוֹ יִשָּׁפֵךְ	Whoever sheds a human's blood, *by* a human shall his blood be shed. Gen 9:6
18.	יָדוֹ בַכֹּל וְיַד כֹּל בּוֹ	His hand (will be) *against* all and everyone's hand *against* him. Gen 16:12
19.	וַיְצַף אֶת־קַרְקַע הַבַּיִת בְּצַלְעוֹת בְּרוֹשִׁים:	He overlaid the floor of the temple *with* boards of cypress.[30] 1 Kgs 6:15
20.	וַתַּעֲלֶה וַתֵּצֵא מֶרְכָּבָה . . . בְּשֵׁשׁ מֵאוֹת כֶּסֶף	A chariot was imported (lit., went up and out) . . . *for* six hundred (sheqels of) silver. 1 Kgs 10:29
21.	הֲדַם הָאֲנָשִׁים הַהֹלְכִים בְּנַפְשׁוֹתָם	Isn't (this) the blood of men who went *at the risk* of their lives? 2 Sam 23:17

27. In Qoh 9:12 *bph* 'in a snare' can be considered either instrument or location.

28. In a negative clause, *beth pretii* used metaphorically can take on quite a different sense: 'How long will they not believe me *bkl h'twt 'šr 'śyty bqrbw* in spite of all the signs which I have performed among them?' (Num 14:11).

On *beth pretii* see Pardee, *UF* 8: 299–300.

29. So Pardee, *UF* 8: 298.

30. The verb *spy* usually governs a double accusative, the second being an accusative of material used in covering (10.2.3c); cf. Pardee, *UF* 9: 225.

e   Other *circumstantial* uses of *b* are common, too. The *beth* of specification serves to qualify the realm with regard to which the verbal action obtains (## 22–24).[31] There are two closely related types: the *beth* of norm ('in the manner of'; # 25) and the estimative *beth*, specifying the range against which an opinion is held (cf. English 'The best little boy *of* all'; # 26).[32] The *beth* of identity (*beth essentiæ*) marks the capacity in which an actor behaves ('as, serving as, in the capacity of'; ## 27–28).[33] Causal *beth* marks the reason or originating force of an action (# 29); it is sometimes hard to distinguish from simple circumstantial uses.[34]

22.   עַל־אַחַת מִכֹּל אֲשֶׁר־יַעֲשֶׂה
      הָאָדָם לַחֲטֹא בָהֵנָּה׃
      in any one of all the things a person might sin (lit., do for sinning) *with regard to* these actions
      Lev 5:22

23.   וְשָׂמַחְתָּ בְכָל־הַטּוֹב
      You shall rejoice *in* all the good. . . .
      Deut 26:11

24.   וַיִּגְוַע כָּל־בָּשָׂר . . . בָּעוֹף
      וּבַבְּהֵמָה וּבַחַיָּה וּבְכָל־הַשֶּׁרֶץ
      All flesh expired . . . *that is*, birds and cattle and beasts and all swarmers.
      Gen 7:21

25.   עַל־כֵּן אֶבְכֶּה בִּבְכִי יַעְזֵר
      Thus I weep *like* Jazer (lit., *in* the weeping of Jazer).
      Isa 16:9

26.   אָרוּם בַּגּוֹיִם
      אָרוּם בָּאָרֶץ׃
      I am exalted *among* the nations,
      I am exalted *in* the earth.
      Ps 46:11

27.   וָאֵרָא אֶל־אַבְרָהָם . . . בְּאֵל
      שַׁדָּי
      I appeared to Abraham . . . *as* El Shaddai.
      Exod 6:3

28.   יהוה לִי בְּעֹזְרָי
      YHWH is with me, (*serving as*) my Helper.
      Ps 118:7

29.   הֲתַשְׁחִית בַּחֲמִשָּׁה אֶת־כָּל־
      הָעִיר
      Will you destroy the whole city *because/on account of* five?
      Gen 18:28

f   A group of more strictly grammatical relations remain. In noun phrases, *b* can mark a distributive (# 30) or a partitive (# 31).[35] The preposition *b* marks the object of a

---

31. The *beth* of specification is used in headings and the like to indicate the topic of a section; see D. W. Baker, "Leviticus 1–7 and the Punic Tariffs," *Zeitschrift für die Alttestamentliche Wissenschaft* 99 (1987) 188–97, esp. 190–91, with references.

32. Cf. *hyph bnšym* 'most beautiful among women,' Cant 1:8; cf. Pardee, *UF* 9: 227. The term "estimative" can also refer to the quality esteemed (e.g., 'innocent' in 'He judged her innocent').

33. Cyrus Gordon, "'In' of Predication or Equivalence," *Journal of Biblical Literature* 100 (1981) 612–13, calls this the *beth* of equivalence and finds the same use with Greek *en* (cf. John 14:10, 17:21); he cites parallels from Arabic (cf. *bi-ʾabi ʾanta wa-ʾummi*, 'you are as my father and mother') and Egyptian.

34. Cf. Pardee, *UF* 8: 312. English 'as' is notoriously difficult in a similar respect.

35. The *b* in 2 Sam 6:6 may be partitive: *wyʾḥz bw* 'and he grabbed *part of* it; in 1 Chr 13:9 we read *wyšlḥ ʿzh ʾt-ydw lʾḥz ʾt-hʾrwn*, 'Uzza extended his hand to grab the ark,' viz., to take hold of it. It is not clear to what extent the versions contrast.

variety of verbs (see 10.2.1); these include verbs of extending, touching; fastening (*on*; # 32), striking (*at*), reaching (*to*), filling (*with*); of exercising authority *over* (# 33); of sense perception (especially seeing; # 34) and of emotion (notably trust; # 35); and of speaking (# 36).

30.	יוֹם בְּיוֹם	day *by* day 2 Chr 30:21
31.	וּבַל־אֶלְחַם בְּמַנְעַמֵּיהֶם׃	And let me not eat (*some*) *of* their dainties.[36] Ps 141:4
32.	וְיָד אַל־תִּשְׁלְחוּ־בוֹ	But you shall not lay a hand *on* him. Gen 37:22
33.	מָשׁוֹל תִּמְשֹׁל בָּנוּ	Will you indeed rule *over* us? Gen 37:8
34.	רָאוּ בַּאֲרוֹן יהוה	They looked *on* the ark of Yhwh. 1 Sam 6:19
35.	בְּךָ יַאֲמִינוּ	They will trust (*in*) you.[37] Exod 19:9
36.	וְדִבַּרְתָּ בָּם בְּשִׁבְתְּךָ בְּבֵיתֶךָ	And talk *about* them when you sit at home. . . . Deut 6:7

בֵּין   **11.2.6**

This preposition is at base a noun meaning 'interval, space between,' though only one   a
occurrence of the noun is certain. In the phrase אִישׁ־הַבֵּנַיִם 'man of the two intervals' (1 Sam 17:4, 23), the 'space between' is that between the two armies; thus the phrase means 'champion.' Singular and plural suffixed pronouns are attached to *bên* and *bênê-* respectively; plural suffixes of the first and third persons may also be attached to the less common *bênôt-*, yielding the forms *bênênû*/*bênôtênû* and *bênêhem* and *bênôtam*. The preposition is paired 126 times in the phrase *bên X ûbên Y* and 30 times in the phrase *bên X ləY*.[38] It has either an inclusive sense (i.e., between or among a quantity of things considered as a group) or an exclusive sense (i.e., between or among two or more diverse things considered as over against one another).

As a one-term expression it has an *inclusive* sense either spatially (simple locative   b
'between,' # 1; manifold locative 'among, amid, within,' ## 2–3) or temporally (# 4). An exceptional distributive sense appears in one late text (# 5).

---

36. See Pardee, *UF* 9: 216.

37. For *b* with psychological predicates that seem to involve the internal organs, see Pardee on Ugaritic *bky bm lb*, which he argues means 'to cry in (*not* from) the heart'; *UF* 8: 217–18. On the question of where tears come from see Terence Collins, "The Physiology of Tears in the Old Testament," *Catholic Biblical Quarterly* 33 (1971) 18–38, 185–97.

38. James Barr, "Some Notes on *Ben* 'Between' in Classical Hebrew," *Journal of Semitic Studies* 23 (1978) 1–24, at 3. Barr includes in his count the expression *bên . . . wə-lə* in Joel 2:17; *bên X wəY* is not a biblical usage. See also Y. Avishur, "Expressions of the Type *byn ydym* in the Bible and Semitic Languages," *Ugarit-Forschungen* 12 (1980) 125–33, on the inclusive use with body parts that occur in pairs.

1. אֲשֶׁר עָבַר בֵּין הַגְּזָרִים הָאֵלֶּה׃   which passed *between* those pieces[39]
   Gen 15:17

2. כִּי הוּא בֵּן אַחִים יַפְרִיא   He thrives *among* (his) brothers.[40]
   Hos 13:15

3. אֲרִי בֵּין הָרְחֹבוֹת׃   (There is) a lion *within* the streets!
   Prov 26:13

4. וְשָׁחֲטוּ אֹתוֹ . . . בֵּין הָעַרְבָּיִם׃   They shall slaughter it . . . *between* the two
   evenings.[41]
   Exod 12:6

5. וּבֵין עֲשֶׂרֶת יָמִים   *every* ten days
   Neh 5:18

c   The *exclusive* sense is expressed by paired phrases. The phrase *bên X ləY* marks the
expression both for *distinction* and for *classes*, except in certain late texts.[42] Not surprisingly it occurs at least twenty-four times in priestly and legal texts (## 6–8).[43]

6. וְהִבְדַּלְתֶּם בֵּין־הַבְּהֵמָה הַטְּהֹרָה   You will separate *between* the clean *and* the unclean
   לַטְּמֵאָה   animals.
   Lev 20:25

7. הַחֻקִּים . . . בֵּין אִישׁ לְאִשְׁתּוֹ   statutes valid . . . *between* a man *and* his wife
   Num 30:17

8. מִשְׁפָּט בֵּין־דָּם לְדָם   legal cases *between* blood *and* blood (i.e., *between*
   one kind of homicide *and* another)
   Deut 17:8

James Barr classifies the uses of the common, unmarked phrase *bên X ûbên Y* as follows: (1) between places named with toponyms (# 9) and other physical locations (# 10);
(2) motion, standing, or separation between persons and the like (# 11); (3) covenants
and oaths (# 12) and war and peace (# 13) between persons and the like; (4) judgments
(# 14); and (5) divisions (## 15–16). Only a few instances fall outside this scheme.[44]

9. בֵּין בֵּית־אֵל וּבֵין הָעָי׃   *between* Bethel *and* Ai
   Gen 13:3

10. וַיַּבְדֵּל בֵּין הַמַּיִם אֲשֶׁר מִתַּחַת   And he divided *between* the waters below the
    לָרָקִיעַ וּבֵין הַמַּיִם אֲשֶׁר מֵעַל   firmament *and* the waters above the firmament.
    לָרָקִיעַ   Gen 1:7

---

39. As Gen 15:10 makes clear, the account refers to two
parallel and opposing lines of sacrificial material.

40. The spelling *bn* is extremely rare.

41. The sense of the expression is unclear; the usual
explanation, based on the sense of *ʿrb* 'entering' (viz., setting, of the sun)' involves one 'entering' at sunset and
another at dark.

42. Barr, "*Ben*," 6. The form *byn X lY* is standard at
Qumran and in Mishnaic Hebrew; see E. Qimron, *The
Hebrew of the Dead Sea Scrolls* (Atlanta: Scholars Press,
1986) 83.

43. But note, e.g., 2 Sam 19:36 (in direct discourse and
perhaps thus dialectal).

44. Barr, "*Ben*," 4.

11.   וְשַׂמְתִּי פְדֻת בֵּין עַמִּי וּבֵין   I will put a distinction *between* my people *and* your
       עַמֶּךָ   people.
                                             Exod 8:19

12.   בְּרִית . . . בֵּין אָבִי וּבֵין אָבִיךָ   a treaty . . . *between* my father *and* your father
                                             1 Kgs 15:19

13.   וַיְהִי שָׁלוֹם בֵּין יִשְׂרָאֵל וּבֵין   And there was peace *between* Israel *and* the
       הָאֱמֹרִי: Amorites.
                                             1 Sam 7:14

14.   יִשְׁפֹּט יְהוה בֵּינִי וּבֵינֶךָ:   May Yʜᴡʜ judge *between* me *and* you.[45]
                                             Gen 16:5 *Sam*

15.   לְהַבְדִּיל בֵּין הַטָּמֵא וּבֵין הַטָּהֹר   distinguishing *between* the unclean *and* the clean
                                             Lev 11:47

16.   וְהֶעֱרִיךְ הַכֹּהֵן אֹתָהּ בֵּין טוֹב   The priest will evaluate it *for* good *and* bad.
       וּבֵין רָע   Lev 27:12

The common pairing, then, can also mark distinction between classes (cf. ## 15–16), as
can the *bên X ləY* pair; note especially ## 6 and 15.

The six suffixed *bênôt*- forms occur only as one-term expressions with, as expected,   d
an inclusive sense (## 17–18); the suffixed *bênê*- forms occur either in one-term phrases
or in paired phrases with definite objects (## 17, 19–20). The sense may be inclusive
(# 19) or exclusive (## 17, 20).[46]

17.   תְּהִי נָא אָלָה בֵּינוֹתֵינוּ בֵּינֵינוּ   There ought to be a sworn agreement *between*
       וּבֵינֶךָ   us—*between* us *and* you.
                                             Gen 26:28

18.   עַל־שְׁבֻעַת יְהוה אֲשֶׁר בֵּינֹתָם   because of the oath to Yʜᴡʜ *between* them, between
       בֵּין דָּוִד וּבֵין יְהוֹנָתָן   David and Jonathan.
                                             2 Sam 21:7

19.   הָיְתָה יְרוּשָׁלַיִם לְנִדָּה בֵּינֵיהֶם: Jerusalem has become an unclean thing *among*
                                             them.
                                             Lam 1:17

20.   וּגְבוּל נָתַן־יְהוה בֵּינֵנוּ   Yʜᴡʜ has made the Jordan a boundary . . . *between*
       וּבֵינֵיכֶם . . . אֶת־הַיַּרְדֵּן   us *and* you.
                                             Josh 22:25

בְּעַד   **11.2.7**

This preposition forms suffixed phrases with both apparently singular and plural   a
bases (e.g., בַּעֲדֵינוּ, בַּעֲדֵנוּ, בַּעֲדוֹ); the form בַּעֲדֵנִי is used alongside בַּעֲדִי. The *locational*

---

45. Read *bynk* with the Samaritan in preference to the   goes astray because he wrongly thinks that the unmarked
MT's *bynyk*.   member, *bênê*-, must be an exact or polar opposite of the
   46. Cf. Barr, "Ben," 15–22. Barr's argument, however,   marked member, *bênôt*- (contra 3.3.5).

sense can be simple ('behind'; # 1) or comprehensive, referring to wherever one turns one's back ('around, about'; # 2). With verbs of motion, b^cd means 'away from, with the back toward,' though English perspective usually demands 'through' or 'over' (# 3).[47] The preposition also designates interest or advantage, arising from the idea of protection *for* ('for the benefit/sake of'; # 4). This last sense rarely entails an exchanged commodity (# 5).

1.   וַיִּסְגְּרוּ בַּעֲדָם   And they shut (the door of the tower) *behind* them.
Judg 9:51

2.   הֲלֹא־אַתָּ שַׂכְתָּ בַעֲדוֹ   Have you not put a hedge *around* him?
Job 1:10

3.   וַתּוֹרִדֵם בַּחֶבֶל בְּעַד הַחַלּוֹן   She let them down by a rope *through* the window.
Josh 2:15

4.   וְיִתְפַּלֵּל בַּעַדְךָ   He will pray *for* you.
Gen 20:7

5.   עוֹר בְּעַד־עוֹר וְכֹל אֲשֶׁר לָאִישׁ יִתֵּן בְּעַד נַפְשׁוֹ:   Skin *for* skin! A person will give up everything *for* his life!
Job 2:4

11.2.8   יַעַן

a   This word is more often used as a conjunction than as a preposition. As a preposition with the sense 'because of,' it governs an infinitive construct (36.2.2b)[48] more often than another nominal form (# 1).

1.   יַעַן כָּל־תּוֹעֲבֹתָיִךְ:   *because of* all your abominable acts
Ezek 5:9

11.2.9   כְּ

a   This preposition is the only extremely common particle of relation that has no basic spatial or temporal sense; it describes comparison and correspondence ('like, as, just as'). In most cases כ is used in ways comparable to other prepositions, but it is distinctive in two of its syntactic features: its capacity to head a noun phrase (e.g., כְּפֶשַׂע '(a distance) like/the like of a footstep,' 1 Sam 20:3) and its ability to "absorb" other prepositions (e.g., כְּהַר 'as on the mountain,' Isa 28:21). It is because of these features that *k* is sometimes referred to as a substantive, 'the like of.' The variant form כְּמוֹ occurs alone and with suffixes, cf. כָּהֵנָה and כָּמוֹךְ. In combination with $^{\circ}šr$, *k* forms the most common temporal conjunction in Hebrew, כַּאֲשֶׁר.[49]

b   There are three facets to the basic use of כ. (1) The preposition may denote *agreement in quantity or measure*, as in 'Moses is *as* tall *as* Joshua' (# 1). Related to this is the use of the preposition before *approximations*, as in 'Moses is *about* that tall' (# 2).

---

47. See 2 Sam 20:21 for the sense 'over,' viz., a wall.
48. See, e.g., 1 Kgs 21:20.

49. Alone, *k* is used rarely as a conjunction; see, e.g., Gen 12:14; *k* in # 7 may better be taken as a conjunction.

(2) *Agreement in kind* is also marked with *k* (# 3), cf. 'Joshua is *like* Moses *as* a prophet.' In this English example, '*as* a prophet' specifies the point of comparison or *tertium quid*, the "third thing" in terms of which the likeness is proposed. The "third thing" need not be specified—it is often evident from the discourse; in poetry the point of comparison may be left vague in order to allow an analogy to open up, inducing the reader to engage the analogy and find not one but many contacts between the things compared.[50] *Agreement in manner or norm* (cf. 'Joshua is a prophet *in the manner of* Moses') is akin to agreement in kind (## 4–7). (3) The logical outcome of comparison is *correspondence* or identity, cf. 'Moses loves Joshua *as* (he does) himself.' The agreement of the things compared is complete, insofar as the discourse is concerned (*kaph veritatis*; # 8). Identity constructions formed with *k* often involve a double use of *k*: in discourse about X, we find either *kX kY* or, more often, *kY kX* (## 9–10); both are used in legal materials. The second of these patterns has come into English: 'Like father, like son.'

1. יהוה . . . יֹסֵף עֲלֵיכֶם כָּכֶם אֶלֶף פְּעָמִים — May Yhwh . . . make you a thousand times *as many as* you are. Deut 1:11

2. וַיֵּשְׁבוּ שָׁם כְּעֶשֶׂר שָׁנִים: — They lived there *about* ten years. Ruth 1:4

3. וִהְיִיתֶם כֵּאלֹהִים יֹדְעֵי טוֹב וָרָע: — You will be *like* divine beings (in being) knowers of good and evil.[51] Gen 3:5

4. נַעֲשֶׂה אָדָם בְּצַלְמֵנוּ כִּדְמוּתֵנוּ — Let us make *ʾādām* in our image *according to* our likeness. Gen 1:26

5. וְהִנֵּה הַמֶּלֶךְ עֹמֵד עַל־הָעַמּוּד כַּמִּשְׁפָּט — There was the king standing by the pillar, *as* the custom was. 2 Kgs 11:14

6. חָנֵּנִי אֱלֹהִים כְּחַסְדֶּךָ — Have mercy on me, God, *in accord with* your unfailing love. Ps 51:3

7. כְּהָנִיף שֵׁבֶט וְאֶת־מְרִימָיו — *like* a rod's wielding him who lifts it up Isa 10:15

8. כִּי־הוּא כְאִישׁ אֱמֶת — For he is *in every way* an honest guy.[52] Neh 7:2

50. Biblical similes and metaphors require both grammatical and theoretical restudy. The character of the problem is becoming more widely appreciated; see, e.g., Michael D. Goulder, *The Song of Fourteen Songs* (Sheffield: JSOT Press, 1986) 4–8, 71, and, on particular passages, e.g.,

32–34, 45. The preposition *k* also plays an important role in ancient exegesis; see M. Fishbane, *Biblical Interpretation in Ancient Israel* (Oxford: Clarendon, 1985) 352–53.

51. See also Gen 44:15.

52. Cf. Hos 5:10.

9.   כְּקוֹנֶה כַּמּוֹכֵר
      [Things will be *as* bad *for* . . . a master *as for* his manservant, *for* a mistress *as for* her maid,] *for* a debtor *as for* (his) creditor (*qwnh*).[53]
Isa 24:2

10.   מוֹת יוּמָת . . . כַּגֵּר כָּאֶזְרָח
      He shall be put to death . . . native *as well as* sojourner.[54]
Lev 24:16

c   Two phenomena related to these points deserve note. First, the use of *k* in making a comparison absorbs other prepositions, as noted above.[55] If we compare Y to X, we have X *kY*; remarkably enough, if the comparison involves *bY*, *ᶜl-Y*, *mn-Y*, etc., we also have simply *kY* (## 11–12). (The other relational term may be expressed, but that is less common.) Second, it is possible for the claim of identity to be vacuous, and *k* then serves as an *emphatic* particle (# 13); in practice it is difficult to be sure when *k* is strictly emphatic.

11.   וְרָעוּ כְבָשִׂים כְּדָבְרָם
      The sheep will graze *as in* their own pastures.
Isa 5:17

12.   שֵׁבֶט הַנֹּגֵשׂ בּוֹ הַחִתֹּתָ כְּיוֹם מִדְיָן׃
      The rod of his oppressor you shattered *as on* the day of Midian['s defeat].[56]
Isa 9:3

13.   בִּהְיוֹתָם מְתֵי מִסְפָּר כִּמְעַט וְגָרִים בָּהּ׃
      When they were few, *indeed* sparse, and strangers there.[57]
Ps 105:12

d   The use of *k* as a quasi-nominal *phrasal head* (## 14–15) was cited earlier;[58] the English use of 'like' as a noun is comparable ('the like(s) of him'). This substantival *k* has something in common with the approximative use, since it tends to be vague; in rhetorical terms it serves as a "hedge," protecting the truth value of a statement from dismissal (cf. # 15). If in English we say, 'He was, like, a prophet,' we aim to protect the claim from misapplied definitions—if he was not precisely a prophet, then he was the like of a prophet.

14.   הֲנִהְיָה כַּדָּבָר הַגָּדוֹל הַזֶּה אוֹ הֲנִשְׁמַע כָּמֹהוּ׃
      Has there been *anything like* this great event? Has *anything like* it been heard of?
Deut 4:32

15.   וְהִנֵּה עֹמֵד לְנֶגְדִּי כְּמַרְאֵה־גָבֶר׃
      There was standing before me *something like* an appearance of a male.
Dan 8:15

---

53. There are six instances of the double *k* construction in Isa 24:2.

54. See Exod 12:48 and Lev 19:34 for related legal formulations.

55. See M. O'Connor, *Hebrew Verse Structure* (Winona Lake, Indiana: Eisenbrauns, 1980) 122, for a preliminary statement.

56. Cf. *kywm bywm* 'day by day' in 1 Sam 18:10.

57. Cf. Obad 11.

58. See also *khnh* in Gen 41:19.

The *temporal* use of *k* is related to its sense either as a marker of approximation   e
('about that time') or of correspondence ('at the (same) time'; # 16) and is found with the
infinitive construct (# 17; 36.2.2b).

16.   כָּעֵת מָחָר אֶשְׁלַח אֵלֶיךָ אִישׁ   *At* this time tomorrow I will send to you a (certain)
                                                 man. . . .
                                                 1 Sam 9:16

17.   וַיְהִי כְּבוֹא אַבְרָם מִצְרָיְמָה   It happened *when* Abram entered Egypt that the
        וַיִּרְאוּ הַמִּצְרִים   Egyptians saw that. . . .
                                                 Gen 12:14

לְ
                                                                                        11.2.10

This preposition, like the other monographic prepositions בְ and כְ, is used in a great   a
many ways (cf. 10.4). A variety of its senses are often rendered by English 'to' in its
diverse meanings. Since a number of the senses of *l* are represented by the dative case in
Latin or Greek or both, many grammars and dictionaries refer to, for example, the
lamed of the ethical dative; such terminology is only acceptable if it be remembered that
Hebrew (like English) has no distinct and interrelated set of dativial functions. The long
form of *l*, לָמוֹ, is used alone (but only in the Book of Job) and with third-person suffixes,
both singular and plural (viz., לָמוֹ for either לָהֶם or לוֹ). The negative particle לֹא may
very occasionally be written without the *aleph* and thus be confused with the preposition,
either in suffixed form or prefixed to another noun.[59] For *l* with the infinitive construct,
see 36.2.3.

The basic senses of *l* are spatial. The preposition may mark location *in* or *at* a point   b
(## 1–2). With verbs of motion *l* marks the object of the motion *toward* (allative; # 3)
and of motion *to* (terminative; # 4).[60] Some phrases with *l* are used as allative adverbials:
לְאָחוֹר 'backward,' לְמַעְלָה 'upward,' לְמִזְרָח 'eastward,' לְפָנִים 'forward.'

1.   וַתֵּשֶׁב לִימִינוֹ:   She sat *at* his right hand.
                                 1 Kgs 2:19

2.   לַפֶּתַח חַטָּאת רֹבֵץ   Sin is a *rōbēṣ at* the door.
                                  Gen 4:7

3.   אִישׁ לְדַרְכּוֹ פָּנִינוּ   We have turned, each (of us), *to* their own way.
                                      Isa 53:6

4.   כִּי הַיּוֹם בָּא לָעִיר   Today he came *to* the city.
                                    1 Sam 9:12

---

59. In 1 Sam 2:16, e.g., the MT has *lw* (*lô*) but the Qere is *lō᾽*, followed by the versions. For the opposite situation, see Ps 100:3.

60. On possible occurrences of *yṣ᾽ l* 'to go out from,' see Pardee, *UF* 8: 237. Note also the metaphorical terminative usage of *l* in Gen 31:30. The preposition *l* is common in nominal clauses and phrases in Inscriptional Hebrew, where it probably designates the recipient of goods; see Pardee, *UF* 7: 336–37 (and references to the extensive and convoluted debate), 8: 301–2.

The *temporal* uses of *l* include a sense like the simple locational (*in, at,* or *during* a period of time; ## 5–7)[61] and a sense like the terminative (*to, by, until,* or *after* a period of time, ## 8–11). The preposition is also used with temporal distributives (*per* or *by* a period of time; # 12; cf. 7.2.3b).[62]

5.	מִתְהַלֵּךְ בַּגָּן לְרוּחַ הַיּוֹם	walking in the garden *at* (*the time of*) the cool (lit., breeze) of the day Gen 3:8
6.	וַתָּבֹא . . . הַיּוֹנָה לְעֵת עֶרֶב	The dove came . . . *at the time of* evening. Gen 8:11
7.	לְיָמִים עוֹד שִׁבְעָה אָנֹכִי מַמְטִיר	*For* seven more days I will cause it to rain. Gen 7:4
8.	וֶהְיֵה נָכוֹן לַבֹּקֶר	Be ready *by* morning. Exod 34:2
9.	לְאֶלֶף דּוֹר	*to/for/unto* a thousand generations Deut 7:9
10.	וַיְהִי לִשְׁנָתַיִם יָמִים	It happened *after* two years. . . . 2 Sam 13:23
11.	וְלֹא־יָלִין מִן־הַבָּשָׂר . . . לַבֹּקֶר:	None of the flesh . . . shall remain *until* morning. Deut 16:4
12.	וְאָנֹכִי אֶתֶּן־לְךָ עֲשֶׂרֶת כֶּסֶף לַיָּמִים	I will give you ten (sheqels) of silver *per* year.[63] Judg 17:10

d   Another set of relations denoted by *l* has a structure similar to the locational : allative spatial set. These relations are based on connections *with regard to*. The quasi-locational group includes possession (## 13–16),[64] authorship (*lamed auctoris*; # 17), specification (## 18–19),[65] manner (# 20; the sense is often best rendered with adverbs in English),[66] class and type (## 21–22),[67] and comparison (# 23). The quasi-allative relations involve the *goal* of an action and are largely of the type sometimes called *datival*. The so-called indirect object of verbs of giving and some verbs of speaking and listening takes *l* (## 24–27).

---

61. For an example with *ywm* see Isa 10:3. Ugaritic *l ym hnd* 'from this day on' is a calque on Akkadian *ištu ūmi annî* 'from this day on' and therefore not evidence of proper Ugaritic usage; so Pardee, *UF* 8: 243. For *l* in the temporal sense 'since,' see perhaps *yhwh lmbwl yšb* 'YHWH has sat (enthroned) since(?) *or* since before(?) the Flood' (Ps 29:10), but the passage is difficult.

62. Cf. also Job 7:18.

63. See Pardee, *UF* 9: 215.

64. See Pardee, *UF* 8: 226. The *lamed* of concern is similar, e.g., *wʾnky lʾ-hyh lkm*, 'I am not concerned with you'

(Hos 1:9); cf. John 2:4 and R. E. Brown, *The Gospel According to John (i–xii)* (Anchor Bible 29; Garden City, New York: Doubleday, 1966) 99.

65. Cf. the accusative of specification (10.2.2e). The *lamed* of specification is used in labels and inscriptions (Isa 8:1, Ezek 37:16—so perhaps not 'for, belonging to'). Sometimes a prepositional phrase of specification is almost causal, e.g., Gen 4:23.

66. Cf. such phrases as *lārōb* 'abundantly' and *lāṭōhar* 'clearly.'

67. Cf. Gen 13:17.

13.	כַּסְפְּךָ וּזְהָבְךָ לִי־הוּא	Your silver and your gold are mine (lit., *to* me). 1 Kgs 20:3
14.	דּוֹדִי לִי וַאֲנִי לוֹ	My beloved is mine and I am his.[68] Cant 2:16
15.	רָאִיתִי בֵּן לְיִשַׁי	I have seen a son *of* Jesse.[69] 1 Sam 16:18
16.	הַמֵּת לְיָרָבְעָם בָּעִיר	anyone *belonging to* Jeroboam who dies in the city 1 Kgs 14:11
17.	לְעֶבֶד יהוה לְדָוִד אֲשֶׁר דִּבֶּר	[A psalm] *by* David, the servant of Yʜwʜ, which he spoke. . . .[70] Ps 18:1
18.	וּלְיִשְׁמָעֵאל שְׁמַעְתִּיךָ	*With regard to* Ishmael, I have heard (what) you (said). Gen 17:20
19.	לֹא־רָאִיתִי כָהֵנָּה . . . לָרֹעַ׃	I haven't seen anything like them . . . *for* ugliness. Gen 41:19
20.	וַיֵּשֶׁב יְהוּדָה וְיִשְׂרָאֵל לָבֶטַח	Judah and Israel dwelt secure*ly*. 1 Kgs 5:5
21.	הִתְיַצְּבוּ . . . לְשִׁבְטֵיכֶם	Present yourselves . . . *according to* your tribes. 1 Sam 10:19
22.	עֵץ פְּרִי עֹשֶׂה פְּרִי לְמִינוֹ	fruit trees (each) producing fruit *according to* its type Gen 1:11
23.	עַד אֲשֶׁר־דַּק לְעָפָר	until it was as fine *as* dust Deut 9:21
24.	תִּתֵּן־לוֹ׃	You shall give *to* him. Deut 15:14
25.	וַיִּקְרָא פַרְעֹה לְאַבְרָם	Pharaoh summoned (lit., called *to*) Abram.[71] Gen 12:18
26.	בָּרוּךְ הוּא לַיהוה	May he be pronounced blessed *to* Yʜwʜ.[72] Ruth 2:20
27.	כִּי שָׁמַעְתָּ לְקוֹל אִשְׁתֶּךָ	Because you listened *to* (or, heeded) the voice of your wife. . . . Gen 3:17

The *lamed* of interest or (dis)advantage (*dativus commodi et incommodi*) marks the person for or against whom an action is directed (## 28–33); the term "benefactive dative" is sometimes used of this *l*.

---

68. See also Cant 6:3.
69. See further below on the indefiniteness of this phrase.
70. This usage is most common in the Psalter, but cf.

also Hab 3:1.
71. Note also the pseudo-passive in 2 Sam 17:16: *whgydw ldwd* 'they told to David' > 'David was told.'
72. Not 'by.' See Pardee, *UF* 8: 221–23, cf. 230; 9: 209.

28. כִּי־נִכְסֹף נִכְסַפְתָּה לְבֵית אָבִיךָ
You long *for* your father's house.
Gen 31:30

29. אַל־תִּבְכּוּ לְמֵת
Do not weep *for* the dead (one).
Jer 22:10

30. וַיֵּהָפֵךְ לָהֶם לְאוֹיֵב
He became their enemy (lit., he turned *against* them to [become] an enemy).[73]
Isa 63:10

31. כִּי יוֹם לַיהוה צְבָאוֹת
There is a day [prepared] *for* YHWH of Hosts.
Isa 2:12

32. הֲלוֹא לָכֶם לָדַעַת אֶת־הַמִּשְׁפָּט׃
Isn't it *your affair* to know the customs?
Mic 3:1

33. לֹא־תַחְמֹד כֶּסֶף וְזָהָב עֲלֵיהֶם וְלָקַחְתָּ לָךְ
You shall not desire the silver and gold that is on them (abandoned idols) and you shall not take (the silver and the gold) *for* yourself.
Deut 7:25

A special variety of the *lamed* of interest is a use that some label *dativus ethicus* or "ethical dative."[74] T. Muraoka points out that this term means that a person other than the subject or object is concerned in the matter, but "the hallmark of the Semitic construction is the identity of grammatical person of the subject of the verb with that of the pronoun suffixed to the preposition."[75] Many scholars refer to this use as "reflexive": *l* marks the action as being of interest to the performer (# 32); the term "ingressive" is also used. Muraoka suggests the nomenclature "centripetal." He explains, "Basically it serves to convey the impression on the part of the speaker or author that the subject establishes his own identity, recovering or finding his own place by determinedly dissociating himself from his familiar surrounding."[76] Perhaps reflexive and centripetal notions should be separated; the former rendered by '-self,' and the latter, with its notions of isolation and seclusion and its use with imperatives and in negative contexts, left untranslated.[77] The centripetal use is found with verbs of motion (## 34–35) and in expressions denoting attitude of mind (## 36–37).

34. וּלְכוּ לָכֶם לְאָהֳלֵיכֶם
Get (you) to your tents.[78]
Josh 22:4

35. וְקוּם בְּרַח־לְךָ אֶל־לָבָן אָחִי
Go flee to my brother, Laban.
Gen 27:43

36. אַל־תִּבְטְחוּ לָכֶם אֶל־דִּבְרֵי הַשֶּׁקֶר
Do not trust in deceptive words.
Jer 7:4

---

73. See also Job 30:21. Cf. Pardee, *UF* 8: 228.
74. GKC § 119s / p. 381; for this treatment we follow T. Muraoka, "On the So-called *Dativus Ethicus* in Hebrew," *Journal of Theological Studies* 29 (1978) 495–98.
75. Muraoka, "*Dativus Ethicus*," 495.

76. Muraoka, "*Dativus Ethicus*," 497.
77. Cf. *LHS* 295.
78. The second *l* is terminative. Cf. Num 22:34; Deut 1:6–7, 5:27–28; 1 Sam 26:11–12; 2 Sam 2:22; Isa 2:22, 40:9; Hos 8:9; Cant 2:10, 13; 2 Chr 25:16.

37.	רַבַּת שָׁכְנָה־לָּהּ נַפְשִׁי עִם שׂוֹנֵא שָׁלוֹם:	Too long I have lived among those who hate peace.[79] Ps 120:6

The "indirect object" *lamed* marks the so-called datival goal, while another sort of goal is marked by the *lamed* of purpose. The goals here include a thing made (with ʿśy, ntn, śym, etc.; ## 38–41) or used (# 42), or a person altered in status or even form (## 43–45, cf. # 38).

38.	וְאֶעֶשְׂךָ לְגוֹי גָּדוֹל	I will make you (*into*) a great nation. Gen 12:2
39.	וְנָתַתִּי אֶת־יְרוּשָׁלַ͏ִם לְגַלִּים	I will make Jerusalem (*into*) a stone heap. Jer 9:10
40.	וְשַׂמְתִּי שֹׁמְרוֹן לְעִי הַשָּׂדֶה	I will make Samaria (*into*) a ruin in the fields. Mic 1:6
41.	הוֹי הָאֹמְרִים לָרַע טוֹב . . . שָׂמִים חֹשֶׁךְ לְאוֹר . . . שָׂמִים מַר לְמָתוֹק	Woe to those who declare good evil . . . who set (i.e., value?) darkness *as* light . . . who set the bitter *as* sweet. Isa 5:20
42.	לָכֶם יִהְיֶה לְאָכְלָה:	It shall be yours *as* food.[80] Gen 1:29
43.	יֵצֵא לַחָפְשִׁי	He shall go out *as* a free man.[81] Exod 21:2
44.	כִּי הָיָה־לִי הַלֵּוִי לְכֹהֵן	This Levite, *as* a priest, belongs to me. Judg 17:13
45.	תְּשִׁיתֵמוֹ לְשָׂרִים	You shall make them princes. Ps 45:17

A great many uses of *l* remain to be elucidated, and their diversity is considerable.   e

Several notable classes of possessive phrases use *l*. An *l* phrase must be used if the   f
phrase must unambiguously refer to an indefinite (## 46–47). Several relevant examples are cited earlier in connection with the *lameds* of specification and of authorship; these may be reviewed: *bēn yišai* means '*the* son *of* Jesse' while *bēn ləyišai* (# 15) means '*a* son *of* Jesse'; note *mizmôr ləḏāwid* 'a psalm *of* David' (Ps 3:1; cf. # 17). In addition, an *l* phrase may be used (*a*) to avoid a three- (or more) term construct phrase (# 48), (*b*) where the possessor is a name (# 49), or (*c*) where the construct form would not be (sufficiently) distinctive (# 50).

46.	וּלְנָעֳמִי מוֹדָע לְאִישָׁהּ	Naomi had a relative *of* her husband's. Ruth 2:1 *Qere*

---

79. Cf. Ezek 37:11, Ps 123:4.
80. Cf. Ugaritic *walp lakl* 'and an ox for food,' cited in

UT § 10.10.
81. Cf. Gen 2:7, 22.

47.	כִּי אֹהֵב הָיָה חִירָם לְדָוִד כָּל־הַיָּמִים:	Hiram had been a longtime ally *of* David's. 1 Kgs 5:15
48.	אִישׁ רֹאשׁ לְבֵית־אֲבֹתָיו הוּא:	each being the head *of* his fathers' house[82] Num 1:4
49.	בִּגְדֵי הַקֹּדֶשׁ אֲשֶׁר לְאַהֲרֹן	the holy garments *of* Aaron Exod 39:1
50.	וְאַרְבַּע כְּנָפַיִם לְאַחַת לָהֶם:	Each one *of* them had four wings.[83] Ezek 1:6

g   The preposition *l* is used to mark the *topic* of a verb of saying (## 51–54, cf. # 26), a use not far removed from the *lamed* of specification. It also denotes the *agent* of a passive verb, usually a *Niphal* (## 55–56);[84] rarely, *l* governs the *subject* of a passive verb (# 57). With an active transitive verb, *l* can mark the object (## 58–60; see 10.4b)[85] or, very rarely, the subject (# 61).

51.	אִמְרִי־לִי אָחִי הוּא:	Say *of* me, "He is my brother." Gen 20:13
52.	וּלְעִתִּים רְחוֹקוֹת הוּא נִבָּא:	He speaks prophecies *about* far distant times. Ezek 12:27
53.	אֲנִי מְדַבֵּר אֹתָךְ לְכָל־חֻקּוֹת בֵּית־יהוה	I am telling you *of* all the rules of YHWH's house. Ezek 44:5
54.	שִׁירוּ לַיהוה שִׁיר חָדָשׁ	Sing *of* YHWH a new song.[86] Ps 96:1, 98:1
55.	הֲלוֹא נָכְרִיּוֹת נֶחְשַׁבְנוּ לוֹ	Aren't we considered foreigners *by* him? Gen 31:15
56.	וְנִבְחַר מָוֶת מֵחַיִּים לְכֹל הַשְּׁאֵרִית	Death will be chosen over life *by* all the remnant. Jer 8:3
57.	וּבַחֲבֻרָתוֹ נִרְפָּא־לָנוּ:	Through his stripes we are healed.[87] Isa 53:5
58.	יַצְדִּיק צַדִּיק עַבְדִּי לָרַבִּים	The just one, my servant, shall adjudge (or, make) many righteous. Isa 53:11

82. On *hwᵓ* here, see 16.3.4a. Note book titles such as *spr dbry hymym lmlky yśrᵓl* (1 Kgs 15:31).

83. The form *ᵓaḥat* is both construct and absolute.

84. R. Althann inconclusively argues that the six occurrences of *lamed* with the *Niphal* of *mwl* 'to circumcise' are all *lameds* of agency; "*MWL*, 'Circumcise' with the *lamedh* of Agency," *Biblica* 62 (1981) 239–40. Note also J. Carmignac, "Le Complément d'agent après un verbe passif dans l'Hébreu et l'Araméen de Qumrân," *Revue de Qumran* 9 (1978) 409–27 (includes a discussion of certain New Testament Greek prepositions).

85. The verb is often a *Hiphil* (as in # 58). The use of *l*

with the direct object may reflect Aramaic influence, and such influence can be seen in some late Akkadian uses of *ana*; see von Soden, *Grundriss der akkadischen Grammatik*, § 114e / p. 164.

86. P. de Boer, "Cantate Domino: An Erroneous Dative?" *Oudtestamentische Studiën* 21 (1981) 55–67, at 62, calls this "a *lāmedh* of reference designating an accusative of theme." Consideration of the associated expressions, e.g., *zmr l*, corroborates his conclusion that the expression should not be translated 'sing to.'

87. There is no agent specified in this passage; the *b* is instrumental.

59.   וְאָהַבְתָּ לְרֵעֲךָ כָּמֹוךָ   You shall love your neighbor as (you do) yourself.
                                            Lev 19:18

60.   לְשַׁחֵת לָעִיר   to destroy the city
                                 1 Sam 23:10

61.   פֶּן יְבֻלַּע לַמֶּלֶךְ   lest the king be swallowed up[88]
                                        2 Sam 17:16

An apposition can be marked with *l*, be it subject (# 62),[89] object (# 63), or preposi-   h
tional object (# 64).

62. כָּל־בֶּן־נֵכָר עֶרֶל לֵב וְעֶרֶל בָּשָׂר   Not one foreigner, be he uncircumcised of heart or
     לֹא יָבֹוא אֶל־מִקְדָּשִׁי לְכָל־בֶּן־   uncircumcised of flesh (*that is*, not one foreigner who
     נֵכָר אֲשֶׁר בְּתֹוךְ בְּנֵי יִשְׂרָאֵל׃   is in the midst of the Israelites) shall enter my
                                                 temple.
                                                 Ezek 44:9

63. אֹו כִי יִגַּע בְּטֻמְאַת אָדָם לְכֹל   Or if anyone touches a human uncleanness, *that is*,
     טֻמְאָתֹו אֲשֶׁר יִטְמָא בָּהּ וְנֶעְלַם   any uncleanness by which he might be rendered
     מִמֶּנּוּ וְהוּא יָדַע וְאָשֵׁם׃   unclean, and he does so without knowing—when he
                                        learns, he is guilty.[90]
                                        Lev 5:3

64. וַאֲנִי הִנֵּה נְתַתִּיךָ הַיֹּום לְעִיר   Today I am appointing you a fortified city . . . over
     מִבְצָר . . . עַל־כָּל־הָאָרֶץ   the whole land, *that is*, the kings of Judah, its
     לְמַלְכֵי יְהוּדָה לְשָׂרֶיהָ לְכֹהֲנֶיהָ   princes, its priests, and the ordinary people.[91]
     וּלְעַם הָאָרֶץ׃   Jer 1:18

In conclusion we turn to the so-called *emphatic lamed*.[92] This particle must be   i
distinguished first of all from the independent hypothetical particle *lû* (written לוּ, לֻא,
לוּא), which introduces optative clauses ('Oh that. . . !') and subordinate clauses of unreal
and concessive force ('even if . . .').[93] Further, it is strongly possible that the emphatic or
asseverative *lamed* is etymologically distinct from the preposition, though the Masoretes
do not distinguish the two. Emphatic *lamed* stands (*a*) before a noun in a verbless clause
(# 65),[94] (*b*) before a verb form in a verbal clause (# 66),[95] and (*c*) before vocatives
(# 67).[96] A different emphatic use involves other prepositions: *l* may follow another

---

88. See also 10.4c and n. 43 there; for a contrasting view
see P. Kyle McCarter, *II Samuel* (Anchor Bible 9; Garden
City, New York: Doubleday, 1984) 388.

89. See also Ezra 1:5.

90. See also Lev 5:4.

91. But W. L. Holladay deletes the phrase with *ᶜl* and
leaves the *l* phrases; see *Jeremiah* (Hermeneia; Philadelphia: Fortress, 1986), 1. 23.

92. On the material discussed in this paragraph, see John
Huehnergard, "Asseverative *la* and Hypothetical *lu/law*
in Semitic," *Journal of the American Oriental Society* 103
(1983) 569–93; a supplementary note dealing with the
shape of the particle is given by R. C. Steiner, "*Lulav*

versus *lu/law*," *Journal of the American Oriental Society*
107 (1987) 121–22.

93. See Huehnergard, "Asseverative *la*," 571.

94. See also Ps 89:19.

95. Huehnergard allows emphatic *lamed* with finite verb
forms except imperatives; "Asseverative *la*," 591.

96. Huehnergard ("Asseverative *la*," 591) and P. D. Miller ("Vocative Lamed in the Psalter," *Ugarit-Forschungen*
11 [1979] 617–37) are dubious about vocative *lamed*. For
an argument that vocative *lamed* is best taken as identical
to the preposition, see O'Connor, *Hebrew Verse Structure*,
80–81. On Ugaritic vocative *lamed* see Pardee, *UF* 7: 371;
8:326.

preposition directly (סָבִיב לְ) or as a complement (בֵּין . . . לְ, Gen 1:6), and its use in such constructions can also be termed emphatic.

65.	כִּי־לְכֶלֶב חַי הוּא טוֹב מִן־ הָאַרְיֵה הַמֵּת:	*Indeed* a live dog is better than a dead lion. Qoh 9:4
66.	יהוה לְהוֹשִׁיעֵנִי	YHWH, *do* save me! Isa 38:20
67.	רַנְּנוּ צַדִּיקִים בַּיהוָה לַיְשָׁרִים נָאוָה תְהִלָּה:	Rejoice, O you just, in YHWH; O you upright, praise is fitting. Ps 33:1

11.2.11   מִן

a   This preposition shows its canonical form מִן before the article regularly and only irregularly otherwise; otherwise, the *nun* assimilates to the following consonant, and the forms -מְ or -מֶ result. There are two long variants: מִנִּי, without suffixes, and -מִמֶּנ, with suffixes (e.g., מִמֶּנִּי). The relations that the preposition designates involve origins and causes.

b   The *spatial* senses of *mn* are both static and dynamic. The *locational mn* describes the place where a thing or person originated (# 1) or the direction where a thing is located (# 2). More basic is the ablative sense of *mn*, designating movement *away from* a specified beginning point (# 3); this sense underlies the designation of origin (cf. # 1). As with other prepositions, several distinct senses may be used together (# 4).

1.	וַיִּשְׁפֹּט . . . אִבְצָן מִבֵּית לָחֶם:	Ibzan, who was *from* Bethlehem, . . . judged. Judg 12:8
2.	וַיָּשִׂימוּ הָעָם אֶת־כָּל־הַמַּחֲנֶה אֲשֶׁר מִצָּפוֹן לָעִיר וְאֶת־עֲקֵבוֹ מִיָּם לָעִיר	They positioned the army—the main force, which was *to* the north of the city, and its rear guard, which was *to* the west of the city. Josh 8:13
3.	לְהוֹצִיאָם מֵאֶרֶץ מִצְרָיִם	to bring them *out of* the land of Egypt Exod 12:42
4.	וַיַּעְתֵּק מִשָּׁם הָהָרָה מִקֶּדֶם לְבֵית־אֵל	And he decamped *from* there to the mountain which is *to* the east of Bethel. Gen 12:8

c   *Temporal* uses of *mn* vary in relation to the beginning point, which may be included ('from, on, in'; # 5) or not ('after'; # 6). Temporal *mn* can also mark a block of time ('after'; # 7).[97]

---

97. Note also *mmḥrt* 'on the next day' (Gen 19:34); *mᵓz* means either 'before then' or 'since.'

5. אִם־מִשְּׁנַת הַיֹּבֵל יַקְדִּישׁ שָׂדֵהוּ
   ... וְאִם־אַחַר הַיֹּבֵל יַקְדִּישׁ
   שָׂדֵהוּ

If someone dedicates his field *from* Jubilee Year
on. . . ; if, in contrast, he dedicates his field after
Jubilee Year. . . .
Lev 27:17–18

6. כַּחֲלוֹם מֵהָקִיץ

as a dream *after* awaking
Ps 73:20

7. יְחַיֵּנוּ מִיֹּמָיִם בַּיּוֹם הַשְּׁלִישִׁי
   יְקִמֵנוּ

He will revive us *after* two days (have passed, i.e., it
will be) on the third day (that) he will raise us up.
Hos 6:2

The *ablative* and *locational* senses of *mn* are similar to another group of the preposition's senses: *mn* marks the material *of* which something is made (# 8) or the author or authority *from* whom a standard or truth originated (# 9). The cause or means of a situation is marked by *mn* (## 10–12), as is an agent (# 13; note the passives in ## 12–13). With verbs of fearing and the like, it is often difficult to distinguish cause and agent (## 14–15).

8. וַיִּצֶר יהוה אֱלֹהִים מִן־הָאֲדָמָה
   כָּל־חַיַּת הַשָּׂדֶה

YHWH God formed all the animals of the field *from*
the ground.
Gen 2:19

9. וְיָדְעוּ ... דְּבַר־מִי יָקוּם מִמֶּנִּי
   וּמֵהֶם:

They will know . . . whose word shall stand, mine or
theirs.
Jer 44:28

10. מֵרֹב עֲוֹנֶיךָ ... חִלַּלְתָּ מִקְדָּשֶׁיךָ

Because of (or, *By*) the multitude of your iniquities
. . . you have profaned your shrines.
Ezek 28:18

11. כִּי לֹא הָיְתָה מֵהַמֶּלֶךְ

It was not (*because of*) the king's will. . . .
2 Sam 3:37

12. וְלֹא־יִכָּרֵת כָּל־בָּשָׂר עוֹד מִמֵּי
    הַמַּבּוּל

All flesh shall not again be cut off *by* the flood
waters.
Gen 9:11

13. וְאִשָּׁה גְּרוּשָׁה מֵאִישָׁהּ

a woman driven out *by* her husband
Lev 21:7

14. מִמִּי אִירָא

Of whom am I afraid?
Ps 27:1

15. וַיִּירְאוּ מִגֶּשֶׁת אֵלָיו:

They were afraid *of* drawing near to him.[98]
Exod 34:30

The preposition has three further uses. (1) It is a *partitive* marker: the phrase with *mn* refers to *part of* the noun (or noun equivalent) after the preposition. The partition

---

98. Infinitives construct can also be used after *mn* to designate temporal or causal relations, as well as in comparative constructions; see 36.2.2b.

may be simple ('some of'; ## 16–17) or comparative/superlative ('the better/best of,' # 18; 'the worse/worst of,' etc.). In negative clauses the *mn* phrase refers to *none of* or *not one of* the prepositional object (## 19–20); such a negative sense can be found in oaths and other rhetorically charged speech (# 21).

16.   יָצְאוּ מִן־הָעָם לִלְקֹט   *Some of* the people went out to gather (it).
Exod 16:27

17.   וְהִזָּה מִדַּם הַחַטָּאת עַל־קִיר   He shall sprinkle *some of* the blood of the
הַמִּזְבֵּחַ   sin-offering on the side of the altar.
Lev 5:9

18.   הַטּוֹב וְהַיָּשָׁר מִבְּנֵי אֲדֹנֵיכֶם   the best and brightest *of* your lord's children
2 Kgs 10:3

19.   וְלֹא־יָלִין מִן־הַבָּשָׂר   *None of* the flesh shall remain overnight.
Deut 16:4

20.   וְלוֹא נַכְרִית מֵהַבְּהֵמָה: We shall cut off *not one of* the cattle.
1 Kgs 18:5

21.   חָלִילָה חַי־יהוה אִם־יִפֹּל   Oh desecration! As YHWH lives, if *even a single*
מִשַּׂעֲרַת רֹאשׁוֹ אַרְצָה   *hair* of his head shall fall earthward. . .!
1 Sam 14:45

(2) The preposition is a *privative* marker, that is, it marks what is missing[99] or unavailable[100] (## 22–23).

22.   בְּצֵל חֶשְׁבּוֹן עָמְדוּ מִכֹּחַ נָסִים   In the shadow of Heshbon the fugitives stand
without strength.
Jer 48:45

23.   בָּתֵּיהֶם שָׁלוֹם מִפָּחַד   Their homes are safe (and) *free from* fear.
Job 21:9

(3) The preposition is a *comparative* marker, prefixed to a standard by which a quality is measured (and thus similar to some English superlatives; # 24) or to a group to which something is compared (and thus comparable to some English comparatives; # 25; 14.4d).

24.   קָטֹנְתִּי מִכֹּל הַחֲסָדִים   I am small *in relation to* (or, *too* small *for*) all the
mercies.
Gen 32:11

25.   דּוֹדִי . . . דָּגוּל מֵרְבָבָה: My beloved . . . is more attractive *than* ten thousand
(other people).
Cant 5:10

99. Cf. Jer 42:4. In Hos 6:6 and Ps 52:5 the sense may be substitutive ('X rather than Y').

100. The verb ʿāṣar 'to restrain' usually governs an infini-   tive with *mn*, viz., 'to keep (someone) from (doing something),' though other prepositions may also follow the verb.

עַד   **11.2.12**

This preposition, also used as a conjunction, may be related to the noun עַד 'future,' a
which occurs only in phrases like לְעֹלָם וָעֶד (Exod 15:18) and לָעַד לְעוֹלָם (Ps 111:8),
'forever and ever.' Two forms of the preposition are used independently, עַד and the
older עֲדֵי, from which the suffixed forms are composed. The basic sense of the preposition is allative (movement toward)-terminative (movement up to).

Some *spatial* uses of the preposition are static (# 1), but the sense of movement *up* b
to is usually present (# 2).[101] *Temporal* uses are more common and more diverse: ᶜd may
mark the time *before* which an event takes place (# 3) or *until* which it takes place
(# 4).[102] Less often, the sense is durative, referring to the time *during* which an event
takes place (# 5).

1.	עַד־צַוָּאר יַגִּיעַ	It (the Euphrates) will (reach *up to* and) touch the neck(s) of the Judahites).[103] Isa 8:8
2.	וַיָּבֹאוּ עַד־חָרָן	They came *as far as* Haran. Gen 11:31
3.	וַיִּפְתַּח אֶת־פִּי עַד־בּוֹא אֵלַי בַּבֹּקֶר	He (God) opened my mouth *before* the coming to me [of the messenger] in the morning. Ezek 33:22
4.	יֵצֵא אָדָם לְפָעֳלוֹ . . . עֲדֵי־עָרֶב:	Man goes out to his work (and he stays at it) . . . *until* evening. Ps 104:23
5.	מָה הַשָּׁלוֹם עַד־זְנוּנֵי אִיזֶבֶל הָרַבִּים: . . .	How can there be peace *as long as* the prostitution of Jezebel . . . abounds? 2 Kgs 9:22

The preposition also expresses *measure or degree* ('as much as, as far as, even to, c
even unto'; # 6), most often in the phrase עַד־מְאֹד 'a great deal.' With a negative the
preposition may take on a privative sense (# 7).

6.	וּמַה־בַּקָּשָׁתֵךְ עַד־חֲצִי הַמַּלְכוּת וְתֵעָשׂ:	What is your request? *Even up to* half the kingdom it shall be granted (lit., done). Esth 5:6

101. The relationship to both the governing verb and other prepositional phrases can be obscure. In 2 Kgs 14:13, we have *wyprṣ bḥwmt yrwšlm bšᶜr ʾprym ᶜd-šᶜr hpnh*, 'He made a breach in the Jerusalem wall (starting) *at* the Ephraim Gate (and *extending*) *as far as* the Corner Gate'; in a synoptic passage the first phrase is given as *mšᶜr ʾprym* '(a breach) *from* the Ephraim Gate' (2 Chr 25:23).

102. Carl Brockelmann, noting parallels in other Semitic languages, explained that "the sense 'up to (a limit)' in a

temporal sense easily shifts into one that places in the foreground the thought of the *period* thus demarcated"; cited by James Barr, "Hebrew עַד, especially at Job i.18 and Neh vii.3," *Journal of Semitic Studies* 27 (1982) 177–88, at 184–85; see also the additional note to Barr's article by J. Hughes, 189–92.

103. On Hebrew ᶜd 'near to,' see Pardee, *UF* 8: 316. The image of water up to the neck is common; cf., e.g., ᶜd-npš 'to the throat' (Jonah 2:6).

7.   לֹא נִשְׁאַר עַד־אֶחָד׃   There remained *not even* one.
                                            Judg 4:16

d   A goal of an abstract sort may be governed by *ᶜd* (# 8), as may a focus or object of interest (# 9).

8.   וְעַד־הַשְּׁלֹשָׁה לֹא־בָא׃   [Even though he was a very good soldier] he did not attain *to* (the level of the elite force) The Three.[104]
                                            2 Sam 23:19

9.   וְעָדֵיכֶם אֶתְבּוֹנָן   I gave my attention *to* you.
                                            Job 32:12

11.2.13   עַל

a   This preposition, also used as a conjunction, may be related to the rare noun עַל 'height' (e.g., הַגֶּבֶר הֻקַם עָל 'the man raised on a height,' 2 Sam 23:1). The suffixed forms of the preposition are derived from the unattested עֲלֵי, for example, עָלַי. The relation 'at or near the top' is basic for this preposition.

b   Of the *spatial* senses, most are locational: simple locational ('upon, on, over'; ## 1–2), contingent locational ('at, beside, by'; # 3), or comprehensive locational ('around, about,' often with verbs of covering and protecting; # 4). With some verbs of motion *ᶜl* has a terminative sense ('on, to, onto'; ## 5–6). (This sense is shared by *ᶜl* and *ᵓl*; from it other senses of the two prepositions come to overlap by analogy. Futile is the tendency to emend the MT in order to eliminate some or all of these senses, although there may be cases in which the prepositions have been confused in the development of the text.)

1.   שְׁכַב עַל־מִשְׁכָּבְךָ   Lie down *on* your bed.
                                            2 Sam 13:5

2.   תְּנָה הוֹדְךָ עַל־הַשָּׁמָיִם׃   (You) set your glory *upon* the heavens.[105]
                                            Ps 8:2

3.   וּשְׁנֵיהֶם עָמְדוּ עַל־הַיַּרְדֵּן׃   And the two of them stopped *at* the Jordan.[106]
                                            2 Kgs 2:7

4.   חוֹמָה הָיוּ עָלֵינוּ   They were a wall *about* us.
                                            1 Sam 25:16

5.   כִּי לֹא הִמְטִיר יהוה אֱלֹהִים   YHWH God had not (yet) made it rain *upon* the
       עַל־הָאָרֶץ   earth.[107]
                                            Gen 2:5

---

104. The sense of the passage is disputed; we follow McCarter, *II Samuel*, 496.

105. The form *tnh* is not an anomalous imperative of *ntn* but an infinitive construct, as if formed from the root *ytn* (the verb 'to give' has this form in Phoenician); compare *yrd*, infinitive construct *rǝdâ*. With *šmym*, *ᶜl* usually

means 'over,' but in the passages with *hwd* it means 'upon' (this passage, Num 27:20, Ps 21:6, Dan 10:8, 1 Chr 29:25).

106. Cf. Ps 1:3. Ernst Jenni associates *ᶜl* meaning 'near' chiefly with deeply sited objects (i.e., rivers, springs, etc.; *LHS* 314).

107. Cf. Gen 15:11.

6.   וְלֹא־תַעֲלֶה בְמַעֲלֹת עַל־מִזְבְּחִי   You shall not go up *to* my altar via steps.[108]
                                                    Exod 20:26

Metaphorically ʿl marks a burden or duty (# 7),[109] when the object feels an incum-   c
bency 'upon' herself or himself, as well as a rank (# 8). With psychological predicates
(verbs of thinking, feeling, rejoicing, grieving, watching) ʿl governs the object of interest
('upon, to, for, over'; ## 9–10). When the subject feels the pathos 'upon' himself or herself, the ʿl-phrase is reflexive (# 11; cf. 11.2.10d). Advantage ('on behalf of, for the sake
of') and disadvantage ('against') are also marked with ʿl (## 12–14).

7.   וְעָלַי לָתֵת לְךָ עֲשָׂרָה כֶסֶף   I would have had to give (lit., *upon* me to give) you
                                                    ten (sheqels) of silver.
                                                    2 Sam 18:11

8.   וְיוֹאָב . . . עַל־הַצָּבָא   Joab . . . was *over* the army.
                                                    2 Sam 8:16

9.   מֵתָה עָלַי רָחֵל   Rachel died *to my sorrow* (lit., *upon* me).
                                                    Gen 48:7

10.   יָשִׂישׂ עָלַיִךְ   He will rejoice *over* you.
                                                    Zeph 3:17

11.   וַתִּתְעַטֵּף עָלַי רוּחִי   My spirit faints *within* me.
                                                    Ps 143:4

12.   אָנֹכִי אֲדַבֵּר עָלַיִךְ אֶל־הַמֶּלֶךְ:   I will speak *on your behalf* to the king.
                                                    1 Kgs 2:18

13.   וַיִּקְצֹף פַּרְעֹה עַל שְׁנֵי סָרִיסָיו   Pharaoh was angry *with* his two officers.
                                                    Gen 40:2

14.   עָלָיו עָלָה שַׁלְמַנְאֶסֶר   Shalmanezer came up *against* him.
                                                    2 Kgs 17:3

The preposition can mark an object of *excess* (cf. 'on top of that'), involving   d
accompaniment ('with, along with, together with'; # 15), addition ('in addition to, to';
16),[110] and even multiplication ('over, above'; # 17).

15.   וַיָּבֹאוּ הָאֲנָשִׁים עַל־הַנָּשִׁים   Men *together with* women came.
                                                    Exod 35:22

16.   כִּי־יָסַפְנוּ עַל־כָּל־חַטֹּאתֵינוּ   For we have added wickedness *to* all our sins.
      רָעָה   1 Sam 12:19

17.   וְהָיָה מִשְׁנֶה עַל אֲשֶׁר־יִלְקְטוּ   And it will be twice *as much as* they gather on other
      יוֹם יוֹם: days.
                                                    Exod 16:5

---

108. But note Pardee's discussion of the idiom *hlk* ʿl 'to   109. On related Ugaritic and Aramaic usages see Pardee,
enter into the presence of'; *UF* 8: 216; and cf. the next   *UF* 8: 250, 302.
paragraph.   110. Cf. Gen 28:9.

e   The preposition may introduce a *norm* (the basis on which an act is performed; 'according to'; # 18), a *cause* (the reason why an act is performed; 'because of'; # 19), or a *goal* (the end for which an act is performed; 'for'; # 20). It is difficult to distinguish norms and causes in some situations, while in others causes and goals are similar.

18.	עַל כָּל־הַדְּבָרִים הָאֵלֶּה׃	*in accordance with* all these words[111] Exod 24:8
19.	הִנְּךָ מֵת עַל־הָאִשָּׁה אֲשֶׁר־לָקַחְתָּ	You are about to die *because* of the woman you have taken. Gen 20:3
20.	עַל מַה־שָּׁוְא בָּרָאתָ כָל־בְּנֵי־אָדָם׃	*For* what futility have you created all people! Ps 89:48

f   An *oppositional sense* is associated with ʿl ('over against'; # 21), from which a concessive sense may be derived ('although, despite, in spite of'; # 22). There may be a rare separative sense (# 23).

21.	לֹא יִהְיֶה־לְךָ אֱלֹהִים אֲחֵרִים עַל־פָּנָי׃	You shall not have other gods *over against* me.[112] Exod 20:3
22.	עַל־מִשְׁפָּטִי אֲכַזֵּב	*Despite* my (being) right, I am considered a liar. Job 34:6
23.	בְּצֵאתוֹ עַל־אֶרֶץ מִצְרָיִם	when he went out *from* the land of Egypt Ps 81:6

g   Also associated with ʿl are certain relations more frequently marked by l; ʿl can mark a topic (often with verbs of speaking; 'about, concerning'; ## 24–25) or a circumstance ('regarding, in connection with'; # 26). In late Biblical Hebrew ʿl sometimes governs an indirect object of the sort that would be governed by l earlier (# 27).[113]

24.	וַאֲנִי שָׁמַעְתִּי עָלֶיךָ	I have heard it said *of* you. . . . Gen 41:15
25.	וְעַל הִשָּׁנוֹת הַחֲלוֹם	Now, *about* the repeating of the dream. . . . Gen 41:32
26.	וְלֹא־תַעֲנֶה עַל־רִב	Do not answer *in connection with* a lawsuit. Exod 23:2
27.	אִם־עֲלֵיכֶם טוֹב	If it seems good *to* you. . . . 1 Chr 13:2

111. For similar adverbials see Lev 5:22, Isa 60:7, Jer 6:14, and Ps 31:24.
112. Most translations reflect a simpler understanding (as in Exod 35:22, # 15 above).
113. Cf. Ezra 7:28. For ṭwb ʿl see also Esth 1:19; the relationship of the three similar syntagms ṭwb + direct object, ṭwb + l, and ṭwb + bʿyny is complex.

עַם   **11.2.14**

This preposition has the base ʿimm-, seen in suffixed forms, for example, עִמָּנוּ; the   a
form עִמָּדִי (1 c.sg.) is of uncertain origin. It expresses a variety of comitative relations
('with').

The most common sense involves *accompaniment* (fellowship and companionship,   b
person + person; 'with'; ## 1–3) or *addition* ('with, along with, and'; # 4); ʿm often
marks a personal complement after verbs ('with, to,' ## 5–7; adversative, 'against,' # 8).
The locus of psychological interest can be marked with ʿm ('with, in'; ## 9–10).

1.	וַיֹּאכְלוּ . . . הוּא וְהָאֲנָשִׁים אֲשֶׁר־עִמּוֹ	They ate. . . , he and the men *with* him.[114] Gen 24:54
2.	כִּי לֹא יִירַשׁ בֶּן־הָאָמָה הַזֹּאת עִם־בְּנִי עִם־יִצְחָק:	That slave woman's son will never share in the inheritance *with* my son, *with* Isaac. Gen 21:10
3.	כִּי־עִם־אֱלֹהִים עָשָׂה הַיּוֹם הַזֶּה	He succeeded *with* (*the help of*) God this day. 1 Sam 14:45
4.	עִם־עָרֵיהֶם הֶחֱרִימָם יְהוֹשֻׁעַ:	And Joshua annihilated them *along with* their cities. Josh 11:21
5.	וַעֲשֵׂה־חֶסֶד עִם אֲדֹנִי אַבְרָהָם:	Show kindness *to* my master Abraham. Gen 24:12
6.	בְּדַבְּרִי עִמָּךְ	when I speak *with* you Exod 19:9
7.	וְלֹא־נְתָנוֹ אֱלֹהִים לְהָרַע עִמָּדִי:	God did not allow him to do evil *to* me. Gen 31:7
8.	כִּי־בְרַבִּים הָיוּ עִמָּדִי	when many are *against* me (or, even though many oppose me)[115] Ps 55:19
9.	וְיָדַעְתָּ עִם־לְבָבֶךָ	Know *in* your heart that. . . . Deut 8:5
10.	הָיְתָה רוּחַ אַחֶרֶת עִמּוֹ	There is another spirit *in* him. Num 14:24

With verbs of motion and the like ʿm marks the end point of an action ('beside,   c
at'; # 11). The preposition is also used in comparative constructions (# 12).

11.	וַיֵּשֶׁב יִצְחָק עִם־בְּאֵר לַחַי רֹאִי:	Isaac settled *near* Beer-lahai-roi.[116] Gen 25:11

---

114. Cf. Gen 13:1.
115. The preposition b here governs the clause rbym hyw ʿmdy.

116. Cf. Gen 35:4. Ugaritic ʿm is more often than its Hebrew cognate used "with verbs of movement to indicate position at the end of a trajectory"; Pardee, *UF* 8: 288.

12.   חָלְפוּ עִם־אֳנִיּוֹת אֵבֶה   They skim past *like* boats of papyrus.
                                    Job 9:26

11.2.15   תַּחַת

a   This preposition is also used occasionally as a noun, 'what is below.'[117] The suffixed forms are largely from a stem *taḥtê-*, for example, תַּחְתֵּיכֶם, but cf. תַּחְתָּם. Location *below* is the basic sense.

b   The *locational* use is usually *under* a place (# 1). The preposition may have the sense 'in place, on the spot' (## 2–3) and, more abstractly, 'in (the) place of, instead of, for' (## 4–5).[118] Authority or control is designated by *tḥt* (# 6).

1.   וַיְכֻסּוּ כָּל־הֶהָרִים הַגְּבֹהִים   All the high mountains *under* the entire heavens
      אֲשֶׁר־תַּחַת כָּל־הַשָּׁמָיִם: were covered.
                                       Gen 7:19

2.   וְעָמַדְנוּ תַחְתֵּינוּ   We will stay *where* we are.
                              1 Sam 14:9

3.   וַיָּמָת תַּחְתָּיו   And he died right *there* (lit., *under* himself).
                           2 Sam 2:23 *Qere*

4.   כִּי שָׁת־לִי אֱלֹהִים זֶרַע אַחֵר   God has granted me another seed *in place of* Abel.
      תַּחַת הֶבֶל   Gen 4:25

5.   וְנָתַתָּה נֶפֶשׁ תַּחַת נָפֶשׁ:   You shall give life *for* life.
                                      Exod 21:23

6.   וְיִצְבְּרוּ־בָר תַּחַת יַד־פַּרְעֹה   Let them store up grain *under* Pharaoh's control.
                                         Gen 41:35

11.3   Compound and Complex Prepositions

a   By *complex prepositions* we mean the combinations of various prepositions and nouns or adverbs to constitute new entities, often with meanings not predictable from the parts. *Compound prepositions* are the result of the piling up of two or more simple prepositions.

b   Prepositions tend to combine formally with the expressions that they govern. This tendency is evident in the inseparable character of ב, כ, ל, and in the frequent use of *maqqeph* to bind independent prepositions to the words they govern. Some combinations of prepositions and nouns become frozen to form prepositions (cf. English 'in place of'). Some adverbials involve combinations of prepositions with adverbs that retain their nominal shape (cf. English 'according to' and 'accordingly'). When compounded with

---

117. Perhaps originally 'place'; Pardee, *UF* 8: 318; 9: 216. Note Ugaritic *qll tḥt* 'to fall at the feet of'; Pardee, *UF* 7: 367; 8: 245. See also J. C. Greenfield, "The Prepositions *b* . . . *taḥat* . . . in Jes 57:5," *Zeitschrift für die Alt-*

testamentliche Wissenschaft 73 (1961) 226–28.

118. Note the conjunctional use: *tḥt ᵓšr qnᵓ lᵓlhyw*, 'in exchange for the fact that (i.e., because) he was zealous for his God' (Num 25:13).

other prepositions the prepositional notion may be made more explicit (cf. English 'into, up to').

Complex Prepositions and Nouns   11.3.1

Some nouns show a frozen union with a preposition. These complex constructions   a
function syntactically as prepositions, that is, they link an ad-verbial noun to the verb
and specify the nature of its relationship to the governed noun. For example, לִפְנֵי 'before'
can be local (cf. Gen 18:22), temporal (cf. Amos 1:1), referential (cf. Gen 7:1), or comparative (cf. 1 Sam 1:16). Similarly מִפְּנֵי (cf. מִלְּפְנֵי) means 'from before' in a locative (cf.
Exod 14:19) or causal (cf. Gen 6:13) sense. Other similar frozen prepositional expressions
are לְמַ֫עַן 'on account of' and עַל־פִּי 'according to the mouth of' > 'according to.'[119]

Complex Prepositions as Adverbials   11.3.2

Some complex prepositional constructions function as adverbials. For example,   a
אֶל־חִנָּם 'in vain, vainly' (Ezek 6:10), אַחֲרֵי־כֵן 'after this, then, afterward' (Gen 6:4),
בְּכֵן 'on this condition, then' (Qoh 8:10), לָכֵן (Num 16:11) and עַל־כֵּן (Gen 20:6) 'therefore,' and עַד־כֵּן 'hitherto' (Neh 2:16). Forms like מִחוּץ 'without,' מִתַּ֫חַת 'below,' מֵרָחוֹק
'far away,' and מֵעַל 'within' arise from the combination of prepositions with nouns of
place to form adverbs. With לְ these adverbs of place become prepositions, for example,
מִחוּץ לְ, 'outside as regards' > 'outside of' and מִתַּ֫חַת לְ 'from under as regards' >
'under. . . .'[120]

Compound Prepositions   11.3.3

Hebrew frequently piles up prepositions to represent more accurately the relation in   a
question, for example, מֵאַחֲרֵי הַצֹּאן, '(Yhwh took me) *from behind* the flock' (Amos
7:15), and אֶל־אַחֲרָי '(turn) *to behind* me' (2 Kgs 9:18).[121] Sometimes complex adverbs are
included in the group: מִבֵּית לְ 'within,' לְמִבֵּית לְ 'within,' אֶל־מִבֵּית לְ 'in, within.' The
combinations and their nuances are too numerous to catalog here.

Aspects of the Syntax of Prepositions   11.4

Verbs with Accusative or Prepositional Objects   11.4.1

The complementary character of some constructions using the accusative case and   a
of those employing a preposition to bind the verb and its nominal modifier can be demonstrated by pairing examples that in one instance do not use the preposition and in
another employ it (cf. 10.2.1c–e).

---

119. For the last, see Mic 3:5 ('he who does not make a donation *according to* their *demands*'); cf. Prov 22:6. Mishnaic Hebrew adds to these complex prepositions others, e.g., *mēḥămat* '(through the fury/energy of,) by, through, because of,' and a *šēm* series: *ləšēm* 'for the sake of,' *miššēm* (~ *miššûm*) 'in the name of,' *ʿal šēm* 'because of';

see Segal, *Mishnaic Hebrew*, 141, 144–45.
120. Cf. GKC § 119c / pp. 377–78. Note that *mtḥt lmdyw* (Judg 3:16) can well be rendered with a pileup of English prepositions, 'up underneath his clothes.'
121. See GKC § 119b / p. 377.

b   The preposition לְ 'to' with its goal orientation matches the goal orientation of the accusative function with transitive verbs (# 1; see 10.2.1, 10.4). Other prepositions also occur with verbs that otherwise govern an object directly (# 2; see 10.2).

1a.   בִּשְׁתַּיִם יְכַסֶּה פָנָיו   With two (wings) it covered its face.
Isa 6:2

1b.   כַּמַּיִם לַיָּם מְכַסִּים: as the waters cover the sea
Isa 11:9

2a.   גָּעַרְתָּ גוֹיִם   You rebuke nations.[122]
Ps 9:6

2b.   וַיִּגְעַר־בּוֹ אָבִיו   His father rebuked him.
Gen 37:10

c   Such pairs can be found for complement accusatives (with intransitive verbs; # 3; 10.2.1h), for adverbial accusatives (# 4; 10.2.2b), and for double accusatives (# 5; 10.2.3c).

3a.   וּפָשַׁט אֶת־בְּגָדָיו וְלָבַשׁ בְּגָדִים   Then he is to take off his garments and put on others.
אֲחֵרִים   Lev 6:4

3b.   לְבוּשׁ מַלְכוּת אֲשֶׁר לָבַשׁ־בּוֹ   a royal garment, which the king has worn
הַמֶּלֶךְ   Esth 6:8

4a.   וַיַּעַל מִשָּׁם פְּנוּאֵל   He went up from there to Penuel.
Judg 8:8

4b.   כִּי־עָלִית כֻּלָּךְ לַגַּגּוֹת: All of you went up on the roof.
Isa 22:1

5a.   וַיִּבְנֶה אֶת־הָאֲבָנִים מִזְבֵּחַ   And he built the stones into an altar.
1 Kgs 18:32

5b.   וַיִּבֶן . . . אֶת־הַצֵּלָע . . . לְאִשָּׁה   And he . . . fashioned the rib . . . into a woman.
Gen 2:22

11.4.2   Prepositions with Multiple Objects

a   When a preposition governs several objects, it is usually repeated with each.

1.   לֶךְ־לְךָ מֵאַרְצְךָ וּמִמּוֹלַדְתְּךָ   Go *from* your native land and *from* your people and
וּמִבֵּית אָבִיךָ   *from* your father's household.
Gen 12:1

It is not rare, however, for the preposition not to be repeated; such a construction is called a *preposition override*.[123]

---

122. On *gᶜr* see Pardee, *UF* 9: 209; on *ʾhz*, with direct object or prepositional object after *b* see Pardee, *UF* 9: 206.

123. See O'Connor, *Hebrew Verse Structure*, 310–11; *UT* § 10.10 n. 2.

2.   הַחֵפֶץ לַיהוה בְּעֹלוֹת וּזְבָחִים   Does Yhwh delight *in* burnt offerings and sacrifices?
    1 Sam 15:22

In adjacent lines of poetry a preposition may govern an object in one line and by   **b**
extension in the next; we can say that a single preposition does *double duty* or that the
second occurrence of the preposition has been removed by *gapping*.[124]

3.   יַעֲשֶׂה חֶפְצוֹ בְּבָבֶל   He will carry out his purpose *against* Babylon;
    וּזְרֹעוֹ כַּשְׂדִּים: his arm will be *against* the Chaldeans.
    Isa 48:14

Supposed Ambiguity and Ellipsis   **11.4.3**

Each of the prepositions of Hebrew has a variety of meanings and uses, as the   **a**
review of many of the simple prepositions in 11.2 makes clear. It is methodologically
unsound to rely on a dictionary to find a small set of translational equivalents to be
"plugged into" a Hebrew text. In some cases English requires no preposition in a construction otherwise similar in Hebrew.[125] Further, some prepositions overlap in sense.
Some uses of על are similar to some uses of אל (11.2.13b), while others are similar to
some uses of ל (11.2.13g); but this does not mean that על, אל, and ל are equivalent or
synonymous as relational terms.[126]

A methodological error similar to these failures involves supposed *ambiguity*. The   **b**
idea that a linguistic unit can have more than one meaning is straightforward, but various kinds of ambiguity can be associated with linguistic units. *Grammatical ambiguity*
arises from certain aspects of the ways in which phrases and clauses are constructed.
Because adjectives and substantives are not ordinarily strictly distinguished, some phrases
of the shape *noun + noun* can be ambiguous; in צַדִּיק עַבְדִּי (Isa 53:11), for example, the
"adjective" צַדִּיק can be construed as a modifier of עַבְדִּי or as a substantive, that is, 'the
Righteous One, (who is) my servant' or 'my servant (who is) righteous.'[127] The ambiguity
of the Hebrew can be exhibited in English, but the grammatical question pertains to the
Hebrew first of all. It is possible to consider the phrase in light of the rest of the passage,
but often in such cases no simple resolution is possible. Nor is it always desirable:
grammatical ambiguity is a genuine and often functional part of language. The other
major type of ambiguity, *lexical ambiguity*, arises from various meanings of a single
term; many very common nouns and verbs have various meanings. In 2 Sam 6:2, we read
וַיֵּלֶךְ דָּוִד וְכָל־הָעָם אֲשֶׁר אִתּוֹ. Does עַם here refer to 'people' or 'army'? This ambiguity is

---

124. The term "double-duty" preposition is favored by,
e.g., M. Dahood; see Dahood and T. Penar, "The Grammar of the Psalter," in M. Dahood, *Psalms III* (Anchor
Bible 17A; Garden City, New York: Doubleday, 1970)
361–456, at 435–37. For "gapping," see O'Connor, *Hebrew
Verse Structure*, 122–27, 405, 422. For the example cited,
see GKC § 119hh / p. 384.

125. On the pseudo-problems created by a failure to
understand both the difference between philology and trans-

lation and the translational task, see, e.g., Pardee, *UF* 7:
335–36; 8: 281–82, 289, 320.

126. It is arguable that *ʾl* and *l* have some etymological
relation (note that Ugaritic lacks *ʾl*), but that possible
historical circumstance has little relevance to actual Hebrew usage; see Pardee, *UF* 8: 290, 314.

127. A similar example is *ʾăḥōtî kallâ* (Cant 4:9, 10, 12;
5:1), 'my sister, (my) bride' or 'my sister-bride.'

resolved by the preceding verse, which mentions David's gathering כָּל־בָּחוּר בְּיִשְׂרָאֵל 'all the picked troops *or* vigorous young men in Israel'; despite uncertainty about the exact reference of בָּחוּר we are dealing with a military expedition and עם means 'force, army.' In vv 3 and 5 the term בֵּית is used; that term is in each case disambiguated by the context: the first בֵּית is בַּגִּבְעָה 'on the hill' and so must be a physical structure, while the second is said to be מְשַׂחֲקִים 'rejoicing' and so must be a group of people.

c   With these two types of ambiguity in mind, let us consider prepositions. It is plain that lexical ambiguity cannot be associated with relational terms: the prepositions, unlike nouns and verbs, do not have the sort of independent senses that lead to lexical ambiguity.[128] To impute to ב a meaning 'in' and a meaning 'from' is to separate the word too drastically from its patterns of use.[129] Ambiguity can be associated with prepositions, but it is structural or grammatical—it is a property of a phrase or a clause rather than the preposition itself.

d   One useful approach to the structural ambiguities associated with prepositions involves considering the perspective from which an action is viewed (11.1). Another approach involves *ellipsis*, the omission of part of a grammatical structure when that part can be recovered from the context. When a preposition appears to be under the immediate government of a verb, but the normal distinctive meanings of the terms exclude such a union, the preposition may be taken to be under the government of an elided verb (usually a verb of motion) appropriate to the preposition.[130]

1.   הָאָרֶץ אֲשֶׁר אַתָּה בָּא עָלֶיהָ   the land into which you are entering [to settle] upon it
Exod 34:12

2.   כִּי־לֵב הַמֶּלֶךְ עַל־אַבְשָׁלוֹם: The king's heart was [set] upon Absalom.
2 Sam 14:1

3.   הַבְעַד עֲרָפֶל יִשְׁפּוֹט: Can he judge [looking out] through the thick clouds?
Job 22:13

4.   וַיֶּאֱהַל עַד־סְדֹם: He [migrated and] pitched his tent until [he came] to Sodom.
Gen 13:12

e   Another source of structural ambiguity associated with prepositions can also be clarified by considering ellipsis. A prepositional phrase may refer to all the actors and the action of a clause in which it occurs, as in # 5.

---

128. The tendency to impute (lexical) ambiguity to the prepositions has some roots in the Jewish exegetical tradition; see Pardee, *UF* 7: 331, 333–34; 8: 321. William Chomsky tried to defend the principle of interchangeability by an appeal to the medieval grammarians as well as to Ugaritic; "The Ambiguity of the Prefixed Prepositions מ, ל, ב in the Bible," *Jewish Quarterly Review* 61 (1970–71) 87–89. C. F. Whitley, basing himself on Chomsky's article,

argued for the interchangeability of emphatic *lamed* with a hypothetical emphatic *beth*; "Some Functions of the Hebrew Particles *Beth* and *Lamedh*," *Jewish Quarterly Review* 62 (1971–72) 199–206.

129. The preference of earlier scholars for wholesale and regular emendation in order to regularize the prepositions is equally insupportable.

130. See GKC § 119ee / p. 384; Pardee, *UF* 8: 246, 283.

5.   לֹא תְנַסּוּ אֶת־יהוה אֱלֹהֵיכֶם   Do not put Yʜᴡʜ your God to the test as you tested
        כַּאֲשֶׁר נִסִּיתֶם בַּמַּסָּה׃   (him) in Massah.
                                            Deut 6:16

Here במסה applies to the testing, the perpetrators, and the victim. Sometimes, however, a prepositional phrase refers only to a subject or an object, and the ambiguity may be said to result from ellipsis of a relative clause.[131]

6.   אֶעֶנְךָ בְּסֵתֶר רַעַם   I (ꜱᴜʙᴊᴇᴄᴛ), [who am] *in* the hidden place of thunder, answer you.[132]
                                        Ps 81:8

7.   כֵּן בַּקֹּדֶשׁ חֲזִיתִיךָ   So I see you (ᴏʙᴊᴇᴄᴛ) [who are] *in* the sanctuary.[133]
                                        Ps 63:3

8.   אֱלֹהִים . . . מוֹצִיא אֲסִירִים   God . . . is the one who brings out prisoners (ᴏʙᴊᴇᴄᴛ)
        בַּכּוֹשָׁרוֹת   [who are] *in* fetters (*not* brings out prisoners *from* fetters).[134]
                                        Ps 68:7

9.   כִּמְעַט כִּלּוּנִי בָאָרֶץ   They almost destroyed me (ᴏʙᴊᴇᴄᴛ) *from* the earth (lit., me [who am] *on* the earth).[135]
                                        Ps 119:87

It is possible for a prepositional phrase to refer to an elided element, usually an object.

10.   שְׁלַח יָדְךָ וֶאֱחֹז בִּזְנָבוֹ   Put out your hand and grasp (it) by its tail.[136]
                                        Exod 4:4

---

131. Earlier scholars occasionally refer to these and similar patterns as "pregnant" constructions, viz., "pregnant with expressed meaning."

132. See Pardee, *UF* 9: 223; note *wyrᶜm bšmym* in Ps 18:14 and *yrᶜm mn-šmym* in the parallel text in 2 Sam 22:14.

133. See Pardee, *UF* 9: 212; on Ugaritic *phy b*, see 7: 365.

134. See Pardee, *UF* 7: 335; 8: 238–39, 241–42, 297; on Ugaritic *bᶜr b*, 7: 342, 8: 220; *wpṯ bṯk*, 8: 229; *ḥdy b*, 7: 346; *ḥsr bn*, 7: 347, 8: 232.

135. See Pardee, *UF* 8: 247; 9: 216.

136. Note that in this case it is not entirely clear whether the antecedent would be *maṭṭeh* or *nāḥāš*.

12

Apposition

12.1 Introduction

a The various syntactic slots associated with nouns can be filled not only by single nouns and pronouns, but also by other, more elaborate types of noun phrases. The most common types of noun phrases in Hebrew are construct phrases (9.1), adjectival phrases (14.1), coordinate phrases (e.g., מֹשֶׁה וְיִתְרוֹ), and appositional phrases. This last group of phrases is distinctive in two ways: the various parts of each phrase are juxtaposed, and they have the same or similar referents.[1] In the phrase יִתְרוֹ חֹתְנוֹ כֹּהֵן מִדְיָן, the three parts, each definite (13.2), stand side by side, and each refers to the same individual, 'Jethro, his (Moses') father-in-law, the priest of Midian' (Exod 3:1). An appositional phrase is thus a sequence of nouns (or noun phrases) with the same syntactic function and agreement and with comparable reference.[2] Sometimes the term *apposition* is used to refer to the whole of an appositional phrase; we, however, use it to describe the second (and later) terms. (*Appositive* has the same meaning.) The first term we will call the *leadword* or head. Thus, יתרו is the leadword and חתנו the apposition (or appositive).

b Appositional phrases are similar to both construct phrases and accusatives of specification; in all three phrase types one noun serves to determine another noun more precisely. Phrases which in English are appositional may correspond to Hebrew genitive phrases, for example, בַּת צִיּוֹן 'daughter Zion' (cf. 9.5.3h). In Biblical Hebrew when an object is *made of gold*, a construct phrase is generally used: עֲטֶרֶת זָהָב 'a crown *of* gold, a golden crown' (Esth 8:15, cf. Ps 21:4; 9.5.3d). But an appositional phrase may be used: שְׁתֵּי הָעֲבֹתֹת הַזָּהָב 'the two gold cords' (Exod 39:17, cf. 2 Kgs 16:17). When *gold itself* is measured, the construction is appositional: שֵׁשׁ־מֵאוֹת זָהָב 'six hundred (units of) gold'

---

1. In some construct phrases the first term shows no shortening or shift of stress, so the parts may also be said to be juxtaposed. On apposition in general see Richter,

GAHG 2. 12–15.

2. The shared case of words in apposition is apparent in Arabic.

(1 Kgs 10:16). When the raw material of gold is being made (ʿśy) into something, an accusative of specification (10.2.2e) is used: וְעָשִׂיתָ שְׁנַיִם כְּרֻבִים זָהָב, 'You shall make two cherubs (of) gold' (Exod 25:18). Because of the similarity and partial overlap of these constructions, we shall be attentive to differences among them.

Like many constructions in Hebrew an appositional phrase has a head-first (*regens-rectum*) shape. It is differentiated from a construct phrase, and similar to an adjectival phrase, in that both parts of such a phrase remain completely distinct words and all its parts agree in definiteness and reference. Occasionally the parts of an appositional phrase agree in their suffixes and in their particles, for example, עַמִּי בְחִירִי 'my people, my elect' (i.e., 'my chosen people'; Isa 43:20), עַל־עַמִּי עַל־יִשְׂרָאֵל 'over my people, over Israel' (i.e., 'over my people Israel'; 2 Sam 7:8). This agreement is not always found; see, for example, בִּירוּשָׁלַיִם הָעִיר 'in Jerusalem, the city' (i.e., 'in the city of Jerusalem'; 2 Chr 12:13), אֶת־בִּנְךָ בְכֹרֶךָ 'your son, your firstborn' (i.e., 'your firstborn son'; Exod 4:23; see also 12.3b). An appositional phrase is differentiated from an adjectival phrase in that substantives and adjectives have distinct sorts of reference. In an appositional phrase the parts have similar or identical reference; as the 'gold' examples show, this differentiation can be problematic.[3] Another differentiation is even more problematic: if two nouns juxtaposed in a phrase are indefinite, is the phrase appositional or an accusative of specification? Since accusatives of specification *may* disagree in definiteness, the indefinite phrase is usually best taken as appositional (10.2.2e).

c

Before we discuss the types of apposition found in Hebrew, we may consider the matter of contrasting linguistic resources and translation. Both English and Hebrew use the resource of apposition, but the two languages use it in different ways, and we need to be aware of the contrast as we go about both grammatical analysis and translation. Consider the ways in which English can join 'Egypt' and 'country': 'the country of Egypt,' 'the country called Egypt,' 'the country Egypt,' 'Egypt, the country.' Apposition, as the last two examples show, is normal in English with certain types of names. The same is true in Hebrew, and thus when such a name is involved in the apposition, the Hebrew text can be rendered word-for-word into English, as, for example, in the case of יְשַׁעְיָהוּ הַנָּבִיא 'Isaiah the prophet' (Isa 39:3), אֶבְיָתָר הַכֹּהֵן 'Abiathar the priest' (1 Sam 23:9), and הַנָּהָר פְּרָת 'the river, (the) Euphrates (1 Chr 5:9).

d

Hebrew, however, employs apposition more extensively than English. In English one does not normally juxtapose a substantival noun with a generic noun of material. Instead of this construction English prefers an attributive adjective that precedes the noun being qualified, for example, not 'the cords, the gold,' but 'the golden cords.' So also, instead of representing by apposition the complex of a substance noun 'tongue' and an abstract noun of quality 'deceitfulness,' as in לָשׁוֹן רְמִיָּה 'tongue, duplicity' (Ps 120:2), English convention requires 'the deceitful tongue,' and whereas Hebrew signifies the compound of 'famine' and 'seven years' by שֶׁבַע שָׁנִים רָעָב 'seven years, famine' (2 Sam 24:13), English represents it by 'seven years of famine.'

e

---

3. Grammarians of Arabic often do not distinguish appositional and adjectival phrases; see W. Wright, *A Grammar of the Arabic Language* (3d ed.; Cambridge: Cambridge University, 1898), 2. 272–74.

f   The wide use of apposition in Hebrew and the Semitic languages generally conforms with the tendency elsewhere within that family of languages to rely on the juxtaposition of elements. It is common in Hebrew to use a verbless clause (or a clause with *hyy*) to join one substantive (as subject) with a generic noun of class or material (as predicate). In such a clause the relationship between subject and predicate is not made as explicit as in a comparable English clause.

1. וַיְהִי כָל־הָאָרֶץ שָׂפָה אֶחָת
All the earth was one tongue. (The earth had one language.) Gen 11:1

2. וְהָיָה כִנּוֹר . . . מִשְׁתֵּיהֶם
Their feast is . . . harp. (They have harps . . . at their banquets.) Isa 5:12

3. מֹר־וַאֲהָלוֹת קְצִיעוֹת כָּל־בִּגְדֹתֶיךָ
All your garments are myrrh, aloes, and cassia. (All your garments are filled with the fragrance of myrrh, aloes, and cassia.) Ps 45:9

4. הַשְּׂעֹרָה אָבִיב וְהַפִּשְׁתָּה גִּבְעֹל׃
The barley was ears of grain, and the flax was bud. (The barley had headed and the flax was in bloom.) Exod 9:31

5. הַדּוּד אֶחָד תְּאֵנִים טֹבוֹת
One basket was (had) good figs. Jer 24:2

Whereas Hebrew prefers to coordinate with the copula or in a verbless clause, English idiom prefers to use such verbs as 'consists of, contains, extends over, measures, weighs,' etc. Similarly, Hebrew, like other Semitic languages, tends to relate clauses by juxtaposition, the placing together of clauses, sentences, phrases without a logically subordinating particle, instead of by subordinating clauses, sentences, phrases by a logical particle.[4]

g   Because of such differences in strategic use of grammatical structures, the Hebrew idiom ought not to be rendered word-for-word into English. At best such a translation would be awkward, and at worst it would actually misrepresent the Hebrew. Rendering ordinary Hebrew idiom with an abnormal English convention might suggest to an English-speaking audience that the Hebrew writer had sought to emphasize or intensify some unlikely aspect of thought. The abnormal English expression 'the ox, the bronze' for הַבָּקָר הַנְּחֹשֶׁת (2 Kgs 16:17) misrepresents the Hebrew, which is a simple apposition. Not infrequently a word-for-word translation, instead of faithfully representing the original text, actually distorts it.

---

4. For a discussion of this point, with good examples, see G. B. Caird, *The Language and Imagery of the Bible* (Philadelphia: Westminster, 1980) 118.

Apposition, Similarity, and Identity   **12.2**

The most difficult point about appositional constructions is the quality of the shared   a
reference. In יִתְרוֹ חֹתְנוֹ 'Jethro, his father-in-law,' there is, if Moses has one wife and she
has one father, complete identity between יתרו and חתנו.[5] In אֶבְיָתָר הַכֹּהֵן 'Abiathar the
priest,' there is a limited but clear overlap: the phrase means a certain Abiathar—no
other—and it does not claim that he was the only priest. The shared reference in שֵׁשׁ־
מֵאוֹת זָהָב is of a different sort: the unit ('six hundred') and the measured thing ('gold')
jointly point to a certain quantity of gold.[6]

It is helpful to review three philosophical distinctions implicitly involved here,   b
though we must not allow metaphysics to dictate grammar.[7] First, Aristotle distinguishes
between "matter" and "form." Every individual thing is said to consist both of matter
and of the particular form imposed upon the physical matter that gives it its identity.
Second, Aristotle also distinguishes between "substance" and "accidence"; substances are
persons or things, of which accidental properties can be predicated. Names, as well as
pronouns and phrases that identify a definite person or thing, are regarded as substantival; accidental properties involve quantity, quality, relation, action, place, state, etc.
Thus, *accidental* properties qualify *substantives*. Third, on another view of ontology, we
can say that *particular* terms are qualified by *universal* (or "generic" or "general") terms,
that is, particular terms mark out *particular* persons or things. Terms for persons or
things do not in themselves denote individuals; rather, they denote either a class of individuals or qualities, states, actions, etc. Some logicians further analyze universal terms
into *sortal* and *characterizing*; *sortals* group persons or things into classes (e.g., 'man,
woman'), while *characterizing* universals include abstract nouns, as well as verbs, adjectives, and adverbs.

Most appositional constructions involve the juxtaposition of nouns distinct in one   c
of these ways. Let us return to the three examples we began with. First, in the phrase שֵׁשׁ־
מאות זהב the leadword is a term for *form* and the appositive זהב is a term for *matter*.
Second, the name יתרו can be taken as a *substance* and חתנו as an *accident* of that
substance. Third, אביתר is a *particular* and הכהן is a qualifying *universal* (or sortal). This
approach to appositional phrases does provide a framework in which to examine the
problems of shared reference.

Noun-Noun Appositional Phrases   **12.3**

Most appositional constructions involve nouns as both leadword (or first term) and   a
apposition (or second term), although pronouns may occur as the leadword. In noun-
noun appositional phrases, the second term identifies or qualifies the first. As a result
some appositional phrases closely resemble the adjectival genitives (9.5.3).

---

5. For the sake of this argument, we assume that *ḥōtēn*
means 'father-in-law' in every sense.

6. The English distinction between restrictive and non-
restrictive modifiers does not match any pattern in Hebrew

usage.

7. See further John Lyons, *Introduction to Theoretical
Linguistics* (Cambridge: Cambridge University, 1968) 403–
5, 424–28.

b   If the leadword is a common noun, the appositive often provides further information about the subclass to which the leadword belongs. The pattern may involve a *sortal*, that is, a broad class term followed by a somewhat narrower term, of the same type.

1.	זְבָחִים שְׁלָמִים	sacrifices, peace-offerings (sacrifices *as peace-offerings*) Exod 24:5
2.	נַעֲרָה בְתוּלָה	a young girl, a virgin (a young *virgin*, *not* a youthful virgin) 1 Kgs 1:2
3.	וְהַמַּזְלֵג שְׁלֹשׁ־הַשִּׁנַּ֫יִם	the fork, the three-prongs (*the three-pronged* fork) 1 Sam 2:13
4.	אֵת כָּל־הַצָּבָא הַגִּבֹּרִים׃	all of the army, the mighty men of valor (the entire army *of fighting men*) 2 Sam 10:7
5.	נַ֫עַר אִישׁ־הָאֱלֹהִים	a young man, *a man of God* 2 Kgs 8:4
6.	מַעֲשֵׂה מִקְשֶׁה	product, hair-do (well-dressed *hair*) Isa 3:24

Indeed, this pattern is found with the broadest possible generic terms for people, אִישׁ and אִשָּׁה (cf. 9.5.3b).

7.	אִישׁ כֹּהֵן	a man, a priest (*a priest*) Lev 21:9
8.	אִשָּׁה אַלְמָנָה	a woman, a widow (*a widow*) 1 Kgs 7:14
9.	שְׁתַּ֫יִם נָשִׁים זֹנוֹת	two women, prostitutes (*two prostitutes*) 1 Kgs 3:16

c   The appositive term may refer to a different kind of categorization than the leadword. The appositive can refer to the *quality or character* of the leadword.

10.	בְּשָׂמִים רֹאשׁ	spices, first (*fine* spices) Exod 30:23
11.	אֲמָרִים אֱמֶת	words, truth (*truthful* words) Prov 22:21
12.	וּמַ֫יִם לַ֫חַץ	water, distress (water *as scanty as in drought*) 1 Kgs 22:27
13.	יַ֫יִן תַּרְעֵלָה	wine, reeling (wine *that makes one stagger*) Ps 60:5

More commonly, the appositive, if it is semantically distinct from the leadword, refers to the *material* of the leadword; both appositives of quality and material tend to involve inanimates.

14.   הַבָּקָר הַנְּחֹשֶׁת   oxen, bronze (*bronze* oxen)
                                      2 Kgs 16:17

15.   אֲשֵׁרָה כָּל־עֵץ   Asherah, every wood (Asherahs *made of any kind of wood*)
                                      Deut 16:21

16.   טוּרִים אָבֶן   rows, stones (rows *of stones*)
                                      Exod 28:17

17.   וְכָל־הָעֵמֶק הַפְּגָרִים וְהַדֶּשֶׁן   all the valley, the corpses and the ashes (the whole valley *where dead bodies and ashes are thrown*)
                                      Jer 31:40

The appositive of *measure* juxtaposes as leadword a measure, weight, or number   d
and as appositive the substance measured, weighed, or counted (## 18–20) or vice versa
(## 21–22).[8]

18. סְאָה־סֹלֶת . . . וְסָאתַיִם שְׂעֹרִים   a seah *of flour* . . . and two seahs *of barley*[9]
                                      2 Kgs 7:1

19.   שְׁלֹשָׁה בָנִים   three *sons*
                                      Gen 6:10

20.   שְׁלֹשֶׁת יָמִים דֶּבֶר   three days *of pestilence*
                                      2 Sam 24:13

21. הוּא־הִכָּה אֶת־אֱדוֹם . . . עֲשֶׂרֶת   he was the one who defeated (from) Edom . . . *ten thousand* (*men*)
     אֲלָפִים   2 Kgs 14:7

22.   וְעַל־יִשְׂרָאֵל כֻּלֹּה: over Israel, *all of it*[10]
                                      2 Sam 2:9

The appositive after a *name* (usually a *personal name*) serves to identify the bearer   e
of the name, by *office* or *relationship*.

23.   יוֹרָם הַמֶּלֶךְ   Joram *the king*
                                      2 Kgs 8:29

---

8. Similarly, if the leadword is price, the appositive is the thing valued. It may be that the leadword is to be understood in some rare instances, e.g., *wyprṣ* [*prṣ*] . . . *ʾrbʿ mʾwt ʾmh*, 'He broke [a breaking] . . . four hundred cubits' (2 Kgs 14:13).

9. Cf. Ruth 2:17.

10. The Arabic cognate of *kol, kull* is "often placed after the definite noun which [it otherwise] might govern in the genitive, in which case a pronominal suffix is appended"; see Wright, *Arabic Language*, 2. 278. See also J. A. Fitzmyer, "The Syntax of כל, כלא, 'All,' in Aramaic Texts from Egypt and in Biblical Aramaic," *Biblica* 38 (1957) 170–84; rpt. in his *A Wandering Aramean* (Missoula: Scholars Press, 1979) 205–17.

24.   וְשָׂרַי אֵשֶׁת אַבְרָם   Sarai, *Abram's wife*
                                         Gen 16:1

In cases in which the name and the identification are equally distinctive,[11] the name may
be used as the apposition; in these examples, it is presupposed that there is only one king
at a time and that *the* river of ancient southwestern Asia was the longest, the Euphrates.

25.   וְהַמֶּלֶךְ דָּוִד   the King, David (King *David*)
                                     2 Sam 3:31

26.   הַנָּהָר פְּרָת   the River *Euphrates*
                                  1 Chr 5:9

f   In cases in which the name is an apposition and the phrase takes a preposition or
אֵת, the particle is generally repeated on leadword and apposition.[12]

27.   לִבְנִי לְיִצְחָק   to my son, to *Isaac* (to my son *Isaac*)
                                    Gen 24:4

28.   לְעַבְדְּךָ לְיַעֲקֹב   to your servant, to *Jacob*
                                       Gen 32:19

29.   אֶת־אָחִיו אֶת־הָבֶל   *his brother*, Abel
                                       Gen 4:2

30.   אֶת־הָעִיר הַזֹּאת אֶת־יְרִחוֹ   this city, *Jericho*
                                               Josh 6:26

If the name is the leadword, the particle is generally not repeated.[13]

31.   אֶל־הֶבֶל אָחִיו   to Abel, *his brother*
                                   Gen 4:8

32.   לְנָחוֹר אָחִיךָ:   to Nahor, *your brother*
                                   Gen 22:20

33.   אֶת־הָגָר הַמִּצְרִית שִׁפְחָתָהּ   Hagar, the Egyptian, *her handmaid*
                                                Gen 16:3

34.   אֵת אוּרִיָּה הַכֹּהֵן   Uriah *the priest*
                                       Isa 8:2

12.4   Pronoun-Noun Appositional Phrases

a   A pronoun may be followed by a noun in apposition.[14] In the case of an independent subject pronoun after a finite verb, it is usual to speak of an emphatic, rather than

---

11. *Not* unique. The relative degree of distinctiveness is a matter of context, not metaphysics.

12. There are exceptions, e.g., Gen 24:12, 1 Sam 25:19, and the expressions ᶜmy (ᶜmk, etc.) yśrʾl. See 12.1c.

13. On preposition override, see 11.4.2.

14. Carl Brockelmann argues that pronouns can occur in apposition to nouns. In fact, only one of his examples is compellingly so understood: štym-ʾnhnw 'the two (of) us' (1 Kgs 3:18); see *Hebräische Syntax* (Neukirchen: Neukirchener Verlag, 1956) 63.

appositional, use; in # 1 the emphatic subject pronoun has its own following apposition, as increasing specificity balances narrative delay (cf. Gen 22:2).

1.	וַיַּעֲשׂוּ גַם־הֵם חַרְטֻמֵּי מִצְרַיִם בְּלַהֲטֵיהֶם כֵּן׃	The Egyptian magicians, they *too* performed (miracles) by their magical arts. Exod 7:11

More often the apposition to an independent pronoun amplifies the subject of the verb (# 2); here, the singular imperative verbs are extended to apply to a larger group—note that אתה, implicit in the imperatives, must be specified before it is amplified.

2.	קוּם עֲבֹר אֶת־הַיַּרְדֵּן הַזֶּה אַתָּה וְכָל־הָעָם הַזֶּה	Cross over this Jordan, *you and all the people.* Josh 1:2

Pronominal suffixes, be they possessive (# 3), objective (# 4–5), or prepositional (# 5), can also serve as leadwords to appositives; for pronoun–pronoun apposition, see 16.3.4a.

3.	בְּבֹאוֹ הָאִישׁ	when he, the man, went in (when *the man* went in) Ezek 10:3
4.	וַתִּרְאֵהוּ אֶת־הַיֶּלֶד	And she saw him, the baby (saw *the baby*). Exod 2:6
5.	תִּשְׂרְפֶנּוּ אֵת אֲשֶׁר־בּוֹ הַנָּגַע׃	You must burn it (the garment), that which is in it, the plague. (You must burn *the plague* in it.) Lev 13:57

Repetitive Apposition   **12.5**

Direct repetition of a noun can serve a variety of purposes; the sense may be distributive (שָׁנָה שָׁנָה 'year by year,' Deut 14:22), diverse (אֶבֶן וָאָבֶן 'two differing weights,' Deut 25:13), or emphatic (זָהָב זָהָב 'pure gold,' 2 Kgs 25:15). Of these senses, discussed earlier (7.2.3, 7.4.1a), the last is closest to appositional use. The second term seems to qualify the leadword; comparable English repetitions, infrequent in writing but common in speech, include 'hot hot' (i.e., hot tasting rather than warm, of food) and 'long long' (i.e., almost unimaginably long).[15]

1.	אַל . . . תְּדַבְּרוּ גְּבֹהָה גְבֹהָה	Do not . . . talk *so* proudly. 1 Sam 2:3
2.	וְעָמֹק עָמֹק מִי יִמְצָאֶנּוּ׃	Deep, deep (i.e., very deep), who can discern it? Qoh 7:24

15. The repetition of the *trisagion* (the seraphs' prayer in Isa 6:3) is similarly emphatic. On the suggestion that it means 'The Holy One, the Holy One, the Holy One is the Lord of Hosts,' see Baruch A. Levine, "The Language of Holiness: Perceptions of the Sacred in the Hebrew Bible," *Backgrounds for the Bible,* ed. M. O'Connor and D. N. Freedman (Winona Lake, Indiana: Eisenbrauns, 1987) 241–55, at 253.

Apposition in the strict sense can also involve repetition: the appositive then repeats the leadword.

3. אָנֹכִי הָאֵל אֱלֹהֵי אָבִיךָ   I am *God*, the *god* of your forebear.[16]
                                       Gen 46:3

4. אֵת־שְׁנֵי הַמְּאֹרֹת הַגְּדֹלִים אֶת־   the two great *lights*, the greater *light* . . . and the lesser
    הַמָּאוֹר הַגָּדֹל . . . וְאֵת־הַמָּאוֹר   *light*
    הַקָּטֹן   Gen 1:16

16. Cf. Exod 3:6.

13

Definiteness and Indefiniteness

Deixis 13.1

Many aspects of the way a clause refers to the world are handled by *pointers*. Using a
pointers, it is possible for speaker and hearer to situate an utterance without explicitly
mentioning all characterizing features. The pointing words are mostly pronouns and
various adverbial expressions; all such grammatical expressions compose a system of
deixis, the Greek word for pointing. The personal pronouns are deictics: the first-person
singular pronoun points to the speaker (the plural points to a group the speaker belongs
to), the second-person singular points to the hearer, and third-person pronouns point to
anything or anyone else. Most other pronouns are also deictics, be they demonstrative
(e.g., '*this* book'), interrogative (e.g., '*who* are you?'), indefinite (e.g., '*whoever* he sends,
goes'), or relative (e.g., 'The book *that/which* I read is good'). Hebrew uses relatively few
deictic adverbial expressions; כֵּן 'thus(ly)' is the most common. In the following chapters
we deal with the pronominal system of Hebrew (Chaps. 16–19), as well as the closely
related topics of adjectives and numerals (Chaps. 14–15); in this chapter we deal with
one of the most basic features of deixis, the *definiteness : indefiniteness* opposition. With
the pronouns this opposition is straightforward: the first- and second-person pronouns
are always definite; the third-person pronouns must be specified to be definite. As we
shall see, the opposition is frequently complex, and significant differences between Biblical Hebrew and English may be observed.

13.2   Definiteness : Indefiniteness

a   In English and other European languages the basic opposition of definite : indefinite is correlated with a pair of articles, English 'the : a, an,' French 'le/la : un/une,' German 'der/die/das : ein/eine.' Two features of the English pair are noteworthy. First, the definite article 'the' begins with a sound that is used initially only in other deictic and similar words: 'this, that, then, their,' etc. Second, the indefinite article is a reduced form of the word 'one'; the original -*n* is preserved before a vowel ('an eye'), otherwise dropped.[1] The articles are not always used in English to mark definites or indefinites. Nouns in some syntactic structures are inherently definite (e.g., 'I went *home*') or indefinite (e.g., '*Tigers* are dangerous animals'). As the examples show, a definite noun or noun phrase may have a *unique* reference (## 1–2) or a *particular* reference (## 3–4); rather infrequently, an English definite may have a *generic* reference (# 5).

> 1. I saw *Moses*.
> 2. I saw *the sun*.
> 3. I saw *the man* I was looking for.
> 4. I saw *the father* of the prophet.
> 5. *The tiger* is a dangerous animal.

An indefinite noun or noun phrase is usually non-specific (# 6), but may be specific (# 7).

> 6. I'm looking for *a tent*, but I can't find one.
> 7. I'm looking for *a tent*, but I can't find it.

In # 6, the pronoun 'one' is non-specific and shows that the phrase 'a tent' is also non-specific; in # 7, 'it' must refer to a particular tent and so also must the phrase 'a tent.'

b   With these facts in mind, we may turn to the Hebrew system, which presents many similarities to the English, so many, in fact, that it is important for students to bear in mind the many differences between the languages.[2] The basic opposition of the categories *definite : indefinite* is similar: in Hebrew, as in English, the definite noun directs attention to the referent's *identity*, while the indefinite noun focuses on the *class* to which the referent belongs, its quality and character. In # 8 the use of an indefinite (or anarthrous) noun emphasizes the class to which the referent belongs, while in # 9 the definite (or arthrous) noun phrase highlights the particularity of the referent.[3]

---

1. German, a close relative of English, uses an unreduced form of 'one,' 'ein,' as the indefinite article; Yiddish shows the same usage as English, 'a.'

2. These similarities are an important basis for the claims of the Reformation translators that Hebrew "goes better" into English than into Latin. Compare Tyndale's famous remark, "The Greek tongue agreeth more with the English than with the Latin [which has no article]. And the properties of the Hebrew tongue agreeth a thousand times more with the English than with the Latin. The manner of speaking is both one; so that in a thousand places thou needest not but to translate into the English, word for word: when thou must seek a compass in the Latin." Quoted by S. L. Greenslade, "English Versions of the Bible, A.D. 1525–1611," *The Cambridge History of the Bible. 3. The West from the Reformation to the Present Day*, ed. S. L. Greenslade (Cambridge: Cambridge University, 1963) 141–74, at 145. On the article in general grammatical theory, see W. P. Schmid, *MPD*, esp. 94–95; in Hebrew, see Richter, *GAHG* 2. 9–11.

3. Greek grammarians used the term *arthron* 'joint' for 'connecting word,' particularly for the article. In modern usage, an *arthrous* noun has the article, an *anarthrous* noun lacks it.

8.   אַתָּה בָּא אֵלַי בְּחֶרֶב   You come against me with *a sword*.
                                         1 Sam 17:45

9.   חֶרֶב גָּלְיָת . . . הִנֵּה־הִיא   *The sword* of Goliath . . . is here.
                                         1 Sam 21:10

The Hebrew system, like the English, includes under the heading of definites both intrinsically definite nouns and those with the article (13.4–6); Hebrew has no indefinite article, though the numeral אַחַת/אֶחָד 'one' is used to mark specific indefinite nouns (13.8). In sum, three categories are relevant to definiteness and indefiniteness as these phenomena are expressed in Hebrew: (1) precise identification ('the house'), (2) class identification ('(a) house'), and (3) specific indefinite identification ('a (certain) house').

Morphology of the Article

                                                  13.3

Before we consider the various syntactic features of definiteness, there are some a
morphological aspects of the article that need to be briefly reviewed.[4] These include the basic consonantal shape of the article, its vocalism, the special form of certain words with the article, and the shortening of it after some prepositions.

    The *basic form* of the article is *ha*- followed by doubling of the first consonant of b
the word to which the article is prefixed. The form is sometimes reconstructed as *han*-; the *n* of this form would account for the doubling, which would be analogous to the doubling of initial-*nun* verbs (e.g., יִפּוֹל, הִפִּיל).[5]

    The *vowel* of the article is usually *a*, as in הַמֶּלֶךְ 'the king,' but there are several c
variants. The vowel may be *lengthened*, *a* to *ā*, or it may be *dissimilated*, *a* to *e*. These changes usually occur if the word begins with a laryngeal or *r*, that is, a consonant that does not permit doubling. Before א and ר, the vowel of the article lengthens (הָ; ## 1–3). Before ה, the vowel is *a* (הַ; # 4), unless the first vowel of the word is *ā*; if that *ā* is stressed, the article has *ā* (הָ; # 5); if that *ā* is not stressed, the vowel of the article is dissimilated to *e* (הֶ; # 6). Before ח, the vowel is *a* (הַ; # 7), unless the first vowel is *ā*

---

4. The article is a West Semitic feature and is only found in dialects attested after 1200 B.C.E. The earlier West Semitic languages and Akkadian do not regularly use a comparable definite : indefinite opposition (see also 9.8b). There are three West Semitic articles: (1) prefix *ha*- + doubling, found in Hebrew, Phoenician-Punic, Moabite, Ammonite, and some Old North Arabic dialects, (2) prefix *al*- (the *l* often assimilates to the following sound), found in Classical Arabic, and (3) postposed and fused *-ā* in Aramaic, on which see Franz Rosenthal, *A Grammar of Biblical Aramaic* (Wiesbaden: Harrassowitz, 1961) §§ 41–43, 46 / pp. 23–24; and G. Bergsträsser, *Introduction to the Semitic Languages*, trans. and sup. Peter T. Daniels (Winona Lake, Indiana: Eisenbrauns, 1983) 88. Two useful sets of examples are Hebrew *hā-ʾāreṣ* ≅ Aramaic *ʾarʿāʾ* ≅ Arabic *ʾal-ʾard* 'the earth'; and Hebrew *haz-zāhāb* ≅ Aramaic *dahăbāʾ* ≅ Arabic *ʾaḏ-ḏahab* 'the gold.' On the background of all three articles, see T. O. Lambdin, "The Junctural Origin of the West Semitic Definite Article," *Near Eastern Studies in Honor of W. F. Albright*, ed. Hans Goedicke (Baltimore: Johns Hopkins, 1971) 315–33. For an attempt to consider a common origin for the Arabic and Hebrew articles, see Edward Ullendorff, "The Form of the Definite Article in Arabic and Other Semitic Languages," in his *Is Biblical Hebrew a Language? Studies in Semitic Languages and Civilizations* (Wiesbaden: Harrassowitz, 1977) 165–71.

For the phonological terminology used below, see, e.g., T. O. Lambdin, *Introduction to Biblical Hebrew* (New York: Scribner, 1971) xvi. The article occurs about 30,000 times (SA/THAT).

5. The form *hal*- is also sometimes reconstructed; it is close to the Arabic article *ʾal*, as well as to certain rare demonstratives in Hebrew, *hallāz*, *hallāzê*, *hallēzû*. The *ha* is at any rate a Semitic demonstrative element. Cf. 17.2a.

(## 8–9) or ŏ (*ḥateph qameṣ*; ## 10–11), in which case the article is הֶ, whether the *ā* is stressed (# 8) or not (# 9). Before ע, the article is generally הָ (## 12–13), unless the first vowel is unstressed *ā*, in which case the article is הֶ (## 14–15).

1.	הָאִישׁ	the man		9.	הֶחָכָם	the wise man
2.	הָרָשָׁע	the wicked man		10.	הֶחֳדָשִׁים	the months
3.	הָרֶגֶל	the foot		11.	הֶחֳרָבוֹת	the wastelands
4.	הַהֵיכַל	the palace		12.	הָעִוֵּר	the blind man
5.	הָהָר	the mountain		13.	הָעִיר	the city
6.	הֶהָרִים	the mountains		14.	הֶעָוֹן	the iniquity
7.	הַחֹדֶשׁ	the month		15.	הֶעָפָר	the dust
8.	הֶחָג	the festival				

In sum, the basic *a* of the article

    a. dissimilates to *e* before הָ, חָ, non-stressed עָ, non-stressed הָ
    b. lengthens to *ā* before א, ר, most other ע, stressed הָ
    c. remains *a* elsewhere (i.e., before other ה, other ח)

d   The form of the article has another variation: words beginning with *yə* or *mə* often form the article without doubling; the word-initial shewa is silent (## 16–19).

16.	הַיְלָדִים	the children	(*haylādîm*)
17.	הַיְסוֹד	the base	(*haysôd*)
18.	הַמְבַקְשִׁים	the searchers	(*hambaqšîm*)
19.	הַמְרַגְּלִים	the spies	(*hamraggəlîm*)

If the consonant after *yə* is ה or ע, this rule is not observed and the doubling is found (## 20–21); if the consonant after *mə* is ה, ע, or ר, the doubling is also usually found (## 22–24).

20.	הַיְּהוּדִים	the Judahites	(*hayyəhûdîm*)
21.	הַיְּעֵפִים	the weary	(*hayyəʿēpîm*)
22.	הַמְּהוּמָה	the confusion	(*hamməhûmâ*)
23.	הַמְּעָרָה	the cave	(*hamməʿārâ*)
24.	בַּמְּרֵעִים	in the evildoers	(*bammərēʿîm*)

e   A few words have a special shape after the article (## 25–29).

25.	הָאָרוֹן	אָרוֹן		28.	עָם / עַם	הָעָם
26.	הָאָ֫רֶץ	אֶ֫רֶץ		29.	פָּר / פַּר	הַפָּר
27.	הֶחָג	חָג / חַג				

In some cases the form of these words with the *ā* is found without the article, but in all cases the article requires the longer vowel.

The article is generally shortened after a monographic preposition, *bə, kə, lə*; the   f
shewa of the preposition and the *h* of the article are elided, so the preposition stands
with the vowel of the article.

30.   לָאִישׁ   to *the* man
31.   בַּשָּׁמַ֫יִם   in *the* heavens

This elision is not strictly phonological, since it does not occur with *wə*, and there are
various exceptions, most in later books (contrast ## 32–33).

32.   לֶחָכָם   to *the* wise man
                                Qoh 7:19

33.   כְּהֶחָכָם   like *the* wise man
                                Qoh 8:1

Definite Nouns

13.4

A noun is definite if it (1) is intrinsically definite, (2) bears the article or a suffix, or   a
(3) is in construct with a noun definite by (1) or (2). Intrinsically definite nouns tend to
have unique referents, while nouns with the article may have particular or unique referents. In this section we deal with the first and third cases of definiteness; in the following
two sections, the arthrous construction is treated.

The largest class of *intrinsically definite nouns* is *names*: divine names (# 1), human   b
names (## 2–3), place names (## 4–6). A name as such has a unique referent.

1.	יהוה	Y<small>HWH</small>		4.	חֶרְמוֹן	Hermon
2.	מֹשֶׁה	Moses		5.	צֹר	Tyre
3.	חַוָּה	Living One, Eve		6.	פְּרָת	Euphrates

Nearly all *pronouns* are also inherently definite, by virtue of their role as pointers to
unique things or persons; definite pronouns may be personal (## 7–8), demonstrative
(## 9–10), or interrogative (# 11).

7.   עֵירֹם אָנֹ֫כִי   *I* am naked.
                                Gen 3:10

8.   אָנֹכִי יהוה אֱלֹהֶ֫יךָ   *I* am Y<small>HWH</small>, your God.
                                Exod 20:2

9.   מַלֵּא שְׁבֻעַ זֹאת   Complete the week of *this one*.
                                Gen 29:27

10.   שִׁלְחוּ־נָא אֶת־זֹאת מֵעָלַי   Send *this one* away from me to the outside.
                הַח֫וּצָה   2 Sam 13:17

11.   מִי הִגִּיד לָךְ   *Who* told you. . . ?
                                Gen 3:11

Also inherently definite are *unique appellatives*, terms that refer to unique individuals or things and are used more or less as names. Terms for the God of Israel tend to be treated as unique appellatives, taking the article rarely (# 12; the anarthrous form is more common in the Pentateuch, while the article is used more often in the Former Prophets) or never (## 13–14).

12.	אֱלֹהִים	God
13.	אֵל עֶלְיוֹן	Most High God
14.	אֵל שַׁדַּי	Ruling (?) God

Certain cosmological elements (## 15–17) and earthly institutions (# 18) are also treated in this way.

15.	תֵּבֵל	The World, Landmass	17.	שְׁאוֹל	The Grave
16.	תְּהוֹם	The Abyss, Deep	18.	אֹהֶל מֹעֵד	The Tent of Meeting

Many earthly place names, for the same reason, lack the article, even if formed with common nouns (## 19–22).

19.	שְׂדֵה כוֹבֵס	Fuller's Field Isa 7:3, 36:2
20.	שְׂדֵה צֹפִים	Watcher's Field Num 23:14
21.	עֵין־גֶּדִי	Kid's Spring 1 Sam 24:1
22.	עֵין שֶׁמֶשׁ	Sun Spring Josh 15:7

Often certain titles are taken as unique (## 23–24).

23.	שַׂר־צָבָא	Chief of the Army[6] 2 Sam 2:8, 19:14; 1 Kgs 16:16
24.	רַב־טַבָּחִים	Captain of the Guard[7] 2 Kgs 25:8, Jer 39:9

c   The *construct relation* usually carries definiteness over from the genitive to the construct: thus, the construct is usually definite if the following genitive is definite as a name (# 25), a pronoun (# 26), a unique appellative (# 27), or because of the article (# 28–29).

25.	אִישׁ נָעֳמִי	*the husband* of Naomi Ruth 1:3
26.	אִישָׁהּ	her *husband* Gen 3:6

---

6. Cf. *śr(-)ḥṣbᵓ* in 1 Sam 17:55, Dan 8:11.   7. Cf. *śr ḥṭbḥym* in Gen 37:36, 39:1.

27.	פְּנֵי תְהוֹם	*the face* of the Abyss Gen 1:2
28.	פְּנֵי הַמָּ֫יִם	*the face* of the water Gen 1:2
29.	מִפְּרִי עֵץ־הַגָּן	from *the fruit of the tree* of the Garden Gen 3:2

There are exceptions, however, in which the construct phrase is indefinite with the following genitive definite as a name (## 30–31), a pronoun (# 32), a unique appellative (# 33), or because of the article (## 34–35; cf. 9.7a).

30.	וָאֵ֫רֶא בַשָּׁלָל אַדֶּ֫רֶת שִׁנְעָר אַחַת טוֹבָה	I saw among the spoil *a certain* beautiful Babylonian *garment.* Josh 7:21 *Qere*
31.	בְּתוּלַת יִשְׂרָאֵל	*a (certain) virgin* of Israel Deut 22:19
32.	אָחִי הוּא	He is *a brother* of mine. Gen 20:5; cf. 8.4.2a
33.	רוּחַ אֱלֹהִים רָעָה	*a (certain)* evil *spirit* of God 1 Sam 18:10
34.	אִישׁ הָאֲדָמָה	*a farmer* Gen 9:20
35.	בִּנְקִיק הַסָּ֫לַע	in *a (certain) cleft* of the rock Jer 13:4

In most of these cases (## 30, 31, 33, 35), it is clear from context that the genitive is a specific indefinite, namely, 'a certain . . .'; in # 30, the addition of ʾaḥat makes this clear. The generic noun of class אִישׁ is used in # 34 with an article of class (cf. 9.5.3b).

Common Nouns with the Article   **13.5**

Common nouns—roughly, all nouns except names and unique appellatives—are a
made definite by the article. The conventions of the Hebrew language regularly call for the use of the article with common nouns in ways similar to the English usage of the article 'the' and in ways that differ noticeably from it. Since the uses of the article may differ in Hebrew and in English, it is necessary to note its normal uses in Hebrew in order to avoid distorting the meaning of the Hebrew; a word-for-word translation would often lead to abnormal English. It is vital to read Hebrew from the Hebrew speaker's point of view; it is also important to consider how that point of view can be represented in English by its normal conventions, without engaging in an extended commentary.

There are two major areas that need to be explored in considering Hebrew articular b
usage. One area involves the referential side: what does the article reveal about the

functioning of the word it modifies? The other area is syntactic: how does the *article* + *noun* combination fit into the clause?

13.5.1   Referential Features

a   The common noun with the article may have a unique, particular, or generic function. Generic usage is vastly more common in Hebrew than it is in English.

b   The common noun with an article may designate a *unique referent*. The uniqueness may be natural, for example, הַשֶּׁמֶשׁ 'the sun' in Exod 17:12 or לַיָּרֵחַ 'to the moon' in Deut 17:3; or theological, for example, הָאֱלֹהִים 'God' in Gen 6:2; or situational, for example, הַמֶּלֶךְ 'the King' in 1 Sam 8:9 or הַכֹּהֵן הַגָּדֹל 'the High Priest' in Num 35:25. The usage conflicts to some extent with the intrinsic definiteness of unique appellatives (13.4b); on the whole, with theological terms and place names the article is rare.

c   Situational uniqueness arises because, for example, the culture allows only one king or high priest at a time. Closely related to this type of definiteness is the use of the *noun + article* to designate *a well-known thing or person*; the combination is close to constituting a name (cf. 13.6). Consider, for example, these English sentences: 'I'm going on holiday in the Rocky Mountains' *versus* 'I will meet you at the rocky hill.' In English we distinguish these two uses in writing by capitalizing the former and writing the latter in lower case. The distinctions involved are sometimes subjective and arbitrary.

1. וַתִּקָּבֵר מִתַּחַת לְבֵית־אֵל תַּחַת הָאַלּוֹן   And she was buried under *the oak* below Bethel.
                                                         Gen 35:8

2. לִפְנֵי הָרָעַשׁ׃   before *the earthquake*
                          Amos 1:1

d   The article most often serves to give a noun a *particular* reference.

3. לֶךְ־לְךָ מֵאַרְצְךָ . . . אֶל־הָאָרֶץ אֲשֶׁר אַרְאֶךָּ׃   Go from your land . . . to *the land* that I will show you.
                                                               Gen 12:1

Particular reference may be based on previous mention of the thing or person; such use is *anaphoric*.

4. וַיִּקַּח בֶּן־בָּקָר . . . וַיִּקַּח . . . בֶּן־הַבָּקָר   And he took a calf . . . and he took . . . *the calf*.
                                                              Gen 18:7–8

5. וַיֵּלֶךְ אִישׁ . . . וְשֵׁם הָאִישׁ אֱלִימֶלֶךְ   And a man went out . . . and the name of *that man* was Elimelech.
                                                          Ruth 1:1–2

6. וַיֹּאמֶר אֱלֹהִים יְהִי אוֹר . . . וַיַּרְא אֱלֹהִים אֶת־הָאוֹר   And God said, "Let there be light." . . . And God saw *the light*.
                                                                       Gen 1:3–4

This usage is weakly demonstrative. A close parallel to # 5 actually uses a demonstrative.

7.	אִישׁ הָיָה בְאֶרֶץ־עוּץ . . . וְהָיָה הָאִישׁ הַהוּא תָּם וְיָשָׁר	There was a man in the land of Uz . . . and *that man* was pure and upright. Job 1:1

Particular reference may also be cataphoric, that is, restricted by what follows; this usage is discussed in 13.5.2d.

The article may also mark *nouns definite in the imagination*, designating either a   e particular person or thing necessarily understood to be present or vividly portraying someone or something whose identity is not otherwise indicated. For a person or thing understood to be present, the English language often also uses the article.

8.	וַיִּקַּח בְּיָדוֹ אֶת־הָאֵשׁ וְאֶת־ הַמַּאֲכֶלֶת	And he took in his hand *the fire* and *the knife*. Gen 22:6
9.	וַתְּעַר כַּדָּהּ אֶל־הַשֹּׁקֶת	And she emptied her jar into *the trough*. Gen 24:20
10.	וַתֹּאמֶר לָהּ הַמְיַלֶּדֶת	And *the midwife* said to her. . . . Gen 35:17; cf. 38:28

At other times English idiom prefers the personal pronoun.[8]

11.	וְלָקַח דָּוִד אֶת־הַכִּנּוֹר	David would take *his* harp. 1 Sam 16:23
12.	וַתִּקַּח הַצָּעִיף	So she took *her* veil. Gen 24:65
13.	וַתִּפֹּל מֵעַל הַגָּמָל׃	She alighted from *her* camel. Gen 24:64

In some cases the proper English rendering is indefinite.[9]

14.	הַמֵּלִיץ בֵּינֹתָם׃	*An interpreter* was between them. Gen 42:23
15.	וַיִּתֵּן אֶל־הַנַּעַר	He gave (it) to *a servant*. Gen 18:7
16.	וַיָּבֹא הַפָּלִיט	*One who had escaped* came. Gen 14:13
17.	וַיָּרָץ הַנַּעַר	*A young man* ran. Num 11:27

---

8. English usage, cited here for comparative purposes, is itself tremendously variable; cf., e.g., *hammiṭṭâ* 'the/his bed' in Gen 47:31, *hakkissēʾ* 'the/his throne' in Judg 3:20.

9. And in some cases the English rendering is open to discussion: a fluent or slightly informal narrative style allows for more situationally understood definite articles.

| 18. | וַיָּבֹא הַמַּגִּיד | *A messenger* came.
2 Sam 15:13 |

This use is also found in the expression וַיְהִי הַיּוֹם.

| 19. | וַיְהִי הַיּוֹם וַיִּזְבַּח אֶלְקָנָה | *One day* Elkanah came to sacrifice.
1 Sam 1:4 |

The analogous English constructions should not mislead: all these occurrences, and others like them, are definite in Hebrew.

f   The use of the article to mark out the particular and unique, as well as the situationally pertinent, is balanced by the *generic* use.[10] The article of class marks out not a particular single person or thing but a class of persons, things, or qualities that are unique and determined in themselves. Sometimes the class is regarded as a unity, while at other times an individual within the species is singled out to represent the genus. This use is much more extensive in Hebrew than in English. The generic article may be used with a *collective singular* (see 7.2.1b).

| 20. | הַבָּקָר | *the cattle* (or, *the herd*)
Gen 18:7 |
| 21. | אֶת־הַצַּדִּיק וְאֶת־הָרָשָׁע | *the righteous* and *the wicked*
Qoh 3:17 |

This use is especially common with animals: an individual of a species may refer to the whole.

| 22. | אַךְ אֶת־זֶה לֹא תֹאכְלוּ . . . אֶת־
הַגָּמָל . . . וְאֶת־הַשָּׁפָן | But these you may not eat . . . *the camel*, . . . *the coney*. . . .
Lev 11:4–5 |
| 23. | שֶׁקֶר הַסּוּס לִתְשׁוּעָה | *A horse* is a vain hope for victory.
Ps 33:17 |

Moreover, it is especially common in comparisons, with (## 24–27) or without animals (## 28–30).

24.	כְּלֵב הָאַרְיֵה	like the heart of *a lion* 2 Sam 17:10
25.	כַּאֲשֶׁר יָלֹק הַכֶּלֶב	as *a dog* laps Judg 7:5
26.	כַּאֲשֶׁר יִרְדֹּף הַקֹּרֵא	as one hunts *a partridge* 1 Sam 26:20
27.	כְּשַׁסַּע הַגְּדִי	as one rends *a kid* Judg 14:6

---

10. Joüon uses the term "imperfect determination" for the generic use; § 137m / p. 425.

28.	כְּקִיטֹר הַכִּבְשָׁן	like the smoke from *a furnace* Gen 19:28
29.	כַּאֲשֶׁר יַחֲלֹם הָרָעֵב	as when someone dreams in *a famine* Isa 29:8
30.	וְנָגֹלּוּ כַסֵּפֶר הַשָּׁמָיִם	And the heavens shall be rolled together as *a scroll*. Isa 34:4

The generic article is also used with plurals.

31.	הַכּוֹכָבִים	*the stars* Gen 15:5; cf. 1:16
32.	הַגּוֹיִם	*the nations* Gen 10:32
33.	לַבְּקָרִים	all *the mornings* Isa 33:2, Ps 73:14
34.	לֹא־כֵן הָרְשָׁעִים	Not so *the wicked*. Ps 1:4

Both singular and plural gentilics regularly take the article in referring to the entire group, for example, הַכְּנַעֲנִי 'the Canaanite(s),' הָעִבְרִים 'the Hebrews.' In gentilics derived from construct-chain names the second term of the chain takes the article, for example, אֲבִי הָעֶזְרִי 'the Abiezrite' (< אֲבִיעֶזֶר;[11] Judg 6:11, 24), בֵּית הַלַּחְמִי 'the Bethlehemite' (< בֵּית לֶחֶם; 1 Sam 17:58). The group term פְּלִשְׁתִּים usually does not take the article; only eight times is הַ used and in only eighteen cases is a preceding preposition given the pointing of the article.

The generic article is found with items other than animals, for example, materials   **g**
(## 35–39; note the comparisons in # 38).[12]

35.	בַּמִּקְנֶה בַּכֶּסֶף וּבַזָּהָב:	in *livestock*, in *silver*, and in *gold* Gen 13:2
36.	בָאֵשׁ	with *fire* Josh 11:9
37.	בַּחֵמָר וּבַזָּפֶת	with *tar* and *pitch*[13] Exod 2:3
38.	אִם־יִהְיוּ חֲטָאֵיכֶם כַּשָּׁנִים כַּשֶּׁלֶג יַלְבִּינוּ	Though your sins be *like crimson*, they shall become as white *as snow*. Isa 1:18

---

11. Abiezer is only attested as a personal name, not as a place name; the analysis of the name as a construct phrase, implicit in the gentilic form, is open to question. The name may in origin be a sentence name, 'My (divine) Father is Help'; cf. 8.2.

12. Other examples in Gen 2:11, 11:3; Amos 2:6; 2 Chr 2:13, 14.

13. For another medium, note *ktb bassēper* 'to write on a scroll' (Exod 17:14, 1 Sam 10:25, Jer 32:10; cf. *ntn bspr* in Job 19:23).

39.   רְבִד הַזָּהָב   *a chain of gold*
                                        Gen 41:42

Measurements and measured units are also so marked.

40.   וְהָעֹמֶר עֲשִׂרִית הָאֵיפָה הוּא׃   *An omer* is one tenth of *an ephah.*
                                        Exod 16:36

41.   צְרוֹר הַמֹּר   *a bag of myrrh*
                                        Cant 1:13

Abstract terms, referring to attributes, qualities, or states, also take the generic article.

42.   בַּסַּנְוֵרִים   with *blindness*
                                        Gen 19:11

43.   הַדָּבֶר   *diseases*[14]
                                        Deut 28:21

44.   בַּתִּמָּהוֹן   with *panic*[15]
                                        Zech 12:4

45.   וְהָאֱמוּנָה אֵזוֹר חֲלָצָיו׃   *Faithfulness* is the sash around his waist.
                                        Isa 11:5

46.   וְיִכּוֹן בַּצֶּדֶק כִּסְאוֹ׃   His throne will be established through *righteousness.*
                                        Prov 25:5

13.5.2   Syntactic Features

a   The article may be used as a demonstrative, as a vocative marker, and as a relative marker. In these uses the referent of the *noun + article* combination is particular.

b   Expressions of *present time* are used adverbially, and the article has a clear *demonstrative* force, though, as noted above, such force can be found elsewhere, too (17.5).

1.   הַיּוֹם   *this day/today*[16]
                                        Gen 4:14

2.   הַלַּיְלָה   *this night/tonight*
                                        Gen 19:5

3.   הַשָּׁנָה   *this year*
                                        2 Kgs 19:29 ≅ Isa 37:30, Jer 28:16

4.   הַפַּעַם   *this time*
                                        Exod 9:27

With a preposition the article does not suffice; the demonstrative pronoun is also needed.

---

14. Other diseases in Lev 13:12; Amos 4:9 ≅ Hag 2:17.
15. Another strong emotion in 2 Sam 1:9.
16. For an extensive discussion of *hayyôm*, see S. J.

DeVries, *Yesterday, Today, and Tomorrow: Time and History in the Old Testament* (Grand Rapids: Eerdmans, 1975) 151–277.

5.   בַּיּוֹם הַזֶּה   in *this day*
                                          Josh 7:25

6.   כַּפַּעַם הַזֹּאת   at *this time*
                                          Exod 8:28

The article is used to mark *a definite addressee*, pointing out a particular individual   c
who is present to the speaker and who is addressed in the *vocative*. English does not use
its definite article in this way. The article may be used when a common noun is in
apposition to a definite noun.

7.   שְׁמַע־נָא יְהוֹשֻׁעַ הַכֹּהֵן הַגָּדוֹל   Listen, *O high priest* Joshua.
                                          Zech 3:8

8.   וַיִּקְרָא אַחֲרֵי־שָׁאוּל לֵאמֹר אֲדֹנִי   And he called to Saul, "My Lord, *O King*."
     הַמֶּלֶךְ   1 Sam 24:9

It is also found when the common noun is in apposition only to a second-person pronoun, implied or stated.

9.   חֵי־נַפְשְׁךָ הַמֶּלֶךְ   As surely as you live, *O King*.
                                          1 Sam 17:55

10.   בֶּן־מִי אַתָּה הַנָּעַר   Whose son are you, *young man*?
                                          1 Sam 17:58

11.   דָּבָר לִי אֵלֶיךָ הַשָּׂר   I have an errand for you, *O Commander*.
                                          2 Kgs 9:5

Quite frequently the article is not used when the reference is to persons not present or
who are more or less imaginary.[17]

12.   שְׂמַח בָּחוּר בְּיַלְדוּתֶיךָ   Be happy, *young man*, when you are young.
                                          Qoh 11:9

13.   לֵךְ־אֶל־נְמָלָה עָצֵל   Go to the ant, *O sluggard*.
                                          Prov 6:6

Anaphoric use of the article is based on the previous mention of the thing referred   d
to (13.5.1d); it is possible for the definiteness to be established in the same clause as the
reference, and such use is called *cataphoric*. Here are two English examples.

anaphoric 'the': I saw a man. *The* man was tall.
cataphoric 'the': *The* man that I saw was tall.

As the English example suggests, cataphoric reference can be associated with relative
clauses, and the comparable Hebrew use of הַ is often likened to the relative pronoun.

---

17. Cf. Isa 22:2, Mic 1:2. But cf. *habbáʿal ʿănēnû* 'O Baal, answer us,' 1 Kgs 18:26.

This so-called relative use of the article (cf. 19.7) is most common with participles, whether used attributively (i.e., adjectivally; ## 14–16; see 37.5) or predicatively (## 17–20).[18]

14.	לַיהוה הַנִּרְאֶה אֵלָיו:	to Yhwh, *who had appeared* to him Gen 12:7
15.	הַשֹּׁלֵחַ	*the one who sent* (you) 2 Kgs 22:18
16.	הַנֶּחֱמָדִים	*the ones to be desired* Ps 19:11
17.	הוּא הַסֹּבֵב	It is *the one that circles around.* . . . Gen 2:11
18.	פִּי הַמְדַבֵּר אֲלֵיכֶם:	It is my mouth *that is speaking to you.* Gen 45:12
19.	עֵינֵיךָ הָרֹאֹת	It is your eyes *that have seen.* . . . Deut 3:21
20.	אָנֹכִי הַבָּא מִן־הַמַּעֲרָכָה	I am *the one who came back* from the battle. 1 Sam 4:16

Other predicates can also take the article; in a sense these predicates are adjectival, but it should be remembered that there is no distinct class of adjectives in Hebrew (14.3.2).

21.	יהוה הַצַּדִּיק וַאֲנִי וְעַמִּי הָרְשָׁעִים:	Yhwh is *the one who is in the right* and I and my people are *the ones who are in the wrong.* Exod 9:27

A predicate adjective with an article often has a superlative sense.

22.	וְדָוִד הוּא הַקָּטָן	Now it was David who was *the youngest.* 1 Sam 17:14
23.	אַתֶּם הָרַבִּים	You are *the ones who are most numerous.* 1 Kgs 18:25

In a few cases, the article is used with a finite verb to form a relative clause, either with an explicit antecedent (## 24–25)[19] or without one (# 26).[20]

24.	קְצִינֵי אַנְשֵׁי הַמִּלְחָמָה הֶהָלְכוּא אִתּוֹ	the army commanders *who had come* with him Josh 10:24
25.	עַמְּךָ הַנִּמְצְאוּ־פֹה	your people *who are present* here 1 Chr 29:17

---

18. Note also Qoh 7:26. Cf. M. H. Segal, *A Grammar of Mishnaic Hebrew* (Oxford: Clarendon, 1927) 181.

19. Same construction in Ezra 8:25, 10:17; with ʾšr in

Judg 5:27, Ezra 10:14.

20. Same construction in 2 Chr 1:4. Note the relative frequency of these usages in Chronicles and Ezra.

26. ‏וַיִּשְׂמַח . . . עַל הַהֵכִין הָאֱלֹהִים‏
    ‏לָעָם‏

And he . . . rejoiced at *what* God *had done* for the people.
2 Chr 29:36

This construction may be compared to English cleft sentences ('It is the prophet that I was seeking') and pseudo-cleft sentences ('The prophet was who I sought'), as well as to French constructions in 'C'est . . . celui qui . . .' ('It is . . . the one who . . .').

Intrinsically Definite Nouns with the Article   13.6

The article is chiefly used with common nouns according to the patterns outlined in 13.5. Normally words that are definite in themselves do not take the article since the article would be redundant. But there is one major class of exceptions. Sometimes, through usage, the article not only points out a particular person or thing, but it also elevates it to such a position of uniqueness that the *noun + article* combination becomes the equivalent of a *proper name* (13.4b). Among English speakers, for example, in some communities 'the city' no longer designates one city out of many, but through usage denotes 'The City,' the only city in that area. In such constructions it is not that the article is added to a name; rather the article makes the combination a name. Such combinations make up toponyms.

1.	‏הַגִּבְעָה‏	the hill	Gibeah
2.	‏הַיְאֹר‏	the stream (*hayʾor*)	the Nile
3.	‏הַכִּכָּר‏	the circuit	the Jordan Circuit
4.	‏הַלְּבָנוֹן‏	the white	(Mt.) Lebanon
5.	‏הַנָּהָר‏	the river	the Euphrates
6.	‏אֶבֶן הָעֵזֶר‏	the rock of help	Ebenezer

They are also used to name individuals.

7.	‏הָאֱלֹהִים‏	the god	God
8.	‏הַבַּעַל‏	the lord	Baal
9.	‏הַשָּׂטָן‏	the adversary	Satan

In addition to this intermediate naming construction, there are other anomalous cases of an article on a noun with a suffix or in construct. In most cases these forms are the result of textual corruption.[21] In Josh 7:21 the form ‏הָאָהֳלִי‏ 'the/my tent' may be a blend of ‏האהל‏ and ‏אהלי‏. The phrase ‏הַמֶּלֶךְ אַשּׁוּר‏ occurs twice in Isa 36:8, 16 but the proper anarthrous form is found in synoptic verses in 2 Kings (18:23, 31). In Isa 24:2 the term ‏כַּגְּבִרְתָּהּ‏ 'like her mistress' may have the pointing *ka* instead of *kǝ* because the syllable *ka* occurs eleven other times in the verse, creating a strong pattern of assonance. In at least one case the suffix on a form has lost its meaning:[22] in addition to the word

---

21. And as such are better dealt with in a commentary than in a grammar. In a few cases the MT is too arresting for simple dismissal, e.g., Mic 2:12.

22. So also W. L. Holladay, *A Concise Hebrew and Aramaic Lexicon of the Old Testament* (Grand Rapids, Michigan: Eerdmans, 1971) 283.

עֵ֫רֶךְ 'value,' Hebrew has a term עֶרְכְּךָ ('your value' >) 'value,' used with the article, הָעֶרְכְּךָ (Lev 27:23), and in construct, כְּעֶרְכְּךָ הַכֹּהֵן 'according to the value (set by) the priest' (Lev 27:12).

13.7   Use and Nonuse of the Article

a The article is not consistently used even according to the best established patterns. Most often it is "omitted," or not used where it would be expected, in *poetry*, and this pattern of nonuse is truer of older poetry, though the pattern is found in relatively late poetic passages and in prose.[23] In studying this pattern scholars have found that the Masoretes tended to regularize articular use where they could, that is, with the monographic prepositions; again, this is only a broad tendency, not a fixed rule.

b Nouns with unique referents furnish some convenient examples. In Gen 1:1 we find the articles in the phrase אֵת הַשָּׁמַיִם וְאֵת הָאָרֶץ, and in 2:1 we find השמים והארץ; in the archaic prayer of Melchisedeq, in contrast, the phrase קֹנֵה שָׁמַיִם וָאָרֶץ lacks the articles (Gen 14:19). Turning back to Genesis 2, we find fluctuation in two neighboring pieces of prose.

1. אֵלֶּה תוֹלְדוֹת הַשָּׁמַיִם וְהָאָרֶץ בְּהִבָּרְאָם   These are the accounts of the cosmos when it was created. Gen 2:4a

2. בְּיוֹם עֲשׂוֹת יהוה אֱלֹהִים אֶרֶץ וְשָׁמָיִם: When Yhwh God made the cosmos. . . . Gen 2:4b

The omission is most common in verse.

3. מַלְכֵי־אָרֶץ   [*the*] kings of [*the*] earth Ps 2:2

4. אַפְסֵי־אָרֶץ   [*the*] ends of [*the*] earth Ps 2:8

5. לִפְנֵי־שֶׁמֶשׁ   before [*the*] sun Ps 72:17

There is fluctuation, however, even in verse.

6. בְּשָׁלוֹם . . . אֶשְׁכְּבָה   I will lie down . . . in peace. Ps 4:9; cf. 55:19

7. יהוה יְבָרֵךְ . . . בַשָּׁלוֹם: May Yhwh bless . . . with peace. Ps 29:11; cf. Job 15:21

23. On the general pattern see Joüon § 137f / 421 n. 3; D. N. Freedman, *Pottery, Poetry, and Prophecy: Studies in Early Hebrew Poetry* (Winona Lake, Indiana: Eisenbrauns, 1980) 2–4; for full details, both theoretical and statistical and counts by individual chapters, see F. I. Andersen and A. Dean Forbes, "'Prose Particle' Counts of the Hebrew Bible," *The Word of the Lord Shall Go Forth: Essays in Honor of David Noel Freedman*, ed. C. L. Meyers and M. O'Connor (Winona Lake, Indiana: Eisenbrauns, 1983) 165–83.

In the archaic invocation to the great lights in Joshua 10, three of the four expected articles are omitted.[24]

8.	וַיֹּאמֶר לְעֵינֵי יִשְׂרָאֵל	He (Yнwн) said in sight of Israel,
	שֶׁמֶשׁ בְּגִבְעוֹן דּוֹם	O sun, stand still over Gibeon.
	וְיָרֵחַ בְּעֵמֶק אַיָּלוֹן:	O moon, over the Valley of Aijalon.
	וַיִּדֹּם הַשֶּׁמֶשׁ	Sun stood still,
	וְיָרֵחַ עָמָד	Moon stood fixed,
	עַד־יִקֹּם גּוֹי אֹיְבָיו	Until he (Yнwн) defeated his enemies' force.
		Josh 10:12–13

Indefinite Nouns

13.8

Indefinite nouns are not as a rule marked in Hebrew, but on occasion specific indefinites may be, with אַחַת/אֶחָד 'one.'[25] As an adjective with a singular noun, it has the force of 'a certain.'[26]

1.	קַח צִנְצֶנֶת אַחַת	Take *a* jar.
		Exod 16:33
2.	אֶבֶן אֶחָת	*a single* stone
		Judg 9:5
3.	אִשָּׁה אַחַת	*a certain* woman
		Judg 9:53
4.	אִישׁ אֶחָד מִצָּרְעָה	*a certain* man of Zorah
		Judg 13:2
5.	וַיְהִי אִישׁ אֶחָד מִן־הָרָמָתַיִם	There was *a certain* man of Ramathaim.
		1 Sam 1:1
6.	וְנָבִיא אֶחָד זָקֵן יֹשֵׁב בְּבֵית־אֵל	*A certain* old prophet was living in Bethel.
		1 Kgs 13:11
7.	וַיִּתֶּן . . . הַמֶּלֶךְ סָרִיס אֶחָד	The king assigned . . . *a certain* official.
		2 Kgs 8:6

As a noun in construct with a plural noun, it has the force of 'one of, a.'

8.	תַּחַת אַחַד הַשִּׂיחִם:	under *one of* the bushes (or, *a* bush)
		Gen 21:15
9.	עַל אַחַד הֶהָרִים אֲשֶׁר אֹמַר אֵלֶיךָ:	on *a* mountain I will tell you of
		Gen 22:2

---

24. On this poem see Robert G. Boling, *Joshua* (Anchor Bible 6; Garden City, New York: Doubleday, 1982) 274, 283–85, who deals with the lexical difficulties of the final line, as well as with the wide range of explanations offered for what the poem describes.

25. See Joüon § 137u–v / p. 428.

26. Note also 1 Sam 7:9, 12. The use is infrequent enough that # 2 and # 3 play a role in the structure of Judges 9.

10.   סְפָחֵנִי נָא אֶל־אַחַת הַכְּהֻנּוֹת   Appoint me to *some* priestly office so that I can have
       לֶאֱכֹל פַּת־לָחֶם: food to eat.
                                        1 Sam 2:36

11.   וּבָאנוּ אֵלָיו בְּאַחַת הַמְּקוֹמֹת   Then we will attack him *wherever* he may be found.
       אֲשֶׁר נִמְצָא שָׁם   2 Sam 17:12

This twist of style is particularly frequent in comparisons.

12.   כְּאַחַד הַצְּבָיִם   as *one of* the wild gazelles
                                      2 Sam 2:18

13.   כְּאַחַד הַנְּבָלִים בְּיִשְׂרָאֵל   like *a* wicked fool in Israel
                                          2 Sam 13:13

b   Indefinite personal nouns may also be marked with a generic noun of class, אִישׁ or an equivalent.

14.   אִשָּׁה־אַלְמָנָה אָנִי   I am *a widow*.
                                      2 Sam 14:5

15.   תָּבֹאנָה שְׁתַּיִם נָשִׁים זֹנוֹת אֶל־   Two *prostitutes* came to the king.
       הַמֶּלֶךְ   1 Kgs 3:16

16.   וַיִּשְׁלַח יהוה אִישׁ נָבִיא אֶל־בְּנֵי   YHWH sent *a prophet* to the Israelites.
       יִשְׂרָאֵל   Judg 6:8

c   A predicate adjective has no article (4.5); it does not identify the subject but categorizes it as belonging to a class.

Adjectives, Numerals, and Pronouns

14

Adjectives

Adjectives and Related Constructions

14.1

Nouns can be modified in a variety of ways (4.6.1), and one major form of adnominal modification involves adjectives. Words of this class describe or qualify nouns by describing their state or condition. Consider the following sentence.   a

יִשְׁמְעוּן אֶת־שִׁמְךָ הַגָּדוֹל וְאֶת־יָדְךָ הַחֲזָקָה וּזְרֹעֲךָ הַנְּטוּיָה	They will hear of your *great* name and your *strong* hand and your *outstretched* arm. 1 Kgs 8:42

In both the Hebrew and English, there are three substantives, each qualified by an attributive adjective.

Hebrew differs from English and other European languages in that it uses adjectival   b modification much less frequently than they do; in Hebrew, noun phrases are often built up in other ways.[1] In the following examples, the English renderings use an adjectival format, while the Hebrew originals use a construct phrase (## 1–3), an accusative of specification (# 4), and an apposition (# 5).

1.	זֶ֫רַע הַמְּלוּכָה	the *royal* seed 2 Kgs 25:25
2.	כִּסֵּא הַמְּלוּכָה	the *royal* throne 1 Kgs 1:46

---

1. On the marginal character of the adjective in the Semitic languages generally, see G. Bergsträsser, *Introduc-* *tion to the Semitic Languages*, trans. and sup. Peter T. Daniels (Winona Lake, Indiana: Eisenbrauns, 1983) 8.

3. בֵּית הַמֶּלֶךְ   the *royal* palace[2]
                        2 Kgs 11:5

4. מַחְסִי־עֹז   my strong refuge (my refuge *as to strength*)
                        Ps 71:7

5. לָשׁוֹן רְמִיָּה   the *deceitful* tongue
                        Ps 120:2

c   Hebrew also differs from English in using adjectives as predicates (as in # 6) less often.

6. טוֹב הַדָּבָר   The word is *good.*
                        1 Kgs 2:38

Hebrew can use a noun alone (# 7) or in a prepositional phrase (# 8) where English relies on an adjectival predicate; most distinctively, Hebrew stative verbs (# 9) often correspond in English to predicate adjectival constructions (but see 27.1c).

7. הֲשָׁלוֹם בֹּאֶךָ   Is your visit *peaceful?*
                        1 Kgs 2:13

8. כִּי לְעוֹלָם חַסְדּוֹ   because his mercy is *eternal*
                        Ps 136:1

9. קָטֹנְתִּי   I am *small.*
                        Gen 32:11

d   Thus, the reliance on adjectival constructions for attribution and predication is limited in Hebrew. Also limited is the morphological distinctiveness of the Hebrew adjective: both substantives and adjectives are formed from the same patterns, for the most part (5.1). Despite these two interrelated limitations, the adjective is an important part of the study of Hebrew syntax. Two classes of adjectives are not considered in this chapter: numerals (Chap. 15) and demonstratives (Chap. 17), both of which present special problems.

14.2 Agreement

a   Adjectives are subordinate to the nouns they qualify in that they mostly *agree* with them in gender and number (## 1–4).

1. שֶׁמֶן זַיִת זָךְ   *pure* olive oil
                        Exod 27:20

2. חֵמָה עַזָּה   *strong* wrath
                        Prov 21:14

2. The gloss 'the palace of the king' is unlikely, since queen Athaliah is in view; cf. 2 Kgs 11:19; so Joüon § 141a / p. 434.

3.   מַ֫יִם אַדִּירִים   *mighty* waters
Exod 15:10

4.   מְנוּחֹת שַׁאֲנַנּוֹת   *secure* dwellings
Isa 32:18

An attributive adjective also agrees with the modified noun (or head) in definiteness (14.3.1).

    Adjectives do not form the *dual number*; dual substantives take plural adjectives.   **b**

5.   עֵינַיִם עִוְרוֹת   *blind* eyes
Isa 42:7

6.   בִּרְכַּ֫יִם כֹּשְׁלוֹת   *failing* knees
Isa 35:3

7.   יָדַ֫יִם רָפוֹת   *feeble* hands
Job 4:3

8.   וִידֵי מֹשֶׁה כְּבֵדִים   The hands of Moses were *heavy*.[3]
Exod 17:12

An adjective often agrees with its noun *ad sensum* (i.e., according to its inherent   **c**
sense) rather than according to its grammatical form. With respect to number, an adjective may be plural with a singular collective noun (## 9–10) or singular with a plural of honorific distinction or intensification (## 11–12; 7.4.3).

9.   צֹאן רַבּוֹת   *large* flocks
Gen 30:43

10.   הָעָם הַנִּמְצָאִים עִמּוֹ   the troop(s) *present* with him[4]
1 Sam 13:15

11.   אֲדֹנִים קָשֶׁה   a *cruel* master
Isa 19:4

12.   אֱלֹהִים צַדִּיק   O *righteous* God[5]
Ps 7:10

With feminine nouns whose plurals are formed with a masculine plural suffix, the adjective agrees with the noun's intrinsic gender (## 13–16; 6.5.2).

13.   הַשָּׁנִים הַטֹּבֹת הַבָּאֹת   these *good* years that are *coming*
הָאֵ֫לֶּה   Gen 41:35

14.   גְּמַלִּים מֵינִיקוֹת   *nursing* camels
Gen 32:16

---

3. Only here is *yd* masculine; cf. Ezek 2:9. For the word order, see 8.4.2d.

4. But cf. *hāʿām hannimṣāʾ ʿimmām* in 1 Sam 13:16,

where the LXX has a plural participle.

5. The plural is rarely used with appellatives for God, but cf. *ʾĕlōhîm qədōšîm* 'holy God' in Josh 24:19.

15.   בֵּיצִים עֲזֻבוֹת   *abandoned* eggs
                                    Isa 10:14

16.   נָשִׁים שַׁאֲנַנּוֹת   *resting* women
                                    Isa 32:9

d   There is *a priority of the masculine gender* (6.5.3). When two adjectives follow a feminine substantive, sometimes only the one standing next to the substantive takes the feminine suffix.[6]

17.   בְּאֶרֶץ־צִיָּה וְעָיֵף   in a *dry* and weary land
                                    Ps 63:2

When an attributive adjective qualifies several substantives of different genders, it agrees with the masculine.

18.   חֻקִּים וּמִצְוֹת טוֹבִים: *good* statutes and commandments
                                    Neh 9:13

e   An adjective normally cannot modify a name directly.

19.   נִינְוֵה הָעִיר הַגְּדוֹלָה   the *great* [city of] Nineveh
                                    Jonah 1:2

f   There is no distinctive form of the adjective to express the comparative and superlative degrees (14.4–5).

14.3   Uses of the Adjective

a   An adjective may be found in one of three syntactic slots: (1) as an attributive modifier of a substantive, (2) as a predicate, and (3) as a substantive. In the last case, it is again apparent that the adjective subclass of nouns is not rigidly defined.

14.3.1   Attributive Use

a   An attributive adjective directly modifies a substantive in such a way that the combined phrase functions as a single syntactic unit in the clause (cf. 37.5b). In this use the adjective normally follows its noun in the order modified-modifier, like nouns in the genitive and in the accusative of specification. It is recognized (1) by its inflection (agreement with its head with respect to gender, number, and determination) and (2) by its position. In verbless clauses an attributive differs from a predicate adjective by its definiteness, if the head noun is definite, and usually by its position after the noun.

1.   מִשְׁתֶּה גָדוֹל   a *great* feast
                                Gen 21:8

---

6. See also 1 Kgs 19:11, Jer 20:9. The apparent clash of *hmʾrt* (masc. noun with *-ôt* plural) *hgdlym* (Gen 1:16) is only formal (cf. ## 13–16).

2.	הַמִּשְׁפָּחָה הָרָעָה הַזֹּאת	this *evil* clan Jer 8:3
3.	שְׁמוֹ הַגָּדוֹל	his *great* name 1 Sam 12:22
4.	בְּחַרְבּוֹ הַקָּשָׁה וְהַגְּדוֹלָה וְהַחֲזָקָה	with his *fierce*, *great*, and *powerful* sword Isa 27:1
5.	אִישׁ אֱלֹהִים קָדוֹשׁ	a *holy* man of God 2 Kgs 4:9
6.	שְׁלֹשֶׁת בְּנֵי־יִשַׁי הַגְּדֹלִים	Jesse's three *oldest* sons 1 Sam 17:13

Sometimes an attributive adjective precedes its noun, notably in the case of the **b** word רֹב in the plural (in the sense of 'many' and not in the sense of 'great'). This use is probably due to a felt affinity with numerals, which may precede their noun (see Chap. 15). Another influence may be מְעַט 'little' and כֹּל 'all,' which, being substantives involving quantity, also precede the noun.[7]

7.	לְדַוָּגִים רַבִּים . . . לְרַבִּים צַיָּדִים	*many* fishermen . . . *many* hunters Jer 16:16
8.	רַבִּים חֲלָלִים הִפִּילָה	*Many* victims she has brought down. Prov 7:26
9.	רַבּוֹת בָּנוֹת עָשׂוּ חָיִל	*Many* women do noble things. Prov 31:29

With רֹב in the masculine singular, it is difficult to decide whether it is an attributive adjective preceding its noun or a nominal use of the adjective.[8]

| 10. | רַב־קָשֶׁב | *great* attention
Isa 21:7 |

Some attributive adjectives, such as the numerals, אַחֵר 'another,' and רַבִּים 'many,'   **c** are definite in themselves and may dispense with the article.

11.	הָרֹאשׁ אֶחָד	*one* company 1 Sam 13:17
12.	אֲחִיכֶם אֶחָד	*one* brother of yours[9] Gen 42:19
13.	הָעַמּוּדִים שְׁנָיִם	the *two* pillars 2 Kgs 25:16

---

7. So Joüon, who also alludes to possible Aramaic influence and to a parallel to appositional constructions; see § 141b / p. 435 n. 2.

8. The feminine singular construct is not ambiguous in

this way; cf. *rabbat ḥelʾātāh* 'the greatness of its rust, its thick rust,' Ezek 24:12.

9. The same phrase with the article in an otherwise close repetition in Gen 42:33.

14.   אֲחִיכֶם אַחֵר   your *other* brother[10]
                              Gen 43:14

15.   הַגּוֹיִם רַבִּים   *many* nations
                              Ezek 39:27

d   Sometimes the attributive adjective is definite and the noun indefinite, especially with numerals (## 16–19; see 15.2.6), with certain quasi-technical terms referring to architectural features (# 18–21; court, gate, entrance, way) and days (# 22), and with unique referents (## 23–24), all of which are definite in themselves.[11]

16.   שֶׁבַע פָּרֹת הַטֹּבֹת   the seven good cows
                              Gen 41:26

17.   שֶׁבַע כְּבָשֹׂת הָאֵלֶּה   these seven lambs[12]
                              Gen 21:29

18.   מָבוֹא הַשְּׁלִישִׁי   the Third Entrance
                              Jer 38:14

19.   מְקוֹם שַׁעַר הָרִאשׁוֹן   the site of the First Gate[13]
                              Zech 14:10

20.   חָצֵר הַגְּדוֹלָה   the Great Courtyard[14]
                              1 Kgs 7:12

21.   דֶּרֶךְ הַטּוֹבָה וְהַיְשָׁרָה: the good and upright way[15]
                              1 Sam 12:23

22.   יוֹם הַשְּׁבִיעִי   the seventh day[16]
                              Exod 20:10

23.   רוּחַ הָרָעָה   the evil spirit
                              1 Sam 16:23

24.   קָנֶה הַטּוֹב   the sweet cane
                              Jer 6:20

14.3.2   Predicate Use

a   A predicate adjective serves in a verbless clause to make an assertion about the subject of the clause. The predicate usually precedes the subject (## 1–3; but cf. 8.4.2 and ## 4–5) and is always indefinite; it otherwise agrees with the subject.[17]

---

10. The Samaritan Pentateuch, which tends to normalize Hebrew grammar, has the article on the adjective. See, too, n. 12.

11. The same apparent discrepancy in definiteness is more common in Mishnaic Hebrew, and all manner of articular "discrepancies" are found in Phoenician-Punic; see M. H. Segal, *A Grammar of Mishnaic Hebrew* (Oxford: Clarendon, 1927) 182–83; and Z. S. Harris, *A Gra-*

mmar of the Phoenician Language (New Haven, Connecticut: American Oriental Society, 1936) 66.

12. The Samaritan Pentateuch has the article.

13. Another gate in Ezek 9:2.

14. Other courtyards in 2 Kgs 20:4 *Qere*; Ezek 40:28, 31.

15. Another way in Jer 6:16.

16. Other days in Gen 1:31, etc.; Exod 12:15.

17. As in the comparable construction in Classical Greek.

1.	צַדִּיק אַתָּה	You are *righteous*. Jer 12:1
2.	וְיָשָׁר מִשְׁפָּטֶיךָ	Your laws are *right*. Ps 119:137
3.	רַבָּה רָעַת הָאָדָם	The wickedness of people is *great*. Gen 6:5
4.	וּזֲהַב הָאָרֶץ הַהִיא טוֹב	Now the gold of that land is *good*. Gen 2:12
5.	וְהֶעָרִים בְּצֻרוֹת גְּדֹלֹת מְאֹד	Now the cites are *fortified, very large*. Num 13:28

We can sharpen our understanding of the opposition between the predicate adjective   b
and the attributive adjective if we consider the classification of the adjective by various
Greek scholars.[18] Plato and Aristotle regard adjectives as a subclass of verbs, while the
Alexandrians treat them as a subclass of nouns. The latter position is supported by the
surface-structure inflection of an adjective like a noun with respect to gender and number,
while the older position sees an adjective as a predication about a subject, as a verb is.
By placing the anarthrous predicate adjective before the subject, the typical position of
the verb, the Hebrew language adds an argument in favor of the position of Plato and
Aristotle, who perceived the "predicate" adjective as functioning like a verb.

Substantive Use   14.3.3

Because the boundary between adjectives and substantives is not fixed or rigid, it is   a
common to find nouns that are most often used as adjectives in substantive slots.
Adjectives may occur as *constructs*, usually with a superlative force (14.5).[19]   b

1.	חַכְמֵי יֹעֲצֵי פַרְעֹה	the *wisest* of Pharaoh's counselors Isa 19:11
2.	רָעֵי גוֹיִם	the *worst* of the nations Ezek 7:24
3.	קְטֹן בָּנָיו	the *youngest* of his sons 2 Chr 21:17
4.	חֲמִשָּׁה חַלֻּקֵי־אֲבָנִים	five *smooth* stones 1 Sam 17:40

They may be used in the *genitive function* after a construct.

5.	חֵיל כָּבֵד	a *great* force 2 Kgs 18:17

---

18. See R. H. Robins, *Ancient and Mediaeval Grammatical Theory in Europe* (London: Bell, 1951) 17–19, 40–41.

19. Other examples in Ps 46:5, Exod 15:16, Ps 65:5. Example # 2 is inherently definite.

6.	יֵין הַטּוֹב	the *best* wine Cant 7:10
7.	צִיצַת נֹבֵל	*withered* flower[20] Isa 28:4
8.	כָּל־בֵּית גָּדוֹל	every *great* house 2 Kgs 25:9
9.	כֹּל כְּלֵי הַקָּטָן	all the *smallest* vessels Isa 22:24
10.	מֵי הַמָּרִים	the *bitter* water Num 5:18
11.	גְּאוֹן עַזִּים	a ferocious beast (lit., the pride of the *strong ones*) Ezek 7:24

c   Adjectives occur in other noun-noun constructions. An adjective used as a substantive in apposition stands *before* its appositive and can thus be distinguished from an attributive adjective.

12.	עֲנִיָּה עֲנָתוֹת	O *poor one*, Anathoth Isa 10:30
13.	הַמְעֻשָּׁקָה בְּתוּלַת בַּת־צִידוֹן	O *crushed one*, Virgin Daughter Sidon Isa 23:12
14.	צַדִּיק עַבְדִּי	a *righteous man*, my servant Isa 53:11
15.	שִׁבְעִים אִישׁ הַזְּקֵנִים	the *seventy* elders Num 11:25

An adjective may serve as an accusative of specification (10.2.2e).

16.	הַזְּרֹעַ בְּשֵׁלָה	the shoulder *when it is boiled* Num 6:19
17.	כַּיָּם נִגְרָשׁ	as the sea *in raging* Isa 57:20
18.	לַחְמָם טָמֵא	their bread *in uncleanness* Ezek 4:13
19.	בְּבָתֵּיכֶם סְפוּנִים	in your houses *with paneling* Hag 1:4
20.	דִּבַּת־הָאָרֶץ רָעָה	a report of the land *with reference to evil* Num 14:37

---

20. The use of a feminine construct with a masculine adjective is strange.

There are some nouns which have a different sense depending on whether they are   d
used as adjectives or substantives.

21a.   עֵירֻמִּם הֵם   They were *naked*.
Gen 3:7

21b.   בְּעֵירֹם   in *nakedness*
Deut 28:48

22a.   מֵאֶרֶץ רְחוֹקָה   from a *distant* land
1 Kgs 8:41

22b.   רָחוֹק יִהְיֶה בֵּינֵיכֶם וּבֵינָיו   There shall be a *space* between you and it.
Josh 3:4 Qere

23a.   וֶהְיֵה תָמִים   and be *blameless*
Gen 17:1

23b.   בְּתָמִים   in *blamelessness*
Judg 9:16

More often, an adjective shows no such variation in sense, and expected accompanying
nouns may be omitted, especially if they are broadly generic.

24.   רַבִּים קָמִים עָלָי׃   *Many* [people] are rising up against me.
Ps 3:2

In some cases the adjective stands where no concrete noun could do duty.

25.   אֲשֶׁר־לָבָן בּוֹ   which had *white* [viz., stuff] on it
Gen 30:35; cf. 30:37

The usage may be poetic: in the figure of antimeria (a type of metonymy) an expected noun
is replaced by an adjective describing some essential characteristic of the elided noun.

26.   וְחָפְרָה הַלְּבָנָה וּבוֹשָׁה הַחַמָּה   *The white* [moon] will be abashed, *the heat* [of the sun] ashamed.
Isa 24:23

27.   עַל־קַל נִרְכָּב   We will ride off on *a swift* (steed).
Isa 30:16

Comparative Degree   14.4

In English and other European languages the adjective forms three degrees by   a
inflection:

degree	example
absolute	young
comparative	younger
superlative	youngest

There are also phrasal equivalents of the two higher degrees, for example, 'more young,' 'most young,' and occasionally there are equivalents with 'less' and 'least.' Hebrew has no inflectional scheme for the higher degrees of adjectives and uses instead a variety of syntactic resources.[21]

b   Uses of the comparative degree involve at least the entities being compared (e.g., '*Joshua* is younger than *Moses*'). In some cases the sphere of the comparison must be made explicit (e.g., 'Moses is greater than Joshua *as a leader/in leadership*, etc.'); the preposition מִן introduces the basis in Hebrew.

c   In a *situational comparison*, the logical structure is often left unspecified and needs to be inferred from the context. The clause מַה־טּוֹב לָכֶם in isolation may be taken as meaning, 'What is good for you?', but if it is followed by a pair of alternatives, טוֹב may be said to have the meaning 'better.'

1.	מַה־טּוֹב לָכֶם הַמְשֹׁל בָּכֶם	Which is *better* for you—seventy men ruling you . . .
	שִׁבְעִים אִישׁ . . . אִם־מְשֹׁל בָּכֶם	or one man ruling you?
	אִישׁ אֶחָד	Judg 9:2

Similarly, בְּקוֹל־גָּדוֹל may be taken to mean 'in a loud voice,' but in a context of prolonged crying, a comparative sense may be discerned.

2.	קִרְאוּ בְקוֹל־גָּדוֹל	Cry *more loudly.*
		1 Kgs 18:27; cf. v 26

Stative verbs can also be used in situational comparisons.

3.	לָרַב תַּרְבֶּה נַחֲלָתוֹ וְלַמְעַט	For the larger group you shall *make* its inheritance
	תַּמְעִיט נַחֲלָתוֹ	*larger,* and for the smaller group you shall *make* its
		inheritance *smaller.*
		Num 26:54

d   When the noun on which the comparison is based is expressed, it is preceded by the preposition מִן, the so-called "comparative *min*" (11.2.11e). This preposition denotes 'away from'; the comparison is viewed from the outside, from a distance. It may indicate a *positive comparison*, wherein both the subject and the thing compared possess the quality expressed by the adjective, with the subject possessing it to a greater degree.

4.	וִירִשְׁתֶּם גּוֹיִם גְּדֹלִים וַעֲצֻמִים	You will dispossess nations *greater* and *more*
	מִכֶּם׃	*powerful* than you.
		Deut 11:23
5.	מַה־מָּתוֹק מִדְּבַשׁ וּמֶה עַז מֵאֲרִי	What is *sweeter* than honey? And what is *stronger*
		than a lion?
		Judg 14:18

---

21. Arabic has the elative or *ʾaqtal* form for both comparative and superlative constructions; compare *ḥasan* 'beautiful' and *ʾaḥsan* 'more/most beautiful'; *jalīl* 'glorious' and *ʾajall* 'more/most glorious.' The few Hebrew adjectives in *ʾaqtāl* may be morphologically related, e.g., *ʾakzāb* 'lying' (cf. 5.6e–f).

Frequently, positive comparisons are framed with stative verbs.

6.	אֶגְדַּל מִמֶּֽךָּ׃	I will be *greater* than you. Gen 41:40
7.	וְגַם־הוּא יִגְדָּל וְאוּלָם אָחִיו הַקָּטֹן יִגְדַּל מִמֶּֽנּוּ	He too will become great. Nevertheless, his younger brother will be *greater* than he. Gen 48:19
8.	וְיִשְׂרָאֵל אָהַב אֶת־יוֹסֵף מִכָּל־ בָּנָיו	Now Israel *loved* Joseph *more* than all his children. Gen 37:3
9.	מִנְּשָׁרִים קַלּוּ מֵאֲרָיוֹת גָּבֵֽרוּ׃	They were *swifter* than eagles; they were *stronger* than lions. 2 Sam 1:23
10.	טוֹב לִי אָז מֵעָֽתָּה׃	It was *better* for me then than now. Hos 2:9
11.	הַנֶּחֱמָדִים מִזָּהָב וּמִפַּז רָב וּמְתוּקִים מִדְּבַשׁ	(They are) *more precious* than gold, than much fine gold; they are *sweeter* than honey. Ps 19:11

Sometimes the adjective on which מִן logically depends is omitted and must be supplied from the context.[22]

12.	וּפְסִילֵיהֶם מִירוּשָׁלָ͏ִם	Their images were (more) than those of Jerusalem. Isa 10:10
13.	יָשָׁר מִמְּסוּכָה	The most upright person (is *worse*) than a thorn hedge. Mic 7:4
14.	וּמִצָּהֳרַיִם יָקוּם חָ֫לֶד	Life will be (*brighter*) than noonday. Job 11:17

In a *comparison of exclusion*, the subject alone possesses the quality connoted by   e
the adjective or stative verb, to the exclusion of the thing compared.

15.	צָדְקָה מִמֶּֽנִּי	She is in the right, *not* I. Gen 38:26
16.	וַיֶּאֱהַב גַּם־אֶת־רָחֵל מִלֵּאָה	He loved Rachel *rather than* Leah. Gen 29:30
17.	אָהַ֫בְתָּ רָּע מִטּוֹב שֶׁקֶר מִדַּבֵּר צֶֽדֶק	You love evil *rather than* good, falsehood *rather than* speaking what is right. Ps 52:5

---

22. Other examples in Isa 40:17, 41:24; Ps 62:10. In # 13, perhaps read *yšrm* 'their most upright.'

18. כִּי . . . חָפַצְתִּי . . . דַּעַת אֱלֹהִים
מֵעֹלוֹת:

For . . . I desire . . . acknowledgment of God, *not*
ʿōlôt.[23]
Hos 6:6

19. וַתִּבְחַר מַחֲנָק נַפְשִׁי מָוֶת
מֵעַצְמוֹתָי:

So I choose strangling and death *rather than* these
bones of mine.
Job 7:15

20. טוֹב פַּת חֲרֵבָה וְשַׁלְוָה־בָהּ
מִבַּיִת מָלֵא זִבְחֵי־רִיב:

A dry crust with peace and quiet is good *rather than*
a house full with strife.
Prov 17:1

f   A third use of comparative *min* appears in those contexts in which the subject is compared with an object or goal to be attained, in which case the subject may be more than equal to the challenge or less than equal to it: such is the *comparison of capability*. In this use stative verbs are much more common than adjectives.

21. וְאִם־יִמְעַט הַבַּיִת מִהְיֹת מִשֶּׂה

If any household be *too small* for a lamb. . . .
Exod 12:4

22. גָּבְרוּ מֶנִּי

They are *too strong* for me.
Ps 65:4

23. יָרוּם מִמֶּנִּי

It is *too high* for me.
Ps 61:3

24. הֲקָצוֹר קָצְרָה יָדִי מִפְּדוּת

Is my hand *too short* to perform redemption?
Isa 50:2

25. הֲיִפָּלֵא מֵיהוה דָּבָר

Is anything *too hard* for Yʜᴡʜ?[24]
Gen 18:14

26. קָטֹנְתִּי מִכֹּל הַחֲסָדִים

I am *unworthy* of all the love.
Gen 32:11

This use is frequent with infinitives.

27. גָּדוֹל עֲוֹנִי מִנְּשֹׂא:

My punishment is *more than I can bear.*
Gen 4:13

28. הָיָה רְכוּשָׁם רָב מִשֶּׁבֶת יַחְדָּו

Their possessions were *too great* for them *to remain*
together.
Gen 36:7

29. מִזְבַּח הַנְּחֹשֶׁת . . . קָטֹן מֵהָכִיל
אֶת־הָעֹלָה

The bronze altar . . . was *too small to hold* the
ʿōlâ. . . .
1 Kgs 8:64

23. This understanding of the verse has a broad base of support in the tradition but has been questioned by F. I. Andersen and D. N. Freedman, who render, 'For I desire . . . the knowledge of God *rather than* ʿōlôt'; see *Hosea* (Anchor Bible 24; Garden City, New York: Doubleday, 1980) 426, 430–31.

24. Other examples with *plʾ* in the *Piel* in Deut 17:8; Jer 32:17, 27.

| 30. | רַב הָעָם . . . מִתִּתִּי אֶת־מִדְיָן בְּיָדָם | The people are *too many* for me . . . *to give* Midian into their hands. Judg 7:2 |

It is sometimes difficult to distinguish between a positive comparison and a comparison of capability.

| 31. | עָצַמְתָּ מִמֶּנּוּ מְאֹד: | You are *much too powerful* for us. / You are *much more powerful than* us. Gen 26:16 |
| 32. | מַר־לִי מְאֹד מִכֶּם | I am *much too bitter* for you. / I have *more bitterness than* you. Ruth 1:13 |

Superlative Degree

14.5

There are two kinds of superlatives, the comparative superlative and the absolute superlative. In the former some person or object is judged to surpass all others in its class with respect to some quality; in the latter some person or thing is judged to excel in some quality, state, or condition. We will analyze these two kinds of superlative and note the expressions employed for each.

a

The *absolute superlative* can be expressed with the anarthrous cognate genitive: a singular cognate noun stands before the same noun in the plural, without an article. (A determined construct chain expresses a comparative superlative; see 9.5.3j and 14.5d.)

b

1.	הֲבֵל הֲבָלִים	futility of futilities, *utter* futility Qoh 1:2
2.	עֶבֶד עֲבָדִים	a slave of slaves, an *abject* slave Gen 9:25
3.	לְנֵצַח נְצָחִים	forever *and ever* Isa 34:10
4.	צְבִי צְבָאוֹת	*most* beautiful Jer 3:19
5.	סָרֵי סוֹרְרִים	*hardened* rebels Jer 6:28

Two nouns of related sense can be similarly used.

6.	חֹשֶׁךְ־אֲפֵלָה	a *thick* darkness Exod 10:22
7.	מֵהֲדַר גְּאֹנוֹ	from his *majestic* splendor Isa 2:10
8.	הַבְלֵי־שָׁוְא	vanities of nothingness, *worthless* vanities Jonah 2:9

9.   שִׂמְחַת גִּילִי   the joy of my rejoicing, my *surpassing* joy
       Ps 43:4

The term מְאֹד (or עַד־מְאֹד) can stand after an adjective used as an absolute superlative.[25]

10.   טוֹב מְאֹד   *very* good
    Gen 1:31

11.   אִישׁ בָּרִיא מְאֹד׃   a *very* fat man
    Judg 3:17

12.   וְהַנַּעֲרָה יָפָה עַד־מְאֹד   The young woman was *extremely* beautiful.
    1 Kgs 1:4

13.   וַתְּהִי הַמִּלְחָמָה קָשָׁה עַד־מְאֹד   The battle was *very* fierce.
    2 Sam 2:17

14.   עֲוֹן . . . גָּדוֹל בִּמְאֹד מְאֹד   The sin . . . is *exceedingly* great.
    Ezek 9:9

Various divine names can be similarly used: "A kind of superlative sense," as A. B. Davidson noted, "is given to a word by connecting it with the divine name. Probably the idea was that God *originated* the thing . . . or that it belonged to Him, and was therefore extraordinary. Sometimes the meaning appears to be 'in God's estimation.'"[26]

15.   נְשִׂיא אֱלֹהִים   a *mighty* prince
    Gen 23:6

16.   חֶרְדַּת אֱלֹהִים   a *very great* trembling
    1 Sam 14:15

17.   הַרְרֵי־אֵל   *mighty* mountains[27]
    Ps 36:7

18.   גַּן־יהוה   a *splendid* garden
    Isa 51:3

19.   עִיר־גְּדוֹלָה לֵאלֹהִים   an *exceedingly great* city
    Jonah 3:3

The same usage can be observed with terms referring to royalty.

20.   בֵּית זְבֻל   a mansion (lit., a *prince's* house)
    1 Kgs 8:13

---

25. The nominal character of *mʾd* is apparent in the structure of the prepositional phrase *ʿd-mʾd* as well as in the two nominal uses of the word ('abundance, strength'). In the remaining three hundred or so uses, *mʾd* serves as an intensifier; the English adverb 'very' (etymologically 'truly, truthfully') is not the sole apt rendering.

26. Quoted by D. Winton Thomas in his review of previous scholarly literature, "A Consideration of Some Unusual Ways of Expressing the Superlative in Hebrew,"

Vetus Testamentum 3 (1953) 209–24, at 219; cf. P. P. Saydon, "Some Unusual Ways of Expressing the Superlative in Hebrew and Maltese," *Vetus Testamentum* 4 (1954) 432–33; Thomas, "The Use of נֵצַח as a Superlative in Hebrew," *Journal of Semitic Studies* 1 (1956) 106–9; Thomas, "Some Further Remarks on Unusual Ways of Expressing the Superlative in Hebrew," *Vetus Testamentum* 18 (1968) 120–24.

27. So the Targum.

Absolute superlatives with a negative sense can be formed with מוּת 'dying,' מָוֶת 'death,' and שְׁאֹל 'Sheol'; compare English 'bored to death, deadly dull, devilishly clever.'[28]

21.   וַתִּקְצַר נַפְשׁוֹ לָמוּת׃
His soul was vexed *to death* (i.e., He could stand it no longer).
Judg 16:16

22.   חָרָה־לִי עַד־מָוֶת׃
I am angered even *to death* (i.e., I couldn't be more angry).
Jonah 4:9

23.   כִּי־עַזָּה כַמָּוֶת אַהֲבָה
Love is as strong *as death* (i.e., Love is exceedingly strong).

קָשָׁה כִשְׁאוֹל קִנְאָה
Jealousy is as cruel *as the grave* (i.e., Jealousy is profoundly cruel).
Cant 8:6

24.   חֶבְלֵי שְׁאוֹל
pains *of Sheol* (i.e., hellish pains)
Ps 18:6

25.   וַתַּשְׁפִּילִי עַד־שְׁאוֹל׃
You debased yourself even *to hell* (i.e., You debased yourself to the lowest depths [with no precise locality in view]).
Isa 57:9

The *comparative superlative* refers to a group, though the group may be discrete   c
and obvious (and thus be left unstated) or diffuse and hard-to-describe (and thus be
unstatable). The simplest such superlative involves a definite adjective.[29]

26.   הַקָּטֹן
the *youngest* [son]
Gen 42:13

27.   בִּתִּי הַגְּדוֹלָה
my *oldest* daughter
1 Sam 18:17

28.   הָעִיר הַקְּרֹבָה
the *nearest* city
Deut 21:3

29.   זֵיתֵיכֶם הַטּוֹבִים
your *best* olive trees
1 Sam 8:14

30.   הֲלֹא אֲחֹתָהּ הַקְּטַנָּה טוֹבָה מִמֶּנָּה
Isn't her *youngest/er* sister better than she?
Judg 15:2

A comparative superlative can also be formed with an adjective made definite by a pronominal suffix (## 31–32) or as the first term of a definite construct chain (## 33–35).

28. Thomas calls attention to a similar use in a Medieval Hebrew letter of Rabbi Ḥisdai ben Shafrūt: "And when I heard this bad news, I was very angry (ḥrh ly ʿd mwt, cf. Jonah 4:9)," parallel to "and I was very distressed (wyṣr ly mʾd)"; see "A Consideration of Some Unusual Ways," 221. The Greek phrase *heōs thanatou* is used in the Christian Gospels (e.g., Matt 26:38 ≅ Mark 14:34).
29. See also Gen 10:21, 29:16; Judg 6:15.

31.	מִקְּטַנָּם וְעַד־גְּדוֹלָם	from the *least* of them to the *greatest* Jer 6:13
32.	מִגְּדוֹלָם וְעַד־קְטַנָּם:	from the *greatest* of them to the *least* Jonah 3:5
33.	גְּדֹלֵי הָעִיר	the *leading* men of the city 2 Kgs 10:6
34.	קְטֹן בָּנָיו	the *youngest* of his sons 2 Chr 21:17
35.	הֲלוֹא בֶן־יְמִינִי אָנֹכִי מִקְּטַנֵּי שִׁבְטֵי יִשְׂרָאֵל	Am I not a Benjaminite, from the *smallest* of the tribes of Israel? 1 Sam 9:21

A similar phrasal type involves a definite adjective, with the group prefixed by בְּ.

36.	הַיָּפָה בַּנָּשִׁים	the *fairest* among women Cant 1:8, 5:9
37.	הָאִישׁ הָרַךְ בְּךָ	the *most delicate* man among you Deut 28:54
38.	כְּשֵׁם הַגְּדֹלִים אֲשֶׁר בָּאָרֶץ:	like the name of the *greatest* (men) in the land 2 Sam 7:9

d   The superlative genitive has a comparative sense if the plural noun, the genitive, is definite.

39.	קֹדֶשׁ הַקֳּדָשִׁים	the *most holy* place Exod 26:33
40.	שִׁיר הַשִּׁירִים	the *most excellent* song Cant 1:1
41.	נְשִׂיא נְשִׂיאֵי הַלֵּוִי	the *chief* leader of the Levites Num 3:32
42.	שְׁמֵי הַשָּׁמַיִם	the *highest* heavens 1 Kgs 8:27

A construct phrase may also be used with מִכֹּל standing before the genitive.

43.	וְהַנָּחָשׁ הָיָה עָרוּם מִכֹּל חַיַּת הַשָּׂדֶה	Now the snake was the *most cunning* of all the beasts. Gen 3:1
44.	אָרוּר אַתָּה מִכָּל־הַבְּהֵמָה	*Cursed* be you *above* all the livestock. Gen 3:14
45.	וְהוּא נִכְבָּד מִכֹּל בֵּית אָבִיו:	He was the *most honored* of all his father's household. Gen 34:19

46. שָׂכַל דָּוִד מִכֹּל עַבְדֵי שָׁאוּל

David met with *more success* than all the rest of Saul's officers.
1 Sam 18:30

Phrases with מכל may also follow stative verbs.

47. עָקֹב הַלֵּב מִכֹּל

The heart is *most deceitful* of all things.
Jer 17:9

48. וַיִּגְבַּהּ מִכָּל־הָעָם

He was found to be the *tallest* of all the people.
1 Sam 10:23

Finally, a comparative superlative may use abstract terms of quality, with a suffix **e** (# 49) or a definite genitive (## 50–53).

49. טוֹבָם כְּחֵדֶק

The *best* of them is like a briar.
Mic 7:4

50. טוּב אֶרֶץ מִצְרַיִם

the *best* of the land of Egypt
Gen 45:18

51. מִבְחַר שָׁלִשָׁיו

his (Pharaoh's) *picked* officers
Exod 15:4

52. רֵאשִׁית גּוֹיִם עֲמָלֵק

Amaleq is a *foremost* nation.[30]
Num 24:20

53. רֵאשִׁית הַגּוֹיִם

the *foremost* nation
Amos 6:1

---

30. The article is often omitted in verse (13.7), though it is probably omitted here because the poet seeks to classify Amaleq rather than to identify it (see 8.4.2). Note further that the article is used in the next example, also in verse.

On *rēʾšît*, see M. Greenberg, *Ezekiel, 1–20* (Anchor Bible 22; Garden City, New York: Doubleday 1983) 375, who cites for the senses 'best' and 'choice' Exod 23:19 = 34:26; Ezek 44:30, cf. Num 18:12.

15

Numerals

15.1 Introduction

a   Numerals or number-words are the linguistic expressions of counting. Just as counting usually involves whole numbers, so the whole numerals are of the greatest interest in language. Similarly, just as counting more often involves small numbers, so the lower numerals show more linguistic complexities.

b   There are two major series of number-words. The more important series, the cardinals, express an amount, 'one, two, three'; in Hebrew these are usually substantives (15.2).[1] The ordinals express degree, quality, or position in a series, 'first, second, third'; in Hebrew these are adjectives (15.3). After reviewing the whole-number ordinals and

---

1. The distinctive qualities of cardinal numbers, from which other series of number-words usually derive, is explored by W. P. Schmid, *MPD* 86–88, 92–93. On the grounds of frequency alone, the Hebrew cardinals are more important than the ordinals; see nn. 5 and 24 below.

For a comparative perspective on the Semitic numerals, see, in addition to the papers cited in nn. 10 and 14, W. von Soden, "Ableitungen von Zahlwörtern im Semitischen," *Language, Literature, and History: Philological and Historical Studies Presented to Erica Reiner*, ed. F. Rochberg-Halton (New Haven, Connecticut: American Oriental Society, 1987) 403–14. On the structure of numeral phrases in Hebrew, see Richter, *GAHG* 2. 26–29.

cardinals, we briefly treat multiplicatives ('double, sevenfold'; 15.4) and fractions ('a half, a third'; 15.5), as well as distributive expressions ('six per person'; 15.6).

Two important points outside our purview require attention. First, in Hebrew and the Semitic languages generally, numerals play almost no role at all in word formation, and the complexities associated with English number-prefixes (e.g., 'monolingual, unicycle; dichotomous, bicycle; tripod; multiracial, polysyllable') are avoided.[2] Second, in the Bible numerals are always spelled out in full. In biblical times, at least two systems of number-signs were in use: hieratic slash-and-punct signs ($//$ = 2) and letter-number signs (ב = 2); there are no traces of either system in the biblical text, however, and all editorial numbers are medieval in date.[3] Students of the Bible are thus never in doubt about the linguistic form of the number, as students of other ancient texts often are.[4]

Cardinals   15.2

The lowest cardinals, 'one,' 'two,' are the most complex. The cardinals 'three–ten' are basically substantives, inflected for gender and used in both absolute and construct forms. The teen cardinals are compounds, and the decimal cardinals are usually plurals of lower numerals. The highest cardinals present a few complexities, but they are basically regular compounds.[5]

Cardinal 'One,' 'Two'   15.2.1

'One' אֶחָד/אַחַת (construct אַחַד/אַחַת) is the most adjectival of the cardinals, although it may be used as a substantive.[6] When it is used as an *attributive adjective*, following the noun it modifies, it has a variety of senses. After an indefinite noun, the sense is most often specific indefinite (cf. 13.8).

1.   שָׂפָה אֶחָת   a *certain* (specific) language[7]
                                  Gen 11:1

---

2. The only exception in Hebrew is *šilšōm/šilšôm* (< *šalôš yôm*) 'three days (ago), i.e., day before yesterday'; at least this is the apparent meaning of the term—in fact, it occurs only in asyndetic combination with *ʾetmôl* (*ʾitmôl/təmôl*) in a phrase meaning 'up to now, recently.'

3. The topic is proper to epigraphy; for convenient illustrations, see Joseph Naveh, *Early History of the Alphabet* (Jerusalem: Magnes, 1982) 85, 108, 119 (slashes in an Elephantine papyrus written in Aramaic, 408 B.C.E.; slashes in a Heshbon ostracon written in Ammonite, late Iron Age II; letters used as numbers on an Alexander Janneus coin, text in Aramaic).

4. For example, most numbers used in Akkadian texts are written with signs rather than words; see W. von Soden, *Grundriss der akkadischen Grammatik* (Analecta Orientalia 33/47; Rome: Pontifical Biblical Institute, 1969) 90. Ugaritic is exceptional in preferring to write numerals

in words; see *UT* § 7.1.

5. The common cardinals are, in order of use, these; the counts (after SA/THAT) include both gender forms, where relevant: *ʾhd* 970 times, *šnym* 762, *mʾh* 583, *ʿšr* 511, *ʾlp* 504, *šlš* 426, *šbʿ* 401, *ḥmš* 346, *ʾrbʿ* 318, *ʿšrym* 315, *šš* 216, *šlšym* 172, *ḥmšym* 163, *ʾrbʿym* 135, *šmnh* 109. The only common non-numeral counting terms are *kōl* (ca. 5,400 times) and *rab* (474 times).

6. The feminine form *ʾaḥat* reflects an original *ʾaḥadt* > *-tt* > *-t*. The apocopated masculine form *ḥad* (Ezek 33:30) agrees with the Aramaic (Franz Rosenthal, *A Grammar of Biblical Aramaic* [Wiesbaden: Harrassowitz, 1961] § 63 / p. 31), though the context suggests the possibility of a scribal error.

7. The usual rendering, 'one single language,' would correspond with the sense discussed immediately below in the text.

2.	אִישׁ אֶחָד	a *certain* man Judg 13:2, 18:19
3.	אִשָּׁה אַחַת	a *certain* woman 2 Kgs 4:1
4.	וַיִּקַּח שְׁמוּאֵל אֶבֶן אַחַת	And Samuel took a *certain* stone. 1 Sam 7:12
5.	לֹא־לְיוֹם אֶחָד וְלֹא לִשְׁנַיִם	not in *one* day or two Ezra 10:13

Less often, an indefinite noun with אחד may have an emphatic, counting force.

6.	בְּיוֹם אֶחָד יָמוּתוּ שְׁנֵיהֶם׃	On a *single* day, they will die—both of them! 1 Sam 2:34
7.	. . . אַחֲרֵי מִי יָצָא מֶלֶךְ יִשְׂרָאֵל אַחֲרֵי פַּרְעֹשׁ אֶחָד׃	After whom does the king of Israel sally forth . . . against a *single* flea? 1 Sam 24:15

The indefinite noun plus אחד has a definite sense in the opening chapter of Genesis: יוֹם אֶחָד 'the first day' (Gen 1:5); this pattern is found nowhere else—even the rest of the account uses indefinite nouns with ordinal numbers (Gen 1:8, 13, etc.).

b   With a definite noun, אחד serves (as an ordinal) to count the first of a small number of things (## 8–9). In this construction the noun may be elided after a recent mention (# 10), the article may be omitted from the adjective (# 11; 14.3.1c).

8.	הַטּוּר הָאֶחָד	the *first* row [out of four rows] Exod 39:10
9.	[הַנָּהָר] הָאֶחָד	the *first* [river out of four rivers] Gen 2:11; cf. vv 13, 14
10.	הָרֹאשׁ אֶחָד	the *one* detachment [out of three detachments] 1 Sam 13:17

c   As an attributive adjective it can also have the sense 'only' (# 11) and as a predicate adjective the sense 'alone' (# 12) or 'integral (i.e., having integrity)' (# 13).

11.	נְצִיב אֶחָד אֲשֶׁר בָּאָרֶץ׃	the *only* governor in the land 1 Kgs 4:19
12.	יִהְיֶה יהוה אֶחָד	Yʜwʜ will be *alone*. Zech 14:9
13.	יהוה . . . אֶחָד׃	Yʜwʜ . . . is one. Deut 6:4

d   The adjective אחד forms a plural. Near a use of the singular form in a specific indefinite construction, the plural has a similar sense (# 14). Elsewhere the plural is used in an expression of time, יָמִים אֲחָדִים; the sense here, too, is specific indefinite, 'a few days, some little while' (# 15).[8]

14.   שָׂפָה אֶחָת וּדְבָרִים אֲחָדִים: a certain language and *certain* vocabulary
                                        Gen 11:1

15.   וַיִּהְיוּ בְעֵינָיו כְּיָמִים אֲחָדִים   They (the seven years) seemed like only *a few* days to him.
                                        Gen 29:20

Related to the attributive adjective use of אחת is a small group of *adverbial* uses.   e

16.   אַחַת נִשְׁבַּ֫עְתִּי   *Once (and for all)* I have sworn.
                              Ps 89:36

17.   לֹא אַחַת וְלֹא שְׁתָּ֫יִם: on a number of occasions (lit., not *once* or *twice*)
                                    2 Kgs 6:10

The *substantive* uses of אחת/אחד chiefly involve construct phrases. The number-   f
word may precede a plural noun (## 18–20) or be in the genitive (## 21–22).

18.   אַחַד הֶהָרִים   *one* of the mountains
                        Gen 22:2

19.   בְּאַחַד הַבֹּרוֹת   in *one* of the pits
                          Gen 37:20

20.   כְּאַחַת שִׁפְחֹתֶ֫יךָ   as *one* of your servants
                              Ruth 2:13

21.   מִשְׁפָּט אֶחָד   *one* judgment
                        Lev 24:22

22.   אֲרוֹן אֶחָד   *a* chest
                      2 Kgs 12:10

Certain *notions of unity* are expressed with words related to אחד, apparently derived   g
from a secondary root, יחד; the key adverbial expression of mutuality is יַחַד, יַחְדּו
'together, as one.' The cardinal number is rarely used in this way.

23.   זְאֵב וְטָלֶה יִרְעוּ כְאֶחָד   The wolf and the lamb will feed *as one*.
                                    Isa 65:25

The numeral 'two' is a morphological puzzle: by tradition, at least, the initial *shewa*   h
in שְׁנַיִם (pausal שְׁנָיִם) and שְׁנֵי is vocal (*šənáyim*), while the *shewa* in שְׁתַּיִם (pausal שְׁתָּיִם)
and שְׁתֵּי is syllable closing (*štáyim*).[9] The numeral is morphologically dual; it agrees in
gender with the noun it refers to, and it can take a suffix.

8. See also Gen 27:44.
9. Compare Arabic ʾiṯnāni and Phoenician ʾšnm, ʾšn,   suggesting *ištáyim*; but this form is dubious. "The feminine numeral 'two' has been a perennial problem of Biblical

i   As a *substantive* the numeral can occur as the first term of a construct chain (## 24–27) or with a pronominal suffix (# 28; cf. 9.5.3f).

24.   שְׁנֵי נְעָרָיו   his *two* servants
       Gen 22:3

25.   שְׁנֵי הָעֹמֶר   *two* omers
       Exod 16:22

26.   שְׁתֵּי־לֶחֶם   *two* (pieces) of bread
       1 Sam 10:4

27.   שְׁתֵּי־אֵלֶּה   *both* of these, these *two* (things)
       Isa 47:9

28.   שְׁנֵיהֶם   *two* of them
       Gen 2:25

The genitive is usually plural; examples ## 25–26 are both exceptional. As with the numeral 'one,' so 'two' can occur as the second term of a construct phrase, though such usage is rare.

29.   עַל־פִּי שְׁנַיִם עֵדִים   at the mouth of *two* witnesses
       Deut 17:6

30.   פִּי שְׁנַיִם   *two* portions (of an inheritance)
       Deut 21:17

The numeral is also substantive in the absolute use: שְׁנַיִם 'a pair' (Gen 7:2), שְׁתַּיִם 'on two occasions' (Job 40:5).

j   The more *adjectival* use of the numeral involves the absolute form standing either before (## 31–32) or after (## 33–34) the plural noun it refers to; the variation in position suggests that such phrases could be termed appositional as well as adjectival.

31.   שְׁנַיִם חֳדָשִׁים   *two* months
       1 Kgs 5:28

32.   שְׁנַיִם כְּרֻבִים   *two* cherubim
       Exod 25:18

33.   וְאֵילִם שְׁנַיִם תְּמִימִם: *two* pure rams
       Exod 29:1

34.   כְּבָשִׂים בְּנֵי־שָׁנָה שְׁנַיִם   *two* yearling lambs
       Exod 29:38

Hebrew orthography and phonology. . . . It . . . must violate at least one of the . . . principles . . . generally assumed to govern the phonetic interpretation" of Hebrew dagesh and shewa; so Robert D. Hoberman, "Initial Consonant Clusters in Hebrew and Aramaic," *Journal of Near Eastern Studies* 48 (1989) 25–29, at 25.

Less often the absolute numeral is used with a singular noun.

35.   נֶפֶשׁ שְׁנָֽיִם   *two* persons
                                        Gen 46:27

Cardinal 'Three–Ten'   **15.2.2**

The cardinal substantives 'three–ten' do not simply agree with the noun enumerated   a
but, following a rule of opposition, have the morphological gender contrary to that
noun.[10]

	with masculine		with feminine	
	absolute	construct	absolute	construct
three	שְׁלֹשָׁה	שְׁלֹשֶׁת	שָׁלֹשׁ	שְׁלֹשׁ
four	אַרְבָּעָה	אַרְבַּֽעַת	אַרְבַּע	אַרְבַּע
five	חֲמִשָּׁה	חֲמֵֽשֶׁת	חָמֵשׁ	חֲמֵשׁ
six	שִׁשָּׁה	שֵֽׁשֶׁת	שֵׁשׁ	שֵׁשׁ
seven	שִׁבְעָה	שִׁבְעַת	שֶֽׁבַע	שְׁבַע
eight	שְׁמֹנָה	שְׁמֹנַת	שְׁמֹנֶה	[שְׁמֹנֶה]
nine	תִּשְׁעָה	תִּשְׁעַת	תֵּֽשַׁע	תְּשַׁע
ten	עֲשָׂרָה	עֲשֶֽׂרֶת	עֶֽשֶׂר	עֶֽשֶׂר

They often do not agree with the noun with respect to definiteness. They may be
attached to the itemized thing in a variety of ways.[11]

These cardinals are used in the construct state before a definite noun.   b

1.   עֲשֶׂרֶת הַדְּבָרִים   the *ten* words
                                     Exod 34:28

2.   עֲשֶׂרֶת הַשְּׁבָטִים   the *ten* tribes
                                     1 Kgs 11:35; cf. v 31

3.   חֲמֵשֶׁת מַלְכֵי מִדְיָן   the *five* kings of Midian
                                     Num 31:8

4.   שִׁבְעַת בָּנָיו   his *seven* sons
                                     1 Sam 16:10

5.   חֲמֵשׁ הַיְרִיעֹת   *five* [of the ten] curtains
                                     Exod 26:3, 9; 36:10, 16

10. This patterning has aroused a great deal of commentary, most of it useless. The general idea that the Semitic
languages rely on certain patterns of polarity has been
rejected by E. A. Speiser, who essays his own explanation
for the cardinal number and gender problem; see "The
Pitfalls of Polarity," *Language* 14 (1938) 187–202, reprinted
in his *Oriental and Biblical Studies*, ed. J. J. Finkelstein
and Moshe Greenberg (Philadelphia: University of Pennsylvania, 1967) 433–54. For a recent explanation using
polarity, see Robert Hetzron, "Agaw Numerals and Incongruence in Semitic," *Journal of Semitic Studies* 12
(1967) 169–97; he alleges that the plural of a masculine
noun was feminine and vice versa.

11. A few morphological facts about these units may be
helpful. In *ʾrbᶜ* 'four,' the *ʾ* is prothetic. The root of *šš* 'six'
is *šdš* (Ugaritic *ṯdṯ*), whence the doubling in *šiššâ* (but not
šḗšet), *šiššî* 'sixth,' *šiššîm* 'sixty.' The doubling in some
forms of *ḥmš* 'five,' e.g., *ḥămiššâ* 'five,' *ḥămiššîm* 'fifty,' is
secondary (i.e., not part of the root), perhaps on analogy
to the *-šš-* of the 'six' forms.

The construct also precedes numbered things taken as a block, notably higher cardinal numbers.

6.   שְׁלֹשֶׁת יָמִים   *three* days (i.e., a trio of days)
2 Sam 24:13

7.   שְׁלֹשׁ מֵאוֹת שָׁנָה   *three* hundred years
Gen 5:22

8.   חֲמֵשֶׁת אֲלָפִים אִישׁ   *five* thousand men
Josh 8:12

9.   חֲמֵשׁ מֵאוֹת אֲתוֹנוֹת   *five* hundred she-donkeys
Job 1:3

These cardinals may appear in *the absolute state* before a plural indefinite noun (## 10–12), especially in lists (## 13–14), or before singular collective nouns (## 15–16). The unit words for commodities may be omitted (## 17–18). Finally, these cardinals may stand after a noun in the absolute state (## 19–21).[12]

10.   שְׁלֹשָׁה בָנִים   *three* sons
Gen 29:34

11.   שְׁלוֹשׁ עָרִים   *three* cities[13]
Deut 19:2

12.   חֲמִשָּׁה אֲנָשִׁים   *five* men
2 Kgs 25:19

13.   שִׁבְעָה בָנִים וְשָׁלוֹשׁ בָּנוֹת׃   *seven* sons and *three* daughters
Job 1:2

14.   אַרְבָּעָה מְלָכִים אֶת־הַחֲמִשָּׁה׃   *four* kings against five
Gen 14:9

15.   חֲמִשָּׁה בָקָר   *five* (head of) cattle
Exod 21:37

16.   שְׁמֹנֶה שָׁנָה   *eight* years
2 Kgs 8:17 *Kethiv*

17.   עֲשָׂרָה זָהָב   *ten* (shekels of) gold
Gen 24:22

---

12. This feature is associated with later Biblical Hebrew; see Robert Polzin, *Late Biblical Hebrew: Toward an Historical Typology of Biblical Hebrew Prose* (Missoula: Scholars Press, 1976) 58–60. The noun + numeral order is found at Qumran, though, as Elisha Qimron notes, the pattern interacts in complex ways with the factor of genre: lists, administrative documents, and texts drawing on them directly would probably have such an order, regardless of date; see *The Hebrew of the Dead Sea Scrolls* (Atlanta: Scholars Press, 1986) 85–86. Aramaic evidence is also complex; see, e.g., J. A. Lund, "The Syntax of the Numeral 'One' as a Noun Modifier in Jewish Palestinian Aramaic of the Amoraic Period," *Journal of the American Oriental Society* 106 (1986) 413–23; 108 (1988) 211–17.

13. ʿārîm is feminine.

18.	שֵׁשׁ־שְׂעֹרִים	six (seahs of) barley Ruth 3:15
19.	יָמִים שְׁלוֹשָׁה	three days 1 Chr 12:40
20.	בָּנוֹת שָׁלוֹשׁ	three daughters 1 Chr 25:5
21.	אַמּוֹת חָמֵשׁ	five cubits 2 Chr 3:11

Cardinal 'Eleven–Nineteen'   **15.2.3**

The numerals 'eleven–nineteen' are normally formed by the juxtaposition of the **a**
units with the numeral in עשׂר. The combined unit-teen phrase usually precedes the
enumerated noun, which is frequently plural, except in the case of the collectives, especially such words as יוֹם, שָׁנָה, אִישׁ, נֶפֶשׁ, and שֶׁקֶל (## 3, 9, 10).[14] The numeral עשׂר in the
teens (in contrast to its use absolutely) agrees with its noun in gender, while the units
follow their own laws of gender agreement (for 'one,' 'two') and gender opposition (for
'three–nine'). The numeral 'two' may be used as an absolute or a construct.

There are three morphological oddities about the teens. (1) The numeral עשׂר has **b**
different vocalisms in combination: עָשָׂר (versus עֶשֶׂר alone) and עֶשְׂרֵה (versus עֲשָׂרָה
alone). (2) The unit used for 'eleven' may be either אחד/אחת or עַשְׁתֵּי, the latter otherwise unused.[15] (3) The unit used for 'twelve' is not a dual but a plural שְׁתֵּים/שְׁנַיִם.

1.	אַחַד עָשָׂר כּוֹכָבִים	eleven stars Gen 37:9
2.	אַחַד עָשָׂר יְלָדָיו	his eleven children Gen 32:23
3.	אַחַד עָשָׂר יוֹם	eleven days Deut 1:2
4.	שְׁנֵים עָשָׂר עֲבָדֶיךָ	your twelve servants Gen 42:13
5.	שְׁתֵּי־עֶשְׂרֵה אֲבָנִים	twelve stones[16] Josh 4:8
6.	שְׁתֵּים עֶשְׂרֵה מַצֵּבָה לִשְׁנֵים עָשָׂר שִׁבְטֵי יִשְׂרָאֵל:	twelve pillars for the twelve tribes of Israel Exod 24:4

14. Hetzron argues, on the basis of Akkadian, that the original Semitic order was teen + unit and that the unit + teen order is secondary, that is, that the basic order is one of decreasing magnitude; see "Innovations in the Semitic Numeral System," *Journal of Semitic Studies* 22 (1977) 167–201; for a dissent, see M. A. Powell, "Notes on Akkadian Numbers and Number Syntax," *Journal of Semitic Studies* 24 (1979) 13–18.

15. Ugaritic and some dialects of Aramaic have the same split between ʾḥd 'one' and ʿšt (ʿšr) 'eleven'. The ʿšty form is cognate to Akkadian ištēn 'one' and Old South Arabic ʿstn; Akkadian uses the ʾḥd root in the adjective (w)ēdu 'alone.'

16. ʾăbānîm is feminine.

7.	שְׁתֵּים עֶשְׂרֵה עֵינֹת מַ֫יִם	*twelve* springs of water Exod 15:27
8.	חֲמֵ֫שֶׁת עָשָׂר בָּנָיו	his *fifteen* sons 2 Sam 19:18
9.	שְׁמוֹנֶה עֶשְׂרֵה שָׁנָה:	*eighteen* years Judg 3:14
10.	תִּשְׁעָה־עָשָׂר אִישׁ	*nineteen* men 2 Sam 2:30

In rare cases, usually in lists, the head noun precedes the numeral.

| 11. | עָרִים שֵׁשׁ־עֶשְׂרֵה וְחַצְרֵיהֶן: | *sixteen* cities with their settlements
Josh 15:41 |

15.2.4 Cardinal Decimals

a   The tens, formed on the basis of the units, are not inflected for gender but always add the masculine plural suffix עֶשְׂרִים :ים- 'twenty,' שְׁלֹשִׁים 'thirty,' etc.[17] A unit may precede (## 1–2, 7) or follow (## 3–6, 9–10); the decimal units follow their own laws of gender agreement and opposition with the enumerated item. If the item follows the numeral, it may be singular (## 1–5) or plural (## 6–7). If the enumerated item is plural, it may precede the numeral (## 8–10); this construction is favored in lists (## 8–9).

1.	שְׁתַּ֫יִם וְשִׁשִּׁים שָׁנָה	*sixty-two* years Gen 5:20
2.	וַיְחִי נָחוֹר תֵּ֫שַׁע וְעֶשְׂרִים שָׁנָה	When Nahor had lived *twenty-nine* years. . . . Gen 11:24
3.	אַרְבָּעִים וּשְׁתַּ֫יִם עִיר:	*forty-two* cities Num 35:6
4.	עֶשְׂרִים וּשְׁנַ֫יִם אֶ֫לֶף	*twenty-two* thousand Judg 7:3
5.	וּשְׁלֹשִׁים וּשְׁנַ֫יִם מֶ֫לֶךְ אִתּוֹ	*thirty-two* kings with him 1 Kgs 20:1
6.	עֶשְׂרִים וְאַרְבָּעָה פָּרִים	*twenty-four* oxen Num 7:88
7.	שָׁלוֹשׁ וּשְׁלֹשִׁים פְּעָמִים	*thirty-three* times[18] Ezek 41:6
8.	פָּרוֹת אַרְבָּעִים וּפָרִים עֲשָׂרָה	*forty* cows and *ten* bulls Gen 32:16

---

17. It is striking that ʿeśrîm is a plural, not a dual.   18. Paʿāmîm is feminine.

9. עָרִים אַרְבָּעִים וּשְׁמֹנֶה   *forty-eight* cities
                                  Josh 21:41

10. הַשָּׁבֻעִים שִׁשִּׁים וּשְׁנַיִם   the *sixty-two* weeks
                                  Dan 9:26

Ordinarily a *decimal + unit numeral* functions as a single entity, but in some in-   **b**
stances the enumerated noun is repeated with each element of the compound numerical
phrase.[19]

11. חָמֵשׁ שָׁנִים וְשִׁבְעִים שָׁנָה   *seventy-five* years
                                  Gen 12:4

12. שְׁלֹשִׁים יוֹם וּשְׁלֹשֶׁת יָמִים   *thirty-three* days[20]
                                  Lev 12:4

Higher Cardinals   **15.2.5**

The substantives for 'one hundred' and its multiples of ten are מֵאָה (fem.) 'one   **a**
hundred,' אֶלֶף (masc.) 'one thousand,' and רְבָבָה, רִבּוֹא, רְבוֹא, רִבּוֹ (fem.) 'ten thousand, a
myriad.' With these and higher numerals the enumerated item may follow the numeral as
a collective singular (## 1–4)[21] or as a plural (## 5–6).

1. בֶּן־מְאַת שָׁנָה   100 years old
                         Gen 11:10

2. מֵאָה־אֶלֶף רַגְלִי   100,000 infantry
                         1 Kgs 20:29

3. בֶּן מֵאָה־שָׁנָה   100 years old
                         Gen 17:17

4. אֶלֶף אַמָּה   1,000 cubits
                         Num 35:4

5. מֵאָה נְבִאִים   100 prophets
                         1 Kgs 18:4

6. אֶלֶף עִזִּים   1,000 he-goats
                         1 Sam 25:2

The higher numerals are used in the plural as vague indicators of great magnitude; in this
use, the numeral usually stands alone.

7. לְאַלְפֵי רְבָבָה   to *thousands* upon *tens of thousands*
                         Gen 24:60

---

19. A well-known Arabic parallel is *ʾAlf Layla wa Layla* 'A Thousand Nights and (One) Night, A Thousand and One Nights.'

20. Cf. 1 Chr 3:4.

21. It seems likely that these numerals are sometimes used to signify social units rather than groups of precisely so many (fighting) men, but this usage seems to have had no effect on the syntax of the terms; such usage is clearest in the case of *ʾelep* 'thousand, company.' See George E. Mendenhall, "The Census Lists of Numbers 1 and 26," *Journal of Biblical Literature* 77 (1958) 52–66; N. K. Gottwald, *The Tribes of Yahweh* (Maryknoll, New York: Orbis, 1979) 270–84; P. K. McCarter, *I Samuel* (Anchor Bible 8; Garden City, New York: Doubleday, 1980) 107.

| 8. | הַפִּיל רְבֹּאוֹת | He shall cast down *myriads*.
 Dan 11:12 |
| 9. | הֵם רִבְבוֹת אֶפְרַיִם וְהֵם אַלְפֵי מְנַשֶּׁה: | Such are the *ten thousands* of Ephraim, such are the *thousands* of Manasseh.
 Deut 33:17 |

b   The numerals for 'two hundred' and 'two thousand' are dual forms, מָאתַיִם and אַלְפַּיִם. Enumerated items follow the numeral in the singular (##10–11) or in the plural (## 12–13).

10.	כְּאַלְפַּיִם אִישׁ	about 2,000 men Josh 7:3
11.	מָאתַיִם לֶחֶם	200 (loaves of) bread 1 Sam 25:18
12.	מָאתַיִם שְׁקָלִים כֶּסֶף	200 sheqels of silver Josh 7:21
13.	אַלְפַּיִם סוּסִים	2,000 horses 2 Kgs 18:23

c   In the higher cardinals, the units take their gender by opposition to the larger number: units three–ten with מאה and רבבה, etc., have masculine form, while those units with אלף have feminine form. These numbers may stand before a singular (## 14–15) or a plural noun (# 16).

14.	אַרְבַּע מֵאוֹת נַעֲרָה בְתוּלָה	400 young women Judg 21:12
15.	מִשְׁתֵּים־עֶשְׂרֵה רִבּוֹ אָדָם	120,000 men Jonah 4:11
16.	שְׁלֹשׁ־מֵאוֹת שׁוּעָלִים	300 foxes Judg 15:4

Mixed coordinated constructions are found, with one noun in the singular, the other in the plural.

| 17. | שְׁלֹשִׁים אֶלֶף רֶכֶב וְשֵׁשֶׁת אֲלָפִים פָּרָשִׁים | 30,000 chariots and 6,000 cavalry[22]
 1 Sam 13:5 |
| 18. | אֶלֶף וּשְׁבַע־מֵאוֹת פָּרָשִׁים וְעֶשְׂרִים אֶלֶף אִישׁ רַגְלִי | 1,700 cavalry and 20,000 infantry
 2 Sam 8:4 |

---

22. The use of *rkb* singular and *pršym* plural is usual; for the pair without numerals, see, e.g., 1 Kgs 1:5, 10:26; 2 Kgs 2:12, 13:14, 18:24; Isa 22:6.

In large counting expressions, the elements are often given in decreasing order: d
thousands → hundreds → decimals → units (## 19–22). The opposite, increasing order is
rare (# 23).

19.	שְׁלֹשָׁה וַחֲמִשִּׁים אֶלֶף וְאַרְבַּע מֵאוֹת:	53,400 Num 1:43
20.	אֲלָפִּים שְׁבַע מֵאוֹת וַחֲמִשִּׁים:	2,750 Num 4:36
21.	שֵׁשֶׁת אֲלָפִים וּמָאתָיִם:	6,200 Num 3:34
22.	אַרְבַּע רִבּוֹא אֲלָפַיִם שְׁלֹשׁ־מֵאוֹת שִׁשִּׁים:	42,360 Ezra 2:64
23.	חֲמִשָּׁה וְשִׁשִּׁים וּשְׁלֹשׁ מֵאוֹת וָאֶלֶף	1,365 Num 3:50

A mixed order is attested also: myriads → thousands → units → decimals → hundreds.

24.	כָּל־בְּכוֹר זָכָר . . . שְׁנַיִם וְעֶשְׂרִים אֶלֶף שְׁלֹשָׁה וְשִׁבְעִים וּמָאתָיִם:	and all the first born males . . . 22,273 Num 3:43

Determination and Cardinals   **15.2.6**

The numerals are deemed to have a certain determination in themselves, and the   a
article is used sparingly with them. When it is used, it has the meanings analyzed above
(see 13.5, 14.3.1d). Apart from the numeral 'one,' the article is rarely used with both the
numeral and the thing enumerated.[23] Generally it is found with the thing numbered, and,
as noted earlier, the numeral may precede (## 1–4) or follow (## 5–6).

1.	בִּשְׁלֹשׁ מֵאוֹת הָאִישׁ	among the *three hundred* men Judg 7:7
2.	שְׁלֹשׁ־מֵאוֹת הַשּׁוֹפָרוֹת	the *three hundred* trumpets Judg 7:22
3.	אֶלֶף־וּמֵאָה הַכֶּסֶף	the *eleven hundred* (sheqels of) silver Judg 17:3
4.	אֶל־מָאתַיִם הָאֲנָשִׁים	to the *two hundred* men 1 Sam 30:21
5.	הָעַמּוּדִים שְׁנַיִם	the *two* columns 2 Kgs 25:16
6.	הַשָּׁבֻעִים שִׁשִּׁים וּשְׁנַיִם	the *sixty-two* weeks Dan 9:26

---

23. Num 16:35, the one instance in which the numeral has the article and the following noun has no article, is textually suspect; the Samaritan Pentateuch lacks the article.

15.3   Ordinals

a   The numbering adjectives or ordinals are distinctive for the lower units only. The most common use of ordinals is in various dating expressions.[24]

15.3.1   Patterns

a   The ordinals 'first–tenth' have special forms. In addition to רִאשׁוֹן, the common primary ordinal אֶחָד is often used with the sense 'first' (15.2.1b). The ordinals 'second–tenth' have the form of gentilic adjectives (5.7c).

1.	הַמַּכָּה הָרִאשֹׁנָה	the *first* slaughter 1 Sam 14:14
2.	וְלֹא־הָיָה דְבָרִי רִאשׁוֹן	Was not my word *first*? 2 Sam 19:44
3.	בַּיּוֹם הָרְבִיעִי	on the *fourth* day Judg 19:5
4.	בַּשָּׁנָה הָרְבִיעִית	in the *fourth* year 2 Kgs 18:9
5.	בַּשָּׁנָה הָרְבִעִית בַּחֹדֶשׁ הַחֲמִישִׁי	in the *fifth* month of the fourth year Jer 28:1 *Qere*

For other ordinal uses, the cardinal numerals are used, standing before the enumerated noun; ordinarily neither numeral nor noun has the article.

6.	וּבְאַרְבַּע עֶשְׂרֵה שָׁנָה	in the *fourteenth* year Gen 14:5
7.	בְּאַרְבָּעִים שָׁנָה	in the *fortieth* year Deut 1:3
8.	בִּשְׁנֵים עָשָׂר חֹדֶשׁ	in the *twelfth* month 2 Kgs 25:27

15.3.2   Dates

a   There are three components to a full date, each numerical. The two simpler elements, day and month, are reckoned absolutely (i.e., by a fixed calendar).[25] Year reckoning is usually by reign (e.g., 2 Kgs 25:1) or by era, for example, of the Exile in Babylonia (e.g., 2 Kgs 25:27). The day and year are usually indicated by cardinal numbers, the month by ordinals.

---

24. The common ordinals are *rʾšwn* 182 times, *šny* 156, *šlšy* 107; *ʾhr* 'another, second' (166 times) can function as a substitute ordinal.

25. Days and months are both usually numbered. Day names are largely post-biblical. Month names follow two calendars, one old calendar (attested in the time of Solomon, 1 Kgs 6:1, 37–38; 8:2, and usually considered pre-exilic) and one more recent (attested in the Persian period, e.g., Neh 2:1; Esth 3:7, 8:9); neither set of month names is fully attested in the Bible, although the later, so-called Babylonian calendar was and remains standard for later Jewish practice.

If the *day* alone is mentioned, there are two common formulas.[26] The first is used   **b**
for the ordinals 'first–tenth' and involves יום with the article, followed by the ordinal
with the article.

1.	בַּיּוֹם הָרִאשׁוֹן	on the *first* day	Exod 12:16, Num 7:12
2.	בַּיּוֹם הַשְּׁבִיעִי	on the *seventh* day	Exod 12:16, Num 7:48
3.	בַּיּוֹם הָעֲשִׂירִי	on the *tenth* day	Num 7:66

For the higher numbered days, the formula is יום + numeral + יום; neither occurrence
of יום has the article.

4.	בְּיוֹם עַשְׁתֵּי עָשָׂר יוֹם	on the *eleventh* day	Num 7:72
5.	בְּיוֹם שְׁנֵים עָשָׂר יוֹם	on the *twelfth* day	Num 7:78

If the *month* is mentioned, there is more variety.

6.	בֶּעָשׂוֹר לַחֹדֶשׁ הַזֶּה	on the *tenth* (day) of this month	Exod 12:3
7.	עַד אַרְבָּעָה עָשָׂר יוֹם לַחֹדֶשׁ הַזֶּה	until the *fourteenth* day of this month	Exod 12:6
8.	בָּרִאשֹׁן בְּאַרְבָּעָה עָשָׂר יוֹם לַחֹדֶשׁ	in the *first* (month), on the *fourteenth* day of the month	Exod 12:18
9.	עַד יוֹם הָאֶחָד וְעֶשְׂרִים לַחֹדֶשׁ	until the *twenty-first* day of the month	Exod 12:18
10.	בַּחֲמִשָּׁה עָשָׂר יוֹם לַחֹדֶשׁ הַשֵּׁנִי	on the *fifteenth* day of the *second* month	Exod 16:1
11.	בִּשְׁנֵים עָשָׂר חֹדֶשׁ בְּעֶשְׂרִים וְשִׁבְעָה לַחֹדֶשׁ	in the *twelfth* month, on the *twenty-seventh* (day) of the month	2 Kgs 25:27

The month is most often specified with the day.

The formulas for the *year* alone are similar to those for the day alone: one is used   **c**
with the lower numbers and another for all the rest. In both, שׁנה is used initially in the
construct. For the lower numbers, the cardinal numeral follows שׁנת.

---

26. Although we are concerned here with dating formulas, we may say that it is rare for a numbered day to be
mentioned outside a dating formula; notably, in Deut 5:14,
yôm haššabîʿî is the subject of a sentence.

12.	בִּשְׁנַת שְׁתַּיִם	in the *second* year
		1 Kgs 15:25, 2 Kgs 15:32
13.	בִּשְׁנַת שָׁלֹשׁ	in the *third* year
		1 Kgs 15:28
14.	בִּשְׁנַת הַתְּשִׁיעִית	in the *ninth* year
		2 Kgs 17:6

For high numbers, a framing construction is used: שְׁנַת + numeral + שָׁנָה.

15.	בִּשְׁנַת שְׁתֵּים־עֶשְׂרֵה שָׁנָה	in the *twelfth* year
		2 Kgs 8:25
16.	בִּשְׁנַת שֵׁשׁ־מֵאוֹת שָׁנָה	in the *six-hundredth* year
		Gen 7:11

In full dates, the elements occur in order of decreasing size: year → month → day.

17.	בִּשְׁנַת שְׁתַּיִם לְדָרְיָוֶשׁ הַמֶּלֶךְ	in the *second* year of King Darius, in the *sixth* month,
	בַּחֹדֶשׁ הַשִּׁשִּׁי בְּיוֹם אֶחָד לַחֹדֶשׁ	on the *first* day
		Hag 1:1

15.4   Multiplicatives

a   The multiplicative expressions are formed in a number of ways.[27] One group of expressions is based on the root for the numeral involved. For 'double' both the cardinal number (# 1) and a derived form, מִשְׁנֶה 'copy, double, second' (## 2–3), are used, both in the absolute. For 'quadruple,' 'septuple,' and perhaps 'ten thousand-fold,' feminine dual forms are used (## 4–6). Cardinal numbers, in the masculine generally, can also be used as multiplicatives; an elided noun, probably פַּעַם, should be understood (# 7).

1.	שְׁנַיִם יְשַׁלֵּם׃	He must pay back *double*.
		Exod 22:3
2.	כֶּסֶף מִשְׁנֶה	*double* the amount of silver
		Gen 43:12
3.	מִשְׁנֶה־כֶּסֶף	*double* the amount of silver[28]
		Gen 43:15
4.	אַרְבַּעְתָּיִם	*four times*
		2 Sam 12:6
5.	שִׁבְעָתַיִם	*seven times, sevenfold*
		Gen 4:15

---

27. Both the multiplicatives and fractions are rather poorly attested in the Bible; cf. Rosenthal, *Grammar of Biblical Aramaic*, §§ 70–71 / p. 33.

28. Note that the MT points *mšnh* as absolute, not a construct, taking *ksp* as an appositive of measure (see 12.3d).

6.	רִבֹּתַיִם	*ten thousand times* (?) Ps 68:18
7.	שֶׁבַע	*seven times* Lev 26:21, 24

The other set of multiplicatives involves a number plus another word conventionally   b
rendered 'time.' Three of the four 'time' words refer to the limbs: פַּעַם (fem.) 'foot' (## 8–
11), רֶגֶל (fem.) 'foot' (# 12), יָד (fem.) 'hand' (## 13–14); the fourth, מֹנֶה, occurs only twice
and its sense is obscure (# 15).[29]

8.	פַּעַם אֶחָת	one *time* Josh 6:3
9.	פַּעֲמַיִם	*two times* Gen 27:36
10.	שָׁלוֹשׁ וּשְׁלֹשִׁים פְּעָמִים	thirty-three *times* Ezek 41:6
11.	מֵאָה פְעָמִים	a hundred *times* 2 Sam 24:3
12.	שָׁלֹשׁ רְגָלִים . . . בַּשָּׁנָה:	three *times* . . . a year[30] Exod 23:14
13.	חָמֵשׁ יָדוֹת	five *times* Gen 43:34
14.	עֶשֶׂר יָדוֹת	ten *times* Dan 1:20
15.	עֲשֶׂרֶת מֹנִים	ten *times* Gen 31:7, 41

Fractions   15.5

There are several patterns used to form fractions, as well as several distinctive   a
words. The terms are usually used as constructs (2 Sam 18:2 is an exception). The
fractions 'one tenth' and greater are feminine ordinals for the corresponding unit: שְׁלִשִׁית
'a third' (2 Sam 18:2), רְבִ(י)עִית 'a fourth' (Num 15:4, 5), עֲשִׂירִית 'a tenth, a tithe' (Num
28:5). There is no such ordinal-based term for 'a half,' but only חֲצִי, apparently from the
root *ḥṣy* 'to divide.' There are terms for several other large fractions which fall outside the
ordinal pattern: רֶבַע and perhaps רֹבַע 'a quarter,' חֹמֶשׁ 'a fifth' (only in Gen 47:26), and
עִשָּׂרוֹן, מַעֲשֵׂר (pl. מַעַשְׂרוֹת), 'tenth, tithe.'

1.	חֲצִי הָעָם הָיָה אַחֲרֵי תִבְנִי	*Half* the people supported Tibni. 1 Kgs 16:21

---

29. It is related to the verb *mānâ* 'to count.'
30. The same phrase is used in Num 22:28, 32, 33; these four are the only multiplicative uses of *régel*.

2.   נִמְצָא בְיָדִי רֶבַע שֶׁקֶל כָּסֶף   There's *a quarter* sheqel of silver in my hand.
                                                   1 Sam 9:8

3.   מִנְחָה סֹלֶת עִשָּׂרוֹן בָּלוּל   an offering (of) fine flour, *a tenth* (of an ephah),
                    בִּרְבִעִית הַהִין שָׁמֶן: moistened with *a quarter* hin (of) oil
                                                    Num 15:4; cf. Exod 29:40

The other pattern, used for fractions under a tenth, involves the cardinal number in construct before the enumerated thing with the article.

4.   מְאַת הַכֶּסֶף   *a hundredth* part of the money
                                                   Neh 5:11

15.6   Distributive Expressions

a   Phrases which associate entities pairwise—'One man, one vote,' 'One for all and all for one'—are called distributives.[31] If the distributed entity is a verbal action, the distributive phrase is adverbial. The preposition בְּ may be used with a repeated noun indicating the distributed entity.

1.   וְלֹא־הֶעֱלָה מִנְחָה . . . כְּשָׁנָה   He did not send tribute . . . as (he had) *year by year*.
                        בְשָׁנָה   2 Kgs 17:4

The preposition לְ may introduce the distributive range.

2.   אַחַת לְשָׁלֹשׁ שָׁנִים תָּבוֹא   It comes once *every three years*.
                                                   1 Kgs 10:22

b   If the distribution is of an entity *to* an entity, לְ again may introduce the range (## 3–6); the phrase for the distributed entity may be repeated (# 4) or the whole may be repeated (## 5–6).

3.   אִישׁ אֶחָד לַשָּׁבֶט: one man *to a* tribe
                                                  Deut 1:23

4.   אִישׁ אֶחָד אִישׁ אֶחָד לְמַטֵּה   one man *for each* tribe of his forebears
                        אֲבֹתָיו   Num 13:2

5.   אֶלֶף לַמַּטֶּה אֶלֶף לַמַּטֶּה   one thousand *to each* tribe
                                                    Num 31:4

6.   שֵׁשׁ כְּנָפַיִם שֵׁשׁ כְּנָפַיִם לְאֶחָד   six wings *to each*
                                                   Isa 6:2

If the distribution is *from* an entity, the preposition מִן is used.

---

31. Cf. 7.2.3b. On the distributive in later Biblical Hebrew, see Polzin, *Late Biblical Hebrew*, 47–51.

7. מִכֹּל הַבְּהֵמָה הַטְּהוֹרָה תִּקַּח־לְךָ
שִׁבְעָה שִׁבְעָה אִישׁ וְאִשְׁתּוֹ

From the clean animals take *seven by seven*, a male
and its female.
Gen 7:2

8. מִן־הַבְּהֵמָה הַטְּהוֹרָה . . . שְׁנַיִם
שְׁנַיִם בָּאוּ

From the clean animals . . . *pair by pair* they came.
Gen 7:8–9

Related to these numerical distributives are universal distributive expressions, mean-   c
ing 'all who' or 'each.' One group of these expressions involves a plural referent (often a
participle) with a singular predicate.

9. מְחַלְלֶיהָ מוֹת יוּמָת

*Anyone who desecrates/all who desecrate/each who
desecrates* it (the Sabbath) shall be put to death.
Exod 31:14

10. תֹּמְכֶיהָ מְאֻשָּׁר:

Any who seizes it (i.e., wisdom) is blessed.
Prov 3:18

Another group of such expressions uses כל before an indefinite singular. (Before a
definite singular *kōl* often signifies an aggregate or totality.)

11. בְּכָל־יוֹם

every day
Ps 7:12

12. סֻגַּר כָּל־בַּיִת מִבּוֹא:

Every house is barred from entering (i.e., The entrance
of *each* house is barred).
Isa 24:10

16

Personal Pronouns

16.1 Pronouns in General

a   Pronouns are words that can stand for (Latin *pro*) a noun (*nomen*) or noun phrase; the major groups of pronouns are personal, demonstrative, interrogative, indefinite, and relative. A variety of expressions can perform the noun role in a clause, including nouns (e.g., 'a boy'), noun phrases ('a boy and a girl'), and clauses ('you know who'), as well as pronouns (see 4.4.1). Grammarians usually limit the word class of pronouns to the groups mentioned. This is in part due to the tradition of the "parts of speech" as first recognized by the Alexandrian grammarians.[1]

b   The traditional segregation of pronouns has certain advantages. The pronoun class, like the deictic system it is part of (13.1),[2] is essentially a closed class (4.2), that is, limited in membership.[3] The pronouns are "workhorses"—they are used frequently and play an important role in all grammatical functioning. The class of pronouns is morphologically diverse: usual categories of Hebrew inflection such as number and gender are manifest, but sometimes in unusual ways. Pronominal shapes are also unusual; the word elements are interlinked in complex ways (cf. 17.2, 19.2).

---

1. R. H. Robins, *Ancient and Mediaeval Grammatical Theory in Europe* (London: Bell, 1951) 39–40, 66; Robins, *A Short History of Linguistics* (Bloomington: Indiana University, 1967) 33–34, cf. 26, 28; John Lyons, *Introduction to Theoretical Linguistics* (Cambridge: Cambridge University, 1968) 12.

2. The deictic quality of pronouns is highlighted in the late antique view of them as "substance (*or* being) without qualities." See Robins, *Short History of Linguistics*, 37, cf. 54, 57–58, 79–80.

3. There are some interesting marginal cases; in some instances *kl* 'each, all' is used as a pronoun, while *ᶜbdk* 'your servant' is a high-style, quasi-honorific substitute for a first-person pronoun. On *ᶜbdk/h* in Ugaritic, see *UT* § 6.15. See also P. Swiggers, *MPD* 60–61.

The four major pronominal groups are each distinct. *Personal pronouns* refer to   c
speaker, to hearer, or to the topic under discussion; they are syntactically the least specialized group. *Demonstratives* single out a person or thing referred to (e.g., English
'*This* is the land'); they share some features of third-person pronouns (e.g., '*This/She* is
the queen') and are also adjectival in character. The *interrogatives* and *indefinites* compose a single correlative group, one part associated with questions (e.g., '*Who* is the
queen?') and the other with a particular sort of reference (e.g., '*Whoever* the queen is,
she must rule'). The indefinite pronouns are only one variety of indefinite usage, just as
questions can be asked without interrogatives (40.3). *Relative pronouns* link up preceding and following elements (e.g., 'The queen ← *who* → rules well will prosper'; 'I visited
the queen ← *who* → called for me').

One special feature of the Hebrew personal pronouns is the extent to which they   d
refer to persons rather than objects, or, more strictly, to animates rather than inanimates.
Only מִי 'who' is comparably restricted among the other pronouns. In the first- and
second-person slots the limitation to animates is complete, and in the third-person slot it
is nearly perfect.

The personal pronouns have been cited in numerous examples in the previous chap-   e
ters, but they are the special concern of this chapter. In succeeding chapters the other
pronominal groups will be treated (Chaps. 17–19).

Personal Pronouns   **16.2**

There are two classes of personal pronouns in Hebrew, and they are distinguished   a
on both formal and functional grounds.[4] The *independent personal pronouns* are both
free-standing words and nominative in function, whereas the *pronominal suffixes* are
never free standing and are in function genitive (with nouns and prepositions) or accusative (with verbs, את, and הנה). From a comparative perspective, this double patterning is
remarkable.[5] Ugaritic, for example, has independent third-person genitive-accusative
pronouns,[6] and some dialects of Akkadian have independent nominative, genitive-
accusative, and dative forms.[7] There are some complexities in the syntax of the independent personal pronouns, involving their use in apposition to nouns in an oblique
function.[8] Such complexities cannot distract from the overwhelmingly basic usage of the
separate pronouns in nominative functions.[9]

---

4. Note especially that Hebrew has no pronominal adjectives, such as are common in the European languages
(English 'mine,' French 'mienne,' German 'mein'); on reflexive usage, see 16.4g.

5. It is occasionally contended that the appositional use
of the independent personal pronouns shows that they are
not strictly nominative, but that use is comparatively marginal. This is apparently the view of T. Muraoka, *Emphatic
Words and Structures in Biblical Hebrew* (Jerusalem:
Magnes/Leiden: Brill, 1985); this volume is an important
contribution, and its influence on our discussion has been
central. On the double patterning, however, the traditional

view has much to commend it.

6. *UT* § 6.4; in Hebrew the role of these pronouns is
played by ʾt + suffixes.

7. E.g., *anāku* 'I'; *jâti* 'me, my'; *jâši* 'to me.' See Wolfram von Soden, *Grundriss der akkadischen Grammatik*
(Rome: Pontifical Biblical Institute, 1969) 41–42.

8. See GKC § 135d–h / p. 438 and below, 16.3.4.

9. There are a very few instances of the independent
pronoun in the oblique cases, apart from the appositional
use; these are all either textually doubtful or to be explained by ellipsis; cf. 2 Kgs 9:18, Isa 18:2, Nah 2:9, etc.
M. Dahood has suggested recognition of some other cases;

16.3   Independent Personal Pronouns

a   Before turning to the topic of the uses of the separate pronouns, we can make a few observations on their shapes.[10]

	singular	plural
first common	אָנֹכִי ,אֲנִי	אֲנַחְנוּ
second masc.	אַתָּה	אַתֶּם
second fem.	אַתְּ	אַתֵּנָה ,אַתֵּן
third masc.	הוּא	הֵמָּה ,הֵם
third fem.	הִיא	הֵנָּה

There are two distinct subgroups. The first- and second-person forms are all formed from a base ʾan with endings;[11] the -n assimilates to the -t- of the second-person endings, yielding -tt-. In contrast, the third-person forms are made up of elements also found in demonstratives and in the article *ha(n?)- (13.3, 17.2). The first-person singular alone has two distinct forms, a short form (ʾănî) and a long form (ʾānōkî); there is no functional difference between them, though it is the long form that eventually disappears, leaving ʾănî only in late Biblical Hebrew, as well as in Mishnaic and later forms of the language.[12] The third-person singular forms[13] seem to be simplified in the monosyllabic MT forms hûʾ-hîʾ; bisyllabic forms[14] are implicit in the Qumran writings הואה, היאה.[15] It is possible that mono- and bisyllabic forms alternated in Classical Hebrew (cf. English 'them' and ''em') and that the Masoretes have preferred consistency on this point.[16]

16.3.1   Uses

a   The independent personal pronouns serve as surrogates for an antecedent or implicit noun, usually referring to a person; they may serve in a variety of linguistic contexts.

---

see, e.g., his paper "The Independent Personal Pronoun in the Oblique Case in Hebrew," *Catholic Biblical Quarterly* 32 (1970) 86–90.

10. The most common pronouns in order of frequency (after SA/THAT) are *hûʾ* 1,390 times, *ʾănî* 870, *ʾattâ* 743, *hēm* and *hēmmâ* 551 (*hēm* 269, *hēmmâ* 282), *hîʾ* 485, *ʾānōkî* 358, *ʾattem* 282, *ʾănaḥnû* 125.

11. As in all the Semitic languages; see, e.g., G. Bergsträsser, *Introduction to the Semitic Languages*, trans. and sup. Peter T. Daniels (Winona Lake, Indiana: Eisenbrauns, 1983) 7; C. Brockelmann, *Grundriss der vergleichenden Grammatik der semitischen Sprachen* (Berlin: Reuter und Reichard, 1908), 1. 297–306.

12. Ugaritic and Phoenician also have the two forms; *UT* § 6.2. Arabic has only the short form, *ʾānā*; Akkadian, only the long form, *anāku*.

In Hebrew there are no occurrences of *ʾnky* in Haggai, Zechariah 1–8, Canticles, Lamentations, Esther, Qoheleth, and Ezra; it is rare in Ezekiel, Daniel, Nehemiah, and Chronicles. On these facts and the Mishnaic usage, see M. H. Segal, *A Grammar of Mishnaic Hebrew* (Oxford:

Clarendon, 1927) 39. For an argument that *ʾny* is the marked member of the pair and is non-predicative in use, while *ʾnky* is often predicative (viz., 'It is I who . . . '), see H. B. Rosén, "*ʾnky* et *ʾny*," in his *East and West: Selected Writings in Linguistics. 2. Hebrew and Semitic Linguistics* (Munich: Fink, 1984) 262–81.

13. In the consonantal text of the Pentateuch, there is only one third-person singular form, *hwʾ*, pointed to agree with the rest of the MT; this may reflect a form of Hebrew in which *hûʾ* was epicene (cf. 6.5.2). There are many other explanations available; see, e.g., Joüon § 39c / p. 91.

14. Cf. Arabic *hūwa*, *hīya* and probably Ugaritic *hw*, *hy*.

15. See E. Qimron, *The Hebrew of the Dead Sea Scrolls* (Atlanta: Scholars Press, 1986) 57, who reports equal use of the long and short forms (*hwʾh* 45 times, *hwʾ* 65 times; *hyʾh* 19 times, *hyʾ* 21 times).

16. Similarly, Qumran (and Samaritan) *ʾtmh* suggests that there was a trisyllabic as well as a bisyllabic form of the second-person masculine plural form, as there seems to have been of the rare corresponding feminine; see Qimron, *Hebrew of the Dead Sea Scrolls*, 58.

Their use is, first of all, a feature of the language's economy (3.2.3). As simple surrogates they relieve the tedious monotony of the same noun being repeated again and again. Such is their normal function, for example, in these verbless clauses.

1.   וְהוּא בֶּן־אִשָּׁה זוֹנָה   *He* was the son of a prostitute ['he' for 'Jephthah'].
                                              Judg 11:1

2.   וְהוּא נַעַר   *He* was a young lad ['he' for 'Joseph'].
                                              Gen 37:2

Sometimes, especially in apposition, personal pronouns signify a mild emphasis on   b
some noun or pronoun in a statement, that is, use of a pronoun makes some difference in meaning in a statement.[17] For example, the meaning of 'Did Mary bring this for me?' depends in part on whether one of the words is emphasized. If the emphasis is on Mary ('Did *Mary* bring this for me?'), the attention is on the fact that Mary was the one who brought the gift; if the emphasis is on one of the pronouns ('Did Mary bring *this* for me?' or 'Did Mary bring this for *me*?') attention falls on either the gift or the speaker. In oral/ aural communication we express such distinctions by stress and tone of voice, but in written expression other means are used. In modern texts these may be strictly typo- graphical, but such devices were not available to ancient writers.[18] They rather had to draw on the syntactic and morphological means in constant service in the spoken lan- guage, marshaling those resources carefully and often more systematically than we might at first suspect.

In the following sections we deal with the independent personal pronouns in both   c
surrogate and emphatic patterns. First, the major classes of clauses, verbal and verbless, will be discussed (16.3.2–3); then the appositional use will be treated (16.3.4). Some minor patterns will be handled last (16.3.5).

Finite Verbal Clauses   **16.3.2**

A finite verb form in Hebrew is intrinsically marked for person, number, and, where   a
relevant, gender: יָצְאוּ is third person, plural, and masculine.[19] If an independent pro- noun were to be used with such a verb, its occurrence would need some explanation: either הֵם יָצְאוּ or יָצְאוּ הֵם seems to be more than is necessary. Two kinds of explanation are advanced for such grammatical structures, neither of them quite adequate. One set of explanations refers to *pleonasm*, literally, overgrowth; it is doubtful that any major lin- guistic element can truly be superfluous or redundant. The second set of explanations refers to *emphasis*: such explanations can be faulted as being overly vague, but they are susceptible of refinement and reconsideration.[20]

---

17. Muraoka is right in complaining, "What annoys us here is that none of these grammarians [who use the con- cept of emphasis] gives us a precise and clear definition of their concept"; *Emphatic Words*, 47.

18. "Modern" here refers to the period since the Renais- sance and the propagation of printing; on this ancient/

modern gap, see, e.g., M. O'Connor, "Writing Systems and Native Speaker Analyses," *Society of Biblical Litera- ture Seminar Papers 1986*, ed. K. H. Richards (Atlanta: Scholars Press, 1986) 536–43.

19. On pronouns with non-finite verbs, see Chaps. 35–37.

20. This is the burden of Muraoka's *Emphatic Words*.

b   There are three reasons why an independent pronoun is used with a finite verb; in all three cases both possible word orders are found, *pronoun + verb* and *verb + pronoun*, although the former is much more common. The first reason involves a syntactic hole in the language—this is neither a pleonastic nor an emphatic use. The other two involve logical contrast and psychological focus—both of these may loosely be termed emphatic.

c   A hole in the syntactic system arises because the verb need not be *fully* marked for the subject.[21] Here are two clauses.

1.   וַיֹּאמֶר יִפְתָּח   And Jephthah said. . . .
                                   Judg 11:7

2.   וַיֹּאמְרוּ זִקְנֵי גִלְעָד   And the elders of Gilead said. . . .
                                   Judg 11:8

In both cases the verb agrees with the subject. The following sentence is also possible, although not attested and thus marked with *.

3.   *וַיֹּאמֶר יִפְתָּח וְזִקְנֵי גִלְעָד   And Jephthah and the elders of Gilead said. . . .

The singular verb before a plural coordinate subject is commonplace. If the preceding discourse concerned the first part of this coordinate subject in such a way that it did not need to be named, we might expect the following clause.

4.   **וַיֹּאמֶר וְזִקְנֵי גִלְעָד   And he and the elders of Gilead said. . . .

This clause type is impossible (and is thus marked with **): in such cases, the independent pronoun must be used to form the coordinate subject.

5.   *וַיֹּאמֶר הוּא וְזִקְנֵי גִלְעָד   And he and the elders of Gilead said. . . .

Here the pronoun is not pleonastic or emphatic; it serves merely to represent the referent of the pronoun as the chief actor among other actors.[22]

6.   בֹּא־אַתָּה וְכָל־בֵּיתְךָ אֶל־הַתֵּבָה   Go, you and all your house, into the ark.
                                   Gen 7:1

7.   וַתֵּלֶךְ הִיא וְרֵעוֹתֶיהָ   She and her women friends went.
                                   Judg 11:38

8.   וַתָּקָם הִיא וְכַלֹּתֶיהָ וַתָּשָׁב   She (Naomi) and her daughters-in-law arose and
           מִשְּׂדֵי מוֹאָב   returned from the fields of Moab.
                                   Ruth 1:6

---

21. Muraoka, *Emphatic Words*, 62–63.

22. The construction under discussion is *verb + subject* (the latter including the pronoun); the superficially similar *subject + pronoun + verb*, where the subject is either coordinate (e.g., Gen 14:24) or complex (e.g., Gen 15:4, 24:7) is a nominative absolute construction of a distinct type (cf. 4.7, 8.4.1, and 16.3.3); contrast Muraoka, *Emphatic Words*, 55.

When another grammatical element intervenes before a subject, it is necessary to add a resumptive personal pronoun.

| 9. | וַיַּעַל אַבְרָם מִמִּצְרַיִם הוּא וְאִשְׁתּוֹ | And Abram went up from Egypt, he and his wife. Gen 13:1 |

An apposition, however, does not constitute such a separation.

| 10. | וַיָּבֹא יִתְרוֹ חֹתֵן מֹשֶׁה וּבָנָיו | And Jethro, Moses' father-in-law, and his sons came. Exod 18:5 |

A second group of uses of independent personal pronouns with finite verbs involves d
logical structure. The referent of the pronoun may be involved in an *explicit antithesis* with another person or group of persons.[23]

11.	דַּבֵּר־אַתָּה עִמָּנוּ וְנִשְׁמָעָה וְאַל־יְדַבֵּר עִמָּנוּ אֱלֹהִים	*You* speak to us, and we will hear; but let not God speak. Exod 20:19
12.	כָּזֹאת וְכָזֹאת יָעַץ אֲחִיתֹפֶל . . . וְכָזֹאת וְכָזֹאת יָעַצְתִּי אָנִי׃	Ahithophel has advised . . . to do such and such, but *I* advised them to do so and so. 2 Sam 17:15
13.	אָנֹכִי חָטָאתִי וְאָנֹכִי הֶעֱוֵיתִי וְאֵלֶּה הַצֹּאן מֶה עָשׂוּ	*I* am the one who has sinned; *I* have done wrong. These are but sheep. What have they done? 2 Sam 24:17
14.	יֵבֹשׁוּ רֹדְפַי וְאַל־אֵבֹשָׁה אָנִי יֵחַתּוּ הֵמָּה וְאַל־אֵחַתָּה אָנִי	Let my persecutors be put to shame, but let *me* not be put to shame; let *them* be terrified, but let *me* not be terrified. Jer 17:18

In some cases both parties to the antithesis are referred to with pronouns.

| 15. | הוּא יְשׁוּפְךָ רֹאשׁ וְאַתָּה תְּשׁוּפֶנּוּ עָקֵב׃ | *He* will crush your head, but *you* will crush his heel. Gen 3:15 |

In other cases the antithesis is only *implicit*; the other, contrasting party is not mentioned.

| 16. | אֲנִי הֶעֱשַׁרְתִּי אֶת־אַבְרָם׃ | *I* [not Yнwн] have made Abram rich. Gen 14:23 |
| 17. | הִיא יָשְׁרָה בְעֵינָי׃ | *She* [not another] is the right one for me. Judg 14:3 |

---

23. Muraoka, *Emphatic Words*, 54–56.

18.   שְׁלֹמֹה בְנֵךְ יִמְלֹךְ אַחֲרַי וְהוּא   Solomon your son shall be king after me, and *he* will
       יֵשֵׁב עַל־כִּסְאִי: sit on my throne [no one else].
                                              1 Kgs 1:17

e   The third group of cases relevant here involves *psychological focus*; most of these
       involve first- and second-person pronouns.[24] In connection with this group Takamitsu
       Muraoka alludes to "strong emotional heightening" and "focused attention or deep self-
       consciousness."[25] Most instances involve the first person, in a state of rapturous eleva-
       tion (# 19), or profound meditation (# 20), or in flashes of self-assertion (## 21–24).

19.   אָנֹכִי לַיהוה אָנֹכִי אָשִׁירָה   *I* will sing to YHWH.
                                              Judg 5:3

20.   דִּבַּרְתִּי אֲנִי עִם־לִבִּי   *I* thought to myself.
                                              Qoh 1:16; cf. 2:1

21.   אָנֹכִי נָתַתִּי שִׁפְחָתִי בְּחֵיקֶךָ   *I* gave my maid to your embrace.
                                              Gen 16:5

22.   אָנֹכִי אֶהְיֶה לָכֶם לְרֹאשׁ:   *I* will really be your chief.
                                              Judg 11:9

23.   וַאֲנִי נָסַכְתִּי מַלְכִּי   *I* installed my king.
                                              Ps 2:6

24.   וַאֲנִי בָּנִיתִי בֵית־זְבֻל לָךְ   *I* have built you an exalted house.
                                              2 Chr 6:2

Self-assertion may be combined with antithesis.

25.   ... אַתָּה עַתָּה תַּעֲשֶׂה מְלוּכָה   Are *you* in charge anymore? . . . *I* will give you the
       אֲנִי אֶתֵּן לְךָ אֶת־כֶּרֶם נָבוֹת   vineyard of Naboth.
                                              1 Kgs 21:7

Pragmatic antithesis arises in cases of answering questions and making promises.

26.   הִשָּׁבְעָה לִּי ... אָנֹכִי אִשָּׁבֵעַ: Swear to me. . . . *I* swear.
                                              Gen 21:23–24

27.   מִי־יֵרֵד אִתִּי ... אֲנִי אֵרֵד עִמָּךְ: Who will go down with me. . . ? . . . *I* will go down
                                              with you.
                                              1 Sam 26:6

In the second-person cases, the pronoun indicates strongly focused attention; the speaker
may be giving a command or leading up to a demand.

28.   וְאַתֵּנָה יְדַעְתֶּן כִּי בְּכָל־כֹּחִי   *You* know that I served your father with all my
       עָבַדְתִּי אֶת־אֲבִיכֶן: strength.
                                              Gen 31:6

---

24. Muraoka, *Emphatic Words*, 58.   25. Muraoka, *Emphatic Words*, 50, 51.

| 29. | וְאַתֶּם עֲזַבְתֶּם אוֹתִי | *You* have forsaken me. |
| | | Judg 10:13 |

30.	וַיֹּאמֶר הַמֶּלֶךְ לְדוֹיֵג סֹב אַתָּה	Then the king said to Doeg, "*You* turn and fall upon
	וּפְגַע בַּכֹּהֲנִים וַיִּסֹּב דּוֹיֵג הָאֲדֹמִי	the priests," and Doeg the Edomite turned and *he* fell
	וַיִּפְגַּע־הוּא בַּכֹּהֲנִים	upon the priests.
		1 Sam 22:18

Verbless Clauses   **16.3.3**

There are two kinds of verbless clauses, identifying (basic word order: subject-predicate) and classifying (basic word order: predicate-subject). A third-person independent personal pronoun may be used in verbless clauses as a so-called copula or pleonastic pronoun, and we have discussed the analysis of such use earlier (8.4). In this section we review our previous treatment and consider the role of the pronoun in particular. **a**

Identifying clauses with independent pronouns in a copula role have the word order **b** subject-pronoun-predicate.

| 1. | עֵשָׂו הוּא אֱדוֹם׃ | Esau is Edom. |
| | | Gen 36:8 |

Such sentences, as noted in 8.4.1, can be analyzed also as nominative absolute (focus or *casus pendens*) constructions: the initial noun (here, עֵשָׂו) is the focus marker and the clause proper has the order subject-predicate (here, הוּא אֱדוֹם). On this analysis, we might paraphrase, 'As for Esau, he is Edom.'

This construction has a "selective-exclusive" force, in Muraoka's term: the subject/ **c** focus is singled out and contrasted with other possible or actual alternatives.[26] In some cases the passage is concerned with the uniqueness of the subject/focus.[27]

| 2. | יהוה הוּא הָאֱלֹהִים אֵין עוֹד | *Yhwh* is God; there is none beside him. |
| | מִלְבַדּוֹ׃ | Deut 4:35 |

3.	יהוה הוּא הָאֱלֹהִים יהוה הוּא	*Yhwh* is God. *Yhwh* is God [in sharp contrast to
	הָאֱלֹהִים׃	Baal].
		1 Kgs 18:39

| 4. | וַיהוה הוּא הַהֹלֵךְ לְפָנֶיךָ | *Yhwh* is the one who walks before you.[28] |
| | | Deut 31:8 |

5.	הָאִישׁ אֲשֶׁר־יִבְחַר יהוה הוּא	*The man whom Yhwh chooses*, he is the one who
	הַקָּדוֹשׁ	is holy.[29]
		Num 16:7

---

26. Muraoka, *Emphatic Words*, 72–74 (quotation from p. 72).

27. Compare the relative clause headed by *hûʾ* in Gen 2:14.

28. In the clause that immediately follows this one, *hûʾ* is the subject and is probably used because the underlying

subject *yhwh* and the verb form *yihyeh* used there are so similar.

29. Contrast the clauses cited here with other identifying clauses that have a predicate with a definite article and lack an independent pronoun, e.g., Exod 9:27, 1 Kgs 3:22*bis*.

In this focus construction the subject/focus can be a pronoun (first- or second-person).[30]

6.   אַתָּה־הוּא הָאֱלֹהִים   *You* are God.
                                       2 Sam 7:28

7.   אָנֹכִי אָנֹכִי הוּא מֹחֶה פְּשָׁעֶיךָ   *I, I* blot out your transgressions.
                                       Isa 43:25

8.   אַתָּה־הוּא מַלְכִּי   *You* are my king.
                                       Ps 44:5

The focus constructions can also be used when there is a change in the center of attention.

9.   וַיָּבֹאוּ בְּנֵי יִשְׂרָאֵל . . . וְיוֹסֵף   And the (other) sons of Israel went . . . but *Joseph*
       הוּא הַשַּׁלִּיט עַל־הָאָרֶץ   was the governor of the land.
                                       Gen 42:5–6

10.   וַיִּהְיוּ בְנֵי־נֹחַ . . . שֵׁם וְחָם   The sons of Noah were . . . Shem, Ham, and Japheth.
       וָיֶפֶת וְחָם הוּא אֲבִי כְנָעַן: Now *Ham* was the father of Canaan.
                                       Gen 9:18

d   In *classifying clauses* with independent personal pronouns, the pronoun follows the basic subject and predicate (8.4.2).

11.   אִישׁ רֹאשׁ לְבֵית־אֲבֹתָיו הוּא: *Each man* is head of his paternal house.
                                       Num 1:4

Here again, under a *casus pendens* analysis, the grammatical mechanism is easier to grasp: the basic or underlying subject is a focus marker (here, אִישׁ), and the rest of the clause has the structure *predicate-subject* (here, רֹאשׁ . . . הוּא).[31] The focus/subject again has a "selective-exclusive" force.

12.   כָּל־הָעֹשֶׁר . . . לָנוּ הוּא וּלְבָנֵינוּ   *All the wealth* . . . is ours, as well as our children's.
                                       Gen 31:16

13.   מִקְנֵהֶם וְקִנְיָנָם וְכָל־בְּהֶמְתָּם   As for *the livestock*, *their property*, and *all their other*
       הֲלוֹא לָנוּ הֵם   *animals*, won't *they* become ours?[32]
                                       Gen 34:23

14.   וְהַלֻּחֹת מַעֲשֵׂה אֱלֹהִים הֵמָּה   *The tablets—they* were the work of God.
                                       Exod 32:16

15.   זוֹבוֹ טָמֵא הוּא: As for *his discharge—it* is unclean.
                                       Lev 15:2

---

30. The demonstrative sense of *hûʾ* is plain here; cf. Muraoka, *Emphatic Words*, 69–70, especially on related patterns in Aramaic. On the interpretation of Ps 44:5 as 'You are *he*—my king,' see pp. 67–69. Other examples of the construction in Isa 37:16; 51:9, 10, 12; 52:6; Jer 14:22, 29:23 *Qere*; the preponderance of Isaianic material is noteworthy.

31. Contrast Muraoka, *Emphatic Words*, 75–76.

32. The interrogative *he* appears in the clause proper, after the focus marker.

| 16. | הָאָרֶץ אֲשֶׁר עָבַרְנוּ בָהּ לָתוּר אֹתָהּ אֶרֶץ אֹכֶלֶת יוֹשְׁבֶיהָ הִיא | *The land we explored—it* devours those living in it. Num 13:32 |

Classifying clauses may have the rare word order predicate-subject or, with a pronoun, predicate-pronoun-subject.[33]

| 17. | שִׁשִּׁים הֵמָּה מְלָכוֹת . . . אַחַת הִיא יוֹנָתִי | Sixty *queens* there may be . . . but my *dove* is unique. Cant 6:8–9 |
| 18. | צַדִּיק הוּא יהוה | *YHWH* is righteous.[34] Lam 1:18 |

Apposition   **16.3.4**

When an independent personal pronoun stands in apposition to a suffixed pronoun,   a
it serves an emphatic role.[35] The suffixed pronoun may be a genitive attached to a noun
(## 1–4) or a preposition (## 5–8).

1.	וּפִגְרֵיכֶם אַתֶּם יִפְּלוּ בַּמִּדְבָּר הַזֶּה:	*Your* damned carcasses shall fall in this desert. Num 14:32
2.	אֲשֶׁר נִשְׁבַּעְנוּ שְׁנֵינוּ אֲנַחְנוּ	what the two of us have sworn, *even we* 1 Sam 20:42
3.	מִי־יִתֵּן מוּתִי אֲנִי תַחְתֶּיךָ	If only *I* had died instead of you. 2 Sam 19:1
4.	אָבַד זִכְרָם הֵמָּה:	The memory of *them* has perished. Ps 9:7
5.	לֹא אֶת־אֲבֹתֵינוּ כָּרַת יהוה אֶת־הַבְּרִית הַזֹּאת כִּי אִתָּנוּ אֲנַחְנוּ	Not with our forebears did *YHWH* make this covenant, but with *us*. Deut 5:3
6.	בִּי־אֲנִי אֲדֹנִי הֶעָוֹן	On *me*, my lord, is the guilt. 1 Sam 25:24
7.	וְלִי אֲנִי־עַבְדְּךָ . . . לֹא קָרָא:	But me, [me of all people] just me, *your servant*, . . . he has not invited.[36] 1 Kgs 1:26
8.	הַעֵת לָכֶם אַתֶּם לָשֶׁבֶת בְּבָתֵּיכֶם סְפוּנִים וְהַבַּיִת הַזֶּה חָרֵב:	Is it time for *you* to be living in your paneled houses while this house is desolate? Hag 1:4

---

33. Muraoka, *Emphatic Words*, 76–77.

34. The predicate is so positioned as to yield the initial *ṣ* required for the acrostic.

35. In these cases, Muraoka alleges, "there was felt a need to bring out the personal element with greater force";

Emphatic Words, 61. The student will appreciate the difficulty of specifying the kind of emphasis involved in any given construction. Note also Mic 7:3.

36. The quasi-pronominal sense of *ʿbdk* as *ʾny* is clear here; cf. n. 3.

Less often, the suffixed pronoun with the apposition is a verbal suffix in an accusative function.[37]

9.	כִּי־צַמְתֶּם . . . הֲצוֹם צַמְתֻּנִי אָנִי: וְכִי תֹאכְלוּ וְכִי תִשְׁתּוּ הֲלוֹא אַתֶּם הָאֹכְלִים וְאַתֶּם הַשֹּׁתִים:	When you fasted, was it for *me* that you fasted? When you ate and when you drank, weren't *you* the eaters, weren't *you* the drinkers? Zech 7:5–6

An apparent obverse of this construction involves an independent pronoun as a *casus pendens* with the same referent as a suffixed pronoun.

10.	אֲנִי יָדַי נָטוּ שָׁמָיִם	*I, my* hands have stretched out the heavens. Isa 45:12

16.3.5   Minor Uses

a   Under this general rubric are considered three quite distinct uses of the independent personal pronouns: with particles, as a neutrum referring to an unspecific antecedent, and as a prepositive marker of names. The last two of these uses involve only third-person forms.

b   The two *particles* of interest are הִנֵּה, usually 'behold' (and the related הֵן), and גַּם, usually 'also' (and the similar אַף). The particles הֵן and הִנֵּה can call special attention either to a certain statement as a whole or to a single word out of the statement.[38] They may stand before the independent pronouns to highlight the pronominal element.[39] A participle commonly follows הנה + pronoun (# 1; cf. 37.6f, 40.2.1d), sometimes with intervening elements (# 2); other forms may follow the combination of הנה + pronoun (# 3).

1.	וַיֹּאמֶר יהוה הִנֵּה־הוּא נֶחְבָּא אֶל־הַכֵּלִים:	Yʜᴡʜ said, "*He* has hidden himself in the baggage." 1 Sam 10:22
2.	כֹּה אָמַר יהוה הִנֵּה אֲשֶׁר־ בָּנִיתִי אֲנִי הֹרֵס	Yʜᴡʜ said this: "What *I* built, *I*'ll tear down." Jer 45:4
3.	וַיֹּאמְרוּ אֵלָיו הִנֵּה אַתָּה זָקַנְתָּ	They said to him, "*You* have gotten old!" 1 Sam 8:5

The particle is suffixed before an independent pronoun only in the combination הִנְנִי־אָנִי.[40]

4.	הִנְנִי־אָנִי וְדָרַשְׁתִּי אֶת־צֹאנִי	*I myself* will search for my sheep. Ezek 34:11

---

37. Muraoka claims that # 9 is a unique case; see *Emphatic Words*, 61–62.

38. Muraoka, *Emphatic Words*, 137–40. For more on the presentative particles, see 40.2.1.

39. In case the personal pronoun stands before *hnh*, it serves as a nominative absolute (see 4.7, 8.3a) to the clause after *hnh*. If *hnh* has no suffix, the clause is usually verbal

(e.g., Num 3:12 = 18:6). If *hnh* is suffixed, the clause is participial (e.g., Gen 6:17). For a personal pronoun before unsuffixed *hnh* introducing a verbless clause, see 40.2.1c # 14.

40. All the examples are first person and in Ezekiel (6:3; 34:11—contrast v 10; 34:20); Muraoka, *Emphatic Words*, 62. Compare Ezek 6:3 and Gen 6:17.

In those instances in which the personal pronoun occurs after גַּם (or, less often, אַף), if it is in apposition to a subject (#5) or in a *casus pendens* construction (#6), it has no special emphasis, and the particle means little more than 'also.' The force of the pronoun may be stronger if it stands in apposition to a prepositional object (#7), a verbal object (#8), or a possessive suffix (#9); see 16.3.4a.[41]

5.	וְצִלָּה גַם־הִוא יָלְדָה	Zillah *also* gave birth.	Gen 4:22
6.	אַף־אֲנִי בַּחֲלוֹמִי	I, *too*, in my dream. . . .	Gen 40:16
7.	וַתְּהִי עָלָיו גַּם־הוּא רוּחַ אֱלֹהִים	The spirit of God *also* came upon him.	1 Sam 19:23
8.	בָּרֲכֵנִי גַם־אָנִי אָבִי:	Bless me, me *too*, father.	Gen 27:34
9.	אֶת־דָּמְךָ גַם־אָֽתָּה:	your blood, yours *also*	1 Kgs 21:19

The third-person singular pronoun, masculine or feminine, may serve as a *neutrum* c
with respect to some vague action or circumstance (6.6). The feminine is usual.

10.	הֲלֹא־הִיא כְתוּבָה עַל־סֵפֶר הַיָּשָׁר	Is *it* not written in the Book of Yashar?	Josh 10:13
11.	אָבִיו וְאִמּוֹ לֹא יָדְעוּ כִּי מֵיהוה הִיא	His parents did not know that *this* was from YHWH.	Judg 14:4

Other modes may be used to express the neutrum; note, in the following example, זֹאת.[42]

12.	וָאֲחַשְּׁבָה לָדַעַת זֹאת עָמָל הוּא בְעֵינָי:	When I tried to understand all this, *it* was painful to me.[43]	Ps 73:16 Qere

Finally, הוּא *precedes a personal name* only in the post-exilic books and has the force d
of 'the same' without special emphasis.[44]

13.	הוּא עֶזְרָא	*the same* Ezra [resumes subject lost track of after a long genealogy]	Ezra 7:6
14.	הוּא שְׁלֹמוֹת	*the same* Shelomoth [refers to previous verse and serves to introduce an explanatory parenthesis]	1 Chr 26:26

---

41. Contrast the treatment of Muraoka, *Emphatic Words*, 63–65, 141–46.

42. The usual understanding of Judg 11:39 is that the verb *wattəhî* shows a neutrum usage, referring to the verbal action described in the next clause (viz., 'It became the custom in Israel that . . . '). P. Trible has proposed that the verb has a true antecedent, Jephthah's daughter herself (viz., 'She became a tradition in Israel'); see *Texts of Terror* (Philadelphia: Fortress, 1984) 106–7.

43. In this verse, both *zōᵓt* and *hûᵓ* are neutrum pronouns.

44. Cf. Muraoka, *Emphatic Words*, 65–66.

16.4   Suffixed Personal Pronouns

a   The uses of the pronominal suffixes is our chief concern here, but a few words about their morphology may be useful to begin with.

	singular	plural
first common	נִי , יִ	נוּ
second masc.	ךָ	כֶם
second fem.	ךְ	כֶן
third masc.	וּ , הָ , וֹ , הוּ	הֶם , םָ
third fem.	הָ , הָ	ןָ , הֶן

The most striking feature of these suffixes is the fact that possessive and objective forms are the same, except in the first-person singular, where -*î* is possessive and -*nî* objective.[45] The phonological development of many of the suffixes is complex, but one point is especially important. The MT form ךָ- (-*kā*) is a blend of an unvoweled suffix -*k* (so the consonantal text) and a final long-vowel form -*kā* (so the vocalization). The long form of the suffix is attested regularly at Qumran in the writing כה- and sporadically in the MT (e.g., בֹּאֲכָה 'your coming,' Gen 10:30). Similarly, ךְ- is a blend of unvoweled -*k* and -*kī*, the form expected on etymological grounds. Qumran regularly uses the suffix in the form כי-, and the MT rarely shows this form, too (e.g., רָעָתֵכִי 'your miseries,' Jer 11:15).[46]

b   The masculine pronoun is often used for a feminine antecedent (## 1–2; 6.5.3).

1.	וּבְרַגְלֵיהֶם תְּעַכַּסְנָה׃	with ornaments jingling on *their* (masc. for בָּנוֹת) ankles Isa 3:16
2.	וְכָל־הַבְּאֵרֹת . . . סִתְּמוּם פְּלִשְׁתִּים וַיְמַלְאוּם עָפָר׃	And as for all the *wells* (fem.) . . . the Philistines stopped *them* (masc.) up and filled *them* (masc.) with earth. Gen 26:15

---

45. The final *yod* has a problematic feature. It is generally accepted that, because *waw* and *yod* are similar in several forms of square script, some confusions of first- and third-person singular suffixes may be found in the MT. (*Waw/yod* variation is the most common source of *Kethiv-Qere* variation; see J. Barr, "A New Look at Kethibh-Qere," *Oudtestamentische Studiën* 21 [1981] 19–37, at 27–28, 33.) M. Dahood, basing himself not only on such possible confusions but also on comparative evidence, alleged that Biblical Hebrew actually had a third-person *î* suffix; see, e.g., *Psalms III* (Anchor Bible 17A; Garden City: Doubleday, 1970) 375–76. There is no evidence for such a suffix that cannot more simply be explained on the basis of (a small number of) scribal errors. For a review, see Z. Zevit, "The Linguistic and Contextual Arguments in Support of a Hebrew 3 m.s. Suffix -*y*," *Ugarit-Forschungen* 9 (1977) 315–28. As for the possessive/objective distribution, it should be noted that the third-person plural forms -*hem*, -*hen* are very rarely used on verbs.

46. On the long forms, see Qimron, *Hebrew of the Dead Sea Scrolls*, 58–59; he reports that the long form -*kh* is found approximately 900 times, the short form -*k* about 160 times. With regard to the feminine -*ky*, note that Jer 11:15 is very difficult; see William L. Holladay, *Jeremiah* (Hermeneia; Philadelphia: Fortress, 1986), 1. 348. The MT pausal form -*āk*, sometimes attributed to specifically Aramaic influence, is rather to be seen as an example of apocope in pause found in both Semitic and non-Semitic languages; on analogy with -*hā* and -*āh* the -*āk* form was extended to general (i.e., non-pausal) use in the three major reading traditions of Hebrew—Tiberian, Babylonian, and Palestinian. See Richard Steiner, "From Proto-Hebrew to Mishnaic Hebrew: The History of ךְ and הָ." *Hebrew Annual Review* 3 (1979) 157–74.

Singular suffixes can have a collective reference (# 3), and, conversely, plural suffixes may be used after collective singulars (# 4; 7.2.1b).

3. וַיְהִי כִּקְרוֹא יְהוּדִי שָׁלֹשׁ   Whenever Jehudi had read three or four *columns* (pl.),
    דְּלָתוֹת וְאַרְבָּעָה יִקְרָעֶהָ   (the king) cut *them* (sing.) off.
                                          Jer 36:23

4. גֵּר יִהְיֶה זַרְעֲךָ בְּאֶרֶץ לֹא לָהֶם   *Your descendants* (sing.) will be *strangers* (sing.) in a
                                          land not *their own* (pl.).
                                          Gen 15:13

Attached to a noun or preposition the suffixes are in the genitive case, while attached   c
to a verb, אֶת, or הִנֵּה they are in the accusative function. We consider first the genitive
usage, then the more complex range of the accusative, and finally the reflexive usages.

The *genitive suffixes* serve the same range of purposes as other genitives (9.5),   d
although the adjectival purposes are rarely relevant. Subjective genitive suffixes are
found, of agency (# 5), authorship (# 6), and relation (# 7; 9.5.1).

5.   בְּיוֹם אֲכָלְכֶם מִמֶּנּוּ   when *you* eat of it
                                          Gen 3:5

6.   בְּרִיתִי   *my* covenant
                                          Gen 9:9

7.   אִשְׁתּוֹ   *his* wife
                                          Gen 2:25

Adverbial genitive suffixes may represent a direct (## 8–9) or a mediated object (## 10–
12; 9.5.2).

8.   אִישׁ הָרַגְתִּי לְפִצְעִי   I have killed a man for wounding *me*.
                                          Gen 4:23

9.   חֲמָסִי   the wrong *I am suffering*, the wrong done *to me*
                                          Gen 16:5, Jer 51:35

10.   אֲנִי אֶתֵּן אֶת־שְׂכָרֵךְ   I will pay *you* (lit., I will give *your* hire).
                                          Exod 2:9

11.   וַיִּתֵּן חִנּוֹ   He granted *him* favor (lit., He gave *his* favor).
                                          Gen 39:21

12.   אֶפֶס כִּי לֹא תִהְיֶה תִּפְאַרְתְּךָ   But the honor will not be *yours* (lit., But it will not
                                          be *your* honor).
                                          Judg 4:9

The pronominal suffix varies with prepositional phrases in *l*, which also indicate possession. Rarely, a noun is marked for possession with both a suffix and a prepositional
(# 13) or relative (## 14–15) phrase.

13.   אֹיְבַי לִי   *my* enemies
                                  Ps 27:2

14.   כַּרְמִי שֶׁלִּי   *my own* vineyard
                                  Cant 1:6

15.   מִטָּתוֹ שֶׁלִּשְׁלֹמֹה   Solomon's *own* carriage
                                  Cant 3:7

Other prepositional suffixes serve the same role as substantive objects of prepositions.

16.   וַיֹּאמֶר לָהֶם אֱלֹהִים   And God said to *them*. . . .
                                  Gen 1:28

e   Since nouns in a construct chain constitute a unified idea, a pronominal suffix attached to the last noun in a chain logically affects the whole construction.

17.   הַר־קָדְשִׁי   *my* holy mountain
                                  Ps 2:6

18.   אֱלִילֵי כַסְפּוֹ   *his* silver idols
                                  Isa 2:20

19.   כְּלֵי מִלְחַמְתּוֹ   *his* weapons
                                  Deut 1:41

20.   יַד־יְמִינוֹ   *his* right hand
                                  Judg 3:15

When a pronominal suffix refers to a noun in a chain that cannot be suffixed, other constructions, such as apposition (## 21–22) or an accusative of specification (# 23), are used to accommodate the desired modifications.

21.   כֻּתָּנְתּוֹ אֶת־כְּתֹנֶת הַפַּסִּים   *his* robe, the richly ornamented robe
                                  Gen 37:23

22.   גְּבִיעִי גְּבִיעַ הַכֶּסֶף   *my* cup, the silver cup
                                  Gen 44:2

23.   מַדּוֹ בַד   *his* garment in linen
                                  Lev 6:3

f   *Accusative suffixes* are used as either direct (## 24–28) or "datival" objects (## 28–29; 10.2.1). In a double-accusative construction, one of the objects can be represented by a suffix (# 27).

24.   וַיְבָרֶךְ אֹתָם אֱלֹהִים   God blessed *them*.
                                  Gen 1:28

25.   סְבָבוּנִי   They surround *me*.
                                  Ps 109:3

26.   תִּמְלָאֵמוֹ נַפְשִׁי   I will gorge myself on *them*.
                              Exod 15:9

27.   וַיַּעֲשֵׂהוּ פֶּסֶל   He made *it* into an image.
                              Judg 17:4

28.   וְהִפְרֵתִי אֹתְךָ . . . וּנְתַתִּיךָ   And I will make *you* fruitful . . . and I am going to
                              give *you*. . . .
                              Gen 17:6

29.   צַמְתֻּנִי   Did you fast *for me*?
                              Zech 7:5

The neutrum or vague referent can be marked with an object pronominal suffix, usually feminine. The action or state is ordinarily described in the preceding clause(s).

30.   וְהֶאֱמִן בַּיהוָה וַיַּחְשְׁבֶהָ לּוֹ   Now he trusted Yʜᴡʜ and he counted *it* to him as
       צְדָקָה: righteousness.
                              Gen 15:6

31.   בָּהּ אֵדַע   By *this* I will know.
                              Gen 24:14

32.   לֹא זָכַרְתְּ אַחֲרִיתָהּ:   You did not reflect on *what* might happen.
                              Isa 47:7

33.   עָלַי הָיוּ כֻלָּנָה: *Everything* is against me.
                              Gen 42:36

In many languages there is a separate series of reflexive pronouns, for example, the   g
English '-self' or French '-même' forms. Hebrew has no such series; rather, with a preposition (or אֵת) a suffix may be used with a reflexive force. In some contexts it has an additional emphatic nuance, but this meaning is recognized more by logic than by formal indicators.

34.   וַיַּעַשׂ לוֹ אֵהוּד חֶרֶב   And Ehud made *for himself* a sword.
                              Judg 3:16

35.   וַיָּבֵא אֹתָהּ אֵלָיו אֶל־הַתֵּבָה: And he brought it (the dove) *to himself* in the ark.
                              Gen 8:9

36.   כִּי־גָמְלוּ לָהֶם רָעָה: For they have brought evil upon *themselves*.
                              Isa 3:9

37.   הֵם יֵלְכוּ וְקֹשְׁשׁוּ לָהֶם תֶּבֶן: They must go and gather straw *for themselves*.
                              Exod 5:7

38.   וַיִּרְאוּ שֹׁטְרֵי בְנֵי־יִשְׂרָאֵל אֹתָם   The Israelite foremen saw *themselves* in trouble.
       בְּרָע   Exod 5:19

17

Demonstratives

17.1 Introduction

a   The demonstratives are independent deictic words that may be used as pronouns, taking the place of a noun, or as adjectives, qualifying or determining a noun. Deictic words point out or call attention to someone or something (13.1). Demonstratives fall into two series. The "near" or "immediate" demonstratives refer to someone or something that is relatively near the speaker or relatively present to the imagination. The "far" or "remote" demonstratives refer to someone or something relatively distant.[1] The near demonstrative in English is 'this,' and the far is 'that'; both are inflected for number, but not otherwise. Hebrew has one class of true demonstratives, those with the *z* element and אלה, and uses the third-person pronouns as quasi-demonstratives; the *z* set has near reference (## 1, 3–4), and the personal pronouns far reference (# 2).[2] Both serve in adjectival roles (## 1–2); the *z* set also has strictly pronominal use (## 3–4).

1.   בַּעַל הַחֲלֹמוֹת הַלָּזֶה   *this* dreamer
       Gen 37:19

2.   הָאָרֶץ הַהִיא   *that* land
       Gen 2:12

---

1. In English there is essentially only one set of forms in each series, but this restriction is not universal. Spanish has one near form ('este') and two far ('ese, aquel,' the latter sometimes rendered 'yonder'); Latin has one near ('hic') and three far ('is, ille, iste'); and Greek has two near ('houtos, hode') and one far ('ekeinos').

2. This doubling of function is also found, e.g., in Akkadian and Syriac; see Sabatino Moscati et al., *An Introduction to the Comparative Grammar of the Semitic Languages* (Wiesbaden: Harrassowitz, 1964) § 13.32 / p. 112. The polysemy reflects the essentially demonstrative quality of the third-person pronouns.

3. לְזֹאת יִקָּרֵא אִשָּׁה כִּי מֵאִישׁ   'Woman' will be used to name *this one* because
      לֻקֳחָה־זֹּאת׃   *this one* was taken from man.
                                                          Gen 2:23

4. הֶן־זֹאת לֹא־צָדַקְתָּ   In *this* you are not right.
                                                          Job 33:12

Morphology   **17.2**

The two major series of *demonstratives* are conventionally set in parallel.   a

	near	*far*
sing. masc.	זֶה	הַהוּא
sing. fem.	זֹה, זוֹ, זֹאת[3]	הַהִיא
pl. masc.	}אֵל, אֵלֶּה	הַהֵם, הַהֵמָּה
pl. fem.		הַהֵנָּה

As we argue in the next section, this near/far arrangement is not precise, as is hinted by
the use of the article in the far demonstrative set. The formative elements in the near
demonstrative set are *z* and *l*.[4] (The formative element *h* is used in the article and is thus
associated with the deictic function of definiteness; see 13.1.) The variants of the feminine
singular are rare;[5] the archaic spelling זוֹ occurs twice, and the spelling זֹה occurs eleven
times.[6] The form אֵל is found nine times, usually with the article; it is possible that אל
should be taken as a variant writing and vocalized אֵל.[7] There is a series of expanded
near demonstratives:[8] הַלָּז (masc., fem.; seven times, all but one use adjectival), הַלָּזֶה
(masc.; only in Gen 24:65, 37:19), הַלֵּזוּ (fem.; only in Ezek 36:35).[9]

There are several groups of related forms. The *determinative pronoun* זוּ (sometimes   b
זֶה) is rare. The so-called *demonstrative adverbs* show the *h* and *l* formative elements
(## 1–2), as well as *n* (## 3–4, 6, 8) and *k* (## 5–8).

1.	הֲלֹם	hither	5.	אַךְ	indeed
2.	הָלְאָה	hence	6.	אָכֵן	indeed
3.	הִנֵּה	behold	7.	כֹּה	here
4.	הֵנָּה	hither	8.	כֵּן	thus

Other adverbs of demonstrative force are אָז 'then,' שָׁם 'there,' and שָׁמָּה 'thither.' The
article (13.5.2b) and את (10.3) are also deictic words that tend to be demonstrative.[10]

---

3. The feminine may be used as a neutrum, cf. 17.4.3b, although it is misleading to speak of a neuter pronoun in Hebrew.

4. The *z* element is etymologically *ð* (*d* or *ḏ*), as in Ugaritic and Arabic (cf. 19.2). The *l* is related to the Arabic article *al-*. The masculine near demonstrative *zeh* occurs 1,169 times, the feminine 605, and the plural 754 (SA/THAT).

5. A further feminine variant, *hz'th*, occurs only in Jer 26:6 *Kethiv*.

6. Six of these occurrences are in Qoheleth, and *z't* is not used in that book.

7. For comparable points of uncertainty involving the personal pronouns, see 16.3.

8. These are used most often in reports of conversation; on related forms in Mishnaic Hebrew, see M. H. Segal, *A Grammar of Mishnaic Hebrew* (Oxford: Clarendon, 1927) 41–42.

9. The *ha-* element is related to the Hebrew article, which has demonstrative uses (13.5.2). The *hallāz(-)* set is cognate to Arabic *hallaðī, hallatī, halladīna* 'that.'

10. On the determinative pronoun, see *UT* § 6.23; cf. below, 17.4.3d. The most common of the adverbs cited are (after SA/THAT) *hinnēh* (1,057 times), *kēn* (695), *šām* (691), *kōh* (581), *'ak* (161), *šammâ* (141), and *'āz* (138).

17.3   True Demonstratives and Quasi-Demonstratives

a   Only the near demonstratives are true demonstratives; the determined personal pronouns (ההוא and its equivalents) are quasi-demonstratives, which serve only in certain
constructions in which the true demonstratives are used. A number of arguments support
this distinction.[11]

b   The first difference between the sets involves *case diversity*: זה[12] can be used in all
functions, nominative (## 1–2), genitive (## 3–4), and accusative (## 5–6).

1.	זֶה הַדָּבָר אֲשֶׁר צִוָּה יהוה:	*This* is what Yhwh commands. Num 30:2
2.	זֶה־יִהְיֶה לָכֶם גְּבוּל יָם:	*This* will be your western border. Num 34:6
3.	שְׁבֻעַ זֹאת	the week of *this one* Gen 29:27
4.	לְזֹאת יִקָּרֵא	It shall be called (to) *this one.* Gen 2:23
5.	קְרָא נָא־זֶה	Read *this.* Isa 29:11
6.	שִׁלְחוּ־נָא אֶת־זֹאת	Send *this person* away. 2 Sam 13:17

הוא, on the other hand, as a personal pronoun, occurs only in the nominative (see 16.2a),
and ההוא occurs only as an attributive adjective.

c   The second difference involves the *functional load* of the two sets of demonstratives;
in all cases where languages with two sets of demonstratives use a contrasting pair (e.g.,
English 'We talked of this and that'), Hebrew uses only זה. Thus, הוא can have the true
demonstrative pronoun as its antecedent (## 7–8), but it is never used in juxtaposition
with it to express 'this one . . . that one.'

7.	וַתֹּאמֶר אֶל־הָעֶבֶד מִי־הָאִישׁ הַלָּזֶה הַהֹלֵךְ בַּשָּׂדֶה לִקְרָאתֵנוּ וַיֹּאמֶר הָעֶבֶד הוּא אֲדֹנִי	And she (Rebekah) asked the servant: "Who is *that* man in the field coming to meet us?" "*He* is my master," the servant answered. Gen 24:65
8.	וְהָיָה אֲשֶׁר אֹמַר אֵלֶיךָ זֶה יֵלֵךְ אִתָּךְ הוּא יֵלֵךְ אִתָּךְ וְכֹל אֲשֶׁר־אֹמַר אֵלֶיךָ זֶה לֹא־יֵלֵךְ עִמָּךְ הוּא לֹא יֵלֵךְ:	And it shall be the case that he of whom I say to you, "*This one* shall go with you," he (or, *that one*) shall go with you; and all those of whom I say to you, "*That one* (or, *This one*) shall not go in your company," he (or, *that one*) shall not go. Judg 7:4

---

11. For the following discussion, see Joüon § 143j–k /
pp. 445–46. From another angle we can say that the true
demonstratives make up the word class that can occur
with the definite article but not with pronominal suffixes.

12. Henceforth, זה stands for the entire *z* set of demonstratives (including ʾēlleh), and ההוא stands for the entire
set of determined third-person pronouns.

By contrast, זה is used for both the "near" object and for the "far" object when a pair is juxtaposed.

9.	זאת אֹמֶ֫רֶת . . . וְזֹאת אֹמֶ֫רֶת	*This* one said . . . and *that* one said. . . . 1 Kgs 3:23
10.	עוֹד זֶה מְדַבֵּר וְזֶה בָּא	*This* one was still speaking when *that* one arrived. Job 1:16

ההוא is never used in this way.

The third argument involves the *direction of reference*. The true demonstrative זה   d
can be used for reference backward (anaphora; # 11) or forward (cataphora; # 12).

11.	זֹאת הָאָ֫רֶץ אֲשֶׁר נִשְׁבַּ֫עְתִּי לְאַבְרָהָם	*This* is the land I promised on oath to Abraham. Deut 34:4; cf. vv 1–3
12.	אֵ֫לֶּה בְנֵי־אֵ֫צֶר בִּלְהָן	*These* are the sons of Ezer: Bilhan. . . . Gen 36:27

הוא and ההוא, on the other hand, refer only to what precedes them.

Even when הזה is bracketed as an attributive, it retains a stronger deictic force than   e
ההוא. Contrast, for example, Jer 25:13 הָאָ֫רֶץ הַהִיא ('*that* land,' of which we have been
speaking) and v 9 הָאָ֫רֶץ הַזֹּאת ('*this* land,' where Jeremiah is found).

True Demonstratives   17.4

Syntactic Properties   17.4.1

זה and its equivalents may be bracketed with other words in a sentence as a nominal   a
equivalent, in any grammatical function, or as an attributive. We have already cited
examples of the former construction (see 17.3b); we need only comment on the attributive
use. As an attributive זה is used in three diverse ways. It may be used like an attributive
adjective (i.e., with the article and after its head; ## 1–2) or like a predicate adjective (i.e.,
anarthrous and preceding its head; ## 3–5).

1.	בַּדּוֹר הַזֶּה	in *this* generation Gen 7:1
2.	הַגּוֹי הַגָּדוֹל הַזֶּה׃	*this* great nation Deut 4:6
3.	זֶה מֹשֶׁה	*this* Moses Exod 32:1
4.	זֹאת קוֹמָתֵךְ	*this* stature of yours Cant 7:8
5.	הֵן אֶ֫רֶץ כַּשְׂדִּים זֶה הָעָם	Look at the land of the Babylonians, *this* people. Isa 23:13

The latter construction occurs usually, but not exclusively (# 5), with proper names (# 3) or with nouns bearing a pronominal suffix (# 4). Finally, with nouns determined by a pronominal suffix, the attributive demonstrative may show a mixture of these two constructions, appearing after its head word but without the article (## 6–8). It may be construed as an apposition in such cases.

6.	אֹתֹתַי אֵלֶּה	*these* (things), miraculous signs of mine Exod 10:1
7.	מִשְּׁבֻעָתִי זֹאת	from *this*, my oath Gen 24:8
8.	וְאִם־תַּגִּידִי אֶת־דְּבָרֵנוּ זֶה	If you tell *this* (thing, the) deed of ours. . . . Josh 2:20

17.4.2   Simple Demonstrative Uses

a   זה can be used in any situation where an object is to be pointed out, whether in reality or imagination. This deictic force informs all its uses, though the relationship between the deixis and the context may vary.

b   A simple deictic force is evident in various *expressions of time* (cf. English 'Do it *this* minute').

1.	לַמּוֹעֵד הַזֶּה	by *this* time Gen 17:21
2.	קוּם כִּי זֶה הַיּוֹם אֲשֶׁר נָתַן יְהוָה אֶת־סִיסְרָא בְּיָדֶךָ	Go—*this* is the day Yhwh has given Sisera into your hands. Judg 4:14
3.	זֹאת הַפַּעַם עֶצֶם מֵעֲצָמַי	*this* time, bone of my bones Gen 2:23

The phrase היום הזה is almost invariably adverbial.[13] It specifies the time when an action occurs (# 4) and is thus equivalent to adverbial היום (13.5.2b).

4.	הַיּוֹם הַזֶּה אָחֵל גַּדֶּלְךָ	*Today* I will begin to exalt you. Josh 3:7

In dating events, היום ההוא is usually used for past and future events, while היום הזה (or בעצם היום הזה) is reserved for present time;[14] the near deictic can, however, be used to refer to far distant time (# 5).[15]

---

13. S. J. DeVries, *Yesterday, Today, and Tomorrow: Time and History in the Old Testament* (Grand Rapids: Eerdmans, 1975) 139. There are exceptions: the phrase is nominative in 2 Kgs 7:9 and accusative in Exod 12:17.

14. The last two phrases are differentiated in cultic descriptions; DeVries, *Yesterday, Today, and Tomorrow*, 151.

15. DeVries, *Yesterday, Today, and Tomorrow*, 141.

5. בִּשְׁנַת שֵׁשׁ־מֵאוֹת שָׁנָה לְחַיֵּי־נֹחַ ... בַּיּוֹם הַזֶּה ...

In the six-hundredth year of Noah's life . . . *on this day*. . . .
Gen 7:11

This association with time is extended to circumstances where there is no immediacy or explicit dating: anarthrous זה (rarely זאת) occurs with numerals in expressions of time and appears to emphasize the time (cf. the English redundancies 'this here' and 'that there').

6. וְעַתָּה הִנֵּה הֶחֱיָה יהוה אוֹתִי כַּאֲשֶׁר דִּבֶּר זֶה אַרְבָּעִים וְחָמֵשׁ שָׁנָה

Now then, Yhwh has kept me alive, just as he promised, these forty-five years.
Josh 14:10

7. וַיְנַסּוּ אֹתִי זֶה עֶשֶׂר פְּעָמִים

They tested me *ten* times.
Num 14:22

8. וְהָיִית כְּאִשָּׁה זֶה יָמִים רַבִּים מִתְאַבֶּלֶת עַל־מֵת:

Act like a woman who has spent *many days* grieving for the dead.
2 Sam 14:2

The simple deictic may refer to *persons*, too; in such cases English idiom tends to   c
use a personal pronoun.[16]

9. כִּי־קָרָא יהוה לִשְׁלֹשֶׁת הַמְּלָכִים הָאֵלֶּה

Has Yhwh called *us* three kings together. . . ?
2 Kgs 3:10

10. הִנֵּה הַשּׁוּנַמִּית הַלָּז:

There is *our* Shunammite.
2 Kgs 4:25

This may be weakened from truly deictic to characterizing.

11. זֶה דּוֹר דֹּרְשָׁיו

Such is the generation of those who seek him.
Ps 24:6 *Qere*

Similar to the simple deictic role is the *paired use* of זה . . . זה cited earlier (17.3c).   d

12. וְקָרָא זֶה אֶל־זֶה

The *one* was calling to *the other*.
Isa 6:3

13. וַיֹּאמֶר זֶה בְּכֹה וְזֶה אֹמֵר בְּכֹה:

One suggested this and *another* that.
1 Kgs 22:20

In the flow of discourse זה may have a deictic *relative* force (17.3d), referring to   e
nouns either preceding (anaphora; ## 14–15) or following (cataphora; ## 16–18).[17]

---

16. As Joüon observes, modern usage allows a demonstrative sense for the first-person pronoun in phrases such as 'a leader for our time/the times,' 'the poetry for our children to study'; § 143e / p. 444.

17. Classical Greek can in certain circumstances distinguish anaphora and cataphora, with *houtos* referring backward and *hode* referring forward, although *houtos* often has both roles.

14. זֹאת . . . וְהָיְתָה הַקֶּשֶׁת בֶּעָנָן   Whenever the rainbow appears in the clouds . . . *this*
     אוֹת־הַבְּרִית   is the sign of the covenant.
                                           Gen 9:16–17

15. וְהָיָה כִּי תָבֹאנָה הָאֹתוֹת הָאֵלֶּה   once *these* signs are fulfilled
                                           1 Sam 10:7 *Qere*; cf. vv 5–6

16. זֶה פִּתְרֹנוֹ שְׁלֹשֶׁת הַשָּׂרִגִים   *This* is its interpretation: The three branches are. . . .
                                           Gen 40:12

17. וְעַתָּה זֶה הַדָּבָר אֲשֶׁר נַעֲשֶׂה   But now *this* is what we'll do to Gibeah: we'll go
     לַגִּבְעָה נַעֲלֶה   up. . . .
                                           Judg 20:9 LXX

18. וְאֵלֶּה תּוֹלְדֹת אַהֲרֹן וּמֹשֶׁה   And *these* are the generations of Aaron and
                                           Moses. . . .[18]
                                           Num 3:1

17.4.3   Other Uses

a   Three uses of זה fall outside the usual range of demonstratives: as a *neutrum* pronoun, for a vague antecedent; as an enclitic with exclamations; and as a relative pronoun.

b   Like the third-person pronouns, the true demonstratives can refer to an action or
circumstance vaguely defined (6.6, 16.3.5c). This *neutrum* pronoun is usually feminine.

1.   זֹאת עֲשׂוּ וִחְיוּ   Do *this* and you will live.
                                           Gen 42:18

2.   בְּזֹאת תִּבָּחֵנוּ   And *this* is how you will be tested.
                                           Gen 42:15

3.   כָּזֹאת וְכָזֹאת יָעַץ אֲחִיתֹפֶל אֶת־   Ahithophel has advised Absalom . . . to do *so and so*
     אַבְשָׁלֹם . . . וְכָזֹאת וְכָזֹאת   and I advised them to do *such and such.*
     יָעַצְתִּי אָנִי: 2 Sam 17:15

4.   וְזֶה אֲשֶׁר תַּעֲשֶׂה אֹתָהּ   And *this* is how you will make it.
                                           Gen 6:15

c   *Enclitic* זה is found with exclamatory questions and presentatives. זה (or, with the
verb עשה, זאת) seems to emphasize the question and is best rendered by an emphatic
adverb or phrase.

5.   מַה־זֶּה מִהַרְתָּ לִמְצֹא בְּנִי   How did you *ever* find it so quickly, my son?
                                           Gen 27:20

6.   מַה־זֶּה רוּחֲךָ סָרָה   Why *in the world* are you so sullen?
                                           1 Kgs 21:5

---

18. This quasi-titling function of *zeh* is most common in genealogies but can be found in other titling positions. Cf.   F. I. Andersen, *The Hebrew Verbless Clause in the Pentateuch* (Nashville: Abingdon, 1970) 40.

7.	וַיֹּאמֶר הָעָם אִישׁ אֶל־רֵעֵהוּ מַה־זֶּה הָיָה לְבֶן־קִישׁ	The people asked each other: "What *in the world* happened to the son of Kish?" 1 Sam 10:11
8.	מַה־זֹּאת עֲשִׂיתֶם:	What *in the world* have you done?[19] Judg 2:2
9.	אֵי־זֶה הַדֶּרֶךְ נַעֲלֶה	By *whatever* route shall we attack? 2 Kgs 3:8

The tautologous זה also occurs with הנה.

10.	וְהִנֵּה־זֶה מַלְאָךְ נֹגֵעַ בּוֹ	Look [here], an angel touches him. 1 Kgs 19:5
11.	הִנֵּה־זֹאת הָרָעָה מֵאֵת יהוה	Look [here], the disaster is from YHWH. 2 Kgs 6:33

The pronoun אשר dominates all *relative* usage, but there are instances in which a   **d**
relative clause is headed by זה (or the closely related זו;[20] 19.5). Most are poetic.

12.	הַר־צִיּוֹן זֶה שָׁכַנְתָּ בּוֹ:	Mount Zion, *where* you dwelt Ps 74:2
13.	כָּל־זֶה קֹלֵעַ	each of *whom* was a slinger Judg 20:16

Quasi-Demonstratives   **17.5**

The determined pronouns, ההוא and the like, share some of the syntactic duties of   **a**
the true demonstratives. ההוא can have a simple deictic force.

1.	אֵת כָּל־הַמִּדְבָּר הַגָּדוֹל וְהַנּוֹרָא הַהוּא	*that* great and awesome wilderness Deut 1:19

It can also be used anaphorically, as a relative deictic.

2.	וְהֵבֵאתִי עַל־הָאָרֶץ הַהִיא	and I brought upon *that* land[21] Jer 25:13

In expressions of time ההוא is frequent.[22] In ordinary narrative, past-time בַּיּוֹם   **b**
הַהוּא occasionally serves to incorporate "supplementary material" (# 3), frequently "functions as part of a concluding formula" (# 4), and in still other places "serves as part of a
transition to a following episode within the pericope" (# 5).[23] Simon DeVries also refers

---

19. Cf. Gen 3:13.

20. In, e.g., the archaic poem Exod 15:13. Note also Ps 104:8, 26. See J. M. Allegro, "Uses of the Semitic Demonstrative Element *z* in Hebrew," *Vetus Testamentum* 5 (1955) 309–12.

21. In # 2 *hʾrṣ hhyʾ* refers to Babylon, just mentioned.

Cf. Jer 25:9, 11 for Judah as *hʾrṣ hzʾt*.

22. The anarthrous phrase *blylh hwʾ* 'in that night' (Gen 19:33, 30:16, 32:23) is both anomalous and textually suspect—the Samaritan Pentateuch read *hhwʾ* in each of the three cases.

23. DeVries, *Yesterday, Today and Tomorrow*, 60–61.

to its use in an epitome, "a summarizing characterization concerning a particular day."[24]
In a small number of passages the phrase serves to mark a synchronism in a recollection
of "exhortation and warning concerning the . . . recent past" (# 6).[25] In cultic or gnomic
(proverbial) contexts it marks a synchronism (# 7).[26] Outside of the prophetic corpus,
ביום ההוא referring to the future creates a synchronism (# 8), an epitome (# 9), or both
(# 10). In 101 future-oriented occurrences in the prophetic corpus,[27] the phrase functions
to include supplementary information (# 11),[28] mark transitions (# 12),[29] and in concluding formulas (## 13–14).[30]

3.	וְלֹא־יָכְלוּ לַעֲשֹׂת־הַפֶּסַח בַּיּוֹם הַהוּא	But some of them could not celebrate the passover on *that day*. Num 9:6
4.	בַּיּוֹם הַהוּא כָּרַת יהוה . . . בְּרִית	On *that day* Yʜᴡʜ made . . . a covenant. Gen 15:18
5.	וַיָּרָץ אִישׁ־בִּנְיָמִן מֵהַמַּעֲרָכָה וַיָּבֹא שִׁלֹה בַּיּוֹם הַהוּא	A Benjaminite ran from the battle line and came to Shiloh on the *same day*. 1 Sam 4:12
6.	וַיֹּאמֶר מֹשֶׁה לִבְנֵי־גָד וְלִבְנֵי רְאוּבֵן . . . וַיִּחַר־אַף יהוה בַּיּוֹם הַהוּא	Moses said to the Gadites and Reubenites, ". . . Yʜᴡʜ's anger was aroused *that day*." Num 32:6, 10
7.	קָבוֹר תִּקְבְּרֶנּוּ בַּיּוֹם הַהוּא	Be sure to bury him the *same day*. Deut 21:23
8.	וְהִפְלֵיתִי בַיּוֹם הַהוּא	I will set off in *that day*. . . . Exod 8:18; see v 17
9.	וְאָנֹכִי הַסְתֵּר אַסְתִּיר פָּנַי בַּיּוֹם הַהוּא	I will certainly hide my face *on that day*. Deut 31:18
10.	וּזְעַקְתֶּם בַּיּוֹם הַהוּא מִלִּפְנֵי מַלְכְּכֶם	*When that day* comes you will cry out for relief from your king. 1 Sam 8:18
11.	בַּיּוֹם הַהוּא יָסִיר אֲדֹנָי	On *that day* the Lord will put aside. . . . Isa 3:18
12.	יִשָּׂא בַיּוֹם הַהוּא	But *in that day* he will cry out. . . . Isa 3:7
13.	הֶחֱזִיקוּ . . . בַּיּוֹם הַהוּא	They will seize . . . on *that day*. . . . Isa 4:1
14.	וְיִנְהֹם עָלָיו בַּיּוֹם הַהוּא	In *that day* he will roar over it. Isa 5:30

24. DeVries, *Yesterday, Today, and Tomorrow*, 136.

25. DeVries, *Yesterday, Today, and Tomorrow*, 118, cf. 126, 283–84.

26. DeVries, *Yesterday, Today, and Tomorrow*, 284–85.

27. DeVries, *Yesterday, Today, and Tomorrow*, 295.

28. DeVries, *Yesterday, Today, and Tomorrow*, 297–310.

29. DeVries, *Yesterday, Today, and Tomorrow*, 310–14.

30. DeVries, *Yesterday, Today, and Tomorrow*, 314–23.

18

Interrogatives and Indefinites

Introduction   18.1

Linguistic markers of uncertainty interact in many different ways with the forms of   a
utterance, that is, declaration, question, exclamation, and the like. Let us begin by considering some facts about English interrogatives. There are five kinds of questions used
in English: (*a*) questions of fact, 'yes-no' or polar questions (# 1), (*b*) questions of circumstance or *wh*-questions (## 2–7), (*c*) alternative questions (# 8), (*d*) exclamatory
questions (# 9), and (*e*) rhetorical questions (# 10).

1. Did Moses travel?
2. Who crossed the steppe?
3. Where did Moses live for forty years?
4. What did Moses cross?
5. When did Moses leave Egypt?
6. Why did Moses leave Egypt?
7. How did Moses leave Egypt?
8. Did Moses or Aaron leave first?
9. How far Moses traveled!
10. Who is like Moses?

The two most common types of questions differ in English in that questions of fact are
formed by word-order changes, while questions of circumstance involve words of a special group, the *wh*- or interrogative words. Alternative questions are similar to questions
of fact, while exclamatory and rhetorical questions (two types of pseudo-question) are
like questions of circumstance.

The class of *wh*-words is not used only in questions; these words can be found in   b
other types of sentences (## 11–16).

11. The man *who* crossed the steppe was Moses.
12. Egypt was *where* Moses was born.
13. Moses took *what* he had in his hand.
14. Moses left *when* he could.
15. Moses asked *why* he should leave.
16. Moses wondered *how* he could leave.

These *wh*-words are used as relative pronouns (##11–12, 14), indefinite pronouns (# 13), and heads of embedded questions (## 15–16). Some of these uses are quite similar to the use in interrogative sentences (## 15–16), while others are rather different (## 11–14).

c   With these facts about English in mind, let us turn to Hebrew usage. Hebrew has a variety of question types, as English does: questions of fact (# 17), questions of circumstance (# 18), alternative questions (# 19), exclamatory questions (# 20), and rhetorical questions (# 21).

17.   הַאֵרֵד אַחֲרֵי פְלִשְׁתִּים   Shall I go down after the Philistines?
                                     1 Sam 14:37

18.   וְלָמֶה יֵרַע לְבָבֵךְ   Why is your heart sick?
                                     1 Sam 1:8

19.   הֲנֵלֵךְ אֶל־רָמֹת גִּלְעָד לַמִּלְחָמָה   Shall we go to Ramoth Gilead to (do) battle or shall
      אִם־נֶחְדָּל   we refrain?
                                     1 Kgs 22:15

20.   מַה־טֹּבוּ אֹהָלֶיךָ יַעֲקֹב   How good are your dwellings, Jacob!
                                     Num 24:5

21.   מִי־כָמֹכָה בָּאֵלִם יהוה   Who is like you among the gods, O Yhwh?
                                     Exod 15:11

As in English, questions of fact and alternative questions are formed similarly: in Hebrew, both types tend to use an interrogative particle הֲ (before a laryngeal, הַ), less often אִם.[1] The other types of questions use interrogative words, מִי, מַה, לָמָה, etc., a group roughly analogous to the *wh*-words of English. Like the *wh*-words, the Hebrew interrogatives are a diverse group: מִי and מַה are pronouns, while some of the other words are better termed adverbials or particles. Like the *wh*-words, too, the Hebrew interrogative pronouns can be used in non-interrogative contexts; in the Hebrew case, they serve as indefinite pronouns, 'whoever, whatever,' etc. The interrogative-indefinite pronouns and some interrogative particles are the topic of this chapter.

d   There are four major parts of the interrogative-indefinite vocabulary of Hebrew: (1) the animate pronoun, (2) the inanimate pronoun,[2] (3) the locative particles, and (4) the temporal particles.

1. Cf. 40.1. The interrogative particles are not necessary; a question of fact need not be specially marked. Its character as a question was presumably signaled in speech by a change in intonation. See Carl Brockelmann, *Grundriss der vergleichenden Grammatik der semitischen Sprachen* (Berlin: Reuter und Reichard, 1913), 2. 192–93.

2. The animate pronoun occurs 422 times and the inanimate 747 times (including prepositional phrases;

The *animate pronoun* is מִי;[3] like מָה, מִי is invariable for gender and number. (Thus the usual masculine/feminine and singular/plural nominal variation in Hebrew is replaced in the interrogative-indefinite category by animate/inanimate variation.) מִי is found in all three case functions, nominative (# 22), genitive (## 23–24), and accusative, always with את (# 25).

22.   מִי הִגִּיד לְךָ   *Who* told you?
      Gen 3:11

23.   בַּת־מִי אַתְּ   *Whose* daughter are you?
      Gen 24:23

24.   לְמִי־אַתָּה   *To whom* do you belong?
      Gen 32:18

25.   אֶת־מִי אֶשְׁלַח   *Whom* shall I send?
      Isa 6:8

The *inanimate pronoun* is מה; the vocalization varies. Essentially, the form is מֶה before א, ה, and ר; מֶה before ח and ע; and מַה elsewhere, with doubling of the following consonant.[4] Whatever the vocalization, מה may take the *maqqeph*.[5] This pronoun is also found in the three case functions, nominative (# 26), genitive, rarely (## 27–28), and accusative (# 29), never with את.

26.   מַה־פִּשְׁעִי   *What* is my crime?
      Gen 31:36

27.   בַּמָּה אֵדַע   *By what* shall I know?
      Gen 15:8

28.   וְחָכְמַת־מֶה לָהֶם: Wisdom *of what sort* (i.e., *What sort* of wisdom) do they have?
      Jer 8:9

29.   מֶה עָשִׂיתָ   *What* have you done?
      Gen 4:10

SA/THAT). The animate : inanimate contrast is widely attested in Semitic, but the pronouns are usually animate *man* : inanimate *mā*. Other terms used as indefinites in Hebrew include animate ʾîš, ʾādām, nepeš 'someone'; lōʾ ʾîš, lōʾ ʾādām, lōʾ nepeš 'no one'; inanimate dābār, məʾûmâ 'something,' as well as various phrases with kōl. The relative ʾšr is rarely used as an indefinite, 19.2 n. 13.

3. The *y* in Hebrew is a vowel lettter, but the Ugaritic form *my* suggests that it was bisyllabic.

4. This account is taken from Thomas O. Lambdin, *Introduction to Biblical Hebrew* (New York: Scribner, 1971) 83. For further discussion, see Paul Joüon, "Études de morphologie hébraïque," *Biblica* 1 (1920) 353–71, esp. 363–65. Particularly striking among many "irregular" pointings

are the cases of *meh* before consonants other than *ḥeth* and *ᶜayin* (note, e.g., Judg 16:5*bis*, 6*bis*, 10, 13, 15).

5. The *h* is a vowel letter (but cf. Ugaritic *mh*) and is sporadically omitted in, e.g., *mhm*, Ezek 8:6 *Kethiv*; the *Qere* restores the vowel letter; cf. Isa 3:15 *Kethiv*. On the Ugaritic, see M. Dietrich and O. Loretz, "Das ugaritische Fragepronomen *mh* und seine Erweiterungen," *Studies in Bible and the Ancient Near East Presented to Samuel E. Loewenstamm*, ed. Y. Avishur and J. Blau (Jerusalem: Rubinstein, 1978) 19–21.

The form *mān* 'what?' in Exod 16:15 is unique, apparently a non-standard form reflecting a popular etymology and corresponding folktale for *mān* 'manna.' On *mn* 'what, who' in Ugaritic, see *UT* § 19.1504.

מה sometimes occurs with a noun which is formally separated from it but syntactically related to it as an accusative of specification (## 30–31).[6]

30.   וּמַה־בְּיָדִי רָעָה׃   *What (with respect to) evil* is in my hand?
                                                 1 Sam 26:18

31.   וּמַה־יֶּשׁ־לִי עוֹד צְדָקָה   *What (with respect to) right* do I yet have?
                                                  2 Sam 19:29

f   The locative adverbs אֵי 'where?' and its derivatives are used in a variety of ways; the adverb אָן 'where?' is less important. The major temporal adverb is מָתַי 'when?', often in the combinations לְמָתַי 'when?' and עַד־מָתַי 'how long?'

g   The remainder of this chapter reviews the animate (18.2) and inanimate pronouns (18.3) and the locative adverbs (18.4).

18.2   The Animate Pronoun

a   One of the basic uses of the pronoun מִי is eliciting the identification or classification of persons (and rarely things) in questions, direct ('*Who* are you?') or indirect, governing another clause ('*Who* are you that you do these things?'), or embedded ('He asked me *who* you are'). Also basic is its use as an indefinite pronoun. מִי is also used in exclamatory and rhetorical questions, preceding a verbal predicate.

b   The interrogative use of מִי as a predicate in verbless clauses can serve to elicit an identification ('I am Moses') or a classification ('I am an Israelite').

1.   מִי־אָתְּ   *Who* are you (identification)?
                                                  Ruth 3:9

2.   מִי־הָאִישׁ הַלָּזֶה   *Who* is that man (classification)?
                                                      Gen 24:65

3.   מִי־אֵלֶּה כָּעָב תְּעוּפֶֽינָה   *Who* are these that fly like a cloud?
                                                      Isa 60:8

The demonstrative זה is sometimes added after מִי (17.4.3c).

4.   בֶּן־מִי־זֶה הַנַּֽעַר   *Whose* son (*I wonder*) is the lad?
                                                      1 Sam 17:55

5.   מִי זֶה מֶלֶךְ הַכָּבוֹד   *Who* is the king of glory!?[7]
                                                      Ps 24:8

6.   וּמִי־זֶה רֹעֶה אֲשֶׁר יַעֲמֹד לְפָנָי׃   *Who* (*I wonder*) is a shepherd who can stand before me?
                                                      Jer 49:19

---

6. See also 1 Sam 20:10, 2 Sam 24:13, 1 Kgs 12:16, Jer 2:5, Qoh 11:2, Esth 6:3.
7. Strictly, a rhetorical question.

The pronoun may be repeated, perhaps for an emphatic purpose.[8]

| 7. | מִי וָמִי הַהֹלְכִים: | *Just who* will be going?
Exod 10:8 |

The pronoun may be associated with various partitive constructions.

8.	וּמִי בְכָל־עֲבָדֶיךָ	*Who of* all your servants. . . ? 1 Sam 22:14
9.	מִי אֶחָד מִשִּׁבְטֵי יִשְׂרָאֵל	*Which* one *of* the tribes of Israel. . . ? Judg 21:8
10.	מִי מִשֶּׁלָּנוּ אֶל־מֶלֶךְ יִשְׂרָאֵל:	. . . *who of* us is for the king of Israel? 2 Kgs 6:11
11.	מִי בְּכָל־אֱלֹהֵי הָאֲרָצוֹת הָאֵלֶּה	*Who among* all the gods of these lands. . . ? Isa 36:20

Most of the clauses we have considered so far in this section are simple clauses. An   c
interrogative clause with מִי can govern another clause (cf. # 3).

12.	מִי אַתָּה קָרָאתָ אֶל־הַמֶּלֶךְ:	*Who* are you, *that* you call to the king? 1 Sam 26:14
13.	מִי אָנֹכִי כִּי אֵלֵךְ אֶל־פַּרְעֹה	*Who* am I, *that* I should go to Pharaoh? Exod 3:11
14.	כִּי מִי כָל־בָּשָׂר אֲשֶׁר	*What* mortal is there who can. . . ? Deut 5:26

An interrogative מִי clause can also be embedded in another clause; the embedded clause
is an *indirect question*.

| 15. | לֹא יָדַעְתִּי מִי עָשָׂה אֶת־הַדָּבָר
הַזֶּה | I don't know *who* has done this.
Gen 21:26 |
| 16. | שְׁאַל אַתָּה בֶּן־מִי־זֶה הָעָלֶם: | Find out *whose* son the young man is.
1 Sam 17:56; cf. # 4 |

This use is sometimes called "the relative use" and presents a blending of a relative with
an interrogative sense.

    Most occurrences of מִי refer to persons in a straightforward way, but some are not   d
so clear. When a thing is closely associated with the person or is pregnant with the idea
of a person, or where persons are understood and implied, מִי may be used. For example,
'What is your name?' can be expressed by מִי שְׁמֶךָ, because the name is conceived of as a

---

8. The repetition may be related to indefinite usage. Akkadian contrasts *man, mannu* 'who?', with the compound (or reduplicating) form *mamman* (< *man-man*) 'who-ever.' See Wolfram von Soden, *Grundriss der akkadischen Grammatik* (Rome: Pontifical Biblical Institute, 1969) 49.

surrogate for the person.[9] Because the inquiry, however, is about some thing (## 17–19) or condition, etc. (## 20–21), English idiom requires other interrogatives: 'what (cf. # 14), how, where,' etc.[10]

17.	מִי שְׁמֶ֔ךָ	*What* is your name (identification)? Judg 13:17
18.	כִּי מִי־גֹוי גָּדֹול	*What* (other) great nation. . . ? Deut 4:7
19.	מִי אָנֹכִי . . . וּמִי בֵיתִי	*Who* am I . . . and *what* is my family. . . ? 2 Sam 7:18
20.	מִי־אַתְּ	*Who* are you (i.e., *How* did it go)? Ruth 3:16
21.	מִי־פֶ֙שַׁע יַעֲקֹב הֲלֹוא שֹׁמְרֹון	*What* is the transgression of Jacob? Is it not Samaria? Mic 1:5

In contrast מה may be used when the circumstance rather than the person is in view.

| 22. | מַה־שְּׁמֶ֔ךָ | *What* is your name?[11] Gen 32:28 |
| 23. | מָה הָעִבְרִים הָאֵ֙לֶּה | *What about* these Hebrews? 1 Sam 29:3 |

e   The *indefinite* uses of מי are chiefly nominative: מי is generally the subject of the main clause and head of a relative clause.

24.	מִי־יָרֵא	*anyone* who is afraid Judg 7:3
25.	מִי לַיהוה אֵלָי	*Whoever* is for Yhwh, [come] to me. Exod 32:26
26.	מִי־בַּעַל דְּבָרִים יִגַּשׁ אֲלֵהֶם:	*Whoever* has a cause, let him approach them. Exod 24:14
27.	מִי חָכָם וְיָבֵן אֵלֶּה	*Whoever* is wise, let him understand these things. Hos 14:10

The relative head אשר may follow מי (# 28) or even מי האיש (## 29–30).

---

9. Aramaic *man* 'who?' can be used the same way; cf. Ezra 5:4, and Franz Rosenthal, *A Grammar of Biblical Aramaic* (Wiesbaden: Harrassowitz, 1961) § 38 / p. 22. On the Hebrew, see Joüon, "Études de morphologie hébraïque," 365.

10. The sense of *mî yāqûm yaᶜăqōb* in Amos 7:2, 5 is not clear; the usual rendering is 'How can Jacob stand?', but more apt may be 'Who is Jacob that he can stand?'

11. A question asking for the meaning of the name. Cf. Exod 3:13 perhaps.

28.   מִי אֲשֶׁר חָטָא־לִי אֶמְחֶנּוּ
      מִסִּפְרִי׃

Whoever has sinned against me I will blot out of my book.[12]
Exod 32:33

29.   מִי הָאִישׁ אֲשֶׁר יָחֵל לְהִלָּחֵם
      בִּבְנֵי עַמּוֹן יִהְיֶה לְרֹאשׁ

Whoever will launch the attack against the Ammonites will be the head. . . .
Judg 10:18

30.   מִי־הָאִישׁ אֲשֶׁר בָּנָה בַיִת־חָדָשׁ
      . . . יֵלֵךְ

Whoever has built a new house . . . let him go [home].
Deut 20:5

Indefinite מי can be used absolutely (with no relative clause following) and as a vocative.

31.   שִׁמְרוּ־מִי

Take care, *whoever* [you may be].
2 Sam 18:12

Indefinite מי can be used in the accusative function.

32.   בַּחֲרוּ . . . אֶת־מִי תַעֲבֹדוּן

Choose . . . *whom* you will serve.
Josh 24:15

Exclamatory and rhetorical questions in מי must be recognized from context, though there are patterns associated with each group. *Exclamatory questions* usually have a non-perfective verb, and the sense is desiderative: 'Who will act?' > 'Oh that someone would act!'   f

33.   מִי יַשְׁקֵנִי מַיִם

Oh that someone would give me water to drink!
2 Sam 23:15

34.   מִי־יֹאמַר

Who would (dare to) say. . . ?
Job 9:12

35.   מִי־יְשִׂמֵנִי שֹׁפֵט

Oh that I were appointed *šopet*!
2 Sam 15:4

The fixed expressions מי יתן and מי יודע convey wish (# 36) or doubt (# 37).[13]

36.   מִי־יִתֵּן עֶרֶב

If only it were evening!
Deut 28:67

37.   מִי יוֹדֵעַ יְחַנַּנִי יהוה

Perhaps Yhwh will be gracious to me.
2 Sam 12:22

Often, as in the last two examples, the outcome is unobtainable.

---

12. These passages illustrate the semantic transition from the interrogative sense to the indefinite sense: 'Who is the one that sinned against me? I will blot him out' > 'Who(ever) sinned against me, I will blot out.' Cf. the

suggestions of Brockelmann, *Grundriss*, 2. 580.
13. See J. L. Crenshaw, "The Expression *mî yôdēaᶜ* in the Hebrew Bible," *Vetus Testamentum* 36 (1986) 274–88.

g   *Rhetorical* questions aim not to gain information but to give information with passion. Properly speaking, this use should be considered in connection with figures of speech. The rhetorical use of the interrogative pronoun מִי, however, for self-abasement or for insult occurs within a consistent grammatical structure and is therefore considered here. According to George W. Coats, the two structural elements in this pattern are

> . . . an introductory question constructed as a noun clause with interrogative particle מָה or מִי and pronoun, name, or noun, and a following assertion, introduced by כִּי, אֲשֶׁר, or a *waw* consecutive imperfect and constructed around a verbal form. The second element regularly picks up the object of the first element as the subject or object of the verb or the object of a preposition. . . . [The pattern] poses a question . . . , then abases the noun or pronoun subject by an implied answer to the question. On the basis of the implied answer, the verb . . . is negated.[14]

This pattern may involve, as noted, self-abasement (# 38; cf. # 13) or insult (## 39–41).

38.   מִי אָנֹכִי . . . כִּי־אֶהְיֶה חָתָן לַמֶּלֶךְ:   *Who* am I . . . *that* I should be the son-in-law of the king?
1 Sam 18:18

39.   מִי יהוה אֲשֶׁר אֶשְׁמַע בְּקֹלוֹ   *Who* is Yнwн *that* I should obey him?
Exod 5:2

40.   כִּי מִי הַפְּלִשְׁתִּי הֶעָרֵל הַזֶּה כִּי חֵרֵף מַעַרְכוֹת אֱלֹהִים חַיִּים: *Who* is this uncircumcised Philistine *that* he should defy the armies of the living God?
1 Sam 17:26

41.   מִי דָוִד   *Who* is David [*that* I should help him]?
1 Sam 25:10

A generalized use of this pattern involves abasing all people, including the speaker, usually in implicit contrast to God.[15]

18.3   The Inanimate Pronoun

a   The range of uses of מה is greater than of מי because מה is frequently combined with prepositions. The kinds of uses are, however, comparable: the interrogative and indefinite patterns are basic, while several exclamatory and rhetorical structures are worthy of note.

b   *Interrogative* מה has a broad repertory of senses, even without prepositional complements. As noted earlier, מה can fulfill any of the major case functions, but it is most common as the direct object of the verb.

---

14. George W. Coats, "Self-Abasement and Insult Formulas," *Journal of Biblical Literature* 89 (1970) 14–26, at 26, cf. 14–15. Parallels from Epigraphic Hebrew (Lachish Letters) and Western Akkadian (El-Amarna letters) are cited, pp. 15–16.

15. Coats, "Self-Abasement and Insult Formulas," 24–26. Note the cases with *mâ* in Ps 8:5 and Job 15:14, related formulas; cf. 18.3g.

1.	מֶה עָשִׂיתָ	*What* have you done? Gen 4:10
2.	מָה אֶתֶּן־לָּךְ	*What* shall I give you? Gen 30:31
3.	מָה רָאִיתָ כִּי עָשִׂיתָ אֶת־הַדָּבָר הַזֶּה׃	*What* was your reason for doing this? Gen 20:10

The use of זה may serve to add "vividness" (17.4.3c, 18.2b).

4.	מַה־זֹּאת עָשִׂית	*What* (*I wonder*) have you done? Gen 3:13

The pronoun may be further specified by an accusative of specification (18.1e).[16]

5.	וּמַה־בְּיָדִי רָעָה׃	*What* (*with reference to*) *evil* is in my hands? 1 Sam 26:18
6.	מַה־מָּצְאוּ אֲבוֹתֵיכֶם בִּי עָוֶל	*What fault* did your forebears find in me? Jer 2:5

Interrogative מה, sometimes with זה, can mean 'why?'

7.	מַה־תִּצְעַק אֵלָי	*Why* are you crying out to me? Exod 14:15
8.	מָה אֲנַחְנוּ יֹשְׁבִים פֹּה	*Why* should we stay here? 2 Kgs 7:3
9.	מַה־זֶּה רוּחֲךָ סָרָה	*Why* (*in the world*) is your spirit so sullen? 1 Kgs 21:5

In a verbless interrogative clause מה can be used with the *lamed of interest* (advantage or disadvantage); the question concerns the object of *l* in a loosely or elliptically defined way. The object is usually personal (## 10–15); double objects are found (## 15–16).

10.	מַה־לָּךְ הָגָר	*What* is to you, Hagar? (i.e., *What troubles* you, Hagar?) Gen 21:17
11.	מַה־לָּךְ׃	*What* (*can I do*) for you? Judg 1:14
12.	מַה־לָּעָם כִּי יִבְכּוּ	*What* is (*wrong*) with the people that they weep? 1 Sam 11:5
13.	מַה־לְּךָ לְסַפֵּר חֻקָּי	*What* (*right have*) you to recite my laws? Ps 50:16

---

16. Note also the "small clause," *mah bésa*ᶜ, 'What (is there with respect to) profit?', in Gen 37:26 and Ps 30:10.

14.	מַה־לִּי וָלָךְ כִּי־בָ֫אתָ	*What* do I have to do with you that you have come? Judg 11:12
15.	מַה־לְּךָ וּלְשָׁלוֹם	*What* do you have to do with peace? 2 Kgs 9:18
16.	מַה־לַתֶּ֫בֶן אֶת־הַבָּר	*What* has straw to do with wheat? Jer 23:28

Such a construction can be given past time reference with the verb *hyy* (# 17).

| 17. | מַה־זֶּה הָיָה לְבֶן־קִישׁ | *What* (*in the world*) happened to the son of Kish?
1 Sam 10:11 |

c   *With prepositions* interrogative מה takes on a variety of senses. The most common combination is למה 'why?', sometimes with זה.[17]

18.	לָ֫מָּה חָרָה לָךְ	*Why* are you angry? Gen 4:6
19.	לָ֫מֶּה תִבְכִּי	*Why* are you crying? 1 Sam 1:8
20.	לָ֫מָּה זֶּה צָחֲקָה שָׂרָה	*Why* (*in the world*) did Sarah laugh? Gen 18:13
21.	וְעַתָּה מֵת לָ֫מָּה זֶּה אֲנִי צָם	Now that he is dead, *why* should I fast? 2 Sam 12:23

In some cases למה is used in a quasi-rhetorical way, introducing an undesirable alternative: 'Do something; למה . . .' = 'why should something else happen?' > 'lest something else happen' *or* 'otherwise something else will happen.'

| 22. | שַׁלְּחֵנִי לָמָה אֲמִיתֶךָ׃ | Send me out; *why* should I kill you? / *lest* I kill you / *otherwise* I'll kill you.
1 Sam 19:17 |
| 23. | לָמָּה יִקְצֹף הָאֱלֹהִים | *otherwise* God will be angry
Qoh 5:5 |

In this use למה may be preceded by a relative pronoun.

| 24. | אֲשֶׁר לָמָּה יִרְאֶה אֶת־פְּנֵיכֶם | *otherwise* he will see you
Dan 1:10 |
| 25. | שַׁלָּמָה אֶהְיֶה כְּעֹטְיָה | *otherwise* I will be like the veiled women
Cant 1:7 |

---

17. The difference between *lmh* 'why (i.e., for what purpose)?' and the slightly less frequent *maddûaᶜ* (< *mâ* + *yaddûaᶜ*) 'why (i.e., for what reason)?' is not entirely firm. For efforts to distinguish the two, see T. W. Nakarai, "LMH and MDUᶜ in the Tanak," *Hebrew Studies* 23 (1982) 45–50; Richter, *GAHG* 3. 179–80.

The other monoliteral prepositions also combine with מה: בַּמֶּה means both 'in, on   d
what?' (# 26) and 'how?' (# 27) and כַּמֶּה both 'how many?' (# 28) and 'how much?'.

26.   בַּמֶּה יִשְׁכָּב   *On what* shall he lie down?
                                        Exod 22:26

27.   בַּמָּה אֵדַע   *How / By what* shall I know?
                                        Gen 15:8

28.   כַּמָּה יְמֵי שְׁנֵי חַיֶּיךָ:   *How* old are you?
                                        Gen 47:8

In combination with עַד, the pronoun has the sense 'how long?' (## 29–30) and with עַל
the sense 'on what basis, why?' (## 31–32).

29.   בְּנֵי אִישׁ עַד־מֶה כְבוֹדִי   *How long*, O high-born men, [will you turn] my
                 לִכְלִמָּה   glory into shame?
                                        Ps 4:3

30.   עַד־מָה יהוה תֶּאֱנַף לָנֶצַח   *How long*, O YHWH? Will you be angry forever?
                                        Ps 79:5

31.   עַל־מָה הִכִּיתָ אֶת־אֲתֹנְךָ   *Why* have you struck your donkey?
                                        Num 22:32

32.   עַל מֶה תֻכּוּ עוֹד   *Why* should you be beaten any more?
                                        Isa 1:5

The *indefinite* use of מה usually involves a clausal object.   e

33.   מַה־תֹּאמַר נַפְשְׁךָ וְאֶעֱשֶׂה־לָּךְ:   *Whatever* you say, I'll do for you.
                                        1 Sam 20:4

34.   מַה־יַּרְאֵנִי וְהִגַּדְתִּי לָךְ   *Whatever* he reveals to me, I will tell you.
                                        Num 23:3; cf. 1 Sam 19:3

35.   וְנִרְאֶה מַה־יִּהְיוּ חֲלֹמֹתָיו: Then we will see *what* comes of his dreams.
                                        Gen 37:20

36.   הִגִּיד לְךָ אָדָם מַה־טּוֹב   He has shown you, O man, *what* is good.
                                        Mic 6:8

Sometimes the relative שׁ follows מה in this usage.[18]

37.   מַה־שֶּׁהָיָה כְּבָר הוּא   *Whatever* is, has already been.
                                        Qoh 3:15

The pronoun can have an indefinite sense in combination with a preposition.[19]

18. In the accusative in Qoh 8:7.
19. Negation in English triggers changes in indefinites: compare 'someone, anyone, no one.' In Hebrew such changes are unknown: *yādəʿâ mmâ* would mean 'She understands something,' and *bal yādəʿâ mmâ* means 'She understands nothing,' Prov 9:13, cf. Neh 2:12.

38. וּרְאֵי בַמֶּה כֹּחוֹ גָדוֹל וּבַמֶּה נוּכַל לוֹ

See wherein *his great strength lies and* how *we can overcome him.*
Judg 16:5

39. כִּי אִם־יִהְיֶה לְבָעֵר קָיִן עַד־מָה אַשּׁוּר תִּשְׁבֶּךָ׃

You Kenites will be destroyed when *Ashur takes you captive.*
Num 24:22

f   The *exclamatory questions* with מה may involve either an adjective (## 40–41) or a verb (## 42–46).

40. מָה־אַדִּיר

how majestic
Ps 8:2

41. מַה־יָּקָר

how priceless
Ps 36:8

42. וּמַה־נִּצְטַדָּק

How can we justify ourselves!
Gen 44:16

43. מָה אֶתֵּן זֶה לִפְנֵי מֵאָה אִישׁ

How can I ever set this before one hundred men!
2 Kgs 4:43

44. מַה־זֶּה מִהַרְתָּ לִמְצֹא

How (in the world) *did you ever find it so quickly!*
Gen 27:20

45. מָה אֶקֹּב לֹא קַבֹּה אֵל

How can I curse what God has not cursed!
Num 23:8

46. כַּמָּה יַמְרוּהוּ בַמִּדְבָּר

How much they rebelled against him in the steppe!
Ps 78:40

g   One of the *rhetorical uses* of מה involves the kind of abasement or insult cited in connection with מי (18.2g).[20]

47. כִּי מָה עַבְדְּךָ הַכֶּלֶב כִּי יַעֲשֶׂה הַדָּבָר הַגָּדוֹל הַזֶּה

What is your servant, the dog, *that* he should do this great thing?[21]
2 Kgs 8:13

48. מָה־אֱנוֹשׁ כִּי־תִזְכְּרֶנּוּ

What is a human life *that* you keep it in mind?
Ps 8:5

Another such use involves rhetorical questions that expect a strongly negative answer.[22]

---

20. Coats, "Self-Abasement and Insult Formulas," 17–19.

21. The self-abasement is heightened by the use of *klb* for the speaker, as well as by the distancing pronominal substitute ʿbdk. See Coats, "Self-Abasement and Insult Formulas," 16–17; and Irene Lande, *Formelhafte Wendungen der Umgangssprache im Alten Testament* (Leiden: Brill, 1949) 101–3.

22. Arabic not only has interrogative-indefinite *mā*, but also a negative *mā*, used alone and in various combina-tions to negate verbs. It has been proposed that Hebrew also has negative *mh*; see M. Dahood, "The Emphatic Double Negative *mᵊyn*," *Catholic Biblical Quarterly* 37 (1975) 458–59; W. Michel, "Job 31:1," *Hebrew Studies* 23 (1982) 59–66, at 60, 64. The exclamatory *mā* noted above is also found in Arabic: *mā afḍal Zaydan*, 'How excellent Zayd is, What an excellent man Zayd is!' See W. Wright, *A Grammar of the Arabic Language* (3d ed.; Cambridge: Cambridge University, 1896–98), 1. 98; 2. 43, 104–5. Compare with # 51 the variant form in 2 Sam 20:1.

49.	בֵּינִי וּבֵינְךָ מַה־הִיא	*What* is *that* between you and me? Gen 23:15
50.	מַה־נִּשְׁתֶּה:	*What* are we to drink? (i.e., We have *nothing* to drink.) Exod 15:24
51.	מַה־לָּנוּ חֵלֶק בְּדָוִד	*What* share do we have in David? (i.e., We have *no* share.) 1 Kgs 12:16

Locative Particles and Related Forms   18.4

An elaborate network of interrogative terms is organized around אֵי 'where?', including a variety of compounds (e.g., אֵי מזה) and related forms (e.g., אֵיפֹה).[23] One apparently related form, אין, is the source of אָן 'where?' and מֵאַיִן 'whence?'[24] Most of these terms are locative in reference and strictly interrogative in use, although they occur in both direct and indirect questions.   a

The core term of the network, אֵי, has two distinct uses. In the simple locative pattern, it can be used absolutely or with זה following.[25]   b

1.	אֵי הֶבֶל אָחִיךָ	*Where* is your brother Abel? Gen 4:9
2.	אֵי אֱלֹהֵימוֹ	*Where* is their god (rhetorical question)? Deut 32:37
3.	אֵי־זֶה הַדֶּרֶךְ הָלַךְ	*Where* is the road he went on?[26] 1 Kgs 13:12
4.	אֵי זֶה סֵפֶר כְּרִיתוּת	*Where* (*I wonder*) is the bill of divorcement? Isa 50:1
5.	אֵי־זֶה דֶּרֶךְ הַטּוֹב	*Where* is the good way?[27] Jer 6:16

אֵי can also be used with pronominal suffixes, sometimes anticipatory (# 8).

6.	אַיֶּכָּה	*Where* are you? Gen 3:9
7.	וְאַיּוֹ	*Where* is he? Exod 2:20
8.	אַיּוֹ מֶלֶךְ־חֲמָת	*Where* is he, the king of Hamath? 2 Kgs 19:13

---

23. On ʾyn and ʾān, see Brockelmann, *Grundriss*, 1. 191.

24. Cf. Arabic ʾayy (fem. ʾayya) 'who?, whoever, what kind of,' alongside of man 'who?, whoever.'

25. The locution ʾê-zeh 'which (of two)?', is found only in indirect questions in Qoh 2:3, 11:6.

26. Same idiom in 2 Kgs 3:8; Job 38:19, 24; 2 Chr 18:23 (cf. 1 Kgs 22:24).

27. The question may represent indirect discourse; see William L. Holladay, *Jeremiah* (Philadelphia: Fortress, 1986), 1. 221.

A directional locative is אֵי מִזֶּה 'whence?'

9.	וְאֵי מִזֶּה אָֽתָּה	*Where* are you *from*? 1 Sam 30:13
10.	וְאֵי־מִזֶּה עַם אָֽתָּה:	*From which* people are you? Jonah 1:8
11.	אֵי־מִזֶּה בָאת	*Where* have you come *from*? Gen 16:8

In # 10 the adverb takes an adverbial accusative, עַם. An apparently analogous phrase אֵי לָזֹאת means not 'whither?' (which would perhaps be אֵי אֶל־זֶה) but 'on what basis, why?'; it is found only in Jer 5:7.

c   Two forms related to אֵי also have the sense 'where?': אַיֵּה and אֵיפֹה, the latter also related to פֹּה 'here.' The first and more common of these two is not used with verbs (## 12–13); אֵיפֹה may be used in either verbal (# 14) or verbless clauses (# 15).

12.	אַיֵּה שָׂרָה אִשְׁתֶּךָ	*Where* is Sarah your wife? Gen 18:9
13.	אַיֵּה שֹׁקֵל	*Where* is the weigher? Isa 33:18
14.	אֵיפֹה שְׁמוּאֵל וְדָוִד	*Where* are Samuel and David? 1 Sam 19:22
15.	אֵיפֹה לֹא שֻׁגַּלְתְּ	*Where* have you not been ravished? Jer 3:2

d   Another set of forms related to אֵי has the sense 'how?', used in both true questions of circumstance and in exclamatory questions; each of these involves a *k* element: אֵיךְ is the most common, while אֵיכָה and אֵיכָכָה are rare.[28] The use in true questions involves all three forms.

16.	אֵיךְ אַתֶּם נֽוֹעָצִים	*How* do you advise me? 1 Kgs 12:6
17.	וְאֵיךְ אָמַ֫רְתָּ אֲחֹתִי הִיא	*How* could you say, "She is my sister"? Gen 26:9
18.	אֵיךְ יָדַ֫עְתָּ כִּי־מֵת שָׁאוּל וִיהוֹנָתָן	*How* do you know that Saul and Jonathan are dead? 2 Sam 1:5
19.	אֵיכָה אֶשָּׂא לְבַדִּי	*How* can I bear you by myself? Deut 1:12
20.	אֵיכָכָה אֶלְבָּשֶׁ֫נָּה	*How* can I put it on? Cant 5:3

---

28. In Cant 1:7*bis*, ʾêkâ is used for 'where?' The form ʾêkōh 'where?' in 2 Kgs 6:13 may be a variant of ʾêkâ.

The *exclamatory use* involves אֵיכָה more often than אֵיךְ; the occurrence of אֵיכָה as   e
the first word of Lamentations (# 22) is the source of the Hebrew name of the book.

21.   אֵיךְ נָפְלוּ גִבּוֹרִים: *How* the mighty have fallen!
                                                 2 Sam 1:19

22.   אֵיכָה יָשְׁבָה בָדָד   *How* it dwells alone!
                                                 Lam 1:1

23.   אֵיכָה הָיְתָה לְזוֹנָה   *How* it has become a whore!
                                                 Isa 1:21

The unattested form אָין* is probably the source of both אָן 'where?' and מֵאַיִן   f
'whence?'[29]

24.   אָן הֲלַכְתֶּם   *Where* did you go?
                                             1 Sam 10:14

25.   מֵאַיִן תָּבֹא   *Whence* have you come?
                                             Job 1:7

There are two related forms which are nearly identical: אָנָה, apparently אָן with the
directional *h*, and אָנָה, apparently an extended form of אָן; both forms usually mean
'whither, where?'

26.   וְאָנָה תֵלֵכִי   *Whither* are you going?
                                         Gen 16:8

27.   וְאָנָה עָשִׂית   *Where* did you work?
                                         Ruth 2:19

28.   אָנָה אֲנַחְנוּ עֹלִים   *Whither* are we going up?
                                             Deut 1:28

The form אָנָה is doubled in a phrase meaning 'here and there,' with no interrogative
force.[30] The locative sense of אָנָה is extended in the phrase עַד־אָנָה 'how long?, till when?'

29.   עַד־אָנָה מֵאַנְתֶּם   *How long* will you refuse?
                                             Exod 16:28

30.   עַד־אָנָה יְנַאֲצֻנִי הָעָם הַזֶּה   *How long* will this people despise me?
                                                     Num 14:11

---

29. The form *mʾn* in 2 Kgs 5:25 is difficult.
30. The doubled phrase *ʾāneh wāʾānâ* occurs in 1 Kgs 2:36, 42; 2 Kgs 5:25.

19

Relatives

19.1   Introduction

a   Most of the clauses discussed so far are simple clauses, that is, clauses that make one predication, verbless or verbal.

1.	וְשֵׁם אִמּוֹ יְדִידָה	His mother's name is Jedidah.
		2 Kgs 22:1
2.	וַיֵּלֶךְ בְּכָל־דֶּרֶךְ דָּוִד	And he followed all David's ways.
		2 Kgs 22:2

It is often necessary to combine more than one predication; in such situations the main (or independent) clause contains one or more subordinate clauses. Relative clauses are a major variety of subordinate clause. The most widely used relative-clause marker is אֲשֶׁר.

3.	וְיַתֵּךְ אֶת־הַכֶּסֶף . . . אֲשֶׁר אָסְפוּ שֹׁמְרֵי הַסַּף	So he can pour out the money . . . *which* the door-keepers have collected.
		2 Kgs 22:4 LXX[L]

In this example הכסף is the object of the main verb ויתך, and it is the object of the verb אספו in the relative clause. Although relative clauses need not be marked, there are several relative-clause markers; some of them are used only in this way and are called *relative pronouns*, while others also serve other roles, notably the article.

b   Relative clauses are in many ways similar to attributive adjectives. They differ in conveying more complex information, that is, information that requires a predication of its own.

4. וַיַּבְדֵּל בֵּין הַמַּ֫יִם אֲשֶׁר מִתַּ֫חַת לָרָקִ֫יעַ וּבֵין הַמַּ֫יִם אֲשֶׁר מֵעַל לָרָקִ֫יעַ	And he divided between the water *which* was below the firmament and the water *which* was above the firmament. Gen 1:7

The two verbless relative clauses here allow the specification of the רקיע as a reference point, as the use of the adjectives תַּחְתִּי 'lower' and עֶלְי 'upper' with מים would not.

It is often said that there are two types of relative clauses in Hebrew, the dependent (or attributive) relative and the so-called "independent relative." The *dependent relative*, which has a close analog in English, contains a head word followed by a relative marker; all the examples so far considered are of this type. In # 4 the head word is המים for both clauses; the relative אשר follows this and introduces the attributive clause. **c**

The "*independent relative*" is really a contradiction in terms because it is independent, that is, it is not relative to anything. In this construction the clause introduced by the "relative" marker functions as a principal part of the main verbal clause, as subject (# 5), object (# 6), or genitive (# 7), or in a verbless clause (# 8). **d**

5. וַיֵּ֫רַע בְּעֵינֵי יהוה אֲשֶׁר עָשָׂה	*What he did* was wicked in Yʜwʜ's eyes. Gen 38:10
6. וְאַגִּ֫ידָה לָכֶם אֵת אֲשֶׁר־יִקְרָא אֶתְכֶם	I will tell you *what will happen* to you. Gen 49:1
7. בְּיַד אֲשֶׁר שָׂנֵאת	into the hands of *those whom you hate* Ezek 23:28
8. רַבִּים אֲשֶׁר־מֵ֫תוּ בְּאַבְנֵי הַבָּרָד מֵאֲשֶׁר הָרְגוּ בְּנֵי יִשְׂרָאֵל בֶּחָֽרֶב׃	*Those who died* by the hailstones were more numerous than *those whom* the Israelites had killed by the sword. Josh 10:11

The "relative" markers indicate in ## 5–8 that the clauses introduced by them are part of a larger sentence.

Types of Relative-Clause Markers   **19.2**

There are four classes of relative-clause markers: (1) אשר, (2) שׁ, (3) the *z* series, and (4) others. The first two are used only as relatives; the *z* series overlaps with the demonstratives, and those gathered under the last heading are grammatical elements used primarily in other ways. The members of the first three groups can be called relative pronouns.[1] **a**

---

1. Both *ʾšr* and *š* are quite often used as conjunctions, but such use is not considered in this chapter. Cf. nn. 10 and 14. On the development of *ʾšr* as a conjunction, and the related problem of the position of the relative pronoun vis-à-vis its head, see M. H. [Goshen-]Gottstein, "Afterthought and the Syntax of Relative Clauses in Biblical Hebrew," *Journal of Biblical Literature* 68 (1949) 35–47.

A fuller account of the problem, set in the context of Mishnaic and Modern Hebrew, is given by T. Givón, "Verb Complements and Relative Clauses," *Afroasiatic Linguistics* 1/4 (1974); he argues in essence that relative clauses evolve from modifying a constituent to modifying a whole clause. There are about 5500 occurrences of *ʾšr* and 138 of *š*, 68 of them in Qoheleth (SA/THAT).

b   The most common relative pronoun, אֲשֶׁר, is etymologically a locative noun, 'a step, place,'[2] and may be considered a noun always used in the construct.[3] There is no trace of the etymological sense,[4] however, and the construct state is useful only in explaining the phonetic shape of the word. Broadly speaking, אשר is rare in poetry, rarer in older poetry than later,[5] and the uses of אשר are more diverse in later prose than in earlier.

c   The relative שֶׁ is pointed in various ways: usually שַׁ or שֶׁ with doubling of the following consonant; שָׁ or שֶׁ, if doubling is not allowed (or before $\bar{o}$ or $\bar{a}$), except for שַׁ before ה. This pronoun presents a curious history: it is attested in the older layer of Biblical Hebrew (e.g., Judg 5:7) and in the later books, but rarely in between.[6] Since most Semitic languages use an $\check{s}$ form for the relative, including Phoenician and Ammonite, and since שׁ is standard in Mishnaic Hebrew, we may suppose that the dominant dialect of Biblical Hebrew was distinctive among Hebrew and South Canaanite dialects in using אשר in preference to שׁ.[7]

d   The relative markers of the z series include the demonstrative זֶה, as well as the rare forms זוּ and זוֹ (זֹה).[8] The diversity of this group of forms is discussed in connection with the demonstratives (17.4.3). The relative use of these forms is primarily poetic. The syntactic patterns of relative clause with אשר and z forms are similar.[9]

1a.	בְּרֶֽשֶׁת־זוּ טָמָ֫נוּ	in the net which they have hidden
		Ps 9:16
1b.	וְרִשְׁתּוֹ אֲשֶׁר־טָמַן	his net which he hid
		Ps 35:8

Like $\check{s}$, z is a frequent element in Semitic relative markers outside Hebrew, and in the Hebrew demonstratives.

e   The final class includes the article, as well as מִי and מַה. The latter uses are cited above (18.2–3); the article as relative is treated below (19.7; cf. 13.5.2d).

f   Markers of the first three groups can be used in forming so-called independent relative clauses. There is a formal distinction between dependent and independent uses of

2. The noun is not attested as such in Hebrew, but cf. Akkadian *ašru* 'place, site' and *ašar* 'where, wherein'; the root *ʾšr/ʾtr* 'to go' is attested in Hebrew and Ugaritic. Only Hebrew and Moabite have *ʾšr*; of the neighboring languages, both Ammonite and Phoenician-Punic have *ʾš* (as does the Canaanite language of the Deir Alla text; see J. A. Hackett, *The Balaam Text from Deir Alla* [Chico: Scholars Press, 1984] 31, 114–15), and many other Semitic languages use *š* forms for the relative. See F. Rundgren, *Über Bildungen mit ʿš)- und n-t-Demonstrativen im Semitischen* (Uppsala: Almqvist & Wiksell, 1955).

3. Cf. BL § 32a / p. 264.

4. Save *perhaps* in Judg 5:27; Ruth 1:17 is dubious.

5. Francis I. Andersen and A. Dean Forbes, "'Prose Particle' Counts of the Hebrew Bible," *The Word of the Lord Shall Go Forth: Essays in Honor of David Noel Freedman*, ed. C. L. Meyers and M. O'Connor (Winona Lake, Indiana: Eisenbrauns, 1983) 165–83.

6. All instances of the relative in Canticles, except one (in the title of the book), involve *š*. In Qoheleth, *š* is used 68 times (often as a conjunction) and *ʾšr* 89 times. *Š* is not, however, frequent in Ezra (only once) or Chronicles (only twice). See Joüon § 38 / p. 89–90.

7. M. H. Segal, *A Grammar of Mishnaic Hebrew* (Oxford: Clarendon, 1927) 42–43.

8. It is strictly correct to say that *zû* is primarily a relative and *zeh* is primarily a demonstrative, but the one is so rare and the other so relatively common that such a flat statement is potentially misleading.

9. Cf. J. M. Allegro, "Uses of the Semitic Demonstrative Element z in Hebrew," *Vetus Testamentum* 5 (1955) 309–12, at 311. On the possibility that *zeh* and *zû* may be confused in the MT, see p. 309.

the relatives: as dependent pronouns they are never bracketed with a preposition or אֵת, but as independent pronouns they may be so bracketed. The independent pronoun is best rendered by the English equivalents: 'he who, he whom, that which, of such a kind as,' etc.

The relative clause may be unmarked, especially in poetry, when the clause clearly functions as part of the sentence.   g

2.   בְּשַׁחַת עָשׂוּ   into the pit (which) they have dug
                                         Ps 9:16

Uses of אשר   19.3

The common relative pronoun is indeclinable.[10] It can introduce dependent or attrib-   a
utive relative clauses, either alone or with a resumptive element, specifying the role of the
relative pronoun in the subordinate clause. Strictly speaking, the structure of the clause
varies, depending on whether the resumptive element is present; the differences are not,
however, crucial to accounting for the use or non-use of the resumptive. In *dependent
relative clauses without resumption*, the pronoun is usually in the nominative function
(## 1–2), although it may be in the accusative (# 3).

1.   הָעֵץ אֲשֶׁר בְּתוֹךְ־הַגָּן   the tree *which* (NOMINATIVE) is in the middle of the
                                         garden
                                         Gen 3:3

2.   אֲנִי יהוה אֲשֶׁר הוֹצֵאתִיךָ   I am YHWH, *who* (NOMINATIVE) brought you out from
              מֵאוּר כַּשְׂדִּים   Ur of the Chaldees.
                                         Gen 15:7

3.   אֱלֹהִים אֲחֵרִים אֲשֶׁר לֹא יָדַעְתָּ   other gods *whom* (ACCUSATIVE) you have not known
                                         Deut 13:7

The most common *resumptive* element is a pronoun, independent for the nomina-   b
tive function (# 4), suffixed otherwise (## 5–9). Note that the head word may be definite
(## 4, 6–9) or indefinite (# 5).

4.   וּמִן־הַבְּהֵמָה אֲשֶׁר לֹא טְהֹרָה   from the animal *which* (NOMINATIVE) (it) is not pure
              הִוא   Gen 7:2

5.   גּוֹי אֲשֶׁר לֹא־תִשְׁמַע לְשֹׁנוֹ:   a nation *whose* (GENITIVE) (the) language (of it) you
                                         will not understand
                                         Deut 28:49

6.   הָאָרֶץ אֲשֶׁר אַתָּה שֹׁכֵב עָלֶיהָ   the land *which* (GENITIVE) you are lying *on* (it)
                                         Gen 28:13

---

10. The conjunctive use of *ʾšr* is not considered here. This use is more common in late Biblical Hebrew; see Robert Polzin, *Late Biblical Hebrew: Toward an Historical Typology of Biblical Hebrew Prose* (Missoula: Scholars Press, 1976) 128. Joüon's apparent view that the conjunctive use is more basic than the pronominal use is ill founded, both on synchronic syntactic and historical grounds; see § 145a / p. 447.

7.   אֲנִי יוֹסֵף אֲחִיכֶם אֲשֶׁר־מְכַרְתֶּם   I am your brother, Joseph, *whom* (ACCUSATIVE) you
אֹתִי מִצְרָיְמָה: sold (me) into Egypt.
Gen 45:4

8.   הַנָּבִיא אֲשֶׁר־שְׁלָחוֹ יהוה   the prophet *which* (ACCUSATIVE) YHWH sent (him)
Jer 28:9

9.   כַּמֹּץ אֲשֶׁר־תִּדְּפֶנּוּ רוּחַ:   like chaff *which* (ACCUSATIVE) the wind drives (it)
away
Ps 1:4

After words of time there is usually no resumptive pronoun, so that אשר appears to be equivalent to 'when.'[11]

10.   עַד־הַיּוֹם אֲשֶׁר־בָּא בְשָׁלוֹם: until the day *when* (*in which*) he came back in safety
2 Sam 19:25

11.   וְעוֹד חָמֵשׁ שָׁנִים אֲשֶׁר אֵין־   (There are) still five years *when* there will be no
חָרִישׁ וְקָצִיר: plowing or reaping.
Gen 45:6

12.   בַּיּוֹם הַהוּא אֲשֶׁר תָּבֹא   on the day *when* you go
1 Kgs 22:25

The resumptive element may also be a locative adverb.

13.   עַד־הַמָּקוֹם אֲשֶׁר־הָיָה שָׁם   to the place *where* (*which*) his tent had been (there)[12]
אָהֳלֹה   Gen 13:3

14.   כָּל־הַמָּקוֹם אֲשֶׁר נָבוֹא שָׁמָּה   every place *to which* we shall come
Gen 20:13

15.   אֶת־הָאֲדָמָה אֲשֶׁר לֻקַּח מִשָּׁם: the ground *from which* he had been taken
Gen 3:23

c   A so-called "*independent relative*" clause may, as noted in 19.1d, serve in a verbal clause as either subject (# 16) or object (# 17), in a verbless clause (# 18), and in a genitive function, either as object of a preposition (## 19–20) or as a second term in a construct chain (# 21).[13]

16.   וַיִּשָּׁאֶר אַךְ־נֹחַ וַאֲשֶׁר אִתּוֹ   Only Noah and *those* with him in the ark were left.
בַּתֵּבָה: Gen 7:23

17.   כִּי יָדַעְתִּי אֵת אֲשֶׁר־תְּבָרֵךְ   I know as blessed *the one whom* you bless.
מְבֹרָךְ   Num 22:6

---

11. This pattern is close to being conjunctive. Joüon includes a greater variety of cases similar to these under the broader heading of prepositional phrases omitted after ʾšr; see § 158i–k / pp. 484–85.

12. The use of *mqwm* shows how completely the etymological sense of ʾšr had faded.

13. Rarely ʾšr is used as an indefinite pronoun, perhaps only in Gen 31:32, 44:9, both times with *mṣʾ*, in related passages. The phrase ʾšr ʿl (h)byt, found in # 19, is also attested in the Silwan or Royal Steward inscription; see H. J. Katzenstein, "The Royal Steward," *Israel Exploration Journal* 10 (1960) 149–54.

18. רַבִּים אֲשֶׁר אִתָּ֫נוּ מֵאֲשֶׁר אִתָּם׃   More are *they who* are with us than they who are with them.
2 Kgs 6:16 *manuscript Kethiv*

19. וַיֹּאמֶר לַאֲשֶׁר עַל־בֵּיתוֹ   He said to *him who* was over his house. . . .
Gen 43:16

20. וּמֵאֲשֶׁר לְאָבִ֫ינוּ   from *what* belonged to our father
Gen 31:1

21. בְּיַד אֲשֶׁר שָׂנֵאת   into the hand of *those* you hate
Ezek 23:28

Uses of שֶׁ   **19.4**

The שֶׁ relative pronoun has a range of uses similar to that of אשר.[14] It can introduce   a
dependent relative clauses without resumption, serving either in the nominative or, less often, in the accusative function in the relative clause.[15]

1. כַּחוֹל שֶׁעַל־שְׂפַת הַיָּם   like the sand *which* (NOMINATIVE) is on the seashore[16]
Judg 7:12

2. יהוה שֶׁלֹּא נְתָנָ֫נוּ טֶ֫רֶף לְשִׁנֵּיהֶם׃   YHWH, *who* (NOMINATIVE) has not made us prey to their teeth
Ps 124:6

3. וּמִן־הַנְּתִינִים שֶׁנָּתַן דָּוִיד . . . לַעֲבֹדַת הַלְוִיִּם   and of the servitors *whom* (ACCUSATIVE) David appointed . . . for service of the Levites
Ezra 8:20

Resumptive elements occur less frequently after שֶׁ, but both pronouns and adverbs are so used.

4. בַּיּוֹם שֶׁיְּדֻבַּר־בָּהּ׃   on the day *on which* she is spoken for (on it)
Cant 8:8

5. שֶׁשָּׁם עָלוּ שְׁבָטִים   *to which* the tribes mount up (there)
Ps 122:4

A so-called *independent relative clause* in שֶׁ may serve as the object (or part of the   b
object) of a verbal main clause (# 6) or as a genitive, either as object of a preposition
(## 7–8) or as the second term of a construct phrase (## 9–10).

6. בִּקַּ֫שְׁתִּי אֵת שֶׁאָהֲבָה נַפְשִׁי   I sought *him whom* I love.
Cant 3:1

---

14. As with *ʾšr*, the conjunctive uses of *š* are not considered here; for examples, see Judg 6:17, Jonah 4:10; the uses of *š* in Judg 5:7*bis* are temporal conjunctions.

15. The *lamed* of possession with *š* combines to yield

the word *šel*; cf. 2 Kgs 6:11; Jonah 1:7, 12; and Polzin, *Late Biblical Hebrew*, 38–40. The word is the standard marker of possession in post-biblical Hebrew.

16. Cf. Judg 8:26.

7. וְעַל שֶׁבַּכְּרָמִים   and in charge of *that which* is in (i.e., the produce of) the vineyards
1 Chr 27:27

8. עַד שֶׁיְּחָנֵּנוּ׃   until he shows us mercy
Ps 123:2

9. אַשְׁרֵי שֶׁיְשַׁלֶּם־לָךְ   the joys of *the one who* pays you back[17]
Ps 137:8

10. אַשְׁרֵי שֶׁאֵל יַעֲקֹב בְּעֶזְרוֹ   the joys of *the one who* (has) the God of Jacob as his help[18]
Ps 146:5

A שׁ clause can also be used as a vocative.

11. הַגִּידָה לִּי שֶׁאָהֲבָה נַפְשִׁי   Tell me, (*you*) *whom* I love.
Cant 1:7

19.5   Uses of *z* Series Forms

a   The three forms of the *z* series relevant here are זֶה, זוּ (זֹה), and זוּ; the forms are not common enough to make it possible to distinguish among them clearly. There are two patterns of use to be discussed: the relative uses are similar to those found with אֲשֶׁר and שׁ, while the quasi-relative or determinative uses are quite different.[19]

b   A *z* form may be used as a *dependent relative pronoun*, usually without a resumptive element.

1. שְׁמַע לְאָבִיךָ זֶה יְלָדֶךָ   Listen to your father, *who* (NOMINATIVE) begot you.
Prov 23:22

2. מִפְּנֵי רְשָׁעִים זוּ שַׁדּוּנִי   from the presence of the wicked *who* (NOMINATIVE) assail me
Ps 17:9

3. לִוְיָתָן זֶה־יָצַרְתָּ   the Leviathan, *which* (ACCUSATIVE) you formed
Ps 104:26

4. וְעֵדֹתִי זוּ אֲלַמְּדֵם   my statues *which* (ACCUSATIVE) I teach to them
Ps 132:12

5. אֶל־מְקוֹם זֶה יָסַדְתָּ לָהֶם׃   to the place *which* (GENITIVE) you assigned for them[20]
Ps 104:8

Less often a *resumptive pronoun* is used.

---

17. Same construction in the following verse, Ps 137:9.
18. The *b* is the *beth* of essence.
19. See Allegro, "Demonstrative Element *z*," 309. Cf.

Ugaritic clauses in *d* (< *ð*).

20. Clauses in *z*, like those in *š*, can stand as the second term of a construct chain.

6.   הִנֵּה אֱלֹהֵינוּ זֶה קִוִּינוּ לוֹ   Behold our God *whom* we have trusted (him).
                                        Isa 25:9

7.   הֲלוֹא יהוה זוּ חָטָאנוּ לוֹ   Was it not YHWH *whom* we have sinned against
                                        (him)?
                                        Isa 42:24

8.   הַר־צִיּוֹן זֶה שָׁכַנְתָּ בּוֹ׃   Mount Zion *which* you dwell on (it)
                                        Ps 74:2

A *z* form can also be used in a so-called *independent relative clause*.

9.   וְזֶה־אָהַבְתִּי נֶהְפְּכוּ־בִי׃   *Those* I love have turned against me.
                                        Job 19:19

10. וְזֶה־חָזִיתִי וַאֲסַפֵּרָה׃   *That which* I have seen I will tell you.
                                        Job 15:17

In considering the *quasi-relative or determinative use* of the *z* forms, we need to   c
reconsider the basic sense of זה.[21] From the use of זה and its equivalents as an attributive
demonstrative (e.g., 'the person, this one'), there developed a substantive use: 'the person,
the one of (something),' which is equivalent to 'the person who. . . .' By definition *z*
forms governing another substantive are not relative pronouns, but since they bracket a
qualifying substantive with a preceding substantive they may be regarded in this use as
quasi-relatives. In such constructions their deictic force and their basic appositive syntax
can still be felt strongly. (It was out of this quasi-relative use that the relative uses treated
above developed.)

The determinative may be used in dependent relative clauses.[22]   d

11. מִפְּנֵי יהוה זֶה סִינַי   before YHWH, *the one* of Sinai[23]
                                        Judg 5:5

12. מִן־הַדּוֹר זוּ לְעוֹלָם׃   from the generation, *the one* of everlasting (i.e., the
                                        everlasting generation)
                                        Ps 12:8

It also occurs in independent relative clauses, in true determinative usage,[24] either as a
predicate in a nominal clause (# 13) or as a construct (# 14).

---

21. Allegro, "Demonstrative Element *z*," 311.

22. Isa 23:13 may be another example, but cf. 17.4.1.

23. Cf. *ʾlhym zh syny* in Ps 68:9. It may be that in origin the phrase *zh syny* was an independent clause, as is assumed by, e.g., F. M. Cross, *Canaanite Myth and Hebrew Epic* (Cambridge: Harvard University, 1973) 164; this would be in conformity with comparable usage in other Semitic languages.

24. The independent use is clearest in Arabic, in such Qurʾanic phrases as *ðū saʿatin* 'he of wealth (i.e., a rich man),' *ðū ʿusrin* 'he of poverty (i.e., a debtor),' *ðū mirratin*

'he of wisdom (i.e., Muhammad),' *ðū haṭṭin ʿaẓīmin* 'he of great fortune,' *ðū l-ʾawtād* 'Lord of Stakes (i.e., Pharaoh),' and the divine titles, *ðū l-faḍli l-ʿaẓīmi* 'Lord of the Grace Unbounded,' *ðū l-qūwati* 'Lord of Power,' and *ðū l-ʿarši (l-majīd)* 'Lord of the (Glorious) Throne.' The dependent use is more common in Aramaic with *d(y)*, e.g., Syriac *rwḥʾ dqwdšʾ* 'the Spirit, the one of Holiness,' a term for the Holy Spirit. See Allegro, "Demonstrative Element *z*," 310; and Franz Rosenthal, *A Grammar of Biblical Aramaic* (Wiesbaden: Harrassowitz, 1961) §§ 35–36, 86 / pp. 21–22, 38.

13.	וְהָיָה זֶה שָׁלֽוֹם	And he will be *the one* of peace.[25] Mic 5:4
14.	זֶה עָנִי קָרָא	*The one* of poverty cried (i.e., The poor man cried).[26] Ps 34:7 *emended*

19.6   Asyndetic Relative Clauses

a   Many relative clauses bear no distinctive relative marker but are juxtaposed directly to the main clause; such unmarked or ∅-marked clauses are common in poetry, particularly as *attributives* (## 1–2) and after time words (## 3–4).

1.	הַבִּיטוּ אֶל־צוּר חֻצַּבְתֶּם וְאֶל־ מַקֶּבֶת בּוֹר נֻקַּרְתֶּם:	Look to the rock (*from which*) you were hewn and to the quarry (*from which*) you were carved. Isa 51:1
2.	עֲצָמוֹת דִּכִּיתָ	the bones (*which*) you broke Ps 51:10
3.	כִּימוֹת עִנִּיתָנוּ	according to the days (*when*) you afflicted us Ps 90:15
4.	מֵעֵת דְּגָנָם וְתִירוֹשָׁם רָבּוּ:	at the time (*when*) their grain and new wine abound Ps 4:8

b   Asyndetic "*independent relative*" clauses occur as prepositional objects (## 5–6).

5.	אַחֲרֵי לֹא־יוֹעִלוּ הָלָכוּ:	They followed (*those who*) cannot help. Jer 2:8
6.	נִדְרַשְׁתִּי לְלוֹא שָׁאָלוּ	I was sought by (*those who*) had not asked. Isa 65:1

19.7   Other Relative Markers

a   In addition to the relative pronouns אשר, שׁ, and זה and the like, there are other relative markers to be considered; the relative use of מי and מה is treated above (18.2–3), while the article remains to be discussed.

b   The article as relative marker must be considered in relation to the participle, to other constructions, and to ambiguous forms. Hebraists sometimes analyze the article with the participle as having a relative force or as investing the participle with this value. For example, Ronald J. Williams lists as one of the uses of the article its use as "equivalent to a relative pronoun . . . with participles,"[27] while A. B. Davidson somewhat more accurately said: "When in apposition with a preceding definite subject the participle with

---

25. Cf. Isa 9:5, *śar-šālôm* 'prince of peace.'
26. Read *ʿŏnî* 'affliction' against the MT's *ʿānî* 'afflicted,' with Allegro, "Demonstrative Element *z*," 311.

27. See the brief treatment in R. J. Williams, *Hebrew Syntax: An Outline* (2d ed.; Toronto: University of Toronto, 1976) 19.

article has the meaning very much of a relative clause. . . . This usage is very common."[28] But even this analysis is not cogent because the participle, as a verbal adjective, *by itself* can serve as a relative clause, 'one who . . . , that which. . . .' Thus a participle can form a subordinate clause even without the article.

| 1. | סְעָרָה בָּאָה מִן־הַצָּפוֹן | a storm *which was coming* from the north Ezek 1:4 |

Thus it is misleading to consider the article as a dependent relative marker with a participle.[29]

The article with a perfective verb, however, does serve as a relative marker; this usage is found chiefly in the later books of the Bible, notably Ezra and Chronicles.[30] c

2.	קְצִינֵי אַנְשֵׁי הַמִּלְחָמָה הֶהָלְכוּא אִתּוֹ	the army commanders *who had come* with him[31] Josh 10:24
3.	וְכֹל אֲשֶׁר בְּעָרֵינוּ הַהֹשִׁיב נָשִׁים נָכְרִיּוֹת	everyone in our towns *who has married* a foreign woman Ezra 10:14
4.	וְכֹל הַהִקְדִּישׁ שְׁמוּאֵל	and everything *which* Samuel *had dedicated* 1 Chr 26:28

An *"independent relative"* clause formed with the article may stand after a preposition.

| 5. | בַּהֵכִין לוֹ דָוִיד | in the (*place*) David *had prepared* for it 2 Chr 1:4 |
| 6. | עַל הַהֵכִין הָאֱלֹהִים | at what God *had brought about* 2 Chr 29:36 |

Unfortunately, it is not always easy to distinguish participles and perfective verbs. d There are forms in older books where the consonants could be read as participles but points or accents indicate perfectives, notably *Niphals* and hollow verb forms. However the pointing or accentuation in the Masorah is to be explained, such forms should probably be read as participles (## 7–8); the article with the perfective is unlikely in early texts.[32]

---

28. A. B. Davidson, *Hebrew Syntax* (3d ed; Edinburgh: T. & T. Clark, 1901) 132–33, abbreviations expanded.

29. With Joüon § 145e / pp. 448–49.

30. The construal of *h* with a preposition in 1 Sam 9:24, though apparently intended by the Masoretes, is dubious; see P. Kyle McCarter, *I Samuel* (Anchor Bible 8; Garden City, New York: Doubleday, 1980) 170, for a conservative solution to the difficult witnesses.

31. The ʾ in *hhlkwʾ* may be a dittograph (note the following ʾ) or an example of a double *mater lectionis* type of writing, found frequently at Qumran; for other biblical examples, see GKC § 23i / p. 81. On the writing, see M.

O'Connor, "Writing Systems, Native Speaker Analyses, and the Earliest Stages of Northwest Semitic Orthography," *The Word of the Lord Shall Go Forth: Essays in Honor of David Noel Freedman*, ed. C. L. Meyers and M. O'Connor (Winona Lake, Indiana: Eisenbrauns, 1983) 439–65, at 450–51.

32. With Joüon § 145e / pp. 448–49; against BL § 32e / p. 265. The noun phrase in Gen 18:21 is anomalous not only because of the modifier *habbāʾâ ʾelay* but also because of the article + preposition + suffixed noun sequence, *hakkaṣaʿăqātāh* 'the according-to-its-outcry that has reached me.'

7. כַּלָּתָהּ עִמָּהּ הַשָּׁבָה מִשְּׂדֵי מוֹאָב

her daughter-in-law with her, *who had returned* from the plains of Moab
Ruth 1:22

8. בְּנוֹ הַנּוֹלַד־לוֹ

his son, *who was born* to him
Gen 21:3

Verbal Stems

20

Introduction to the Verbal System

Multifunctionality

20.1

Language is a system that uses finite means for infinite expressiveness, and therefore **a** many aspects of a language's working are called on to perform a variety of functions. We have seen this multifunctional quality exemplified over and over again in Biblical Hebrew grammar, but the greatest multifunctionality involves the verbal system. The verbal system is at the core of the expression of predication; while Hebrew uses non-verbal clauses (8.4) and interjections and exclamations are found intermittently (40.2), the central role in predication is played by the various verbal stems (*Qal*, *Piel*, etc.) and forms (perfective conjugation רָעָשָׂה, non-perfective conjugation אֱזְמָר, imperative שִׁמְעוּ, etc.). Prior to treating the stems and forms, we outline the wide variety of categories relevant to predication in this chapter.

Before turning to these categories, however, let us consider again the notion of **b** multifunctionality. In his analysis of the development of a child's language, M. A. K. Halliday notes that in the speech act of a very young child each utterance serves just one function, for example, 'I want my toy.'[1] In adult language, in contrast, speakers are able to objectify themselves in relation to their experiences and audiences, and each utterance is very complex, for example, 'There's my last duchess hanging on the wall.' Halliday refers to adult language as having three components: "ideational" (i.e., representing a thought or an experience), "interpersonal" (i.e., expressing the speaker's side of the utterance, the choice of roles for the addressee, the conveyance of judgments and predictions, etc.), and "textual" (i.e., filling "the requirement that language should be operationally relevant—that it should have a texture, in real contexts of situation.").[2] These three components or "macro-functions" are "highly abstract linguistic reflexes of the multiplicity of social uses of language."

---

1. M. A. K. Halliday, *Explorations of the Functions of Language* (London: Edward Arnold, 1973) 42.

2. Halliday, *Functions of Language*, 36.

Whereas with the child, in the first beginnings of the [grammatical] system, the functions remain unintegrated . . . with one utterance having just one function, the linguistic units of the adult language serve all (macro-)functions at once. A clause in English is the simultaneous realization of ideational, interpersonal and textual meanings. But these components are not put together in discrete fashion such that we can point to one segment of the clause as expressing one type of meaning and another segment as expressing another. The choice of a word may express one type of meaning, its morphology another and its position in sequence another; and any element is likely to have more than one structural role, like a chord in a polyphonic structure which participates simultaneously in a number of melodic lines.[3]

c   Given that an "element is likely to have more than one structural role," we may speak of the multifunctionality of the element: a grammatical form has many meanings at one and the same time.[4] Of all the word classes the verb is the most multifunctional and thus the one most likely to determine a variety of macro-functions.[5]

d   Consider the form וַיַּכּוּהָ, which would conventionally be glossed 'And they (the members of the tribe of Judah) smote it (the city of Jerusalem)' (Judg 1:8). The verb expresses:

1. the action of smiting (root *nky*)
2. the subject, here the actor (3 m.pl.)
3. the object, here the patient (3 f.s.)
4. voice (the subject is an actor and so the voice is active, not passive; the subject and object are different and so the voice is active, not reflexive; etc.)
5. case frame (the verb is transitive, not intransitive; it is singly transitive, i.e., has one object, rather than doubly transitive; etc.)
6. type of action (the verb is *Hiphil*, though the relevance of the stem is not obvious in this case; cf. English simple action, 'He raged against his audience,' *versus* causative action, 'He enraged his audience')
7. time of action relative to time of speaking (the smiting precedes the reference to it; contrast יַכֶּכָּה 'he smites/will smite you,' in which the time of action does not precede the speaking)
8. the quality of action (the action, though cumulatively made up of smaller actions, has an endpoint, though not necessarily an endproduct)
9. mood or modality (the action is independent; though consequent on another predicate, the verb is not subordinate to it; further, the verb makes an assertion rather than, say, a request)

e   These notions and various others are all bound up in וַיַּכּוּהָ. This form involves both a conjunction and a verb form; some of the features of the predicate arise from the combination of the two and are thus syntactic in character. Others involve the suffix *-hā*.

---

3. Halliday, *Functions of Language*, 42.
4. Multifunctionality should be distinguished from *polysemy*, which designates the capacity of a lexeme or morpheme to have various distinct meanings, only one of which is used in an utterance (unless a pun is intended).

Multifunctionality is a grammatical matter, polysemy a lexical one. See also 3.2.3.
5. This is true of virtually all languages with a distinct class of verbs and of Hebrew and its sibling Semitic languages in particular.

In the form *yakkû* (and in all finite verbs), we have four bound morphemes.   f

1. the verbal root, signifying the state or action being represented, here *nky*
2. the pronominal affix(es), signifying the person, gender, and number of the subject of the action, here *ya-û*
3. the prefix and/or lengthening of the root's medial consonant, signifying voice and causitivity, that is, the markers of the "verbal stem," here the *Hiphil*
4. the vocalic infix signifying tense/aspect and mood/modality, that is, the "verbal conjugation," here the prefixing form (as used after *waw*)

In fact, the conjunctive morpheme *waw* prefixed to a verbal form may show the   g
relationship of the situation represented by the verbal form to other situations. It therefore plays a special role in verbal morphology. Although these four morphemes are in some sense discrete elements in the verbal form, they are bound together so that the shape of each depends on the shape of the others. The infix pattern of the verbal conjugation is affected by the presence of the affixes pertaining to the verbal stems, etc. These four morphemes are found in finite verbs. When the verbal root is stripped of the pronominal affixes indicating the person, gender, and number of the subject and the concomitant infix patterns of the verbal conjugations signifying tense/aspect and mood/modality, the resulting form is no longer a true verb but a hybrid. With no additional prefix or suffix it is a verbal noun, that is, an infinitive; Hebrew has two contrasting patterns, the so-called "infinitive construct" and "infinitive absolute."[6] Another stripped-down form may add suffixes of the sort used with adjectives along with other affixes, in which case it is a verbal adjective, that is, a participle.

The difficult task in describing the Hebrew verbal system involves mapping. How do   h
phenomena like the nine noted above map onto the elements of the verb? In some cases, we know things about the working of a verb form from its syntax, namely, the conjunctions preceding, the order of words in a clause, the verb form in the preceding (and to a lesser extent following) clauses, etc. In other cases, we know things from the lexicon, that is, the way a given root is regularly and distinctively used. It is a third group of cases that concerns us here: what does the derivational morphology actually tell us? This is not a matter of translational equivalence, but a prior matter of linguistic study. It is only after we understand how the Hebrew verbal system works that we can properly debate how to express that information in a fluent translation, using the verbal categories of a target language. In all this a real-world appreciation of how predicates work is useful, but appeals to common sense must not be allowed to replace careful study. Common sense has often been used to beat the Hebrew verbal system into a system like those of English, German, or Classical Greek.

---

6. This terminology is well established, but it is somewhat misleading in the implicit comparison to European languages. In fact, Modern Hebrew uses as a citation form an infinitive type drawn from the languages of Europe, incorporating a prepositional infinitive marker, e.g., *liktob* 'to write.'

20.2   Categories Relevant to Predication

a   Before we consider how the Hebrew verbal system works, we would do well to pause and consider some of the categories which are reflected in predicates in various languages. Our purpose is not to survey linguistic systems, but to have a glance at systems that have features which are relevant to Hebrew or which are not relevant but might seem to be.[7] This survey is somewhat arbitrary, just as the above list of nine connotations of ויכוה was arbitrary to some extent.

b   A number of relevant categories require little attention. The features of *person*, *number*, and *gender* are associated with the subject of the verb, be it an incorporated pronominal element (וַיֹּאמֶר 'and *he* said') or an expressed subject (ויאמר גִּדְעוֹן 'and *Gideon* said'). If there is an object, the same features are relevant for it. These three features have certain distinctive aspects in Hebrew (cf. Chaps. 6, 7), but they present no major obstacles or keys to understanding the verb.

c   Categories demanding attention are *tense, modality, voice,* and the two types of *aspect*. The English word "aspect" refers to two entirely separate sets of grammatical categories, aspect as the contour of action (perfective, progressive, etc.; German *Aspekt*) and aspect as the type of action (causative, stative, etc.; German *Aktionsart*, literally 'type of action'). For example, in the predication 'He sang' the *Aspekt* is preterite (complete, past, definite) and the *Aktionsart* of the verb 'sing' is strongly iterative. Many languages of the world have complex systems for representing one or the other of these categories;[8] the Semitic languages have well developed expressions of *both* systems, in that they formally distinguish *Aspekt* through the conjugations and *Aktionsart* by the stems. Thus the English reader must always be wary of the naked term "aspect" in connection with Semitic studies; further, many authors are idiosyncratic in their use of the terms (and, unavoidably, so are we). In this chapter we resort to the expedient of using the German terms wherever confusion might arise.

d   *Tense* refers to the category of morphological phenomena that locate a situation[9] in the course of time. Tenses always refer to both the time of the action and the time of the utterance: 'He ran' uses a past-tense verb to refer to an action before the time of speaking. Tenses may also refer to the time of another action: 'Having run, he rested'

7. Relevant surveys include John Lyons, *Introduction to Theoretical Linguistics* (Cambridge: Cambridge University, 1968); Bernard Comrie, *Aspect: An Introduction to the Study of Verbal Aspect and Related Problems* (Cambridge: Cambridge University, 1976); Comrie, *Tense* (Cambridge: Cambridge University, 1985). See also Richter, *GAHG* 1. 139–48; R. Bartelmus, *HYH: Bedeutung und Funktion eines hebräischen "Allerweltswortes"* (St. Ottilien: EOS, 1982), and D. Pardee's review, *Catholic Biblical Quarterly* 47 (1985) 107–10; S. Segert, "Verbal Categories of Some Northwest Semitic Languages," *Afroasiatic Linguistics* 2 (1975) 83–94; H. Rosén, "On the Uses of the Tenses in the Aramaic of Daniel," in his *East and West: Selected Writings in Linguistics. 2. Hebrew and Semitic Linguistics* (Munich: Fink, 1984) 286–305.

8. Comrie's book *Aspect* deals exclusively with *Aspekt*. Both *Aspekt* and *Aktionsart* are treated in Ernest N. McCarus, "A Semantic Analysis of Arabic Verbs," *Michigan Oriental Studies in Honor of George G. Cameron*, ed. L. L. Orlin et al. (Ann Arbor: Department of Near Eastern Studies, University of Michigan, 1976) 3–28.

9. A situation may be (1) a state, (2) an event (which is both dynamic and seen as a whole), or (3) a process (which is both dynamic and seen as ongoing). If states are divided into two types, one refers to long-term or permanent qualities and the other to short-term or transitory qualities; the differentiation of these types of statives (see 22.3–4) is extremely vestigial in Hebrew.

uses two past-tense verbs to refer to situations prior to the utterance, and one of them ('having run') is anterior in time to the other. Tenses may be simple, using one form ('runs, ran'), or periphrastic, using two verbs, one an auxiliary ('will run').

Biblical Hebrew has no tenses in the strict sense; it uses a variety of other means to express time relations. This is not a rare situation. "Many languages lack tenses, i.e. do not have grammaticalised time reference, though probably all languages can lexicalise time reference, i.e. have temporal adverbials that locate situations in time."[10] Hebrew uses adverbials to some extent, but much more important are various syntactic means. Because these means are so well known and because the pressure of real-world understanding is so great, we are tempted to say that, for example, *wayyíqtol* is a past tense. As we shall see, the grammar is more complex.[11]

Modality refers to the category of morphological phenomena that locate a situation in the discourse; informally, we can say that they reflect the mood of the speaker. Some modal categories are directly involved in Hebrew morphology: a clause in the imperative mood may take an imperative verb; a cohortative clause may have a cohortative verb. Some categories that are modal in many languages have no morphological trace in Hebrew; interrogative clauses, for example, are only formed with syntactic or lexical devices in Hebrew (18.1; cf. 40.3). The mood of most Hebrew verbs is indicative (or declarative); the jussive may be distinct. There are traces of two other moods. It appears that stages immediately prior to Hebrew had a subjunctive; this mood is of great historical importance in explaining the extant verb system of Biblical Hebrew. Further, there are a variety of forms with *nun* either between the stem and suffix (the energic forms) or after the stem (the forms with paragogic *nun*); these forms, too, reflect an earlier stage of the language. As in other languages the subjunctive, energic, and paragogic forms are used in syntactically complex constructions, though the contrast with declarative verbs is now often obscure.

Aspect (*Aspekt*) refers to the category of morphological phenomena that describe the contour of a situation in time. In English there are two sets of aspectual markers, both fused to some extent with tense markers. The progressive aspect indicates that a situation is ongoing, and there are present progressive forms ('I am running'), past progressives ('I was running'), future progressives ('I will be running'), etc. The perfective aspect indicates that a situation is complete, whether in present time ('I love') or in past time ('I loved'). Perfective aspect needs to be distinguished from the English perfect tense, which combines perfective aspect and anterior time reference, again, whether in present time (present perfect 'I have run') or in past time (past perfect 'I had run'). As in English, tense and aspect systems are fused in the Romance languages (French, Spanish, etc.), but in many languages aspect is an independent category. The Slavic languages (e.g., Russian) use full imperfective and perfective verbal structures; the perfective is a marked structure (i.e., use of these forms asserts that a situation is complete or finished),

---

10. Comrie, *Aspect*, 6.

11. Mishnaic and Modern Hebrew are much closer to being strictly tensed languages, as a result of a reanalysis of the conjugations and a shift in use of the participle. See M. H. Segal, *A Grammar of Mishnaic Hebrew* (Oxford: Clarendon, 1927) 150–65.

while the imperfective is unmarked (i.e., use of these forms asserts nothing about the completeness).[12] Classical Greek uses a three-way aspectual system: the perfect asserts that the situation is complete as against the imperfect and aorist forms, while the imperfect asserts that the situation is not complete and the process is ongoing as against the aorist.[13]

h   Hebrew aspectual marking is similar to the Slavic imperfective/perfective system, but its operation is simpler because there is no system of forms marked for tense under the two aspectual rubrics. The deictic time reference of Hebrew verb forms is determined largely by syntax, though it is time reference that dictates whether the non-perfective conjugation signifies imperfective aspect (as with past or present time) or not (as with future time).

i   Other phenomena related to aspect (*Aspekt*) are of less importance than the progressive and perfective phenomena. They include iterativity or frequentativity (marking a verb as designating a repeated action) and the closely related category of habituality (marking a verb as designating a habitual action); cf. English 'I *used to* run.' These aspectual categories are in Hebrew closely tied to non-perfective expressions. Other aspectual categories refer to punctuality (or momentariness) and inception (or ingression or inchoation), that is, to verbs describing the entirety of a brief event and those describing the beginning of a situation ('I *began* to run'). These categories are relevant to some minor operations of the stem system.

j   *Aspect* (*Aktionsart*) refers to the category of morphological phenomena that describe the kind of situation a verb refers to. A well-known group of aspectual phenomena are the *voices* of the European languages. English recognizes two voices, active ('I ran') and passive ('I was beaten'). With an active verb the subject is an agent or actor, while with a passive verb the subject is a patient (one who undergoes or suffers the action). Other languages, for example, Classical Greek, recognize a third voice, called middle; the subject of a middle verb acts on itself or acts in a way concerning itself. (The reflexives of English and other European languages are analogous.) The *voices* may serve to sort out various grammatical features of Hebrew, as we shall see in the next chapter.

k   Another group of aspect (*Aktionsart*) phenomena involve *fientivity* and *transitivity*. The first of these terms refers to the type of movement or activity inherent in the verb.[14] A verb may be stative (describe a state) or fientive (describe an activity). This differentiation is related to the age-old question of how closely adjectives are related to verbs.[15] In

---

12. "In discussing aspect it is important to grasp that the difference between perfectivity and imperfectivity is not necessarily an objective difference between situations"; Comrie, *Aspect*, 4.

13. The aorist is the verb form which is without a boundary (*a-horos*). The gnomic aorist is the use that corresponds most closely to the English generic present; both designate general rules or invariant patterns, often in proverbs (*gnōmai*).

14. Benno Landsberger coined the term *fientive* from the Latin *fiens* 'becoming.' Peter T. Daniels notes, "It

came to be used, if at all, to designate both verbs that are non-stative in inherent meaning, and inflections of a verb that are not permansive (stative) in form"; see his notes to G. Bergsträsser, *Introduction to the Semitic Languages*, trans. and sup. P. T. Daniels (Winona Lake, Indiana: Eisenbrauns, 1983) 10. We use the term in the first of these senses.

15. The earlier Greek philosophers tended to associate verbs and adjectives, as modern linguists incline to; Hellenistic grammarians tied adjectives to nouns; see the references in 4.2.2. From another perspective, verbal clauses

languages with a progressive aspect, fientive verbs may be progressive (cf. 'He was learn-ing Hebrew'), while statives cannot (cf. the unacceptability of **'He was knowing He-brew'). Fientive verbs are sometimes called dynamic verbs, which is an acceptable term, or active verbs, which should not be used, for it is liable to confusion with the sense of active that refers to the subject's role.[16]

Transitivity refers to the contour of movement or activity inherent in the verb. An | intransitive verb is one which customarily takes no object; all pure statives (cf. 30.5.3) and many fientives (cf. 'I ran') are intransitive. A transitive verb is one which takes object(s); a singly transitive verb takes one object (cf. 'Saul struck David'), while a doubly transitive verb takes two objects (cf. 'David gave Saul his armor'). Another way to describe these three groups is based on counting the number of nouns directly tied to the verb. Thus, an intransitive verb is a "one-place" verb (subject only); a singly transitive verb is a "two-place" verb (subject, object); a doubly transitive verb is a "three-place" verb (subject, object$_1$, object$_2$).

There are two major types of *causation constructions*. These may be conceived of as m passive and active counterparts. In sentences like 'She makes me tired' and 'She makes me learned,' *me*, as the object of the causation, is caused to be in an *effected* state; such a construction is called *factitive* (with adjectival stative verbs) or *resultative* (with fientive verbs). In contrast take these sentences: 'She tires me' and 'She makes me learn.' Here the object *me* is seen as active, and such a construction is called *causative*. The semantic con-trast of these English examples is weak, precisely because the contrast is not especially important in English. Let us restate the difference from a morphological point of view. If a transitive verb, in which the object participates in the action, is formed from an intransi-tive fientive verb by the addition of a morphological element, the verb is called a *causative*. Most causation is expressed in English by distinct words or by various syn-tactic constructions (e.g., 'He *made* me run,' 'She *caused* me to go,' 'They *had* me write'). If a transitive verb is from an adjectival stative verb (e.g., כבד 'to be heavy') by the addition of a morphological element, the verb is called a *factitive*. English *en* is factitive as a suffix ('whiten, quicken, sadden, gladden') and causative as a prefix ('enable, enrich, enclose'; 'enlighten' is doubly marked). Closely related to factitive verbs is a class involv-ing not a stative verb but an adjective proper; this class is variously *declarative* (cf. 'He declared me just'), *estimative* (cf. 'He thought it silly'), or *putative* (cf. 'He belittled the venture'). The relationship of causation constructions and voice is dealt with in 21.2.2.

Another set of aspectual determinants involves *double-status actions*. *Reflexive* con- n structions, as noted, involve the subject (singular or plural) acting on itself. *Reciprocal* constructions (plural) involve a variety of individual subjects performing actions on each

---

can be seen as ultimately derived from nominal clauses and thus "verbs" can be taken as reinterpreted nouns; see C. T. Hodge, "The Nominal Sentence in Semitic," *Afro-asiatic Linguistics* 2 (1975) 69–75. It can also be argued that there is no unitary class of verbs, i.e., that finite verbs do not belong to the same word class as infinitives, and so on; see W. P. Schmid, *MPD* 90–97.

16. Compare S. Segert's remark: "The usual terms, 'active' and 'stative,' express the character of Semitic verbs better than 'transitive' and 'intransitive.' A slight inconve-nience arises from the fact that the word 'active' is also used for the active voice, but it does not seem necessary to introduce any new term, such as 'verb of action,' 'progres-sive' or 'non-progressive'"; "Verbal Categories," 86.

other. *Tolerative* constructions (usually singular) involve an agent (usually human) allowing itself to undergo an action (cf. 'He let himself be chosen').

o   The parameters treated under the heading of aspect (*Aktionsart*) can be summarized in this list.

> 1. *voice:* active passive middle   (20.2j)
> 2. *type of movement/activity:* fientive stative   (20.2k)
> 3. *contour of movement/activity:* transitive intransitive   (20.2l)
> 4. *causation:* causative resultative/factitive declarative   (20.2m)
> 5. *double-status action:* reflexive reciprocal tolerative   (20.2n)

We have not commented on the relevance to Hebrew of these sets of terms; each plays an important part in the stem system.

20.3   The Hebrew Verbal System

a   The verbal system of Hebrew is a system of derivational morphology that realizes many of the categories we have just surveyed. In the following chapters we set forth the grammatical subsystems of morphemes essential to the true verb. We arrange our material in order of rank, considering the more inclusive morpheme as having the higher rank. On this basis we begin with the verbal stems, because no stem subsumes another but each one subsumes the verbal conjugations. We do not handle the pronominal affixes again, because for our purposes the grammatical subsystems to which they belong have been sufficiently set forth in the preceding chapters. Further, we do not deal with the differences between strong (triradical) verbs and weak verbs, except where a phenomenon historically obscured in the strong verbs is still apparent in the weak verbs.[17] After analyzing the subsystems pertaining to the essential morphemes of the true verb, we address ourselves to its conjunctive prefixes and the special role of *waw* and stress in syntax. We treat the verbal hybrids last. The dense interactions of morphology both with individual roots and with basic syntactic phenomena concern us throughout. Despite the ties of verbal morphology to other parts of grammar, however, the morphology is in itself systematic, and, as with any linguistic system, the meaning of one element is relative to those of others.

---

17. There are several systems of terms for the weak verbs, more or less traditional. In one system a roman numeral is used to indicate the position in the root of the "weakness": I-*nun* (or Prima-*nun*) verbs are those with the first radical *nun*, II-weak or II-*w/y* those with medial *w* or *y* (also called Hollow), III-ʾ those with a final radical ʾaleph, and so on; in this system geminates are called II/III or II=III. In another system, the template verb *pʿl* 'to make' is used, and so we have Pe-*nun*, Ayin-*waw/yod*, Lamed-*aleph*, Ayin-Ayin (for geminates), and so on. For good surveys of weak-verb morphology, see A. Ungnad, *Hebräische Grammatik* (Tübingen: J. C. B. Mohr, 1912) 130–85; and H. S. Nyberg, *Hebreisk Grammatik* (Uppsala: Geber, 1952) 64–65, 91–147.

21

The System of Verbal Stems

Terminology

The central phenomenon of Hebrew verbal derivational morphology is the modification of the root[1] or consonantal skeleton by various vocalic and consonantal affixes. The latter include prefixed *n* and *h*, infixed *t*, and lengthening or doubling of the middle radical of the root. Grammarians label these patterns of affixation in various ways; the major patterns themselves are called *Qal, Niphal, Piel, Pual, Hithpael, Hiphil*, and *Hophal*. The early Hebrew grammarians called these verbal patterns בנינים *binyanim* 'formatives' (lit., 'buildings'), and in the earliest grammars presented with Hebrew and Latin *en face* the Latin term *conjugatio* appears opposite Hebrew *binyan*. The term "conjugation" for these patterns is still used.[2] However, misgivings have long been expressed about this term because it means something different in Latin-influenced grammars than "formative." Some modern scholars protest against this usage for the further reason that they wish to reserve "conjugation" for the suffixed and prefixed verbal forms.[3] A large number of comparative/historical grammars group together the stems other than the *Qal* as "derived stems" (cf. the Hebrew term *Kabed* 'heavy');[4] the term

1. In calling the consonantal skeleton of the verbs a root, we follow the practice of the early Jewish grammarians, who used the term *šōreš*. Many moderns prefer the term "stem" (e.g., GKC § 31 / p. 103).

2. E.g., GKC §§ 39–39 / pp. 114–16; Joüon §§ 51–59 / pp. 113–28; T. O. Lambdin, *Introduction to Biblical Hebrew* (New York: Scribner, 1971) 175.

3. E.g., Frithiof Rundgren, "Das Verbalpräfix *yu-* im Semitischen und die Entstehung der faktitiv-kausativen Bedeutung des D-Stammes," *Orientalia Suecana* 12 (1964) 99–114, at 104; cf. M. H. Goshen-Gottstein, "The System of Verbal Stems in the Classical Semitic Languages," *Proceedings of the International Conference on Semitic*

Studies Held in Jerusalem, 19–23 July 1965 (Jerusalem: Israel Academy of Sciences and Humanities, 1969) 70–91, at 70 n. 1.

4. E.g., BL § 38 / pp. 279–94; *UT* § 9.32; Carl Brockelmann, *Grundriss der vergleichenden Grammatik der semitischen Sprachen* (Berlin: Reuter und Reichard, 1908), 1. 504–44; S. Moscati et al., *An Introduction to the Comparative Grammar of the Semitic Languages* (Wiesbaden: Harrassowitz, 1964) 122–31; I. M. Diakonoff, *Semito-Hamitic Languages: An Essay in Classification* (Moscow: Nauka, 1965) 97. It is correct to see a split between the *Qal* and the other stems, but there can be no doubt that all the stems are of the same order of phenomenon.

may be misleading if it is allowed to obscure the relationship of the *Qal* to the system as a whole. Other scholars call the *binyanim* "verbal patterns," "modifications," "themes," or "stirpes" (Latin *stirps* 'stalk, stock'). We use the now common term "verbal stems," though even it, too, has the potential to be misleading.[5]

b   The traditional names for the verbal stems themselves derive from the oldest Jewish grammarians. They called the first stem *Qal* 'light' because it is unaugmented in comparison with the other stems. They named the remaining verbal stems after the verbal stem's third masculine singular form in the suffix conjugation, with the root פעל, their paradigmatic verb; thus the terms נִפְעַל *Niphal*, פִּעֵל *Piel*, etc.[6] Later grammarians have retained these terms, though they rarely use פעל as the paradigm verb because of its middle guttural, preferring instead קטל 'to kill' or כתב 'to write.'[7]

c   After the advent of the comparative/historical method, scholars sought general names for the cognate verbal stems corresponding to one another in both form and function across the Semitic languages; these would ignore individual idiosyncrasies within each language. The unaugmented stem corresponding to Hebrew *Qal* they called "G stem" (from German "*Grundstamm*") or "B stem" ("Base-stem") because it appears to be the verbal stem on which the others were built. The *Niphal* is called the "N stem" because of its characteristic *n* prefix in the cognate languages; the *Piel* is dubbed "D stem" from its characteristic doubling; etc. Most of the Semitic languages add a *-t-* to one or more of these verbal stems, which leads to the labels "Gt stem," "Dt stem," etc. Unfortunately, the cognates of Hebrew *Hiphil* vary tremendously (*š* [Akkadian], *h* [Hebrew], *ʾ* [Syriac, Arabic], etc.),[8] and no term is universally accepted.[9]

21.2   The System

21.2.1   The Problem

a   Three unfortunate problems have marred discussions of the stem system. First, scholars have tended to describe the system as based formally on the *Qal* stem. Second,

---

5. On the use of "stem" in other contexts, see, e.g., GKC § 30d / p. 100.

6. The paradigm verb *fʿl* was first used by the Arab grammarians.

7. For general Semitic studies the choice of a paradigm verb is problematic. The root *qtl* is not a possible root of Akkadian, so its use has been found objectionable. The root *ktb* shows Hebrew and Syriac spirantization, but it is not found in Akkadian. P. T. Daniels, in preparing the paradigms for G. Bergsträsser, *Introduction to the Semitic Languages* (Winona Lake, Indiana: Eisenbrauns, 1983), used the "non-existent root *pdk* . . . in order to maximize comparability among the paradigms without prejudicing the data in the direction of any one language, and so that spirantization of stops may be fully displayed in Hebrew and Syriac" (p. 225). Rainer M. Voigt objects because the root *pdk* is not attested and is probably not a possible Semitic root; see his "Review of Bergsträsser-Daniels," *Welt des Orients* 14 (1983) 262–67, at 262.

8. See Voigt, "Review of Bergsträsser-Daniels," 263. It has been proposed that the earliest stages of Semitic had a sibilant-initial causative in *š* (a *Šaphel*) and a laryngeal-initial causative in *h* (*Hiphil*, etc.; later in *ʾ* or *y*, thus Aramaic *Aphel*, Phoenician *Yiphil*). See C. Rabin, "The Origins of the Subdivisions of Semitic," *Hebrew and Semitic Studies Presented to Godfrey Rolles Driver*, ed. D. W. Thomas and W. D. McHardy (Oxford: Clarendon, 1963) 103–15. This problem is related to that of the third-person singular pronouns (cf. Akkadian *šū, šī*, Hebrew *hûʾ, hîʾ*). On Hebrew *Yiphils* and *Šaphels*, see nn. 27 and 34.

9. The Arabic system of numerals is useful. The stems (Arabists prefer the term "forms") with Hebrew correspondents are:

Qal (G or B)	I
Piel / *Pual* (D)	II
Hiphil / *Hophal* (H)	IV
Hithpael (tD)	V
Niphal (N)	VII

they have described the stems notionally in an atomistic way, that is, assigning a meaning or set of meanings to each stem independently. Third, they have neglected the very systemic character of the system. M. H. Goshen-Gottstein's complaint about Sabatino Moscati's *Introduction to the Comparative Grammar of the Semitic Languages* is true of many other Semitistic works: "This description steers clear (consciously?) of any systematic presentation and presents the facts atomistically. In this it follows to some extent C. Brockelmann, *Grundriss der vergleichenden Grammatik der semitischen Sprachen.*"[10] Now obviously the scientific method requires the analysis and systematic classification of the uses of the individual verbal stems, but the atomistic approach often fails to take adequate note of the fact that the verbal stems constitute a system, a system of clearly differentiated morphemes, which, by definition, involves both form and function.[11]

Recently Goshen-Gottstein attempted to correct the atomistic approach to the Semitic verbal stems by constructing a diagram of the verbal stem system that would throw into relief the known facts about these verbal stems.[12] His diagram concerns itself with forms rather than meanings. If, however, the individual verbal stems serve particular functions, and if they together constitute a system, then we may with good reason attempt to study the function of the system as a whole. In fact, such an abstraction can be of help in understanding the functions or meanings of the individual parts and of their relationships to one another.

All grammarians agree that the verbal stems in part denote voice, the relationship of the subject to the situation, discussed in 20.2j. The passive character of several of the stems was recognized in the *Maʿaseh Ephod* of Profiat Duran (ca. 1400 C.E.); in the treatment of the *binyanim* of the verb, the *Pual* and *Hophal* are called the stems whose agents are not mentioned.[13] Moshe Greenberg offers a model of the verbal stems, based on a "grid" or system of coordinates ("axes"), with one of the coordinates pertaining to voice.[14]

10. Goshen-Gottstein, "System of Verbal Stems," 72 n. 8, cf. 79; he cites the Brockelmann passage referred to above in n. 4.

11. It should be noted that an atomistic approach is not particularly successful at dealing with the semantic anomalies and subpatterns that affect any study of the Hebrew verb. Some usages are unpredictable and thus a matter of the lexicon. A half-hearted or timid grammar is no better a complement to the lexicon than a serious one. For other approaches to the topic of the system, see Richter, *GAHG* 3. 94–142; S. Segert, "Verbal Categories of Some Northwest Semitic Languages," *Afroasiatic Linguistics* 2 (1975) 83–94. The system of verbal stems in Modern Hebrew, though vastly restricted, reveals some interesting patterns; see the studies of R. A. Berman, "Lexical Decomposition and Lexical Unity in the Expression of Derived Verbal Categories in Modern Hebrew," *Afroasiatic Linguistics* 6 (1979) 117–42; and S. Bolozky, "Semantic Productivity and Word Frequency in Modern Hebrew Verb Formation," *Hebrew Studies* 27 (1986) 38–46.

12. Goshen-Gottstein, "System of Verbal Stems," 83–91. Note also Diakonoff's comment that these morphologically distinct stems have their "own semantics, variously characterizing the action or state from the point of view of quality, quantity, or direction"; *Semito-Hamitic Languages*, 97.

13. David Tene, "Linguistic Literature, Hebrew," *Encyclopedia Judaica* (Jerusalem: Keter, 1971), 16. 1374.

14. After Moshe Greenberg, *Introduction to Hebrew* (Englewood Cliffs, New Jersey: Prentice-Hall, 1965) 42; cf. August Dillmann, *Grammatik der äthiopischen Sprache* (Leipzig: Tauchitz, 1857; 2d ed. in 1899). For similar schemata for the other Semitic languages, see Goshen-Gottstein, "System of Verbal Stems," esp. 74–75; Bergsträsser/Daniels, *Introduction to the Semitic Languages*; and Voigt, "Review of Bergsträsser-Daniels."

	I	II	III
Active	שָׁמַר	סִפֵּר	הִזְכִּיר
Passive	נִשְׁמַר	סֻפַּר	הָזְכַּר
Reflexive (Double-status)[15]	נִשְׁמַר	הִתְאַפֵּק	—

Greenberg's diagram helps to present the functions of the verbal system, but it also serves to highlight the difficulties of abstracting the features of the system. The vertical set of coordinates pertains to voice, but what about the horizontal axis? This axis is usually described in terms of the verbal action itself, that is, I = "simple," II = so-called "intensive," III = "causative." The second column, the "intensive" is, however, a problematic entry; the common morphological basis of *Piel*, *Pual*, and *Hithpael* is clear, but the semantic basis is much less certain. A reconsideration of these stems is crucial to understanding the relationship between the two axes and thus the system as a whole.

21.2.2   Toward a Solution

a   There are various approaches to elucidating the stem system; more traditional grammarians stress the *Qal : Piel* relation as key, while recently the *Piel : Hiphil* relation has been emphasized. The *Piel* is the key to the system,[16] and the first major step toward unlocking the system was taken by Albrecht Goetze in his survey of the Akkadian D stem; his work has been extended to West Semitic by Ernst Jenni and others.[17] To some extent, scholars prior to Goetze and Jenni failed to perceive the function of the Hebrew verbal stem system because they thought that the *Piel* signified primarily intensive action. Jenni's study of the Hebrew *Piel* demonstrates that it fundamentally entails a notion related to the basic active : passive dichotomy of voice. This new insight offers an opportunity to see the system in its entirety, though we believe Jenni fails to catch the full significance of his thesis because he excludes the notion of causation from his understanding of the *Piel*.[18]

b   The horizontal axis in the Greenberg diagram pertains to causation. Let us reconsider the role relations of constructions involving causation. The English sentence 'John cooked the cabbage' may have only slight causation nuance ("In your mind's eye picture John as he cooked the cabbage"); with a stronger causation nuance, it may mean either 'John made the cabbage cooked,' in which case the cabbage is presented as being in the "passive" state of being cooked, or 'John caused the cabbage to cook,' with the more

---

15. Double-status situations include reflexive, reciprocal, and tolerative situations; see 20.2n.

16. "D is exceptional in its form/function problems"; M. H. Goshen-Gottstein, "Problems of Semitic Verbal Stems," *Bibliotheca Orientalis* 42 (1985) 278–83, at 283 n. 19.

17. A. Goetze, "The So-called Intensive of the Semitic Languages," *Journal of the American Oriental Society* 62 (1942) 1–8; Ernst Jenni, *Das hebräische Piᶜel* (Zürich: EVZ, 1968); Jenni, "Zur Funktion der reflexiv-passiven

Stammformen im Biblisch-Hebräischen," *Proceedings of the Fifth World Congress of Jewish Studies* (Jerusalem: World Union of Jewish Studies, 1973), 4. 61–70; Stuart A. Ryder II, *The D-Stem in Western Semitic* (The Hague: Mouton, 1974); F. Leemhuis, *The D and H Stems in Koranic Arabic* (Leiden: Brill, 1977).

18. For the purposes of this discussion, the term "causation (predicate)" refers to both causative and factitive/resultative aspects (*Aktionsarten*); see the preliminary exposition in 20.2m.

"active" sense that the cabbage is somehow participating in the action. Bound up with the notion of causation, there can be various degrees of agency ("activeness") or patiency ("passiveness").

Causation is expressed in many of the European languages by constructions with   c
two verbs. For example, German, French, and English use the auxiliary verbs 'lassen,' 'faire,' 'make/cause,' respectively. The English auxiliaries 'make' and 'cause' tend to introduce a suggestion of force or coercion, a notion not crucial to causation formations, and, along with that, the similarly foreign idea that some other agent besides the subject may be involved in the action. This is not generally so in German and French, which tend to use their broader causation constructions more extensively. An English verb which can be intrinsically causative, such as 'to cook,' avoids the extra baggage of the causation auxiliary construction. It thus comes closer to the morphological causation forms of Hebrew. Roughly stated, it is our proposal that the verb 'cooked' in the sentence 'John cooked the cabbage' in the sense 'John made the cabbage cooked' would be rendered in Hebrew by the *Piel*, and in the sense 'John caused the cabbage to cook' by the *Hiphil*. *Piel* tends to signify causation with a patiency nuance, and *Hiphil* causation notion with an agency nuance. The two types of causation forms differ from one another with reference to the status of the subject being acted upon by the main verb, that is, the voice associated with the undersubject or secondary subject.

$$
\begin{array}{ll}
\text{John} & \text{cause} \\
\text{subject}_1 & \text{verb}_1 \\
\end{array}
$$

$$
\begin{array}{ll}
\text{cabbage} & \text{cook} \\
\text{subject}_2 & \text{verb}_2 \\
\end{array}
$$

Roughly stated, the differences between *Qal, Niphal,* and *Hithpael,* etc. (the vertical differences in Greenberg's diagram) refer to the voice of subject$_1$, the primary subject; the differences between *Qal, Piel,* and *Hiphil,* etc., refer to the voice of subject$_2$, where there is one.[19] We use English sentences here to suggest the stems' differences in meaning; in the following chapters we illustrate them from Biblical Hebrew.

The example of English 'to cook' with its various senses is reminiscent of the   d
complexities of Hebrew verbs used in various stems. Another English verb with similar diversity is 'to fly,' which may be used transitively or intransitively, in similar but varying contexts; an examination may be of heuristic value. In the following admittedly rather far-fetched examples we have indicated in parentheses the Hebrew verbal stem that would have been used in each instance. In most instances the English verb remains unchanged even as the Hebrew stem varies. We have already indicated one reason for this; in the comments that follow the sentences we will give others.

1. Sarah flies (*Qal*) the airplane.
2. Sarah flies (*Qal*) tonight. / Sarah flies (*Qal*) off into the sky.
3. Sarah flies (*Niphal*) to Egypt, when Abraham offers to fly her there.

---

19. The examples here are fientives; we omit statives from this preliminary discussion.

4. Sarah is being flown (*Niphal*) to Egypt.
5. Sarah flies (*Niphal*) to Egypt, instead of taking her mule.
6. Sarah is flying (*Niphal*) to Egypt in order to appeal her case to the Pharaoh.
7. Sarah is flying (*Piel*) the airplane in spite of the dust storm.
8. Sarah is flown (*Pual*) to Egypt, when the Pharaoh snaps his fingers.
9. Sarah flies (*Hithpael*) to Egypt.
10. Sarah flies the airplane higher (*Hiphil*) / causes it to fly (*Hiphil*) higher.
11. Sarah flew (*Hiphil*) higher in the airplane.
12. Sarah is made to fly (*Hophal*) the airplane higher.

e   *Sentence 1* represents the active voice with a transitive verb. Sarah is the actor or agent, performing the action expressed by the verb. *Sentence 2* also represents the active voice. Like (1), it answers the question "What is Sarah doing?", but unlike (1) the verb here is intransitive. These sentences illustrate that transitive and intransitive actions are not necessarily related to the function of voice. The *Qal* expresses both (1) and (2).

f   In *sentence 3*, Sarah is no longer the agent performing the action. Instead of answering the question "What is Sarah doing?", the first clause implicitly answers the question "What is happening to Sarah?" Here Sarah is implicitly the object of the syntactic equivalent "Abraham flies Sarah." The intransitive verb in (3) has as its grammatical subject the noun that would be the object of the corresponding transitive verb.[20] In the *Niphal* construction the subject is not the performer of the action but only a participator in it. English, lacking a construction indicating the syntactic relationship between the goal-word of a transitive verb and the non-agent subject of an intransitive equivalent, does not formally distinguish between (1), if the object were omitted—as it can be—and (3). *Sentence 4* represents the simple passive voice. As in (3), Sarah is a non-agent, but unlike (3) she is viewed not as participating in the act but as in the *state* of "being acted upon" or "suffering the effects of the action." In this construction the agent may or may not be expressed. The *Niphal* is used in (3) and (4) because in both cases the subject is not the performer of the action but the undergoer of it, more (sentence 4) or less (sentence 3) explicitly.

g   In *sentences 5 and 6* a reflexive notion is implicit. The full senses are: (5) 'Sarah flies herself . . .' and (6) 'Sarah flies in her own interests. . . .'[21] Since the action affects the

---

20. In some languages of the world the subject of an intransitive verb and the object of a transitive verb take the same case, the "ergative"; the "absolutive" case is used for the subject of a transitive verb. Such languages are called ergative languages. See John Lyons, *Introduction to Theoretical Linguistics* (Cambridge: Cambridge University, 1968) 351–52, 354–57. In other languages, some ergative features are combined with standard Indo-European-type inflection (called, in this respect, an "accusative" system); languages which are so mixed (e.g., Hindi-Urdu) are called split-ergative languages. There were ergative languages in the ancient Near East (Hurrian and its close relative Urartian; perhaps Sumerian), and it is not surpris-ing to find some signs of split ergativity in the Semitic N stems, as we shall argue below. Ten years after our discussion was initially drafted, a parallel set of observations was made independently by Hans-Peter Müller, "Ergativ-elemente im akkadischen und althebräischen Verbalsystem," *Biblica* 66 (1985) 385–417. An earlier discussion of erga-tivity in Hebrew is provided by F. I. Andersen, "Passive and Ergative in Hebrew," *Near Eastern Studies in Honor of William Foxwell Albright*, ed. H. Goedicke (Baltimore: Johns Hopkins University, 1971) 1–15, who focuses chiefly on the anomalous verb *yld* 'to bear, beget.'

21. Actions on oneself and in one's interest are both in the middle voice in Classical Greek.

subject of the verb (sentence 5) or her interests (sentence 6), the *Niphal* would be used. In the English, the reflexive would often be redundant and is therefore left out.

In *sentence 7* we have an example of a causation construction with a passive nuance. As in the case of 'John cooked the cabbage,' the English speaker would probably say 'Sarah flies the airplane . . .' rather than the long-winded, and potentially misleading, circumlocution 'Sarah gets the airplane flown.' The meaning in (7) is quite different from the one intended in (1) though the expressions are formally identical. In (1) the event, the happening of Sarah flying the airplane, is intended; in (7) the achieved state of the airplane flying is meant, that is, the plane was placed in the passive state of being flown. The same nuance could have been expressed by 'Sarah makes her airplane flown,' except that statement would normally mean 'She causes someone else to fly the airplane.' Here 'cause' implies coercion and another agent. With some verbs the causation notion is more readily indicated in English. Such is the case with 'shine.' The equivalent to (1) with 'shine' would be 'Sarah shines the airplane' and to (7) 'Sarah makes the plane shined-up [= shiny]' or more simply 'Sarah shines up the airplane.' (The equivalent is not 'Sarah makes the airplane shine'; that notion belongs to sentence 10.)

Sentence 8 is the syntactic equivalent to 'Abraham gets Sarah flown to Egypt,' without the agent necessarily in view; in very awkward English it means 'Sarah is made flown.' The English speaker uses in (8) a construction similar to that in (4) and allows the context to differentiate between 'Sarah is flown' as an accomplished state and 'Sarah is being flown' as a happening.

In *sentence 9* Sarah makes herself flown to Egypt, perhaps in her own interests. (Here, too, the use of 'makes' would run the risk of introducing the notion of coercion.) The sense can scarcely be represented in English. The reflexive sense in (5) or (6) involves a happening, but in (9) it denotes an achieved state. As (5) and (6) are the reflexive counterparts of (1), so (9) is the reflexive counterpart of (7).

In *sentence 10* Sarah causes the airplane to participate in the act of flying. Here the object of the "causing" is the subject of the flying, as in (7), but unlike (7) the second subject has a more agential role. This notion of causing a (grammatical) object to participate as a subject in the action is represented by the *Hiphil*.

In *sentence 11* both causative and reflexive notions are implicit. The full sense is 'Sarah caused herself to fly higher in the airplane.' Such an "internal" *Hiphil* would be distinguished from other *Hiphils* by being a one-place predicate.

In *sentence 12* we have the passive counterpart of (10). One syntactical equivalent might be 'The highjackers made Sarah fly the plane higher.' In contrast to (8), where 'Sarah' undergoes both the "causing" and the verbal idea, here she is both passive and active—passive with reference to the "causing" ('is made') and active with reference to the verb ('she flies the plane higher'). *Hophal* conveys this passive counterpart to *Hiphil*.

We can now return to the chart presented earlier and define both axes with reference to voice. The vertical axis represents the voice of the primary subject, the horizontal axis represents the voice of the secondary subject, the object of the "causing" predicate, if there is one. On the horizontal axis I represents the absence of a causation notion;

II, causation with a passive state ('made flown'); III, causation with active participation ('made to fly'). The numbers in parentheses indicate the sentence that illustrates the basic relations.

		VOICE OF UNDERSUBJECT		
		I. ∅	II. *Passive*	III. *Active*
VOICE OF PRIMARY SUBJECT	I. *Active*	Qal (1–2)	Piel (7)	Hiphil (10)
	II. *Middle/Passive* (Subject < object of transitive verb)	Niphal (3–4)	Pual (8)	Hophal (12)
	III. *Reflexive* (Double-status)	Niphal (5–6)	Hithpael (9)	Hiphil ("internal," 11)

o   Thus the Hebrew stem system functions to connote *Aktionsarten* (voice, causation, transitivity; 20.2). The various interrelated inflections serve to represent varying categories of relationships between the subject and the predicate(s). The system is far more complex than the one familiar to us in English. In Hebrew, unlike English, the inflected forms of the verb indicate whether a non-agential subject of an intransitive verb would be the object in an equivalent clause with a transitive verb; and whether causation, with either a passive or active role for the secondary subject, is meant.

p   The English verb system does not differentiate between underlying transitivity and intransitivity, so that (1) and (3) may assume the same verbal shape. Moreover, English tends to elide the reflexive when the subject acts in its own interest or for its own benefit, and so (5) and (6) along with (9) and (10) take on the same shape as (1) and (3). Also, the English auxiliaries 'make, cause,' etc., with many verbs make the claim that the subject is coercing someone else to perform the action, with the result that the corresponding non-coercive sentences (7) and (8)—we have already mentioned (9) and (11)—fall together with (1), (3), (5), (6). In sum, six or seven of the twelve sentences have similar English shapes though they mean different things. Further, while (10) brings out the causative force without ambiguity, it, too, can be expressed by 'Sarah flies. . . .' For the most part the English speaker depends on the context in recognizing notions of agency, causativity, and reflexivity. Without context 'Sarah flies . . .' is a very ambiguous statement in English; the same applies to 'Sarah is flown.'

q   One can sympathize with scholars who have expressed doubts about the view that each stem indicates a difference in meaning. Alexander Sperber claimed, "I am going to disprove this notion by demonstrating that the so-called verbal stems were interchangeably used in order to indicate one and the same meaning, without implying the slightest differentiation."[22] His lists of forms from different stems used in similar contexts are of great interest, but ultimately his evidence carries no conviction because he fails to take

---

22. Alexander Sperber, *A Historical Grammar of Biblical Hebrew* (Leiden: Brill, 1966) 6, cf. 5–14, drawing on his "Hebrew Grammar: A New Approach," *Journal of Biblical Literature* 62 (1943) 137–262.

note of the verb's full context in each passage. His argument amounts to little more than holding up sentences 1, 5, etc. and proclaiming: "See, there's no difference in meaning between the Hebrew verbal stems. They all mean 'Sarah flies' and can be used interchangeably."

Because English and other European-language verbal systems are impoverished in   r morphological treatments of transitivity, causativity, and reflexivity, most modern Hebrew lexicons also fail to show adequately the subtle differences in meaning among the verbal stems. The lexicographers are often forced to assign similar "meanings" of a verb to the different verbal stems. For example, William L. Holladay, in his fine lexicon, presents נקם as follows.[23]

> Qal: take revenge
> Niphal: be avenged, take revenge, avenge oneself
> Piel: avenge
> Hophal: be avenged, suffer vengeance
> Hithpael: take one's vengeance

No wonder certain aspects of the study of Hebrew seem hopeless or make the language seem nonsensical. English and similar languages can hardly begin to convey its shape. Many students will be tempted to endorse this candid comment by Sperber:

> I must confess to utter ignorance of Hebrew; for these . . . pages of verbal forms [in Hebrew grammars], which were allegedly "Hebrew" while the language of the Bible was a living tongue, are as many pages of mysteries and unsurmountable difficulties to me. How my forebears could have mastered them is to me a real miracle![24]

As we have seen, the real problem lies in the way other languages cover up the Hebrew structures.

Awareness of the ambiguities within the English verbal system when set *vis-à-vis* the   s subtle distinctions used in the Hebrew verbal stem system with regard to causation and voice, should warn the researcher against giving priority to the stem's apparent function over its manifest form in trying to decide its functions. Prejudged categories, dictated by the "cruder" English structures, are inadequate for interpreting the Hebrew categories; we must be guided by the Hebrew forms and usages rather than by those of English.

Minor Features   21.2.3

How many stems are there? The basic medieval tradition recognized seven stems,   a though there was discussion over whether to add or subtract one. David Qimḥi in his influential *Mikhlol* opted for eight, adding *Poel*.[25] Although modern scholars disagree

---

23. William L. Holladay, *A Concise Hebrew and Aramaic Lexicon of the Old Testament* (Grand Rapids: Eerdmans, 1971) 245. We do not mean to suggest that there is any simple, straightforward, and practical alternative.

24. Sperber, *Historical Grammar*, 6.

25. Cf. Goshen-Gottstein, "System of Verbal Stems," 72; William Chomsky, *David Ḳimḥi's Hebrew Grammar (Mikhlol)* (New York: Bloch, 1952) 54.

about the number of verbal stems represented by rare forms, they essentially agree that there are seven major stems, those based on triradical roots, and a dozen or so minor ones, most based on biradical roots.[26] The minor stems are, for the most part, morphemic variants of the major. Thus along with *Piel*, there are *pôʿēl*, *piʿlēl* and *pəʿalʿal*, and *pilpēl*; *Pual* is complemented by *pôʿal*, *puʿlal*, and *polpal*; and *Hithpael* by *hitpôʿēl*, *hitpaʿlel*, *hitpaʿlal*, and *hitpalpel*.

b   Some rare and disputed forms may be mentioned.[27] (1) *Hithpael*, without the typical lengthening or doubling of the second radical characterizing the *Hithpael* and the lengthening of the *a* before a non-guttural, is found in Judg 20:15, 17 and 21:9; it is interpreted by Paul Joüon as a variant byform of the *Hithpael*,[28] but by Carl Brockelmann as a reflexive of the *Qal*, comparable to a so-called Gt form found in the other Semitic languages.[29]

c   (2) *Hippael* forms are controversial: the doubling of an initial *nun* or *kaph* with some roots[30] is treated by some as a sign of *Hithpael* forms in which the infixed -*t*- has been assimilated to the root's initial radical.[31] Israel Eitan considers some of the forms as evidence of a נ-reflexive stem,[32] and David Yellin has identified some of them as part of a heretofore unidentified *Hippael* stem.[33]

d   (3) *Hištaphʿel*: The important word השתחוה, which occurs about 170 times, has been interpreted by most moderns, on the basis of the Ugaritic *š* form (comparable to the *Hiphil*), as an *Št* stem;[34] J. A. Emerton thinks there is evidence to tip the balance of

---

26. On some of the complexities of biradical roots, see F. I. Andersen, "Biconsonantal Byforms of Weak Hebrew Roots," *Zeitschrift für die Alttestamentliche Wissenschaft* 82 (1970) 270–74; J. Blau, "Studies in Hebrew Verb Formation," *Hebrew Union College Annual* 42 (1971) 133–58.

27. Some of the rare and minor stems have close analogs in Arabic. It has been alleged that Hebrew has a *Yiphil* (as Phoenician does) alongside the *Hiphil*; see M. Dahood, "Hebrew Lexicography: A Review of W. Baumgartner's *Lexikon*, Volume II," *Orientalia* 45 (1976) 327–65, at 333, 342, 344; Dahood, "Yiphil Imperative *yaṭṭī* in Isaiah 54,2," *Orientalia* 46 (1977) 383–84; Dahood, "Two Yiphil Causatives in Habakkuk 3,13a," *Orientalia* 48 (1979) 258–59. The allegation is open to serious doubt. The non-assimilated-*nun* forms are problematic, e.g., *ninʿartî* Ps 109:23 (cf. *ʾinnāʿēr* Judg 16:20) and *yinṣōrû* Deut 33:9 (cf. *yiṣṣərû* Prov 20:28).

28. Joüon § 53g / p. 120; cf. GKC § 54*l* / p. 151. The forms are *y/hitpāqədû*, *yitpāqēd*; note also a corresponding passive *hotpāqədû* (Num 1:47, 2:33, 26:62; 1 Kgs 20:27).

29. Brockelmann, *Grundriss*, 1. 529–30, citing the Moabite Gt form *hltḥm* 'to wage war.'

30. The forms are, for *n*, (1) *hinnābēʾ*, Ezek 37:9; (2) *hinnabbēʾtî*, Ezek 37:10; (3) *hinnabbəʾû*, Jer 23:13; (4) *hinnéḥāmtî*, Ezek 5:13; (5) *tinnaśśēʾ*, Num 24:7; (6) *yinnaśśēʾ*, 2 Chr 32:23; (7) *yinnaśśəʾû*, Dan 11:14; and, for *k*, (8) *tikkônēn*, Num 21:27; (9) *tikkasseh*, Prov 26:26. Of the nine forms, five (## 1, 2, 4, 6, 7) are in prose, four in verse.

31. GKC § 54c / p. 149.

32. I. Eitan, "Light on the History of the Hebrew Verb," *Jewish Quarterly Review* 12 (1921–22) 25–32, referring to the *nšʾ* forms, ## 5–7 in n. 30.

33. David Yellin, "The Hippaʿel-Nifʿal Conjugation in Hebrew and Aramaic: The Assimilation of ת in the Hitpaʿel Conjugation," *Journal of the Palestine Oriental Society* 4 (1924) 85–106, esp. 89–97, referring to the *nbʾ* forms, ## 1–3 in n. 30.

34. E.g., *UT* § 19.847, identifying the root as **hwy* 'to strike,' Št 'to throw oneself down (striking the earth)'; others refer to the root *hyy* 'to live,' Št 'to cause oneself to live (by worship).' Cf. Lambdin, *Introduction to Biblical Hebrew*, 254; J. A. Soggin, *Old Testament and Oriental Studies* (Rome: Biblical Institute, 1975) 188–202 (on *š* causatives), esp. 190–92, 195, 203–9 (on *hwy*); G. I. Davies, "A Note on the Etymology of *hištaḥᵃwāh*," *Vetus Testamentum* 29 (1979) 493–95 (a reply to Emerton's paper cited in n. 35). Actually, the etymology was originally made by Martin Hartmann in 1875 on the basis of other comparative evidence.

On the rarity of infixed-*t* forms in general, see J. Blau, "Über die t-form des Hifʿil in Bibelhebräisch," *Vetus Testamentum* 7 (1957) 385–88; S. B. Wheeler, "The Infixed -*t*- in Biblical Hebrew," *Journal of the Ancient Near Eastern Society* 3 (1970–71) 20–31. On *š* causatives, see, in addition to Soggin, L. Wächter, "Reste von Šafʿel-Bildungen im Hebräischen," *Zeitschrift für die Alttestamentliche Wissenschaft* 83 (1971) 380–89.

probability in favor of the more or less traditional view that it is a *Hithpael* from the root שחה.[35] In any case the unusual shape of the word hints at its extraordinary cultural significance.

A statistical summary of the uses of the verb stems may be useful.[36]

e

	Occurrences		Roots used[37]	
	N	%	N	%
Qal	49,180	68.8	1,115	71.2
Niphal	4,140	5.8	435	27.8
Piel	6,450	9.0	415	26.5
Pual	460	0.6	190	12.1
Hithpael	830	1.2	175	11.2
Hiphil	9,370	13.1	505	32.2
Hophal	400	0.6	100	6.4
Other	680	0.9	130	8.3
Total	71,510		1,565	

The statistics do not provide any direct clues to the stem system, but they do afford a rough overview of how it is used.

35. J. A. Emerton, "The Etymology of *hištaḥᵃwāh*," *Oudtestamentische Studiën* 20 (1977) 41–55; cf. GKC § 75kk / p. 215. The existence of a root *šḥy* 'to bow' is not in question; what is in question is whether it is primary (so Emerton) or secondary to *hštḥwy*; for the verb see Isa 51:23, Prov 12:25.

36. From SA/THAT.

37. The number 1,565 represents the total number of verbal roots used in Biblical Hebrew; since many roots occur in more than one stem (though only a few occur in all seven stems), this number is substantially less than the sum of the roots used in each stem. The figures in the last column represent the percentage of all verbal roots (that is, of 1,565) used in each stem.

22

Qal Stem

22.1 Introduction

a   The most commonly used verbal stem is the *Qal* or "light" stem, also known as the G (*Grundstamm*) or B (Basic) stem. The *Qal* stem is appropriately called "simple," in the sense that the root bears no consonantal affixes; it is simple semantically in that notions of causation are absent.

b   Before analyzing the stem's forms and meanings with respect to the basic division between fientive and stative verbs, we first rehearse its form and meaning as a whole. We then turn to explore the fundamental division of this stem into fientive and stative verbs with reference to meaning (22.2) and form (22.3). Having sketched the difference between the two kinds of *Qal* verbs, we go on to consider more particularly the classes within *Qal* statives (22.4). Next we consider the use of the *Qal* to mold denominatives (22.5). Finally we review the evidence for the existence of a *Qal* passive and its forms (22.6), and *Qal* impersonal constructions (22.7).

22.2 Semantics

a   In contrast to the other five major stems, the *Qal* and *Niphal* stems ordinarily have no element of causation in their predication. Aligning *Pual* and *Hithpael* with *Piel*, and *Hophal* with *Hiphil*, we posit a three-way *Qal : Piel : Hiphil* contrast. Consider these English examples: 'Moses split (cf. *Qal*) the rock,' 'Moses split up (cf. *Piel*) the rock,' and 'Moses split (cf. *Hiphil*) the rock' (i.e., 'Moses caused the rock to split'). Consider further these Hebrew examples contrasting *Qal* and *Piel*.

| 1a. | בָּקַע יָם | He (God) *split* (*Qal*) the sea. |
| | | Ps 78:13 |

| 1b. | יְבַקַּע צֻרִים בַּמִּדְבָּר | He (God) *split up* (*Piel*) rocks in the desert. |
| | | Ps 78:15 |

The first of these two utterances represents a situation with God as the agent and the sea as the object of the splitting action. The second utterance represents God as the agent and the rocks as having been caused to be put into the state of being *split up*.

The *Qal* and *Niphal* differ with respect to the role of the subject; the *Qal* subject is   b active, as can be seen by comparing # 1a and # 2.

| 2. | וַתִּבָּקַע הָאֲדָמָה אֲשֶׁר תַּחְתֵּיהֶם׃ | The ground under them *split open* (*Niphal*). |
| | | Num 16:31 |

The *Qal* example represents the subject as the agent, implicitly answering the question 'What is God doing?' The *Niphal* by contrast answers the question 'What happened to the ground?' It does not represent the subject as the actor or agent. It rather represents the subject as having been acted upon by an unstated agent; the subject is merely participating in the action.

Fientive and Stative Verbs   22.2.1

Verbs in the *Qal* stem (setting aside the rare passive forms) fall into two form/   a function groups. Grammarians have called them "voluntaria" (*freiwillig*) and "involuntaria" (*unfreiwillig*),[1] "active" and "neutral" (*neutrisch*),[2] and "active" and "stative."[3] Since the term "active" is also used for voice, it is inappropriate to use in referring to type of action, so we use the term "fientive" (20.2k, 30.2.3).[4]

A *fientive verb* is one that designates a dynamic situation. With this kind of verb a   b clause answers the implicit question 'What does X do?', where X is a nominal expression and *do* is a fientive verb. A fientive verb may be either transitive or intransitive; a few, such as b‹r, may be both.[5]

1. E.g., Paul Haupt, "Transitive and Intransitive Verbs in Semitic," *Journal of the American Oriental Society* 16 (1894) ci–cii, cited in GKC § 43a n. 1 / pp. 118–19; and Brockelmann (see next note).

2. E.g., Carl Brockelmann, *Grundriss der vergleichenden Grammatik der semitischen Sprachen* (Berlin: Reuter und Reichard, 1908), 1. 505, where the "neutral" verb is said to describe states (*Zustände*); cf. GB 2. 75 (§ 14b).

3. E.g., Joüon § 41 / p. 95 ("verbes d'action," "verbes statifs"); S. Moscati et al., *An Introduction to the Comparative Grammar of the Semitic Languages* (Wiesbaden: Harrassowitz, 1964) 122; cf. T. O. Lambdin, *Introduction to Biblical Hebrew* (New York: Scribner, 1971) 93.

4. With, e.g., R. J. Williams, *Hebrew Syntax: An Outline* (2d ed.; Toronto: University of Toronto, 1976) 27.

5. Others are *sāpâ* 'to be snatched away (intransitive), snatch away (transitive)'; *rāʿâ* 'to graze, pasture'; *ṣāpan* 'to hide (i.e., lie hidden), hide (something).' Note also *pānâ* 'to turn (intransitive), turn oneself (reflexive)'; and *rāḥaṣ* 'to wash (transitive), wash oneself (reflexive).'

1a.   גֶּחָלִים בָּעֲרוּ מִמֶּֽנּוּ׃   Burning coals *blazed* (intransitive) out of it (his mouth).
Ps 18:9

1b.   כְּאֵשׁ תִּבְעַר־יָֽעַר   as fire *consumes* (transitive) the forest
Ps 83:15

With fientive verbs the subject may be described as an "actor."

c   A *stative verb* is one that describes a circumstance or state, whether external and physical, or psychological, or perceptual. Sentences with this kind of verb implicitly answer the question 'What is X's characteristic, quality, circumstance, state (physical or mental)?', where *X* is a nominal expression and the characterizing situation is a stative verb, for example, *zāqēn dāwîd* 'David was old.'

d   The difference between the two kinds of verbs can sometimes be tested in one of two ways. First, verbs may be tested for transitivity (20.2l), since transitives tend to be fientives. Transitivity means that the effects of the action expressed by the verb pass over from the subject (the "agent" or "actor") to the object (or "goal").[6]

e   English offers a second convenient test for distinguishing stative and fientive verbs: stative verbs in English do not occur in progressive forms. For example, a fientive verb like 'read' freely forms the progressive, as in 'I am reading this book.' By contrast, one cannot freely say 'I am loving this book.' Since 'love' describes a stative situation (in this case, a psychological state), one freely says 'I love this book.' This test may be of use in considering difficult cases.

22.2.2   Stative Verbs and Adjectives

a   English does not discriminate between stative verbs and predicate adjective constructions, as Hebrew does, and this discrepancy is worth exploring. Hebrew uses the *Qal*, for example, in חָכַמְתָּ 'you are wise' (Prov 9:12), שָׁכֹלְתִּי 'I am bereaved' (Gen 43:14), and וַיִּכְבַּד 'it (Pharaoh's heart) was heavy' (Exod 9:7). In these instances English accurately renders the Hebrew by inserting a form of the "dummy verb" *to be*, marking the situation represented by the utterance with respect to those meanings carried by the macrofunctional verb (see 4.8, 20.2).

b   The ease with which Hebrew represents "adjectival states" by means of verbal forms reflects the relationship philosophers and grammarians have alleged to exist between adjectives and verbs. We may say that the Hebrew structures reveal the similarity of function between verb and adjective found in all languages.

c   Earlier Hebrew grammarians supposed that stative verbs had evolved from adjectives. Hans Bauer and Pontus Leander, for example, contend that the vocalic patterns **qatil* and **qatul* were originally those of adjectives; the suffixes of the perfective conjugation were later affixed to them.[7] Carl Brockelmann similarly speaks of statives as

6. Cf. John Lyons, *Introduction to Theoretical Linguistics* (Cambridge: Cambridge University, 1968) 350.
7. BL § 42a–c / pp. 307–8.

adjectives that developed into a verbal flexion.[8] Despite the reasonableness of these views, most scholars now think that the forms of the inflected stative verbs, *qatila* and *qatula*, were already present in the earliest stages of Semitic.[9]

How do the stative constructions differ from the predicate-adjective constructions? **d** The *Qal* stative constructions mark the situation represented with all the values of a verbal form (aspect, mood, *Aktionsart*), while the adjectival construction is unmarked for these values. English cannot render the latter representation; it must add the "dummy verb" *to be*, thereby making it appear as though there is no difference between the two Hebrew constructions.

1a.	וַיִּרְאוּ בְנֵי־הָאֱלֹהִים אֶת־בְּנוֹת הָאָדָם כִּי טֹבֹת הֵנָּה	The sons of *hā'ĕlōhîm* saw that the daughters of *hā'ādām* were beautiful (adjective). Gen 6:2
1b.	מַה־טֹּבוּ אֹהָלֶיךָ	How beautiful (verb) are your tents! Num 24:5

In the first example, the sense of the second clause טבת הנה (in terms of aspect and time reference) is more determined by its syntactic context (as an embedded clause after a form of the verb *r'y* with *ky*, 'to see that . . .'), than is the sense of the second example, מה־טבו. This discrepancy between the Hebrew and English idioms leads to English "covering up" the workings of two different Hebrew constructions.[10]

Fientive and Stative with the Same Root   22.2.3

Both English and Hebrew treat certain verbs sometimes as stative, sometimes as **a** fientive, depending on the particular meaning they have in a sentence. Bernard Comrie illustrates the point by contrasting the verb 'be' in 'Fred is silly' and 'Fred is being silly.' In the first sentence Fred is in a state, but in the second 'he is acting silly,' a dynamic (i.e., fientive) situation.[11] Compare these sentence pairs.

1a.	וַיֶּחְכַּם מִכָּל־הָאָדָם	And he (Solomon) *was wiser* (stative) than anyone. 1 Kgs 5:11
1b.	בְּכָל־עֲמָלִי שֶׁעָמַלְתִּי וְשֶׁחָכַמְתִּי	all my work, into which I *have poured* my effort and *skill* (fientive) Qoh 2:19

8. Carl Brockelmann, *Hebräische Syntax* (Neukirchen: Neukirchener Verlag, 1956) 35.

9. W. L. Moran, *A Syntactical Study of the Dialect of Byblos as Reflected in the Amarna Tablets* (Johns Hopkins University Dissertation, 1950) 114; T. L. Fenton, "The Hebrew 'Tenses' in the Light of Ugaritic," *Proceedings of the Fifth World Congress of Jewish Studies* (Jerusalem:

World Union of Jewish Studies, 1973), 4. 31–39, at 35–36.

10. There are some cases where the Hebrew adjective and stative verb coincide and are undistinguishable, but this parsing problem is essentially minor.

11. Bernard Comrie, *Aspect: An Introduction to the Study of Verbal Aspect and Related Problems* (Cambridge: Cambridge University, 1976) 36.

2a.   וִיהוֹשֻׁעַ . . . מָלֵא רוּחַ חָכְמָה   Now Joshua . . . *was filled* (stative) with the spirit of
                                              wisdom.
                                              Deut 34:9

2b.   וּכְבוֹד יהוה מָלֵא אֶת־הַמִּשְׁכָּן׃   And Yʜᴡʜ's glory *filled* (fientive) the tabernacle.
                                              Exod 40:34

b   Some verbs, especially those denoting a mental perception or an emotional state,
exhibit both stative and fientive characteristics at one and the same time. Often, as in the
sentence וָאֹהַב אֶת־יַעֲקֹב וְאֶת־עֵשָׂו שָׂנֵאתִי, 'I *love* Jacob but Esau I *hate*' (Mal 1:2–3),
stative forms are used, and they are rendered by non-progressive forms in English. On
the other hand, as in the above sentence, they may be bound with direct objects, coloring
them with a fientive notion, and may even occur in the participle, which tends to have a
progressive and thus fientive sense. For example:

3a.   וְכָל־יִשְׂרָאֵל וִיהוּדָה אֹהֵב אֶת־   And all Israel and Judah *loved* (lit., *was loving*)
          דָּוִד   David.
                                              1 Sam 18:16

3b.   וְהוּא לֹא־שֹׂנֵא לוֹ מִתְּמוֹל   and he *did* not *hate* (lit., *was* not *hating*) him
          שִׁלְשׁוֹם   previously
                                              Deut 4:42

Strictly speaking, however, even though bound with an object, the verbs are not notionally transitive, for no action passes over from the agent to the goal word. In the clause
וַיִּשְׁמַע אֱלֹהִים אֶת־נַאֲקָתָם, 'and God heard their groaning' (Exod 2:24), though the syntactical relation between the subject and the object is the same as in וַיַּךְ אֶת־הַמִּצְרִי, 'and he
(Moses) killed the Egyptian' (Exod 2:12), notionally no action passes over from the
subject to the object. R. H. Robins observes:

> The weakness of semantic definitions is well illustrated here: *hit*, in *I hit you* is syntac-
> tically a transitive verb . . . ; but *hear* in *I hear you* is involved in exactly the same
> syntactic relations with the two pronouns, and is regarded as a transitive verb, though
> in this case, the "action," if any action is in fact referred to, is the other way around.[12]

Nevertheless, in spite of their stative forms and the semantic equivocation with these
verbs of mental state when bound with a goal word, they are best construed as quasi-
fientive when they occur either implicitly or explicitly with an object and as stative when
they are free. The occurrence with an object, in contrast to other statives, suggests that
they were felt as fientives. Compare these sentences:

4a.   וָאִירָא   I *was afraid* (stative).
                                              Gen 3:10

4b.   אַל־תִּירְאוּ אֶת־עַם הָאָרֶץ   *Do* not *fear* (quasi-fientive) the people of the land.
                                              Num 14:9

---

12. R. H. Robins, *General Linguistics: An Introductory Survey* (London: Longmans, 1964) 266; cited in Lyons,
Theoretical Linguistics, 350.

| 5a. | וַיֶּחֱזַק הָרָעָב | The famine *became severe* (stative).
Gen 41:56 |
| 5b. | וְלֹא חֲזָקוֹ: | He did not *give* him *strength* (fientive).
2 Chr 28:20 |

Some verbs have both a stative (*qātēl*) and a fientive (*qātal*) form in the *Qal* stem.   c

| 6a. | לָבֵשׁ יהוה עֹז | Yнwн *is clothed* (stative) with might.
Ps 93:1 |
| 6b. | אֲשֶׁר לָבַשׁ בְּבֹאוֹ אֶל־הַקֹּדֶשׁ | which he *put on* (fientive) when he entered the sanctuary
Lev 16:23 |

More frequently, Hebrew formally contrasts comparable differences by using the verbal root in both *Qal* and either *Piel* or *Hiphil*.

Some verbs with differentiation appear to have lost one of the potential meanings.   d
For example, קָרֵב originally meant 'to be near,' at least to judge from the alternate form קָרַב and Arabic cognates, but in Hebrew both forms have a fientive meaning.

| 7a. | אֶל־אֱלֹהֶיהָ לֹא קָרֵבָה: | She *does* not *draw near* to God.
Zeph 3:2 |
| 7b. | וַאֲבִימֶלֶךְ לֹא קָרַב אֵלֶיהָ | Now Abimelek *had* not *gone near* to her.
Gen 20:4 |

Some scholars think the stative forms of these pairs are older than fientive forms. For   e
example, G. R. Driver proposed that in verbs where an intransitive suffix conjugation can take either *i* or *a* in the final syllable, the *qātēl* form represents an older layer in the language than the *qātal* form (cf. 22.3f*v*).[13] T. L. Fenton argues the opposite, contending that where both exist the *Qal* fientive is older than the *Qal* stative.[14] It is clear, at any rate, that the number of *Qal* fientive/stative pairs is small, and their differentiation is of only marginal synchronic importance.

Morphology   22.3

All the West Semitic languages provide evidence of a three-way split in the *Qal*   a
suffix conjugation, a fact that suggests that this split is basic to the languages.[15] The suffix pattern $*C_1aC_2aC_3a$ (prefix $*yaC_1C_2uC_3u$) was used for fientives, $*C_1aC_2iC_3a$ (prefix $*yaC_1C_2aC_3u$) for statives designating a temporary state, and $*C_1aC_2uC_3a$ (prefix $*yaC_1C_2u/aC_3u$) for statives designating a lasting state. Thus we have these Arabic forms.[16]

---

13. G. R. Driver, *Problems of the Hebrew Verbal System* (Edinburgh: T. & T. Clark, 1936) 48.

14. Fenton, "Hebrew 'Tenses,'" 36.

15. Cf. n. 9; Brockelmann, *Grundriss*, 1. 504–8.

16. Classical Arabic sometimes uses one root in two classes; there is one (and only one) root attested for all three cases: *baṭana* 'to hide,' *baṭina* 'to be full,' *baṭuna* 'to be paunchy.' We owe this example to Ernest N. McCarus. On these matters, see Driver, *Hebrew Verbal System*, in general.

naẓara ~ *yanẓuru*	to look at, see
salima ~ *yaslamu*	to be safe, well
ḥasuna ~ *yaḥsunu*	to be beautiful

The fientive (*a/u*) pattern is the most common in Arabic, while the temporary stative (*i/a*) and the permanent stative (*u/u*) patterns are less frequent. Similar distributions of comparable forms are found in Hebrew.

b   Hebrew *Qal* has six patterns, three like the Arabic and three others resulting from diverse minor patterns and mergers.

(1)	*qātal* (< *qatala)	*yiqtōl* (< **ya/iqtulu*)	
	כָּתַב	יִכְתֹּב	to write
(2)	*qātēl* (< *qatila)	*yiqtal* (< **ya/iqtalu*)	
	חָמֵץ	יֶחְמַץ	to be sour, leavened
(3)	*qātōl* (< *qatula)	*yiqtal* (< **ya/iqta/u?lu*)	
	קָטֹנְתִּי	תִּקְטַן	to be small

(4)	*qātal*	*yiqtal*	
	לָמַד	יִלְמַד	to learn
(5)	*qātal*	*yēqtēl* (< **ya/iqtilu*)	
	יָלַד	תֵּלֵד	to bear, beget
(6)	*qātēl* (< *qatila)	*yiqtōl*	
	נָבֵל	יִבּוֹל	to droop

We will review these patterns in turn.

c   *Pattern # 1: qātal/yiqtōl.*   The first pattern, by far the most common, is associated chiefly with fientives. The suffix-conjugation *ā-a* is also used for various classes of weak verbs; these are differentiated in the prefix conjugation, with some fientives showing a *yaqtol* (< *yaqtulu) form and thus conforming to pattern # 1, for example, geminate סָבַב ~ יָסֹב 'to turn,' II-*waw* קָם ~ יָקוּם 'to rise,' I-guttural עָמַד ~ יַעֲמֹד 'to stand.' (Statives and fientives of other weak verbs in *qātal* conform to patterns ## 4–5.)

d   *Pattern # 2: qātēl/yiqtal.*   The stative patterns, ## 2–3, are much smaller than # 1, but # 2 is still used with a clearly defined class of verbs.[17] Though most are intransitive (e.g., זָקֵן ~ יִזְקַן 'to be old,' יָרֵא ~ יִירָא 'to be afraid,' כָּבֵד ~ יִכְבַּד 'to be heavy,' מָלֵא ~ ימלא 'to be filled,' שָׁפֵל ~ יִשְׁפַּל 'to be(come) low'), a few are transitives, involving psychological states (e.g., שָׂנֵא ~ יִשְׂנָא 'to hate').

e   *Pattern # 3: qātōl/yiqtal.*   The original permanent stative pattern is almost dead and survives with only a few verbs. These include קטן ~ יקטן 'to be small,' יגר 'to fear,' יקש 'to lay a bait,' and שכל (cf. אֶשְׁכָּל) 'to be bereaved.' The two stative patterns (## 2–3) use the same prefix-conjugation forms. According to some, this pattern is also attested in

---

17. For fientive *qatila-yiqtal* verbs in Ugaritic, see J. Huehnergard, *Ugaritic Vocabulary in Syllabic Transcription* (Atlanta: Scholars Press, 1987) 132–33.

some II-*waw* verbs (אוֹר 'to be light,' בּוֹשׁ ~ יֵבוֹשׁ 'to be ashamed,' etc.),[18] but in general hollow verbs do not readily conform to the patterns discussed here.

Pattern # 4: qātal/yiqtal. The fourth pattern is composite in origin and its sources   f need to be analyzed further. The pattern seems to be mixed, with the suffix conjugation of # 1 (*qātal*) and the prefix conjugation of ## 2–3 (*yiqtal*).

(*i*) *Fientive II- and III-gutturals.* Almost all II- and III-gutturals belong to this   g pattern; some of them, at least to judge from their meaning as well as from the suffix-conjugation forms, are in fact fientive verbs (e.g., בָּלַע ~ יִבְלַע 'to swallow,' and פָּתַח ~ יִפְתַּח 'to open').

(*ii*) *Stative II- and III-gutturals.* In other verbs with II- and III-gutturals exhibiting   h pattern # 4 one can detect in suffix-conjugation pausal forms or the forms with suffixed pronouns (especially vocalic) an original (or alternative) stative form (*qātēl*). The dominance of the fientive pattern, *qātal*, may be due to three factors: (1) the guttural, (2) the analogical penetration of the fientive pattern, and (3) a partially fientive meaning.

1.	צָלַח	(צָלְחָה)	~	יִצְלַח	to prosper
2.	שָׂבַע	(שָׂבְעוּ)	~	יִשְׂבַּע	to be sated
3.	שָׂמַח	(שָׂמֵחַ)	~	יִשְׂמַח	to be glad
4.	שָׁאַל	(שְׁאֵלוּנוּ)	~	יִשְׁאַל	to ask
5.	שָׁכַח	(שְׁכֵחָנִי)	~	יִשְׁכַּח	to forget
6.	שָׁמַע	(שָׁמֵעַ)	~	יִשְׁמַע	to hear

(*iii*) *Other fientive weak verbs.* Pattern # 4 is common for fientive I-*yod* verbs.   i

7.	ינק ~ יָנַק	יִינַק	to suck
8.	יָעַץ ~ יעץ	יִיעַץ	to advise
9.	יקץ ~ יָקַץ	יִיקַץ	to awake
10.	יָרַשׁ ~ ירשׁ	יִירַשׁ	to inherit

(*iv*) *Other stative weak verbs.* A variety of weak verb classes use this pattern for   j statives: geminate קלל ~ תֵּקַל 'to be light,' חַת ~ יֵחַת to be shattered,' יָרַע ~ רַע 'to be evil,' I-guttural חָזַק ~ יֶחֱזַק 'to be strong,' and perhaps some hollow verbs.

(*v*) *Stative regular verbs.* Aside from these weak verbs, pattern # 4 is used with   k regular verbs. Many of these betray an earlier stative form in the suffix conjugation by their pausal forms and forms with verbal suffixes, or by a parallel adjectival form of the type *qātēl* with the same root. With these verbs it appears as though the dominant fientive pattern is penetrating into the stative patterns, for if pattern # 3 is almost dead, pattern # 2 is dying. Verbs exhibiting an earlier stative suffix form in their pausal (and similar) forms include:

11.	אָשַׁם	(אָשֵׁמוּ)	~	יֶאְשַׁם	to be guilty
12.	גָּבַר	(גָּבְרוּ)	~	יִגְבַּר	to be strong

---

18. GB 2. 75 (§ 14b).

13.	דָּבַק	(דְּבֵק)	~	יִדְבַּק	to cling
14.	לָבַשׁ	(לָבֵשׁ)	~	יִלְבַּשׁ	to put on
15.	קָדַשׁ	(קָדְשׁוּ)	~	יִקְדַּשׁ	to be holy

A verb exhibiting an earlier stative form by its shape with verbal suffixes is גָּדַל (גְּדֵלַנִי) ~ יִגְדַּל 'to be(come) great.' Verbs exhibiting an earlier stative form by a parallel *qātēl* form include:

16.	אָבֵל	אָבַל	~	תֶּאֱבַל	mourning, to mourn
17.	חָרֵד	חָרַד	~	יֶחֱרַד	trembling, to tremble
18.	קָצֵר	קָצַר	~	תִּקְצַר	short, to be short

(*vi*) *Other regular verbs.* A few strong verbs with this pattern give no indication of an earlier stative form. In some instances, therefore, pattern # 4 may represent an original but rare pattern for fientive verbs. In other instances one may suspect that an original stative form was lost.

19.	יִלְמַד ~ לָמַד	to learn
20.	יִרְבַּץ ~ רָבַץ	to lie stretched out, to lie down
21.	יִרְכַּב ~ רָכַב	to ride
22.	יִשְׁכַּב ~ שָׁכַב	to lie down

Pattern # 5: qatal/yēqtēl. The fifth pattern is found with I-*yod* verbs and *nātan*. Verbs with this pattern should be regarded as fientive; their form is to be contrasted with that of I-*yod* verbs that follow pattern # 4.

23.	יֵלֵד ~ יָלַד	to bear
24.	יֵרֵד ~ יָרַד	to descend
25.	יֵשֵׁב ~ יָשַׁב	to dwell
26.	יִתֵּן ~ נָתַן	to give[19]

Pattern # 6: qātēl/yiqtōl. The pattern, like # 4, seems to be mixed, with the suffix conjugation of # 2 (*qātēl*) and the prefix conjugation of # 1 (*yiqtōl*). This mixture can be accounted for in one of two ways: either the dominant fientive pattern is penetrating into this pattern (cf. pattern # 4*v*) or phonological conditioning is at work. The latter explanation is based on the observation that of the sixty verb forms vocalized in this pattern, thirty-six of them have *b, p, m, h, g, k, q,* as the second or third consonant of the root, and these consonants could condition a shift from *a* to *u* (> *ō*).[20] In any case the pattern is mixed.

---

19. Phoenician and Ugaritic use the root *ytn* for Hebrew *ntn*; *UT* § 9.48 n. 2. This may reflect a secondary formation based on the prefix form.

20. GB 2. 74 (§ 14a). Probably also part of pattern # 6 are the mixed inflections of *qṣr* 'to be short' and *škn* 'to dwell.'

27. יַחְפֹּץ ~ חָפֵץ   to delight in
28. יִבּוֹל ~ נָבֵל   to droop
29. יִשֹּׁם ~ שׁמם   to be desolate

In sum. Patterns ## 1 and 5 are fientive in form and meaning. Patterns ## 2 and 3   o
are stative in form and meaning, though pattern # 2 allows fientive notions. Patterns ## 4
and 6 mix fientive and stative features both in form and meaning. To judge from the
cognate languages, and from the evidence of stative forms used for customary fientive
forms when the verb is in pause or bound with a verbal suffix, it appears that the dominant # 1 is supplanting earlier stative forms. We do not need to establish in detail the
historical development of these forms. We content ourselves with the realization that
verbs displaying patterns ## 4 and 6 are mixed both in form and meaning, while verbs in
pattern # 2 are unmixed as to form, but somewhat mixed as to meaning (i.e., they can
behave as notionally fientive verbs).

Verb Classes   22.4

Sometimes an attempt is made to classify the verbs used in the *Qal* stem. For fien-   a
tives, that attempt is for practical and theoretical reasons unimportant. Practically, fientive verbs with pattern # 1 are too numerous and varied, and theoretically, the study is
more lexical than grammatical, for even so fundamental a division of fientive verbs into
transitive and intransitive is not indicated by distinct forms. To reinforce this point,
made earlier (see 22.2.1), contrast the verbs in this verse.

1. וְכִי־יִפְתַּח אִישׁ בּוֹר . . . וְנָפַל־   If a man opens (transitive) a pit . . . and an ox
    שָׁמָּה שׁוֹר   falls (intransitive) into it. . . .
                                                      Exod 21:33

The *Qal* is used for both kinds of fientive verb, with no contrast.

The case of stative verbs is somewhat different; this smaller group can more profit-   b
ably be analyzed. Formal and notional stative verbs are of three kinds: those that describe a characteristic, an external circumstance, or an emotional state. The distinction is
helpful in understanding the meaning of stative verbs in general, particularly in connection with verbal conjugations. Some verbs, as already mentioned, are stative in form but
fientive in meaning; the lines dividing these meanings are not sharp. Some examples will
serve to indicate the three groups.

2.   יֶעֱרַב עָלָיו שִׂיחִי   Let my meditation *be pleasing* (characteristic) to him.
                                                  Ps 104:34

3.   לֹא חָסֵרוּ   They *were* not *lacking* (circumstance).
                                                  Neh 9:21

4. וְגַם אֶל־שֹׁפְטֵיהֶם לֹא שָׁמֵעוּ   But they *did* not *listen* (psychological state) to their
                                                  judges.
                                                  Judg 2:17

c   Verbs that designate a *characteristic* may refer to an inherent quality (e.g., *qṣr*),[21] an achieved quality (e.g., *zqn*), or a temporary or contingent capacity (e.g., *ykl*).

5. יִזְקַן ~ זָקֵן	to be(come) old	15. יִכְבַּד ~ כָּבֵד	to be heavy
6. יֶחֱזַק ~ חָזַק	to be firm	16. יִכְשָׁר ~ כָּשֵׁר	to be suitable
7. יֶחְכַּם ~ חָכַם	to be wise	17. יִנְעָם ~ נעם	to be pleasant
8. יחמץ ~ חָמֵץ	to be sour	18. יֶעֱרַב ~ ערב	to be sweet
9. תֶּחֱנַף ~ חנף	to be polluted	19. יִצְדַּק ~ צדק	to be just
10. יֶחֱרַב ~ חרב	to be dry	20. יִקְדַּשׁ ~ קָדַשׁ	to be holy
11. יֶחֱרַשׁ ~ חרשׁ	to be silent	21. יקטן ~ קטן	to be small
12. תֶּחְשַׁךְ ~ חָשַׁךְ	to be(come) dark	22. תִּקְצַר ~ קָצֵר	to be short
13. יִיבַשׁ ~ יָבֵשׁ	to be dry	23. יִשְׁפַּל ~ שָׁפֵל	to be low
14. יוּכַל ~ יָכֹל	to be able		

d   Statives can also be used to describe a *circumstance* or an *accident* (in the philosophical sense); the reference involves, to some extent, the transitory.

24.	הַבֹּקֶר אוֹר	The morning *grew light*. Gen 44:3
25.	וַתָּאֹרְנָה עֵינָיו:	And his eyes *brightened*. 1 Sam 14:27 *Qere*
26.	וְטָמֵא עַד־הָעֶרֶב וְטָהֵר:	and it will be unclean until evening and then it *will be(come) clean* Lev 11:32

Some circumstantial verbs (some of them not well attested) may be listed.

27. אָפֵס	to cease[22]	33. יָמוּת ~ מֵת	to die
28. בָּצֵק	to swell	34. ימלא ~ מָלֵא	to be filled
29. יֶחְסַר ~ חָסֵר	to be lacking	35. יִצְלַח ~ צלח	to prosper
30. יֵקַד	to be kindled	36. יִרְקַב	to rot
31. יִיקַץ	to awake	37. יִשְׁכַּב ~ שָׁכַב	to lie down
32. יִישַׁן ~ ישן	to sleep	38. יִשְׁלָם ~ שלם	to be complete

Similar are verbs of temporary physical state.

39. יֶחֱרַד ~ חָרַד	to tremble	42. יִרְעַב ~ רָעֵב	to be hungry
40. יִיעַף ~ יעף	to be weary[23]	43. יִשְׂבַּע ~ שָׂבֵעַ	to be sated
41. יִצְמָא ~ צמא	to be thirsty		

e   An important class of temporary states is *psychological* (emotional or mental).

---

21. There are two roots 'to be good': suffix conjugation *ṭwb* and prefix conjugation *yṭb*.

22. Cf. also *pss*.

23. Cf. also *ygᶜ*.

44.   אַל־תִּירָאֵם   *Do* not *fear* them (the people of the land).
Num 14:9

45.   יָגֹרְתִּי מִפְּנֵי הָאַף   I *feared* before the anger.
Deut 9:19

Other psychological statives are these.

46.	תֶּאֱבַל ~ אָבַל	to mourn		52.	יגר	to be afraid
47.	יֶאֱהַב ~ אָהֵב	to love		53.	יִפְחָד ~ פָּחַד	to fear
48.	יֵבוֹשׁ ~ בּוֹשׁ	to be ashamed		54.	יִרְגַּז ~ רָגַז	to be agitated
49.	יַחְפֹּץ ~ חָפֵץ	to delight in		55.	יִשְׂנָא ~ שָׂנֵא	to hate
50.	יחפר ~ חפר	to be abashed		56.	יֵשֹׁם ~ שׁמם	to be appalled
51.	יֵחַת ~ חתת	to be aghast				

Denominatives

The *Qal* stem forms denominative verbs, verbs based on nouns (cf. also 24.4), with an either fientive or stative notion. The *fientives* designate some action implicit in the noun.[24]   a

1.	אהל	to tent	<	אֹהֶל	tent
2.	אזר	to gird (for battle)	<	אֵזוֹר	waistband
3.	אצל	to lay aside	<	אֵצֶל	side
4.	חגג	to celebrate a festival	<	חַג	festival
5.	חמר	to stop with pitch	<	חֵמָר	pitch
6.	חרף	to winter	<	חֹרֶף	winter
7.	לבן	to mold bricks	<	לְבֵנָה	brick
8.	מלח	to salt	<	מֶלַח	salt
9.	משׁל	to make up a *mašal*	<	מָשָׁל	saying
10.	שׂער	to bristle	<	שֵׂעָר	hair
11.	שׁבר	to buy grain	<	שֶׁבֶר	grain

The *statives* signify being or becoming that which is expressed by the noun.[25]

12.	בעל	to be(come) a lord	<	בַּעַל	lord
13.	בער	to be stupid	<	בַּעַר	stupid(ity)
14.	הבל	to be(come) *hebel*	<	הֶבֶל	breath, void
15.	מלך	to be(come) a king	<	מֶלֶךְ	king
16.	פתה	to be simple	<	פֶּתִי	simplicity

Qal Passive

The Masoretes recognized *Qal* only as an active stem, but there is much evidence   a
that Biblical Hebrew also had a passive counterpart.[26] On comparative grounds a *Qal*

---

24. GB 2. 74 (§ 14a).
25. GB 2. 75 (§ 14a).

26. See Mayer Lambert, "L'emploi du *nifal* en hébreu,"
Revue des études juives 41 (1900) 196–214, esp. 200–206;

passive is easily justified. A simple passive stem is attested in some of the cognate languages: in Arabic, where it is in full use;[27] in Ugaritic, where it cannot be readily distinguished in the prefix conjugation from the passive stem with prefix *n*; in the Tell Amarna glosses; and possibly in some Aramaic dialects. Moreover, some putative *Qal* passives are pointed as *Pual* suffix forms, but the *Piel* and *Hithpael* of the root are either unattested or attested only in a different sense. Others are pointed as *Hophal* prefix forms, but similarly the *Hiphil* of the root is unattested or attested only in a different sense. Also, in some cases, the MT has *Niphal* prefix forms that must be parsed as *Qal*-passive suffix forms. Participles have forms improper for *Niphal*, *Pual*, or *Hophal*. These and various resulting asymmetries (e.g., *Pual* suffix forms and *Hophal* prefix forms from the same root in the same sense) suggest the existence of a *Qal* passive stem, as do the semantics of the forms. The anomalous *l* assimilation of *lqḥ* also suggests that its passive forms are *Qal*. Assignment on the basis of sense alone is problematic.[28]

b   The *Qal* passive of some roots is found for the suffix conjugation (pointed as *Pual*) and the prefix conjugation and participles (pointed as *Hophal*), for example, *lqḥ*.[29]

1a.   אֲשֶׁר לֻקַּח מִשָּׁם׃   from which he was taken
                                      Gen 3:23

1b.   יֻקַּח־נָא מְעַט־מַיִם   Let a little water be taken.
                                      Gen 18:4

1c.   אִם־תִּרְאֶה אֹתִי לֻקָּח מֵאִתָּךְ   If you see me being taken from you. . . .
                                      2 Kgs 2:10

Some verbs show only the *Qal*-passive suffix conjugation (pointed as *Pual*), for example, *bzz* and *zrᶜ*.[30]

2.   וּבֻזָּזוּ   And they will be plundered.
                        Jer 50:37

H. L. Ginsberg, "Studies on the Biblical Hebrew Verb: Masoretically Misconstrued Internal Passives," *American Journal of Semitic Languages and Literatures* 46 (1929) 53–56; R. J. Williams, "The Passive *Qal* Theme in Hebrew," *Essays on the Ancient Semitic World*, ed. J. W. Wevers and D. B. Redford (Toronto: University of Toronto, 1970) 43–50; Joüon § 58 / pp. 125–27; BL § 38l′–r′ / pp. 285–88; Lambdin, *Introduction to Biblical Hebrew*, 253; and especially GB 2. 87–89 (§ 15), from which our lists are substantially drawn. The pioneering modern study was that of F. Böttcher in his *Ausführliches Lehrbuch der hebräischen Sprache* (2 vols.; Leipzig: Barth, 1866–68); on the widespread (though not universal) medieval recognition of *Qal* passive, see William Chomsky, *David Ḳimḥi's Hebrew Grammar (Mikhlol)* (New York: Bloch, 1952) xvi, xvii–xix, 89, 103. Note also E. Y. Kutscher, "Contemporary Studies in North-western Semitic," *Journal of Semitic Studies* 10 (1965) 21–51, at 51.

27. The Arabic forms are *qutila/yuqtalu*.

28. Lambdin, *Introduction to Biblical Hebrew*, 253.

29. The root *lqḥ* shows an apparent *Pual* eight times and an apparent *Hophal* six times; the participle occurs in the cited instance, though some of the *Pual* finite forms could also be parsed as participles. The root *šdd* shows both *šuddad* (Isa 15:1*bis*; "*Pual*" twenty times total) and *yûššad* (Hos 10:14; cf. Isa 33:1 for another "*Hophal*").

30. Cf. cases for these roots: *zwr* 'to press out' (*zōrû*, Isa 1:6); *zny* (*zûnnâ*, Ezek 16:34); *zrq* (*zōraq*, Num 19:13, 20); *ḥpś* (*ḥupǎśâ*, Lev 19:20; no *Qal* active attested); *yld* (*yullad*, Gen 4:26; twenty-six *Pual* suffix forms total; see below, nn. 34 and 37, on participles); *yṣr* (*yuṣṣǎrû*, Ps 139:16); *krt* (*korrat*, Ezek 16:4; *korǎtâ*, Judg 6:28); *mrq* (*mōraq*, Lev 6:21); *nph* (*nuppāḥ*, Job 20:26); *ᶜbd* (*ᶜubbad*, Deut 21:3, Isa 14:3); *ᶜzb* (*ᶜuzzāb*, Isa 32:14; *ᶜuzzǎbâ*, Jer 49:25); *ᶜśy* (*ᶜuśśêtî*, Ps 139:15); *qrᵓ* (*qōrāᵓ*, Isa 48:8; five "*Pual*" suffix forms; cf. the true *Pual* participle *məqōrāᵓî*, Isa 48:12); *špk* (*šuppak*, Num 35:33; three *Pual* forms total; the Hithpael has a different sense).

3.   בַּל־זֹרָ֫עוּ   They are not (quite) sown.
                                        Isa 40:24

Prefix forms are pointed as *Niphal* alongside *Pual* suffix forms for some roots, for example, *ḥṣb*, where both sets are plainly *Qal* passive.[31]

4a.   הַבִּ֫יטוּ אֶל־צוּר חֻצַּבְתֶּם   Look to the rock from which you were hewn.
                                        Isa 51:1

4b.   בַּצּוּר יֵחָצְבוּן׃   They were engraved in rock.
                                        Job 19:24

A fourth group of roots show only *Qal*-passive prefix forms, pointed as *Hophal*.[32]

5.   מִי־יִתֵּן בַּסֵּ֫פֶר וְיֻחָ֑קוּ׃   Oh that they were written on a scroll!
                                        Job 19:23

6.   כִּי שִׁבְעָתַ֫יִם יֻקַּם־קָ֑יִן   If Cain is avenged seven times. . . .
                                        Gen 4:24[33]

There are two *Qal* passive participles, *quṭṭal* (pointed as if shortened from *Pual*   c
məquṭṭal)[34] and *qiṭṭōl* (apparently parsed by the Masoretes as an adjectival form).[35]

7.   וְהַסְּנֶה אֵינֶ֫נּוּ אֻכָּל׃   But the bush was not being burned up.[36]
                                        Exod 3:2

8.   כָּל־הַבֵּן הַיִּלּוֹד הַיְאֹרָה   Every boy that is born you must throw into the
                      תַּשְׁלִיכֻ֫הוּ   river.[37]
                                        Exod 1:22

The finite forms of the *Qal* passive stem are treated by the Masoretes as follows.   d
Where both suffix and prefix forms occur, the suffix forms are *Pual*; the prefix forms are either *Hophal* (in the case of two roots) or *Niphal* (in the case of nine roots). If only the

---

31. Cf. cases for these roots: *ʾsr* (*Pual ʾussərû, ʾussắrû*, both in Isa 22:3; *Niphal yēʾāsēr*, Gen 42:19; *tēʾāsēr*, Judg 16:6, 10, 13); *dḥy* (*Pual dōḥû*, Ps 36:13; *Niphal yiddāḥeh*, Prov 14:32); *hrg* (*Pual hōrāg*, Isa 27:7; *horágnû*, Ps 44:23; *Niphal yēhārēg*, Lam 2:20; *tēharagnâ*, Ezek 26:6, cf. v 15); *ṭrp* (*Pual ṭārōp ṭōrap*, Gen 37:33; *ṭārōp ṭōrāp*, Gen 44:28; *Niphal ṭārōp yiṭṭārēp*, Exod 22:12; *yiṭṭārēp*, Jer 5:6); *mrṭ* (*Pual morắṭṭâ*, Ezek 21:15, 16; cf. participles below, n. 34; *Niphal yimmārēṭ*, Lev 13:40, 41); *śrp* (*Pual śōrāp*, Lev 10:16; *Niphal yiśśārēp*, Josh 7:15; fourteen forms total); *šgl* (*Pual šuggalt*, Jer 3:2 *Kethiv*; *Niphal tiššāgalnâ*, Isa 13:16 *Kethiv*, Zech 14:2 *Kethiv*); *šṭp* (*Pual šuṭṭap*, Lev 6:21; *Niphal yiššāṭēp*, Lev 15:12; *yiššāṭəpû*, Dan 11:22).
32. Cf. cases for these roots: *ʾrr* (*tāʾōr yûʾār*, Num 22:6); *dwš* (*yûdaš*, Isa 28:27); *ḥwl* 'to writhe' (*yûḥal*, Isa 66:8); *ḥnn* (*yuḥan*, Isa 26:10, Prov 21:10); *ysr* (*yûsar*, Isa 54:17); *ktt* (*yûkkat*, Isa 24:12; *yukkattû*, Mic 1:7, Jer 46:5, Job 4:20); *ntn* (*yuttan*, 1 Kgs 2:21; eight forms total); *ntṣ* (*yuttaṣ*,

Lev 11:35); *ntš* (*tuttaš*, Ezek 19:12); *swk* 'to pour' (*yûssāk?*, Exod 30:32 *Sam*); *śym* (*yûśam*, Gen 24:33 *Qere*); *šyr* (*yûšar*, Isa 26:1); *šyt* (*yûšat*, Exod 21:30).
33. The "*Hophal*" of *nqm* is also found in Gen 4:15, Exod 21:21.
34. Note also cases for *yld* (*yûllād*, Judg 13:8), *lqḥ* (*luqqāḥ*, 2 Kgs 2:10), and *mrṭ* (*môrāṭ*, Isa 18:2, 7; cf. the true *Pual məmōrāṭ*, 1 Kgs 7:45).
35. Note also cases for *zrʿ* (*zērûaʿ*, perhaps for *zērôaʿ*, Lev 11:37, Isa 61:11) and *škr* (*šikkōr*, 1 Sam 25:36; thirteen times total).
36. The *Qal* passive of *ʾkl* occurs three times in suffix conjugation (Nah 1:10; Neh 2:3, 13), and in the prefix conjugation in Isa 1:20; the participle is found in Exod 3:2. All are pointed as *Pual*.
37. The form *yillôd* (and plural) is used ten times; cf. n. 34.

suffix forms are used, they are pointed as *Pual* (for sixteen roots); if only the prefix forms are used, they are pointed as *Hophal* (for fifteen roots).

Qal passive

Suffix	Prefix	Prefix
(= MT *Pual*)	(= MT *Hophal*)	(= MT *Niphal*)
לֻקַּח	יֻקַּח	—
יֻלַּד	—	—
שֹׁרַף	—	יִשָּׂרֵף
—	יֻתַּן	

Forty-two roots are involved (forty-five if we include the participles), and approximately 160 forms (nearly 200 with the participles).[38] The majority of the forms are found in verse.[39]

22.7   *Qal* Impersonal Constructions

a   The vast majority of Hebrew verbs have personal subjects; they may be definite, as usual, or indefinite, as with the pseudo-passive use of the third-person masculine plural or, less often, singular (4.4.2). A small group of verbs is used impersonally, that is, with no topic in view other than the condition or action expressed by the predicate; nearly all are found in the *Qal*.[40] Such constructions are familiar from English environmental verbs, for example, '*It's raining*,' '*It's hot* out.' One category of Hebrew impersonal constructions is the *environmentals* (## 1–2).[41]

1.	וְאוֹר לָכֶם וָלֵכוּ׃	When *it is light* (enough) for you (to go), go. 1 Sam 29:10
2.	תַּשְׁלֵג בְּצַלְמוֹן׃	*It snows* on (Mount) Zalmon. Ps 68:15

b   A larger category of impersonals involves a range of emotions and experiences; in these constructions the undergoer of the emotion or experience is specified by a following prepositional phrase in *l*.[42] The *emotionals* represent the emotion as coming to the undergoer from outside (## 3–4), but this point should not be exaggerated. The *experientials* describe a circumstance (## 5–6) or fate (# 7). The verb *ṭwb* can be used as either an

---

38. The root *ʾkl* is excluded. There are disputed cases; Williams, for example, omits *ḥpś* and *ktt* and includes forms of *hgw*, *hgy*, *hry*, *yqś*, *yśb*, *nṭś*, *ʿmm*, *qbr*, *qrṣ*, *rʾy*, and *rᶜᶜ* 'to break' for a total of fifty-two roots; see "Passive *Qal*," 46–47. Some of these show only *Qal* passive infinitives, a problematic form altogether; see BL § 38r′ / p. 288.
39. Cf. Williams, "Passive *Qal*," 50.
40. Cf. GKC § 144b–g / pp. 459–60. Ruth Berman distinguishes seven classes of impersonal constructions in Modern Hebrew, all but the last two of them with close biblical analogs: (*a*) existential and possessive *yēš* and *ʾên*, (*b*) what we have called the pseudo-passive (only the mas-

culine plural is used in modern Hebrew), (*c*) experientials, (*d*) environmentals, (*e*) various passive usages, (*f*) various modal predicates, and (*g*) true subjectless clauses (no agent, no action). See "The Case of an (S)VO Language: Subjectless Constructions in Modern Hebrew," *Language* 56 (1980) 759–76.
41. The impersonal use of *śᶜr* 'to storm' is *Niphal*, the *Qal* in Ps 58:10 being difficult. Although it rains more than it snows in the Levant, *mṭr* has no *Qal*, but only *Niphal* ('to be rained on') and *Hiphil* ('to send rain').
42. In Esth 8:5 *ᶜal* may be used in a phrase preceding *ṭôb*, but that form may be an adjective rather than a verb.

emotional or experiential, a fact that suggests that there is little difference between the groups.[43]

3.   וַיִּ֫חַר לוֹ:   And he was mad (lit., *it was kindled* to him).
                                    Jonah 4:1

4.   וְרָוַח לְשָׁאוּל וְטוֹב לוֹ   Saul was relieved (lit., *it was broad* to Saul) and felt good (lit., *it was good* to him).[44]
                                    1 Sam 16:23

5.   יֵ֫צֶר לוֹ   He will be in distress (lit., *it will be narrow* to him).[45]
                                    Job 20:22

6.   יָשַׁ֫נְתִּי אָז יָנ֫וּחַ לִי: Now I would be asleep, at rest (lit., *it would be at rest* to me).
                                    Job 3:13

7.   וְלַמּוֹכִיחִים יִנְעָם   *It will be well* for those who reprove (the guilty).
                                    Prov 24:25

---

43. It could be argued that the same is true of *ṣrr*. Other verbs used in these constructions include *rʕʕ* 'to be evil,' *mrr* 'to be bitter,' *ḥmm* 'to be hot.'

44. The *Qal* impersonal of *rwḥ* is also used in Job 32:20.

45. The masculine of *ṣrr* is more common as an impersonal but the feminine is used in Judg 10:9 and 1 Sam 30:6.

23

Niphal Stem

23.1   Form and Meaning

a   The *Qal* and *Niphal* stems are distinguished from the other stems in that they essentially lack any element of causation (cf. 23.4h). The two are distinguished from each other in that the *Qal* or G stem is unmarked, while the *Niphal* or N stem is marked, both morphologically (with *n*) and semantically. The characteristic *n* augment of the stem functioning principally as the marked counterpart of the G stem is attested over the entire Semitic area with the exception of Aramaic.[1] In Hebrew the *nun* appears initially in the suffix conjugation *niqtal*, participle *niqtāl*, and one form of the infinitive absolute, *niqtôl*; it appears in an assimilated form with the first root consonant in the prefix conjugation *yiqqātēl* and related forms with a so-called protective *h*, for example, imperative *hiqqātēl*, infinitive construct *hiqqātēl*, and another form of the infinitive absolute, *hiqqātōl*.[2]

b   Concerning the origin of the *n* prefix nothing definite can be said. Hans Bauer and Pontus Leander suppose that the **na* and **ta* affixes in the *Niphal* and *Hithpael* stems respectively represent the original Proto-Semitic pronouns of the first-person plural

1. S. Moscati et al., *An Introduction to the Comparative Grammar of the Semitic Languages* (Wiesbaden: Harrassowitz, 1964) 126–27; G. Bergsträsser, *Introduction to the Semitic Languages*, trans. and sup. P. T. Daniels (Winona Lake, Indiana: Eisenbrauns, 1983) 84–85.

2. The secondary *h* in these forms presumably results from analogy with comparable forms in the inflection of the *Hiphil* stem.

cf. Hebrew *ʾănáḥnû*) and of the second person (cf. Hebrew *ʾattâ*, etc.). They further suppose that these affixes originally indicated reflexives for just these persons and that they were generalized secondarily throughout the conjugations for the expression of the reflexive. They defend their suggestion by pointing to the Scandinavian and Slavic languages, where the third-person reflexive pronoun penetrated into the remaining persons in expressions of the passive.[3]

The suggestion that the *na* augment originated with the first-person plural pronoun   c
is plausible, but the further suggestion that it was originally used to express a reflexive idea goes beyond the formal evidence. Of greater importance than the etymological problem is the actual usage of the *Niphal.*

Grammarians have sought to determine the *Niphal*'s meaning in three different   d
ways: (1) by categorizing the stem's values, (2) by abstracting a meaning common to all its values in translation, and (3) by theorizing one original meaning from which others secondarily were developed. Gotthelf Bergsträsser essentially opted for the first approach:

> The *Niphal* is related according to its meaning mostly to the *Qal*; it is (*a*) reflexive of the *Qal*—occasionally (*b*) in a reciprocal sense—still more frequently (*c*) passive. From the passive meaning is derived the sense of 'to allow something to be done to someone.'[4]

The task of categorizing is a necessary preliminary, but Bergsträsser's analysis neither exhausts the *Niphal*'s functions nor does it attempt to penetrate to the meaning of the stem in Semitic categories.

Thomas O. Lambdin went beyond basic efforts by abstracting a medio-passive   e
meaning from what he considered to be the four categories of *Niphal* use: (1) *incomplete passive*, (2) *middle*, (3) *reflexive*, and (4) *resultative*: "These four categories have been defined on the basis of English. In Hebrew, however, they are one: the medio-passive as expressed by the Niphal form."[5] Ernst Jenni also sought one essential meaning and found no equivalent category of thought in the Indo-European languages:

> An exact equivalent to the *Niphal*'s category of meaning does not exist in our languages, so that we are compelled to take two different categories to help in the rendering of the uniform stem—namely, passive and reflexive, to which sometimes must be added a so-called tolerative use. . . .[6]

His conclusion is thus similar to Bergsträsser's.

We shall attempt to follow the third approach, namely, we shall abstract as best we   f
can a primary meaning from the stem's many uses and theorize the course of secondary

3. BL § 38c / p. 280.
4. GB 2. 89 (§ 16b); see the similar treatment of Mayer Lambert, "L'emploi du *nifal* en hébreu," *Revue des études juives* 41 (1900) 196–214. On the use of forms of the *Qal* and *Niphal* stems of the same root in neighboring lines of verse, see Moshe Held, "The Action-Result (Factitive-Passive) Sequence of Identical Verbs in Biblical Hebrew and Ugaritic," *Journal of Biblical Literature* 84 (1965) 272–82.
5. T. O. Lambdin, *Introduction to Biblical Hebrew* (New York: Scribner, 1971) 177, cf. 175–78.
6. *LHS* 131.

developments. Since such an approach goes beyond the descriptive evidence, we need to justify it. We need to approximate the Hebrew structures (in contradistinction to those of English), and we need to establish the meaning of the grammatical category (in contradistinction to lexical meanings).

g   Our aim being to establish the meaning(s) of the *Niphal* stem in Hebrew, we may begin by classifying the species of the *Niphal*. We may consult the categories of thought known to us as English speakers, but the categories of English are not necessarily those of Hebrew. By abstracting an essential notion behind all these specific uses we may come closer to the Hebrew category. The stem's values differ according to a word's meaning in context. By abstracting the common notion behind these uses we may, however, come close to the grammatical form's significance apart from the lexical values. Some grammarians referred to the *reflexive* idea as primary, but they do not adequately define this notion.[7] If, when we attempt to trace the development of a primary meaning into its secondary uses, we find a plausible development, it will tend to corroborate our starting point.

h   The stem's specific meanings can be classified as (1) middle, (2) passive, (3) adjectival (simple adjectival, ingressive, gerundive), and (4) double-status (reflexive, benefactive, reciprocal, tolerative, causative-reflexive). There are some unclassified uses and some *Niphal* denominatives. We abstract from these specific meanings a medio-reflexive notion. In all the specific uses of the *Niphal*, we find the common notion(s) that the action or state expressed by the verb affects the subject (as in the middle voice) or its interests (as in the reflexive).[8] Species 1, 2, and 3 can plausibly be associated with the middle notion, and the others with the reflexive. Even in the double-status uses, where the subject is both actor and patient of the action, the primary notion is that the subject is affected by the action.

i   The *Niphal* normally functions as a counterpart of the *Qal* rather than of any of the causation stems, but sometimes it becomes confused with values normally attributed to the *Qal* itself or serves as a medio-reflexive counterpart to a causation stem (23.6).

j   The *Niphal*'s functions depend on the verb's meaning and its context. Hebrew, as we shall see, groups together the three senses of 'move' in the sentences, 'Ruth moved,' 'Ruth was moved,' and 'Ruth moved herself.' All of these would be *Niphals*. Few English verbs, however, show the syntactic flexibility of 'move.' The verb 'cut,' for instance, cannot be used intransitively (as in 'Ruth moved'); 'Ruth cut . . . ' demands an object, be it reflexive ('herself') or not ('the bread'). The English equivalents of Hebrew *Niphal* forms will therefore be diverse. Consider these sentences:

1a.   וּבְנָבִיא נִשְׁמָר׃   By a prophet it (Israel) *was guarded.*
                                            Hos 12:14

---

7. Carl Brockelmann, *Grundriss der vergleichenden Grammatik der semitischen Sprache* (Berlin: Reuter und Reichard, 1908), 1. 536; Brockelmann, *Hebräische Syntax* (Neukirchen: Neukirchener Verlag, 1956) 37; BL § 38b–e,

s′ / pp. 279–80, 288; Joüon § 51c / p. 115.

8. GKC § 51c / p. 137 mentions the similarity of the *Niphal* to the Greek middle, which has medio-passive sense.

1b. וַעֲמָשָׂא לֹא־נִשְׁמַר בַּחֶרֶב   But Amasa *did* not *guard himself* against the sword.
                                        2 Sam 20:10

The English diversity is a translational matter and should not be confused with the Hebrew diversity, the proper subject of our study.

Basic Species of the *Niphal*   23.2

The two most common categories of *Niphal* usage are the middle or quasi-ergative, **a** and the passive, which developed from the middle. The middle is not necessarily the most common kind of *Niphal*; it is rather the most general, affording the common denominator of meaning, more abstract than the other varieties.

Middle   23.2.1

The basis of the systemic role of the *Niphal* stem is its contrast with the *Qal*. The **a** elementary *Qal : Niphal* pair involves, we shall argue, a construction with a *Qal* transitive verb governed by an agentive subject and governing an object and a corresponding *Niphal* intransitive verb where the *Qal* object serves as the subject and the *Qal* agent is unexpressed. Contrast these two uses of בקע 'to split open, burst.'

1a. וַיִּבְקַע אֱלֹהִים אֶת־הַמַּכְתֵּשׁ   Then God *split open* (*Qal*) the hollow.
                                           Judg 15:19

1b. נִבְקְעוּ כָּל־מַעְיְנֹת תְּהוֹם רַבָּה   And all the springs of the great abyss *burst open*
                                             (*Niphal*).
                                             Gen 7:11

In the first sentence 'God' is the "actor" or "agent" and the verb is transitive with an "object" or "goal" word. In the second sentence, which means approximately 'God split open all the springs,' the construction requires that the water source is the subject and the verb is an intransitive, expressing no agency. Here is another pair of clauses with *bqᶜ*.

2a. כְּמוֹ פֹלֵחַ וּבֹקֵעַ בָּאָרֶץ   as one who plows and *breaks up* (*Qal*) the earth
                                      Ps 141:7

2b. וַתִּבָּקַע הָאָרֶץ בְּקוֹלָם׃   and the earth *split* (*Niphal*) with their sound
                                     1 Kgs 1:40

A similar pair can be found with שבר 'to break.'

3a. וַיִּשְׁבְּרוּ הַכַּדִּים   And they (Gideon's three hundred) *broke* (*Qal*) the
                                jars.
                                Judg 7:20

3b. וְהָאֳנִיָּה חִשְּׁבָה לְהִשָּׁבֵר׃   And the ship threatened *to break* (*Niphal*).
                                          Jonah 1:4

The *Niphal* is used in conjunction with intransitive *Qal* verbs.

4.   בִּנְפֹל אוֹיִבְךָ אַל־תִּשְׂמָח   When your enemy *falls* (*Qal*) do not gloat; when he
      וּבִכָּשְׁלוֹ אַל־יָגֵל לִבֶּךָ׃   *stumbles* (*Niphal*) do not let your heart rejoice.
                                        Prov 24:17 *Qere*

In fact, כשל normally occurs in *Qal* with the suffix conjugation and in *Niphal* with the prefix conjugation, so that the two stems mutually complement (or supplete) one another in the conjugation of that verb.[9]

b   One tool in understanding pairs like those cited for *bqᶜ* and *šbr* is the concept of *ergativity*. As noted earlier (21.2.2f n. 20), in many languages (e.g., Basque, the Eskimo languages, those of European Georgia) the subject of an intransitive verb is marked with the same case inflection as the object of an equivalent transitive verb. For example, in Eskimo the sentence 'Boaz moved Naomi,' which implicitly answers the question 'What did Boaz do?', becomes, in answer to the question 'What happened to Naomi?', 'Her moved,' not 'She moved.' This case function is called the ergative. The middle use of the *Niphal* has some similarities to the ergative patterning, the most striking involving אֶת־.

5a.   וְאָכְלוּ אֶת־הַבָּשָׂר   And they ate (*Qal*) *the flesh*.
                                 Exod 12:8

5b.   וְלֹא יֵאָכֵל אֶת־בְּשָׂרוֹ   *Its flesh* shall not be eaten (*Niphal*).
                                       Exod 21:28

Normally את marks the goal word after a transitive verb, but in the *Niphal* construction here it marks the subject. Strictly speaking this is not an ergative construction because *yēʾākēl* 'be eaten' is passive, assuming an agent, whereas an ergative construction refers to intransitive verbs, but the resemblance of the Hebrew *Niphal* is suggestive. An ergative system highlights the participant in the verbal situation that is most directly affected, the "object" of a transitive and the "subject" of an intransitive. The *Niphal* is the stem in Hebrew that performs a similar highlighting role; the middle sense of the *Niphal*, in fact, is based on "object/subject" mutuality. Similar to the "ergative *Niphal*" is the use of the *Niphal* with an internal accusative.[10]

6.   וַיִּנָּקְמוּ נָקָם בִּשְׁאָט בְּנֶפֶשׁ   They took vengeance with malice of heart.
                                              Ezek 25:15

23.2.2   Passive

a   The passive sense of the *Niphal* is arguably the most common. By "passive" we mean that the subject is in the *state* of being acted upon or of suffering the effects of an action by an implicit or explicit agent. As with the middle, so also with the passive the

---

9. Some common *Qal* intransitives have no *Niphal*, notably *hlk* 'to walk' (save perhaps in Ps 109:23), *npl* 'to fall,' *ᶜmd* 'to stand,' and *qwm* 'to rise.'

10. David Toshio Tsumura, "Niphal with an Internal Object in Habakkuk 3:9a," *Journal of Semitic Studies* 31 (1986) 11–16; cf. Jer 14:17, Isa 45:17, Hab 3:9.

Niphal subject would correspond to a *Qal* object. Thus, וַיִּקָּבֵר יוֹאָשׁ, 'And Joash *was buried*' (2 Kgs 13:13), is equivalent to וַיִּקְבְּרוּ אֶת־יוֹאָשׁ, 'And they *buried* Joash.' The middle differs from the passive in two ways: (1) it is more "process" oriented, whereas the passive is more "state" oriented, and (2) whereas the middle is non-agent oriented, the passive is agent oriented.

The middle readily merges with the passive in some verbs.   b

1. וַיּוֹלֶךְ יהוה אֶת־הַיָּם . . . וַיָּשֶׂם   And Yʜwʜ drove back the sea . . . and turned the
    אֶת־הַיָּם לֶחָרָבָה וַיִּבָּקְעוּ הַמָּיִם: sea into dry land, and so the waters *were divided*.
                                               Exod 14:21

Here we see juxtaposed the syntactic pattern *agent* ('Yʜwʜ') + *transitive verb* ('drove back') + *goal word* ('sea') with the pattern *Niphal* + *goal word*. The second pattern is incomplete (the agent is omitted). The form of *bq^c* can be treated as a middle, namely, 'the waters divided,' but the agentive nuance of the third clause is so strongly present from the first two that it is best classified as passive. The same phenomenon can be observed with פתח 'to open.'

2. וַיִּפְתַּח אֶת־פִּי . . . וַיִּפָּתַח פִּי   And he *opened* (*Qal*) my mouth . . . and my
                                               mouth *was opened* (*Niphal*).
                                               Ezek 33:22

Often no distinction is possible.

3a. הָפַךְ לִבָּם לִשְׂנֹא עַמּוֹ   He (God) *changed* (*Qal*) their (the Egyptians')
                                      heart to hate his people.
                                      Ps 105:25

3b. וַיֵּהָפֵךְ לְבַב פַּרְעֹה וַעֲבָדָיו   And the heart of Pharaoh and his officials
     אֶל־הָעָם   *changed* (or, *was changed*) (*Niphal*) toward
                                            the people.
                                            Exod 14:5

In historical terms, it was through the "merging" of the "non-agentive" nuance with   c
the "agentive" that the *Niphal* took on the passive sense and in due course ousted the old *Qal* passive (22.6), even with an expressed agent. It is instructive to note that in Classical Arabic a comparable development was resisted: "It is a rule that in High Arabic a passive cannot be bound by a preposition with the corresponding active subject. . . . Therefore the 'rule' can be established, 'the passive construction in Arabic is only used where the actor is not mentioned.'"[11] Even in Hebrew the agent with the *Niphal* is only rarely indicated by a prepositional phrase.

In the Indo-European languages a similar merger of the non-agentive middle with   d
the agentive passive occurred. Indeed, John Lyons notes, "this seems to have been the

11. E. König, *Historisch-kritisches Lehrgebäude der hebräischen Sprache* (Leipzig: Hinrichs, 1897), 3. 34 (§ 100).

point de départ for the subsequent development of passive constructions in the Indo-European languages."[12] So, for example, in Latin one finds (letting *A* stand for agent and *B* for object):

active	*A movet B*	'A moves B'
passive	*B movetur*	'B moves' or 'B is moved'

That is, the Latin passive has a middle sense. In Greek, "the opposition of voice . . . is primarily one of active *v.* 'middle.' The passive was a later development."[13]

e   Passive constructions in Hebrew may be incomplete or complete. In the *incomplete passive* the agent is not indicated.

4.	וְאַנְשֵׁי־חֶסֶד נֶאֱסָפִים	Devout men *are taken away*.[14] Isa 57:1
5.	שַׁעֲרֵי הַנְּהָרוֹת נִפְתָּחוּ	The river gates *are opened*.[15] Nah 2:7
6.	לְעוֹלָם נִשְׁמָרוּ	Forever they *will be protected*. Ps 37:28
7.	וּמַרְאֵה הָעֶרֶב וְהַבֹּקֶר אֲשֶׁר נֶאֱמַר אֱמֶת הוּא	The evening and morning vision which *was told* you is true.[16] Dan 8:26
8.	אִם־אֵין לוֹ וְנִמְכַּר בִּגְנֵבָתוֹ׃	If he (the thief) has nothing, then he must *be sold* (to pay) for his theft.[17] Exod 22:2

A special form of the incomplete passive involves the third-person singular form without an expressed subject. To reflect this kind of *impersonal construction*, with its pattern *subject + verb*, English usually demands the insertion of the "dummy" pronoun *it*.

9.	לְזֹאת יִקָּרֵא אִשָּׁה	To this one *it shall be called* woman. Gen 2:23
10.	עַל־כֵּן יֵאָמַר בְּסֵפֶר מִלְחֲמֹת יהוה	Thus *it is said* in the Book of the Wars of Yʜwʜ. Num 21:14
11.	וּבַחֲבֻרָתוֹ נִרְפָּא־לָנוּ׃	By his stripes we *were healed* (lit., *it was healed* to us). Isa 53:5

As with other passive usages, the subject of a *Niphal* may be marked with את.[18]

---

12. John Lyons, *Introduction to Theoretical Linguistics* (Cambridge: Cambridge University, 1968) 375.
13. Lyons, *Theoretical Linguistics*, 373.
14. Cf. 1 Sam 14:19.
15. Cf. Ps 78:23.

16. For the sense, cf. Ezek 13:7.
17. Cf. Gen 37:27.
18. Cf. *wayyimaḥ* in Gen 7:23, where the proper form may be a *Niphal*. Note the use of ʾt with a *Hophal* in Exod 10:8.

| 12. | וַיִּוָּלֵד לַחֲנוֹךְ אֶת־עִירָד | *Irad* was born to Enoch. Gen 4:18 |
| 13. | כַּאֲשֶׁר יֵאָכֵל אֶת־הַצְּבִי וְאֶת־הָאַיָּל | as *the gazelle and deer* are eaten Deut 12:22 |

In the *complete passive*, the agent may be indicated by a prepositional phrase in בּ   f
(## 14–16) or ל (## 17–19); the means or instrument may be given after בּ (# 20) or מִן
(# 21).[19]

14.	עַם נוֹשַׁע בַּיהוה	a people saved *by Yhwh* Deut 33:29
15.	שֹׁפֵךְ דַּם הָאָדָם בָּאָדָם דָּמוֹ יִשָּׁפֵךְ	Whoever sheds human blood, *by a human* shall his blood be shed. Gen 9:6
16.	כָּל־מְלָאכָה לֹא־יֵעָשֶׂה בָהֶם	No work may be done *by them.* Exod 12:16
17.	הֲלוֹא נָכְרִיּוֹת נֶחְשַׁבְנוּ לוֹ	Are we not counted as strangers *by him*? Gen 31:15
18.	אֲשֶׁר יֵאָכֵל לְכָל־נֶפֶשׁ	which is eaten *by everyone* Exod 12:16
19.	וְלֹא־נִפְקַד לָהֶם מְאוּמָה	And nothing has been missed *by them.* 1 Sam 25:7
20.	כִּי בְּאֵשׁ קִנְאָתִי תֵּאָכֵל כָּל־הָאָרֶץ:	Because the whole earth will be consumed *by the fire* of my zeal.[20] Zeph 3:8
21.	וְלֹא־יִכָּרֵת כָּל־בָּשָׂר עוֹד מִמֵּי הַמַּבּוּל	All flesh shall not again be cut off *by the water* of the flood. Gen 9:11

Adjectival Species of the *Niphal*   23.3

The *Niphal* has several uses which may loosely be called adjectival: these include the   a
simple adjectival (cf. 'The wall *is* broken'), the ingressive-stative (cf. 'Naomi *grew* sad')
and the gerundive (cf. 'Jonathan *is to be* loved'). As the examples below suggest, the
ingressive and gerundive are used with both personal and non-personal subjects, while
the simple adjectival is found with non-personal subjects.

In the *simple adjectival Niphal*, the subject is in an adjectival state described by the   b
verb; such a form is "essentially a stative verb." Lambdin contrasts comparable English
passive and simple adjectival forms: "In the passive *It was broken*, *was* is an auxiliary

---

19. The preposition *b* is most common for agency. For other examples with *l*, see Josh 17:16, Jer 8:3, Neh 6:1.
20. Cf. Lev 6:3.

verb in the unit *was-broken*," whereas in the adjectival, "*It was broken, was* is the verb *to be* followed by an adjective/participle."[21]

1.	וְלֹא נִפְתַּח אֵזוֹר חֲלָצָיו וְלֹא נִתַּק שְׂרוֹךְ נְעָלָיו:	Not a belt *is loose* at his waist, not a sandal-thong *is broken*. Isa 5:27
2.	נִשְׁבְּרוּ בְרִיחֶיהָ:	The bars of its (Babylon's) gates *are broken*. Jer 51:30
3.	שַׁעַר . . . יִהְיֶה סָגוּר . . . יִפָּתֵחַ	The gate . . . will be shut [for six days . . . , then] *will be open*. Ezek 46:1

c   The *ingressive-stative Niphal* describes the subject coming to be in a particular state.[22] If the subject is non-personal, the *Niphal* also has a middle sense.

4.	וְהִנֵּה־מַיִם בָּאִים מִדֶּרֶךְ אֱדוֹם וַתִּמָּלֵא הָאָרֶץ אֶת־הַמָּיִם:	There it was—water flowing from the Way of Edom, and the land *became filled* with water. 2 Kgs 3:20

With a personal subject, the ingressive-stative also has a reflexive sense, for it refers to emotions and the like, which react upon the psyche.

5.	כִּי־נִכְמְרוּ רַחֲמָיו אֶל־אָחִיו	And his compassion *grew hot* toward his brother. Gen 43:30
6.	כִּי נִבְהֲלוּ מִפָּנָיו:	because they *became terrified* at his presence Gen 45:3
7.	וַיָּקָם יְהוֹנָתָן מֵעִם הַשֻּׁלְחָן בָּחֳרִי־אָף . . . כִּי נֶעֱצַב אֶל־דָּוִד	Jonathan got up from the table in fierce anger . . . because he *became grieved* (or, *hurt*) for David. 1 Sam 20:34
8.	נִלְאֵיתִי הִנָּחֵם:	I have *become too weary to be moved to pity*. Jer 15:6
9.	נִלְאָה לַהֲשִׁיבָהּ אֶל־פִּיו:	He (the sluggard) *gets weary* by returning it (his hand) to his mouth. Prov 26:15
10.	הִיא נֶאֶנְחָה	It (Jerusalem) *is groaning*. Lam 1:8

---

21. Lambdin groups together the simple adjective and gerundive *Niphals* as "resultative," a term we reserve for one use of the *Piel*. Note his English examples: passive 'to be opened' *versus* simple adjectival 'to be open'; passive 'It is being broken' *versus* simple adjectival 'It is broken.' See *Introduction to Biblical Hebrew*, 177. English illustrations only suggest the relevant distinctions.

22. In Akkadian the N stem with stative verbs is predominantly ingressive, e.g., G stem *ibašši* 'he is' *versus* N stem *ibbašši* 'he becomes.' See Moscati et al., *Comparative Grammar*, 126–27; W. von Soden, *Grundriss der akkadischen Grammatik* (Rome: Pontifical Biblical Institute, 1969) 118. Von Soden allows for an ingressive fientive, but such a form is at best rare in Akkadian.

By "*gerundive*" we mean verbs in the *Niphal* (often participles) signifying that the   d
adjectival state is necessary, or proper, or possible.[23] In English the adjectival suffixes
-*able*/-*ible*/-*ful*/-*ly* signify these notions.

11.	לַבַּ֫יִת הַנִּבְנֶה לְשֵׁם־יהוה:	the house that *is to be built* to the name of YHWH 1 Chr 22:19
12.	כָּל־הַמִּדְבָּר הַגָּדוֹל וְהַנּוֹרָא	all that vast and *dreadful* steppe Deut 1:19
13.	מֵאֶ֫רֶץ נוֹרָאָה:	from a *terrible* land Isa 21:1
14.	עַד־בֹּאָם אֶל־אֶ֫רֶץ נוֹשָׁ֫בֶת	until they came to a land that *was inhabitable* Exod 16:35
15.	וַיַּכּוּם לְפִי־חֶ֫רֶב . . . כָּל־הַנִּמְצָא	And they struck them with the sword . . . all *who were found*. Judg 20:48
16.	אֵין אֶ֫בֶן נִרְאָה:	Not a stone *was visible*. 1 Kgs 6:18
17.	וּבֵין הַחַיָּה הַנֶּאֱכֶ֫לֶת וּבֵין הַחַיָּה אֲשֶׁר לֹא תֵאָכֵל:	between living creatures that *are edible* and those that *are inedible* Lev 11:47
18.	עֲשֹׂה צְדָקָה וּמִשְׁפָּט נִבְחָר לַיהוה מִזָּ֫בַח:	To do what is right and just is more *acceptable* to YHWH than sacrifice. Prov 21:3
19.	שָׁאוּל וִיהוֹנָתָן הַנֶּאֱהָבִים וְהַנְּעִימִם	Saul and Jonathan *were lovely* and gracious. 2 Sam 1:23

Double-Status Species of the *Niphal*   23.4

In the double-status uses of the *Niphal*, the subject (almost always personal) is at   a
the same time agent and patient (or undergoer) of the verbal action. These correspond to
reflexives and related constructions in the European languages, for example, English 'I
wash myself,' French 'Je me brosse les dents,' German 'Ich setze mich.' As these examples suggest, reflexive actions are not a closed or fixed category: English does not use
a reflexive for brushing the teeth, as French does, and ordinarily it does not do so for
sitting down (but cf. 'Set yourself down'). The double-status categories other than reflexive arise from various kinds of semantic complexity.

A *reflexive construction* is one in which the subject and object of the verb refer to   b
the same person or thing. *Niphal* reflexives in the singular work straightforwardly; in the

---

23. The term gerundive is derived from Latin grammar;
the future passive participle, which signifies comparable notions, corresponds in form with the gerund. Note *agenda*,

Latin, 'those things that are to be done.' Lambdin refers in
connection with these forms to "the nuance of potentiality"; *Introduction to Biblical Hebrew*, 177.

plural the sense tends to be distributive (cf. English 'We washed ourselves,' 'We each washed ourselves,' 'Each of us washed herself'). Some *Niphals* are essentially reflexive; thus, נִשְׁמַר almost always signifies 'to guard oneself,' נָקַם 'to avenge oneself,' נִשְׁעַן 'to lean (oneself),' נֶחְנַק 'to hang oneself.'[24]

1.	וְאִנָּקְמָה מֵאוֹיְבָי׃	I *will avenge myself* on my enemies. Isa 1:24
2.	יִסָּמֵךְ אִישׁ עָלָיו	If a man *supports himself* on it. . . . Isa 36:6
3.	וּבְכֹל אֲשֶׁר־אָמַרְתִּי אֲלֵיכֶם תִּשָּׁמֵרוּ	And, with regard to everything I said to you, *take care to yourselves.* Exod 23:13

In other cases the reflexive sense is found alongside others, for example, נִצַּל may signify 'to deliver oneself' or 'to be delivered.'

c   In many situations where other languages use reflexive constructions, Hebrew does not use the *Niphal*. Sometimes the reflexive relationship is expressed by means of the prepositions ל (11.2.10d), כ, etc., with a personal pronoun or some circumlocution, such as לבב or נפש.

4.	וַיִּקַּח־לוֹ לֶמֶךְ שְׁתֵּי נָשִׁים	Then Lamech took *for himself* two wives. Gen 4:19
5.	וְאָהַבְתָּ לְרֵעֲךָ כָּמוֹךָ	You shall love your neighbor *as yourself.* Lev 19:18
6.	כִּי־אַהֲבַת נַפְשׁוֹ אֲהֵבוֹ׃	He loved him with the love (he had) *for himself.* 1 Sam 20:17
7.	כִּי תֹאמַר בִּלְבָבְךָ	If you say in the heart (i.e., *to yourself*). . . . Deut 7:17

A reflexive construction may also involve a *Niphal* along with a prepositional phrase, as in the frequent injunction הִשָּׁמֶר לְךָ, 'Guard yourself for yourself' (Deut 4:9).

d   In a *benefactive construction* the subject acts for its own benefit or interest; the verb is usually transitive. This construction, as noted above, also occurs with the Greek middle (e.g., *endysasthai khitōna* 'to put on [oneself] a tunic'). Compare French reflexive 'Je me lave' ('I am washing myself') and benefactive 'Je me lave une chemise' ('I am washing [myself] a shirt'). The *Niphal* benefactive is not common.

8.	נִשְׁאֹל נִשְׁאַל מִמֶּנִּי דָוִד לָרוּץ בֵּית־לֶחֶם	David *earnestly asked* (*for himself*) leave of me to hurry to Bethlehem. 1 Sam 20:6; cf. v 28

---

24. Lambdin, *Introduction to Biblical Hebrew*, 177.

A *reciprocal construction* is a plural variety of reflexive, where the action is mutual.   e
Sometimes the subjects act in relationship with one another, and at other times the
subjects interact hostilely. The close relationship between the reflexive and reciprocal
notions is sometimes evident, as in the *Niphal* of אסף.[25]

9.   וַיִּקְרָא יַעֲקֹב אֶל־בָּנָיו וַיֹּאמֶר   Then Jacob called his sons and said: '*Gather
     הֵאָסְפוּ   (yourselves) together.* . . .
                                          Gen 49:1

Action in concert can be self-contained (# 10) or directed outward (# 11).

10. הֲיֵלְכוּ שְׁנַיִם יַחְדָּו בִּלְתִּי אִם־   Do two walk together unless they *agree*?
     נוֹעָדוּ:   Amos 3:3

11. וַיִּלָּחֲמוּ עָלֶיהָ:   And they *waged war* against it.
                                          Josh 10:5

Hostile action may include single combat (## 12–13) or judicial procedure (# 14).

12. וְכִי־יִנָּצוּ אֲנָשִׁים   If men *struggle with each other.* . . .
                                          Exod 21:22

13. תְּנוּ־לִי אִישׁ וְנִלָּחֲמָה יָחַד: Give me a man and *let us fight together.*
                                          1 Sam 17:10

14. וְאִשָּׁפְטָה אִתְּכֶם לִפְנֵי יהוה   so that I *may go to court with you* before Yнwн.
                                          1 Sam 12:7

In a transitive sentence the reciprocal merges with the benefactive.

15. וַיִּוָּעַץ הַמֶּלֶךְ רְחַבְעָם אֶת־   Then King Rehoboam *consulted* the elders.
     הַזְּקֵנִים   1 Kgs 12:6

A *tolerative construction* is one which combines the reflexive notion with the notion   f
of permission. The subject allows an implicit or explicit agent to effect upon him the
action denoted by the verb: 'X (subject) allows himself to be Y (verb).' If in a passive the
subject is non-willing and in a reflexive the subject is willing, then in a tolerative the subject is half-willing. Hebrew often uses the *Niphal* for such constructions. A passive
rendering of such *Niphals* is often possible; for example, בְּנִי הִזָּהֵר (Qoh 12:12) may be
rendered 'Be warned, my son' or 'Allow/Suffer yourself to be warned, my son.' Indeed,
other languages use the passive and similar forms for tolerative constructions, for example, the Greek middle form in *Anebē de kai Iōsēph . . . apograpsasthai*, 'Joseph then
went up . . . to be registered (i.e., to allow himself to be registered)' (Luke 2:4–5).
    The tolerative *Niphal* often involves the element of efficacy: what the subject allows   g
to happen can indeed be carried through. Thus Paul Joüon glosses נִדְרָשׁ as "'to let

oneself be questioned,' and that efficaciously so that it practically means 'to answer' (when speaking of God); נִזְהַר, 'to let oneself be warned' and that efficaciously and so practically 'to bear in mind the warning'; נוֹסַר, 'to let oneself be corrected, to be corrected'; נֶעְתַּר, 'to let oneself be entreated (efficaciously), to grant.'"[26] The tolerative is often used of the deity.

16. וְנֶעְתַּר לָהֶם
And he *will respond to* their *pleas* (< *allow himself to be entreated* by them).
Isa 19:22

17. נִדְרַשְׁתִּי לְלוֹא שָׁאָלוּ נִמְצֵאתִי לְלֹא בִקְשֻׁנִי
I *answered* (< *allowed myself to be sought by*) those who did not ask (for me); I *revealed myself to* (< *allowed myself to be found by*) those who did not seek me.
Isa 65:1

18. וַיֶּעְתַּר יִצְחָק לַיהוה . . . וַיֵּעָתֶר לוֹ יהוה
And Isaac entreated (*Qal*) Yhwh . . . and Yhwh *answered* (< *allowed himself to be entreated by*) him.
Gen 25:21

19. וַאֲנִי אִדָּרֵשׁ לָכֶם בֵּית יִשְׂרָאֵל חַי־אָנִי . . . אִם־אִדָּרֵשׁ לָכֶם:
Am I *to let myself be inquired of* by you (or, *answer* you), O House of Israel? As surely as I live, . . . I will not *let myself be inquired of* by you (or, *answer* you).
Ezek 20:31

The notion of efficacy is not always present.

20. הָאֲנָשִׁים הָאֵלֶּה הֶעֱלוּ גִלּוּלֵיהֶם עַל־לִבָּם . . . הַאִדָּרֹשׁ אִדָּרֵשׁ לָהֶם
These men have mounted idols on their hearts. . . . *Should I really let myself be consulted* by them?
Ezek 14:3

h   The *causative-reflexive scheme* in Hebrew is usually *Hithpael*, but in some cases the *Niphal* is used. In these verbs the subject causes the action to happen to himself: 'X (subject) gets himself to be Y (verbal notion).' Greek uses the middle for comparable senses, for example, *misthoumai* 'I get myself hired, I take a job, I sign on (as a mercenary soldier),' *didaskomai* 'I get myself taught.' Thus in Hebrew we have נוֹדַע 'to make oneself known.'

21. אַל־תִּוָּדְעִי לָאִישׁ
But *do* not *make yourself known* to the man.
Ruth 3:3

22. וְנוֹדַע יהוה לְמִצְרַיִם וְיָדְעוּ מִצְרַיִם אֶת־יהוה
So Yhwh *will make himself known* to the Egyptians, and so the Egyptians will know Yhwh.
Isa 19:21

---

26. Joüon § 51c / p. 115, comparing also *šʾl Hiphil*, with a sense similar to *ʿtr Niphal*. See also J. H. Eaton, "Some Misunderstood Hebrew Words for God's Self-Revelation," *Bible Translator* 25 (1974) 331–38.

23. וָאֵרָא אֶל־אַבְרָהָם . . . בְּאֵל שַׁדָּי
וּשְׁמִי יהוה לֹא נוֹדַעְתִּי לָהֶם:

I *appeared* (< *made myself to be seen*) to Abraham
. . . as El Shaddai, but by my name YHWH I *did* not
make myself known to them.
Exod 6:3

Since this function of the *Niphal* corresponds with the *Hithpael*'s primary function, the
two stems may be used similarly with some verbs. In at least one case, the older *Niphal* is
replaced by a later *Hithpael* (with a change in the preposition used).[27]

24a.   וַיִּרְאוּ בְּנֵי עַמּוֹן כִּי נִבְאֲשׁוּ
בְּדָוִד
2 Sam 10:6

24b.   וַיִּרְאוּ בְּנֵי עַמּוֹן כִּי הִתְבָּאֲשׁוּ
עִם־דָּוִיד
1 Chr 19:6

The Ammonites realized that they *had made themselves foul-smelling* to David.

Isolated and Denominative *Niphals*   23.5

Two groups of *Niphals* break with the schemata we have elaborated. One group   a
includes verb roots attested only in the *Niphal*; these isolates are left unclassified because
the other verbal stems are lacking to serve as points of reference. Among these are אבק
'to wrestle' (only in Gen 32:25–26), אות 'to consent,' אלח 'to be corrupt.' The first two
are apparently reciprocal, the third adjectival.[28]

The rare denominative use of the *Niphal* is probably related to its ingressive-stative   b
and causative-reflexive functions.

> אחז *Niphal*, 'to possess' < אֲחֻזָּה 'possession' (cf. Josh 22:9)
> יאל *Niphal*, 'to become foolish' < אֱוִיל 'fool' (cf. Isa 19:13; cf. v 11)
> לבב *Niphal*, 'to get a heart' < לֵבָב 'heart' (hapax in Job 11:12)
> נבא *Niphal*, 'to prophesy' < נָבִיא 'prophet' (cf. 1 Sam 10:11)
> צמד *Niphal*, 'to attach oneself' < צֶמֶד 'pair' (cf. Num 25:3)
> שבע *Niphal*, 'to swear'[29] < שֶׁבַע 'seven' (cf. Gen 21:24)

Mixed Forms   23.6

The systematic character of the Hebrew stem system is occasionally compromised.   a
Carl Brockelmann notes that, in contrast to Classical Arabic and Aramaic, the verbal
stems in Hebrew tend to become confused: "The system of verbal stems . . . purely
preserved in Classical Arabic and Aramaic—is stifled with all kinds of cross-overs in
several modern Arabic dialects, in Hebrew, but especially in Ethiopic and Akkadian."[30]

---

27. The *Hithpael* of *bʾš* is found only in the 1 Chron-
icles passage; for the *Niphal* see also, e.g., 2 Sam 16:21.
Note, too, *brk* Hithpael in Gen 22:18 and *brk* Niphal in
Gen 12:3; see 23.6.4. For *Niphal*/*Hithpael* similarities in
later Hebrew, see, e.g., E. Qimron, *The Hebrew of the
Dead Sea Scrolls* (Atlanta: Scholars Press, 1986) 49.

28. On isolated *Niphals*, see Lambert, "L'emploi du *nifal*
en hébreu," 213–14.

29. The sense of *šbʿ* is evidently 'to seven onself, bind
oneself by seven things'; this is the most common denominative *Niphal*.

30. Brockelmann, *Grundriss*, 1. 540.

Specifically, some verbs in the *Niphal* with its various functions become confused with *Qal, Piel, Hiphil,* and *Hithpael.*

23.6.1 Mixture with *Qal*

a   We have already noted the correspondence between the *Niphal*'s "middle" function and the use of some *Qal* intransitive verbs (23.2.1a). The ingressive-stative *Niphal* function is obviously similar to that of *Qal* statives. With some roots *Qal* and *Niphal* exhibit no noticeable difference in meaning; in the conjugation of some others the *Qal* and *Niphal* combine to form one paradigm. The *Niphal* also becomes mixed with the old *Qal* passive.

b   Where no difference in meaning is apparent, the stems seem interchangeable.[31]

1a.   כִּי חָלִיתִי הַיּוֹם שְׁלֹשָׁה׃   because I *became sick* (*Qal*) three days ago
1 Sam 30:13

1b.   וְלֹא נֶחְלוּ עַל־שֵׁבֶר יוֹסֵף׃   But they *do* not *become sick* (*Niphal*) over the ruin of Joseph.
Amos 6:6

2a.   וּבְמוֹט הָרִים בְּלֵב יַמִּים׃   and when the mountains *will totter* (*Qal*) into the heart of the sea
Ps 46:3

2b.   בַּל־תִּמּוֹט   It *will* not *totter* (*Niphal*).
Ps 46:6

c   Some verbs build their suffix conjugation with *Niphal* and their prefix conjugation with *Qal.* Mayer Lambert explains this phenomenon:

> In the case of rare verbs one could believe that it is an accident that one finds *Niphal* for one tense and *Qal* for another. But this explanation is not possible for other verbs, which are so used frequently. It is likely that both the *Niphal* and the *Qal* have their own special origin, but the difference in sense has been effaced and the analogy of sound led to the tenses which resemble one another in one or the other form being preferred, as נִגַּשׁ and יִגַּשׁ.[32]

This pattern is an example of suppletion.[33]

3.   וְנִגַּשׁ מֹשֶׁה לְבַדּוֹ אֶל־יהוה   And Moses alone *is to approach* (*Niphal*) Yʜᴡʜ;
וְהֵם לֹא יִגָּשׁוּ   the others *must* not *approach* (*Qal*).
Exod 24:2

---

31. Note also these pairs: *mwṭ* (*Qal* Ps 60:4, *Niphal* Ps 104:5), *qll* 'to be insignificant' (*Qal* Gen 16:4, *Niphal* 2 Sam 6:22), *śgb* 'to be lofty' (*Qal* Job 5:11, *Niphal* Prov 18:10); cf. GB 2. 90 (§ 16c) and cf. Lambert, "L'emploi du *nifal* in hébreu," 210–11.

32. Lambert, "L'emploi du *nifal* in hébreu," 212.

33. In addition to *kšl* mentioned above (23.2.1a), the fol-lowing verbs have *Qal* prefix (and imperative) forms and *Niphal* suffix (and participial) forms (with examples): *lʾy* 'to be weary' (*Qal* Gen 9:11, *Niphal* Jer 9:4), *ngš* 'to approach' (*Qal* Gen 27:22, *Niphal* Deut 25:9), *ntk* 'to be poured out' (*Qal* Jer 44:6, *Niphal* Jer 42:18), *pwṣ* 'to be scattered' (*Qal* 1 Sam 11:11, *Niphal* Gen 10:18). This list follows GB 2. 90 (§ 16c).

4. נָפֹצוּ ... וַתְּפוּצֶ֫ינָה מִבְּלִי רֹעֶה צֹאנִי		They (my flock) *scattered* (*Qal*) because there was no shepherd. . . . My flock *scattered* (*Niphal*). Ezek 34:5–6
5a.	הַנּוֹגֵעַ בָּאָ֫רֶץ וַתָּמוֹג	he who touches the earth and it *melts* (*Qal*) Amos 9:5
5b.	וְכִי נָמֹגוּ כָּל־יֹשְׁבֵי הָאָ֫רֶץ מִפְּנֵיכֶם׃	because all that live in the land *melt* (*Niphal*) before you Josh 2:9

It is likely that sometimes the *Qal* passive and the *Niphal* were confounded by the   d
Masoretes, as, for example, with the I-*nun* verbs in their prefix conjugation, where the
old *Qal* passive would have a *šureq* instead of the *Niphal*'s *ḥireq*. Lambert reasons: "It is
probable that in the case of I-*nun* where the *Niphal* is not encountered apart from the
past [the suffix conjugation], the *Niphal* past, if it has the passive sense, might be considered as an ancient passive of the *Qal*."[34] Three examples he cites are *ngś Niphal* 'to be
hard pressed,' נִגַּשׁ (e.g., # 3; 1 Sam 13:6); *nṭ* *Niphal* 'to be planted,' only in נִטָּעוּ (Isa
40:24); *nsḥ Niphal* 'to be torn away,' only in וְנִסַּחְתֶּם (Deut 28:63; cf. יִסְחוּ, probably *Qal*
passive יִסְחוּ in Prov 2:22 as in a Cairo Geniza text).

Lambert also alleges that the gradual substitution of the *Niphal* for the *Qal* passive   e
can be seen with some verbs which show a *Qal* infinitive absolute before a *Niphal* prefix
form, as, for example, סָקוֹל יִסָּקֵל, 'He will surely be stoned' (Exod 19:13) and שָׁקוֹל
יִשָּׁקֵל, 'It will be weighed' (Job 6:2). He rightly acknowledges that one cannot be certain
with which verbs this substitution took place (cf. 35.2.1d).[35]

Mixture with *Piel*   23.6.2

Although *Niphal* normally stands in juxtaposition to *Qal*, with some verbs it serves   a
as the middle-reflexive counterpart to *Piel*; the usual passive and reflexive stems are *Pual*
and *Hithpael*, respectively. The mixture is clearest with verbs whose *Qal* is unattested;
this is the case with all verbs paired here.[36]

1a.	וְהַגֶּד־נָא לִי מֶה עָשִׂיתָ אַל־ תְּכַחֵד מִמֶּ֫נִּי׃	Tell me what you did. *Do* not *hide* (*Piel*) from me. Josh 7:19
1b.	וְאַשְׁמוֹתַי מִמְּךָ לֹא־נִכְחָ֫דוּ׃	And my sins *were* not *hidden* (*Niphal*) from you. Ps 69:6
2a.	וּבִעֲתַ֫תּוּ רוּחַ־רָעָה מֵאֵת יהוה׃	And an evil spirit from YHWH *terrified* (*Piel*) him. 1 Sam 16:14

---

34. Lambert, "L'emploi du *nifal* en hébreu," 203.
35. Lambert, "L'emploi du *nifal* en hébreu," 205. Just as
the *Qal* passive shifts to the *Niphal*, so the *Niphal* shifts to
the *Hithpael*.

36. Verbs showing *Piel : Niphal* forms with no *Qal* or
only marginal usage include *dbr* (*Niphal* reciprocal), *kbd*
(*Niphal* passive), *ksy* (*Niphal* passive), *mlṭ* (*Niphal* unclear), *qdš* (*Niphal* reflexive and passive).

2b.   כִּי נִבְעַת מִפְּנֵי חֶרֶב מַלְאַךְ   because he *was terrified* (*Niphal*) by the presence of
        יהוה׃   the Angel of Yʜᴡʜ's sword
                                          1 Chr 21:30

3.   וּבַת אִישׁ כֹּהֵן כִּי תֵחֵל לִזְנוֹת   If a priest's daughter *defiles herself* (*Niphal*) by play-
        אֶת־אָבִיהָ הִיא מְחַלֶּלֶת   ing the harlot, she *defiles* (*Piel*) her father.
                                          Lev 21:9

23.6.3   Mixture with *Hiphil*

a   As with *Piel : Niphal* roots, the *Niphal* of some verbs stands closer to the *Hiphil*
than to the *Qal*.[37]

1a.   וְהִכְחַדְתִּיו   And I *will destroy* (*Hiphil*) them.
                                          Exod 23:23

1b.   אִם־לֹא נִכְחַד קִימָ֫נוּ   Surely our foes *are destroyed* (*Niphal*).
                                          Job 22:20

2a.   וְאֵין מֹשִׁיעַ   There was none *to save* (*Hiphil*) them.
                                          2 Sam 22:42

2b.   וּמֵאֹיְבַי אִוָּשֵׁעַ׃   I *am saved* (*Niphal*) from my enemies.
                                          2 Sam 22:4

3a.   וַיַּכְנִיעֵם   And he (David) *subdued* (*Hiphil*) them (the
                                          Philistines).
                                          2 Sam 8:1

3b.   וַיִּכָּנְעוּ הַפְּלִשְׁתִּים   So the Philistines *were subdued* (*Niphal*).
                                          1 Sam 7:13

4a.   בְּצֵל יָדוֹ הֶחְבִּיאָ֫נִי   In the shadow of his hand he *hid* (*Hiphil*) me.
                                          Isa 49:2

4b.   וַיִּוָּתֵר יוֹתָם . . . כִּי נֶחְבָּא׃   But Jotham escaped . . . because he *hid himself*
                                          (*Niphal*).
                                          Judg 9:5

5.   וְאַתָּה כִּי הִזְהַרְתּוֹ צַדִּיק לְבִלְתִּי   But if you *warn* (*Hiphil*) the righteous one not
        חֲטֹא . . . וְהוּא לֹא־חָטָא חָיוֹ   to sin . . . , and he does not sin, he will surely
        יִחְיֶה כִּי נִזְהָר   live, because he *allowed himself to be*
                                          warned (*Niphal*).
                                          Ezek 3:21

---

37. Verbs showing *Hiphil : Niphal* stems with no *Qal*   *Hiphil : Niphal* include *bhl*, *qdš*; for *bhl*, note Job 23:16
include *zhr*, *ḥbᵓ*, *yšᶜ*, *kwn*, *knᶜ*, *šmd*; verbs showing *Piel* +   (*Hiphil*), 15 (*Niphal*).

6.   . . . :וַהֲכִינֹתִי אֶת־מַמְלַכְתּוֹ
וְכֹנַנְתִּי אֶת־כִּסֵּא מַמְלַכְתּוֹ עַד־
עוֹלָם: . . . כִּסְאֲךָ יִהְיֶה נָכוֹן עַד־
עוֹלָם:

And I *will establish* (*Hiphil*) his kingdom . . . and I *will establish* (*Polel*) the throne of his kingdom forever . . . your throne *will be established* (*Niphal*) forever.
2 Sam 7:12, 13, 16

Mixture with *Hithpael* 23.6.4

Since the *Hithpael* historically tends to take on the passive functions of the *Niphal*   a (26.1.3, 26.3), it is not surprising that the stems are occasionally confounded.

1a.   וְהִתְבָּרֲכוּ בְזַרְעֲךָ כֹּל גּוֹיֵי
הָאָרֶץ

And through your offspring all nations of the earth *will be blessed* (*Hithpael*).
Gen 22:18

1b.   וְנִבְרְכוּ בְךָ כֹּל מִשְׁפְּחֹת
הָאֲדָמָה:

And through you all peoples on earth *will be blessed* (*Niphal*).
Gen 12:3

The passive import of both verbs is clear from the context: it is God who blesses (Gen 12:3a, 22:17), that is, who fills the potency for life, albeit through an agent.[38] With some verbs the *Niphal* suffix conjugation and the *Hithpael* prefix conjugation supplete or complement one another, forming one paradigm; the verbs are טמא and יצב.

2.   אַל־תִּטַּמְּאוּ בְּכָל־אֵלֶּה כִּי בְכָל־
אֵלֶּה נִטְמְאוּ הַגּוֹיִם

Do not *defile yourselves* (*Hithpael*) in any of these ways because in all these ways the nations *defiled themselves* (*Niphal*).
Lev 18:24

---

38. For a careful analysis of the clause structures in Gen 12:1–4 (and of their means of signifying), see P. D. Miller, Jr., "Syntax and Theology in Genesis XII 3a," *Vetus Testamentum* 34 (1984) 472–76.

24

Piel Stem

24.1 Form and Meaning

a   The classical Semitic languages have a stem characterized by the *doubling* (or lengthening) of the middle radical, whence the term D stem; the characterization of these stems in the various languages has proved to be difficult.[1] Before Albrecht Goetze's revolutionary study of the Akkadian D stem Hebraists commonly claimed that the *Piel* primarily signified an "intensification" of the root's meaning. In addition, it was thought, the *Piel* signified a "causative" (and on occasion "declarative" or "estimative") meaning with some roots; a denominative meaning was found with other roots. Among the verbs regularly cited in the grammars to display these uses were these.[2]

---

1. We have relied in this chapter on Ernst Jenni, *Das hebräische Pi‘el: Syntaktisch-semasiologische Untersuchung einer Verbalform im Alten Testament* (Zurich: EVZ, 1968)—among major reviews of the book, note T. O. Lambdin, *Catholic Biblical Quarterly* 31 (1969) 435–37; and J. F. A. Sawyer, *Journal of Semitic Studies* 14 (1969) 260–62—and on Stuart A. Ryder II, *The D-Stem in Western Semitic* (The Hague: Mouton, 1974). Other relevant papers by Jenni include "Factitiv [*Piel*] und Kausativ [*Hiphil*] von אבד 'zugrunde gehen,'" *Hebräische Wortfor-*

schung: Festschrift Walter Baumgartner (Supplements to Vetus Testamentum 16; Leiden: Brill, 1967) 143–57; and the paper cited in n. 17.

2. See the general surveys given in GKC § 52f–s / pp. 141–43; BL § 38d″–t″ / pp. 290–93; Joüon § 52 / pp. 115–18; GB 2. 93–98 (§ 17); C. Brockelmann, *Hebräische Syntax* (Neukirchen: Neukirchener Verlag, 1956) 35–36; Brockelmann, *Grundriss der vergleichenden Grammatik der semitischen Sprachen* (Berlin: Reuter und Reichard, 1908), 1. 508–10.

Root	Qal Meaning	Piel Meaning	Classification
שׁבר	to break	to shatter	intensive
למד	to learn	to teach	causative
צדק	to be right	to declare right	declarative
קדשׁ	to be holy	to pronounce holy	estimative
כהן	priest (participle; no other *Qal* forms)	to fill a priest's office	denominative

Such a diversity of functions for a morphologically unified stem perplexed most gram-   b
marians.[3] They tried either to abstract a common basis for all these meanings or to explain
some of them as having developed secondarily from an original meaning. The Gesenius-
Kautzsch-Cowley grammar opted for the first approach and regarded the notion of intensification as the basic meaning: "The fundamental idea of *Pi^el*, to which all the various
shades of meaning in this conjugation may be referred, is *to busy oneself eagerly* with the
action indicated by the stem."[4] As this formulation suggests, such an approach is awkward, and earlier grammarians reached no fundamental consensus regarding the stem's
sense. Customarily, they awarded the vague notion of "intensification" first place because
they saw a connection between form (the doubling of the root's middle radical) and sense
(a supposed heightening of the root's meaning).[5] But they could not advance a plausible
explanation for the link between such notions as diverse as "intensive" and "causative."
Hans Bauer and Pontus Leander, for example, state resignedly: "The question as to how
the Semitic intensive gained a causative meaning cannot be answered at present."[6] Goetze
similarly remarks: "The causative-factitive force of the form is customarily said to be an
outgrowth of the intensive force. But nobody has ever been able to demonstrate in a satisfactory manner how this development should have been possible."[7]

Goetze in 1942 labeled the semantic interpretation of the doubled middle radical a   c
"romantic notion" and called for a study establishing the *Piel*'s meaning according
to modern linguistic principles.[8] Ernst Jenni accepted the challenge; instead of content-
ing himself with repeating the dozen or so verbs cited in the traditional grammars, he

---

3. Moshe Greenberg makes a plausible virtue of necessity when he writes, "In the *pi^el*, the verbal idea of the *qal*
is made more complex or given a special nuance"; *Introduction to Hebrew* (Englewood Cliffs, New Jersey:
Prentice-Hall, 1965) 43, cf. 58. Jacob Weingreen formu-
lates the effect of the *Piel* on verbs of action or motion as
"the active promotion of the state, condition or situation"
or "being energetically or habitually engaged in the act"
indicated by the *Qal*, and on stative verbs "the active
promotion of the state, situation or condition" denoted by
the *Qal*; see "The Pi^el in Biblical Hebrew: A Suggested
New Concept," *Henoch* 5 (1980) 21–29.

4. GKC § 52f / p. 141.

5. Cf. V. Christian, "Die kausative Bedeutung des semitischen Steigerungsstammes," *Miscellanea Orientalia dedicata Antonio Deimel* (Analecta Orientalia 12; Rome:
Pontifical Biblical Institute, 1935) 41–45. The Akkadian

iparras form has also been cited as relevant to the medial
lengthening; see 29.4d n. 67.

6. BL § 38t″ / p. 293.

7. A Goetze, "The So-called Intensive of the Semitic
Languages," *Journal of the American Oriental Society* 62
(1942) 1–8, at 3.

8. The correlation of doubling and intensiveness is tech-
nically a matter of iconicity, in which the formal means is
taken as an icon for or to stand for the semantic matter.
There are iconic aspects to language, but they are not so
straightforward as this correlation would be. See Roman
Jakobson and Linda Waugh, *The Sound Shape of Lan-
guage* (Bloomington: Indiana University, 1979); and M.
O'Connor, "'Unanswerable the Knack of Tongues': The
Linguistic Study of Verse," *Exceptional Language and
Linguistics*, ed. L. K. Obler and L. Menn (New York:
Academic Press, 1982) 143–68.

investigated all 415 Biblical Hebrew verbs attested in the *Piel*. He gives special attention to verbs which occur in *Qal : Piel* or *Piel : Hiphil* pairs, in similar contexts as much as possible; he is thus able to offer for the *Piel* stem a unified semantic description and to set it apart from the other stems.

d   Jenni begins his study by turning away from the venerable tradition behind Arabic and Hebrew grammars, looking instead to recent developments in Akkadian grammar, where Goetze established a close connection between the stative meaning of the G stem (~ Hebrew *Qal*) and the D stem. According to Goetze, the Akkadian D stem does not modify the verbal root, as is the case with the Akkadian Š and N stems (~ Hebrew *Hiphil* and *Niphal*). Rather, the D stem is to be associated with the adjectival use of the G stem. Among the finite forms of the Akkadian, five are important (the examples are from the root *parāsu* 'to separate, cut'): present *iparras* 'he is cutting,' perfect *iptaras* 'he has cut,' preterite *iprus* 'he cut,' imperative *purus* 'cut!', and permansive or stative *paris* 'he is cut.'[9] The last of these is relevant here; the Akkadian permansive or *stative* verb form should not be confused with the class of *stative* verbs, that is, verbs which refer to a state or quality (22.2.1). The Akkadian permansive form is used when the subject has a quality or has undergone an action associated with the root. (In the latter case the form is rendered as a passive.) Goetze's proposal associates the G stem permansive *arik* 'it is long' with the D stem *urrukum* 'to make (to be) long.' Wolfram von Soden, in his standard grammar of Akkadian, follows Goetze in describing the stem: "The chief function of the D stem is factitive, that is, it expresses above all the bringing about of a situation which would be designated by the permansive of the G stem, . . . (e.g., *damiq* 'he is good' : *dummuqum* 'to make good'; *baliṭ* 'he is alive' : *bulluṭum* 'to make (to be) living, keep alive'; *salim* 'he is friendly' : *sullumum* 'to make (to be) friendly, reconcile')."[10] Thus, in von Soden's grammar, the "intensive" concept is not used to explain the D stem.

e   Jenni's argument about the sense of the Hebrew *Piel* is modeled on Goetze's treatment, though the shape of it is different for a number of reasons.[11] First, Hebrew has no finite verb form like the Akkadian permansive. Second, *Piel* forms are used with a greater variety of verbs than are D-stem forms in Akkadian; specifically more verbs which are fientive (usually transitive) in the G stem use the D stem. (For such groups, we shall use terms such as *Qal* fientive or *Qal* transitive.)

f   The *Piel*, according to Jenni, expresses the notion of effecting or causing a state corresponding to the basic meaning of the root; this state can be expressed in terms of an

---

9. The first three of these forms are treated below (Chaps. 29–31); for the moment, it is sufficient to note that the labels attached to them are conventional and the glosses somewhat arbitrary.

10. W. von Soden, *Grundriss der akkadischen Grammatik* (Rome: Pontifical Biblical Institute, 1969) 115. A factitive meaning for the Akkadian D stem is also recognized by (A. Ungnad–)L. Matouš, *Grammatik des Akkadischen* (Munich: Beck, 1964) 74–75; K. K. Riemschneider,

Lehrbuch des Akkadischen (Leipzig: Verlag Enzyklopädie, 1969) 83; F. Rundgren, "Das Verbalpräfix *yu-* im Semitischen und die Entstehung der faktitiv-kausativen Bedeutung des D-Stammes," *Orientalia Suecana* 12 (1964) 99–114.

11. Jenni emphasizes the systematic character of the Hebrew stems; see 21.2.2q and contrast the views of Sperber cited there. Our hesitation in following Jenni entirely does not diminish our admiration of his goal.

adjectival construction.[12] With *Qal* intransitive verbs (often stative) this meaning is labeled "factitive," and with *Qal* transitive verbs (usually fientive), "resultative." For example, the *Qal* intransitive verb גָּדַל 'to be great' becomes in the *Piel* 'to make great'; the *Qal* transitive שָׁבַר 'to break' becomes in the *Piel* 'to make (to be) broken.'

Stuart A. Ryder II also takes up Goetze's insight into the meanings of the Semitic   g
D stems. Six years after the publication of Jenni's work, though independently of him, Ryder wrote: "Goetze gives us the means for discerning the nature of the associations which evolved, the means of introducing order into what is otherwise a scene of linguistic confusion.... The several functions which [the D stem] assumed [in the various West Semitic languages] are mutually consistent from the standpoint of the stem's denominative-factitive orientation."[13] In contrast to Jenni, who tends to force all relevant roots into a model stipulating that the *Piel* transforms the notion defined by the *Qal*, Ryder recognizes that not all roots need present a "correct" relationship to the verbal stems. Variations, he argues, are to be expected.[14] Taking up the dubious view that the stems arose independently and then came to be associated and contrasted with one another, Ryder emphasizes the genuine overlap of the various stems, as well as the idiosyncratic side of the individual lexical items.

Though in the remainder of the chapter we follow Jenni quite closely, we shall   h
depart from him at various points, and it is thus proper to offer his own summary of his work.[15] He begins by insisting that each of the various stems in Hebrew is morphologically unified both in form and semantic function. Each functions in distinctive opposition to the other stems in the system. The meaning of the *Piel* stem is neither intensive nor causative (in the sense that it is practically equivalent in meaning to the *Hiphil*).

---

12. Lambdin summarizes Jenni's philosophical argument in this way: "J[enni] begins by characterizing the difference between adjectival and verbal predication as adjectival : verbal :: subjective : objective :: synthetic : analytic. That is, in an adjectival predication, the adjective lexeme (or root) itself represents the subjective opinion of the speaker, while in the verbal predication the lexical substance is a *datum* (objective) and only the modality of the verb reflects the speaker's role. Since . . . the piel and hiphil are viewed respectively as the factitive/causative transforms of adjectival and verbal predication, and since, in regard to the subject, adjectival predication is accidental, while verbal predication is substantial or essential . . . , piel and hiphil verbs of the type under discussion should differ from one another by expressing accidental and substantial factivizations, respectively." Thus *Piel* > synthetic > accidental, while *Hiphil* > analytic > substantial. See *Catholic Biblical Quarterly* 31 (1969) 436.

13. Ryder, *D-Stem*, 97, 167.

14. Ryder, *D-Stem*, 97.

15. Some of Jenni's arguments are weak and speculative, but his is nonetheless a coherent and suggestive account. As Sawyer emphasizes, it is also a surprising account, for "until now we have been, to use Sapir's celebrated imagery,

prisoners of our European language systems. We did not expect to find in Old Testament Hebrew grammar a set of fairly subtle distinctions, not available in our own language without the clumsy insertion of adverbial phrases." See *Journal of Semitic Studies* 14 (1969) 262. Similarly, T. N. D. Mettinger in an overview of studies on the verb evaluates Jenni's work as excellent, even if not convincing in every detail; see "The Hebrew Verb System," *Annual of the Swedish Theological Institute* 9 (1973) 68–84, at 69. F. Leemhuis supports Jenni's thesis in general and Ryder's investigation of the D stem in the Arabic of the Qurʾān in particular: "On the whole [Ryder's] presentation . . . appears as quite convincing"; *The D and H Stems in Koranic Arabic* (Publications of the Netherlands Institute of Archaeology and Arabic Studies in Cairo; Leiden: Brill, 1977) 7. Among the various dissenting voices are J. Blau, *A Grammar of Biblical Hebrew* (Wiesbaden: Harrassowitz, 1976) 52, who quite pointedly retains the term intensive; W. T. Claassen, "On a Recent Proposal as to a Distinction between Piʿel and Hiphʿil," *Journal of Northwest Semitic Languages* 1 (1971) 3–10, who focuses on Jenni's review of ʾbd (see n. 1); and R. Degen, "Zur neueren hebräistischen Forschung," *Die Welt des Orients* 6 (1971) 47–79.

Rather, it expresses the bringing about of a state. With *Qal* intransitive verbs the *Piel* is factitive: it designates without regard to the process the bringing about of the state depicted by an adjective. The object experiences this action as an "accident" (a philosophical term signifying that a quality or situation is not essential to the person or thing in question). The difference between a true factitive meaning and a declarative-estimative meaning consists in whether the effected state, described in terms of an adjective, is experienced externally (by the senses) or subjectively (in the mind). With *Qal* transitive verbs the *Piel* is resultative: it designates the bringing about of the outcome of the action designated by the base root, which action can be expressed in terms of an adjective, and without regard to the actual process of the event. The species of the resultative (metaphorical meaning, indirect action, summarizing successive action with plural objects, etc.) are to be understood in contrast to the actual action, which is presented by the base root. Denominative verbs in the *Piel* have either a factitive or resultative meaning. More specifically, the denominative expresses itself in terms of productive, or successive iterative, or privative verbal meanings, rather than in terms of an actual event or a causative meaning.[16]

i   The *Piel* is associated with causation: the *Piel* causes a state rather than an action (as the *Hiphil*, for which we reserve the term causative, does). Since the object of causation is in a state of suffering the effects of an action, it is inherently passive in part. Both these features, emphasized earlier (21.2.2), comport well with Jenni's analysis and continue that scholar's basic project of discovering the "living" unity of the stem system.[17]

24.2   Factitive

a   The class of verbs with the basic profile (*Qal* intransitive) :: *Piel* factitive :: (*Hiphil*-causative) includes, according to Jenni, about a hundred verbs, which may be divided into four groups.[18]

I.	*Qal-Piel-Hiphil* attested (ca. 45 verbs)	examples: צדק, כבד, גדל
II.	*Qal-Piel* attested (ca. 25 verbs)	examples: ישן, טהר, דשן
III.	*Piel-Hiphil* attested (ca. 8 verbs)	examples: פלא, מלט
IV.	*Piel* attested (ca. 20 verbs)	examples: רמה, טנף, חדש

The last two groups may be treated as *Qal* intransitive on the basis of evidence from cognate languages and semantic patterns.[19] For example, Hebrew *glḥ Piel* 'to shave' has no corresponding *Qal*, but Arabic has the simple stem *jaliḥa* 'to be bald.'[20]

---

16. Paraphrased and in part translated from Jenni, *Piʿel*, 275.

17. Cf. Jenni's paper, "Zur Funktion der reflexiv-passiven Stammformen im Biblisch-Hebräischen," *Proceedings of the Fifth World Congress of Jewish Studies* (Jerusalem: World Union of Jewish Studies, 1973), 4. 61–70.

18. Jenni, *Piʿel*, 20–21, gives the list. Ryder's comparable groups are *Piel* transformative :: *Qal* durative stative (39 verbs; e.g., *šālēm* 'to be whole,' *šillēm* 'to make whole') and *Piel* transformative :: *Qal* perfect stative (52 verbs; e.g., *lāmad* 'to learn,' *limmēd* 'to teach'); see *D-Stem*, 94, 97–104.

19. Ryder, *D-Stem*, 107.

20. Ryder, *D-Stem*, 98.

In the *Piel* of this class of verbs, the basic sense of the *Qal* is transformed: the *Piel*   b
designates an effected state and governs an object. This class of verbs includes chiefly *Qal* intransitives (verbs that do not govern a direct object), most of them statives; but quasi-
fientives (22.2.3) and a few transitives (of a historically different type) are also included (the
case of למד is discussed below). The verbs denote at base a condition, whether a general
condition (e.g., 'to be wealthy') or an attained one (e.g., 'to be worn out'). We exclude, in
contrast to Jenni, *Qal* intransitives that refer to physical effort (e.g., נתר 'to leap'), vocal
projection (e.g., צעק 'to cry out'), and expectation (e.g., קוה 'to wait for'); see 24.5 for these.

The difference between *Qal*, *Piel*, and *Hiphil* can be seen in connection with the verb   c
למד. Grammars often cite this verb as an example of the causative function of *Piel* since
the *Qal* means 'to learn' (always transitive) and the *Piel* 'to teach (something to someone),' a use very much like the *Hiphil* double accusative. But למד was originally intransitive, to judge from its thematic *a* vowel with the *Qal* prefix conjugation, and from
Ethiopic, where it means 'to be accustomed.' The step between this intransitive sense and
its transitive sense in Hebrew can be seen in Aramaic, where the verb means 'to be
accustomed (to something).' The Hebrew *Piel* builds on the original intransitive meaning,
and from this base the sense can be extrapolated to 'to make (someone) accustomed (to
something), i.e., to teach (something to someone),' a meaning distinct from the sense of
the *Hiphil*, as we shall see.

The factitive *Piel* can be the result of a sensory causation, a "real" result available to   d
the physical senses, or of a psychological or linguistic causation, a mental change or a
speech act that reflects a mental change.

A *"real" factitive* refers to an objective event, an event that can be seen or felt apart   e
from the participants. The verb חלה is the only *Qal* intransitive attested in all seven
stems,[21] and it furnishes apt examples for the *Qal : Piel* contrast.[22]

1a.	חָלִיתִי הַיּוֹם שְׁלֹשָׁה׃	I *became sick* (*Qal*) three days ago. 1 Sam 30:13
1b.	אֲשֶׁר־חִלָּה יהוה בָּהּ׃	(the sickness) with which YHWH *will have made* (the land) *sick* (*Piel*) Deut 29:21

The *Qal* form is a stative, and the action of the *Piel* involves putting the object (here, the
prepositional object of *b*) into the state described by the *Qal*. Consider this contrasting
pair.

2a.	וְקָדַשׁ הוּא וּבְגָדָיו	And he *will be holy* (*Qal*) along with his clothes. Exod 29:21
2b.	קַדֶּשׁ־לִי כָל־בְּכוֹר	*Consecrate* (*Piel*) to me every first-born. Exod 13:2

---

21. See Jenni, "Funktion der reflexiv-passiven Stammformen," 66.

22. Note also *ḥyy Qal* 'to live, be alive' (e.g., Deut 8:3)
and *Piel* 'to keep alive' (e.g., Gen 12:12).

The intransitive *Qal* 'to be holy' becomes in *Piel* 'to make to be holy = transfer to a state of holiness = consecrate,' which takes an object. The proper understanding of this example depends on an appreciation of "holiness" itself as a physical attribute and of "consecration" as the result of various gestures of touching and sprinkling.[23] Consider another pair involving a *Qal* intransitive.

| 3a. | וַאֲבִימֶלֶךְ לֹא קָרַב אֵלֶיהָ | Now Abimelech *had* not *gone near* (*Qal*) her (Sarah). Gen 20:4 |
| 3b. | קֵרַבְתִּי צִדְקָתִי | I am *bringing* my righteousness *near* (*Piel*). Isa 46:13 |

The glosses may be misleading. The *Qal* form, though it may be glossed 'to go near, approach,' represents an ingressive stative event; the burden of the story is that Abimelech did not infringe on Sarah's protected status as a married woman by *becoming near* her. In the passage with the *Piel* example the object *ṣdqty* enters the state of 'being near.' Finally, compare these verbs that are fientive in the *Qal* with their *Piel* counterparts.

4a.	עַל־הָאָרֶץ יֵשֵׁבוּ	They *will sit* (*Qal*) on the ground. Ezek 26:16
4b.	וְיִשְׁבוּ טִירוֹתֵיהֶם	They *will set up* (*Piel*) their camps. Ezek 25:4
5.	בְּטֶרֶם תָּבוֹא אֲלֵהֶן הַמְיַלֶּדֶת וְיָלָדוּ׃	Before the *midwife* (*Piel*) (lit., one who *makes brought forth*) comes to them, they *will have given birth* (*Qal*). Exod 1:19.

f   A "*psychological/linguistic*" *factitive* refers to a subjective event. The salient feature of that event is open to discussion. Jenni refers to such verbs as declarative-estimative, by which he means that the state described is attained by a declaration (i.e., 'to declare someone to be in a state') or as a result of an estimation (i.e., 'to esteem someone as being in a state'). Delbert Hillers prefers to call the so-called declarative verbs "delocutive verbs."[24] He correctly notes that with some of these verbs the *Piel* usage is based on a locution rather than on an adjectival or even a verbal use. The verb קלל, for example, in the *Qal* means 'to be light, slight, trifling.'

| 6a. | וּבֹזַי יֵקָלּוּ׃ | Those who despise me *are trifling*. 1 Sam 2:30 |

---

23. See, e.g., Baruch A. Levine, "The Language of Holiness," *Backgrounds for the Bible*, ed. M. O'Connor and D. N. Freedman (Winona Lake, Indiana: Eisenbrauns, 1987) 241–55.

24. See D. R. Hillers, "Delocutive Verbs in Biblical Hebrew," *Journal of Biblical Literature* 86 (1967) 320–24. For a *Qal : Hiphil* pair, see *ṣdq Qal* (e.g., Job 10:15) and delocutive *Hiphil* (Deut 25:1, Prov 17:15).

The *Piel* usage is often glossed 'to curse,' but more strictly it means 'to declare to be trifling.'

6b. הֲתַחַת זֹאת לֹא יוּמַת שִׁמְעִי כִּי קִלֵּל אֶת־מְשִׁיחַ יהוה:	Is it not the case that Shimei should be put to death for this: that he *declared* the anointed of Yнwн *to be trifling*? 2 Sam 19:22

The offense in view is not cursing or even thinking poorly of someone; it is publicly declaring him of no importance. Shimei's crime, that is, is sedition (verging on *lèse majesté*), not nastiness. A clear example of a delocutive *Piel* is אִשֵּׁר 'to pronounce blessed'; it cannot be based on the verbal notion of אשׁר 'to march' but must be derived from the locution אַשְׁרֵי 'blessed.' On the lexical level, if the simple verb is attested, it can occur in a locution. Since the delocutive use of the *Piel* is based on a statement, it can be grouped with the denominatives (24.4g); because of the experiential basis, which is physical, it can be grouped with the "real" factitives. In point of fact, however, the pronouncement depends on a prior subjective assessment, and some *Piels* are simply estimative; we ought not to insist too strongly on the difference between Hillers's "delocutive" and Jenni's "declarative."

The relationship between the "real" factitive and the delocutive-estimative *Piel* can   g
be seen in these examples.

7a. וַיֹּאמֶר יהוה אֶל־יְהוֹשֻׁעַ הַיּוֹם הַזֶּה אָחֵל גַּדֶּלְךָ בְּעֵינֵי כָל־ יִשְׂרָאֵל	Yнwн said to Joshua, "Today I will begin *to make you great* (*Piel*) in the eyes of all Israel." Josh 3:7
7b. גַּדְּלוּ לַיהוה אִתִּי	*Make* Yнwн *great* (or, *Declare* that Yнwн is *great*) (*Piel*) along with me. Ps 34:4

The first example is a "real" factitive because Israel is to experience physically Yнwн's making Joshua great; in the second case the action is a declaration, specifically pronounced and based on a prior subjective judgment. Judgments about the status of a "psychological/linguistic" factitive are difficult, unless the speech act is clearly documented, as in the priestly laws.

8. וְטִהֲרוֹ אֹתוֹ	He *will pronounce* him (ritually) *clean*. Lev 13:34

In some cases the verb refers primarily to the estimation reflected in the speech acts.[25]

---

25. Here are some further examples of *Piel* verbs which are est(imative), deloc(utive), and fact(itive), drawn from Jenni's lists: *gdl* mostly fact. 'to make great,' rarely deloc. 'to praise' and est. 'to esteem (as) great'; *dmy* deloc.-est. 'to liken, compare,' est. 'to hold as suitable, devise, imagine'; *dšn* deloc.-est. 'to consider (an offering) fat (enough, i.e., acceptable),' also fact. 'to make fat, anoint' and privative (see 24.4f) 'to clear of fat drippings'; *ṭhr* deloc. 'to declare purely,' rarely fact.; *ṭmʾ* deloc. 'to declare impure' (Lev 13:3–59, 20:25), otherwise fact.; *kbd* est. 'to

9a.	עַל־צַדְּקוֹ נַפְשׁוֹ מֵאֱלֹהִים׃	on account of his *holding* himself as *being* more *righteous* (*Piel*) than God Job 32:2
9b.	צָדְקָה נַפְשָׁהּ מְשֻׁבָה יִשְׂרָאֵל מִבֹּגֵדָה יְהוּדָה׃	Turncoat Israel *has esteemed* herself more *righteous* (*Piel*) than Treacherous Judah.[26] Jer 3:11
9c.	וַתְּצַדְּקִי אֶת־אֲחוֹתַיִךְ בְּכָל־תּוֹעֲבוֹתַיִךְ אֲשֶׁר עָשִׂית׃	You *have made* your sister *appear* (or, *have declared*) more *righteous* (*Piel*) through all the abominations which you have committed. Ezek 16:51 *Qere*

h   Given that the factitive is associated with adjectival state, the *comparative use* is not surprising.[27] The examples given above of *ṣdq* are all comparative, the object of comparison governed by *mn* (## 9a–b) or unexpressed (# 9c). Such comparative use is found in simple estimative examples.

| 10. | וַתְּכַבֵּד אֶת־בָּנֶיךָ מִמֶּנִּי | You *have honored* your sons more than me.
1 Sam 2:29 |

The comparative may involve a "real" factitive.

| 11. | וִיגַדֵּל אֶת־כִּסְאוֹ מִכִּסֵּא אֲדֹנִי הַמֶּלֶךְ דָּוִד׃ | And may he *make* his throne *greater* than the throne of my master, King David.
1 Kgs 1:37 |
| 12. | וַתְּחַסְּרֵהוּ מְּעַט מֵאֱלֹהִים | You *have made* it (humanity) *lack* [only] a little of divine beings.
Ps 8:6 |

24.3   Resultative

a   The majority of the *Piel* verbs present a resultative profile, or more strictly (*Qal* transitive) :: *Piel* resultative :: (*Hiphil* causative). According to Jenni, about 180 verbs are attested in *Qal* : *Piel* (:: *Hiphil*), and 135 in *Piel* (:: *Hiphil*).[28] Jenni's category of *Qal* transitives is largely made up of fientives, and in fact it could better be so called, because Jenni extends the class of transitives to include verbs which "notionally" take an

honor (i.e., regard as heavy),' rarely fact.; *nbl* only est. 'to regard as contemptible'; *nqy* deloc.-est. 'to declare/regard as guiltless'; *qdš* deloc. 'to declare holy,' est. 'to hold as holy,' fact. 'to consecrate'; *ṣdq* usually deloc. 'to hold as right(eous)'; *qll* only deloc. 'to revile as trifling.' It is in connection with delocutive and estimative uses that the proposals of E. Rubinstein go astray; see "Adjectival Verbs in Biblical Hebrew," *Israel Oriental Studies* 9 (1979) 55–76.
26. On the epithets of Judah and Israel, see W. L. Hol-

laday, *Jeremiah* (Philadelphia: Fortress, 1986), 1. 59, 116.
27. Jenni, *Piʿel*, 72–74.
28. Jenni, *Piʿel*, 123–26. Ryder's somewhat different classification, allowing for comparative evidence (*D-Stem*, 108–18), yields different counts. Some *Piel* verbs without *Qal* correspondents do find simple-stem cognates in Arabic, e.g., *ʾzn Piel* 'to weigh' (Qoh 12:9), cf. Arabic *wazana* 'to weigh'; and *gšš Piel* 'to touch' (Isa 59:10), cf. Arabic *jassa* 'to handle.' Cf. Ryder, *D-Stem*, 108, 110.

"imagined" object, for example, *hlk* 'to go, i.e., make a trip' and *ṣ*ᶜ*q* 'to cry, i.e., utter a cry.' This device seems to beg the issue. The approximately forty *Qal* intransitive fientive verbs are best treated separately (24.5).

The *Piel* stems of *Qal* transitive verbs signal the bringing about of a state corre-   b
sponding to the verbal meaning of the *Qal* stem, a state that can be described in terms of an adjectival construction. In most instances this involves transforming the verb into a form that corresponds to the English past participle, for example, שׁבר *Qal* 'to break' becomes *Piel* 'to make broken' and זרה *Qal* 'to scatter' becomes *Piel* 'to make scattered.' Jenni calls this use of the *Piel* resultative. Ryder prefers the term "transformative" for the *Piel* of both stative and transitive verbs.

The distinction between *Qal* and *Piel* for transitive fientive verbs can scarcely be   c
recognized in English; the "meaning" 'to make broken' is a "longwinded circumlocution" for the more simple 'to break.' This similarity is reflected in some patterns of occurrence, for example, the use of *Qal* and *Piel* in neighboring lines of verse with no noticeable difference in meaning. The distinction, Jenni reasons, must have been important in Hebrew because the two stems are distinct. More reasonably, Ryder concedes that

> the distinction between "do something" and "have something done" is not clearcut. . . .
> Where the difference in meaning between [the *Qal*] and [the *Piel*] is scarcely notice-
> able, the choice between them may be determined by lexical classification . . . or [it
> may be] a question of stylistic effectiveness on the part of an individual writer.[29]

This view is notably apt for roots that display mixed forms (24.6), those that occur regularly in *Piel* and only rarely in *Qal* (and then as participles or infinitives), and those that are so rare in the *Piel* as to suggest that they may be *ad hoc* formations.

The *Qal* : *Piel* distinction can be seen with some English verbs through particle   d
usage. For example, English contrasts 'break' and 'break up,' 'cut' and 'cut off' or 'cut down,' 'run' and 'run away,' 'fall' and 'fall down,' 'walk' and 'walk out,' 'bore' and 'bore through,' etc. In each case the simple form signifies the action itself and the form with the particle denotes the state achieved. Incidentally, this analogy may help to explain why the *Piel* is traditionally thought of as intensive, for the effected state put this way seems more intensive, though in fact the way of expressing it does not "mirror" the situation.[30] The term "resultative" refers to the state into which the verbal notion of the transitive is brought as an end state, a result. Jenni's terminology agrees with that of von Soden, who writes of Akkadian:

> In transitive fientive verbs the D stem sometimes has a kind of resultative meaning
> (e.g., *ṣabātum* 'to grasp' : *ṣubbutum* 'to keep grasped'; *paṭārum* 'to discharge' :
> *puṭṭurum* 'to break up'; *zâzum* 'to divide' : *zuʾʾuzu* 'to distribute'; *ṭarādum* 'to send' :
> *ṭurrudum* 'to send away').[31]

---

29. Jenni, *Piᶜel*, 125; Ryder, *D-Stem*, 122.   31. Von Soden, *Grundriss der akkadischen Grammatik*,
30. This relationship would also be iconic; see n. 8.   116.

In Jenni's view, the *Qal* stem of fientive verbs signifies the verbal idea as an act, an event. In contrast to the *Piel* stem, which has an achieved result in view, the *Qal* sees the action in its execution, in its course, "*in actu.*" Jenni employs the term *actualis*. It is also possible to conceive of the *Qal* as the unmarked stem and the *Piel* as the marked (cf. 23.1).

24.3.1   Simple Resultative

a   The contrast of the *Qal* and simple resultative *Piel* can be illustrated by the case of שבר mentioned above or that of חלק *Qal* 'to apportion,' *Piel* 'to make apportioned.'

1a.	כֵּן עָשׂוּ בְנֵי יִשְׂרָאֵל וַיַּחְלְקוּ אֶת־הָאָרֶץ׃	So the Israelites did and they *apportioned* (*Qal*) the land. Josh 14:5
1b.	וַיְכַלּוּ מֵחַלֵּק אֶת־הָאָרֶץ׃	They completed *apportioning* (or, *making apportioned*) (*Piel*) the land. Josh 19:51

The distinction is scarcely discernible in our language. Jenni notes that only the *Qal* of *ḥlq* is negated, as might be expected of the form referring to the action. Contrast, for example, these cases.

1c.	אֲשֶׁר לֹא־חָלְקוּ אֶת־נַחֲלָתָם	who had *not* yet *apportioned* (*Qal*) their possession Josh 18:2
1d.	וַיְחַלֶּק־שָׁם יְהוֹשֻׁעַ אֶת־הָאָרֶץ	Joshua *apportioned* (*Piel*) there the land. Josh 18:10

There is a similar case with בתר.

2.	וַיִּקַּח־לוֹ אֶת־כָּל־אֵלֶּה וַיְבַתֵּר אֹתָם בַּתָּוֶךְ . . . וְאֶת־הַצִּפֹּר לֹא בָתָר׃	He took all these (heifer, goat, ram) and *cut* (*Piel*) them in two . . . but the bird he did *not cut* (*Qal*). Gen 15:10

b   One type of simple resultative is associated with bodily movement: the *Qal* specifies the movement as an event (processual aspect/*Aktionsart*), and the *Piel* as at an end (terminal *Aktionsart*).

3a.	אִם . . . פָּרַשְׂתָּ אֵלָיו כַּפֶּךָ׃	If . . . you *stretch out* (*Qal*) your hands to him. . . . Job 11:13
3b.	כְּצֵאתִי אֶת־הָעִיר אֶפְרֹשׂ אֶת־כַּפַּי אֶל־יְהוָה	When I have gone out of the city, I *will spread* (*Qal*) my hands to Yʜwʜ. Exod 9:29

3c.	וּבְפָרִשְׂכֶם כַּפֵּיכֶם אַעְלִים עֵינַי מִכֶּם	When you *spread out* (*Piel*) your hands (in prayer), I will hide my eyes from you (i.e., because of the outstretched hands). Isa 1:15
3d.	פֵּרַשְׂתִּי יָדַי כָּל־הַיּוֹם אֶל־עַם סוֹרֵר	All day I *hold* my hands *outstretched* (*Piel*) to a rebellious folk. Isa 65:2

The contrast is found with other verbs of spreading or stretching; both פשׂק and שׂטח are rare.

4.	פֹּשֵׂק שְׂפָתָיו מְחִתָּה־לוֹ׃	Whoever *opens* (*Qal*) wide his lips comes to ruin. Prov 13:3
5.	שִׂטַּחְתִּי אֵלֶיךָ כַפָּי׃	I hold my hands *spread out* (*Piel*) to you. Ps 88:10

Irreal Resultative   24.3.2

Some verbs use a *Qal : Piel* contrast that is best summed up by the terms *realis : irrealis*. If the *Piel* describes an irreal version of the action of the *Qal*, the *Piel* may be metaphorical or may signify indirect action.[32] Thus if 'He built a bridge' were *Qal*, then 'He built a bridge between old enemies' would be metaphorical, and 'He built thousands of bridges' would be indirect (since others actually built the bridges). Let us consider first the metaphorical use and then the indirect.

It was Gotthelf Bergsträsser who observed that the *Qal* and *Piel* stems sometimes distinguish themselves in that the former has an actual or literal sense and the latter a *metaphorical* one: "One of the two forms is used in the more essential sense, the other in the more metaphorical sense."[33] Jenni reasons that the *Qal* focus on the event itself fits in with the natural sense, while the *Piel* focus on the end state comports better with the metaphorical. The argument is interesting but not compelling. Here are some examples.

1a.	וַיִּזֶר עַל־פְּנֵי הַמַּיִם	He *scattered* (*Qal*) (the ground up calf) upon the water. Exod 32:20
1b.	מְזָרֶה רְשָׁעִים מֶלֶךְ חָכָם	A wise king is one who *winnows* (*Piel*) (lit., *makes scattered*) the wicked. Prov 20:26

---

32. Jenni, *Piᶜel*, 135–40.   33. GB 2. 93 (§ 17a).

1c.	וְהַשְּׁלִשִׁית תִּזְרֶה לָרוּחַ	A third (of the hair) you *shall scatter* (*Qal*) to the winds. Ezek 5:2
1d.	וְהַשְּׁלִישִׁית לְכָל־רוּחַ אֱזָרֶה	A third (of the people) I *will scatter* (*Piel*) to every wind. Ezek 5:12

c   In a similar way, the *Qal* with its concrete, actual meaning may be bracketed with earthly subjects, while the metaphorical *Piel*, which takes only the end state in view, may be bracketed with God.

2a.	וַתִּדְלֶנָה	And they (the daughters of Midian) *drew* (*Qal*) (water). Exod 2:16
2b.	כִּי דִלִּיתָנִי	For you (Yhwh) *drew* me *out* (*Piel*) (of the chaotic waters). Ps 30:2

Regarding the use of the *Piel* with such anthropomorphisms, Jenni comments: "The *Piel* succeeds in leading the results back to Yhwh without having to describe more exactly the course of events. Naturally, a strict rule cannot be derived from that."[34]

d   Under the heading of *direct-indirect action*, as Jenni recognizes, the difference is not the kind of action so much as the way in which the subject is related to the action. In the *Qal*, he argues, the subject is directly involved in the action, while in the *Piel* the subject is only indirectly involved in the bringing about of the action. In this action the subject effects the resulting state through a person or instrument that may be named or only implied. Here are some examples.

3a.	רוּחַ הַקָּדִים שְׁבָרֵךְ	And the east wind *broke* (*Qal*) you. Ezek 27:26
3b.	בְּרוּחַ קָדִים תְּשַׁבֵּר אֳנִיּוֹת תַּרְשִׁישׁ:	You *broke* (*Piel*) with an east wind the ships of Tarshish. Ps 48:8
4a.	עַל־בִּקְעָם הָרוֹת	because they (the Ammonites) *ripped open* (*Qal*) pregnant women Amos 1:13
4b.	וְהָרֹתֵיהֶם תְּבַקֵּעַ:	And you (Hazael) *will rip open* (*Piel*) their pregnant women. 2 Kgs 8:12

---

34. Jenni, *Piʿel*, 137. Note *ʾzr* 'to arm, gird,' *Qal* of humans (reflexive?, passive?) in 1 Sam 2:4, *Piel* of God in Ps 18:33.

Concerning the difference between # 4a and # 4b Jenni comments:

> In connection with the complaint of Amos the Ammonites themselves are named as actors; the verb therefore stands in the *Qal*. On the other hand, Hazael will accomplish his predicted atrocities not with his own hands but indirectly through his soldiers; therefore the resultative verb in the *Piel*.[35]

Other   24.3.3

Traditionally, the uses of the *Qal* and *Piel* (a) to transmit action to one object (*Qal*)   a
versus numerous objects (*Piel*) or (b) for a single/simple movement (*Qal*) *versus* successive movements (*Piel*) or (c) for occasional (*Qal*) *versus* professional (*Piel*) activities were regarded as special nuances of the intensive notion of the *Piel*. Jenni contends rather that these plural patterns are in keeping with his thesis that the *Qal* : *Piel* difference for fientives is due to the opposition of *actualis* and resultative. He argues that with a single object or with a single movement, for example, the event is represented *in actu*, while in the case of many objects or many movements a series of successive events can be represented only as an achieved result.

We present Jenni's arguments but confess we do not find them compelling, for a   b
plurality of actions, it seems to us, can be presented *in actu*.[36] It may be worth noting again that *Piels* of these types are similar to the English verbs bracketed with a particle. For example, contrast 'he cut the loaf' (a single act) and 'he cut up the loaf' (a multiplicity of acts leading to several pieces). Contrast again, 'he broke the stick' and 'he broke up the stick.' Both of these offer a contrast, comparable to the *Qal* : *Piel* contrast. This use of the *Piel* may represent an analogical extension of the frequentative from (a relatively few) intransitive verbs to transitive verbs (see 24.5). In any case, though scholars differ in their analyses and explanations, they agree that for a few roots the *Piel* is used in connection with multiple objects or actions.

The *Piel* of multiple objects can be illustrated with the verbs נשׁך (twice in *Piel*) and   c
נשׁק (five times in *Piel*). For the first, consider these cases.

1a.	יְהִי־דָן נָחָשׁ עֲלֵי־דֶרֶךְ . . . הַנֹּשֵׁךְ עִקְּבֵי־סוּס וַיִּפֹּל רֹכְבוֹ אָחוֹר׃	Dan is a serpent by the roadside . . . that *bites* (*Qal*) the horse's heels so that its rider tumbles backward. Gen 49:17
1b.	הִנְנִי מְשַׁלֵּחַ בָּכֶם נְחָשִׁים צִפְעֹנִים . . . וְנִשְּׁכוּ אֶתְכֶם	I am sending venomous snakes among you . . . and they *will bite* (*Piel*) you. Jer 8:17

---

35. Jenni, *Piʿel*, 143. Contrast *škḥ Qal* in Ps 44:25, where Yʜᴡʜ forgets, and *škḥ Piel* in Lam 2:6, where it cannot be Yʜᴡʜ who forgets; so Ryder, *D-Stem*, 117.

36. It may be that the argument would be better reformulated to claim, e.g., that the *Piel* cannot represent isolated events. See 24.5.

Here the *Qal* describes a single incident, with one (plural) object in view, while the *Piel* refers to a plurality of incidents and objects.[37] There is no sense that the *Piel* biting is more intense.[38] Here are two cases of נשׁק.

2a.	אֶשָּׁקְךָ	I *would kiss* (*Qal*) you.
		Cant 8:1
2b.	וְלֹא נְטַשְׁתַּ֫נִי לְנַשֵּׁק לְבָנַי	You (Jacob) *would* not *let* me (Laban) *kiss* (*Piel*)
	וְלִבְנֹתָי	my sons and daughters.
		Gen 31:28

Jenni rightly argues that the difference in stems here cannot be due to any difference in the strength (either passionately or profusely) of the kissing![39]

24.4 Denominative

a   Since the *Piel* is the stem most commonly used to form denominatives in Hebrew, it is appropriate that we consider that class more broadly than we did in connection with denominative *Qals* (22.5) and *Niphals* (23.5). By "denominative" we mean those verbs which do not belong to an *original* verbal root, be it transitive or intransitive, but to another part of speech, especially a substantive, adjective, or numeral; in living languages, this relationship is recognized by the speakers of a language. From this definition it is apparent that one ascertains whether or not a verb is denominative on descriptive, semantic, and historical linguistic grounds: the nominal form is primary and the verbal secondarily derived from it. In practice this decision is not so easily made. In a living language verbs are constantly being developed from nouns (cf. English 'He *wolfed* down his food') and vice versa (cf. English 'The players went on *strike*'), so that the lexicographer and grammarian are sometimes uncertain whether the nominal or verbal form is primary.[40] Then too, they are uncertain which is primary because denominatives assume all kinds of meanings; for example, denominatives of the English noun 'root' include the notions found in 'The prejudices of parents usually *take root* in their children,' 'We *were rooted* to the spot by surprise,' 'Good manners *were rooted* in him like second nature,' and 'The new district attorney *rooted out* the city's criminal element.' This kind of polysemy in Hebrew sometimes makes it difficult to distinguish denominatives from primary verbs. For our purposes we must be satisfied to explain and illustrate the denominative use of the *Piel* stem with those verbs that are regarded as such by the recent scholarly consensus. Jenni argues that the historical issue is not crucial from a

---

37. For more biting, see Num 21:6–9. Cf. Jenni, *Pi‘el*, 148.

38. It is, however, possible that it is metaphorical; see Holladay, *Jeremiah*, I. 292.

39. Jenni argues, too, for a definite resultative, his chief example being *dbr* (*Qal* 41 times, *Piel* 1,081 times); the *Qal*, he alleges, means 'to speak (in general)' and the *Piel* 'to say (something in particular).' Since *dbr Qal* is confined

to the participle (39 times) and the infinitive (2 times), other factors seem to be involved. Other definite resultative verbs are those of hoping (see 24.5). See Jenni, *Pi‘el*, 164–73.

40. English has tremendous flexibility in this respect, and this fact, combined with its simple morphology, makes comparison with Hebrew potentially misleading, especially in relation to the issue of productivity.

descriptive point of view because the *Piel* exhibits the same essential function with denominative verbs as it does with other roots. Ryder, in contrast, believes that the *Piel*'s transformative force is missing with nominal roots.[41]

Although the *Piel* stem expresses the essential notion of bringing about the adjectivally declared state corresponding to the base root, the denominative meaning can be shaped in many ways, depending on the root in question. For example, כֹּהֵן 'priest' becomes כהן *Piel* 'to serve as priest' (intransitive) but יָבָם 'levirate brother' becomes יבם *Piel* 'to perform for someone the duty of the levirate brother' (transitive). Jenni argues against overemphasizing this diversity: "The varying types of relationships between the denominative verbal meaning and the noun in question on the whole have only an indirect relationship to the function of the *Piel* stem as such."[42] Jenni's thesis is supported by the fact that the *Piel* stem is not the only stem in which denominatives are formed. One finds denominatives in the *Qal* (e.g., ברך *Qal* 'to kneel' from בִּרְכַּיִם 'knee,' חמר *Qal* 'to pitch' from חֵמָר 'asphalt,' שבר *Qal* 'to purchase (grain)' from שֶׁבֶר 'grain'); in the *Niphal* (e.g., אחז *Niphal* 'to be settled (in a possession)' from אֲחֻזָּה 'possession,' שבע *Niphal* 'to swear' from שֶׁבַע 'seven'); and in the *Hiphil* (e.g., ימן *Hiphil* 'to turn oneself to the right' from יָמִין 'right hand,' אזן *Hiphil* 'to hear' from אֹזֶן 'ear').[43]

It is the *Piel* that is used in connection with many denominative verbs. Certainly the *Piel* stem, which expresses the effecting of an adjectival state, is most suited for making adjectives into verbs. Jenni defends his overall thesis by juxtaposing denominative verbs that occur in both *Qal* and *Piel* stems over against each other; the meaning gleaned from these juxtapositions he plausibly extends to those *Piel* denominatives that lack a *Qal* counterpart.

It is necessary to reckon with the fact that in some instances where denominatives occur in more than one stem the differences among them may no longer be apparent; the denominatives in one stem or the other may, in contrast, have been formed over an extended period of time during which the relevant root showed a variety of meanings. This is the case, for example with חטא *Qal* 'to miss the mark; to sin,' *Hiphil* 'to cause to sin,' and *Piel* 'to recognize something as missed' (estimative, Gen 31:39), 'to purify from sin' (privative), and 'to present as a sin-offering' (productive). The root עצם offers yet another example of denominatives with varying meanings related to variety in the base words: עצם has an adjectival meaning 'strong' (cf. עָצוּם 'mighty') and becomes in the *Qal* 'to be strong, mighty,' and a nominal meaning 'bone' (cf. עֶצֶם) that becomes in *Piel* 'to gnaw bones' (privative).

The denominative *Piel* may be analyzed into several basic types. It may be resultative with the notion of either producing the mass designated by the noun or the taking away of it. The former we call "the productive *Piel*" and the latter "the privative *Piel*." Many denominative *Piel*s connote the notion of producing something (cf. English 'to wall [in]'). Concerning this use Jenni explains: "This productivity, as one could call it,

---

41. Jenni, *Pi*ᶜ*el*, 264–67; Ryder, *D-Stem*, 128–30.
42. Jenni, *Pi*ᶜ*el*, 265.

43. See both Jenni, *Pi*ᶜ*el*, 265, and the discussion of other denominative verbs here.

designates the producing of the thing from the designation of which the verbs are derived, not as an actual event but as a resultative, from the outcome of it."[44] This small group of verbs includes the following.

1.	בִּכֵּר	firstborn	יְבַכֵּר	It will bear early fruit. Ezek 47:12
2.	?דבר	descendant[45]	יְדַבֵּר	He will leave behind descendants. Prov 21:28
3.	חַטָּאָה	sin-offering	הַמְחַטֵּא	one who presents a sin offering Lev 6:19
4.	לְבִבָה	(heart-shaped) cake	וַתְּלַבֵּב	And she baked cakes. 2 Sam 13:6, 8
5.	עָנָן	cloud	בְּעַנְנִי עָנָן	when I form clouds Gen 9:14
6.	עָפָר	dust	וְעִפַּר בֶּעָפָר	He threw dirt. 2 Sam 16:13

f   In contrast to the productive nuance, the denominative *Piel* can also denote the taking away of the mass designated by the noun (cf. English 'to skin, to behead, to root out, to uproot, to bone,' etc.). Concerning this use Jenni explains: "Here the *Piel* is very understandable if an abiding outcome is created by the taking away of a designated mass. Also here it is a matter, however, not of a special privative function but of the general factitive-resultative meaning of the *Piel*."[46] Among the many privative *Piel* verbs are these.[47]

7.	דֶּשֶׁן	fat drippings[48]	לְדַשְּׁנוֹ	to clear/clean it (the altar) of fat Exod 27:3
8.	זָנָב	tail	וַיְזַנֵּב	He cut off at the rear. Deut 25:18; cf. Josh 10:19
9.	חֵטְא	sin	וְחִטְּאוֹ	He (the clean person) shall de-sin him (the unclean).[49] Num 19:19
10.	לֵבָב	heart	לִבַּבְתִּנִי	You (fem.) have taken away my heart. Cant 4:9

---

44. Jenni, *Piʿel*, 270.
45. For the evidence for this word, see Jenni, *Piʿel*, 270.
46. Jenni, *Piʿel*, 273.
47. No noun *sql* 'stone' is attested, but a privative *Piel* 'to clear of stones' is found in Isa 5:2.

48. Hebrew does not distinguish 'fat' and 'fat drippings' (the phrase 'fatty ashes,' used in handbooks, is hardly English); for the delocutive of *dšn*, see 24.2g n. 25.
49. The verb is only here used of persons; elsewhere it is used of things.

11.	סָעִיף	branch	מְסָעֵף	one who cuts down branches Isa 10:33
12.	עֶ֫צֶם	bone	עִצְּמוֹ	He gnaws his bones. Jer 50:17
13.	שֹׁרֶשׁ	root	וְשֵׁרֶשְׁךָ	He will uproot you. Ps 52:7

With other nominal roots, the denominative *Piel* denotes effecting a state by acting   g
on an object or quality that already exists (## 14–16). A denominative from an adjective
describes the result of a process, usually the process of coming to be in the state denoted by the adjective; thus there are denominatives from עִוֵּר 'blind (or one-eyed?)'
(# 17), מָהִיר 'skilled, dextrous,' (# 18), and יָדוֹעַ 'expert' (# 19). A similar formation
comes from the preposition קֶ֫דֶם 'in front of' (# 20). From an agentive noun a denominative means 'to act as' (## 21–22). With other nouns the *Piel* may be delocutive (# 23) or
estimative (# 24).

14.	וְלֹא־יַהֵל [> יָאֳהֵל] שָׁם עֲרָבִי	No Arab will *pitch* his *tent* there. Isa 13:20
15.	וְנִחֵשׁ	And he *practiced sorcery* (lit., he *used a serpent*). 2 Kgs 21:6
16.	כִּי־יְחַנֵּן קוֹלוֹ	Though he *makes* his voice (to be) *charming*. . . . Prov 26:25
17.	הַשֹּׁחַד יְעַוֵּר פִּקְחִים	A bribe *blinds* those who see. Exod 23:8
18.	וַיְמַהֵר אַבְרָהָם הָאֹהֱלָה	So Abraham *hastened* (lit., *made* [the going] *quick*) into the tent. Gen 18:6
19.	יִדַּ֫עְתָּ הַשַּׁחַר מְקֹמוֹ׃	*Have* you ever *guided* the dawn to its place? Job 38:12 *Qere*
20.	לֹא־קִדְּמוּ אֶתְכֶם	They did not come *to meet* you (lit., to effect a situation of being over against you). Deut 23:5
21.	וְכִהֵן לִי׃	He *will serve* me *as a priest*. Exod 40:13
22.	וְיַבֵּם אֹתָהּ	*Fulfill your duty* to her *as a brother-in-law*. Gen 38:8
23.	כָּל־גּוֹיִם יְאַשְּׁרוּהוּ׃	All nations *will call* him *blessed*. Ps 72:17

24.   וְתַעֵב תְּתַעֲבֶ֫נּוּ   You *shall* utterly *detest* it (lit., *regard* it *as*
                                        an abomination).
                                        Deut 7:26

h   In the numeral denominatives, the *Piel* seems to pertain to fractional numbers and
the verbs behave as verbs of dividing or partitioning, for example, חמשׁ *Piel* 'to take a
fifth (as a tax)' (Gen 41:34), שׁשׁ *Piel* 'to divide into sixths' (perhaps in Ezek 45:13), שׁלשׁ
Piel 'to divide into thirds' (Deut 19:3). The last of these may also have the sense 'to do a
third time' (1 Kgs 18:34; cf. 1 Sam 20:19).

i   To illustrate the frequentative aspect of *Piel* as over against *Qal* the case of עשׂר is
useful.

25a.   וְזַרְעֵיכֶם וְכַרְמֵיכֶם יַעְשֹׂר   He *will take a tithe* (*Qal*) of your grain and of your
                                                        vintage.
                                                        1 Sam 8:15; cf. v 17

25b.   וְכֹל אֲשֶׁר תִּתֶּן־לִי עַשֵּׂר   And of all that you give me, I *will give a tenth* (*Piel*)
            אֲעַשְּׂרֶ֫נּוּ לָךְ:   of it to you.
                                                    Gen 28:22

The difference in meaning here between the *Qal* and the *Piel* stems does not involve the
contrast of 'to take a tithe' (*Qal*) and 'to give a tithe' (*Piel*), for that distinction cannot be
carried through consistently. The *Piel* can also mean 'to take a tenth.'

25c.   וְהֵם הַלְוִיִּם הַמְעַשְּׂרִים בְּכֹל   The Levites are the ones who *collect the tithe* (*Piel*)
            עָרֵי עֲבֹדָתֵ֫נוּ:   in all the cities where we work.
                                                        Neh 10:38

Jenni explains the difference between the *Qal* and *Piel* as the difference between a single
act (*Qal*) and multiple acts (*Piel*), that is, *actualis* versus resultative. In this case, such a
view seems dubious.

24.5   Frequentative

a   There is a group of verbs that in the *Qal* are intransitive and denote physical
movement or effort, voice projection, or expectation; the *Piel* of these denotes a frequentative aspect, either iterative over time or plural through space. Ryder finds about forty of
these roots.[50] Whereas earlier grammarians wrongly built their theory of the stem's
intensive meaning largely on the narrow base of this relatively small group, Jenni over-
reacts by minimizing the iterative meaning. He tries to explain these verbs in terms of the
resultative *Piel*, either as a plural resultative (the *Piel* reflects a multiplicity of actions or
objects; the corresponding *Qal* designates a single action or object) or as a definite

---

50. Ryder, *D-Stem*, 130–35.

resultative (the *Qal* designates an activity with no definite outcome or product; the *Piel* refers to a definite outcome or product). Jenni fails, however, to take adequate account of certain facts: these words are intransitive in the *Qal* and tend not to take an object in the *Piel*. Because of their distinctive lexical and syntactic features, we prefer with Goetze and Ryder to interpret them as denoting frequentative aspect in the *Piel*. If we suppose that the *Qal* is the unmarked form and the *Piel* the marked form, then we can say that the *Qal* means anything other than the frequentative.

One major group of these verbs includes verbs of movement or physical effort   b (## 1–2).

1a.	וַיֵּלְכוּ שְׁנֵיהֶם יַחְדָּו׃	And the two of them *went* (*Qal*) together. Gen 22:6
1b.	הִלְּכוּ בְּלִי לְבוּשׁ	They (the defrauded poor) *go about* (*Piel*) without clothes.[51] Job 24:10
2a.	כָּל־הַדּוֹלֵג עַל־הַמִּפְתָּן	all who *leap* (*Qal*) over the threshold Zeph 1:9
2b.	הִנֵּה־זֶה בָּא מְדַלֵּג עַל־הֶהָרִים	Here he comes *leaping* (*Piel*) over the mountains. Cant 2:8

Some verbs of vocal expression also present this profile.

| 3a. | הֵן אֶצְעַק חָמָס | Though I *cry* (*Qal*): "(I've been) wrong(ed). . . ."
Job 19:7 |
| 3b. | וְהוּא מְצַעֵק אָבִי אָבִי רֶכֶב יִשְׂרָאֵל וּפָרָשָׁיו | And he *was crying out* (*Piel*): "My father, my father! The chariots and cavalry of Israel!"
2 Kgs 2:12 |

With verbs of hoping and expecting the *Qal* expresses any kind of action other than the frequentative indicated by the *Piel*. Jenni explains ## 4a–b as involving a contrast of general hoping, without a goal (*Qal*) *versus* carrying the action forward to a definite goal (*Piel*); they might better be explained as frequentative action *versus* non-frequentative. Both stems are found in # 5.

| 4a. | וְקוֹיֵ יהוה | those who *hope* (*Qal*) in Yʜᴡʜ
Isa 40:31 |
| 4b. | וַיְקַו לַעֲשׂוֹת עֲנָבִים | Then he *looked for* (*Piel*) it to produce grapes.
Isa 5:2 |

---

51. See Jenni, *Piᶜel*, 151–56, on *hlk* and related verbs.

5. וְלָכֵן יְחַכֶּה יהוה לַחֲנַנְכֶם וְלָכֵן יָרוּם לְרַחֶמְכֶם כִּי־אֱלֹהֵי מִשְׁפָּט יהוה אַשְׁרֵי כָּל־חוֹכֵי לוֹ׃

Therefore Y<small>HWH</small> *tarries* (*Piel*) to be gracious to you, and therefore he raises himself that he might be merciful to you, because Y<small>HWH</small> is a God of justice. Blessed are all who *tarry* (*Qal*) for him.
Isa 30:18

c   The *Piel* stem, especially its participle, is used with conspicuous frequency for designating professional activity and other actions practiced habitually.[52] With ארב the *Qal* means 'to lie in wait,' while the *Piel* refers to a '(professional) ambusher, sniper.'[53]

6a. וְעַתָּה קוּם לַיְלָה אַתָּה וְהָעָם אֲשֶׁר־אִתָּךְ וֶאֱרֹב בַּשָּׂדֶה׃

Now then, during the night you and your men come and *lie in wait* (*Qal*) in the fields.
Judg 9:32

6b. וַיָּשִׂימוּ לוֹ בַעֲלֵי שְׁכֶם מְאָרְבִים עַל רָאשֵׁי הֶהָרִים

In opposition to him the citizens of Shechem set men on the hilltops as *ambushers* (*Piel*).
Judg 9:25

Regarding נאף 'to commit adultery,' Jenni comments: "The *Qal* (16 times) designates the individual, actual case of adultery. . . . In the *Piel* (15 times) a customary behavior with several different partners is almost always meant."[54] The *Qal* of כתב means 'to write,' while the *Piel* describes the actions of a professional caste (## 7a–b).[55] The professional sense of the *Piel* is sometimes extended to roots which are transitive in the *Qal* (cf. ## 8a–b).

7a. וַאֲנִי כֹּתֵב עַל־הַסֵּפֶר בַּדְּיוֹ׃

I *wrote* (*Qal*) on the scroll with ink.
Jer 36:18

7b. הוֹי . . . מְכַתְּבִים עָמָל כִּתֵּבוּ׃

Woe . . . to the *scribes* (*Piel* participle) *who write out* (decrees of) hard labor.
Isa 10:1

8a. וַיִּתְפְּרוּ עֲלֵה תְאֵנָה

They *sewed* (*Qal*) fig leaves.
Gen 3:7

8b. הוֹי לִמְתַפְּרוֹת כְּסָתוֹת

Woe to the women who *sew* (*Piel*) magic charms.
Ezek 13:18

24.6   Mixed Forms

a   The *Qal* and *Piel* can be confounded in various ways (24.3.1). *Pual* forms that lack *Piel* counterparts may well be *Qal* passive forms (22.6). Sometimes the *Piel* applies its factitive force to verbs attested not in the *Qal* but in the *Niphal*.

---

52. Cf. 5.3b, 25.3d; Jenni, *Pi^cel*, 156–64.
53. Jenni, *Pi^cel*, 160.
54. Jenni, *Pi^cel*, 161.

55. Some *Qal* participles do have a (quasi-)professional sense, e.g., *šōpēṭ*, *kōhēn*. The latter is a common West Semitic term for priest.

1a.   כַּפֵּיכֶם נְגֹאֲלוּ בַדָּם   Your hands *are defiled* (*Niphal*) with blood.
                                                          Isa 59:3

1b.   בַּמֶּה גֵאַלְנוּךָ   How *have* we *defiled* (*Piel*) you?
                                                          Mal 1:7

25

Pual Stem

25.1 Form and Meaning

a   The *Piel* and *Pual* stems stand in active : passive opposition; essentially, the object of a *Piel* would serve as the subject of a corresponding *Pual*.[1] This straightforward relation is entirely distinct from the *Qal : Niphal* relation (23.1), but it is comparable to the *Qal* : passive *Qal* relation.

$$Qal \ : \ \text{passive } Qal$$
$$Piel \ : \ Pual$$

This analogy is obscured by the fact that many passive *Qal* forms are pointed in the MT as *Pual* (22.6). In this chapter we are concerned with the forms that properly belong to the *Pual* stem.

b   These forms as a whole present one striking contrast to the stems so far studied: the *Pual* is a strongly participial stem. Ernst Jenni reviews the statistics.

> The *Niphal* shows a remarkably high rate of participles in comparison to the *Qal*. Almost 20% of all *Niphal* forms are participles; infinitives make up 5%. The situation of the *Pual* is entirely different. Since the foregrounded interest is not in an event that happens to the subject but rather in a condition attained by it, the participle has a good chance of being used frequently. In the *Pual* the participle ("a thing or person for/in which a new condition has been attained") comprises no less than 40% of all *Pual* forms. . . . That this is no mere coincidence is shown by a crosscheck of the infinitive as *nomen actionis*. Because the infinitive would mean the act of "being put in

---

1. See, in addition to the references given above for the *Piel*, Klaus Beyer, *Althebräische Grammatik* (Göttingen: Vandenhoeck und Ruprecht, 1969) 56.

a condition" and because the *Pual* is not concerned with an act but an attained condition, the *Pual* infinitive is essentially a contradiction.[2]

This participial quality of the *Pual* reflects its structure as an essentially adjectival causation predicate (like the *Piel*) and as passive. This structure is apparent even in nonparticipial uses. *Qal* intransitive גדל in the *Pual* גֻּדַּל means 'was made [causation] : to be great [adjective]' > 'was made grown (i.e., brought up)'; *Qal* transitive בקש in the *Pual* בֻּקַּשׁ means 'was made : to be sought' > 'was (made) sought.' The presentation of the *Pual* essentially follows the format of the *Piel* chapter. It is important to note that the *Piel* frequentative verbs (of physical motion, expectation, and vocal projection) are largely lacking, consistent with the character of the *Pual*.[3] The frequent use of the *Piel* participle to form an agent noun is also lacking.

Factitive   25.2

Qal intransitive verbs form *Pual* factitives. Such a *Pual* may reflect a sensible   a
causation and thus be a "*real*" *factitive*.[4]

1.	וּבָשֵׁל מְבֻשָּׁל בַּמָּיִם	or boiled (meat) (adjective) *boiled* (*Pual* participle; lit., which *was made to be boiled*) in water Exod 12:9
2.	גַּם־אַתָּה חֻלֵּיתָ כָמֹונוּ	You *have been made as weak* as we are. Isa 14:10

A psychological or linguistic causation is at the base of an *estimative or delocutive*   b
Pual.

3.	אַתְּ אֶרֶץ לֹא מְטֹהָרָה	You are a land that *has* not *been pronounced clean*.[5] Ezek 22:24
4.	וְהַחֹוטֶא בֶּן־מֵאָה שָׁנָה יְקֻלָּל׃	And he who fails to reach one hundred years *will be declared* (or, *regarded as*) *cursed*. Isa 65:20

---

2. Ernst Jenni, "Zur Funktion der reflexiv-passiven Stammformen im Biblisch-Hebräischen," *Proceedings of the Fifth World Congress of Jewish Studies* (Jerusalem: World Union of Jewish Studies, 1973), 4. 61–70, at 66. The only example Jenni allows of a *Pual* infinitive (construct) is in Ps 132:1, which he regards as questionable; GKC § 52r / p. 143 adds one infinitive absolute, in Gen 40:15.

3. See S. A. Ryder II, *The D-Stem in Western Semitic* (The Hague: Mouton, 1974) 130–33, for the list of *Piel* intransitives; the only verb on the list that is used in the passive is wrongly given there: *nph* (Job 20:26).

4. Other examples include *ṭmʾ Pual* 'to be defiled' (Ezek

4:14, participle), *yšr Pual* 'to be evened out (in hammering)' (1 Kgs 6:35, participle), *kbd Pual* 'to be honored' (Prov 13:18, 27:18; estimative in Isa 58:13), *kly Pual* 'to be completed' (Gen 2:1, Ps 72:20), *lmd Pual* 'to be instructed' (Jer 31:18, etc.), *mlʾ Pual* 'to be set with (of jewels)' (Cant 5:14, participle), *ʿny Pual* 'to be humbled' (Isa 53:4, participle; for the apparent reflexive elsewhere, see 25.5b), *pty Pual* 'to be seduced (seducible)' (Jer 20:10, etc.). Note also *bʿr Pual* in Jer 36:22, where the subject is marked with *ʾt* (cf. 23.2.2e).

5. The context suggests that the LXX reading *brechomenē*, from *brechō* 'to (get) wet, steep (in water),' reflecting a *Pual* of *mṭr*, may be correct.

25.3   Resultative

a   The *Qal* transitive verbs are associated with resultative uses of the *Pual*.[6] The *simple resultative* may be illustrated with חלק and other verbs.

1.   וְאַדְמָתְךָ בַּחֶבֶל תְּחֻלָּק   And your land *will be apportioned* by the measuring
                                          line.
                                          Amos 7:17

2.   כִּי לֹא פֹרַשׁ מַה־יֵּעָשֶׂה לוֹ:   What should be done to him *had* not *been distinctly
                                          declared.*
                                          Num 15:34

3.   שְׁמָרִים מְזֻקָּקִים   *filtered* wine
                                          Isa 25:6

4.   תַּמְנוּ חֵפֶשׂ מְחֻפָּשׂ   We have devised a *perfect* (lit., *searched out*) plan.
                                          Ps 64:7

5.   יְזֹרֶה עַל־נָוֵהוּ גָפְרִית: Burning sulphur *has been scattered* over his dwelling.[7]
                                          Job 18:15

b   The *irreal resultative* is also expressed with the *Pual*. In the *Pual* אכל is always used figuratively (# 6); the figurative use of בלע is concentrated in the *Piel* and *Pual* (# 7). In the *Piel* נקר may be literal (Judg 16:21) or metaphorical (Job 30:17); its one occurrence in the *Pual* is figurative (# 8).

6.   וְהִנֵּה הַסְּנֶה בֹּעֵר בָּאֵשׁ וְהַסְּנֶה   Though the bush was on fire, it was not *consumed.*
      אֵינֶנּוּ אֻכָּל: Exod 3:2

7.   פֶּן יְבֻלַּע לַמֶּלֶךְ   lest the king *be destroyed* (lit., lest it *be made
                                          swallowed up* with reference to the king)[8]
                                          2 Sam 17:16

8.   וְאֶל־מַקֶּבֶת בּוֹר נֻקַּרְתֶּם: to the quarry from which you *were hewn*
                                          Isa 51:1

If the implicit action is indirect ('He built a bridge' ~ 'He had a bridge built'), the *Pual* may be used.

9.   כְּהֶרֶג הֲרֻגָיו הֹרָג: *Has* he *been slain* like the slaying of his people who
                                          were slain?
                                          Isa 27:7

---

6. Note the context of the *Pual* forms of *nts* and *krt* in Judg 6:28—the setting is clearly the morning after and the topic is the present state of the ravaged cultic equipment. Cf. Jenni, "Funktion der reflexiv-passiven Stamm-

formen," 68.

7. Here *zry* is not metaphorical, though the *Piel* is (e.g., 1 Kgs 14:15, Ps 139:3).

8. See 22.7 on the impersonal construction.

10. עֹלְלֵיהֶם יְרֻטָּשׁוּ וְהָרִיּוֹתָיו יְבֻקָּעוּ׃   Their little ones *will be dashed* to the ground, their pregnant women *ripped open*.
Hos 14:1

11. וְחֻלַּק שְׁלָלֵךְ בְּקִרְבֵּךְ׃   And your plunder *will be apportioned* in your midst.
Zech 14:1

The *plural resultative* of *Qal* intransitive is, on Jenni's view, found in the *Pual* as well as the *Piel*: as with the *Piel*, the *Pual* of certain roots refers to a plurality of events, where the *Qal* refers to one such event. In the *Pual* such verbs have multiple subjects.[9] In a few cases Jenni's examples are plausible; we discuss one other relevant verb as a frequentative (25.5a).

12. שָׁמָּה קֻבַּר אַבְרָהָם וְשָׂרָה אִשְׁתּוֹ׃   There Abraham and his wife Sarah *were buried*.
Gen 25:10

13. בְּהֹנוֹת יְדֵיהֶם וְרַגְלֵיהֶם מְקֻצָּצִים   their thumbs and big toes *hacked off*
Judg 1:7

14. שִׁקְמִים גֻּדָּעוּ   The fig trees *have been felled*.
Isa 9:9

The *Pual*, in contrast to the *Piel*, is not often used to designate professional activity (cf. 5.3b). But like its counterpart the *Pual* is used extensively with the *technical vocabulary of building and crafts*. Concerning this use of the *Piel* Jenni notes: "Also here the resultative is the starting point for the meaning which is transformed by professional activity, an activity which is performed successively and, for the most part, on numerous objects."[10] Such words listed by Jenni as occurring frequently in the *Piel* occur with relatively high frequency in the *Pual* stem as well.

15. וְחֻבָּר   And it (the ephod) *will be made fast*.
Exod 28:7

16. כָּל־עַמּוּדֵי הֶחָצֵר סָבִיב מְחֻשָּׁקִים כֶּסֶף   All the posts around the courtyard are *to be bound* with silver.
Exod 27:17

17. עַל־אַרְבָּעָה עַמּוּדֵי שִׁטִּים מְצֻפִּים זָהָב   upon four posts of acacia wood which are *overlaid* with gold
Exod 26:32

18. כֶּסֶף מְרֻקָּע מִתַּרְשִׁישׁ יוּבָא   *Hammered* (*Pual*) silver is brought up (*Hophal*) from Tarshish.
Jer 10:9

9. Jenni's notion of a definitive resultative is unlikely; his chief examples are *dbr* in Ps 87:3 and Cant 8:8.
10. E. Jenni, *Das hebräische Piᶜel* (Zurich: EVZ, 1968)

163. The texts not surprisingly refer to religious architecture or commerce.

25.4   Denominative

a   The denominative *Pual* verbs are of the same types as corresponding *Piels*. Substantives (e.g., דֶּשֶׁן 'fat' and the unattested סקל 'stone'), as well as adjectives (e.g., חָכָם 'skilled'), form "*real*" *factitive Puals*.

1.	וַעֲפָרָם מֵחֵלֶב יְדֻשָּׁן׃	And their dust *will be saturated* (lit., *made fat*) with fat. Isa 34:7
2.	סֻקַּל נָבוֹת	Naboth *has been stoned*.[11] 1 Kgs 21:14
3.	חוֹבֵר חֲבָרִים מְחֻכָּם׃	an *expert* (lit., *one instructed*) caster of spells Ps 58:6

b   The *productive Pual* may point to a result (## 4–5) or to an "object" already in existence (זְמָן 'appointed time'; # 6). The *Pual* of ברך (בִּרְכַּיִם 'knees') may be processual (# 7) or delocutive (# 8; cf. # 9).[12]

4.	לֹא גֻשְׁמָה	It *has* not *been rained on*.[13] Ezek 22:24 emended
5.	וְעָשִׂיתָ אֹתָהּ קְטֹרֶת . . . מְמֻלָּח	You shall make it as incense . . . *seasoned with salt*. Exod 30:35
6.	לְעִתִּים מְזֻמָּנִים	at the times which *have been appointed* Ezra 10:14
7.	וְעַתָּה הוֹאֵל וּבָרֵךְ אֶת־בֵּית עַבְדְּךָ . . . וּמִבִּרְכָתְךָ יְבֹרַךְ בֵּית־עַבְדְּךָ לְעוֹלָם׃	Now be pleased to bless (*Piel*) the house of your servant . . . and with your blessing the house of your servant *will be blessed* (*Pual*) forever. 2 Sam 7:29
8.	יְהִי שֵׁם יהוה מְבֹרָךְ׃	*Blessed be* the name of YHWH. Job 1:21
9.	יְאֻשַּׁר בָּאָרֶץ	He *will be called blessed* in the land. Ps 41:3

c   The *numerical Pual* is a specialized multiplicative in some uses from שׁלשׁ *Pual*, yielding the sense 'to be three years old.'

10.	קְחָה לִי עֶגְלָה מְשֻׁלֶּשֶׁת וְעֵז מְשֻׁלֶּשֶׁת וְאַיִל מְשֻׁלָּשׁ	Fetch me a heifer, a goat, and a ram, each *three* (years old). Gen 15:9

---

11. Contrast privative *Piel* of *sql* 'to clear of stones' (Isa 5:2; 24.4f n. 47).

12. For an estimative case, see the conjectured *mətoʿab* in Isa 49:7.

13. Read so, against the MT, which has *gušmāh* (*he* with *mappiq*), as if 'its rain, rain for it' (< *góšem*?, other-wise unknown); on the first half of the verse, see n. 5. On the emendation here, see C. Rabin, "Lexical Emendation in Biblical Research," *Fucus: A Semitic/Afrasian Gathering in Remembrance of Albert Ehrman*, ed. Y. L. Arbeitman (Amsterdam: John Benjamins, 1988) 379–418, at 399; Rabin favors retention of the MT.

As the passive of the *Piel* 'to do three times,' the *Pual* means 'being done three times, having been done three times.'

11.	הַחוּט הַמְשֻׁלָּשׁ	a *three-fold* cord Qoh 4:12
12.	מְשֻׁלָּשׁוֹת הֵנָּה	These are *three-storied* chambers. Ezek 42:6

Frequentative and Mixed Forms   25.5

The only intransitive *Piel* with a *Pual* counterpart is רנן 'to give a ringing shout.'   a
Consider this cento of examples.

1a.	צַהֲלִי וָרֹנִּי	Cry aloud and *give a shout of joy* (*Qal*). Isa 12:6
1b.	הָקִיצוּ וְרַנְּנוּ	Wake up and *give shouts of joy* (*Piel*). Isa 26:19
1c.	לֹא־יְרֻנָּן לֹא יְרֹעָע	*Shouts of joy shall* not *be given* (*Pual*), no shouting (*Polal*). Isa 16:10

There is one case of a *Pual* which seems to be reflexive rather than passive, from   b
ענה, and so has apparently been confounded with *Hithpael*.[14]

2.	כִּי כָל־הַנֶּפֶשׁ אֲשֶׁר לֹא־תְעֻנֶּה	anyone who *does* not *afflict himself* Lev 23:29

---

14. See n. 4. It may be that the construction is better taken (as C. John Collins suggests to us) in association with the *Piel* idiom ʿinnâ ʾet-hannépeš 'to humble oneself (by fasting),' as in Lev 16:29, 31.

26

Hithpael Stem

26.1 Form and Meaning

26.1.1 Morphological Diversity

a   There is a large group of Semitic verbal stems using an infixed or prefixed *t*,[1] and this group is represented in Hebrew chiefly by the *Hithpael* or tD stem, which serves primarily as the double-status (reflexive-reciprocal) counterpart of the *Piel* and secondarily as a passive form. So many morphological and semantic complexities attend the *Hithpael* that some scholars have suggested that the stem is the result of the convergence of a number of minor stems. We argue that the stem exhibits a basic unity.

b   Certain features of the stem result from the prefixed *t*; these are not irregularities but merely the effects of some relatively rare rules of Hebrew phonology. If the root begins with a sibilant, the *t* and the sibilant metathesize (## 1–17).[2] If the sibilant is

---

1. Aramaic has three *t* stems (*Ethpeel*, related to *Peal* ~ Hebrew *Qal*; *Ethpaal*, related to *Pael* ~ Hebrew *Piel*; *Ettaphal*, related to *Aphel* ~ Hebrew *Hiphil*), all passive. Arabic has four (VIII Form, related to I Form ~ Hebrew *Qal*; V Form, cognate to *Hithpael*; and two others), all basically reflexive. See G. Bergsträsser, *Introduction to the Semitic Languages*, trans. and sup. P. T. Daniels (Winona Lake, Indiana: Eisenbrauns, 1983) 15. Ugaritic has at least two *t* stems, Gt and tD (the latter similar to the *Hithpael*), and perhaps also an Št; see *UT* § 9.32–33, 39. Hebrew preserves one clear *Qal* infixed-*t* (Gt) form, *maštîn* in the expression *maštîn bəqîr* 'male, one who pisses on a wall' (1 Sam 25:22, 34, etc.; six times total). This is in line with the fact that taboo words often have anomalous shapes.

2. There are no clear cases of the *Hithpael* of a I-*z* root; note *hizzakkû* in Isa 1:16 and the discussion in William Chomsky, *David Ḳimḥi's Hebrew Grammar (Mikhlol)* (New York: Bloch, 1952) 94, 106. If the metathesis rule would lead to a sequence of *dental stop* + *vowel* + *dental stop*, it is usually blocked; thus the exceptional form *hitšôṭāṭnâ* (Jer 49:3); contrast ## 4, 18 below. The metathesis rule is not entirely operative in Qumran Hebrew; see E. Qimron, *The Hebrew of the Dead Sea Scrolls* (Atlanta: Scholars Press, 1986) 55–56. The *š* + *t* metathesis is attested in Ugaritic for a form of the root *šʾl* (not used in *Hithpael* in Hebrew); see John Huehnergard, "A Dt Stem in Ugaritic?" *Ugarit-Forschungen* 17 (1985) 402.

In the lists below all occurrences are given unless *etc.* is added after the references.

emphatic (i.e., צ), the metathesis is accompanied by emphatic assimilation of the *t* (ת → ט; ## 18–19). If the root begins with a dental stop, the prefix *t* assimilates to it (תד → ד; תט → ט; of course, תת → ת; ## 20–25).[3]

	Root	*Hithpael*	
1.	סבל	יִסְתַּבֵּל	Qoh 12:5
2.	סלל	מִסְתּוֹלֵל	Exod 9:17
3.	ספח	הִסְתַּפֵּחַ	1 Sam 26:19
4.	סתר	מִסְתַּתֵּר	1 Sam 23:19, etc.
5.	שכר	הַמִּשְׂתַּכֵּר	Hag 1:6*bis*
6.	שרר	הִשְׂתָּרֵר	Num 16:13*bis*
7.	שבח	הִשְׁתַּבֵּחַ	Ps 106:47 = 1 Chr 16:35
8.	שגע	מִשְׁתַּגֵּעַ	1 Sam 21:15; cf. v 16
9.	שחח	תִּשְׁתּוֹחֲחִי	Ps 42:6, etc.
10.	שכח	יִשְׁתַּכְּחוּ	Qoh 8:10
11.	שכר	תִּשְׁתַּכָּרִין	1 Sam 1:14
12.	שלל	מִשְׁתּוֹלֵל	Isa 59:15, etc.
13.	שמם	יִשְׁתּוֹמֵם	Ps 143:4, etc.
14.	שמר	אֶשְׁתַּמֵּר	2 Sam 22:24 = Ps 18:24, etc.
15.	שנה	הִשְׁתַּנִּית	1 Kgs 14:2
16.	שעה	נִשְׁתָּעָה	Isa 41:23, etc.
17.	שפך	תִּשְׁתַּפֵּךְ	Job 30:16, etc.
18.	צדק	נִצְטַדָּק	Gen 44:16
19.	ציד	הִצְטַיָּדְנוּ	Josh 9:12
20.	דבר	מְדַבֵּר	2 Sam 14:13, etc.
21.	דדה[4]	אֲדַדֶּה	Isa 38:15
22.	דמה	אֲדַמֶּה	Isa 14:14
23.	טהר	הִטַּהֲרֵנוּ	Josh 22:17, etc.
24.	טמא	יִטַּמָּא	Lev 21:1, etc.
25.	תמם	תִּתַּמָּם	2 Sam 22:26 = Ps 18:26

The morphology of the *Hithpael* has certain complexities. Variant related stems c include the rare *Hithpāel* without doubling (# 26) and the *Hippael* (## 27–28), both discussed in 21.2.3. The so-called *Hippael* forms are used alongside *Hithpael* forms (## 29–30) and may be considered examples of irregular assimilations, תנ → נ (hardly surprising) and תכ → כ. Only five roots are involved in the *Hippael*, three I-*n* and two I-*k*. There are two other apparent variant stems. The *Hithpoel* is found once (# 31); the *Hithpaal* is frequent, usually in roots that either begin or end with a guttural (## 32–34, cf. ## 23, 35).[5] Thus the *Hippael*, *Hithpoel*, and *Hithpaal* are unremarkable variants of the *Hithpael*, as are the *Hithpolel* and *Hithpalpel* of geminate roots (for *Hithpolel*, see ## 2, 9, 12, 13 above; for *Hithpalpel*, see ## 36–39).

---

3. These rules also apply to minor stem forms, e.g., ## 2, 9, 12, 13.

4. The root shape *ddy* (with the first two consonants

identical) is anomalous.

5. Joüon § 52b / p. 119 refers rather to Aramaic influence; both factors may be relevant.

	Root	*Hithpael*	
26.	פקד	יִתְפָּקֵד	Judg 21:9, etc.
27.	נבא	הִנַּבֵּאתִי	Ezek 37:10, etc.
28.	כסה	תְּכַסֶּה	Prov 26:26, etc.
29.	נבא	הִתְנַבִּיתָ	1 Sam 10:6, etc.
30.	כסה	יִתְכַּסּוּ	Isa 59:6, etc.
31.	געש	הִתְגֹּעֲשׁוּ	Jer 25:16, etc.
32.	אפק	יִתְאַפַּק	Gen 43:31, etc.
33.	אנף	הִתְאַנַּף	Deut 1:37, etc.
34.	חכם	תִּתְחַכָּם	Qoh 7:16, etc.
35.	פלא	תִּתְפַּלָּא	Job 10:16
36.	מרר	יִתְמַרְמַר	Dan 11:11; cf. 8:7
37.	שעע	אֶשְׁתַּעֲשָׁע	Ps 119:16; cf. v 47[6]
38.	שקק	יִשְׁתַּקְשְׁקוּן	Nah 2:5
39.	תעע	מִתַּעְתְּעִים	2 Chr 36:16

d   These variant guises of *Hithpael* are unremarkable,[7] or they would be so except for further complexities. Although the *Hithpael* is associated with the *Piel*, some *Hithpael* forms have no counterpart in the *Piel* but do find one in the *Qal* or *Hiphil* stems: thus הִתְנַדֵּב 'to present oneself voluntarily' matches נָדַב *Qal* 'to urge on,' הִתְאַבֵּל 'to observe mourning rites' matches אָבַל *Qal* 'to mourn,' etc. Second, some verbs in the *Hithpael* do not have a sense related to the primary reflexive meaning of the *Hithpael*. For example, הִתְוַדָּה 'to confess,' whose counterpart is attested only in the *Hiphil* ידה 'to acknowledge,' does not readily display itself as a reflexive counterpart to a *Piel* stem.[8] The presence of passive *Hithpael*-like forms, the *Hothpael*, further compounds the problem (26.3b).

26.1.2   Comparative Semitic Proposals

a   Partially in response to this diversity and partially by reasoning analogically from the many *t*-prefixed and -infixed stems in the other Semitic languages, some scholars have come to regard the *Hithpael* stem not as an original morphological unity with one function in the stem system, but as a composite of heterogeneous stems which in the course of time fell together into one common stem. These earlier stems for the most part cannot be recognized formally but must be uncovered by their atypical meanings. E. A. Speiser argued this view:

> The Hithpaᶜel . . . combines several independent *t*-stems, their merger being due on the one hand to the successful competition on the part of the Nifᶜal and the Hofᶜal, and on the other hand to specific phonologic and morphologic circumstances. . . .

6. Forms ## 37–38 show metathesis.

7. So also Ernst Jenni, "Zur Funktion der reflexiv-passiven Stammformen im Biblisch-Hebräischen," *Proceedings of the Fifth World Congress of Jewish Studies* (Jerusalem: World Union of Jewish Studies, 1973), 4. 61–70, at 69.

8. On the "indistinct" *Hithpaels* being older and more common in verse, see Paul Mazars, "Sens et usage de l'hitpael dans le Bible hebraïque," *Divinitas* 12 (1968) 351–64, at 362–64 (on *hlk, hll, pll*, 358–60; others, 360–62).

[There is] a residue of Hebrew *t*-forms in which the function of the infix can hardly be reflexive, middle, or reciprocal. Most of these are immediately betrayed as atypical by the fact that the corresponding stems without a *t*-morpheme—in the Qal or the Piᶜel, as the case may be—appear to perform the same duty as the *t*-forms.[9]

By comparing some of these atypical uses of the *Hithpael* stem with the *t*-prefixed stems in the cognate Semitic languages, especially Akkadian, Speiser (and Bruno Dombrowski independently)[10] detects a durative-iterative *t* stem homonymous with the reflexive *t* stem. Such a stem is represented in Akkadian by a *tan* infix (Gtn, Dtn, etc.).[11] In Hebrew it would tend to merge with the "normal" *Hithpael* stem.[12] Speiser cites these illustrations with the shared root הלך/*alāku* 'to go' in its various meanings (the Akkadian forms are Gtn stems, and the Hebrew forms are *Hithpael*).[13]

    (i)   in the meaning 'to walk about'
         Akk.: [Lord,] wanderer in the night (*muttallik muši*)
         Heb.: [God] walking in the garden (*mithallēk*) toward the cool of the day
              (Gen 3:8)
    (ii) in the meaning 'to wander (aimlessly)'
         Akk.: [chariots with their riderless horses] wandered to and fro (*ittanallakā mithāriš utirrā*)
         Heb.: [from roaming over the earth] and wandering on it to and fro (*ûmēhithallēk bāh*) (Job 1:7, 2:2)
    (iii) in the meaning 'to walk with, commune'
         Akk.: [If he rejected sin,] his god will walk with him (*ilšu ittišu ittanallak*)
         Heb.: And Enoch walked with God (*wayyithallēk ḥănôk ᵓet-hāᵓĕlōhîm*) (Gen 5:22, 24; cf. Gen 6:9)

Speiser supports his theory with three arguments. First, the comparative argument that the other Semitic languages have more than one *t* form. Second, a morphological argument that the traditional vocalization still reflects vestiges of a *Qal t* stem in הִתְפָּקְדוּ (Judg 20:15). Third, a semantic argument that a group of Hebrew *Hithpael* forms has a

---

9. E. A. Speiser, "The Durative Hithpaᶜel: A *tan* Form," *Journal of the American Oriental Society* 75 (1955) 118–21, rpt. in his *Oriental and Biblical Studies*, ed. J. J. Finkelstein and Moshe Greenberg (Philadelphia: University of Pennsylvania, 1967) 506–14, at 507, cited from the reprint.

10. Bruno W. W. Dombrowski, "Some Remarks on the Hebrew Hithpaᶜel and Inversative -*t*- in the Semitic Languages," *Journal of Near Eastern Studies* 21 (1962) 220–23. Dombrowski refers not to the Akkadian *tan* forms, but to the durative sense of *t* forms elsewhere in the Semitic languages. He argues that the *t* infix "defines what is radically different from thinking and speaking man— what is *other* than himself" (p. 223); the import of this essentially undemonstrated view is unclear.

11. Akkadian regularly uses a G-Gt-Gtn and a D-Dt-Dtn series, as well as an Š-Štn and an N-Ntn series. "The

basic function of the *tan* stems is that of an iterative to the relevant simple main stems (e.g., *aštanappar* 'I am continually writing'; . . . *šitakkun* 'he is over and over supplied with'; . . . *tuqtanattar* 'you are always perfumed'. . .; *uštanaṣbat* 'he is ever again causing to seize'; *ittanabriq* 'it continually flashes'). The meaning of the iterative stems is often habitual (e.g., . . . *aktanarrabakkum* 'I am accustomed always to pray for you'. . .)." See W. von Soden, *Grundriss der akkadischen Grammatik* (Rome: Pontifical Biblical Institute, 1969) 119–20.

12. A certain amount of homonymy is found among the Akkadian verb forms; the G perfect (*iptaras*) corresponds to the Gt preterite (*imtaḫaṣ*), and the Gt present (*imtaḫḫaṣ*) to the Gtn preterite (*iptarras* < *iptanras*). See von Soden, *Grundriss der akkadischen Grammatik*, 12*–13*.

13. Speiser, "Durative Hithpaᶜel," 510–11; examples abridged and transliteration modified.

distinctive aspectual sense. Thus, Speiser argues, some *Hithpael* forms should be treated as if they were *tn* (or *tan*) forms.[14] According to this view one should translate these forms as iterative or durative.

1.   וַיִּתְגָּעֲשׁוּ וְלֹא יוּכָלוּ   Although (its waves) *batter continuously*, they cannot prevail.
Jer 5:22

2.   וְהָאִישׁ מִשְׁתָּאֵה לָהּ   The man (Eliezer) *gazed fixedly* at her (Rebekah).
Gen 24:21

Speiser assigned to his *tn* durative stem אבל 'to mourn,' אוה 'to desire,' אנף 'to be angry,' געש 'to shake,' הלך 'to move about,' נחל 'to inherit,' עלל 'to act (often adversely),' עטף 'to grow/be weak, faint,' and שאה and שעה 'to gaze,' because these verbs show "no trace of the ordinary uses of the [Hebrew] *t*-stems." Speiser implies that he disallows Goetze's notion of a frequentative use of the *Piel* (24.5) on the grounds that only tD stems like the *Hithpael* can show this meaning. In fact, the frequentative *Piel* could be taken as indirect support for Speiser's view, in that it allows for more diversity within a stem than, say, Ernst Jenni would (24.1h).

c   Not all of Speiser's nine roots need be construed as iterative. It is difficult to construct a grammar on the basis of apparent meaning, and the verbs assigned by Speiser to this stem may only seem not to fit the typical meaning of the *Hithpael*. Curiously, the "non-reflexive" use is presented, in one linguistically naïve description, as the most frequent use of the stem—the typical use! A. F. Bean came to this erroneous conclusion by analyzing the functions of the stem in a purely "descriptive way," apparently unaware that he described his sample according to the structures of the English language; he draws the conclusion that most of the occurrences of the *Hithpael* have a "simple, non-specific meaning," by which he means that they behave like fientive verbs in the *Qal* or *Piel* stems.[15] Bean includes in his lists of *Hithpael* verbs with "simple" senses פלל 'pray' and נבא 'prophesy.'[16] Speiser, however, excludes these from his list of "atypical" *Hithpaels* because he realizes that in Hebrew they describe reflexive actions: פלל *Hithpael* means 'to seek a mediation for oneself' with a true reflexive force,[17] and נבא *Hithpael* means 'to appear/conduct oneself as a prophet,' again a typical *Hithpael* reflexive notion. In short, although 'pray' and 'prophesy' from the English perspective do not seem to have a reflexive force, yet reflection discloses that they do.

d   On balance, the *Hithpael* probably denotes iterative or frequentative aspect with אבל, געש, עטף, and שאה and שעה. These roots show no *t*-stem sense in the *Hithpael* and have *Qal* rather than *Piel* as a correspondent to the *Hithpael*. The verb הלך may be

---

14. A similar view is taken by Samuel B. Wheeler, "The Infixed -t- in Biblical Hebrew," *Journal of the Ancient Near Eastern Society* 3 (1970–71) 20–31; cf. A. M. L. Boyle, *Infix-t Forms in Biblical Hebrew* (Boston University Dissertation, 1969).

15. A. F. Bean, *A Phenomenological Study of the*

Hithpaᶜel Verbal Stem in the Hebrew Old Testament (Louisville, Kentucky: Southern Baptist Theological Seminary Dissertation, 1975) 139–47, 157–66, 172–73.

16. Bean, *Hithpaᶜel Verbal Stem*, 159.

17. E. A. Speiser, "The Stem *PLL* in Hebrew," *Journal of Biblical Literature* 82 (1963) 301–6.

judged to present special problems; it is even possible that the *Hithpael* of this root is an "Akkadianism" borrowed into Hebrew.[18]

Distribution   26.1.3

There are over 825 occurrences of the *Hithpael*, involving 175 roots, many of them   a
used only once.[19] Bean's study offers some observations on the sporadic use of the
stem.[20] He shows that attempts at explaining this spotty use by geographical, form-
critical, or semantic factors are nugatory.[21]

Bean's study does demonstrate that the stem was used throughout the historical   b
period represented by the literature in the Bible and that its use was changing from the
pre-exilic through the exilic and on into the post-exilic periods. Although modern scholarship has not been able to assign dates to all segments of the biblical literature and
therefore Bean's conclusions are of necessity somewhat arbitrary, the overall impact of
the evidence is such that Bean has established with certitude that the stem is growing in
popularity in the biblical literature and that it was becoming less a reflexive stem and
more a passive one.[22] His study supports the theory that the *Hithpael*'s original meaning
was reflexive and that the passive uses represent a secondary development within the
Hebrew language.

Double-Status Use   26.2

The *Hithpael* is used primarily as the double-status (reflexive/reciprocal) counterpart   a
of the *Piel* stem. The object of causation in the *Piel* is the subject of the *Hithpael* and
transforms itself/is transformed into the effected state signified by the root. Such meanings harmonize both with its form (*t prefix + Piel*) and its contextual use.

In the analysis given below we further refine the reflexive use into direct reflexive,   b
indirect reflexive, benefactive reflexive, and estimative-declarative reflexive. In the illustrations given below for these varying usages it should be borne in mind that although
we have rendered the verbs into idiomatic English, in fact, in addition to its reflexive (or
reciprocal or passive) force, the *Hithpael* is usually either factitive or resultative. Thus,
for example, the verb in # 1 means '*make* yourselves *girded.*'

---

18. Thomas O. Lambdin cites *hlk* as the only example of the iterative use of the *Hithpael*; see *Introduction to Biblical Hebrew* (New York: Scribner, 1971) 250. For another explanation of *hlk Hithpael*, see S. A. Ryder II, *The D-Stem in Western Semitic* (The Hague: Mouton, 1974) 131. Note, too, that David Qimḥi remarks that "the reflexive sense . . . is not always apparent, e.g., הִתְהַלֶּךְ־נֹחַ Gn 6:9. . . . The sense being: he made himself worthy (by his good deeds) of walking with God." See Chomsky, *Mikhlol*, 93 and n. *a.* J. A. Soggin discusses *hlk Hithpael* in 1 Sam 23:13 in his *Old Testament and Oriental Studies* (Rome: Biblical Institute, 1975) 235–36. An iterative sense

may be proper to the root *šqq*, not cited by Speiser; compare the *Qal* in Prov 28:15 and the *Hithpalpal* in Nah 2:5. The other verbs cited by Speiser are probably double-status verbs: *ʾwh* and *nḥl* (benefactive), *ʾnp* (estimative-declarative), *ʿll* (simple reflexive).

19. See SA/THAT. Bean, *Hithpaʿel Verbal Stem*, 29, 44–48, gives a slightly higher count.

20. Bean, *Hithpaʿel Verbal Stem*, 129.

21. Bean, *Hithpaʿel Verbal Stem*, 132.

22. Bean, *Hithpaʿel Verbal Stem*, 152. There are sixty-three *Hithpael* forms in the Hebrew of Daniel; see Mazars, "Sens et usage de l'hitpael," 354.

c   In the *direct reflexive*, the subject is also the direct object of the verbal notion.

1.   הִתְאַזְּרוּ   *Gird yourselves* (for battle).
Isa 8:9

2.   לֹא תִתְנַקֵּם נַפְשִׁי׃   *Should* not my soul *avenge itself*?
Jer 5:9

3.   וַאֲדֹנִיָּה . . . מִתְנַשֵּׂא   Now Adonijah . . . *exalted himself.*
1 Kgs 1:5

4.   הֲלוֹא דָוִד מִסְתַּתֵּר עִמָּנוּ   Is not David *hiding* (*himself*) with us?
1 Sam 23:19

d   In the *indirect reflexive* use the subject is also the indirect object of the action; often a direct object is expressed.

5.   וַיִּתְפָּרְקוּ כָּל־הָעָם אֶת־נִזְמֵי   And all the people *took off* (*from themselves*)
הַזָּהָב   their gold earrings.
Exod 32:3

6.   וַיִּתְפַּשֵּׁט יְהוֹנָתָן אֶת־הַמְּעִיל   And Jonathan *stripped off* (*from himself*) the
robe.
1 Sam 18:4

e   The *benefactive reflexive* refers to an action done on one's own behalf.[23]

7.   וְהִתְפַּלְלוּ וְהִתְחַנְּנוּ אֵלֶיךָ   They *pray* and *implore* you *for favor* (lit., *make
a mediation* [*by asking* you] *for themselves*).
1 Kgs 8:33

8.   וְיִתְפַּלֵּל בַּעַדְךָ   And he *will pray* for you (lit., he *will cause a
mediation* [*by seeking* or *asking*] *for himself* on
your *behalf*).
Gen 20:7

9.   עַל־שָׁרְשֵׁי רַגְלַי תִּתְחַקֶּה׃   You *put slave markings* (*for yourself*) on the soles
of my feet.
Job 13:27

10.   זֶה לַחְמֵנוּ חָם הִצְטַיַּדְנוּ אֹתוֹ   This is our bread—it was hot—we *packed* it *as
provisions* (*for ourselves*).[24]
Josh 9:12

f   The *estimative-declarative reflexive* is the counterpart to the *Piel*'s use to esteem someone as in a state or to declare someone as existing in a state; the *Hithpael* may

23. See John Lyons, *Introduction to Theoretical Linguistics* (Cambridge: Cambridge University, 1968) 374; and

11.2.10.
24. A denominative from *ṣáyid* 'provisions.'

denote esteeming or presenting oneself in a state, sometimes without regard to the question of truthfulness (## 12–13, 15?).

11.	וְהִתְגַּדִּלְתִּי וְהִתְקַדִּשְׁתִּי וְנוֹדַעְתִּי לְעֵינֵי גּוֹיִם רַבִּים	And I *will show* my *greatness* and *display* my *holiness*, and I will make myself known before the eyes of many nations. Ezek 38:23
12.	שְׁכַב עַל־מִשְׁכָּבְךָ וְהִתְחָל	Lie down on your bed and *act/pretend to be sick*. 2 Sam 13:5
13.	יֵשׁ מִתְעַשֵּׁר וְאֵין כֹּל	There is a man who *pretends to be rich*, yet has nothing. Prov 13:7
14.	וַיִּתְעַבָּר	And he *showed himself angry*.[25] Ps 78:21
15.	וְרַבִּים מֵעַמֵּי הָאָרֶץ מִתְיַהֲדִים	And many of the peoples of the land *pretended to be Jews*.[26] Esth 8:17

g When two or more subjects act in relationship to each other according to the notion expressed by the verbal root, the action is *reciprocal*. Although the *Hithpael* is used to designate such action, it is rare.

16.	לָמָּה תִּתְרָאוּ:	Why *do* you *look on one another*? Gen 42:1
17.	וְלֹא יִתְבֹּשָׁשׁוּ:	And they *felt* no *shame before each other*. Gen 2:25
18.	וַיִּשְׁמַע אֶת־הַקּוֹל מִדַּבֵּר אֵלָיו	He heard the voice (of someone) *conversing* with him. Num 7:89

Passive Use, Passive Forms   26.3

a The passive uses of the *Hithpael* may express either (*a*) the notion that the subject is transformed into a state by an unexpressed agent or (*b*) the notion that the subject transforms itself into such a state. Thus, # 1 can be taken as either (*a*) 'she is made/caused to be praised' (cf. the *Pual*) or (*b*) 'she makes herself such as to be praised' (cf. the benefactive *Hithpael*). The second view finds theoretical support in that it maintains the differences among the various stems; the first view is supported by the growing popularity of the *Hithpael* during the history of Biblical Hebrew.

---

25. This verb is a denominative from *ʿebrâ* 'arrogance, fury.'

26. This verb is a denominative from *yəhûdâ/yəhûdî*.

Some scholars render the verb 'they converted to be Jews'; NJPS is appropriately ambiguous, 'And many of the people of the land professed to be Jews.'

1.   :הִיא הִתְהַלָּל   She *is praised.*
                                   Prov 31:30

2.   כְּלֵיל הִתְקַדֶּשׁ־חָג   as on the night when a holy festival *is celebrated*
                                   Isa 30:29

3.   כֻּלָּם הִתְיַחְשׂוּ בִּימֵי יוֹתָם   All these *were registered* in the days of Jotham.[27]
                                   1 Chr 5:17

4.   וַיָּשָׁב לְהִתְרַפֵּא   And he returned *to be healed.*
                                   2 Chr 22:6

5.   וְיִשְׁתַּכְּחוּ   And they *are forgotten.*
                                   Qoh 8:10

As examples ## 3–5 suggest, the passive sense tends to be found in later biblical literature.

b   In the earlier literature there are a few *Hothpael* forms.[28]

6.   וְרָאָה הַכֹּהֵן אַחֲרֵי הֻכַּבֵּס אֶת־   The priest shall look after the diseased thing *has been*
      הַנֶּגַע . . . וְהִנֵּה כֵּהָה הַנֶּגַע   *washed* . . . and if the disease is dim after it *has been*
      אַחֲרֵי הֻכַּבֵּס אֹתוֹ   *washed.* . . .[29]
                                       Lev 13:55–56

7.   הֻטַּמָּאָה   She *has been defiled.*
                                       Deut 24:4

8.   חֶרֶב . . . הָדַּשְׁנָה מֵחֵלֶב   The sword *is gorged* with fat.
                                       Isa 34:6

Since the stem is found only in verse and technical priestly writing, it is hard to believe that it was common.

26.4   Denominative Use

a   The *Hithpael* pattern with one of its more specific meanings is sometimes imposed on a nominal form. For example, the estimative-declarative nuance is attached to נביא 'prophet' and אנף 'anger,' yielding הִתְנַבֵּא 'to appear as a prophet' and הִתְאַנַּף 'to show oneself angry.'[30] A benefactive reflexive value is attached to ציד 'provision, food' and so becomes הִצְטַיַּד 'to supply oneself with provisions' (Josh 9:12).

---

27. A denominative from *yáḥaś* 'genealogical record.'
28. All the following forms show assimilation of the *t* prefix.

29. Note *ʾt* twice with the subject of a passive verb.
30. Cf. the examples from *ʿebrâ*, n. 25, and *yəhûdî*, n. 26. Cf. also n. 27.

27

Hiphil Stem

Form and Meaning 27.1

The stem system of the Hebrew verb works *as a system*, and the two major points of   a
system stress and development involve the *Qal : Piel* contrast and the *Piel : Hiphil* contrast. These two contrasts are discussed in 21.2.2; we treat the relevant points more
briefly here. Hebrew grammars traditionally represent the *Hiphil* stem as the causative of
the *Qal* stem. Since they also teach that the *Piel* stem sometimes signifies this same
notion, they cannot effectively distinguish the two stems; for some verbs at least they
assert that there is no practical distinction. Thus, writes one grammar, "The meaning of
Hiphʿîl is primarily, and even more frequently than in *Piʿēl*, . . . *causative* of *Qal*. . . . In
some verbs, *Piʿēl* and *Hiphʿîl* occur side by side in the same sense. . . ."[1] The use of both
stems for the so-called "*declarative* sense" further exacerbates the confusion.

Ernst Jenni, beginning with the assumption that the two morphologically distinct   b
stems have different semantic values, undertook an exhaustive study of the *Piel*, focusing
on the *Piel* and *Hiphil* stems of the same verbal root in similar contexts. According to
Jenni, the *Piel* signifies *to bring about a state*, and the *Hiphil, to cause an event.*[2] His
distinction involves two contrasting ideas: *state* versus *event*, and *to bring about* versus
to cause actively.[3] According to Jenni, the differences between *Piel* and *Hiphil* can be
understood by appealing to deep differences: the *Piel* is analogous to a nominal clause,
the *Hiphil* to a verbal clause.

---

1. GKC § 53c / p. 144; cf. R. J. Williams, *Hebrew Syntax: An Outline* (2d ed.; Toronto: University of Toronto, 1976) 28. Due to the complex morphology of the *Hiphil* the weak verbs are largely straightforward. The contrast of I-*w* and I-*y* verbs is best preserved in the *Hiphil*; the I-*w* group is much larger than the I-*y* group, of which only *yṭb* is common. Cf. also n. 10.

2. Ernst Jenni, *Das hebräische Piʿel* (Zurich: EVZ, 1968) 20–52. Cf. W. T. Claassen, "On a Recent Proposal as to a Distinction between Piʿel and Hiphʿil," *Journal of Northwest Semitic Languages* 1 (1971) 3–10.

3. There are cases in which the sense of the *Hiphil* is lexicalized, i.e., distinctively specified for the root; see below, 27.4b, on *škm*.

c   In our discussion of stative verbs we contrasted the Hebrew predicate-adjective construction with the stative construction (22.2.2). The former predicates a state or condition without any verb, that is, without marking for aspect, mood, *Aktionsart*. In the latter construction, by contrast, the root has all the markings of a verb. Thus, the predicate-adjective construction presents the subject's *state* or condition and the stative construction presents a *situation* involving a state or condition. Consider these pairs.

1a.	גְּדֹלִים מַעֲשֵׂי יהוָה	*Great* (are) Yʜwʜ's works. Ps 111:2
1b.	מַה־גָּדְלוּ מַעֲשֶׂיךָ יהוָה	How *great are* your works, O Yʜwʜ! Ps 92:6
2a.	וַאדֹנִי חָכָם	My lord is *wise*. 2 Sam 14:20
2b.	לוּ חָכְמוּ	If they *were wise*. . . . Deut 32:29

Jenni notes two fundamental differences between the nominal and verbal clauses:[4]

    1. The nominal clauses [## 1a, 2a] represent a state, whereas the verbal clauses [## 1b, 2b] represent an event. The former is rigid, a non-activity; the latter an activity, a movement, a happening, a deed.

    2. In the nominal clauses the speaker regards the predicate as a feature added to the subject (a synthetic judgment); in the verbal sentences he regards the predicate as closely joined together with the subject and as established in one situation (an analytic judgment). The former expresses a subjective judgment about the subject; the latter an objective event.

English and most other European languages cannot formally distinguish the relevant notions because for both notions they must employ the verb 'to be' (or the like) and allow contextual considerations to indicate whether 'be' is a "dummy" verb with a predicate adjective or a true verb. Speakers of the English language can appreciate the difference between the notions of state and event by juxtaposing 'he is alive' with 'he lives,' though strictly speaking the former may usually be experienced as an event as well as the latter.

d   Though both stems involve causation, the factitive-resultative *Piel* generally has to do with the bringing about of a state or condition, and the causative *Hiphil* with the causing of an event. The *Piel* can often be translated by an adjectival construction: an adjective (with stative verbs), a passive past participle (with fientive verbs). Superficially considered, the relationship between subject and object in both *Piel* and *Hiphil* stems is often that of a transitive *making* or *causing* which proceeds from the subject to the object. The object, however, experiences this action quite differently in the two stems.

---

4. Paraphrased from Jenni, *Piᶜel*, 25–33.

With the *Piel*, the object is transposed passively into a new state or condition. Philosophers would refer to this transposition as "accidental" because the object makes no contribution to the verbal notion. With the *Hiphil*, however, the object participates in the event expressed by the verbal root. Let us illustrate the difference Jenni has plausibly established between the stems by juxtaposing cases of אבד, a root often used to support the view that the stems have the same sense.[5]

3a. :וַתְּאַבֵּד אֵת כָּל־זֶ֫רַע הַמַּמְלָכָה   She (Athaliah) *made destroyed* (*Piel*) the whole royal seed.
2 Kgs 11:1

3b. וְהַאֲבַדְתִּי אֶת־הַנֶּ֫פֶשׁ הַהִיא   I (YHWH) *will cause* that soul *to perish* (*Hiphil*).
Lev 23:30

Admittedly, for the sake of "good" English we would probably translate אבד in both instances 'destroy,' but in doing that we would gloss over a fundamental distinction in Hebrew. In the first example, the writer conceptualizes the object, the royal family, as "accidentally" transferred into the state of perdition, but in the second example, the lawgiver presents the object, that soul, as an actor in the event of perishing. Without the causative notion of the *Hiphil*, the sentence would read as a *Qal*, just as in:

3c.   וַאֲבַדְתֶּם   You *will perish* (*Qal*).
Deut 11:17

Whereas the *Piel* represents the subject as transposing an object into the state or   e
condition corresponding to the notion expressed by the verbal root, the *Hiphil* represents the subject as causing an object to participate indirectly as a second subject in the notion expressed by the verbal root.[6] In fact, this notion probably accounts for the *Hiphil*'s distinctive form. The *Hiphil* stem's characteristic *h* preformative, derived from a third-person personal pronoun, reflects a designation of a second subject's participation in the action.[7] In E. A. Speiser's view the *Hiphil* originally signified: 'X (the subject) caused that Y (the second subject) be or do something.'[8]

---

5. Jenni, *Pi⁽el*, 65–67; GKC § 53c / p. 144.

6. Jenni emphasizes, too, that the *Piel* tends to be habitual, while the *Hiphil* tends to refer to occasional or one-time situations; this difference is especially relevant to the participles; *Pi⁽el*, 55–65.

7. "The Semitic personal pronouns for the third person exhibit virtually the same variations of initial sounds that we have found in the causative prefixes," i.e., *š* in, e.g., Akkadian ~ *h* in, e.g., Hebrew. See E. A. Speiser, "Studies in Semitic Formatives," *Journal of the American Oriental Society* 56 (1936) 22–46, esp. 23–33; rpt. in his *Oriental and Biblical Studies*, ed. J. J. Finkelstein and Moshe Greenberg (Philadelphia: University of Pennsylvania, 1967) 403–32, at 409, cited from the reprint. See 21.1c n. 8. There may be some old causatives in *š* in Biblical Hebrew (as there are *š* causatives in Aramaic, the result of loans from Akkadian; e.g., Biblical Aramaic *šêzîb* 'to rescue').

On these forms, see J. A. Soggin's essay "Traces of Ancient Causatives in *š*- Realized as Autonomous Roots in Biblical Hebrew," in his *Old Testament and Oriental Studies* (Rome: Biblical Institute, 1975) 188–202.

8. Speiser proposes: "The phrase 'A orders (wishes, etc.) that B build a house' was actually construed as 'A orders, B builds the house.' In such asyndetic *that*-clauses particular emphasis was needed to make clear that a given action was to be performed by someone, or that a given quality was attributed to someone or something. The pronoun of the third person, a demonstrative in origin, was evidently the only available means of conveying this idea. It was unavoidable, therefore, that this pronoun should become associated with the *that*-clause in the linguistic consciousness of the speaker." See Speiser, "Studies in Semitic Formatives," 414. This type of shift, from an analytic to a synthetic construction, is common in many languages.

f   The fundamental causative notion of the *Hiphil* can be nuanced by consideration of the kind of verbal root to which it is affixed and by the modal relationship that exists between the subject and the object(s). We broadly distinguish between roots that are *Qal* or *Niphal* intransitive (27.2), *Qal* transitive (27.3), and denominative or isolated (27.4).[9] In 27.5 we discuss the modal relationships that may exist between the subject and the object.

27.2   *Hiphils* of *Qal* and *Niphal* Verbs Used Intransitively

a   *Qal* and *Niphal* fientive roots used intransitively are one-place predicates (involving only a subject; see 20.2l); they tend to form transitive or two-place *Hiphils*, with a subject and an object. Less often, such roots form one-place or internal *Hiphils*.

b   In linking one-place *Qal* and *Niphal* intransitive fientives and *Hiphil* two-place transitives, we must be careful to maintain the distinction of the *Hiphil* from the *Piel*.[10] For the difference between these two stems with this kind of root contrast these sentences.

1a.	וַיְעַבֵּר בְּרַתּוּקוֹת זָהָב לִפְנֵי הַדְּבִיר	And he *extended* (*Piel*) (lit., *made passed over*) gold chains across the front of the inner sanctuary. 1 Kgs 6:21 Qere
1b.	וַיַּעֲבֵר אֱלֹהִים רוּחַ עַל־הָאָרֶץ	And God *caused* a wind *to pass over* (*Hiphil*) the earth. Gen 8:1

In the *Piel* construction the verb of motion denotes an accomplished state, while in the *Hiphil* construction an event is described in which the object/second subject ('a wind') participates. In the first construction the effect is direct and immediate; in the second it is indirect and mediated. The same difference can be seen with שׁוב.[11]

2a.	לְשׁוֹבֵב יַעֲקֹב אֵלָיו	to restore (*Polel* for *Piel*) (lit., *make restored*) Jacob to him Isa 49:5
2b.	וַהֲשִׁבֹתִיךָ אֶל־הָאֲדָמָה הַזֹּאת	And I *will bring* you *back* (*Hiphil*) (lit., *cause* you *to return*) to this land. Gen 28:15

A major group of *Qal* intransitive fientives is the verbs of motion, including these:[12]

---

9. For the various shapes of the *Hiphil* in Greek translation, see E. Tov, "The Representations of the Causative Aspects of the *Hiphʿil* in the LXX: A Study in Translation Technique," *Biblica* 63 (1982) 417–24.

10. The morphological opposition of stative and fientive roots is confined almost entirely to the *Qal*, but there is a trace of it in the *Hiphil* inflection of geminate roots; stative geminates have the vowel *a* in the second syllable (*mrr* 'to be bitter,' *hēmar*; *ṣrr* 'to be cramped,' *hēṣar*; *qll* 'to be slight,' *hēqal*; *rkk* 'to be soft,' *hērak*), while fientive geminates have *ē* (*ḥll Hiphil* 'to begin,' *hēḥēl*; *sbb* 'to go around,' *hēsēb*; *prr Hiphil* 'to break,' *hēpēr*). See P. Joüon, "Études de morphologie hébraïque," *Biblica* 1 (1920) 353–71, esp. 353–54.

11. Cf. also *nṭy Qal* (the donkey's turning aside) and *Hiphil* (the master's turning the donkey back) in Num 22:23.

12. T. O. Lambdin, *Introduction to Biblical Hebrew* (New York: Scribner, 1971) 212.

3.	בָּא	הֵבִיא	to bring (take, lead, send) in, to, into
4.	יָצָא	הוֹצִיא	to bring (take, lead, send) out
5.	יָרַד	הוֹרִיד	to bring (take, lead, send) down
6.	עָבַר	הֶעֱבִיר	to bring (take, lead, send) across
7.	עָלָה	הֶעֱלָה	to bring (take, lead, send) up
8.	שָׁב	הֵשִׁיב	to bring (take, lead, send) back

As these verbs and the examples suggest, the *Hiphil* is often associated with personal or human objects, since humans are more readily able to serve as objects of verbal causation. The extent of the association should not be exaggerated: in example # 2a, a *Piel* has a human object (though it is metaphorical), while in # 1b, and # 9, the object of a *Hiphil* is non-personal.[13]

9.	וְכָל־עֵץ טוֹב תַּפִּילוּ	You *will cut down* (lit., *cause to fall*) every good tree. 2 Kgs 3:19

Some intransitive verbs are attested in *Niphal* but not in *Qal*; the *Hiphil* of these   c
follows the pattern of roots with *Qal* intransitive usage. Thus נגר, a one-place *Niphal*, 'to be poured,' forms a two-place *Hiphil*, 'to cause (something) to be poured, pour.'

10.	וְהִגַּרְתִּי לַגַּי אֲבָנֶיהָ	I *will pour* (lit., *cause to be poured*) her stones into the valley. Mic 1:6

Qal stative verbs tend to form two-place *Hiphils* usually rendered as transitives. The   d
sense is often ingressive, describing the object entering into a state. It can be difficult for the English speaker to distinguish a factitive (*Piel*) and a causative (*Hiphil*) that are derived from a stative, intransitive root. Contrast these clauses.

11a.	גָּדוֹל כְּבוֹדוֹ	His glory (is) *great* (predicate adjective). Ps 21:6
11b.	גָּדַ֫לְתָּ	You *are great* (*Qal* stative). 2 Sam 7:22
11c.	גִּדַּל יהוה אֶת־יְהוֹשֻׁעַ	Yhwh *made* Joshua *great* (*Piel*). Josh 4:14
11d.	הִגְדַּ֫לְתָּ . . . אִמְרָתֶךָ׃	You *caused* your word . . . *to be great* (*Hiphil*). Ps 138:2

Above (27.1c) we touched on the difference between # 11a and # 11b; given that the fundamental distinction between *Piel* and *Hiphil* is that the former signifies the *bringing about of a state* and the latter *the causing of an event*, we can plausibly suppose that # 11c is the factitive counterpart of # 11a and that # 11d is the causative counterpart of # 11b. Once

---

13. Cf. Ezek 17:24, # 14 below.

again proper usage in English leads to blurring of a fundamental Hebrew distinction by leveling both constructions with the verb *exalt*: 'Yнwн exalted Joshua' and 'You exalted your word.' Again, contrast these pairs of sentences.

12a.	וְלָמָּה תְכַבְּדוּ אֶת־לְבַבְכֶם כַּאֲשֶׁר כִּבְּדוּ מִצְרַיִם וּפַרְעֹה אֶת־לִבָּם	Why *do* you *harden* (*Piel*) your hearts (lit., *make your hearts to be hard*) as the Egyptians and Pharaoh hardened their hearts? 1 Sam 6:6
12b.	וְהַכְבֵּד אֶת־לִבּוֹ	And he (Pharaoh) *hardened* (*Hiphil*) his heart (lit., *caused* his heart *to become hard*). Exod 8:11
13a.	בְּנוֹ קִדְּשׁוּ	They *consecrated* (*Piel*) (lit., *made consecrated*) his son. 1 Sam 7:1
13b.	וְאִם מִשְּׂדֵה אֲחֻזָּתוֹ יַקְדִּישׁ אִישׁ לַיהוה	If someone *consecrates* (*Hiphil*) (lit., *causes to become consecrated*) to Yнwн part of his family land. . . . Lev 27:16

In these instances the English tends to blur the distinction between the *Piel*'s factitive notion and the *Hiphil*'s causative meaning. The *Piel* verbs here direct attention to the results of the situation apart from the event (the hearts' being hardened, the son's being consecrated), and the *Hiphils* refers to the process (the making hard of the hearts, the making holy of the land). The emphasis on event can be seen in this example.

14.	אֲנִי יהוה הִשְׁפַּלְתִּי עֵץ גָּבֹהַּ הִגְבַּהְתִּי עֵץ שָׁפָל	I, Yнwн, *bring down* the tall tree and *cause* the low tree *to grow tall*. Ezek 17:24

Verbs that can be used in the *Qal* as either intransitive or transitive form two-place *Hiphils* with the former use.

15a.	גַּם־עָבִים נָטְפוּ מָיִם:	The clouds *drop* (*Qal* transitive) water. Judg 5:4
15b.	וְעָלֵימוֹ תִּטֹּף מִלָּתִי:	On them my words *dropped* (*Qal* intransitive). Job 29:22
15c.	לֹא־יַטִּפוּ לָאֵלֶּה	They *will* not *drop* (*Hiphil*) (words) about these things. Mic 2:6

e   *Qal* statives can also yield putative-delocutive *Hiphils*.[14] Just as the *Piel* can denote that an object is subjectively regarded or declared by the speaker(s) as having attained a

---

14. The delocutive *Hiphils* are based on locutions such as 'He is just'; see D. R. Hillers, "Delocutive Verbs in Bib-

lical Hebrew," *Journal of Biblical Literature* 86 (1967) 320–24. As noted in connection with *Piels* (24.2f), delocutives

certain state (the so-called "estimative-declarative *Piel*," 24.2), so also the *Hiphil* can denote the causing of an event in which a person or object is esteemed or declared through a judicial sentence or some other kind of recognition to be in a state.[15] The *Piel* delocutive use pertains to the making of a state, while the *Hiphil* delocutive pertains to the causing of an event.

16.　　　אֲשֶׁר יַרְשִׁיעֻן אֱלֹהִים　　he whom God *declares* (lit., *causes to be declared*) *in the wrong*
Exod 22:8

To illustrate the difference between the delocutive-factitive *Piel* and the delocutive-causative *Hiphil*, contrast these clauses.

17a.　　　דַּבֵּר כִּי־חָפַצְתִּי צַדְּקֶךָּ׃　　Speak, for I *want to declare* you *righteous* (*Piel*) (lit., *to make* you *declared righteous*).
Job 33:32

17b.　　חָלִילָה לִּי אִם־אַצְדִּיק אֶתְכֶם　　Far be it from me—I *will* never *declare* you *righteous* (*Hiphil*) (lit., *cause you to be declared righteous*).
Job 27:5

In some cases the delocutive causative is hard to distinguish from a simple causative.

18a.　לְהַרְשִׁיעַ רָשָׁע לָתֵת דַּרְכּוֹ
בְּרֹאשׁוֹ וּלְהַצְדִּיק צַדִּיק לָתֶת
לוֹ כְּצִדְקָתוֹ׃　　*to condemn* the wicked by bringing down on his head what he deserves and *to acquit* the righteous by rewarding him according to his righteousness
1 Kgs 8:32

18b.　מַצְדִּיק רָשָׁע וּמַרְשִׁיעַ צַדִּיק
תּוֹעֲבַת יהוה גַּם־שְׁנֵיהֶם׃　　*He who acquits* the guilty and *he who condemns* the righteous—both are an abomination to Yʜwʜ.
Prov 17:15

18c.　　　כִּי לֹא־אַצְדִּיק רָשָׁע׃　　For I *will* not *declare* the wicked *righteous*.
Exod 23:7

In these instances the person is probably recognized as becoming either righteous or wicked by some observable act of judgment imposed on him.

Qal intransitives, usually *statives*, can form intransitive *Hiphils*; these are called　f
one-place or inwardly transitive or internal *Hiphils*. As illustrations of one- and two-place *Hiphils* from the same root contrast these.[16]

---

have an intermediate character; a *Hiphil* delocutive is in part causative and in part denominative. See also W. T. Claassen, "The Declarative-Estimative Hiphᶜil," *Journal of Northwest Semitic Languages* 2 (1972) 5–16.

15. For further uses, see *qll* in 2 Sam 19:44 (referring to esteem in the mind of the speaker) and Isa 8:23 (with *kbd*

Hiphil) and 23:9 (both referring to esteem in the mind of others).

16. Internal *Hiphils* (like the cognate Arabic verb stem ʾafᶜala) are sometimes associated with the Arabic superlative or elative form ʾafᶜal; see Speiser, "Studies in Semitic Formatives," 32.

| 19a. | מַגְדִּל יְשׁוּעוֹת מַלְכּוֹ | He *magnifies* (lit., *causes to become great*) his king's victories. Ps 18:51 |
| 19b. | יִלְבְּשׁוּ־בֹשֶׁת וּכְלִמָּה הַמַּגְדִּילִים עָלָי: | May all who *magnify* (*themselves*) over me be clothed with shame and disgrace. Ps 35:26 |

In # 19a the subject causes someone else to be taken as great or proved great, but in # 19b the subject causes himself to be regarded as great (i.e., 'to talk big').[17] Often in the one-place *Hiphil* the subject and the object are the same; the double-status subject causes itself to be or do something, and since the object is elided the verb is formally intransitive. Sometimes the elided object is not the subject itself but is closely connected with the subject, as in # 20b; these two examples are similar in sense.

| 20a. | לְהַחֲזִיק הַמַּמְלָכָה בְּיָדוֹ: | *to strengthen* in his hand (lit., *cause* his hand *to be strengthened*) on the kingdom 2 Kgs 15:19 |
| 20b. | כִּי הֶחֱזִיק עַד־לְמָעְלָה: | because he *had become powerful* (lit., *had caused* his hand *to be strengthened*) tremendously 2 Chr 26:8 |

In the internal *Hiphil* the subject works in connection with itself as the causer of the action, even when an object other than the subject is elided. In contrast to the *Piel* stem, to which is attached the reflexive *Hithpael* stem, the *Hiphil* has no reflexive stem form. The double-status use of the *Niphal* is also germane to such *Hiphils*.

g   The difference between the two-place *Hiphil* as over against the internal *Hiphil* can be observed with other *Qal*-stative verbs as well.[18]

21a.	לְמַעַן הַרְחִיק אֶתְכֶם מֵעַל אַדְמַתְכֶם	so as *to remove* you (lit., *cause* you *to be far*) *from your land* Jer 27:10
21b.	לֹא הִרְחִיקוּ	they *had* not *gone far* (lit., *had* not *caused* [*themselves*] *to be far*) Gen 44:4
22a.	וַיַּקְרֵב אֶת־הַמִּנְחָה לְעֶגְלוֹן	He *presented* (lit., *caused to be near*) the tribute to Eglon. Judg 3:17

---

17. For *gdl* in this sense, see Jer 48:26, 42; Ezek 35:13; Zech 2:8, 10; Ps 35:26, 38:17, 55:13; Job 19:5; Lam 1:9; Dan 8:4, 8, 11, 25.

18. The internal *Hiphil* may have an inchoative or ingressive sense, referring to entering into a state, e.g., *ḥly*

'to become ill,' *zyd* 'to (come to a) boil.' The internal *Hiphil* also occurs with verbs for expressing or receiving a quality: *ʾhl*, *zhr*, *ypᶜ* 'to be clear, bright' versus *ḥšk* 'to be dark,' *ʾmṣ* to be strong' versus *ᶜṭp* 'to be weak'; see GKC § 53d / p. 145.

| 22b. | וּפַרְעֹה הִקְרִיב | And Pharaoh *approached* (lit., *caused* [*himself*] *to be near*). Exod 14:10 |

As the examples with גדל reveal, the internal *Hiphil* can be metaphorical; the subjects here are non-personal.

| 23. | גַּם־חֹשֶׁךְ לֹא־יַחְשִׁיךְ מִמֶּךָ | Even the darkness *will* not *be* (too) *dark* (lit., *cause itself to be dark*) for you. Ps 139:12 |
| 24. | וְהַבַּיִת לִבְנוֹת לַיהוה לְהַגְדִּיל | And the house to be built for Yʜᴡʜ *should be magnificent*. 1 Chr 22:5 |

Lambdin remarks that these inwardly transitive usages constitute a translation problem since nearly all of the verbs have a transitive causative meaning as well.[19] In fact, the senses are rarely confused with one another because the internal *Hiphil* is formally intransitive, whereas the transitive causative *Hiphil* generally has an expressed object clearly different from the subject.

Hiphils of *Qal* Verbs Used Transitively

27.3

Roots that are transitive in *Qal* (i.e., roots that take a direct object in that stem) in the *Hiphil* tend to be causative. Most often, such constructions are three-place predicates, with a subject and two accusatives, the object of the causing (usually a person) and the object of the basic or root verb.[20]

a

| 1. | וַיַּפְשִׁיטוּ אֶת־יוֹסֵף אֶת־כֻּתָּנְתּוֹ | They *stripped* Joseph (lit., they *caused* Joseph *to put off*) of his coat. Gen 37:23 |

The object of causing here is יוסף, while the object of the stripping is כתנתו.

Three-place *Hiphil* constructions vary in the way the two objects are introduced. Both may be marked by את (## 1–2), or only the object of "causing" by את (# 3), or only the object of the root verb by את (# 4).[21] The object of "causing" may be marked by a preposition (## 5, 7) and so can the object of the root verb (# 6; cf. # 7). The object of causing may be a relative אֲשֶׁר, with or without את (## 8–9).[22]

b

| 2. | כִּי אַתָּה תַּנְחִיל אֶת־הָעָם הַזֶּה אֶת־הָאָרֶץ | You shall cause *this people* to inherit *the land*. Josh 1:6 |

19. Lambdin, *Introduction to Biblical Hebrew*, 212.

20. In addition to the roots cited in the examples, note ʾkl, byn, ynq, nḥl, qny, rʾy, rwy, śbʿ, and škḥ. See the catalogue provided in Mordechai Ben-Asher, "Causative

Hipʿil with Double Objects in Biblical Hebrew," *Hebrew Annual Review* 2 (1978) 11–19.

21. For a suffix and an unmarked object, see Isa 48:6.

22. For a clause headed by *mh*, see Zech 1:9.

3.   וַיַּלְבֵּשׁ אֹתוֹ בִּגְדֵי־שֵׁשׁ   And he clothed *him* in (lit., caused *him* to put on) *vestures of fine linen.*
                                            Gen 41:42

4.   הַשְׁמִיעִנִי אֶת־קוֹלֵךְ   Let *me* hear *your voice.*[23]
                                            Cant 2:14

5.   וְהוֹדַעְתָּ לָהֶם אֶת־הַדֶּרֶךְ   You will show *them the way.*
                                            Exod 18:20

6.   וַתַּשְׁקֵמוֹ בִּדְמָעוֹת שָׁלִישׁ:   You made *them* drink *tears* by the bowlful.
                                            Ps 80:6

7.   מִמּוּל שַׂלְמָה אַדֶּרֶת תַּפְשִׁטוּן   You strip off *the rich robe of those who pass by.*[24]
        מֵעֹבְרִים   Mic 2:8 *emended*

8.   לֹא הוֹדַעְתַּנִי אֵת אֲשֶׁר־תִּשְׁלַח   But you did not let *me* know *whom you will send with me.*[25]
        עִמִּי   Exod 33:12

9.   וְהוֹרֵיתִיךָ אֲשֶׁר תְּדַבֵּר: I will teach *you what you shall say.*
                                            Exod 4:12

c   Just as a verb that is ordinarily transitive in the *Qal* may appear without an object, so a verb that is usually a three-place *Hiphil* may show only one object. With these two-place *Hiphils*, that object is usually a person.

10.   הֲלֹא . . . הִשְׁמַעְתִּיךָ   *Did* I not *inform you* (lit., *cause you to hear*). . . .
                                            Isa 44:8

11.   כַּאֲשֶׁר הֶרְאָה אֹתְךָ בָּהָר   just as he *showed you* (lit., *caused you to see*) on the mount
                                            Exod 27:8

12.   הוֹדַעְתִּיךָ הַיּוֹם   I *teach you* (lit., *cause you to know*) today.
                                            Prov 22:19

Such a construction may have a non-personal object, and in such cases the sense of the causing is a stative event. The objects of causation in these cases are either abstract nouns or speech acts.

13.   אַזְכִּיר צִדְקָתְךָ לְבַדֶּךָ:   I *will make mention of your righteousness* (lit., *cause your righteousness to be remembered*) alone.[26]
                                            Ps 71:16

14.   הוֹדִיעַ יהוה יְשׁוּעָתוֹ   YHWH *has made known* (lit., *caused to be known*) his salvation.
                                            Ps 98:2

---

23. Cf. Exod 33:18, Deut 4:10. With ## 4, 6, 8, cf. 27.5b.
24. Emend the pointing, taking the *athnach* with the following word; for MT ʾdr (perhaps taken as an accusa-

tive of material, 'richness(?)'), read ʾdrt b̥ haplography.
25. On the permissive sense of the *Hiphil*, see 27.5.
26. Cf. 2 Sam 18:18.

| 15. | מִי הִשְׁמִיעַ זֹאת מִקֶּדֶם | Who *foretold* this (lit., *caused* this *to be heard*) from of old?
Isa 45:21 |
| 16. | יהוה הִשְׁמִיעַ . . . אִמְרוּ לְבַת־
צִיּוֹן | YHWH *has proclaimed* (lit., *caused to be heard*). . . :
"Say to Daughter Zion. . . ."
Isa 62:11 |

Denominative and Isolated *Hiphils*   **27.4**

Like the *Niphal* (23.5) and the *Piel* (24.4), the *Hiphil* has a denominative function. **a**
The causative value is always present in this use but with a wide range of meanings, and
extended meanings, depending on the root. One important group refers to generation
(e.g., בְּכֹר 'firstborn'), growth (e.g., שֹׁרֶשׁ 'root,' קֶרֶן 'horn(s),' פַּרְסָה 'hoof'), and the
atmosphere (e.g., אוֹר 'light,' מָטָר 'rain').[27]

1.	צָרָה כְּמַבְכִּירָה	a groan as of *one bearing her first child* (lit., *causing a first born to come forth*)[28] Jer 4:31
2.	יַשְׁרֵשׁ יַעֲקֹב	Jacob *will take root* (lit., *cause a root to come forth*). Isa 27:6
3.	פָּר מַקְרִן מַפְרִיס:	a bull which *has horns* (and) *hoofs* Ps 69:32
4.	לְהָאִיר עַל־הָאָרֶץ	*to give light* on the earth Gen 1:15
5.	כִּי לֹא הִמְטִיר יהוה אֱלֹהִים עַל־הָאָרֶץ	because YHWH God *had* not yet *caused it to rain* upon the earth Gen 2:5

Another group refers to the use of *body parts* (cf. English 'to make eyes').

6.	וְלֹא הֶאֱזִין אֲלֵיכֶם:	He *turned a deaf ear* to you (or, He *did* not *prick up* his ears for you). Deut 1:45
7.	אִם־אֵשׁ לְהֵמִין וּלְהַשְׂמִיל מִכֹּל אֲשֶׁר־דִּבֶּר אֲדֹנִי הַמֶּלֶךְ	No one *can turn to the right* (hand) or *to the left* (hand) from anything my lord the king says. 2 Sam 14:19
8.	אַל־תַּלְשֵׁן עֶבֶד אֶל־אֲדֹנָיו	Do not *slander* (lit., *use a tongue* on) a servant to his master. Prov 30:10 *Qere*

---

27. Note also *higšîm* 'to rain' (Jer 14:22); *hizrîaʿ* 'to form seed' (Gen 1:11, etc.), 'to conceive' (Lev 12:2); *hišlîg* 'to snow' (Ps 68:15). Participles and infinitives are notably common among productive *Hiphils*.

28. On the difficult form *ṣrh*, see W. L. Holladay, *Jeremiah* (Philadelphia: Fortress, 1986), 1. 145.

Sometimes a denominative from an abstract noun may denote execution of the root notion (e.g., חֵרֶם 'ban').

9.	אֲשֶׁר לֹא־יָכְלוּ בְּנֵי יִשְׂרָאֵל לְהַחֲרִימָם	upon whom the Israelites *could* not *execute the ban* 1 Kgs 9:21

Most often, however, abstract denominatives in the *Hiphil* stem (often figurative) tend to behave like the inwardly transitive *Hiphil* (cf. 27.2g), that is, the subject causes itself to behave according to the nominal notion (e.g., perhaps, שֵׂכֶל 'insight,' and certainly זֹהַר 'brightness' and לָבָן 'white'; cf. 27.2g ## 23–24).

10.	וְהַמַּשְׂכִּלִים יַזְהִרוּ כְּזֹהַר הָרָקִיעַ	And they *who are wise* shall *shine* like the brightness of the firmament. Dan 12:3
11.	כַּשֶּׁלֶג יַלְבִּינוּ	They (your sins) *shall become* as *white* as snow (lit., as snow *causes* [*itself*] *to be white*). Isa 1:18

A denominative *Qal* can also yield a *Hiphil*: רַע 'evil' yields both רעע *Qal* 'to be evil' and *Hiphil* 'to cause to be evil, to make (one's actions) evil, to act evilly.'

b   Constructions may develop due to *figurative expressions* in which the force of the basic term or grammatical form is no longer clearly visible. Thus שְׁכֶם 'shoulder' developed the form הִשְׁכִּים 'to shoulder (i.e., to use the shoulder)' and with pack animals 'to load the backs'; since this happened early in the morning, by metonymy הִשְׁכִּים came to mean 'to break up camp early in the morning.'

12.	וְהִשְׁכַּמְתֶּם מָחָר לְדַרְכְּכֶם	And you can *get up early tomorrow* (and go) on your way. Judg 19:9

The opposite is הֶעֱרִיב 'to act in the evening,' from עֶרֶב 'evening.'

13.	וַיִּגַּשׁ הַפְּלִשְׁתִּי הַשְׁכֵּם וְהַעֲרֵב	The Philistine approached *morning* and *evening*. 1 Sam 17:16

Note also נגד *Hiphil* 'to act in front of, to declare,' a reflection of the basic stance of speaking to or reporting *néged* the addressee. Such lexicalizations are unpredictable isolated areas of the stem system where semantic specialization has overtaken systematic force.

c   The function of the *Hiphil* with some roots cannot be classified with certainty into any of the above types because the root is otherwise unknown. In these unclassified instances, however, the basic semantic value of the stem is usually evident, and one can often discern whether the form functions as a transitive or inwardly transitive, etc.

14.   יָרֵחַ וְלֹא יַאֲהִיל   The moon *is* not *bright* (lit., the moon *does* not *cause* [*itself*] *to be bright*).[29]
                                         Job 25:5

15.   וְהֶאֶזְנִיחוּ נְהָרוֹת   The canals *will stink*.[30]
                                         Isa 19:6

Modal Senses   27.5

The *Hiphil*'s causative notion can assume various nuances or functions not only   a
because of the nature of the root but also because of the relationship that may exist
between the principal subject and the subject of the caused action (the undersubject).
Because the expression of such functions is associated with the non-indicative moods in
languages that use them (e.g., Classical Greek, Latin), they are called modal functions.
English expresses them with a small category of irregular verbs, called the modals (e.g.,
'can, could, should, would, may, might,' etc.).

If, for example, the "causing" occasions an event unacceptable to the undersubject,   b
the verb takes on the nuance of *compulsion*.

1.   אֲהָהּ בִּתִּי הַכְרֵעַ הִכְרַעְתִּנִי   Alas, my daughter, you *have brought* me *to my knees*.
                                               Judg 11:35

2.   קוּמָה יהוה קַדְּמָה פָנָיו   Arise, YʜᴡH, confront him (the foe), *make* him *bow*.
         הַכְרִיעֵהוּ   Ps 17:13

If, on the other hand, the "causing" notion is right and welcome or agreeable to the
participating subject, then the *Hiphil* may denote *solicitude*, 'to take care that.'

3.   וָאַשְׂבִּעַ אוֹתָם   And I *took care to satisfy* them.
                                         Jer 5:7

Sometimes the action is welcome or agreeable to the object but is not regarded as a
propriety. Here the *Hiphil* denotes *permission*.

4. אַחֲרֵי הוֹדִיעַ אֱלֹהִים אוֹתְךָ אֶת־   Since God *let* you *know* all this. . . .
    כָּל־זֹאת   Gen 41:39

A similar sense is found with non-personal objects.

5.   אָז אַשְׁקִיעַ מֵימֵיהֶם וְנַהֲרוֹתָם   Then I *will let* her waters *settle*, and her streams *flow*
        כַּשֶּׁמֶן אוֹלִיךְ   like oil.
                                         Ezek 32:14

---

29. The examples in the text are both hapaxes. There are a number of more common *Hiphil*-only roots which are apparently isolates: *ybl* Hiphil 'to conduct,' *ydy* Hiphil 'to praise' (probably not the same root as *ydy* Qal, Piel 'to throw'), *ykḥ* Hiphil 'to decide,' *šlk* Hiphil 'to throw,' perhaps *šqy* Hiphil 'to (give) water (to drink).'

30. The form is anomalous, perhaps from an elative variant root or perhaps a double causative (Hebrew *h* + Aramaizing *ʾ*). Cf. n. 16 above. A convenient example of double formative is Modern Hebrew *braksim* 'brakes.'

c   If the caused activity is welcome to the undersubject but unacceptable or dis-
agreeable to a third party, then the notion of *toleration* comes into view.

6.   הִשְׂמַחְתָּ כָּל־אוֹיְבָיו: You *have allowed* all his enemies *to rejoice*.
                                                 Ps 89:43

In certain instances the caused activity is agreeable to both subject and undersubject and
the undersubject becomes an indirect object of the "causing," in which case that notion
becomes equivalent to *bestowal*.

7.   הִצְלִיחוֹ הָאֱלֹהִים: God *gave* him *success*.
                                                 2 Chr 26:5

8.   וְלֹא תַצְלִיחִי לָהֶם: You *will* not *grant success* to them.
                                                 Jer 2:37

28

Hophal Stem

Form and Meaning   28.1

Like the *Piel* and *Pual*, the *Hiphil* and *Hophal* stems stand in active : passive oppo-   a
sition.[1] The *Pual* and *Hophal* are the rarest of the seven major stems, and the *Hophal* is
the rarer of the two. As with the *Pual*, certain *Qal* passive forms are pointed as *Hophal*
(22.6).

Both the *Pual* and *Hophal* stems represent the subject as being caused to be acted   b
upon or to suffer the effects of having been acted upon (usually by an unnamed agent).
Whereas in *Pual* the subject is made into a state represented by the root, in *Hophal* it is
caused, or suffers the effects of having been caused, to be in the event signified by the
root. Compare and contrast, for example, these cases with ילד and כון (which has
Polel/Polal instead of *Piel/Pual*).

1a.	בְּיַלֶּדְכֶן אֶת־הָעִבְרִיּוֹת	When you *help* the Hebrew women *in childbirth* (*Piel*) (lit., when you *make* the Hebrew women *to be delivered of child*). . . . Exod 1:16
1b.	אָרוּר הַיּוֹם אֲשֶׁר יֻלַּדְתִּי בּוֹ	Cursed be the day in which I *was born* (*Pual*) (lit., *was made to be born* [as a state]). Jer 20:14
1c.	וַיּוֹלֶד בָּנִים וּבָנוֹת׃	He *begat* (*Hiphil*) sons and daughters (lit., *caused* sons and daughters *to be born* [as an event]). Gen 5:4

---

1. The original or basic first vowel of the *Qal* passive, *Pual*, and *Hophal* is *u*, but in the last stem *o* is more common; for the two vowels, note *wəhomlēaḥ loʾ humláḥat*, 'You were not rubbed with salt' (Ezek 16:4).

1d.   יוֹם הֻלֶּ֫דֶת אֶת־פַּרְעֹה   on Pharaoh's *birth*day (*Hophal*) (lit., on the day of Pharaoh's *having been caused to be born* [as an event])[2]
Gen 40:20

2a.   וְכֹנַנְתִּי אֶת־כִּסֵּא מַמְלַכְתּוֹ   And I *will establish* (*Polel*) the throne of his kingdom (lit., I *will make* the throne of his kingdom *established* [as a state]).
2 Sam 7:13

2b.   מֵיהוה מִצְעֲדֵי־גֶ֫בֶר כּוֹנָ֑נוּ   The steps of a man *are made firm* (*Polal*) (lit., *are made to be firm* [as a state]) by YHWH.
Ps 37:23

2c.   יהוה בַּשָּׁמַ֫יִם הֵכִין כִּסְאוֹ   YHWH *established* (*Hiphil*) his throne in the heavens (lit., *caused* his throne *to be established* [as an event]).
Ps 103:19

2d.   וְהוּכַן בַּחֶ֫סֶד כִּסֵּא   In unfailing love a throne *will be established* (*Hophal*) (lit., *will be caused to be established* [as an event]).
Isa 16:5

These examples show that the *Hophal* represents the subject as the undergoer of a causative situation involving an event. The object of the active causative notion with the *Hiphil* stem becomes the subject with the *Hophal* stem; the agent, expressed in the *Hiphil*, is normally unexpressed in the *Hophal*. For example, 'throne' in # 2c is the object of the causative notion, with God as agent, but in # 2d 'throne' is the subject, and the agent is not mentioned.

c   The distinctiveness of the *Hophal* vis-à-vis the other passive stems can be seen in these illustrations using בקע.

3a.   וַתִּבָּקַע הָעִיר   The city *was breached* (*Niphal*).
2 Kgs 25:4

3b.   כִּמְבוֹאֵי עִיר מְבֻקָּעָה: like the entering of a city that *is breached* (*Pual*) (lit., *was made to be breached*)
Ezek 26:10

3c.   הָבְקְעָה הָעִיר: The city *was breached* (*Hophal*) (lit., *was caused to be breached*).
Jer 39:2

Each of these passives reflects a corresponding active form in which the city is the object of the breaching. In the passive stems, the city is the subject being acted upon or suffering the effects of the action; the agent is not mentioned. In # 3a the *Niphal* represents the

---

2. The *Hophal* infinitive construct is found only in this form and in several forms of *šmm*; *hŏššammâ* (Lev 26:34), *hoššammâ* (Lev 26:35, 2 Chr 36:21), (*bā*)*hšammâ* (Lev 26:43). The infinitive absolute in the second syllable has an *ē* vowel against the *a* elsewhere, e.g., *hohṭēl* (Ezek 16:4) as in the *Hiphil*.

simple action, without a causation notion. In # 3b and # 3c the *Pual* and *Hophal* signify causation; in the *Pual* the city is represented as being made into a state of being breached, while in the *Hophal* the city is represented as being caused to suffer the effects of the event of being breached.

Hophals of *Qal* and *Niphal* Verbs Used Intransitively   28.2

Since the *Hiphil* is much more widely used than the *Hophal*, virtually all roots   a
which form *Hophals* also form *Hiphils*, and it is convenient to exhibit the two stems
together.

Qal and *Niphal* intransitive fientive verbs and their corresponding *Hophals* are one-   b
place predications; in the *Hophal* the agent of the *Hiphil* is not represented, and the
subject is the patient or undergoer of the action.

1a.	וַיִּשְׁכַּב עַל־הַיֶּלֶד	And he *lay* (*Qal*) upon the boy. 2 Kgs 4:34
1b.	וַתַּשְׁכִּבֵהוּ	And she *laid* (*Hiphil*) him *down*. 2 Kgs 4:21
1c.	מֻשְׁכָּב עַל־מִטָּתוֹ:	who *had been laid* (*Hophal*) (lit., *had been caused to lie*) on his bed 2 Kgs 4:32
2a.	וַיָּשָׁב מֹשֶׁה אֶל־יהוה	And Moses *returned* (*Qal*) to Y<small>HWH</small>. Exod 5:22
2b.	וַיָּשֶׁב יָדוֹ אֶל־חֵיקוֹ	So he *put back* (*Hiphil*) his hand (lit., *caused* his hand *to return*) into his bosom. Exod 4:7
2c.	וַיּוּשַׁב אֶת־מֹשֶׁה וְאֶת־אַהֲרֹן אֶל־פַּרְעֹה	And Moses and Aaron *were brought back* (*Hophal*) (lit., *were caused to return*) to Pharaoh.[3] Exod 10:8
3a.	כַּמַּיִם הַנִּגָּרִים אַרְצָה	as water *poured* (*Niphal*) on the ground 2 Sam 14:14
3b.	וַיַּגֵּר	He *pours* (it) *out* (*Hiphil*) (lit., *causes* [it] *to be poured*) Ps 75:9
3c.	כְּמַיִם מֻגָּרִים בְּמוֹרָד:	as water *poured* (*Hophal*) (lit., *caused to be poured*) into a gorge Mic 1:4
4a.	וְנָשַׁמּוּ דַּרְכֵיכֶם:	Your roads *will be laid waste* (*Niphal*). Lev 26:22

---

3. For ʾ*t* with the subject of a passive verb, see 10.3.2.

4b.	וַהֲשִׁמֹּתִי אֲנִי אֶת־הָאָרֶץ	And I *will lay waste* (*Hiphil*) your land (lit., *will cause* your land *to be deserted*). Lev 26:32
4c.	כָּל־יְמֵי הָשַּׁמָּה	all the time that [it] *lies desolate* (*Hophal*) (lit., of [its] *being caused to be deserted*)[4] Lev 26:35
5a.	תִּדְבַּק־לְשׁוֹנִי לְחִכִּי	May my tongue *stick* (*Qal*) to the roof of my mouth. Ps 137:6
5b.	וּלְשׁוֹנְךָ אַדְבִּיק אֶל־חִכֶּךָ	And I *will make* your tongue *stick* (*Hiphil*) to the roof of your mouth. Ezek 3:26
5c.	וּלְשׁוֹנִי מֻדְבָּק מַלְקוֹחָי	And my tongue *sticks* (*Hophal*) (lit., *is caused to stick*) to my palate. Ps 22:16

c   *Qal* stative verbs rarely form passive causatives, none of the putative-delocutive type. None of the stative verbs cited in 22.4 occurs unambiguously with a stative meaning in the *Hophal* stem, though some appear in the *Hiphil*. In the case of verbs with both a *Qal* stative and *Qal* fientive force (e.g., שׁמם 'to be desolate; to lay waste,' מות 'to be dead; to die') it seems best to construe *Hophal* forms as fientives.

d   There is no *Hophal* analogue to the internal *Hiphil*. Even a verb that may be inwardly transitive in the *Hiphil* is passive in the *Hophal*, with an implied agent other than itself. This lack of use is easy to understand: the subject of the *Hophal* stem is normally an implied object of a causative notion other than the agent, but in the case of the internal *Hiphil* there is no such object. Contrast חלה *Qal*, *Hiphil*, and *Hophal*.

6a.	וְחָלִיתִי	And I *will be(come) weak* (*Qal*). Judg 16:17
6b.	הֶחֱלוּ שָׂרִים חֲמַת מִיָּיִן	The princes *are inflamed* (*Hiphil*) with wine (lit., *cause themselves to be(come) sick* with fever from wine). Hos 7:5
6c.	כִּי הָחֳלֵיתִי׃	because I've *been wounded* (*Hophal*) (lit., *have been caused to be wounded*) 1 Kgs 22:34

28.3   *Hophals* of *Qal* Verbs Used Transitively

a   The *Hophal* forms of roots that are transitive in *Qal* are passive causatives. In addition to the examples in 28.1, consider these.

4. The LXX reads a suffix on the infinitive.

1a. וַיִּרְאוּ אֵת אֱלֹהֵי יִשְׂרָאֵל

And they *saw* (*Qal*) the God of Israel.
Exod 24:10

1b. כְּכֹל אֲשֶׁר אֲנִי מַרְאֶה אוֹתְךָ

according to all that I *show* you (*Hiphil*) (lit., *cause you to see*)
Exod 25:9

1c. אֲשֶׁר־אַתָּה מָרְאֶה בָּהָר:

which you *were shown* (*Hophal*) (lit., *were caused to see*) on the mount[5]
Exod 25:40

2a. וְלָקַחְתָּ אֶת־שֶׁמֶן הַמִּשְׁחָה וְיָצַקְתָּ עַל־רֹאשׁוֹ

And you shall take the anointing oil and *pour* (*Qal*) [it] on his head.
Exod 29:7

2b. וְהִיא מוֹצֶקֶת:

And she *kept on pouring* (*Hiphil*) [the oil] (lit., *causing* [the oil] *to be poured*).
2 Kgs 4:5 *Qere*

2c. אֲשֶׁר־יוּצַק עַל־רֹאשׁוֹ שֶׁמֶן הַמִּשְׁחָה

upon whose head the anointing oil *was poured* (*Hophal*) (lit., *was caused to be poured*)
Lev 21:10

Denominative and Isolated *Hophals*

28.4

The denominative role of the *Hiphil* is also found with the *Hophal*. Consider these sets, from נֶגֶד 'before,' שָׁלוֹם 'peace,' and מֶלַח 'salt'; for the last, no *Hiphil* forms are attested.

a

1a. וְהַגֶּד־נָא לִי מֶה עָשִׂיתָ

Tell (*Hiphil*) me what you have done.
Josh 7:19

1b. הֻגֵּד הֻגַּד לַעֲבָדֶיךָ

Your servants *were clearly told* (*Hophal*).
Josh 9:24

2a. וּשְׁלָם

And *be at peace* (*Qal*).
Job 22:21

2b. וְאִם־לֹא תַשְׁלִים עִמָּךְ

And if it *will* not *make peace* (*Hiphil*) with you (lit., *will* not *cause to be at peace* with you [as an event]). . . .
Deut 20:12

2c. וְחַיַּת הַשָּׂדֶה הָשְׁלְמָה־לָךְ:

And the wild animals *will be caused to be at peace* (*Hophal*) with you.
Job 5:23

---

5. T. O. Lambdin uses the example *horʾâ hāʾîš ʾet-hāʾôr,* 'The man was shown the light,' but such *Hophal* clauses are rare at best; see *Introduction to Biblical Hebrew* (New York: Scribner, 1971) 244.

3a. וְכָל־קָרְבַּן מִנְחָתְךָ בַּמֶּלַח תִּמְלָח   *Season* (*Qal*) all your grain offerings with salt. Lev 2:13

3b. וְהָמְלֵחַ לֹא הֻמְלַחַתְּ   To be sure, you *were* not *rubbed with salt* (*Hophal*) (lit., *were* not *caused to be salted*). Ezek 16:4

b   Isolated or unclassified *Hiphils* also form *Hophals*.

4a. וַיַּשְׁלִכוּ אֶל־יוֹאָב   And they *threw* (*Hiphil*) (the head) to Joab. 2 Sam 20:22

4b. רֹאשׁוֹ מֻשְׁלָךְ אֵלֶיךָ   His head *will be thrown* (*Hophal*) to you. 2 Sam 20:21

5a. בְּצֵל יָדוֹ הֶחְבִּיאָנִי   In the shadow of his hand he *hid* (*Hiphil*) me. Isa 49:2

5b. וּבְבָתֵּי כְלָאִים הָחְבָּאוּ   And they *were hidden* (*Hophal*) in prisons. Isa 42:22

6a. וְהֵטַלְתִּי אֹתְךָ . . . עַל הָאָרֶץ אַחֶרֶת   I *will hurl* (*Hiphil*) you . . . into another country. Jer 22:26

6b. מַדּוּעַ הוּטֲלוּ הוּא וְזַרְעוֹ וְהֻשְׁלְכוּ עַל־הָאָרֶץ   Why *will* he and his seed *be hurled out* (*Hophal*) and *be cast* (*Hophal*) into a land. . . ? Jer 22:28

28.5   Modal Senses

a   Just as the *Hiphil* can take on modal nuances when the will of the participants is felt to be involved, so also the *Hophal* can take on the same nuances when such an object becomes the passive subject of the causative notion. For example, one feels the nuance of compulsion in this command with the root שׁכב (see 27.5).

1. וְהָשְׁכְּבָה אֶת־עֲרֵלִים: and *be laid* (lit., *be caused* [against your will] *to be laid*) among the uncircumcised[6] Ezek 32:19

---

6. This form is a *Hophal* imperative, a semantic anomaly. *Pual* and *Hophal* imperatives do not essentially exist in the system of the language. This form may be considered a literary creation—note that *škb* occurs eight times in Ezekiel 31–32. L. Boadt remarks that "*šākab* often refers euphemistically to dying"; see *Ezekiel's Oracles against Egypt: A Literary and Philological Study of Ezekiel 29–32* (Rome: Biblical Institute, 1980) 164. This imperative may then be likened to the anomalous English passive imperative 'Drop dead.' For the only other *Hophal* imperative, see *hopnû* 'Be turned back!' in Jer 49:8, also in a passage suggesting that the form is an *ad hoc* creation.

Verbal Conjugations
and Clauses

29

Introduction to the Conjugations

The Variety of Verb Forms   29.1

There are three overlapping groups of verb forms in Hebrew, the *conjugations*, the   a
modals, and the *non-finites*, and we discuss them in this grammar in that order. For the
moment, let us review them in reverse order. The *non-finite forms* include the participle
(# 1) and the two infinitives (or verbal nouns), the construct (# 2) and the absolute (# 3).
The *modal forms* include the cohortative (first-person modal, # 4), the imperative
(second-person modal, # 5), and the jussive (third-person modal, # 6). The conjugations
may have some bearing on the modal forms, for all the modals are related to or derived
from one of the conjugations.[1]

1.	participle	עֹמֵד	עוֹלֶה
2.	infinitive construct	לַעֲמֹד	כַּעֲלוֹת
3.	infinitive absolute	עָמֹד	עָלֹה
4.	cohortative	אֶזְמְרָה	אֶעֱלֶה
5.	imperative	עֲמֹד	עֲלִי
6.	jussive	יַעֲמֹד	יַּעַל

There are two major *conjugations*, the suffix(ing), perfective (perfect, *qatal*, *qtl*) and   b
the prefix(ing), non-perfective (imperfect, *yiqtol*, *yqtl*).[2] The variety of terms used for the

---

1. The *yqtl* form; see, e.g., Leslie McFall, *The Enigma of the Hebrew Verbal System: Solutions from Ewald to the Present Day* (Sheffield: Almond, 1982) 105–6; some earlier scholars associate the imperative with the *qtl* form.

2. Other, older names include *qtl* = Latin *preteritum* = Arabic *al-māḍī* = Hebrew ʿabar; *yqtl* = Latin *futurum* =

Arabic *al-mustaqbal* = Hebrew ʿatîd. Joüon uses perfect and future, "terms vulgar and unmatched, for want of anything better; they at least have the advantages of being short and of usually matching the reality"; Joüon § 111b/ p. 290. For simplicity's sake, we omit the diacritics from the terms *qatal*, etc.

conjugations gives a hint of the controversy that has surrounded modern study of them. At the heart of the controversy is the fact that conjugations have a variety of syntactic roles, related in part to the use of the conjunction *waw*.[3] Five major combinations are usually reckoned with. These include the perfective without *waw* (# 7) and with *waw* (# 8), that is, *qatal* and *wǝqatal*; and the non-perfective without *waw* (*yiqtol*, # 9), with *waw* and doubling (*wayyiqtol*, # 10), and with simple *waw* (*wǝyiqtol*, # 11).

7.	*qatal*	עָמַ֫דְתִּי	עָלְתָה
8.	*wǝqatal*	וְעָמַד	וְעָלָה
9.	*yiqtol*	תַּעֲמֹד	נַעֲלֶה
10.	*wayyiqtol*	וַיַּעַמְדוּ	וַיַּ֫עַל
11.	*wǝyiqtol*	וְיַעַמְדוּ	וְנַעֲלֶה

These five combinations have been the basis of much study, for it is not obvious in what ways they are independent of each other. Other questions about the conjugations involve their relations with the non-finite forms (particularly the relation of the infinitives and the prefix conjugation), their time reference, and their relationship to "tense" and aspect systems in other languages.

c   The combinations are not equally common, as the following list of occurrences reveals.[4]

qatal	13,874	27%	} 20,252	40%
wǝqatal	6,378	13%		
yiqtol	14,299	28%	} 30,606	60%
wayyiqtol	14,972[5]	29%		
wǝyiqtol	1,335	3%		
	50,858			

The prefix forms are appreciably more common than the suffix forms. Although the most frequent combination is *wayyiqtol*, the forms without *waw* are altogether more common, 28,173 forms (55%), as opposed to those with *waw*, 22,685 forms (45%).[6] Also noteworthy is the dominance of three of the combinations, *qatal*, *yiqtol*, and *wayyiqtol*, which account for 85% of the Hebrew conjugational forms of the Bible (43,145).

d   Hebraists are not agreed about the significance of the conjugations and their constructions with *waw*. Various theories, each with strengths and weaknesses, have been

---

3. Hans Bauer remarked that the Hebrew verbal system is one "which reasoning men would never have thought of . . . since it came about through the blind force of linguistic laws" (quoted in McFall, *Hebrew Verbal System*, 104). The same is true of all linguistic systems, and all the various parts of linguistic systems, but the observation does have a certain edge.

4. The list is based on McFall, *Hebrew Verbal System*, 186–88, cf. 150. The last three lines of the list include cohortative and jussive forms. For slightly different counts and a further breakdown, see Bo Johnson, *Hebräisches Perfekt und Imperfekt mit vorangehendem wᵉ* (Lund: Gleerup, 1979).

5. According to SA/THAT, the ca. 15,000 cases of *waw* with *wayyqtl* account for 30% of the 50,000 cases of *waw* in the Hebrew Bible.

6. These occurrences of *waw* constitute about 45% of all cases; see previous note.

advanced. In their study of the conjugations Hebraists have been something like the proverbial five blind men examining an elephant. Each of them has described a portion of the beast accurately, but they differed in their conclusions because they tried to describe the whole by generalizing from a part. In order to avoid the reductionistic abstractions that have plagued this most difficult area of Hebrew grammar, it seems advisable to begin by surveying the theories; after we critically appraise them we shall be able to construct a provisional scaffold from which to pursue the investigation.

Leslie McFall has recently reviewed the literature on the subject from the earliest   e
medieval Jewish grammarians to T. W. Thacker's study of 1954, concentrating on "solutions from Ewald to the present day."[7] We follow McFall's review closely up to the introduction of the comparative-historical approach to the subject, around 1900. From that point on his work must be supplemented, because he neglected some significant studies (e.g., Brockelmann, Sperber, Hughes, and Michel).[8]

Some features of any modern view of the conjugations represent a break with the   f
terms of the traditional debate. From the time of the Renaissance to the late nineteenth century, there was a consistent tendency to regard the Hebrew verbal system as intrinsically "primitive," Biblical Hebrew being an archaic tongue unable to approach the complexities of languages attested later.[9] No modern solution could be based on such a suspicious and misleading notion of Hebrew as a language. Further, prior to the rise of modern linguistic thinking, the verbal system of Hebrew was measured against European languages, and it was the discrepancies that seemed to require explanation. A special form of this view is based on the concerns of translation, but no absolutely consistent equivalence system exists for rendering the Hebrew verbs into another language.[10] Modern scholars seek to explain Hebrew as much as possible on its own terms.

Every phase of the modern study of comparative Semitics has stimulated new   g
theories of the Biblical Hebrew verb, although some of these theories have been unacceptable as ideas about *one* language. As we shall see, comparative Semitic information can be used both to clarify and to create a major muddle in Hebrew grammar. It is impossible to explain Hebrew by alleging that it is a mongrel or monster among its Semitic cousins, for, although Hebrew is different from them, it is not different *in kind*.[11]

Two differences about Hebrew *are* relevant. The first involves what is in the Bible: h
because there are certain types of writing in Biblical Hebrew which are not well represented in extrabiblical Semitic, especially Northwest Semitic, texts, we must be careful about comparisons. The preponderance of continuous narrative prose in the Bible is unparalleled in the ancient Near East; even the Akkadian annals of the Neo-Assyrian kings present major differences. As we shall see, there are distinctive features of narrative

---

7. McFall, *Hebrew Verbal System*.

8. See references in nn. 29, 33, 36, 49, 74. McFall claims that "no fundamentally new solution to the [Hebrew verbal system] has appeared since 1954 that has received significant support from Hebraists and Semitists" (*Hebrew Verbal System*, 27, cf. 185), but this is unjust to the work of

several scholars. Michel is cited in passing, p. 225.

9. On the "primitive" character of Hebrew, see, e.g., McFall, *Hebrew Verbal System*, 41, 45, 50, 55, 85, 146, 177.

10. See McFall, *Hebrew Verbal System*, 17–21, 53.

11. See 29.4 on Hans Bauer and G. R. Driver.

prose as well as of prophetic speech, and these "genre effects" need to be borne in mind in evaluating the verb system.[12] A second difference involves the way in which Hebrew is preserved. Any notion of major distortion in the MT can play no serious role in explaining the verbs.[13] This should be clear from the separation of וַיִּקְטֹל and וְיִקְטֹל forms, cited earlier, and from the variation in accentuation of the *wǝqatal* combination in certain persons (e.g., וְאָמַרְתָּ, Isa 14:4, but וְאָמַרְתָּ, Ezek 29:3; cf. וְאָמַרְתִּי, Deut 32:40).[14]

i   The chief, indeed only, idea behind the earliest views on the Hebrew verb was *tense* (29.2); the nineteenth century added the idea (though not the vocabulary) of *aspect* (29.3). The decipherment of cuneiform and the recovery of other ancient Semitic monuments contributed funds of new data (29.4). The integration of this material is only part of the ongoing efforts at comprehension (29.5–6).

29.2   Theories Based on Tense

a   Time reference may be indicated in language in various ways. It may be *lexicalized*, that is, expressed with individual words (such as the English adverbs 'now, soon, formerly'), or it may be *grammaticalized*, that is, expressed morphologically as part of or in conjunction with verb forms. Grammaticalized time reference is called *tense*.[15] English uses the category of tense, distinguishing present tense 'I run' from past tense 'I ran.' Biblical Hebrew has no such simple tense forms,[16] but because Mishnaic Hebrew[17] and most European languages do, for at least eight centuries, from ca. 1000 C.E. on, the medieval Jewish grammarians and Christian scholars of the Hebrew Scriptures thought that *qtl, qôtēl, yqtl* signified past, present, and future times respectively.[18] Such a system is basically that of Mishnaic (and later) Hebrew, which is thus a tense language. This view can hardly accommodate the facts of Biblical Hebrew, and a stratagem was needed to explain the "past" reference of *wayyqtl* and the "present/future" reference of *wǝqtl*.

b   The earliest Jewish grammarians (2.2) thought that the conjugations signified tense and that a prefixed *waw* could "convert" the signification to its opposite. Japeth ha-Levi,

---

12. On genre effects, see, e.g., McFall, *Hebrew Verbal System*, 58, 72, 82–83, 125, 185, 193, 201. On the peculiarities of narrative in general, see Bernard Comrie, *Tense* (Cambridge: Cambridge University, 1985) 61–62, 67, 104. Note that the opposition of discursive and narrative use found in W. Schneider is *not* generic—the two patterns are intertwined in various genres (cf. Gell's views); see E. Talstra, "Text Grammar and Hebrew Bible. I. Elements of a Theory," *Bibliotheca Orientalis* 35 (1978) 169–74. For a further reference to Schneider's work, see n. 91.

13. See 1.6 and McFall, *Hebrew Verbal System*, 125–26.

14. Cf. McFall, *Hebrew Verbal System*, 145–46, 189–210.

15. Comrie, *Tense*, 1, 9–13.

16. This does not mean, as we shall see, that the verbs do not convey information about time or that the Hebrews had no concept of time; contrast the passage from Herder cited in 29.3b and Comrie, *Tense*, 3–4.

17. On the virtual loss of the special *waw* combinations, as well as the cohortative and jussive forms, see M. H. Segal, *A Grammar of Mishnaic Hebrew* (Oxford: Clarendon, 1927) 72–73; on Mishnaic Hebrew as a tense language, see pp. 150, 155–56. The situation in Qumranic Hebrew is not clear; see, e.g., E. Qimron, *The Hebrew of the Dead Sea Scrolls* (Atlanta: Scholars Press, 1986) 45–46, but the participle is shifting toward more strictly verbal use (p. 70). Note also the discussion of Qumranic Hebrew in Beat Zuber, *Das Tempussystem des biblischen Hebräisch* (Beiheft zur Zeitschrift für die Alttestamentliche Wissenschaft 164; Berlin: de Gruyter, 1986) 147–52. The *waw* combinations are found in Biblical Aramaic (Zuber, *Tempussystem*, 69–71), in a few cases in Moabite, and perhaps in Phoenician-Punic.

18. McFall, *Hebrew Verbal System*, 2–20. No grammatical analysis of the Classical Hebrew verbal system has a native-speaker basis; cf. McFall, p. 16.

the tenth-century Qaraite grammarian of Jerusalem, calls the *waw* with the suffix conjugation *waw ʿatīdī*, 'waw of the future.' David Qimḥi (1160–1235), in his *Mikhlol*, "the Gesenius' grammar of his age," like his predecessors thought in terms of tenses. He calls the *waw* that "substitutes" the past for the future and vice versa the *waw haššārût* 'waw of service.'[19] Elijah Levita (1468–1549) may have coined the term that became standard for this "type" of *waw*, *waw hippûk*, 'waw-conversive.' The ordinary *waw*, the simple conjunction, he called *waw ḥibbûr*, 'waw of joining.'

The medieval Jewish grammarians thus saw three tenses: *qtl* past, *qôtēl* present, and   c
yqtl future; the *waw hippûk* could convert the first and third. The earliest Christian Hebraists accepted the medieval Jewish view. They called *waw ḥibbûr*, *conjunctivum*, and *waw hippûk*, *conversivum*.

Until 1827 the traditional view prevailed in the Christian universities of Europe, but   d
some began to refine, criticize, and modify it. Johannes Buxtorf's grammar (1653), for example, denied that the Hebrews had a present tense.[20] McFall cites, as typical of bewilderment over the *tempora* (Latin 'tenses') in Hebrew, C. Bayly's statement of 1782: "The Tenses are often used promiscuously especially in the poetic and prophetic books."[21] Nevertheless, the tense and *waw-conversive* theory survived. W. Gesenius in his thirteen editions of his grammar (1813–1842) did not abandon it.

The tense and *waw-conversive* theory represented such a venerable tradition that it   e
would have seemed foolhardy to challenge it. Some statistics certainly support it. In 14,202 instances of *wayyqtl* (out of a total of 14,972) RSV translates with a past tense.[22] Furthermore, a tense theory appeals to "common sense."[23] F. R. Blake argued, for example, that it seems a priori unlikely that a verb would be without tense.[24] Finally, the necessity of rendering the Hebrew verb into the tense structures of European languages abets the tense theory.

The theory has, however, tremendous weaknesses. While it may be true that *wayyqtl*   f
most often designates past time, it does not always have this value (see 31.2). When we turn to other forms the statistical pattern is not elegant. According to McFall the RSV translators render *yqtl* as a past tense 774 times, a present tense 3,376 times, a future tense 5,451 times, a non-past modal 1,200 times, a past modal 423 times, an imperative 2,133 times, a jussive/cohortative 789 times, and non-verbally 153 times. With regard to *qtl*, RSV renders it in Job, a good source for comparison because of its non-historical character, as a past tense 252 times and as a present tense 244 times; in its bound form *wqtl* as a past 12 times, a present 23 times, and a future 14. Clearly, the RSV translators

19. William Chomsky, *David Ḵimḥi's Hebrew Grammar (Mikhlol)* (New York: Bloch, 1952) 62, 78. Chomsky's modernization of grammatical terminology means his translation must be used with caution.

20. McFall, *Hebrew Verbal System*, 12.

21. McFall, *Hebrew Verbal System*, 15.

22. The counts here and below are from McFall, *Hebrew Verbal System*, 186–88. For some lively argumentation based on translations, ancient and modern, see Zuber, *Tempussystem*, 5–33 (modern), 34–58, 72–77, 169–70, 179–83 (LXX and Vulgate).

23. The common sense, that is, of speakers of languages with tense systems. There are some truly tenseless languages; see McFall, *Hebrew Verbal System*, 220, citing West African examples (Yoruba, Igbo); and Comrie, *Tense*, 40, 45, 49–52, 126, citing an Australian example (Dyirbal).

24. F. R. Blake, *A Resurvey of Hebrew Tenses* (Rome: Biblical Institute, 1951) 2.

needed all three principal tenses of English to render the two conjugations with and without *waw*. How can forms each of which "represent" all three English major tenses have a primarily temporal value?

g   N. W. Schröder in 1766 offered an alternative explanation for the "promiscuous" use of the Hebrew verb forms by introducing the concept of relative time.[25] According to this theory the time of a situation is not located absolutely in relation to the present moment of the speaker's time; rather, it is related to the time of the preceding verb. In application this means that *wayyqtl* is future relative to a preceding past event represented by *qtl*. With this suggestion he replaced the "barbarism," as some had called it, that *waw* could "convert" tense forms into their opposites; he thereby laid the foundations for the later *waw-consecutive* theory. Schröder's theory did not solve the weaknesses of the tense theory pointed out above, and it introduced new problems. Could the Hebrews have had the mental agility constantly and easily to shift back and forth between the past and future? Why do the *qtl* ~ *wayyqtl* and *yqtl* ~ *wqtl* constructions occur under stringent syntactic conditions? Does not *wqtl* continue to convert the past into the future?

h   In 1818 Philip Gell, independently of Schröder, offered a similar solution, but instead of the term "relative future *waw*" he used "inductive *waw*." McFall summarizes his view:

> Philip Gell suggested that every genre or category of literature was comprised of major and minor systems. A major system, for example, may be an historical narrative. It will commence with a governing verb that sets the narrative in its true historic period. This will be followed by subordinate verb forms which retain their own individual tense. The temporal power of the governing, or initial, verb is inducted, or passed on, to the subordinate verbs by means of the *waw* conjunctive.[26]

In Gell's view the *waw* communicated the effect flowing from the whole to the part.

i   Gell's study is seminal for discourse study. His appreciation of the genre effect and distinction between major and minor literary systems offer valuable insights into the syntactic structure of Hebrew narrative (see 31.2). Furthermore, he opened the door to see the bound *waw* constructions as denoting consequence (see 32.2) and epexegetical situations (see 32.2.2). But we are still left with the problems inherent in any tense theory and with the problem of *wqtl*, for which Gell confessed his principle did not operate.

j   In 1827 Samuel Lee (1783–1852), Regius Professor of Hebrew at Cambridge, tried to introduce a historical view into the debate. He analyzed the conjugated verbs as consisting of pronominal affixes and nominal roots. He contended that *qtl*, formed on concrete nouns, represented the past tense, and that *yqtl*, formed on the abstract infinitive, signified the present tense.[27] Like Schröder he thought the *wayyqtl* signified relative time,

---

25. McFall, *Hebrew Verbal System*, 21–24. A recent advocate of a similar scheme is O. L. Barnes, *A New Approach to the Problem of the Hebrew Tenses* (Oxford:

Thornton, 1965).

26. McFall, *Hebrew Verbal System*, 15–16, cf. 24–26.

27. McFall, *Hebrew Verbal System*, 28–37.

but he defined it differently. For him the form worked like the historical present tense encountered in Greek and Latin, where the present tense is used to refer to a past situation.[28] A simple English example would be: 'I was sitting on the veranda when up comes John and says. . . .' This offers a more vivid narrative than 'I was sitting on the veranda when up came Kathy and said. . . .' A relative present in the *wayyqtl* construction fits his theory nicely, for he did not distinguish the meaning of *yqtl* in its free form from its bound one with *waw*-relative.

Lee's work must be judged revolutionary. He first moved scholarship away from the venerable tradition that *yqtl* signifies only the present-future tense. His morphological analysis of the conjugations into affixes and nominal roots is foundational for the later comparative-historical approach. In fact, some comparative Semitists still support his theory that the *yqtl* form is based on the infinitive.[29] His distinction between concrete and abstract actions looks forward to Diethelm Michel's distinction between accidental and substantial actions. Although he challenged the tradition, in fact he merely substituted one notion of tense for another, and no view based exclusively on tense is adequate. In a way this failure is surprising since Lee recognized that what he called Oriental thought differed from Occidental.

Elementary Aspect Theories

29.3

Given the defects of theories based on tense, it is not surprising that scholars looked to other explanatory factors, which may be grouped together under the heading of aspect. In addition to the strictly aspectual views of Heinrich Ewald and William Turner, we consider the "universal tense" theory as an aspectual theory by default.

The "universal tense" theory, which has surely been held briefly by every student of elementary Biblical Hebrew, alleges that the two conjugations cannot strictly be separated. The great German romantic critic Johann Gottfried von Herder (1744–1803) was one of the first modern appreciators of Hebrew literature. In his book *Vom Geist der Ebräischen Poesie* (*On the Spirit of Hebrew Poetry*, 1783), he suggested that Hebrew had only one tense, or rather that the two tenses are essentially undefined tenses, both aorists, that is, unbounded tenses.[30] Herder's view is based on his attribution to the "primitive" and "serene and open" Hebrew mind the quality of immediacy: "All the Hebrew songs in praise of [creation] . . . were . . . formed, as it were, in the immediate view of those very scenes [described]."[31] The desire to present vivid impressions at first hand led the Hebrews "like children" to rely on unbounded verb forms.[32]

28. Latin "perfectum historicum"; cf. GKC § 111a / p. 326. See Zevit's paper cited in n. 73 for a similar view.

29. His idea that the *qtl* form is based on concrete nouns must be seen in light of the Akkadian permansive or stative form; cf. W. von Soden, *Grundriss der akkadischen Grammatik* (Rome: Pontifical Biblical Institute, 1969) 100–101; G. R. Driver, *Problems of the Hebrew Verbal System* (Edinburgh: T. & T. Clark, 1936) 11, 17, 20, 22, 26; C. Brockelmann, "Die 'Tempora' des Semitischen," *Zeitschrift für Phonetik und allgemeine Sprachwissenschaft* 5 (1951) 133–54, esp. 140–44; G. Buccellati, "An Interpretation of the Akkadian Stative as a Nominal Sentence," *Journal of Near Eastern Studies* 27 (1968) 1–14. See also 30.1.

30. McFall, *Hebrew Verbal System*, 14.

31. See the passage given in Burton Feldman and R. D. Richardson, eds., *The Rise of Modern Mythology* (Bloomington: Indiana University, 1972) 236–40, quotation at 238.

32. McFall, *Hebrew Verbal System*, 14.

c   Oddly, such views can be found in our own time, albeit with different rationales. Alexander Sperber (1897–1971), an erratic but diligent scholar, essentially agreed with Herder.[33] He argued that the two conjugations were used interchangeably on the basis of pentateuchal passages where he alleged such jumbling could be found (e.g., הוּסַר in Lev 4:31, יוּסַר in 4:35). He also collected a number of verses where the perfect was continued by imperfect (e.g., Num 9:15), where the imperfect was continued by perfect (cf. Lev 6:21), etc. He therefore proposed:

> Each of these tenses . . . may indicate any and every time. Thus, they do not complement one another in order to form a complete verbal conjugation expressing past and future, respectively, but they run parallel to one another, representing two possibilities of expressing one and the same time.[34]

For this reason he called for a new terminology, the suffix tense and the prefix tense. Why then are there two tense forms? Sperber explained the phenomenon by his comprehensive theory that Biblical Hebrew is not a unified language but a confluence of dialects: "The combined use of both tenses, which runs through our Biblical literature, is further evidence for our assertion that the language of our Bible is of a mixed type."[35]

d   James Hughes reached a similar conclusion (without denying the text's unity): "There seems to be no difference between the two tenses—form excepted—as they appear in the Hebrew Scriptures."[36] Tense, according to Hughes, is indicated by the particles occurring with the "afformative aorist [i.e., *qtl*]" and the "preformative aorist [i.e., *yqtl*]."

e   Sperber's and Hughes's studies have the salient values of describing the text and of correcting overgeneralizations. In the light of the lack of consensus regarding the meaning of the text, Sperber's appeal for a neutral, descriptive terminology based on form rather than meaning makes sense. Accordingly scholars have taken up the terms prefix conjugation and suffix conjugation. Moreover, "universal" is an apt term for describing the range of the prefix conjugation. But Sperber's profound skepticism regarding the trustworthiness of the Masoretic vocalization and of the language's essential unity is unjustified (see 1.6). The phenomenon on which he based his dissection of the text into dialects, namely, the mixture of the tenses in neighboring lines of poetry, also occurs in Ugaritic. Is Ugaritic, too, a "mixed language?" Furthermore, it is methodologically unsound to build a theory on isolated difficulties rather than on a comprehensive synchronic and diachronic study of the verbal system. The "universal tense" theories, whether

---

33. Sperber's views on the conjugations were first published in a long essay in 1943 ("Hebrew Grammar: A New Approach," *Journal of Biblical Literature* 62: 137–262), substantially reprinted in his *A Historical Grammar of Biblical Hebrew* (Leiden: Brill, 1966); see esp. pp. 591–92.

34. Sperber, *Historical Grammar*, 592; examples from pp. 587–88.

35. Sperber, *Historical Grammar*, 592.

36. James A. Hughes, "Another Look at the Hebrew Tenses," *Journal of Near Eastern Studies* 29 (1970) 12–24, at 13; the essay is based on his Glasgow dissertation. Hughes does map out some syntactic patterns in the use of the conjugations and offers some useful observations on common particles. Note the summary of J. Hoftijzer's somewhat similar views in F. Charles Fensham, "The Use of the Suffix Conjugation and the Prefix Conjugation in a Few Old Hebrew Poems," *Journal of Northwest Semitic Languages* 6 (1978) 9–18, at 12; and see n. 88 below.

defended by Herder or Sperber, offer no final solution to the problem of the verbal system.

Aspectual theory proper begins in the 1820s, contemporary with Samuel Lee's f studies. Heinrich Ewald (1803–1875) in 1827 wrote of the two conjugations: "The first aorist [*qtl*] conveys a completed (*perfectam*) thing, whether present, preterite, or future. The second aorist [*yqtl*] conveys a non-completed (*imperfectam*) thing, whether present, preterite, or future."[37] Although he used the Latin terms *modi* 'moods' and *tempora* 'tenses (lit., times),' Ewald's conception is aspectual. It was in accord with Ewald's views that the Hebrew conjugations became known as the perfect and imperfect;[38] these, as he said, represent "the two grand and opposite aspects under which every conceivable action may be regarded." By the perfect Ewald meant that the speaker represents the action as finished and thus before him; the imperfect represents the action as unfinished and non-existent, but possibly becoming and coming. McFall summarizes Ewald's view of the perfect thus:

> It is used of actions which the speaker from his *present* regards as actually past and therefore complete. [And] it is used of actions which are regarded as finished but which reach right into the present.[39]

Regarding Ewald's view of the imperfect, McFall remarks:

> From the basic idea of Incompleteness there arise two distinct meanings which are very widely different from one another. Firstly, what is stated absolutely to be incomplete refers to time and is therefore a mere time-form or tense. Secondly, what is stated to be dependent on something else is set forth as in a particular "*kind* of being, which hence becomes more a *mood* than a *tense*."[40]

Now that Ewald had freed the study of the Hebrew verb from tense, the *waw*- g conversive theory also came into question. In its place Ewald advanced the notion of *waw*-relative as understood by Lee. Ewald erroneously speculated that ·נ (i.e., *way*-) prefixed to the historical present *yqtl* was comprised of ו 'and' and אז 'then' and thought that it indicated more emphatically the consequence of an action.[41] For this interpretation of the form Ewald (like most moderns) adopted F. Böttcher's term, *waw*-consecutive. Ewald further rightly proposed that *wqtl* functions as the antithesis of *wayyqtl*. Of great importance to later research based on the comparative-historical method was Ewald's observation that the *wayyqtl* form is based wherever possible on the jussive form. Here,

37. McFall, *Hebrew Verbal System*, 44; on Ewald generally, pp. 43–57.

38. E. Rödiger took over the task of updating Gesenius's grammar with the 14th edition and "immediately adopted Ewald's grammatical terms, Perfect and Imperfect"; McFall, *Hebrew Verbal System*, 15.

39. McFall, *Hebrew Verbal System*, 45.

40. McFall, *Hebrew Verbal System*, 46.

41. The idea that *way*(*yiqtol*) conceals some (other) morphological element has persisted into our own day but

has never done much explanatory duty, as noted by E. J. Revell, "Stress and the *Waw* 'Consecutive' in Biblical Hebrew," *Journal of the American Oriental Society* 104 (1984) 437–44, at 443; for recent efforts to accord special status to the element, see, e.g., J. F. X. Sheehan, "Egypto-Semitic Elucidation of the Waw Conversive," *Biblica* 52 (1971) 39–43; C. H. Gordon, "Eblaitica," *Eblaitica*, ed. C. H. Gordon, G. A. Rendsburg, and N. H. Winter (Winona Lake, Indiana: Eisenbrauns, 1987), 1. 19–28, at 21–22. Cf. 33.1.2.

however, he overgeneralized; McFall calls attention to instances where it is built on the so-called longer imperfect form.[42]

h   Ewald's study considerably narrowed the gap between text and interpretation. In scientific thought a theory is created by imagination from the data being investigated, and the theory is then tested by logic against the data. Ewald's aspect theory, in the minds of many, better satisfied the data than any tense theory; in most grammars the terms "perfect" and "imperfect" replaced the temporal terms. Standard works on the other Semitic languages came to employ similar concepts and terms.[43] The term "aspect" has gradually been applied to these forms.[44]

i   Ewald's views were in some respects deficient. Like many of his successors, he confused the concept of *complete* with that of *completed*. As a result he felt compelled to explain the prophets' use of the perfect for future events as the result of ecstatic experiences, in which they saw the future as completed. Qimḥi had explained the same phenomenon similarly six centuries earlier: "The matter is as clear as though it had already passed."[45] Ewald substituted "finished" for "passed."

j   Moreover, Ewald is guilty of reductionism, for it is questionable whether the abstraction "imperfect aspect" can include future-time references and modal nuances. Thomas O. Lambdin rightly cautions, "It is not entirely accurate . . . to describe such action [general, non-specific, habitual, potential, or to some degree probable] as incomplete or unfinished, as is often done."[46]

k   Finally, in our appraisal of Ewald, we take note of Péter Kustár's allegations that *qtl* can designate action which is not completed, as in יָעַצְתִּי (2 Sam 17:11), זָכַרְנוּ (Num 11:5), and אָהַבְתָּ (Gen 22:2), and that *yqtl* can designate completed action as in Job 3:3 (אִוָּלֶד) and Judg 2:1 (אַעֲלֶה). The observations cannot be wholly sustained, as we shall see in the following chapters.[47]

l   The reception and popularization of Ewald's theory by the influential British scholar S. R. Driver (1846–1914) represents a setback. Though both a great scholar in his own right and a major mediator of German scholarship, Driver made no considerable independent contribution to the study of the tenses.[48] Driver largely accepted Ewald's view, except that, as noted by Carl Brockelmann, he sought to explain the two conjugations in Hebrew by relating them to the aspects "perfect" and "imperfect" as interpreted by G. Curtius for Greek.[49] This led him to claim that the imperfect always signified nascent or incipient action, whereas Ewald had suggested such meanings as only one possibility. Driver wrote:

42. McFall, *Hebrew Verbal System*, 54–55.

43. Some scholars use, instead of "imperfect(um/ive)," either *fiens* (Latin 'acting, i.e., ongoing') or *infectum* (Latin 'un-done, i.e., unfinished').

44. E.g., S. Moscati et al., *An Introduction to the Comparative Grammar of the Semitic Languages* (Wiesbaden: Harrassowitz, 1964) 131.

45. McFall, *Hebrew Verbal System*, 8.

46. T. O. Lambdin, *Introduction to Biblical Hebrew*

(New York: Scribner, 1971) 100.

47. Péter Kustár, *Aspekt im Hebräischen* (Basel: Reinhardt, 1972).

48. McFall, *Hebrew Verbal System*, 60–77; Fensham ("Suffix Conjugation," 11) incorrectly attributes the introduction of aspectual theory to S. R. Driver.

49. Brockelmann, "'Tempora' des Semitischen," 135–36; Brockelmann, *Hebräische Syntax* (Neukirchen: Neukirchener Verlag, 1956) 38.

It is ... of the utmost consequence to understand and bear constantly in mind the fundamental and primary facts ... : (1) that the Hebrew verb notifies the character without fixing the date of an action, and (2) that, of its two forms ... , one is calculated to describe an action as *nascent* and so as imperfect; the other to describe it as *completed* and so as perfect.[50]

As might be anticipated from this citation, he accepted the concept of a "prophetic perfect."

[With] ease and rapidity [the speaker] *changes his standpoint*, at one moment speaking of a scene as though still in the remote future, at another moment describing it as though present to his gaze.[51]

Driver demonstrated that *qtl* in its bound form (*wqtl*) lost its individuality and passed under the sway of the verb to which it is connected.[52] In Driver's view *wayyqtl* also represented a "becoming" and "incomplete" activity, but relatively rather than absolutely, namely, in relationship to the preceding verbal expression to which it subordinated itself. E. König referred to such a connection as an *annexum* (i.e., a "consequence").

Driver's views were widely accepted, but his theory cannot be endorsed.[53] He   m
inherited the weakness of Ewald's reductionism and exacerbated it. Further, as McFall cogently argues, some complicated situations demand that we interpret the *yqtl* as describing completed action: "Nascent action is too narrow a view of an action for it to be a fit medium to describe a total event made up of a number of individually complete actions, *e.g.* 2 Chr. 28:15."[54] In fact, Driver is forced to abandon his theory of *yqtl* in connection with the combination *wayyqtl*: "The use of [*wayyqtl*] in the historical books ... renders it inconceivable that it should have suggested anything except the idea of a *fact done*."[55] McFall also points out the same inconsistency in Ewald.[56] Driver, writing more than a century ago, did not have the advantage of ancient comparative Semitic materials in preparing his survey, and his reliance on Greek is perhaps understandable.

The response to Ewald by William Turner of Edinburgh was in the nature of a   n
rebuttal, but his theory was at base aspectual and philosophical.[57] Turner sought to counter Ewald's theory with the view that *qtl* represents the act or state of the verb as an objective fact and that the *yqtl* describes the process. In his view *qtl* is objective fact, *yqtl*

---

50. S. R. Driver, *A Treatise on the Use of the Tenses in Hebrew* (3d ed.; Oxford: Clarendon, 1892) 5. Note the acknowledgment of Ewald: "By his originality and penetration [he] was the founder of a new era in the study of Hebrew grammar" (p. x).
51. S. R. Driver, *Tenses in Hebrew*, 5.
52. S. R. Driver, *Tenses in Hebrew*, 114–57.
53. Brockelmann ("'Tempora' des Semitischen," 136–37) cites as accepting S. R. Driver's views Johannes Pedersen, Marcel Cohen, and, in part, Henri Fleisch. (Cohen's *Le Système verbal sémitique et l'expression du temps* [Paris: Imprimerie Nationale, 1924] remains especially valuable for its survey of Semitic compound tenses.) The approach

of S. R. Driver is carried to an extreme in J. Wash Watts, *A Survey of Syntax in the Hebrew Old Testament* (Grand Rapids: Eerdmans, 1964).
54. McFall, *Hebrew Verbal System*, 71.
55. S. R. Driver, *Tenses in Hebrew*, 94, cf. p. 98.
56. McFall, *Hebrew Verbal System*, 53.
57. See McFall, *Hebrew Verbal System*, 77–86, on Turner (McFall confuses this scholar with the London-born American William Wadden Turner, p. 57, as D. P. Aiken points out to us); McFall, like Turner himself, does not regard Turner as an aspectualist. The views of Bo Johnson are similar to those of Turner; see *Hebräisches Perfekt und Imperfekt*.

subjective representation; *qtl* focuses on the historical results, *yqtl* on the forging of history. Turner sees no essential difference between *qtl* with roots denoting a state *versus* an activity; neither one represents the subject as putting forth energy but rather both mark the subject with an attribution. He distinguished *qtl* from the participle (*qôtēl*) by suggesting that the latter emphasizes the person and the former the fact. Both the free and bound forms of *yqtl* expressed the element of personal life and activity.

o   Turner presents us once again with an interesting but reductionistic view. He anticipates Michel's theories as well as modern views of aspect and the subjective representation of reality. Though Turner contrasted his views with aspectual theory, his analysis is not entirely different. Note Brockelmann's explanation that both conjugations represent aspect:

> The tempora are to be explained as subjective aspects, as can be observed in many languages according to whether the speaker wishes simply to state that which happened as an event (perfect) or its progress (cursive) (imperfect).[58]

Turner seems to observe the aspects out of focus.

p   Of the three groups of theories sketched here, it is Ewald's view which represents the most permanent contribution. The "universal tense" theory is not a serious view, and the English-speaking post-Ewaldians do not advance on their German master. As Ewald, S. R. Driver, and Turner were writing, fresh data was becoming available from ancient monuments. Such data inform most more recent studies.

29.4   Comparative-Historical Theories

a   By the opening decade of this century, the major features of Akkadian grammar were understood and could be brought to bear on the problems of Hebrew verbal conjugations.[59] Hans Bauer, in his 1910 dissertation, took up the new comparative-historical method.[60] He found S. R. Driver's interpretation artificial and returned to the concept that the two Semitic conjugations referred to periods of time. Even though all the cognate Semitic languages exhibit at least two conjugations, Bauer hypothesized that the Semites originally had only one verbal form, the prefix conjugation. This form was originally timeless, and therefore he named it "aorist." The suffix conjugation originated out of a nominal clause construction (see 8.4) involving the participle, and therefore he called it "nominal"; he believed this proto-form must be assigned the meaning of a verb, either that of a perfect (e.g., *qatal* 'he is a murderer,' which is equated with 'he murdered') or a present (e.g., *yada*ᶜ 'he is skillful,' an equivalent of 'he knows'). The perfect meaning of the suffix conjugation prevailed in the West Semitic languages, with the

58. Brockelmann, *Hebräische Syntax*, 39.

59. Certain features of Akkadian grammar only came into focus with the studies of Benno Landsberger in the 1920s, but earlier scholars were well advanced. J. A. Knudtzon's theory of the Hebrew verb (McFall, *Hebrew Verbal System*, 87–93) is the earliest to reflect the impact of Akkadian grammar; unfortunately he studied the Hebrew verbal system before his work on the Amarna letters (see references to the Amarna verb studies, all crucially indebted to Knudtzon, in n. 71).

60. Hans Bauer, "Die Tempora im Semitischen," *Beiträge zur Assyriologie und semitischen Sprachwissenschaft* 81 (1910) 1–53; cf. Brockelmann, *Hebräische Syntax*, 38–39; McFall, *Hebrew Verbal System*, 93–115.

result that there the prefix conjugation became restricted to the present and future periods. By contrast, in Akkadian the suffix conjugation underwent a metamorphosis to emerge as a prefix form (supposed *iparas*) and was used for the present tense, with the result that the old prefix form (*iprus*) became restricted to the past. Since the preterite meaning for *yqtl* is also found in Hebrew, Bauer was forced to allege that Hebrew in its *wayyqtl* form must preserve this Akkadian preterite conjugation; the *waw* of this form is thus the *waw-conservative*.

To explain the presence in Hebrew of both West Semitic and East Semitic prefix conjugations Bauer proposed that the wandering Hebrews brought with them the East Semitic conjugations and later mixed them with the West Semitic conjugations of the resident Canaanites. Hebrew is not strictly a West Semitic language, but a mixed language. In sum, Bauer, holding that Hebrew *qtl* = perfect tense, *yqtl* = present/future tense, *wayyqtl* = past tense, returned dramatically to the medieval Jewish view but for different reasons.

Bauer's theory was accepted without the hypothesis of language mixture by Gotthelf Bergsträsser.[61] By contrast, G. R. Driver sought to defend precisely the assumption of language mixture.[62] F. R. Blake also essentially followed Bauer.[63] Most recently J. F. A. Sawyer also has harked back to such a tense interpretation.[64]

But Bauer's hypothesized development could not be maintained. The suffix conjugation is found in other Afroasiatic languages, which were in the earliest period connected with Proto-Semitic. Moreover, later research showed that the so-called present of Akkadian originally had a doubled middle radical and therefore could not be related to the West Semitic perfect,[65] but should be related to the similarly constructed imperfect indicative of the Ethiopic languages.[66] The Akkadian present (*iparras*) and the Ethiopic indicative imperfect (*yeparres*) express imperfective aspect; the form was eliminated in the other languages on account of its similarity to the D stem (i.e., *Piel*).[67]

61. GB 2. 9–14 (§ 3).

62. G. R. Driver, *Problems of the Hebrew Verbal System* (Edinburgh: T. & T. Clark, 1936); the son of S. R. Driver, G. R. Driver begins his study by confessing "a hereditary interest" in the subject, p. v; he summarizes his views in a note to J. Weingreen, *A Practical Grammar for Classical Hebrew* (Oxford: Clarendon, 1961) 252–53. Although he did important work on Ugaritic and other early Northwest Semitic materials, Driver's study antedates that work. See in general McFall, *Hebrew Verbal System*, 116–51; on Driver's use of Akkadian, see David Marcus, "The Stative and the *Waw*-Consecutive," *Journal of the Ancient Near Eastern Society* 2 (1969) 37–40.

63. Blake, *Hebrew Tenses.*

64. J. F. A. Sawyer, *A Modern Introduction to Biblical Hebrew* (Stocksfield: Oriel, 1976) 82; Sawyer's attempt to use ideas of tense, aspect, and mood as comparable factors is too great an oversimplification to be useful. Cf. M. H. Silverman, "Syntactic Notes on the *Waw* Consecutive," *Orient and Occident: Essays Presented to Cyrus H. Gordon*, ed. H. A. Hoffner (Alter Orient und Altes Testa-

ment 22; Kevelaer: Butzon und Bercker/Neukirchen-Vluyn: Neukirchener Verlag, 1973) 167–75. Both Brockelmann and S. Segert see an originally aspectual system shifting to an essentially tensed system; Brockelmann, "'Tempora' des Semitischen," looks to Aramaic influence. See Segert, "Verbal Categories of Some Northwest Semitic Languages," *Afroasiatic Linguistics* 2 (1975) 83–94, at 90–92.

65. As assumed by J. Barth, "Das semitische Perfect im Assyrischen," *Zeitschrift für Assyriologie* 2 (1887) 375–86.

66. As Paul Haupt had argued in "The Oldest Semitic Verb-Form," *Journal of the Royal Asiatic Society* 10 (1878) 244–52; cited in McFall, *Hebrew Verbal System*, 108.

67. So, e.g., Brockelmann, "'Tempora' des Semitischen"; and T. W. Thacker, *The Relationship of the Semitic and Egyptian Verbal System* (Oxford: Oxford University, 1954) 189.

Otto Rössler and Rudolf Meyer have argued that Hebrew had a *yeqattel* durative form, evidenced by remnants like *ynṣrw* (MT *yinṣórû*, Deut 33:9), for *yenaṣṣerū* or the like, and by some Qumranic forms. See Rössler,

e   Bauer's work, despite its defects, provides the crucial outline of a modern view of the Hebrew tenses. It is, first of all, a theory grounded in comparative data. Since we now have available vastly improved descriptions of Akkadian, as well as of Egyptian, and new material from various sites, notably Amarna and Ugarit, we have a much broader field of comparison against which to study Hebrew. Second, Bauer recognized that Hebrew *yqtl/wayyqtl* was at base a mixed lot, and most scholars accept his view that the Hebrew prefix conjugation is (or better, contains remnants of) two older prefix conjugations, one denoting the present/future tense (as Bauer would have it) or a cursive/durative aspect (as, e.g., Rudolf Meyer describes it), and the other a past narrative form. Unquestionably, the Proto-Semitic language had at least two prefix conjugations, including a "longer"(?) form signifying non-perfective aspect, future tense, etc., and a "shorter"(?) form for past narrative. Let us review some of the comparative data.[68]

f   In Akkadian one finds a long prefix conjugation (the "present"—*iparras*, *irappud*, *ikabbit*) to express incomplete or habitual action in past time, a historical present or actual present, and simple future, as well as modal nuances. As we shall see, this range of uses comports almost exactly with that of the Hebrew *yqtl* (historically **yaqtula*). Akkadian also has a short prefix conjugation (the "preterite"—*iprus*, *iplaḫ*, *ikbit*) for either preterite action or the jussive mood.[69] The discovery of this form led philologists to see West Semitic *yaqtul* (i.e., Hebrew jussive and *wayyqtl*) as both preterite and jussive.

g   In Arabic one also finds a long prefix conjugation (*yaqtulu*), signifying imperfect aspect, circumstantial action, and (with the particle *sawfa*) future time. The short prefix conjugation (*yaqtul*) signifies either the jussive mood or (with the negative *lam*) preterite action.[70]

h   As for the evidence from Early Northwest Semitic, Ugaritic is problematic because it is unvocalized. In the Amarna correspondence the long form (*yaqtulu*, pl. *yaqtuluna*)

"Eine bisher unbekannte Tempusform im Althebräischen," *Zeitschrift der Deutschen Morgenländischen Gesellschaft* 111 (1961) 445–51; and "Die Präfixkonjugation Qal der Verbae Iᵃᵉ Nûn im Althebräischen und das Problem der sogennanten Tempora," *Zeitschrift für die Alttestamentliche Wissenschaft* 74 (1962) 125–41; and the following works by Meyer: *Hebräische Grammatik* (3d ed.; Berlin: de Gruyter, 1969), 2. 134–35; "Probleme der hebräischen Grammatik," *Zeitschrift für die Alttestamentliche Wissenschaft* 63 (1951) 221–35, at 224–25; "Zur Geschichte des hebräischen Verbums," *Vetus Testamentum* 3 (1953) 225–35, at 229; "Das hebräische Verbalsystem im Lichte der gegenwärtigen Forschung," *Congress Volume: Oxford 1959* (Vetus Testamentum Supplement 7; Leiden: Brill, 1960) 309–17, at 311–12; "Aspekt und Tempus im althebräischen Verbalsystem," *Orientalistische Literaturzeitung* 59 (1964) 117–26; "Zur Geschichte des hebräischen Verbums," *Forschungen und Fortschritte* 40 (1966) 241–43. Although T. N. D. Mettinger is sympathetic to this view ("The He-brew Verb System," *Annual of the Swedish Theological Institute* 9 [1973] 64–84, at 69–73), most scholars are not; see A. Bloch, "Zur Nachweisbarkeit einer hebräischen Entsprechung der akkadischen Form *iparras*," *Zeitschrift der Deutschen Morgenländischen Gesellschaft* 113 (1963) 41–50; T. L. Fenton, "The Absence of a Verbal Formation **yaqattal* from Ugaritic and North-west Semitic," *Journal of Semitic Studies* 15 (1970) 31–41; Revell, "Stress and Waw 'Consecutive,'" 442.

68. See N. Waldman, "The Hebrew Tradition," *Current Trends in Linguistics. 13. Historiography of Linguistics*, ed. T. A. Sebeok et al. (The Hague: Mouton, 1975) 1285–1330, at 1285–87.

69. Von Soden, *Grundriss der akkadischen Grammatik*, 102–3.

70. W. Wright, *A Grammar of the Arabic Language* (3d ed.; Cambridge: Cambridge University, 1898), 2. 18–22; W. Fisher, *Grammatik des klassischen Arabisch* (Wiesbaden: Harrassowitz, 1972) 96.

denotes imperfective aspect, unreal mood, or general present and future actions. The short form (*yaqtul*, pl. *yaqtulu*) denotes either jussive mood or preterite action.[71]

How does this evidence help us in understanding Hebrew? Ewald observed that in   i Hebrew verbs, where prefix forms vary, the *wayyqtl* form has the same shape as the jussive. It may be argued from the comparative Semitic evidence that these forms represent a historically short form in contrast to the regular *yqtl*. For example, in the *Hiphil* stem the "imperfect" is *yaqtîl* (<*yaqtilu) but the jussive/*waw*-relative form is *yaqtēl* (<*yaqtil). A similar distinction can be observed in the II-*waw* (e.g., קוּם) and geminate roots (e.g., סבב): *yāqûm* (<*yaqūmu) versus *yāqōm* (<*yaqum) and *yāsōb* (<*yasubbu) versus *yāsob* (<*yasub). An archaic short prefix conjugation thus may have survived in the *wayyqtl* form of narrative. Some think it also survived in a free form, especially in poetry (31.6).[72]

In spite of the apparent correlation in form and meaning between the longer and   j shorter prefix conjugations in other Semitic languages and the Hebrew forms, the theory nevertheless has its own set of problems. The major problem is the alleged split between long and short forms. With most verbs one cannot distinguish between the two alleged prefix conjugations. This is explained by the fact that around 1100 B.C.E. the language lost all its final short vowels, causing most *yaqtulu and *yaqtul forms to *fall together as homonyms*. But can a language tolerate such a homonymy? Can a language tolerate over an extended period the same form representing opposing aspects or tenses? One could reply that Hebrew (as well as some other Semitic languages) uses a common prefix conjugation to express both the jussive and indicative moods. (The same confusion sometimes also overtakes the cohortative and indicative moods.) If the same form can signify opposite moods, can the same form not also express opposite aspects? The comparative Semitic evidence and the two distinct uses of the Hebrew prefix conjugation suggest that in fact *yaqtulu* and *yaqtul* have *merged* in Hebrew to form a (nearly) common conjugation.[73]

71. *UT* § 9.10 and n. 73 below. The most intensively studied part of the Amarna correspondence is the body of letters from Byblos (background in P. Swiggers, "Byblos dans les lettres d'el Amarna," *Studia Phoenicia. 3. Phoenicia and Its Neighbors*, ed. E. Lipiński [Leuven: Peeters, 1985] 45–58). See in general on the language W. L. Moran, "The Hebrew Language in Its Northwest Semitic Background," *The Bible and the Ancient Near East: Essays in Honor of William Foxwell Albright*, ed. G. E. Wright (Garden City, New York: Doubleday, 1961; rpt. Winona Lake, Indiana: Eisenbrauns, 1979) 54–66, esp. 63–66; and, on the Byblian letters, Moran, "Early Canaanite *yaqtula*," *Orientalia* 29 (1960) 1–19, esp. 7–8. Moran's full study has never been published: *A Syntactical Study of the Dialect of Byblos as Reflected in the Amarna Tablets* (Johns Hopkins University Dissertation, 1950); see there esp. pp. 43–51. See also A. F. Rainey, "Morphology and the Prefix-Tenses of West Semitized El Amarna Tablets," *Ugarit-Forschungen* 7 (1975) 395–426.

72. See, e.g., Meyer, *Hebräische Grammatik* (1972), 3. 39–44; Hughes, "Another Look at the Hebrew Tenses," 13.

73. Cf., e.g., Meyer, *Hebräische Grammatik*, 3. 39–44; Meyer, "Das hebräische Verbalsystem," 313–15. Note that the formulation in the text does not require that the survival be directly reflected in the morphology, especially the accentuation, of the two types of prefix form (see Richter, *GAHG* 1. 99–101). The arguments against such a survival are presented by Revell, "Stress and *Waw* 'Consecutive.'" For another view on stress survival, see R. Hetzron, "The Evidence for Perfect **y'aqtul* [= *yáqtul*] and Jussive **yaqt'ul* [= *yaqtúl*] in Proto-Semitic," *Journal of Semitic Studies* 14 (1969) 1–21. On the historical/synchronic problem, note the formulations of H. B. Rosén, "The Comparative Assignment of Certain Hebrew Tense Forms," *East and West: Selected Writings in Linguistics. 2. Hebrew and Semitic Languages* (Munich: Fink, 1984) 229–51; A. F. Rainey, "The Ancient Prefix Conjugations in the

The syntactic consequences of the merger are not obvious. Studies of the text itself must be decisive in reviewing the results of the comparative evidence.

29.5   Philosophical Theories

a   Diethelm Michel in his 1960 study of the conjugations in the Psalter took a different tack.[74] He rejects the older aspectual theories as well as historical-comparative theories of the type pioneered by Bauer. A reconsideration based on a polar opposition between *qtl* and *yqtl* forms is necessary, he believes.

b   Michel begins his study by justifying the use of poetry rather than prose and in the process deals with the problem of genre effects. He rejects using prose narrative as the major source of data because the verb in such literature almost always refers to past tense or completed action. In addition, according to him, the available theories do not fit the data. He writes of standard theories of the working of poetry:

> Suddenly in poetry there is an "archaic narrative imperfectum with past meaning"; in poetry one must accept a "prophetic perfectum" and apply psychology in order to explain its existence; in poetry there is in direct address a "perfectum of execution," also called "declarative perfectum," which accompanies an action and therefore designates an uncompleted, present action.[75]

Michel then turns to the so-called consecutive *tempora* (conjugations):

> It appears unexpected and odd, to say the least, that a *tempus* should be turned around into its opposite by the mere prefixing of ו. And if one further considers that this same form ו plus perfectum is said to be used on one occasion as a "perfectum copulativum," like the customary perfectum, and on another occasion as "perfectum consecutivum," like the customary imperfectum, the questions become unbearably loud.[76]

Light of Amarnah Canaanite," *Hebrew Studies* 27 (1986) 4–19; and several related papers: E. L. Greenstein, "On the Prefixed Preterite in Biblical Hebrew," *Hebrew Studies* 29 (1988) 7–17 (note esp., on the Ugaritic situation, 12–14); J. Huehnergard, "The Early Hebrew Prefix-Conjugations," *Hebrew Studies* 29 (1988) 19–23; Z. Zevit, "Solving a Problem of the *Yaqtúl* Past Tense," *Hebrew Studies* 29 (1988) 25–33; A. F. Rainey, "Further Remarks on the Hebrew Verbal System," *Hebrew Studies* 29 (1988) 35–42 (on Ugaritic, 37–38). On the necessary separation between the history of the system (the etymology, as it were) and the working of the system, note Greenstein's formula: "Sense is determined not on the basis of forms [alone] but on the basis of the contrast or opposition of forms" ("Prefixed Preterite," 14); and Zevit's: "Etymological explanations that purport to describe the origins of the Hebrew verbal system are inadequate as descriptions of how this system works in fact" ("*Yaqtúl* Past Tense," 27).

74. Diethelm Michel, *Tempora und Satzstellung in den Psalmen* (Bonn: Bouvier, 1960); see Mettinger, "Hebrew Verb System," 77–78, for a summary.

75. Michel, *Tempora und Satzstellung*, 11. For other studies of poetic texts, see Fensham, "Suffix Conjugation," 14–18, on Pss 29, 82, and 93; and W. Gross, *Verbform und Funktion: Wayyiqtol für die Gegenwart?* (St. Ottilien: EOS, 1976). Michel neglects the use of the *qtl* and *yqtl* of the same root in neighboring lines; on the phenomenon, see Moshe Held, "The *YQTL-QTL (QTL-YQTL)* Sequence of Identical Verbs in Biblical Hebrew and in Ugaritic," *Studies and Essays in Honor of Abraham A. Neuman*, ed. M. Ben-Horin (Leiden: Brill, 1962) 281–90.

76. Michel, *Tempora und Satzstellung*, 12.

He then takes up the discrepancy noted by all students when they turn from the grammars to the text.

> We must test and discuss all the verb forms that occur. It makes no sense to cite as evidence only those passages which support our thesis and to conceal the others. Such an eclectic approach as the grammars must of necessity use by reason of space must rely on advanced work which has tested all the evidence, and this advanced work we will provide here by investigating the Psalms.[77]

He also rejects the results of the comparative-historical school.

> We do not take over . . . the results of comparative linguistic studies concerning the meaning of the Semitic verb forms. Where one can end up, if he takes his starting point here, Brockelmann has now shown very beautifully with the help of Bauer's theories. Comparative linguistics is only possible if the languages to be compared are understood on their own.[78]

c This iconoclast launches his investigation with the "imperfectum consecutivum" (*wayyqtl*). Having studied its occurrences after "perfectum" (*qtl*), after "imperfectum" (*yqtl*), in a chain of "imperfecta consecutiva," and after nominal sentences, participles, and infinitives, he draws the conclusion that it always denotes *consequence* or *dependence*, regardless of time (hence the term the *waw-consequential theory*):

> It has been shown that the so-called imperfectum consecutivum gives a consequence, and in fact does so without regard to time. To be sure, the majority of passages have to be translated in the past, yet we also find a considerable group which cannot be categorized in any time period.[79]

d Next he studies the "perfectum" in various kinds of psalms and situations. Here he discovers that it can refer to perfect, present, and future actions, and that it can be used in constructions which append explanatory facts to something pictured earlier. From this study he draws the conclusion that the "perfectum" does not serve to refer to a period of time but rather "reports an event which stands in no dependent relationship but which is important in itself." He argues that this can be proved in three ways:

1. If a perfectum stands in isolation or at the beginning of a clause it expresses a fact. . . .
2. If a perfectum follows syndetically or asyndetically on an imperfectum or a participle, it does not advance them but rather sets an explicating fact alongside of them. . . .
3. If several perfecta stand unconnected alongside of one another, they do not advance the action, but itemize equally important facts. . . .

77. Michel, *Tempora und Satzstellung*, 13.
78. Michel, *Tempora und Satzstellung*, 14; the last sentence has an attractive ring, but it is not true in a straightforward way, especially of ancient written languages, especially those with no continuous tradition.
79. Michel, *Tempora und Satzstellung*, 41.

By contrast, he notes, "Of the imperfectum it can be said right at the start that it does not do all this; it reports an action that stands in a relationship."[80]

e   Michel then turns to the significance of the conjugations in view of the acting subject. After an in-depth examination of Psalm 1 he provisionally advances his thesis in philosophical terms: the "perfectum" and "imperfectum" have an "accidental" and "substantial" character, respectively:

> The typical actions expressed by the perfecta designate facts, which a person does but can also theoretically not do. The actions could be called typical to the extent that the person who does them manifests his belonging to a certain type of individual. If the person acted otherwise, he would exhibit himself as belonging to another type of individual. Accordingly, the actions are not reported under the point of view that they proceed from a definite kind of person, but that they make this kind of being first manifest. In short: the actions designated by the perfectum with regard to the acting person have an accidental character.
>
> On the other hand, the kind of tree in [Ps 1:]3 is established from what precedes: it is a matter of a tree planted by streams of water. That this tree brings fruit in its season, that its leaves do not wither are not actions which it can or cannot do; rather they result with necessity from the character [*Wesen*] of the tree. In short: the actions designated by the imperfectum with regard to the acting subject have a substantial character.[81]

Michel attempts to validate this provisional distinction through a comprehensive study of the Psalter. He summarizes his conclusions thus: "The criteria for the choice of the *tempus* do not lie in the action itself (period of time, *Aktionsart*, or the like), but in the relationship which the speaker wishes to see expressed."[82]

f   Michel now studies *yqtl* forms in isolation. He commences his research with the view that if *qtl* designates an independent fact, then *yqtl* must designate dependent actions. He validates his view by examining *yqtl* forms with respect to (1) negative consequences, the so-called poetic aorist, (2) corresponding occurrences—"where a second action interprets the first," (3) the modal use, (4) iterative use, (5) expressions of request, and (6) conjunctions. Some of his results deserve mention. In connection with "the so-called poetic aorist" he denies, against Stade, Bauer, Bergsträsser, Gunkel, and others, that an ancient use of *yqtl* for past actions has survived in the Psalter. For Michel no significant difference exists between the *yqtl* and *wayyqtl*—both express a consequence:

> Between the imperfectum [*yqtl*] and imperfectum consecutivum [*wayyqtl*] no distinction exists with regard to their meaning. . . . The two *tempora* are distinguished only by the fact that with the so-called imperfectum consecutivum a closer connection is effected by the prefixed *וַ*.[83]

---

80. Michel, *Tempora und Satzstellung*, 98–99.   82. Michel, *Tempora und Satzstellung*, 127.
81. Michel, *Tempora und Satzstellung*, 110.   83. Michel, *Tempora und Satzstellung*, 132.

With regard to modal use he argues that if an action occurs as a consequence of the essence of the acting person or from the givenness of the situation, *yqtl* designates a modal notion and in effect is "substantial." "The expression 'he does this' is independently important, but the expressions 'he can, wants to, may, . . .' are meaningful only in relation to another given."[84] He reasons that *yqtl* is understandably used for repeated actions since with an action that repeats itself an ever-new happening is being reported rather than a fact. The "substantial" theory, he argues, also works with the use of *yqtl* for requests and commands because an action which is either demanded or forbidden is not important in itself but has its significance through its connection with the person making the command. It is therefore "substantial."

Unquestionably, Michel has advanced and enriched considerably this central, and   g yet most difficult and debated, area of Hebrew grammar with his comprehensive study of a selected portion of the text. Future scholarship stands in his debt, and we draw on his work in the following chapters. He has demonstrated beyond reasonable doubt that the *waw*-relative construction (*wayyqtl*) can signify consequence or dependence. But if "event" refers to dynamic situations in contrast to static ones, then his statement is inadequate for stative verbs.[85] His view of the suffix conjugation strongly resembles that of Turner (whom he does not cite), and our criticism of Turner (29.3) applies here as well. Michel, like Turner, seems to be out of focus, seeing nuances that accompany the conjugations while missing their aspectual features.

His work contains flaws in its account of prefix forms. It is not true that the con-   h jugations present a philosophical contrast between situations that are accidental and factual and those that are substantial and less factual (contrast *ʾmr yqtl* in Isa 40:1 and *ʾmr qtl* in Ps 83:5: is the first quotation less "factual" than the second?) Many actions represented by the *wayyqtl* construction signify self-important, independent acts (cf. the creation narrative, Gen 1:3ff.). Although the prefix conjugation sometimes represents "substantial" acts, acts which of necessity proceed from the subject, it does not always do so. Consider # 1.

1.   יָבֵשׁ חָצִיר נָבֵל צִיץ כִּי רוּחַ   The grass withers and the flowers fade because
            יהוה נָשְׁבָה בּוֹ   Yʜᴡʜ's wind blows on them.
                                     Isa 40:7

According to Michel's theory we should have expected the prefix conjugation with the first two verbs, for, if the tree planted by streams of water *of necessity* bears fruit (Ps 1:3), so grass withers and the flowers wilt *of necessity* before the divine wind.

In general terms, too, Michel's work can be faulted. The focus on poetry, often   i elevated and idiosyncratic, ignores one set of (possible) genre effects to avoid being misled by another set, those of narrative prose. Further, while Bauer's theories proved far too speculative, and important features could not stand further inquiry, to dismiss

---

84. Michel, *Tempora und Satzstellung*, 143.
85. Cf. 20.2k and Bernard Comrie, *Aspect: An Intro-*   *duction to the Study of Verbal Aspect and Related Problems* (Cambridge: Cambridge University, 1976) 13.

the whole historical-comparative method for this reason seems unwarranted. Michel, in introducing his method, says that he wishes to avoid a priori assumptions, and yet he fails on just that score when he alleges that the prefix conjugation must be the precise opposite of the suffix conjugation. An unmarked grammatical form is not necessarily the (logical) opposite of a marked form. We will argue, in fact, that the prefix conjugation represents everything non-perfective.[86] Michel has also fallen into the same trap as researchers before him, the trap of reductionism through abstraction. A form does not necessarily have just one meaning; it may cover several meanings which speaker and audience distinguish by context.

j   A few specific points can be noted. It appears forced to say that repeated acts are lacking in factuality. Consider # 2.

2. וַיַּרְא וְהִנֵּה בְאֵר בַּשָּׂדֶה וְהִנֵּה־ שָׁם שְׁלֹשָׁה עֶדְרֵי־צֹאן רֹבְצִים עָלֶיהָ כִּי מִן־הַבְּאֵר הַהִוא יַשְׁקוּ הָעֲדָרִים	There he saw a well in the field with three flocks of sheep by it, because from that well they watered the flocks. Gen 29:2

The prefix conjugation form יַשְׁקוּ is not necessary here because of the dependent causal clause (cf. סָגַר in 1 Sam 1:5). Rather, the storyteller by means of the prefix form is giving the audience necessary facts, as also happens with the suffix conjugation. It is far more probable that the prefix conjugation denotes here, as it does in other Semitic languages, imperfective aspect and that factuality is not the issue. Remarkably, Michel's study lacks a consideration of wqtl, which is the apparent opposite of wayyqtl, and therefore might help in clarifying the latter form's functions. It seems unlikely, in light of the strict syntax that governs the use of the free and bound forms in prose, that yqtl and wayyqtl differ not in kind but only in degree, while wqtl and wayyqtl are utterly distinct.

k   A variant of Michel's thesis is worth noting. Péter Kustár proposes conclusions similar to Michel's.[87] But whereas Michel refers to qtl and yqtl as representing independent and dependent actions respectively, Kustár refers to them as representing determining and determined aspects. He writes:

> The basic law of the use of the aspect categories is the following: the speaker, through the use of qtl and yqtl aspect categories, distinguishes the actions, according to which some are to be considered in the immediate relationship of the actions to one another as determining and some as determined, that is, the speaker wants to point to some actions as the originating point, the basis, the determining moment, the purpose, result, or concluding point of the other actions, and to other actions as having their

---

86. A statement of principle may be quoted on this point: "When a linguist investigates two morphological categories in mutual opposition, he often starts from the assumption that both categories should be of equal value, and that each of them should possess a positive meaning of its own. . . . In reality, the *general meanings* of correlative categories are distributed in a different way: if Cate-

gory I announces the existence of A, then Category II does not announce the existence of A, i.e., it does not state whether A is present or not"; Roman Jakobson, *Russian and Slavic Grammar: Studies, 1931–1981*, ed. Linda R. Waugh and Morris Halle (Berlin: Mouton, 1984) I. The diversity of opposition is crucial to the Prague school.

87. Kustár, *Aspekt im Hebräischen*.

basis, purpose, or moment determined. The determining actions are designated through the *qtl* forms, the determined actions by *yqtl* forms.[88]

His thesis falls under many of the same censures as Michel's, notably the insistence on a *polar* opposition of the *qtl* and *yqtl* forms.

A Further Conception   29.6

All of the theories outlined here represent informed and considered efforts to come   a
to grips with the use of the Hebrew conjugations.[89] If it seems that the number of factors and systems too grotesquely outstrips the complexity of the usages, it may be worth recalling that some subparts of the English tense system are obscure. The operation of the sequence of tenses, for example, and the relationship of the perfect and pluperfect tenses are the subject of much controversy in a language that is not only living and widely spoken but also quite intensively studied.[90] Thus, a little patience is needed for work on the Hebrew conjugations. The studies considered so far suggest that the basic structure of the system, though it allows for time reference, is aspectual;[91] let us review that structure.

With the advocates of the aspectual theory we base our study of the suffix conjuga-   b
tion on the hypothesis that it designates perfective aspect (*Aspekt*).[92] Bernard Comrie defines aspects as "different ways of viewing the internal temporal constituency of a situation."[93] Consider the sentence: 'John was reading when I entered.' Comrie explains:

> The first verb presents the background to some event, while that event itself is introduced by the second verb. The second verb presents the totality of the situation referred to (here, my entry) without reference to its internal temporal constituency: the whole of the situation is presented as a single unanalysable whole, with beginning, middle, and end rolled into one; no attempt is made to divide this situation up into the various individual phases that make up the action of entry. Verbal forms with this meaning will be said to have perfective meaning, and where the language in question

88. Kustár, *Aspekt im Hebräischen*, 55. Cf. Fensham, "Suffix Conjugation," 12–13. Another polar-opposition theory is Hoftijzer's conception based on dependent/independent functions; see Fensham, p. 13.

89. G. R. Driver was perhaps ungenerous in his comment, "The problem of the Semitic tenses is complicated, though not so complicated as some of the solutions of it which have been propounded"; *Hebrew Verbal System*, 1.

90. Comrie, *Tense*, 104–21.

91. Most current textbooks are aspectualist; see, e.g., Weingreen, *Classical Hebrew*, 56; R. J. Williams, *Hebrew Syntax: An Outline* (2d ed.; Toronto: University of Toronto, 1976) 29–34; Moshe Greenberg, *Introduction to Hebrew* (Englewood Cliffs, New Jersey: Prentice-Hall, 1965) 45, allowing for *yaqtul/yaqtulu* coalescence. G. S. Ogden alleges that all Hebrew verbs are inflected for aspect, except *hyy*, which is tensed; see "Time, and the Verb היה in O. T. Prose," *Vetus Testamentum* 21 (1971)

451–69. For a recent extension of an aspectual approach in the framework of W. Schneider's text linguistics (3.3.4d and this chapter, n. 12), see A. Niccacci, *Sintassi del verbo ebraico nella prosa biblica classica* (Jerusalem: Franciscan Printing Press, 1986).

92. McFall, *Hebrew Verbal System*, 180–82.

93. Comrie, *Aspect*, 3; *Tense*, 6; on tense-aspect fusion, see *Tense*, 7. Classical Arabic has "two verb tense-aspects, conventionally called imperfect and perfect [the convention being that established by Ewald's work]. In addition to aspectual values, the imperfect has the time reference meaning component of relative non-past, while the perfect has the time reference meaning component of relative past"; Comrie, *Tense*, 63, cf. 21–22 (on Maltese), 76–77. Biblical Hebrew differs from Arabic in having only marginal time reference meaning components to its aspects. Cf. also J. Kuryłowicz, "Verbal Aspect in Semitic," *Orientalia* 42 (1973) 114–20.

has special verbal forms to indicate this, we shall say that it has perfective aspect. The other forms, i.e. those referring to the situation of John's reading, do not present the situation in this way, but rather make explicit reference to the internal temporal constituency of the situation. In these examples, in particular, reference is made to an internal portion of John's reading, while there is no explicit reference to the beginning or to the end of his reading. This is why the sentences are interpreted as meaning that my entry is an event that occurred during the period that John was reading, i.e. John's reading both preceded and followed my entry. Another way of explaining the difference between perfective and imperfective meaning is to say that the perfective looks at the situation from outside, without necessarily distinguishing any of the internal structure of the situation, whereas the imperfective looks at the situation from inside, and as such is crucially concerned with the internal structure of the situation, since it can both look backwards towards the start of the situation, and look forwards to the end of the situation, and indeed is equally appropriate if the situation is one that lasts through all time, without any beginning and without any end.[94]

Several points in this passage need to be noted in the light of the study of the Hebrew conjugations. Crucially, Comrie does not define perfective as *completed* (perfect) action.

There is an important semantic distinction which turns out to be crucial in discussing aspect. The perfective does indeed denote a complete situation, with beginning, middle, and end. The use of "completed", however, puts too much emphasis on the termination of the situation, whereas the use of the perfective puts no more emphasis, necessarily, on the end of the situation than on any other part of the situation.[95]

c   Significantly, Comrie speaks not of an action but of a situation, which may be either stative or dynamic. If perfective aspect is defined in terms of a *complete situation*, the term is applicable to both stative and fientive verbs.

d   The second verb in the example above, 'entered,' is conventionally called simple past, while the first, 'was reading,' is a past progressive. The asymmetry of these terms suggests that the perfective and progressive aspects in English are not polar opposites, even though their meanings are distinct. The search for polar opposition, we argue, led Michel astray, and in Hebrew we have found that masculine and feminine genders are not simple opposites (6.3–5). These lessons will be useful in considering the *yqtl* form, in relation to perfective *qtl*.[96]

e   The (historically long) prefix conjugation (*yaqtulu*) cannot be described solely in the terms of imperfective aspect. In this form the notions of aspect and time both blend (imperfective aspect in past and present time) and separate (aorist in future time).

94. Comrie, *Aspect*, 3–4.
95. Comrie, *Aspect*, 18. A perfective verb "encodes an event globally"; time reference is "not part of the meaning of the perfective"; *Tense*, 28.
96. This point, the core of Jakobsonian theory, is well appreciated by F. Rundgren, *Das althebräische Verbum:*

Sperber and Hughes are partially right in describing it as a universal tense. And it may signify more than a blending of tense and aspect or pure tense; it may also signify either real or unreal moods—the indicative as well as degrees of dubiety and volition. In short: a form that can signify any time, any mood, and imperfective aspect (but not perfective), is not imperfective but non-perfective, "a more than opposite" of the suffix conjugation. (The term "aorist," meaning without limits or boundaries, is not inappropriate.)

The *wayyqtl* (from historically short *yaqtul*) and *wqtl*, traditionally named *waw-* f *consecutive* forms, are better named *waw-resultative* forms, though not in the sense that Schröder, Lee, or Ewald attached to that term.[97] These *waw* constructions principally occur in relationship to a preceding verb and signify two notions at one and the same time: the bound prefix form has the values of the suffix conjugation and the bound suffix form has the values of the non-perfective conjugation and both bound forms represent a situation subordinate to that of the preceding clause, either as a (con)sequence or explanation of it. The terms *waw-conversive* and *waw-consecutive* are too restrictive. The term *waw-relative*, by contrast, suggests the relationship with the preceding verb and leaves open the possibilities of subordinate meaning. As we have already noted, the origin of this system may lie with the *yqtl* ~ *wayyqtl* forms, the first derived from a long prefix form with non-perfective sense and the second from a short prefix form used as a narrative preterite. But whatever the origin of the system, there has eventuated in Hebrew a quite different system of *yqtl* with relative *waw* used as a perfective. As we shall argue, this new system (32.1.2b) was developed at first in opposition to the *wəqtl* combination used to introduce the apodosis after a conditional protasis (e.g., 'If this be so, *wəqtl* = then so is/will be this') and later led, by analogy, to the development of the *wəqtl* combination used as a non-perfective. Our view of the relative *waw* combines and enriches the old notion of *waw hippûk* and Ewald's consequential *waw*.

Abriss der Aspektlehre (Stockholm: Almqvist & Wiksell, 1961) 101; his aspectual opposition is based on *qtl* stative (*qām*) versus unmarked, neutral *yqtl* (*yaqum/yaqom*). For a summary of Rundgren's view, see Mettinger, "Hebrew Verb System," 74–77; and Meyer, "Aspekt und Tempus im althebräischen Verbalsystem." T. J. Finley misrepresents Rundgren when he summarizes his view by saying that "since the perfective has both a negative and a neutral value with respect to the imperfective, it is the unmarked member of the opposition whereas the imperfective is marked"; see "The *Waw*-Consecutive with 'Imperfect' in Biblical Hebrew: Theoretical Studies and Its Use in Amos," *Tradition and Testament: Essays in Honor of Charles Lee Feinberg*, ed. J. S. Feinberg and P. D. Feinberg (Chicago: Moody, 1981) 241–62, at 251. In fact, Rundgren says (p. 101), "Das althebräische Verbalsystem hat somit als Achse die aspektuelle privative Opposition *Stativ/Fiens*, wobei der Stativ als der mekmalhafte [sic] Term der Opp. zu gelten hat. . . . Als merkmalloser Term hat dann das Fiens zwei Werte: non-stativisch (negativer Wert) und

weder stativisch noch kursiv (neutraler Wert)." ("The Old Hebrew verb system thus has as its axis the aspectual privative opposition *stative/fiens* [cf. n. 43], in which the stative is valued as the marked term of the opposition. . . . As the unmarked term the *fiens* thus has two values: non-stative [the negative value] and again stative-yet-cursive [the neutral value].") Another, implicitly markedness-based approach is that of R. Bartelmus: *qatal* (previous time reference, perfect aspect) opposed to the subsequent-time-reference forms, *yiqtol* and *wəqatal* (imperfect aspect) and *wayyiqtol* (perfect aspect); see *HYH: Bedeutung und Funktion eines hebräischen "Allerweltswortes"* (St. Ottilien: EOS, 1982). A. Loprieno reconstructs a primary aspectual system for Afroasiatic as a whole in *Das Verbalsystem im Ägyptischen und im Semitischen* (Wiesbaden: Harrassowitz, 1986).

97. McFall, *Hebrew Verbal System*, 50, 57. Joüon refers to the energ(et)ic *waw*, comparing Arabic *fa* 'and then'; Joüon § 115b / p. 313, but cf. § 117a / p. 319 for other suggestions.

g   We set forth our views provisionally, leaning heavily on prior critical studies, to provide a framework within which to study the forms. The framework, however, must not be so heavy that it imposes itself on reluctant texts. Rather, it must be tested, refined, and filled in by the text.

30

Suffix (Perfective) Conjugation

Form and Meaning

30.1

The Hebrew conjugations *qtl* and *yqtl* are opposed as perfective (pfv.) and non- a
perfective (non-pfv.). The morphological marking of this aspectual opposition is complex. Many languages mark only one of a given pair of aspects, with a prefix (*mi-* for
Persian imperfective [impfv.]; *pro-*, *na-*, etc., for Russian pfv.) or a suffix (*-zhe* for Chinese progressive). English usually uses a simple verb form for perfective (e.g., 'she read')
and a compound form for progressive (e.g., 'she was reading').[1] The Hebrew opposition
is marked in several ways. The morphological distinction between perfective and non-
perfective is shown by (1) distinct infix patterns (e.g., *qātal-* versus *-qtōl-*), (2) distinct sets
of affixes indicating person (first, second, third), number (singular, plural), and gender
(masculine, feminine), and (3) the use of suffixing (pfv.) versus affixing (both suffixing
and prefixing for non-pfv.). Thus: *qātal-tā* versus *ti-qtōl*, *ti-qtəl-û*. The perfective also
differs from the non-perfective, which is closely related to the various modal and volitional forms (Chap. 34), in not being closely associated with other parts of the verb
system.

---

1. Bernard Comrie, *Aspect: An Introduction to the Study of Verbal Aspect and Related Problems* (Cambridge: Cambridge University, 1976) 88–94.

b   As the names suggest, the *perfective conjugation* is more specialized in meaning than the *non-perfective conjugation*. The suffix form of the verb announces that a certain category (perfectivity) is relevant, while the prefix form does not invoke this category. *Perfectivity* involves viewing a situation as a whole, viewing it globally (29.6). If the verb is fientive, the perfective form refers to an *event*.

c   The perfective and non-perfective conjugations are complementary parts of the verb system. There is an opposite to perfective verb aspect, imperfective; many but not all uses of the Hebrew non-perfective conjugation show imperfective aspect. If a verb is fientive, an imperfective view of it describes a *process* (rather than an event). Imperfectivity directs attention to the internal distinctions of various separate phases making up the situation.[2]

d   Two negative points about perfectivity are important. First, perfectivity does not pertain to the duration of the situation. The situation represented by the perfective form may last a moment or years. This can be made clear by showing both the perfective and non-perfective conjugations being employed in reference to the same extended duration.

1.   וּבְנֵי יִשְׂרָאֵל אָכְלוּ אֶת־הַמָּן
      אַרְבָּעִים שָׁנָה

      The Israelites *ate* (pfv.) manna for forty years.
      Exod 16:35

2.   אַרְבָּעִים שָׁנָה אָקוּט בְּדוֹר

      For forty years I *loathed* (non-pfv.; or, *was loathing*) (that) generation.
      Ps 95:10

When the perfective form gathers together an extended internal situation, we refer to it as a *constative perfect*.[3] Second, the perfective does not emphasize the completedness of a situation. Earlier researchers commonly erred in characterizing the suffix conjugation as indicating completed action, instead of indicating a *complete* situation. Expressed in that erroneous way, the theory that the suffix conjugation indicates perfective aspect is open to objection. In # 3 the suffix form does not represent a completed action.

3.   בִּשְׁנַת שְׁתֵּים־עֶשְׂרֵה שָׁנָה
      לְיוֹרָם . . . מָלַךְ אֲחַזְיָהוּ

      In the twelfth year of Joram . . . Ahaziah *became king*.
      2 Kgs 8:25

---

2. Comrie, *Aspect*, 16. F. Rundgren (cf. 29.6d n. 96) takes a similar view: he designates the suffix conjugation as the marked member, arguing that the prefix conjugation has both a negative value (i.e., imperfective) and a neutral value; see *Das althebräische Verbum: Abriss der Aspektlehre* (Stockholm: Almqvist & Wiksell, 1961) 84–104.

It is generally recognized that the perfective form developed in the West Semitic languages, including Hebrew, from a form cognate to the one known in Akkadian as the permansive (or stative); see G. Bergsträsser, *Introduction to the Semitic Languages*, trans. and sup. Peter T. Daniels (Winona Lake, Indiana: Eisenbrauns, 1983) 20–23; H. Y. Priebatsch, "Der Weg des semitischen Perfekts," *Ugarit-Forschungen* 10 (1978) 337–47. The interpretation of the Akkadian form is, however, so controverted that it can shed little light on the working of the Hebrew system. See J. Huehnergard, "'Stative,' Predicative Form, Pseudo-Verb," *Journal of Near Eastern Studies* 46 (1987) 215–32; and G. Buccellati, "The State of the 'Stative,'" *Fucus: A Semitic/Afrasian Gathering in Remembrance of Albert Ehrman*, ed. Y. L. Arbeitman (Amsterdam: John Benjamins, 1988) 153–89. On the Amarna evidence for the use of the ENWS suffix form, see (in addition to the references at 29.4j n. 71), W. L. Moran, "The Death of ʿAbdi-Aširta," *Eretz-Israel* 9 (1969) 94–99.

3. GB 2. 25 (§ 16b).

We discuss such examples as this one below. The faulty completedness definition also necessitated inventing an abnormal prophetic psychology to explain the prophets' use of the suffix conjugation for future events. Perfective aspect may occur in reference to any time period.[4]

Varieties of Perfective Aspect   30.2

A number of factors, such as the inherent meaning of the verb, adverbial and adjec- a tival modification, and the stative or fientive character of a verb, modify the perfective aspect. The variations caused by these factors may be hidden by the Hebrew conjugation but find overt expression in the richer and more complex English verbal system.

Lexical Variation   30.2.1

The inherent meaning of a word in the larger context of discourse may single out a either the beginning, or the extension, or the end of the internal structure of the situation represented as a single event.

Sometimes the inherent value of a word and the context in which the single situa- b tion is set entail that the perfective form is *ingressive*; that is, it refers to the beginning of the situation.

1a.	מָלַךְ דָּוִד עַל־יִשְׂרָאֵל אַרְבָּעִים שָׁנָה	David *reigned* (constative) over Israel forty years. 1 Kgs 2:11
1b.	בִּשְׁנַת שְׁתֵּים־עֶשְׂרֵה שָׁנָה לְיוֹרָם . . . מָלַךְ אֲחַזְיָהוּ	In the twelfth year of Joram . . . Ahaziah *became king* (ingressive). 2 Kgs 8:25

The perfective form in # 1a is constative, that in # 1b ingressive. Stative verbs, inherently implying duration, when they are used in a perfective situation, often have an ingressive force.

2.	וַיֵּלֶךְ הָלוֹךְ וְגָדֵל עַד כִּי־גָדַל מְאֹד:	And he kept on becoming wealthier until he *became very rich*. Gen 26:13
3.	וְאִם־טָהֲרָה מִזּוֹבָהּ	when she *has become cleansed* from her discharge Lev 15:28

A *constative* meaning, as noted above, may be shown by external modifiers that c extend the internal structure of the perfective situation; in other cases the word's inherent meaning extends the internal temporal structure of a single situation.

---

4. As patterns of verb usage in the Slavonic (or Slavic) languages show; note that "in the East and West Slavonic languages (including Russian, Polish, Czech, but not Bul- garian or Serbo-Croatian), and also in Georgian . . . the Perfective non-Past is primarily a future tense"; Comrie, *Aspect*, 66–67.

4.   וַיִּהְיוּ כָּל־יְמֵי אָדָם אֲשֶׁר־חַי   Altogether, Adam's life comprised 930 years.
      תְּשַׁע מֵאוֹת שָׁנָה וּשְׁלֹשִׁים שָׁנָה   Gen 5:5

5.   אַבְרָם יָשַׁב בְּאֶרֶץ־כְּנָעַן   Abram *dwelt* in Canaan.
                                                  Gen 13:12

d   Other verbs have built into them a telos or terminal point (e.g., 'kill' is telic).

6.   כִּי אִישׁ הָרַגְתִּי לְפִצְעִי   I *kill* a man for wounding me.
                                                  Gen 4:23

A *telic* meaning can be found if the inherent meaning of the word entails that the perfective form represents the end of the internal situation to which the action is pointing. For
example, there is an important difference between 'he was reigning' and 'he was being
made king' with regard to the internal structure of the situation. In the second case,
there eventually comes a point at which the subject enters the state described by 'being
made king' (cf. Dan 9:1). One can inspect the first situation at any point and find the
same action occurring, but inspecting the second at selected intervals before the terminal
point would reveal different actions in progress. The first situation ('was reigning'), in
contrast to the second, has no goal in view. Situations like 'was reigning' are named
atelic, those like 'being made king,' *telic*. Bernard Comrie comments, "A telic situation is
one that involves a process [within a perfective situation] that leads up to a well-defined
terminal point, beyond which the process cannot continue."[5] The perfective form may
signify the attainment of the terminal point of the telic situation.

7.   וַאֲנִי־בָאתִי בִּדְבָרֶיךָ:   And I *came* in response to your words.
                                                  Dan 10:12

30.2.2   Syntactic Variation

a   The perfective form, representing a situation as a single whole, cannot by itself
represent internal structuring; however, by means of modifiers a single event can be
unfolded into parts.

1.   וְלֹא־קָרַב זֶה אֶל־זֶה כָּל־   And the one *did* not *approach* the other all night
        הַלָּיְלָה: long.
                                              Exod 14:20

The single situation in which the pillar of cloud stood between the two opposing armies
of Israel and Egypt is broken up in space by זה . . . זה and in time by כל־הלילה.
Similarly, בבקר בבקר in the next example extends the action in view.

2.   וְהֵם הֵבִיאוּ אֵלָיו עוֹד נְדָבָה   And they *continued to bring* to him freewill offerings
        בַּבֹּקֶר בַּבֹּקֶר: every morning.
                                              Exod 36:3

---

5. Comrie, *Aspect*, 45.

Sometimes a perfective situation is represented by a point (.) in contrast to an   b
imperfective situation, which is represented by either a series of points (....) or a line
(_____). Comrie suggests rather that we view the perfective situation as a blob:

> Since the notion of a point seems to preclude internal complexity, a more helpful
> metaphor would perhaps be to say that the perfective reduces a situation to a blob,
> rather than to a point: a blob is a three-dimensional object, and can therefore have
> internal complexity, although it is nonetheless a single object with clearly circum-
> scribed limits.[6]

Stative *versus* Fientive   30.2.3

Stative verbs differ from fientive ones by capturing the subject in a state of being   a
rather than in a state of activity (22.2.1).[7] We have observed that English uses its progressive
construction with fientive verbs (e.g., 'he is running,' imperfective *versus* 'he runs,' perfective) but not with statives (e.g., 'he knows' but not 'he is knowing'). With fientive
verbs the dynamic situation only continues as long as the subject or agent continually
puts new energy into it, whereas in static situations no effort is required on its part (e.g.,
'he fills,' dynamic *versus* 'he is full,' stative). Further, in dynamic situations the internal
structure of the situation entails different phases, but this is generally not so in static
situations, where the internal phases tend to be uniform. If we say 'God formed the man,'
the dynamic situation entails that God took up the clay, molded the flesh, etc., but if we
say 'she fears' (stative) or 'he knows best' (quasi-fientive), the internal structure of the
situation is the same wherever we inspect it.

When a durative state is expressed by a verb with a perfective aspect, the focus may   b
be on the inceptual moment (ingressive perfective) or on both inception and continuation
(constative perfective). Either way a certain dynamism is entailed, for reference to the internal structure of the situation implies some change. Thus even a stative situation may
become an event.

Perfective Aspect and the Perfect State   30.3

The terms *perfective* and *perfect* are used in different senses. By perfect (abbreviated   a
pf.) we mean a past, present, or future state related to a preceding situation or a past
situation relevant to a continuing later state. Contrast, for example, these two sentences.

1.	וְהָאָרֶץ הָיְתָה תֹהוּ וָבֹהוּ	Now the earth *was* chaotic. Gen 1:2
2.	הֵן הָאָדָם הָיָה כְּאַחַד מִמֶּנּוּ	Adam *has become* as one of us. Gen 3:22

---

6. Comrie, *Aspect*, 18.
7. See Comrie, *Aspect*, 48–51; F. R. Blake, "The So-
called Intransitive Verbal Forms in Hebrew," *Journal of
the American Oriental Society* 24 (1903) 145–204. For

another approach to the material, see T. L. Fenton, "The
Hebrew 'Tenses' in the Light of Ugaritic," *Proceedings of
the Fifth World Congress of Jewish Studies* (Jerusalem:
World Union of Jewish Studies, 1973), 4. 31–39.

In # 1 a single situation is in view; in # 2 there are two things in view, both an earlier situation and the resulting state. It would change the sense of both verses radically if we interpreted them vice versa.

b   Traditionally the perfect has been characterized as a tense. In fact, however, it represents a state flowing from an earlier situation, and it therefore seems better to think of it as a nuance that may be related to aspect. Since the perfect nuance, with its double focus on past event and present state, seems at first glance to differ significantly from the other uses of the perfective conjugation, it may seem incredible to speakers of English, which may formally distinguish the perfect notion, that speakers of Hebrew tolerated such diversity to be wrapped up in one conjugation. How can the same form represent such divergent situations as are found in, for example, ## 1–2? Perhaps we can dispel our incredulity by noting that in both Greek and English perfect forms come very close to other, tensed verb forms in actual usage. Indeed, in Modern Greek the perfect and the aorist of the classical language have practically blended, and in English the use of the perfect is often optional. Compare, for example, two translations of the clause וּשְׁמוּאֵל מֵת (1 Sam 28:3): 'Now Samuel had died' (RSV), and 'Now Samuel was dead' (NIV, AV). In this example RSV gives overt expression to the perfect notion, whereas AV and NIV allow the reader to infer it. Similarly, when the perfect sense is relevant Hebrew employs the perfective form and allows other contextual considerations to indicate that a resulting state attended the situation. The more time-oriented English language, in contrast to Hebrew, may distinguish between past perfect, present perfect, and future perfect states. Contrast, for example, these cases.

3. וְהַגָּדִי לָקְחוּ נַחֲלָתָם אֲשֶׁר נָתַן
    לָהֶם מֹשֶׁה
    The Gadites took the inheritance Moses *had given* them.
    Josh 13:8

4. וְלָמָּה נָפְלוּ פָנֶיךָ:
    Why *has* your countenance *fallen*?
    Gen 4:6

5. וּבֵרַכְתָּ אֶת־יהוה אֱלֹהֶיךָ עַל־
    הָאָרֶץ הַטֹּבָה אֲשֶׁר נָתַן־לָךְ:
    And you will bless Yʜwʜ your God in the good land he *will have given* you.
    Deut 8:10

6. וַאדֹנָי יהוה יַעֲזָר־לִי . . . עַל־כֵּן
    שַׂמְתִּי פָנַי כַּחַלָּמִישׁ
    My Master Yʜwʜ will help me, . . . therefore, I *have set* my face like flint.
    Isa 50:7

Here we see the same Hebrew conjugation rendered by the three perfect tenses of English. Speakers of English, in a less formal register, tend to replace the past and future perfects with the simple past and future tenses, and, like Hebrew, allow listeners to infer the more precise perfect notion from the context. We could just as well render # 3 by '. . . Moses *gave* them' and # 5 by '. . . the good land he *will give* you.' Perfectivity is a part of the Hebrew verb system; the perfect notion is one that can be explicit in English and one that is relevant to actions described in Hebrew. Thus if we talk about a perfective verb having a perfect meaning, we are talking about interpretation or about translation, a special form of interpretation.[8]

Perfective Aspect and Time Reference   **30.4**

The time frame in which a perfective situation occurs influences the significance of   a
the form. Referring to past time the perfective form signifies completed events. Clear
temporal modifiers can characterize Hebrew narrative of past events.

Sometimes the perfective conjugation is used for *present-time situations*. This com-   b
bination creates notional tensions because the form entails a single aspect, but present
time tends to entail imperfective aspect. We gain insight into this use of the Hebrew perfective from the Bulgarian form which overtly expresses both perfective aspect and
present tense. The form in question may be used with habitual meaning in the sense that
a single instance exemplifies a recurrent situation. Comrie illustrates this use and explains it:

> The Present Tense is used to express a habitual situation by presenting one instance to
> exemplify the recurrent situation, as in: *spoglednat* (Pfv. Present) *se, pousmixnat* (Pfv.
> Present) *devojki, ponadevat* (Pfv. Present) *zarumeni lica . . .* 'the girls look at one
> another, smile at one another, incline their reddened faces. . . .' The sense is not, how-
> ever, that this is what they are doing at the present moment, but rather that this is
> what happens whenever a certain set of circumstances holds (and, indeed, it is quite
> likely that this particular set of circumstances does not hold precisely at the present
> moment).[9]

Hebrew may use its perfective form with the same, present/habitual significance ("the
gnomic perfective").

1. וְתֹר . . . וְעָגוּר שָׁמְרוּ אֶת־עֵת   The dove . . . and the bulbul *observe* the time of
    בֹּאָנָה   their migration.[10]
    Jer 8:7

Hebrew also uses its perfective form for a present situation in which a speaker resolves on
a future action (hence, "perfective of resolve"). The Bulgarian perfective present has a use
somewhat similar to this one: *iskam da kupja* (perfective present) *kniga*, 'I-want that
I-buy book.'

We have already noted that in other languages which are aspectually oriented the   c
perfective aspect may be associated with *future situations*. The same holds for Hebrew.
Temporal indicators mark the future time in which the temporal situation occurs.[11]

---

8. The matter of mood is similar. A speaker may have in mind an irreal perfective situation. The suffix conjugation indicates the perfective sense, while other markers in the context signify the mood. In English, by contrast, the form of the verb itself signifies the mood.

9. Comrie, *Aspect*, 69–70.

10. For the birds, see W. L. Holladay, *Jeremiah* (Philadelphia: Fortress, 1986), 1. 280.

11. J. A. Hughes would argue that it is the particle ʿd-mty in #2 that signifies the tense; "Another Look at the Hebrew Tenses," *Journal of Near Eastern Studies* 29 (1970) 12–24; cf. *LHS* 265.

2.   עַד־מָתַי מֵאַנְתָּ לֵעָנֹת מִפָּנָי   How long *will* you *refuse* to humble yourself before
me?
Exod 10:3

d   Both the suffix and prefix conjugations may be used in connection with absolute
future time. How do they differ? The suffix conjugation marks the situation as complete:
the prefix conjugation does not do so, but rather marks the situation as dependent.
Representing a future action or situation as complete and independent leads to a certain
dramatic quality of representation.

30.5   Species of Perfective Usage

a   The rich English verbal system often overtly expresses nuances associated with factors analyzed above. In this section we attempt to relate to the English verbal system
various nuances potentially proper to the Hebrew perfective form. We also expose other
nuances not formally represented in English. (We often allow the illustrations themselves
to suggest the ways in which the perfective situation might be rendered in English.)

30.5.1   Fientive Verbs

a   Perfective forms of *fientive verbs* may refer to any block of time, past, present, or
future.

b   *Past-time reference* is shown either by particles such as *waw*-relative (combined with
other verbs in the context) or by adverbial modifiers. The perfective sense may be *definite*
("*preterite*"; ## 1–2), *ingressive* (# 3), *constative* (# 4), *complex* (# 5), or *telic* (# 6).

1.   וְלַחֹשֶׁךְ קָרָא לָיְלָה   He *called* the darkness "Night."
Gen 1:5

2.   וַתְּכַחֵשׁ שָׂרָה לֵאמֹר לֹא צָחַקְתִּי   Sarah lied and said, "I *did* not *laugh*."
Gen 18:15

3.   מִן־הַיּוֹם הָרִאשׁוֹן אֲשֶׁר נָתַתָּ   from the first day that you *set* your heart to
אֶת־לִבְּךָ לְהָבִין   understand
Dan 10:12

4.   שְׁתֵּים עֶשְׂרֵה שָׁנָה עָבְדוּ אֶת־   For twelve years they *served* Chedorlaomer.
כְּדָרְלָעֹמֶר   Gen 14:4

5.   וַיְהִי מִדֵּי צֵאתָם שָׂכַל דָּוִד מִכֹּל   As often as they came out, David *met with* more
עַבְדֵי שָׁאוּל   *success* than all the (other) servants of Saul.
1 Sam 18:30

6.   אֲשֶׁר־מְכַרְתֶּם אֹתִי מִצְרָיְמָה: the one whom you *sold* (me) into Egypt
Gen 45:4

When the perfective form represents a situation that occurred in the recent past, English idiom often requires the use of the auxiliary 'has/have.'[12] Though the form appears to be perfect, the idea is simple past ("*recent perfective*").

7.	וַיֹּאמֶר מֶה עָשִׂיתָ	And he said, "What *have* you *done*?" Gen 4:10
8.	הַיּוֹם הַזֶּה רָאִינוּ	Today we *have seen*. . . . Deut 5:21
9.	אֲנִי הַיּוֹם יְלִדְתִּיךָ:	Today I *have begotten* you. Ps 2:7

The perfective form may represent a past situation which the speaker is either unwilling or unable to specify precisely ("*indefinite perfective*"). For this use, too, English idiom normally adds the auxiliary 'has/have.'[13]

10.	תַּאֲוַת לִבּוֹ נָתַתָּה לּוֹ	You *have given* him his heart's desire. Ps 21:3
11.	רָאִיתִי רָשָׁע עָרִיץ	I *have seen* a ruthless wicked person. Ps 37:35

The context may suggest an emphasis on the uniqueness of an act in the indefinite past. In this case, the translation may be assisted by adding an English adverb, 'ever' or 'never.'

12.	אֶת־שׁוֹר מִי לָקַחְתִּי	Whose ox *have* I *ever taken*? 1 Sam 12:3
13.	מִי־שָׁמַע כָּזֹאת	Who *has ever heard* such a thing? Isa 66:8
14.	לֹא־נִהְיְתָה וְלֹא־נִרְאֲתָה כָּזֹאת	Such a thing *has never been seen* or *done*. Judg 19:30
15.	קֶשֶׁת יְהוֹנָתָן לֹא נָשׂוֹג אָחוֹר	The bow of Jonathan *never turned* back. 2 Sam 1:22

A number of Hebrew perfective uses can be correlated with *present-time reference*   c as it is understood in English; it should be borne in mind that the English simple present tense is rarely used to refer to present time. In the *persistent (present) perfective*, the suffix conjugation represents a single situation that started in the past but continues (persists) into the present. English often uses its perfect form here but in fact the form does not juxtapose a past situation with a present state.

---

12. On this and the next several points, see both Joüon § 112c–e / pp. 296–97 and S. R. Driver, *A Treatise on the Use of the Tenses in Hebrew* (3d ed.; Oxford: Clarendon, 1892) 14–16.

13. Comrie refers to the "experiential perfect," which indicates "that a given situation has held at least once during some time in the past leading up to the present"; *Aspect*, 58.

16. לִי לֹא נָתַתָּה זָּרַע   You *have* not *given* me children.
Gen 15:3

17. וְאָנֹכִי לֹא־חָטָאתִי לָךְ   I *have* not *wronged* you [from the past right up to now].
Judg 11:27

18. לְטוֹבָה כֹּל אֲשֶׁר־עָשִׂיתִי   for all the good which I *have done*
Neh 5:19

The *gnomic* or *proverbial perfective* in Hebrew often corresponds to present-tense forms in English.[14]

19. כָּלָה עָנָן   (as) a cloud *vanishes*
Job 7:9

20. יָבֵשׁ חָצִיר נָבֵל צִיץ   Grass *withers*, flowers *fade*.
Isa 40:7

d   An *instantaneous perfective* represents a situation occurring at the very instant the expression is being uttered. This use appears chiefly with *verba dicendi* ('verbs of speaking,' swearing, declaring, advising, etc.) or gestures associated with speaking.

21. הִגַּדְתִּי הַיּוֹם   I *declare* today. . . .
Deut 26:3

22. כִּי יָעַצְתִּי   I *advise* you. . . .
2 Sam 17:11

23. אָמַרְתִּי אַתָּה וְצִיבָא תַּחְלְקוּ   I *order* that you and Ziba divide up the land.
אֶת־הַשָּׂדֶה: 2 Sam 19:30

24. הֲרִימֹתִי יָדִי אֶל־יְהוָה   I *lift* my hand to Yнwн.
Gen 14:22

25. פֵּרַשְׂתִּי יָדַי אֵלֶיךָ   I *spread out* my hands to you.
Ps 143:6

This use of the perfective form also occurs with other kinds of words.

26. כִּי קָנִיתִי   I *acquire* (here and now).[15]
Ruth 4:9

27. הִשְׁתַּחֲוֵיתִי   I *humbly bow*.
2 Sam 16:4

28. וַיֹּאמֶר אֲרַוְנָה . . . הַכֹּל נָתַן   Araunah said, . . . "Araunah *gives* all . . . to the king."
אֲרַוְנָה . . . לַמֶּלֶךְ   2 Sam 24:22–23

---

14. Driver, *Tenses in Hebrew*, 17.   15. Cf. Ruth 4:4; Driver, *Tenses in Hebrew*, 17.

An *epistolary perfective* represents a situation in past time from the viewpoint of the recipient of a message.[16] To judge from the use of "epistolary aorist" in Latin and Greek, the writer uses the perfective form in this context as a delicate courtesy—he assumes the perspective of the recipient and thus regards the communique as having been sent in the past. English idiom, however, employs a present progressive form, a form that obscures the force of the Hebrew.

29a.	שָׁלַחְתִּי לְךָ שֹׁחַד	I *am sending* you a gift. 1 Kgs 15:19
29b.	שָׁלַחְתִּי אִישׁ־חָכָם	I *am sending* a craftsman. 2 Chr 2:12

The epistolary perfective may be seen as a special case of the instantaneous perfective. Another, overlapping subtype is the *performative*, in which not only are speaking and acting simultaneous, they are identical.[17] Of the examples above # 23 is performative, and ## 26 and 28 (*ntn*) probably are also. Another present-time use of the suffix conjugation is the *perfective of resolve*.

30.	מָכְרָה נָעֳמִי	Naomi *is going to sell*. . . . Ruth 4:3
31.	וַיַּעַן עֶפְרוֹן הַחִתִּי אֶת־אַבְרָהָם . . . הַשָּׂדֶה נָתַתִּי לָךְ . . . וַיְדַבֵּר אֶל־עֶפְרוֹן . . . נָתַתִּי כֶּסֶף הַשָּׂדֶה	And Ephron the Hittite replied to Abraham . . . , "I *will give* you the field. . . ." And he (Abraham) said to Ephron . . . , "I *will pay* the price of the field." Gen 23:10–11, 13
32.	פְּתַחְתִּיךָ הַיּוֹם מִן־הָאזִקִּים	I *will release* you from your chains today. Jer 40:4

Referring to absolute future time, a perfective form may be *persistent* or *accidental*.[18] A *persistent (future) perfective* represents a single situation extending from the present into the future.

e

---

16. See Dennis Pardee, "The 'Epistolary Perfect' in Hebrew Letters," *Biblische Notizen* 22 (1983) 34–40; Pardee and R. M. Whiting, "Aspects of Epistolary Verbal Usage in Ugaritic and Akkadian," *Bulletin of the School of Oriental and African Studies* 50 (1987) 1–31; cf. *LHS* 265.

17. A test for performativity in English is provided by 'hereby'; contrast 'I hereby renounce title to the estates' and 'I renounce title to the estates by marrying the woman I love.' On performativity, see Pardee and Whiting, "Epistolary Verbal Usage," 23–31; E. Talstra, "Text Grammar and Hebrew Bible. II. Syntax and Semantics," *Bibliotheca Orientalis* 39 (1982) 26–38. D. R. Hillers, in "Some Performative Utterances in Biblical Hebrew" (unpublished), has a

fairly full list, including the following examples from roots that are not entirely obvious candidates for performativity: ʾhb 'to love, declare allegiance to' (Exod 21:5), bḥr 'to choose' (Hag 2:23), ḥrp 'to defy' (1 Sam 17:10), nsk 'to appoint' (Ps 2:6), ʿbr Hiphil (Zech 3:4), and pqd Hiphil (Jer 1:10). Many of the instantaneous perfectives noted here may be taken as performatives.

18. Cf. Joüon § 112g–i / pp. 298–300; *LHS* 265. The role of what B. Zuber calls the "uncertainty at first blush" of the sense of certain forms would be worth exploring; see *Das Tempussystem des biblischen Hebräisch* (Beiheft zur Zeitschrift für die Alttestamentliche Wissenschaft 164; Berlin: de Gruyter, 1985) 140–41.

33. עַד־מָתַי מֵאַנְתָּ לֵעָנֹת מִפָּנָי

Until when *will* you *refuse* to humble yourself before me?
Exod 10:3

With an *accidental perfective* a speaker vividly and dramatically represents a future situation both as complete and as independent.

34. וּלְיִשְׁמָעֵאל . . . הִנֵּה בֵּרַ֫כְתִּי אֹתוֹ

And concerning Ishmael . . . I *will bless* him.
Gen 17:20

35. אִשְּׁר֫וּנִי בָּנוֹת

Women *will call* me *happy*.
Gen 30:13

36. הֵן גָּוַ֫עְנוּ אָבַ֫דְנוּ כֻּלָּ֫נוּ אָבָֽדְנוּ׃

We *will die*. We *are lost*, we *are* all *lost*.
Num 17:27

This use is especially frequent in prophetic address (hence it is also called the "prophetic perfect" or "perfective of confidence").

37. אֶרְאֶ֫נּוּ וְלֹא עַתָּה אֲשׁוּרֶ֫נּוּ וְלֹא קָרוֹב דָּרַךְ כּוֹכָב מִיַּעֲקֹב

I see him, but not now; I behold him, but not near. A star *will come* out of Jacob.
Num 24:17

38. כָּעֵת הָרִאשׁוֹן הֵקַל . . . וְהָאַחֲרוֹן הִכְבִּיד . . . הָעָם הַהֹלְכִים בַּחֹ֫שֶׁךְ רָאוּ אוֹר גָּדוֹל

In the past he humbled . . . in the future he will honor. . . . The people walking in darkness *will see* a great light.
Isa 8:23–9:1

30.5.2 Fientive Verbs, Perfect State

a   The various uses of the perfective form in connection with the perfect state are revealed clearly by the time-oriented character of the English verbal system.

b   The *past perfect* (*pluperfect*) signifies a resulting state in time that is past relative to the speaker. This use is frequent in (1) relative, causal, or temporal clauses, when the main clause pertains to a past situation (## 1–2) and (2) after a *waw*-disjunctive introducing parenthetical material (# 3).

1. וַיָּ֫שָׁב יִצְחָק וַיַּחְפֹּר אֶת־בְּאֵרֹת הַמַּ֫יִם אֲשֶׁר חָפְרוּ בִּימֵי אַבְרָהָם

Isaac reopened the wells which *had been dug* in the time of Abraham.
Gen 26:18

2. וְלֹא־יָדַע יַעֲקֹב כִּי רָחֵל גְּנָבָתַם׃

Jacob did not know that Rachel *had stolen* them.
Gen 31:32

3. וּשְׁמוּאֵל מֵת . . . וְשָׁאוּל הֵסִיר הָאֹבוֹת

Now Samuel *had died* . . . and Saul *had put away* those that had a familiar spirit.
1 Sam 28:3

The *present perfect* signifies a resulting perfect state in present time relative to the speaker.

4. אָמַר בְּלִבּוֹ שָׁכַח אֵל הִסְתִּיר פָּנָיו

He says to himself, "God *has forgotten*; he *has covered* his face."
Ps 10:11

5. אֱלֹהִים זְנַחְתָּנוּ

God, you *have rejected* us.
Ps 60:3

The *future perfect* signifies a resulting perfect state in future time relative to the speaker. In Hebrew, this use of the perfective form is especially frequent with עד and compounds with it (e.g., עַד אֲשֶׁר אִם ,עַד אִם).

6. כִּי לֹא אֶעֱזָבְךָ עַד אֲשֶׁר אִם־
עָשִׂיתִי אֵת אֲשֶׁר־דִּבַּרְתִּי לָךְ:

I will not leave you until I *shall have done* what I promised you.
Gen 28:15

7. וְהִצְלִיחַ עַד־כָּלָה זַעַם

He will be successful until (the time of) wrath *is completed*.
Dan 11:36

8. וְנִבְחַר מָוֶת . . . בְּכָל־הַמְּקֹמוֹת
. . . אֲשֶׁר הִדַּחְתִּים שָׁם

They will prefer death . . . in all the places . . . I *shall have driven* them.
Jer 8:3

Stative Verbs

30.5.3

The perfective form of stative verbs can signify most of the uses suggested for fientive verbs, but statives present a special set of problems in the perfective form. A stative inherently denotes a situation with an extended internal structure, while a perfective form conceptualizes a situation from without, as a single whole. In this section we are concerned only with those points of grammar unique to statives. Before turning to the suffix conjugation's more precise nuances in stative situations, we should note first that translation in these situations depends on the nature of the verb. Statives can be analyzed into three kinds: (1) those that denote an adjectival quality without taking an object, which often take a copula verb plus adjective in English (e.g., 'I *am unworthy* [קָטֹנְתִּי] of any love,' Gen 32:11); (2) those that denote a quality and take a complementary object (10.2.1), which are often translated like those without an object (e.g., 'your hands *are full* [מָלֵאוּ] of blood,' Isa 1:15); and (3) quasi-fientives (22.2.3), those that exhibit both stative and fientive characteristics; these denote a mental or psychological state *and* take an object (e.g., 'Israel loved [אָהַב] Joseph,' Gen 37:3). The relationship between these three kinds of statives can be seen in the English trio: 'she is afraid,' 'she is afraid of him,' 'she fears him.'

a

The uses of the suffix forms of statives are similar to those of fientives. In *past time* a stative situation may be telic (## 1–3), ingressive (## 4–6), or constative (## 7–8). These situations take on a somewhat dynamic quality because the reference is to an event; the dynamic quality increases when the verb is transitive (viz., quasi-fientive; # 7).

b

1.   כָּלָה הַבַּיִת   The temple *was finished.*
                          1 Kgs 6:38

2.   כָּלוּ בֶעָשָׁן כָּלוּ׃   They *vanish,* in smoke, they *vanish.*
                          Ps 37:20

3.   כִּי־כָלְתָה הָרָעָה מֵעִמּוֹ׃   (An) evil (fate) *has been determined* by him.
                          1 Sam 20:7

4.   וְאַבְרָהָם זָקֵן   Abraham *had become old.*
                          Gen 24:1

5.   וְעֵינֵי יִשְׂרָאֵל כָּבְדוּ מִזֹּקֶן   Israel's eyes *became heavy* because of old age.
                          Gen 48:10

6.   גַּם־רָעֵב וְאֵין כֹּחַ   He *got hungry* and had no strength.
                          Isa 44:12

7.   וְלֹא זָכְרוּ . . . אֶת־יהוה   They *did* not *remember* . . . Yhwh.
                          Judg 8:34

8.   וְאָנֹכִי לֹא יָדָעְתִּי׃   I *was* not *aware* (of it).
                          Gen 28:16

c   In a *present-time frame,* stative situations may be similar to those encountered in dynamic situations. The situation, for example, may be gnomic (## 9–10; # 10 is also ingressive).

9.   חָכָם יָרֵא וְסָר מֵרָע   The wise man *fears* (Yhwh) and *shuns* evil.
                          Prov 14:16

10. כְּפִירִים רָשׁוּ וְרָעֵבוּ   The lions *grow weak* and *hungry.*
                          Ps 34:11

In the *adjectival present perfective,* the use of the verb form directs attention to the subject's involvement more than would a comparable construction with an adjective (27.1c).

11. מַה־יָּפִית   How *lovely* you *are!*
                          Cant 7:7

12. וְיֶלֶד זְקֻנִים קָטָן   The son born to him in his old age *is young.*
                          Gen 44:20

Stative verbs denoting an effected state in the perfective may be ingressive in past time (# 4) or may signify a present state that implicitly came about through an earlier situation (## 13–15). In this use it approximates the perfect state, which refers to the preceding situation as bringing about the effected state. We can argue indirectly that stative verbs in the suffix conjugation may signify a present (effected) state by noting the historical connection in many languages between the perfective tense and the passive voice, and between the passive voice and stative forms. Comrie has shown that the perfect state and passive voice frequently go together because both refer to such an effected state. He also notes that "the older forms of the passive in many languages are likewise stative."[19] This historical connection displayed in many languages suggests that stative verbs in the perfective represent a present state and not a perfect event.

13.	לָבְשׁוּ כָרִים הַצֹּאן	The meadows *are covered* with flocks. Ps 65:14
14.	יְדֵיכֶם דָּמִים מָלֵאוּ׃	Your hands *are full* of blood. Isa 1:15
15.	זָקַנְתִּי לֹא יָדַעְתִּי יוֹם מוֹתִי׃	I *am old* (or, *have become old*) and *do* not *know* the day of my death (i.e., I may die any day now). Gen 27:2

The *durative stative perfective* is found with quasi-fientive verbs, indicating an ongoing emotional response.

| 16. | כַּאֲשֶׁר אָהַבְתִּי | such as I *love* Gen 27:4 |
| 17. | דְּבַר־הַתֹּעֵבָה הַזֹּאת אֲשֶׁר שָׂנֵאתִי׃ | this detestable thing I *hate* Jer 44:4 |

Irreal Mood   **30.5.4**

The perfective form does not denote mood, either real (i.e., indicative in Greek and   a
Latin) or irreal (i.e., subjunctive, optative, or imperative in the classical languages). These notions are communicated in Hebrew by particles or other features in the context, but perfective verbs are often used in such contexts.

Hypothetical ('if') clauses use the perfective in (1) contrary-to-fact sentences (## 1–3),   b
(2) clauses of hypothetical assertion (# 4), and (3) expressions of a wish that is not expected to be realized (# 5). In contrary-to-fact sentences, the second ('then') clause also uses a perfective. We may presume that the suffix conjugation in a conditional clause has a perfective value even though that value is not obvious. Thomas O. Lambdin is dubious about such a view:

> It is always possible to justify the use of the perfect in the protasis ['if'-clause] as representing a completed action of accomplished state in the mind of the speaker. It is difficult within Hebrew itself to predict the choice between the perfect and the imperfect in the construction with the same meaning. Whatever the original distinction was, it has become obscured in Hebrew of the biblical period, so that both verbs will have, in general, the same range of translational values.[20]

It seems unlikely that the conjugations, otherwise distinct, became confused in this one class of sentences, though that is possible.

19. Comrie, *Aspect*, 86.   20. T. O. Lambdin, *Introduction to Biblical Hebrew* (New York: Scribner, 1971) 277.

1. כִּי לוּלֵא הִתְמַהְמָ֫הְנוּ כִּי־עַתָּה
    שַׁ֫בְנוּ זֶה פַעֲמָ֫יִם:
    If we *had* not *delayed*, we *could have* [gone and] *returned* twice.
    Gen 43:10

2. לוּ הַחֲיִתֶם אוֹתָם לֹא הָרַ֫גְתִּי
    אֶתְכֶם:
    If you *had spared* their lives, I *would* not *kill* you.
    Judg 8:19

3. לוּ חָפֵץ יהוה לַהֲמִיתֵ֫נוּ לֹא־
    לָקַח מִיָּדֵ֫נוּ עֹלָה
    If Yhwh *had meant to kill* us, he *would* not *have accepted* from our hands a burnt offering.
    Judg 13:23

4. כִּמְעַט שָׁכַב אַחַד הָעָם אֶת־
    אִשְׁתֶּ֫ךָ
    One of the people easily *might have slept* with your wife.
    Gen 26:10

5. לוּ־מַ֫תְנוּ בְּאֶ֫רֶץ מִצְרַ֫יִם
    If only we *had died* in Egypt!
    Num 14:2

c   A distinctive use of the irreal perfective is the *precative perfective* or perfective of prayer. In contrast to the use of the perfective form for situations which the speaker expresses as a wish without expectation of fulfillment, the perfective can be used with reference to situations the speaker prays for and expects to be realized. This use of the perfective form can be recognized by the presence of other unambiguous forms in the context signifying a volitional mood.[21] As Moses Buttenwieser has noted, this use of the perfective was recognized over a century ago by Heinrich Ewald and F. Böttcher. Such a use is known in several of the cognate Semitic languages: in Aramaic, Arabic, and Ugaritic.[22] According to H. L. Ginsberg, "one of the original functions of the perfect was that of an optative and precative."[23] S. R. Driver cautioned against basing the case for this Hebrew use on the Arabic evidence because in Arabic the form in question all but universally stands first in the sentence; for this reason he ruled out the possibility that the suffix conjugation could be used in Hebrew as a precative.[24] But far more significant than the Arabic word order is the fact that Arabic uses the form in connection with the volitional mood.

d   The precative perfective can be recognized contextually; Buttenwieser set forth the conditions: "The precative perfect proper . . . is invariably found alternating with the imperfect or the imperative; it is by this outward sign that the precative perfect may unfailingly be identified."[25] Unfortunately several modern translations and editions of the Bible ignore this point or waffle on it.[26] Once this use is admitted, it would be far

---

21. This discussion follows Moses Buttenwieser, *The Psalms: Chronologically Treated with a New Translation* (Chicago: University of Chicago, 1938) 18–25.

22. See Buttenwieser, *Psalms*, 21–23; *UT* § 13.28. In Inscriptional Hebrew, note the precative perfective in M. O'Connor, "The Poetic Inscription from Khirbet el-Qôm," *Vetus Testamentum* 37 (1987) 224–30.

23. H. L. Ginsberg, "The Rebellion and Death of Baᶜlu," *Orientalia* 5 (1936) 161–98, at 177.

24. Driver, *Tenses in Hebrew*, 25–26; so also GKC § 106n n. 2 / p. 312.

25. Buttenwieser, *Psalms*, 21.

26. In some obvious passages, e.g., the 1978 edition of the NIV concedes its use, but unless the context absolutely demands a precative sense, it translates the perfective as a past; compare Ps 3:8 and 4:2. (The inconsistency was corrected in 1984.) In Ps 7:7, the MT has *hinnāśēʾ*, and *BHS* considers *wəhinnāśēʾ*.

better to follow Buttenwieser's observations. Some exegetes, too, force some other uses of the perfective form on the text. No reason exists to deny this use of the suffix conjugation when all recognize that it is used in connection with hypothetical conditions. Why should it be strange that the perfective is used in prayers? This use occurs about twenty times, in the Psalms.

6.   בְּקָרְאִי עֲנֵנִי אֱלֹהֵי צִדְקִי
                 בַּצָּר הִרְחַבְתָּ לִּי
             חָנֵּנִי וּשְׁמַע תְּפִלָּתִי׃

When I cry out, answer me, O my righteous God.
In my distress, *bring* me *relief*.
Be gracious to me and hear my prayer.[27]
Ps 4:2

7.   הוֹשִׁיעֵנִי מִפִּי אַרְיֵה וּמִקַּרְנֵי
                    רֵמִים עֲנִיתָנִי׃

Rescue me from the mouth of the lions, *save* me from the horns of the wild oxen.
Ps 22:22

8. . . . תּוֹצִיאֵנִי מֵרֶשֶׁת זוּ טָמְנוּ לִי
        פָּדִיתָה אוֹתִי יהוה אֵל אֱמֶת׃

Free me from the trap that is set for me. . . .
Redeem me, O YHWH, the God of truth.
Ps 31:5–6

---

27. RSV renders, following the usual sense of the perfective, against the sense of the passage, 'Answer me. . . . Thou hast given me room. . . . Be gracious to me, and hear. . . .' *BHS* proposes two emendations of *hirḥábtā*. In fact, the verb is precative, as, e.g., M. Dahood notes in *Psalms I: 1–50* (Anchor Bible 16; Garden City, New York: Doubleday, 1966) 23.

31

Prefix (Non-Perfective) Conjugation

31.1   Form and Meaning

a   The non-perfective conjugation has a broader range of meaning than the perfective. It is also historically a more complex form, both in itself and in relation to the jussive and cohortative moods. Some of the history of the verbal system is outlined in Chapter 29; we must, however, take up the topic again before proposing a working view of the Biblical Hebrew non-perfective.[1]

31.1.1   A Historical View

a   The Amarna letters from Byblos, from the fourteenth century B.C.E., provide what is often judged a reliable guide to a verbal system like the one possessed by Biblical Hebrew's ancestor (29.4). Byblian Canaanite has at least three prefix conjugations, including *yaqtulu* and *yaqtul*, the forms of interest here, and subjunctive *yaqtula*, the antecedent to the Hebrew cohortative. (Amarna Canaanite and other forms of ENWS show traces of an energic pattern, too, related to the Arabic heavy energic *yaqtulanna*

---

1. For bibliography, see the notes to 29.4 and 29.6.

and the light energic *yaqtulan*.)[2] These forms help to explain the background of various Biblical Hebrew forms.

On the usual understanding, an understanding based on comparative Semitic grammar, the longer form, *yaqtulu*, signifies (1) the present-future and (2) the iterative past in main clauses, and (3) is used in subordinate or circumstantial clauses. The shorter form, *yaqtul*, signifies usually jussive mood or preterite action, commonly when bound with *waw*-relative and rarely when free. These two forms would have largely fallen together when *yaqtulu* lost its final short vowel, *u*. It has been argued that formal vestiges of the distinction between two such prefix conjugations survive in the *Hiphil* stem of the regular verb: *yaqtîl* (signifying the non-perfective values associated with *yaqtulu*) versus *yāqtēl* (signifying the jussive value of *yaqtul* in its free form and the preterite value of *yaqtul* when bound with *waw*-relative). Similar distinctions occur in the *Qal* stem with III-*he* verbs (*yibnéh* [corresponding to *yaqtulu*] versus *yíben* [corresponding to *yaqtul*]); with hollow verbs (i.e., II-*waw*/*yodh*; *yāqûm* [non-perfective] versus *yā́qom* [jussive/preterite with relative *waw*]); and with geminate verbs (*yāsṓb* [non-perfective] versus *yā́sōb* [jussive/preterite with relative *waw*]).[3]

If this historical reconstruction of the "proto-Hebrew" prefix conjugations be correct, then the jussive value of the historical short form *yaqtul* was associated with the later morphologically unified conjugation. As we explained in 29.4, the correctness of this reconstruction and its relevance to Biblical Hebrew have been doubted. To the question, Did the preterite value of *yaqtul* become a part of the later, largely morphologically unified prefix conjugation of Hebrew, Hans Bauer, Gotthelf Bergsträsser, and others have answered affirmatively. But Carl Brockelmann, Diethelm Michel, and others have denied that the prefix conjugation, whether in its free form or bound with relative *waw*, signifies a preterite notion (i.e., serves as a past perfective form).

The following arguments, based on Hebrew usage, favor the view that (some part of) the prefix conjugation may denote preterite action. (1) If we accept the view that the *jussive value* of *yaqtul* was incorporated into the prefix conjugation, then we might expect that the preterite value of *yaqtul* was also part of the conjugation. (2) The prefix conjugation *bound with waw-relative*, the form that most clearly shows its probable historical origin in *yaqtul*, most frequently seems to refer to preterite action. (3) In *Ugaritic* (ca. 1400 B.C.E.), another Early Northwest Semitic dialect, the prefix conjugation may have referred to past tense as well as had the meanings we normally associate

---

2. The Amarna and Ugaritic materials also raise the question of sporadic cases of a *t*-prefix third-person masculine plural prefix verb in Hebrew (e.g., *tqrbwn* in Deut 5:23, *tʾmrw* in Deut 5:24, *tqrbw* in Ezek 37:7), a possibility recently rejected by R. Ratner, "Does a *t*- Preformative Third Person Masculine Plural Verbal Form Exist in Hebrew?" *Vetus Testamentum* 38 (1988) 80–88. The *t* prefix (rather than *y*) is standard in Ugaritic; see D. L. Dobrusin, "The Third Masculine Plural of the Prefixed Form of the Verb in Ugaritic," *Journal of the Ancient Near Eastern Society* 13 (1981) 5–14. The occurrence of a *t* prefix in the singular in Hebrew (e.g., perhaps *tśym* in Isa 53:10) is more problematic; see W. L. Moran, "*Taqtul*—Third Masculine Singular?" *Biblica* 45 (1964) 80–82, rejecting the form in Amarna Canaanite; and H. van Dijk, "Does Third Masculine Singular *Taqtul* Exist in Hebrew?" *Vetus Testamentum* 19 (1969) 440–47.

3. H. J. Polotsky established semantic categories for Egyptian by considering the variant forms apparent only in weak verbs, as noted by A. F. Rainey, "The Ancient Hebrew Prefix Conjugation in Light of Amarnah Canaanite," *Hebrew Studies* 27 (1986) 4–19, at 5.

with the non-perfective. In both Ugaritic and Hebrew poetry one finds the alternation of *qtl/yqtl* or *yqtl/qtl* of the same verb in associated lines. Moshe Held explained both as preterites, supposing the poet exchanged the forms for stylistic reasons.[4] (4) In some prose texts it seems that some prefix forms without *waw* must be taken as *preterites*.[5]

1.   אַעֲלֶה אֶתְכֶם מִמִּצְרַיִם   I *brought* you *up* from Egypt.
                                       Judg 2:1

(5) After the *adverbials* אז, טרם, and בטרם it seems that some prefix forms must be taken as preterites.[6] This is a conditioned use, however, as will be seen. (6) In *poetic texts recounting history* the unbound prefix conjugation seems sometimes to signify preterite situations. David Robertson argues that in such poetic texts (e.g., Exodus 15, Amos 2:9–12) unbound *yqtl* is used of the past where no habitual or frequentative notion is relevant.[7] Walter Gross finds a similar pattern in such material; he also finds that short *yqtl* (< *yaqtul*) forms tend to occur clause initially (e.g., *yṣb* in Deut 32:8) and long *yqtl* (< *yaqtulu*) forms tend to occur clause internally (e.g., *tšth* in Deut 32:14). The clause-initial forms Gross associates with *wayyiqtol*, a form with perfective meaning; the non-clause-initial forms he assigns a "historical imperfect aspect."[8] (7) A comparison of the *synoptic psalms* Psalm 18 and 2 Samuel 22 reveals that the remains of the historically short prefix conjugation apparently alternate between the free and bound forms. If the bound form of *yqtl* signifies preterite action, then we have strong evidence that the free form can also signify preterite action. Compare, for example:

2a.   וַיָּשֶׁת חֹשֶׁךְ . . . סֻכּוֹת   *And he made*(?) darkness . . . his covering.
                                          2 Sam 22:12

2b.   יָשֶׁת חֹשֶׁךְ . . . סִכָּתוֹ   *He made*(?) darkness . . . his covering.
                                          Ps 18:12

The same phenomenon occurs in vv 7, 39, 44, and the opposite is found in v 14. This is an impressive range of arguments from morphological development and from usage that the Hebrew prefix conjugation contains at least two paradigms, the long (< *yaqtulu*) signifying imperfective and dependent situations and the short (< *yaqtul*) signifying a jussive when unbound and a preterite, especially when bound with relative *waw*.

---

4. Moshe Held, "The *YQTL-QTL (QTL-YQTL)* Sequence of Identical Verbs in Biblical Hebrew and in Ugaritic," *Studies and Essays in Honor of Abraham A. Neuman*, ed. M. Ben-Horin et al. (Leiden: Brill, 1962) 281–90; note these examples: Ps 29:10, 38:12; Prov 11:7; Amos 7:4.

5. This case is discussed by Péter Kustár, *Aspekt im Hebräischen* (Basel: Reinhardt, 1972) 7. S. R. Driver cites some other examples, e.g., 1 Kgs 7:8 (*yᶜsh*), 21:6 (*ᵓdbr*); 2 Kgs 8:29 (*ykhw*); see *A Treatise on the Use of the Tenses in Hebrew* (3d ed.; Oxford: Clarendon, 1892) 32–33.

6. R. Meyer, *Hebräische Grammatik* (Berlin: de Gruyter, 1972), 3. 43–44.

7. D. A. Robertson, *Linguistic Evidence in Dating Early*

Hebrew Poetry (Society of Biblical Literature Dissertation Series 3; Missoula: Scholars Press, 1972) 17–55; he does not distinguish long and short *yqtl* forms.

8. W. Gross, *Verbform und Funktion: Wayyiqtol für die Gegenwart?* (St. Ottilien: EOS, 1976) 143–46. Another morphological pattern may be relevant: M. Lambert argued that the energic suffixes occur on non-perfective forms (e.g., *lōᵓ yišmərénnû* 'he has not been keeping it in,' Exod 21:29), while suffixes without *nun* are attached to jussive/preterite forms (e.g., *ᵓōhăbêhû* 'I loved it,' Hos 11:1). See further 31.7.2; M. Lambert, "De l'emploi des suffixes pronominaux avec *noun* et sans *noun*," *Revue des études juives* 46 (1903) 178–83, cited by Rainey, "Ancient Hebrew Prefix Conjugation," 10–12.

On the other side of the ledger, however, the following arguments (which we present with some critical appraisal) convince some scholars that an alleged preterite value of *yaqtul* did not come over into the prefix conjugation or at least the unbound form of it.[9] (1) The jussive value of the historical *yaqtul* could readily be merged with the values of the non-perfective *yaqtulu* conjugation. As we shall see, the non-perfective form often signifies volitional or contingent situations, both notions also entailed by the jussive mood. By contrast, the preterite value hardly comports with the range of the non-perfective's senses. (2) Correlatively, one would not suppose that the (preterite paradigm of the) prefix conjugation could have a value also associated with the suffix conjugation. Michel argues:

> It must be accepted that every verb form must have had its own meaning. A language does not develop varying verb forms if they do not serve to express varying meanings. And if a language develops only two verb forms, it has to be accepted that these two express basic differences, perhaps even contrasts. . . . Should one really accept that a language in which obviously only two points of view were decisive in connection with actions, later mixed these up to such an extent that it uses the same verb form for the two points of view?[10]

On the other hand, in Byblian Canaanite, both *qatala* and *yaqtul* are preterite. Further, we may wonder whether the morphological and syntactic factors distinguishing the off-spring of *yaqtulu* and *yaqtul* do not drastically reduce the number of prefix forms actually "competing" with suffix forms. (The diversity of these two factors does not, it should be noted, militate against their working together.) (3) *Wayyqtl* in even the most ancient poetry does not always represent a preterite, and this fact suggests that it does not preserve the alleged preterite notion of *yaqtul*. For example, in Psalm 29, an ancient poem, we find the following.

3. קוֹל יהוה שֹׁבֵר אֲרָזִים
   וַיְשַׁבֵּר יהוה אֶת־אַרְזֵי הַלְּבָנוֹן:

The voice of Yʜwʜ breaks (participle) the cedars;
Yʜwʜ *breaks up* (wayyqtl) the cedars of Lebanon.
Ps 29:5

4. קוֹל יהוה יְחוֹלֵל אַיָּלוֹת
   וַיֶּחֱשֹׂף־יְעָרוֹת
   וּבְהֵיכָלוֹ כֻּלּוֹ אֹמֵר כָּבוֹד:

The voice of Yʜwʜ twists (*yqtl*) the oaks
and *strips* (wayyqtl) the forest *bare*,
and in his temple all cry (participle), "Glory!"
Ps 29:9

F. C. Fensham thinks that the *wayyqtl* forms in this psalm are later innovations of the Masoretes.[11] We do not think so, but, be that as it may, the text we have in hand—the

9. We leave out of account the phonological and morphological objections.

10. D. Michel, *Tempora und Satzstellung in den Psalmen* (Bonn: Bouvier, 1960) 12. Michel's objection seems to treat "preterite" and "perfective" as synonyms, but they are not: preterite refers to an event or state exclusively in past time; perfective refers to a complete situation irrespective of time.

11. F. C. Fensham, "The Use of the Suffix Conjugation and the Prefix Conjugation in a Few Old Hebrew Poems," *Journal of Northwest Semitic Languages* 6 (1978) 9–18, at 15.

object of our study—does not seem to treat them as preterites, or even as having past time reference. (4) Unquestionably the prefix conjugation both in ENWS and in Biblical Hebrew could represent past situations in narrative, but that does not necessarily mean that it functioned as a preterite. As we shall see, the prefix conjugation can signify imperfective past action. So also in Hebrew poetry the prefix conjugation in parallel with the suffix conjugation may signify one of its non-perfective past meanings. For example, perhaps we should find an ingressive and a telic sense in these lines.

5.   תְּהֹמֹת יְכַסְיֻמוּ   The deep waters *began to cover* them;
       יָרְדוּ בִמְצוֹלֹת כְּמוֹ־אָבֶן: they *sank* to the depths like a stone.
                                         Exod 15:5

On a historical view, however, the prefix conjugation form here would be associated not with *yaqtul* but with *yaqtulu*. (5) The same event can be described either as a perfective or as a non-perfective situation, depending solely on the subjective view of the speaker. This is not so in the case of a tense system, for notions of absolute time stand apart from the speaker's views: an event either took place prior to the time of speaking or not. There is much more to the Hebrew system than time: the speaker enjoys the latitude of representing the same event by both the prefix and suffix conjugations. Because they are often used subjectively to represent a situation, it is possible for a poet to juxtapose complementary uses of the conjugations over against one another. We can demonstrate the complementary use of the conjugations with reference to present-time uses. For example, the poet may set a gnomic perfective over against a habitual non-perfective, as in # 6.

6.   בְּמוֹת אָדָם רָשָׁע תֹּאבַד תִּקְוָה   When a wicked person dies, his hope *perishes*;
       וְתוֹחֶלֶת אוֹנִים אָבָדָה: all he expected from his power *perishes*.
                                         Prov 11:7

Or, the poet may juxtapose the instantaneous perfective with the incipient-progressive non-perfective, as in # 7.

7.   כִּי־אֶשָּׂא אֶל־שָׁמַיִם יָדִי   For I *lift up* my hand to heaven,
       וְאָמַרְתִּי   and I *say*. . . .
                                         Deut 32:40

If the two conjugations can refer in juxtaposition to present time, we should expect the same phenomenon with reference to past time. For this reason it seems unlikely that when the two conjugations are nearby they both represent a perfective state in past time. Again, however, the historical view contends that this is true, but that these cases reflect the historical *yaqtulu* and thus do not disprove that historical *yaqtul* with its preterite value was preserved in other cases.

(6) The prose passages in which the unbound prefix form signifies a preterite are not f
without difficulties. The form in # 1 is the long form, not the short form the theory
predicts. Such passages may, however, be conditioned in some non-obvious way or may
simply be exceptional.[12] The few passages with an unexpected prefix conjugation in
prose cannot override the overwhelming evidence in the opposite direction. S. R. Driver
thought that some of them were frequentative and Bergsträsser that some were used as a
historical present for vivid description of the event.[13] Leslie McFall rightly calls for an
examination of the 775 simple *yqtl* forms used of past events.[14] (7) The use of the long
prefix forms of weak verbs with a preterite value after אז, טרם, and בטרם is syntactically
conditioned and cannot be used as evidence for the same use in other situations.
(8) McFall notes that the short prefix form is not consistently used with relative *waw* and
that both the long and short form may have the same sense. He cites as an example a
partially duplicated phrase in Jeremiah, וַיַּעֲלֶה נְשָׂאִים (10:13) and וַיַּעַל נשׂאים (51:16),
'and he makes the mist rise,' as showing that the "shortening is not due to the prefixed ·ו,
but to style, or variety, or some other such reason."[15] To be sure, the long form of a
weak verb can be used as a jussive (e.g., *trʾh* in Gen 1:9; cf. Chap. 34.4), yet no one
denies that the jussive and the non-perfective can be distinguished.

Whether or not the prefix conjugation (as a whole, apart from the *yaqtul*/*yaqtulu*   g
distinction) can serve as a preterite, especially in its unbound form in Hebrew poetry,
cannot be decided beyond reasonable doubt at present. Two factors complicate the
discussion and prevent us from coming to a decisive answer. First, since the Hebrew
conjugations do not simply represent absolute time but the speaker's subjective representation of a state or an event, the interpretation of the forms is also subjective. It is
instructive to note, for example, that whereas Held thinks the two forms of differing
conjugations in Ps 93:3 both signify preterite action, Fensham thinks that both signify
habitual activity.[16] Second, etymology and usage are related in complex ways. While the
comparative-historical evidence favors the view that earlier *yaqtul*, which signified preterite action, survived in Hebrew *wayyqtl*, in actual usage the bound form seems to have
taken on the values of the suffix conjugation, including those involving other time
periods. In short, it lost its original value in the bound form to take on new values, and
we may suppose that the same may have happened in the case of the unbound form.

On balance the comparative-historical evidence seems to demand some respect, and   h
we believe that vestiges of historical *yaqtul* survive in the prefix conjugation beyond the
jussive. In prose the *waw*-relative is normally bound with the offspring of preterite
yaqtul, a form not consistently differentiated from the descendants of *yaqtulu*. The basically similar situation in poetry is complicated by stylistic and idiosyncratic usage as well
as by variation. Poetry, especially early poetry, occasionally preserves a *yaqtul* preterite
in unbound form, as an archaic or archaizing usage (1.4.1).

---

12. C. Brockelmann, *Hebräische Syntax* (Neukirchen:
Neukirchener Verlag, 1956) 44.

13. Driver, *Tenses in Hebrew*, 31; GB 2. 39 (§ 9a).

14. L. McFall, *The Enigma of the Hebrew Verbal*

System (Sheffield: Almond, 1982) 54–55.

15. McFall, *Hebrew Verbal System*, 55.

16. Fensham, "Suffix Conjugation," 16. Such disparate
views are not infrequent.

31.1.2   A Working View

a   In Chapter 29 we noted that most grammarians have erred in trying to abstract one meaning from the several uses of the prefix conjugation, and we suggested that the only possible generalization had to be expressed negatively: the non-perfective conjugation stands over against the perfective conjugation. The non-perfective prefix conjugation has two major values: to signify either an imperfective situation in past and present time, or a dependent situation. In the latter use, the situation may be dependent on the speaker, the subject, or another situation.

b   We analyze the use of the prefix conjugation first according to time: past time (31.2) and present time (31.3). We group its uses to represent dependent situations into those involving the speaker or the subject, and those dependent on another situation. We divide the first group into those situations where speakers do *not* impose their will on the subject (the *modal* uses, 31.4) and those in which they do (the *volitional* uses, 31.5). Finally, we discuss other contingent uses, including its use in the less frequent past-time frame with certain particles (31.6), and some morphological relics (31.7).

31.2   Non-Perfective and Past Time

a   A clear demonstration of non-perfective and past-time relations is provided by an Arabic example.

> *wā ttabaᶜū* (pfv., *tbᶜ*) *mā tatlū* (impfv., *tly*) *š-šayāṭīnu ᶜalā mulki sulaymān*[17]
> And they followed that which the demons used to recite (or, follow) in Solomon's reign.

The time reference of the prefix conjugation *tatlū* 'they used to recite' is past and absolute because it occurred in a time prior to the event of speaking; the aspect is imperfective, more specifically customary (iterative), because explicit reference is made to the internal temporal structure of the situation, viewing the situation from within, in contrast to *ʾittabaᶜu* 'they followed,' whereby explicit reference is made to the situation as a single whole, viewing the situation from without. The same combination of time reference and aspect occurs in Hebrew, in several patterns.

b   In the *customary non-perfective* the internal structure of a situation is conceived of as extended over an indefinite period in the time prior to the act of speaking. Bernard Comrie remarks that the view may be "so extended in fact that the situation referred to is viewed not as an incidental property of the moment but, precisely, as a characteristic

---

17. The first verb is an VIIIth Form (*ʾiqtatala*), with the initial *ʾi-* elided after the conjunction *wa*. The sentence is discussed by W. Wright, *A Grammar of the Arabic Language* (Cambridge: Cambridge University, 1898), 2. 21; and by B. Comrie, *Aspect* (Cambridge: Cambridge University, 1976) 80 (where the transliteration of the first verb should be corrected). The sense of the sentence can be paraphrased in Hebrew: *wayyišmǝrû ʾet-ʾăšer yǝdabbǝrû haggillûlîm bimlōk šǝlōmōh* (cf. *ʾet kol-ʾăšer taᶜăśûn*, Deut 29:8; cf. Exod 4:15).

feature of a whole period."[18] The past customary non-perfective, in contrast to what we call the present non-perfective, implies that the situation described no longer holds at the time of the utterance. With active situations the customary non-perfective is essentially a statement of iterativity (i.e., 'he used to do X'; ## 1–4). This usage is less frequent with stative situations, in which it represents the situation as existing without interruption (## 5–6; note that the verbs in question are not stative).[19]

1. וְאֵד יַעֲלֶה מִן־הָאָ֑רֶץ   Streams(?) *would come up* from the ground.
                              Gen 2:6

2. כָּכָה יַעֲשֶׂה אִיּוֹב כָּל־הַיָּמִים׃   Thus Job *would* always *do*.
                                          Job 1:5

3. וְכֵן יַעֲשֶׂה שָׁנָה בְשָׁנָה   And so he *used to do* annually.
                                  1 Sam 1:7

4. אֲשֶׁר יַחְדָּו נַמְתִּיק ס֗וֹד   . . . with whom we *used to enjoy* fellowship;
    בְּבֵית אֱלֹהִים נְהַלֵּךְ בְּרָֽגֶשׁ׃   we *used to walk* together in the throng into the house
                                          of God.[20]
                                      Ps 55:15

5. וּבְלוּלִים יַעֲלוּ עַל־הַתִּֽיכֹנָה   A stairway *led up* to the middle level.
                                      1 Kgs 6:8

6. כָּל־יְמֵי אֲשֶׁר יִשְׁכֹּן הֶעָנָן עַל־   All the days the cloud *stayed* over the tabernacle,
    הַמִּשְׁכָּן יַחֲנוּ׃   they *would camp*.
                        Num 9:18

In the *incipient past non-perfective* the speaker has in view the initial and continu-   c
ing phases within the internal temporal structure of a past situation. In contrast to the participle, which represents a situation as continuing without interruption or progressing but does not focus on the inception of the situation, the prefix conjugation in this use combines the notions of commencement and continuation. Like the participle, this use lends itself to circumstantial clauses. Brockelmann seems to have had this use in mind when he wrote: "The imperfect can designate past events with a lively sympathy. . . . In poetry the imperfect can also vividly visualize unique actions of the past."[21] Driver, though mistakenly viewing this function as the one essential meaning of the prefix conjugation, described it more precisely:

> The imperfect does not imply *mere* continuance as such (which is the function of the participle), though, inasmuch as it emphasizes the process introducing and leading to completion, it expresses what may be termed *progressive* continuance; by thus seizing

---

18. Comrie, *Aspect*, 28.
19. Cf. Joüon § 113f / p. 303; contrast Driver, *Tenses in Hebrew*, 27–28.

20. Cf. Ps 42:5 for a conceptually and grammatically similar passage.
21. Brockelmann, *Hebräische Syntax*, 43–44.

upon an action while nascent, and representing it under its most striking and impressive aspect (for it is just when a fresh object first appears upon a scene that it exhibits greater energy, and is, so to speak, more aggressive, than either while it simply continues or after it has been completed), it can present it in the liveliest manner possible.[22]

7. וַיָּבֹא חוּשַׁי . . . הָעִיר וְאַבְשָׁלֹם יָבֹא יְרוּשָׁלָיִם

And Hushai . . . came into the city while Absalom *entered* (*began entering*) Jerusalem. 2 Sam 15:37

8. וַיָּנֻעוּ אַמּוֹת הַסִּפִּים . . . וְהַבַּיִת יִמָּלֵא עָשָׁן:

The doorposts shook . . . and the temple *filled* (*began filling*) with smoke. Isa 6:4

9. וַיַּעֲלוּ אִישׁ יִשְׂרָאֵל: הוּא קָם וַיַּךְ בַּפְּלִשְׁתִּים . . . וְהָעָם יָשֻׁבוּ אַחֲרָיו אַךְ־לְפַשֵּׁט:

And the men of Israel retreated. He (Eleazar) stood his ground and struck the Philistines . . . and the troops *returned* (*began returning*) after him but only to strip the dead. 2 Sam 23:9–10

10. וַתִּתְפַּלֵּל עַל־יהוה וּבָכֹה תִבְכֶּה:

She prayed to Yʜᴡʜ and *began weeping* bitterly. 1 Sam 1:10

31.3 Non-Perfective and Present Time

a   Under the heading of present time we consider the range of uses associated with English present tenses, including certain habitual or gnomic patterns.

b   By *progressive non-perfective* we mean a pattern similar to the *customary non-perfective*, but in a present-time frame with reference to the act of speaking. Here the non-perfective, instead of implying that a specific situation has ceased, represents it as ongoing. This pattern is more common with dynamic situations. Contrast, for example, אֵי־מִזֶּה בָאת, 'Where have you come from?', with וְאָנָה תֵלֵכִי, 'Where are you going?', in Gen 16:8. Regarding pairs like these William Turner surprisingly confessed:

> It is, at the same time, to be freely granted that there are many instances in which in our apprehension, there exists no apparent reason why the one form rather than the other should be employed, as *e.g.* . . . . מֵאַיִן תָּבוֹא, and . . . מֵאַיִן בָּאתָ.[23]

McFall, however, nicely explains the difference.

> The verb forms have been determined by the actual situation then prevailing, for in Gen. 16:8 Hagar was resting when the angel asked her, 'Whence camest thou?' (אֵי־מִזֶּה בָאת). It would have been inappropriate to have used the *yqtl* form since that would have implied that she was going somewhere at that moment; though it is possible that Hagar could have been viewed as on a journey, and her present situation ignored.

---

22. Driver, *Tenses in Hebrew*, 27.   23. Quoted in McFall, *Hebrew Verbal System*, 84.

Joseph uses the *qtl* form in Gen. 42:7, 'Whence came ye?' (מֵאַ֫יִן בָּאתֶ֑ם), because at that precise moment it was obvious they were not on a journey, but had arrived. Notice, however, the difference in Jos. 9:8, 'Who are you? And where do you come from?' (וּמֵאַ֫יִן תָּבֹֽאוּ). It is obvious to Joshua that these men *are* on a journey, that is their present activity. Joshua's question is: From where did you start out on your journey? He does not know yet that he is the goal of their journey; but this comes out in the choice of verb form they use: 'From a very far country *your* servants have come,' בָּ֫אוּ . . . , implying that they had finished their journey and had reached their destination.[24]

Progressive non-perfective forms in poetry can be used in association with similar forms (## 1–2) or with a persistent (present) perfective form (# 3; 30.5.1c).

1.   יִפְרְצֵ֫נִי פֶ֫רֶץ עַל־פְּנֵי־פָ֑רֶץ   Again and again he *bursts* upon me;
               יָרֻ֖ץ עָלַ֣י כְּגִבּֽוֹר׃   he *rushes* at me like a warrior.
                                       Job 16:14

2.   יוֹם לְיוֹם יַבִּ֣יעַ אֹ֑מֶר   Day after day they (the heavens) *pour forth* speech;
      וְלַ֥יְלָה לְּ֝לַ֗יְלָה יְחַוֶּה־דָּֽעַת׃   night after night they *display* knowledge.
                                         Ps 19:3

3.   אֱלֹהִ֥ים נִצָּ֥ב בַּעֲדַת־אֵ֑ל   God *presides* (pfv.) in the great assembly;
            בְּקֶ֖רֶב אֱלֹהִ֣ים יִשְׁפֹּֽט׃   he *gives judgment* (non-pfv.) among the divine beings.
                                         Ps 82:1

     A *stative non-perfective* represents the internal temporal structure of a stative (non-changing) present situation. This use differs from the participle in that the latter occurs in dynamic situations.   **c**

4.   בְּצוּר־יָר֖וּם מִמֶּ֣נִּי תַנְחֵֽנִי׃   Lead me to a rock that *is higher* than I.
                                         Ps 61:3

This use forms a fitting complement for stative situations represented by the perfective conjugation (30.5.3c).

5.   לֹ֤א יָדְע֣וּ וְלֹ֣א יָבִ֔ינוּ   They *do* not *know* (pfv.) and *do* not *understand*.
                                         Ps 82:5

     In the *incipient present non-perfective* the internal temporal structure of a situation   **d** is conceived of as beginning and continuing in the non-past (## 6–8). It is like the incipient past non-perfective, except that the situation exists not prior to the time of speaking but at the same time. In verse, this type of non-perfective can be associated with an instantaneous perfective (# 9; 30.5.1d).

---

24. McFall, *Hebrew Verbal System*, 84–85.

6.   הַקְשִׁיבָה לְקוֹל שַׁוְעִי . . .
כִּי־אֵלֶיךָ אֶתְפַּלָּל׃

Pay attention to my cry for help, . . .
because to you I *pray* (*begin praying*).
Ps 5:3

7.   שְׁמַע־יהוה קוֹלִי אֶקְרָא

Hear, YHWH, as I *call* (*begin calling*) aloud.
Ps 27:7

8.   נַחֲמוּ נַחֲמוּ עַמִּי יֹאמַר
אֱלֹהֵיכֶם׃

"Comfort, comfort my people," your God *begins to
say*.
Isa 40:1

9.   אָמְרוּ לְכוּ וְנַכְחִידֵם מִגּוֹי . . .

They *say* (pfv.), "Come, let us efface them from
(being) a nation. . . .

כִּי נוֹעֲצוּ לֵב יַחְדָּו
עָלֶיךָ בְּרִית יִכְרֹתוּ׃

They *plot together* (pfv.) with one mind,
they *form* (non-pfv.) an alliance against you.
Ps 83:5-6

e   By *habitual non-perfective* we mean the representation of a repeated general, non-specific situation. Rarely in prose, but rather frequently in poetry and proverbial expressions, the non-perfective is used to denote habitual activity with no specific tense value. It forms a fitting parallel with the gnomic perfective (30.5.1c).[25] Whereas the gnomic perfective conceives of a universal state or event as a single event, the habitual non-perfective represents the internal temporal phases of the general situation as occurring over and over again, including the time present to the act of speaking.

10.   כֹּל אֲשֶׁר־יָלֹק בִּלְשׁוֹנוֹ . . .
כַּאֲשֶׁר יָלֹק הַכֶּלֶב

whoever *laps* with his tongue . . . as a dog *laps*
Judg 7:5

11.   עַל־כֵּן לֹא־יֹאכְלוּ בְנֵי־יִשְׂרָאֵל
אֶת־גִּיד הַנָּשֶׁה אֲשֶׁר עַל־כַּף
הַיָּרֵךְ עַד הַיּוֹם

Therefore to this day the Israelites *do* not *eat* the
tendon attached to the socket of the hip.
Gen 32:33

12.   הַשֹּׁחַד יְעַוֵּר פִּקְחִים

A bribe *blinds* officials.
Exod 23:8

13.   בֵּן חָכָם יְשַׂמַּח־אָב

A wise son *makes* his father *glad*.
Prov 10:1

31.4   Modal Uses of the Non-Perfective

a   Whereas tense (Latin *tempus*) refers to the absolute temporal relationship of the situation to the speaker, mood refers to a subjective judgment about the factuality of the situation. It may be regarded as real (i.e., indicative in the classical languages) or other than real (irreal or unreal mood, i.e., subjunctive and optative in the classical languages). A situation may be regarded as irreal for one of two reasons: (1) because the speaker is uncertain about the reality of the situation itself, or (2) because the speaker is uncertain

25. T. O. Lambdin, *Introduction to Biblical Hebrew* (New York: Scribner, 1971) 39.

about the reality existing between the subject and its predicate in the situation. That is, the situation may be contingent on the relationship (1) of the speaker to the statement or (2) of the subject of the statement to that predicated of it. For example, the speaker, wishing the subject to sing, may say, 'Tubal-Cain should start singing now,' but the situation proposed is not real, for it depends on the subject's willingness to accede to the speaker's will. On the other hand, the speaker, uncertain about the subject's wish to sing, may say, 'Tubal-Cain may sing when he sees Jubal.' In either case the mood is irreal.

In the Germanic languages (including English) the nature of the irreality is often **b** expressed by adding modals such as 'can, should, must, may,' etc., to the infinitive of the verb in question.[26] In Hebrew, while a construction involving a finite verb[27] with an infinitive may be used, more often the simple prefix conjugation suffices, allowing other indications in the context to decide its precise value.

The *non-perfective of capability* denotes the subject's capability to perform the **c** action expressed by the root. This use often overlaps with "consequential situations."

1.	אֵיכָה אֶשָּׂא לְבַדִּי טָרְחֲכֶם	How *can* I *bear* your problems all by myself? Deut 1:12

The expression לֹא־אוּכַל לְבַדִּי שְׂאֵת אֶתְכֶם in Deut 1:9 shows that this value is relevant for the prefix conjugation in # 1.

2.	וְחָרָשׁ לֹא יִמָּצֵא	Not a blacksmith *could be found.* 1 Sam 13:19
3.	וְאַתָּה קַח־לְךָ מִכָּל־מַאֲכָל אֲשֶׁר יֵאָכֵל	You, take every kind of food that *is edible.* Gen 6:21
4.	וְאִם בְּאֶבֶן יָד אֲשֶׁר־יָמוּת בָּהּ הִכָּהוּ	If he struck him with a hand stone which *could kill.* . . . Num 35:17
5.	וְלֹא יְקוּמוּן	They *could* not *rise.*[28] 2 Sam 22:39
6.	וַאֲנִי כְחֵרֵשׁ לֹא אֶשְׁמָע	I am like a deaf person, who *cannot hear.* Ps 38:14

RSV renders # 6 as 'I am like a man who *does* not *hear,*' thereby showing the close connection between the modal nuance and consequential results; the relative clause in either case depends on the situation in the primary clause.

The *non-perfective of permission* denotes the speaker's permission for the subject to **d** perform an action.

---

26. The verb *ykl* 'to be able' is perhaps most similar to a Germanic modal. See discussion of ## 1, 5.

27. See 36.2.3l. Cf. GB 2. 35–36 (§ 7i); Joüon § 113l–n /

pp. 304–6.

28. The synoptic parallel in Ps 18:39 reads *walōʾ-yukəlû qûm.*

7.	אֶת־שְׁנֵי בָנַי תָּמִית	You *may kill* my two sons. Gen 42:37
8.	אֶת־הַנָּכְרִי תִּגֹּשׂ	You *may require payment* from a foreigner. Deut 15:3
9.	יהוה מִי־יָגוּר בְּאָהֳלֶךָ מִי־יִשְׁכֹּן בְּהַר קָדְשֶׁךָ׃	YHWH, who *may dwell* in your tent? Who *may live* on your holy hill? Ps 15:1

e   The *non-perfective of possibility* denotes the possibility that the subject may perform an action.

10.	כָּל־מָקוֹם אֲשֶׁר תִּדְרֹךְ כַּף־ רַגְלְכֶם בּוֹ	every place where you *may set* your foot Josh 1:3

This use is common in the protasis of conditional clauses (see 38.6).

f   The *non-perfective of deliberation* denotes the speaker's or subject's deliberation as to whether a situation should take place. This use normally involves questions of doubt and thus resembles the Greek subjunctive in questions. Strictly speaking, deliberative questions ask not about the factuality of the action but about the desirability or necessity of it.

11.	וּלְשֹׂנְאֵי יהוה תֶּאֱהָב	*Should* you *love* the enemies of YHWH?[29] 2 Chr 19:2
12.	לָמָה אֶשְׁכַּל גַּם־שְׁנֵיכֶם	Why *should* I *lose* both of you? Gen 27:45
13.	הַכְזוֹנָה יַעֲשֶׂה אֶת־אֲחוֹתֵנוּ׃	*Should* he *have treated* our sister like a prostitute? Gen 34:31
14.	כִּי־נִתֵּן לִצְבָאֲךָ לָחֶם׃	. . . that we *should give* bread to your troops? Judg 8:6

g   The *non-perfective of obligation* refers to either what the speaker considers to be the subject's obligatory or necessary conduct or what the subject considers to be an obligation. This use is similar to the one above, but instead of occurring in an interrogatory clause it occurs in a declarative statement. This use is closely related to both the use of the prefix conjugation to express volition and to its use for consequential results.

15.	בְּרֹב עֻזְּךָ יְכַחֲשׁוּ לְךָ אֹיְבֶיךָ׃	So great is your power that your enemies (*must*) *cringe* before you. Ps 66:3
16.	וְהוֹרֵיתִי אֶתְכֶם אֵת אֲשֶׁר תַּעֲשׂוּן׃	I will teach you what you *should do*. Exod 4:15

---

29. Cf. *ʾăšer-ʾāhábtā* 'whom you love,' in Gen 22:2.

| 17. | אֲחַטֶּ֫נָּה מִיָּדִי תְּבַקְשֶׁ֫נָּה | I *would have to bear* the loss of it myself.
Gen 31:39 |
| 18. | מַעֲשִׂים אֲשֶׁר לֹא־יֵעָשׂוּ עָשִׂ֫יתָ
עִמָּדִי: | You have done things to me that *should* not
be done.
Gen 20:9 |

The *non-perfective of desire* denotes a desire or wish of the subject.   h

19.	הֲתֵלְכִי עִם־הָאִישׁ הַזֶּה	*Will* you (i.e., *do* you *wish to*) *go* with this man? Gen 24:58
20.	אִם־אֹתָהּ תִּקַּח־לְךָ קָח	If you *want to take* it, do so. 1 Sam 21:10
21.	וְלֹא יִשְׁמְרֶ֫נּוּ בְּעָלָיו	yet the owner *would* not *keep* it penned up Exod 21:36

Volitional Uses of the Non-Perfective   31.5

Closely related to the modal nuances of the non-perfective, which express a situa-   a
tion wherein the action of the subject is contingent on the will of the speaker, is its use in
situations wherein the speaker imposes an obligation on the subject addressed. In this
use it approximates the imperative mood and is, in fact, frequently found in conjunction
with an imperative form. The force with which the speaker is able to make the imposition
depends on the social distance between speaker and addressee. If an inferior addresses a
superior the obligation takes the force of a request, but if the communication proceeds
from a superior to an inferior it has the force of a command. The volitional non-
perfective is closely related both morphologically and semantically to the volitional
paradigms (Chap. 34), including the cohortative and the jussive as well as the imperative.
These forms emphasize the will of the speaker, whereas the non-perfectives to be treated
here emphasize the action enjoined or forbidden.

A *non-perfective of injunction* expresses the speaker's will in a positive request or   b
command.

1.	תְּחַטְּאֵ֫נִי בְאֵזוֹב וְאֶטְהָר תְּכַבְּסֵ֫נִי וּמִשֶּׁ֫לֶג אַלְבִּין:	*Cleanse* me with hyssop, and I will be clean; *wash* me, and I will be whiter than snow.[30] Ps 51:9
2.	וְתֵרָאֶה הַיַּבָּשָׁה	*Let* the dry ground *appear.* Gen 1:9
3.	הַט אָזְנְךָ וּשְׁמַע דִּבְרֵי חֲכָמִים וְלִבְּךָ תָּשִׁית לְדַעְתִּי:	Incline your ear and hear the words of the wise; *pay attention* to my knowledge. Prov 22:17

---

30. Note the imperatives in Ps 51:11–14.

c   A *non-perfective of instruction* expresses the speaker's will in a context of legislation or teaching.

| 4. | מִפְּנֵי שֵׂיבָה תָּקוּם | (You *shall*) *rise* in the presence of the aged. Lev 19:32 |

| 5. | אָדָם כִּי־יַקְרִיב מִכֶּם קָרְבָּן לַיהוָה מִן־הַבְּהֵמָה מִן־הַבָּקָר וּמִן־הַצֹּאן תַּקְרִיבוּ אֶת־קָרְבַּנְכֶם׃ | When any of you bring a *qorban*-offering to Yнwн, you *shall bring* your *qorban*-offering from cattle, be it from herd or flock. Lev 1:2 |

| 6. | דַּבְּרוּ אֶל־כָּל־עֲדַת יִשְׂרָאֵל לֵאמֹר . . . וְיִקְחוּ לָהֶם אִישׁ שֶׂה | Speak to all the congregation of Israel, saying, ". . . they *shall take* for themselves, each one, a lamb." Exod 12:3 |

d   A *non-perfective of prohibition* expresses negative instruction in legal literature. The use of לֹא with the non-perfective is common in legislative contexts.

| 7. | וְלֹא־תוֹתִירוּ מִמֶּנּוּ עַד־בֹּקֶר | *Do not leave* any of it till morning. Exod 12:10 |

| 8. | לֹא תִּרְצָח׃ | You *shall not murder.* Exod 20:13 |

31.6   Further Contingent Uses of the Non-Perfective

a   Three uses of the non-perfective verb form may be gathered under the heading of other uses based on contingency. Two of the three are related to the irreal senses, and two of the three are associated with particles.

31.6.1   With Particles Expressing Contingency

a   Related to the use of the unmarked prefix conjugation with irreal modal nuances (31.4) is its use with particles expressing uncertainty or contingency. These may be divided into conditional particles introducing the protasis (the 'if' clause in an 'if-then' sentence) and telic particles introducing the apodosis (the 'then' clause).

b   The most common of the conditional particles is אִם 'if.' The conjunction כִּי can be similarly used. The counterfactual conditional particle is לוּ 'if only (. . . but it is not so).'[31]

| 1. | אִם־אֶצְדָּק | If I *were innocent.* . . . Job 9:20 |

---

31. The particle *ʾm* occurs 1,060 times (SA/THAT); *lû* (in various spellings) occurs about 22 times. Note that *ʾm* is gapped over four clauses in Ps 139:8–9.

2. אִם־אֶמְצָא . . . חֲמִשִּׁים צַדִּיקִם   If I *find* . . . fifty righteous people. . . .
                                           Gen 18:26

3.   כִּי יִפְגָּשְׁךָ עֵשָׂו אָחִי   When my brother Esau *meets* you. . . .
                                           Gen 32:18

4.   לוּ שָׁקוֹל יִשָּׁקֵל כַּעְשִׂי   If only my anguish *could be weighed*!
                                           Job 6:2

The telic particles may be positive (לְמַעַן, בַּעֲבוּר, 'so that'; אֲשֶׁר is also so used) c
or negative (פֶּן, לְבִלְתִּי, 'so that not = lest').[32] In Latin, telic particles are used not with
the indicative mood, the mood of certainty, but with the subjunctive, the mood of
contingency.

5.   לְמַעַן יִיטַב־לִי   . . . so that I *will be treated well*.
                                           Gen 12:13

6.   וּבַעֲבוּר תִּהְיֶה יִרְאָתוֹ עַל־   . . . so that the fear of him (God) *will be* with you.
                   פְּנֵיכֶם   Exod 20:20

7.   פֶּן־תְּמֻתוּן   . . . lest you (*will*) *die*.
                                           Gen 3:3

8.   לְבִלְתִּי תֶחֱטָאוּ:   . . . lest you (*will*) *sin*.
                                           Exod 20:20

Future Time   31.6.2

The prefix conjugation is used to represent a real situation which arises as a con- a
sequence of some other situation. Whereas the suffix conjugation may dramatically
represent a future situation as an accidental event, the prefix conjugation represents it as
a logical consequence of some expressed or unexpressed situation. Though Michel over-
extends the concept of dependency to all uses of the prefix conjugation, he has plausibly
suggested that substantiality in contrast to accidence is one of the differences between the
conjugations.

> The imperfectum . . . must designate an action which is not important in itself, but
> which stands in relationship to something else, and in this relationship has its mean-
> ing. In brief: it is dependent.[33]

This use overlaps with some of the modal nuances, which also involve dependency, especially those of capability, of obligation, and of deliberation.

1.   כִּי בְּיוֹם אֲכָלְךָ מִמֶּנּוּ מוֹת   . . . because when you eat of it you *shall* surely *die*.
                   תָּמוּת: Gen 2:17

---

32. Cf. GKC § 107q / p. 318; *lmᶜn* occurs 270 times   85 times and *bᶜb(w)r* about 50 times.
(SA/THAT) and *pn* 133 times (SA/THAT); *lblty* is found   33. Michel, *Tempora und Satzstellung*, 128.

2. עֹשֵׂה־אֵלֶּה לֹא יִמּוֹט לְעוֹלָם:

He who does these things *will* (or, *can*) never *be shaken*.
Ps 15:5

3. וְלֹא נִשְׁבַּע לְמִרְמָה:
    יִשָּׂא בְרָכָה מֵאֵת יְהוָה

Who does not swear by what is false,[34]
he *will* (*must*) *receive* blessing from Yʜwʜ.
Ps 24:4–5

4. גַּם כָּל־קוֶֹיךָ לֹא יֵבֹשׁוּ
    יֵבֹשׁוּ הַבּוֹגְדִים רֵיקָם:

All who hope in you *will* (*can*) not *be put to shame*;
they *will* (*must*) *be put to shame* who are vainly treacherous.
Ps 25:3

5. יְהוָה אוֹרִי וְיִשְׁעִי
    מִמִּי אִירָא

Yʜwʜ is my light and my salvation;
whom *shall* (*should*) I *fear*?
Ps 27:1

b   These examples and many more suggest that the prefix conjugation may represent a future situation as dependent or contingent on some other expressed or unexpressed situation. With reference to the time of speaking, the situation may be future or past. If the action is in the future, the sense is of a *specific future*.

6. . . . כֻּלָּם נִקְבְּצוּ בָאוּ־לָךְ
    כִּי כֻלָּם כָּעֲדִי תִלְבָּשִׁי

All of them (your sons) gather and come to you . . .
you *will wear* them all as ornaments.
Isa 49:18

7. בַּחֲשֵׁכָה יִתְהַלָּכוּ
    יִמּוֹטוּ כָּל־מוֹסְדֵי אָרֶץ:

They walk about in darkness
(*so that*) the foundation of the earth *shakes* (*will shake*).
Ps 82:5

8. הַמַּשְׂבִּיעַ בַּטּוֹב עֶדְיֵךְ
    תִּתְחַדֵּשׁ כַּנֶּשֶׁר נְעוּרָיְכִי:

He who satisfies your desires with good things,
(*so that*) your youth *is renewed* like the eagle's.
Ps 103:5

This use can be fittingly associated with the suffix conjugation used for future events.

9. לָכֵן כֹּה־אָמַר יְהוָה
    שַׁבְתִּי לִירוּשָׁלַיִם בְּרַחֲמִים
    בֵּיתִי יִבָּנֶה בָּהּ

Therefore, this is what Yʜwʜ says,
"I will return to Jerusalem with mercy,
and in it my house *will be built*."
Zech 1:16

A negated form can be used with a corresponding sense.

10. וּבַיהוָה בָּטַחְתִּי לֹא אֶמְעָד:

In Yʜwʜ I trusted (pʀ . .) (*so that*) I *will* (*do*) not *waver*.
Ps 26:1

---

34. The phrase *nšbᶜ lmrmh* can be glossed 'swear falsely *or* by what is false *or* by Falsehood/the False One.'

11.   יְהוָה רֹעִי לֹא אֶחְסָר׃   Yhwh is my shepherd, I *will (do)* not *lack* (anything).
Ps 23:1

The consequent situation may in fact be past with reference to the absolute time of   c
the speaker but future to some other situation. This use is found only in dependent
clauses.[35]

12.   וַיָּבֵא אֶל־הָאָדָם לִרְאוֹת מַה־   And he brought (them) to Adam to see what he
יִּקְרָא־לוֹ   *would name* them.
Gen 2:19

13.   וּבֵיתוֹ אֲשֶׁר־יֵשֶׁב שָׁם   and the house in which he *was to live*
1 Kgs 7:8

Past Time with Particles   31.6.3

The non-perfective verb form regularly (but not always) has a past time reference   a
after אָז, טֶרֶם, and בְּטֶרֶם.[36] David Qimḥi appeals to Arabic to explain this unexpected
use.

> And with the particle אָז 'then', a future usually comes in the place of a past, as
> אָז יָשִׁיר מֹשֶׁה [Exod. 15:1 'then sang Moses']. . . . And the sage Rabbi Abraham Aben
> Ezra wrote that this is the custom in the language of Ishmael [i.e., Arabic].[37]

Arabic *yaqtulu* may function as a verbal complement to *qatala* (suffix conjugation). In
this construction *yaqtulu* retains the force of the perfective conjugation, for example,
jalasa (pfv.) *nnasu yašrabûna* (impfv.) *lḥamra*, 'The men sat, *drinking* wine.'

In Hebrew these particles are sometimes used with the prefix conjugation to denote   b
a past situation. Most common of them is אָז.

1.   אָז יָשִׁיר־מֹשֶׁה   Then Moses *sang*.
Exod 15:1

2.   אָז תָּבֹאנָה שְׁתַּיִם נָשִׁים זֹנוֹת   Now two prostitutes *came* to the king.
אֶל־הַמֶּלֶךְ   1 Kgs 3:16

Isaac Rabinowitz agrees with traditional grammarians that *ʾāz* followed by a non-
perfective verb form may express a future-temporal or logical consequence, while with
the perfective *ʾāz* "marks a consecution in an uninterrupted narration of past actions
or events: first so-and-so did such-and-such, *then* (*ʾāz*) so-and-so did (perfect) such-
and-such." He further notes that in fifteen instances when it refers to the past, the
non-perfective with *ʾāz* indicates that the context of narrated past events is "approximately the time when, the time or circumstances in the course of which, or the occasion

---

35. Cf. GB 2. 30 (§ 7a).
36. Joüon § 113i–j / p. 304.

37. Quoted in McFall, *Hebrew Verbal System*, 8. The
construction is one type of circumstantial (*ḥāl*) clause.

upon which the action designated by the imperfect verb-form went forward: *this was when* (*ʾāz* . . .) so-and-so *did* (imperfect) such-and-such." The action introduced by אז is to be thought of as having taken place before the completion of the preceding action and in this sense the non-perfective describes relative action.[38]

3. אָז יֵחָלֵק הָעָם יִשְׂרָאֵל לַחֵצִי   *This was when* the army-host, Israel, *became divided.*[39]
1 Kgs 16:21

c   The particle טרם, most often preceded by ב, is usually used in temporal clauses.[40]

4. וַיָּלִנוּ שָׁם טֶרֶם יַעֲבֹרוּ:   They stayed the night there before *they crossed over.*
Josh 3:1

5. וַיִּשָּׂא הָעָם אֶת־בְּצֵקוֹ טֶרֶם יֶחְמָץ   The people took their dough before *it was leavened.*
Exod 12:34

6. וָאֹכַל מִכֹּל בְּטֶרֶם תָּבוֹא   I ate it all just before *you came.*[41]
Gen 27:33

7. וּבְטֶרֶם יִקְרַב אֲלֵיהֶם   before *he reached* them . . .
Gen 37:18

Brockelmann has suggested on the basis of the occurrences of this construction that it is dying out in Biblical Hebrew.[42] Compare these cases.

8a. אָז יִבְנֶה יְהוֹשֻׁעַ מִזְבֵּחַ לַיהוה   Then Joshua *built* an altar for YHWH.
Josh 8:30

8b. אָז בָּנָה אֶת־הַמִּלּוֹא: Then he *built* the Millo.
1 Kgs 9:24

The Chronicler uses אז with the prefix conjugation only twice.[43]

31.7   *Nun*-Bearing Forms

a   Some non-perfective forms in Biblical Hebrew bear an atypical *nun.*[44] As with other non-perfective forms, it is easier to figure out where these might have come from than

38. Isaac Rabinowitz, "ʾāz Followed by Imperfect Verb-Form in Preterite Contexts: A Redactional Device in Biblical Hebrew," *Vetus Testamentum* 34 (1984) 53–62, quotations at 54. The sense in # 1 is that the song was sung when Israel saw the Egyptians lying dead on the shore and therefore came to trust YHWH (cf. Exod 14:30–31); the sense in # 2 is that the women came while the king was still at Gibeon (1 Kgs 3:5), before he went to Jerusalem. Cf. E. L. Greenstein, "On the Prefixed Preterite in Biblical Hebrew," *Hebrew Studies* 29 (1988) 7–17, at 8, 11 n. 13.
39. That is—before the entire army made Omri king, it

had been divided between Tibni and Omri.
40. Contrast GB 2. 31 (§ 7b).
41. The sense of *mkl* is uncertain.
42. Brockelmann, *Hebräische Syntax*, 42.
43. Arno Kropat, *Die Syntax des Autors der Chronik* (Beiheft zur Zeitschrift für die Alttestamentliche Wissenschaft 16; Giessen: Töpelmann, 1909) 17.
44. R. J. Williams groups all these forms together under the headings of energics; we follow standard practice in separating them into two groups, though Williams's view is plausible (and it is certainly hard to insist that the two

how they work in Hebrew. One set of them, the paragogics, is related to the *yaqtulu/yaqtul* problem treated in 29.4 and 31.1.1; the other set, the energics, is probably related to a set of non-perfective energic forms found in Amarna Canaanite and Ugaritic. The etymology of the Hebrew forms can be grasped if we review some features of the Arabic non-perfective paradigm.[45]

	indicative	jussive	heavy energic	light energic
2 m.s.	*taqtulu*	*taqtul*	*taqtulanna*	*taqtulan*
2 f.s.	*taqtulīna*	*taqtulī*	*taqtulinna*	*taqtulin*
3 m.s.	*yaqtulu*	*yaqtul*	*yaqtulanna*	*yaqtulan*
2 m.pl.	*taqtulūna*	*taqtulū*	*taqtulunna*	*taqtulun*
3 m.pl.	*yaqtulūna*	*yaqtulū*	*yaqtulunna*	*yaqtulun*

The feminine singular and masculine plural indicative and jussive forms differ in that the *-na* ending is not found in the jussive. Recalling that the earlier *yaqtul* and *yaqtulu* (and subjunctive *yaqtula*) forms largely merged with the loss of final short vowels in Hebrew, we might wonder about the fate of comparable forms in *-na*. In fact, there are some Hebrew cases that preserve the final *n* of earlier forms, the final short *a* having disappeared; these cases attest to the complex origins of the Hebrew prefix paradigm(s) from a different angle than the *yāqōm/yāqûm* contrast and the syntactic uses. These morphological relics present a somewhat different profile than the factors discussed earlier, and so we present them here. The final *n* in Hebrew is called *paragogic* (Greek '[word-]extending'), and the forms themselves may loosely be called paragogics.[46]

The Arabic paradigm also shows two series of energic forms, a heavy form in *-anna*, etc., and a light form in *-an*, etc.[47] These energic forms also have analogs in Hebrew, revealing (as do Amarna and Ugaritic materials) that the dialects ancestral to Hebrew used the energic endings. Curiously, however, these endings survive with Hebrew prefix forms only if a suffix follows. Such forms are said to have an energic ending; it is not clear that there were (as there are in Arabic) two different endings in question.

b

---

groups are absolutely inseparable; relic forms are rarely so well behaved). See "Energic Verbal Forms in Hebrew," *Studies on the Ancient Palestinian World Presented to F. V. Winnett*, ed. J. W. Wevers and D. B. Redford (Toronto: University of Toronto, 1972) 75–85. The forms are also dealt with in Rainey, "Ancient Hebrew Prefix Conjugation."

45. Wright, *Grammar of the Arabic Language*, 1. 60–61, 298.

46. The term paragogic is occasionally used of other morphological elements in Hebrew.

47. There are also energic imperative forms in Arabic. Aramaic dialects, like Hebrew, use the energic ending before suffixes; it is sufficiently standard that, e.g., F. Rosenthal, *A Grammar of Biblical Aramaic* (Wiesbaden: Harrassowitz, 1961) 54–55, does not use the term. Both in Arabic and Ugaritic the energics are frequent in verse (see, e.g., *UT* § 9.11).

31.7.1   Paragogic Non-Perfective Forms

a   There are three classes of Hebrew forms with the *nun paragogicum*. The second-person masculine plural (# 1)[48] and the feminine singular (# 2) are rare, while the third-person masculine plural form (# 3) is much more common.[49]

1a.	תִּתֹּצוּן	Exod 34:13	1f.	וַתִּקְרְבוּן	Deut 1:22, 4:11
1b.	תְּשַׁבֵּרוּן	Exod 34:13	1g.	וַתַּעַמְדוּן	Deut 4:11
1c.	תִּכְרֹתוּן	Exod 34:13	1h.	וַתְּשִׂימוּן	Ezek 44:8
1d.	תִּשְׁמָעוּן	Deut 1:17	1i.	תֶּאֱהָבוּן	Ps 4:3
1e.	תַּקְרִבוּן	Deut 1:17			
2a.	תִּשְׁתַּכָּרִין	1 Sam 1:14	2c.	תִּתְחַמָּקִין	Jer 31:22[50]
2b.	תְּחִילִין	Isa 45:10	2d.	תִּדְבָּקִין	Ruth 2:8, 21[51]
3a.	יִרְגָּזוּן	Exod 15:14	3d.	יְחִילוּן	Isa 13:8
3b.	יְרִיבֻן	Exod 21:18[52]	3e.	וַיֶּאֱתָיוּן	Isa 41:5
3c.	יֹאחֵזוּן	Isa 13:8	3f.	וּתְדַכְּאוּנַנִי	Job 19:2[53]

According to J. Hoftijzer's counts, there are 6,900 cases of forms that could show the ending, 23% of the 30,606 non-perfective forms in Biblical Hebrew; of these 6,900, about 300 do show the *nun* (4% of the forms that could bear it; 1% of the non-perfective forms).[54] The paragogics tend to occur in pause.[55] Hoftijzer believes that there is in prose a difference between יכתבו and יכתבון, with the longer form marking contrast;[56] other scholars treat the longer form as durative. In line with its origin as long-form non-perfective, the paragogic form is never found after אל (which governs the jussive) and rarely after *w* (in either *wǝyiqtol* or *wayyiqtol* shape; but note ## 1f–h, 3e–f).[57] The forms are more common in earlier texts; thus, for the synoptic passages, paragogics in Kings are not found in Chronicles (# 4),[58] and Qoheleth and the Hebrew of Daniel have no paragogics.[59]

4a.	לְמַעַן יֵדְעוּן כָּל־עַמֵּי הָאָרֶץ אֶת־שְׁמֶךָ	so that all the peoples of the earth know your name 1 Kgs 8:43

---

48. Some forms are ambiguous between second-person plural and third-person plural with prefix *t* (see n. 2), e.g., the form in Deut 5:23 is taken as second person by AV, RSV, NJPS, NAB, and J. Hoftijzer, *The Function and Use of the Imperfect Forms with Nun Paragogicum in Classical Hebrew* (Assen: Van Gorcum, 1985) 4, and as third person by NIV; Amos 6:3, pace most current translations, may be third person.

49. There are three perfective forms in *-ûn*, presumably the result of analogy to the non-perfectives: *yādǝ῾ûn* (Deut 8:3, 16; the Samaritan in both places lacks the *n*), *ṣāqûn* (Isa 26:16); see GKC § 44l / p. 121.

50. Examples ## 2a–c all occur in questions, # 2a and # 2c after ῾d-mty and # 2b after *mh*; cf. Hoftijzer, *Nun Paragogicum*, 5–6.

51. The cases not listed here are also in Ruth (3:4, 18); all the cases in Ruth are used in dialogue. On *kh* in Ruth 2:8, see Hoftijzer, *Nun Paragogicum*, 18–19, 99. On the seven cases total, see GKC § 47o / p. 129.

52. Defective spellings of the ending are rare.

53. Forms with a suffix are rare; GKC § 60e / p. 161.

54. Hoftijzer, *Nun Paragogicum*, 2.

55. Hoftijzer, *Nun Paragogicum*, 98 n. 27.

56. Hoftijzer, *Nun Paragogicum*, 55–56; for other views, see pp. 96–97 n. 10.

57. Hoftijzer, *Nun Paragogicum*, 2–3, 97 n. 17.

58. GKC § 47m / pp. 128–29; cf. Hoftijzer, *Nun Paragogicum*, 43–44, etc.

59. Hoftijzer, *Nun Paragogicum*, 21, 89; they are rare in P material, p. 23; cf. *LHS* 99.

4b. לְמַעַן יֵדְעוּ כָל־עַמֵּי הָאָרֶץ   so that all the peoples of the earth know
     אֶת־שְׁמֶךָ   your name
                                         2 Chr 6:33

Certain features of Hoftijzer's study of the paragogics deserve note.[60] He is clear   b
that while the paragogics may mark "contrastivity," their absence does not signal the
absence of the feature; rather, it leaves the matter open. The substance of contrastivity
involves "exceptions to normal practice, contradictions, deviations from normal expectation, . . . [and] statements . . . which are contrary to the wishes . . . of other people."[61]
The pattern of contrastivity that he discerns in prose texts is generally less clear in verse,
prophetic or not.[62] In poetry the paragogics mark, among other things, contrastivity or
certainty; and they also mark that a volitional sense is excluded. Though Hoftijzer does
not discuss the matter, it is reasonable to suppose that poetic syntactic patterns make a
feature such as contrastitivity difficult to recognize.

Energic Non-Perfective Forms   31.7.2

The non-perfective forms that show an energic -an- ending before a suffix are   a
slightly more common than paragogic forms; about 450 forms show such a suffix, in one
of a variety of forms.[63] There is a further small group of other forms that have an energic
ending.[64] The endings occur on non-perfective forms with singular suffixes,[65] first (# 1),

---

60. Of Hoftijzer's important monographs (including those on the *he*-locale and on the nominal clause), *Nun Paragogicum* may be the most accessible.

61. Hoftijzer, *Nun Paragogicum*, 55–56. For example, in Num 11:19 "the possibility that the people will have meat to eat for one or two days is contrasted with the possibility that they will have meat for a month" (p. 10). Note also the use of paragogics in independent clauses, in questions (never rhetorical) associated with anger or frustration (e.g., Exod 17:3, Ps 4:2); prescriptions (e.g., Judg 2:2, Deut 1:17); interdictions (e.g., 1 Kgs 12:24); consequences (Deut 17:13); and in dependent clauses stating consequences (positive with *lmᶜn*, e.g., Exod 20:12; negative with *pn*, e.g., Gen 3:3).

62. Hoftijzer, *Nun Paragogicum*, 94.

63. The count is from Williams, "Energic Verbal Forms," 82; see also GKC § 58i–l / pp. 157–58. The connection of the Hebrew energics with the Arabic (and other) energics has been affirmed most recently by John Huehnergard, "The Early Hebrew Prefix-Conjugation," *Hebrew Studies* 29 (1988) 19–23, at 22–23; and (apparently) denied by Rainey, "Ancient Hebrew Prefix Conjugation." The suggestion that energic endings appear not on forms analogous to *yaqtulanna* but rather on *yaqtulu* (and thus not on *yaqtul*) forms, which originated in the nineteenth

century, has recently been revived by Rainey, "Ancient Hebrew Prefix Conjugation," 14–15; see also Greenstein, "Prefixed Preterite," 9–11.

There are some cases of a *nâ* ending on third feminine singular forms (Judg 5:26, Job 17:16) and one on a second masculine plural form (Obad 13, identical to the Judg 5:26 form), perhaps energics. It has been suggested that the *nāʾ* precative particle (40.2.5c) is related to the energic. Williams, "Energic Verbal Forms," 85, is dubious about both proposals. On *nāʾ* as etymologically related to the energic, see recently H. Gottlieb, "The Hebrew Particle -*nāʾ*," *Acta Orientalia* 33 (1971) 47–54; and T. O. Lambdin, "The Junctural Origin of the West Semitic Definite Article," *Near Eastern Studies in Honor of William Foxwell Albright*, ed. Hans Goedicke (Baltimore: Johns Hopkins University, 1971) 315–33.

64. There are energic imperatives, e.g., 1 Sam 16:11, 20:21 (forms of *lqḥ*), 21:20 (*ntn*); for a list, see Williams, "Energic Verbal Forms," 83. There are also energic infinitives construct (pp. 83–84) and participles (p. 84), and, as a result of analogy, perfectives (Gen 30:6, Deut 24:13, Ps 118:18; cf. GKC § 59f / p. 160).

65. On possible first-person plural examples, see GKC § 58k / p. 158; cf. § 100o / pp. 296–97.

second (# 2), or third person (## 3–4). The *n* may be unassimilated (## 1a, 2a, 3a) or assimilated (# 1b, *n* + *n* > *nn*; # 2b, *n* + *k* > *kk*; ## 3b–4, *n* + *h* > *nn*).[66]

	unassimilated			*assimilated*	
1a.	יְכַבְּדָ֫נְנִי	Ps 50:23	1b.	תְּבַעֲתַ֫נִּי	Job 7:14
2a.	אֶתְּקֶ֫נְךָ	Jer 22:24[67]	2b.	יַטֶּ֫ךָּ	Job 36:18
				יִשְׂנָאֶ֑ךָּ	Prov 9:8
				יַכֶּ֫כָּה	Isa 10:24
3a.	יְסֹבְבֶ֫נְהוּ	Deut 32:10	3b.	יִשְׁמְרֶ֫נּוּ	Exod 21:29
	יְבָרֲכֶ֫נְהוּ	Ps 72:15		אֲרִיצֶ֫נּוּ	Jer 49:19
				תִּזְכְּרֶ֫נּוּ	Ps 8:5
				יְסוֹבְבֶ֫נּוּ	Ps 32:10
4.				וְנַעֲשֶׂ֫נָּה	Deut 30:12
				יִשָּׂאֶ֫נָּה	Prov 18:14

b The energic forms are found with past- (# 5) and present-time reference (# 6) and in expressions of wishes, positive (# 7) and negative (# 8). The variety of uses leads many to contend that no special sense attaches to the non-perfective energic forms.[68]

5.	יִצְּרֶ֫נְהוּ כְּאִישׁוֹן עֵינוֹ׃	He guarded it (Israel) like the apple of his eye.[69] Deut 32:10
6.	אֶרְאֶ֫נּוּ וְלֹא עַתָּה אֲשׁוּרֶ֫נּוּ וְלֹא קָרוֹב	I see him but not yet, I spy him but not nearby. Num 24:17
7.	כָּל־הַיּוֹם יְבָרֲכֶ֫נְהוּ׃	May he bless him all day. Ps 72:15
8.	וְאֵמָתוֹ אַל־תְּבַעֲתַ֫נִּי׃	O that his terror did not frighten me! Job 9:34

---

66. The unassimilated third feminine form is not attested; the unassimilated forms are rare in general; cf. n. 67.

67. This unassimilated second-person form is unique; see W. L. Holladay, *Jeremiah* (Philadelphia: Fortress,

1986), 1. 606, for a possible explanation.

68. GKC § 58l / p. 158 refers to emphasis; cf. Williams, "Energic Verbal Forms," 84–85; and *LHS* 146, 148.

69. See Rainey, "Ancient Prefix Conjugation," 16.

32

Waw + Suffix Conjugation

32.1

Form and Meaning

32.1.1

Diversity

a   The suffix conjugation preceded by *waw* is associated with two semantically distinct constructions, one with *relative* force and the other with *coordinate* force. Contrast these sentences.

| 1a. | וְהָיָה כְּקָרָבְכֶם אֶל־הַמִּלְחָמָה
וְנִגַּשׁ הַכֹּהֵן וְדִבֶּר אֶל־הָעָם: | It will be that when you are about to go into battle, the priest will come forward *and will speak* to the army.
Deut 20:2 |
| 1b. | הַהוּא אָמַר וְלֹא יַעֲשֶׂה
וְדִבֶּר וְלֹא יְקִימֶנָּה: | Does he (God) promise and not act?
And does he *speak* and not fulfill it?
Num 23:19 |

In # 1a the priest's speaking is relative and future to the preceding situation, in which he steps forward. In # 1b God's speaking is not relative to the preceding situation, in which he made a promise; rather, the same situation is expressed in another way. We call the first construction *waw-relative* and the second *waw-copulative*. (Traditionally the former has been called either *waw-conversive* or *waw-consecutive*.) These two semantically distinct constructions are similar in form in that the conjunction *wə* is inseparably prefixed to the suffix conjugation, and this bound form begins the clause. Are the two constructions formally distinguished in any way? David Qimḥi thought they could be distinguished by the preceding verb. According to him, if the preceding verb was in the suffix conjugation, then *wqtl* would be copulative; otherwise, it would be relative. He wrote:

> The [*waw*-relative] prefixed to a verb in the Perfect indicates action in the future, e.g. וְשָׁמַר Dt 7:12, etc. When preceded by a verb in the Perfect the Waw with Perfect has merely copulative force, e.g. פָּעַל וְעָשָׂה Is 41:4, אָכַל וְשָׁתָה וְעָשָׂה Jr 22:15.[1]

Although Qimḥi's distinction holds in his examples, it does not obtain for all relevant cases.

b   Rather, the two constructions are formally distinguished by accentuation, though only in some forms: *waw*-relative in first-person singular and second-person masculine singular throws the accent forward to the final syllable as much as possible (# 2b), whereas *waw*-copulative does not (# 2a).

2a.	וְהִצַּלְתִּי מִפִּיו	*And* I *rescued* (the sheep) from its mouth. 1 Sam 17:35
2b.	וְהִצַּלְתִּי אֶתְכֶם מֵעֲבֹדָתָם	*And* I *will rescue* you from being slaves to them. Exod 6:6

S. R. Driver compared this contrast through stress with similar phenomena in English and German.

> Exactly, therefore, as in English and German, we do not stultify ourselves by reading *con′vict, inva′lid, pre′sent, geb′et* (give!), where the context demands *convict′, in′valid′, present′, gebet′* (prayer), so in Hebrew we must beware of saying *wᵉqatálta* when grammar and logic call for *wᵉqátaltá*.[2]

Many forms of the suffix conjugation, however, always bear the accent on the last syllable (i.e., *milraᶜ*): for example, קָטְלוּ, אֲמַרְתֶּם, רָעוּ (from רעה), שָׁתָה, etc., and with such, no change is possible.

c   Even with the remaining forms (1 c.s. and 2 m.s.) there are many exceptions. The source of variation is semantic rather than strictly syntactic. "It is," as E. J. Revell notes, "often not possible to provide a precise, objective description of the conditioning of the

---

1. William Chomsky, *David Ḳimḥi's Hebrew Grammar (Mikhlol)* (New York: Bloch, 1952) 62. For verb sequencing elsewhere in Afroasiatic, see A. Loprieno, "The Sequential Forms in Late Egyptian and Biblical Hebrew," *Afroasiatic Linguistics* 7 (1980) 143–62.

2. S. R. Driver, *A Treatise on the Use of the Tenses in Hebrew* (3d ed.; Oxford: Clarendon, 1892) 115–16. The consonantal forms of (*a*) w + *infinitive absolute* and (*b*) w + *third-person masculine singular perfective* may be identical, and there may be cases in which the forms have been confused in the MT (*b* read as *a*, the less frequent combination, is likely to be more common). See J. Huesman, "The Infinitive Absolute and the Waw + Perfect Problem," *Biblica* 37 (1956) 410–34.

variations." For the most part these exceptions can be grouped into three categories. The stress is *usually* not thrown forward with *waw*-relative when (1) the suffix conjugation is followed immediately by a stressed syllable in the succeeding word (this phenomenon is known as *nesiga* or *nasog ʾaḥor*), (2) the penult is an open syllable, or (3) the word is in pause.[3] We can illustrate the first two points.

3.   אֶרֶץ כִּי תֶחֱטָא־לִי . . . וְנָטִ֫יתִי   If a country sins against me . . . and I stretch out my
     יָדִי . . . וְשָׁבַ֫רְתִּי לָהּ מַטֵּה־לֶחֶם   hand . . . and I break its food supply . . . and I cut
     . . . וְהִכְרַתִּ֫י מִמֶּ֫נָּה   off from it. . . .
                                          Ezek 14:13

Note that the stress shifts forward with והכרתי but not with ונטיתי and ושברתי because the penult is open in the former and the latter is followed immediately by a stressed syllable in the following word. In addition to these groups of exceptions, the form fluctuates in both the *Qal* and *Niphal* of geminate verbs and in forms from hollow (II-*waw*) roots that end in ו or הָ. Thus distinguishing between the two constructions involves not only formal distinctions but also contextual considerations.

The *wəqtl* combination (in all forms) occurs 6,378 times (13% of the conjugation forms; cf. 29.1c). It is most frequent in Leviticus, Amos, Zechariah, Deuteronomy, and Ezekiel.[4] Leviticus exhibits a high number because it contains many prescriptions. The combination is frequent in the first two sections of the canon, namely, the legal and prophetic books, and less frequent in the Writings, though it is common in Daniel and Qoheleth. The combination occurs much more frequently in the so-called Deuteronomistic work (Deuteronomy through 2 Kings) as over against the works of the so-called Chronicler (Chronicles through Ezra). This suggests that *wəqtl* (like *wayyqtl*) is dying.

Comparative Evidence   32.1.2

Two bodies of comparative data are useful in considering the constructions in   a
wə + *suffix form*, one from the Amarna texts, the other from Arabic.

The relative *waw* with suffix conjugation may be the descendant of a construction   b
found in Byblian Canaanite. The apodosis *waw* introduces a consequential independent clause (apodosis) after a conditional dependent clause (protasis). W. L. Moran writes, "In the Byblos letters there are thirty-three cases where the [Akkadian] perfect [reflecting the Canaanite usage] is used with reference to the future. Of these, twenty-four are

---

3. See Driver, *Tenses in Hebrew*, 122–23, for a fuller account; cf. E. J. Revell, "Stress and the *Waw* 'Consecutive' in Biblical Hebrew," *Journal of the American Oriental Society* 104 (1984) 437–44, esp. 439–40; and especially Revell, "The Conditioning of Stress Position in *Waw* Consecutive Perfect Forms in Biblical Hebrew," *Hebrew Annual Review* 9 (1985) 277–300, quotation at 280. Revell proposes that "stress position in perfect forms with *waw* consecutive is . . . conditioned by the intonation patterns

characteristic of the speech units" (p. 299). Qoheleth is exceptional for the *wqtl* form: there, even when the stress shifts in the *waqataltí* forms, the value is simple (copulative) *waw* with perfective aspect. On the first category above, see Revell, "Stress Position in *Waw* Consecutive," 279.

4. For this and the following statistics, see the tables in Bo Johnson, *Hebräisches Perfekt und Imperfekt mit vorangehendem wᵉ* (Lund: Gleerup, 1979) 24–29.

preceded by the conjunction *u*, 'and,' and are comparable, therefore, to the [*waw*-conversive with the perfect] of Hebrew."[5] Most of these twenty-four instances occur in sentences which are either explicitly or implicitly conditional: "the apparent inversion of the tenses is chiefly confined to the apodosis of conditional sentences and imperative sentences."[6] For example:

- (a) with a stative verb (after an imperative that is implicitly conditional): *dûkūmi eṭlakunu u ibaššātunu kīma yatinu u pašḫātunu*, 'Kill your lord, *and then* you *will be* like us *and have peace*'
- (b) with a fientive verb: *allu paṭārima awīlūt ḫupši u ṣabtū GAZ āla*, 'Behold! if the serfs desert, *then* the Hapiru *will seize* the city'

Because the force of *u*-relative with the suffix conjugation in Byblos is clearly 'and then,' Moran labeled it the "and of *succession*."

> In conditional sentences the force of the conjunction is clearly 'and then,' like Arabic *fa*. When used before a perfect with future meaning, its force, we believe, is the same, emphasizing that the following perfect is successive to the previous action.[7]

However, not all the Byblian cases of *u* + *perfect* signify succession; *u* in some cases simply marks coordination.

> We have . . . very many examples of a perfect preceded by *u* where there is clearly no inversion of tenses. Thus *u palḫātī anāku* "and I am afraid" . . . ; *u laqû ālānišu*, "and they have taken his cities."[8]

In sum, we find both relative and copulative *wqtl* in a Canaanite dialect shortly before the emergence of Hebrew. Moran has proposed that the relative *waw* in Biblical Hebrew developed its many diversified uses from an original function of introducing the apodosis after a conditional clause. In these uses the *wə* never lost its notion of succession 'then, and so' (temporal or logical).

c   Classical Arabic expresses two different notions of 'and' in a way which may help us to understand Hebrew. Arabic has two forms, *wa* and *fa*.[9] *Wa* is employed for "simple" (i.e., copulative) 'and,' *fa* for the "energic" (i.e., succession, result, purpose) 'and.' For the 'and' of succession, *fa* (rarely *wa*) is used with the indicative; for the purpose-consecutive 'and,' *fa* is used with the subjunctive.[10]

---

5. W. L. Moran, "The Hebrew Language in Its Northwest Semitic Background," *The Bible and the Ancient Near East: Essays in Honor of William Foxwell Albright*, ed. G. E. Wright (Garden City, New York: Doubleday, 1961; rpt. Winona Lake, Indiana: Eisenbrauns, 1979) 54–72, at 64; cf. W. F. Albright and W. L. Moran, "A Reinterpretation of an Amarna Letter from Byblos (EA 82)," *Journal of Cuneiform Studies* 2 (1948) 239–48.

6. Cf. Moran, "Hebrew Language," 64–65.

7. Cf. Moran, "Hebrew Language," 65.

8. Cf. Moran, "Hebrew Language," 65.

9. Arabic *fa* has a cognate in the rare Northwest Semitic conjunction *p* 'and (then),' attested in Ugaritic (*UT* § 12.1), in a variety of Aramaic dialects (C.-F. Jean and Jacob Hoftijzer, *Dictionnaire des inscriptions sémitiques de l'ouest* [Leiden: Brill, 1965] 225), and perhaps in Biblical Hebrew; on the last, see 39.2.6c.

10. Joüon § 115 / pp. 312–14.

Hebrew lacks this differentiation. The "simple" and "energic" 'and' are both ex-   d
pressed with וְ. With the suffix conjugation the two senses are sometimes distinguished by
stress. But even with the shift of stress no distinction is made between indicative (chronological) and subjunctive (logical) succession. And apart from the spotty stress shifts, we
can only distinguish the different meanings through careful study.

Meaning   **32.1.3**

Scholars are agreed that the *wə* in the *wəqataltí* construction usually (though not   a
always) signifies succession (temporal or logical), but they are not agreed about the
meaning of the suffix conjugation in this construction. Diethelm Michel, Bo Johnson,
and others think that it retains the same significance as in its unbound form,[11] while
S. R. Driver, Paul Joüon, Gotthelf Bergsträsser, Thomas O. Lambdin, Ernst Jenni, and
others think its value comes under the sway of the preceding verb to which it is appended.[12] The second view reflects a modern understanding of the medieval notion that
prefixed *waw* "converts" the conjugations.

A. O. Schulz laid the foundation for the view that relative *waw* does not alter the   b
function of the conjugations.[13] Johnson has recently restated it.

> In narrative the pure perfect is used in most instances as a "Tempus of the past." A
> perfect with a prefixed *wə*- is not used in these instances, since *wa* + imperfect already
> dominated in this sphere. Bobzin here draws the conclusion that *wa* + perfect, seen
> diachronically, cannot be derived from the meaning of the perfect but is rather totally
> dependent on its position in the system. But are these two alternatives incompatible?
> The pure perfect has a greater sphere than the *wə* + perfect. The *wə* + perfect is
> confined to the areas where *wa* + imperfect could not be used, for example, with 'and'
> and events which stand in a final or consecutive relation to the preceding. That does
> not mean, however, that the perfect here would have assumed a new final or consecu-
> tive meaning—this meaning lies in the whole construction with 'and' + the perfect and
> at the same time naturally also in the fact that *wa* + imperfect exists in the system.
> Both the *wə* + perfect and the perfect have the character of completed, concluded
> action, an action which is seen from without as something whole. At first glance that
> does not comport well with the final or consecutive function of the perfect, where a
> *wə* + perfect emphasizes the non-independence of the action and its dependence on
> the preceding. But even here the character of the perfect comes to the surface: the final
> or consecutive action in question is seen from without as a whole. The whole event is
> already there at one moment. With 'and' + perfect the following happening is seen as

11. D. Michel, *Tempora und Satzstellung in den Psalmen* (Bonn: Bouvier, 1960); Johnson, *Hebräisches Perfekt und Imperfekt.* Scholars occasionally try to use the problematic status of *wəqtl* forms as an entry into other, not strictly related spheres of research; see, e.g., R. Bartelmus, "Ez 37, 1–14, die Verbform *wᵉqatal* und die Anfänge der Auferstehungshoffnung," *Zeitschrift für die Alttestamentliche Wissenschaft* 97 (1985) 366–89.

12. Driver, *Tenses in Hebrew*, 116–18; Joüon § 115 / pp. 312–14; GB 2. 39–45 (§ 9); T. O. Lambdin, *Introduction to Biblical Hebrew* (New York: Scribner, 1971) 108–9; LHS 96–98, 264.

13. A. O. Schulz, *Über das Imperfekt und Perfekt mit* ·וְ (וַ) *im Hebräischen* (Königsberg Inaugural Dissertation, 1900).

a finished, complete whole. One does not enter into the following action in order to picture the initiative or intention of the acting subject, but one sees the happening as a finished moment, which is pointed out from without in its connections.[14]

c   Driver expressed the second view, which is closer to the traditional view.

> Whatever . . . be the shade of meaning borne by the first or "*dominant*" verb, the perfect following, inasmuch as the action it denotes is conceived to take place under the *same* conditions, assumes it too: be the dominant verb a jussive, frequentative, or subjunctive, the perfect is virtually the same. To all intents and purposes the perfect, when attached to a preceding verb by means of this waw consecutive, *loses its individuality*: no longer maintaining an independent position, it passes under the sway of the verb to which it is connected.[15]

As we shall see, Driver has overstated the situation; there are occasions, such as when *wǝqataltí* succeeds a perfective form (see 32.2.3), in which it does not take on a value of the dominant verb but rather of the non-perfective. More recently Jenni also represented the more traditional view.

> The *waw*-perfectum, like the *waw*-imperfectum, is a sequential tempus: through the perfectum consecutivum an action or an event is expressed which follows temporally or logically an imperfectum or imperative (or a nominal form with an equivalent value). . . . If the imperfectum designates repeated or enduring actions and events in the present or past time . . . , then the *waw*-perfectum also has this meaning.[16]

Two arguments favor this more traditional view. First, when a negative or other word comes between the *waw* and the perfective, the discourse returns to the non-perfective.

אִם תִּהְיוּ כָמֹנוּ . . . וְנָתַנּוּ אֶת־
בְּנֹתֵינוּ לָכֶם וְאֶת־בְּנֹתֵיכֶם נִקַּח־
לָנוּ וְיָשַׁבְנוּ אִתְּכֶם וְהָיִינוּ לְעַם
אֶחָד: וְאִם־לֹא תִשְׁמְעוּ אֵלֵינוּ
. . . וְלָקַחְנוּ אֶת־בִּתֵּנוּ וְהָלָכְנוּ:

If you become like us . . . then we will give you our daughters and *take* yours to ourselves. We will dwell with you and become one people (with you). But if you will not listen to us . . . , we will take our daughter and depart. Gen 34:15–17

Though it is true that *qtl* can refer to the future, does it not seem strange that the supposed switch of viewpoint from non-perfective to perfective occurs only with the relative-*waw* construction and that even the smallest insertion separating the *waw* from the verb form effects a switch such that the action is no longer looked at from without as complete but from within as incomplete? Further, as we shall see, the *wǝqataltí* construction not infrequently carries on the imperfective aspect of a preceding verb. Though the suffix conjugation can denote a gnomic notion (see 30.5.1c), it never by itself signifies customary activity in past time; that meaning is signified by the prefix conjugation.

---

14. Johnson, *Hebräisches Perfekt und Imperfekt*, 32.   16. *LHS* 106–7.
15. Driver, *Tenses in Hebrew*, 118.

Johnson, with his working hypothesis that the suffix conjugation has the same value both with and without relative *waw*, cites many examples where *wəqataltí* had an iterative meaning in past time.[17] The unbound suffix conjugation, however, does not have this value.

We are defending the traditional use both in terms of future time reference and in   d
terms of imperfective aspect in past and present time. The perfective/non-perfective opposition remains functional. Further, Driver and Jenni overgeneralize the matter when they contend without qualification that relative *waw* always comes under the sway of the dominant verb. Elsewhere Driver remarks: "If, for instance, the principal verb involve *will, would,* or *let . . . ,* the subordinate verbs connected with it by ו consecutive must be understood in the same tense or mood."[18] Driver's comment is apt if *yqtl* precede *wəqataltí*, for after *yqtl*, *wəqataltí* takes on the specific value of *yqtl*. But his statement is not accurate if a *qtl* form with preterite value, for example, precedes the *waw*-relative. As Driver himself notes elsewhere, *wəqataltí* in that connection may also signify the same non-perfective values as in its connection with *yqtl*.[19]

Relative *wqtl* is subordinate to a primary verb (or equivalent) and in that connection   e
it represents either an epexegetical situation with imperfective aspect (only in past or present time) or a consequential (logical and/or temporal) situation. Since imperfective aspect and future-time reference are primary associations of the non-perfective conjugation, relative *waw* can be thought of as a "*waw*-conversive," though that label does not do justice to its subordinating function. The term "*waw*-consecutive" also does not do justice to all uses of the form in question. As we shall see, after the perfective conjugation, for example, *waw*-relative does not represent a chronologically successive situation but rather explicates the one represented as a single whole. In sum, *wəqataltí* has the values of the prefix conjugation and represents a situation relative (that is subordinate) to the leading verb (or equivalent).

Relative *Waw* + Suffix Conjugation   **32.2**

The proposed original function of the *wəqataltí* construction to signify the apodosis   a
of a conditional clause shines through almost all of its uses in Biblical Hebrew. In most instances *wə* in this construction is equivalent to English 'then.' This primary function becomes more apparent if we accept Lambdin's broad definition of a conditional sentence: "Any two clauses, the first of which states a real or hypothetical condition, and the second of which states a real or hypothetical consequence thereof, may be taken as a conditional sentence."[20] Conditional sentences represent one situation as logically contingent on another and entail a temporal sequence as well. Sometimes, in fact, the notion of logical succession gives way to chronological succession, though often the line of distinction between the two ideas is blurred, just as with the English 'then.' Furthermore, the notion of logical contingency may also develop into expressing a final or consecutive idea.

---

17. Johnson, *Hebräisches Perfekt und Imperfekt*, 38–41.
18. Driver, *Tenses in Hebrew*, 123–24.
19. Driver, *Tenses in Hebrew*, 139–40.

20. Lambdin, *Introduction to Biblical Hebrew*, 276; cf. Joüon § 167 / pp. 512–18 on temporal and conditional clausal connections.

Because these ideas cannot always be sharply demarcated from one another, Johnson groups together under one heading uses with "future, final or consecutive meaning."[21]

b   As Johnson also notes, in many instances the distinct meanings can be more exactly differentiated.[22] Here we aim to analyze the uses more strictly, but it should be remembered that the essential meaning involves clausal subordination. When the connection with what precedes is not focal, the construction is dropped and the non-perfective conjugation reappears. *Wəqataltí* in a chain either takes on the value of a preceding *wəqataltí* form or functions as an apodosis *waw*.[23]

32.2.1   After Prefix-Conjugation Forms

a   We have already analyzed the meanings and values that characterize the prefix conjugation (Chap. 31). Here we present the common uses of that form as they affect the construction under investigation.

b   If the protasis of a conditional clause has a non-perfective form with a contingent-future sense (after אִם, כִּי, etc.),[24] the apodosis is introduced by *wəqataltí*; the *waw* has the apparently archaic role of the "apodosis *waw*" (## 1–4).

1.	אִם־יִהְיֶה אֱלֹהִים עִמָּדִי . . . וְהָיָה יְהוָה לִי לֵאלֹהִים׃	If God will be with me . . . *then* Yhwh *will be* my God. Gen 28:20–21
2.	אִם־יַעַבְרוּ . . . אִתְּכֶם . . . וּנְתַתֶּם לָהֶם	If they cross over . . . with you, . . . you *shall give* them. . . . Num 32:29
3.	וְעַתָּה אִם־שָׁמוֹעַ תִּשְׁמְעוּ בְּקֹלִי . . . וִהְיִיתֶם לִי סְגֻלָּה	And now if you obey me fully . . . , *then* you *will be* my *segullâ*. Exod 19:5
4.	כִּי־יִהְיֶה לָהֶם דָּבָר בָּא אֵלַי וְשָׁפַטְתִּי . . . וְהוֹדַעְתִּי אֶת־חֻקֵּי הָאֱלֹהִים	Whenever they have a matter that comes to me, I *judge* . . . and *make known* the statutes of God. Exod 18:16

c   Often *waw*-relative with the suffix conjugation represents a situation as a simple (con)sequence, whether logical, temporal, or both, of a preceding situation represented by the non-perfective conjugation. This *simple (con)sequential wəqataltí* can be illustrated (# 5; cf. # 1).

---

21. Johnson, *Hebräisches Perfekt und Imperfekt*, 35–38.

22. Johnson, *Hebräisches Perfekt und Imperfekt*, 35.

23. For the survey that follows, cf. GB 2. 40 (§ 9b–d). On the apodosis *waw*, see Joüon § 176 / pp. 529–32.

24. For a catalog of the particles involved, see Driver, *Tenses in Hebrew*, 129–36. The protasis usually has a non-perfective form in Biblical Hebrew, but in Qumranic Hebrew "*qtl* in the protasis is much more common"; see E. Qimron, *The Hebrew of the Dead Sea Scrolls* (Atlanta:

Scholars Press, 1986) 84. Rodney K. Duke has recently contended that after such a protasis, the *wəqataltí* form can serve to continue the protasis and need not represent the apodosis; even if we admit that Deut 18:6–8 is problematic, the other passages he cites in Deuteronomy (notably 17:14–15) hardly constitute compelling counterexamples to the pattern described above; see "The Portion of the Levite," *Journal of Biblical Literature* 106 (1987) 193–201, at 196.

5. אִם־יִהְיֶה אֱלֹהִים עִמָּדִי וּשְׁמָרַ֫נִי
בַּדֶּ֫רֶךְ הַזֶּה . . . וְנָֽתַן־לִי לֶ֫חֶם
לֶאֱכֹל וּבֶ֫גֶד לִלְבֹּשׁ: וְשַׁבְתִּ֫י
בְשָׁלוֹם . . . וְהָיָה יהוה לִי
לֵאלֹהִים:

If God will be with me *and will watch* over me on this way . . . *and will give* me food to eat and clothes to wear *so that* I return safely . . . , then Yʜᴡʜ will be my God.
Gen 28:20–21

In this example, וּשְׁמרני and ונתן represent chronologically (and logically) successive situations; וּשבתי is a situation logically successive to all three preceding situations; and והיה expresses the apodosis to this extended protasis. In # 6 (cf. # 3) the protasis is also expanded by a (con)sequential *wqtl*.

6. וְעַתָּה אִם־שָׁמ֫וֹעַ תִּשְׁמְעוּ בְּקֹלִי
וּשְׁמַרְתֶּם אֶת־בְּרִיתִי וִהְיִיתֶם

If you obey me fully *and keep* my covenant, then you will be. . . .
Exod 19:5

On the other hand, (con)sequential *wqtl* expands the apodosis in # 7 (cf. # 4).

7. וְשָׁפַטְתִּ֫י בֵּין אִישׁ וּבֵין רֵעֵ֫הוּ
וְהוֹדַעְתִּ֫י

. . . then I judge between the parties *and make known* to them. . . .
Exod 18:16

The (con)sequential *wqtl* usually takes on the sense of the preceding non-perfective, which may be imperfective (## 8–13), modal (## 14–16), legislational (## 17–18), volitional (# 19), future (## 20–25), or telic (## 26–29).   d

8. וְאֵד יַעֲלֶה מִן־הָאָ֫רֶץ וְהִשְׁקָה

Streams would come up from the earth *and would water*. . . .
Gen 2:6

9. . . . כִּי מִן־הַבְּאֵר הַהִיא יַשְׁקוּ
וְנֶאֶסְפוּ־שָׁ֫מָּה כָל־הָעֲדָרִים
וְגָלֲלוּ אֶת־הָאֶ֫בֶן . . . וְהִשְׁקוּ
אֶת־הַצֹּאן וְהֵשִׁ֫יבוּ אֶת־הָאֶ֫בֶן

From that well they (people) would water . . . and all the flocks *would gather* there, *and* they *would roll away* the stone . . . , *and* they *would water* the sheep; *and* they *would return* the stone.
Gen 29:2–3

10. עַל־כֵּן יַעֲזָב־אִישׁ אֶת־אָבִיו
וְאֶת־אִמּוֹ וְדָבַק בְּאִשְׁתּוֹ

Therefore a man leaves his father and mother *and clings* to his wife.
Gen 2:24

11. אַף־יַשִּׂיק וְאָ֫פָה לָ֫חֶם

He kindles a fire *and bakes* bread.
Isa 44:15

12. תִּרְאֵ֫נִי וּבָחַנְתָּ לִבִּי

You see me *and test* my heart.
Jer 12:3

13. כֻּלָּם יֵחַ֫מּוּ כַּתַּנּוּר וְאָכְלוּ אֶת־
שֹׁפְטֵיהֶם

All of them are as hot as an oven *and they devour* their judges.
Hos 7:7

14. אִם־יָבוֹא עֵשָׂו אֶל־הַמַּחֲנֶה הָאַחַת וְהִכָּהוּ וְהָיָה הַמַּחֲנֶה הַנִּשְׁאָר לִפְלֵיטָה:

If Esau comes (i.e., should come) to one camp *and smites* it, then the remaining camp will be a fugitive.[25]
Gen 32:9

15. וּבַמֶּה נוּכַל לוֹ וַאֲסַרְנֻהוּ לְעַנֹּתוֹ

How can we prevail over him *and tie* him up to subdue him?
Judg 16:5

16. דֶּרֶךְ שְׁלֹשֶׁת יָמִים נֵלֵךְ בַּמִּדְבָּר וְזָבַחְנוּ לַיהוה אֱלֹהֵינוּ

We must go a three days' journey into the wilderness *and sacrifice* to Yнwн our God.
Exod 8:23

17. אֶל־פֶּתַח אֹהֶל מוֹעֵד יַקְרִיב אֹתוֹ . . . וְסָמַךְ יָדוֹ

At the entrance of the Tent of Meeting he will offer it . . . *and he will lay* his hand. . . .
Lev 1:3–4

18. שֵׁשֶׁת יָמִים תַּעֲבֹד וְעָשִׂיתָ כָּל־מְלַאכְתֶּךָ

Six days you shall labor *and do* all your work.
Exod 20:9

19. כִּי אֶל־אַרְצִי . . . תֵּלֵךְ וְלָקַחְתָּ אִשָּׁה

To my land you shall go *and take* a wife. . . .
Gen 24:4

20. אוּלַי יְמֻשֵּׁנִי אָבִי וְהָיִיתִי

Perhaps my father will feel me, *and I shall be*. . . .
Gen 27:12

21. אוֹ־יוֹמוֹ יָבוֹא וָמֵת אוֹ בַמִּלְחָמָה יֵרֵד וְנִסְפָּה:

. . . or his day will come *and he will die*, or he will go into battle *and perish*.
1 Sam 26:10

22. אֶהְיֶה עִמָּךְ וְהִכִּיתָ

I will be with you, *and you will strike down*. . . .
Judg 6:16

23. עַבְדְּךָ יֵלֵךְ וְנִלְחַם

Your servant will go *and fight*.
1 Sam 17:32

24. וְאֵיךְ אֶעֱשֶׂה הָרָעָה הַגְּדֹלָה הַזֹּאת וְחָטָאתִי לֵאלֹהִים:

How could I do this great evil *and sin* against God?
Gen 39:9

25. נָכוֹן יִהְיֶה הַר בֵּית־יהוה בְּרֹאשׁ הֶהָרִים וְנִשָּׂא מִגְּבָעוֹת וְנָהֲרוּ אֵלָיו כָּל־הַגּוֹיִם: וְהָלְכוּ עַמִּים רַבִּים וְאָמְרוּ

The mountain of Yнwн's temple will be established as the highest mountain; it *will be raised* above the hills, *and* all nations *will stream* to it. Many *will come and say*. . . .
Isa 2:2–3

26. וּלְמַעַן תְּסַפֵּר . . . וִידַעְתֶּם כִּי־אֲנִי יהוה:

. . . so that you may tell . . . *and know* that I am Yнwн.
Exod 10:2

27. אֲשֶׁר יִשְׁמְעוּן שִׁמְעֲךָ וְרָגְזוּ

. . . so that they will hear reports about you *and tremble*.
Deut 2:25

---

25. Note the two distinct uses of *wəqtl* in this chain.

28. לְמַ֫עַן יִֽיטַב־לִי . . . וְחָיְתָ֥ה
     נַפְשִׁ֖י בִּגְלָלֵֽךְ׃

. . . so that it may go well with me . . . *and* my life *will be spared* for your sake.
Gen 12:13

29. פֶּן־יִשְׁלַ֣ח יָד֗וֹ וְלָקַח֙ . . . וְאָכַ֖ל

. . . lest he reach out his hand *and take* . . . *and eat.* . . .
Gen 3:22

Sometimes the non-perfective is used in anticipatory (*casus pendens*) clauses (4.7) **e** and *wəqataltí* functions as a main clause (## 30–33), often with a resumptive pronoun (## 30, 32).[26] The *casus pendens* resembles a conditional clause.

30. אֲשֶׁר־יַכֶּ֥ה אֶת־קִרְיַת־סֵ֖פֶר
     וּלְכָדָ֑הּ וְנָתַ֥תִּי ל֛וֹ אֶת־עַכְסָ֥ה
     בִתִּ֖י לְאִשָּֽׁה׃

As for him who smites Qiryath-sepher and seizes it, I *shall give* him my daughter Aksah in marriage.
Judg 1:12

31. וַאֲשֶׁ֙ר לֹ֣א צָדָ֔ה . . . וְשַׂמְתִּ֥י לְךָ֖
     מָק֕וֹם אֲשֶׁ֥ר יָנ֖וּס שָֽׁמָּה׃

As for him who did not lie in wait . . . , I *shall provide* you a place whither he may flee.
Exod 21:13

32. וְטַפְּכֶ֗ם אֲשֶׁ֤ר אֲמַרְתֶּם֙ לָבַ֣ז יִהְיֶ֔ה
     וְהֵבֵיאתִ֖י אֹתָ֑ם

As for your little ones whom you thought would become prey, I *shall cause* them to enter. . . .
Num 14:31

33. מַה־יַּרְאֵ֖נִי וְהִגַּ֥דְתִּי לָֽךְ

Whatever he reveals to me, I *will tell* you.
Num 23:3

After Volitional Forms

32.2.2

Wəqataltí may express a consequent (logical and/or chronological) situation to a **a** situation represented by a volitional form (cohortative, imperative, jussive; #1 b). By contrast, a construction involving *wə* bound to an imperative after another imperative does not signify a directly consequent situation (# 1a; cf. 34.6a).

1a. הִתְיַצְּב֗וּ וּרְאוּ֙ אֶת־יְשׁוּעַ֣ת
     יְהוָ֔ה

Stand firm *and see* (imperative) YHWH's deliverance.
Exod 14:13

1b. עֲל֥וּ זֶה֙ בַּנֶּ֔גֶב . . . וּרְאִיתֶ֥ם
     אֶת־הָאָ֖רֶץ מַה־הִֽוא

Go up through the Negev . . . *and (so) see* (wqtl) what the land is like.
Num 13:17–18

---

26. Phoenician-Punic furnishes examples of this sentence type. See C. R. Krahmalkov, "The *Qatal* with Future Tense Reference in Phoenician," *Journal of Semitic Studies* 31 (1986) 5–10. Since the *w* is not always present in the Punic examples, Krahmalkov contends "that the presence of the conjunction is purely stylistic, serving the sole function of co-ordinating the clauses. That is, there is no inherent syntactic force in *w*- that 'converts' a perfect (past) into an imperfect (future). The *qatal* is, in other words, unmarked for tense, its future tense reference a factor of the syntactic structure in which it is embedded" (p. 10). We would propose that historically *w* was necessary for this construction and only came to be omitted at a relatively advanced stage in development.

Succession as in # 1a may be implied by lexical considerations, but it is not grammatically indicated, as in # 1b. For example, in English, 'divide and conquer' signifies a consecutive relationship between the two imperatives, but that is not so with the command 'eat and drink.' These two statements are grammatically similar, but they represent different relationships for lexical reasons; the same is true in Hebrew.

b   The most important of the volitional forms is the imperative (## 2–3), and, as Driver notes, *wəqatalti* is "by far the most common construction after an imperative: sometimes, however, a succession of imperatives is preferred, and sometimes the perfect and imperative alternate."[27] It is also found after cohortatives (## 4–6) and jussives (## 7–8).

2.	לֵךְ וְאָמַרְתָּ֙ אֶל־עַבְדִּי	Go *and tell* my servant. 2 Sam 7:5
3.	עֲשֵׂה לְךָ תֵּבַת עֲצֵי־גֹפֶר . . . וְכָפַרְתָּ֣ אֹתָהּ	Make yourself a gopherwood ark . . . *and pitch* it. Gen 6:14
4.	וַאֲבָרֲכָה מְבָרְכֶ֑יךָ . . . וְנִבְרְכוּ בְךָ כֹּל מִשְׁפְּחֹת הָאֲדָמָה׃	I will bless the ones blessing you . . . *and (so)* all the clans of the earth *will be blessed* in you.[28] Gen 12:3
5.	אֲלַקֳטָה־נָּא וְאָסַפְתִּ֖י	Let me glean *and (so) gather*. Ruth 2:7
6.	וְנִקְרְבָה בְּאַחַד הַמְּקֹמֹות וְלַ֖נּוּ	Let us approach one of these places *and spend the night.* . . . Judg 19:13
7.	יְהִי מְאֹרֹת . . . וְהָיוּ	Let there be lights . . . *and let* them *be* for. . . . Gen 1:14
8.	וְנֹ֤ועַ יָנֻ֣ועוּ בָנָיו וְשִׁאֵ֑לוּ	Let his children wander about *and beg*. Ps 109:10

32.2.3   After Suffix-Conjugation (and *wayyqtl*) Forms

a   *Waw*-relative suffix forms used after a suffix form do not take on that conjugation's perfective aspect. Rather, in that connection *wəqatalti* signifies either a consequent (logical and/or chronological) situation (without aspect, in future time) to the one represented by *qtl* or an epexegetical situation (with an imperfective aspect in past or present time). The consequent meaning attaches to *wəqatalti* when it functions in an apodosis after a conditional clause, or when the situation represented by *qtl* constitutes the basis for the one envisioned by relative *wəqatalti*, which may thus be volitional. The clause with *qtl* may be a conditional clause, which may be unmarked or introduced by a particle such as אם. Relative *wqtl* normally signifies an epexegetical situation with imperfective aspect after *qtl* forms (or *wayyqtl*) representing a past situation. In this connection it unpacks

---

27. Driver, *Tenses in Hebrew*, 125.
28. On the grammar of this difficult verse, see P. D.

Miller, Jr., "Syntax and Theology in Genesis XII 3a," *Vetus Testamentum* 34 (1984) 472–76.

the situation represented as a single event, thereby specifying the perfective situation as constative (30.1d).

In the *apodosis-waw construction* the suffix conjugation preceding the apodosis **b** *waw* has a value which characterizes that conjugation (30.5.4). The protasis may be marked with a particle (## 1–3) or not (## 4–6); a stative verb may be used in the protasis (# 2).

1. אִם־גֻּלַּחְתִּי וְסָר מִמֶּנִּי כֹחִי
   וְחָלִיתִי וְהָיִיתִי כְּכָל־הָאָדָם:

   If I were shaved, my strength *would leave* me, and I would become weak and become like any other man.[29]
   Judg 16:17

2. אִם־חָפֵץ בָּנוּ יהוה וְהֵבִיא אֹתָנוּ
   אֶל־הָאָרֶץ הַזֹּאת

   If Yhwh is pleased with us, he *will lead* us into this land.
   Num 14:8

3. אִם עָבַרְתָּ אִתִּי וְהָיִתָ עָלַי
   לְמַשָּׂא:

   If you go with me, you *will be* a burden to me.
   2 Sam 15:33

4. וּדְפָקוּם יוֹם אֶחָד וָמֵתוּ כָּל־
   הַצֹּאן:

   If they drive them hard for just one day, all the flock *will die*.
   Gen 33:13

5. וְעָזַב אֶת־אָבִיו וָמֵת:

   And if he left his father, he (his father) *would die*.
   Gen 44:22

6. וְשָׁמַע שָׁאוּל וַהֲרָגָנִי

   And if Saul heard (about it), he *would kill* me.
   1 Sam 16:2

In a *simple (con)sequential situation*, the independent clause represented by *qtl* also **c** constitutes the logical basis or cause for the situation expressed by relative *wqtl* (see 32.2.1). This pattern can involve any use of the perfective, with past-time reference (## 7–8), or the recent past or present perfect situation (## 9–12); the *qtl* form may be a stative (# 13), an epistolary perfective (# 14), a perfective of resolve (# 15), or an accidental future perfective (## 16–17).

7. גַּם אֶת־הָאֲרִי גַּם־הַדּוֹב הִכָּה
   עַבְדֶּךָ וְהָיָה הַפְּלִשְׁתִּי . . . כְּאַחַד
   מֵהֶם

   Your servant smote both the lion and the bear *and* the Philistine *will be* . . . like one of them.
   1 Sam 17:36

8. כִּמְעַט שָׁכַב אַחַד . . . אֶת־
   אִשְׁתֶּךָ וְהֵבֵאתָ עָלֵינוּ אָשָׁם:

   Someone . . . might have slept . . . with your wife *and* you *would have brought* trouble on us.[30]
   Gen 26:10

9. כִּי־עַתָּה הִרְחִיב יהוה לָנוּ
   וּפָרִינוּ בָאָרֶץ:

   Now Yhwh has given us room *and* we *will flourish* in the land.
   Gen 26:22

---

29. Note the two different uses of *wqtl* in this chain.   30. Note the implicit condition.

10. קָרַע יהוה אֶת־מַמְלְכוּת . . . מֵעָלֶיךָ הַיּוֹם וּנְתָנָהּ
YHWH has rent the kingdom . . . from you today *and* he *will give* it. . . .
1 Sam 15:28

11. הִנֵּה נָגַע זֶה עַל־שְׂפָתֶיךָ וְסָר עֲוֹנֶךָ וְחַטָּאתְךָ תְּכֻפָּר:
This has touched your lips *and so* your guilt *shall depart* and your sin will be atoned for.
Isa 6:7

12. אֲנִי יהוה דִּבַּרְתִּי וְעָשִׂיתִי:
I YHWH have spoken *and will do* (it).
Ezek 17:24, 22:14, etc.

13. נָקֵל . . . וּנְתַתִּיךָ
It is too small a thing . . . I *will make* you. . . .
Isa 49:6

14. הִנֵּה שָׁלַחְתִּי אֵלֶיךָ אֶת־נַעֲמָן . . . וַאֲסַפְתּוֹ
I am sending Naaman to you . . . *so that* you *might cure* him.
2 Kgs 5:6

15. חַי־יהוה כִּי־אִם־רַצְתִּי אַחֲרָיו וְלָקַחְתִּי מֵאִתּוֹ מְאוּמָה:
As YHWH lives: I will run after him *and get* something from him.
2 Kgs 5:20

16. הִנֵּה בֵּרַכְתִּי אֹתוֹ וְהִפְרֵיתִי אֹתוֹ
I will bless him *and make* him *fruitful.*
Gen 17:20

17. שָׁלַחְתִּי בָבֶלָה וְהוֹרַדְתִּי בָרִיחִים כֻּלָּם
I will send to Babylon *and bring* them all *down* as fugitives.
Isa 43:14

d In some contexts, especially in legal literature, relative *wqtl* with a consecutive notion takes on a subordinate volitional force. This force may also characterize the non-perfective conjugation, the non-subordinate equivalent of *wəqataltí* (31.5).

18. רַק בַּאֲבֹתֶיךָ חָשַׁק יהוה לְאַהֲבָה אוֹתָם וַיִּבְחַר . . . כַּיּוֹם הַזֶּה: וּמַלְתֶּם אֵת עָרְלַת לְבַבְכֶם וְעָרְפְּכֶם לֹא תַקְשׁוּ עוֹד:
Yet on your forebears YHWH set his affections and he chose . . . as it is today. *So circumcise* the foreskins of your hearts, and do not be stiff-necked any longer.
Deut 10:15–16

According to the theology of Deuteronomy, Israel should offer God future obedience on the basis of past gracious acts to them, and here as elsewhere *wəqataltí* represents the entreaty form (ומלתם), and *qtl* + *wayyqtl* the past acts (חשק . . . ויבחר).[31]

19. רָאוּ עֵינֶיךָ . . . וָאוֹלֵךְ . . . וּשְׁמַרְתֶּם
Your eyes have seen . . . and I led you . . . *so carefully follow.* . . .
Deut 29:2, 4, 8

---

31. Sometimes it is not clear whether an imperative sense is intended; consider *hwṣyʾ . . . wydʿt* in Deut 7:8–9: is it
'He brought you . . . so that you might know' or ' . . . (so) know!'?

20.   הַחַיִּים וְהַמָּוֶת נָתַתִּי לְפָנֶיךָ . . .   Life and death I set before you . . . *so choose* life.
        וּבָחַרְתָּ בַּחַיִּים   Deut 30:19

This use is not confined to Deuteronomy.

21.   כִּי אִם־זְכַרְתַּנִי אִתְּךָ . . . וְעָשִׂיתָ   But if you remember me . . . *then show mercy* to me
        נָּא עִמָּדִי חָסֶד וְהִזְכַּרְתַּנִי   . . . *and remember* me.[32]
                                                Gen 40:14

22.   עַתָּה שַׁבְנוּ אֵלֶיךָ וְהָלַכְתָּ עִמָּנוּ   Now we have turned to you. *So come* with us.
                                                Judg 11:8

After *qtl* (or *wayyqtl*) representing a situation in past time, subordinate *wqtl* rep-   e
resents an imperfective situation within the single event, the *epexegetical wǝqataltí* construction (cf. 33.2.2; see also 32.2.1d # 9).

23.   וַיִּבְחַר מֹשֶׁה אַנְשֵׁי־חַיִל . . .   Moses chose capable men . . . and he placed them as
        וַיִּתֵּן אֹתָם רָאשִׁים . . . וְשָׁפְטוּ . . .   heads . . . *and* they *would judge*. . . . The difficult cases
        אֶת־הַדָּבָר הַקָּשֶׁה יְבִיאוּן אֶל־   they would bring to Moses, but all the simple ones
        מֹשֶׁה וְכָל־הַדָּבָר הַקָּטֹן יִשְׁפּוּטוּ   they decided on their own.
        הֵם׃   Exod 18:25–26

We prefer to interpret the *wqtl* construction as epexegetical with an imperfective meaning
rather than as copulative with perfective value for two reasons.[33] First, epexegetical
wǝqataltí may signify a (future) consequence, a primary meaning of the non-perfective
conjugation, after *qtl*. We see no reason for denying the possibility that it might also
express imperfective aspect, the other primary value of the non-perfective conjugation, in
the same syntactical construction. Second, when the chain is broken the text reverts to
yqtl, which signifies imperfective aspect in past time (see, e.g., # 23). In this connection
the situation represented by *wǝqataltí* does not chronologically follow that expressed by
the suffix conjugation, but rather explains the leading situation. The aspectual value of
epexegetical *wǝqataltí* after *qtl* can be seen by contrasting that construction with *wayyqtl*
after היה. Lambdin contrasts the two constructions with these examples.[34]

הָיָה רָעָב בָּאָרֶץ וְיָרַד מִצְרָיְמָה   There was a famine in the land and he used to go
                                          down to Egypt (customary).

הָיָה רָעָב בָּאָרֶץ וַיֵּרֶד מִצְרָיְמָה   There was a famine in the land and he went down to
                                          Egypt (specific, punctual).

By this contrast Lambdin rightly aims to show the difference in aspect between the two
sentences. The first is imperfective, more specifically customary, the second perfective,
more specifically preterite. But the sentences also differ with respect to temporal sequence.

32. Note the particle of entreaty *nāʾ/nnāʾ*, usually used   33. With Driver, *Tenses in Hebrew*, 117–18.
with modal forms (40.2.5c).   34. Lambdin, *Introduction to Biblical Hebrew*, 279.

The verb וְיָרַד is contemporary with the primary situation, while וַיֵּרֶד is probably chronologically successive to the first. Lambdin confines the contemporary/sequential differentiation to sentences with היה in the main clause. In any narrative sequence, however, relative *waqataltí* signifies a past situation that is subordinate or epexegetical to a situation represented by *wayyqtl* or *qtl* in the leading clause.

24.	וַיִּשְׁפֹּט שְׁמוּאֵל אֶת־יִשְׂרָאֵל . . . וְהָלַךְ	And Samuel judged Israel . . . *and would go*. . . . 1 Sam 7:15–16
25.	וּמֵישַׁע . . . הָיָה נֹקֵד וְהֵשִׁיב . . . כָּרִים	Now Mesha . . . was a sheep breeder *and* he *would supply* . . . lambs. 2 Kgs 3:4
26.	וְהַכְּשָׁבִים הִפְרִיד יַעֲקֹב . . . וְהָיָה	Now Jacob set apart the young of the flock. . . . *And* there *would be*. . . . Gen 30:40–41
27.	וְגַם אָנֹכִי מָנַעְתִּי מִכֶּם אֶת־ הַגֶּשֶׁם . . . וְהִמְטַרְתִּי עַל־עִיר אֶחָת וְעַל־עִיר אַחַת לֹא אַמְטִיר חֶלְקָה אַחַת תִּמָּטֵר וְחֶלְקָה אֲשֶׁר־ לֹא־תַמְטִיר עָלֶיהָ תִּיבָשׁ׃ וְנָעוּ שְׁתַּיִם שָׁלֹשׁ עָרִים אֶל־עִיר אַחַת	I also withheld rain from you. . . . I *would send rain* on one city, but would withhold it from another. One field would have rain; another, which would have none, would dry up. People of two or three cities *would stagger* to one city. . . . Amos 4:7–8

32.2.4   After Nominal Clauses

a   The *waqataltí* form after nominal clauses shows the same range of meanings as after suffix-conjugation forms: it is found in the apodosis after a conditional clause (# 1); in a consequent situation (## 2–9), which may be volitional (# 9); or with an imperfective sense (# 10–11).

1.	וְאִם־אֵין מוֹשִׁיעַ אֹתָנוּ וְיָצָאנוּ אֵלֶיךָ׃	If there is none to save us, we *will surrender* to you. 1 Sam 11:3
2.	הַעוֹד־לִי בָנִים בְּמֵעַי וְהָיוּ לָכֶם לַאֲנָשִׁים׃	Do I still have sons in my womb *that* they *may become* husbands for you? Ruth 1:11
3.	הֲכִי־אָחִי אַתָּה וַעֲבַדְתַּנִי חִנָּם	Because you are a relative of mine, *should* you *serve* me for nothing? Gen 29:15
4.	אֲנִי יהוה וְהוֹצֵאתִי אֶתְכֶם . . .	I am Yʜᴡʜ, *and* I *will bring* you *out*. . . . Exod 6:6
5.	אֵין־יִרְאַת אֱלֹהִים . . . וַהֲרָגוּנִי	There is no fear of God . . . *and* they *will kill* me. Gen 20:11
6.	הִנֵּה־נָא אַתְּ־עֲקָרָה וְלֹא יָלַדְתְּ וְהָרִית וְיָלַדְתְּ בֵּן׃	You are sterile and have not borne a child, *but* you *will become pregnant and bear* a son. Judg 13:3

7. וּמִי בֶן־יִשַׁי . . . וְלָקַחְתִּ֫י . . .
וְנָתַתִּ֫י

Who is this son of Jesse . . . *that I should take . . . and give. . . .*
1 Sam 25:10–11

8. מָחָר חֹ֫דֶשׁ וְנִפְקַ֫דְתָּ

Tomorrow is New Moon, *and* you *will be missed.*
1 Sam 20:18

9. זֹאת עֲבֹדַת בְּנֵי־קְהָת . . . וּבָא
אַהֲרֹן וּבָנָיו

This is the work of the Kohathites . . . Aaron and his sons *will enter.* . . .[35]
Num 4:4–5

10. כִּי חֹק לַכֹּהֲנִים מֵאֵת פַּרְעֹה
וְאָכְלוּ אֶת־חֻקָּם

. . . because the priests had an allotment from Pharaoh *and would eat* from their allotment.
Gen 47:22

11. אֵ֫שֶׁת כְּסִילוּת הֹמִיָּה . . .
וְיָשְׁבָה לְפֶ֫תַח בֵּיתָהּ

The woman Folly is loud . . .
and sits at the entrance of her house.
Prov 9:13–14

With Non-Finite Verb Forms   32.2.5

Wəqataltí forms can be used with all three types of non-finite verb forms. After a **a**
participle used in a conditional clause, relative *wəqtl* can serve in the apodosis (# 1). The
participle used as a *casus pendens* (## 2–4) is similar to a conditional clause. The *wəqtl*
form can be used to describe a consequent situation, whether temporal (# 5) or logical
(## 6–7; # 6 with a volitional force), or an imperfective situation (cf. # 12). Both *wayyqtl*
and relative *wəqtl* may follow a participle. How do the two constructions differ? Driver
rightly noted that the latter construction occurs in connection with indefinite situations
whereas the former occurs with concrete ones:

> Wherever the [participle] or [infinitive] asserts something indefinite or undetermined—
> wherever, therefore, it may be resolved into *whoever, whenever, if ever* etc. . . . —we
> find the *perfect* with ‫ו‬ consecutive employed: where, on the contrary, the [participle] or
> [infinitive] asserts an actual concrete event, we find the following verbs connected with
> it by the *imperfect* and ·‫ו‬.[36]

This contrast between *wayyqtl* and *wəqataltí* after the participle is consistent with the
theory that *qtl* inverts its value with *waw*-relative and that *wayyqtl* preserves a preterite
value.

1. הַנֹּגֵעַ בְּמֵת . . . וְטָמֵא

Whoever touches one who has died . . . *will be unclean.*
Num 19:11

2. כִּי כָּל־אֹכֵל חָמֵץ וְנִכְרְתָה
הַנֶּ֫פֶשׁ הַהִיא

As for anyone who eats leavened bread (i.e., if anyone eats leavened bread), that soul *will be cut off.* . . .
Exod 12:15

---

35. Cf. Deut 18:3.   36. Driver, *Tenses in Hebrew*, 137.

3.	הַמְדַבֵּר אֵלֶיךָ וַהֲבֵאתוֹ אֵלִי	As for the one who speaks to you (i.e., if anyone speaks to you), *bring* him to me. 2 Sam 14:10
4.	אִישׁ אֲשֶׁר יִרְקַח כָּמֹהוּ . . . וְנִכְרַת מֵעַמָּיו:	As for a man who makes perfume like it . . . he *will be cut off* from his people. Exod 30:33
5.	הִנֵּה הָעַלְמָה הָרָה וְיֹלֶדֶת בֵּן וְקָרָאת	The *ʿalmâ* will be pregnant and will bear a son *and will call.* . . . Isa 7:14
6.	כִּי יהוה . . . הוּא אֱלֹהֵי הָאֱלֹהִים . . . וְאֹהֵב גֵּר . . . וַאֲהַבְתֶּם אֶת־הַגֵּר	Because Yhwh . . . is God of gods . . . and one who loves the sojourner . . . *so you are to love* the sojourner. Deut 10:17–19
7.	הִנְנִי מַפְרְךָ וְהִרְבִּיתִךָ	I will make you fruitful *and numerous.* Gen 48:4

b   Unlike the use of relative *wəqataltí* in the above constructions, where it retains in varying degrees its apodosis force, with a *substantival participle* the situation represented by *wəqataltí* may represent a simple chronologically subsequent situation (## 8–11).[37] *Wəqataltí* after a *predicate participle* in past time represents an explanatory, imperfective situation (# 12). For a consequential situation in future time, see 37.7.2a.

8.	וְהַיּוֹצֵא וְנָפַל	The one who goes out *and surrenders.* . . . Jer 21:9
9.	מַכֵּה אִישׁ וָמֵת מוֹת יוּמָת:	Whoever strikes a man, *and he dies,* will be put to death. Exod 21:12
10.	וְגֹנֵב אִישׁ וּמְכָרוֹ . . . מוֹת יוּמָת:	Whoever kidnaps a man *and sells* him . . . will be put to death. Exod 21:16
11.	הָאֹמְרִים נְאֻם־יהוה וַיהוה לֹא שְׁלָחָם וְיִחֲלוּ לְקַיֵּם דָּבָר:	Those who say: "Thus says Yhwh," but Yhwh has not sent them, *and they expect* to establish [their] word. . . . Ezek 13:6
12.	וִיהוֹנָתָן וַאֲחִימַעַץ עֹמְדִים . . . וְהָלְכָה הַשִּׁפְחָה וְהִגִּידָה לָהֶם	Now Jonathan and Ahimaaz were staying . . . *and a servant girl would go and inform* them. 2 Sam 17:17

c   The *wəqataltí* construction after an *infinitive construct* functions in ways similar to those we have observed in connection with other leading verbs. The line between an apodosis and a consequent situation is often fuzzy in the construction (## 13–18). The

---

37. Lambdin, *Introduction to Biblical Hebrew*, 276–77.

examples can be taken as conditional sentences; for example, # 14 can readily be taken as 'when the wrath of your brother subsides, then. . . .' In some cases, the *wəqtl* relative form is consequential (## 16, 19–21),[38] in others imperfective (cf. # 17), or, subordinate to an adverbial expression of time (# 22).

13.	כִּי בְּיוֹם אֲכָלְכֶם מִמֶּ֫נּוּ וְנִפְקְחוּ עֵינֵיכֶם	When you eat from it, your eyes *will be opened*. Gen 3:5
14.	עַד־שׁוּב אַף־אָחִ֫יךָ . . . וְשָׁלַחְתִּ֫י וּלְקַחְתִּ֫יךָ	until the wrath of your brother subsides . . . *then* I *will send* for you Gen 27:45
15.	לְהָמִית צַדִּיק עִם־רָשָׁע וְהָיָה כַצַּדִּיק כָּרָשָׁע	to kill the righteous with the wicked *and so* the righteous *become* as the wicked Gen 18:25
16.	. . . בְּעָבְרְכֶם אֶת־בְּרִית יהוה וַהֲלַכְתֶּם וַעֲבַדְתֶּם אֱלֹהִים אֲחֵרִים . . . וְחָרָה אַף־יהוה בָּכֶם	If you violate the covenant of Yʜᴡʜ . . . and go and serve other gods . . . , *then* Yʜᴡʜ's anger *will burn* against you. Josh 23:16
17.	עַל־רָדְפוֹ . . . וְשִׁחֵת רַחֲמָיו	because he pursued . . . *and* [repeatedly] *ruined* mercy Amos 1:11
18.	בְּשִׁבְרִי לָכֶם מַטֵּה־לֶחֶם וְאָפוּ עֶ֫שֶׂר נָשִׁים . . . בְּתַנּוּר אֶחָד	When I cut off your supply of bread, ten women *will bake* . . . in one oven. Lev 26:26
19.	עַד־בֹּאִי אֵלֶ֫יךָ וְהוֹדַעְתִּ֫י לְךָ	until I come to you *and tell* you . . . 1 Sam 10:8
20.	כְּטוֹב לֵב־אַמְנוֹן . . . וְאָמַרְתִּ֫י אֲלֵיכֶם	when Amnon's heart becomes merry . . . *and* I *tell* you . . . 2 Sam 13:28
21.	. . . וְהָיָה בְּיוֹם צֵאתְךָ וְעָבַרְתָּ֫ יָדֹעַ תֵּדַע כִּי מוֹת תָּמוּת	On the day you go forth *and cross over* . . . , know that you will die. 1 Kgs 2:37
22.	וּבְיוֹם פָּקְדִי וּפָקַדְתִּ֫י עֲלֵיהֶם חַטָּאתָם:	When I punish, *then* I *will punish* them for their sin. Exod 32:34

d After an *infinitive absolute* the relative *waw* + suffix conjugation construction denotes, as in its other grammatical connections, either a consequent or an explanatory imperfective situation. It may have the former notion when the infinitive absolute functions as a surrogate for a finite verb; the latter notion adheres to it when it functions

---

38. Note *ləmáʿan* with an infinitive in 1 Kgs 8:60–61.

adverbially in the postpositive position. As we shall see, the infinitive absolute can function as a finite verb for various reasons (see 35.5.2). Not surprisingly, the *wəqataltí* construction can represent a situation consequent to that envisioned by the infinitive absolute (## 23–24). These sentences could also be classified as apodoses because the leading situation usually implies the condition for the subsequent situation. We shall also see that a postpositive infinitive absolute which is concordant with the finite verb denotes action either simultaneous or quasi-simultaneous with the finite verb (see 35.4). In this way the internal structure of the finite verb is unpacked in its progress even if it be presented as a single whole by the finite verb. The *wəqataltí* construction, with its potential to represent an imperfective and epexegetical situation, may occur with an infinitive absolute concordant with the finite verb to represent a situation subordinate to the situation represented by the finite verb (## 25).

23. הָסֵר מְשׂוּכָּתוֹ וְהָיָה לְבָעֵר
      פָּרֹץ גְּדֵרוֹ וְהָיָה לְמִרְמָס׃

I will remove its hedge, *and* it *will be* consumed;
I will break down its wall, *and* it *will become* trampled ground.
Isa 5:5

24. נָאוֹף וְהָלֹךְ בַּשֶּׁקֶר
      וְחִזְּקוּ יְדֵי מְרֵעִים

They commit adultery and walk in a lie *and* they *strengthen* the hands of evildoers.
Jer 23:14

25. וַתֵּלֶךְ הָלוֹךְ וְזָעָקָה׃

And she kept on going *and crying out.*
2 Sam 13:19

32.2.6   Two Further Points

a   Relative *waw* with a suffix form occurs chiefly in the environments noted above, but two adjunct matters require comment.

b   We noted the temporal expression formed with infinitives (32.2.5c ## 21–22). Not surprisingly, the dependent notion of (con)sequence can be subordinated to adverbial expressions of time (## 1–4). Sometimes the future time is emphasized by the addition of היה (# 5; for יהי, see 33.2.4).

1. עֶרֶב וִידַעְתֶּם . . . וּבֹקֶר וּרְאִיתֶם

In the evening you *will know* . . . *and* in the morning you *will see.* . . .
Exod 16:6–7

2. בַּצַּר לְךָ וּמְצָאוּךָ כֹּל הַדְּבָרִים הָאֵלֶּה

(When) in your distress all these things *will have happened.* . . .
Deut 4:30

3. בְּשָׁלֹשׁ שָׁנִים . . . וְנִקְלָה כְּבוֹד מוֹאָב

Within three years . . . Moab's splendor *will be despised.*
Isa 16:14

4. עַד־אוֹר הַבֹּקֶר וַהֲרַגְנֻהוּ׃

At dawn's light we *will kill* him.
Judg 16:2

| 5. | אִם־לֹא תַגִּידוּ . . . וְהָיָה בְּתֵת־
יהוה לָנוּ אֶת־הָאָרֶץ וְעָשִׂינוּ
עִמָּךְ חֶסֶד וֶאֱמֶת: | If you do not tell . . . then it will be that when
Yhwh *gives* us the land we *will treat* you justly
and honestly.
Josh 2:14 |

The second point is also associated with the existential verb. Sometimes הָיָה func-   c
tions either to introduce a discourse or to advance it by introducing a situation that is
only more or less loosely connected with the preceding situation. Gottfried Vanoni has
studied the two most common existential verb forms. He alleges that וַיְהִי does not
ordinarily introduce an independent temporal sentence in itself but is rather synchronic
with what follows, while וְהָיָה usually has a deictic temporal function.[39] In this use the
time is often specified by a temporal adverbial construction and followed by another
wǝqataltí or by *yqtl*. In this construction *wǝqataltí* signifies either future time (## 6–9) or,
in past time, imperfective aspect (## 10–12).

6.	הַדָּבָר אֲשֶׁר חָזָה יְשַׁעְיָהוּ . . . וְהָיָה בְּאַחֲרִית הַיָּמִים נָכוֹן יִהְיֶה הַר בֵּית־יהוה	The word which Isaiah saw. . . : It *will be* in the last days that the mountain of Yhwh's temple will be established. Isa 2:1–2
7.	וְהָיָה בְּעַנְנִי עָנָן עַל־הָאָרֶץ וְנִרְאֲתָה הַקֶּשֶׁת בֶּעָנָן: וְזָכַרְתִּי אֶת־בְּרִיתִי	It *will be* whenever I bring clouds over the earth and a rainbow appears in the clouds, that I will remember my covenant. . . . Gen 9:14–15
8.	וְהָיָה בְּיוֹם הָנִיחַ יהוה לְךָ . . . וְנָשָׂאתָ הַמָּשָׁל הַזֶּה	It *will be* when Yhwh gives you relief . . . that you will take up this taunt. Isa 14:3–4
9.	הִנֵּה אָנֹכִי נִצָּב עַל־עֵין הַמָּיִם וְהָיָה הָעַלְמָה הַיֹּצֵאת	I am standing by a spring of water; *and* it *will be* that the *ᶜalmâ* who comes out. . . . Gen 24:43
10.	וַיֵּדַע אוֹנָן כִּי לֹא לוֹ יִהְיֶה הַזָּרַע וְהָיָה אִם־בָּא אֶל־אֵשֶׁת אָחִיו וְשִׁחֵת	But Onan knew the offspring would not be his. *So* it *would be* that when (i.e., whenever) he went to his brother's wife, he would destroy. . . . Gen 38:9
11.	וְהָיָה כְּצֵאת מֹשֶׁה אֶל־הָאֹהֶל יָקוּמוּ כָּל־הָעָם	*And* it *would be* that when (i.e., whenever) Moses went out to the tent, all the people would rise. Exod 33:8
12.	וְהָיָה אִם־זָרַע יִשְׂרָאֵל וְעָלָה מִדְיָן	*And whenever* Israel planted their crops, Midian would attack. Judg 6:3

---

39. Gottfried Vanoni, "Ist die Fügung HYY + Circumstant der Zeit im Althebräischen ein Satz?" *Biblische
Notizen* 17 (1982) 73–86. On these forms in Chronicles,

see R. Polzin, *Late Biblical Hebrew: Toward an Historical
Typology of Biblical Hebrew Prose* (Missoula: Scholars
Press, 1976) 56–58.

32.3   Copulative *Waw* + Suffix Conjugation

a   Whereas relative *wəqtl* represents one situation as subordinate to another, copulative *wəqtl* represents two situations as coordinate with one another. The two constructions are distinguished by stress (in first singular and second masculine singular) and by semantics. Two rather restricted sets of circumstances where *wqtl* has the value of *qtl* with simple *waw* have been established by Revell; these are:

(a) As the second of a pair or longer series of perfect forms acting as a semantic unit, that is, representing different aspects of the same event, not different actions in a sequence of events, as *bānîm giddáltî werômámtî* ("Children have I reared and raised", Isa 1:2).

(b) Where verbs semantically related in the same way occur in a series of short parallel clauses, as *hôbáštî ᶜēṣ lāḥ wehipráḥtî ᶜēṣ yābēš* ("I have dried up the fresh tree, and cause the dried tree to sprout", Ezek 17:24).[40]

Thus, if semantic pertinence demands that the situation represented by *wəqtl* is perfective in aspect and not subordinate to the preceding situation, then the construction should be construed as a *waw*-copulative. Contrariwise, if the same factor demands that *wəqtl* represents a subordinate situation, be it (con)sequential and/or imperfective aspect, then it should be interpreted as a *waw*-relative construction. Copulative *wqtl* is used in at least four different ways.

b   The copulative construction sometimes serves in a *hendiadys*, to represent two aspects of a complex situation (cf. Revell's first set).

1.	וַאֲנִי זָקַנְתִּי וָשַׂבְתִּי	I am old *and gray*. 1 Sam 12:2
2.	הַהוּא אָמַר . . . וְדִבֶּר	Does he speak. . . ? *Does he promise*. . . ? Num 23:19
3.	הֵתֶל בִּי וְהֶחֱלִף אֶת־מַשְׂכֻּרְתִּי	He has cheated me *by changing* my wages. Gen 31:7
4.	כִּי־הִקְשָׁה יהוה . . . אֶת־רוּחוֹ וְאִמֵּץ אֶת־לְבָבוֹ	YHWH . . . made his spirit stubborn *and* his heart *obstinate*. Deut 2:30
5.	וְהֵשִׁיבוּ אֶל־לְבָּם . . . וְשָׁבוּ וְהִתְחַנְּנוּ	And if they have a change of heart . . . *and repent and plead*. . . . 1 Kgs 8:47

c   On other occasions the *qtl wəqtl* forms function in juxtaposition, *contrasting two situations* rather than presenting two sides of the same one (cf. Revell's second set).

---

40. Revell, "Stress Position in *Waw* Consecutive," 279.

6. וְהִנֵּה נָטַשׁ אָבִיךָ אֶת־דִּבְרֵי
    הָאֲתֹנוֹת וְדָאַג לָכֶם

Your father has stopped thinking about the donkeys *and has become worried* about you.
1 Sam 10:2

7. וְלֹא־שָׁאַלְתָּ . . . וְשָׁאַלְתָּ

You have not asked for . . . *but* you *have asked for.* . . .
1 Kgs 3:11

8. אִם־חָכַמְתָּ . . . וְלַצְתָּ

If you are wise . . . , *but if you are a mocker.* . . .
Prov 9:12

The copulative may simply serve in *coordination* to link two points in the discourse.   d

9. הוּא־הִכָּה אֶת־אֱדוֹם . . . וְתָפַשׂ
    אֶת־הַסֶּלַע בַּמִּלְחָמָה

He smote Edom . . . *and captured* Sela in the battle.
2 Kgs 14:7

10. וַיִּבֶן אֶת־הַבָּמוֹת . . . וּבָנָה
    מִזְבְּחֹת בְּבֵית יְהוָה

He built the high places . . . *and built* altars in the House of YHWH.
2 Kgs 21:3–4

11. . . . וַיִּשְׂרְפֵם מִחוּץ לִירוּשָׁלַיִם
    וְנָשָׂא אֶת־עֲפָרָם בֵּית־אֵל:

He burned them outside of Jerusalem . . . *and took* their ashes to Bethel.
2 Kgs 23:4

This use tends to replace the common *wayyqtl* in the later books, in part as the language comes more and more under the influence of Aramaic, which lacks the *wayyqtl* form.

12. עָשִׂיתִי לִי גַּנּוֹת וּפַרְדֵּסִים
    וְנָטַעְתִּי בָהֶם עֵץ כָּל־פֶּרִי:

And I made for myself gardens and parks *and I planted* all kinds of fruit trees in them.
Qoh 2:5

13. . . . וְגָדַלְתִּי וְהוֹסַפְתִּי מִכֹּל

And I became greater by far than. . . .[41]
Qoh 2:9

The *wəqatāltî* form may indicate a disjunction, *signaling a situation out of chronological sequence* (39.2.3). As Johnson notes, "In several instances a parenthetical remark—a parenthetically inserted particular or preliminary remark—is designated by *wə* + perfect. If this occurs in a narration of past time, *wə* + perfect corresponds ordinarily to our pluperfect."[42]   e

14. וַיַּרְא עֵשָׂו כִּי־בֵרַךְ יִצְחָק אֶת־
    יַעֲקֹב וְשִׁלַּח אֹתוֹ פַּדֶּנָה אֲרָם

And Esau saw that Isaac had blessed Jacob *and had sent* him to Paddan-Aram.
Gen 28:6

---

41. Note the hendiadys. On Qoheleth, see n. 3.
42. Johnson, *Hebräisches Perfekt und Imperfekt*, 41. In ## 14–15, the *wəqtl* could be seen as simply consecutive.

15. וַיְמַהֵר שִׁמְעִי . . . וַיֵּרֶד עִם־אִישׁ
יְהוּדָה . . . וְאֶלֶף אִישׁ עִמּוֹ
מִבִּנְיָמִן . . . וְצָלְחוּ הַיַּרְדֵּן לִפְנֵי
הַמֶּלֶךְ:

And Shimei . . . hurried and went down with the men
of Judah. . . . Now there were with him one thousand
Benjaminites . . . *and* they *had rushed* to the Jordan
before the king.
2 Sam 19:17–18

16. וַיִּתְאַנַּף יְהוה בִּשְׁלֹמֹה כִּי־נָטָה
לְבָבוֹ . . . וְצִוָּה אֵלָיו

And Yнwн became angry with Solomon because
his heart had turned . . . *and* (Yнwн) *had
commanded* him. . . .
1 Kgs 11:9–10

33

Waw + Prefix Conjugation

Waw-Relative + Short Prefix Conjugation   **33.1**

Form   **33.1.1**

Waw-relative with the short prefix conjugation (*wayyqtl*), the most frequent conju-   a
gational form in Hebrew narrative, exhibits five formal characteristics: (1) the *waw* is
vocalized with *pathaḥ* and the prefix consonant is doubled (·וַ); (2) the *waw* is normally
prefixed to the short prefix-conjugation form, where available (e.g., וַיִּבְךְ and not וַיִּבְכֶּה);
(3) the stress is thrown back toward the *waw* as much as possible (e.g., וַיָּקָם and not
וַיָּקָם); (4) the construction normally begins its clause; and (5) it does not take an energic
ending (31.1.1d, 31.7.2). The relationship between the *wayyqtl* and the jussive forms is
clear in Gen 1:3: וַיְהִי . . . יְהִי, 'Let there be . . . and there was. . . .' In contrast to *waw*-
relative as used with the suffix conjugation (*wəqtl*), *waw*-relative in the bound form
wayyqtl is always pointed differently from the *waw*-copulative that occurs with the non-
perfective conjugation. The phonologically conditioned variants of ·וַ—for example, וָ
with א—do not disguise this fact.

Two prefix-conjugation forms, long and short, are distinguished in the cases of   b
(1) the *Hiphil* of all verbs; (2) every verbal stem of III-*he* verbs except *Pual* and *Hophal*;

(3) the *Qal* of geminates, hollow roots (II-*waw*/*yodh*), I-*aleph* verbs, and I-*waw*/*yodh* verbs. As Leslie McFall rightly points out, *waw*-relative with the prefix conjugation does not always occur with the short form: "וַתִּבְכֶּה *and she wept* occurs alongside וַתֵּבְךְ, וַיִּבֶן alongside וַיָּשִׂתְּה, וַיְשֶׁתָּ alongside וַיֵּשֶׁתְ, וַיַּעֲלֶה and וַיַּעַל, וַיַּעֲנֶה and וַיַּעַן, וַיַּעֲשֶׂה and וַיַּעַשׂ, וַיִּרְאֶה and וַיַּרְא, וַיִּרְבֶּה and וַיֶּרֶב, etc."[1] If there were originally two sets of prefix conjugations and these are reflected in the long and short forms of Biblical Hebrew, it may be that the accentuation of the biblical short form reflects the accentuation of the form from which it is descended. The rare long forms used after *wa*(*y*)- would represent secondary, analogical developments, as the two prefix forms came to be seen as variants of one form.

c   The frequency of the *wayyiqtol* form hardly requires comment: 29% of the finite verbs in the Hebrew Bible show this form (14,972 cases; cf. 29.1c). In about ninety cases the *waw*-relative occurs with the pseudo-cohortative, principally in the parts of Daniel, Ezra, and Nehemiah where the narrative is in the first person, and rarely elsewhere (34.5).[2] This is not necessarily a late feature of the language: it is not used by the post-exilic writer of Chronicles, but it is used by the earlier Deuteronomist (cf. 1 Chr 17:8 with 2 Sam 7:9). Moreover, it is not found in Zechariah 1–8 or Esther, both of which are post-exilic.

33.1.2   Origins and Meanings

a   The understanding of the origin of the *wayyqtl* form may influence the interpretation of its meaning. Scholars have not reached a consensus regarding the origin of either the *wa*(*y*)- or of the *yqtl* portions of the compound form, though the weight of scholarly opinion is tipped in favor of recognizing a distinctive source for the short prefix form.

b   The history of speculation about the origin of *wa*(*y*)- is colorful; here is Péter Kustár's summary.

> Storr (1779) perceived in the fixed *dagesh forte* of the *wa* the remains of the *he*-interrogativum. Schultens (1737), the founder of Hebrew linguistic research in Holland, sought to explain the *dagesh forte* of the *wa* by a *he*-demonstrativum that dropped out. Other grammarians believed they could recognize in the *waw* with *pathaḥ* and the following *dagesh forte* a syncope either from *whyh* or from *hyh* (*hwh*) and correspondingly in the imperfect with *wa* an analogy to Arabic *kāna yaqtulu*. Scholze first proposed this hypothesis (1735); he found numerous followers. . . .

---

1. Leslie McFall, *The Enigma of the Hebrew Verbal System* (Sheffield: Almond, 1982) 54–55, accentuation modified. See also F. R. Blake, *A Resurvey of Hebrew Tenses* (Rome: Pontifical Biblical Institute, 1951) 46; and E. Qimron, "Consecutive and Conjunctive Imperfect: The Form of the Imperfect with *Waw* in Biblical Hebrew," *Jewish Quarterly Review* 77 (1986–87) 149–61, arguing that the *waw* tends to trigger use of the short form.

2. "It seems . . . likely that the use of the [-*ah*] affixed form with *waw* consecutive reflects the fact that this form was perceived [in later Biblical Hebrew] as the equivalent,

in the 1st person, of the short imperfect form in the 2nd and 3rd person"; so E. J. Revell, "First Person Imperfect Forms with *Waw* Consecutive," *Vetus Testamentum* 38 (1988) 419–26, at 422. Cf. S. R. Driver, *A Treatise on the Use of the Tenses in Hebrew* (3d ed.; Oxford: Clarendon, 1892) 74–75; T. J. Finley, "The *Waw*-Consecutive with 'Imperfect' in Biblical Hebrew: Theoretical Studies and Its Use in Amos," *Tradition and Testament: Essays in Honor of Charles Lee Feinberg*, ed. J. S. Feinberg and P. D. Feinberg (Chicago: Moody, 1981) 241–62, at 260.

Gesenius himself adopted the view (1817) . . . [but] gave it up entirely in the 12th edition of the grammar (1839). Ewald (1863) supposed that *we* and *ʾaz* had merged in the *wa*, while Grimme (1896) sought in the permanent *dagesh* after *wa* a *le* which assimilated to the prefixes. From this historical survey we can see that already at that time every conceivable, fantastic hypothesis existed, instead of an adequate understanding of the phenomenon. A quite necessary and also noteworthy reaction, therefore, can be seen in the opinion of Jahn, who ascribed the diverse punctuations of the forms with *waw* to a "subtle ingenuity" of the punctuator.

The latest research, by contrast, can be characterized as an attempt for objectivity. Scholars have tried to understand the function of the *waw* on the basis of the form with *waw* itself. To achieve this they often took parallel phenomena of the other Semitic languages to help clarify it. From such a linguistic relationship the *wa* was explained as the modification of the *wĕ*-copula. S. R. Driver (1881) explained it in this way; he thought the *waw*-copula had a demonstrative character. Accordingly he designated the *waw*-copula as signifying "a direct consequence of the event thus referred to." To render the viewpoint of König (1897), the following may be cited: the *waw* "most probably is an 'and' that became solemn, which connects the consequence that depends on a preceding event; the consequence therefore was something which had not happened in relationship to that past moment." And Bauer (1910) thinks "there must exist in these connections with *waw* an archaic style." The imperfect with *waw* "is timeless just like the Proto-Semitic *yaqtul* and can therefore include any temporal moment which can be conceived of in any way with a verb connected with 'and'; therefore, present, past, future as the connection in question demands it. . . . If the relationship to the past predominates, then that is due to the fact that in the narration of past events the series with 'and' is preferred." Essentially G. R. Driver (1936) says nothing more than this. He sought the origin of the *wa* in the Akkadian connective *ma* or in the Assyrian *uma* and showed that in Assyrian, for example, *m* can change into *w*. G. Douglas Young (1953) sees the origin of the imperfect with *waw* in the merging of the Egyptian connective *iw* and of *n*, the sign of the past tense (*wan*/*wanyiqtol* = *wayyiqtol*).[3]

Similar views can be found. V. Maag, for example, has suggested that the form originated with the deictic or demonstrative particle *han*. According to him, when a simple *shewa* stands before *h* both syncopate (thus, *wəhanyiqtul > *wanyiqtul > *wayyiqtul*).[4] The fact that no theory based on a special origin for *wa(y)*- has gained acceptance suggests that the meaning of the compound construction cannot be decided on this basis. All agree, however, that the *wa(y)*- element is related to the conjunction ו, and connects one situation with another.

The origin of the (*way*)*yiqtol* element is similarly problematic, but at least here there is more data to work with. We noted earlier that Hebraists differ in their evaluation of the comparative Semitic data (see 29.4). The issue is important here because the   c

---

3. Péter Kustár, *Aspekt im Hebräischen* (Basel: Reinhardt, 1972) 28–29, silently abridged by omission of references.

4. V. Maag, "Morphologie des hebräischen Narrativs," *Zeitschrift für die Alttestamentliche Wissenschaft* 65 (1953) 86–88.

meaning of *wayyqtl* is partially determined by the approach to this data. Researchers who hold that Hebrew preserves only one prefix conjugation, which signifies non-perfective notions, tend to minimize this data. Diethelm Michel, for example, writes: "Regarding the relationship of the imperfectum and imperfectum consecutivum it can be stated that no distinction exists between the two 'tempora' with respect to meaning. . . . The imperfectum consecutivum only expresses a closer connection with the preceding verbal form."[5] In contrast, researchers who allow for the preservation of two prefix forms relate the construction to the short prefix conjugation, that is, to the historical short form *yaqtul*, which signifies either preterite action or jussive mood; thus *wayyqtl* may well express a notion contrary to the prefix conjugation not bound with the *waw*-relative, that is, with the descendant of the historical long form *yaqtulu*. Comparative Semitic grammar, the form itself, and use recognize the truth of the second view. As noted in the earlier discussions, various Semitic languages had at least two prefix conjugations, the shorter of which indicated both the jussive and preterite notions. Furthermore, as also noted earlier, *wayyqtl* seems to share essentially the jussive form, just as in the cognate languages. Recall, too, that the unbound short-prefix form may be used as a preterite in some early texts; compare, for example, יָשֶׁת 'he made' (Ps 18:12) and וַיָּשֶׁת 'and he made' in a synoptic text (2 Sam 22:12). Finally, the form with *waw*-relative does not generally signify the distinctive uses of the non-perfective conjugation, namely, dependent modal nuances or customary action in past time. Rather, it signifies perfective aspect, as both W. Gross (arguing from a range of poetic texts) and T. J. Finley (basing himself on Amos) have recently contended.[6]

d   These two studies rightly suggest that *wayyqtl* signifies other notions than that of a preterite. In addition to occurring after the suffix conjugation, *wayyqtl* also occurs with the prefix conjugation, participles, nominal clauses, and infinitives; in all of these connections it may refer to either present or future time as well as past.

e   Whether *wayyqtl* originated in the short prefix conjugation, *yaqtul*, it shows in Hebrew meanings equivalent to those of the suffix conjugation. Like that conjugation it tends to represent concrete and specific situations according to the perfective aspect. As we shall see, it may signify a past constative situation, a perfect state, or a present state with stative verbs, a persistent or gnomic perfective, etc. When a chain of *waw*-relatives is broken, the verb reverts to the suffix conjugation, a phenomenon strongly suggesting that the two forms are equivalent, apart from the value of the *waw*-relative bound to it.

1.	וַיִּקְרָא אֱלֹהִים לָאוֹר יוֹם	And God called the light day,
	וְלַחֹשֶׁךְ קָרָא לָיְלָה	and the darkness *he called* night.
		Gen 1:5

The apparent equivalency of *wayyqtl* with *qtl* with respect to aspect finds an analogy in the equivalency of relative *wqtl* with the prefix conjugation. In fact, relative *wqtl* may

---

5. D. Michel, *Tempora und Satzstellung in den Psalmen* (Bonn: Bouvier, 1960) 51.
6. W. Gross, *Verbform und Funktion: Wayyiqtol für die*
Gegenwart? (St. Ottilien: EOS, 1976); Finley, "*Waw*-Consecutive with 'Imperfect.'" Related studies are discussed in Chap. 29.

have influenced the development of *wayyqtl* as an "alternative" suffix conjugation, to be used when the situation is conceived of as dependent on a prior one.

This evidence strongly favors interpreting those instances of *wayyqtl* which must be   f
taken as referring to the present or future according to the meaning and uses of the suffix conjugation rather than according to those of the prefix conjugation; that is, instead of regarding a form as representing a customary situation or a dependent future situation, etc., we prefer to interpret it as denoting a gnomic perfective or specific future, etc. It should be underscored that such a gnomic perfective interpretation, for example, does not derive solely from a descriptive analysis of the passages in question, but also from the other evidence that *wayyqtl* functions as an equivalent of the suffix conjugation.

In sum, *wayyqtl* subjectively represents a situation according to the perfective aspect   g
and subordinates it to a preceding statement. Since these two features, subordination and perfective aspect, are distinct and yet always present, we analyze separately the diverse kinds of subordinate connection (33.2) and the diverse functions of the perfective aspect (33.3). Since the perfective conjugation was studied in depth in Chapter 30, we do not aim here to be exhaustive but only to comment on a sufficient number of cases to justify, explain, and illustrate our interpretation of the most frequent verbal form in the Hebrew Scriptures.

Waw-Relative: Varieties of Connection   **33.2**

Relative *waw* with a prefix form represents a situation that is usually successive and   a
always subordinate to a preceding statement. The succession may be either absolute or subjective, and often the distinction between them is blurred. Temporal sequence depends on objective fact outside the control of the speaker; logical sequence, by contrast, subjectively exists in the way a speaker sees the relationship between situations. Sometimes with *wayyqtl* a situation is represented as a logical entailment from (a) preceding one(s) or a logical contrast with it/them or as a summarizing statement of it/them. If the explanatory situation in fact occurred prior to the leading one, it may be necessary to translate *wayyqtl* by a pluperfect. *Wayyqtl* may be used after any clause which provides a starting point for development, as happens when *wayyqtl* is used epexegetically, after a circumstantial clause or phrase.

Succession   **33.2.1**

Situations described with *wayyqtl* are mostly temporally or logically succeeding.   a
"The most obvious and frequent relation is," as S. R. Driver notes, "that of simple chronological succession [# 1] . . . but of this there is no need to give . . . examples, as they abound throughout the historical portions of the Old Testament."[7] *Wayyqtl* signifies logical succession where a logical entailment from (a) preceding situation(s) (## 2–4) is expressed.

---

7. Driver, *Tenses in Hebrew*, 80.

1. וְהָאָדָם יָדַע אֶת־חַוָּה . . . וַתַּהַר
    וַתֵּלֶד אֶת־קַיִן

Adam knew Eve . . . *and* she *conceived and gave birth* to Cain.
Gen 4:1

2. וַיְהִי יהוה אֶת־יוֹסֵף וַיְהִי אִישׁ
    מַצְלִיחַ

YHWH was with Joseph *and so* he *was* prosperous.
Gen 39:2

3. יַעַן מָאַסְתָּ אֶת־דְּבַר יהוה
    וַיִּמְאָסְךָ מִמֶּלֶךְ׃

Because you have rejected the word of YHWH, he *has rejected* you as king.
1 Sam 15:23

4. לֹא־מוֹתְתַנִי מֵרָחֶם וַתְּהִי־לִי אִמִּי
    קִבְרִי

He did not kill me in the womb, *so that* my mother *would have become* my tomb.
Jer 20:17

One may question whether the notion of succession is signified by the grammatical form or by the associations of the words. That the form and not the words signifies succession becomes clearer in those instances where a chain is broken (# 5) and where several perfectives are followed by *wayyqtl* (cf. # 6).

5. קַוֹּה קִוִּיתִי יהוה
    וַיֵּט אֵלַי
    וַיִּשְׁמַע שַׁוְעָתִי׃
    וַיַּעֲלֵנִי מִבּוֹר שָׁאוֹן . . .
    וַיָּקֶם עַל־סֶלַע רַגְלַי
    כּוֹנֵן אֲשֻׁרָי׃
    וַיִּתֵּן בְּפִי שִׁיר חָדָשׁ

I waited for YHWH;
then he *turned* to me
and heard my cry.
Then he *lifted* me out of the pit . . .
and set my feet upon a rock.
He made my steps firm.
Then he *put* a new song in my mouth.
Ps 40:2–4

Concerning the *waw*-relative constructions in this passage Michel has this comment.

> The imperfecta consecutiva picture a chain of actions arising the one out of the other ('he turned to me,' 'heard my cry,' 'lifted me out of the pit . . . ,' 'set my feet upon a rock' 'put a new song in my mouth . . .'), which are as a whole the consequence of the cry for help. Highly exceptional, then, is the perfect כּוֹנֵן in the midst of this chain. This change certainly cannot be explained as due to a varying period of time because the action 'he made my steps firm' is as past as 'he set my feet upon a rock.' If one considers these two sentences closely, one must say that in essence they are expressing the same thing; one cannot assert that there is an advance in the development of the thanksgiving. Here, in our opinion, lies the basis for the varying use of the tempora; we cannot see any other possibility.
>   Summarizing 40:2–4 we can therefore say: the chain of the imperfecta consecutiva arising one out of another expresses an advance in action; it designates actions that arise consecutively out of one another. The perfectum is not a member of this consecutive action; it explicates the preceding imperfecta consecutiva and so introduces to a certain extent a retarding moment in the action.[8]

8. Michel, *Tempora und Satzstellung*, 17–18.

Michel's explanation is confirmed by many similar passages in the Hebrew Bible.   b
We content ourselves with but one more example.

6.   כִּי רָדַף אוֹיֵב נַפְשִׁי   The enemy pursues me,
      דִּכָּא לָאָרֶץ חַיָּתִי   he crushes me to the ground;
      הוֹשִׁיבַנִי בְמַחֲשַׁכִּים . . .   he makes me dwell in darkness. . . .
      וַתִּתְעַטֵּף עָלַי רוּחִי   *So* my spirit *grows faint* within me;
      בְּתוֹכִי יִשְׁתּוֹמֵם לִבִּי: my heart within me is dismayed.
                                      Ps 143:3–4

Here, too, Michel offers an apt comment:

> Psalm 143 is an individual lament; vv 3–4 picture the happenings that lead the
> psalmist to his complaint. The defeats by the enemy have naturally already taken
> place, but they have not ended since otherwise the lament would be baseless. The
> perfecta in v 3 are therefore best translated as presents. The same is true, however, also
> of the distress and despair . . . in v 4. One can hardly explain the differentiation of the
> tempora by varying periods of time.
>
> But also one cannot derive from this passage the idea that a description begun in
> the perfectum is advanced by an imperfectum consecutivum. If that were so, it would
> not be clear why an imperfectum consecutivum could not and would not have to stand
> also already in connection with the second and third action of v 3.
>
> Possibly one could establish that a description begun in the perfectum can be
> advanced by an imperfectum consecutivum, but it is unnecessary. . . .
>
> The actions of v 3 are similar to one another; they constitute a certain kind of
> enumeration; they are placed as facts alongside of one another, without being con-
> nected logically or temporally. Verse 4 [beginning with וַתִּתְעַטֵּף], by contrast, does not
> advance the enumeration, but turns the gaze to the psalmist. Obviously the description
> here pertains to the action effected by the enemy; there lies, therefore, between v 3 and
> v 4 the relationship of cause and effect, ground and consequence. I cannot see any
> other difference between the actions of v 3 and v 4a. That leads to the conclusion, that
> here the imperfectum consecutivum is used in order to express a consequence.[9]

Most noteworthy in narrative is the way *wayyqtl* traces the thread of discourse (see   c
also 39.2).

7.   וַיָּבֹאוּ שְׁנֵי הַמַּלְאָכִים סְדֹמָה   *And* the two angels *entered* (*wayyqtl*) Sodom in the
      בָּעֶרֶב וְלוֹט יֹשֵׁב בְּשַׁעַר־סְדֹם   evening, while Lot was sitting (participle) in the
      וַיַּרְא־לוֹט וַיָּקָם לִקְרָאתָם   gateway to Sodom. *And* Lot *saw* (*wayyqtl*) them *and
      וַיִּשְׁתַּחוּ אַפַּיִם אָרְצָה: got up* (*wayyqtl*) to greet them *and bowed down*
                                        (*wayyqtl*) with his face to the ground.
                                        Gen 19:1

---

9. Michel, *Tempora und Satzstellung*, 15–16.

Often a minor sequence developed with *wqtl* (in # 8 after the imperative) operates within the major narrative sequence indicated by *wayyqtl*.

8. וַיֹּאמֶר הִנֶּה נָּא־אֲדֹנַי סוּרוּ נָא אֶל־בֵּית עַבְדְּכֶם וְלִינוּ וְרַחֲצוּ רַגְלֵיכֶם וְהִשְׁכַּמְתֶּם וַהֲלַכְתֶּם לְדַרְכְּכֶם וַיֹּאמְרוּ לֹא	And he said (*wayyqtl*), "My lords, please *turn aside* to your servant's house *and spend the night* (*wqtl*) *and wash* (*wqtl*) your feet *and then go* (*wqtl*) *early* (*wqtl*) on your way." And they said (*wayyqtl*), "No." Gen 19:2

The development of the major chain often relies heavily on the minor one (cf. 32.2.3e for *wqtl* here).

9. וַיְהִי אִישׁ אֶחָד . . . וּשְׁמוֹ אֶלְקָנָה . . . וַיְהִי הַיּוֹם וַיִּזְבַּח . . . וְנָתַן לִפְנִנָּה אִשְׁתּוֹ וּלְכָל־בָּנֶיהָ וּבְנוֹתֶיהָ מָנוֹת: וּלְחַנָּה יִתֵּן מָנָה אַחַת אַפָּיִם . . . וַתִּבְכֶּה וְלֹא תֹאכַל: וַיֹּאמֶר	There was a certain man . . . and his name was Elqanah. . . . One day he *offered a sacrifice* (*wayyqtl*). . . . He would give (*wqtl*) portions (of the meat) to his wife Peninah and to all her sons and daughters but to Hannah he would give (*yqtl*) a double portion. . . . *And* [on that particular day] she *wept* (*wayyqtl*) and could not eat (*yqtl*). *And* he *said* (*wayyqtl*). . . . 1 Sam 1:1, 4–5, 7–8

d   Under the heading of logical relation we can consider a number of more or less distinct links. Sometimes the situation represented as a logical consequence occurred in absolute time prior to the first situation (# 10). The two situations may be logically contrasted (*w* has the sense 'and yet'; ## 11–12).[10] The *wayyqtl* statement can be a summary remark (## 13–15).

10. כִּי־זֶה שְׁנָתַיִם הָרָעָב בְּקֶרֶב הָאָרֶץ וְעוֹד חָמֵשׁ שָׁנִים אֲשֶׁר אֵין־חָרִישׁ וְקָצִיר: וַיִּשְׁלָחֵנִי אֱלֹהִים לִפְנֵיכֶם	For two years now there has been famine in the land, and for the next five years there will not be plowing and reaping. *So* God *sent* me ahead of you. . . . Gen 45:6–7
11. כִּי־רָאִיתִי אֱלֹהִים פָּנִים אֶל־פָּנִים וַתִּנָּצֵל נַפְשִׁי:	I have seen God face to face *and yet* my soul *is delivered*. Gen 32:31
12. וַיּוֹאֶל הָאֱמֹרִי לָשֶׁבֶת בְּהַר־חֶרֶס . . . וַתִּכְבַּד יַד בֵּית־יוֹסֵף	The Amorites were determined to dwell in the hills of Heres(?) . . . *and yet* the power of the House of Joseph *increased*. Judg 1:35
13. וַיְכֻלּוּ הַשָּׁמַיִם וְהָאָרֶץ	*Thus* the heavens and the earth *were completed*. Gen 2:1
14. וַיָּקָם הַשָּׂדֶה וְהַמְּעָרָה אֲשֶׁר־בּוֹ לְאַבְרָהָם	*So* the field and the cave in it *were confirmed* for Abraham. Gen 23:20

---

10. Driver, *Tenses in Hebrew*, 80.

15. וַיִּקְרָא שֵׁם הַמָּקוֹם הַהוּא גִּלְגָּל   *So* that place *has been called* Gilgal to this day.
עַד הַיּוֹם הַזֶּה: Josh 5:9

Epexegesis   **33.2.2**

Sometimes the situation represented by ·וַ does not succeed the prior one either in **a**
time or as a logical consequence; rather it explains the former situation (cf. 33.2.3e). In a
sense, this *epexegetical* use of *wayyqtl* is the opposite of the summarizing use. The major
fact or situation is stated first, and then the particulars or details, component or concomitant situations are filled in.[11]

1. אֲבָל אִשָּׁה־אַלְמָנָה אָנִי וַיָּמָת   I am, alas, a widow; my husband *died*.
אִישִׁי: 2 Sam 14:5

2. וַתְּלַקֵּט בַּשָּׂדֶה . . . וַיִּקֶר מִקְרֶהָ   She gleaned in the field . . . *and* it *turned out to be* a
חֶלְקַת הַשָּׂדֶה לְבֹעַז   portion of the field of Boaz.
Ruth 2:3

This use is common after היה in the leading clause. If a narrative sequence begins **b**
with a clause containing the verb היה, the following relative-*waw* clause explains the
overall situation represented by it. Whereas relative *wqtl* may signify customary event(s)
within the situation (32.2.1d), relative *wayyqtl* represents specific, concrete events (## 3–
4). The same phenomenon occurs in connection with other grammatical forms (# 5; the
wayyqtl form is perhaps a pluperfect) and is especially common with verbs of speaking
(## 6–7) and doing (## 8–10), in which relation the subordinate situation is often simultaneous with the leading situation.

3. וְאֵלֶּה הָיוּ בְּנֵי אָהֳלִיבָמָה . . .   These were the sons of Oholibamah . . . ; she *bore*
וַתֵּלֶד לְעֵשָׂו   to Esau. . . .[12]
Gen 36:14

4. אִישׁ הָיָה . . . וַיִּוָּלְדוּ לוֹ   There was a man . . . *and* there *was born* to him. . . .
Job 1:1–2

5. הֲלוֹא אִם־קָטֹן אַתָּה בְּעֵינֶיךָ   Although you were small in your own eyes, were you
רֹאשׁ שִׁבְטֵי יִשְׂרָאֵל אָתָּה   not the head of the tribes of Israel?—Yʜwʜ
וַיִּמְשָׁחֲךָ יהוה לְמֶלֶךְ עַל־   *anointed* you king over Israel.
יִשְׂרָאֵל: 1 Sam 15:17

6. וְסַרְנֵי פְלִשְׁתִּים נֶאֶסְפוּ לִזְבֹּחַ   Now the rulers of the Philistines assembled to offer a
זֶבַח־גָּדוֹל לְדָגוֹן . . . וַיֹּאמְרוּ   great sacrifice to Dagon . . . , *saying*. . . .
Judg 16:23

7. וַתִּקְרָא שְׁמוֹ מֹשֶׁה וַתֹּאמֶר כִּי   She called his name Moses, *saying*, "I drew him out of
מִן־הַמַּיִם מְשִׁיתִהוּ:   the water."
Exod 2:10

---

11. Driver, *Tenses in Hebrew*, 82–83. Epexegetical *wqtl*   serves as a preterite.
represents a customary situation; epexegetical *wayyqtl*   12. Cf. Gen 36:31–32.

8.   מֶה עָשִׂיתָ וַתִּגְנֹב אֶת־לְבָבִי

What have you done? You *have deceived* me?
Gen 31:26

9.   כְּכָל־הַמַּעֲשִׂים אֲשֶׁר־עָשׂוּ מִיּוֹם
הַעֲלֹתִי אֹתָם מִמִּצְרַיִם וְעַד־
הַיּוֹם הַזֶּה וַיַּעַזְבֻנִי וַיַּעַבְדוּ
אֱלֹהִים אֲחֵרִים כֵּן הֵמָּה עֹשִׂים
גַּם־לָךְ׃

As they have done from the day I brought them up
out of Egypt until this day, they *forsook* me *and
served* other gods. So they are doing to you.
1 Sam 8:8

10.   וְגַם אַתָּה יָדַעְתָּ אֵת אֲשֶׁר־
עָשָׂה לִי יוֹאָב . . . אֲשֶׁר עָשָׂה
לִשְׁנֵי־שָׂרֵי צִבְאוֹת יִשְׂרָאֵל . . .
וַיַּהַרְגֵם וַיָּשֶׂם דְּמֵי־מִלְחָמָה
בְּשָׁלֹם

You know what Joab . . . did to me—what he did to
the two commanders of Israel's armies. . . . He *killed*
them and so shed the blood of battle in times of peace.
1 Kgs 2:5

33.2.3   Pluperfect

a   The use of *wayyqtl* to represent pluperfect situations can be seen as a subvariety of
epexegetical use, but it has been controversial. Driver denied such use apart from instances occurring at the beginning of a narrative or paragraph. He tried to explain the
exceptions to this rule as due to a redactor who joined originally distinct literary units
together without regard to formal unity. But W. J. Martin and D. W. Baker have argued
otherwise. Driver seems inconsistent here, since he allows for the epexegetical use of
waw-relative, which may entail a pluperfect situation.[13] Moreover, *wayyqtl* in the received
text, the object of our grammatical investigation, must be understood to represent the
pluperfect. David Qimḥi in the early period of Hebrew studies already pointed out this
use.[14]

1.   וְהַלְוִיִּם לְמַטֵּה אֲבֹתָם לֹא
הָתְפָּקְדוּ בְּתוֹכָם׃ וַיְדַבֵּר יהוה
אֶל־מֹשֶׁה לֵּאמֹר׃ אַךְ אֶת־מַטֵּה
לֵוִי לֹא תִפְקֹד

The families of the tribe of Levi, however, were not
counted along with the others. YHWH *had said* to
Moses: "You must not count the tribe of Levi."
Num 1:47–49

2.   וַיֹּאמֶר יהוה אֵלָיו מִי שָׂם פֶּה
לָאָדָם . . . וְעַתָּה לֵךְ וְאָנֹכִי אֶהְיֶה
עִם־פִּיךָ וְהוֹרֵיתִיךָ אֲשֶׁר תְּדַבֵּר׃
. . . וַיֵּלֶךְ מֹשֶׁה וַיָּשָׁב אֶל־יֶתְרוֹ
חֹתְנוֹ וַיֹּאמֶר לוֹ אֵלְכָה נָּא
וְאָשׁוּבָה אֶל־אַחַי אֲשֶׁר־
בְּמִצְרַיִם . . . וַיֹּאמֶר יהוה אֶל־
מֹשֶׁה בְּמִדְיָן לֵךְ שֵׁב מִצְרָיִם כִּי־
מֵתוּ כָּל־הָאֲנָשִׁים הַמְבַקְשִׁים
אֶת־נַפְשֶׁךָ׃

YHWH said to him, "Who gave people mouths? . . .
Now go; I will help you speak. . . ." Then Moses
went back to Jethro his father-in-law and said to him,
"Let me go back to my own people in Egypt. . . ."
YHWH *had said* to Moses in Midian, "Go back to
Egypt, for all the men who wanted to kill you are
dead."
Exod 4:11–12, 18[*Sam*]–19

---

13. See Driver, *Tenses in Hebrew*, 84–85; A. B. Davidson, *Hebrew Syntax* (3d ed.; Edinburgh: T. & T. Clark,
1901) 72–73; and, for the alternative view, W. J. Martin,
"'Dischronologized' Narrative in the Old Testament," *Congress Volume: Rome 1968* (Vetus Testamentum Supplement 17; Leiden: Brill, 1969) 179–86; D. W. Baker, *The
Consecutive Nonperfective as Pluperfect in the Historical
Books of the Hebrew Old Testament* (Regent College
Thesis, 1973).

14. Cited by McFall, *Hebrew Verbal System*, 8–9.

3. וַיְדַבֵּר אֲלֵהֶם אֲבִיהֶם אֵי־זֶה   Their father asked them, "Which way did he go?" His
    הַדֶּרֶךְ הָלָךְ וַיִּרְאוּ בָנָיו אֶת־   sons *had seen* the way. . . .
    הַדָּרֶךְ   1 Kgs 13:12

After Circumstantial Phrases and Clauses

33.2.4

Even as relative *wqtl* can represent a dependent (con)sequential situation in future   **a**
time after adverbial expressions (32.2.6), so also *wayyqtl* can express a dependent (con)se-
quential situation in past time. The function of *wayyqtl* after non-finite verbal constructions is similar to its use after היה in the leading clause (33.2.2b). The preceding expression provides "a starting-point for a development" and represents the circumstance in
which the narrative unfolds.[15] In most cases the expression is temporal (## 1–5), but
other phrases, used in *casus pendens*, are found (## 6–8; 33.3.4).

1. בַּיּוֹם הַשְּׁלִישִׁי וַיִּשָּׂא אַבְרָהָם   On the third day Abraham *looked up*.
    אֶת־עֵינָיו   Gen 22:4

2. בִּשְׁנַת־מוֹת הַמֶּלֶךְ עֻזִּיָּהוּ   In the year King Uzziah died I *saw* the Lord.
    וָאֶרְאֶה אֶת־אֲדֹנָי   Isa 6:1

3. וּכְעֵת מוּתָהּ וַתְּדַבֵּרְנָה הַנִּצָּבוֹת   As she was dying, the women by her *said*. . . .
    עָלֶיהָ   1 Sam 4:20

4. כִּי נַעַר יִשְׂרָאֵל וָאֹהֲבֵהוּ   When Israel was a child I *loved* him.
        Hos 11:1

5. בְּיוֹם קָרָאתִי וַתַּעֲנֵנִי   When I called, you *answered* me.
        Ps 138:3

6. וּפִילַגְשׁוֹ . . . וַתֵּלֶד   As for his concubine . . . , she *also bore*. . . .
        Gen 22:24

7. וְגַם אֶת־מַעֲכָה אִמּוֹ וַיְסִרֶהָ   And also Maacah his grandmother—he *deposed* her.
        1 Kgs 15:13

8. וּבְנֵי יִשְׂרָאֵל . . . וַיִּמְלֹךְ עֲלֵיהֶם   But as for the Israelites . . . Rehoboam *ruled over*
    רְחַבְעָם: them.
        1 Kgs 12:17

A circumstantial clause introduced by ויהי may be followed by a *wayyqtl* form.[16]   **b**

9. וַיְהִי־אִישׁ מֵהַר־אֶפְרַיִם . . .   Now a man from the hill country of Ephraim . . .
    וַיֹּאמֶר   *said*. . . .
        Judg 17:1–2

10. וַיְהִי־אִישׁ מִבֶּן־יָמִין . . .   There was a Benjaminite. . . . The she-donkeys
    וַתֹּאבַדְנָה הָאֲתֹנוֹת   *were lost*.
        1 Sam 9:1, 3 *Kethiv*

---

15. Davidson, *Hebrew Syntax*, 74.

16. This usage is rare in late Biblical Hebrew, a development reflecting a variety of other shifts in later texts; see

R. Polzin, *Late Biblical Hebrew: Toward an Historical
Typology of Biblical Hebrew Prose* (Missoula: Scholars
Press, 1976) 56.

11. וַיְהִי בִּימֵי שְׁפֹט הַשֹּׁפְטִים וַיְהִי
רָעָב בָּאָֽרֶץ

In the days when the *šopetim* ruled, there *was* a famine in the land.
Ruth 1:1

12. וַיְהִי אַחֲרֵי הַדְּבָרִים הָאֵלֶּה וַיֻּגַּד

Sometime later he *was told*. . . .
Gen 22:20

Thomas O. Lambdin analyzed this frequent construction with temporal clauses and phrases:

> Within a narrative sequence temporal modifiers are very frequently placed before the clause they modify and are introduced by *waw-conversive* + a form of the verb הָיָה. In the past tense narrative this is uniformly וַיְהִי. . . . The temporal [form] is then followed by the expected sequential form of the main narrative.[17]

This construction introduces the books of Joshua, Judges, 1 Samuel, 2 Samuel, Ezekiel, Ruth (# 11 above), Esther, and Nehemiah.[18] *Wayyqtl* apart from וַיְהִי introduces the books of Leviticus, Numbers, 2 Kings, and 2 Chronicles, but these are best regarded as secondary beginnings; that is, the books have a connection with the ones that precede them. This use of *wayyqtl* after ויהי stands in polarity over against relative *wqtl* after והיה (cf. 32.2.6b).

33.3   *Waw*-Relative: Aspectual Matters

a   An inductive study of *wayyqtl*'s uses confirms the presumption that *wayyqtl* represents a situation subjectively as perfective. We cite uses with forms of the suffix and the prefix conjugations and verbless clauses, participles, and infinitives. Lacking an adequate understanding of aspect, A. B. Davidson, for example, taught the common error that the "conversive tenses" have "the meaning of the preceding tenses."[19] In fact, however, *wayyqtl* after the non-perfective conjugation does not have the meaning of that conjugation; rather it signifies perfective aspect in addition to the subordinate values analyzed above. When *wayyqtl* follows a prefix conjugation it possesses a complementary perfective value, even as a suffix conjugation can complement a prefix conjugation in a pair of poetic lines. Significantly, there are no instances of *wayyqtl* after a prefix conjugation denoting either customary aspect in past time or a dependent modal situation. After the other grammatical forms *wayyqtl* also signifies notions associated with the suffix conjugation.

33.3.1   After Suffix-Conjugation Forms

a   *Wayyqtl*, after a suffix form, usually expresses a perfective value. If the time reference is to the past, the *wayyqtl* form may be a definite ("preterite"; # 1, cf. # 9), ingressive (# 2), constative (# 3), complex (## 4–5), telic (## 6–7), indefinite perfective (# 8), or unique definite past (# 9).

17. T. O. Lambdin, *Introduction to Biblical Hebrew* (New York: Scribner, 1971) 123.

18. Cf. GB 2. 37 (§ 8a*).

19. Davidson, *Hebrew Syntax*, 70.

1.	הַנָּחָשׁ הִשִּׁיאַנִי וָאֹכֵל:	The serpent deceived me, *and so* I *ate*. Gen 3:13
2.	לֹא שָׁעָה וַיִּחַר לְקַיִן מְאֹד	He (God) did not respect (his offering), *and* Cain *became* very *angry*. Gen 4:5
3.	עִם־לָבָן גַּרְתִּי וָאֵחַר עַד־עָתָּה:	I have been staying with Laban *and have remained* until now. Gen 32:5
4.	וְהַמַּיִם גָּבְרוּ מְאֹד מְאֹד עַל־הָאָרֶץ וַיְכֻסּוּ כָּל־הֶהָרִים הַגְּבֹהִים	The waters rose exceedingly greatly on the earth *and covered* all the high mountains. Gen 7:19
5.	וְשִׁחֵת רַחֲמָיו וַיִּטְרֹף לָעַד אַפּוֹ	He destroyed all his fellow feeling and his anger *raged* continually. Amos 1:11
6.	וְלֹא־מָצְאָה הַיּוֹנָה מָנוֹחַ . . . וַתָּשָׁב אֵלָיו	But the dove did not find a resting place . . . *and so returned* to him. Gen 8:9
7.	לֹא־מָצְאוּ מַעֲנֶה וַיַּרְשִׁיעוּ אֶת־אִיּוֹב:	They did not find an answer *and yet* they *condemned* Job. Job 32:3
8.	הֲשָׁמַע עָם קוֹל אֱלֹהִים . . . וַיֶּחִי:	Has a people ever heard the voice of God . . . *and lived*? Deut 4:33
9.	רָאִיתִי אֶת־אֲדֹנָי נִצָּב עַל־הַמִּזְבֵּחַ וַיֹּאמֶר	I saw the Lord standing by the altar, *and* he *said*. . . . Amos 9:1

If the time reference is present, *wayyqtl* may take on the range of meanings asso-   **b**
ciated with the perfective conjugation with the same time reference (30.5.1). These include
notably persistent present (# 10–11) and gnomic (## 12–14) perfectives, as well as present
statives (## 15–16). These usages may be found together, for example, persistent fientives
with present *qtl* statives (## 16–17).

10.	וַאֲנִי בְּתֻמִּי תָּמַכְתָּ בִּי וַתַּצִּיבֵנִי לְפָנֶיךָ לְעוֹלָם:	In my integrity you uphold me *and set* me in your presence forever. Ps 41:13
11.	יֶלֶק פָּשַׁט וַיָּעֹף:	[Like] locusts they have stripped (the land) *and flown away*. Nah 3:16
12.	וְגַם־נָשַׁף בָּהֶם וַיִּבָשׁוּ	He blows upon them *and* they *wither*. Isa 40:24
13.	כָּלָה עָנָן וַיֵּלַךְ	The cloud wastes away *and vanishes*. Job 7:9

14.	בָּא־זָדוֹן וַיָּבֹא קָלוֹן	When pride comes, *so does* disgrace. Prov 11:2
15.	אָהַבְתָּ צֶּדֶק וַתִּשְׂנָא רֶשַׁע	You love righteousness and *so hate* wickedness. Ps 45:8
16.	כִּי מָלְאוּ מִקֶּדֶם . . . וַתִּמָּלֵא אַרְצוֹ כֶּסֶף וְזָהָב	They are full of (things) from the east [superstitions]; . . . their (lit., its) land *is full of* silver and gold. Isa 2:6–7
17.	שַׂמְתִּי פָנַי כַּחַלָּמִישׁ וָאֵדַע כִּי־ לֹא אֵבוֹשׁ:	I have set my face like a flint *for I know* that I will not be put to shame. Isa 50:7
18.	יַעַן כִּי גָבְהוּ בְּנוֹת צִיּוֹן וַתֵּלַכְנָה	Because the women of Zion are haughty *and walk*. . . . Isa 3:16
19.	לָכֵן שָׂמַח לִבִּי וַיָּגֶל כְּבוֹדִי	Therefore my heart is glad *and* my glory *rejoices*. Ps 16:9

c   *Wayyqtl* forms can signify a perfect state after suffix forms with that meaning. For example, the time structures may be present perfect (## 20–22) or pluperfect (past perfect; ## 23–24). Here, too, the perfect state may complement other meanings of the suffix conjugation, for example, after past-tense references (## 25–26) or present-time references (# 27).

20.	יַעַן מָאָסְכֶם בַּדָּבָר הַזֶּה וַתִּבְטְחוּ בְּעֹשֶׁק	Because you have rejected this word *and have relied* on oppression. . . . Isa 30:12
21.	הִקְשַׁבְתִּי וָאֶשְׁמָע	I have listened *and heard*. Jer 8:6
22.	כִּי־יִתְרִי פִתַּח וַיְעַנֵּנִי	He (God) has unstrung my bow *and afflicted* me. Job 30:11 *Qere*
23.	וְרָחֵל לָקְחָה אֶת־הַתְּרָפִים וַתְּשִׂמֵם בְּכַר הַגָּמָל וַתֵּשֶׁב עֲלֵיהֶם	Now Rachel *had* taken the *teraphim*, *and put* them in the camel's saddle, *and sat* upon them. Gen 31:34
24.	כִּי־עָזַב בִּגְדוֹ . . . וַיָּנָס	He had left his garment . . . *and had fled*. Gen 39:13
25.	כּוֹנַנְתָּ אֶרֶץ וַתַּעֲמֹד:	You established the earth *and it stands*. Ps 119:90
26.	וּשְׁתֵּים עֶשְׂרֵה אֲבָנִים הֵקִים יְהוֹשֻׁעַ . . . וַיִּהְיוּ שָׁם עַד הַיּוֹם הַזֶּה:	Joshua set up twelve stones . . . , *and* they *are* there until this day. Josh 4:9
27.	וְלֹא־נִפְקַד מִמֶּנּוּ אִישׁ: וַנַּקְרֵב אֶת־קָרְבַּן יהוה	Not one of them is missing, *so we have brought* an offering to Yʜᴡʜ. Num 31:49–50

Whereas a suffix-conjugation form can represent an objective future situation as a   d
single, accidental event, a following *wayyqtl* represents the situation according to the
uses of relative *waw*, but nevertheless as a single, perfective whole (## 28–32).

28.   כִּי־יֶ֤לֶד יֻלַּד־לָ֙נוּ֙ . . . וַתְּהִ֤י   For to us a child will be born . . . *and* the government
       הַמִּשְׂרָה֙ עַל־שִׁכְמ֔וֹ וַיִּקְרָ֥א שְׁמ֖וֹ   *will be* on his shoulders. *And* he *will be called.* . . .
                                           Isa 9:5

In this case the first relative *waw* signifies a (con)sequential event and the second, with a
verb of speaking, an explanatory one. Often, chronological succession is in view.

29.   פָּרְצ֖וּ וַֽיַּעֲבֹ֑רוּ   They will break through *and go out.*
                                       Mic 2:13

30.   חָתֻ֣ם בִּצְר֣וֹר פִּשְׁעִ֑י   My offense will be sealed up in a bag,
            וַתִּטְפֹּ֥ל עַל־עֲוֺנִֽי׃   *and* (so) you *will cover* over my sin.
                                       Job 14:17

31.   אָכְל֬וּ וַיִּֽשְׁתַּחֲו֨וּ ׀ כָּל־דִּשְׁנֵי־אֶ֗רֶץ   All the wealthy of the earth will eat *and worship.*
                                       Ps 22:30

32.   קָ֤מוּ ׀ וַיֵּבֹ֑שׁוּ   (When) they attack, they *will be put to shame.*
                                       Ps 109:28

Wayyqtl is also used after a suffix form that is a hypothetical or conditional perfec-   e
tive (## 33–35).

33.   כִּ֣י לוּלֵ֤י מִהַ֙רְתְּ֙ וַתָּבֹ֔את   If you had not made haste *and come.* . . .
                                       1 Sam 25:34 *Qere*

34.   אִם־נִטְמְאָ֥ה וַתִּמְעֹ֖ל מַ֑עַל   If she has defiled herself *and been unfaithful.* . . .
                                       Num 5:27

35.   אִם־קָרָ֥אתִי וַיַּֽעֲנֵ֑נִי   If I summoned (him) *and he responded.* . . .
                                       Job 9:16

It is very rare that *wayyqtl* refers to a time other than that of the preceding suffix   f
conjugation, apart from its use as pluperfect or to indicate the perfect state in present
time. Excluding these groups of exceptions we are left with only one instance from Gotthelf Bergsträsser's list of alleged examples of instances where *wayyqtl* has no connection
with a preceding perfective conjugation of a different time period.[20]

36.   וְגַם־אָמְנָ֗ה אֲחֹתִ֤י . . . הִוא֙ . . .   She really is my sister . . . *and* she *became* my wife.
            וַתְּהִי־לִ֖י לְאִשָּֽׁה׃   Gen 20:12

Another example of a perfective conjugation in a time period different from that of the
leading verb is the following.

---

20. GB 2. 37 (§ 8a*).

37. אֵת אֲשֶׁר־הִשְׁלִ֖יכוּ אֶל־הַבּ֑וֹר   . . . in that they have thrown him into the cistern
     וָיָּ֖מָת   *and* he *will die.*
     Jer 38:9

Both of these apparently epexegetical uses are exceptional.

33.3.2   After Short Prefix-Conjugation Forms

a   After a short prefix form, *wayyqtl* expresses a situation that is subordinate, logically, temporally, or epexegetically, and has a perfective value that is the same as or complementary to that of the leading verb. Note, for example, preterite (## 1–2) and gnomic (# 3) values.

1. יַרְכִּבֵ֙הוּ֙ עַל־בָּ֣מֳותֵי אָ֔רֶץ   He made him ride on the heights of the land
    וַיֹּאכַ֖לֵ֔הוּ תְּנוּבֹ֣ת שָׂדָ֑י   *and fed* him with the fruit of the field
    וַיֵּנִקֵ֤הוּ דְבַשׁ֙ מִסֶּ֔לַע   *and* he *nourished* him with honey from the crag.
    Deut 32:13 *Kethiv/Sam*

2. צ֥וּר יְלָדְךָ֖ תֶּ֑שִׁי   You deserted the Rock, who fathered you,
    וַתִּשְׁכַּ֖ח אֵ֥ל מְחֹלְלֶֽךָ׃   *and forgot* the God who gave you birth,
    וַיַּ֥רְא יְהוָ֖ה וַיִּנְאָ֑ץ   *and* Yhwh *saw* this *and rejected* them.
    Deut 32:18–19

3. תָּשֵׁ֣ב אֱ֭נוֹשׁ עַד־דַּכָּ֑א וַתֹּ֖אמֶר   You turn men back to the dust, *saying.* . . .
    Ps 90:3

33.3.3   After Prefix-Conjugation Forms

a   *Wayyqtl* after a prefix-conjugation (non-perfective) form may signify either a (con)sequential or an explanatory situation, in accord with the uses of perfective aspect forms after prefix-conjugation forms.

b   After a prefix conjugation signifying a past situation, *wayyqtl* signifies a (con)sequent or explanatory situation in the past time, according to one of the specific uses of the suffix conjugation in that time frame, normally definite perfective; this arrangement is found after ʾāz (## 1–2), stative situations (# 3), and incipient progressive imperfective situations (# 4).

1. אָ֣ז יִבְנֶ֤ה יְהוֹשֻׁ֙עַ֙ מִזְבֵּ֔חַ . . .   Then Joshua built an altar . . . *and* they *offered*
    וַיַּעֲל֨וּ   *up.* . . .
    Josh 8:30–31

2. אָ֣ז יְדַבֵּ֤ר יְהוֹשֻׁ֙עַ֙ . . . וַיֹּ֖אמֶר   Then Joshua spoke . . . *and said.* . . .
    Josh 10:12

3. אַרְבָּעִ֣ים שָׁנָ֤ה אָק֙וּט . . . וָאֹמַ֔ר   For forty years I was angry . . . *so* I *said.* . . .
    Ps 95:10

4. תְּגָרֵ֣שׁ גּוֹיִ֖ם וַתִּטָּעֶֽהָ׃   You drove out the nations *and planted* it.
    Ps 80:9

Likewise, after regular *yqtl* referring to a present-time situation, *wayyqtl* represents   c
a (con)sequential or explanatory situation in the same time frame according to a perfective aspect. Presuming that the prefix forms (excluding unbound short forms) set the
structure of the verb sequence, we find that frequently *wayyqtl*, after a present progressive
yqtl, has the sense of a persistent present perfective (## 5–9). After a habitual *yqtl* imperfective, *wayyqtl* may have the value of a gnomic perfective (# 10).

5. וְיִשְׁתַּמֵּר חֻקּוֹת עָמְרִי . . . וַתֵּלְכוּ
    בְּמֹעֲצוֹתָם

You observe the statutes of Omri, . . . *and so* you
follow their (the Ahabites') traditions.
Mic 6:16

6. לָמָּה תִבְעֲטוּ בְּזִבְחִי . . . וַתְּכַבֵּד
    אֶת־בָּנֶיךָ מִמֶּנִּי

Why do you scorn my sacrifice . . . *and honor* your
sons more than me?
1 Sam 2:29

7. אַלְמָנָה וְגֵר יַהֲרֹגוּ . . . וַיֹּאמְרוּ

They slay widow and alien . . . , *saying.* . . .
Ps 94:6–7

8. קוֹלִי אֶל־יְהוה אֶקְרָא וַיַּעֲנֵנִי

I cry aloud to Yʜᴡʜ, *and* he *answers* me. . . .
Ps 3:5

9. זִבְחֵי הַבְהָבַי יִזְבְּחוּ בָשָׂר
    וַיֹּאכֵלוּ

They offer sacrifices given(?) to me *and eat* the meat.
Hos 8:13

10. חָרָשׁ בַּרְזֶל מַעֲצָד וּפָעַל בַּפֶּחָם
    וּבַמַּקָּבוֹת יִצְּרֵהוּ וַיִּפְעָלֵהוּ
    בִּזְרוֹעַ כֹּחוֹ

The blacksmith (with) an iron tool(?)—he works
(with it) in the coals; he shapes it with hammers,
and forges it with the strength of his arm. . . .
Isa 44:12

Suffix and prefix forms with the same time reference probably complement one another
(31.3c). In # 11 a progressive imperfective is associated with a persistent present perfective, and *wayyqtl* continues the persistent perfective; in # 12–13 a *wayyqtl* form continues
a progressive imperfective and in # 12 precedes a persistent present perfective.

11. אֹהֲבַי . . . מִנֶּגֶד נִגְעִי יַעֲמֹדוּ
    וּקְרוֹבַי מֵרָחֹק עָמָדוּ׃
    וַיְנַקְשׁוּ מְבַקְשֵׁי נַפְשִׁי

My friends . . . stand apart (from me) for my disease,
my neighbors stand far away,
(*so*) those who seek my life *set* traps.
Ps 38:12–13

12. כִּי לֹא שָׁלוֹם יְדַבֵּרוּ . . .
    וַיַּרְחִיבוּ עָלַי פִּיהֶם אָמְרוּ הֶאָח
    הֶאָח

They do not speak peaceably . . . *and* they *open wide*
their mouths against me; they say, "Alas! Alas!"
Ps 35:20–21

13. יָגוֹדּוּ עַל־נֶפֶשׁ צַדִּיק . . .
    וַיְהִי יהוה לִי לְמִשְׂגָּב

They band together against the righteous . . .
so Yʜᴡʜ *has become* my fortress.
Ps 94:21–22

So also *wayyqtl* may have a persistent perfective meaning (## 14–15) or a present-time
stative meaning (## 16–17) after an incipient imperfective.

14.	יִקְרָא אֶל־הַשָּׁמַ֫יִם . . . וַיַּגִּ֫ידוּ שָׁמַ֫יִם צִדְקוֹ	He summons the heavens . . . *and* the heavens *proclaim* his righteousness. Ps 50:4, 6
15.	יִרְאָה וָרַ֫עַד יָבֹא בִי וַתְּכַסֵּ֫נִי פַּלָּצוּת׃	Fear and trembling came upon me, *and* horror *overwhelms* me. Ps 55:6
16.	כִּי עַתָּה תָּבוֹא אֵלֶ֫יךָ וַתֵּ֫לֶא	But now it (trouble) comes to you, *and* you *are discouraged.* Job 4:5
17.	תִּרְאוּ חֲתַת וַתִּירָ֫אוּ׃	You see a horror *and are afraid.* Job 6:21

33.3.4 After Nominal Clauses

a   The use of *wayyqtl* after circumstantial nominal clauses is discussed earlier (33.2.4), but other features of nominal clause + *wayyqtl* verb require attention.

b   After a nominal clause with past-time reference, *wayyqtl* tends to represent a definite perfective situation in past time, a use in harmony with its perfective aspect.

1.	וְלוֹ שְׁתֵּי נָשִׁים . . . וַיְהִי לִפְנִנָּה יְלָדִים	He had two wives; . . . Peninnah *had* children. 1 Sam 1:2
2.	וְהִנֵּה רֶ֫כֶב־אֵשׁ וְסוּסֵי אֵשׁ וַיַּפְרִ֫דוּ בֵּין שְׁנֵיהֶם	Suddenly (there were) a chariot and horses of fire *and* the two of them *separated.* 2 Kgs 2:11
3.	וּבִתּוֹ שֶׁאֱרָה וַתִּ֫בֶן	His daughter was Sheerah; she *built.* . . . 1 Chr 7:24

c   If the time frame of the nominal clause corresponds to that of the English present tenses, the *wayyqtl* form may be present persistent (# 4), gnomic (## 5–7), or stative present (# 8).

4.	יהוה אֲדֹנָי חֵילִי וַיָּ֫שֶׂם רַגְלַי כָּאַיָּלוֹת	The Lord Yhwh is my strength *and so* he *makes* my feet like a hind's. Hab 3:19
5.	אֵל יהוה וַיָּ֫אֶר לָ֫נוּ	Yhwh is God *and so* he *makes* his light shine on us. Ps 118:27
6.	יהוה מָה־אָדָם וַתֵּדָעֵ֫הוּ	O Yhwh, what is a person *that* you *care* for him? Ps 144:3
7.	הַנְּמָלִים עַם לֹא־עָז וַיָּכִ֫ינוּ . . . לַחְמָם׃	Ants are creatures of no strength, *yet* they *store up* . . . their food. Prov 30:25

8.   מִי־אַתְּ וַתִּירְאִי   Who are you *that* you *fear*?
                                         Isa 51:12

With Non-finite Verb Forms   33.3.5

The *wayyqtl* form is more common after participles than infinitives.   a

Wayyqtl after a *relative participle* (usually with ה; 'the one who . . .'; 13.5.2d) b
represents a situation that complements the participle. Thus, if the participle refers to the
past, *wayyqtl* may represent a subordinate preterite situation (## 1–4), in contrast to a
wqtl form, which, after a relative participle, represents an indefinite situation (32.2.5b).
Wayyqtl may represent a logical consequence persisting into the present (# 5). Subordinate to a relative participle denoting a perfect state, *wayyqtl* may represent a perfect state
or some nuance of perfective aspect in present time, such as persistent perfective (# 6).
Subordinate to a relative participle referring to present time, *wayyqtl* also represents a
perfective situation, be it persistent (# 7) or gnomic (# 8) perfective.

1.   מִי־אֵפוֹא הוּא הַצָּד־צַיִד וַיָּבֵא   Who was it that hunted game *and brought* it to me?
                                      לִי   Gen 27:33

2.   לָאֵל הָעֹנֶה אֹתִי בְּיוֹם צָרָתִי   to God who answered me in the day of my distress
    וַיְהִי עִמָּדִי בַּדֶּרֶךְ אֲשֶׁר הָלָכְתִּי: *and was* with me on the road I (just) traveled
                                         Gen 35:3

3.   וְהַנִּשְׁבֶּרֶת וַתַּעֲמֹדְנָה אַרְבַּע   and the broken (horn) and the four (horns) *that arose*
                             תַּחְתֶּיהָ   in its place
                                           Dan 8:22

4.   הַקֹּרֵא לְמֵי־הַיָּם   He who summoned the waters of the sea
    וַיִּשְׁפְּכֵם עַל־פְּנֵי הָאָרֶץ   *and then* poured them *out* over the earth.[21]
                                         Amos 9:6

5.   . . . מַשְׁבִּיחַ שְׁאוֹן יַמִּים   who stilled the roaring of the seas . . .
    וַיִּירְאוּ יֹשְׁבֵי קְצָוֹת   *so that* those dwelling far away *fear*
                                         Ps 65:8–9

6.   הִנֵּה הָעָם הַיֹּצֵא מִמִּצְרַיִם וַיְכַס   Look, a people that has come out of Egypt (*and*)
    אֶת־עֵין הָאָרֶץ   *covers* the land.
                                         Num 22:11

7.   הָאֵל הַמְאַזְּרֵנִי חָיִל   The God who arms with strength
    וַיִּתֵּן תָּמִים דַּרְכִּי: *and so makes* my way perfect.
                                         Ps 18:33

8.   גֹּעֵר בַּיָּם וַיַּבְּשֵׁהוּ   He who rebukes the sea *and so dries* it *up*.
                                         Nah 1:4

After a *participle used as a predicate* in present time, subordinate *wayyqtl* may have c
a stative present sense (# 9) or a persistent perfective sense (## 10–12).[22]

---

21. Amos 5:8 has a nearly identical reference to the Noahic flood; see Finley, "*Waw*-Consecutive with 'Imperfect,'" 256.
22. Davidson, *Hebrew Syntax*, 73.

9.   הִנֵּה הַמֶּ֫לֶךְ בֹּכֶה וַיִּתְאַבֵּל   The king is weeping *and mourns*.
     2 Sam 19:2

10.   נֹצְרִים בָּאִים . . . וַיִּתְּנוּ   Blockaders are coming . . . *raising* . . .
     קוֹלָם: their voice.
     Jer 4:16

11.   כֻּלּוֹ עֹשֶׂה שָּׁקֶר: All practice deceit
     וַיְרַפְּאוּ אֶת־שֶׁ֫בֶר עַמִּי   *and so dress* the wound of my people.
     Jer 6:13–14

12.   חֹנֶה מַלְאַךְ־יהוה . . .   The angel of Yʜwʜ encamps . . . *and so*
     וַיְחַלְּצֵם: *delivers* them.
     Ps 34:8

d   After an *infinitive* representing a situation in the past, *wayyqtl* tends to represent a definite perfective situation in past time.

13.   בְּבָרְכוֹ אֹתוֹ וַיְצַו עָלָיו לֵאמֹר   when he blessed him and *commanded* him, saying . . .
     Gen 28:6

14.   בְּקָרְבָתָם לִפְנֵי־יהוה וַיָּמֻ֫תוּ:   when they approached Yʜwʜ and *died*
     Lev 16:1

15.   בַּעֲלֹתִי הָהָ֫רָה . . . וָאֵשֵׁב בָּהָר   When I went up on the mountain . . . I *stayed* on the mountain.
     Deut 9:9

In present-time reference, the *wayyqtl* can have a variety of senses, including complex (# 16) and gnomic (## 17–18).

16.   מַה־לְּךָ לְסַפֵּר חֻקָּי   What right have you to recite my statutes
     וַתִּשָּׂא בְרִיתִי עֲלֵי־פִ֫יךָ:   *and so take* my covenant on your mouth?
     Ps 50:16

17.   לְקוֹל תִּתּוֹ . . . וַיַּעֲלֶה נְשִׂאִים   When he thunders . . . he *makes clouds rise.*
     Jer 10:13

18.   בִּפְרֹחַ רְשָׁעִים . . .   When the wicked spring up . . .
     וַיָּצִ֫יצוּ כָּל־פֹּעֲלֵי אָ֫וֶן   *and* evildoers *flourish.* . . .
     Ps 92:8

33.4   Simple *Waw + Prefix Conjugation*

a   *Wəyqtl* differs from *wayyqtl* with reference to both elements of the compound, the conjunction and the verb form. In 39.2 the coordinator is discussed; here we note only some salient features of the use of *wəyqtl*.

b   The conjunction does not mark *wəyqtl* as successive or subordinate; it is rather an unmarked connector, though it may introduce (for lexical rather than grammatical reasons) a clause that is logically or temporally subordinate to its predecessor (# 1). In post-exilic Hebrew *wəyqtl* tends to replace sequential *wəqtl* (# 2). After a volitional (cohortative, imperative, jussive) form *wəyqtl* has a consequential force (# 3; cf. 39.2.2). The prefix conjugation in this combination is usually imperfective, for example, in a habitual usage (# 4).

1.   תַּעְתִּיר אֵלָיו וְיִשְׁמָעֶ֑ךָ

You will pray to him, *and* he *will hear* you.
Job 22:27

2.   וְנִזְעַק אֵלֶיךָ מִצָּרָתֵ֫נוּ וְתִשְׁמַע
וְתוֹשִׁיעַ׃

And we will cry out to you in our distress *and* you *will hear* (us) *and save* (us).
2 Chr 20:9

3.   שִׁמְעוּ אֵלַי בַּעֲלֵי שְׁכֶם וְיִשְׁמַע
אֲלֵיכֶם אֱלֹהִים׃

Listen to me, citizens of Shechem, *so that* God *may listen* to you.
Judg 9:7

4.   כִּי הַשֹּׁחַד יְעַוֵּר פִּקְחִים וִיסַלֵּף
דִּבְרֵי צַדִּיקִים׃

A gift blinds those who see, *and twists* the words of the righteous.
Exod 23:8

34

Jussive, Imperative, Cohortative

34.1 Volitional Forms

a   The largest class of clauses is the declarative, that is, those that make an assertion or claim (e.g., 'Baruch wrote the scroll'), but other simple clauses are also found, and the most important group of these is the volitional. In the classical languages, Greek and Latin, volitional forms are associated with verbal moods such as the imperative, subjunctive, and optative. English has a distinct grammatical form for the imperative (the second-person volitional), but other volitional forms are composed of auxiliaries (e.g., 'let, shall, may') with simple verb forms. In Hebrew there is a set of volitional forms, the cohortative, imperative, and jussive. These do not make up a mood, however, since they are morphologically independent; in antecedent forms of the language, the jussive (< *yaqtul*) and cohortative (< *yaqtula*) formed distinct conjugations in all persons. The Hebrew volitionals rather form a functional class.[1]

b   Because the jussive (chiefly third person), imperative (second person), and cohortative (first person) forms do not overlap extensively in their uses, the three forms together

---

1. See Joüon § 114 / pp. 307–12; W. L. Moran, "Early Canaanite *Yaqtula*," *Orientalia* 29 (1960) 1–19, at 12; and A. Niccacci, *Sintassi del verbo ebraico nella prosa biblica classica* (Jerusalem: Franciscan Printing Press, 1986) 55– 59, all of whom take the forms together as a group. For a more broadly based approach to modality, see E. Talstra, "Text Grammar and Hebrew Bible. II. Syntax and Semantics," *Bibliotheca Orientalis* 39 (1982) 26–38, esp. 30–35.

comprise one unified system for the expression of the speaker's will. The once separate forms now work together to form a volitional class.

first person	cohortative
second person *positive*	imperative / non-perfective
negative	ᵓl + jussive / lᵓ + non-perfective
third person	jussive

The forms do overlap to a limited degree, most notably in the use of the jussive form for the negative imperative role. Further, the uses overlap because of surrogates for the personal pronouns, for example, words for 'soul,' 'heart,' etc. Constructions that differ in grammar on the surface level of the language (e.g., 'May I . . . ,' first person; 'O my soul, may you . . . ,' second person; 'May my soul . . . ,' third person) are at a deeper level semantically equivalent.

The terms imperative and jussive refer etymologically to absolute expressions of will   c (Latin *impero* 'to command,' *jubeo* 'to order'). In fact, these forms may express varying degrees of volition (Latin *volo* 'to wish'), as do comparable constructions in other languages. Through the volitional forms a speaker aims to impose his or her will on some other person (or, in figurative language, thing). The force with which that will is exerted depends on various factors, including the speaker's social standing *vis-à-vis* the addressee, the social context of the discourse, and the meaning of the verb. For these reasons the precise nuances of the volitional forms may range from command, advice, and permission to request, wish, etc.

The class of volitional forms is the basis for the syntactic study of volitional expres-   d sions, but it is only the basis.[2] Some descriptions of commands or exhortations involve the perfective conjugation (30.5.4) and others the non-perfective conjugation (31.5). The jussive form is not always morphologically distinct from other prefix forms (33.1). The cohortative is hardly ever marked for final-*he* verbs, rarely for final-*aleph* verbs, and is indistinguishable before suffixes.[3] An ᵓqtl form may be taken to denote volition (i.e., may be taken as cohortative) in an environment where a cohortative would occur, for example, after אל or נא or after an imperative (34.6–7). Sometimes the imperative is replaced by an infinitive absolute (35.5.1). Because of these and related complexities, we discuss the morphology of the volitional forms before treating usage.

---

2. Joüon § 114b / p. 307 suggests that it is necessary to distinguish cohortative mood (i.e., sense or syntactic role) from cohortative form because, on the one hand, the prefix conjugation may connote notions that we associate with the cohortative mood, and, on the other, the cohortative form is used for the indicative mood. On this point, see also P. D. Miller, "Syntax and Theology in Genesis XII 3a," *Vetus Testamentum* 34 (1984) 472–76, at 475–76; and 34.5.3.

3. On final-*he* verbs, see E. J. Revell, "First Person Imperfect Forms with *Waw* Consecutive," *Vetus Testamentum* 38 (1988) 419–26, at 419–20 (cf. 424–25 on the phonology in general); GKC § 75l / p. 210, § 108a n. 2 / p. 319. For final-*aleph* verbs, note ᵓemṣāᵓ-ḥēn 'let me find favor' (Gen 33:15, 34:11, etc.); niqrāᵓ 'let's call' (Gen 24:57); ᵓal-nāᵓ ᵓeśśāᵓ 'let me not lift' (Job 32:21); waᵓērāpēᵓ 'that I may be healed' (Jer 17:14, with waᵓiwwāšēᶜâ 'that I may be saved'); ᵓeśśāᵓ '(if) I rise' (Ps 139:9, followed by ᵓeškanâ 'if I dwell'); wanēṣēᵓ 'let us go' (1 Kgs 20:31); ᵓābôᵓ 'I would go' (Gen 38:16); but note waᵓēṣaᵓâ 'that I may go out' (2 Chr 1:10, before waᵓābôᵓâ 'and that I may go'). Suffixed forms are also not marked as cohortative, e.g., lakî ᵓîᶜāṣēk nāᵓ ᶜēṣâ 'Come now, let me advise you' (1 Kgs 1:12). See also Miller, "Syntax and Theology," 475–76.

34.2   Morphological Background

34.2.1   Jussive

a   The Canaanite dialects antecedent to Hebrew distinguished prefix forms *yaqtulu* and *yaqtul*, as we have noted (29.4, 31.1.1, 33.1.2). The Hebrew *jussive* in some sense derived from the short *yaqtul* form. Whatever the historical facts, there are two groups of *yiqtol* forms in Biblical Hebrew, the long and short, for certain verbal stems and roots. In cases where the differentiation is found, the short form is the jussive (as well as the *wayyqtl* form).[4]

long form	jussive
יַכְרִית	יַכְרֵת
יִגְלֶה	יֶגֶל
יִרְאֶה	יֵרֶא, יֵרֶא
יֶחֱרֶה	יִחַר
יָקוּם	יָקֶם
יָקִים	יָקֵם

The differentiation is not common, however, and there is no morphological distinction between jussive and non-jussive forms with most roots. For example, in the Aaronide blessing, only two of the six verbs are formally jussives, yet all have the same volitional sense.

יְבָרֶכְךָ יהוה וְיִשְׁמְרֶךָ׃	YHWH bless you and keep you.
יָאֵר יהוה פָּנָיו אֵלֶיךָ וִיחֻנֶּךָּ׃	YHWH *make* his face *shine* upon you and be gracious to you.
יִשָּׂא יהוה פָּנָיו אֵלֶיךָ	YHWH turn his face to you.
וְיָשֵׂם לְךָ שָׁלוֹם׃	And *give* you peace.
	Num 6:24–26

In such a situation all the verbs are to be taken as jussives.[5] In some instances the distinctive form of the jussive is not used even when it could appear (cf. 1 Sam 25:25, אַל־נָא יָשִׂים), a phenomenon we already observed with *wayyqtl* (see 33.1.1b). The longer form is more common before a pausal form or in pause (e.g., וְתֵרָאֶה, Gen 1:9; and וְיִרְאֶה, 2 Kgs 6:17). This sporadic split between form and meaning advises us to distinguish between *jussive form* and *jussive sense*; it is the latter we are chiefly concerned with. Because of the widespread polysemy of *yqtl* forms the interpreter must in most instances judge on the basis of semantic pertinence whether the form is jussive or non-perfective (see 3.2.3).

---

4. For the development of the jussive (*versus* "indicative") in West Semitic, the Aramaic dialects are more revealing than Hebrew; see A. M. R. Aristar, "The Semitic Jussive and the Implications for Aramaic," *Maarav* 4 (1987) 157–89; J. Huehnergard, "The Feminine Plural Jussive in Old Aramaic," *Zeitschrift der Deutschen Morgenländischen Gesellschaft* 137 (1987) 266–77.

5. The contrary position, that all the forms are indicatives, is argued by H. Jagersma, "Some Remarks on the Jussive in Numbers 6, 24–26," *Von Kanaan bis Kerala: Festschrift . . . J. P. M. van der Ploeg*, ed. W. C. Delsman et al. (Alter Orient und Altes Testament 211; Kevelaer: Butzon und Bercker/Neukirchen-Vluyn: Neukirchener Verlag, 1982) 131–36.

In earlier stages of Northwest Semitic the short prefix conjugation could be used with   b
all three persons, but in Biblical Hebrew it is mostly restricted to the third person (in either
positive or negative clauses) and to the second person (chiefly in negative clauses). With
both second- and third-person jussive forms, the negative particle is usually אַל rather than
לֹא.[6] The combination of אַל with the second-person jussive constitutes the negative
imperative; the imperative form itself cannot be preceded by a negative particle. A non-
perfective form with לֹא can have a similar sense. The construction with אַל tends to reflect
urgency and that with לֹא legislation. With a third-person jussive אַל marks a negative
jussive.

Rarely, a jussive form occurs where we would expect a non-perfective conjugation   c
form (cf. Ps 25:9, 47:4, 90:3, 107:29; Isa 12:1; Joel 2:2, etc.). These unexpected jussive
forms may be due to the confusion between the form groups or to textual corruptions; or
they may represent vestiges of an earlier verbal system. Some grammarians explain them
on rhythmical grounds.[7] Because of this minor formal confounding, it is best in problem
passages of this nature to be governed by sense rather than by form. A similar approach
is warranted in the few passages where the vocalization that characterizes the jussive
occurs with the first person (cf. Isa 42:6).[8]

Similarly, although the negative particle with the jussive form in a jussive clause is   d
normally אַל, sometimes לֹא is found (cf. 1 Kgs 2:6, Ezek 48:14). These examples further
suggest that the forms are, to a slight degree, confounded within the Masoretic tradition.

The particle אַל, like לֹא, regularly stands immediately before the verb, but occa-   e
sionally it occurs before a strongly emphasized member of the sentence other than the
verb (cf. Isa 64:8; Jer 10:24, 15:15; Ps 6:2, 38:2).

Imperative and Cohortative   34.2.2

All the Semitic languages express the *imperative*, the form denoting volitional mood   a
for second person, by a form similar to that of the second person of the prefix conjugation.[9] This is clearest in Hebrew in the *Piel*: contrast תְּדַבֵּר and דַּבֵּר. The apparent

---

6. The combination *ʾl + jussive* is sometimes called the
vetitive (Latin *veto* 'to not permit'); e.g., R. J. Williams,
Hebrew Syntax: An Outline (2d ed.; Toronto: University
of Toronto, 1976) 35. The relationship between the vetitive and the *lʾ yqtl* syntagm (sometimes called the prohibitive, Latin *prohibeo* 'to forbid') is disputed (see, e.g., Joüon
§ 114i / p. 310, who is agnostic; GKC § 107o–p / p. 317
refers to the prohibitive as more emphatic, cf. § 109d /
p. 322); the role of the genre cannot be discounted. The
contrast of the two syntagms is most vivid in 1 Kgs 3:25–
26, as Anson F. Rainey has pointed out to us. The rare
negative particle *bal* (found 68 times, chiefly in verse) can
be used as equivalent to either *ʾl yqtl* (as in Ps 10:18) or *lʾ
yqtl* (Ps 93:1); see N. J. Tromp, "The Hebrew Particle
בַּל," *Oudtestamentische Studiën* 21 (1981) 277–87.

7. E.g., GKC § 109k / p. 323.

8. On these forms, see GKC § 48g n. 1 / p. 131; Moran,
"Early Canaanite *Yaqtula*," 12.

9. Sabatino Moscati et al., *An Introduction to the Comparative Grammar of the Semitic Languages* (Wiesbaden:
Harrassowitz, 1964) 136. Scholars debate whether the imperative stem (*qtul/qutul*) is primary, with personal affixes
added later to form the prefix conjugation, or whether the
prefix conjugation is primary, with the affixes later dropped
to form the imperative. The latter view is dominant (see,
e.g., M. M. Bravmann, *Studies in Semitic Philology*
[Leiden: Brill, 1977] 195–99), but Hans Bauer (among
others) held the former; see Leslie McFall, *The Enigma of
the Hebrew Verbal System* (Sheffield: Almond, 1982) 106–
7, cf. 131, 172. Mishnaic (and, infrequently, Biblical) Hebrew and Aramaic form a compound imperative with the
verb 'to be' (Hebrew *hyy*) and the participle; see M. H.
Segal, *A Grammar of Mishnaic Hebrew* (Oxford: Clarendon, 1927) 157; J. C. Greenfield, "The 'Periphrastic Imperative' in Aramaic and Hebrew," *Israel Exploration
Journal* 19 (1969) 199–210.

"dropping" of the 'you' prefix is not unlike the English imperative, which also normally deletes the pronoun, for example, 'Go!', not 'You [will] go!' In the *Niphal*, *Hiphil*, and *Hithpael* stems a prothetic *he* is added to "protect" the characteristic infix patterns of these stems, for example, הִשָּׁמֵר, הוֹשַׁע, הִתְחַזַּק, etc. The *Pual* and *Hophal* do not regularly form imperatives. The situation in the *Qal* is somewhat complex. As with other non-perfective forms (22.3), *Qal* fientive and stative verbs are distinguished: קְטֹל fientive *versus* קְטַל stative. The feminine plural form קְטֹלְנָה uses the same base as the masculine singular, while the feminine singular and masculine plural forms (those with endings involving a vowel) use a number of other bases (קָטְלִי/וּ, קִטְלִי/וּ, pausal קְטֹלִי/וּ), which also are found with forms bearing pronominal suffixes. A long form of the imperative, with final הָ-, is found with the masculine singular.[10] The *-ā* morpheme is related to the *-ā* of the cohortative. Prohibition in the second person is expressed by a negative particle with the jussive (34.2.1b), rather than with the imperative form.[11]

b   The *cohortative*, like the alternative *Qal* imperative with הָ- suffix, is derived from an earlier Canaanite *yaqtula* volitional conjugation.[12] In Hebrew, the form is found almost exclusively in the first-person singular and plural.

34.3   Uses of the Jussive

a   Third-person expressions of volition are found in a variety of discourse settings. If the jussive is used with its ordinary pragmatic force, it may be directed from a superior to an inferior or vice versa. A special case of the former situation is presented by divine jussives; these have the force of a command. A jussive directed to the divine realm (explicitly or implicitly) may be a benediction or a malediction. The jussive may also be used rhetorically, conveying a distinctive pragmatic force.

b   The sense of a jussive in simple discourse usually follows from the status relations of the speaker and addressee. When a superior uses the jussive with reference to an inferior the volitional force may be command (human, # 1; divine, # 2), exhortation (# 3), counsel (# 4), or invitation or permission (# 5). Sometimes the jussive qualifies or circumscribes an imperative (# 6). A second-person jussive may have the sense of an order (# 7). When an inferior uses the jussive with reference to a superior, it may denote an urgent request (# 8), prayer (# 9), or request for permission (## 10–11). Frequently it is followed by נָא (## 4, 8, 10; see 34.7).

1.   אַךְ אִישׁ אַל־יָרֵב וְאַל־יוֹכַח   *Let* none *contend* and none *reprove*.
           אִישׁ   Hos 4:4

2.   יְהִי אוֹר   *Let* there *be* light.
                                            Gen 1:3

---

10. This *h* is sometimes called paragogic ('extending') *he*.
11. GKC § 48i–j / pp. 131–32. On the "third-person cohortatives," see GKC § 48d / p. 130.

12. Moran, "Early Canaanite *Yaqtula*." See also J. Blau, "Studies in Hebrew Verb Formation," *Hebrew Union College Annual* 42 (1971) 133–58, at 133–44.

3. יֵלֵךְ וְיָשֹׁב לְבֵיתוֹ
    Let him *go* home (lit., *Let* him *go* and return to his house).
    Deut 20:5

4. תְּהִי־נָא לְךָ תַּחְתֶּֽיהָ:
    Have her (the younger sister) instead of her (Samson's wife).
    Judg 15:2

5. אִתִּי יַעֲבֹר כִּמְהָם
    Let Kimham *cross over* with me.
    2 Sam 19:39

6. אַל־יֵרַע בְּעֵינֶיךָ . . . שְׁמַע בְּקֹלָהּ
    Let it not *be* evil in your eyes . . . *listen* to her.
    Gen 21:12

7. וִיהִי בְּשָׁמְעֲךָ אֶת־קוֹל צְעָדָה בְּרָאשֵׁי הַבְּכָאִים אָז תֶּחֱרָץ
    And *let* it *be* that as soon as you hear the sound of marching in the tops of the balsam trees, *move*. . . .
    2 Sam 5:24

8. יַעֲבָר־נָא אֲדֹנִי
    Let my lord *go* on ahead.
    Gen 33:14

9. אַל־יִתֵּן לַמּוֹט רַגְלֶךָ
    May he not *permit* your foot to slip.
    Ps 121:3

10. יֵלֶךְ־נָא אֲדֹנָי בְּקִרְבֵּֽנוּ
    Let the Lord *go* with us.
    Exod 34:9

11. יֹסֵף יהוה לִי בֵּן אַחֵר:
    May YHWH *add* to me another son.
    Gen 30:24

A benediction (## 12–15) or malediction (## 16–18) can take the form of a jussive   c
clause.

12. יְחִי הַמֶּֽלֶךְ:
    Long live the king!
    1 Sam 10:24; cf. 1 Kgs 1:25, etc.

13. כֹּה תְבָרֲכוּ אֶת־בְּנֵי יִשְׂרָאֵל אָמוֹר לָהֶם: . . . יָאֵר יהוה פָּנָיו אֵלֶיךָ
    This is how you are to bless the Israelites. Say to them: ". . . YHWH *make* his face *shine* upon you."
    Num 6:23, 25

14. וִיהִי אֱלֹהִים עִמָּךְ
    May God *be* with you.[13]
    Exod 18:19

15. יְחִי רְאוּבֵן וְאַל־יָמֹת
    May Reuben *live* and not *die*.
    Deut 33:6

16. וִיהִי כְנַֽעַן עֶבֶד לָֽמוֹ:
    May Canaan *be* his (Shem's) slave.
    Gen 9:26

17. תִּגַּל עֶרְוָתֵךְ
    Let your nakedness *be* exposed.
    Isa 47:3

18. יוֹם אֲשֶׁר־יְלָדַתְנִי אִמִּי אַל־יְהִי בָרוּךְ:
    May the day my mother bore me not *be* blessed.
    Jer 20:14

13. Cf. 1 Sam 20:13.

d   The jussive's usual pragmatic force may be lost in poetic contexts or in literary prose. In some cases this loss arises from projecting feelings onto nature, as S. R. Driver notes.[14]

> To the poet, whatever be his language or country, the world is animated by a life, vibrating in harmony with his own, which the prosaic eye is unable to discern: for him, not merely the animal world, but inanimate nature as well, is throbbing with human emotions, and keenly susceptible to every impression from without (e.g. Ps. 65:14, 104:19, 114:3–6; Isa. 35:1f.); he addresses boldly persons and objects not actually present (e.g. Isa. 13:2, 23:1f., 4; 40:9 etc.; Ps. 98:7f., 114:7f.), or peoples a scene with invisible beings, the creations of his own fancy (Isa. 40:3, 57:14, 62:10); he feels, and expresses, a vivid sympathy with the characters and transactions with which he has to deal. The result is that instead of describing an occurrence in the language of bare fact, a poet often loves to represent it under the form of a command proceeding from himself.[15]

The specific literary devices involved are personification (## 19–20) and metonomy (## 21–22); in the latter cases a place stands for the people who live in it (note the plural in # 22). The jussive is also used to vary verb sequences and literary texture, creating *oratio variata* (## 23–24). One form of such *oratio* is based on apostrophe, direct address *to* a person, after a passage talking *about* that person (# 25).

19. יִרְעַם הַיָּם וּמְלֹאוֹ׃
Let the sea *resound*, and all that is in it.
Ps 96:11

20. נְהָרוֹת יִמְחֲאוּ־כָף
Let the rivers *clap* (their) hands.
Ps 98:8

21. תָּגֵל הָאָרֶץ יִשְׂמְחוּ אִיִּים רַבִּים׃
Let the earth *be glad*; *let* the many shores *rejoice*.
Ps 97:1

22. יִירְאוּ מֵיהוה כָּל־הָאָרֶץ
Let all the earth *fear* YHWH.
Ps 33:8

23. אַשְׁרֵי מַשְׂכִּיל אֶל־דָּל . . . וְאַל תִּתְּנֵהוּ בְּנֶפֶשׁ אֹיְבָיו׃
Blessed is he who has regard for the weak . . . and *may* he not *surrender* him to the desire of his foe.
Ps 41:2–3

24. מִצִּיּוֹן . . . אֱלֹהִים הוֹפִיעַ׃ יָבֹא אֱלֹהֵינוּ וְאַל־יֶחֱרַשׁ
From Zion . . . God shines forth. *May* our God *come* and not *be silent*.
Ps 50:2–3

25. יֹאכְלוּ עֲנָוִים וְיִשְׂבָּעוּ יְהַלְלוּ יהוה דֹּרְשָׁיו יְחִי לְבַבְכֶם לָעַד׃
The poor will eat and be satisfied; they who seek him will praise YHWH— *may* your hearts *live* forever!
Ps 22:27

14. Driver's contemporary John Ruskin dubbed such projection the "pathetic fallacy." For a discussion with biblical examples, see the selections from *Modern Painters III* (1856) in *The Literary Criticism of John Ruskin*, ed. H. Bloom (New York: Norton, 1971) 62–78.

15. S. R. Driver, *A Treatise on the Use of Tenses in Hebrew* (3d ed.; Oxford: Clarendon, 1892) 59–60.

Uses of the Imperative   **34.4**

Second-person expressions of volition are formed with the imperative or non-   a
perfective, if positive; if negative, the jussive with אל or the non-perfective with לא is
used. The positive imperative differs from the regulative or legislative non-perfective in
being more urgent or in demanding immediate, specific action on the part of the addressee (## 1–2); the differentiation is not precise.[16] No differentiation is possible between
the regular and long (ה‎ָ-) forms of the imperative, since they occur in similar contexts
(## 3–4).[17] With some verbs the longer form has become the fixed imperative form, for
example, הַקְשִׁיבָה 'hasten,' עוּרָה 'awake,' הַגִּישָׁה 'bring near,' הִשָּׁבְעָה 'swear,' חוּשָׁה
'listen.'[18]

1.	וַיֹּאמֶר לָהּ בֹּעַז לְעֵת הָאֹכֶל גֹּשִׁי הֲלֹם	At mealtime Boaz said to her, "*Come over* here." Ruth 2:14
2.	וְכַאֲשֶׁר תִּרְאֶה עֲשֵׂה עִם־עֲבָדֶיךָ׃	And *treat* your servants in accordance with what you see. Dan 1:13
3.	וַיֹּאמְרוּ לַזַּיִת מָלְכָה עָלֵינוּ׃	They said to the olive tree, "*Be our king.*" Judg 9:8 *Qere*
4.	וַיֹּאמְרוּ כָל־הָעֵצִים אֶל־הָאָטָד לֵךְ אַתָּה מְלָךְ־עָלֵינוּ׃	All the trees said to the thornbush, "Come, *be our king.*" Judg 9:14

The dominant use of the imperative, as suggested, involves direct commands (## 5–   b
7). An imperative can also grant permission (## 8–10) or convey a request (## 11–13) or
a wish (## 14–15). Imperatives may be used sarcastically (## 16–17).

5.	הִפָּרֶד נָא מֵעָלָי	*Separate yourself* from me. Gen 13:9
6.	שִׂים־נָא יָדְךָ תַּחַת יְרֵכִי׃	*Put* your hand under my thigh. Gen 24:2
7.	שִׁפְטוּ־דַל	*Defend the cause* of the weak. Ps 82:3
8.	וִיהִי־מָה אָרוּץ וַיֹּאמֶר לוֹ רוּץ	(Ahimaaz said:) "Come what may, I want to run." So he (Joab) said: "*Run.*" 2 Sam 18:23
9.	וַיִּפְצְרוּ־בוֹ עַד־בֹּשׁ וַיֹּאמֶר שְׁלָחוּ	But they persisted until he was too ashamed to refuse. So he said: "*Send* (them)." 2 Kgs 2:17

---

16. For Ugaritic commands in *tqtl* versus imperatives, see T. L. Fenton, "Command and Fulfillment in Ugaritic— '*TQTL:YQTL*' and '*QTL:QTL*,'" *Journal of Semitic Studies* 14 (1969) 34–38.

17. Joüon § 48d / pp. 108–9, § 114m / p. 311; T. O. Lambdin, *Introduction to Biblical Hebrew* (New York: Scribner, 1971) 114.

18. The short form *haqšēb* occurs in Job 33:31.

10.	עֲלֵה וּקְבֹר אֶת־אָבִיךָ כַּאֲשֶׁר הִשְׁבִּיעֶךָ׃	*Go up* and *bury* your father, as he made you swear (to do). Gen 50:6
11.	וְאִישׁ יְהוּדָה שִׁפְטוּ־נָא בֵּינִי וּבֵין כַּרְמִי׃	People of Judah, *judge* between me and my vineyard. Isa 5:3
12.	תְּנָה־נָא לָהֶם כִּכַּר־כֶּסֶף	*Give* them a talent of silver. 2 Kgs 5:22
13.	קוּמָה אֱלֹהִים שָׁפְטָה הָאָרֶץ	*Arise*, O God, *judge* the earth. Ps 82:8
14.	וַיְבָרֲכוּ אֶת־רִבְקָה . . . אַתְּ הֲיִי לְאַלְפֵי רְבָבָה	And they blessed Rebekah . . . , "*May* you *increase* to vast multitudes." Gen 24:60
15.	הִנָּקִי מִמֵּי הַמָּרִים הַמְאָרֲרִים הָאֵלֶּה׃	*May* this bitter water that brings a curse *leave* (you) *innocent*. Num 5:19
16.	וְשַׁאֲלִי־לוֹ אֶת־הַמְּלוּכָה כִּי הוּא אָחִי הַגָּדוֹל מִמֶּנִּי	*Request* the kingdom for him (Adonijah)—after all, he is my older brother! 1 Kgs 2:22
17.	בֹּאוּ בֵית־אֵל וּפִשְׁעוּ	Go to Bethel and *sin*! Amos 4:4

c   The imperative, like the jussive, has uses in which its ordinary force is lost. The figure of *heterosis* involves the exchange of one grammatical form for another; with the imperative, heterosis creates a promise or prediction to be fulfilled in the future, made more emphatic and vivid than would be the case were the prefix conjugation used (## 18–20).

18.	אָכוֹל הַשָּׁנָה סָפִיחַ וּבַשָּׁנָה הַשֵּׁנִית סָחִישׁ וּבַשָּׁנָה הַשְּׁלִישִׁית זִרְעוּ וְקִצְרוּ וְנִטְעוּ כְרָמִים וְאִכְלוּ פְרְיָם׃	This year you will eat what grows by itself, and the second year what springs from that. But in the third year *sow* and *reap*, *plant* vineyards and *eat* their fruit. 2 Kgs 19:29
19.	מַטֵּה־עֻזְּךָ יִשְׁלַח יהוה מִצִּיּוֹן רְדֵה בְּקֶרֶב אֹיְבֶיךָ׃	Yhwh will extend your mighty scepter from Zion; *rule* in the midst of your enemies. Ps 110:2
20.	בִּצְדָקָה תִּכּוֹנָנִי רַחֲקִי מֵעֹשֶׁק	In righteousness you will be established; *be far* from tyranny. Isa 54:14

Apostrophe with the imperative is usually directed to unspecified or indefinite persons (## 21–22); the personifying jussive is comparable (34.3d).

21.	עַל הַר־נִשְׁפֶּה שְׂאוּ־נֵס הָרִימוּ קוֹל לָהֶם	Raise a banner on the bare hilltop, *shout* to them. Isa 13:2

22.   הָכִ֫ינוּ לְבָנָיו מַטְבֵּחַ   *Prepare a place* to slaughter his sons.
                                            Isa 14:21

Uses of the Cohortative   34.5

The first-person volitional form presents many more complexities than the jussive or   a
the imperative. In his work on the Byblian dialect of Late Bronze Age Canaanite, W. L.
Moran isolates two uses of *yaqtula* as primary, accounting for about two-thirds of the
examples: (*a*) the "direct volitive," to express a wish, request, or command, and (*b*) the
"indirect volitive," in clauses of purpose or intended result. Both of these have analogs
among the uses of the Hebrew cohortative.[19] Byblian *yaqtula* is also found in conditional
sentences, in protasis or apodosis.[20] The Hebrew *-â* forms (cf. 34.1d) can be distinguished
according to their occurrence in independent or dependent clauses.

Cohortative in Independent Clauses   34.5.1

The cohortative expresses the will or strong desire of the speaker. In cases where the   a
speaker has the ability to carry out an inclination it takes on the coloring of resolve ('I
will . . .'; ## 1–4). In other cases, where the speaker cannot effect a desire without the
consent of the one addressed, it connotes request ('May I . . .'; ## 5–7). The sense is
optative when the speaker's will involves dubiety, an indefinite potentiality ('I might/
can . . .'; ## 8–9). Finally, in first-person plural, the speakers usually seek to instigate or
encourage each other to some action ('Let us . . .'; ## 10–12). By etymology the term
"cohortative" is applicable only to this last use (Latin *cohortor* 'to encourage'), but the
term has been expanded to cover the other uses mentioned here. The negative particle
with the cohortative is אל (# 2).

1.   אֵלְכָה וְאֶרְאֶ֫נּוּ   I *will go* and *see* him.
                                       Gen 45:28

2.   אַל־אֶרְאֶה בְּמוֹת הַיָּ֫לֶד   I *will* not *watch* the boy die.
                                       Gen 21:16

3.   וַאֲזַמְּרָה שֵׁם־יהוה עֶלְיוֹן: I *will praise* YHWH Elyon.
                                       Ps 7:18

4.   וַאֲנִי וְהַנַּ֫עַר נֵלְכָה עַד־כֹּה   As for me and the boy, we *will go* there and *worship*.
          וְנִשְׁתַּחֲוֶה   Gen 22:5

---

19. See in general Moran, "Early Canaanite *Yaqtula*";
more briefly, Moran, "The Hebrew Language in Its Northwest Semitic Background," *The Bible and the Ancient Near
East: Essays in Honor of William Foxwell Albright*, ed.
G. E. Wright (Garden City, New York: Doubleday, 1961;
reprinted, Winona Lake, Indiana: Eisenbrauns, 1979) 54–
72, at 64.

20. Arabic contrasts indicative *yaktubu* and subjunctive
yaktuba; the subjunctive "occurs only in subordinate

clauses. It indicates an act which is dependent upon that
mentioned in the previous clause, and future to it in point
of time"; see W. Wright, *A Grammar of the Arabic Language* (3d ed.; Cambridge: Cambridge University, 1898),
2. 24, cf. 2. 34–35. For a Palestinian Aramaic contrast of
first-person indicative *ʾeqtol* and (again, confined to subordinate clauses) subjunctive *neqtol*, see J. W. Wesselius,
"A Subjunctive in the Aramaic of the Palestinian Targum,"
Journal of Jewish Studies 35 (1984) 196–99.

5.   וְאָמַרְתָּ֫ אֹכְלָה בָשָׂר   And you will say, "I *would like to eat* meat."
                                Deut 12:20

6.   בְּרַגְלַי אֶעֱבֹ֫רָה: *Let* me *pass through* on foot.
                                Num 20:19

7.   נִפְּלָה־נָּא בְיַד־יהוה . . . וּבְיַד־   *Let us fall* into the hands of YHWH . . . but *let* me
     אָדָם אַל־אֶפֹּ֫לָה: not *fall* into the hands of men.
                                2 Sam 24:14

8.   עַל־מִי אֲדַבְּרָה וְאָעִ֫ידָה   Against whom *can I speak* and *give* a warning?
                                Jer 6:10

9.   אוּלַי אֲכַפְּרָה בְּעַד חַטַּאתְכֶם: Perhaps I *can make atonement* for you (lit.,
                                atonement for your sin).[21]
                                Exod 32:30

10. נֵלְכָה דֹּתָ֫יְנָה   *Let's go* to Dothan.
                                Gen 37:17

11. נֵלְכָה אַחֲרֵי אֱלֹהִים אֲחֵרִים   *Let* us *follow* other gods.
                                Deut 13:3

12. נְנַתְּקָה אֶת־מוֹסְרוֹתֵ֫ימוֹ   *Let* us *break* their chains.
                                Ps 2:3

The effect of the plural cohortative is frequently heightened by a verb of motion in the imperative, which functions as an auxiliary or interjection. The verbs used include *hlk* (## 13–16), *bwᵓ* (# 17), and *qwm* (## 18–20); the verb *yhb* 'to give' occurs only in the imperative, sometimes in this role (# 21). Such an imperative may be linked to the cohortative with a *waw* (## 13–15, 18–20) or it may be juxtaposed asyndetically (## 16–17, 21).

13. לְכָה וְנִקְרְבָה בְּאַחַד הַמְּקֹמוֹת   *Come, let's try to reach* one of these places.
                                Judg 19:13 Qere; cf. v 11

14. לְכוּ וְנֵלְכָה עַד־הָרֹאֶה   *Come, let's go* to the seer.
                                1 Sam 9:9

15. לְכוּ־נָא וְנִוָּכְחָה   *Come* now, *let's reason* together.
                                Isa 1:18

16. לְכוּ נְרַנְּנָה לַיהוָה   *Come, let* us *sing* to YHWH.
                                Ps 95:1

17. בֹּאוּ נִשְׁתַּחֲוֶה וְנִכְרָ֫עָה   *Come, let* us *bow down* in worship.
                                Ps 95:6

18. ק֫וּמָה וְנָשֻׁ֫בָה   *Get up, let's go back.*
                                Jer 46:16

19. ק֫וּמִי וְנֵלֵ֫כָה   *Get up, let's go.*
                                Judg 19:28

20. ק֫וּמוּ וְנִבְרָ֫חָה   *Get up, let's flee.*
                                2 Sam 15:14

---

21. A similar idiom occurs in Gen 32:21.

| 21. | הָ֫בָה נֵרְדָה | *Come, let* us *go down.*[22] |
| | | Gen 11:7 |

Cohortative in Dependent Clauses   34.5.2

a In sentences made up of more than one clause, the cohortative may be found in dependent purpose clauses and in the protasis ('if') or apodosis ('then') clauses of conditional sentences. These uses are closely related to its role in independent clauses to express self-inclination with the mood of dubiety.

b With the nuance of purpose or intended result the cohortative form often occurs after another volitional form (## 1–3; cf. 34.6) and sometimes after a question (## 4–6).

1.	וְהָבִ֫יאָה לִּי וְאֹכֵ֫לָה	And *bring* it to me *so that* I *may eat.*
		Gen 27:4
2.	חָנְנֵ֫נִי . . . לְמַ֫עַן אֲסַפְּרָה כָּל־ תְּהִלָּתֶ֫יךָ	Have mercy on me . . . that I *may recite* all your praises.
		Ps 9:14–15
3.	אַל־נָא יִ֫חַר לַאדֹנָי וַאֲדַבֵּ֫רָה	Let not my Lord be angry, *that I may speak.*[24]
		Gen 18:30; cf. v 32
4.	הַאֵין פֹּה נָבִיא לַיהוה . . . וְנִדְרְשָׁה מֵאוֹתוֹ׃	Is there not a prophet of YHWH here . . . *that* we *might inquire* of him?
		1 Kgs 22:7
5.	מִי־הִגִּיד מֵרֹאשׁ וְנֵדָ֫עָה	Who told of this from the beginning, *so* we *could hear?*
		Isa 41:26
6.	מָתַי יַעֲבֹר הַחֹ֫דֶשׁ וְנַשְׁבִּ֫ירָה שֶּׁ֫בֶר	When will the New Moon be over *that* we *may sell* grain?
		Amos 8:5

In conditional sentences, the cohortative can be used in either the protasis (## 7–9)[23] or the apodosis (## 10–12).

7.	אִם . . . וְאַצִּ֫יעָה שְּׁאוֹל הִנֶּ֑ךָּ׃	If . . . I *make* my *bed* in Sheol, you are there.
		Ps 139:8
8.	אִם־אֲדַבְּרָה לֹא־יֵחָשֵׂךְ כְּאֵבִי	If I *speak*, my pain is not relieved.
		Job 16:6
9.	אָק֫וּמָה וַיְדַבְּרוּ־בִי׃	*When* I *appear*, they ridicule me.
		Job 19:18
10.	מִי־יִתְּנֵ֫נִי שָׁמִיר שַׁ֫יִת בַּמִּלְחָמָה אֶפְשְׂעָה בָהּ	If only there were briars and thorns confronting me I *would march* against them in battle.[25]
		Isa 27:4

---

22. The combination *hbh* with the cohortative is used in Gen 11:3, 4 by the conspirators at Babel and here by God.

23. Blau, "Hebrew Verb Formation," 134, says that there are no further examples.

24. The sequence in Judg 6:39 is nearly identical.

25. For the idiom in this and the following example, see

11. מִי־יִתְּנֵנִי בַמִּדְבָּר מְלוֹן אֹרְחִים
וְאֶעֶזְבָה אֶת־עַמִּי

Oh that I had in the desert a lodging place for travelers, *then* I *would leave* my people.
Jer 9:1

12. אוּלַי יְפֻתֶּה וְנוּכְלָה לוֹ וְנִקְחָה
נִקְמָתֵנוּ מִמֶּֽנּוּ׃

Perhaps he will be deceived; *then* we *will prevail* over him and *take* our retribution on him.
Jer 20:10

34.5.3   Pseudo-Cohortative

a   The cohortative form is sometimes used where an appropriate sense is lacking. The use of a single form to denote both the volitional and indicative moods cannot be readily explained. Similar divergent patterns of *yaqtula* are attested in the Amarna letters from Byblos; Moran cautiously offers this explanation: "We can only suggest that in clauses of intended result the idea of actual accomplishment has begun to supersede that of intention, not completely however, and thus (*u* ['and']) *yaqtula*, still felt as indicating a willed result, expresses actual result only after a clause in the first person."[26] This use in early Canaanite rules out the suggestion of some earlier Hebraists that in certain passages the cohortative does not denote internal impulse but external compulsion and should be rendered by 'must.' (Driver had earlier ruled out this suggestion as both unnecessary and unlikely.)[27]

b   The pseudo-cohortative (as we may call this form) can be used to refer to past time, without *waw*-relative (## 1–3) or with it (## 4–6).[28] The latter combination is relatively common (about ninety occurrences) and has an erratic distribution in the Bible. The presence of this construction in a text cannot be used to date it because, on the one hand, *yaqtula* is used in Byblian Canaanite for past tense, and, on the other hand, the combination is used extensively in the Dead Sea Scrolls.[29] The combination also occurs in some pre-exilic texts but not in some post-exilic books (and is even lacking in post-exilic texts synoptic with pre-exilic texts evincing the form).[30] The combination is also used in gnomic situations (rendered with an English present tense; ## 7–8) and with future-time reference (# 9).

B. Jongeling, "L'Expression *my ytn* dans l'Ancien Testament," *Vetus Testamentum* 24 (1974) 32–40.

26. Moran, "Early Canaanite *Yaqtula*," 18.

27. Driver, *Tenses in Hebrew*, 55–56; see W. L. Holladay, *Jeremiah* (Hermeneia; Philadelphia: Fortress, 1986), 1. 161–62, for a defense of the earlier view.

28. Note also *ʾerdəpâ* in 2 Sam 22:38 and *ʾerdōp* in Ps 18:38.

29. For biblical occurrences, see McFall, *Hebrew Verbal System*, 211–14; for Qumran, see E. Qimron, *The Hebrew of the Dead Sea Scrolls* (Atlanta: Scholars Press, 1986) 44, cf. 45–46. S. Morag has recently argued that the *wᵊqtlh* forms in Qumranic Hebrew are to be taken not as archaisms but as reflections of a later stage of Hebrew, "a continuation . . . not necessarily . . . literary"; see "Qumran Hebrew: Some Typological Observations," *Vetus Testamentum* 38 (1988) 148–64, at 163, cf. 154–55. Similarly Revell, "First Person Imperfect Forms," 423, argues that the biblical cases are not archaizing. See also E. Qimron, "Consecutive and Conjunctive Imperfect: The Form of the Imperfect with *Waw* in Biblical Hebrew," *Jewish Quarterly Review* 77 (1986–87) 149–61, esp. 161.

30. See R. Polzin, *Late Biblical Hebrew: Toward an Historical Typology of Biblical Hebrew Prose* (Missoula: Scholars Press, 1976) 54–55. Cf. Qimron, *Dead Sea Scrolls*, 44.

1.	נָשָׂאתִי אֵמֶיךָ אָפֽוּנָה׃	I have borne your terrors (and) I *am in despair*. Ps 88:16
2.	הָפַךְ יָם לְיַבָּשָׁה . . . שָׁם נִשְׂמְחָה־בּֽוֹ׃	He turned the sea into dry land, . . . there we *rejoiced* in him. Ps 66:6
3.	וָאֵרֶא בַפְּתָאיִם אָבִינָה בַבָּנִים	I saw among the simple, I *noticed* among the young men. . . . Prov 7:7
4.	וָאַצִּל אֶתְכֶם מִיַּד מִצְרַיִם . . . וָאֶתְּנָה לָכֶם אֶת־אַרְצָם׃ וָאֹמְרָה	And I snatched you from the power of Egypt . . . *and* I *gave* you their land, *and* I *said*. . . . Judg 6:9–10
5.	וַיְהִי כִּי־בָאנוּ אֶל־הַמָּלוֹן וַנִּפְתְּחָה אֶת־אַמְתְּחֹתֵינוּ	At the place where we stopped for the night, we *opened* our sacks. Gen 43:21
6.	וָאֲשַׁבְּרָה מְתַלְּעוֹת עַוָּל	I *broke* the fangs of the wicked. Job 29:17
7.	נְגַשְׁשָׁה כַעִוְרִים קִיר וּכְאֵין עֵינַיִם נְגַשֵּׁשָׁה	Like the blind we *grope* along the wall, we *grope* like those without eyes. Isa 59:10
8.	נַפְשִׁי בְּתוֹךְ לְבָאִם אֶשְׁכְּבָה	I *lie* among lions. Ps 57:5
9.	עַד־מָתַי אֶרְאֶה־נֵּס אֶשְׁמְעָה קוֹל שׁוֹפָר׃	How long will I *see* the battle standard and *hear* the sound of the trumpet? Jer 4:21

Jussive and Cohortative after Imperative   **34.6**

After an imperative a verbal form not preceded by its subject or a negative particle   a
is normally either a jussive (## 1–2) or a cohortative (## 3–5; cf. 34.5.2b).[31] Where a
prefix-conjugation form is not morphologically marked in such a context, it may be
taken as having jussive (# 6) or cohortative (# 7) force (34.1d n. 3). The second volitional
form signifies purpose or result, in contrast to the sequence *imperative + imperative* (cf.
3, 10).[32] A chain of jussives or cohortatives can follow an imperative. When the verb
after an imperative is preceded by its own subject (## 8–9) or by a negative particle
(# 10), it is usually a non-perfective form, with a volitional sense.[33]

| 1. | הַעְתִּירוּ אֶל־יהוה וְיָסֵר הַצְפַרְדְּעִים מִמֶּנִּי וּמֵעַמִּי | Pray to Yʜᴡʜ *that* he *take* the frogs away from me and my people. Exod 8:4 |

---

31. H. M. Orlinsky, "On the Cohortative and Jussive after an Imperative or Interjection in Biblical Hebrew," *Jewish Quarterly Review* 31 (1940–41) 371–82; 32 (1941–

42) 191–205, 273–77.
32. Cf. Lambdin, *Introduction to Biblical Hebrew*, 119.
33. Orlinsky, "Cohortative and Jussive," 32:273–77.

2.	הוֹצֵא אֶת־בִּנְךָ וְיָמֹת	Bring out your son *that* he *might die.* Judg 6:30
3.	הִתְהַלֵּךְ לְפָנַי וֶהְיֵה תָמִים: וְאֶתְּנָה בְרִיתִי	Walk before me and be perfect *and* I *will confirm* my covenant. Gen 17:1–2
4.	הָבָה נִלְבְּנָה לְבֵנִים וְנִשְׂרְפָה לִשְׂרֵפָה	Come, *let's make bricks* and bake them thoroughly. Gen 11:3
5.	קַח מִמֶּנִּי וְאֶקְבְּרָה אֶת־מֵתִי	Accept (it) from me *so that* I *can bury* my dead. Gen 23:13
6.	הֲשִׁבֵהוּ אִתְּךָ . . . וְיֹאכַל לֶחֶם וְיֵשְׁתְּ מָיִם	Bring him back with you . . . *so that* he *might eat* bread and drink water. 1 Kgs 13:18
7.	לֶךְ־לְךָ מֵאַרְצְךָ . . . וְאֶעֶשְׂךָ לְגוֹי גָּדוֹל וַאֲבָרֶכְךָ וַאֲגַדְּלָה שְׁמֶךָ	Leave your country . . . *and* I *will make* you a great nation *and bless* you *and magnify* your name. Gen 12:1–2
8.	וֶהְיֵה־לִי לְאָב וּלְכֹהֵן וְאָנֹכִי אֶתֶּן־לְךָ	Be a father-priest to me *and* I *will give* you. . . . Judg 17:10
9.	לֵךְ וַיהוה יִהְיֶה עִמָּךְ:	Go *and may* Yhwh *be* with you. 1 Sam 17:37
10.	רְדוּ־שָׁמָּה וְשִׁבְרוּ־לָנוּ מִשָּׁם וְנִחְיֶה וְלֹא נָמוּת:	Go down there, buy us (some grain) there, *so that* we *might live* and not die. Gen 42:2

## 34.7	The Particle נָא

a	The particle נָא, frequently associated with volitional forms, is generally known as a precative particle and translated into English by 'please.'[34] Thomas O. Lambdin has argued that it is a logical rather than a precative particle and is better left untranslated: "The particle seems . . . to denote that the command in question is a logical consequence, either of an immediately preceding statement or of the general situation in which it is uttered."[35] He bases his insight on its use with הִנֵּה, which he argues is also often a logical particle in direct speech and as such is used to introduce a fact on which a following statement or command is based. His understanding finds further support in the use of נא with the logical particles אם and עַתָּה, and in its use with the cohortative of resolve in passages where a precative use is unlikely.

b	The particle is found with a volitional form and הנה (## 1–2), אם (# 3), and עתה (# 4); -nāʾ is attached to the logical particle for הנה and אם and to the verb for עתה (and

---

34. The particle occurs, in the forms -nāʾ and -nnāʾ, 405 times (SA/THAT). The origin of the particle is a matter distinct from its usage: it may well have arisen from reanalysis of the underused energic forms of earlier

stages of the older language (compare the heavy energic *yaqtulanna* and the light energic *yaqtulan* of Arabic); see 31.7.

35. Lambdin, *Introduction to Biblical Hebrew,* 170.

often also for הנה; ## 1–2). It may also be attached to the negative אל (# 3). The combination הנה־נא is found in non-volitional contexts (## 5–6). The cohortative of resolve is
followed by נא (## 7–8). In commands that are preceded or followed by a reason (## 9–
11), נא is also found. The *n* is sometimes doubled after a syllable ending in a vowel
(## 7–8, contrast ## 9, 11).

1.	הִנֵּה־נָא דִבְרֵי הַנְּבִיאִים פֶּה־ אֶחָד טוֹב אֶל־הַמֶּלֶךְ יְהִי־נָא דְבָרְךָ כִּדְבַר אַחַד מֵהֶם	*Since* the words of the (other) prophets are uniformly good for the king, *let* your words agree with theirs. 1 Kgs 22:13 *Kethiv*
2.	הִנֵּה־נָא עֲצָרַנִי יהוה מִלֶּדֶת בֹּא־נָא אֶל־שִׁפְחָתִי	*Because* YHWH has kept me from having children, *go* to my handmaid. Gen 16:2
3.	אִם־נָא מָצָאתִי חֵן בְּעֵינֶיךָ אַל־ נָא תַעֲבֹר מֵעַל עַבְדֶּךָ:	*If* I have found favor in your eyes, *do* not *pass* your servant by. Gen 18:3
4.	. . . וְעַתָּה קַח־נָא אֶת־הַחֲנִית וְנֵלְכָה לָּנוּ:	*Now get* the spear . . . and let's go! 1 Sam 26:11
5.	הִנֵּה־נָא מָצָא עַבְדְּךָ חֵן בְּעֵינֶיךָ . . . וְאָנֹכִי לֹא אוּכַל לְהִמָּלֵט	*Even though* your servant has found favor . . . I can't flee. Gen 19:19
6.	. . . הִנֵּה־נָא מוֹשַׁב הָעִיר טוֹב וְהַמַּיִם רָעִים	*Even though* the city site is good . . . the waters are bad. 2 Kgs 2:19
7.	אֵרֲדָה־נָּא וְאֶרְאֶה	I *will go down* and see. Gen 18:21
8.	אָסֻרָה־נָּא וְאֶרְאֶה אֶת־הַמַּרְאֶה הַגָּדֹל הַזֶּה	I *will go over* and see this strange sight. Exod 3:3
9.	הֲלֹא אֲחֹתָהּ הַקְּטַנָּה טוֹבָה מִמֶּנָּה תְּהִי־נָא לְךָ תַּחְתֶּיהָ:	Isn't her younger sister more attractive than she? *Marry* her instead of her (the older sister). Judg 15:2
10.	הֲלֹא כָל־הָאָרֶץ לְפָנֶיךָ הִפָּרֶד נָא מֵעָלָי	Is not all the land before you? *Separate* youself from me. Gen 13:9
11.	אִמְרִי־נָא אֲחֹתִי אָתְּ לְמַעַן יִיטַב־לִי בַעֲבוּרֵךְ	*Say* you are my sister that I may be well treated for your sake. Gen 12:13

35

Infinitive Absolute

35.1 Non-finite Verb Forms

a   The Semitic languages generally distinguish two categories of non-finite verb forms, the *infinitive*, which designates the *action* or *situation* of the verb, and the *participle*, which refers to the *actor* or *patient* of the verb.[1] Neither infinitives nor participles are inflected for aspect (*Aspekt*). Number and gender inflections refer to the noun-like features of the form; participles are regularly marked for number and gender, while infinitives rarely are so marked, usually with possessive suffixes. Hebrew (along with a few closely related languages)[2] is distinctive in having not one but two infinitive types. The

---

1. See in general J. M. Solá-Solé, *L'Infinitif sémitique* (Paris: Champion, 1961). The term "verbal noun" is properly restricted to the infinitives or, better, the infinitive construct; in Arabic the form corresponding to the infinitive construct is called the verbal noun, the Arabic term being *maṣdar* 'source.' In Hebrew, the infinitive absolute can be described as a nominal with no inflectional properties; the infinitive construct as a nominal that can occur with a genitive noun or a pronominal suffix.

2. Notably Phoenician and Ammonite; see Z. S. Harris, *A Grammar of the Phoenician Language* (New Haven:

American Oriental Society, 1936) 41; K. P. Jackson, *The Ammonite Language of the Iron Age* (Chico: Scholars Press, 1983) 10; and n. 9. The infinitive absolute is rare in Qumranic Hebrew and largely absent from Mishnaic Hebrew; see R. Polzin, *Late Biblical Hebrew: Toward an Historical Typology of Biblical Hebrew Prose* (Missoula: Scholars Press, 1976) 44; E. Qimron, *The Hebrew of the Dead Sea Scrolls* (Atlanta: Scholars Press, 1986) 47–48; and, allowing for greater frequency of the form at Qumran, J. Carmignac, "L'Infinitif absolu chez Ben Sira et à Qumran," *Revue de Qumran* 12 (1986) 251–61.

simpler infinitive type is the infinitive construct, used as infinitives and gerunds are used in Latin and modern European languages. The infinitive absolute is, as Gotthelf Bergsträsser remarks, "a peculiarly Hebrew hybrid of verbal noun and verbal interjection of imperative character."[3]

The terms infinitive absolute and infinitive construct are open to objection.[4] They   b should not be construed to mean that the "absolute" is reduced in certain linguistic environments to the "construct," as happens in the case of a noun standing before another noun in the genitive case (see 9.2). Rather, to judge from their historically distinctive nominal patterns, from their functions in Biblical Hebrew, and from similar uses of the infinitive in other Semitic languages, these two forms are historically distinct and unrelated. In earlier Semitic the nominal pattern that developed in Hebrew into the *Qal* infinitive absolute *qātōl/qātôl* was **qatāl*, and the nominal pattern that developed into the infinitive construct *qətōl* was either **qtul* or **qutul*.[5]

The Masoretic vocalization clearly distinguishes two types of infinitives, and much   c external evidence supports the distinction.[6] The correctness of the Masoretic vocalization is supported indirectly by the recognition of the different functions of the infinitives in Biblical Hebrew. For these reasons E. Hammershaimb rightly objects to the rejection of the Masoretic vocalization, saying: "Only a partisan judgement on Hebrew alone combined with profound scepticism as to the Masoretic vocalization can lead to a repudiation of the functional difference between the two infinitives."[7]

Form and Meaning   35.2

Form   35.2.1

Among its many uses in Biblical Hebrew the infinitive absolute may intensify a finite   a verb, serve as a word of command, or function as a finite verb.[8] Related forms in Akkadian, Arabic, and Ugaritic similarly serve to intensify a finite verb or as a word of command; and in the Northwest Semitic languages (Ugaritic, Phoenician, and Amarna Canaanite) such forms may function as finite verbs.[9]

The pattern of the *Qal* infinitive absolute, *qātôl*, is carried over to some other stems,   b for example, *Niphal nilḥōm* 'to fight' and *Piel yassôr* 'to set right.'[10] Elsewhere in the

---

3. G. Bergsträsser, *Introduction to the Semitic Languages*, trans. and sup. P. T. Daniels (Winona Lake, Indiana: Eisenbrauns, 1983) 56.

4. Thus we have the alternative terms "(usual) infinitive" (for infinitive construct) and "fixed infinitive" (for infinitive absolute) used by BL §36b′ / p. 277.

5. C. Brockelmann, *Grundriss der vergleichenden Grammatik der semitischen Sprachen* (Berlin: Reuter und Reichard, 1913), 1. 399, 345–46.

6. Note the Latin and Greek vocalizations of infinitive forms given by A. Sperber, *A Historical Grammar of Biblical Hebrew* (Leiden: Brill, 1966) 184–85, 190.

7. E. Hammershaimb, "On the So-called *Infinitivus Absolutus* in Hebrew," *Hebrew and Semitic Studies Presented to Godfrey Rolles Driver*, ed. D. W. Thomas and

W. D. McHardy (Oxford: Clarendon, 1963) 85–94, at 86.

8. There are about 500 cases of the intensifying infinitive (35.3.1) and about 300 others, according to Burton L. Goddard, *The Origin of the Hebrew Infinitive Absolute in the Light of the Infinitive Uses in the Related Languages and Its Use in the Old Testament* (Harvard Dissertation, 1943) v, cf. 125–42.

9. See J. Huesman, "Finite Uses of the Infinitive Absolute," *Biblica* 37 (1956) 271–95, at 281–83; Brockelmann, *Grundriss*, 1. 168.

10. The *Qal* infinitives absolute and construct occasionally merge in form, yielding, e.g., inf. abs. *qōb*, Num 23:25 (inf. cstr. *lāqōb*, Num 23:11); inf. abs. (*rôb*, the usual form for medial-*waw* verbs but also) *rîb*, Jer 50:34 (inf. cstr. *rîb*, Isa 3:13).

so-called derived stems, perhaps reflecting the use of the *Qal* infinitive absolute as a word of command, infinitives absolute are identical to the imperatives, for example, *Niphal himmāṣēʾ, Piel bārēk, Hiphil haśkēl, Hithpael hitnaśśēʾ.*[11] The *Niphal* and *Piel* are the only stems with variant infinitive-absolute patterns.

c   As we shall see (35.3.1), the infinitive absolute usually occurs paronomastically with a finite verb. Used in this way, it usually shares the stem of the finite verb, for example, *Qal* (Gen 2:16), *Niphal* (Exod 22:3), *Piel* (Gen 22:17), *Pual* (Gen 40:15), *Hithpael* (Num 16:13), *Hiphil* (Gen 3:16), and *Hophal* (Ezek 16:4).

d   Sometimes the *Qal* infinitive absolute is so used with a form of a different stem. This is common with the *Niphal* (Exod 19:13; 21:20, 22, 28; 22:11, 12; 2 Sam 23:7; Isa 40:30; Jer 10:5; 34:3; 49:12;[12] Mic 2:4; Nah 3:13; Zech 12:3; Job 6:2); note the *Hophal* in the usual expression מוֹת יוּמָת (Exod 19:12, etc.). The *Qal* infinitive absolute is also bracketed with other stems, for example, with the *Piel* (2 Sam 20:18), *Hiphil* (Gen 46:4, 1 Sam 23:22, Isa 31:5), and *Hithpoel* (Isa 24:19).[13]

e   Apart from this mixture of *Qal* infinitives absolute with other stems, an infinitive absolute is rarely used with a finite verb in a stem different from itself; exceptions occur, for example, *Hophal* with *Niphal* (2 Kgs 3:23), *Hophal* with *Pual* (Ezek 16:4), *Piel* with *Hiphil* (1 Sam 2:16), and *Pilpel* with *Hithpael* (Jer 51:58).

35.2.2   Meaning

a   Infinitives, in contrast to finite verb forms, do not require affixes that limit the situation denoted by the root with regard to the agent or circumstances under which the action takes place. Rather, they denote the bare verbal action or state in the abstract.[14] Since the Hebrew infinitives occur in verbal stems, they are restricted with respect to stem-defining *Aktionsart*, though as we have seen the infinitive absolute of the *Qal* is used with other stems.

b   Infinitives are hybrids, verbal nouns, and as such are bracketed with the other words in settings where we would expect either a verb or a noun. Sometimes they are bracketed as both at one and the same time. Consider this example:

1.   מוֹת יוּמַת הָאִישׁ רָגוֹם אֹתוֹ   This man must die—the whole assembly *stoning* him.
     בָּאֲבָנִים כָּל־הָעֵדָה   Num 15:35

The infinitive absolute רגום is bracketed with the main verb יומת as an adverbial accusative, qualifying how the action will be performed, and at the same time it is bracketed with both its own subject and object.

c   The infinitive absolute and infinitive construct are distinguished in part by their syntax. Although both are used in ways associated with both verbs and nouns, they differ in the following respects.

---

11. Brockelmann, *Grundriss*, 1. 346.
12. For *nqy Niphal finite form* + *Niphal infinitive absolute*, see Jer 25:29.
13. The use of the *Qal* infinitive absolute with a finite

form of a different stem suggests to Bergsträsser that the infinitives absolute of the other stems derive from a later stage in the language; see GB 2. 64 (§ 12f).
14. Hammershaimb, "*Infinitivus Absolutus*," 86.

a. Only the infinitive absolute regularly takes the place of a finite verb.

b. Only the infinitive construct is regularly used with a preposition.

c. Only the infinitive construct can take a pronominal suffix.

d. If the subject of the verbal action expressed by the infinitive absolute is stated, it is always an independent noun; with the infinitive construct it may be a pronominal suffix.

e. The infinitive absolute is used much less rarely than the infinitive construct in the most frequent uses of the noun, namely, as a subject in the nominative function, as a genitive, or in the accusative function.

The infinitive absolute also takes the place of other parts of speech in a clause   d besides those of the noun and verb; notably it serves as an adverb.[15] It can be used as a word of command and even functions where we expect an infinitive construct. We broadly classify the uses of the infinitive absolute by these parts of speech:[16]

a. as a noun, especially as an absolute or adverbial complement (35.3)

b. as a frozen adverb (35.4)

c. as a word of command (35.5.1)

d. as a finite verb (35.5.2)

e. as a participle (35.5.3)

f. as an infinitive construct (35.5.4)

Within these broad classifications according to word classes we can specify its more precise values.

Before turning to these species, we need to note further that the infinitive absolute is   e not normally negated; a negative particle, where needed, is normally placed before the finite verb.

| 2. | וְנַקֵּה לֹא יְנַקֶּה פֹּקֵד עֲוֹן | Yet he will *by no means* leave the guilty unpunished. Exod 34:7 |
| 3. | וּמָכֹר לֹא־תִמְכְּרֶנָּה | You *must not* sell her. Deut 21:14 |

Nominal Uses   35.3

The infinitive absolute is used most often as a noun in two distinctive roles: as an   a absolute complement to a clause (in the nominative function; 35.3.1)[17] and as an adverbial

---

15. The distinction between an independent adverb (cf. 39.3) and an "ad-verbial" use is most nearly obscured with the infinitive.

16. Bergsträsser cites some instances where the influence of the infinitive absolute on the meaning of the sentence can perhaps no longer be perceived (GB 2. 63 [§ 12f]). While it is true that the nuance of the form is sometimes slight (and difficult to translate, but that is another matter), the instances cited by him can be understood along the lines sketched out here.

17. Thus, e.g., 40 of the 51 infinitives absolute in Genesis are absolute complements, according to S. J. P. K. Riekert, "The Struct [sic] Patterns of the Paronomastic and Co-ordinated Infinitives Absolute in Genesis," *Journal of Northwest Semitic Languages* 7 (1979) 69–83, at 69. This use is virtually unknown in late Biblical Hebrew; see, e.g., Polzin, *Late Biblical Hebrew*, 43.

complement, that is, a complement to the verb (35.3.2). The infinitive absolute may occur syntactically where a noun is expected, namely, as a subject in the nominative case, or as a genitive, or in an accusative role (35.3.3).

35.3.1   Absolute Complement

a   The earlier grammarians did not have any doubt that when the infinitive absolute intensifies a verb it is used as a kind of *internal accusative*. As recently as 1978 Ernst Jenni still referred to such a form as *an inner object*.[18] In Ugaritic, however, where case can be formally identified in forms from final-*aleph* roots, which indicate the final vowel, this use of the infinitive absolute occurs with the nominative case; for example, *ǵmʾu ǵmʾit* (to be vocalized **ǵamāʾu*, infinitive absolute with nominative u, *ǵamiʾtī*), 'you (fem.) are certainly thirsty.'[19] In this light Rudolf Meyer appropriately treats the corresponding Hebrew use of the infinitive absolute as "a verbal-nominal apposition, which stands in the isolated nominative."[20] For this reason the construction can be analyzed as an *absolute* in the nominative function.

b   Because in this use the infinitive absolute shares the verbal root and (usually) stem of the accompanying finite verb, the use is said to be paronomastic, that is, based in word play, or to exhibit the *schema etymologicum*.[21] By bracketing the paronomastic infinitive with the verb, the verbal idea is intensified. The effect of the infinitive refers to the entire clause, whence comes the term absolute complement. The infinitive *usually* emphasizes not the meaning denoted by the verb's root but the force of the verb in context. When the verb makes an assertion, whatever its aspect, the notion of certainty is reinforced by the infinitive (e.g., with affirmation, contrast, concession, or climax). By contrast, if the verb in context is irreal, the sense of irreality (e.g., dubiety, supposition, modality, or volition) becomes more forceful. Both verbal conjugations may express either assertion or irreality. Usually the intensifying infinitive with the perfective conjugation forcefully presents the certainty of a completed event,[22] as in טָרֹף טֹרָף, 'Without a shadow of a doubt he has been torn to pieces' (Gen 37:33). With the non-perfective conjugation the infinitive absolute often emphasizes that a situation was, or is, or will take place. Since the non-perfective is used for irreality and volition, the infinitive absolute can intensify the sense of irreality in connection with that conjugation. There is, however, no precise match between the infinitive's force and the finite verb's conjugation. Both conjugations may represent a situation as real or irreal and therefore the infinitive may emphasize either sense with either conjugation. We refer to this use of the infinitive as the *intensifying infinitive*.

---

18. *LHS* 117–18.
19. *UT* § 9.27.
20. R. Meyer, *Hebräische Grammatik* (Berlin: de Gruyter, 1972), 3. 63, 75; contrast the approach of Hammershaimb, "*Infinitivus Absolutus*," 89.
21. The cases in which the stems differ are noted below (cf. 35.2.1c–e). For further examples as well as the latter term, see GKC § 113m / p. 342, § 117q–r / p. 367.

T. Muraoka usefully insists that it is misleading to call the infinitive absolute as such *emphatic*; it is the doubling up in the paronomastic construction that is emphatic; see *Emphatic Words and Structures in Biblical Hebrew* (Leiden: Brill, 1985) 86, 92.

22. Goddard reckons with 81 cases of the intensifying infinitive with the perfective; see *Hebrew Infinitive Absolute*, 31.

Scholars debate whether the infinitive absolute can ever intensify the verbal root.   c
Jenni denies it, while Paul Joüon and S. Riekert affirm it.[23] We agree with the latter
scholars, though noting that such use is rare.

The earlier grammarians divide the uses of the absolute or intensifying infinitive into   d
two categories, prepositive (that is, before the other verb) and postpositive (that is, after
the other verb), while allowing that the difference in meaning between them is slight.
Many of them also allege that the paronomastic infinitive more frequently signifies intensification in the more common prepositive position and continuation or repetition in
the postpositive position. Riekert, however, rightly demurs on the basis of a close study
of the intensifying infinitive in Genesis: "The author is convinced that we have here an
artificial distinction between the prepositive and postpositive inf[initive] and that the
latter is incorrectly credited with this aspect of expressing duration."[24] Over a half
century earlier, Joüon had also called the distinction into question.[25] In our opinion the
paronomastic infinitive is always an intensifying infinitive, and so we do not recognize
this traditional distinction. Nevertheless, where we can identify a specific use of the intensifying infinitive in only one or the other of these positions, we note that fact in our
analysis; otherwise we exemplify under a single heading a species of the intensifying infinitive which shows both positions. The intensifying infinitive almost always occurs
postpositively with *wayyqtl*, the imperative, and the participle.

The precise nuance of intensification must be discovered from the broader context;   e
it can usually be rendered into English by an intensifying adverb appropriate to the
clause (e.g., 'certainly, really'). The potential species of emphasis are too diverse to
classify; it is more important to grasp the contextual meaning of the infinitive absolute.[26]
Riekert makes the point well: "Although the emphasis on the verb is brought about 'in
various ways' . . . , it is not different kinds of uses. It is rather a differentiation caused by
being used in a richly diversified field of contextual situations."[27]

Affirmation is the most straightforward role for an infinitive absolute (## 1–5);   f
sometimes the particle אַף is added for emphasis (# 6); the infinitive generally stands in prepositive position. The affirmation may form a strong contrast to what precedes (## 7–8)[28]

23. Jenni remarks, "The determination consists in a strengthening of the modus of the expression (not of the root's meaning as such) and can only be decided upon from context"; *LHS* 117; contrast Joüon § 123j / p. 351 and Riekert, "Infinitives Absolute in Genesis," 71.

24. Riekert, "Infinitives Absolute in Genesis," 77.

25. Joüon § 123d / pp. 348–49. As he notes, the *Hith-pael* infinitive is always postpositive. The intensifying infinitive precedes the finite verb in Amarna Canaanite, Ugaritic (with one exception), and Old Aramaic. Such infinitives following the verb are found notably in the Mari texts, with the verb *raṭāpu* 'to continue (doing something)' (perhaps under Amorite—rather than Canaanite, *pace* Hammershaimb—influence); see Hammershaimb, "*Infini-tivus Absolutus*," 87–88. Goddard, *Hebrew Infinitive*

Absolute, 125–42, takes a similar view; further, he counts in his class of single uses of the intensifying infinitive abso-lute (468 cases), only about 30 in which the infinitive fol-lows the verb or participle it refers to. Muraoka, too, is dubious (*Emphatic Words*, 89); he notes also that the *pre-positive infinitive + verb* syntagm can only be interrupted by a negative (## 5, 10, 36), while the reverse allows for other insertions (see ## 13–15, 34).

26. Contrast, e.g., GKC § 113 / pp. 339–47, and Joüon § 123 / pp. 347–58 and cf. A. Reider, *Die Verbindung des Infinitivus Absolutus mit dem Verbum Finitum des selbes Stammes im Hebräischen* (Leipzig: Metzger und Wittig, 1872).

27. Riekert, "Infinitives Absolute in Genesis," 76.

28. Note also 1 Sam 6:3.

or follows (# 9), or infinitives may be used in both members of a pair (# 10).[29] The contrast may involve a concession qualifying what follows (## 11–12) or precedes (# 13).

1.	מוֹת תָּמוּת׃	You will *surely* die. Gen 2:17
2.	שׁוֹב אָשׁוּב אֵלֶיךָ	I will *surely* return to you. Gen 18:10
3.	כִּי־בָרֵךְ אֲבָרֶכְךָ	I will *surely* bless you. Gen 22:17
4.	כֹּל אֲשֶׁר־יְדַבֵּר בּוֹא יָבוֹא	All that he says will *surely* happen. 1 Sam 9:6
5.	וְהָמְלֵחַ לֹא הֻמְלַחַתְּ וְהָחְתֵּל לֹא חֻתָּלְתְּ׃	*To be sure*, you were not rubbed with salt or wrapped in cloth (*Pual* perf. + *Hophal* inf. abs.). Ezek 16:4
6.	אַךְ נָגוֹף נִגָּף הוּא לְפָנֵינוּ	*Surely* he is fleeing before us. Judg 20:39
7.	לֹא כִּי־קָנוֹ אֶקְנֶה מֵאִתְּךָ	No, I *insist* on paying you (for it). 2 Sam 24:24 *manuscripts*
8.	לָקֹב אֹיְבַי לְקַחְתִּיךָ וְהִנֵּה בֵּרַכְתָּ בָרֵךְ׃	I brought you to curse my enemies but you *have done nothing but* bless them. Num 23:11
9.	שִׁמְעוּ שָׁמוֹעַ וְאַל־תָּבִינוּ	Hear *indeed*, but do not comprehend! Isa 6:9
10.	כִּי־אָסֹר נֶאֱסָרְךָ . . . וְהָמֵת לֹא נְמִיתֶךָ	We will *only* tie you up . . . ; we will *not* kill you. Judg 15:13
11.	וַתֹּאמֶר הָלֹךְ אֵלֵךְ עִמָּךְ אֶפֶס כִּי	"*Very well*," she said, "I will go with you. But. . . ." Judg 4:9
12.	אָמוֹר אָמַרְתִּי בֵּיתְךָ . . . יִתְהַלְּכוּ לְפָנַי עַד־עוֹלָם וְעַתָּה	*Indeed* I had promised that your family would forever minister before me. But now. . . . 1 Sam 2:30
13.	אָנֹכִי אֵרֵד עִמְּךָ מִצְרַיְמָה וְאָנֹכִי אַעַלְךָ גַם־עָלֹה	I will go down with you to Egypt, and I will *surely* bring you up (again). Gen 46:4

The climax of a series of situations may be marked with the postpositive infinitive absolute, preceded by גַם (## 14–15).[30]

14.	וַיֹּאכַל גַּם־אָכוֹל אֶת־כַּסְפֵּנוּ׃	He has *even* used up the money paid (to him) for us. Gen 31:15
15.	כִּי־תִשְׂתָּרֵר עָלֵינוּ גַּם־הִשְׂתָּרֵר׃	*Now* you *even* want to set yourself up as ruler over us! Num 16:13

---

29. Cf., too, Ps 126:6.   30. The particle *gm* is also used in # 13.

The intensifying effect of the infinitive absolute is found in a variety of *non-affirming*   g
contexts. In impassioned questions the prepositive infinitive shows doubt or the improb-
ability of an affirmative answer (## 16–18). A preposed infinitive may also be used in a
conditional clause (## 19–21) or a counterfactual expression ('O that . . . , if only . . .';
22–23). Various modal nuances are also associated with preposed infinitives absolute
(## 24–25).[31]

16.	הֲמָלֹךְ תִּמְלֹךְ עָלֵינוּ אִם־מָשׁוֹל תִּמְשֹׁל בָּנוּ	Will you *actually* reign over us and rule us? Gen 37:8
17.	הֶאָכוֹל אָכַלְנוּ מִן־הַמֶּלֶךְ אִם־נִשֵּׂאת נִשָּׂא לָנוּ׃	Have we eaten *anything* from the king('s holdings) or has he *ever* lifted away (tax obligations) for us? 2 Sam 19:43
18.	הֲקָצוֹר קָצְרָה יָדִי מִפְּדוּת	*Really*, is my arm too short to be redeemed? Isa 50:2
19.	וְאָבִיהָ יָרֹק יָרַק בְּפָנֶיהָ	If her father *had happened to* spit in her face. . . . Num 12:14
20.	אִם־הִפָּקֵד יִפָּקֵד	If he *should happen to be* missing. . . . 1 Kgs 20:39
21.	אִם־אָמֹר אָמַר	*If* I say. . . . 1 Sam 20:21
22.	אַף כִּי לוּא אָכֹל אָכַל הַיּוֹם הָעָם	*If only* the troops had eaten today. . . . 1 Sam 14:30
23.	לוּ שָׁקוֹל יִשָּׁקֵל כַּעְשִׂי	*If only* my anguish could be weighed (*Qal* inf. abs. + *Niphal* non-perf.). . . . Job 6:2
24.	הֲיָדוֹעַ נֵדַע כִּי	How could we *possibly* have known that. . . ?[32] Gen 43:7
25.	מִי־יִתֵּן הַחֲרֵשׁ תַּחֲרִישׁוּן	*Would to God* you would be silent! Job 13:5

Related to both the affirmative and volitional uses of the infinitive is its use *with*   h
orders and admonitions; as we shall see below, the infinitive may stand alone as a word of
command. With other orders, the infinitive is generally prepositive with prefix forms
(## 26–29) and postpositive with imperatives (# 30; cf. # 9).

26.	וַיְצַו אֲבִימֶלֶךְ אֶת־כָּל־הָעָם לֵאמֹר הַנֹּגֵעַ בָּאִישׁ הַזֶּה וּבְאִשְׁתּוֹ מוֹת יוּמָת׃	So Abimelech gave orders to all the people, "Whoever molests this man or his wife shall *surely* be put to death (*Qal* inf. abs. + *Hophal* non-perf.)." Gen 26:11

---

31. The sense of *ʾākōl tōʾkēl* (Gen 2:16) may be 'You *may* eat.' Cf. 31.4d.

32. Contrast *yādōaʿ tēdaʿ kî*, 'It is absolutely necessary that you know that . . .' (Gen 15:13).

27.	הוֹכֵחַ תּוֹכִיחַ אֶת־עֲמִיתֶךָ וְלֹא־ תִשָּׂא עָלָיו חֵטְא:	*Be sure* to rebuke your neighbor frankly so you will not share in his guilt. Lev 19:17
28.	סָקוֹל יִסָּקֵל הַשּׁוֹר	The bull *must* be stoned (*Qal* inf. abs. + *Niphal* non-perf.). Exod 21:28
29.	שָׁמוֹר תִּשְׁמְרוּן אֶת־מִצְוֹת	*Be sure* to keep the commands. . . . Deut 6:17
30.	שִׁמְעוּ שָׁמוֹעַ אֵלַי וְאִכְלוּ־טוֹב	*Listen*, listen to me and eat what is good. Isa 55:2

i   In some cases it is difficult to focus on the force of the infinitive absolute. Occasionally it seems to intensify the root situation (usually postpositive, ## 31–32; prepositive, # 33).[33] Elsewhere the effect is to stress a negation (# 34) or a relevant time boundary (## 35–36).

31.	בְּכוּ בָכוֹ לַהֹלֵךְ	Weep *bitterly* for him who goes (into exile). Jer 22:10
32.	וַיִּשְׁטְחוּ לָהֶם שָׁטוֹחַ סְבִיבוֹת הַמַּחֲנֶה:	They spread them (the quail) out for themselves *all over* around the camp. Num 11:32
33.	כִּי־נִכְסֹף נִכְסַפְתָּה לְבֵית אָבִיךָ	You yearned *intensely* (to return) to your father's house. Gen 31:30
34.	וְסוֹךְ לֹא־סָכְתִּי	I used no lotions *at all.* Dan 10:3
35.	וַיְהִי אַךְ יָצֹא יָצָא יַעֲקֹב מֵאֵת פְּנֵי יִצְחָק . . . וְעֵשָׂו . . . בָּא	It was *just after* Jacob left Isaac's presence that . . . Esau . . . came in! Gen 27:30
36.	אַךְ הָקֵם הֵקִימוּ אֶת־הַשֹּׁמְרִים	They had *just then* installed the guards. Judg 7:19

35.3.2   Adverbial Complement

a   When a *non-paronomastic* infinitive absolute is bracketed with a verb, the infinitive qualifies the verb in ways other than by intensifying it. In this use the infinitive may be an adverbial accusative (see 10.2.2) and is then referred to as the *adverbial infinitive* or complement. An adverbial infinitive adds a qualification to the situation represented by the finite verb. More specifically, it describes the manner or the attendant circumstance of that situation; it is not joined by a copula to the finite verb (## 1–5). The main verb

---

33. Other alleged prepositive cases include Gen 43:3, 1 Sam 20:6 (*š²l*), Joel 1:7, Prov 27:23.

may be active (## 1–3) or passive (## 4–5) in sense. The final example here (# 5) is noteworthy in that the infinitive has its own subject and governs a prepositional phrase.

1.	וְסַבֹּתֶם אֶת־הָעִיר כֹּל־אַנְשֵׁי הַמִּלְחָמָה הַקֵּיף אֶת־הָעִיר פַּעַם אֶחָת	March around the city with all the warriors, *circling* it one time. Josh 6:3
2.	אָקִים . . . אֶת כָּל־אֲשֶׁר דִּבַּ֫רְתִּי . . . הָחֵל וְכַלֵּה:	I will accomplish . . . all that I have said . . . *from the beginning to the end.* 1 Sam 3:12
3.	וַיְמַדְּדֵם בַּחֶ֫בֶל הַשְׁכֵּב אוֹתָם	He measured them off with a length of cord *by making* them *lie down.* 2 Sam 8:2
4.	קְבוּרַת חֲמוֹר יִקָּבֵר סָחוֹב וְהַשְׁלֵךְ	He will have the burial of a donkey— *dragged off* and *thrown away.* Jer 22:19
5.	מוֹת יוּמַת הָאִישׁ רָגוֹם אֹתוֹ בָאֲבָנִים כָּל־הָעֵדָה	This man must die—the whole assembly *stoning* him. Num 15:35

A finite verb may be bracketed with a paronomastic infinitive absolute which is   b
coordinated with another, non-paronomastic infinitive absolute (## 6–15).[34] Hebraists are not agreed about the meaning of the two infinitives in this kind of construction. Some think the compound invariably expresses continuance, continuous action, or repetition of action denoted by the main verb,[35] while others suggest simply that the non-paronomastic infinitive expresses some other qualification to the action.[36] Joüon suggests that the infinitives represent actions simultaneous or quasi-simultaneous with the main verb.[37] In this construction we can see the coordination of an intensifying infinitive (the paronomastic member)[38] and an adverbial infinitive (the non-paronomastic member).

Most cases involve *main verbs of motion*, and with these the intensifying infinitive   c
does signify repetition or continuance. One of the infinitives is often *hālôk*, and, where the main verb is *hlk*, it serves as the intensifying infinitive (## 6–10).[39] The infinitives are both usually postpositive, but one (# 10) or both (# 9) can be prepositive. With other verbs of motion the adverbial complement can be *hālôk* (## 11–12) or, indicating repetition, *šôb* (# 13, cf. # 11) or *haškēm* (## 14–15).

---

34. There are about thirty cases involved; see Goddard, *Hebrew Infinitive Absolute*, 41. More than a third of these, especially with *haškēm*, occur in Jeremiah; see S. J. P. K. Riekert, "The Co-ordinated Structs [sic] of the Infinitive Absolute in Jeremiah and Their Bearing on the Stylistics and Authenticity of the Jeremianic Corpus," *Journal of Northwest Semitic Languages* 13 (1987) 98–106.

35. BL § 36e′ / p. 277; R. J. Williams, *Hebrew Syntax: An Outline* (2d ed.; Toronto: University of Toronto, 1976) 38; F. R. Blake, *A Resurvey of Hebrew Tenses* (Rome: Pontifical Biblical Institute, 1951) 23.

36. GKC § 113s / p. 343; Ewald as cited by Riekert,

"Infinitives Absolute in Genesis," 81; C. Brockelmann, *Hebräische Syntax* (Neukirchen: Neukirchener Verlag, 1956) 82.

37. Joüon § 123m / p. 352; cf. Goddard, *Hebrew Infinitive Absolute*, 27–28.

38. Following the formulation of Riekert, "Infinitives Absolute in Genesis," 81.

39. There are a few related minor patterns: (*a*) two infinitives with a verbless clause (2 Kgs 2:11); with a finite verb (*b*) an infinitive absolute followed by a verbal adjective (Gen 26:13) and (*c*) an infinitive absolute followed by a participle (2 Sam 18:25).

6.	וַיֵּלֶךְ הָלוֹךְ וְאָכֹל	He *ate as he went along.* Judg 14:9
7.	בִּמְסִלָּה אַחַת הָלְכוּ הָלֹךְ וְגָעוֹ	They *kept* on the road, *lowing* all the way. 1 Sam 6:12
8.	וַיֵּלֶךְ דָּוִד הָלוֹךְ וְגָדוֹל	And David grew stronger *and stronger.* 2 Sam 5:10
9.	הָלוֹךְ וְטָפֹף תֵּלַכְנָה	They *trip along with mincing steps.* Isa 3:16
10.	הָלוֹךְ יֵלֵךְ וּבָכֹה	He who (regularly) *goes out weeping.* . . .[40] Ps 126:6
11.	וַיָּשֻׁבוּ הַמַּיִם . . . הָלוֹךְ וָשׁוֹב	The water receded *steadily.* Gen 8:3
12.	וַיִּסַּע אַבְרָם הָלוֹךְ וְנָסוֹעַ הַנֶּגְבָּה׃	Abram *kept on moving* toward the Negev. Gen 12:9
13.	וַיֵּצֵא יָצוֹא וָשׁוֹב	And it *kept flying back and forth.* Gen 8:7
14.	וָאֲדַבֵּר אֲלֵיכֶם הַשְׁכֵּם וְדַבֵּר	I spoke to you already for a long period (lit., *rising up early* and speaking).[41] Jer 7:13
15.	הַנְּבִאִים אֲשֶׁר אָנֹכִי שֹׁלֵחַ אֲלֵיכֶם וְהַשְׁכֵּם וְשָׁלֹחַ	the prophets whom I sent to you *again and again* . . . Jer 26:5

d   A smaller group of double infinitives absolute involve an intensifying paronomastic infinitive and an adverbial infinitive in a combination which serves to qualify the goal or character of the principal verb (## 16–18).[42]

16.	וַיַּכֵּהוּ הָאִישׁ הַכֵּה וּפָצֹעַ׃	So the man struck him (the prophet) *in such a way as to wound* him. 1 Kgs 20:37
17.	וְנָתַשְׁתִּי אֶת־הַגּוֹי הַהוּא נָתוֹשׁ וְאַבֵּד	I will uproot that nation *in such a way as to destroy* it. Jer 12:17
18.	וְנָגַף יהוה אֶת־מִצְרַיִם נָגֹף וְרָפוֹא	YHWH will strike Egypt with a plague; he *will strike* them *and heal* them. Isa 19:22

The broader narrative of # 16 shows clearly that the prophet intended the man to strike him in such a way that he would not be recognized. In the context of # 17 two kinds of uprootings are in view: an uprooting that is not beyond recovery (vv 14–17) and an

---

40. Note that the adjacent line *bᵓ-ybwᵓ brnh* also begins with an infinitive absolute.

41. Cf. Jer 35:15. See Riekert, "Jeremiah," 98.

42. See again Joüon § 123m / p. 352.

uprooting beyond recovery (v 17). The threat to strike Egypt in # 18 is expressed in a context that promises the restoration of Egypt. The thought might be better expressed in English by a negative: 'I will not strike Egypt beyond recovery.' Nothing in these contexts suggests that the paronomastic infinitive signifies continuous or iterative action. The identification of the paronomastic infinitive as the intensifying infinitive that gives prominence to the verbal idea, which is then qualified by the coordinate adverbial construction, is apposite in each context.

Other Nominal Uses   **35.3.3**

The infinitive absolute is only rarely used in grammatical roles other than the complements. In a nominative frame, it is found as subject of a verbal clause (## 1–2) or subject (## 3–4) or predicate (# 5; cf. צום in # 13) of a verbless clause.[43] An infinitive can be the object of a preposition (## 6–7) or the genitive in a construct phrase (## 8–10).[44]   a

1.	וְגַם־הַרְבֵּה נָפַל מִן־הָעָם	*Many* of the people fell. 2 Sam 1:4
2.	וּמַה־יּוֹכִיחַ הוֹכֵחַ מִכֶּם:	What does *reproving* from you reprove? Job 6:25
3.	אָכֹל דְּבַשׁ הַרְבּוֹת לֹא־טוֹב	*To eat* too much honey is not good. Prov 25:27
4.	כִּי חַטַּאת־קֶסֶם מֶרִי וְאָוֶן וּתְרָפִים הַפְצַר	For rebellion is (like) the sin of divination and *arrogance* (like) the evil of idolatry. 1 Sam 15:23
5.	וַעֲבֹדַת הַצְּדָקָה הַשְׁקֵט וָבֶטַח	The work of righteousness is *quiet* and security. Isa 32:17
6.	וְהִכִּיתָ אֶת־אֲרָם בַּאֲפֵק עַד־כַּלֵּה:	You will *completely* (lit., unto *completion*) destroy the Arameans at Aphek.[45] 2 Kgs 13:17
7.	וְאַחֲרֵי שָׁתֹה	and after *drinking* 1 Sam 1:9
8.	בְּמַטְאֲטֵא הַשְׁמֵד	with the broom *of destruction* Isa 14:23
9.	לָקַחַת מוּסַר הַשְׂכֵּל	to acquire the discipline *of being prudent* Prov 1:3
10.	מִדֶּרֶךְ הַשְׂכֵּל	from the path *of understanding* Prov 21:16

---

43. There are about eight nominative cases all told, and the predicate nominative case here is unique, according to Goddard, *Hebrew Infinitive Absolute*, 50, 71–72.

44. The infinitive is called absolute because it cannot be the construct term in a construct phrase (see, e.g., GB 2. 61 [§ 12a*]); but cf. Joüon § 49a n. 1 / p. 110.

45. The phrase ʿad-kallēh is also used in 2 Kgs 13:19 and Ezra 9:14 and may be a frozen phrase.

b   An infinitive absolute can be used in a variety of accusative roles: direct object (## 11–13), adverbial accusative of state (# 14) or specification (# 15), and in a double accusative construction (# 16). Such adverbial accusative uses differ from those discussed above (35.3.2) in that there the infinitive describes the attendant circumstances of the verb.

11.	לִמְדוּ הֵיטֵב	Learn *to do good*. Isa 1:17
12.	נָתַן לָהֶם הָאֱלֹהִים מַדָּע וְהַשְׂכֵּל	God gave them knowledge and *understanding*. Dan 1:17
13.	הֲלוֹא זֶה צוֹם אֶבְחָרֵהוּ פַּתֵּחַ חַרְצֻבּוֹת רֶשַׁע	Is this not the (kind of) fasting I have chosen: *to loose* the chains of injustice. . . . Isa 58:6
14.	וּמָה־יהוה דּוֹרֵשׁ מִמְּךָ . . . וְהַצְנֵעַ לֶכֶת	*What* does Yhwh require of you? . . . *to walk* prudently. . . . Mic 6:8
15.	וַעֲוֹנֹתֵינוּ יְדַעֲנוּם: פָּשֹׁעַ וְכַחֵשׁ	And as for our iniquities, we know them: *rebellion* and *treachery*. . . . Isa 59:12–13
16.	סְחִי וּמָאוֹס תְּשִׂימֵנוּ	You made us scum and *refuse*. Lam 3:45

35.4   Adverbial Uses

a   Some infinitives absolute (mostly *Hiphils*) have become adverbs; these are similar to adverbial complements such as הָלוֹךְ (35.3.2), differing in that they can occur with a variety of verb types. Such infinitives include הֵיטֵב 'well, thoroughly' (## 1–2), הַרְבֵּה 'much' (often with מְאֹד; # 3),[46] הַרְחֵק 'at a distance' (# 4), הַשְׁכֵּם 'early' (# 5),[47] and מַהֵר 'quickly' (# 6). An adverbial infinitive can modify an adverbial-complement infinitive (# 2).

1.	וְשָׁאַלְתָּ הֵיטֵב	You shall investigate *thoroughly*. Deut 13:15
2.	וָאֶכֹּת אֹתוֹ טָחוֹן הֵיטֵב	Then I crushed it, grinding it *thoroughly*. Deut 9:21
3.	וָאֶשְׁגֶּה הַרְבֵּה מְאֹד:	I have erred *greatly*. 1 Sam 26:21
4.	קָמוּ נֵד־אֶחָד הַרְחֵק מְאֹד	It piled up in a heap *a great distance away*. Josh 3:16

---

46. Goddard, *Hebrew Infinitive Absolute*, 50, 67, proposes to distinguish from the adverbial uses a set of adjec-

tival uses of *hrbh*, e.g., 2 Sam 12:2, Neh 4:13, 2 Chr 25:9.

47. Note also the pair *haškēm wahaʿărēb* in 1 Sam 17:16.

5. מְבָרֵךְ רֵעֵהוּ בְּקוֹל גָּדוֹל בַּבֹּקֶר הַשְׁכֵּים

(A man) loudly blessing his neighbor when he *rises early* in the morning. . . .
Prov 27:14

6. סָרוּ מַהֵר מִן־הַדֶּרֶךְ

They have turned aside *quickly* from the road.
Exod 32:8

Verbal Uses   35.5

The infinitive absolute can be used to "stand for" a variety of other verb forms; such **a** replacement use is a function of the non-finite character of the form.[48] It can "replace" command forms, finite verbs, participles, or infinitives construct.

As a Command Form   35.5.1

The infinitive absolute used as a word of command or as an interjection is asyndetic **a** and begins its clause. The use of the form as a volitional is extremely old, to judge from comparable usages in other Semitic languages.[49] In later Hebrew it disappeared, as shown by its absence in the Chronicler (in contrast to the Deuteronomist) and from the Samaritan Pentateuch.[50] In this use it predominantly expresses divine and/or prophetic commands: legislative commands (## 1–2), divine commands (## 3–6), or legislative jussive (# 7).[51]

1. וָאֲצַוֶּה אֶת־שֹׁפְטֵיכֶם בָּעֵת הַהִיא לֵאמֹר שָׁמֹעַ בֵּין־אֲחֵיכֶם וּשְׁפַטְתֶּם צֶדֶק

And I commanded your *šopeṭim* at that time, "*Hear* the disputes between your kinfolk and judge fairly."
Deut 1:16

2. זָכוֹר אֶת־יוֹם הַשַּׁבָּת

Remember the Sabbath day.[52]
Exod 20:8

3. נָשֹׂא אֶת־רֹאשׁ בְּנֵי קְהָת

Take a census of the Kohathites.
Num 4:2

---

48. This point is stressed by Amikam Gai, "The Reduction of the Tense (and Other Categories) of the Consequent Verb in North-west Semitic," *Orientalia* 51 (1982) 254–56; but Gai exaggerates the unmarked character of the infinitive absolute and does not account for the relative rarity of its use for a finite verb; he cites some interesting Indo-European parallels from Paul Kiparsky, "Tense and Mood in Indo-European Syntax," *Foundations of Language* 4 (1968) 30–55.

49. See Brockelmann, *Grundriss*, 1. 345; Huesman, "Infinitive Absolute," 281; W. Wright, *A Grammar of the Arabic Language* (3d ed.; Cambridge: Cambridge University, 1896), 1. 62.

50. See Polzin, *Late Biblical Hebrew*, 43; A. Kropat, *Die Syntax des Autors der Chronik verglichen mit der seiner Quellen* (Beiheft zur Zeitschrift für die Alttestamentliche Wissenschaften 16; Giessen: Töpelmann, 1909) 23; B. K. Waltke, "The Samaritan Pentateuch and the Text of the Old Testament," *New Perspectives on the Old Testa-*

ment, ed. J. B. Payne (Waco, Texas: Word, 1970) 212–39, at 215–16.

51. J. D. W. Watts argues that the infinitive absolute serves "as an imperative" only if there is an adjacent imperative; he thus denies that sense to Exod 20:8; see "Infinitive Absolute as Imperative and the Interpretation of Exodus 20:8," *Zeitschrift für die Alttestamentliche Wissenschaft* 74 (1962) 141–47.

52. The MT of Deut 5:12 has *šāmôr ᵓt-ywm hšbt* and the Samaritan Pentateuch of Exod 20:8 has *šmwr*. It may be that it is "in legal texts of rather general, not immediate application" that this usage is found—so alleges Muraoka, *Emphatic Words*, 85. The further suggestion that there are distinct grammatical structures for positive and negative commands is less clear, though his proposed scheme works in some texts, notably the second Decalogue: positive commands have the infinitive absolute (Deut 5:12, 16) and negative commands have the non-perfective with *lōᵓ* (Deut 5:17–21).

4.	הָלוֹךְ וְדִבַּרְתָּ אֶל־דָּוִד	*Go* and say to David. . . .[53] 2 Sam 24:12
5.	עֲשֹׂה הַנַּחַל הַזֶּה גֵּבִים גֵּבִים׃	*Make* this valley full of ditches. 2 Kgs 3:16
6.	הֵילִילִי שַׁעַר זַעֲקִי־עִיר נָמוֹג פְּלֶשֶׁת כֻּלֵּךְ	Wail, O Gate! Howl, O City! *Melt away*, all you Philistines. Isa 14:31
7.	הִמּוֹל לוֹ כָל־זָכָר	*Let* every male of his *be circumcised*. Exod 12:48

35.5.2   As a Finite Verb

a   The role of the infinitive absolute as a finite verb varies, depending on the use of *waw*.[54] *Without the conjunction* the infinitive has no formal or clear conceptual connection with the preceding statement. It can be used for the cohortative (## 1–2), jussive (# 3), perfective (# 4), and non-perfective (# 5), and in proverbial sayings (## 6–8, cf. ## 2–3). All the narrative examples cited here (## 1, 4–5) occur in direct speech.

1.	וַיֹּאמֶר מֶלֶךְ יִשְׂרָאֵל . . . הִתְחַפֵּשׂ וָבֹא בַמִּלְחָמָה	And the king of Israel said . . . , "I *will disguise myself* and *enter* into the battle." 1 Kgs 22:30 = 2 Chr 18:29
2.	אָכוֹל וְשָׁתוֹ כִּי מָחָר נָמוּת׃	*Let* us *eat* and drink because tomorrow we die. Isa 22:13
3.	פָּגוֹשׁ דֹּב שַׁכּוּל בְּאִישׁ	*Let* a bear robbed of its whelps *meet* a man. Prov 17:12
4.	וַיֹּאמֶר מֵהָחֵל הַתְּרוּמָה לָבִיא בֵית־יהוה אָכוֹל וְשָׂבוֹעַ	And he said, "Since the contributions began to come(?) into Yʜᴡʜ's house, we *have eaten and been satisfied*." 2 Chr 31:10
5.	כִּי כֹה אָמַר יהוה אָכֹל וְהוֹתֵר׃	This is what Yʜᴡʜ says, "They *will eat and have some left over*." 2 Kgs 4:43
6.	הָרֹה עָמָל וְיָלֹד אָוֶן	They *conceive* trouble and *give birth* to wickedness. Job 15:35
7.	הָפֵר מַחֲשָׁבוֹת בְּאֵין סוֹד	Plans *fail* for lack of counsel. Prov 15:22
8.	פָּקוֹחַ אָזְנַיִם וְלֹא יִשְׁמָע׃	He *opens* his ears but hears nothing. Isa 42:20

---

53. The parallel text in 1 Chr 21:10 has *lēk wǝdibbartā*.
54. This use, too, is rare in later texts; see Polzin, *Late Biblical Hebrew*, 44–45.

Sometimes such infinitives seem to function as *interjections*, that is, as bare roots in hurried and animated speech exclaiming a point. The infinitive absolute without *waw* may serve in place of a finite verb in making emphatic expressions and indignant questions (## 9–11).[55] When the infinitive absolute is used as an interjection the reader must supply the appropriate person and aspect on the basis of semantic pertinence. The distinction between the use of the infinitive as interjection or as an adverbial is somewhat blurred and subjective. For example, in # 11, the infinitives could be rendered as below (or as 'You rely. . . . You conceive. . . . '), or they could be interpreted as qualifying adverbials and rendered, 'No one calls for justice . . . , relying on empty argument and speaking lies, conceiving trouble and giving birth to evil!'

9.   הֲגָנֹב רָצֹחַ וְנָאֹף . . . וְהָלֹךְ   *Will you steal, murder, and commit adultery* . . . and
    אַחֲרֵי אֱלֹהִים אֲחֵרִים   *follow* after other gods?
                                            Jer 7:9

10.   פָּנֹה אֶל־הַרְבֵּה וְהִנֵּה לִמְעָט   *You expected* much, but see, it turned out to be little.
                                            Hag 1:9

11.   אֵין־קֹרֵא בְצֶדֶק וְאֵין נִשְׁפָּט   No one calls for justice, no one pleads his case with
    בֶּאֱמוּנָה בָּטוֹחַ עַל־תֹּהוּ וְדַבֶּר־   integrity. They *rely on* empty argument and *speak* lies!
    שָׁוְא הָרוֹ עָמָל וְהוֹלֵיד אָוֶן: They *conceive* trouble and *give birth* to evil!
                                              Isa 59:4

According to A. Rubinstein *the infinitive absolute with the conjunction* at the   **b** beginning of its clause continues a preceding finite verb in about forty-five passages.[56] This usage belongs to a later stage of the language, to judge from the relatively greater frequency of this construction in Jeremiah (ten times), Zechariah (three times), Esther (nine times), and Nehemiah (four times) and from the rarity of this construction in the Pentateuch (twice) and in the earlier prophets.

The purpose served by this construction can just as well be served by other constructions;[57] its use has been explained as an expression of a desire for stylistic variation, but   **c** this explanation does not account for its predominance in late Biblical Hebrew. Rubinstein suggests that it is the result of the disappearance of *waw-consecutive* forms in late Hebrew: "It is at least significant that in the preponderant majority of our instances the inf. abs. occurs precisely at the point where one would expect a transition to the appropriate consecutive form of the verb."[58] His further thesis that the substitution belongs not to the original text but to the work of scribes and copyists lacks convincing evidence.[59]

---

55. Cf. also Isa 5:5, Ps 17:5, Job 40:2. On the origin of this usage, see Goddard, *Hebrew Infinitive Absolute*, 87.

56. A. Rubinstein, "A Finite Verb Continued by an Infinitive Absolute in Hebrew," *Vetus Testamentum* 2 (1952) 362–67; cf. Hammershaimb, "*Infinitivus Absolutus*," 90; cf. also Sperber, *Historical Grammar*, 73–75; Huesman, "Infinitive Absolute."

57. Note the variety attested in these cases: *hakbēd* in Exod 8:11 MT and *wykbd* in Exod 8:11 *Sam*; *wənātōn* in

Isa 37:19 and *wənatənû* in 2 Kgs 19:18; *wəhassēk* in Jer 19:13 and *wəhissikû* in Jer 32:29; *šābtî wərāʾōh* in Qoh 9:11 and *wəšabtî ʾănî wāʾerʾeh* in Qoh 4:1, 7. Further, Qumran biblical manuscripts often shift infinitive absolute forms to finite forms; see, e.g., Rubinstein, "Finite Verb," 365–67; Hammershaimb, "*Infinitivus Absolutus*," 91.

58. Rubinstein, "Finite Verb," 365.

59. So also, for example, Hammershaimb, "*Infinitivus Absolutus*," 91.

d   This use of the infinitive absolute, bound with *waw* and functioning in place of a finite verb, closely approximates its use as an adverbial complement, for in both constructions the infinitive qualifies a leading verb. The constructions are distinguished by the presence or absence of a conjunctive *waw*. Without *waw* the infinitive is adverbial, qualifying the same situation as the verb; with *waw* the infinitive is used as a finite verb and represents a situation subordinate to the leading verb. In Jer 22:19 (35.3.2 # 4), for example, the adverbial infinitives סָחוֹב וְהַשְׁלֵךְ 'dragged off and thrown away,' though coordinate with one another, are not coordinated with the verb and thus directly qualify the situation יִקָּבֵר 'will be buried.' In the present construction the infinitive is coordinated with the main verb and represents a situation distinct from though subordinate to it; the infinitive absolute with *waw* introduces a separate situation from that represented by the finite verb, though that verb specifies the person and aspect of the infinitive.[60] The infinitive can be found in sequence with a perfective form (## 12–13), a non-perfective form (## 14–15), a jussive (# 16), a *wəqtl* form (# 17), a *wayyqtl* form (# 18), a participle (35.5.3), or an infinitive construct (35.5.4).

12.	הֲנִגְלֹה נִגְלֵיתִי אֶל־בֵּית אָבִיךָ וּבָחֹר אֹתוֹ . . .	Did I reveal myself to your father's house . . . and *choose* it. . . . 1 Sam 2:27–28
13.	כִּי־צַמְתֶּם וְסָפוֹד	when you fasted and *mourned* Zech 7:5
14.	וְכִי־תִמְכְּרוּ . . . אוֹ קָנֹה	If you sell . . . or *buy*. . . . Lev 25:14
15.	אִישׁ כִּי־יִדֹּר נֶדֶר . . . אוֹ־הִשָּׁבַע שְׁבֻעָה	When someone makes a vow . . . or *takes an oath*. . . . Num 30:3
16.	יְבַקְשׁוּ . . . וְיַפְקֵד הַמֶּלֶךְ	Let a search be made . . . and *let* the king *appoint*. . . . Esth 2:2–3

---

60. But cf. # 16. There is a systematic exception to this pattern: in a few passages a pronoun follows the infinitive absolute and qualifies it, e.g., *wəšabbēaḥ ʾănî* 'I praised' (Qoh 4:2), *wənahăpôk hûʾ* 'it has been changed' (Esth 9:1, cf. 3:13; Exod 36:7; 1 Chr 5:20; Esth 2:3). This is called the *qatāli anāku* construction and is most common in the first person; it is found in Hebrew, Phoenician, and Amarna Canaanite. See W. L. Moran, "'Does Amarna Bear on Karatepe?'—An Answer," *Journal of Cuneiform Studies* 6 (1952) 76–80; Moran, "The Hebrew Language in Its Northwest Semitic Background," *The Bible and the Ancient Near East: Essays in Honor of William Foxwell Albright*, ed. G. E. Wright (Garden City, New York: Doubleday, 1961; reprinted, Winona Lake, Indiana: Eisenbrauns, 1979) 54–72, at 61–62. Despite the clear examples in prose, this construction has been controversial; see G. R. Driver, "Some Uses of *qtl* in the Semitic Languages," *Proceedings of the International Conference on Semitic Studies Held in Jerusalem, 19–23 July 1965* (Jerusalem: Israel Academy of Sciences and Humanities, 1969) 49–64 (all Hebrew examples are "really" perfectives); Hammershaimb, "*Infinitivus Absolutus*," 91–93; David Marcus, "Studies in Ugaritic Grammar I," *Journal of the Ancient Near East Society* 1/2 (1968) 55–61; Samuel Loewenstamm, "Remarks upon the Infinitive Absolute in Ugaritic and Phoenician," *Journal of the Ancient Near East Society* 2 (1969) 53. On occurrences of the infinitive absolute used as a finite verb in verse, see Moran, "Hebrew Language," 62; M. O'Connor, *Hebrew Verse Structure* (Winona Lake, Indiana: Eisenbrauns, 1980) 170, 181, 210, 227, 289. The unusual construction *śāś* (perfective) *ʾānōkî*, Ps 119:162, is distinct, as Philip C. Schmitz observes to us, since the infinitive absolute would be *śōś* (cf. the form used in Isa 61:10).

17.	וְהִבִּיטוּ אֵלַי . . . וְסָפְדוּ . . . וְהָמֵר	They will look on me . . . and mourn . . . and *grieve. . . .* Zech 12:10
18.	וַיַּרְא פַּרְעֹה כִּי . . . וְהַכְבֵּד אֶת־לִבּוֹ	Pharaoh saw that . . . and he *hardened* his heart. Exod 8:11

As a Participle   35.5.3

The infinitive absolute may stand as a participle, although this use is difficult to   a
distinguish from an adverbial-accusative use. The distinctive cases involve either a verbless clause (# 1) or a mixture of infinitives and participles together (## 2–3).

1.	וְהַחַיּוֹת רָצוֹא וָשׁוֹב	And the living creatures were *running* and *returning*. Ezek 1:14
2.	כְּתָב אֲשֶׁר־נִכְתָּב בְּשֵׁם־הַמֶּלֶךְ וְנַחְתּוֹם בְּטַבַּעַת הַמֶּלֶךְ	the writing which is written in the name of the king and *sealed* with the king's ring Esth 8:8
3.	הַבָּנִים מְלַקְּטִים עֵצִים וְהָאָבוֹת מְבַעֲרִים אֶת־הָאֵשׁ וְהַנָּשִׁים לָשׁוֹת בָּצֵק . . . וְהַסֵּךְ נְסָכִים	The children are gathering wood and the fathers are lighting the fire and the women knead the dough . . . and they *pour out* offerings. Jer 7:18

As an Infinitive Construct   35.5.4

The precise nuance of the infinitive absolute when it is used in lieu of an infinitive   a
construct depends in part on the presence or absence of *waw*. When not bound with the
conjunction the infinitive absolute may show the infinitive construct's use as a verbal
complement (# 1),[61] while bound with *waw* it has the same use as a preceding infinitive
construct (## 2–3).

1.	וְלֹא־אָבוּ בִדְרָכָיו הָלוֹךְ	They were not willing *to walk* in his ways. Isa 42:24
2.	וַיֵּשֶׁב הָעָם לֶאֱכֹל וְשָׁתוֹ	And the people sat down to eat and *drink*. Exod 32:6
3.	בְּתִתְּךָ לוֹ לֶחֶם וְחֶרֶב וְשָׁאוֹל לוֹ בֵּאלֹהִים	when you gave him food and a sword and *inquired* of God for him[62] 1 Sam 22:13

In addition to אָבָה (# 1), the unbound infinitive absolute may function as a verbal   b
complement with חָפֵץ 'to desire' (Job 13:3), אָהַב 'to love' (Prov 15:12), נָסָה 'to try' (Deut
28:56), חָדַל 'to stop' (Isa 1:16).[63]

---

61. Compare the adverbial complement use treated in 35.3.2.

62. Cf. 1 Sam 25:26.

63. Perhaps also *ykl* in Isa 57:20 = Jer 49:23; *ydᶜ* in Isa 7:15, 16.

36

Infinitive Construct

36.1   Form and Meaning

36.1.1   Form

a   The ordinary Hebrew infinitive, called the infinitive construct,[1] is a verbal noun used in the ways that English uses its infinitive ('to go') and its gerund ('going'). It is typically presented as the "real" infinitive of Biblical Hebrew, in contradistinction to the infinitive absolute (35.1). Like the infinitive absolute, but to an even greater degree, it is not unbounded, despite the etymology of "infinitive" (Latin 'non-limited'). Rather, it can be suffixed, used as the first term of a construct phrase, and governed by a preposition.

b   The infinitive construct is not consistently morphologically distinct from the imperative (in some stems) or the infinitive absolute (in the so-called derived stems). Thus, for example, the form *hitqattēl* serves as both infinitives and the imperative of the *Hithpael* stem. In the *Hiphil* the infinitive construct generally has an *ī*, written *plene* (הַקְטִיל), while the absolute usually has an *ē* and is written defectively (הַקְטֵל). In some cases a form with an *ē* and *plene* spelling is used in both roles (הַשְׂכֵּיל in Job 34:35, infinitive construct; in Jer 3:15, infinitive absolute). A form with *ē* written defectively is found as an infinitive construct (e.g., Deut 32:8, Jer 44:19). Such homophonous forms must be distinguished on the basis of semantic pertinence and syntax.

---

1. See 35.1b on the term "infinitive construct" and for references.

The infinitive construct of the *Qal* is morphologically more complex than that of   c
other stems; a number of base forms are used. These may be derived from an earlier
*qutul form,[2] though **qtul* has also been proposed by scholars.[3] There are a number of
Hebrew variants of the infinitive. One group of variants is essentially graphic: קְטֹל is
free-standing (and קְטוֹל is a rare alternant of that) while קְטָל־ occurs before *maqqeph*.
Another group involves the base: the base קְטֹל is used independently and with consonantal suffixes (‑ךְ, ‑כֶם, ‑כֶן), for example, כָּתׇבְךָ *kǝtobka*, while the base קְטׇל־ is used with
vocalic suffixes, for example, כָּתְבִי *kotbî* (with *shewa medium*).

For some roots the independent form reflects a **qtul* base, while suffixed forms   d
show a **qatl/qitl* base, for example, בְּשַׁחֲטָם/לִשְׁחֹט, בִּלְעִי/לִבְלֹעַ, בְּבִגְדוֹ/לִבְגֹד.[4] Occasionally, two forms are found for the suffixed infinitive of the same root, for example,
נׇפְלָם/נׇפְלוֹ.[5] The feminine forms of the infinitive take the shapes קְטֹלֶת, קׇטְלׇה, קִטְלׇה, and קְטֻלׇה,
for example, לֶכֶת, יִרְאׇה, דׇּבְקׇה; less frequent forms include those that have, instead of *o*
in the first syllable, *a*, *e*, and *u* (e.g., חֶמְלׇה, חֶמְלַת, אַהֲבׇה). All CVCCâ infinitives can be
identified as independent nouns rather than infinitives, and the dictionaries vary on this
point; many of the roots with such infinitives are statives.[6] The segholate infinitives are
chiefly from I-*yod* and I-*nun* roots, though these roots may form other infinitives.[7]
Another source of variation involves the prepositions; the forms בִּכְתֹב and כִּכְתֹב have
shewa medium, while the most common combination, לִכְתֹב, has a silent *shewa*.[8] Note, too,
the contrast of בֶּאֱמֹר and לֵאמֹר.

Only with the first-person singular and second masculine singular suffixes is there a   e
distinction between the possessive suffix (genitive) and the verbal suffix (accusative).

First-person singular

Possessive	עַד‑בֹּאִי	until *I* come (2 Kgs 18:32)
Verbal	לְרַמּוֹתַנִי	to betray *me* (1 Chr 12:18)
	לְעׇזְרֵנִי	to help *me* (1 Chr 12:18)

Second-person masculine singular

Possessive	זַעֲקֶךָ	*your* crying for help (= *you* cry for help) (Isa 30:19)
Verbal	גַּדֶּלְךָ	to exalt *you* (Josh 3:7)

2. GKC § 45b / p. 123; BL § 43b / p. 316; C. Brockelmann, *Grundriss der vergleichenden Grammatik der semitischen Sprachen* (Berlin: Reuter und Reichard, 1908), 1. 18,
338, 579; GB 2. 83 (§ 14p); Joüon § 49a / pp. 109–10;
S. Moscati et al., *An Introduction to the Comparative
Grammar of the Semitic Languages* (Wiesbaden: Harrassowitz, 1964) 147.

3. R. Meyer, "Zur Geschichte des hebräischen Verbums,"
Vetus Testamentum 3 (1953) 225–35, at 230–32; cf. *UT*
§ 9.20, 26. In any case, the *o* vowels of the two infinitives
have distinct origins, as the infinitive absolute is from
*qatāl and the construct from **q(u)tul*.

4. On the morphological tangles, see the sure guide of
H. M. Orlinsky, "The Qal Infinitive Construct and the
Verbal Noun in Biblical Hebrew," *Journal of the Ameri-
can Oriental Society* 67 (1947) 107–26. On the mixed pat-
tern of the verb *škb*, see his "The Hebrew Root ŠKB,"
Journal of Biblical Literature 63 (1944) 19–44, at 42–44.

5. Orlinsky argues that the **qitl* forms are segholate
nouns rather than infinitive nouns; see "Qal Infinitive
Construct," 119–20.

6. Orlinsky, "Qal Infinitive Construct," 117; for other
supposed *Qal* infinitives, see pp. 118–19.

7. A number of roots, especially weak roots, use a
variety of infinitives construct, possibly with some semantic specialization; see again Orlinsky, "Hebrew Root ŠKB."

8. On this pointing, see W. Weinberg, "'Before' and
'After' in the Teaching of Hebrew Grammar," *Hebrew
Studies* 23 (1982) 127–44, at 129–31; S. Levin, "Defects,
Alleged or Real, in the Tiberias Pointing," *Hebrew Studies*

Elsewhere the forms of the possessive suffixes are used, and contextual considerations must decide whether a subjective or objective genitive is intended (see 9.4).[9]

1. עַל־רָדְפוֹ . . . אָחִיו   because of *his* pursuing his brother (< *he* pursued)
Amos 1:11

2. וַיָּטֶל שָׁאוּל אֶת־הַחֲנִית עָלָיו
לְהַכֹּתוֹ   But Saul hurled his spear at him for the smiting of *him* (i.e., to smite *him*).
1 Sam 20:33

Sometimes ambiguity is avoided by using אֶת after the infinitive, for example, לָדַעַת אֹתִי 'to know *me*' (Jer 24:7). Sometimes, for the objective role, a long verbal suffix (-*ēhû* rather than -*ô*) is used for the third-person masculine and an energic verbal suffix for the second-person masculine (-*kka* < -*nka*; cf. 31.7.2).[10]

3. לְהוֹצִאֵהוּ   to take *him* out
Jer 39:14

4. לְיַסְּרֶךָ   to discipline *you*
Deut 4:36

36.1.2   Meaning

a   The infinitive construct is a true infinitive, a verb and a noun, and thus a form without necessary restriction as to agency. As a verbal noun the infinitive may function where a nominal constituent might be expected or as a verbal predicator; it may function in both ways at the same time. It is best construed nominally (36.2) if it is used (1) absolutely, or (2) in the construct state, or (3) with a pronominal suffix without an additional object or prepositional phrase. On the other hand, it is best construed as a verbal predicator (36.3) if it governs an object or prepositional phrase. The infinitive occurs often in the genitive with prepositions, and with the preposition לְ an extensive range of uses has developed. Rarely it seems to take the place of a finite verb, notably after לְ.

36.2   Nominal Uses

36.2.1   Syntactic Features

a   The basic syntactic features of nouns are relevant to the infinitive construct when it is positioned as a noun, as it usually is, and so are some verbal features, such as negation.[11] We begin with the nominal categories of case frame and definiteness.

---

23 (1982) 67–84, at 72–76. In Mishnaic and later Hebrew, only the infinitive construct with *l* is used; see M. H. Segal, *A Grammar of Mishnaic Hebrew* (Oxford: Clarendon, 1927) 165–66; and W. J. Van Bekkum, "The Origins of the Infinitive in Rabbinical Hebrew," *Journal of Semitic Studies* 28 (1983) 247–72.

9. Thus *kotběnî* 'writing to me' versus *kotbî* 'my writ-

ing,' but *kotbô* 'writing to him, his writing.' See *LHS* 118. Mishnaic Hebrew eliminates this source of ambiguity: "The pronominal suffixes . . . are . . . always of an objective force"; Segal, *Mishnaic Hebrew*, 166.

10. For other examples of -*kkā*, see Deut 23:5, Job 33:32 (all three are pausal).

11. Other verbal features are treated in 36.3.1.

The infinitive construct can represent every nominal part of a clause. In a nomina-   b
tive frame, it is usually found in a verbless clause, as subject (## 1–4)[12] or predicate (# 5).
The predicate is masculine even if the infinitive subject has a feminine form (## 1–2). It is
appropriate to translate an infinitive construct with an English gerund in rare cases, such
as these.

1.   לֹא־טוֹב הֱיוֹת הָאָדָם לְבַדּוֹ   *The being* of the man alone is not *good* (i.e., It is
                                           not *good* for hā'ādām *to be* alone).
                                           Gen 2:18

2.   רַב־לָכֶם שֶׁבֶת בָּהָר הַזֶּה: Too much for you (is the) *staying* at this mountain
                                           (i.e., You *have stayed* at this mountain too long).
                                           Deut 1:6

3.   וְלָנוּ הַסְגִּירוֹ בְּיַד הַמֶּלֶךְ:   To us will be *the turning* him *over* into the king's
                                           hand (i.e., It will be our responsibility *to hand* him
                                           over to the king).
                                           1 Sam 23:20

4.   מַה־טּוֹב לָכֶם הַמְשֹׁל בָּכֶם   What is good for you—that (the) *ruling* over you be
      שִׁבְעִים אִישׁ   seventy men (i.e., that seventy men *rule* over you). . . .
                                           Judg 9:2

5.   וְזֶה הַחִלָּם לַעֲשׂוֹת   And this is *the beginning* of them to do (i.e., And this
                                           is what they *have begun* to do).
                                           Gen 11:6

The infinitive occurs as a genitive after a preposition or a noun in the construct   c
state; we consider its use with prepositions separately (36.2.2). After a noun in the construct state (## 6–9) it is also often best translated not by a gerund but by some other
construction. In ## 8–9 the infinitives govern direct objects.

6.   בֶּן הַכּוֹת הָרָשָׁע   a son *of being smitten* is the guilty man (i.e., the guilty
                                           man *deserves to be smitten*)
                                           Deut 25:2

7.   אֵשֶׁת לֵדָה   a woman *of childbearing* (i.e., a woman *in labor*)
                                           Jer 13:21

8.   עֵת הֵאָסֵף הַמִּקְנֶה   time *for* the *gathering of the cattle* (i.e., time for the
                                           cattle *to be gathered*)
                                           Gen 29:7

9.   יוֹם הֻלֶּדֶת אֶת־פַּרְעֹה   the day *of the being born* the Pharaoh (i.e., on
                                           Pharaoh's *birthday*)
                                           Gen 40:20

12. For other examples, see Ps 17:3; Prov 16:19, 17:26;   quasi-adverbial example, see 2 Sam 15:20 (təmôl bô'ēkā,
for the infinitive in a construct phrase, see Isa 7:13; for a   'Your coming was yesterday, i.e., you came yesterday').

d   In an accusative frame, infinitives construct are common as objects or as adverbial accusatives. The infinitive may occur as a goal word with a verb; this construction is customarily called a *verbal complement* because the infinitive is an obligatory constituent to "complete" the situation of the verb (## 10–12).

10.   לֹא־תֹסֵף תֵּת־כֹּחָהּ לָךְ   It will not *add giving* of its strength to you (i.e., *will* no *longer give* its strength). Gen 4:12

11.   לֹא נוּכַל דַּבֵּר אֵלֶיךָ   We are un*able to speak* to you. Gen 24:50

12.   אָחֵל תֵּת פַּחְדְּךָ   I will *begin to put terror* of you. . . . Deut 2:25

Other verbs that govern verbal complements include אבה 'to be willing' (Deut 2:30, 10:10), בקש *Piel* 'to seek' (Exod 4:24), ידע 'to know (how)' (1 Kgs 3:7), מאן 'to refuse' (Num 20:21), נתן 'to allow, cause' (Num 20:21).[13] When the infinitive construct occurs with verbs which have a distinctly adverbial force (denoting place, time, manner, etc.),[14] it is best construed as an *adverbial accusative* (## 13–15); the construction is usually to be translated by rendering the infinitive as a finite verb and the finite verb or participle by an adverb.[15]

13.   עַתָּה הִסְכַּלְתָּ עֲשׂוֹ׃   Now you have played a fool *with respect to doing* (it) (i.e., you *have done* foolishly). Gen 31:28

14.   מַדּוּעַ מִהַרְתֶּן בֹּא הַיּוֹם׃   Why did you hasten *with respect to coming* today (i.e., why *did* you *come* so quickly today)? Exod 2:18

15.   וּמֵטִב נַגֵּן   one who does well *with respect to playing* (i.e., one who *plays* well) Ezek 33:32

e   As a substantive the infinitive construct may be *definite*, occurring not only with suffixes but also with the article, כֹּל (notably in late Biblical Hebrew), etc.

16.   כָּל־כְּלֵי הַשָּׁרֵת   all the articles (used) *for (the) ministering*[16] Num 4:12

17.   כָּל־הִתְנַדֵּב׃   *all* (of) the freewill offering(s) Ezra 1:6

18.   עֵץ הַדַּעַת טוֹב וָרָע׃   the tree of *the knowing* of good and evil Gen 2:9

---

13. See GB 2. 54–55 (§ 14d*) for other relevant verbs.
14. Often denominatives in *Piel* or *Hiphil*.

15. For other relevant verbs, see GB 2. 54–55 (§ 14d*).
16. The phrase occurs without the article in 2 Chr 24:14.

The substantival quality of the infinitive construct varies. Some infinitives function f
entirely as substantives: דַּ֫עַת 'knowledge,' שְׂחוֹק 'laughter,' הִתְיַחֵשׂ 'enrollment.'[17] Other
infinitives, closer to their origins in the verbal system, are used as unmarked forms in
striking ways. Active infinitives may have a passive sense (## 19–20), and the personal
reference of some forms may be surprising (## 21–22).

19.	וַיְהִי הַשַּׁ֫עַר לִסְגּוֹר	The gate was about *to be shut.* Josh 2:5
20.	נִמְכַּ֫רְנוּ . . . לְהַשְׁמִיד	For we have been sold . . . *to be destroyed.* Esth 7:4
21.	לֹא־יֵעָשֶׂה כֵן בִּמְקוֹמֵ֫נוּ לָתֵת	It is not done in our land *to give* (i.e., *that we give*). . . . Gen 29:26
22.	הַרְאֹתְךָ אֶת־כֹּחִי	*to show* you (i.e., *that I might show* you) my strength Exod 9:16

The *negative* with the infinitive construct is mostly (לְ)בִּלְתִּי (rarely בְּלִי), a nominal g
form with the archaic genitive ending î (# 23).[18] בְּלֹא is used, essentially with the meaning
'without' (# 24). In late Hebrew one finds וְלֹא לְ,[19] אֵין לְ,[20] and אֵין.[21]

23.	אֲשֶׁר צִוִּיתִיךָ לְבִלְתִּי אֲכָל־ מִמֶּ֫נּוּ	of which I have commanded you *not to eat* Gen 3:11
24.	בְּלֹא רְאוֹת	*without seeing* (him) Num 35:23

With Prepositions
36.2.2

"The most important use of the infinitive construct," as Ernst Jenni notes, "is its use a
after prepositions in place of a subordinate clause (with conjunction and finite verb)." He
compares the following examples.[22]

1a.	עַד־בּוֹא אֲדֹנָיו אֶל־בֵּיתוֹ:	*until the coming* of his lord into his house (i.e., *until his lord comes* home) Gen 39:16
1b.	עַד אֲשֶׁר־אָבֹא אֶל־אֲדֹנִי	*until I come* to my lord Gen 33:14

17. See GB 2. 55 (§ 14e).
18. See Joüon § 124e / p. 360. The form *biltî* occurs 112 times (SA/THAT).
19. For examples, see 1 Chr 5:1, 2 Chr 12:12.
20. For an example, see 2 Chr 5:11.
21. For an example, see 2 Chr 20:25; for ʾyn with ʿôd 'no longer,' see Mal 2:13.
22. *LHS* 119. The infinitive construct with *b* and *k* is rarer in late Biblical Hebrew, while that with *l* is more common; see R. Polzin, *Late Biblical Hebrew: Toward an Historical Typology of Biblical Hebrew Prose* (Missoula: Scholars Press, 1976) 45–46, 60–61.

These temporal clauses are equivalent in sense, and, since the gerund construction is awkward in English, the first construction is best translated like the second, employing a subordinate clause construction.

b   The preposition used most commonly with infinitives is לְ, and for this reason, we discuss it separately (36.2.3). The construction occurs with every preposition, but most frequently with בְּ and כְּ, especially with a temporal sense. With the infinitive construct, בְּ denotes in general the temporal proximity of one event to another, כְּ more specifically the more immediately preceding time.[23]

2.	בֶּן־שְׁלֹשִׁים שָׁנָה דָוִד בְּמָלְכוֹ	David was thirty years old *when* he *became king.* 2 Sam 5:4
3.	וַיְהִי כְמָלְכוֹ הִכָּה אֶת־כָּל־בֵּית יָרָבְעָם	*Right when* he (Baasha) *became king* he killed off the whole house of Jeroboam. 1 Kgs 15:29
4.	בְּבוֹא־אֵלָיו נָתָן הַנָּבִיא כַּאֲשֶׁר־בָּא אֶל־בַּת־שָׁבַע׃	*when* the prophet Nathan *came* to him right after he had gone into Bathsheba Ps 51:2

The most common infinitive clauses are, as noted, *temporal*, involving בְּ (## 2, 4, 5), כְּ (## 3, 6, 7), עד (## 1a, 8), אחר and אחרי (# 9), and מן (# 10).[24] Another group of clauses denotes logical relations, specifying a cause or a goal. *Causal* clauses are governed by בְּ (# 11), מן (# 12), יען (# 13), and על (# 14). *Final* or result clauses are governed by למען (# 15). There are two negative clause types, *separative* in מן (# 16) and *concessive* ('although') in על (# 17). Thus, בְּ may be temporal (## 2, 4, 5) or causal (# 11); על may be causal (# 14) or concessive (# 17); and מן may be temporal (# 10), causal (# 12), or separative (# 16);[25] the rest of the prepositions have only one major role in infinitive clauses.

5.	וַיְהִי בִּהְיוֹתָם בַּשָּׂדֶה	and *while* they *were* in the field Gen 4:8
6.	וַיְהִי כִּרְאֹת אֶת־הַנֶּזֶם . . . וַיָּבֹא אֶל־הָאִישׁ	*When* he *had seen* the ring . . . he went out to the man. Gen 24:30
7.	כְּבוֹא הַשֶּׁמֶשׁ	*when* the sun *sets* Deut 16:6
8.	עַד־בֹּאֲכֶם עַד־הַמָּקוֹם הַזֶּה׃	*until* you *reached* this place Deut 1:31

---

23. *LHS* 119.

24. On the prevalence of infinitives construct in Deuteronomy and thus in the examples here, see C. H. Miller, "The Infinitive Construct in the Lawbooks of the Old Testament," *Catholic Biblical Quarterly* 32 (1970) 222–26. On temporal clauses with ʿm in Qumranic Hebrew, see E.

Qimron, *The Hebrew of the Dead Sea Scrolls* (Atlanta: Scholars Press, 1986) 73–74.

25. In Gen 4:13 (36.2.1 # 18) it is not clear whether the sense is separative or comparative: *gādôl ʿăwōnî minnaśōʾ*, 'My guilt is (too) great *for bearing*' or '. . . is too great *to bear*.'

9.	אַחֲרֵי הַכֹּתוֹ אֵת סִיחֹן	*after* he *had defeated* Sihon Deut 1:4
10.	מֵהָחֵל חֶרְמֵשׁ בַּקָּמָה	*from* the time you *begin* to put sickle to harvest Deut 16:9
11.	בְּשִׂנְאַת יהוה אֹתָ֫נוּ	*because* YHWH *hates* us Deut 1:27
12.	כִּי מֵאַהֲבַת יהוה אֶתְכֶם	*because* YHWH *loved* you Deut 7:8
13.	יַ֫עַן מָאָסְכֶם	*because* you *refused* Isa 30:12
14.	עַל־אָמְרֵךְ	*because* you *say* Jer 2:35
15.	לְמַ֫עַן תִּתּוֹ בְיָדֶךָ	*so as to hand* him over to you Deut 2:30
16.	מִתֵּת לְאַחַד מֵהֶם	*so that* he *will* not *give* to one of them Deut 28:55
17.	עַל־דַּעְתְּךָ	*although* you *know* Job 10:7

With the Preposition ל

The combination of *l* + *infinitive construct* is common in a variety of uses.[26] Some **a** are similar to those of the infinitive without preposition, while others are specialized along the lines of infinitive clauses with ב, כ, and other prepositions. The special role of this combination is indicated by the non-*raphe* status of the opening of the second syllable, *liktob* not *liktob*.

The combination can be found in any *nominal* role in a clause.[27] In a nominative **b** frame, it is usually used as a subject, in verbless clauses (## 1–2) or in clauses with היה (## 3–4).

1.	טוֹב לְהֹדוֹת לַיהוָה	*To praise* YHWH is good. Ps 92:2
2.	וְאִם רַע בְּעֵינֵיכֶם לַעֲבֹד אֶת־ יהוה	If it is evil in your eyes *to worship* YHWH.... Josh 24:15
3.	כִּי מֵאֵת יהוה הָיְתָה לְחַזֵּק אֶת־ לִבָּם	Because from YHWH was *the hardening* (of) their heart (i.e., because YHWH *hardened*).... Josh 11:20

---

26. See I. Soisalon-Soinenen, "Der Infinitivus construc-tus mit ל im Hebräischen," *Vetus Testamentum* 22 (1972)

82–90; cf. n. 22 on late Biblical Hebrew.
27. Except in a genitive role.

| 4. | כִּי לֹא הָיְתָה מֵהַמֶּלֶךְ לְהָמִית אֶת־אַבְנֵר | the killing (of) Abner was not from the king
2 Sam 3:37 |

Infinitives with *l* can also serve as *verbal complements*, supplying a verb to "complete" the main finite verb (## 5–9). Some finite verbs generally govern complements in לְ (e.g., ירא, # 5), while others can govern infinitives with or without לְ (e.g., מאן, # 6; cf. 36.2.1d). Rarely an infinitive with לְ serves as an *adverbial* after a noun (## 10–11).[28]

5.	יָרֵא לָשֶׁבֶת בְּצוֹעַר	He *was afraid to stay* in Zoar. Gen 19:30
6.	וַיְמָאֵן לְהִתְנַחֵם	He *refused to be comforted.* Gen 37:35
7.	וְאִם־לֹא יַחְפֹּץ הָאִישׁ לָקַחַת אֶת־יְבִמְתּוֹ	If a man *does* not *want to marry* his brother's widow. . . . Deut 25:7
8.	יוֹדֵעַ לַעֲשׂוֹת בַּזָּהָב־וּבַכֶּסֶף	one who *knows* [how] *to work* in gold and silver 2 Chr 2:13
9.	הִפְגִּעוּ בַמֶּלֶךְ לְבִלְתִּי שְׂרֹף אֶת־הַמְּגִלָּה	They *urged* the king not *to burn* the scroll. Jer 36:25
10.	גַּם־מָקוֹם לָלוּן:	as well as *room to spend the night* Gen 24:25
11.	כִּי הוּא הַנֹּתֵן לְךָ כֹּחַ לַעֲשׂוֹת חָיִל	For it is he who gives you *the strength to produce wealth.* Deut 8:18

c   Infinitive clauses with לְ are of various types. Some of these types are analogous to those formed with other prepositions, that is, purpose, result, and temporal clauses. Others reflect the distinctiveness of the *l* combination, that is, gerundive, modal, and immanent clauses.

d   Purpose, result, and temporal clauses or phrases can be seen as serving the role of verbal complements, though with complements of a type that can also be specified by a subordinate clause with a finite verb. Infinitive purpose or final clauses (# 12a) are similar to purpose clauses with finite verbs (# 12b).[29]

| 12a. | לִשְׁמֹעַ אֵת חָכְמַת שְׁלֹמֹה | *in order to listen to* the wisdom of Solomon
1 Kgs 5:14 |
| 12b. | לְמַעַן יִשְׁמְעוּ כָּל־עֲדַת בְּנֵי יִשְׂרָאֵל: | *in order that* the whole Israelite community *will listen* (to him)
Num 27:20 |

28. This use may be blurred with the epexegetical use.
29. *LHS* 119–20. On *hinnēh* with infinitive purpose clauses, see D. J. McCarthy, "The Uses of *wᵉhinnēh* in Biblical Hebrew," *Biblica* 61 (1980) 330–42, at 339–40.

The line of demarcation between the purpose infinitive clause and the complementary infinitive is somewhat blurred (# 13). (With verbs of commanding, the infinitive is best taken as an object accusative.)

13a.　　　וְלָבָן הָלַךְ לִגְזֹז אֶת־צֹאנֽוֹ　　　Laban went *to shear* his sheep.
Gen 31:19

13b.　　　וַיֵּרֶד יהוה לִרְאֹת אֶת־הָעִיר　　　Yʜwʜ went down *to see* the city.
Gen 11:5

The subject of the infinitive may be subject of the main verb (## 12a, 13a, 14) or a noun not involved in that clause (# 15).

14.　　　וַיֵּצֵא הָאֱמֹרִי . . . לִקְרַאתְכֶם　　　The Amorite came out . . . *to confront* you.
Deut 1:44

15.　　　שִׂים־לְךָ שְׁנַיִם דְּרָכִים לָבוֹא חֶרֶב　　　So now, mark out two roads for the sword . . . *to come*.
Ezek 21:24

Result clauses express a consequence of the main verb ('and so; so that'; ## 16–19).

16.　　　לַעֲשׂוֹת הָרַע בְּעֵינֵי יהוה לְהַכְעִיסֽוֹ׃　　　by doing evil in Yʜwʜ's eyes *and so provoking* him
Deut 9:18

17.　　　וַאדֹנִי חָכָם . . . לָדַעַת אֶת־כָּל־אֲשֶׁר בָּאָֽרֶץ׃　　　My lord is wise . . . *so that* he *knows* everything in the world.
2 Sam 14:20

18.　　　לָמָה אַתֶּם עֹשִׂים רָעָה גְדוֹלָה אֶל־נַפְשֹׁתְכֶם . . . לְבִלְתִּי הוֹתִיר לָכֶם שְׁאֵרִית׃　　　Why do you bring great disaster on yourselves . . . *and so leave* yourselves without a remnant?
Jer 44:7

19.　　　מַדּוּעַ מָצָאתִי חֵן בְּעֵינֶיךָ לְהַכִּירֵנִי　　　Why have I found such favor in your eyes *that* you *notice* me?
Ruth 2:10

Temporal clauses in ל can mark a point in time or an extent in time. Signaling a point is chiefly associated with the verb *pny* 'to turn,' yielding the expressions לפנת בקר 'at the turning of (the) day' (## 20–21) and לפנת ערב 'at the turning of evening' (## 22). Extent in time can be marked with ל (# 23), and, with עד, this pattern can also be used with spatial reference (## 24–25).[30]

---

30. The spatial extension of meaning reflects the language of tours and so is ultimately temporal; cf. the language of English tours such as 'You walk *until* you see a big tree, *then* you turn. . . .' See M. O'Connor, "The Grammar of Finding Your Way in Palmyrene Aramaic," *Fucus:*　　　*A Semitic/Afrasian Gathering in Remembrance of Albert Ehrman*, ed. Y. L. Arbeitman (Amsterdam: John Benjamins, 1988) 353–69. Thus the sense in # 24 (and similar phrases) is 'up to the point where you (*or* one) enters (the area of) Hamath.'

20. וַיָּ֫שָׁב הַיָּם לִפְנוֹת בֹּ֫קֶר לְאֵיתָנוֹ   The sea went back to its flow *at daybreak*.
                                               Exod 14:27

21. וַתָּבֹא הָאִשָּׁה לִפְנוֹת הַבֹּ֫קֶר   The woman came in *at daybreak* and collapsed at the
     וַתִּפֹּל פֶּ֫תַח . . . עַד־הָאוֹר: door . . . (remaining there) until (it was) light.
                                               Judg 19:26

22. וַיֵּצֵא . . . בַּשָּׂדֶה לִפְנוֹת עָ֫רֶב   He went out . . . to the field *at evening time*.
                                               Gen 24:63

23. וַיִּֽתְנַבְּאוּ עַד לַעֲלוֹת הַמִּנְחָה   They prophesied *until* (the time of) *the offering* of
                                               the sacrifice.
                                               1 Kgs 18:29

24. עַד לְבוֹא חֲמָת: up *to the entering* of Hamath
                                               Josh 13:5

25. וְלַמִּזְרָח יָשַׁב עַד־לְבוֹא מִדְבָּ֫רָה   To the east he occupied the land *up to the entering* of
                                               the steppe.
                                               1 Chr 5:9

Temporal phrases or clauses can complement verbs that denote a period of time drawing near (קרב; # 26)[31] or being completed (כלה; ## 27–28).

26. וַיִּקְרְבוּ יְמֵי־יִשְׂרָאֵל לָמוּת   The time *drew near* for Israel *to die*.
                                               Gen 47:29

27. וּכְכַלּוֹת לְהַעֲלוֹת כָּרְעוּ   *Having completed* (the time of) *sacrifice*, they
                                               knelt.
                                               2 Chr 29:29

28. וְכַלָּתוֹ . . . לָלַת   *the* (time of) *delivering* being completed
                                               1 Sam 4:19

e   As a *gerundive, explanatory or epexegetical*, the construction ל + *infinitive* often explains the circumstances or nature of a preceding action. In developing the thought of a finite verb it resembles the Latin gerundive (e.g., *faciendo* 'doing'), the English "in [do]ing something." The construction is found frequently in the Qumranic Hebrew;[32] there and in Biblical Hebrew[33] it is used in oratorical phrasing. Under this heading may be included the very frequent לֵאמֹר, used to introduce direct discourse after verbs of saying and of mental activity (thinking, praying, etc.).

29. שָׁמוֹר אֶת־יוֹם הַשַּׁבָּת לְקַדְּשׁוֹ   Keep the Sabbath day *by sanctifying* it.
                                               Deut 5:12

---

31. Note a comparable verbless clause in Isa 56:1.
32. R. Meyer, *Hebräische Grammatik* (Berlin: de Gruy-

ter, 1969), 2. 130; cf. Qimron, *Dead Sea Scrolls*, 72–73.
33. Joüon § 124o / pp. 363–64.

30.   כִּי תִשְׁמַע בְּקוֹל יהוה . . .   If you obey YHWH . . . *by keeping* all his
       לִשְׁמֹר אֶת־כָּל־מִצְוֹתָיו . . .   commandments . . . *by doing* what is right. . . .
       לַעֲשׂוֹת הַיָּשָׁר   Deut 13:19

31.   הֵן הָאָדָם הָיָה כְּאַחַד מִמֶּנּוּ   *Hāʾādām* has become as one of us *in knowing* good
       לָדַעַת טוֹב וָרָע   and evil.
                            Gen 3:22

32.   בַּמֶּה יְזַכֶּה־נַּעַר אֶת־אָרְחוֹ   How can a young man keep his way pure?
       לִשְׁמֹר כִּדְבָרֶךָ:   *By living* according to your word.
                            Ps 119:9

The *modal* senses of *l* clauses are found in verbless clauses or clauses with יֵשׁ or   f
אֵין.[34] Usually a prepositional phrase is also used, generally with *l* (to indicate possibility
or permission; ## 33–38) or *ʿl* (to indicate obligation or permission; ## 39–40), though
other prepositions are found, too (## 41–43). Modal clauses with no prepositional phrase
tend to be used in poetry (## 44–45).

33.   מֶה לַעֲשׂוֹת לָךְ הֲיֵשׁ לְדַבֶּר־לָךְ   What can be done for you? *Can* we *speak* on your
       אֶל־הַמֶּלֶךְ   behalf to the king?
                            2 Kgs 4:13

34.   מַה־לְּךָ לְסַפֵּר חֻקָּי   What *right* have you *to recite* my statutes?
                            Ps 50:16

35.   לֹא לָכֶם לְהִלָּחֵם בָּזֹאת   You *are* not *to fight* in this (battle).
                            2 Chr 20:17

36.   לֹא־לְךָ עֻזִּיָּהוּ לְהַקְטִיר   It is not *right* for you, Uzziah, *to burn* incense.
                            2 Chr 26:18

37.   יֵשׁ לַיהוה לָתֶת לְךָ הַרְבֵּה מִזֶּה: YHWH *can give* you much more than that.
                            2 Chr 25:9

38.   וְאֵין־לָנוּ אִישׁ לְהָמִית בְּיִשְׂרָאֵל   None of us has *a right to kill* an Israelite citizen.
                            2 Sam 21:4

39.   וְעָלַי לָתֶת לְךָ עֲשָׂרָה כָסֶף   Then I *would have had to give* you ten shekels of
                            silver.
                            2 Sam 18:11

40.   עָלָיו אֵין לְהוֹסִיף וּמִמֶּנּוּ אֵין   Nothing *can be added* to it and nothing *can be taken*
       לִגְרֹעַ   from it.
                            Qoh 3:14

41.   אִם־יֵשׁ אֶת־נַפְשְׁכֶם לִקְבֹּר אֶת־   If you are *ready to bury* my dead. . . .
       מֵתִי   Gen 23:8

42.   וְאֵין עִמְּךָ לְהִתְיַצֵּב: And no one *can stand* against you.
                            2 Chr 20:6

---

34. A precative use of *l* + *infinitive* is common at Qumran; see Qimron, *Dead Sea Scrolls*, 70–72.

43.   כִּי אֵין זוּלָתְךָ לִגְאוֹל   And none has *the right to redeem* (it) except you.
                                      Ruth 4:4

44.   מַה־לַּעֲשׂוֹת עוֹד לְכַרְמִי   What more *could* I *do* for my vineyard?
                                      Isa 5:4

45.   הָס כִּי לֹא לְהַזְכִּיר בְּשֵׁם   Hush, we *must* not *mention* the name.
                                      Amos 6:10

g   The *immanent* sense of the infinitive with *l* describes a non-perfective event, usually one "about to" happen (*tempus instans*); the clause may be verbless (## 46–48) or governed by a form of היה, if the reference is to the past (# 49).[35]

46.   יהוה לְהוֹשִׁיעֵנִי   YHWH *will save* me.
                            Isa 38:20

47.   גַּם־בָּבֶל לִנְפֹּל   Babylon *will fall.*
                            Jer 51:49

48.   שֹׁמֵר תְּבוּנָה לִמְצֹא־טוֹב׃   He who cherishes understanding *will find* what is good.
                                        Prov 19:8

49.   וַיְהִי הַשֶּׁמֶשׁ לָבוֹא   The sun was *about to set.*
                                  Gen 15:12

36.3   Verbal Uses

36.3.1   Syntactic Features

a   An infinitive construct can manifest its verbal character in various ways.[36] It may be associated with its subject only (## 1–2) or its object only (## 3–5) or a preposition only (## 6–7). Less often both subject and object follow the infinitive; the object may be unmarked (# 8) or signaled by את (# 9) or a prepositional phrase may be used (# 10; cf. 10.2.1c–d).[37]

1.   לָנֻס שָׁמָּה הָרֹצֵחַ   so that *the killer* can flee there
                              Num 35:6

2.   לָמוּת שָׁם אֲנַחְנוּ וּבְעִירֵנוּ׃   so that *we and our cattle* might die there
                                            Num 20:4

---

35. If the reference is to the future, the clause is either descriptive (e.g., Ezek 30:16) or jussive (e.g., Ps 109:13). C. R. Krahmalkov alleges that in this use "the infinitive expresses neither purpose nor obligation but is . . . a true periphrasis of the imperfect," citing # 48, Hos 9:13, and Qoh 3:15; see "The Periphrastic Future Tense in Hebrew and Phoenician," *Rivista degli Studi Orientali* 61 (1987) 73–80, at 73.

36. Many of the examples cited above are relevant here

and may be consulted. In Biblical Hebrew, the nouns governed by an infinitive follow it, while in Aramaic and in Qumranic Hebrew the opposite order is attested for objects; see Qimron, *Dead Sea Scrolls,* 74.

37. For an infinitive with two objects, note *harʾōtəkā ʾet-kōḥî* 'that (I) make *you* see *my strength*' (Exod 9:16). The object of an infinitive may itself be an infinitive governing an object with ʾt, e.g., *hamʿaṭ qaḥtēk ʾet-ʾîšî,* 'Isn't it enough that you took my husband?' (Gen 30:15).

3.	לְיַסְּרָה אֶתְכֶם	to punish *you*[38] Lev 26:18
4.	לְיִרְאָה אֹתִי	to fear *me* Deut 4:10
5.	לְהָמִית אֶת־דָּוִד	to kill *David* 1 Sam 19:1
6.	לְנַשֵּׁק לְבָנַי וְלִבְנֹתָי	to kiss *my sons and daughters* Gen 31:28
7.	מַה־טּוֹב לָכֶם הַמְשֹׁל בָּכֶם	What is better for you—that the ruling *over you*. . . ? Judg 9:2
8.	בְּיוֹם עֲשׂוֹת יהוה אֱלֹהִים אֶרֶץ וְשָׁמָיִם׃	when *Yhwh God* made *earth and heaven* Gen 2:4
9.	בְּשָׁמְעוֹ אֶת־הַדְּבָרִים הָאֵלֶּה	when *he* heard *these words* 1 Sam 11:6
10.	בְּפִגְעוֹ־בוֹ	when *he* meets *him* Num 35:19

As a Finite Form

Sometimes in poetic speech or in late Hebrew the infinitive construct after וְל is used   a
as an equivalent of a finite verb (or of a nominal construction) to represent a situation
successive to that represented by a finite verb (# 1) or participle (# 2).[39]

1.	וְאָרַח לְחֶבְרָה עִם־פֹּעֲלֵי אָוֶן וְלָלֶכֶת עִם־אַנְשֵׁי־רֶשַׁע׃	He keeps company with evildoers; he *associates* with wicked men. Job 34:8
2. . . .	וְרַבִּים מֵהַכֹּהֲנִים . . . בֹּכִים וְרַבִּים . . . לְהָרִים קוֹל׃	Many of the priests . . . were weeping . . . and many . . . *were shouting.* Ezra 3:12

In many of its uses the infinitive construct is continued by a finite verb.

3.	עַל־עָזְבָם אֶת־תּוֹרָתִי . . . וְלֹא־ שָׁמְעוּ בְקוֹלִי	because they *have forsaken* my law . . . and have not obeyed my voice Jer 9:12

---

38. The shape of the feminine endings here and in # 4
reinforces the Masoretic conviction that such forms are

not construct.
39. Jouön § 124p / p. 364.

37

Participles

37.1   Form and Meaning

a   The participle is so called because it *participates* in both nominal and verbal characteristics; it is a non-finite verb form used as a noun (specifically, as an adjective).[1] English has two participles, the present participle (in *-ing*; used to form the progressive verbs, # 1, and in noun clauses, # 2) and the past participle (in *-ed*; used to form the perfective verbs with the auxiliary 'have,' # 3, and passive verbs with the auxiliary 'be,' # 4). According to traditional grammarians, the *-ing* form in English can serve either as a participle, an adjectival form (## 5–6), or as a gerund, a substantival form (## 7–8, cf. # 2). Modern grammarians sometimes question the usefulness of this distinction.[2] The various uses of the two participles depend on semantic features as well as syntactic patterns.

> 1. Abraham *was walking* from Ur.
> 2. *Walking* from Ur was pleasant.
> 3. He *had closed up* his house.
> 4. He *was persuaded* to leave.
> 5. *Running* camels are dangerous.
> 6. I watched the camels *running* from Ur.
> 7. *Running* camels is dangerous.
> 8. I watched the camels' *running* from Ur.

---

1. R. H. Robins, P. Swiggers, and A. Martinet in *MPD* 21, 26–27, 41, 44, 50, 59, 81.

2. R. Quirk et al., *A Grammar of Contemporary English* (Harlox, Essex: Longman, 1972) 135.

The infinitives of Hebrew correspond to the English gerund and the participles to the English (adjectival) participle.

Hebrew has two kinds of participles, active and passive; the passive feature of the derived stems denoting passive voice (i.e., *Niphal, Pual, Hophal*) is independent of this distinction in participles, and the occurrence of a passive participle in a given stem is not entirely predictable. The *Qal* masculine singular participles have these forms: active fientive קֹטֵל and stative קָטֵל, passive קָטוּל (rarely קְטָל or קְטוֹל).[3] Participles are inflected for number and gender and are used in both absolute and construct states; in the absolute they have a more verbal character and may govern nouns.

The active participle has four principal functions in Biblical Hebrew: as a substantive (# 9; cf. # 12), an adjective (## 10–11), a relative (# 12), and a predicate (# 13).[4] The relative use is the most clearly intermediate form, both an adjective and a predicate. The passive participle is rare as a substantive, but it is common in the other functions.

9.	וַיְהִי בִּימֵי שְׁפֹט הַשֹּׁפְטִים	When *the šopetim* judged. . . . Ruth 1:1
10.	וְנָתַתָּ לְעַבְדְּךָ לֵב שֹׁמֵעַ	So give your servant a *hearing* heart. 1 Kgs 3:9
11.	לֹא־הָיָה דָּבָר נֶעְלָם מִן־הַמֶּלֶךְ	Nothing was *hidden* from the king. 1 Kgs 10:3
12.	עַל־הָרֹעִים הָרֹעִים אֶת־עַמִּי	against the shepherds *who tend* my people Jer 23:2
13.	אָנָה אַתָּה הֹלֵךְ	Where *are* you *going*? Zech 2:6

Does one "meaning" attach to all these functions? A. B. Davidson, representing a traditional view, claims that the participle denotes linear aspect: "The [participle] or *nomen agentis* . . . presents the person or subj[ect] in the continuous exercise or exhibition of the action or condition denoted by the verb."[5] Along the same lines, S. R. Driver carefully distinguishes this linear aspect from the broken, repetitive aspect of the non-perfective conjugation: "*Mere* continuance in the sense of duration *without progress* is never expressed by the imp[erfect]. . . . The participle is the form which indicates continued action. . . . Thus while the imp[erfect] multiplies an action, the participle prolongs it."[6]

This presentation needs qualifying. One can scarcely speak of the purely substantival participle (*nomen agentis*) in terms of action (see 37.2); in this use the *qōtēl* form points not so much to an action as to a person. Further, the stative participle functions as an adjective, connoting a fixed and permanent quality; as M. Greenberg states: "Stative

---

3. The stative active *qātēl* form (e.g., *kābēd*) is often called a verbal adjective; see, e.g., GKC § 116b / p. 356. For passive *quttāl* forms, note, e.g., *ʾukkal* 'consumed' (Exod 3:2), for passive *qittôl*, e.g., *yillôd* 'born' (Exod 1:22).

4. *LHS* 93.

5. A. B. Davidson, *Hebrew Syntax* (3d ed.; Edinburgh: T. & T. Clark, 1901) 130.

6. S. R. Driver, *A Treatise on the Use of the Tenses in Hebrew* (3d ed.; Oxford: Clarendon, 1892) 35–36.

participles are pure adjectives."[7] E. Kautzsch claims that the language is "fully conscious of the difference between a state implying action" and one not implying it, for quasi-fientive roots, that is, roots with transitive stative participles (e.g., שָׂנֵא 'to hate') in contrast to intransitive stative roots (e.g., כָּבֵד 'to be heavy'; see 22.2.3), may form a participle not after the stative but after the fientive pattern; only with this form can such roots denote continued activity.[8] Further, progressive aspect is not crucial in the participle's use as a relative. T. O. Lambdin notes that in this use the participle connotes "completed action": "In English, therefore, a relative clause with a perfect or preterite verb is often required in translation" (37.5).[9] The passive participle, too, tends to describe a situation not implying progressive activity but resulting from some earlier action.[10] Finally, the participle is sometimes used where one would expect a finite form. This is especially true in the post-exilic books: "The participle is sometimes used—especially in the later books . . .—where we should expect the action to be divided up into its several parts, and consequently should expect the finite verb."[11]

f   Thus the characterization of the participle as denoting unbroken aspect is true only in the case of the participle's almost purely verbal use as predicative.[12] We cannot abstract from the participle's four functions one basic meaning. If, however, we leave the substantival use aside, we can say that as a verbal adjective the participle tends to describe a state of affairs rather than to present a bare event.

37.2   Substantival Use

a   Some words with the *qōṭēl* pattern (5.2) are used only as nouns, while others are sometimes used as nouns or participles. B. Kedar-Kopfstein has suggested that syntactic, etymological, and semantic considerations are relevant in deciding both when a participle is used substantively (as a *nomen agentis* or actor noun) and the extent of its substantive quality.[13] The parts-of-speech classification of words describes their distribution, that is, their potential for occurring in a clause relative to the occurrence of other words in the same clause (4.2.2). When a participle is related to the other words in a clause in a way which we associate with nouns, it often functions as a *nomen agentis*. Consider this example.

1.   שֹׁפְטִים וְשֹׁטְרִים תִּתֶּן־לְךָ   You shall appoint *šopetim* and *officials.*
Deut 16:18

The two *qōṭēl* nouns could readily be replaced by other nominal forms but not so readily by other verbal forms. On the other hand, in # 2, another verb, in contrast to some other parts of speech, could readily be substituted for שֹׁפֵט.

---

7. Moshe Greenberg, *Introduction to Hebrew* (Englewood Cliffs, New Jersey: Prentice-Hall, 1965) 55.
8. GKC § 116b / p. 356.
9. T. O. Lambdin, *Introduction to Biblical Hebrew* (New York: Scribner, 1971) 158.
10. BL § 361' / p. 278.
11. GKC § 116c / p. 356.

12. GKC § 116b / p. 356.
13. B. Kedar-Kopfstein, "Die Stammbildung *qôṭel* als Übersetzungsproblem," *Zeitschrift für die Alttestamentliche Wissenschaft* 93 (1981) 254–79, at 256; cf. also his "Semantic Aspects of the Pattern *Qôṭēl*," *Hebrew Annual Review* 1 (1977) 155–76.

2.   וְהִגַּ֣דְתִּי ל֔וֹ כִּי־שֹׁפֵ֥ט אֲנִ֛י אֶת־   And I told him that I *would judge* his family forever.
      בֵּית֖וֹ עַד־עוֹלָ֑ם   1 Sam 3:13

Syntax, the distribution of words in a clause or sentence, is decisive in describing the use of a participle.

The relationship of the *qōtēl* pattern and the class of active fientive participles is   b
problematic. "Isolated" *qōtēl* forms (i.e., forms from verbal roots that exist in the *Qal* only in the *qōtēl* form) are best taken as substantives; for example, כֹּהֵן 'priest,' רֹזֵן 'ruler,' שֹׁטֵר 'officer,' נֹקֵד 'sheep-breeder,' etc. Some scholars cite these purely nominal forms in connection with participles.[14] Kedar-Kopfstein argues that the participial character adheres more clearly to forms like שֹׁפֵט 'judge' and יֹצֵר 'potter' because corresponding finite forms are attested.[15] E. König has said that an overgrowth of the more frequent *qōtēl* pattern should be recognized in the case of adjectives like נֹסֵס 'sick (person),' זוֹלֵל 'rubbish,' קֹדֵר 'squalid,' etc.[16] A third class of *qōtēl* forms that do not properly belong among the participles is made up of denominatives; words like בּוֹקֵר 'cowpoke' (from בָּקָר 'cattle'),[17] כֹּרֵם 'vinedresser' (from כֶּ֫רֶם 'vineyard'), יֹגֵב 'farmer' (from יֶגֶב 'field'), שׁוֹעֵר 'gatekeeper' (from שַׁ֫עַר 'gate') possess a clear substantival character.[18] Kedar-Kopfstein points up the distinction between a *qōtēl* form lacking a clear verbal origin from one with a verbal base by contrasting אוֹיֵב with שׂוֹנֵא.

> With אויב the importance lies in the person, therefore it is a substantive in the fullest sense; the signified sense belongs to it uninterruptedly. With שׂונא it is a matter of the deportment and action which characterize a person, perhaps temporarily.[19]

Another group of words can be judged on semantic rather than etymological grounds   c
to be distinct from the *qōtēl* participles.[20] These are terms for professions, for example, יֹצֵר etymologically 'fashioner' becomes the professional 'potter'; צוֹרֵף 'smelter' becomes 'goldsmith'; רֹפֵא 'healer' becomes 'doctor.' Other activities, however, are of a more transitory nature, for example, שׁוֹטֵף 'flooding,' צוֹעֵק 'crying out,' נֹבֵל 'fading.' The profession terms are more substantival than these participial terms for passing phenomena.

Participial Syntax: Accusative and Genitive   37.3

The participle displays its dual participation in verbal and nominal (specifically,   a
adjectival) characteristics in constructions with modifying words. We have seen that nouns are modified by the genitive case and verbs by the accusative case or by a prepositional phrase (see 9.2, 10.2, 11.1). The participle can occur with modifying words in either case frame; it also occurs with both possessive and verbal pronominal suffixes.

---

14. So GKC § 84ᵃs / p. 232.
15. Kedar-Kopfstein, "Stammbildung *qôṭel*," 259.
16. E. König, *Historisch-comparative Syntax der hebräischen Sprache* (Leipzig: Hinrichs, 1897) 128.

17. Only in Amos 7:14 and questioned there.
18. Kedar-Kopfstein, "Stammbildung *qôṭel*," 259.
19. Kedar-Kopfstein, "Stammbildung *qôṭel*," 259.
20. Kedar-Kopfstein, "Stammbildung *qôṭel*," 259.

b   The participle in the *absolute state* can govern an accusative object, an adverbial accusative, or a prepositional phrase; such a participle may be an active fientive participle (with objects: ## 1–2; with prepositional phrases: ## 3–4), a quasi-fientive stative participle (## 5–6), a stative participle (or verbal adjective; with adverbial accusative, ## 7–8), or a passive participle (with adverbial accusative, ## 9–11).

1.	כָּל־הַקֹּרֹת אֹתָם	all that (i.e., the events that) befell *them* Gen 42:29
2.	וְהִנֵּה בָרָק רֹדֵף אֶת־סִיסְרָא	Barak was pursuing *Sisera*. Judg 4:22
3.	יהוה הַדֹּבֵר אֵלֶיהָ	YHWH who spoke *to her* Gen 16:13
4.	נִלְחָמִים עִם־פְּלִשְׁתִּים׃	fighting *with the Philistines* 1 Sam 17:19
5.	וְרִבְקָה אֹהֶבֶת אֶת־יַעֲקֹב׃	But Rebekah (was one who) loved *Jacob*. Gen 25:28
6.	כִּי־יָרֵא אָנֹכִי אֹתוֹ	I fear *him*. Gen 32:12
7.	וּשְׂמֵחִים שִׂמְחָה גְדוֹלָה	rejoicing *with* great *joy* 1 Kgs 1:40
8.	חָפֵץ רֶשַׁע	that has pleasure *in wickedness* Ps 5:5
9.	חָגוּר כְּלֵי מִלְחָמָה׃	armed *with weapons* for battle[21] Judg 18:11
10.	קָרוּעַ כֻּתָּנְתּוֹ	rent *as regards* his *coat* 2 Sam 15:32
11.	לָבֻשׁ בַּדִּים	clothed *in linen*[22] Ezek 9:2

c   In the *construct state*, a participle governs an object or some other specification in the genitive (9.5). The active fientive participle chiefly governs adverbial genitives, for example, objects (## 12–13)[23] and, with verbs of motion, genitives of location (## 14–15), where an accusative (10.2) might be expected. In poetry the genitive may refer to "other specifications (especially of space) which otherwise [viz., in prose] can only be made to depend on the verb in question by means of a preposition" (## 16–18).[24] A quasi-fientive stative participle can govern a genitive (# 19), as can a passive participle. With a passive, the genitive may be of agency (# 20) or instrument (## 21–23). T. O. Lambdin notes,

---

21. Compare similar phrases in Judg 18:16, 17.

22. Note also *hā'îš hallābuš habbadîm* (Ezek 9:3); and M. O'Connor, "The Grammar of Getting Blessed in Tyrian-Sidonian Phoenician," *Rivista di studi fenici* 5

(1977) 5–11, at 10–11.

23. For an example in a longer construct phrase, note *'ereṣ zābat ḥālāb ûdbāš* (Exod 3:8); cf. 1 Kgs 18:19.

24. GKC § 116h / p. 358.

"The addition of a prepositional phrase to express an agent, as in 'the man who was slain by his enemies,' is virtually unknown in Hebrew, but like any adjective it [the passive participle] may be in construct with a following qualifying noun."[25] Other kinds of genitives, especially the epexegetical (9.5.3c), may also follow the passive participle (## 24–26; cf. ## 10–11).

12.	נֹתְנֵי לַחְמִי וּמֵימַי	who give (me) *my bread and my water* Hos 2:7
13.	מְשִׁיבֵי מִלְחָמָה שָׁעְרָה:	those who turn back *the battle* at the gate Isa 28:6
14.	בָּאֵי שַׁעַר־עִירוֹ	who had come *to the gate* of his town Gen 23:10
15.	יֹצְאֵי הַתֵּבָה	that departed *from the ark* Gen 9:10
16.	יוֹרְדֵי־בוֹר	they that go down *into the pit* Isa 38:18
17.	שֹׁכְבֵי קֶבֶר	that lie *in the grave* Ps 88:6
18.	כְּאֵלָה נֹבֶלֶת עָלֶהָ	like an oak fading *in its leaf* Isa 1:30
19.	יְרֵא אֱלֹהִים	one who fears *God*[26] Gen 22:12
20.	מֻכֵּה אֱלֹהִים	smitten *by God* Isa 53:4
21.	וּשְׁדוּפֹת קָדִים	scorched *by the east wind* Gen 41:6
22.	עָרֵיכֶם שְׂרֻפוֹת אֵשׁ	your cities burnt *with fire* Isa 1:7
23.	מְטֹעֲנֵי חָרֶב	those pierced *by the sword* Isa 14:19
24.	קְרֻעֵי בְגָדִים:	rent *in respect of clothes* 2 Sam 13:31
25.	וְהִנֵּה הָאִישׁ לְבֻשׁ הַבַּדִּים	the man clothed *with linen* Ezek 9:11
26.	נְשׂוּי־פֶּשַׁע	forgiven *in respect of sin* Ps 32:1

Just as a participle may be followed by an object in the accusative (the participle   d
being absolute) or by a genitive (the participle being construct), so *suffixes* to the

25. Lambdin, *Introduction to Biblical Hebrew*, 158.   26. The phrase occurs in the plural in Exod 18:21.

participle may be genitive or accusative.[27] The possessive and the accusative suffixes exhibit different forms only in the first-person singular, *-î* possessive, *-[ē]nî* objective.

27. אַיֵּה אֱלוֹהַּ עֹשָׂי   Where is God *my* Maker?[28]
                                Job 35:10

28. הֲלֹא־בַבֶּטֶן עֹשֵׂנִי עָשָׂהוּ   Did not he who made *me* in the womb make him?
                                            Job 31:15

29. אֵין רֹאָנִי   There is none who sees *me*.
                        Isa 47:10

But even here caution is needed: "In fact, this distinction is erased, inasmuch as the possessive suffix *-ī*, according to the analogy of the remaining suffixes, can also assume an objective meaning."[29] This leveling is apparent in the following examples (## 30–32, objective *-ēnî* expected).

30. לֹא־תְשׁוּרֵנִי עֵין רֹאִי   The eye that (now) sees *me* will see me no longer.
                                    Job 7:8

31. כָּל־מֹצְאִי   all who find *me*
                        Gen 4:14

32. קָמַי   those that rise up *against me*[30]
                Ps 18:40

Although the *-î* suffix is more common, a similar confusion may occur with the accusative first-person suffix used as a possessive (contrast עֹשֵׂנִי in Job 32:22 with # 27). The objective use of the suffixes is common (## 33–35); rarely, a participle with a suffix governs another, independent object (## 36–37).

33. מְבָרְכֶיךָ   those that bless *you*
                      Gen 12:3

34. יֹדְעָיו   those who knew *him*
                    Job 42:11

35. הַמַּעֲלֵם   who brought *them* up
                      Isa 63:11

---

27. Note that the MT has *môrîš ᵓōtām* in Deut 18:12, while the Samaritan has *mwryšm*, as does the Qumran Temple Scroll in a synoptic passage. In Qumranic Hebrew, singular participles can govern either an object or possessive suffix, but plural participles can govern only possessive suffixes. See E. Qimron, *The Hebrew of the Dead Sea Scrolls* (Atlanta: Scholars Press, 1986) 76.

28. The use of participial titles for God is especially important in the old poetry of the Pentateuch (e.g., Deut 32:39) and Former Prophets (e.g., 1 Sam 2:6–8) and in some of the prophets (e.g., Amos 4:13, 5:8–9, 9:5–6; Isa 43:1; 44:2, 24; 44:7, 9, 11, 18) and in Job (e.g., 5:9, 9:9–10, 25:2).

29. BL § 48y' / p. 343.

30. Ordinarily *qûm* 'to arise (with hostility against)' governs an object with *ᶜal* or another preposition, but in verse the plural participle ('those who arise against') takes a suffix.

36.   הִנְנִי מַאֲכִילָם ... לַעֲנָה   I will make *them* eat . . . *wormwood*.
                                           Jer 9:14

37.   הַמַּלְבִּשְׁכֶם שָׁנִי   who clothed *you with scarlet*
                                           2 Sam 1:24

Is there a difference between participles with accusative regimens and those with genitive regimens? Grammarians are divided. For example, Kedar-Kopfstein has argued that no distinction exists.[31] In contrast, E. Sellin has claimed that the genitive-governing participles pertain to more enduring situations while accusative- or preposition-governing forms refer to more transitory states. **e**

> By an exhaustive examination of the statistics, Sellin . . . shows that the participle when construed as a *verb* expresses a single and comparatively transitory act, or relates to particular cases, historical facts, and the like, while the participle construed as a *noun* . . . indicates repeated, enduring, or commonly occurring acts, occupations, and thoughts.[32]

In fact, this differentiation is not so straightforward. There are cases in which Sellin's view seems clear (contrast, e.g., ## 1–4, 6–7, but not # 5 or # 8, with ## 12–13, 19, but not # 14 or # 24). A variety of other factors seems to be involved, for example, definiteness (contrast # 11 and # 25), so further study seems warranted.

Adjectival Use   **37.4**

By adjectival is meant the use of a participle in a clause where it could be replaced **a**
by an adjective, either attributive or predicate, rather than by some other part of speech. Since the passive participle has some distinctive features in this function, we analyze the active and passive participles separately.

The modifying *active participle* is usually used as a relative (see 37.5). In some **b**
instances, however, it occurs where an attributive adjective would be found (# 1).

1. כִּי יהוה אֱלֹהֶיךָ אֵשׁ אֹכְלָה הוּא   As for YHWH your God, he is a *consuming* fire.[33]
                                              Deut 4:24

The *passive participle* can be used as either an attributive (# 2)[34] or predicate adjec- **c**
tive (## 3–5).

2.   וּבְיָד חֲזָקָה וּבִזְרוֹעַ נְטוּיָה   by a mighty hand and by an *outstretched* arm
                                                Deut 4:34

3.   עֲזֻבוֹת עָרֵי עֲרֹעֵר   The cities of Aroer are *deserted*.
                                         Isa 17:2

---

31. Kedar-Kopfstein, "Stammbildung *qōṭel*," 256.   33. Cf. Deut 9:3.
32. GKC § 116f / p. 357, after Sellin.   34. The attribute is negated by *lōʾ*, cf., e.g., Jer 2:2.

4.	וִיהוֹשֻׁעַ הָיָה לָבֻשׁ	Now Joshua was *dressed*. . . . Zech 3:3
5.	גְּדֹלִים מַעֲשֵׂי יהוה דְּרוּשִׁים לְכָל־חֶפְצֵיהֶם:	The works of YHWH are great, *pondered* by all who delight in them. Ps 111:2

d   The participles of the reflexive or passive stems, especially the *Niphal*, correspond occasionally to an English *-ible/-able* term or a Latin gerundive (23.3d; ## 6–8), for example, נוֹרָא 'metuendus, to be feared, terrible,' נֶחְמָד 'desiderandus, desirable,' נֶחְשָׁב 'aestimandus, estimable,' מְהֻלָּל 'laudandus, to be praised.' (See 25.1 for such uses of the *Pual*.)[35] The gerundive meaning is also attested with the relative (# 9) and predicate participles.

6.	בַּת־בָּבֶל הַשְּׁדוּדָה	O Daughter Babylon, *doomed to destruction* Ps 137:8
7.	לְעַם נוֹלָד	to a people *to be born* Ps 22:32
8.	הַחַיָּה הַנֶּאֱכֶלֶת	the *edible* game Lev 11:47
9.	אֶת־כָּל־הַכֶּסֶף הַנִּמְצָא בְאֶרֶץ־ מִצְרַיִם	all the money *which was to be found* in Egypt Gen 47:14

e   The closely related forms *qāṭûl* and *qāṭîl*, according to König, can be distinguished.[36] The passive participle *qāṭûl* has an inchoative sense, that is, it focuses on the coming of the subject into a modified state, in contrast to *qāṭîl*, which refers to the state proper. For example, אָסוּר draws attention to the moment of being taken to prison, while אָסִיר abstracts from each moment and looks to the circumstance dating from it.

10a.	מְקוֹם אֲשֶׁר יוֹסֵף אָסוּר שָׁם:	the place where Joseph had (recently) been *imprisoned* Gen 40:3
10b.	אֵת כָּל־הָאֲסִירִם אֲשֶׁר בְּבֵית הַסֹּהַר	all the *prisoners* who were in the prison Gen 39:22
10c.	אֶל־בֵּית הַסֹּהַר מְקוֹם אֲשֶׁר־ אֲסִירֵי הַמֶּלֶךְ אֲסוּרִים	to the prison, the place where the *prisoners* of the king were imprisoned Gen 39:20 *Qere*

Only rarely, according to König, does *qāṭûl* designate the abstract quality originating in the modification, for example, יְדֻעִים 'experienced, respected' (Deut 1:13)[37] and סוּר 're-jected' (cf. Isa 49:21).

---

35. See GKC § 116g / p. 357. The participle *nôšāᶜ* in Zech 9:9, conventionally rendered 'victorious,' is difficult; it may have the sense 'saveable, (worthy) of being saved.'

36. König, *Historisch-comparative Syntax*, 129. The *Qere/Kethiv* variation in # 10c puts this view in doubt.
37. Cf. also Isa 53:3.

Relative Use   **37.5**

The participle can be used as the equivalent of relative clauses (cf. English 'hearer,   a
one who hears'). A relative clause can be either independent or dependent (19.1c–d). An
independent relative clause with a participle can occur in any part of a main clause, for
example, as subject (# 1), *casus pendens* (# 2), predicate nominative in a verbless clause
(## 3–4), or object (## 5–7). As a dependent relative, such a participle can serve as an
attributive to a word in any function, for example, in a prepositional phrase (# 8).

1.	וַיֹּאמֶר הַמֶּלֶךְ הַמְדַבֵּר אֵלַיִךְ	And the king said, "*Whoever speaks* to you. . . ." 2 Sam 14:10
2.	שֹׁפֵךְ דַּם הָאָדָם בָּאָדָם דָּמוֹ יִשָּׁפֵךְ	As for *him who sheds human blood*, his blood will be shed by a human. Gen 9:6
3.	מִי הָאֹמֵר שָׁאוּל יִמְלֹךְ עָלֵינוּ	Who is *he who said*, "Saul shall reign over us"? 1 Sam 11:12
4.	עֵינֶיךָ הָרֹאֹת אֵת כָּל־אֲשֶׁר עָשָׂה	Your eyes are *the ones that saw* all he did. Deut 3:21
5.	וָאֶשְׁמַע אֵת מִדַּבֵּר אֵלָי׃	I heard *one speaking* to me. Ezek 2:2
6.	וַיַּגִּידוּ לוֹ אֵת כָּל־הַקֹּרֹת אֹתָם	And they told him all *that had happened* to them. Gen 42:29
7.	שָׁמַעְתִּי אֹמְרִים נֵלְכָה דֹּתָיְנָה	I heard (*them*) *say*, "Let's go to Dothan." Gen 37:17
8.	כַּמַּיִם הַנִּגָּרִים אַרְצָה	like water *spilled* on the ground 2 Sam 14:14

The relative participle, unlike the predicative, often has the article (19.6). Like an   b
adjective, the attributive relative (which functions as a dependent relative clause) agrees
with its noun in definiteness (definite: ## 9–11; indefinite: # 12), though in later style
exceptions occur (## 13–14). Because of this agreement, it is possible for the relative
participle to be separated from its antecedent (## 11, 15).[38]

9.	עַל־הַמִּזְבֵּחַ הַבָּנוּי׃	upon *the altar which had been built* Judg 6:28
10.	לַיהוה הַנִּרְאֶה אֵלָיו׃	*YHWH*, *who had appeared* to him Gen 12:7

---

38. On the definiteness disagreements, see Davidson, *Hebrew Syntax*, 133; on the separation, note also Ps 19:8–11 and
137:7, pointed out to us by Paul Mosca; cf. Ps 70:4.

11.　מִשְׁפְּטֵי־יהוה אֱמֶת צָדְקוּ
יַחְדָּו: הַנֶּחֱמָדִים מִזָּהָב

The statutes of Yʜᴡʜ are true, altogether righteous,
that are more desirable than gold.
Ps 19:10–11

12.　רוּחַ סְעָרָה בָּאָה מִן־הַצָּפוֹן

a stormy wind that was coming from the north
Ezek 1:4

13.　בְּיַד מַלְאָכִים הַבָּאִים יְרוּשָׁלָ͏ִם

through *the envoys who have come* to Jerusalem
Jer 27:3

14.　עַם נָגִיד הַבָּא

(the) people of (*the*) *ruler who will come*
Dan 9:26

15.　כָּל־הַנֶּפֶשׁ לְבֵית־יַעֲקֹב הַבָּאָה
מִצְרָיְמָה

all the *folk* of the house of Jacob, *who came* into
Egypt
Gen 46:27

When relative participial clauses are used in succession, the first may have the article and the other(s) not (## 16–17), though sometimes all have the article (# 18).[39]

16.　הוֹי הָאֹמְרִים לָרַע טוֹב . . .
שָׂמִים חֹשֶׁךְ לְאוֹר

Woe to those who call evil good . . .
who put darkness for light. . . .
Isa 5:20

17.　הַשֹּׁכְבִים עַל־מִטּוֹת שֵׁן . . .
וְאֹכְלִים כָּרִים מִצֹּאן

those who lie on beds inlaid with ivory . . .
who dine on choice lambs
Amos 6:4

18.　הַיֹּשֵׁב עַל־חוּג הָאָרֶץ . . .
הַנּוֹטֶה כַדֹּק שָׁמַיִם . . .
הַנּוֹתֵן רוֹזְנִים לְאָיִן

the one who sits enthroned above the earth's circle . . .
who stretches out the heavens as a canopy . . .
who brings rulers to nothing
Isa 40:22–23

c　　The participial relative with the article can take on a generic indefinite sense (cf. 'whoever hears'). This sense is similar to the use of a substantival participle with the article to refer to a class of agents, for example, הַכֹּרֵת 'the hewer (of trees)' (Isa 14:8), namely, 'all those who hew down (trees), woodsmen.' As a relative, the definite participle refers to a transitory quality (## 19–20).

19.　הַנֹּגֵעַ בָּאִישׁ הַזֶּה

whoever touches this man
Gen 26:11

20.　הַמַּאֲמִין לֹא יָחִישׁ:

Whoever trusts will not be put to shame.
Isa 28:16

d　　When the relative participle as predicate receives the article, it identifies the subject (8.4.1); this construction corresponds to the French 'C'est . . . celui qui' (## 21–22; cf. # 20).

---

39. Davidson, *Hebrew Syntax*, 133.

| 21. | הוּא הַסֹּבֵב אֵת כָּל־אֶרֶץ הַחֲוִילָה | It is *the one that goes around* the land of Havilah. Gen 2:11 |
| 22. | כִּי־פִי הַמְדַבֵּר אֲלֵיכֶם: | My mouth is *the one that speaks* to you. Gen 45:12 |

The relative participle is a non-finite form and thus, as Paul Joüon remarks, "it   e
expresses by itself neither time nor even aspect; . . . thus הָאִישׁ הַבָּא can signify, according to context, *the man who comes, who will come, who has come, and these once or
often, in an instantaneous or durative fashion.*"[40] The relative participle occurs predominantly in connection with time contemporary with the main verb (# 23), or overlapping
with it (# 24) and less often for action completed in the past (## 25–26).

23.	וְהָיָה הָעַלְמָה הַיֹּצֵאת לִשְׁאֹב	Let it be that the ʿalmâ *who comes out* to draw water. . . . Gen 24:43
24.	כִּי יהוה אֱלֹהֶיךָ מְבִיאֲךָ אֶל־אֶרֶץ טוֹבָה . . . עֲיָנֹת וּתְהֹמֹת יֹצְאִים בַּבִּקְעָה וּבָהָר:	For Yнwн your God *is bringing* you into a good land . . . with springs and pools *that flow* in the valleys and the hills. Deut 8:7
25.	הַכֶּסֶף הַשָּׁב בְּאַמְתְּחֹתֵינוּ בַּתְּחִלָּה	the silver *that had been put back* into our sacks the first time Gen 43:18
26.	וַיִּבֶן שָׁם מִזְבֵּחַ לַיהוה הַנִּרְאֶה אֵלָיו:	He built there an altar to Yнwн, *who had appeared* to him. Gen 12:7

The relative participle is negated either by the clausal adverb אֵין, a predicator of   f
non-existence (# 27), even as יֵשׁ is used with it as a predicator of existence (# 28;
39.3.2a), or by the item adverb לֹא (# 29).

27.	אֵין יוֹצֵא וְאֵין בָּא:	*There was none* who went out *or* came in. Josh 6:1
28.	יֵשׁ מְפַזֵּר	*There is* one who scatters. Prov 11:24
29.	בְּאֶרֶץ לֹא זְרוּעָה	in a land *not* sown Jer 2:2

Predicate Use   37.6

A participle is often used as the predicate of a verbless clause. The subject is usually   a
expressed, often as an independent pronoun (## 1–2) or as a suffix with יֵשׁ or אֵין (## 3–4).

---

40. Joüon § 121i / p. 341.

Rarely the subject is not expressed, notably after הנה (## 5–6) or if the referent has just been mentioned (# 7).[41]

1.	הֵ֫מָּה עֹלִים	*They* were going up. 1 Sam 9:11
2.	מָחָר אַתָּה מוּמָת׃	Tomorrow *you* will be killed. 1 Sam 19:11
3.	אִם־יֶשְׁךָ מוֹשִׁיעַ	If *you* will save. . . . Judg 6:36
4.	וְאִם־אֵינְךָ מְשַׁלֵּחַ	If *you* will not send. . . . Gen 43:5
5.	וַיָּבֹא אֶל־הָאִישׁ וְהִנֵּה עֹמֵד	He came to the man, and, behold, [*he* was] standing. Gen 24:30
6.	וַיִּמְצָאֵהוּ אִישׁ וְהִנֵּה תֹעֶה בַּשָּׂדֶה	A man found him, and behold, [*he* was] wandering in the field. Gen 37:15
7.	כִּי יֹאמְרוּ נָסִים לְפָנֵ֫ינוּ	They will say, "[*They* are] fleeing before us." Josh 8:6

b   Although the usual syntactic structure for a participial predicate is a verbless clause, the verbal character of the participle is not thereby effaced, as the examples above show. In its workings, the predicate participle approximates the prefix conjugation (cf. 37.7.2a), but distinguishes itself by emphasizing a durative circumstance and thus by not representing modal/temporal or volitional action, though the ongoing state of affairs may involve repeated action. The participle exhibits its adjectival origin in its essential use to express circumstances, states of affairs, facts, etc., rather than events. In circumstantial clauses it focuses on the figures moving in the background, contemporaneous with the main action; it is frequent in *causal clauses* (## 8–9).[42]

8.	כִּי יֹדֵעַ אֱלֹהִים כִּי	because God (is *one who*) *knows* that . . . Gen 3:5
9.	כִּי אֹתָהּ אַתֶּם מְבַקְשִׁים	because you *have been asking* for it Exod 10:11

c   The participle does not function in Biblical Hebrew as a finite verb with a distinct time reference,[43] though such use is regular in Mishnaic and later Hebrew; thus the

---

41. With # 7, cf. Neh 9:3. On the particle *hnh*, see D. J. McCarthy, "The Uses of *weḥinnēh* in Biblical Hebrew," *Biblica* 61 (1980) 330–42. Examples ## 5–6 fit McCarthy's category of "excited perception," pp. 332–33.

42. Cf. Carl Brockelmann, *Hebräische Syntax* (Neukirchen: Neukirchener Verlag, 1956) 46.

43. Contrast, e.g., König, *Historisch-comparative Syntax*, 129; and Davidson, *Hebrew Syntax*, 134.

words יוֹדֵעַ אֲנִי would in Biblical Hebrew have the sense 'I am one who knows,' while in Mishnaic they mean simply 'I know.'[44]

    With reference to a *past* state of affairs, a participle may describe the circumstances   d accompanying a principal event (## 10–12). Sometimes, the adverb עוֹד is used with the participle to emphasize the simultaneity (# 13). More often, the participle describes an ongoing state of affairs, involving repeated (## 14–15) or continuous (## 16–17) action.

10. וִיהוֹנָתָן וַאֲחִימַעַץ עֹמְדִים בְּעֵין־רֹגֵל וְהָלְכָה הַשִּׁפְחָה

While Jonathan and Ahimaaz *were staying* at En Rogel, a servant girl would go. . . .
2 Sam 17:17

11. הִיא בָּאָה בְסַף־הַבַּיִת וְהַנַּעַר מֵת:

As she *crossed* the threshold of the house, the child died.
1 Kgs 14:17

12. הִיא מוּצֵאת וְהִיא שָׁלְחָה

As she *was being brought forth*, she sent (word).
Gen 38:25

13. עוֹד זֶה מְדַבֵּר וְזֶה בָּא

While this one *was still speaking*, another came.
Job 1:16

14. וּמַלְכַּת־שְׁבָא שֹׁמַעַת אֶת־שֵׁמַע שְׁלֹמֹה . . . וַתָּבֹא

Now the Queen of Sheba *was hearing* of Solomon's fame . . . and so she came.
1 Kgs 10:1

15. רַק הָעָם מְזַבְּחִים בַּבָּמוֹת

Only, the people *were sacrificing* at the high places.
1 Kgs 3:2

16. וְנָהָר יֹצֵא מֵעֵדֶן

Now, a river *was flowing* from Eden.
Gen 2:10

17. הִנֵּה חָמִיךְ עֹלֶה תִמְנָתָה לָגֹז צֹאנוֹ:

Your father-in-law *is going up* to Timnath to shear his sheep.
Gen 38:13

Two varieties of this pattern require notice. With הנה the participial clause usually describes immediate circumstances (## 18–20; cf. # 17); because these generally require observation the translation 'behold' has established itself in English.[45] A clause with הלך indicates a long-term state of affairs (# 21).

---

44. See M. H. Segal, *A Grammar of Mishnaic Hebrew* (Oxford: Clarendon, 1927) 156. In Modern Hebrew, the participle is clearly either nominal or verbal in any given context. In the tense system of Modern Hebrew, the *pronoun + participle* serves as the present tense. The participial construction involves the word order subject-verb-object (SVO), and it has contributed to the dominance of that word order. See A. Gordon, "The Development of the Participle in Biblical, Mishnaic, and Modern Hebrew," *Afroasiatic Linguistics* 8 (1982) 121–79; Gordon's survey of Biblical Hebrew usage is somewhat skewed by his use of verse and prose materials as strictly comparable.

45. Again, compare McCarthy's "excited perception," in "Uses of wᵉhinnēh," 332–33.

18. וְהִנֵּה אֵינֶנּוּ פֹתֵחַ דַּלְתוֹת הָעֲלִיָּה
וַיִּקְחוּ אֶת־הַמַּפְתֵּחַ

And *behold*, he *was* not *opening* the doors of the upper room, so they took the key.
Judg 3:25

19. וַיִּשָּׂא עֵינָיו וַיַּרְא וְהִנֵּה שְׁלֹשָׁה
אֲנָשִׁים נִצָּבִים עָלָיו

He looked up and saw, and *behold* three men *were standing* by him.
Gen 18:2

20. וַיִּישָׁן וַיַּחֲלֹם . . . וְהִנֵּה שֶׁבַע
שִׁבֳּלִים עֹלוֹת

He slept and dreamt . . . and *behold*, seven heads of grain *were coming up*.
Gen 41:5

21. וְדָוִד הֹלֵךְ וְחָזֵק וּבֵית שָׁאוּל
הֹלְכִים וְדַלִּים:

David *grew stronger and stronger*, while the House of Saul *grew weaker and weaker*.
2 Sam 3:1

e   In reference to *present* time the participle also approximates the prefix conjugation but distinguishes itself by denoting a continuing state of affairs (rather than iterative aspect) without any modal or volitional meaning (## 22–25), sometimes in a purely circumstantial (relative) expression (## 26–27), and sometimes in a durative circumstance involving repeated actions (## 28–29).[46] Such a state of affairs is rarely introduced by הנה (# 30).

22. קוֹל דְּמֵי אָחִיךָ צֹעֲקִים אֵלַי

Your brother's blood *is crying out* to me.[47]
Gen 4:10

23. אָנֹכִי בֹּרַחַת:

I *am fleeing*.
Gen 16:8

24. כִּי יהוה נִלְחָם לָהֶם

Yʜᴡʜ *is fighting* for them.
Exod 14:25

25. וְהָאָרֶץ לְעוֹלָם עֹמָדֶת:

The earth *endures* forever.
Qoh 1:4

26. מִבְּנוֹת הַכְּנַעֲנִי אֲשֶׁר אָנֹכִי יוֹשֵׁב
בְּקִרְבּוֹ:

from the daughters of the Canaanites *among whom* I *am dwelling*
Gen 24:3

27. כִּי הַמָּקוֹם אֲשֶׁר אַתָּה עוֹמֵד
עָלָיו

the place *where* you *are standing*
Exod 3:5

28. . . . תֶּבֶן אֵין נִתָּן לַעֲבָדֶיךָ . . . , yet they
אֹמְרִים

Straw *is* not *being given* to your servants . . . , yet they *say*. . . .
Exod 5:16

29. עַל־כֵּן אֲנִי זֹבֵחַ לַיהוה כָּל־פֶּטֶר
רֶחֶם הַזְּכָרִים

Therefore I *am sacrificing* to Yʜᴡʜ every first male offspring. . . .
Exod 13:15

46. Cf. also 1 Kgs 3:3 (cf. # 15), 4:20.
47. The subject *qôl* is singular; the participle is plural by attraction to *dəmê* (cf. 7.4.1b).

הִנֵּה פְלִשְׁתִּים נִלְחָמִים בִּקְעִילָה .30 וְהֵמָּה שֹׁסִים אֶת־הַגֳּרָנוֹת:	*Look*, the Philistines *are fighting* against Keilah and *are looting* the threshing floors. 1 Sam 23:1

With reference to situations which are in fact *future*, the participle may denote   f
merely a circumstance accompanying a future event (# 31). Usually, however, it denotes
the full range of ideas connoted by English 'I am going to . . . ,' namely, certainty, often
with immanency—the so-called *futurum instans* participle (## 32–37). In this function it
also occurs in a main clause with some logical connection to other clauses (## 38–41) or
in a temporal/conditional clause in connection with a future event (## 42–44). הנה often
occurs with all these constructions because that particle calls attention to a situation
either for vividness (## 31–33, 35) or for its logical connection with some other event
(## 38, 40, 44).

.31	לֵךְ אֶל־פַּרְעֹה בַּבֹּקֶר הִנֵּה יֹצֵא הַמַּיְמָה	Go to Pharaoh in the morning *as he goes* to the river.[48] Exod 7:15
.32	וַאֲנִי הִנְנִי מֵבִיא אֶת־הַמַּבּוּל	I *am going to send* a flood. Gen 6:17
.33	הִנֵּה אָנֹכִי עֹשֶׂה דָבָר בְּיִשְׂרָאֵל	I *am going to do* something in Israel. 1 Sam 3:11
.34	מֶלֶךְ אֲרָם עֹלֶה עָלֶיךָ:	The king of Aram *is going to attack* you. 1 Kgs 20:22
.35	הִנְכָה רֹאֶה בְּעֵינֶיךָ	You *are going to see* (it) with your own eyes. 2 Kgs 7:2
.36	אֵת אֲשֶׁר הָאֱלֹהִים עֹשֶׂה הִגִּיד לְפַרְעֹה:	God has told Pharaoh what he *is going to do*. Gen 41:25
.37	צֹאנְךָ נְתֻנוֹת לְאֹיְבֶיךָ	Your flock *will be given* to your enemies. Deut 28:31
.38	עוֹדְךָ מִסְתּוֹלֵל בְּעַמִּי . . . הִנְנִי מַמְטִיר	You still set yourself against my people. . . . *Therefore*, I *am going to send* rain. . . . Exod 9:17–18
.39	הַיֶּלֶד אֵינֶנּוּ וַאֲנִי אָנָה אֲנִי־בָא:	The boy isn't there, so as for me, where *am* I *going to go*? Gen 37:30
.40	הִנְּךָ מֵת עַל־הָאִשָּׁה . . . וְהִיא בְּעֻלַת בָּעַל:	You *are going to die* on account of this woman . . . ; she is a married woman.[49] Gen 20:3

---

48. Cf. Exod 8:16.

49. On this verse, see C. H. J. van der Merwe, "Hebrew   Grammar, Exegesis and Commentaries," *Journal of Northwest Semitic Languages* 11 (1983) 143–46, at 145–46.

41.	וְגַם אֶת־הַגּוֹי אֲשֶׁר יַעֲבֹדוּ דָּן אָנֹכִי	The nation whom they serve I *am going to judge*. Gen 15:14
42.	אֲנִי נֶאֱסָף אֶל־עַמִּי קִבְרוּ אֹתִי	I *am about to be gathered* to my people, (so) bury me. . . . Gen 49:29
43.	אָנֹכִי הֹלֵךְ בְּדֶרֶךְ כָּל־הָאָרֶץ וְחָזַקְתָּ	I *am about to go* in the way of all the earth, so be strong. . . . 1 Kgs 2:2
44.	הִנֵּה יהוה עֹשֶׂה אֲרֻבּוֹת בַּשָּׁמַיִם הֲיִהְיֶה הַדָּבָר הַזֶּה	If YHWH *opens up* the windows of heaven, could this happen? 2 Kgs 7:2

37.7   Use with Finite Verbs

37.7.1   With היה

a   The verb היה serves as an independent verb with participles used as substantives (# 1) or adjectives (# 2), including all passive participles (## 3–4).[50]

1.	וַיְהִי־לוֹ נֹשֵׂא כֵלִים:	And he *became* his armor bearer. 1 Sam 16:21
2.	וְהָיוּ נְכֹנִים לַיּוֹם הַשְּׁלִישִׁי	And *be* ready on the third day. Exod 19:11
3.	כִּי־מֻלִים הָיוּ כָל־הָעָם	For all the people *had been* circumcised. Josh 5:5
4.	יְהִי מַכִּירֵךְ בָּרוּךְ	*May* the one who took note of you *be* blessed. Ruth 2:19

b   By connecting a finite form of היה with a following predicate participle, an aspectual and / or modal index is assigned to the participle, yielding forms that are past progressive (## 5–7), perfect progressive (## 8–10), future progressive (# 11), or jussive progressive (# 12).[51]

5.	וָאֶשְׁמַע מִדַּבֵּר אֵלָי . . . וְאִישׁ הָיָה עֹמֵד אֶצְלִי:	And I heard someone speaking to me . . . while the man *was standing* beside me. Ezek 43:6
6.	וְאַבְנֵר הָיָה מִתְחַזֵּק בְּבֵית שָׁאוּל:	Now Abner *was* (or, *had been*?) *strengthening* himself in the House of Saul. 2 Sam 3:6

---

50. In 37.7 we follow closely GB 2. 72–74 (§ 13i–l).
51. Contrast GKC § 116r / p. 360. Usually when the participle precedes *hyy*, it is either an adjective (Deut 9:22, Ps 122:2) or a substantive (Deut 9:7 = 9:24 = 31:27).

7.	וַיִּהְיוּ יָמִים שְׁלוֹשָׁה בֹּזְזִים	And so three days they *were plundering*. 2 Chr 20:25
8.	כִּי עַד־הַיָּמִים הָהֵמָּה הָיוּ בְנֵי־ יִשְׂרָאֵל מְקַטְּרִים לוֹ	For up to that time the Israelites *had been burning* incense to it. 2 Kgs 18:4
9.	וַיִּהְיוּ מַכְעִסִים אֹתִי מִן־הַיּוֹם	And they *have been provoking* me from the day. . . . 2 Kgs 21:15
10.	גַּם־תְּמוֹל גַּם־שִׁלְשֹׁם הֱיִיתֶם מְבַקְשִׁים אֶת־דָּוִד לְמֶלֶךְ	For some time you *have been seeking* to make David king. 2 Sam 3:17
11.	וְהָיִיתָ מְמַשֵּׁשׁ בַּצָּהֳרַיִם	You *will be groping* at midday. Deut 28:29
12.	יְהִי רָקִיעַ . . . וִיהִי מַבְדִּיל בֵּין מַיִם לָמָיִם:	Let there be a firmament . . . (*let it be*) *dividing* water from water. Gen 1:6

Sometimes the temporal notion seems to be more precisely 'at just that time . . .' (## 13–14); the aspectual notion may be inchoative ('begin to . . .'; # 15).

13.	יוֹסֵף בֶּן־שְׁבַע־עֶשְׂרֵה שָׁנָה הָיָה רֹעֶה . . . וַיָּבֵא	Joseph, a young man of seventeen, *was at one time tending* the flocks . . . and he brought. . . . Gen 37:2
14.	וּמֶלֶךְ אֲרָם הָיָה נִלְחָם בְּיִשְׂרָאֵל וַיִּוָּעַץ אֶל־עֲבָדָיו	The king of Aram *being then at war* with Israel, he took counsel with his staff. 2 Kgs 6:8
15.	וַיֵּלֶךְ אֶלְקָנָה הָרָמָתָה עַל־בֵּיתוֹ וְהַנַּעַר הָיָה מְשָׁרֵת אֶת־יהוה	Elqanah went home to Ramah, and the lad *began to minister* to Yʜwʜ. 1 Sam 2:11

In later Biblical Hebrew, the combination היה + *participle* substitutes for a perfective verb form; this "periphrastic construction" is probably the result of Aramaic influence, as Joüon notes.

> In the later language one finds the periphrastic הָיָה קֹטֵל construction with the sense of a pure perfect *he killed*. . . . This free use (or abuse), which is usual in post-biblical Hebrew, is due to the influence of Aramaic. In that language the periphrastic construction, which asserts itself for a durative or frequentative action (cf. Dan 5:19) is also employed, very freely, for an instantaneous or unique act.[52]

Lacking firm formal criteria to distinguish the full range of roles noted here, we must sometimes hesitate over identifying precise nuances.

---

52. Joüon § 121g / pp. 340–41; cf. G. Bergsträsser, *Introduction to the Semitic Languages*, trans. and sup. P. T. Daniels (Winona Lake, Indiana: Eisenbrauns, 1983) 84.

16. וְשָׁם הָיוּ לְפָנִים נֹתְנִים אֶת־הַמִּנְחָה

And they had formerly *stored* the grain offerings there.
Neh 13:5

17. וַיִּהְיוּ נִקְרָאִים

And they (the chronicles) *were read*.[53]
Esth 6:1

18. וָאֹמְרָה לַלְוִיִּם אֲשֶׁר יִהְיוּ מִטַּהֲרִים וּבָאִים

Then I commanded the Levites *to purify themselves* and *come*. . . .
Neh 13:22

37.7.2   In Association with Finite Verbs

a   When a perfective or non-perfective verb is used to describe an action, a closely related action with the same actor is generally described with the same type of verb. Participles often break such patterns. A participial predicate can be followed by a prefix form, with similar sense (# 1), or can be used where a prefix form would be expected (compare ## 2a–b), or can be followed by *waw*-relative and a suffix form with either an epexegetical notion in past time (cf. 37.6d) or a (con)sequential situation in future time (## 3–4; cf. 32.2.5b).

1. אֲנִי זֹבֵחַ לַיהוה כָּל־פֶּטֶר רֶחֶם הַזְּכָרִים וְכָל־בְּכוֹר בָּנַי אֶפְדֶּה:

I *sacrifice* to Yʜᴡʜ the first male offspring of every womb and *redeem* each of my firstborn sons.
Exod 13:15

2a. וְאַרְאֶךָּ אֶת־הָאִישׁ אֲשֶׁר־אַתָּה מְבַקֵּשׁ

I will show you the man you *are looking for*.
Judg 4:22

2b. וְאוֹלִיכָה אֶתְכֶם אֶל־הָאִישׁ אֲשֶׁר תְּבַקֵּשׁוּן

I will lead you to the man you *are looking for*.
2 Kgs 6:19

3. כִּי לְיָמִים עוֹד שִׁבְעָה אָנֹכִי מַמְטִיר . . . וּמָחִיתִי . . . .

Seven days from now I *will send* rain . . . and I *will blot out*. . . .
Gen 7:4

4. שָׂרָה . . . יֹלֶדֶת לְךָ בֵּן וְקָרָאתָ אֶת־שְׁמוֹ

Sarah . . . *will bear* you a son and you *will call* his name.
Gen 17:19

Similarly, a relative participle may be continued by a non-perfective form (# 5), a *waw*-relative with short prefix form (## 6–7), or a suffix form (## 8–9).

5. הוֹי מַגִּיעֵי בַיִת בְּבַיִת שָׂדֶה בְשָׂדֶה יַקְרִיבוּ

Woe to those *who join* house to house and *lay* field to field.[54]
Isa 5:8

---

53. Cf. Esth 9:21, 27.   54. Cf. Ps 147:14–15.

6. מִי־אֵפוֹא הוּא הַצָּד־צַיִד וַיָּבֵא לִי   Who then was it *that hunted game* and *brought* (it) to me?
Gen 27:33

7. הָעֹנֶה אֹתִי בְּיוֹם צָרָתִי וַיְהִי עִמָּדִי   the one *who answered* me in the day of distress and *has been* with me
Gen 35:3

8. הוֹי בֹּנֶה עִיר בְּדָמִים
וְכוֹנֵן קִרְיָה בְּעַוְלָה: Woe to him *who builds* a city with bloodshed
and *establishes* a town by crime!
Hab 2:12

9. הַנִּשְׁבָּעִים . . . וְאָמְרוּ   those *who swear . . . and say*[55]
Amos 8:14

---

55. Cf. Mic 3:5.

38

Subordination

38.1   Textual Organization

a   The principal subjects of this grammar are the internal organization of phrases and clauses; we have considered these in the larger context of the biblical discourse but without close attention to the ways in which that discourse works (3.3.4). The basis for larger textual organization is furnished by various classes of markers, notably particles, including conjunctions such as וְ and אַף and exclamations such as הוֹי, and by various verb and noun forms such as וַיְהִי and אַשְׁרֵי. It is with these and similar markers that the three final chapters are concerned. In this chapter we discuss some aspects of subordination, namely, the grammatical control of one clause by another clause, that is, by a main clause; in the next chapter we discuss some features of coordination, that is, the grammatical association of two or more clauses; and in Chapter 40 we discuss exclamations and interrogative clauses.

b   Much of the Masoretic system is focused on textual organization, and a few of the relevant features may be mentioned.[1] Modern grammarians of Biblical Hebrew have, until recently, tended to slight the study of the Masorah, viewing that mass of observations and notes as the result of study undertaken long after the biblical text was recorded. It has become increasingly clear that the Masoretes were first of all recorders and preservers of tradition and only then scholars interested in reconstructing the shape of that tradition (cf. 1.6.3g–m).[2]

---

1. We rely here on Israel Yeivin, *Introduction to the Tiberian Masorah*, ed. and trans. E. J. Revell (Masoretic Studies 5; Missoula: Scholars Press, 1980).

2. Two groups of materials are relevant: Qumranic texts that witness to the antiquity of certain aspects of the

Masorah, and modern grammatical studies that show that the complexities of Masoretic study could not be the result of later reconstruction; for this latter group, see the various studies of phonology cited in the Bibliography (§ 1d–e), especially those of J. L. Malone and E. J. Revell.

The Masoretes supplied the preserved text with four features which assist the exe- c
gete in analyzing both the discourse's units of thought and the relationships among
clauses and words. To stay within the scope of this grammar we limit ourselves to a
simple presentation. (1) *Paragraphs* (based on content) called *pisqot* or *parashiyyot*, are
marked by spaces in the text. The *pisqot* seem to have been marked in early (Jewish)
manuscripts of the Greek translation, showing that they were a feature of the text before
the turn of the era.[3] (2) The division into *verses* was formalized later than that into
pisqot. Nevertheless, it seems that the Bible was divided into verses in talmudic times,
since there are *halakot* (legal findings) which depend on this feature.[4] (3) *Column and
line* divisions are also useful. "In a synagogue scroll, care is taken to begin every column
with some word beginning with *waw*, with the exception of six columns which must
begin with particular words," including notably בראשית (Gen 1:1).[5] The "songs" in the
Torah are written in a distinctive format, described in the Talmud. The manner in which
the other biblical poems and lists are written is less rigidly fixed.[6] (4) The *accents* constitute the most complex of these features. Whereas the first three contribute to understanding a variety of linguistic facts, the accentuation system is most important for
understanding the relationship of words and clauses within a given verse. Such understanding, however, is not strictly the first goal of the accents. Rather, as Israel Yeivin
notes, they supplement the text.

> Their primary function . . . is to represent the musical motifs to which the Biblical text
> was chanted in the public reading. This chant enhanced the beauty and solemnity of
> the reading, but because the purpose of the reading was to present the text clearly and
> intelligibly to the hearers, the chant is dependent on the text, and emphasizes the
> logical relationships of the words. Consequently the second function of the accents is
> to indicate the interrelationship of the words in the text. The accents are thus a good
> guide to the syntax of the text; but . . . accentuation marks semantic units, which are
> not always identical with syntactic units.[7]

The medieval rabbinical interpreters and the ancient versions generally understood d
the text in a way consistent with the accents. To make this point, Yeivin cites Abraham
ibn Ezra: "You should not listen to, or agree with, any interpretation which is not consistent with the accentuation."[8] The complex accentual systems added to the text by the
Masoretes represent an important understanding of the text, one that complements the
study of Hebrew grammar but one that needs to be taken up independently.[9]

---

3. Yeivin, *Tiberian Masorah*, 42.
4. Yeivin, *Tiberian Masorah*, 42.
5. Yeivin, *Tiberian Masorah*, 43.
6. Yeivin, *Tiberian Masorah*, 43.
7. Yeivin, *Tiberian Masorah*, 158.
8. Yeivin, *Tiberian Masorah*, 218.
9. For a preliminary analysis of the Masoretic accent system as a native-speaker grammatical analysis, see M. Aronoff, "Orthography and Linguistic Theory: The Syntactic Basis of Masoretic Hebrew Punctuation," *Language* 61 (1985) 28–72. For more on the concept of native-speaker analyses, see M. O'Connor, "Writing Systems, Native Speaker Analyses, and the Earliest Stages of Northwest Semitic Orthography," *The Word Of The Lord Shall Go Forth: Essays in Honor of David Noel Freedman*, ed. C. L. Meyers and M. O'Connor (Winona Lake, Indiana: Eisenbrauns, 1983) 439–65; O'Connor, "Writing Systems and Native Speaker Analyses," *Society of Biblical Literature Seminar Papers 1986*, ed. K. H. Richards (Atlanta: Scholars Press, 1986) 536–43.

e   If we seek to systematize our understanding of textual organization, we need to introduce the notion of different levels and types of organization. Not every verse, for example, works in the same way in itself and in relation to the verses around it. We may recognize a class of major textual markers or macrosyntactic signs, by which we mean conjunctions and other expressions that bind together the sentences constituting a larger span of text. Wolfgang Schneider defines macrosyntactic signs, the basis of his discourse analysis, as follows:

> Macrosyntactic signs are words, particles, and expressions which serve . . . to mark out the major divisions of a text. . . . The speaker inserts such macrosyntactic signs in order to highlight for the hearer the beginning, transitions, climaxes, and conclusions of his address. . . . Even if the spoken (colloquial) language is the essential sphere of such macrosyntactic signs, nevertheless its influence can be also observed in the literary, fixed linguistic forms, such as we encounter in the Bible, especially in contexts involving dialogue.[10]

Schneider lists the following macrosyntactic signs as introductory and transitional signals in dialogue: הֵן, הִנֵּה, וְהִנֵּה, and וְעַתָּה. He cites the following as signals for breaking up narrative: וַיְהִי as introductory and transitional and וְהִנֵּה as transitional. As Schneider cautions, his study is only an initial step in identifying and systematizing macrosyntactic signs. Like the Masoretic accent system, this method of analyzing textual organization requires independent study (cf. 3.3.4).

f   A simpler approach may be offered. Sometimes a sign may serve on more than one *level*. Consider, for example, וְ in these two sentences:

1a.	הַבְאֵשׁ הִבְאִישׁ . . . וְהָיָה לִי לְעָבֶד	He has made himself so odious [elsewhere] . . . that he will be my servant. 1 Sam 27:12
1b.	וְהָיָה בְּעַנְנִי עָנָן עַל־הָאָרֶץ	And it will be, whenever I bring clouds over the earth. . . . Gen 9:14

In the first sentence וְ is an *interclausal* conjunction, introducing a logically dependent clause within a sentence; in the second it adds another, separate provision to the Noahic covenant, and joins it to what precedes, on a macrosyntactic or intersentential level.[11] Strictly speaking, relative *waw* with the short prefix conjugation is a macrosyntactic conjunction, binding together sentences within a larger span of discourse, whereas relative

---

10. Wolfgang Schneider, *Grammatik des biblischen Hebräisch* (Munich: Claudius, 1974) 261. The terms *discourse analysis* (North America) and *text-linguistics* and *text-grammar* (Europe) are more or less interchangeable. See Egon Werlich, *Typologie der Texte* (Heidelberg: Puelle und Meyer, 1975); as well as several papers by E. Talstra, on Schneider's work, "Text Grammar and Hebrew Bible," *Bibliotheca Orientalis* 35 (1978) 169–74, 39 (1982) 26–38;

and on clause types, "Towards a Distributional Definition of Clauses in Classical Hebrew: A Computer-Assisted Description of Clauses and Clause-Types in Deut 4, 3–8," *Ephemerides Theologicae Lovanienses* 63 (1987) 95–105.

11. The combination *wəhāyâ* is the most common particle or particle combination found on both the interclausal and macrosyntactic levels, but others are also so used, e.g., *raq*.

waw with the suffix conjugation is often a interclausal conjunction, binding together clauses within a sentence.[12] A rough distinction between the intersentential and interclausal conjunctions enables us to discuss the latter more discretely.

Even if we limit our focus to interclausal connections, complexities abound. Two   g
types of conjunctions bind clauses together: the coordinating conjunction *waw* 'and' and the subordinating conjunctions.[13] The latter class includes אֲשֶׁר and the *š* and *z* elements, various other subordinating words, and prepositions. The important clausal signal אֲשֶׁר, along with other signals of relative clauses, is treated in Chapter 19. This conjunction and the other relatives may also subordinate to a main clause conditional clauses, final clauses, consequence clauses, causal clauses, comparative clauses, temporal clauses, and noun clauses.

The system expressed in the text may skew the unexpressed semantic system; for   h
example, the conjunction ו and the deictic particle הִנֵּה may conceal the logically subordinate relationship of the clauses which they introduce.[14] With regard to the former, compare, for example, these two synoptic sentences.

2a.   עֲלֵה וּנְתַתִּים בְּיָדֶךָ:   Go up, *and* [i.e., *because*] I will hand them over to
                                            you.
                                            1 Chr 14:10

2b.   עֲלֵה כִּי־נָתֹן אֶתֵּן אֶת־   Go up, *because* I will hand the Philistines over to you.
           הַפְּלִשְׁתִּים בְּיָדֶךָ:   2 Sam 5:19

The discourse system in # 2b expresses the logical connection between the clauses, which is veiled by the ו in # 2a. We discuss the words ו and הנה in part in order to uncover the skewing between the text's syntax and its semantic system (39.2, 40.2.1). Asyndetic constructions, those without conjunctions, omit any linking word or expression, depending totally on the semantic system operating behind the text to establish the interpropositional relationships.

In this chapter we survey some of the major types of subordinate clauses and con-   i
junctions, leaving aside relative clauses (Chap. 19) and infinitive clauses (Chap. 36).[15]

---

12. We must assume that authors or editors of biblical books, though they may have used sources with differing macrosyntactic features, created a final text that was intelligible to their audiences. Contrast the views expressed in the influential study of W. Richter, *Traditionsgeschichtliche Untersuchungen zum Richterbuch* (Bonn: Peter Hanstein, 1963), early, we add, in the astonishing range of that scholar's work.

13. Two common particles found in the clauses discussed here (and found elsewhere) are *ky* (used 4,470 times) and *gm* (767 times; SA/THAT). On *ky* in general, see A. Schoors, "The Particle כִּי," *Oudtestamentische Studiën* 21 (1981) 240–76.

Unlike many languages, Hebrew does not use a different word order for main and subordinate clauses; the general preference for verb-subject-object obtains in both groups, with many exceptions.

14. Traditional grammars, though not clearly expressing the point, have defined syntactic units by function and not solely by form, and we follow that practice, with appropriate caution. On the relationship between *ᵓšr* as a pronoun and as a conjunction, see the study of M. H. [Goshen-]Gottstein, "Afterthought and the Syntax of Relative Clauses in Biblical Hebrew," *Journal of Biblical Literature* 68 (1949) 35–47.

15. In addition to the grammars, e.g., Richter, *GAHG* 3. 190–202, see J. Hoftijzer, *The Function and Use of the Imperfect Forms with Nun Paragogicum in Classical Hebrew* (Assen: Van Gorcum, 1985) 25–57, for another classification of subordinate clauses. Cf. also A. Niccacci, *Sintassi del verbo ebraico nella prosa biblica classica* (Jerusalem: Franciscan Printing Press, 1986) 83–100.

Most conjunctions have both a cohesive function (they tie the text together) and a subordinating function (they signal the hierarchical relationships of the units within the text). In Chapter 39 we survey the use of ו and related adverbial usage; in Chapter 40 the workings of הנה and similar exclamatory terms, as well as of interrogative ה, are treated.

38.2   Conditional Clauses

a   One of the most common types of logical relation between clauses is the conditional. "Any two clauses, the first of which states a real or hypothetical condition, and the second of which states a real or hypothetical consequence thereof, may be taken as a conditional sentence," T. O. Lambdin states.[16] Note the following alignment of relevant terms.

situation	condition	consequence
logic	protasis	apodosis
clause	subordinate	main
English	'If . . .	then. . . .'

b   In our discussion of the *wəqataltí* construction (32.2.1) we noted that the *waw*-relative in that construction often serves as an apodosis *waw*, introducing the consequential independent clause (the apodosis) after the conditional dependent clause (the protasis). Many of the uses of *wəqataltí* discussed there satisfy the definition of a conditional sentence. We will not review all of those constructions here. Moreover, in that chapter we also noted the various constructions that occur in the protasis.[17]

c   There are two classes of conditionals, depending on whether the condition is *real* (whether fulfilled in the past or still capable of being fulfilled) or *irreal* (whether contrary to the facts of a previous situation or incapable of fulfillment).[18]

d   The protasis of a *real conditional* is usually introduced by אם (## 1–2)[19] or, in the negative, אם לא (## 1, 3); the verb of the protasis may be non-perfective (# 1) or perfective (## 2–3).

1.
אִם תִּהְיוּ כָמֹנוּ . . .   —   *If* you become like us . . . ,
וְנָתַנּוּ אֶת־בְּנֹתֵינוּ לָכֶם   —   *then* we will give you our daughters
וְאֶת־בְּנֹתֵיכֶם נִקַּח־לָנוּ   —   and take your daughters;
וְיָשַׁבְנוּ אִתְּכֶם   —   and we will dwell with you
וְהָיִינוּ לְעַם אֶחָד: —   and become one people.
וְאִם־לֹא תִשְׁמְעוּ אֵלֵינוּ . . .   —   *But if* you do *not* listen to us . . . ,
וְלָקַחְנוּ אֶת־בִּתֵּנוּ   —   we will take our daughter
וְהָלָכְנוּ:   —   and go.
Gen 34:15–17

16. T. O. Lambdin, *Introduction to Biblical Hebrew* (New York: Scribner, 1971) 276.

17. On the use of both *yqtl* and *qtl* forms in the protases of conditional sentences, see Joüon § 167 / pp. 512–18; note also the variation in the Ugaritic hippiatric texts—see

D. Pardee, *Les Textes hippiatriques* (Paris: Editions Recherche sur les Civilisations, 1985) 17–18, 41–42.

18. Lambdin, *Introduction to Biblical Hebrew*, 276–77. Some scholars distinguish from real conditionals a class of concessive clauses (*anglice* 'though, even though, even if');

2.   וְאִם־יָשַׁבְנוּ פֹה וָמָתְנוּ   And *if* we stay here, we shall die.
2 Kgs 7:4

3.   וְהָיָה אִם־לֹא חָפַצְתָּ בָּהּ   And *if* you are *not* pleased with her, you can send
וְשִׁלַּחְתָּהּ   her away.
Deut 21:14

The particle כִּי can introduce a protasis, too, standing either first (# 4) or directly after the subject (# 5), which may thus be taken as a *casus pendens*.[20]

4.   כִּי־תִמְצָא אִישׁ לֹא תְבָרְכֶנּוּ   *If* you encounter someone, do not greet him, and *if*
וְכִי־יְבָרֶכְךָ אִישׁ לֹא תַעֲנֶנּוּ   anyone greets you, do not answer.
2 Kgs 4:29

5. . . . אָדָם כִּי־יַקְרִיב מִכֶּם קָרְבָּן   *When* any one of you brings an offering . . . , bring
מִן־הַבְּהֵמָה מִן־הַבָּקָר וּמִן־   your offering from the beasts or the herd or the
הַצֹּאן תַּקְרִיבוּ   flock. . . .
Lev 1:2

A protasis can also be introduced by אֲשֶׁר (# 6, note the negative in אִם־לֹא), הֵן (# 7), or asyndetically (# 8). Conditional sentences may consist of two *waw*-relative clauses in juxtaposition (32.2.3).

6.   רְאֵה אָנֹכִי נֹתֵן לִפְנֵיכֶם הַיּוֹם   Look: I am giving you a choice today, blessing or
בְּרָכָה וּקְלָלָה: אֶת־הַבְּרָכָה אֲשֶׁר   curse—the blessing (will obtain) *if* you listen . . . and
תִּשְׁמְעוּ . . . וְהַקְּלָלָה אִם־לֹא   the curse (will obtain) *if* you do *not* listen. . . .
תִּשְׁמְעוּ   Deut 11:26–28

7.   וְכִי תֹאמְרוּ מַה־נֹּאכַל . . . הֵן   And if you say, "What shall we eat . . . *if* we may not
לֹא נִזְרָע . . . וְצִוִּיתִי אֶת־בִּרְכָתִי   sow . . . ?", [you should realize that] I will command
לָכֶם   my blessing for you.
Lev 25:20–21

8.   תִּתֵּן לָהֶם יִלְקֹטוּן   (*When/if*) you give it to them, they gather it up.[21]
Ps 104:28

The protasis of an *irreal conditional* may be introduced by לוּ (## 9–11) or, in the negative, לוּלֵא/לוּלֵי (< לוּ + לֹא; # 12).[22] The particle לוּ may introduce a free-standing   e

see, e.g., R. J. Williams, *Hebrew Syntax: An Outline* (2d ed.; Toronto: University of Toronto 1976) 88.

19. On this particle, see C. van Leeuwen, "Die Partikel אִם," *Oudtestamentische Studiën* 18 (1973) 15–48; on conditional clauses, see pp. 16–27. There are 1,060 occurrences of *ʾm* (SA/THAT). On the Ugaritic particles *ʾim* (prose only) and *hm* (verse and prose), see Kjell Aartun, *Die Partikeln des Ugaritischen. 2. Präpositionen, Konjunktionen* (Kevelaer: Butzon und Bercker/Neukirchen-Vluyn: Neukirchener Verlag, 1978) 95–97.

20. In case law, *ky* can introduce the major circumstance

and *ʾm* the minor circumstances, e.g., Exod 21:28 (*ky*)–29 (*ʾm*); cf. *LHS* 184, citing the sequence of Exod 21:37 (*ky*), 22:1 (*ʾm*), 22:2 (*ʾm*).

21. Note, too, the second half of the verse.

22. There are a few cases in which *lûlē(ʾ)* is not counterfactual; note the verse example in Judg 14:18. On *lû*, see J. Huehnergard, "Asseverative *la and Hypothetical *lu/law in Semitic," *Journal of the American Oriental Society* 103 (1983) 569–93, esp. 570–71; with the phonological addendum of R. C. Steiner, "Lulav versus *lu/law," *Journal of the American Oriental Society* 107 (1987) 121–22.

protasis, one without an apodosis (# 13); the sense is then 'oh (I wish) that, would that.'[23] The particle כי can also introduce an irreal conditional (# 14).

9.	לוּ יֶשׁ־חֶרֶב בְּיָדִי כִּי עַתָּה הֲרַגְתִּיךְ׃	*If* there were a sword in my hand, I would surely now kill you. Num 22:29
10.	לוּ חָכְמוּ יַשְׂכִּילוּ זֹאת	*If* they were wise, they would understand this. Deut 32:29
11.	לוּ חָפֵץ יהוה לַהֲמִיתֵנוּ לֹא־לָקַח . . . עֹלָה	*If* YHWH had wanted to kill us, he would not have taken . . . the offering. . . . Judg 13:23
12.	לוּלֵי אֱלֹהֵי אָבִי . . . הָיָה לִי כִּי עַתָּה רֵיקָם שִׁלַּחְתָּנִי	*If* the God of my father . . . had *not* been on my side, you would have sent me away empty-handed. Gen 31:42
13.	וְלוּ הוֹאַלְנוּ וַנֵּשֶׁב בְּעֵבֶר הַיַּרְדֵּן׃	*Would that* we had been content to dwell on the other side of the Jordan! Josh 7:7
14.	גַּם כִּי־אֵלֵךְ בְּגֵיא צַלְמָוֶת לֹא־אִירָא רָע	Even if I were walking in the valley of death's shadow, I would not fear (anything) evil. Ps 23:4

38.3 Final and Result Clauses

a   In Hebrew (as in many languages) expressions of purpose and consequence are not always readily distinguished; the precise sense of the relevant constructions and particles must be determined from context.[24] The main clause expresses a situation, and the subordinate clause either a purpose (final or telic clause) or a consequence (result clause). We have already considered the common use of *l* + *the infinitive* to form a purpose clause (36.2.2–3). Here we take up other markers of final and result clauses, positive and negative.

b   The relative conjunction אשר is common in a variety of final and result clauses. In positive clauses אשר alone can introduce either a final (# 1) or a result clause (# 2). Final clauses are introduced by למען,[25] with or without אשר (## 3–6), or by בעבור, with or without אשר (## 7–8); למען can govern a finite verb (## 3–4) or an infinitive construct

23. Lambdin, *Introduction to Biblical Hebrew*, 279. On the relation of the conditional sense and the other, which he calls optative, see Huehnergard, "Asseverative *la*," 573–74; he suggests that at base the particle marks that "a statement [is] hypothetical, that a proposition [is] deemed by the speaker to be contrary to known fact or to reasonable expectation" (p. 574).

24. Similarly Joüon § 168a / p. 518, § 169i / p. 521. On

ky in such clauses, see W. T. Claassen, "Speaker-Oriented Functions of kî in Biblical Hebrew," *Journal of Northwest Semitic Languages* 11 (1983) 29–46.

25. See H. A. Brongers, "Die Partikel לְמַעַן in der biblisch-hebräischen Sprache," *Oudtestamentische Studiën* 18 (1973) 84–96. Brongers suggests that *lmʿn* introduces a result clause in a few cases (Lev 20:3, 2 Kgs 22:17, Amos 2:7; p. 89); he also notes that sometimes the particle is

(## 5–6). A result clause can be introduced by כִּי (## 9–11), notably after a question (## 9–10).

1.	וְאַשְׁמִעֵם אֶת־דְּבָרָי אֲשֶׁר יִלְמְדוּן לְיִרְאָה אֹתִי	I will make them hear my words, *so that* (i.e., with the goal that) they may learn to fear me. Deut 4:10
2.	וַיִּקְרָא . . . שֵׁם־הַמָּקוֹם הַהוּא . . . אֲשֶׁר יֵאָמֵר הַיּוֹם	He called . . . the place . . . *so that* (i.e., with the result that) to this day it is said. . . . Gen 22:14
3.	לְמַעַן יַאֲמִינוּ כִּי	*so that* they might believe that . . . Exod 4:5
4.	לְמַעַן אֲשֶׁר יְצַוֶּה אֶת־בָּנָיו	*so that* he will direct his children Gen 18:19
5.	לְמַעַן זְבֹחַ לַיהוה	*so that* they (the people) might sacrifice to Yhwh 1 Sam 15:15
6.	לְמַעַן הַדִּיחִי אֶתְכֶם	*so that* I will banish you Jer 27:15
7.	בַּעֲבוּר יִשְׁמְרוּ חֻקָּיו	*so that* they might keep his precepts Ps 105:45
8.	בַּעֲבֻר אֲשֶׁר יְבָרֶכְךָ	*so that* he may bless you Gen 27:10
9.	מָה־אֱנוֹשׁ כִּי־תִזְכְּרֶנּוּ	What is man *that* you think of him? Ps 8:5
10.	הַאֱלֹהִים אָנִי . . . כִּי־זֶה שֹׁלֵחַ אֵלַי	Am I God . . . *that* this person sends to me. . . ? 2 Kgs 5:7
11.	לֹא־עָשִׂיתִי מְאוּמָה כִּי־שָׂמוּ אֹתִי בַּבּוֹר׃	I have done nothing *that* they should have put me in the pit. Gen 40:15

Negative final and result clauses also use אשר, with לֹא (# 12, final; # 13, result).   c
Negative final clauses may be introduced by פֶּן (# 14), לְבִלְתִּי (# 15), and לְמַעַן לֹא (# 16).[26]
Negative result clauses may be infinitive clauses after מִן (# 17).

12.	אֲשֶׁר לֹא יִשְׁמְעוּ אִישׁ שְׂפַת רֵעֵהוּ׃	*so that* they will *not* understand each other Gen 11:7
13.	אֲשֶׁר לֹא־יֹאמְרוּ זֹאת אִיזָבֶל׃	*so that no* one will be able to say, "This is Jezebel" 2 Kgs 9:37

---

elliptical in sense and a paraphrase is necessary: "the consequence of which will be." The form *lmᶜn* occurs 270 times (SA/THAT).

26. In Ezek 19:9 *lmᶜn lᵓ* introduces a result clause (contrast the final clauses in 14:11, 25:10, 26:20). The particle *pn* occurs 133 times (SA/THAT).

14.	שְׁלֹף חַרְבְּךָ וּמוֹתְתֵנִי פֶּן־יֹאמְרוּ לִי אִשָּׁה הֲרָגָתְהוּ	Unsheath your sword and slay me, *lest* (people) say of me, "A woman slaughtered him." Judg 9:54
15.	בָּא הָאֱלֹהִים . . . לְבִלְתִּי תֶחֱטָאוּ׃	God has come . . . *in order that* you might *not* sin. Exod 20:20
16.	לְמַעַן לֹא אֶחֱטָא־לָךְ׃	*in order that* I might *not* sin against you Ps 119:11
17.	כִּי־שִׁלַּחְנוּ אֶת־יִשְׂרָאֵל מֵעָבְדֵנוּ׃	that we have let the Israelites go *with the result* that they will no longer serve us Exod 14:5

38.4   Causal Clauses

a   If one situation constitutes the basis for another, that first or causal situation can be described with an infinitive clause (36.2.2–3), a clause with relative *waw* and suffix form (32.2.3), or by a clause introduced by one of a number of particles. The most common are כִּי (## 1–2) and אֲשֶׁר (# 3). Both of these can be used with יַעַן (11.2.8), which can also be used alone (## 4–7); יען can govern a finite form (## 4–6) or an infinitive construct (# 7).[27] Like (לְ)מַעַן, יען is derived from the root of the verb ענה 'to answer.'

1.	כִּי־מַיִם עַל־פְּנֵי כָל־הָאָרֶץ	*because* there was water over all the surface of the earth Gen 8:9
2.	כִּי עָשִׂיתָ זֹּאת אָרוּר אַתָּה	*Because* you did this, may you be cursed. Gen 3:14
3.	אֲשֶׁר שָׁכְבָה עָלָיו׃	*because* she lay on top of him 1 Kgs 3:19
4.	יַעַן מָאַסְתָּ אֶת־דְּבַר יהוה	*because* you have rejected the word of Yʜᴡʜ 1 Sam 15:23
5.	יַעַן כִּי־מְאַסְתֶּם אֶת־יהוה	*because* you have rejected Yʜᴡʜ Num 11:20
6.	כִּי יַעַן אֲשֶׁר עָשִׂיתָ אֶת־הַדָּבָר הַזֶּה	*because* you did this thing Gen 22:16
7.	יַעַן אֲמָרְכֶם אֶת־הַדָּבָר הַזֶּה	*because* you use this word Jer 23:38

Less frequent combinations are numerous. The preposition עַל (11.2.13) can introduce causal clauses with other particles, yielding עַל־דְּבַר אֲשֶׁר, עַל־כִּי, and עַל אֲשֶׁר (# 8), 'through the fact that.' The preposition מִן (11.2.11) is also so used, in מֵאֲשֶׁר (# 9) or מִפְּנֵי

---

27. See M. J. Mulder, "Die Partikel יַעַן," *Oudtestamentische Studiën* 18 (1973) 49–83, esp. pp. 56–80; on other causal conjunctions, see pp. 80–82.

אֲשֶׁר, as are תחת (11.2.15), in תַּחַת אֲשֶׁר (# 10) and תַּחַת כִּי, and בְּ, in בַּאֲשֶׁר (# 11). The term עֵ֫קֶב 'consequence,' related to עָקֵב 'heel,' is also combined with אשר to introduce causes (# 12).

8.	עַל אֲשֶׁר הֵמִית אֶת־עֲשָׂהאֵל	*because* he had killed Asahel 2 Sam 3:30
9.	מֵאֲשֶׁר יָקַ֫רְתָּ בְעֵינַי	*because* you are precious in my eyes Isa 43:4
10.	תַּ֫חַת אֲשֶׁר־לֹא־שָׁמְעוּ אֶל־דְּבָרַי	*because* they have not hearkened to my words Jer 29:19
11.	בַּאֲשֶׁר יהוה אִתּוֹ	*because* YHWH was with him Gen 39:23
12.	עֵ֫קֶב אֲשֶׁר שָׁמַ֫עְתָּ בְּקֹלִי:	*because* you obeyed me Gen 22:18

Comparative Clauses   **38.5**

Clauses comparing one situation with another often use particles to introduce both the situation compared (in the subordinate clause or protasis) and the present situation (in the main clause or apodosis). The most common pairing is כַּאֲשֶׁר + protasis—כֵּן + apodosis (## 1–4), usually in that order, although the reverse may be found (# 4). The protasis may be introduced by כְּ before either an infinitive (# 5) or a verbless clause (# 6), with כן in the apodosis.[28] (For comparative עם, see 11.2.14.)

1.	וַיְהִי כַּאֲשֶׁר פָּתַר־לָ֫נוּ כֵּן הָיָה	And it was the case that *as* he interpreted for us, *so* it was. Gen 41:13
2.	וְכַאֲשֶׁר יְעַנּוּ אֹתוֹ כֵּן יִרְבֶּה וְכֵן יִפְרֹץ	*The more* they (the Egyptians) oppressed them (the Israelites), *the more* they multiplied and burst forth. Exod 1:12
3.	כַּאֲשֶׁר יֶהְגֶּה הָאַרְיֵה . . . עַל־טַרְפּוֹ . . . לֹא יֵחָת . . . כֵּן יֵרֵד יהוה . . . עַל־הַר־צִיּוֹן	*As* a lion . . . growls over its prey (and) . . . is not frightened off . . . , *so* YHWH . . . will come down on Mount Zion. Isa 31:4
4.	כֵּן תַּעֲשֶׂה כַּאֲשֶׁר דִּבַּ֫רְתָּ:	*So* do, *according to* what you say. Gen 18:5
5.	כְּרֻבָּם כֵּן חָטְאוּ־לִי	*As* [*the more*] they multiplied, *so* [*the more*] they sinned against me. Hos 4:7

---

28. Apparently the protasis in Jer 3:20 has no introductory particle, but ʾākēn there is suspect; perhaps read ʾak

kə, with W. L. Holladay, *Jeremiah* (Philadelphia: Fortress, 1986), 1. 60–61. See also Joüon § 174e / p. 528.

| 6. | הִנֵּה כְעֵינֵי עֲבָדִים אֶל־יַד אֲדוֹנֵיהֶם ... כֵּן עֵינֵינוּ אֶל־ יהוה | *As* the eyes of slaves (look) to the hand of their master . . . *so* our eyes (look) to Yʜwʜ. Ps 123:2 |

The particle כ can be used with two compared things, the effect being that the situation of one of them is likened to that of the other. The present situation (i.e., the situation under discussion) is usually given first (## 7–8), though the reverse is found (## 9–10).[29]

7.	וְהָיָה כַצַּדִּיק כָּרָשָׁע	And the (state of the) righteous would be *like* the (state) of the wicked. Gen 18:25
8.	כִּי כָמוֹךָ כְּפַרְעֹה:	Indeed, you are *like* Pharaoh. Gen 44:18
9.	כַּחַטָּאת כָּאָשָׁם תּוֹרָה אַחַת לָהֶם	The guilt offering (ʾšm) is *like* the sin offering (ḥṭʾt): there is one set of rules for (both of) them. Lev 7:7
10.	כָּכֶם כַּגֵּר יִהְיֶה לִפְנֵי יהוה:	*As* you are, *so* shall the sojourner be before Yʜwʜ. Num 15:15

38.6   Exceptive Clauses

a   There is a small class of dependent clauses which presents exceptions to the situation described in the corresponding main clauses. Exceptive dependent clauses are similar in function to restrictive independent clauses, marked by such sentential adverbs as רַק (39.3.5); the clauses differ in that the independent clauses refer to a longer stretch of preceding text, while the dependent clauses refer only to the immediately preceding main clause.[30]

b   The particle אם is frequent in exceptive clauses, with בִּלְתִּי (# 1) or כי (## 2–4); בלתי is found without אם (# 5).

1.	הֲיִתֵּן כְּפִיר קוֹלוֹ ... בִּלְתִּי אִם־לָכָד:	Does a lion roar . . . *unless* it has vanquished (its prey)?[31] Amos 3:4
2.	לֹא אֲשַׁלֵּחֲךָ כִּי אִם־בֵּרַכְתָּנִי:	I won't release you *unless* you bless me. Gen 32:27
3.	כִּי לֹא יַעֲשֶׂה אֲדֹנָי יהוה דָּבָר כִּי אִם־גָּלָה סוֹדוֹ אֶל־עֲבָדָיו הַנְּבִיאִים:	The Lord Yʜwʜ does nothing *unless* he has revealed his plan to his servants, the prophets.[32] Amos 3:7

---

29. See also Lev 24:16, *kaggēr kāʾezrāḥ*. The two *k*-phrases may together be seen as a type of "small clause," the rule of thumb.

30. Compare the treatment of Williams, *Hebrew Syntax*, 92–94, who keeps such clauses together; see also van Leeuwen, "Die Partikel אם," 42–47, esp. 46–47.

31. Note also *blty ʾm* in Amos 3:3 and *ky ʾm* in 3:7.

32. The occurrences of *blty ʾm* in Amos 3:3–4 are both governed by the interrogative particle; this otherwise similar clause with *ky ʾm* is declarative.

4. ‫וְלֹא יֹאכַל מִן־הַקֳּדָשִׁים כִּי אִם־‬
‫רָחַץ בְּשָׂרוֹ בַּמָּיִם:‬

He shall not eat of the holy things *unless* he washes himself in water.
Lev 22:6

5. ‫לֹא־תִרְאוּ פָנַי בִּלְתִּי אֲחִיכֶם‬
‫אִתְּכֶם:‬

You will not see my face *unless* your brother is with you.
Gen 43:3

Temporal Clauses

The majority of dependent temporal clauses are formed with an infinitive introduced
by a preposition (36.2.2–3; 11.2.5, 9–11). There are a variety of other temporal clause types, however, introduced by other particles. These may be classified according to the temporal relation of the main clause situation and that of the subordinate clause. If the situations are *contemporary*, the conjunction is usually ‫כַּאֲשֶׁר‬ (# 1) or ‫כִּי‬ (# 2); ‫אם‬ is rarely used in this way (# 3).[33] If the subordinate clause refers to a *later* situation, the conjunction is most commonly ‫עַד‬ (11.2.12), alone (# 4) or in combination, ‫עד אשר‬ (# 5), ‫טרם‬, ‫עד כי‬; ‫עד אם‬, or ‫עד אשר אם‬, alone (# 6) or with ‫ב‬ (# 7), is also used (cf. 31.6.3 on the use of prefix forms). For a *preceding* situation, the conjunction is most often ‫אַחַר‬ or ‫אַחֲרֵי‬ (# 8; 11.2.1), either of which can be used with ‫אשר‬ (# 9); ‫מֵאָז‬ is also used (# 10).

1. ‫וַיְהִי כַּאֲשֶׁר כִּלָּה לְהַקְרִיב אֶת־‬
‫הַמִּנְחָה וַיְשַׁלַּח אֶת־הָעָם‬

When he (Ehud) had presented the tribute, he sent the people away.
Judg 3:18

2. ‫כִּי־אֶרְאֶה שָׁמֶיךָ‬

When/as often as I see your heavens. . . .
Ps 8:4

3. ‫וְהָיָה אִם־זָרַע יִשְׂרָאֵל וְעָלָה‬
‫מִדְיָן‬

Whenever the Israelites had planted their crops, the Midianites attacked.
Judg 6:3

4. ‫תָּמִים אַתָּה . . . עַד־נִמְצָא‬
‫עַוְלָתָה בָּךְ:‬

You were blameless . . . *until* iniquity was found in you.
Ezek 28:15

5. ‫וְלֹא־הֶאֱמַנְתִּי לַדְּבָרִים עַד‬
‫אֲשֶׁר־בָּאתִי וַתִּרְאֶינָה עֵינַי‬

I did not believe (such) things *until* I came and saw (them) with my own eyes.
1 Kgs 10:7

6. ‫וַיָּלִנוּ שָׁם טֶרֶם יַעֲבֹרוּ:‬

They camped there *before* they crossed over.
Josh 3:1

7. ‫בְּטֶרֶם יָבֹא הַמַּלְאָךְ אֵלָיו וְהוּא‬
‫אָמַר‬

Before the messenger came to him, he had said. . . .
2 Kgs 6:32

---

33. See van Leeuwen, "Die Partikel ‫אם‬," 47–48.

8. וְאִם־יָשׁוּב הַנֶּגַע וּפָרַח בַּבַּיִת אַחַר חִלֵּץ אֶת־הָאֲבָנִים וְאַחֲרֵי הִקְצוֹת אֶת־הַבַּיִת וְאַחֲרֵי הִטּוֹחַ׃ וּבָא הַכֹּהֵן וְרָאָה

If the infection returns and again breaks out in the house, *after* he has pulled out the stones and *after* scraping(?) the house and *after* plastering, the priest shall go inspect.
Lev 14:43–44

9. בְּאַרְבַּע עֶשְׂרֵה שָׁנָה אַחַר אֲשֶׁר הֻכְּתָה הָעִיר

in the fortieth year *after* the city was captured
Ezek 40:1

10. וַיְהִי מֵאָז הִפְקִיד אֹתוֹ בְּבֵיתוֹ וַיְבָרֶךְ יהוה אֶת־בֵּית הַמִּצְרִי . . .

And from the time that he (the master) had set him (Joseph) over his house . . . , Yʜᴡʜ blessed the Egyptian's house.
Gen 39:5

38.8   Constituent Noun Clauses

a   It is common for a clause to stand in a case frame usually occupied by a noun; such a dependent clause is called a *noun clause* or a constituent noun clause.[34] (A verbless clause, also called a *nominal clause*, is an independent clause with subject and predicate; see 8.4.) A noun clause is often prefaced by כִּי, אֲשֶׁר, or (in the accusative case frame) אֵת; those clauses preceded by כִּי or אֲשֶׁר are often called "'that' clauses" (since the particle involved is often translated 'that'), while many noun clauses are called "object clauses."

b   In a *nominative* case frame, a clause can serve as the subject of a main clause (## 1, 3–4) or as a predicate nominative (# 2). The noun clause can be an infinitive construct (often with לְ; # 1), an אֲשֶׁר clause (## 2–3), or a כִּי clause (# 4); a clause in apposition is usually asyndetic (# 5). The noun clause may be masculine (## 2–5) or feminine (# 1).

1. כִּי מֵאֵת יהוה הָיְתָה לְחַזֵּק אֶת־לִבָּם

From Yʜᴡʜ was *the hardening (of) their heart.*
Josh 11:20

2. וְזֶה אֲשֶׁר תַּעֲשֶׂה אֹתָהּ

This is *how you are to build it.*
Gen 6:15

3. טוֹב אֲשֶׁר לֹא־תִדֹּר

Better *that you do not vow* than . . . (lit., it is better *that you do not vow* than . . .).
Qoh 5:4

4. וּלְשָׁאוּל הֻגַּד כִּי־נִמְלַט דָּוִד מִקְּעִילָה

That David had left Keilah was told to Saul (lit., it was told Saul *that David . . .*).
1 Sam 23:13

5. וְהִנֵּה אֱמֶת נָכוֹן הַדָּבָר נֶעֶשְׂתָה הַתּוֹעֵבָה הַזֹּאת

If the matter is established as true *that this detestable thing was done. . . .*[35]
Deut 13:15

---

34. See Williams, *Hebrew Syntax*, 80–82; M. O'Connor, *Hebrew Verse Structure* (Winona Lake, Indiana: Eisenbrauns, 1980) 314–15.

35. The subject is *hdbr* and the clause *nᶜśth htwᶜbh hzᵓt*

is in apposition to it. Cf. also Ps 99:4, also a verbless main clause, with the dependent clause *mšpṭ ᵓhb*, 'He loves justice.' Note also *zmty bl yᶜbr py*, 'I have resolved: my mouth will not transgress' (Ps 17:3).

A noun clause may occur after a noun in the construct, that is, in a *genitive* frame. c
The clause may be introduced by אֲשֶׁר (## 6–7) or it may be asyndetic (## 8–9).[36] Similarly, a noun clause can follow a preposition, with אֲשֶׁר (# 10) or without it (## 11–12).

6.	אֶל־בֵּית הַסֹּהַר מְקוֹם אֲשֶׁר־ אֲסִירֵי הַמֶּלֶךְ אֲסוּרִים	to the prison, the place *where the king's prisoners were confined* Gen 39:20 *Qere*
7.	כָּל־יְמֵי אֲשֶׁר הַנֶּגַע בּוֹ יִטְמָא טָמֵא הוּא	All the time *he has the infection* he is unclean. Lev 13:46
8.	כָּל־יְמֵי הִתְהַלַּכְנוּ אִתָּם	all the days *we went about with them* 1 Sam 25:15
9.	תְּחִלַּת דִּבֶּר־יְהוָה בְּהוֹשֵׁעַ	When Yhwh began *to speak through Hosea*.... Hos 1:2
10.	אַחֲרֵי אֲשֶׁר־הֵנִיחַ יהוה לְיִשְׂרָאֵל	after *Yhwh had given Israel rest* Josh 23:1
11.	וַיִּגְנֹב יַעֲקֹב אֶת־לֵב לָבָן . . . עַל־בְּלִי הִגִּיד לוֹ כִּי בֹרֵחַ הוּא:	Jacob deceived Laban . . . by *not telling him* that he was fleeing. Gen 31:20
12.	עַל לֹא־חָמָס בְּכַפָּי	though *there is no violence in my hands* Job 16:17

In an *accusative* frame, a clause may stand as an object of a verb or as an adverbial d
accusative. As an object, a constituent noun clause is frequent after verbs of perceiving
(often with כִּי, ## 13, 18; less often with אֲשֶׁר, # 14; or asyndetic, # 15) and saying (generally asyndetic, # 16; sometimes with אֲשֶׁר, # 17).[37] The logical subject of the subordinate
noun clause may be raised out of that clause and appear as the object of the main clause
(# 18; cf. # 15). An adverbial-accusative noun clause may be juxtaposed to the main
clause it depends on (# 19).

13.	וַיַּרְא יהוה כִּי רַבָּה רָעַת הָאָדָם	Yhwh saw *that human wickedness was great.* Gen 6:5
14.	וַיַּרְא שָׁאוּל אֲשֶׁר־הוּא מַשְׂכִּיל	Saul saw *that he was successful (how successful he was).*[38] 1 Sam 18:15
15.	מָה רְאִיתֶם עָשִׂיתִי מַהֲרוּ עֲשׂוּ כָמוֹנִי:	*What* you have seen *that I do*, hasten to do like me. Judg 9:48

36. Note also *'m hyšr hwlk* 'with he who behaves up-rightly' (Mic 2:7), where *hyšr* is an adverbial accusative governed by the participle *hwlk*. The doubts expressed by L. H. Glinert about this use of clauses after a construct are overstated; see "The Preposition in Biblical and Modern Hebrew," *Hebrew Studies* 23 (1982) 115–25, at 120.

37. This is not to sidestep the enormous problems of direct discourse in the Bible; see, provisionally, K. R. Crim, "Hebrew Direct Discourse as a Translation Problem," *Bible Translator* 24 (1973) 311–16; O'Connor, *Hebrew Verse Structure*, 409–20.

38. Cf. 1 Sam 24:11.

16.   כִּי אָמַר אִיּוֹב אוּלַי חָטְאוּ בָנַי

Job said, "*Perhaps my children have sinned.*"
Job 1:5

17.   וַיְהִי הוּא מְסַפֵּר לַמֶּלֶךְ אֵת
       אֲשֶׁר־הֶחֱיָה אֶת־הַמֵּת

He (Gehazi) was telling the king *that he (Elisha)
revived the dead.*[39]
2 Kgs 8:5

18.   וַיַּרְא מְנֻחָה כִּי טוֹב
       וְאֶת־הָאָרֶץ כִּי נָעֵמָה

He saw *that* rest *was good*
and the land *was sweet.*
Gen 49:15

19.   וַיָּבֹא אֲלֵיהֶם יְהוֹשֻׁעַ פִּתְאֹם
       כָּל־הַלַּיְלָה עָלָה מִן־הַגִּלְגָּל׃

Joshua came upon them suddenly (*after*) *he had gone
up from Gilgal throughout the night.*
Josh 10:9

---

39. The rendering of # 16 as direct discourse and of # 17 as indirect discourse should not be taken to suggest that Hebrew distinguishes these two formats in the way English (along with other European languages) does.

39

Coordination and Clausal Adverbs

Textual Organization   39.1

The continuity of Hebrew discourse, especially narrative, is the result of two factors. **a** The first is the dominance of a single clausal *coordinating conjunction* over all others. So pervasive is *wə* that the discourse is largely organized around this single particle, which, it should be noted, has other roles to play, notably as the particle joining nouns in sequence. The duty of clausal coordination is shared only with the rare *ɔô* 'or' and possibly the extremely rare *p* 'and so.' The second factor responsible for discourse continuity is the class of *clausal adverbs*, particles that modify an entire clause, either in itself (notably the negative particles) or in relation to the surrounding discourse (the emphatic and restrictive particles).

In this chapter these two factors are considered. First, we take up the coordinators, **b** filling in gaps in our earlier considerations of *waw* and discussing briefly *ɔô* and *p*. The amorphous category of adverbs is then discussed, before we discuss the various types of clausal adverb.[1]

---

1. For a survey of much comparable Ugaritic material, see Kjell Aartun, *Die Partikeln des Ugaritischen. 1. Ad-*   *verbien, Verneinungspartikeln, Bekräftigungspartikeln, Hervorhebungspartikeln; 2. Präpositionen, Konjunktionen*

39.2   Coordination

a   The three coordinating particles, *w*, *ʾô*, and *p*, form a closely united phonological class, but in terms of use, only one is of major importance. Insofar as *ʾô* and (if it occurs in Hebrew) *p* have defined roles, they can apparently everywhere be replaced by *w*.[2]

39.2.1   Basic Functions of *Waw*

a   The conjunction *w* has two basic roles to play in Hebrew: it conjoins nouns on the phrasal level and it conjoins clauses. That these are different roles is suggested by a variety of languages that distinguish them; that they are similar is shown by the greater number of languages (including English) that combine them.

b   *Phrasal w* is usually found on each item in a series (# 1) but sometimes only on the last of a series (# 2); it is rarely distributed irregularly through the series (# 3) and still more rarely omitted (# 4).

1.	הַדָּגָן וְהַתִּירוֹשׁ וְהַיִּצְהָר	the grain *and* the must *and* the oil Hos 2:10
2.	חַגָּהּ חָדְשָׁהּ וְשַׁבַּתָּהּ	her festival, her new-moon (feast), *and* her sabbath[3] Hos 2:13
3.	נֹתְנֵי לַחְמִי וּמֵימַי צַמְרִי וּפִשְׁתִּי שַׁמְנִי וְשִׁקּוּיָי׃	those who give my bread *and* my water, my wool *and* my flax, my oil *and* my drink[4] Hos 2:7
4.	בִּימֵי עֻזִּיָּה יוֹתָם אָחָז יְחִזְקִיָּה מַלְכֵי יְהוּדָה	in the time of Uzziah-Jotham-Ahaz-Hezekiah, kings of Judah Hos 1:1

After a clausal negative, *waw* with a noun often has an alternative force (# 5); as with the operation of simple conjoining, the operation of specifying alternatives can be either phrasal or clausal. The sense of # 5 is 'I will not save by the bow and (I will) not (save) by the sword,' etc. Normally a noun phrase specifying or glossing another noun phrase stands juxtaposed to it in apposition (12.1), but sometimes *waw* intervenes (# 6). In some

---

(Kevelaer: Butzon und Bercker/Neukirchen-Vluyn: Neukirchener Verlag, 1974–78); supplemented by Aartun's "Die Belegten Partikelformen in den ugaritischen Texten aus Ras Ibn Hani," *Ugarit-Forschungen* 12 (1980) 1–6. The topic of parenthetical expressions, not treated here, is discussed by M. H. [Goshen-]Gottstein, "Afterthought and the Syntax of Relative Clauses in Biblical Hebrew," *Journal of Biblical Literature* 68 (1949) 35–47.

2. The *waw* occurs about 50,000 times and *ʾô* occurs 319 times (of which 136, 43%, are found in Leviticus; SA/THAT). On the form *waw* + *enclitic mem*, originally recognized by F. I. Andersen, see the several essays by C. H. Gordon, Constance Wallace, and G. A. Rendsburg

in *Eblaitica*, ed. C. H. Gordon, G. A. Rendsburg, and N. H. Winter (Winona Lake, Indiana: Eisenbrauns, 1987), 1. 29–41; examples include Ruth 4:5 and Neh 5:11 (both have *wmʾt*, with *ʾt* the sign of the direct object), as well as Ps 147:3. Aartun takes as the class of Ugaritic coordinating conjunctions the set *w*, *p*, *ʾp*, and *u* (*Partikeln*, 2. 63–91). For *ʾp* here, see 39.3.4d.

3. The omission of *w* here may be called a *conjunction override*; see 9.3b on construct override (see # 3 here, too) and 11.4.2 on preposition override.

4. This passage is in verse, and the genitive nouns are in pairs, though these facts do not in themselves explain the patterning of *w*.

cases this *explicative waw* occurs on a non-appositional part of a clause; in such cases it may be called *emphatic waw* (# 7).[5] Phrasal *waw* pointed as *wā* indicates a close bond between the parts of the phrase (# 8).[6]

5. וְלֹא אוֹשִׁיעֵם בְּקֶשֶׁת וּבְחֶרֶב
    וּבְמִלְחָמָה בְּסוּסִים וּבְפָרָשִׁים׃

    I will not save them by bow *or* by sword *or* by battle, by horses *or* charioteers.
    Hos 1:7

6. וַיָּשֶׂם אֹתָם בִּכְלִי הָרֹעִים אֲשֶׁר־
    לוֹ וּבַיַּלְקוּט

    He put them in the shepherds' vessel he had, *that is*, in the pouch.
    1 Sam 17:40

7. וַאֲעֲלֶה בְאֹש מַחֲנֵיכֶם וּבְאַפְּכֶם

    I will make the stench of your camp ascend *even* into your nostrils.
    Amos 4:10

8. וְנִין וָנֶכֶד

    and offspring *and* descendant (or, kith *and* kin)
    Isa 14:22

Clausal waw is a simple conjunction, that is, it places propositions or clauses one   c
after another, without indicating the hierarchical relation between them. Biblical Hebrew frequently joins logically subordinate clauses to a main clause either asyndetically or, more often, syndetically with this conjunction. G. B. Caird justly censors philologists who have inferred from this feature of the language that the Hebrews were intellectually naïve.

> Yet there are eminent philologists who have drawn strangely faulty inferences from it. "The Semitic sentence is a succession of short sentences linked together by simple co-ordinate conjunctions. The principal mark, therefore, of Hebrew and especially of classical Hebrew style is that it is what the Greeks called *lexis eiromenê* 'speech strung together' like a row of beads. . . . It will, therefore, be readily understood that philosophical reasoning and sustained argument were beyond the grasp of the Hebrew intellect or, at any rate, beyond its power of expression" [G. R. Driver].
>
> Driver is on sounder ground when he describes this as a feature of Hebrew style than when he attempts to deduce from it the limitations of Hebrew thought. Hebrew possesses words for 'if', 'because' and 'therefore'; and any language which has such words is capable of being used for logical thought.[7]

Although Hebrew relies heavily on *waw*, other indicators in the text's surface grammar sometimes mark out more precise logical values. Moreover, the patterns of the use of *waw* allow for precision.

---

5. See D. W. Baker, "Further Examples of the *Waw Explicativum*," *Vetus Testamentum* 30 (1980) 129–36. Note the conjoint hendiadys *gēr wətôšāb* '(resident alien or temporary alien =) alien' and the juxtaposed hendiadys *gēr tôšāb* 'alien' (both in Lev 25:47; the first also occurs in Gen 23:4, Lev 23:35).

6. Usually but not always nouns; see E. J. Revell, "Ne-

siga and the History of the Masorah," *Estudios masoreticos . . . dedicados a Harry M. Orlinsky*, ed. E. Fernández Tejero (Madrid: Instituto "Arias Montano," 1983) 37–48, at 38.

7. G. B. Caird, *The Language and Imagery of the Bible* (Philadelphia: Westminster, 1980) 117.

d   We have already considered *waw*-relative clauses (Chaps. 32, 33); here we primarily treat other types of clauses joined by *wə* (וְ). A starting point is provided by T. O. Lambdin, who analyzes clauses joined by *wə* into two types.

> (1) *conjunctive-sequential*, in which the second clause is temporally or logically posterior or consequent to the first, and
>
> (2) *disjunctive*, in which the second clause may be in various relations, all non-sequential, with the first.

The major device in Hebrew for signalling the difference between conjunctive and disjunctive clauses is the type of word which stands immediately after the *wə-*:

> *wə-* (or *wa-*) + verb is conjunctive[-sequential]
> *wə-* + non-verb is disjunctive.[8]

We have already seen that *waw + the suffix conjugation* can be purely conjunctive (32.3)[9] and that relative *waw* with the verb can be epexegetical (32.2.3e, 33.2.2). To the two uses of *wə/wa* joining clauses cited by Lambdin, we accordingly add epexegetical and conjunctive.[10]

39.2.2   Conjunctive-sequential *Waw*

a   Most conjunctive-sequential uses of *waw* have been discussed in connection with *waw*-relative constructions with the suffix and prefix conjugations; there is no need to rehearse or sample that material here. We may recall one important construction: *volitional form* (i.e., cohortative, imperative, or jussive) + *wə* + *prefix conjugation* (## 1–2). In this use the second clause expresses a purpose or result ('so that'; 34.6).[11] It is often difficult to distinguish examples of this construction from cases with two volitional forms in a row (39.2.5).

1.   אֵלְכָה נָּא וְאַכֶּה אֶת־יִשְׁמָעֵאל   Let me go *so that* I can kill Ishmael.
                                       Jer 40:15

2.   יָשָׁב־נָא עַבְדְּךָ וְאָמֻת בְּעִירִי   Let your servant return, *so that* I can die in my own city.
                                         2 Sam 19:38

39.2.3   Disjunctive *Waw*

a   Interclausal *waw* before a non-verb constituent has a disjunctive role. There are two common types of disjunction. One type involves a continuity of scene and participants, but a change of action, while the other is used where the scene or participants shift.

---

8. T. O. Lambdin, *Introduction to Biblical Hebrew* (New York: Scribner, 1971) 162.

9. Lambdin, *Introduction to Biblical Hebrew*, 165.

10. For analyses of extended prose passages, carefully surveying syntactic patterns and alternations, see Lamb-

din, *Introduction to Biblical Hebrew*, 281–82; and E. J. Revell, "The Battle with Benjamin (Judges xx 29–48) and Hebrew Narrative Techniques," *Vetus Testamentum* 35 (1985) 417–33, which deals with the entire book of Judges.

11. Lambdin, *Introduction to Biblical Hebrew*, 119.

If the disjunctive *waw* is used in a situation with *continuity of setting*, the clause it   b
introduces may *contrast* with the preceding (## 1–2),[12] specify contemporary *circum-*
stances (usually verbless clauses; ## 3–5) or *causes* (## 6–7), or provide a *comparison*
(## 8–9).

1.	וַיָּשֶׁב אֶת־שַׂר הַמַּשְׁקִים עַל־ מַשְׁקֵהוּ . . . וְאֵת שַׂר הָאֹפִים תָּלָה	He returned the chief butler to his butlership, . . . *but* he hanged the chief baker. Gen 40:21–22
2.	וַיְהִי רָעָב בְּכָל־הָאֲרָצוֹת וּבְכָל־ אֶרֶץ מִצְרַיִם הָיָה לָחֶם:	There was famine in all the (other) lands, *but* throughout Egypt there was food. Gen 41:54
3.	נִבְנֶה־לָּנוּ עִיר וּמִגְדָּל וְרֹאשׁוֹ בַשָּׁמַיִם	Let us build a city and a tower, *with* its top reaching into the sky. Gen 11:4
4.	וְהִנֵּה רִבְקָה יֹצֵאת . . . וְכַדָּהּ עַל־שִׁכְמָהּ:	Rebekah was coming out . . . *with* her pitcher on her shoulder. Gen 24:15
5.	וַיָּבֹא הַבַּיְתָה לַעֲשׂוֹת מְלַאכְתּוֹ וְאֵין אִישׁ מֵאַנְשֵׁי הַבַּיִת שָׁם בַּבָּיִת:	And he came into the house to do his work *while* none of the household staff were there in the house. Gen 39:11
6.	אַל־תְּאַחֲרוּ אֹתִי וַיהוה הִצְלִיחַ דַּרְכִּי	Do not detain me *since* Yʜᴡʜ has made my journey successful. Gen 24:56
7.	וְגֵר לֹא תִלְחָץ וְאַתֶּם יְדַעְתֶּם אֶת־נֶפֶשׁ הַגֵּר	You shall not oppress a stranger *because* you yourselves know the feelings of a stranger. Exod 23:9
8.	מַיִם קָרִים עַל־נֶפֶשׁ עֲיֵפָה וּשְׁמוּעָה טוֹבָה מֵאֶרֶץ מֶרְחָק:	[Like] cold water to a weary soul, *so* is good news from a far land.[13] Prov 25:25
9.	הַדֶּלֶת תִּסּוֹב עַל־צִירָהּ וְעָצֵל עַל־מִטָּתוֹ:	[As] the door turns on its hinges, *so* a sluggard on his bed. Prov 26:14

A disjunctive-*waw* clause may also shift the scene or refer to new participants; the   c
disjunction may come at the beginning or end of a larger episode or it may "interrupt"
one. The "interruptive" use, better called explanatory or parenthetical, "break[s] into the
main narrative to supply information relevant to or necessary for the narrative" (# 10).[14]
The disjunction may also indicate "either the completion of one episode or the beginning

---

12. Note also Gen 2:17; cf. v 16.   14. Lambdin, *Introduction to Biblical Hebrew*, 164, cit-
13. Cf. Prov 25:3.   ing 1 Sam 1:9, Gen 29:16; note also Gen 13:7.

of another."[15] At the beginning of a story episode, new characters are often first mentioned (# 11); at the conclusion, further developments are briefly sketched or the narrated episode is put in context (# 12).

10. וַיֹּאמֶר הַגֹּאֵל . . . גְּאַל־לְךָ אַתָּה
     אֶת־גְּאֻלָּתִי . . . וְזֹאת לְפָנִים . . .
     עַל־הַגְּאוּלָּה . . . לְקַיֵּם כָּל־דָּבָר
     שָׁלַף אִישׁ נַעֲלוֹ . . . וַיֹּאמֶר
     הַגֹּאֵל לְבֹעַז קְנֵה־לָךְ וַיִּשְׁלֹף
     נַעֲלוֹ:

The redeemer said, ". . . Redeem my redemption for yourself. . . ." *Now* in the past this was . . . (the procedure) for redemption . . . : to establish any matter a man would draw off his sandal. . . . So when the redeemer said to Boaz, "Acquire (it) for yourself," he drew off his sandal.
Ruth 4:6–8

11. וּלְנָעֳמִי מוֹדַע לְאִישָׁהּ . . .
     וּשְׁמוֹ בֹּעַז:

Now, Naomi had a relative on her husband's side . . . named Boaz.
Ruth 2:1 *Qere*

12. וְאֵלֶּה תּוֹלְדוֹת פָּרֶץ . . . וְשַׂלְמוֹן
     הוֹלִיד אֶת־בֹּעַז וּבֹעַז הוֹלִיד
     אֶת־עוֹבֵד: . . . וְיִשַׁי הוֹלִיד אֶת־
     דָּוִד:

Now, these are the generations of Perez. . . . Salmon begot Boaz and Boaz begot Obed . . . and Jesse begot David.
Ruth 4:18, 21–22

39.2.4   Epexegetical *Waw*

a   *Waw* may stand before clauses which serve to clarify or specify the sense of the preceding clause; the common use of the epexegetical *waw*, in prose, as the *waw*-relative has been discussed (e.g., 32.2.3, 33.2.2).

b   In verse the epexegetical *waw* is more problematic. H. A. Brongers has pointed out that where neighboring lines have nearly identical sense, the *waw* cannot be copulative but probably functions to intensify the poetry (## 1–2).[16] He further suggests that in some cases it compensates for gapping of the initial verb (# 3)[17] or as an emphatic *waw* ('yea') (# 4). When it intensifies the poetic expression, it is often best left untranslated in English. These three usages should be considered together because the distinction between them is subjective.

1. הִנֵּה שְׂכָרוֹ אִתּוֹ
    וּפְעֻלָּתוֹ לְפָנָיו:

See, his reward is with him,
his recompense [goes] before him.
Isa 40:10

2. יַעַבְדוּךָ עַמִּים
    וְיִשְׁתַּחֲווּ לְךָ לְאֻמִּים

May nations serve you,
peoples bow down to you.
Gen 27:29 *Qere*

---

15. Lambdin, *Introduction to Biblical Hebrew*, 164, citing Gen 3:1, 4:1, 16:1, and 21:1.

16. H. A. Brongers, "Alternative Interpretationen des sogennanten Waw copulativum," *Zeitschrift für die Alttestamentliche Wissenschaft* 90 (1978) 273–77.

17. Brongers, "Waw copulativum," 275–76. On verb gapping in Hebrew verse, see M. O'Connor, *Hebrew Verse Structure* (Winona Lake, Indiana: Eisenbrauns, 1980) 122–27. On emphatic seconding, see James Kugel, *The Idea of Biblical Poetry* (New Haven: Yale University, 1981) 51.

3.	וְעַתָּה שְׁמַע יַעֲקֹב עַבְדִּי וְיִשְׂרָאֵל בָּחַרְתִּי בוֹ:	But now listen, O Jacob, my servant, [listen,] Israel, whom I have chosen. Isa 44:1
4.	אֵין־קָדוֹשׁ כַּיהוה . . . וְאֵין צוּר כֵּאלֹהֵינוּ:	There is no one holy like YHWH . . . *yea*, there is no Rock like our God. 1 Sam 2:2

c The epexegetical *waw* on the clausal level may serve the goal of introducing a clause restating or paraphrasing the previous clause;[18] it may be found in either prose (## 5–6) or verse (## 7–8). The precise nuance of *waw* in these and similar cases is often hard to pin down.

5.	וַיֹּאמְרוּ כֹּל אֲשֶׁר־דִּבֶּר יהוה נַעֲשֶׂה וְנִשְׁמָע:	They said, "All that YHWH has said, we will do, *that is*, we will obey." Exod 24:7
6.	אֲבָל אִשָּׁה־אַלְמָנָה אָנִי וַיָּמָת אִישִׁי:	Alas, I am a widow, *that is*, my husband has died. 2 Sam 14:5
7.	כִּי־גוֹי אֹבַד עֵצוֹת הֵמָּה וְאֵין בָּהֶם תְּבוּנָה:	They are a nation without sense, *that is*, there is no discernment in them. Deut 32:28
8.	נַפְתָּלִי שְׂבַע רָצוֹן וּמָלֵא בִּרְכַּת יהוה	Napthali is abounding with favor, *that is*, full of YHWH's blessing. Deut 33:23

Conjunctive *Waw*   39.2.5

a   Conjunctive *waw* serves to join two clauses which describe interrelated or overlapping situations not otherwise logically related. Pairs of such clauses may form a *hendiadys*. There is a tendency, both in translation and commentary, to assign to the conjunctive *waw* a more logically distinct value where possible; this tendency may obscure the distinctive shape of Hebrew narrative.[19] We have already discussed the use of conjunctive (or copulative) *waw* before suffix forms (32.3) and prefix forms (33.4); here we treat conjunctive *waw* before volitionals and some non-volitional prefix forms.

b   Conjunctive *waw* can connect *volitional forms*: imperatives (## 1–2), jussives (# 3), or cohortatives (# 4), or various combinations (cohortative + jussive, # 5; imperative + cohortative, # 6; 34.6). It can also join a clause beginning with a prefix form to a preceding clause (## 7–9).

1.	עֲלֵה אֱכֹל וּשְׁתֵה	Go, eat *and* drink. 1 Kgs 18:41

18. See further Baker, "*Waw Explicativum*."
19. See T. J. Meek, "The Syntax of the Sentence in

Hebrew," *Journal of Biblical Literature* 64 (1945) 1–13;
or the passage from Driver cited by Caird (see n. 7).

2.   וּדְעִי וּרְאִי כִּי־רַע וָמָר

Know *and* see that it is evil and bitter.
Jer 2:19

3.   יַפְתְּ אֱלֹהִים לְיֶפֶת
וְיִשְׁכֹּן בְּאָהֳלֵי־שֵׁם
וִיהִי כְנַעַן עֶבֶד לָמוֹ׃

May God extend the territory of Japheth;
may Japheth live in the tents of Shem;
and may Canaan be his slave.
Gen 9:27

4.   וְאֶתְּנָה בְרִיתִי בֵּינִי וּבֵינֶךָ
וְאַרְבֶּה אוֹתְךָ בִּמְאֹד מְאֹד׃

I will make my covenant between me and you *and*
will greatly increase you.
Gen 17:2

5.   נַעֲשֶׂה אָדָם בְּצַלְמֵנוּ כִּדְמוּתֵנוּ
וְיִרְדּוּ

Let us make humans in our image . . . *and* let
them rule.
Gen 1:26

6.   לְכוּ וְנַעֲלֶה אֶל־הַר־יְהוה

Go *and* let us ascend Yhwh's mountain.
Isa 2:3 = Mic 4:2

7.   אַכֶּנּוּ בַדֶּבֶר וְאוֹרִשֶׁנּוּ

I will strike them down with the plague *and* destroy
them.
Num 14:12

8.   וְכָל־הָעָם יִשְׁמְעוּ וְיִרָאוּ

All the people will hear *and* be afraid.
Deut 17:13; cf. 19:20, 21:21

9.   הֵן יֵבֹשׁוּ וְיִכָּלְמוּ
כֹּל הַנֶּחֱרִים בָּךְ

All who rage against you
will be ashamed *and* disgraced.
Isa 41:11

39.2.6 Other Coordinating Conjunctions

a   Other than *waw*, the only coordinating conjunction established in Hebrew is אוֹ 'or,' used to join alternatives. It is alleged that *p* 'and then' is to be found in Hebrew.

b   The coordinator אוֹ is found separating alternatives in main clauses (## 1–2)[20] and, more often, in subordinate clauses (## 3–4);[21] subordinate clauses are common in legal materials where the precision of אוֹ is desired.[22] As a coordinator, אוֹ works by reducing identical material associated with two conjoined clauses, leaving only what is different; thus the basic structure of # 1 is תֵּשֵׁב . . . יָמִים אוֹ תֵּשֵׁב . . . עָשׂוֹר, 'Let the girl stay with us a few days *or* let the girl stay with us ten days.'[23]

1.   תֵּשֵׁב הַנַּעֲרָה אִתָּנוּ יָמִים אוֹ
עָשׂוֹר

Let the girl stay with us a few days *or* ten.
Gen 24:55 *Qere*

---

20. Joüon § 175 / pp. 528–29. Compare *w* in main clauses (e.g., 2 Sam 2:19; cf. # 2) and with alternatives within a construct phrase (e.g., Exod 21:17).

21. Compare *w* in subordinate clauses (e.g, Exod 21:16, Deut 24:7); note also *ʾm . . . ʾm* in Ezek 2:5. See R. J.

Williams, *Hebrew Syntax: An Outline* (2d ed.; Toronto: University of Toronto, 1976) 71.

22. See M. Fishbane, *Biblical Interpretation in Ancient Israel* (Oxford: Clarendon, 1985) 170–72, 211–12.

23. There is no conjunction reduction in # 4.

2.   נְטֵה לְךָ עַל־יְמִינְךָ אוֹ עַל־ שְׂמֹאלֶךָ   Turn yourself to your right *or* your left. 2 Sam 2:21

3.   וְכִי־יִגַּח שׁוֹר אֶת־אִישׁ אוֹ אֶת־ אִשָּׁה וָמֵת   If an ox gores (*either*) a man *or* a woman who (later) dies.... Exod 21:28

4.   אוֹ־בֵן יִגָּח אוֹ־בַת יִגָּח   (If) it gores *either* a son *or* a daughter....[24] Exod 21:31

The conjunction *p* 'and so (then)' is attested commonly in Arabic (*fa*) and in a   c variety of Northwest Semitic dialects.[25] It has been alleged that it occurs in the Bible, its use neglected by the Masoretes.[26] Consider these verses.

5.   כִּי־לִי כָל־חַיְתוֹ־יָעַר בְּהֵמוֹת בְּהַרְרֵי־אָלֶף: יָדַעְתִּי כָּל־עוֹף הָרִים וְזִיז שָׂדַי עִמָּדִי: All the forest creatures are mine, the beasts on hills.... I know every mountain bird, and all that shakes(?) the fields is at home with me. Ps 50:10–11

The phrase הררי־אלף is problematic; the Masoretes read אָלֶף 'a thousand,' while the Greek has *ktēnē en tois oresin kai boes* 'herds on the mountains and cattle,' reflecting בהמות בהר(ר) ואלף (the Peshitta is similar). Neither of these senses of אָלֶף, 'thousand' or 'cattle,' seems apposite. A phrase in Ps 36:7, כְּהַרְרֵי־אֵל 'mighty hills,'[27] suggests that the last word of Ps 50:10 is אל, while פ is the conjunction; the sense would be, 'the animals are mine *and so* I know them all.' There is a small number of difficult passages for which similar arguments have been offered.[28] The question of Biblical Hebrew *p* is not settled.

Clausal Adverbs   39.3

Adverbs in General   39.3.1

The class of adverbs includes words that modify other words or clauses. In any   a grammar the class presents numerous problems: "The adverb class is the least satisfactory of the traditional parts of speech; [it is an] especially mixed [class], ... having small and fairly well-defined groups of closed-system items [cf. English 'very, well, yet'] alongside the indefinitely large open-class items [cf. English 'briefly, largely, frankly,

---

24. Cf. also Exod 21:32, Lev 5:1.

25. For the Arabic, see W. Wright, *A Grammar of the Arabic Language* (3d ed.; Cambridge: Cambridge University, 1896), 1. 290–91; for the other languages, see the references in the next note.

26. The particle has been most often discussed by M. Dahood, in, e.g., *Psalms I: 1–50* (Garden City, New York: Doubleday, 1966) 293, 307–8, where the example given below is treated (pp. 307–8); all the alleged examples are

rejected by K. Aartun in his review, "Textüberlieferung und Vermeintliche Belege der Konjunktion *pV* im Alten Testament," *Ugarit-Forschungen* 10 (1978) 1–13 (this example at pp. 5–7).

27. Noted by P. Craigie, *Psalms 1–50* (Waco, Texas: Word, 1983) 363.

28. Notably in Job 9:20; see the firm discussion of M. H. Pope, *Job* (3d ed.; Garden City, New York: Doubleday, 1973) 72–73.

timewise'].["29] Further, the items called adverbs often fit into other part-of-speech categories, for example, English 'round' is not only an adverb, but also a noun, an adjective, and a verb.[30] All of these problems are especially acute for Hebrew (and the other Semitic languages); the class of adverbs is extremely small, extremely heterogeneous, and its members are often used in other ways. Many grammars of Hebrew in fact pass over the adverbs, treating some important subclasses in detail while neglecting the class as a whole.[31]

b   The adverbial functions of various European languages afford no guide to Hebrew adverbial use, for in Hebrew other *syntactic approaches* are taken to those functions.[32] The two most important are the "adverbial" accusative (10.2.2) and the "adverbial use" of the infinitive absolute (35.4); both these terms bear the imprint of European grammarians and reflect an alien approach to Hebrew. Nonetheless, the patterns of use are clear, and it is useful to retain such terminology in a grammar for English speakers. Another syntactic approach is based on the use of two Hebrew verbs in sequence, corresponding to a *verb + adverb* construction in other languages; the two Hebrew verbs may have the same form or they may differ in form. (Occasionally, the verb that is similar to an English adverb is called by grammarians an auxiliary or quasi-auxiliary; this terminology is rather dubiously relevant.) Examples of such usage are furnished by verbs such as שׁוב and יסף, which are often rendered with adverbs such as 'again, further, continually,' etc. This syntactic approach to what European languages take as an adverbial function is properly a matter for the Hebrew lexicon; once the pattern is appreciated as an integral part of Hebrew, it requires little grammatical notice.[33]

c   Setting aside constructions that can be called adverbial from an external viewpoint, we are still left with a class of Hebrew adverbs.[34] It is a class that overlaps with other word groups in the language, and one that reveals only modest regularities, but one that demands a brief review before we turn to the subject at hand, the subclass of clausal adverbs.

d   There are three *subgroups* of adverbs in Hebrew: clausal adverbs, item adverbs, and constituent adverbs; the first two groups include largely particles, while the third is more

---

29. R. Quirk et al., *A Grammar of Contemporary English* (Harlow, Essex: Longman, 1972) 267, 47.

30. Quirk et al., *Contemporary English*, 271.

31. For some treatments, see Joüon § 102 / pp. 267–73; K. Beyer, *Althebräische Grammatik* (Göttingen: Vandenhoeck und Ruprecht, 1969) 67–85; H. S. Nyberg, *Hebreisk Grammatik* (Uppsala: Geber, 1952) 53–55. A. B. Davidson, *Hebrew Syntax* (3d ed.; Edinburgh: T. & T. Clark, 1901) 87, is minimal, while on the Ugaritic side, Aartun, *Partikeln I* is full. The best review of basic issues, though brisk, is provided by J. Blau, *An Adverbial Construction in Hebrew and Arabic* (Jerusalem: Israel Academy of Sciences and Humanities, 1977) 1–18; note that he distinguishes, as we do, "between 'adverbs', being a part of speech, and the syntactic [or functional] notion 'adverbial'"

(p. 2 n. 3).

32. Thus Joüon's class of "adverbs of suppletion" (including, e.g., *mar* 'bitterly,' *ləbad* 'apart,' *hêṭēb* 'well') is too mixed a bag to be useful; but our own classification is not proof against the same criticism; see Joüon § 102c–g / pp. 268–70. The grammar of GKC (§ 100b–f / pp. 294–95) draws together adverbs and "forms of other parts of speech, which are used adverbially"; the latter group is another mixed bag and includes prepositional phrases, substantives in the accusative (10.2.2), adjectives (notably feminines, 6.4.2; note, e.g., *rabbâ* 'mightily' in Ps 89:8), infinitives absolute (35.4), etc.

33. Contrast Davidson, *Hebrew Syntax*, 100, 113–16.

34. Note Davidson's desperate phrase "real adverbs," *Hebrew Syntax*, 100.

heterogeneous, including nouns and verbs as well as particles.[35] Clausal and item adverbs modify, respectively, clauses and individual words in a way related to the discourse, that is, they negate, emphasize, or restrict what they modify in relation to some other grammatical feature.[36] Constituent adverbs modify clauses (and, rarely, individual words) but, in contrast to clausal and item adverbs, they modify the predicate, that is, they specify the time, place, or manner of the predicated situation. Consider this pair of clauses.

קְרָא שְׁמָהּ לֹא רֻחָמָה כִּי לֹא אוֹסִיף
עוֹד אֲרַחֵם אֶת־בֵּית יִשְׂרָאֵל

Call her name *Not*-Pitied, *for indeed* I will *not* continue *any longer* to have pity on the House of Israel.[37]
Hos 1:6

The form עוֹד is a constituent adverb, qualifying the time extent of the predicate, while לֹא (אוֹסִיף) is a clausal adverb, negating the entire clause. The particle כִּי is another clausal adverb, this one emphasizing the clause it introduces. Traditionally כִּי is considered a conjunction (cf. 'for'), but we consider it rather to be an emphatic adverb (cf. 'indeed'). The question is not primarily one of translation (though the standard translation 'for' is sometimes illogical and often tedious), but rather of aligning כִּי with other forms that work similarly. The fourth adverb, לֹא (רחמה), is an item adverb, negating only the adjective that immediately follows.

In terms of frequency, clausal and constituent adverbs are common, while item adverbs are rare. In terms of grammatical difficulty, clausal and item adverbs are of considerable interest, while constituent adverbs require less attention.

A listing of *constituent adverbs* should enable the student to grasp the character of the class and prepare to observe its workings. There are four types of constituent adverbs, each with internal dynamics and with significant overlapping with other word groups.[38]

Adverbs of location are of two semantic types. The most common are *deictics*, those which point to a place relative to the situation of the speaking; the senses are 'here' and 'there' (static) and 'hither' and 'thither' (dynamic).[39] The other type of locational adverb has *independent* reference, that is, reference independent of the situation in which the clause is spoken; relevant markers include 'above'—'below,' 'inside'—'outside,' 'around,' and 'behind.'

---

35. In the discussion that follows we concentrate on individual adverbs, slighting all but the most common compound adverbs. Joüon includes all interrogatives, § 102i / p. 271. For expository purposes, we leave out here interrogative pronouns and phrases (18.1) and the polar particle *h* (40.3); the last is certainly a clausal adverb, and it may be that some of the other interrogatives (e.g., *mdw^c*) are also.

36. Aartun, *Partikeln 1*, uses a related principle of classification, referring to "forms for intensification (Bekräftigung)/emphasis (Hervorhebung) of individual words or complete sentences" *versus* "forms for the intensification of complete sentences (only)" and "forms for the negation

(Verneinung) of complete sentences" *versus* "forms for the negation of individual words and complete sentences."

37. There is a sense in which *ʾôsîp* might be said to function adverbially or as an auxiliary to *ʾărahēm*, but that sense is not an important one; see 39.3.1b.

38. There is no clear rule about the placement of constituent adverbs, though temporal adverbs (and adverbial phrases, especially with prepositions) tend to occur initially; for some discussion, see W. Gross, *Die Pendenskonstruction im biblischen Hebräisch* (St. Ottilien: EOS, 1987) 43–77 (on temporals), 78–87 (on locatives).

39. Nyberg groups *ph* and *šm* with *kh* as demonstrative adverbs; see *Hebreisk Grammatik*, 53.

1.	הֲלֹם	hither	7.	מָטָּה	below
2.	הֵנָּה	hither	8.	פְּנִימָה	inside
3.	כֹּה	here	9.	חוּץ	outside
4.	פֹּה	here	10.	מֵסַב	around
5.	שָׁם/שָׁמָּה	there, thither[40]	11.	סָבִיב	around
6.	מַעַל	above	12.	אַחַר	behind

Some of these are derived from roots (## 6–12, all the independents), while others are composed of elements found in other grammatical words (## 1–5, all the deictics).[41] The independent adverbs are also used as prepositions (## 6, 12) or as nouns, often with prepositions (## 8–12). Most of these adverbs have only locational senses, though several also have a rare temporal sense (## 2, 5), and כה is also found as a clausal adverb.

h   *Temporal adverbs* are similarly of two semantic types. *Deictics*, referring to the situation of speaking, may be stative ('now, then') or dynamic ('not yet, previously, already'). The stative temporal deictics עתה and אז share with the English counterparts 'now' and 'then' a logical force ('Now we can see . . . , then we can say . . .'), but the temporal and logical uses are best kept distinct. The dynamic deictics are rare. *Independent* temporal adverbs, those that do not derive their reference from the situation of speaking, can be either local in sense ('by day, tomorrow, afterward') or extensive ('always/still, for a long time, forever'). The frequent phrase יוֹמָם וָלַיְלָה 'by day and by night' (e.g., Ps 1:2) is a good illustration of an adverb and an adverbial accusative being used together.

13.	עַתָּה	now[42]	20.	כְּבָר	already[46]
14.	הֵנָּה	now (cf. # 2)	21.	יוֹמָם	by day
15.	אָז/אֲזַי	then[43]	22.	מָחָר/מָחֳרָת	tomorrow
16.	שָׁם	then (cf. # 5)	23.	אַחַר	then, afterward (cf. # 12)
17.	טֶרֶם	not yet	24.	עוֹד	still[47]
18.	אֶתְמוֹל שִׁלְשׁוֹם	previously[44]	25.	רַבַּת	for a long time
19.	עֶדֶן/עֲדֶנָה	previously[45]	26.	עוֹלָם	forever
			27.	נֶצַח	forever

The etymological diversity noted for the locational adverbs is evident here, too. Only one of these forms (# 23) is used as a preposition, but the last three are used as nouns; רבת (# 24) is the feminine of רב 'much.' Another form of derivation can be seen in יומם and

---

40. The forms *šm* and *šmh* are found 691 and 141 times, respectively, in all senses (SA/THAT; in what follows, we supply the count for the most common words from this source; the most common words are those that occur more than one hundred times).

41. Aartun similarly contrasts "adverbs derived from deictic elements" and "adverbs derived from roots."

42. Occurs 433 times (SA/THAT).

43. *ʾāz* occurs 138 times (SA/THAT).

44. The phrase never has the supposed "literal" sense 'yesterday (*ʾtmwl*) or the day before (*šlšwm*, lit., the third day ago [counting today]).'

45. Only in Qoh 4:2 (*ʿdnh*), 4:3 (*ʿdn*), derived from *ʿad*, suggesting a basic sense 'until now.'

46. Only in Qoheleth, where it occurs nine times.

47. Occurs 490 times (SA/THAT).

שִׁלְשׁוֹם; though the -*ām* "adverbial" ending is no longer productive in Biblical Hebrew, it has yielded several important forms (5.7e).[48]

Scalar adverbs make up a more diverse group than either locational or temporal adverbs. One group of scalars refers to grades of *degree*, on a scale from 'much, very, extremely, abundantly' (amplifiers) down to 'a little, almost' (diminishers). Another group of scalars refers to grades of *identity of action*; a situation may be repeated ('again') or uninterrupted ('continually').

28.	מְאֹד	very[49]		32.	מְעַט	a little, almost
29.	הַרְבֵּה	very[50]		33.	עוֹד	again, continually (cf. # 24)
30.	יוֹתֵר	extremely[51]		34.	תָּמִיד	continually
31.	רַבַּת	abundantly (cf. # 25)				

All but one of these (# 32) is used as a noun (including הרבה!). Although מעט is common (it occurs ca. 100 times), the relative rarity of diminishers is striking.

The *manner adverbs* are the most diverse group of constituent adverbs: they can describe the manner of an action with regard to (*a*) action ('quickly, suddenly'), (*b*) the actors ('together, secretly'), (*c*) their motives ('falsely'), or (*d*) the results ('vainly').

35.	מְהֵרָה	quickly		40.	חֶרֶשׁ	secretly
36.	פִּתְאֹם	suddenly, abruptly[52]		41.	שָׁוְא	falsely
37.	פֶּתַע	suddenly		42.	חִנָּם	in vain, gratis[53]
38.	רֶגַע	suddenly		43.	רֵיקָם	vainly[54]
39.	יַחַד/יַחְדָּו	together				

Except for the three forms with adverbial -*ā/ōm* ending (## 36, 42, 43), all these adverbs are also used as nouns, and it should be plain that there is no strict line separating these manner adverbs from a variety of other adverbial accusative uses of nouns.

Clausal and Item Adverbs   39.3.2

The two groups of clausal adverbs and item adverbs overlap to a large extent, but the overlap is largely the result of another fact: item adverbs are rare in Hebrew. The grammatical tasks of negation, emphasis, and restriction are usually associated with the entire clause, rather than an item within it. This relationship is most easily recognized with negation: the common, clausal type is shown in ## 1–2, rare, item types in ## 3–4.

---

48. This -*ām/ōm* element may be (related to) the enclitic *mem* (9.8); cf., e.g., Aartun, *Partikeln*, 1. 51–61.

49. More frequently an item adverb. For its unique use as a noun in Deut 6:5, see S. D. McBride, "The Yoke of the Kingdom," *Interpretation* 27 (1973) 273–306, at 304. *Mᵊʾd* occurs 300 times (SA/THAT).

50. Strictly, an infinitive absolute. See 35.4.

51. Only in Qoheleth and Esther as an adverb.

52. It is common to derive *ptʾm* from *ptᶜ* (e.g., Jouon § 102b / p. 268), but the weakening of ᶜ*ayin* to *ʾaleph* is rare.

53. From *ḥēn* with adverbial -*ām*; compare Latin *gratia* and *gratis* (Jouon § 102b / p. 268).

54. From *rēq* 'empty,' with adverbial -*ām*.

1. וְאֶת־הָאָרֶץ הַזֹּאת לֹא־יִרְאֶה
עֽוֹד׃

And this land he shall *no more* see / see *no more*.
Jer 22:12

2. וְרָעָה לֹא רָאִֽינוּ׃

And evil we did *not* see / we saw *no* evil.
Jer 44:17

3. עֹרֶף וְלֹא־פָנִים אֶרְאֵם

I will show them (my) neck and *not* (my) face.
Jer 18:17 *Oriental manuscripts*[55]

4. מִכֹּל הַבְּהֵמָה הַטְּהוֹרָה תִּקַּח־לְךָ
שִׁבְעָה שִׁבְעָה אִישׁ וְאִשְׁתּוֹ וּמִן־
הַבְּהֵמָה אֲשֶׁר לֹא טְהֹרָה הִוא
שְׁנַיִם אִישׁ וְאִשְׁתּֽוֹ׃

Take with you seven male-female pairs of every kind of clean animal and a male-female pair of every kind of *not* clean animal.
Gen 7:2

In the first two examples the negative לֹא stands before the verb, though in the first the negated element is the adverb עוד and in the second the negated element is the object רעה. In ## 3–4, the item negative לֹא stands before the specific item negated.[56] The preference for emphasis and restriction on the clausal level, rather than on the item level, is similar to the treatment of negation. Indeed Hebrew has only one important item adverb that is not principally a clausal adverb and more commonly used as such, מאד (## 5–6).[57]

5. וַיְנִיחֵנִי אֶל־הַר גָּבֹהַּ מְאֹד

He led me to a *very* high mountain.
Ezek 40:2

6. וַיַּעַמְדוּ . . . חַיִל גָּדוֹל מְאֹד־
מְאֹד׃

They stood up . . . a *very*, *very* great troop.
Ezek 37:10

A variety of clausal adverbs can be used as item adverbs, usually in a heightened sense and often in poetry; some of these uses are mentioned below.

b   There are three groups of clausal adverbs. The negatives are best considered in connection with the constructions they occur in, and we provide only a brief summary here. The emphatic and restrictive adverbs, both often treated as types of conjunctions, require more discussion here.

39.3.3   Negative Adverbs

a   There are five principal negative adverbs; each is specialized in function, though some crossover is found with all but the rarest.[58] Independent verbal clauses are negated with לֹא (# 1), unless the verb is a negative imperative, which requires אל before the jussive (# 2).[59]

---

55. MT has the *Qal*, ᵓerᵓēm.

56. Compare # 3 with Jer 2:27.

57. Note that postposed *hûᵓ* and *hîᵓ* are also used as item adverbs ('precisely').

58. See Joüon § 160 / pp. 488–95. The other negative particles are largely confined to verse: *bal* is a clausal negative used as *lōᵓ* is, while *bəlî* is used largely as *ᵓên* is; *biltî* is usually an item adverb ('except'). On the positive force of

bal, see C. F. Whitley, "The Positive Force of the Hebrew Particle בל," *Zeitschrift für die Alttestamentliche Wissenschaft* 84 (1972) 213–19; the best example is probably Isa 44:8. All Whitley's examples are doubted by T. Muraoka, *Emphatic Words and Structures in Biblical Hebrew* (Leiden: Brill, 1985) 125–27.

59. *Lōᵓ* occurs 5,200 times and *ᵓal* 730 times (SA/ THAT). For *lōᵓ* as an item adverb, note (a) compounds,

1. לֹא־יִשָּׂא גוֹי אֶל־גוֹי חֶרֶב   *No* nation shall lift a sword against a(nother) nation.
    Isa 2:4

2. וְאַל־תִּשָּׂא לָהֶם: Do *not* forgive them!
    Isa 2:9

Dependent verbal clauses may be negated with פֶּן for a finite purpose clause (# 3), and
לְבִלְתִּי or מִן for an infinitive clause (# 4);[60] otherwise לֹא is used (# 5).

3. וְעֵינָיו הָשַׁע פֶּן־יִרְאֶה בְעֵינָיו   Seal its eyes *lest* it see with its eyes.
    Isa 6:10

4. וְאַתֶּם הֲרֵעֹתֶם לַעֲשׂוֹת
    מֵאֲבוֹתֵיכֶם . . . לְבִלְתִּי שְׁמֹעַ
    אֵלָי: You have been more evil in your behavior than your
    forebears . . . in that you did *not* listen to me.
    Jer 16:12

5. אִם לֹא תַאֲמִינוּ כִּי לֹא תֵאָמֵנוּ:   If you do *not* remain faithful, you will indeed
    not remain standing.
    Isa 7:9

Verbless clauses are negated with אֵין (in the construct; ## 6–7) or rarely אַיִן (in the   **b**
absolute; # 8).[61] Two frequent negative verbless clause types are אֵין followed by a participle (# 9) and אֵין with a possessive suffix denoting the subject (## 10–11). Various negative types may occur together (# 12).

6. אַל־תַּעֲלוּ כִּי אֵין יהוה
    בְּקִרְבְּכֶם   Don't attack! YHWH is *not* in your midst!
    Num 14:42

7. אֵין־בּוֹ מְתֹם   There's *no* health in it!
    Isa 1:6

8. וְכֹחַ אַיִן לְלֵדָה: There's *no* strength to give birth!
    Isa 37:3

9. וּשְׁכַבְתֶּם וְאֵין מַחֲרִיד   You shall lie down and there will be *no one* to
    terrorize (you).
    Lev 26:6

---

e.g., *lōʾ-ʾēl* 'no god' (Deut 32:21), *lōʾ-ḥākām* 'non- (or
anti-)wise' (Deut 32:6; cf. further GKC § 152a / p. 478),
as well as (*b*) simple adverbial use (e.g., Jer 18:17 [39.3.2
3], Gen 32:29, Job 13:16). For *ʾal* as an item adverb,
note (*a*) compounds, e.g., *ʾal-māwet* 'no death' (Prov
12:28), and (*b*) simple use (e.g., Jer 10:24). The variation
between *lʾ* and *lw* is an important source of *Kethiv-Qere*
variation; see J. Barr, "A New Look at *Kethibh-Qere*,"
Oudtestamentische Studiën 21 (1981) 19–37, at 31. Both
lōʾ and *ʾal* are used alone, as the equivalent of reduced
verbal clauses, with the sense 'no!' (*lōʾ* in Gen 42:10 and
so read for *lô* in 1 Sam 10:19; *ʾal* in Gen 33:10). See Ziony
Zevit, "Expressing Denial in Biblical Hebrew and Mishnaic Hebrew, and in Amos," *Vetus Testamentum* 29 (1979)
505–9. On the semantics of negation, see G. E. Whitney,

"*Lōʾ* ('Not') as 'Not Yet' in the Hebrew Bible," *Hebrew
Studies* 29 (1988) 43–48.

60. The preposition *mn* is used to form negative infinitive (notably result) clauses (e.g., Isa 5:6); cf. the examples
cited in 38.3c.

61. *ʾáyin*/ *ʾên* occurs 789 times; its conventional anto-
nym *yēš* occurs 140 times (SA / THAT). The latter is often
considered an adverb (e.g., GKC § 100o / pp. 296–97). For
ʾên as an item adverb, note compounds such as *ʾên-qēṣ*
'endless' (Isa 9:6), *ʾên qēṣeh* 'endless' (Isa 2:7*bis*), *ʾên
mispār* 'innumerable' (Jer 2:32, 1 Chr 22:4), *ʾên mišqāl*
'beyond weighing' (1 Chr 22:3). Note the discussion of
J. Carmignac, "L'emploi de la négation אֵין dans la Bible
et à Qumrân," *Revue de Qumrân* 8 (1974) 407–13, who
emphasizes the increase in item-adverbial use at Qumran.

10.	אֵינֶ֫נִּי נֹתֵן לָכֶם תֶּֽבֶן׃	I am *not* giving you straw. Exod 5:10
11.	בַּעֲמַל אֱנוֹשׁ אֵינֵ֫מוֹ	They are *not* (involved) in human pain. Ps 73:5
12.	אֵין־עָיֵף וְאֵין־כּוֹשֵׁל בּוֹ	There is *no one* who is weary, *no one* who stumbles in it (the road?),
	לֹא יָנוּם וְלֹא יִישָׁן	*no one* dozes, *no one* slumbers. Isa 5:27

39.3.4   Emphatic Adverbs

a   The category of emphatic clausal adverbs includes adverbs that modify the clause in itself (as negatives do), those that modify the clause in relation to preceding or following clauses (dependent or independent), and those that modify the clause in relation to the whole discourse. In traditional Hebrew grammars, some of these are called particles and others adverbs;[62] some are associated with clause types, while others are relegated to the lexicon.[63] The group is not itself a strict unity, but these adverbs are best considered together.

b   The *disjuncts* are those adverbs which modify a clause in relation to the act of speaking.[64] Hebrew has few disjuncts, all rare. English has a great many disjuncts, in contrast, and they are used frequently and imprecisely in rendering Hebrew; for this reason, the category deserves some extra attention. English disjunct adverbs convey the speaker's attitude toward the form of the utterance ('truly, truthfully, roughly') or its content ('definitely, indeed, surely, plainly, actually, really'). Both types are regularly used to render the whole range of Hebrew emphatic adverbs, especially when a given form has no other English correspondent. It is important to note this disparity between English and Hebrew, so that translational practice does not obscure grammatical fact. The two Hebrew disjuncts referring to form are אָמְנָה and אָמְנָם[65] (אֻמְנָם in polar questions with ה),[66] 'verily, truly' (## 1–3). The two that refer to content are אוּלַי 'perhaps' (## 4–5) and מְעַט 'a little, somewhat' (# 6).[67]

1.	אָמְנָה אָנֹכִי חָטָ֫אתִי	*In truth* (I tell you that) I have sinned. Josh 7:20

62. See Joüon § 164 / pp. 502–3.

63. And the lexicons usually do a wonderful job with them. We leave out of account here a variety of emphatics much discussed in recent scholarly literature. On the emphatic *l*, see Muraoka, *Emphatic Words*, 113–23, whose findings are largely negative. Contrast, e.g., J. A. Soggin, *Old Testament and Oriental Studies* (Rome: Biblical Institute, 1975) 219–24.

64. The term is from Quirk et al., *Contemporary English*, 507. They could also be called "metapropositional" adverbs in that they comment on how the proposition is to be understood. Blau refers to "sentence adverbials denoting judgement on the rest of the sentence," which "may be considered logical predicates"; see *Adverbial Construction*, 15.

65. Again, we have the -*ām* adverbial ending. On *ʾomnām kî*, see Blau, *Adverbial Construction*, 26.

66. In, e.g., Gen 18:13.

67. Blau (*Adverbial Construction*, 30) notes also *kimʿaṭ šе-* 'hardly' in Cant 3:4. The understanding of these disjunct adverbs depends in part on the understanding of the associated action, in particular whether, say, 'worship' is a scalar phenomenon.

2.   אָמְנָם יהוה הֶחֱרִיבוּ מַלְכֵי   *Of a truth*, (I tell you,) YHWH, (that) the Assyrian
      אַשּׁוּר אֶת־כָּל־הָאֲרָצוֹת   kings have wasted all the lands.[68]
                                        Isa 37:18

3.   כִּי־אָמְנָם לֹא־שֶׁקֶר מִלָּי   *Truly* (I claim that) my words are not lies.
                                        Job 36:4

4.   בֹּא־נָא אֶל־שִׁפְחָתִי אוּלַי אִבָּנֶה   Go to my maid. *Perhaps* I shall be built up from her.
      מִמֶּנָּה   Gen 16:2

5.   עִמְדִי־נָא בַחֲבָרַיִךְ . . .   Stand fast in your spells. . . .
      אוּלַי תּוּכְלִי הוֹעִיל   *Perhaps* you'll be able to benefit.
                                        Isa 47:12

6.   וָאֱהִי לָהֶם לְמִקְדָּשׁ מְעַט   I have been to *some extent* a sanctuary for them.
                                        Ezek 11:16

The role of disjuncts can be performed by non-adverbs, for example, the prepositional
phrase באמת 'in truth.'[69]

The adverbs that modify a clause in relation to what follows or, less often, precedes   c
fall into three categories: particles recognized as coordinators (אף, גם), a series of particles in כ usually taken as logical markers (כי, כן, כה, ככה), and the common temporal
adverbs (אז, עתה).[70] Hebrew grammars tend to assign well-defined roles to these words,
but as the lexicons usually recognize, such assignments do not describe the usages adequately. All these terms have quite broad emphatic uses as well as the specific senses to
be discussed. The notion that the broad or hard-to-define use grew out of the narrow or
easy-to-define use is attractive, but probably misleading.

Of the two major *coordinators*, אף is the simpler and closer to ו, sometimes scarcely   d
distinct from it (# 7); אף can also serve as a correlative, lining up the situation of its
clause with that of the previous clause.[71] The clauses in such correlation are independent
(# 8), and thus such a pair is distinct from the כ protasis + כֵּן apodosis combination
(38.5). Followed by כי, אף can have emphatic role (## 8–9).[72] The second major coordinator גם, though it is used as an item adverb,[73] generally has more distinctly logical force
than אף, though it can be used as an emphatic (## 10–11), often with a pronoun following. It can signal a final climax in an exposition (## 12–13) and is the only Hebrew
adverb that marks a discourse ending—all others mark beginnings or middles.[74] The
particle can serve as a correlative, in an apodosis after יען (## 14–15) or after an independent clause (# 16).

---

68. Cf. the synoptic verse, 2 Kgs 19:17.

69. Thus, *b'mt* serves an adverbial role but is not an
adverb; cf. n. 31.

70. We omit interrogatives here; see n. 35.

71. Occurs 134 times (SA/THAT).

72. The related particle *'ēpô* is an enclitic used after
interrogatives, *'im*, and imperatives (for an example of the
last, see Job 19:6); cf. Muraoka, *Emphatic Words*, 137.

73. In, e.g., Isa 49:25; Jer 2:33, 25:14; see in general
Muraoka, *Emphatic Words*, 143–46; and C. J. Labu-
schagne, "The Emphasizing Particle *GAM* and Its Con-
notations," *Studia Biblica et Semitica: Theodoro Christiano
Vriezen . . . Dedicata*, ed. W. C. van Unnik (Wageningen:
Veenman en Zonen, 1966) 193–203.

74. Though it is hardly a strict marker, rather a rhythmic
indicator.

7.   אֲמַצְתִּ֫יךָ אַף־עֲזַרְתִּ֫יךָ

I will strengthen you *and* help you.
Isa 41:10

8.   הִנֵּ֣ה בִּֽהְיוֹת֣וֹ תָמִ֔ים לֹ֥א יֵעָשֶׂ֖ה
     לִמְלָאכָ֑ה אַ֣ף כִּי־אֵ֤שׁ אֲכָלַ֙תְהוּ֙
     . . . וְנֵחָ֔ר וְנַעֲשָׂ֥ה ע֖וֹד לִמְלָאכָֽה:

When it (such wood, the wood of the vine) is whole, it is not used for anything. *How much less*, when fire has consumed it . . . , is it ever used for anything?
Ezek 15:5

9.   אַ֣ף כִּֽי־אַרְבַּ֣עַת שְׁפָטַ֣י הָרָעִ֗ים
     . . . שִׁלַּ֣חְתִּי

How much more when I send my four evil judgments. . . .[75]
Ezek 14:21

10. כֻּלָּ֤ם יַֽעֲנוּ֙ וְיֹאמְר֣וּ אֵלֶ֔יךָ גַּם־
     אַתָּ֛ה חֻלֵּ֥יתָ כָמֹ֖ונוּ אֵלֵ֥ינוּ נִמְשָֽׁלְתָּ:

All of them will speak (lit., answer) and say to you, "You are *indeed* as sick as we are—you are like us!"[76]
Isa 14:10

11. שׁוֹחֵ֤ט הַשּׁוֹר֙ מַכֵּה־אִ֔ישׁ
     . . . זֹבֵ֤חַ הַשֶּׂה֙ עֹ֣רֵֽף כֶּ֔לֶב
     גַּם־הֵ֗מָּה בָּֽחֲרוּ֙ בְּדַרְכֵיהֶ֔ם

He who slaughters an ox is a manslayer.
He who sacrifices a sheep is a dog killer. . . .
They have *plainly* chosen their paths.[77]
Isa 66:3

12. נָ֥חָה שָׁקְטָ֖ה כָּל־הָאָ֑רֶץ פָּצְח֖וּ
     רִנָּ֑ה: גַּם־בְּרוֹשִׁ֛ים שָׂמְח֥וּ לְךָ֖

It rests, is peaceful, all the earth. Then they (the inhabitants of the earth) break out in shouts. *Even* the cypresses exult over you.
Isa 14:7–8

13. בְּחַלְּקֵֽי־נַ֣חַל חֶלְקֵ֔ךְ הֵ֥ם הֵ֖ם
     גּוֹרָלֵ֑ךְ גַּם־לָהֶ֗ם שָׁפַ֙כְתְּ֙ נֶ֔סֶךְ
     הֶעֱלִ֖ית מִנְחָֽה

Your inheritance is among the wadi's rocks. They, they are your portion. To them you *even* pour out libations; you offer up grain gifts.
Isa 57:6

14. . . . יַ֣עַן אֶת־מִקְדָּשִׁי֙ טִמֵּ֔את
     וְגַם־אֲנִ֖י אֶגְרַ֑ע

Since you defiled my sanctuary . . . I will *in recompense* diminish (you).[78]
Ezek 5:11

15. יַ֣עַן אֲשֶׁ֤ר לֹֽא־זָכַרְתְּ֙ אֶת־יְמֵ֣י
     נְעוּרַ֔יִךְ . . . וְגַם־אֲנִ֗י הָ֤א דַרְכֵּךְ֙
     בְּרֹ֣אשׁ נָתַ֔תִּי

Since you have not kept in mind your youth . . . *in recompense* I will certainly put (the burden of) your ways on your head.[79]
Ezek 16:43

16. שִׁמְע֤וּ מַטֶּה֙ . . . אֲשֶׁ֣ר עֲשִׁירֶ֗יהָ
     מָלְא֤וּ חָמָס֙ וְיֹשְׁבֶ֣יהָ דִּבְּרוּ־שָׁ֔קֶר
     וּלְשׁוֹנָ֖ם רְמִיָּ֣ה בְּפִיהֶ֑ם: וְגַם־אֲנִ֛י
     הֶחֱלֵ֥יתִי הַכּוֹתֶֽךָ

Listen, tribe . . . whose rich men are full of violence and whose inhabitants speak lies and their tongues are deceitful in their mouths! I will *in recompense* make your wound worse (lit., make sore your smiting).
Mic 6:9, 12–13

---

75. The clausal structures in Ezekiel are always complex; see here the context.

76. The English adverb appears to be a disjunct of content rather than an emphatic coordinator.

77. Cf. RSV, 'These have chosen their *own* ways.'

78. Four oath and exclamatory formulas precede this.

78. The interjection *hēʾ* is otherwise found only in Gen 47:23.

The four important *adverbs in k* are usually treated as logical markers, rendered   e
'for, thus, therefore,' etc., but such an approach can be misleading. Each of the three
most common is associated with a specific point in the discourse—כֹה is initial, while כִּי
and כֵּן are medial; only כָּכָה can occupy either position.[80] This consistency does not mean
that a rigid logical or translational understanding is desirable. The most problematic of
these four particles is כִּי, used not only as a clausal adverb but also as a conjunction
introducing various types of subordinate clauses (37.2–4, 7–8).[81] There are two clause-
adverbial uses of כִּי: the emphatic (## 17–18) and the logical (twice in # 19). The second
of these overshadows the first through the dominance of the translation 'for' in "Biblical
English." This translation is often used where it, and the understanding behind it, are
simply wrong, that is, where there is no evident logical link of the clause to what precedes. Further, 'for' suggests that כִּי is a subordinating conjunction, which it often is not
when used in the logical sense. The two clausal uses, which can occur in adjacent clauses
(# 20, first logical, then emphatic), should not be too strictly separated.

17.   צִיּוֹן בְּמִשְׁפָּט תִּפָּדֶה . . . כִּי   Zion shall be redeemed justly. . . . They (its
      יֵבֹשׁוּ מֵאֵילִים . . . כִּי תִהְיוּ   inhabitants) shall *indeed* be ashamed of oaks. . . .
      כְּאֵלָה   You shall *indeed* be like an oak.
                                                      Isa 1:27, 29–30

18.   קוּמָה יהוה   Arise, Yнwн,
      הוֹשִׁיעֵנִי אֱלֹהַי   Deliver me, O my God.
      כִּי־הִכִּיתָ אֶת־כָּל־אֹיְבַי לֶחִי   *Indeed*, strike all my enemies on the cheek.
                                                      Ps 3:8

19.   אַל־תִּשְׂמְחִי פְלֶשֶׁת כֻּלֵּךְ   Do not rejoice, all of you, Philistia
      כִּי נִשְׁבַּר שֵׁבֶט מַכֵּךְ   (*over the fact*) *that* the rod of your smiting is
                                                         broken—
      כִּי־מִשֹּׁרֶשׁ נָחָשׁ יֵצֵא צֶפַע   (*because of the fact*) *that* an adder will emerge from
                                                         the serpent root.
                                                      Isa 14:29

20.   הֲשִׁיבֵנִי וְאָשׁוּבָה   Bring me back so I can come back,
      כִּי אַתָּה יהוה אֱלֹהָי: *because* you are Yнwн my God.
      כִּי־אַחֲרֵי שׁוּבִי נִחַמְתִּי   *Indeed* after I turned away I repented.
                                                      Jer 31:18–19

---

80. *Ky* occurs 4,470 times, *kn* 695 times, *kh* 581 times (SA/THAT), and *kkh* 37 times.

81. It is used as an item adverb in, e.g., Hos 8:6; cf. Jouon § 164b / p. 503. The classic studies of *ky* by James Muilenburg are available in his *Hearing and Speaking the Word*, ed. T. F. Best (Chico: Scholars Press, 1984) 208–33, 27–44, esp. 39–40; J. L. Kugel, "The Adverbial Use of *kî ṭôb*," *Journal of Biblical Literature* 99 (1980) 433–35, claims that the cited phrase is adverbial, 'greatly, how great'; G. Janzen offers a rebuttal in the same journal,

"Kugel's Adverbial *kî ṭôb*: An Assessment," 102 (1983) 99–106. Closely related to *ky* is emphatic *k* (pointed as if identical to the preposition, perhaps correctly); see the basic review of cases by R. Gordis, "The Asseverative *Kaph* in Ugaritic and Hebrew," *Journal of the American Oriental Society* 63 (1943) 176–78, reprinted in his *The Word and the Book* (New York: Ktav, 1976) 211–13. For a cautious approach to emphatic uses, see A. Schoors, "The Particle כִּי," *Oudtestamentische Studiën* 21 (1981) 240–76, at 243–53; he also surveys the subordinating uses, pp. 252–73.

The particle כֵּן is regularly used in the apodosis of a comparative sentence ('thus'; 38.5); when it stands in a clause that is not a comparative apodosis, it has a general comparative sense with no specific referent (## 21–22); the referent is usually clear from context. Adverbial כֵּן is common in the two combinations לָכֵן and עַל־כֵּן.[82] The first of these usually introduces a proposed or anticipated response after a statement of certain conditions ('the foregoing being the case, therefore'; ## 23 twice, 24). In contrast, עַל־כֵּן usually introduces a statement of later effects (# 25), notably the adoption of a name or a custom (# 26).

21. כֵּן יֹאבְדוּ כָל־אוֹיְבֶיךָ יהוה

Thus perish all your enemies, O YHWH.
Judg 5:31

22. כֵּן אָהֲבוּ לָנוּעַ

Thus have they loved to wander.
Jer 14:10

23. וְאֵת פֹּעַל יהוה לֹא יַבִּיטוּ
וּמַעֲשֵׂה יָדָיו לֹא רָאוּ׃ לָכֵן גָּלָה
עַמִּי מִבְּלִי־דָעַת וּכְבוֹדוֹ מְתֵי
רָעָב וַהֲמוֹנוֹ צִחֵה צָמָא׃ לָכֵן
הִרְחִיבָה שְּׁאוֹל נַפְשָׁהּ

YHWH's actions they do not look at. The work of his hands they do not see. (*That being so,*) *therefore* my people go into exile lacking knowledge. Its glory is starving men and its crowd is dry with thirst. (*That being so,*) *therefore* Sheol has widened its gullet.
Isa 5:12–14

24. מֵתִים בַּל־יִחְיוּ . . . לָכֵן פָּקַדְתָּ
וַתַּשְׁמִידֵם

(Being) dead, they (other gods) cannot live . . . *that being so*, you have visited them with destruction.
Isa 26:14

25. כִּי מַעֲלֵה הַלּוּחִית בִּבְכִי יַעֲלֶה־
בּוֹ כִּי דֶּרֶךְ חוֹרֹנַיִם זַעֲקַת־שֶׁבֶר
יְעֹעֵרוּ׃ . . . כִּי־יָבֵשׁ חָצִיר . . .
עַל־כֵּן יִתְרָה עָשָׂה . . . יִשָּׂאוּם׃

Item: Luhith Ascent—they mount it in tears. Item: Horonaim Road—they raise[83] a cry of destruction. . . . Item: the grass is parched. . . . *As a result*, the surplus they made . . . they bear off.
Isa 15:5–7

26. כִּי אֶת־מַעְשַׂר בְּנֵי־יִשְׂרָאֵל . . .
נָתַתִּי לַלְוִיִּם לְנַחֲלָה עַל־כֵּן
אָמַרְתִּי לָהֶם . . . לֹא יִנְחֲלוּ
נַחֲלָה׃

Indeed the Israelites' tithe . . . I give to the Levites as an inheritance. *As a result*, I ordered of them . . . that they inherit no (other) inheritance.
Num 18:24

In addition to serving as a constituent adverb of place ('here'), כֹּה is used to introduce speech (especially with אמר) and action (especially with עשה); it thus initiates a section of discourse (# 27; cf. # 28). The closely related particle כָּכָה can introduce speech which points back to what precedes (# 28) or it can summarize preceding material (# 29).[84]

---

82. On *kn*, see the articles of M. J. Mulder, "Die Partikel כֵּן im Alten Testament," and E. Talstra, "The Use of כֵּן in Biblical Hebrew," *Oudtestamentische Studiën* 21 (1981) 201–27, 228–39. The combinations are discussed here because of their frequency: *lkn* occurs 188 times and *ᶜl-kn* 145 times. See also H. Lenhard, "Über den Unterscheid zwischen לכן und עַל־כֵן," *Zeitschrift für die Alttestamentliche Wissenschaft* 95 (1983) 269–72; B. Jongeling, "*Lākēn* dans l'Ancien Testament," *Oudtestamentische Studiën* 21 (1981) 190–200.

83. The root and stem of *yᶜrw* are obscure.

84. On *kkh*, see L. Glinert, "The Preposition in Biblical and Modern Hebrew," *Hebrew Studies* 23 (1982) 115–25, at 121–22.

27. כֹּה תְבָרֲכוּ אֶת־בְּנֵי יִשְׂרָאֵל
אָמוֹר לָהֶם: יְבָרֶכְךָ יהוה

In the following way will you bless the Israelites, by saying to them, "May Yнwн bless you. . . ."
Num 6:23–24

28. . . . וְשָׁבַרְתָּ הַבַּקְבֻּק . . . וְאָמַרְתָּ
כֹּה־אָמַר יהוה צְבָאוֹת כָּכָה
אֶשְׁבֹּר אֶת־הָעָם הַזֶּה

You shall break the flask. . . . You shall say . . . , "*In the following way* (*kh*) speaks Yнwн Ṣbᵓwt: '*In the foregoing way* (*kkh*) I will break this people. . . .'"
Jer 19:10–11

29. זֹאת אֲשֶׁר לַלְוִיִּם מִבֶּן חָמֵשׁ
וְעֶשְׂרִים שָׁנָה וָמַעְלָה יָבוֹא . . .
כָּכָה תַּעֲשֶׂה לַלְוִיִּם בְּמִשְׁמְרֹתָם:

This is what concerns the Levites: from age twenty-five on (each of them) shall go in. . . . *In the foregoing way* you shall handle the Levites in their duties.
Num 8:24, 26

The temporal adverbs עתה and אַזִי/אָז have, in addition to their temporal use, a logical or emphatic use; these two uses merge in translation and commentary, because many languages assign logical value (cf. English 'now . . . , then . . .') or even emphatic value (cf. English 'Now then . . .') to time words. The sets of uses are, however, best distinguished, in order to avoid misunderstanding the overall sense of a passage. The logical force of עתה is usually confined to the combination ועתה, introducing a shift in argumentative tack with a continuity in subject and reference (# 30 twice). In the example, ועתה separates three stages of discussion of a single topic.[85] The particle אז is more diverse. It can mark a logical turn (## 31–32) or, in verse, serve an emphatic role (# 33). The emphatic role is problematic because almost any pair of clauses in (grammatical) sequence can be understood as being in temporal sequence. Both אז and אזי can introduce the apodosis of a conditional sentence (# 34).

30. כֶּרֶם הָיָה לִידִידִי . . . וַיְעַזְּקֵהוּ
. . . וַיִּטָּעֵהוּ שֹׂרֵק . . . וַיְקַו
לַעֲשׂוֹת עֲנָבִים וַיַּעַשׂ בְּאֻשִׁים:
. . . וְעַתָּה יוֹשֵׁב יְרוּשָׁלַיִם
שִׁפְטוּ־נָא בֵּינִי וּבֵין כַּרְמִי: מַה־
לַעֲשׂוֹת עוֹד לְכַרְמִי וְלֹא עָשִׂיתִי
בּוֹ . . . וְעַתָּה אוֹדִיעָה־נָּא אֶתְכֶם
אֵת אֲשֶׁר־אֲנִי עֹשֶׂה לְכַרְמִי

My lover had a vineyard. . . . He weeded it . . . and he planted it with vines. . . . And he expected (it) to yield grapes and it made weeds. *And now (that you know these basic facts)*, Jerusalemites, render judgment between my vineyard and me: What more was there to do for my vineyard that I did not do . . . ? *And now (that you have formed a judgment)*, I will reveal to you what I am going to do with my vineyard.
Isa 5:1–5

31. הַיּוֹם יָדַעְנוּ כִּי־בְתוֹכֵנוּ יהוה
אֲשֶׁר לֹא־מְעַלְתֶּם בַּיהוה הַמַּעַל
הַזֶּה אָז הִצַּלְתֶּם אֶת־בְּנֵי יִשְׂרָאֵל
מִיַּד יהוה:

Today we know that Yнwн is in our midst in that you did not act arrogantly against Yнwн. (*As a result we can conclude*), *now*, (*that*) you saved the Israelites from Yнwн's power.
Josh 22:31

---

85. See H. A. Brongers, "Bemerkungen zum Gebrauch des adverbiellen *weᶜattāh* im Alten Testament," *Vetus Testamentum* 15 (1965) 289–99.

32.   לָמָּה לֹא מֵרֶחֶם אָמוּת . . . כִּי־
עַתָּה שָׁכַבְתִּי וְאֶשְׁקוֹט יָשַׁנְתִּי אָז
יָנוּחַ לִי:

Why did I not die just out of the womb?[86] . . . *Had that been the case (ᶜth), I would have lain down and been quiet, I would have slept (and) as a result* everything would have been fine with me.[87]
Job 3:11, 13

33.   יִגְּשׁוּ אָז יְדַבֵּרוּ

They approach *and then* they speak.
Isa 41:1

34.   לוּלֵי יהוה שֶׁהָיָה לָנוּ בְּקוּם
עָלֵינוּ אָדָם: אֲזַי חַיִּים בְּלָעוּנוּ

Had YHWH not been for us when people rose against us, *then* they would have swallowed us alive.[88]
Ps 124:2–3

g   The intensifying adverb מאד is more frequent as an item adverb than as a clausal adverb, but since in that capacity it almost always modifies stative verbs (## 35–37), there is no need to separate the uses too strictly. With forms of כבד, for example, we find the adjective כָּבֵד used with מאד for 'extremely wealthy' (Abraham, Gen 13:2) or 'oppressively severe' (famine, Gen 41:31), and we also find כָּבְדָה with מאד for 'egregiously serious' (sin, Gen 18:20).

35.   וַיִּבְטְחוּ . . . וְעַל פָּרָשִׁים כִּי־
עָצְמוּ מְאֹד

They trust in . . . cavalry—they are *very* numerous.
Isa 31:1

36.   עַל־זָקֵן הִכְבַּדְתְּ עֻלֵּךְ מְאֹד:

On the elderly you have made your yoke *exceedingly* heavy.
Isa 47:6

37.   יָרוּם וְנִשָּׂא וְגָבַהּ מְאֹד:

He is high and lifted up and *extremely* exalted.
Isa 52:13

39.3.5   Restrictive Adverbs

a   The category of restrictive clausal adverbs includes a range of particles said to function as restrictive, exceptive, adversative, or limitative entities.[89] These adverbs are intermediate in sense between negative and emphatic adverbs: they are often essentially negators of continuity between clauses, and they highlight the special status of the clause they occur in. Indeed, it could well be argued that these constitute a special class of the emphatic adverbs; they certainly show a greater unity than the emphatic class as a whole. Further, as we shall see, these adverbs often have strictly emphatic functions.

b   The position of the restrictive adverbs is always, in some sense, medial to the discourse. Let us say that there are two situations, A and B. Clause B with a restrictive adverb describes situation B. The three uses of restrictive adverbs are these: (1) Situation

---

86. Negative lōʾ is here an item adverb.

87. On the structure of the entire chapter, see M. O'Connor, "The Pseudosorites: A Type of Paradox in Hebrew Verse," *Directions in Biblical Hebrew Poetry*, ed. E. R.

Follis (Sheffield: JSOT Press, 1987) 161–72.

88. The whole sentence spans vv 1b–5, with three occurrences of ʾzy.

89. Williams, *Hebrew Syntax*, 92–94.

A is described in the immediately preceding clause (= clause A); the adverb (e.g., *raq*) follows, and it has the sense 'only, except.' (2) Situation A is described in the preceding group of clauses; the adverb follows, with the sense 'however, nevertheless, only.' (3) Situation A is not described but may be inferred from context; the adverb follows, with the sense 'I thought/It seemed to be otherwise *but now* I realize/it is obvious that. . . .' This diverse set of relationships between the anterior or restricted situation and the restricting clause accounts for the usual polar glosses for, for example, *ʾăbāl* 'of a truth' and 'but.' Of these two glosses, the second is more basic; the 'surely' senses of these adverbs are secondary.[90]

The full range of uses is evident with רק, which with אך is the most common of these adverbs.[91] The immediate restrictive sense of רק is found when it stands initially (## 1–2) or medially (# 3) in its clause; the standard English glosses reflect the polarity of the preceding clause: after a positive clause, 'only,' and after a negative, 'but, except.' The general restrictive sense is found in two settings: *raq* may introduce a summary (often with instructions; # 4) or a clarification (## 5–6) of what precedes.[92] The unspecified restrictive sense (i.e., where the situation to be qualified is not described) has with רק, as with other adverbs of this group, an emphatic effect (# 7).

   c

1. רַק . . . וְסָרוּ הַצְפַרְדְּעִים מִמְּךָ
   בַּיְאֹר תִּשָּׁאַרְנָה׃

The frogs will depart from you. . . . *Only* they shall remain in the Nile.
Exod 8:7

2. וַעֲשׂוּ לָהֶן כַּטּוֹב בְּעֵינֵיכֶם רַק
   לָאֲנָשִׁים הָאֵל אַל־תַּעֲשׂוּ דָבָר

Do what you like to these (women). *Only* do nothing to these men.
Gen 19:8

3. פְּרִי אַדְמָתְךָ . . . יֹאכַל עַם אֲשֶׁר
   לֹא־יָדָעְתָּ וְהָיִיתָ רַק עָשׁוּק
   וְרָצוּץ כָּל־הַיָּמִים׃

A people you don't know will consume your land's fruit. . . . You shall be *nothing but* squeezed and crushed forever.
Deut 28:33

4. וְעַתָּה יִשְׂרָאֵל שְׁמַע אֶל־הַחֻקִּים
   . . . לַעֲשׂוֹת לְמַעַן תִּחְיוּ . . . לֹא
   תֹסִפוּ עַל־הַדָּבָר . . . וְאַתֶּם
   הַדְּבֵקִים בַּיהוה . . . רַק הִשָּׁמֶר
   לְךָ

Now, Israel, hearken to the statutes . . . by carrying them out, so that you can live. . . . Do not add to the message. . . . You are those who have clung to Yʜᴡʜ. . . . *Only* [*the most important thing is/the upshot is*], take heed.
Deut 4:1–2, 4, 9

---

90. The relationship among the various functions is recognized by Muraoka for *ʾak* (*Emphatic Words*, 129–30) and *raq* (pp. 130–32), but only with two stipulations: that the emphatic force of *ʾak* is "original" and the "restrictive-adversative use" is a secondary development with "a slight residue of the original force . . . still preserved originally" (p. 130) and that the reverse (from restrictive to emphatic) is true for *raq*. The developments are not historical, however, but semantic, and no one sense has an assignable priority.

91. The adverb *raq* is found 109 times, and *ʾak* 161 times (SA/THAT). On the former, see B. Jongeling, "La particule רַק," *Oudtestamentische Studiën* 18 (1973) 97–107; his account overemphasizes the importance of position. Rare in verse, *raq* is also used as an item adverb (e.g., Gen 6:5, 41:40). For *rq* and *ʾk* together, see Num 12:2.

92. See also 1 Kgs 8:9.

5. הִשָּׁ֣מֶר לְךָ֗ פֶּֽן־תַּעֲלֶ֖ה עֹלֹתֶ֑יךָ
בְּכָל־מָק֖וֹם . . . רַ֗ק בְּכָל־אַוַּ֤ת
נַפְשְׁךָ֙ תִּזְבַּ֣ח וְאָכַלְתָּ֣ בָשָׂ֔ר . . .
בְּכָל־שְׁעָרֶֽיךָ

Take heed lest you offer ῾ōlôt offerings in every
site. . . . *However* [only ῾ōlôt offerings are so
restricted—]whenever your soul desires you can
slaughter and eat meat . . . in any city gate.
Deut 12:13, 15

6. וַיֶּאֱהַ֥ב שְׁלֹמֹ֖ה אֶת־יהוה לָלֶ֕כֶת
בְּחֻקּ֖וֹת דָּוִ֣ד אָבִ֑יו רַ֗ק בַּבָּמ֛וֹת
ה֥וּא מְזַבֵּ֖חַ וּמַקְטִֽיר׃

Solomon loved Yнwн (and showed it) by following
the practices of his father David. *However* [this
devotion was not perfect—]he offered sacrifices and
incense on the high places.
1 Kgs 3:3

7. וּשְׁמַרְתֶּם֮ . . . כִּ֣י הִ֤יא חָכְמַתְכֶם֙
. . . לְעֵינֵ֖י הָעַמִּ֑ים אֲשֶׁ֣ר יִשְׁמְע֗וּן
אֵ֚ת כָּל־הַֽחֻקִּ֣ים הָאֵ֔לֶּה וְאָמְר֗וּ
רַ֚ק עַם־חָכָ֣ם וְנָב֔וֹן הַגּ֥וֹי הַגָּד֖וֹל
הַזֶּֽה׃

Observe them . . . for such will be your wisdom . . . in
the eyes of the peoples, who will hear (of) all these
statutes and will say, "[On the face of it we might have
thought otherwise] *but* this great nation is a wise and
discerning people."
Deut 4:6

d   As with the emphatic adverbs, there is a series of *restrictive adverbs in k*: אַךְ and
אָכֵן; some uses of כִּי also deserve notice here. The most common of the restrictive
adverbs, אַךְ, is used as an item adverb[93] and a clausal adverb restricting what precedes
generally, offering clarification (# 8) or instruction (## 9–10),[94] or highlighting an unexpected conclusion (# 11).[95] The two uses can be found together in a single passage
(# 12). Unlike אַךְ, אכן reverses or restricts what *immediately* precedes (## 13–14);[96] like
אַךְ, אכן has a general emphatic sense (# 15),[97] indicating "a sudden recognition in contrast to what was theretofore assumed."[98]

8. כָּל־רֶ֙מֶשׂ֙ אֲשֶׁ֣ר הוּא־חַ֔י לָכֶ֥ם
יִהְיֶ֖ה לְאָכְלָ֑ה . . . אַךְ־בָּשָׂ֕ר
בְּנַפְשׁ֥וֹ דָמ֖וֹ לֹ֥א תֹאכֵֽלוּ׃

Every moving thing with life in it is yours for
food. . . . *Nevertheless* [this is on the understanding
that] you shall not eat flesh with its life force (i.e.),
its blood (still in it).
Gen 9:3–4

9. עָלַ֥י קִלְלָתְךָ֖ בְּנִ֑י אַ֛ךְ שְׁמַ֥ע בְּקֹלִ֖י

Your curse be on me, my son, [and that being
understood], *just* obey me.
Gen 27:13

10. בֹּ֣אִי עֲשִׂ֣י כִדְבָרֵ֗ךְ אַ֣ךְ עֲשִׂי־לִ֣י
. . . עֻגָ֨ה קְטַנָּ֤ה בָרִאשֹׁנָה֙

Go, do as you say, *but* first make me . . . a little
pancake.
1 Kgs 17:13

---

93. In the senses 'even, only, surely'; see, e.g., Gen 18:32,
Isa 34:14–15; see Williams, *Hebrew Syntax*, 65.

94. See also 1 Sam 18:17.

95. See also Gen 44:28. For the sense 'on the contrary,'
see N. H. Snaith, "The Meaning of the Hebrew אַךְ," *Vetus
Testamentum* 14 (1964) 221–25. On ʾk 'however' in exegesis, see Fishbane, *Biblical Interpretation*, 184–85, 197–99.

96. See also Ps 66:19, Job 32:7–8.

97. See also Gen 28:16, 1 Kgs 11:2, Isa 40:7.

98. So W. Holladay on Jer 3:23, a difficult text; see
Jeremiah (Philadelphia: Fortress, 1986), 1. 124. Holladay's
treatment of ʾkn agrees with ours, as does, for the most
part, that of Muraoka, *Emphatic Words*, 132–33; note
also F. J. Goldbaum, "Two Hebrew Quasi-Adverbs: לכן
and אכן," *Journal of Near Eastern Studies* 23 (1964)
132–35.

11. וַיַּרְא אֶת־אֱלִיאָב וַיֹּאמֶר אַךְ
נֶגֶד יהוה מְשִׁיחוֹ:

And he looked at Eliab and said, "[Before I didn't know who I was looking for, but here he is—]*surely*, Yʜᴡʜ's messiah is before him."[99]
1 Sam 16:6

12. חָזְקוּ פְנֵיהֶם מִסֶּלַע מֵאֲנוּ
לָשׁוּב: וַאֲנִי אָמַרְתִּי אַךְ־דַּלִּים
הֵם נוֹאֲלוּ כִּי לֹא יָדְעוּ דֶּרֶךְ יהוה
. . . אֵלְכָה־לִּי אֶל־הַגְּדֹלִים . . .
כִּי הֵמָּה יָדְעוּ דֶּרֶךְ יהוה . . . אַךְ
הֵמָּה יַחְדָּו שָׁבְרוּ עֹל

They had hardened their faces harder than rock, refused to repent. I said, "*But* [I was wrong to look there—] there are the poor, who are foolish. They clearly don't know Yʜᴡʜ's path. . . . I'll go to the great. . . . They surely will know Yʜᴡʜ's path. . . ." *But surely* [that was misguided of me—] they all together [poor and rich] have broken the yoke.
Jer 5:3–5

13. . . . וַאֲנִי אָמַרְתִּי לְרִיק יָגַעְתִּי
אָכֵן מִשְׁפָּטִי אֶת־יהוה

I said, "I've labored in vain" . . . *but* [I was wrong to say that, because] my judgment is with Yʜᴡʜ.
Isa 49:4

14. וְלֹא חֲשַׁבְנֻהוּ: אָכֵן חֳלָיֵנוּ הוּא
נָשָׂא

We did not esteem him, *but* [we were wrong because] he carried our weakness.
Isa 53:3–4

15. אָנֹכִי עָשִׂיתִי אֶרֶץ . . . אָכֵן אַתָּה
אֵל מִסְתַּתֵּר

"I made the earth," [says Yʜᴡʜ and it might be thought that Yʜᴡʜ would therefore be visible,] . . . *but* [that is not so—]you are a god who hides himself.
Isa 45:12, 15

Related to the uses of אכן to restrict the immediately preceding clause is the restrictive use of כי (# 16)[100] and כי אם (# 17) in a clause after a negative clause; the combination כי אם can be used to restrict generally preceding material (# 18).[101]

16. שָׂרַי אִשְׁתְּךָ לֹא־תִקְרָא אֶת־
שְׁמָהּ שָׂרָי כִּי שָׂרָה שְׁמָהּ:

As for your wife Sarai—you shall *not* call her Sarai. *Rather*, her name is Sarah.[102]
Gen 17:15

17. וְלֹא תִתְחַתֵּן בָּם . . . כִּי־אִם־כֹּה
תַעֲשׂוּ לָהֶם

You shall *not* intermarry with them. . . . *Rather*, you shall treat them in the following way.
Deut 7:3, 5

18. וַיֹּאמְרוּ לֹא כִּי אִם־מֶלֶךְ יִהְיֶה
עָלֵינוּ:

They said, "No! *Rather*, let there be a king over us."
1 Sam 8:19

Of the remaining, less frequent restrictive adverbs, only אֲבָל exhibits the three patterns seen earlier: it can restrict an immediately preceding clause (# 19) or generally

e

---

99. It is irrelevant that the speaker is wrong; the force of ʾkn derives from his beliefs.
100. Cf. Amos 7:14.

101. Cf. Ps 1:2.
102. The accompanying and parallel name change for Abraham in Gen 17:5 has w.

preceding materials (## 20–21), and it can mark a reversal in expectations or beliefs (# 22).[103] This last, emphatic use is missing from אפס and אולם.[104] Both אפס and אפס כי restrict general preceding material, offering clarifications (## 23–25), and the latter combination can also restrict the immediately preceding clause (# 26). The particle אולם serves only to restrict a clause in relation to a preceding clause (## 27–28).[105]

19. וְרָאִיתִי . . . לְבַדִּי אֶת־הַמַּרְאָה וְהָאֲנָשִׁים אֲשֶׁר הָיוּ עִמִּי לֹא רָאוּ אֶת־הַמַּרְאָה אֲבָל חֲרָדָה גְדֹלָה נָפְלָה עֲלֵיהֶם וַיִּבְרְחוּ בְּהֵחָבֵא:	I alone . . . saw the vision. The men who had been with me did not see the vision. *Rather*, great terror fell on them, and they fled into hiding. Dan 10:7
20. וַיֹּאמֶר אֱלֹהִים אֲבָל שָׂרָה אִשְׁתְּךָ יֹלֶדֶת לְךָ בֵּן	God said, "[Don't focus your hopes on Ishmael—] *rather*, your (primary) wife Sarah will bear you a son." Gen 17:19
21. וַיֹּאמֶר הֲיָדַעְתָּ לָמָּה־בָּאתִי אֵלֶיךָ וְעַתָּה אָשׁוּב לְהִלָּחֵם עִם־שַׂר פָּרָס . . . אֲבָל אַגִּיד לְךָ אֶת־הָרָשׁוּם	And he said, "Do you know why I have come to you? I must return now to fight with the Persian prince. . . . *Nevertheless*, I will tell you what is written down." Dan 10:20–21
22. וַיֹּאמְרוּ אִישׁ אֶל־אָחִיו אֲבָל אֲשֵׁמִים אֲנַחְנוּ עַל־אָחִינוּ	Each said to his brother, "[We believed wrongly that we had gotten away with disposing of our brother] *but* we are (now) found to be at fault in the matter of our brother." Gen 42:21
23. גַּם־יהוה הֶעֱבִיר חַטָּאתְךָ לֹא תָמוּת: אֶפֶס כִּי־נִאֵץ נִאַצְתָּ אֶת [דְּ]בַר יהוה בַּדָּבָר הַזֶּה גַּם הַבֵּן הַיִּלּוֹד לְךָ מוֹת יָמוּת:	Indeed Yhwh [on his part] has transferred your sin. You shall not die. *Nevertheless*, since you profaned Yhwh's word in this matter, the son to be born to you will die.[106] 2 Sam 12:13–14 *4QSam^a*
24. בָּאנוּ אֶל־הָאָרֶץ . . . אֶפֶס כִּי־עַז הָעָם	We entered the land. . . . *Nevertheless*, the people are strong. Num 13:27–28
25. הָלֹךְ אֵלֵךְ עִמָּךְ אֶפֶס כִּי לֹא תִהְיֶה תִּפְאַרְתְּךָ	I will go with you, *but* [contrary to your expectations] there will be no glory for you. Judg 4:9

---

103. The standard view (see, e.g., Muraoka, *Emphatic Words*, 128–29) that ʾbl has an "early" meaning (in Genesis) and a distinct "late" meaning (in Daniel, cf. 2 Chr 1:4) is dubious; cf. n. 90. The particle *biltî* is apparently an item restrictive adverb in Num 11:6 and a clausal restrictive adverb in Isa 10:4.

104. The adverbial ending -ām is found on ʾwlm.

105. With ʾwlm, contrast the related particle ʾwly 'perhaps' (39.3.4b). For ʾwlm, see also the cases in Gen 48:19, Exod 9:16.

106. Note that the construction may be haplologic (two identical neighboring items are reduced to one): ʾepes kî kî > ʾepes kî. On the Qumran reading, see P. K. McCarter, Jr., *II Samuel* (Garden City, New York: Doubleday, 1984) 296; McCarter himself reads nʾṣt ʾt yhwh, with versional support.

26. וְהִשְׁמַדְתִּי אֹתָהּ . . . אֶפֶס כִּי לֹא
     הַשְׁמֵיד אַשְׁמִיד אֶת־בֵּית יַעֲקֹב

I will destroy it (the errant kingdom). . . .
Nevertheless, I won't [in the process] destroy the
House of Jacob.
Amos 9:8

27. וַיִּקְרָא אֶת־שֵׁם־הַמָּקוֹם הַהוּא
     בֵּית־אֵל וְאוּלָם לוּז שֵׁם־הָעִיר
     לָרִאשֹׁנָה:

He called that place Bethel. In the past, *however*, the
name of the city was Luz.
Gen 28:19

28. וְכֹל אֲשֶׁר לָאִישׁ יִתֵּן בְּעַד
     נַפְשׁוֹ: אוּלָם שְׁלַח־נָא יָדְךָ וְגַע
     אֶל־עַצְמוֹ

All that a person has he will give for his life. Extend
your hand, *however*, and touch his bones. . . .[107]
Job 2:4–5

---

107. See also Job 1:11.

40

Exclamations and Polar Questions

40.1   Introduction

a   A standard feature of syntactic study is the functional classification of clauses and sentences. Any such sorting-out is problematic. One traditional scheme distinguishes statements or assertions ('It is good'), commands ('Be good'), questions ('How good is it?', 'Is it good?'), and exclamations ('How good it is!', 'Good!'). In terms of the basic structures of Hebrew, statements, commands, and most questions draw on comparable resources, and these have been treated throughout. One class of questions, polar or 'yes-no' questions, remains to be treated, as does the broad class of exclamations. The considerable overlap among the four functional classes, notably of interrogative clauses and exclamations, is not our special concern here.[1] Evaluation of difficult cases is a matter of more specialized study.

40.2   Exclamations

a   Under the rubric of exclamations we include a variety of utterances.[2] Four groups require attention because of the syntactic complexities associated with them: presentative exclamations (e.g., those with הנה), wish and oath formulas (e.g., those with חי), nominal exclamations (e.g., those with אשרי), and woe cries (e.g., those with הוי). Other types of exclamation can be treated more briefly.[3]

---

1. Joüon § 162a / pp. 499–500.
2. J. Blau discusses a number of what are here called exclamations under the heading "minor clauses"; his approach may prove fruitful for further study; see *A Gram-* *mar of Biblical Hebrew* (Wiesbaden: Harrassowitz, 1976) 82–83.
3. We leave out of account here greeting formulas and "block language" (titles and headings)

Presentative Exclamations

40.2.1

The presentative exclamations are those that begin with the presentative particles,   **a**
הִנֵּה and הֵן;[4] the two particles do not differ in their use.[5] Both introduce exclamations of immediacy and fuller exclamations of perception, cause, circumstance, etc.

In *exclamations of immediacy*, הנה is frequently inflected with a pronoun (# 1),[6]   **b**
often in answer to a summons (# 2). With or without the pronoun it "emphasizes the immediacy, the here-and-now-ness, of the situation,"[7] either in direct discourse (## 1–2) or in narrative (# 3).

1.	הִנְנוּ אָתָנוּ לָךְ	*Here we are.* We come to you.
		Jer 3:22
2.	וָאֹמַר הִנְנִי שְׁלָחֵנִי:	And I said, "*Here I am.* Send me."
		Isa 6:8
3.	וַיֻּגַּד לַמֶּלֶךְ . . . כִּי נָס יוֹאָב אֶל־	The king . . . was told that Joab had fled to
	אֹהֶל יהוה וְהִנֵּה אֵצֶל הַמִּזְבֵּחַ	YHWH's tent and *there he was*, next to the altar.
		1 Kgs 2:29

Presentative הנה has this nuance of vivid immediacy often in clauses with participles (## 4–5), sometimes quite elaborate (# 6), as well as in verbal clauses (# 7).

4.	הִנֵּה חָמִיךְ עֹלֶה תִמְנָתָה	Your father-in-law is *now* on his way up to Timnah.
		Gen 38:13
5.	הִנֵּה אָבִיךָ חֹלֶה	Your father is *now* sick.
		Gen 48:1
6.	כִּי הִנֵּה הָאָדוֹן יהוה צְבָאוֹת	The Lord, YHWH *Ṣbᵓwt*, is *now* taking from
	מֵסִיר מִירוּשָׁלַיִם . . . מַשְׁעֵן	Jerusalem . . . support and staff. . . .[8]
	וּמַשְׁעֵנָה	Isa 3:1
7.	הִנֵּה אֲנָשִׁים בָּאוּ הֵנָּה הַלַּיְלָה	Some men came here *just* tonight.
		Josh 2:2

---

4. The form *hnh* occurs 1,057 times (SA/THAT), about a third of the time preceded by *w*; *hn* occurs 100 times and is frequent in Job and Isaiah 40–66. The term presentative is Blau's; see *Biblical Hebrew*, 105–6, and *An Adverbial Construction in Hebrew and Arabic* (Jerusalem: Israel Academy of Sciences and Humanities, 1977) 18–22. On *hnh* and *whnh*, see L. Alonso-Schökel, "Nota estilistica sobre la particula הִנֵּה," *Biblica* 37 (1956) 74–80; D. J. McCarthy, "The Uses of *wᵉhinnēh* in Biblical Hebrew," *Biblica* 61 (1980) 330–42; A. Niccacci, *Sintassi del verbo ebraico nella prosa biblica classica* (Jerusalem: Franciscan Printing Press, 1986) 59–64; Richter, *GAHG* 1. 193–94, 3. 203–5 (*hnh* as *Satz-Deitikon* 'sentential deictic'); note also James Muilenburg, "Form Criticism and Beyond," *Journal of Biblical Literature* 88 (1969) 1–18, esp.

14–15, rpt. in *Hearing and Speaking the Word*, ed. T. F. Best (Chico: Scholars Press, 1984) 27–44, at 40–41. The presentative *raᵓēh* 'look!' is rare in the Bible (e.g., Deut 4:5); the other presentatives, *hn* and *hnh*, though they are conventionally rendered with visual predicates like 'behold!,' do not have any essential reference to vision. The phrase *lāhēn* is an emphatic adverb, usually 'therefore.'

5. C. J. Labuschagne, "The Particles הֵן and הִנֵּה," *Oudtestamentische Studiën* 18 (1973) 1–14.

6. On the suffix pronoun *versus* independent pronoun after *hnh*, see T. Muraoka, *Emphatic Words and Structures in Biblical Hebrew* (Leiden: Brill, 1985) 138–40.

7. T. O. Lambdin, *Introduction to Biblical Hebrew* (New York: Scribner, 1971) 168.

8. A total of sixteen objects follow the participle.

Related to this sense of immediacy is the use of והנה *as a bridge* to introduce with emotion a noun clause (38.8) or perception, either after a verb of perception (# 8) or after a new situation of perception is described (## 9–10).[9] In the latter cases the verb is usually said to be omitted for the sake of "vividness." In such uses והנה is often best left untranslated.

8. וְלֹא־הֶאֱמַ֫נְתִּי לַדְּבָרִים עַד אֲשֶׁר־בָּ֫אתִי וַתִּרְאֶ֫ינָה עֵינַי וְהִנֵּה לֹא־הֻגַּד־לִי הַחֵ֫צִי	I didn't believe the reports until I came and my own eyes saw [*to my astonishment*] that I hadn't been told half the truth.[10] 1 Kgs 10:7
9. וַיָּבֹא דָוִד וַאֲנָשָׁיו אֶל־הָעִיר וְהִנֵּה שְׂרוּפָה בָּאֵשׁ	David and his men came to the city and (saw [*to their indignation*] that) it was burned down. 1 Sam 30:3
10. וָאָקֻם בַּבֹּ֫קֶר לְהֵינִיק אֶת־בְּנִי וְהִנֵּה־מֵת	I got up in the morning to nurse my son and (saw [*to my horror*] that) he was dead. 1 Kgs 3:21

c   Presentatives introducing *longer or fuller exclamations* serve to ground and define the material that follows them. The distinction between exclamations of immediacy and exposition may be blurred (as in # 10). D. J. McCarthy in his discussion of והנה offers some English examples for comparison.

> Take the sentences: "Look! Uncle Joe is coming. We'll go!". This can reassure, say, a child anxious to be off, and so be equivalent to "*When* Uncle Joe comes etc." without the force of the colloquial original. It can imply doubt: "*If* Uncle Joe etc.". . . . It can even express a purpose: perhaps Uncle Joe is not a favorite so that it implies: "*To avoid* Uncle Joe we'll go away!". And so on. . . . In all this the expression remains exclamatory with an emotional note and we miss the language-user's full meaning if we simply *equate* the sentences with the suggested temporal or conditional or causal or purpose clauses. We get the meaning but not the feeling, and the two must be grasped to get the full force of the language.[11]

The presentative הנה is common in direct speech, while the combination והנה is frequent in narrative. With or without ו, הנה serves "to *introduce a fact* upon which a following statement or command is based."[12] Thus it can stand before either a verbless clause (# 11) or a verbal clause (## 12–13). With reference to future time, הנה clauses can stand before a clause with a volitional form (## 11–12; sometimes with ועתה, # 13), or before a suffix conjugation form with relative *waw* (# 14). For past time *waw*-relative with the short prefix conjugation is found (# 15). This use is also often best left untranslated.

---

9. See also Judg 3:25; cf. Jer 26:14.   11. McCarthy, "Uses of *weḥinnēh*," 331.

10. Cf. Judg 18:9.   12. Lambdin, *Introduction to Biblical Hebrew*, 169.

11. הִנֵּה־נָא דִּבְרֵי הַנְּבִיאִים פֶּה־
אֶחָד טוֹב אֶל־הַמֶּלֶךְ יְהִי־נָא
דְבָרְךָ כִּדְבַר אַחַד מֵהֶם וְדִבַּרְתָּ
טוֹב:

Okay, now: the findings of the (other) prophets are uniformly favorable to the king. Let your finding be like one of those, so that you can speak favorably.
1 Kgs 22:13 *Qere*

12. הִנֵּה־נָא שָׁמַעְנוּ כִּי מַלְכֵי בֵּית
יִשְׂרָאֵל כִּי־מַלְכֵי חֶסֶד הֵם
נָשִׂימָה נָּא שַׂקִּים בְּמָתְנֵינוּ

[*Since*] we've heard, regarding Israelite kings, that they are merciful kings—let's put sackcloth round our middles. . . .
1 Kgs 20:31

13. הִנֵּה בַּעַל הַחֲלֹמוֹת הַלָּזֶה בָּא:
וְעַתָּה לְכוּ וְנַהַרְגֵהוּ

[*Since*] that dreaming lord is here—come on, now, let's kill him.
Gen 37:19–20

14. אֲנִי הִנֵּה בְרִיתִי אִתָּךְ וְהָיִיתָ
לְאַב הֲמוֹן גּוֹיִם:

My covenant is with you and (or, *as for me*, because my covenant is with you) you shall become father of a throng of nations.
Gen 17:4

15. וְהִנֵּה אֵין־יוֹסֵף בַּבּוֹר וַיִּקְרַע
אֶת־בְּגָדָיו:

Because Joseph was not in the pit, he rent his clothes.
Gen 37:29

Similar to these causal connections, the presentative forms הנה and והנה also *intro-* d *duce* clauses expressing a temporal connection (# 16) or the occasion or condition (## 17–18) for the ensuing clause, using either a verbless construction (## 16–17) or a verbal (# 18). Other semantic functions include adversative (# 19) and concessive notions (# 20).

16. וְהִנֵּה־הוּא וְהָעָם אֲשֶׁר־אִתּוֹ
יֹצְאִים אֵלֶיךָ וְעָשִׂיתָ לּוֹ כַּאֲשֶׁר
תִּמְצָא יָדֶךָ:

When he and the people who are with him attack you, do to them whatever your hands find to do.
Judg 9:33

17. הִנֵּה יָמִים בָּאִים וְגָדַעְתִּי אֶת־
זְרֹעֶךָ

There will come a time when I will put a stop to your strength (or, *when* in the future. . .).
1 Sam 2:31

18. וְהִנֵּה אָנֹכִי בָא . . . וְהָיָה
כַּאֲשֶׁר־אֶעֱשֶׂה כֵּן תַּעֲשׂוּן:

When I arrive . . . let it be that whatever I do, you do.
Judg 7:17

19. הִנֵּה הָאֵשׁ וְהָעֵצִים וְאַיֵּה הַשֶּׂה
לְעֹלָה:

Here are the fire and the wood, but where is the lamb for the ʿōlâ?
Gen 22:7

20. וְהִנֵּה יהוה עֹשֶׂה אֲרֻבּוֹת
בַּשָּׁמַיִם הֲיִהְיֶה כַּדָּבָר הַזֶּה

Even if Yhwh opened the floodgates of heaven, could this happen?
2 Kgs 7:19

In addition to serving as a bridge to introduce a noun clause of perception, הנה can e also function *as a bridge* for a logical connection between a preceding clause and the clause it introduces, whether verbal (## 21, 27, 28, 31)[13] or participial (## 22–24, 26,

13. See also 2 Sam 19:21.

29–30) or verbless (# 25).[14] This bridging role may involve a causal relation (# 21), a condition (# 22)[15] or circumstance (## 23–24), a reversal of expectations (# 25),[16] the apodosis to a dependent temporal clause (## 26–27), a result (## 28–30),[17] or a concession (# 31).

21.	וַיָּרָץ . . . וְהִנֵּה הֵחֵל הַנֶּגֶף בָּעָם	And he ran . . . *because* the plague had already begun (to spread) among the people. Num 17:12
22.	וְעָמַדְתָּ . . . וְהִנֵּה יהוה עֹבֵר	Stand still . . . *because* Yhwh is about to pass by. 1 Kgs 19:11
23.	וַיָּבֹא אֶל־הָאִישׁ וְהִנֵּה עֹמֵד עַל־הַגְּמַלִּים	He came to the man *while* he was standing by the camels. Gen 24:30
24.	עוֹד שָׁאַר הַקָּטָן וְהִנֵּה רֹעֶה בַּצֹּאן	There remains yet the youngest, tending the sheep. 1 Sam 16:11
25.	וַיִּקְרָא אֲדֹנָי . . . לִבְכִי . . . וְהִנֵּה שָׂשׂוֹן	My lord . . . called for weeping . . . and (or, *but*) there was rejoicing. Isa 22:12–13
26.	וַיְהִי־הוּא טֶרֶם כִּלָּה לְדַבֵּר וְהִנֵּה רִבְקָה יֹצֵאת	Before he had finished speaking, Rebecca emerged. Gen 24:15
27.	וַיְהִי כְּכַלֹּתוֹ לְהַעֲלוֹת הָעֹלָה וְהִנֵּה שְׁמוּאֵל בָּא	When he had finished offering the ʿōlâ, Samuel arrived. 1 Sam 13:10
28.	וַיַּכּוּ הָאֶחָד אֶת־הָאֶחָד וַיָּמֶת אֹתוֹ : וְהִנֵּה קָמָה כָל־הַמִּשְׁפָּחָה	The one struck the other and killed him. *So now* the whole clan has risen up. . . . 2 Sam 14:6–7
29.	הֵן לִי לֹא נָתַתָּה זָרַע וְהִנֵּה בֶן־בֵּיתִי יוֹרֵשׁ אֹתִי :	You have given me no children; *so* a house-born servant will be my heir. Gen 15:3
30.	תֶּבֶן אֵין נִתָּן לַעֲבָדֶיךָ . . . וְהִנֵּה עֲבָדֶיךָ מֻכִּים	Your servants are given no straw . . . *and so* your servants are being beaten. Exod 5:16
31.	וּבָזָה אָלָה לְהָפֵר בְּרִית וְהִנֵּה נָתַן יָדוֹ	He has reviled an oath in breaking the covenant *even though* he had given his hand to it. Ezek 17:18

40.2.2   Oath and Wish Exclamations

a   The expression of wishes and oaths does not require the use of any sort of exclamation, but a diverse set of exclamations are used, some protases without apodoses and

---

14. See also Deut 17:4–5.
15. Note also Lev 13:3–5, 1 Sam 9:7.
16. Note also Zech 11:6.

17. McCarthy's examples of purpose clauses (2 Sam 15:32, 16:1; 1 Kgs 18:7) are such because of their infinitives rather than other features of their syntax.

some phrases headed up by substantives. The particles אם and לא are involved in a number of these exclamations, not always in a comprehensible way. While Paul Joüon argues that the unpredictable usages are the result of contamination among the various patterns, it may be better to confess that the calculus of the particles is beyond our specification.[18]

An oath need not be introduced by an exclamation.[19] It may have no introduction   b
or it may be preceded only by the particles כי ('certainly,' 39.3.4e; positive, # 1), אם (negative; # 2),[20] אם לא (positive; # 3), or כי אם (positive; # 4); with the particles only, the oath has the form of a protasis with no apodosis. An oath can also be preceded by the term חי + a name (or some powerful or sacred substitute); the term is sometimes pointed חֵי (perhaps a verb[21] but probably a noun[22]), and sometimes חֵי (< חַיִּים).[23] The חי + name combination is followed by a clause with כי (positive; # 5), אם (negative; # 6), אם לא (positive; # 7), or כי אם (positive; # 8); the two items are grammatically independent (note # 9), despite the standard translation of the ḥy phrase as a protasis and of the ʾm clause as its apodosis ('As Yahweh lives, may . . .').

1.	נִשְׁבַּע אֲדֹנָי יהוה בְּקָדְשׁוֹ כִּי הִנֵּה יָמִים בָּאִים	The Lord Yhwh swears by his holiness: "*Surely*, the time will come. . . ." Amos 4:2
2.	הִנְנִי נִשְׁבַּעְתִּי בִּשְׁמִי הַגָּדוֹל אָמַר יהוה אִם־יִהְיֶה עוֹד שְׁמִי נִקְרָא בְּפִי כָּל־אִישׁ יְהוּדָה אֹמֵר חַי־אֲדֹנָי יהוה בְּכָל־אֶרֶץ מִצְרָיִם:	"I hereby swear by my great name," says Yhwh—"my name shall *no* more be invoked in the mouth of every Judahite in the land of Egypt who says '(By) the Lord Yhwh's life.' " Jer 44:26
3.	נִשְׁבַּע יהוה צְבָאוֹת לֵאמֹר אִם־ לֹא כַּאֲשֶׁר דִּמִּיתִי כֵּן הָיָתָה	Yhwh Ṣbʾwt swears, "As I have *surely* intended it, so shall it be." Isa 14:24
4.	נִשְׁבַּע יהוה צְבָאוֹת בְּנַפְשׁוֹ כִּי אִם־מִלֵּאתִיךְ אָדָם	Yhwh Ṣbʾwt swears by himself: "I will *surely* fill you with people." Jer 51:14
5.	חַי־יהוה כִּי בֶן־מָוֶת הָאִישׁ הָעֹשֶׂה זֹאת:	Yhwh's life! *Surely* the man who did this is a dead man. 2 Sam 12:5
6.	וַיִּשָּׁבַע שָׁאוּל חַי־יהוה אִם־ יוּמָת:	Saul swore, "Yhwh's life! He shall not die!" 1 Sam 19:6

---

18. Joüon § 165a–j / pp. 503–5 implicates in the contamination the forms treated here and the self-curse (or imprecation) formula (e.g., kōh-yaʿăśeh-llî ʾĕlōhîm wəkōh yôsīp ʾim yaʿămōd rōʾš ʾĕlîšāʿ . . . ʿālāyw, 'Thus [with a gesture?] may God do to me and thus may he continue (to do) if Elisha's head . . . stands on his shoulders,' 2 Kgs 6:31).

19. Joüon § 165b / p. 504.
20. The oath exemplifies what it forbids.
21. Joüon § 79s / p. 164.
22. M. Greenberg, "The Hebrew Oath Particle ḥay/ḥê," *Journal of Biblical Literature* 76 (1957) 34–39; cf. W. L. Holladay, *Jeremiah* (Philadelphia: Fortress, 1986), I. 128.
23. Joüon § 165e / p. 504.

7.   חַי־אָנִי אִם־לֹא אָלָתִי אֲשֶׁר
בָּזָה . . . וּנְתַתִּיו בְּרֹאשׁוֹ:
     My (Yhwh's) life! I will *surely* bring down on his head my oath that he despised. . . .
Ezek 17:19

8.   וַיֹּאמֶר דָּוִד חַי־יהוה כִּי אִם־
יהוה יִגֳּפֶנּוּ אוֹ־יוֹמוֹ יָבוֹא וָמֵת
     David said, "Yhwh's life! Yhwh will *surely* strike him or his day will come and he'll die."
1 Sam 26:10

9.   וְנִשְׁבַּעְתָּ חַי־יהוה בֶּאֱמֶת
בְּמִשְׁפָּט וּבִצְדָקָה
     You shall swear "Yhwh's life!" truly, justly,
and rightly.
Jer 4:2

c   A *negative oath* may be introduced by the phrase חָלִילָה לִּי, conventionally 'far be it from me,'[24] followed by a dependent clause specifying the undesired outcome; this clause begins with מִן (# 10) followed by an infinitive or אִם (# 11) followed by a prefix form.

10.   חָלִילָה לִּי מֵעֲשׂוֹת זֹאת
     Far be it from me to do that!
Gen 44:17

11.   חָלִילָה לִּי מֵיהוה אִם־אֶעֱשֶׂה
אֶת־הַדָּבָר הַזֶּה
     Yhwh *forbid me* to do that thing!
1 Sam 24:7

d   Wishes may be expressed in complete independent clauses (e.g., with מִי יִתֵּן or אַחֲלַי with a prefix form)[25] or in protases lacking apodoses, introduced by אִם (# 12) or, more often לוּ (## 13–15).[26]

12.   יִשְׂרָאֵל אִם־תִּשְׁמַע־לִי:
     O Israel, *would that* you would hear me!
Ps 81:9

13.   לוּא הִקְשַׁבְתָּ לְמִצְוֹתָי
     Would that you had heard my commandments!
Isa 48:18

14.   לוּ שָׁקוֹל יִשָּׁקֵל כַּעְשִׂי
     Oh that my anguish could be measured!
Job 6:2

15.   לוּ־מַתְנוּ בְּאֶרֶץ מִצְרַיִם
     Would that we had died in Egypt!
Num 14:2

40.2.3   Nominal Exclamations

a   There are three groups of nominal exclamations.[27] One group consists of ad-hoc creations, that is, nouns or noun phrases used according to need (# 1).[28]

---

24. Joüon § 105f / p. 288, § 165k / p. 505.

25. Joüon § 163d / p. 502; B. Jongeling, "L'Expression *my ytn* dans l'Ancien Testament," *Vetus Testamentum* 24 (1974) 32–40.

26. Cf. 38.2e. The apparently similar particle ʾăbî is used in Job 34:36 and not clearly elsewhere.

27. See also 39.3.4.

28. Joüon § 162c / p. 500. Note also *laʾōholêkā yiśrāʾēl*

'to your tents, O Israel' (1 Kgs 12:16); cf. W. J. Martin, "Some Notes on the Imperative in the Semitic Languages," *Rivista degli studi orientali* 32 (1957) 315–19, at 316–17. A famously difficult example may be found in Qoh 8:2: ʾănî pî-mélek šəmôr, in which the initial pronoun and the final imperative seem to float freely of each other. C. Rabin has suggested that the pronoun may be a topic marker and thus that "the MT phrase could possibly be translated 'As

1.   וַיֹּאמֶר אֶל־אָבִיו רֹאשִׁי רֹאשִׁי   And he said to his father, "*My head! my head!*"
                                          2 Kgs 4:19

Another consists of nouns or noun phrases used independently of their grammatical context; a number of these are important: (*a*) נְאֻם יהוה 'declaration(?) of YHWH,' almost always used as a closing formula in the prophets;[29] (*b*) אָמֵן 'amen!';[30] (*c*) בִּי 'pardon me,' perhaps with the sense 'on me be any guilt arising from what I say / do,' always followed by אֲדֹנִי or אֲדֹנָי in conversation;[31] and perhaps (*d*) סֶלָה, a word of unknown sense found only in the Psalter and in the psalm of Habakkuk 3 and apparently some sort of exclamation. These two groups of exclamations involve contained units.

A third group of nominal exclamations is more complex: the nouns in this group   b
introduce phrases of some complexity. Among these are אַשְׁרֵי 'O the blessings of, enviable the situation of,' a petrified plural noun found only in construct phrases (# 2–3) or with suffixes (# 4), and קוֹל 'O the voice of, hark!', a noun ('voice') widely used elsewhere but capable of heading an independent phrase (# 5).[32] Other nouns that form nominal exclamations are חֲלִילָה and, if it is a noun, חַי (40.2.2).

2.   אַשְׁרֵי הָאִישׁ אֲשֶׁר לֹא הָלַךְ   *To be envied* is the person who does not walk in the
      בַּעֲצַת רְשָׁעִים   evildoers' counsel!
                                          Ps 1:1

3.   אַשְׁרֵי אֲנָשֶׁיךָ אַשְׁרֵי עֲבָדֶיךָ   *The joys of* your men, *the joys of* these your aides
      אֵלֶּה הָעֹמְדִים לְפָנֶיךָ תָּמִיד   who stand before you always!
                                          1 Kgs 10:8

4.   אַשְׁרֶיךָ יִשְׂרָאֵל   You are *to be envied*, Israel.
                                          Deut 33:29

5.   אֲנִי יְשֵׁנָה וְלִבִּי עֵר   I slept while my heart stirred.
      קוֹל דּוֹדִי דוֹפֵק   *Hark!* My beloved knocks!
                                          Cant 5:2

Woe Cries   40.2.4

There are half-a-dozen cries that are conventionally associated with woe. Only two   a
are common, הוֹי (about fifty times, always in the prophets) and אוֹי (about twenty-five

---

far as I am concerned, it [the rule of conduct] is "watch the king's mouth!".'" See "Lexical Emendation in Biblical Research," *Fucus: A Semitic/Afrasian Gathering in Remembrance of Albert Ehrman,* ed. Y. L. Arbeitman (Amsterdam: John Benjamins, 1988) 379–418, at 391–92.

29. The term *nʾm* is used 376 times (SA/THAT), almost always with *yhwh.* The closure may be slight.

30. Joüon § 105f / p. 288. Used repeatedly in Deut 27:15–26 and elsewhere; as a noun in Isa 65:16*bis.*

31. Joüon § 105c / p. 287.

32. The *ʾśry* phrase is followed by a statement contain-

ing the basis for the pronouncement; cf. W. Janzen, "*ʾašrê* in the Old Testament," *Harvard Theological Review* 58 (1965) 213–26. On *qwl,* see Joüon § 162e / p. 500. M. H. Pope contends that *qôl* "does not mean 'voice,' but 'noise' or 'sound' and is often used as an exclamation, as in Isa 40:3 . . . 'Hark! one cries: "In the wilderness etc."'" See *Song of Songs* (Garden City, New York: Doubleday, 1977) 512, cf. 389. On some other, unusual uses of *qwl,* see A. B. Davidson, *Hebrew Syntax* (3d ed.; Edinburgh: T. & T. Clark, 1901) 154–55; GKC § 144l–m / p. 461; Rabin, "Lexical Emendation," 391–92.

times). The הוֹי cry can be followed by a vocative (# 1)[33] or a topic (# 2); in either case the following noun is juxtaposed to הוֹי. In a number of cases the particle has no woe sense at all; it is merely a summons, conventionally rendered 'ho!' (# 3).[34] Sometimes the cry introduces further speech, without the personal focus of the cry being specified (# 4). Though it is usually uttered, the cry may be quoted (# 1).

1. לֹא־יִסְפְּדוּ לוֹ הוֹי אָחִי וְהוֹי
    אָחוֹת לֹא־יִסְפְּדוּ לוֹ הוֹי אָדוֹן
    וְהוֹי הֹדֹה׃

They shall not lament for him, "*Alas*, my brother," and "*Alas*, my sister." They shall not lament for him, "*Alas*, Lord," and "*Alas*, His Majesty."
Jer 22:18

2. הוֹי עֲטֶרֶת גֵּאוּת שִׁכֹּרֵי אֶפְרַיִם

Woe to the crown of the pride of the drunks in Ephraim!
Isa 28:1

3. הוֹי כָּל־צָמֵא לְכוּ לַמַּיִם

Ho! All you who are thirsty, come to the water!
Isa 55:1

4. הוֹי אַשּׁוּר שֵׁבֶט אַפִּי
    וּמַטֶּה־הוּא בְיָדָם זַעְמִי׃

Woe! Assyria is the rod of my anger!
My fury is a staff in their hand.
Isa 10:5

The אוֹי cry[35] is usually followed by a topic; if the topic is a pronoun, it takes לְ (# 5),[36] but if it is a noun phrase, it is simply juxtaposed (# 6). It, too, is usually uttered, but may be quoted (# 7, the only occurrence of אֲבוֹי, another woe cry).

5. אוֹי לָךְ יְרוּשָׁלַיִם לֹא תִטְהֲרִי

Woe to you, O Jerusalem! You are not clean!
Jer 13:27

6. אוֹי עִיר הַדָּמִים

Woe to the bloody city!
Ezek 24:6, 9

7. לְמִי אוֹי לְמִי אֲבוֹי
    לְמִי מִדְוָנִים לְמִי שִׂיחַ

Whose is "*Woe!*"? Whose is "*Oy!*"?
Whose are quarrels? Whose is angst?
Prov 23:29

b   The remaining cries are rare. The form אַלְלַי (Mic 7:1) / אַלְלָי (Job 10:15) is always followed by לִי; once it is uttered (Mic 7:1) and once quoted. In Qoheleth אִי is used in the forms אִילוֹ (4:10, followed by an apposition, followed by a relative clause) and אִי־לָךְ (10:16, followed by a vocative, followed by a relative clause). The cry אֲהָהּ can stand

---

33. See D. R. Hillers, "*Hôy* and *Hôy*-Oracles: A Neglected Syntactic Aspect," *The Word of the Lord Shall Go Forth: Essays in Honor of David Noel Freedman*, ed. C. L. Meyers and M. O'Connor (Winona Lake, Indiana: Eisenbrauns, 1983) 185–88; and Hillers, *Micah* (Philadelphia: Fortress, 1984) 16; on the meaning of *hôy*, see Waltke in D. W. Baker, T. D. Alexander, and B. K. Waltke, *Obadiah, Jonah, Micah* (Downers Grove, Illinois: Inter-

Varsity, 1988) 156–57.

34. See the discussion in R. J. Clifford, "Isaiah 55: Invitation to a Feast," *The Word of the Lord Shall Go Forth: Essays in Honor of David Noel Freedman*, ed. C. L. Meyers and M. O'Connor (Winona Lake, Indiana: Eisenbrauns, 1983) 27–35.

35. The long form *ʾôyâ* is found only in Ps 120:5.

36. For a first-person example, see Isa 6:5.

alone (e.g., Judg 11:35) or before a vocative (e.g., Ezek 4:14); once it is followed by לְיוֹם (Joel 1:15).

Other Exclamations

40.2.5

The exclamations that remain, most of them interjections, are not a homogeneous group: a few have straightforward etymologies, while most are phonologically marginal.[37] In the case of the forms that seem to represent odd sounds—אָח, הֶאָח, הָס, נָא־, אָנָּא, and הָא—it is important to bear in mind that the shape of the word is likely to be a convention. Exclamations, that is, tend to use sounds not ordinarily part of a language's sound system, as in the sounds written in English as 'whew, tch, tut-tut, tisk-tisk, ugh, argh.'[38] This group of Hebrew exclamations is semantically hard to pin down, because most of the items are rare.

a

Three of these exclamations may be classed as *cries or impolite utterances.* אָח is a cry of pain or grief (uttered in Ezek 21:20; quoted in Ezek 6:11).[39] A cry associated with a horse going into battle (# 1), הֶאָח is apparently a human cry of joy (sometimes mean spirited). It is always preceded by אמר and may stand with nothing following (e.g., Ps 40:16) or be followed by a phrase (Ps 35:25) or a clause (# 2). A *Niphal* participle of יאש 'to despair,' the form נוֹאָשׁ is used as a cry of despair (# 3).[40]

b

1.	הֲתִתֵּן לַסּוּס גְּבוּרָה . . . בְּדֵי שֹׁפָר יֹאמַר הֶאָח וּמֵרָחוֹק יָרִיחַ מִלְחָמָה רַעַם שָׂרִים וּתְרוּעָה:	Did you give the horse strength. . . ? As often as the trumpet sounds, he says "he ʾah" and from afar smells battle, officers' thunder and taratantara.[41] Job 39:19, 25
2.	וְיֹאמַר הֶאָח חַמּוֹתִי רָאִיתִי אוּר:	He says, "*Aha!* I am warm! I can see the fire!" Isa 44:16
3.	וַתֹּאמְרִי נוֹאָשׁ לוֹא כִּי־אָהַבְתִּי זָרִים וְאַחֲרֵיהֶם אֵלֵךְ:	You said, "*I quit!* No! I've loved strangers and I'll follow them."[42] Jer 2:25

Several exclamations are *polite,* more like promptings than cries. The need for silence is marked by הָס (e.g., Amos 6:10); apparently at base an exclamation, this word came to be treated as a verb (only twice: *Qal* in Neh 8:11, *Hiphil* in Num 13:30). The opposite process is illustrated by a hortatory term הַב (e.g., Exod 1:10): the root יהב 'to give,' common in Aramaic, is rare in Hebrew, occurring only in the imperative (e.g.,

c

---

37. They are also, like most of the elements treated in this chapter, syntactically marginal. As W. Richter remarks, "The vocative and the interjection are syntactically bound only to a slight degree; they enter into no phrases. Further, they often have no regular role in a syntagma or sentence, can frequently be entirely isolated, and belong among the extremely rare entities that can stand without a sentence or sentence-substitute" (*GAHG* 3. 158).

38. R. Quirk et al., *A Grammar of Contemporary En-* glish (Harlow, Essex: Longman, 1972) 413. These spellings, though they can be pronounced, actually correspond to quite different grunts and groans.

39. The apparent occurrence in Ezek 18:10 is dubious.

40. See Holladay, *Jeremiah,* 1. 53–54, 102, 517.

41. Does the trumpet also "say" "*he ʾah*"? The metaphorical use of ʾ*mr* for the horse is related to the synesthesia in the rest of the verse, viz., the smelling of noise.

42. See Holladay (cited in n. 40) further on this verse.

Gen 29:21), from which the hortatory use ('Come on, . . .') developed. The enclitic particle נָא־ is often used after imperatives and other volitional forms (e.g., Isa 1:18, 5:5), as well as after הנה and other exclamations and adverbs. As Lambdin observes, "the particle seems . . . to denote that the command [or the like] in question is a logical consequence, either of an immediately preceding statement or of the general situation in which it is uttered."[43] A related term, אָנָּה/אָנָּא, is used before imperatives (e.g., Gen 50:17) and in similar contexts.

d   The sense of the exclamation הֵא is unknown; its context is different in both its occurrences (Gen 47:23, Ezek 16:43).[44]

40.3   Polar Questions

a   There are two types of questions in Hebrew. The words used for *question-word questions* have been discussed (18.1): מִי, מָה, מָתַי, מַדּוּעַ form one group ('who, what, when, why?'), and אַיִן, אָן, אָיֵה, אֵיכֹה, אֵיפֹה, אֵי ('where?') and אֵיךָ, אֵיךְ, אֵיכָה ('how?') form another. *Polar questions*, known in English as 'yes-no' questions, differ from question-word questions in that the entire proposition is questioned rather than just one feature of it.

b   Polar questions may be unmarked as questions or marked with the interrogative הֲ (the first question in # 1 is unmarked; the second has ה).[45] The same question is found with and without the ה (# 2).[46] As with other questions, polar questions with ה can have an exclamatory sense (# 3).[47] In double or triple questions, the first question has ה and the others אם (# 4), ואם, ה, or או. Questions in verse are often rhetorical, requiring assent rather than reply (# 5).[48]

1. חֲסַר מְשֻׁגָּעִים אָנִי כִּי־הֲבֵאתֶם אֶת־זֶה לְהִשְׁתַּגֵּעַ עָלָי הֲזֶה יָבוֹא אֶל־בֵּיתִי:	Am I short on lunatics that you bring that one to throw fits at me? Should such a person enter my house? 1 Sam 21:16

---

43. Lambdin, *Introduction to Biblical Hebrew*, 170. For the possible etymology of *-nāʾ* in the energic form, see 31.7.2 n. 63; note that the particle occurs in a variety of positions but almost never after a suffix form (GKC § 105b / p. 308).

44. The Mishnaic analog apparently means 'behold'; see M. H. Segal, *A Grammar of Mishnaic Hebrew* (Oxford: Clarendon, 1927) 148.

45. The interrogative *h* is used 746 times (SA/THAT). On its initial position, see W. Gross, *Die Pendenskonstruktion im biblischen Hebräisch* (St. Ottilien: EOS, 1987) 180. On unmarked questions, see Joüon § 161a / p. 495; A. Sperber, *A Historical Grammar of Biblical Hebrew* (Leiden: Brill, 1966) 622—note also Sperber's treatment of the vocalization of *h*, pp. 623–25.

46. Note also (*hă*)*tiślāḥ* 'will it thrive?' in Ezek 17:9–10.

47. Joüon § 161b / pp. 495–96.

48. Moshe Held, "Rhetorical Questions in Ugaritic and Biblical Hebrew," *Eretz-Israel* 9 (1969) 71–79. The combination *hălōʾ* is often likened to the Latin particle *nonne*, a double negative used to indicate that an affirmative answer is expected; in English such an expectation is shown by a tag question, e.g., 'isn't that so?' Most cases of *hlʾ* fit that description, but there are cases that do not; see H. A. Brongers, "Some Remarks on the Biblical Particle *hălōʾ*," *Oudtestamentische Studiën* 21 (1981) 177–89, who attributes to the form a politeness usage, assigning it sometimes the force of 'as you know' (p. 177, citing Deut 11:30) and sometimes 'please' (pp. 187–88, citing 1 Sam 26:14). He also discusses presentative and emphatic uses. M. L. Brown, reviewing some difficult cases, has proposed that Hebrew (like Ugaritic and Aramaic) has a particle *ʾhălû* 'surely' in, e.g., Ezek 38:14; see "'Is It Not?' or 'Indeed!': HL in Northwest Semitic," *Maarav* 4 (1987) 201–19.

2a.   הֲשָׁלוֹם לַנַּעַר לְאַבְשָׁלוֹם   Is the young man Absalom all right?
                                            2 Sam 18:32

2b.   שָׁלוֹם לַנַּעַר לְאַבְשָׁלוֹם   Is the young man Absalom all right?
                                            2 Sam 18:29

3.   הַזְּבָחִים וּמִנְחָה הִגַּשְׁתֶּם־לִי   O Israel, you brought me sacrifices and offerings for
      בַּמִּדְבָּר אַרְבָּעִים שָׁנָה בֵּית   forty years in the wilderness?!
      יִשְׂרָאֵל׃   Amos 5:25

4.   הֲלָנוּ אַתָּה אִם־לְצָרֵינוּ׃   Are you for us *or* for our enemies?
                                            Josh 5:13

5.   הֲלוֹא תֵדְעוּ הֲלוֹא תִשְׁמָעוּ   Didn't you know? Haven't you heard?
      הֲלוֹא הֻגַּד מֵרֹאשׁ לָכֶם   Weren't you told from the start?
      הֲלוֹא הֲבִינֹתֶם מוֹסְדוֹת הָאָרֶץ׃   Haven't you understood since the earth's foundations?
                                            Isa 40:21

Glossary, Bibliography, and Indexes

Glossary

ablative direction or movement away from

accidence *see* inflection

accident (philosophical sense) that which is present but nonessential; a quality not crucial to an understanding of a thing or being; *see also* substance

accusative *see* case (function)

active *see* voice; *elsewhere* used for fientive

adjunct an optional or less important element in a grammatical construction, notable groups of adjuncts being adverbs and some prepositional phrases

affix a form attached to another form (root or base), before (prefix), after (suffix), or internally (infix)

agent a form identifying who is responsible for a situation, usually an action

agreement the condition of grammatical elements sharing a corresponding inflectional category, e.g., number or gender; *also called* concord or congruence

Aktionsart (German 'type of action') the way in which the structure of a situation is understood in relation to causation, voice, transitivity, reflexivity, repetition, and similar factors; *see also* aspect and *Aspekt*

allative direction or movement to or toward

ambiguous unclear with a small number of variant interpretations possible; *see also* vague

analogy a type of linguistic change in which a larger class of forms influences or even overtakes a smaller class

anaphora reference of a grammatical element to something mentioned earlier, e.g., in 'Moses fled and Jethro helped *him*,' *him* is an anaphoric pronoun; *see also* cataphora

anaptyxis the intrusion of a vowel between two consonants, in Hebrew, often a *seghol*

anarthrous lacking the article

aorist (Greek 'without + boundaries') a verb form indicating a situation without regard to absolute time; the actual use of the aorist form in, e.g., Greek involves a variety of factors

apocope the shortening of a form at the end and the resulting changes in syllable structure

apodosis the 'then' clause of an 'if-then' or conditional sentence, a term used *here* in the broadest sense; *see also* protasis

apposition juxtaposition of a noun (or noun phrase) to another noun (or noun phrase) with the same reference and in the same grammatical slot

archaic marked by characteristics of an earlier time

archaizing a process by which the characteristics of an earlier time are imitated

argument a noun (or noun phrase) slot in a sentence, i.e., subject, object, etc.

aspect the marking of a verb form to indicate chiefly the structure over time of the situation described; *see* Aspekt and Aktionsart

Aspekt (German) the way in which the internal structure of a situation is understood in relation to time, as either complete or not; *see also* Aktionsart and aspect

asyndetic lacking a(n expected) conjunction or other connector

attributive adjective an adjective that posits an attribute of the substantive it modifies, e.g., *hammā᾿ôr haggādōl* 'the *great* light'; *see also* predicate adjective

base *here* a form of a root intermediate in specification between the root and a word, e.g., *qtl* is a root, *-qtōl-* is the prefix conjugation base, and *yiqtōl* is a word

biconsonantal root a root composed of two consonants, e.g., *bn*, the root of *bên* 'between' and *bn(y)*, the source of *bny* 'to build'

binyan (Hebrew 'building') stem

case (function) *here* a group of semantic and syntactic phenomena that can plausibly be grouped together, on the basis of both internal and comparative data; *elsewhere* an inflection of a noun or pronoun reflecting various semantic and syntactic phenomena; the Semitic cases include the nominative (the case of subject, vocative, predicate in verbless clauses), accusative (the case of nouns modifying the verb, notably of direct object), and genitive (the case of nouns modifying other nouns, notably of possessor, and of prepositional object), as well as, marginally, the dative (case of indirect object, usually a recipient)

casus pendens (Latin 'hanging case')   *see* nominative absolute

cataphora   reference of a grammatical element to something mentioned later, e.g., in 'When *he* fled, Moses was afraid,' *he* is a cataphoric pronoun; *see also* anaphora

causative   *see* factitive

citation form   the form of a word given in isolated citation, as in a lexicon; *also* dictionary form

cognate forms   words that are ultimately derived from the same source, e.g., Hebrew *šēm*, Akkadian *šumu*, and Arabic *ism* are cognates

colon   *see* line

complement   an element in a grammatical construction that completes the predicate, notable types being objects and some adverbials

complex sentence   a sentence made up of a main clause and one or more dependent clauses; *see also* compound sentence

compound sentence   a sentence made up of several coordinate clauses; *see also* complex sentence

concord   *see* agreement

congruence   *see* agreement

conjugation   a major inflectional category of verbs, the principal Hebrew conjugations being the *qatal* (or perfective or suffix) conjugation and the *yiqtol* (or non-perfective or prefix) conjugation

constative   referring to remaining or persisting in a state

construct chain   a phrase involving a construct (*regens*) term followed by a genitive or absolute (*rectum*) term, often of a possessed-possessor type, e.g., *bêt hammélek* 'the king's house'

contrastive analysis   identification of differences between two languages or families of languages, such differences being seen as points of potential difficulty in learning and understanding

copula (Latin 'rope, thong')   a verb that joins the subject and predicate of an equational verb clause, e.g., 'She *is* tall'; or a pronoun that joins the subject and predicate of a verbless clause, e.g., 'Miriam, *she* (is) tall'

customary   *see* habitual

dative   *see* case (function)

declarative   *see* indicative

deixis (Greek 'pointing')   the system of words that shift their reference depending on the speech situation (especially personal, temporal, and locational features), including prominently pronouns; e.g., the reference of *I* depends on who is speaking, that of *there* depends on where one is pointing (directing attention)

delocutive   a verb form referring to a speech act; *see also* performative utterance

denominative   a verb derived from a noun

dictionary form   *see* citation form

double-status action   an action involving a person in two different roles, i.e., subject and (direct or prepositional or implicit) object

dummy   a grammatical element that is semantically empty and is used chiefly to fill a needed syntactic slot, e.g., *it* in '*It*'s raining' is a dummy pronoun, with no true antecedent; *also* pleonasm

enclitic (Greek 'leaning on')   a word or element that carries no stress of its own and depends on the preceding word; in Hebrew, an element written together with the preceding word

epexegesis (Greek 'in addition + explanation')   the function of glossing or clarifying immediately preceding material

epigraphy   the study of ancient written remains on durable, hard materials (as opposed to manuscripts, on papyrus, cloth, wood, parchment, or paper)

ergative system   a case-marking system in which the object of a transitive verb and the subject of an intransitive verb govern the same case (the absolutive) and the subject of a transitive verb governs a different case (the ergative); some languages are predominantly ergative (e.g., Basque), some are partially so (e.g., split-ergative languages like Hindi), and others display traces of ergativity

etymology   the origins or sources of the elements of a word or phrase as well as the study of the developments of its shape and meaning; an origin or source is called an etymon (pl. etyma)

factitive   a construction in which a cause produces a state, e.g., if *kill* meant 'cause to be dead,' it would be factitive; factitive is contrasted with causative, a construction in which a cause produces an event, e.g., if *kill* meant 'cause to die,' it would be causative

fientive   a verb describing motion or change of state; *see also* stative

finite   a verb form that can stand as a predicate in an independent clause and is inflected for aspect and mood; non-finite forms can stand as a predicate in dependent clauses and are not inflected for aspect or mood

focus marker   *see* nominative absolute

function   *see* case (function)

gapping   the omission of an item in the second of two adjacent clauses of similar structure

generic statement   a statement referring to a class of entities or events; *see also* gnomic

genitive   *see* case (function)

genre   a category of compositions with common qualities, e.g., prayer, parable, letter

gnomic   having the character of a rule, proverb, or byword; *see also* generic statement

habitual   characteristic of an extended period of time extending up to or into the present, as of a verb form used to describe regular repetition of an action; a verb form used to describe such action in the past is called customary

hapax legomenon (Greek 'once read'; pl. *hapax legomena* or, less formally, hapaxes)   a word, form, or combination of words found only once in a given body of literature

head   the main element in a phrase

hemistich   *see* line

hendiadys (Greek 'one through two')   a single expression of two apparently separate parts, e.g., 'kith and kin'

homonyms   words of the same shape (pronunciation and spelling) but different meanings; homophones are words of the same pronunciation but different meanings; in languages with complex spelling traditions, e.g, English, homophone is used for words with different spellings and homonym for words with identical spelling

homophones   *see* homonyms

imperfective   an aspect (*Aspekt*) in which a situation is understood as ongoing, whatever its temporal relation to the time of speaking; *see also* non-perfective *and* perfective

impersonal   an active construction with no specified agent

inceptive   referring to the beginning of a situation; *also* inchoative

inchoative   *see* inceptive

indicative   the mood of a simple statement or assertion; *also* declarative

indirect action   an action in which the subject is the originating or motivating force but not the agent, i.e., not the immediate mover or actor; indirect action may be mediated by an animate or inanimate intermediary (e.g., by a servant or a tool)

infix   *see* affix

inflection   a systematic morphological marking signaling a grammatical relationship; *also* accidence

ingressive   referring to entering into a state; *compare* inceptive

intransitive verb   a verb that (usually) does not govern an object; stative verbs are generally intransitive; *see also* transitive verb

irreal   other than real or actual, e.g., hypothetical, dubious; *see also* mood

line   the basic unit of Hebrew verse; *also* colon, hemistich, verset

maqqeph (Hebrew 'binder')   the Masoretic equivalent of a dash, often also serving as a sign that one of the two or three elements joined has no independent stress

markedness analysis   an analysis based on the presence or absence of a particular linguistic feature

metathesis   a change in the sequence of sounds or syllables, reflecting a slip of the tongue, phonological change, or copyist error

mater lectionis (Latin 'mother of reading'; pl. *matres lectionis*)   a letter used in a consonantal script to indicate a vowel

middle   *see* voice

mimation   the ending *m* added after the case endings of many nouns in older dialects of Akkadian (Old Akkadian, Old Babylonian, Old Assyrian)

mišqal (Hebrew 'weight')   noun pattern, e.g., CéCeC is the *mišqal* of *kéleb* and *mélek*

modernizing   a process by which older or archaic characteristics are replaced by corresponding newer ones

mood   a major inflectional category of the verb marking orientation to fact, either real (indicative mood) or irreal (the volitional moods, cohortative, imperative, jussive)

neutrum   a grammatical element of vague or broad reference, often in Hebrew a feminine pronoun; analogous to the vague "neuter" of 'Don't do *it*' or '*This* is a mess'

nominal clause   *see* verbless clause

nominative   *see* case (function)

nominative absolute   a grammatical element isolated outside a clause, usually at the start of the clause; *also* known as focus marker, *casus pendens*, topic

non-finite   *see* finite

non-perfective   an aspect (*Aspekt*) in which the structure of a situation over time is not specified, i.e., in which a situation is not specified as to perfectivity; relevant situations often include those set in future time or displaying irreal mood; *see also* imperfective *and* perfective

non-perfective conjugation   *see* prefix conjugation

noun (Latin *nomen* 'name')   the class of naming words, including substantives (names of things or beings) and adjectives, as well as participles in some uses

noun clause   a dependent clause that is the object of a verb of speaking or perception, e.g., 'He saw *that he was alone*'

orthography   the study of the way in which words and word elements are spelled

paradigm   a set of inflectional forms of a word; *or* a class of words that can perform similar syntactic functions

paragogic (Greek 'leading past')   an element that is added at the end of a word

paronomasia (Greek 'word play, play involving similar-sounding words')   a figure of speech involving punning or playing on different senses of the same word or of similar-sounding words; the related term

schema etymologicum refers to word play involving etymologically related words; both terms are sometimes applied to the use of the infinitive absolute with a corresponding finite verb in Biblical Hebrew

particle   a class of words that connects and subjoins nouns and verbs (including prepositions, some adverbs, the article, etc.) or exists on the margins of utterances (e.g., exclamations and interjections)

partitive   a construction indicating some or a part of a larger entity

passive   *see* voice

patient   a form identifying who undergoes an action

pause   the break in Masoretic verse division associated with the end of a verse (marked with *silluq* and *sop pasuq*) or the middle of a verse (usually marked with *athnach*); a form in pause may show various phonological shifts, in accentuation or vocalization or both

perfect   a verb form indicating a past situation with present relevance; *see also* preterite

perfective   an aspect (*Aspekt*) in which a situation is understood as complete (rather than completed), as a whole; *see also* imperfective *and* non-perfective

perfective conjugation   *see* suffix conjugation

performative utterance   an utterance that performs the act it describes, e.g., 'I now pronounce you husband and wife'; *see also* delocutive

phrase   words that stand in agreement with one another; *or* words that form a single grammatical unit

pleonasm (Greek 'redundancy')   *see* dummy

polarity   a positive : negative contrast, positing total, exclusive contrast, as of *A* and *not-A*

polar question   a question demanding a yes or no response

polysemous   showing several distinct meanings

postpositive   occurring after a specified position; *see* prepositive

predicate adjective   an adjective that predicates an attribute of a substantive in a clause, e.g., *gādôl kəbôdô* '*great* is his glory'; *see also* attributive adjective

prefix   *see* affix

prefix conjugation   the conjugation characterized by prefixing, e.g., *yi-qtōl* (and suffixing, e.g., *yi-qtəl-û*), and *here* associated with non-perfective aspect; *also* non-perfective conjugation and *yiqtol* conjugation; *see also* suffix conjugation

prepositive   occurring before a specified position; *see* postpositive

preterite   a form describing a simple past situation; *see also* perfect

privative   a verb indicating removal of something, e.g., 'to skin, poll'

proclitic (Greek 'leaning forward')   a word or element that carries no stress of its own and depends on the following word; in Hebrew an element written together with the following word or attached to it by a *maqqeph*

progressive   a common term for tenses marked for imperfective aspect, e.g., the English present progressive 'I *am running*'

prose   language without the numerical regulation of verse

prosthesis   *see* prothesis

protasis   the 'if' clause of an 'if-then' sentence; *see also* apodosis

prothesis (Greek 'placing before')   the addition of an initial syllable before a word; prothetic ʾ in Hebrew appears to be used to break up an initial consonant cluster; *sometimes* the term prosthesis (Greek 'placing with, adding') is so used

***qatal* conjugation**   *see* suffix conjugation

rectum (Latin 'governed')   the modifying or defining term in a phrase or less often a clause; *see also regens* and construct chain

reference   any aspect of meaning associated with the external world; in contrast to sense, any aspect of meaning arising from the lexical and grammatical relations of language

regens (Latin 'governing')   the modified or defined word in a phrase or less often a clause; *see also rectum* and construct chain

regens-rectum   a structure of the modified-modifier type, as in construct-absolute, noun–attributive adjective, possessed-possessor; verb-object; particle (i.e., preposition)-object

relative clause   a dependent clause that modifies a noun phrase in the main clause and may be introduced by a relative pronoun ('the king *that* I saw') or left unintroduced ('the king I saw')

resumptive   a grammatical element connecting a clause to a preceding nominative absolute, e.g., *him* in 'As for Moses, I saw *him*' (resumptive pronoun) or *there* in 'As for Midian, he left *there*' (resumptive adverb)

rhetorical question   a question to which no answer is expected

root   *here* the consonantal skeleton of a word, e.g., *mlk* is the root of *mélek* and *yimlōk*; *elsewhere* the base form of a word, from which the word and cognates are derived, e.g., *move* is the root of *move, movement, immovable, mobile*; *or* the historical base form of a word, e.g., Latin *moveo* is the root of English *move*

sense   *see* reference

short prefix form   a prefix conjugation form displaying, where possible, stress shift and syncope, and associated with jussive and preterite senses

sibilant   a hissing or hushing fricative sound; Hebrew *s, š, z, ṣ, ś*

signifiant (French)   that which signifies; the word as a sound; *see also* signifié

signifié (French)   that which is signified; the word as an element of meaning and grammar; *see also* signifiant

situation   an action, event, state, or process described by a verb

substance (philosophical sense)   a thing or being that is distinct in itself; that which is essential and in which accidents inhere; *see also* accident

smoothing   an effort to remove deviant (archaic, dialectal, geographical, etc.) characteristics

stative   a verb or verb form describing a state or quality; *see also* fientive

stem   *here* a major inflectional category of the verb marking *Aktionsart*, e.g., *himlîk* is a *Hiphil* stem form; *elsewhere* a form of the root intermediate in specification between the root and a word, e.g., *malk-* is the stem of *mélek, malkî, malkâ*; *or* a form of a root to which affixes are attached, e.g., *-mov-* is the stem of *im-mov-able*

substance (philosophical sense)   a thing or being that is distinct in itself; that which is essential and in which accidents inhere; *see also* accident

substantive   *see* noun

suffix   *see* affix

suffix conjugation   the conjugation characterized by suffixing, e.g., *qāṭal-tî*, and associated with perfective aspect; *also* perfective conjugation and *qatal* conjugation; *see also* prefix conjugation

syncope   shortening a word from the end

synoptic text   a text preserved in two (or more) versions, thus Psalm 18 and 2 Samuel 22 are synoptic texts, and sections of Kings are synoptic with sections of Isaiah, Jeremiah, and Chronicles

syntagm   a series of different elements forming a syntactic unit

telic   possessing a goal or endpoint

tempus (Latin 'time')   tense

tense   the marking of a verb form to indicate chiefly the time of the situation described relative to the time of speaking

topic-comment   *here* a particular construction involving a topic (cf. nominative absolute) followed by a comment; *elsewhere* an analytic approach to an informational unit (e.g., a clause) distinguishing old or given information (topic, theme) and new information (comment, rheme)

transitive verb   a verb that (usually) governs a (direct) object (one-place or singly transitive) or, less often, two objects (two-place or doubly transitive); *see also* intransitive verb

triconsonantal root   a root composed of three consonants; usually excluded as biconsonantal are medial and final weak roots, among others

vague   unclear as a result of restricted or unspecified information, capable of an unspecifiable range of variant interpretations; *see also* ambiguous

valency   the number of links a grammatical element, especially a verb, has other elements

verbal noun   an infinitive, in Hebrew, of either type

verbless clause   a clause that connects a subject and predicate with no verb, used for classification or identification; *also* nominal clause

verse   numerically regulated language; verse may be regulated in terms of the sound material of language (as in English) or in terms of the syntactic material (as in Hebrew); the numerical regulation always involves small numbers (an iambic foot in English includes two syllables; a pentameter line includes five feet, etc.)

verset   *see* line

vetitive   a form expressing negative prohibition

vocative   a form used in address, e.g., *hammélek* 'O king'

voice   an inflectional category of the verb referring to the relationship of the agent (actor) and patient (undergoer): in active voice the agent is the subject and the patient is the object; in passive voice the patient is the subject; in middle voice the agent is both subject and object

word order   patterns of meaningful arrangement of words in a given language; a VSO language tends to use clauses with the elements verb-subject-object in that order

yiqtol **conjugation**   *see* prefix conjugation

Bibliography

1. Biblical Hebrew

a. Grammars, Lexicons, and Concordances

Francis I. Andersen. 1970. *The Hebrew Verbless Clause in the Pentateuch.* Journal of Biblical Literature Monograph 14. Nashville: Abingdon.

_____. 1974. *The Sentence in Biblical Hebrew.* Janua Linguarum, Series Practica 231. The Hague: Mouton.

Hans Bauer and Pontus Leander. 1918–22. *Historische Grammatik der hebräischen Sprache des Alten Testamentes.* Halle: Niemeyer. Rpt., Hildesheim: Olms, 1962.

Walter Baumgartner et al. 1967–. *Hebräisches und aramäisches Lexikon zum Alten Testament.* Leiden: Brill.

Gotthelf Bergsträsser. See Gesenius-Bergsträsser 1918–29.

Klaus Beyer. 1969. *Althebräische Grammatik: Laut- und Formenlehre.* Göttingen: Vandenhoeck und Ruprecht.

Joshua Blau. 1976. *A Grammar of Biblical Hebrew.* Porta Linguarum Orientalium N.S. 12. Wiesbaden: Harrassowitz.

Friedrich Böttcher. 1866–68. *Ausführliches Lehrbuch der hebräischen Sprache.* 2 vols. Leipzig: Barth.

G. Johannes Botterweck and Helmer Ringgren, eds. 1970–. *Theologisches Wörterbuch zum Alten Testament.* Stuttgart: Kohlhammer.

_____. 1974–. *Theological Dictionary of the Old Testament.* Grand Rapids: Eerdmans.

Carl Brockelmann. 1956. *Hebräische Syntax.* Neukirchen: Neukirchener Verlag.

Francis Brown, S. R. Driver, and C. A. Briggs. 1907. *A Hebrew and English Lexicon of the Old Testament.* Oxford: Clarendon.

William Chomsky. 1952. *David Ḳimḥi's Hebrew Grammar (Mikhlol)*. New York: Bloch.

A. B. Davidson. 1900. *Introductory Grammar*. Edinburgh: T. & T. Clark.

_____. 1901. *Hebrew Syntax*. 3d ed. Edinburgh: T. & T. Clark.

_____. 1925. *An Introductory Hebrew Grammar*. 22d ed. Edinburgh: T. & T. Clark.

A. B. Davidson–John Mauchline. 1966. *An Introductory Hebrew Grammar*. 26th ed. Edinburgh: T. & T. Clark.

Heinrich Ewald. 1870. *Ausführliches Lehrbuch der hebräischen Sprache des Alten Bundes*. 8th ed. Leipzig: Hinrichs.

Wilhelm Gesenius. 1812. *Hebräisch-deutsches Handwörterbuch über die Schriften des Alten Testaments*. Leipzig: Vogel.

_____. 1813. *Hebräische Grammatik*. Halle: Renger.

[Wilhelm Gesenius-]Gotthelf Bergsträsser. 1918–29. *Hebräische Grammatik*. 29th ed. 2 vols. Leipzig: Vogel. Rpt., Hildesheim: Olms, 1962.

[Wilhelm Gesenius-]F. Buhl. 1915. *Hebräisches und aramäisches Handwörterbuch über das Alte Testament*. 16th ed. Leipzig: Vogel.

[Wilhelm Gesenius-]Emil Kautzsch. 1909. *Hebräische Grammatik*. 28th ed. Leipzig: Vogel.

_____. 1910. *Gesenius' Hebrew Grammar*. Translated by A. E. Cowley. Oxford: Clarendon.

Moshe Greenberg. 1965. *Introduction to Hebrew*. Englewood Cliffs, New Jersey: Prentice-Hall.

W. R. Harper. 1888. *Elements of Hebrew Syntax*. New York: Scribner.

[W. R. Harper-]J. M. Powis Smith. 1959. *Introductory Hebrew: Method and Manual*. Chicago: University of Chicago.

R. Laird Harris, Gleason L. Archer, Jr., and Bruce K. Waltke, eds. 1980. *Theological Wordbook of the Old Testament*. 2 vols. Chicago: Moody.

William L. Holladay. 1971. *A Concise Hebrew and Aramaic Lexicon of the Old Testament Based upon the Lexical Work of Ludwig Koehler and Walter Baumgartner*. Grand Rapids: Eerdmans.

H. Irsigler. 1978. *Einführung in das biblische Hebräisch*, vol. 1. St. Ottilien: EOS.

Ernst Jenni. 1981. *Lehrbuch der hebräischen Sprache des Alten Testaments*. Basel: Helbing und Lichtenhahn.

Ernst Jenni with Claus Westermann. 1971–76. *Theologisches Handwörterbuch zum Alten Testament*. 2 vols. Munich: Chr. Kaiser.

Paul Joüon. 1923. *Grammaire de l'hébreu biblique*. 2d ed. Rome: Pontifical Biblical Institute.

Emil Kautzsch. See Gesenius-Kautzsch 1909 and 1910.

B. P. Kittel, V. Hoffer, and R. A. Wright. 1989. *Biblical Hebrew: A Text and Workbook*. New Haven: Yale University.

Ludwig Koehler and Walter Baumgartner. 1953. *Lexicon in Veteris Testamenti Libros*. Leiden: Brill.

_____. 1958. *Supplementum ad Lexicon in Veteris Testamenti Libros*. Leiden: Brill.

Eduard König. 1881–97. *Historisch-kritisches Lehrgebäude der hebräischen Sprache*. 2 vols. in 3. Leipzig: Hinrichs.

_____. 1897. *Historisch-Comparative Syntax der hebräischen Sprache*. Leipzig: Hinrichs [vol. 2.2 of previous entry].

Arno Kropat. 1909. *Die Syntax des Autors der Chronik verglichen mit der seiner Quellen: Ein Beitrag zur historischen Syntax des Hebräischen*. Beiheft zur Zeitschrift für die Alttestamentliche Wissenschaft 16. Giessen: Töpelmann.

Thomas O. Lambdin. 1971. *Introduction to Biblical Hebrew*. New York: Scribner.

Mayer Lambert. 1972. *Traité de grammaire hébraïque*. Hildesheim: Gerstenberg. Originally Paris: Leroux, 1931–38.

Jaakov Levi. 1987. *Die Inkongruenz im biblischen Hebräisch*. Wiesbaden: Harrassowitz.

Saul Levin. 1966. *Hebrew Grammar*. Binghampton: State University of New York at Binghampton.

G. Lisowsky. 1958. *Konkordanz zum hebräischen Alten Testament*. Stuttgart: Privilegierte Württembergische Bibelanstalt.

S. Mandelkern. 1971. *Veteris Testamenti: concordantiae, hebraicae atque chaldaicae*. Jerusalem: Schocken. Originally, Leipzig: Veit, 1896.

Rudolf Meyer. 1966–72. *Hebräische Grammatik*. 3d ed. 4 vols. Sammlung Göschen. Berlin: de Gruyter.

Diethelm Michel. 1977. *Grundlegung einer hebräischen Syntax*, vol. 1. Neukirchen-Vluyn: Neukirchener Verlag.

T. W. Nakarai. 1951. *Biblical Hebrew* [Philadelphia:] Bookman Associates.

H. S. Nyberg. 1952. *Hebreisk Grammatik*. Uppsala: Geber.

Justus Olshausen. 1861. *Lehrbuch der hebräischen Sprache*. 2 vols. Braunschweig: Vieweg.

Wolfgang Richter. 1978–80. *Grundlagen einer althebräischen Grammatik*. 3 vols. St. Ottilien: EOS.

John F. A. Sawyer. 1976. *A Modern Introduction to Biblical Hebrew*. Stocksfield: Oriel.

Wolfgang Schneider. 1974. *Grammatik des biblischen Hebräisch*. Munich: Claudius.

C. L. Seow. 1987. *A Grammar for Biblical Hebrew*. Nashville: Abingdon.

Alexander Sperber. 1943. Hebrew Grammar: A New Approach. *Journal of Biblical Literature* 62:137–262.

_____. 1959. *A Grammar of Masoretic Hebrew: A General Introduction to the Pre-Masoretic Bible*. Corpus Codicum Hebraicorum Medii Aev: Pars II [Supplement]. Copenhagen: Ejnar Munksgaard.

_____. 1966. *A Historical Grammar of Biblical Hebrew*. Leiden: Brill.

Baruch Spinoza. 1962. *Hebrew Grammar* [*Compendium Grammatices Linguae Hebraeae*]. Translated by M. J. Bloom. New York: Philosophical Library.

B. Stade. 1879. *Lehrbuch der hebräischen Grammatik*. Leipzig: Vogel.

Arthur Ungnad. 1912. *Hebräische Grammatik*. Tübingen: J. C. B. Mohr.

Jacob Weingreen. 1957. *Classical Hebrew Composition*. Oxford: Clarendon.

_____. 1959. *A Practical Grammar for Classical Hebrew*. 2d ed. Oxford: Clarendon.

Samuel B. Wheeler. 1969. Review of Sperber, *Historical Grammar of Biblical Hebrew* (1966). *Journal of the Ancient Near Eastern Society* 2:66–73.

b. Individual Morphemes and Particles

Kjell Aartun. 1978. Textüberlieferung und Vermeintliche Belege der Konjunktion *pV* im Alten Testament. *Ugarit-Forschungen* 10:1–13.

Karl Albrecht. 1929. את vor dem Nominativ und beim Passiv. *Zeitschrift für die Alttestamentliche Wissenschaft* 47:274–83.

John M. Allegro. 1955. Uses of the Semitic Demonstrative Element *z* in Hebrew. *Vetus Testamentum* 5:309–12.

L. Alonso-Schökel. 1956. Nota estilistica sobre la particula הִנֵּה. *Biblica* 37:74–80.

R. Althann. 1981. *MWL*, "Circumcise" with the *lamedh* of Agency. *Biblica* 62:239–40.

Francis I. Andersen. 1969. A Short Note on Construct *k* in Hebrew. *Biblica* 50:68–69.

Francis I. Andersen and A. D. Forbes. 1983. "Prose Particle" Counts of the Hebrew Bible. Pp. 165–83 in *The Word of the Lord Shall Go Forth: Essays in Honor of David Noel Freedman*, ed. C. L. Meyers and M. O'Connor. Winona Lake, Indiana: Eisenbrauns.

Y. Avishur. 1980. Expressions of the Type *byn ydym* in the Bible and Semitic Languages. *Ugarit-Forschungen* 12:125–33.

David W. Baker. 1980. Further Examples of the *Waw Explicativum*. *Vetus Testamentum* 30:129–36.

James Barr. 1978. Some Notes on *Ben* 'Between' in Classical Hebrew. *Journal of Semitic Studies* 23:1–22.

———. 1982. Hebrew עד, especially at Job i.18 and Neh vii.3. *Journal of Semitic Studies* 27:177–88.

Mordechai Ben-Asher. 1978. The Gender of Nouns in Biblical Hebrew. *Semitics* 6:1–14.

Joshua Blau. 1954. Zum angeblichen Gebrauch von את vor dem Nominativ. *Vetus Testamentum* 4:7–19.

———. 1956. Gibt es ein emphatisches ʾēt im Bibelhebräisch? *Vetus Testamentum* 6:211–12.

———. 1980. The Parallel Development of the Feminine Ending -*at* in Semitic Languages. *Hebrew Union College Annual* 51:17–28.

P. A. H. de Boer. 1981. Cantate Domino: An Erroneous Dative? [*šîr ləyhwh* 'cantate dominum, sing about/of the Lord']. *Oudtestamentische Studiën* 21:55–67.

M. Bogaert. 1964. Les suffixes verbaux non accusatifs dans le sémitique nord-occidental et particulièrement en hébreu. *Biblica* 45:220–47.

H. A. Brongers. 1965. Bemerkungen zum Gebrauch des adverbiellen *wᵉᶜattāh* im Alten Testament. *Vetus Testamentum* 15:289–99.

———. 1973. Die Partikel לְמַעַן in der biblisch-hebräischen Sprache. *Oudtestamentische Studiën* 18:84–96.

———. 1978. Alternative Interpretationen des sogennanten Waw copulativum. *Zeitschrift für die Alttestamentliche Wissenschaft* 90:273–77.

———. 1981. Some Remarks on the Biblical Particle *hᵃlōʾ*. *Oudtestamentische Studiën* 21:177–89.

Ronald J. Williams. 1976. *Hebrew Syntax: An Outline*. 2d ed. Toronto: University of Toronto.

M. L. Brown. 1987. "Is It Not?" or "Indeed!": *HL* in Northwest Semitic. *Maarav* 4:201–19.

William Chomsky. 1970–71. The Ambiguity of the Prefixed Prepositions מ, ל, ב in the Bible. *Jewish Quarterly Review* 61:87–89.

W. T. Claassen. 1983. Speaker-Orientated Functions of *kî* in Biblical Hebrew. *Journal of Northwest Semitic Languages* 11:29–46.

Mitchell Dahood. 1970. The Independent Personal Pronoun in the Oblique Case in Hebrew. *Catholic Biblical Quarterly* 32:86–90.

———. 1975. The Emphatic Double Negative *mʾyn*. *Catholic Biblical Quarterly* 37:458–59.

D. N. Freedman. 1972. The Broken Construct Chain. *Biblica* 53:534–36.

G. Garbini. 1985. Il relativo *š* in Fenicio e in Ebraico. Pp. 185–99 in *Mélanges linguistiques offerts à Maxime Rodinson*, ed. C. Robin. Paris: Geuthner.

Stanley Gevirtz. 1982. Formative ע in Biblical Hebrew. *Eretz-Israel* 16:57*–66*.

D. Gill. 1982. Case Marking, Phonological Size, and Linear Order [on ʾt]. *Syntax and Semantics*. 15. *Studies in Transitivity*, ed. P. J. Hopper and S. A. Thompson. New York: Academic Press.

L. H. Glinert. 1982. The Preposition in Biblical and Modern Hebrew. *Hebrew Studies* 23:115–25.

F. J. Goldbaum. 1964. Two Hebrew Quasi-Adverbs: לכן and אכן. *Journal of Near Eastern Studies* 23:132–35.

Robert Gordis. 1943. The Asseverative *Kaph* in Ugaritic and Hebrew. *Journal of the American Oriental Society* 63:176–78. Rpt. as pp. 211–13 in his *The Word and the Book*. New York: Ktav, 1976.

Cyrus H. Gordon. 1981. "In" of Predication or Equivalence. *Journal of Biblical Literature* 100:612–13.

H. Gottlieb. 1971. The Hebrew Particle -*nāʾ*. *Acta Orientalia* 33:47–54.

Moshe Greenberg. 1957. The Hebrew Oath Particle *ḥay/ḥê*. *Journal of Biblical Literature* 76:34–39.

J. C. Greenfield. 1961. The Prepositions *b . . . taḥat . . .* in Jes 57:5. *Zeitschrift für die Alttestamentliche Wissenschaft* 73:226–28.

D. R. Hillers. 1983. *Hôy* and *hôy*-Oracles: A Neglected Syntactic Aspect. Pp. 185–88 in *The Word of the Lord Shall Go Forth: Essays in Honor of David Noel Freedman*, ed. C. L. Meyers and M. O'Connor. Winona Lake, Indiana: Eisenbrauns.

J. Hoftijzer. 1965. Remarks Concerning the Use of the Particle ʾ*t* in Classical Hebrew. *Oudtestamentische Studiën* 14:1–99.

——— et al. 1981. *A Search for Method: A Study in the Syntactic Use of the H-Locale in Classical Hebrew*. Studies in Semitic Languages and Linguistics 12. Leiden: Brill.

Horace D. Hummel. 1957. Enclitic *Mem* in Early Northwest Semitic, especially Hebrew. *Journal of Biblical Literature* 76:85–107.

S. Izreʾel. 1978. *ʾet* 'to, towards' in Biblical Hebrew. *Shnaton* 3:203–12.

B. Jongeling. 1973. La particule רַק. *Oudtestamentische Studiën* 18:97–107.

———. 1981. *Lākēn* dans l'Ancien Testament. *Oudtestamentische Studiën* 21:190–200.

Paul Joüon. 1920. Etudes de morphologie hébraïque. *Biblica* 1:353–71.

C. R. Krahmalkov. 1970. The Enclitic Particle *TA/I* in Hebrew. *Journal of Biblical Literature* 89:218–19.

C. J. Labuschagne. 1966. The Emphasizing Particle *GAM* and Its Connotations. Pp. 193–203 in *Studia Biblica et Semitica: Theodoro Christiano Vriezen . . . Dedicata*, ed. W. C. van Unnik. Wageningen: Veenman en Zonen.

———. 1973. The particles הֵן and הִנֵּה. *Oudtestamentische Studiën* 18:1–14.

Thomas O. Lambdin. 1971. The Junctural Origin of the West Semitic Definite Article. Pp. 315–33 in *Near Eastern Studies in Honor of William Foxwell Albright*, ed. H. Goedicke. Baltimore: Johns Hopkins.

C. van Leeuwen. 1973. Die Partikel אִם. *Oudtestamentische Studiën* 18:15–48.

H. Lenhard. 1983. Über den Unterschied zwischen לכן und עַל־כֵן. *Zeitschrift für die Alttestamentliche Wissenschaft* 95:269–72.

D. J. McCarthy. 1980. The Uses of *wᵉhinnēh* in Biblical Hebrew. *Biblica* 61:330–42.

John Macdonald. 1964. The Particle את in Classical Hebrew: Some New Data on Its Use with the Nominative. *Vetus Testamentum* 14:264–75.

Rudolf Meyer. 1973. Bemerkungen zur syntaktischen Funktion der sogenannten Nota accusativi. Pp. 137–42 in *Wort und Geschichte: Festschrift für Kurt Elliger*, ed. H. Gese and H.-P. Rüger. Kevelaer: Butzon und Bercker/Neukirchen-Vluyn: Neukirchener Verlag.

P. D. Miller, Jr. 1979. Vocative *Lamed* in the Psalter. *Ugarit-Forschungen* 11:617–37.

J. Muilenburg. 1961. The Linguistic and Rhetorical Usages of the Particle כי in the Old Testament. *Hebrew Union College Annual* 32:135–60. Rpt. as pp. 208–33 in *Hearing and Speaking the Word*, ed. T. F. Best. Chico: Scholars Press, 1984.

M. J. Mulder. 1973. Die Partikel יַעַן. *Oudtestamentische Studiën* 18:49–83.

———. 1981. Die Partikel כֵּן im Alten Testament. *Oudtestamentische Studiën* 21:201–27.

T. Muraoka. 1978. On the So-called *Dativus Ethicus* in Hebrew. *Journal of Theological Studies* 29:495–98.

A. F. Rainey. 1966. Private Seal-Impressions: A Note on Semantics [preposition *l*]. *Israel Exploration Journal* 16:187–90.

N. M. Sarna. 1959. The Interchange of the Prepositions *Beth* and *Min* in Biblical Hebrew. *Journal of Biblical Literature* 78:310–16.

P. P. Saydon. 1964. Meanings and Uses of the Particle את. *Vetus Testamentum* 14:192–210.

Anton Schoors. 1981. The Particle כִּי. *Oudtestamentische Studiën* 21:240–76.

Harald Schweizer. 1975. Was ist ein Akkusativ?—Ein Beitrag zur Grammatiktheorie. *Zeitschrift für die Alttestamentliche Wissenschaft* 87:133–45.

N. H. Snaith. 1964. The Meaning of the Hebrew אַךְ ['on the contrary']. *Vetus Testamentum* 14:221–25.

Ilmari Soisalon-Soininen. 1977/78. Die Wiedergabe einigen hebräischer, mit der Präpositionen *be* ausgedruckter Zeitangaben in der Septuaginta. *Annual of the Swedish Theological Institute* 11:138–46.

Richard C. Steiner. 1987. *Lulav* versus **lu/law*. *Journal of the American Oriental Society* 107:121–22.

Edmund F. Sutcliffe. 1955. A Note on ʿal, lᵉ, and *from*. *Vetus Testamentum* 5:436–39.

P. Swiggers. 1983. Review of Hoftijzer et al., *A Search for Method* (1981). *Biblica* 64:279–82.

E. Talstra. 1981. The Use of כֵּן in Biblical Hebrew. *Oudtestamentische Studiën* 21:228–39.

N. J. Tromp. 1981. The Hebrew Particle בַּל. *Oudtestamentische Studiën* 21:277–87.

Edward Ullendorff. 1977. The Form of the Definite Article in Arabic and Other Semitic Languages. Pp. 165–71 in *Is Biblical Hebrew a Language?* Wiesbaden: Harrassowitz.

Norman Walker. 1955. Concerning the Function of ʾ*ēth*. *Vetus Testamentum* 5:314–15.

Jacob Weingreen. 1954. The Construct-Genitive Relation in Hebrew Syntax. *Vetus Testamentum* 4:50–59.

C. F. Whitley. 1971–72. Some Functions of the Hebrew Particles *Beth* and *Lamedh*. *Jewish Quarterly Review* 62:199–206.

———. 1972. The Positive Force of the Hebrew Particle בל. *Zeitschrift für die Alttestamentliche Wissenschaft* 84:213–19.

———. 1975. Some Remarks on *lû* and *loʾ* [emphatic]. *Zeitschrift für die Alttestamentliche Wissenschaft* 87:202–4.

G. E. Whitney. 1988. *Lōʾ* ('Not') as 'Not Yet' in the Hebrew Bible. *Hebrew Studies* 29:43–48.

Alfred M. Wilson. 1889–90. The Particle אֵת in Hebrew. *Hebraica* 6:139–50, 212–24.

Ziony Zevit. 1977. The Linguistic and Contextual Arguments in Support of a Hebrew 3 m.s. Suffix -*y*. *Ugarit-Forschungen* 9:315–28.

———. 1979. Expressing Denial in Biblical Hebrew and Mishnaic Hebrew, and in Amos. *Vetus Testamentum* 29:505–9.

c. Semantics and Individual Words

James Barr. 1961. *The Semantics of Biblical Language*. Oxford: Oxford University. Rpt., Philadelphia: Fortress, 1984.

———. 1972. Semantics and Biblical Theology—a Contribution to the Discussion. Pp. 11–19 in *Congress Volume: Uppsala 1971*. Vetus Testamentum Supplement 22. Leiden: Brill.

James Barr. 1973. Ugaritic and Hebrew "ŠBM"? *Journal of Semitic Studies* 18:17–39. Rpt. as pp. 388–411 in *Comparative Philology and the Text of the Old Testament*. Winona Lake, Indiana: Eisenbrauns, 1987.

———. 1974. Etymology and the Old Testament. *Oudtestamentische Studiën* 19:1–28.

———. 1983. Limitations of Etymology as a Lexicographical Instrument in Biblical Hebrew. *Transactions of the Philological Society* 1983: 41–65. Rpt. as pp. 412–36 in *Comparative Philology and the Text of the Old Testament*. Winona Lake, Indiana: Eisenbrauns, 1987.

Athalya Brenner. 1982. *Colour Terms in the Old Testament*. Journal for the Study of the Old Testament Supplement 21. Sheffield: JSOT Press.

G. B. Caird. 1980. *The Language and Imagery of the Bible*. Philadelphia: Westminster.

H. R. Cohen. 1978. *Biblical Hapax Legomena in the Light of Akkadian and Ugaritic*. Society of Biblical Literature Dissertation Series 37. Missoula: Scholars Press.

J. L. Crenshaw. 1986. The Expression *mî yôdēa*^{c} in the Hebrew Bible. *Vetus Testamentum* 36:274–88.

Mitchell Dahood. 1970. Hebrew-Ugaritic Lexicography VIII. *Biblica* 51:391–404.

———. 1976. Hebrew Lexicography: A Review of W. Baumgartner's *Lexikon*, Volume II. *Orientalia* 45:327–65.

Peter T. Daniels. 1984. Virtuous Housewife or Woman of Valor? [*ʾēšet ḥáyil*] On Sexist Language in the Hebrew Bible. *Proceedings [of the] Eastern Great Lakes and Midwest Biblical Societies* 4:99–106.

G. I. Davies. 1979. A Note on the Etymology of *hištaḥᵃwāh*. *Vetus Testamentum* 29:493–95.

Otto Eissfeldt. 1974. אָדוֹן *ʾādhôn*. Vol. 1, pp. 59–72 in *Theological Dictionary of the Old Testament*, ed. G. Johannes Botterweck and Helmer Ringgren. Grand Rapids: Eerdmans.

Maximilian Ellenbogen. 1962. *Foreign Words in the Old Testament*. London: Luzac.

J. A. Emerton. 1977. The Etymology of *hištaḥᵃwāh*. *Oudtestamentische Studiën* 20:41–55.

Aloysius Fitzgerald. 1975. *BTWLT* and *BT* as Titles for Capital Cities. *Catholic Biblical Quarterly* 37:167–83.

D. N. Freedman and M. O'Connor. 1980. יהוה JHWH. Vol. 3, pp. 533–54 in *Theologisches Wörterbuch zum Alten Testament*, ed. G. Johannes Botterweck and Helmer Ringgren. Stuttgart: Kohlhammer.

———. 1986. יהוה YHWH. Vol. 5, pp. 500–521 in *Theological Dictionary of the Old Testament*, ed. G. Johannes Botterweck and Helmer Ringgren. Grand Rapids: Eerdmans.

D. R. Hillers. 1987. Dust: Some Aspects of Old Testament Imagery. Pp. 105–9 in *Love and Death in the Ancient Near East: Essays in Honor of Marvin H. Pope*, ed. J. H. Marks and R. M. Good. Guilford, Connecticut: Four Quarters.

W. Janzen. 1965. *ʾašrê* in the Old Testament. *Harvard Theological Review* 58:213–26.

B. Jongeling. 1974. L'Expression *my ytn* dans l'Ancien Testament. *Vetus Testamentum* 24:32–40.

H. J. Katzenstein. 1960. The Royal Steward. *Israel Exploration Journal* 10:149–54.

Benjamin Kedar. 1981. *Biblische Semantik: Eine Einführung*. Stuttgart: Kohlhammer.

Baruch A. Levine. 1987. The Language of Holiness [*qdš*]. Pp. 241–55 in *Backgrounds for the Bible*, ed. M. O'Connor and D. N. Freedman. Winona Lake, Indiana: Eisenbrauns.

O. Loretz. 1983. Ugaritische und hebräische Lexikographie (IV). *Ugarit-Forschungen* 15:59–64.

Tryggve N. D. Mettinger. 1972. The Nominal Pattern *qᵉtullā* in Biblical Hebrew. *Journal of Semitic Studies* 16:2–14.

Rudolf Meyer. 1979. Gegensinn und Mehrdeutigkeit in der althebräischen Wort- und Begriffsbildung. *Ugarit-Forschungen* 11:601–12.

T. W. Nakarai. 1982. LMH and MDU^c in the Tanak. *Hebrew Studies* 23:45–50.

H. M. Orlinsky. 1944. The Hebrew Root ŠKB. *Journal of Biblical Literature* 63:19–44.

C. Rabin. 1988. Lexical Emendation in Biblical Research. Pp. 379–418 in *Fucus: A Semitic/Afrasian Gathering in Remembrance of Albert Ehrman*, ed. Y. L. Arbeitman. Amsterdam: John Benjamins.

R. Ratner. 1987. *Derek*: Morpho-Syntactical Considerations. *Journal of the American Oriental Society* 107:471–73.

Katherine Doob Sakenfeld. 1977. *The Meaning of Ḥesed in the Hebrew Bible*. Missoula: Scholars Press.

John F. A. Sawyer. 1967. Root Meanings in Hebrew. *Journal of Semitic Studies* 12:37–50.

P. P. Saydon. 1954. Some Unusual Ways of Expressing the Superlative in Hebrew and Maltese. *Vetus Testamentum* 4:432–33.

J. J. Scullion. 1971. *Ṣedeq-ṣedaqah* in Isaiah cc. 40–66. *Ugarit-Forschungen* 3:335–48.

Moisés Silva. 1983. *Biblical Words and Their Meaning*. Grand Rapids: Zondervan.

E. A. Speiser. 1963. The Stem *PLL* in Hebrew. *Journal of Biblical Literature* 82:301–6.

W. F. Stinespring. 1976. Zion, Daughter of. P. 985 in *The Interpreter's Dictionary of the Bible: Supplementary Volume*, ed. K. Crim. Nashville: Abingdon.

P. Swiggers. 1981. The Meaning of the Root *LḤM* "Food" in the Semitic Languages. *Ugarit-Forschungen* 13:307–8.

———. 1981. The Word *šibbōleṯ* in Jud. XXII.6. *Journal of Semitic Studies* 26:205–7.

D. Winton Thomas. 1953. A Consideration of Some Unusual Ways of Expressing the Superlative in Hebrew. *Vetus Testamentum* 3:209–24.

———. 1956. The Use of נֶצַח as a Superlative in Hebrew. *Journal of Semitic Studies* 1:106–9.

———. 1968. Some Further Remarks on Unusual Ways of Expressing the Superlative in Hebrew. *Vetus Testamentum* 18:120–24.

d. The Verb

Francis I. Andersen. 1970. Biconsonantal Byforms of Weak Hebrew Roots. *Zeitschrift für die Alttestamentliche Wissenschaft* 82:270–74.

———. 1971. Passive and Ergative in Hebrew. Pp. 1–15 in *Near Eastern Studies in Honor of William Foxwell Albright*, ed. H. Goedicke. Baltimore: Johns Hopkins.

David W. Baker. 1973. *The Consecutive Nonperfective as Pluperfect in the Historical Books of the Hebrew Old Testament*. Regent College Thesis.

O. L. Barnes. 1965. *A New Approach to the Problem of the Hebrew Tenses*. Oxford: Thornton.

Rüdiger Bartelmus. 1982. *HYH: Bedeutung und Funktion eines hebräischen "Allerweltswortes": Zugleich ein Beitrag zur Frage des hebräischen Tempussystems*. St. Ottilien: EOS.

———. 1985. Ez 37,1–14, die Verbform *wᵉqatal* und die Anfänge der Auferstehungshoffnung. *Zeitschrift für die Alttestamentliche Wissenschaft* 97:366–89.

Hans Bauer. 1910. Die Tempora im Semitischen. *Beiträge zur Assyriologie und semitischen Sprachwissenschaft* 81:1–53.

A. F. Bean. 1975. *A Phenomenological Study of the Hithpaᶜel Verbal Stem in the Hebrew Old Testament*. Southern Baptist Theological Seminary [Louisville, Kentucky] Dissertation.

Mordechai Ben-Asher. 1978. Causative *Hipᶜil* with Double Objects in Biblical Hebrew. *Hebrew Annual Review* 2:11–19.

F. R. Blake. 1903. The So-called Intransitive Verbal Forms in Hebrew. *Journal of the American Oriental Society* 24:145–204.

———. 1951. *A Resurvey of Hebrew Tenses*. Rome: Pontifical Biblical Institute.

Josua Blau. 1957. Über die t-Form des Hifᶜil im Bibelhebräisch. *Vetus Testamentum* 7:385–88.

———. 1971. Studies in Hebrew Verb Formation. *Hebrew Union College Annual* 42:133–58.

A. Bloch. 1963. Zur Nachweisbarkeit einer hebräischen Entsprechung der akkadischen Form *iparras*. *Zeitschrift der Deutschen Morgenländischen Gesellschaft* 113:41–50.

A. M. L. Boyle. 1969. *Infix-t Forms in Biblical Hebrew*. Boston University Dissertation.

W. T. Claassen. 1971. On a Recent Proposal as to a Distinction between Piᶜel and Hiphᶜil. *Journal of Northwest Semitic Languages* 1:3–10.

———. 1972. The Declarative-Estimative Hiphᶜil. *Journal of Northwest Semitic Languages* 2:5–16.

Mitchell Dahood. 1977. Yiphil Imperative *yaṭṭī* in Isaiah 54,2. *Orientalia* 46:383–84.

———. 1979. Two Yiphil Causatives in Habakkuk 3,13a. *Orientalia* 48:258–59.

H. J. van Dijk. 1969. Does Third Masculine *taqtul* Exist in Hebrew? *Vetus Testamentum* 19:440–47.

Bruno W. W. Dombrowski. 1962. Some Remarks on the Hebrew Hithpaᶜel and Inversative -t- in the Semitic Languages. *Journal of Near Eastern Studies* 21:220–23.

G. R. Driver. 1936. *Problems of the Hebrew Verbal System*. Edinburgh: T. & T. Clark.

———. 1969. Some Uses of *qtl* in the Semitic Languages. Pp. 49–64 in *Proceedings of the International Conference on Semitic Studies Held in Jerusalem, 19–23 July 1965*. Jerusalem: Israel Academy of Sciences and Humanities.

S. R. Driver. 1892. *A Treatise on the Use of the Tenses in Hebrew*. 3d ed. Oxford: Clarendon.

J. H. Eaton. 1974. Some Misunderstood Hebrew Words for God's Self-Revelation [*Niphal*]. *Bible Translator* 25:331–38.

I. Eitan. 1921–22. Light on the History of the Hebrew Verb (נִפְעַל or intensive נִפַּעַל). *Jewish Quarterly Review* 12:25–32.

F. C. Fensham. 1978. The Use of the Suffix Conjugation and the Prefix Conjugation in a Few Old Hebrew Poems [Pss 29, 82, 93]. *Journal of Northwest Semitic Languages* 6:9–18.

Terry L. Fenton. 1970. The Absence of a Verbal Formation *yaqattal* from Ugaritic and North-west Semitic. *Journal of Semitic Studies* 15:31–41.

———. 1973. The Hebrew "Tenses" in the Light of Ugaritic. Vol. 4, pp. 31–39 in *Proceedings of the Fifth World Congress of Jewish Studies*. Jerusalem: World Union of Jewish Studies.

T. J. Finley. 1981. The *WAW*-Consecutive with "Imperfect" in Biblical Hebrew: Theoretical Studies and Its Use in Amos. Pp. 241–62 in *Tradition and Testament: Essays in Honor of Charles Lee Feinberg*, ed. J. S. Feinberg and P. D. Feinberg. Chicago: Moody.

A. Fitzgerald. 1972. A Note on G-Stem ינצר Forms in the Old Testament. *Zeitschrift für die Alttestamentliche Wissenschaft* 84:90–92.

Amikam Gai. 1982. The Reduction of the Tense (and Other Categories) of the Consequent Verb in North-west Semitic. *Orientalia* 51:254–56.

H. L. Ginsberg. 1929. Studies on the Biblical Hebrew Verb: Masoretically Misconstrued Internal Passives. *American Journal of Semitic Languages and Literatures* 46:53–58.

Burton L. Goddard. 1943. *The Origin of the Hebrew Infinitive Absolute in the Light of the Infinitive Uses in the Related Languages and Its Use in the Old Testament*. Harvard University Dissertation.

A. Goetze. 1942. The So-called Intensive of the Semitic Languages. *Journal of the American Oriental Society* 62:1–8.

Amnon Gordon. 1982. The Development of the [Active] Participle in Biblical, Mishnaic, and Modern Hebrew. *Afroasiatic Linguistics* 8:121–79.

M. H. [Goshen-]Gottstein. 1949. Afterthought and the Syntax of Relative Clauses in Biblical Hebrew. *Journal of Biblical Literature* 68:35–47.

J. C. Greenfield. 1969. The "Periphrastic Imperative" in Aramaic and Hebrew. *Israel Exploration Journal* 19:199–210.

Edward L. Greenstein. 1988. On the Prefixed Preterite in Biblical Hebrew. *Hebrew Studies* 29:7–17.

W. Gross. 1976. *Verbform und Funktion: Wayyiqtol für die Gegenwart?* St. Ottilien: EOS.

E. Hammershaimb. 1963. On the So-called *Infinitivus Absolutus* in Hebrew. Pp. 85–94 in *Hebrew and Semitic Studies Presented to Godfrey Rolles Driver*, ed. D. W. Thomas and W. D. McHardy. Oxford: Clarendon.

Moshe Held. 1962. The *YQTL-QTL* (*QTL-YQTL*) Sequence of Identical Verbs in Biblical Hebrew and in Ugaritic. Pp. 281–90 in *Studies and Essays in Honor of Abraham A. Neuman*, ed. M. Ben-Horin, B. D. Weinryb, and S. Zeitlin. Leiden: Brill.

———. 1965. The Action-Result (Factitive-Passive) Sequence of Identical Verbs in Biblical Hebrew and Ugaritic. *Journal of Biblical Literature* 84:272–82.

D. R. Hillers. 1967. Delocutive Verbs in Biblical Hebrew. *Journal of Biblical Literature* 86:320–24.

———. Unpublished. Some Performative Utterances in Biblical Hebrew.

J. Hoftijzer. 1985. *The Function and Use of the Imperfect Forms with Nun Paragogicum in Classical Hebrew*. Studia Semitica Neerlandica 21. Assen: Van Gorcum.

John Huehnergard. 1988. The Early Hebrew Prefix-Conjugations. *Hebrew Studies* 29:19–23.

J. Huesman. 1956. Finite Uses of the Infinite Absolute. *Biblica* 37:271–95.

———. 1956. The Infinitive Absolute and the Waw + Perfect Problem. *Biblica* 37:410–34.

James A. Hughes. 1970. Another Look at the Hebrew Tenses. *Journal of Near Eastern Studies* 29:12–24.

Ernst Jenni. 1967. Faktitiv und Kausativ von אבד "zugrunde gehen." Pp. 143–57 in *Hebräische Wortforschung: Festschrift . . . Walter Baumgartner*. Vetus Testamentum Supplement 16. Leiden: Brill.

———. 1968. *Das hebräische Piᶜel: Syntaktisch-semasiologische Untersuchung einer Verbalform im Alten Testament*. Zurich: EVZ.

———. 1973. Zur Funktion der reflexiv-passiven Stammformen im Biblisch-Hebräischen. Vol. 4, pp. 61–70 in *Proceedings of the Fifth World Congress of Jewish Studies*. Jerusalem: World Union of Jewish Studies.

Bo Johnson. 1979. *Hebräisches Perfekt und Imperfekt mit vorangehendem wᵉ*. Lund: Gleerup.

Benjamin Kedar-Kopfstein. 1977. Semantic Aspects of the Pattern *Qôṭel*. *Hebrew Annual Review* 1:155–76.

———. 1981. Die Stammbildung *Qôṭel* als Übersetzungsproblem. *Zeitschrift für die Alttestamentliche Wissenschaft* 93:254–79.

C. R. Krahmalkov. 1987. The Periphrastic Future Tense [*l* + infinitive construct] in Hebrew and Phoenician. *Rivista degli Studi Orientali* 61:73–80.

Péter Kustár. 1972. *Aspekt im Hebräischen*. Theologische Dissertationen 9. Basel: Reinhardt.

Thomas O. Lambdin. 1969. Review of Jenni, *Das hebräische Piᶜel* (1968). *Catholic Biblical Quarterly* 31:435–37.

———. 1980. Review of Johnson, *Hebräisches Perfekt und Imperfekt mit vorangehendem wᵉ* (1979). *Catholic Biblical Quarterly* 42:388–89.

Mayer Lambert. 1900. L'emploi du *nifal* en hébreu. *Revue des études juives* 41:196–214.

Samuel Loewenstamm. 1969. Remarks upon the Infinitive Absolute in Ugaritic and Phoenician. *Journal of the Ancient Near Eastern Society* 2:53.

———. 1984. *Yštql*. *Ugarit-Forschungen* 16:357–58.

A. Loprieno. 1980. The Sequential Forms in Late Egyptian and Biblical Hebrew. *Afroasiatic Linguistics* 7:143–62.

V. Maag. 1953. Morphologie des hebräischen Narrativs. *Zeitschrift für die Alttestamentliche Wissenschaft* 65:86–88.

Leslie McFall. 1982. *The Enigma of the Hebrew Verbal System: Solutions from Ewald to the Present*. Sheffield: Almond.

David Marcus. 1969. The Stative and the *Waw* Consecutive. *Journal of the Ancient Near Eastern Society* 2:37–40.

W. J. Martin. 1969. "Dischronologized" Narrative in the Old Testament. Pp. 179–86 in *Congress Volume: Rome 1968*. Vetus Testamentum Supplement 17. Leiden: Brill.

Paul Mazars. 1968. Sens et usage de l'hitpael dans le Bible hébraïque. *Divinitas* 12:353–64.

T. J. Meek. 1929. The Co-ordinate Adverbial Clause in Hebrew. *Journal of the American Oriental Society* 49:157–59.

———. 1945. The Syntax of the Sentence in Hebrew. *Journal of Biblical Literature* 64:1–13.

———. 1955–56. Result and Purpose Clauses in Hebrew. *Jewish Quarterly Review* 46:40–43.

C. H. J. van der Merwe. 1983. Hebrew Grammar, Exegesis and Commentaries. *Journal of Northwest Semitic Languages* 11:143–56.

Tryggve N. D. Mettinger. 1973. The Hebrew Verb System. *Annual of the Swedish Theological Institute* 9:64–84.

Rudolf Meyer. 1953. Zur Geschichte des hebräischen Verbums. *Vetus Testamentum* 3:225–35.

———. 1960. Das hebräische Verbalsystem im Lichte der gegenwärtigen Forschung. Pp. 309–17 in *Congress Volume: Oxford 1959*. Vetus Testamentum Supplement 7. Leiden: Brill.

———. 1964. Aspekt und Tempus im althebräischen Verbalsystem [on Rundgren, *Das althebräische Verbum* (1961)]. *Orientalische Literaturzeitung* 59:117–26.

———. 1966. Zur Geschichte des hebräischen Verbums. *Forschungen und Fortschritte* 40:241–43.

Diethelm Michel. 1960. *Tempora und Satzstellung in den Psalmen*. Abhandlungen zur evangelischen Theologie 1. Bonn: Bouvier.

C. H. Miller. 1970. The Infinitive Construct in the Lawbooks of the Old Testament. *Catholic Biblical Quarterly* 32:222–26.

Hans-Peter Müller. 1985. Ergativelemente im akkadischen und althebräischen Verbalsystem. *Biblica* 66:385–417.

T. Muraoka. 1979. On Verb Complementation in Biblical Hebrew. *Vetus Testamentum* 29:425–35.

A. Niccacci. 1986. *Sintassi del verbo ebraico nella prosa biblica classica*. Jerusalem: Franciscan Printing Press.

G. S. Ogden. 1971. Time, and the Verb היה in O.T. Prose. *Vetus Testamentum* 21:451–69.

H. M. Orlinsky. 1940–41, 1941–42. On the Cohortative and Jussive after an Imperative or Interjection in Biblical Hebrew. *Jewish Quarterly Review* 31:371–82; 32:191–205, 273–77.

———. 1947. The Qal Infinitive Construct and the Verbal Noun in Biblical Hebrew. *Journal of the American Oriental Society* 67:107–26.

Dennis G. Pardee. 1983. The "Epistolary Perfect" in Hebrew Letters. *Biblische Notizen* 22:34–40.

Dennis G. Pardee. 1985. Review of Bartelmus, *HYH: Bedeutung und Funktion eines hebräischen "Allerweltswortes"* (1982). *Catholic Biblical Quarterly* 47:107–10.

E. Qimron. 1986–87. Consecutive and Conjunctive Imperfect: The Form of the Imperfect with *Waw* in Biblical Hebrew. *Jewish Quarterly Review* 77:149–61.

Isaac Rabinowitz. 1984. *ʾāz* Followed by Imperfect Verb-Form in Preterite Contexts: A Redactional Device in Biblical Hebrew. *Vetus Testamentum* 34:53–62.

A. F. Rainey. 1986. The Ancient Hebrew Prefix Conjugation in the Light of Amarnah Canaanite. *Hebrew Studies* 27: 4–19.

———. 1988. Further Remarks on the Hebrew Verbal System. *Hebrew Studies* 29:35–42.

R. Ratner. 1988. Does a *t*- Preformative Third Person Masculine Plural Verbal Form Exist in Hebrew? *Vetus Testamentum* 38:80–88.

A. Reider. 1872. *Die Verbindung des Infinitivus Absolutus mit dem Verbum Finitum des selbes Stammes im Hebräisch.* Leipzig: Metzger und Wittig.

E. J. Revell. 1984. Stress and the *Waw* "Consecutive" in Biblical Hebrew. *Journal of the American Oriental Society* 104:437–44.

———. 1985. The Battle with Benjamin (Judges xx 29–48) and Hebrew Narrative Techniques. *Vetus Testamentum* 35:417–33.

———. 1985. The Conditioning of Stress Position in *Waw* Consecutive Perfect Forms in Biblical Hebrew. *Hebrew Annual Review* 9:277–300.

———. 1988. First Person Imperfect Forms with Waw Consecutive. *Vetus Testamentum* 38:419–26.

S. J. P. K. Riekert. 1979. The Struct [sic] Patterns of the Paronomastic and Co-ordinated Infinitives Absolute in Genesis. *Journal of Northwest Semitic Languages* 7:69–83.

———. 1987. The Co-ordinated Structs [sic] of the Infinitive Absolute in Jeremiah and Their Bearing on the Stylistics and Authenticity of the Jeremianic Corpus. *Journal of Northwest Semitic Languages* 13:97–106.

O. Rössler. 1961. Eine bisher unbekannte Tempusform im Althebräischen. *Zeitschrift der Deutschen Morgenländischen Gesellschaft* 111:445–51.

———. 1962. Die Präfixkonjugation Qal der Verba Iᵃᵉ Nûn im Althebräischen und das Problem der sogennanten Tempora. *Zeitschrift für die Alttestamentliche Wissenschaft* 74: 125–41.

A. Rubinstein. 1952. A Finite Verb Continued by an Infinitive Absolute in Hebrew. *Vetus Testamentum* 2:362–67.

E. Rubinstein. 1979. Adjectival Verbs in Biblical Hebrew. *Israel Oriental Studies* 9:55–76.

Frithiof Rundgren. 1961. *Das althebräische Verbum: Abriss der Aspektlehre.* Stockholm: Almqvist & Wiksell.

———. 1963. Das Verbalpräfix *yu-* im Semitischen und die Entstehung der faktitiv-kausativen Bedeutung des D-Stammes. *Orientalia Suecana* 12:99–114.

Stuart A. Ryder II. 1974. *The D-Stem in Western Semitic.* Janua Linguarum, Series Practica 131. The Hague: Mouton.

John F. A. Sawyer. 1969. Review of Jenni, *Das hebräische Piʿel* (1968). *Journal of Semitic Studies* 14:260–62.

P. P. Saydon. 1962. The Conative Imperfect in Hebrew. *Vetus Testamentum* 12:124–26.

A. O. Schulz. 1900. *Über das Imperfekt und Perfekt mit ·ן (ן) im Hebräischen.* Königsberg Inaugural Dissertation.

Stanislav Segert. 1975. Verbal Categories of Some Northwest Semitic Languages: A Didactic Approach. *Afroasiatic Linguistics* 2:83–94.

J. F. X. Sheehan. 1971. Egypto-Semitic Elucidation of the Waw Conversive. *Biblica* 52:39–43.

M. H. Silverman. 1973. Syntactic Notes on the *Waw Consecutive*. Pp. 167–75 in *Orient and Occident: Essays Presented to Cyrus H. Gordon*, ed. H. A. Hoffner, Jr. Alter Orient und Altes Testament 22. Kevelaer: Butzon und Bercker/ Neukirchen-Vluyn: Neukirchener Verlag.

Ilmari Soisalon-Soininen. 1972. Der Infinitivus constructus mit ל im Hebräischen. *Vetus Testamentum* 22:82–90.

E. A. Speiser. 1955. The Durative Hithpaʿel: A *tan* Form. *Journal of the American Oriental Society* 75:118–21. Rpt. as pp. 506–14 in *Oriental and Biblical Studies*, ed. J. J. Finkelstein and Moshe Greenberg. Philadelphia: University of Pennsylvania, 1967.

N. Stern. 1986. The Infinitive as a Complement of a Predicate of Incomplete Predication. *Hebrew Annual Review* 10: 337–49.

T. W. Thacker. 1954. *The Relationship of the Semitic and Egyptian Verbal System.* Oxford: Oxford University.

E. Tov. 1982. The Representations of the Causative Aspects of the *Hiphʿil* in the LXX: A Study in Translation Technique. *Biblica* 63:417–24.

D. T. Tsumura. 1986. Niphal with an Internal Object in Habakkuk 3:9a. *Journal of Semitic Studies* 31:11–16.

Gottfried Vanoni. 1982. Ist die Fügung HYY + Circumstant der Zeit im Althebräischen ein Satz? *Biblische Notizen* 17:73–86.

Ludwig Wächter. 1971. Reste von Šafʿel-Bildungen im Hebräischen. *Zeitschrift für die Alttestamentliche Wissenschaft* 83:380–89.

J. D. W. Watts. 1962. Infinitive Absolute as Imperative and the Interpretation of Exodus 20:8. *Zeitschrift für die Alttestamentliche Wissenschaft* 74:141–47.

J. Wash Watts. 1964. *A Survey of Syntax in the Hebrew Old Testament.* Grand Rapids: Eerdmans.

Jacob Weingreen. 1980. The Piʿel in Biblical Hebrew: A Suggested New Concept. *Henoch* 5:21–29.

P. Wernberg-Møller. 1959. Observations on the Hebrew Participle. *Zeitschrift für die Alttestamentliche Wissenschaft* 71:54–67.

Samuel B. Wheeler. 1970–71. The Infixed -*t*- in Biblical Hebrew. *Journal of the Ancient Near Eastern Society* 3: 20–31.

Ronald J. Williams. 1970. The Passive *Qal* Theme in Hebrew. Pp. 43–50 in *Essays on the Ancient Semitic World*, ed. J. W. Wevers and D. B. Redford. Toronto: University of Toronto.

———. 1972. Energic Verbal Forms in Hebrew. Pp. 75–85 in *Studies on the Ancient Palestinian World Presented to Professor F. V. Winnett*, ed. J. W. Wevers and D. B. Redford. Toronto: University of Toronto.

David Yellin. 1924. The Hippaʿel-Nifʿal Conjugation in Hebrew and Aramaic: The Assimilation of ח in the Hitpaʿel

Conjugation. *Journal of the Palestine Oriental Society* 4:85–106.

Ziony Zevit. 1988. Solving a Problem of the *YAQTÚL* Past Tense. *Hebrew Studies* 29:25–33.

B. Zuber. 1986. *Das Tempussystem des biblischen Hebräisch.* Beiheft zur Zeitschrift für die Alttestamentliche Wissenschaft 164. Berlin: de Gruyter.

e. Phonology, Orthography, and Writing

Francis I. Andersen and A. Dean Forbes. 1986. *Spelling in the Hebrew Bible.* Biblica et Orientalia 41. Rome: Biblical Institute.

Mark Aronoff. 1985. Orthography and Linguistic Theory: The Syntactic Basis of Masoretic Hebrew Punctuation. *Language* 61:28–72.

James Barr. 1967. St. Jerome and the Sounds of Hebrew. *Journal of Semitic Studies* 12:1–36.

———. 1981. A New Look at *Kethibh-Qere. Oudtestamentische Studiën* 21:19–37.

Ze'ev Ben Hayyīm. 1954. *Studies in the Traditions of the Hebrew Language.* Madrid: Consejo Superior de Investigaciones Cientificas/Instituto "Arias Montano."

Harris Birkeland. 1940. *Akzent und Vokalismus in Althebräischen.* Oslo: Dybwad.

S. A. Birnbaum. 1954–71. *The Hebrew Scripts.* 2 vols. Leiden/London: Brill/Palaeographia.

Joshua Blau. 1970. *On Pseudo-corrections in Some Semitic Languages.* Jerusalem: Israel Academy of Science and Humanities.

———. 1977. "Weak" Phonetic Change and the Hebrew *Sîn. Hebrew Annual Review* 1:67–119.

———. 1978. Hebrew Stress Shifts, Pretonic Lengthening, and Segolization: Possible Cases of Aramaic Interference in Hebrew Syllable Structure. *Israel Oriental Studies* 8:91–106.

———. 1979. Non-Phonetic Conditioning of Sound Change and Biblical Hebrew. *Hebrew Annual Review* 3:7–15.

———. 1979. Some Remarks on the Prehistory of Stress in Biblical Hebrew. *Israel Oriental Studies* 9:49–54.

———. 1981. On Pausal Lengthening, Pausal Stress Shift, Philippi's Law and Rule Ordering in Biblical Hebrew. *Hebrew Annual Review* 5:1–13.

E. Brønno. 1943. *Studien über hebräische Morphologie und Vokalismus auf Grundlage der mercatischen Fragmente der zweiten Kolumne der Hexapla des Origenes.* Leipzig: Brockhaus.

———. 1970. *Die Aussprache der hebräischen Laryngale nach Zeugnissen des Hieronymus.* Copenhagen: University of Aarhus.

Miles B. Cohen. 1972. Masoretic Accents as a Biblical Commentary. *Journal of the Ancient Near Eastern Society* 4:2–11.

F. M. Cross and D. N. Freedman. 1952. *Early Hebrew Orthography.* American Oriental Series 36. New Haven: American Oriental Society.

Alice Faber. 1986. On the Origin and Development of Hebrew Spirantization. *Mediterranean Language Review* 2:117–38.

A. Fitzgerald. 1978. The Interchange of *L, N,* and *R* in Biblical Hebrew. *Journal of Biblical Literature* 97:481–88.

D. N. Freedman. 1962. The Masoretic Text and the Qumran Scrolls: A Study in Orthography. *Textus* 2:87–102. Rpt. as

pp. 196–211 in *Qumran and the History of the Biblical Text,* ed. F. M. Cross and S. Talmon. Cambridge: Harvard University, 1975.

W. Randall Garr. 1987. Pretonic Vowels in Hebrew. *Vetus Testamentum* 37:129–53.

———. 1989. The *Seghol* and Segholation in Hebrew. *Journal of Near Eastern Studies* 48:109–16.

J. C. L. Gibson. 1974. The Massoretes as Linguists. *Oudtestamentische Studiën* 19:86–96.

C. D. Ginsburg. 1966. *Introduction to the Massoretico-Critical Edition of the Hebrew Bible.* Prolegomenon by H. Orlinsky. New York: Ktav. Originally London: Trinitarian Bible Society, 1894.

A. Goetze. 1939. Accent and Vocalism in Hebrew. *Journal of the American Oriental Society* 59:431–59.

Edward L. Greenstein. 1973. Another Attestation of Initial *h > ʾ* in West Semitic. *Journal of the Ancient Near Eastern Society* 5:157–64.

———. 1983. An Introduction to a Generative Analysis of Biblical Hebrew Phonology. Pp. 301–8 in *Society of Biblical Literature 1983 Seminar Papers,* ed. K. H. Richards. Chico: Scholars Press.

Zellig S. Harris. 1941. Linguistic Structure of Hebrew. *Journal of the American Oriental Society* 61:143–67.

———. 1948. Componential Analysis of a Hebrew Paradigm. *Language* 24:87–91.

C. D. Isbell. 1978. Initial ʾalef-yod Interchange and Selected Biblical Passages. *Journal of Near Eastern Studies* 37:227–36.

Stephen A. Kaufman. 1986. The Pitfalls of Typology: On the Early History of the Alphabet. *Hebrew Union College Annual* 57:1–14.

E. A. Knauf. 1979. Dagesh agrammaticum im Codex Leningradensis. *Biblische Notizen* 10:23–35.

E. Y. Kutscher. 1965. Contemporary Studies in North-western Semitic. *Journal of Semitic Studies* 10:21–51.

Thomas O. Lambdin. 1985. Philippi's Law Reconsidered. Pp. 135–45 in *Biblical and Related Studies Presented to Samuel Iwry,* ed. A. Kort and S. Morschauser. Winona Lake, Indiana: Eisenbrauns.

Saul Levin. 1979. The מתג according to the Practice of the Early Vocalizers. *Hebrew Annual Review* 3:129–39.

———. 1982. Defects, Alleged or Real, in the Tiberias Pointing. *Hebrew Studies* 23:67–84.

J. L. Malone. 1971. Wave Theory, Rule Ordering and Hebrew-Aramaic Segholation. *Journal of the American Oriental Society* 91:44–66.

———. 1972. A Hebrew Flip-Flop Rule and Its Historical Origins. *Lingua* 30:422–48.

———. 1975. Systematic vs. Autonomous Phonemics and the Hebrew Grapheme *Dagesh. Afroasiatic Linguistics* 2:113–29.

J. L. Malone. 1979. Textually Deviant Forms as Evidence for Phonological Analysis: A Service of Philology to Linguistics. *Journal of the Ancient Near Eastern Society* 11:71–79.

K. A. Mathews. 1983. The Background of the Paleo-Hebrew Texts at Qumran. Pp. 549–68 in *The Word of the Lord Shall Go Forth: Essays in Honor of David Noel Freedman*, ed. C. L. Meyers and M. O'Connor. Winona Lake, Indiana: Eisenbrauns.

Shelomo Morag. 1962. *The Vocalization Systems of Arabic, Hebrew, and Aramaic*. The Hague: Mouton.

———. 1971. Pronunciations of Hebrew. Vol. 13, cols. 1120–45 in *Encyclopedia Judaica*. Jerusalem: Keter.

———. 1974. On the Historical Validity of the Vocalization of the Hebrew Bible. *Journal of the American Oriental Society* 94:304–15.

A. Murtonen. 1986. *Hebrew in Its West Semitic Setting. I. A Comparative Lexicon. A. Proper Names*. Leiden: Brill.

———. 1986. On Structural Growth in Language. *Abr-Nahrain* 24:139–54.

Joseph Naveh. 1982. *Early History of the Alphabet*. Jerusalem: Magnes.

M. O'Connor. 1983. Writing Systems, Native Speaker Analyses, and the Earliest Stages of Northwest Semitic Orthography. Pp. 439–65 in *The Word of the Lord Shall Go Forth: Essays in Honor of David Noel Freedman*, ed. C. L. Meyers and M. O'Connor. Winona Lake, Indiana: Eisenbrauns.

———. 1986. Writing Systems and Native Speaker Analyses. Pp. 536–43 in *Society of Biblical Literature Seminar Papers 1986*, ed. K. H. Richards. Atlanta: Scholars Press.

H. M. Orlinsky. 1960. The Origin of the Kethib-Qere System. Pp. 184–92 in *Congress Volume: Oxford 1959*. Vetus Testamentum Supplement 7. Leiden: Brill.

H. Y. Priebatsch. 1980. Spiranten und Aspiratae in Ugarit, AT und Hellas. *Ugarit-Forschungen* 12:317–33.

E. Puech. 1986. Origine de l'alphabet: Documents en alphabet linéaire et cunéiforme du IIe millénaire. *Revue biblique* 93:161–213.

E. J. Revell. 1970. *Hebrew Texts with Palestinian Vocalization*. Toronto: University of Toronto.

———. 1970. Studies in the Palestinian Vocalization of Hebrew. Pp. 51–100 in *Essays on the Ancient Semitic World*, ed. J. W. Wevers and D. B. Redford. Toronto: University of Toronto.

———. 1971–72. The Oldest Evidence for the Hebrew Accent System. *Bulletin of the John Rylands Library* 54:214–22.

———. 1972. The Placing of the Accent Signs in Biblical Texts with Palestinian Pointing. Pp. 34–45 in *Studies on the Ancient Palestinian World Presented to Professor F. V. Winnett*, ed. J. W. Wevers and D. B. Redford. Toronto: University of Toronto.

———. 1974. Aristotle and the Accents. *Journal of Semitic Studies* 19:19–35.

———. 1974. The Hebrew Accents and the Greek Ekphonetic Neumes. *Studies in Eastern Chant* 4:140–70.

———. 1975. The Diacritical Dots and the Development of the Arabic Alphabet. *Journal of Semitic Studies* 20:178–90.

———. 1976. Biblical Punctuation and Chant in the Second Temple Period. *Journal for the Study of Judaism* 7:181–98.

———. 1977. *Biblical Texts with Palestinian Pointing and Their Accents*. Missoula: Scholars Press.

———. 1980. Pausal Forms in Biblical Hebrew. *Journal of Semitic Studies* 25:165–79.

———. 1981. Pausal Forms and the Structure of Biblical Poetry. *Vetus Testamentum* 31:186–99.

———. 1981. Syntactic/Semantic Structure and the Reflexes of Original Short *a* in Tiberian Pointing. *Hebrew Annual Review* 5:75–100.

———. 1983. *Nesiga* and the History of the Masorah. Pp. 37–48 in *Estudios masoreticos . . . dedicados a Harry M. Orlinsky*, ed. E. Fernández Tejero. Textos y Estudios "Cardenal Cisneros" 33. Madrid: Instituto "Arias Montano."

———. 1986. Pausal Phenomena and the Biblical Tradition in Texts with Palestinian Pointing. Pp. 235–44 in *Salvación en la Palabra: Targum, Derash, Berith; En memoria del profesor Alejandro Diez Macho*, ed. D. Muñoz León. Madrid: Ediciones Cristiandad.

Wolfgang Richter. 1983. *Transliteration und Transkription: Objekt- und metasprachliche Metazeichensysteme zur Wiedergabe hebräischer Texte*. St. Ottilien: EOS.

G. Sampson. 1973. Duration in Hebrew Consonants. *Linguistic Inquiry* 4:101–4.

G. M. Schramm. 1964. *The Graphemes of Tiberian Hebrew*. Berkeley: University of California.

Richard C. Steiner. 1979. From Proto-Hebrew to Mishnaic Hebrew: The History of ךְ֡ and הּ֡. *Hebrew Annual Review* 3:157–74.

John Strugnell. 1969. Notes and Queries on "The Ben Sira Scroll from Masada." *Eretz-Israel* 9:109–19.

W. Weinberg. 1982. "Before" and "After" in the Teaching of Hebrew Grammar. *Hebrew Studies* 23:127–44.

———. 1985. *The History of Hebrew Plene Spelling*. Cincinnati: Hebrew Union College.

———. 1985. Observations about the Pronunciation of Hebrew in Rabbinic Sources. *Hebrew Union College Annual* 41:117–43.

J. W. Wevers. 1970. *Heth* in Classical Hebrew. Pp. 101–12 in *Essays on the Ancient Semitic World*, ed. J. W. Wevers and D. B. Redford. Toronto: University of Toronto.

W. Wickes. 1970. *Two Treatises on the Accentuation of the Old Testament*. Prolegomenon by A. Dotan. New York: Ktav. Originally Oxford: Clarendon, 1881, 1887.

Israel Yeivin. 1980. *Introduction to the Tiberian Masorah*. Edited and translated by E. J. Revell. Masoretic Studies 5. Missoula: Scholars Press.

f. Commentaries and Discussions of Particular Passages

Francis I. Andersen. 1976. *Job: An Introduction and Commentary*. Tyndale Old Testament Commentaries. Downers Grove, Illinois: InterVarsity.

———. 1987. On Reading Genesis 1–3. Pp. 137–50 in *Backgrounds for the Bible*, ed. M. O'Connor and D. N. Freedman. Winona Lake, Indiana: Eisenbrauns.

Francis I. Andersen and D. N. Freedman. 1980. *Hosea*. Anchor Bible 24. Garden City, New York: Doubleday.

David W. Baker. 1987. Leviticus 1–7 and the Punic Tariffs. *Zeitschrift für die Alttestamentliche Wissenschaft* 99:188–97.

David W. Baker, T. Desmond Alexander, and Bruce K. Waltke. 1988. *Obadiah, Jonah, Micah*. Tyndale Old Testament Commentaries. Downers Grove, Illinois: InterVarsity.

Lawrence Boadt. 1980. *Ezekiel's Oracles against Egypt: A Literary and Philological Study of Ezekiel 29–32*. Biblica et Orientalia 37. Rome: Biblical Institute.

Robert G. Boling. 1975. *Judges*. Anchor Bible 6A. Garden City, New York: Doubleday.

———. 1982. *Joshua*. Anchor Bible 6. Garden City, New York: Doubleday.

Moses Buttenwieser. 1938. *The Psalms Chronologically Treated with a New Translation*. Chicago: University of Chicago.

R. J. Clifford. 1983. Isaiah 55: Invitation to a Feast. Pp. 27–35 in *The Word of the Lord Shall Go Forth: Essays in Honor of David Noel Freedman*, ed. C. L. Meyers and M. O'Connor. Winona Lake, Indiana: Eisenbrauns.

Peter Craigie. 1983. *Psalms 1–50*. Word Biblical Commentary. Waco, Texas: Word.

F. M. Cross and D. N. Freedman. 1953. A Royal Song of Thanksgiving: II Samuel 22 = Psalm 18. *Journal of Biblical Literature* 72:15–34.

Mitchell Dahood. 1966. *Psalms I: 1–50*. Anchor Bible 16. Garden City, New York: Doubleday.

———. 1968. *Psalms II: 51–100*. Anchor Bible 17. Garden City, New York: Doubleday.

———. 1970. *Psalms III: 101–150*. Anchor Bible 17A. Garden City, New York: Doubleday.

———. 1973. Northwest Semitic Notes on Dt. 32,20. *Biblica* 54:405–6.

———. 1976. Jeremiah 5,31 and *UT* 127:32. *Biblica* 57:106–8.

Mitchell Dahood and Tadeusz Penar. 1970. The Grammar of the Psalter. Pp. 361–456 in *Psalms III: 101–150*. Anchor Bible 17A. Garden City, New York: Doubleday.

S. R. Driver. 1913. *Notes on the Hebrew Text and the Topography of the Books of Samuel*. Oxford: Clarendon.

Rodney K. Duke. 1987. The Portion of the Levite: Another Reading of Deuteronomy 18:6–8. *Journal of Biblical Literature* 106:193–201.

Michael V. Fox. 1985. *The Song of Songs and the Ancient Egyptian Love Songs*. Madison: University of Wisconsin.

M. H. Goshen-Gottstein. 1973. Hebrew Syntax and the History of the Bible Text: A Pesher in the MT of Isaiah [Isa 9:13–14]. *Textus* 8:100–106.

Michael D. Goulder. 1986. *The Song of Fourteen Songs*. Journal for the Study of the Old Testament Supplement 36. Sheffield: JSOT Press.

Moshe Greenberg. 1983. *Ezekiel, 1–20*. Anchor Bible 22. Garden City, New York: Doubleday.

A. E. Hill. 1983. Dating the Book of Malachi: A Linguistic Reexamination. Pp. 77–89 in *The Word of the Lord Shall Go Forth: Essays in Honor of David Noel Freedman*, ed. C. L. Meyers and M. O'Connor. Winona Lake, Indiana: Eisenbrauns.

D. R. Hillers. 1984. *Micah*. Hermeneia. Philadelphia: Fortress.

William L. Holladay. 1986. *Jeremiah*, vol. 1. Hermeneia. Philadelphia: Fortress.

Avi Hurvitz. 1982. *A Linguistic Study of the Relationship between the Priestly Source and the Book of Ezekiel*. Paris: Gabalda.

H. Jagersma. 1982. Some Remarks on the Jussive in Numbers 6,24–26. Pp. 131–36 in *Von Kanaan bis Kerala: Festschrift . . . J. P. M. van der Ploeg*, ed. W. C. Delsman et al. Alter Orient und Altes Testament 211. Kevelaer: Butzon und Bercker/Neukirchen-Vluyn: Neukirchener Verlag.

J. Gerald Janzen. 1985. *Job*. Interpretation. Atlanta: John Knox.

———. 1987. On the Most Important Word in the Shema (Deuteronomy VI 4–5). *Vetus Testamentum* 37:280–300.

G. M. Landes. 1982. Linguistic Criteria and the Date of Jonah. *Eretz-Israel* 16:147*–70*.

R. E. Longacre. 1989. *Joseph, a Story of Divine Providence: A Text Theoretical and Textlinguistic Analysis of Genesis 37 and 39–48*. Winona Lake, Indiana: Eisenbrauns.

S. Dean McBride. 1973. The Yoke of the Kingdom: An Exposition of Deuteronomy 6:4–5. *Interpretation* 27:273–306.

P. Kyle McCarter, Jr. 1980. *I Samuel*. Anchor Bible 8. Garden City, New York: Doubleday.

———. 1984. *II Samuel*. Anchor Bible 9. Garden City, New York: Doubleday.

W. J. Martin. 1965. The Hebrew of Daniel. Pp. 28–30 in *Notes on Some Problems in the Book of Daniel*, by D. J. Wiseman et al. London: Tyndale.

George E. Mendenhall. 1958. The Census Lists of Numbers 1 and 26. *Journal of Biblical Literature* 77:52–66.

W. Michel. 1982. Job 31:1. *Hebrew Studies* 23:59–66.

P. D. Miller, Jr. 1984. Syntax and Theology in Genesis XII 3a. *Vetus Testamentum* 34:472–76.

———. 1986. *Interpreting the Psalms*. Philadelphia: Fortress.

T. Muraoka. 1986. Hosea V in the Septuagint Version. *Abr-Nahrain* 24:120–38.

K. Oberhuber. 1953. Zur Syntax des Richterbuches: Der einfache Nominalsatz und die sog. Nominale Apposition. *Vetus Testamentum* 3:2–45.

Marvin H. Pope. 1973. *Job*. 3d ed. Anchor Bible 15. Garden City, New York: Doubleday.

———. 1977. *Song of Songs*. Anchor Bible 7C. Garden City, New York: Doubleday.

G. Rendsburg. 1980. Late Biblical Hebrew and the Date of "P." *Journal of the Ancient Near Eastern Society* 12:65–80.

Wolfgang Richter. 1963. *Traditionsgeschichtliche Untersuchungen zum Richterbuch*. Bonn: Peter Hanstein.

Bruce K. Waltke. 1975. The Creation Account in Genesis 1:1–3. *Bibliotheca Sacra* 132:216–28.

R. N. Whybray. 1987. *The Making of the Pentateuch*. Journal for the Study of the Old Testament Supplement 53. Sheffield: JSOT Press.

Walther Zimmerli. 1983. *Ezekiel*, vol. 2. Hermeneia. Philadelphia: Fortress.

g. Text Criticism

B. Albrektson. 1978. Reflections on the Emergence of a Standard Text of the Hebrew Bible. Pp. 49–65 in *Congress Volume: Göttingen 1977*. Vetus Testamentum Supplement 29. Leiden: Brill.

D. Barthélemy. 1953. Redécouverte d'un chaînon manquant de l'histoire de la Septante. *Revue biblique* 60:18–29. Rpt. as pp. 38–50 in his *Etudes d'histoire du texte d'Ancien Testament*. Fribourg: Editions Universitaires, 1978. Rpt. as pp. 127–39 in *Qumran and the History of the Biblical Text*, ed. F. M. Cross and S. Talmon. Cambridge: Harvard University, 1975.

_____. 1963. *Les Devanciers d'Aquila*. Vetus Testamentum Supplement 10. Leiden: Brill.

_____. 1978. *Etudes d'histoire du texte d'Ancien Testament*. Orbis Biblicus et Orientalis 21. Fribourg: Editions Universitaires.

M. H. Goshen-Gottstein. 1979. The Aleppo Codex and the Rise of the Massoretic Bible Text. *Biblical Archeologist* 42: 145–63.

Sidney Jellicoe. 1978. *The Septuagint and Modern Study*. Ann Arbor, Michigan: Eisenbrauns. Originally Oxford: Clarendon, 1968.

Stephen A. Kaufman. 1982. The Temple Scroll and Higher Criticism. *Hebrew Union College Annual* 53:29–43.

P. de Lagarde. 1863. *Anmerkungen zur griechischen Übersetzung der Proverbien*. Leipzig: Brockhaus.

_____. 1891–92. *Septuaginta Studien*. 2 vols. Göttingen: Dieter.

P. Kyle McCarter, Jr. 1986. *Textual Criticism: Recovering the Text of the Hebrew Bible*. Philadelphia: Fortress.

Judith E. Sanderson. 1986. *An Exodus Scroll from Qumran*. Atlanta: Scholars Press.

N. M. Sarna. 1971. Bible Text. Vol. 4, cols. 816–36 in *Encyclopedia Judaica*. Jerusalem: Keter.

A. Schenker. 1982. *Psalmen in den Hexapla*. Studi e testi 295. Vatican City: Bibliotheca Apostolica Vaticana.

S. Talmon. 1964. Aspects of the Textual Transmission of the Bible in Light of Qumran Manuscripts. *Textus* 4:95–132. Rpt. as pp. 226–63 in *Qumran and the History of the Biblical Text*, ed. F. M. Cross and S. Talmon. Cambridge, Harvard University, 1975.

E. Tov. 1981. *The Text-critical Use of the Septuagint in Biblical Research*. Jerusalem: Simor.

_____. 1988. Hebrew Biblical Manuscripts from the Judaean Desert. *Journal of Jewish Studies* 39:5–37.

Bruce K. Waltke. 1965. *Prolegomena to the Samaritan Pentateuch*. Harvard University Dissertation.

_____. 1970. The Samaritan Pentateuch and the Text of the Old Testament. Pp. 212–39 in *New Perspectives on the Old Testament*, ed. J. Barton Payne. Waco, Texas: Word.

_____. 1979. Textual Criticism of the Old Testament. Vol. 1, pp. 211–28 in *Expositor's Bible Commentary*, ed. F. E. Gaebelein. Grand Rapids: Zondervan.

_____. 1989. Aims of OT Textual Criticism. *Westminster Theological Journal* 51:93–108.

_____. 1989. The *New International Version* and Its Textual Principles in the Book of Psalms. *Journal of the Evangelical Theological Society* 32:17–26.

h. Other Studies and Collections

Elizabeth Achtemeier. 1988. The Impossible Possibility: Evaluating the Feminist Approach to Bible and Theology. *Interpretation* 42:45–57.

P. R. Ackroyd and C. F. Evans, eds. 1970. *The Cambridge History of the Bible. 1. From the Beginnings to Jerome*. Cambridge: Cambridge University.

W. J. Adams, Jr., and L. LaMar Adams. 1977. Language Drift and the Dating of Biblical Passages. *Hebrew Studies* 18:160–64.

Karl Albrecht. 1895–96. Das Geschlecht der hebräischen Hauptwörter. *Zeitschrift für die Alttestamentliche Wissenschaft* 15:313–25, 16:41–121.

W. F. Albright. 1957. *From the Stone Age to Christianity*. Garden City, New York: Anchor/Doubleday.

N. Avigad. 1982. A Hebrew Seal Depicting a Sailing Ship. *Bulletin of the American Schools of Oriental Research* 246:59–62.

Y. Avishur. 1976. Studies of Stylistic Features Common to the Phoenician Inscriptions and the Bible. *Ugarit-Forschungen* 8:1–22.

James Barr. 1968. *Comparative Philology and the Text of the Old Testament*. Oxford: Clarendon. Rpt. with additions, Winona Lake, Indiana: Eisenbrauns, 1987.

_____. 1969. The Ancient Semitic Languages—the Conflict between Philology and Linguistics. *Transactions of the Philological Society* 1968: 37–55.

_____. 1974. Philology and Exegesis. Pp. 39–61 in *Questions disputées d'Ancien Testament*, ed. C. Brekelmans. Gembloux: Duculot. Rpt. as pp. 362–87 in *Comparative Philology and the Text of the Old Testament*. Winona Lake, Indiana: Eisenbrauns, 1987.

_____. 1975. The Nature of Linguistic Evidence in the Text of the Bible. Pp. 35–57 in *Language and Texts: The Nature of Linguistic Evidence*, ed. H. H. Paper. Ann Arbor: Center for Coördination of Ancient and Modern Studies, University of Michigan.

John Beekman and John Callow. 1974. *Translating the Word of God*. Grand Rapids: Zondervan.

Adele Berlin. 1985. *The Dynamics of Biblical Parallelism*. Bloomington: Indiana University.

Joshua Blau. 1977. *An Adverbial Construction in Hebrew and Arabic: Sentence Adverbials in Frontal Position Separated from the Rest of the Sentence*. Proceedings—Israel Academy of Sciences and Humanities 6.1. Jerusalem: Israel Academy of Sciences and Humanities.

_____. 1978. Hebrew and North West Semitic: Reflections on the Classification of the Semitic Languages. *Hebrew Annual Review* 2:21–44.

Walter R. Bodine. 1987. Linguistics and Philology in the Study of Ancient Near Eastern Languages. Pp. 39–54 in *"Working with No Data": Semitic and Egyptian Studies Presented to Thomas O. Lambdin*, ed. D. M. Golomb. Winona Lake, Indiana: Eisenbrauns.

Brevard S. Childs. 1979. *Introduction to the Old Testament as Scripture*. Philadelphia: Fortress.

D. J. A. Clines. 1972. X, X *ben* Y, *ben* Y: Personal Names in Hebrew Narrative Style. *Vetus Testamentum* 22:266–87.

George W. Coats. 1970. Self-Abasement and Insult Formulas. *Journal of Biblical Literature* 89:14–26.

Jeffery M. Cohen. 1981. *A Samaritan Chronicle* [Samaritan Chronicle no. II]. Studia Post-Biblica 30. Leiden: Brill

Terence Collins. 1971. The Physiology of Tears in the Old Testament. *Catholic Biblical Quarterly* 33:18–38, 185–97.

———. 1978. *Line Forms in Hebrew Poetry*. Studia Pohl, Series Maior 7. Rome: Pontifical Biblical Institute.

K. R. Crim. 1973. Hebrew Direct Discourse as a Translation Problem. *Bible Translator* 24:311–16.

F. M. Cross. 1970. The Cave Inscriptions from Khirbet Beit Lei. Pp. 299–306 in *Near Eastern Archaeology in the Twentieth Century: Essays in Honor of Nelson Glueck*, ed. J. A. Sanders. Garden City, New York: Doubleday.

———. 1973. *Canaanite Myth and Hebrew Epic: Essays in the History of the Religion of Israel*. Cambridge: Harvard University.

R. Degen. 1971. Zur neueren hebräistischen Forschung. *Welt des Orients* 6:47–79.

S. J. DeVries. 1975. *Yesterday, Today, and Tomorrow: Time and History in the Old Testament*. Grand Rapids: Eerdmans.

J. D. Douglas, ed. 1962. *The New Bible Dictionary*. Grand Rapids: Eerdmans.

Michael Fishbane. 1985. *Biblical Interpretation in Ancient Israel*. Oxford: Clarendon.

E. R. Follis, ed. 1987. *Directions in Biblical Hebrew Poetry*. Journal for the Study of the Old Testament Supplement 40. Sheffield: JSOT Press.

A. Dean Forbes. 1987. Syntactic Sequences in the Hebrew Bible. Pp. 59–70 in *Perspectives on Language and Text: Essays and Poems in Honor of Francis I. Andersen*, ed. E. W. Conrad and E. G. Newing. Winona Lake, Indiana: Eisenbrauns.

D. N. Freedman. 1980. *Pottery, Poetry, and Prophecy: Studies in Early Hebrew Poetry*. Winona Lake, Indiana: Eisenbrauns.

R. M. Frye. 1989. Language for God and Feminist Language: A Literary and Rhetorical Analysis. *Interpretation* 43:45–57.

G. Gerleman. 1948. *Synoptic Studies in the Old Testament*. Lunds Universitets Årsskrift 1/44. Lund: Gleerup.

Robert Gordis. 1976. *The Word and the Book: Studies in Biblical Language and Literature*. New York: Ktav.

Cyrus H. Gordon. 1955. North Israelite Influence on Postexilic Hebrew. *Israel Exploration Journal* 5:85–88.

N. K. Gottwald. 1979. *The Tribes of Yahweh*. Maryknoll, New York: Orbis.

———. 1985. *The Hebrew Bible—A Socio-Literary Introduction*. Philadelphia: Fortress.

Edward L. Greenstein. 1983. Theories of Modern Bible Translation. *Prooftexts* 3:9–41.

———. 1986–87. Aspects of Biblical Poetry. *Jewish Book Annual* 44:33–42.

W. Gross. 1987. *Die Pendenskonstruction im biblischen Hebräisch*. Studien zum althebräischen Satz I. Arbeit zu Text und Sprache im Alten Testament 27. St. Ottilien: EOS.

Daniel Grossberg. 1979–80. Nominalizations in Biblical Hebrew. *Hebrew Studies* 20–21:29–33.

A. R. Guenter. 1977. *A Diachronic Study of Biblical Hebrew Prose Syntax*. University of Toronto Dissertation.

Moshe Held. 1969. Rhetorical Questions in Ugaritic and Biblical Hebrew. *Eretz-Israel* 9:71*–79*.

J. Hoftijzer. 1973. The Nominal Clause Reconsidered. *Vetus Testamentum* 23:446–510.

J. H. Hospers. 1973. Some Observations about the Teaching of Old Testament Hebrew. Pp. 188–98 in *Symbolae biblicae et Mesopotamicae Francisco Mario Theodoro de Liagre Böhl dedicatae*, ed. M. A. Beek et al. Leiden: Brill.

Avi Hurvitz. 1968. The Chronological Significance of Aramaisms in Biblical Hebrew. *Israel Exploration Journal* 18: 234–40.

Ernst Jenni. 1985. Hebraistiche Neuerscheinungen. *Theologische Rundschau* 50:313–26.

Barbara Bakke Kaiser. 1987. Poet as "Female Impersonator": The Image of Daughter Zion as Speaker in Biblical Poems of Suffering. *Journal of Religion* 67:164–82.

C.-A. Keller. 1970. Probleme des hebräischen Sprachunterrichte. *Vetus Testamentum* 20:278–86.

K. A. Kitchen. 1966. *Ancient Orient and the Old Testament*. London: Tyndale/Chicago: InterVarsity.

James Kugel. 1981. *The Idea of Biblical Poetry*. New Haven: Yale University.

E. Y. Kutscher. 1977. *Hebrew and Aramaic Studies*. Edited by Z. Ben Hayyim, A. Dotan, and G. Sarfatti. Jerusalem: Magnes.

G. W. H. Lampe, ed. 1969. *The Cambridge History of the Bible. 2. The West from the Fathers to the Reformation*. Cambridge: Cambridge University.

Irene Lande. 1949. *Formelhafte Wendungen der Umgangssprache im Alten Testament*. Leiden: Brill.

André Lemaire. 1988. Recherches actuelles sur les sceaux nord-ouest sémitiques [including a survey of Hebrew inscriptions]. *Vetus Testamentum* 38:220–30.

John Macdonald. 1969. *The Samaritan Chronicle No. II (or: Sepher Ha-Yamin): From Joshua to Nebuchadnezzar*. Beiheft zur Zeitschrift für die Alttestamentliche Wissenschaft 107. Berlin: de Gruyter.

John Macdonald and A. J. B. Higgins. 1971. The Beginnings of Christianity according to the Samaritans [from Samaritan Chronicle no. II]. *New Testament Studies* 18:54–80.

Stanley B. Marrow. 1976. *Basic Tools of Biblical Exegesis: A Student's Manual*. Rome: Biblical Institute.

T. J. Meek. 1940. The Hebrew Accusative of Time and Place. *Journal of the American Oriental Society* 60:224–33.

Rudolf Meyer. 1951. Probleme der hebräischen Grammatik. *Zeitschrift für die Alttestamentliche Wissenschaft* 63:221–35.

W. L. Moran. 1961. The Hebrew Language in Its Northwest Semitic Background. Pp. 54–72 in *The Bible and the Ancient Near East: Essays in Honor of William Foxwell*

Albright, ed. G. E. Wright. Garden City, New York: Double-day. Rpt., Winona Lake, Indiana: Eisenbrauns, 1979.

James Muilenburg. 1969. Form Criticism and Beyond. *Journal of Biblical Literature* 88:1–18. Rpt. as pp. 27–44 in *Hearing and Speaking the Word*, ed. T. F. Best. Chico: Scholars Press, 1984.

_____. 1984. *Hearing and Speaking the Word: Selections from the Works of James Muilenburg.* Edited by T. F. Best. Chico: Scholars Press.

T. Muraoka. 1985. *Emphatic Words and Structures in Biblical Hebrew.* Leiden: Brill/Jerusalem: Magnes.

E. A. Nida. 1972. Implications of Contemporary Linguistics for Biblical Scholarship. *Journal of Biblical Literature* 91: 73–89.

_____. 1981. Problems of Cultural Differences in Translating the Old Testament. Pp. 297–307 in *Mélanges Dominique Barthélemy*, ed. P. Casetti, O. Keel, and A. Schenker. Göttingen: Vandenhoeck und Ruprecht.

M. O'Connor. 1980. *Hebrew Verse Structure.* Winona Lake, Indiana: Eisenbrauns.

_____. 1982. "Unanswerable the Knack of Tongues": The Linguistic Study of Verse. Pp. 143–68 in *Exceptional Language and Linguistics*, ed. L. K. Obler and L. Menn. New York: Academic Press.

_____. 1986. "I only am escaped alone to tell thee": Native American and Biblical Hebrew Verse. *Religion and Intellectual Life* 3:121–32.

_____. 1987. The Pseudosorites: A Type of Paradox in Hebrew Verse. Pp. 161–72 in *Directions in Biblical Hebrew Poetry*, ed. E. R. Follis. Sheffield: JSOT Press.

_____. 1987. The Pseudosorites in Hebrew Verse. Pp. 239–53 in *Perspectives on Language and Text: Essays and Poems in Honor of Francis I. Andersen*, ed. E. W. Conrad and E. G. Newing. Winona Lake, Indiana: Eisenbrauns.

_____. 1987. The Poetic Inscription from Khirbet el-Qôm. *Vetus Testamentum* 37:224–30.

M. O'Connor and D. N. Freedman, eds. 1987. *Backgrounds for the Bible.* Winona Lake, Indiana: Eisenbrauns.

Dennis G. Pardee. 1978. Letters from Tel Arad. *Ugarit-Forschungen* 10:289–336.

Dennis G. Pardee, S. D. Sperling, J. D. Whitehead, and P. E. Dion. 1982. *Handbook of Ancient Hebrew Letters.* Chico: Scholars Press.

Robert Polzin. 1976. *Late Biblical Hebrew: Toward an Historical Typology of Biblical Hebrew Prose.* Missoula: Scholars Press.

J. Pritchard, ed. 1969. *Ancient Near Eastern Texts Relating to the Old Testament.* 3d ed. Princeton: Princeton University.

D. A. Robertson. 1972. *Linguistic Evidence in Dating Early Hebrew Poetry.* Society of Biblical Literature Dissertation Series 3. Missoula: Scholars Press.

H. B. Rosén. 1984. *East and West: Selected Writings in Linguistics. 2. Hebrew and Semitic Linguistics.* Munich: W. Fink.

H. Rosenberg. 1905. Zum Geschlecht der hebräischen Hauptwörter. *Zeitschrift für die Alttestamentliche Wissenschaft* 25:325–39.

G. B. Sarfatti. 1982. Hebrew Inscriptions of the First Temple Period. *Maarav* 3:55–83.

William R. Scott. 1987. *A Simplified Guide to BHS: Critical Apparatus, Masora, Accents, Unusual Letters, and Other Markings.* Berkeley: Bibal.

Patrick W. Skehan. 1971. *Studies in Israelite Poetry and Wisdom.* Washington: Catholic Biblical Association of America.

J. Alberto Soggin. 1975. *Old Testament and Oriental Studies.* Biblica et Orientalia 29. Rome: Biblical Institute.

E. Talstra. 1978. Text Grammar and Hebrew Bible. I. Elements of a Theory. *Bibliotheca Orientalis* 35:169–74.

_____. 1982. Text Grammar and Hebrew Bible. II. Syntax and Semantics. *Bibliotheca Orientalis* 39:26–38.

E. Tov. 1988. Computers and the Bible. *Bible Review* 4:38–43.

Phyllis Trible. 1976. God, Nature of. Pp. 368–69 in *The Interpreter's Dictionary of the Bible: Supplementary Volume*, ed. K. Crim. Nashville: Abingdon.

_____. 1978. *God and the Rhetoric of Sexuality.* Philadelphia: Fortress.

_____. 1986. *Texts of Terror.* Philadelphia: Fortress.

D. T. Tsumura. 1983. Literary Insertion (A×B Pattern) in Biblical Hebrew. *Vetus Testamentum* 33:468–82.

_____. 1986. Literary Insertion, A×B Pattern, in Hebrew and Ugaritic. *Ugarit-Forschungen* 18:351–61.

Edward Ullendorff. 1977. *Is Biblical Hebrew a Language? Studies in Semitic Languages and Civilizations.* Wiesbaden: Harrassowitz.

Dieter Vetter and Johanna Walter. 1971. Sprachtheorie und Sprachvermittlung: Erwägungen zur Situation des hebräischen Sprachstudiums. *Zeitschrift für die Alttestamentliche Wissenschaft* 83:73–96.

Clarence Vos. 1968. *Woman in Old Testament Worship.* Delft: Judels en Brinkman.

Max Wagner. 1966. *Die lexikalischen und grammatikalischen Aramaismen im Alttestamentlichen Hebräisch.* Beiheft zur Zeitschrift für die Alttestamentliche Wissenschaft 96. Berlin: Töpelmann.

W. G. E. Watson. 1980. Gender-Matched Synonymous Parallelism in the Old Testament. *Journal of Biblical Literature* 99:321–41.

Werner Weinberg. 1980. Language Consciousness in the Old Testament. *Zeitschrift für die Alttestamentliche Wissenschaft* 92:185–204.

J. W. Wevers. 1961. Semitic Bound Structures. *Canadian Journal of Linguistics* 7:9–14.

2. Post-Biblical Hebrew (Qumranic, Mishnaic, Medieval, and Modern), the History of the Study of Hebrew, and Related Matters

Moshe Bar-Asher. 1987. The Different Traditions of Mishnaic Hebrew. Pp. 1–38 in *"Working with No Data": Semitic and Egyptian Studies Presented to Thomas O. Lambdin*, ed. D. M. Golomb. Winona Lake, Indiana: Eisenbrauns.

James Barr. 1971. Hebrew Linguistic Literature [from the Sixteenth Century to the Present]. Vol. 16, cols. 1390–1401 in *Encyclopedia Judaica*. Jerusalem: Keter.

W. J. van Bekkum. 1983. Observations on Stem Formations (Binyānīm) in Rabbinical Hebrew. *Orientalia Lovaniensia Periodica* 14:167–98.

———. 1983. The Origins of the Infinitive in Rabbinical Hebrew. *Journal of Semitic Studies* 28:247–72.

Ruth Aronson [Berman]. 1969. The Predictability of Vowel Patterns in the [Modern] Hebrew Verb. *Glossa* 3:127–45.

Ruth [Aronson] Berman. 1978. *Modern Hebrew Structure*. Tel Aviv: University Publishing Projects.

———. 1979. Lexical Decomposition and Lexical Unity in the Expression of Derived Verbal Categories in Modern Hebrew. *Afroasiatic Linguistics* 6:117–42.

———. 1980. The Case of an (S)VO Language: Subjectless Constructions in Modern Hebrew. *Language* 56:759–76.

Joshua Blau. 1981. *The Renaissance of Modern Hebrew and Modern Standard Arabic*. Berkeley: University of California.

S. Bolozky. 1986. Semantic Productivity and Word Frequency in Modern Hebrew Verb Formation. *Hebrew Studies* 27:38–46.

Chaim Brovender, Yehoshua Blau, E. Y. Kutscher, Esther Goldenberg, and Eli Eytan. 1971. Hebrew Language. Vol. 16, cols. 1560–1662 in *Encyclopedia Judaica*. Jerusalem: Keter.

T. Carmi. 1981. *The Penguin Book of Hebrew Verse*. New York: Penguin.

J. Carmignac. 1974. L'Emploi de la négation אין dans la Bible et à Qumrân. *Revue de Qumran* 8:407–13.

———. 1978. Le Complément d'agent après un verbe passif dans l'Hébreu et l'Araméen de Qumrân. *Revue de Qumran* 9:409–27.

———. 1986. L'Infinitif absolu chez Ben Sira et à Qumrân. *Revue de Qumran* 12:251–61.

William Chomsky. 1957. *Hebrew: The Eternal Language*. Philadelphia: Jewish Publication Society.

Eve V. Clark and Ruth A. Berman. 1984. Structure and Use in the Acquisition of Word Formation. *Language* 60:542–90.

E. A. Coffin. 1968. *Ibn Janāḥ's Kitāb al-Lumaᶜ: A Critique of Medieval Grammatical Tradition*. University of Michigan Dissertation.

———. 1976. Ibn Janāḥ's *Kitāb al-Lumaᶜ*: An Integration of Medieval Grammatical Approaches. Pp. 65–79 in *Michigan Oriental Studies in Honor of George G. Cameron*, ed. L. L. Orlin et al. Ann Arbor: Department of Near Eastern Studies, University of Michigan.

Peter Cole, ed. 1976. *Studies in Modern Hebrew Syntax and Semantics*. Amsterdam: North-Holland Publishing.

F. M. Cross. 1961. *The Ancient Library of Qumran and Modern Biblical Studies*. 2d ed. Garden City, New York: Doubleday.

F. M. Cross and S. Talmon, eds. 1975. *Qumran and the History of the Biblical Text*. Cambridge: Harvard University.

Alexander Di Lella. 1966. *The Hebrew Text of Sirach*. The Hague: Mouton.

P. E. Dion. 1977. The Hebrew Particle את in the Paraenetic Part of the "Damascus Document." *Revue de Qumran* 9:197–205.

Jerome Friedman. 1983. *The Most Ancient Testimony: Sixteenth-Century Christian-Hebraica in the Age of Renaissance Nostalgia*. Athens: Ohio University.

Amikam Gaï. 1988. Structural Similarities between Tannaitic Hebrew and Arabic. *Le Muséon* 101:43–49.

T. H. Gaster. 1976. *The Dead Sea Scriptures*. 3d ed. Garden City, New York: Anchor/Doubleday.

T. Givón. 1974. Verb Complements and Relative Clauses. *Afroasiatic Linguistics* 1/4.

———. 1975. On the Role of Perceptual Clues in [Modern] Hebrew Relativization. *Afroasiatic Linguistics* 2:131–47.

M. H. Goshen-Gottstein. 1983. Humanism and the Rise of Hebraic Studies: From Christian to Jewish Renaissance. Pp. 691–96 in *The Word of the Lord Shall Go Forth: Essays in Honor of David Noel Freedman*, ed. C. L. Meyers and M. O'Connor. Winona Lake, Indiana: Eisenbrauns.

S. L. Greenslade, ed. 1963. *The Cambridge History of the Bible. 3. The West from the Reformation to the Present Day*. Cambridge: Cambridge University.

Frederick Greenspahn. 1985–86. Abraham Ibn Ezra and the Origin of Some Medieval Grammatical Terms. *Jewish Quarterly Review* 76:217–27.

Edward L. Greenstein. 1984. Medieval Bible Commentaries. Pp. 213–59 in *Back to the Sources: Reading the Classic Jewish Texts*, ed. Barry W. Holtz. New York: Summit.

Hermann Greive. 1978. Die hebräische Grammatik Johannes Reuchlins De rudimentis hebraicis. *Zeitschrift für die Alttestamentliche Wissenschaft* 90:395–409.

J. Gruntfest. 1979. Spinoza as a Linguist. *Israel Oriental Studies* 9:103–28.

Herman Hailperin. 1963. *Rashi and the Christian Scholars*. Pittsburgh: University of Pittsburgh.

B. W. Holtz, ed. 1984. *Back to the Sources: Reading the Classic Jewish Texts*. New York: Summit.

G. Lloyd Jones. 1983. *The Discovery of Hebrew in Tudor England: A Third Language*. Manchester: Manchester University.

K. G. Kuhn et al. 1960. *Konkordanz zu den Qumrantexten*. Göttingen: Vandenhoeck und Ruprecht.

———. 1963. Nachträge zur "Konkordanz zu den Qumrantexten." *Revue de Qumran* 4:163–234.

E. Y. Kutscher. 1982. *A History of the Hebrew Language*. Edited by Raphael Kutscher. Jerusalem: Magnes.

Pinchas E. Lapide. 1984. *Hebrew in the Church*. Grand Rapids: Eerdmans.

Malachi Martin. 1958. *The Scribal Character of the Dead Sea Scrolls*. Louvain: Publications Universitaires.

C. H. J. van der Merwe. 1987. A Short Survey of Major Contributions to the Grammatical Description of Old Hebrew since 1800 A.D. *Journal of Northwest Semitic Languages* 13:161–90.

Rudolf Meyer. 1957. Das Problem der Dialektmischung in den hebräischen Texten von Chirbet Qumrān. *Vetus Testamentum* 7:139–48.

Rudolf Meyer. 1958. Bemerkungen zu den hebräischen Aussprachetraditionen von Chirbet Qumrān. *Zeitschrift für die Alttestamentliche Wissenschaft* 70:39–48.

J. Milgrom. 1978. The Temple Scroll. *Biblical Archeologist* 41:105–20.

Shelomo Morag. 1988. Qumran Hebrew: Some Typological Observations. *Vetus Testamentum* 38:148–64.

T. V. Parfitt. 1972. The Use of Hebrew in Palestine, 1800–1882. *Journal of Semitic Studies* 17:237–52.

J. J. Petuchowski. 1978. *Theology and Poetry: Studies in the Medieval Piyyut*. London: Routledge and Kegan Paul.

Elisha Qimron. 1986. *The Hebrew of the Dead Sea Scrolls*. Atlanta: Scholars Press.

C. Rabin. 1943. *The Evolution of the Syntax of Post-Biblical Hebrew*. Oxford University Dissertation.

———. 1970. Hebrew. Pp. 304–46 in *Current Trends in Linguistics. 6. Linguistics in South West Asia and North Africa*, ed. T. A. Sebeok et al. The Hague: Mouton.

———. [1973.] *A Short History of the Hebrew Language*. Jerusalem: Orot.

———. 1976. Hebrew and Aramaic in the First Century. Pp. 1007–39 in *The Jewish People in the First Century. 2. Historical Geography, Political History, Social, Cultural and Religious Life and Institutions*, ed. S. Safrai and M. Stern. Assen: Van Gorcum.

Isaac Rabinowitz. 1983. *The Book of the Honeycomb's Flow . . . by Judah Messer Leon*. Ithaca, New York: Cornell University.

C. del Valle Rodríguez. 1982. *Die grammatikalische Terminologie der frühen hebräischen Grammatikern*. Madrid: Consejo Superior de Investigaciones Científicas.

S. Rosenblatt. 1985. Materials toward a Biblical Grammar in the Biblical Exegesis of the Tosefta. Pp. 219–26 in *Biblical and Related Studies Presented to Samuel Iwry*, ed. A. Kort and S. Morschauser. Winona Lake, Indiana: Eisenbrauns.

Norman Roth. 1982. "Seeing the Bible through a Poet's Eyes": Some Difficult Biblical Words Interpreted by Moses Ibn Ezra. *Hebrew Studies* 23:111–14.

Ángel Saénz-Badillos. 1988. *Historia de la Lengua Hebrea*. Barcelona: Editorial AUSA.

N. M. Samuelson. 1984. Medieval Jewish Philosophy. Pp. 261–303 in *Back to the Sources: Reading the Classic Jewish Texts*, ed. Barry W. Holtz. New York: Summit.

M. H. Segal. 1927. *A Grammar of Mishnaic Hebrew*. Oxford: Clarendon.

Solomon Skoss. 1955. *Saadiah Gaon, the Earliest Hebrew Grammarian*. Philadelphia: Dropsie College.

Beryl Smalley. 1952. *Study of the Bible in the Middle Ages*. Oxford: Basil Blackwell. Rpt., Notre Dame, Indiana: University of Notre Dame, 1964.

S. Strousma. 1987. From Muslim Heresy to Jewish-Muslim Polemics. *Journal of the American Oriental Society* 107: 767–72.

P. Swiggers. 1979. L'Histoire de la grammaire hébraïque jusqu'au xvie siècle. *Orientalia Lovaniensia Periodica* 10:183–93.

David Tene. 1971. Hebrew Linguistic Literature [up to the Sixteenth Century]. Vol. 16, cols. 1352–90 in *Encyclopedia Judaica*. Jerusalem: Keter.

Y. Thorion. 1981. The Use of Prepositions in 1 Q Serek. *Revue de Qumran* 10:405–33.

Yosef Tobi. 1984. Saadia's Biblical Exegesis and His Poetic Practice. *Hebrew Annual Review* 8:241–57.

Isidore Twersky. 1980. *Introduction to the Code of Maimonides*. New Haven: Yale University.

N. Waldman. 1975. The Hebrew Tradition. Pp. 1285–1330 in *Current Trends in Linguistics. 13. Historiography of Linguistics*, ed. T. A. Sebeok et al. The Hague: Mouton.

———. 1989. *The Recent Study of Hebrew: A Survey of the Literature with Selected Bibliography*. Winona Lake, Indiana: Eisenbrauns.

Pinchas Wechter. 1964. *Ibn Barun's Arabic Works on Hebrew Grammar and Lexicography*. Philadelphia: Dropsie College.

P. Wexler. 1986. Review of Kutscher, *A History of the Hebrew Language* (1982). *Language* 62:687–90.

3. Other Semitic Languages

a. Second-Millennium Northwest Semitic

Kjell Aartun. 1974. *Die Partikeln des Ugaritischen. 1. Adverbien, Verneinungspartikeln, Bekräftigungspartikeln, Hervorhebungspartikeln*. Alter Orient und Altes Testament 21/1. Kevelaer: Butzon und Bercker/Neukirchen-Vluyn: Neukirchener Verlag.

———. 1978. *Die Partikeln des Ugaritischen. 2. Präpositionen, Konjunktionen*. Alter Orient und Altes Testament 21/2. Kevelaer: Butzon und Bercker/Neukirchen-Vluyn: Neukirchener Verlag.

———. 1980. Die Belegten Partikelformen in den ugaritischen Texten aus Ras Ibn Hani. *Ugarit-Forschungen* 12:1–6.

———. 1982. Präpositionale Ausdrücke im Ugaritischen als Ersatz für semitisch *min*. *Ugarit-Forschungen* 14:1–14.

W. F. Albright. 1969. *The Proto-Sinaitic Inscriptions and Their Decipherment*. 2d ed. Harvard Theological Studies 22. Cambridge: Harvard University.

W. F. Albright and W. L. Moran. 1948. A Re-interpretation of an Amarna Letter from Byblos (EA 82). *Journal of Cuneiform Studies* 2:239–48.

A. Altman (with J. Klein). 1977. The Fate of Abdi-Ashirta. *Ugarit-Forschungen* 9:1–11.

M. Dietrich and O. Loretz. 1978. Das ugaritische Fragepronomen *mh* und seine Erweiterungen. Pp. 19–21 in *Studies in Bible and the Ancient Near East Presented to Samuel E. Loewenstamm*, ed. Y. Avishur and J. Blau. Jerusalem: Rubinstein.

M. Dietrich and O. Loretz. 1980. Zweifelhafte Belege für ug. *m(n)* "von": Zur ugaritischen Lexikographie (XVI). *Ugarit-Forschungen* 12: 183–87.

———. 1984. Ugaritisch *ʾṯr, aṯr, aṯryt* und *aṯrt. Ugarit-Forschungen* 16:57–62.

M. Dietrich, O. Loretz, and J. Sanmartín. 1976. Die angebliche ug.-he. Parallele *spsg//sps(j)g(jm). Ugarit-Forschungen* 8: 37–40.

D. L. Dobrusin. 1981. The Third Masculine Plural of the Prefixed Form of the Verb in Ugaritic. *Journal of the Ancient Near Eastern Society* 13:5–14.

Terry L. Fenton. 1969. Command and Fulfillment in Ugaritic— "*TQTL : YQTL*" and "*QTL : QTL.*" *Journal of Semitic Studies* 14:34–38.

D. Freilich. 1986. Is There an Ugaritic Deity *Bbt? Journal of Semitic Studies* 31:119–30.

Stanley Gevirtz. 1973. On Canaanite Rhetoric: The Evidence of the Amarna Letters from Tyre. *Orientalia* 42:162–77.

———. 1986. Of Syntax and Style in the "Late Biblical Hebrew"-"Old Canaanite" Connection. *Journal of the Ancient Near Eastern Society* 18:25–29.

H. L. Ginsberg. 1936. The Rebellion and Death of Baᶜlu. *Orientalia* 5:161–98.

Cyrus H. Gordon. 1965. *Ugaritic Textbook.* Analecta Orientalia 38. Rome: Pontifical Biblical Institute.

———. 1966. *Ugarit and Minoan Crete.* New York: Norton.

F. Gröndahl. 1967. *Die Personennamen der Texte aus Ugarit.* Studia Pohl 1. Rome: Pontifical Biblical Institute.

Andrée Herdner. 1963. *Corpus des tablettes en cunéiformes alphabétiques.* 2 vols. Paris: Geuthner.

John Huehnergard. 1981. Akkadian Evidence for Case-Vowels on Ugaritic Bound Forms. *Journal of Cuneiform Studies* 33:199–205.

———. 1985. A Dt Stem in Ugaritic? *Ugarit-Forschungen* 17:402.

———. 1987. *Ugaritic Vocabulary in Syllabic Transcription.* Atlanta: Scholars Press.

———. 1987. Northwest Semitic Vocabulary in Akkadian Texts. *Journal of the American Oriental Society* 107:713–25.

Herbert B. Huffmon. 1965. *Amorite Personal Names in the Mari Texts.* Baltimore: Johns Hopkins University.

J. A. Knudtzon, O. Weber, and E. Ebeling. 1907–15. *Die El-Amarna-Tafeln.* 2 vols. Vorderasiatische Bibliothek 2. Leipzig: Hinrichs.

C. R. Krahmalkov. 1969. The Amorite Enclitic Particle *TA/I. Journal of Semitic Studies* 14:201–4.

———. 1971. Northwest Semitic Glosses in Amarna Letter No. 64:22–23. *Journal of Near Eastern Studies* 30:140–43.

André Lemaire. 1984. Mari, the Bible, and the Northwest Semitic World. *Biblical Archaeologist* 47:101–9.

David Marcus. 1968. Studies in Ugaritic Grammar 1. *Journal of the Ancient Near Eastern Society* 1/2:55–61.

———. 1970–71. The *Qal* Passive in Ugaritic. *Journal of the Ancient Near Eastern Society* 3:102–11.

Baruch Margalit. 1983. Lexicographical Notes on the *Aqht* Epic (Part I: KTU 1.17–18). *Ugarit-Forschungen* 15:65–103.

G. E. Mendenhall. 1985. *The Syllabic Inscriptions from Byblos.* Beirut: American University of Beirut.

W. L. Moran. 1950. *A Syntactical Study of the Dialect of Byblos as Reflected in the Amarna Tablets.* Johns Hopkins University Dissertation.

———. 1950. The Use of the Canaanite Infinitive Absolute as a Finite Verb in the Amarna Letters from Byblos. *Journal of Cuneiform Studies* 4:169–71.

———. 1951. New Evidence on Canaanite *taqtulū(na)* [3 m.pl.]. *Journal of Cuneiform Studies* 5:33–35.

———. 1952. "Does Amarna Bear on Karatepe?"—An Answer. *Journal of Cuneiform Studies* 6:76–80.

———. 1953. Amarna *šumma* in Main Clauses. *Journal of Cuneiform Studies* 7:78–80.

———. 1960. Early Canaanite *yaqtula. Orientalia* 29:1–19.

———. 1964. **Taqtul*—Third Masculine Singular? [Not in Amarna.] *Biblica* 45: 80–82.

———. 1969. The Death of ᶜAbdi-Aširta. *Eretz-Israel* 9:94*–99*.

———. 1973. The Dual Personal Pronouns in Western Peripheral Akkadian. *Bulletin of the American Schools of Oriental Research* 211:50–53.

G. del Olmo Lete. 1981. *Mitos y leyendas de Canaan según la tradición de Ugarit.* Institución san Jerónimo para la investigación bíblica. Fuentes de la ciencia bíblica 1. Madrid: Ediciones Cristiandad.

———. 1984. *Interpretación de la mitología cananea: Estudios de semántica ugarítica.* Institución san Jerónimo para la investigación bíblica. Fuentes de la ciencia bíblica 2. Valencia: Institución san Jerónimo.

Dennis G. Pardee. 1975, 1976. The Preposition in Ugaritic. *Ugarit-Forschungen* 7:329–78, 8:215–322.

———. 1977. Attestations of Ugaritic Verb/Preposition Combinations in Later Dialects. *Ugarit-Forschungen* 9:205–31.

———. 1979. More on the Preposition in Ugaritic. *Ugarit-Forschungen* 11:685–92.

———. 1985. *Les Textes hippiatriques.* Paris: Editions Recherche sur les Civilisations.

Dennis G. Pardee and J. T. Glass. 1984. The Mari Archives. *Biblical Archaeologist* 47:88–100.

Dennis G. Pardee and R. M. Whiting. 1987. Aspects of Epistolary Verbal Usage in Ugaritic and Akkadian. *Bulletin of the School of Oriental and African Studies* 50:1–31.

A. F. Rainey. 1975. Morphology and the Prefix-Tenses of West Semitized El Amarna Tablets. *Ugarit-Forschungen* 7:395–426.

Stanislav Segert. 1984. *A Basic Grammar of the Ugaritic Language.* Berkeley: University of California.

———. 1985. Polarity of Vowels in the Ugaritic Verbs II /ʾ/. *Ugarit-Forschungen* 15:219–22.

D. Sivan. 1984. *Grammatical Analysis and Glossary of the Northwest Semitic Vocables in Akkadian Texts of the 15th–13th C. B.C. from Canaan and Syria.* Alter Orient und Altes Testament 214. Kevelaer: Butzon und Bercker/Neukirchen: Neukirchener Verlag.

P. Swiggers. 1985. Byblos dans les lettres d'el Amarna. Pp. 45–58 in *Studia Phoenicia. 3. Phoenicia and Its Neighbors,* ed. E. Lipiński. Leuven: Peeters.

E. Vereet. 1984. Beobachtungen zum Ugaritischen Verbalsystem. *Ugarit-Forschungen* 16:307–21.

b. First-Millennium Northwest Semitic (except Aramaic)

Francis I. Andersen. 1966. Moabite Syntax. *Orientalia* 35: 81–120.

H. Donner and W. Röllig. 1962–73. *Kanaanäische und aramäische Inschriften.* 3 vols. Wiesbaden: Harrassowitz.

A. Dotan. 1971–72. Vowel Shift in Phoenician and Punic. *Abr-Nahrain* 12:1–5.

Johannes Friedrich with Wolfgang Röllig. 1970. *Phönizisch-punische Grammatik.* 2d ed. Analecta Orientalia 46. Rome: Pontifical Biblical Institute.

W. Randall Garr. 1985. *Dialect Geography of Syria-Palestine, 1000–586 B.C.E.* Philadelphia: University of Pennsylvania.

J. C. L. Gibson. 1971. *Textbook of Syrian Semitic Inscriptions. 1. Hebrew and Moabite Inscriptions.* Oxford: Clarendon.

———. 1982. *Textbook of Syrian Semitic Inscriptions. 3. Phoenician Inscriptions.* Oxford: Oxford University.

Jo Ann Hackett. 1984. *The Balaam Text from Deir Alla.* Harvard Semitic Monographs 31. Chico: Scholars Press.

Zellig S. Harris. 1936. *A Grammar of the Phoenician Language.* American Oriental Series 8. New Haven: American Oriental Society.

———. 1939. *Development of the Canaanite Dialects.* American Oriental Series 16. New Haven: American Oriental Society.

J. Hoftijzer and G. van der Kooij et al. 1976. *Aramaic Texts from Deir ʿAlla.* Leiden: Brill.

John Huehnergard. 1987. Review of Garr, *Dialect Geography of Syria-Palestine, 1000–586 B.C.E.* (1985). *Journal of Biblical Literature* 106:529–33.

K. P. Jackson. 1983. *The Ammonite Language of the Iron Age.* Chico: Scholars Press.

C.-F. Jean and J. Hoftijzer. 1965. *Dictionnaire des inscriptions sémitiques de l'ouest.* Leiden: Brill.

C. R. Krahmalkov. 1970. Observations on the Affixing of Possessive Pronouns in Punic. *Rivista degli Studi Orientali* 44:181–86.

———. 1970. Studies in Phoenician and Punic Grammar. *Journal of Semitic Studies* 15:181–88.

———. 1972. Comments on the Vocalization of the Suffix Pronoun of the Third Feminine Singular in Phoenician and Punic. *Journal of Semitic Studies* 17:68–75.

———. 1974. The Object Pronouns of the Third Person of Phoenician and Punic. *Rivista di Studi Fenici* 2:39–43.

———. 1979. On the Third Feminine Singular of the Perfect in Phoenician-Punic. *Journal of Semitic Studies* 24:25–28.

———. 1986. The *QATAL* with Future Tense Reference in Phoenician. *Journal of Semitic Studies* 31:5–10.

M. O'Connor. 1977. The Grammar of Getting Blessed in Tyrian-Sidonian Phoenician. *Rivista di Studi Fenici* 5:5–11.

———. 1977. The Rhetoric of the Kilamuwa Inscription. *Bulletin of the American Schools of Oriental Research* 226:15–29.

Stanislav Segert. 1976. *A Grammar of Phoenician and Punic.* Munich: Beck.

P. Swiggers. 1987. Phoenician *b* "from"? *Aula Orientalis* 5: 152–54.

c. Aramaic

A. M. R. Aristar. 1987. The Semitic Jussive and the Implications for Aramaic. *Maarav* 4:157–89.

Hans Bauer and Pontus Leander. 1927. *Grammatik des Biblisch-Aramäischen.* Halle: Niemeyer.

Klaus Beyer. 1984. *Die aramäischen Texte vom Toten Meer.* Göttingen: Vandenhoeck und Ruprecht.

———. 1986. *The Aramaic Language: Its Distribution and Subdivisions.* Translated by J. F. Healey. Göttingen: Vandenhoeck und Ruprecht. [Partial translation of Beyer, *Die aramäischen Texte vom Toten Meer* (1984).]

Daniel Boyarin. 1982. Review of Sabar, *Pǝšaṭ Wayǝhi Bǝšallaḥ* (1976). *Maarav* 3:99–114.

J. A. Fitzmyer. 1957. The Syntax of כל, כלא, "All," in Aramaic Texts from Egypt and in Biblical Aramaic. *Biblica* 38:170–84. Rpt. as pp. 205–17 in *A Wandering Aramean.* Missoula: Scholars Press, 1979.

———. 1979. *A Wandering Aramean.* Missoula: Scholars Press.

J. C. L. Gibson. 1975. *Textbook of Syrian Semitic Inscriptions. 2. Aramaic Inscriptions.* Oxford: Clarendon.

Robert Hetzron. 1977. Innovations in the Semitic Numeral System. *Journal of Semitic Studies* 22:167–201.

Robert D. Hoberman. 1989. *The Syntax and Semantics of Verb Morphology in Modern Aramaic: A Jewish Dialect of Iraqi Kurdistan.* American Oriental Series 69. New Haven: American Oriental Society.

John Huehnergard. 1987. The Feminine Plural Jussive in Old Aramaic. *Zeitschrift der Deutschen Morgenländischen Gesellschaft* 137:266–77.

Stephen A. Kaufman. 1974. *The Akkadian Influences on Aramaic.* Assyriological Studies 19. Chicago: The Oriental Institute.

———. 1984. On Vowel Reduction in Aramaic. *Journal of the American Oriental Society* 104:87–95.

Georg Krotkoff. 1982. *A Neo-Aramaic Dialect of Kurdistan: Texts, Grammar, and Vocabulary.* American Oriental Series 64. New Haven: American Oriental Society.

E. Y. Kutscher. 1970. Aramaic. Pp. 347–412 in *Current Trends in Linguistics. 6. Linguistics in Southwest Asia and North Africa,* ed. T. A. Sebeok et al. The Hague: Mouton. Rpt. as pp. 90–155 in *Hebrew and Aramaic Studies,* ed. Z. Ben Hayyim, A. Dotan, and G. Sarfatti. Jerusalem: Magnes, 1977.

———. 1971. Aramaic. Vol. 3, cols. 259–87 in *Encyclopedia Judaica.* Jerusalem: Keter.

J. A. Lund. 1986, 1988. The Syntax of the Numeral "One" as a Noun Modifier in Jewish Palestinian Aramaic of the Amoraic Period. *Journal of the American Oriental Society* 106:413–23, 108:211–17.

W. S. Morrow and E. G. Clarke. 1986. The *Ketib/Qere* in the Aramaic Portions of Ezra and Daniel. *Vetus Testamentum* 36:406–22.

T. Muraoka. 1987. *Classical Syriac for Hebraists*. Wiesbaden: Harrassowitz.

M. O'Connor. 1986. The Arabic Loanwords in Nabatean Aramaic. *Journal of Near Eastern Studies* 45:213–29.

———. 1986 [appeared 1989]. Northwest Semitic Designations for Elective Social Affinities. *Journal of the Ancient Near Eastern Society* 18:67–80.

———. 1988. The Grammar of Finding Your Way in Palmyrene Aramaic. Pp. 353–69 in *Fucus: A Semitic/Afrasian Gathering in Remembrance of Albert Ehrman*, ed. Y. L. Arbeitman. Amsterdam: John Benjamins.

Bezalel Porten. 1968. *Archives from Elephantine*. Berkeley: University of California.

F. Rosenthal. 1961. *A Grammar of Biblical Aramaic*. Porta Linguarum Orientalium N.S. 5. Wiesbaden: Harrassowitz.

Yona Sabar. 1976. *Pəšaṭ Wayəhi Bəšallaḥ: A Neo-Aramaic Midrash on Beshallaḥ (Exodus)*. Wiesbaden: Harrassowitz.

Stanislav Segert. 1975. *Altaramäische Grammatik*. Leipzig: VEB.

J. W. Wesselius. 1984. A Subjunctive in the Aramaic of the Palestinian Targum. *Journal of Jewish Studies* 35:196–99.

d. Other Semitic Languages, Comparative Semitics, and Afroasiatic Languages

Jacob Barth. 1887. Das semitische Perfect im Assyrischen. *Zeitschrift für Assyriologie* 2:375–86.

———. 1894. *Die Nominalbildung in den semitischen Sprachen*. 2d ed. Leipzig: Hinrichs.

———. 1913. *Die Pronominalbildung in den semitischen Sprachen*. Leipzig: Hinrichs.

A. F. L. Beeston. 1984. Reflections on Verbs "To Be." *Journal of Semitic Studies* 29:7–13.

M. Lionel Bender, ed. 1976. *The Non-Semitic Languages of Ethiopia*. Committee on Ethiopian Studies 5. East Lansing: African Studies Center, Michigan State University.

Gotthelf Bergsträsser. 1983. *Introduction to the Semitic Languages*. Translated and supplemented by Peter T. Daniels. Winona Lake, Indiana: Eisenbrauns. Originally Munich: Hueber, 1928.

M. M. Bravmann. 1977. *Studies in Semitic Philology*. Leiden: Brill.

Carl Brockelmann. 1903. *Die Femineneendung t im Semitischen*. Breslau: G. P. Aderholz.

———. 1908. *Kurzgefasste vergleichende Grammatik der semitischen Sprachen*. Porta Linguarum Orientalium 21. Berlin: Reuter und Reichard.

———. 1908–13. *Grundriss der vergleichenden Grammatik der semitischen Sprachen*. 2 vols. Berlin: Reuter und Reichard. Rpt., Hildesheim: Olms, 1961.

———. 1910. *Précis de linguistique sémitique*. Paris: Geuthner.

———. 1951. Die "Tempora" des Semitischen. *Zeitschrift für Phonetik und allgemeine Sprachwissenshaft* 5:133–54.

Giorgio Buccellati. 1968. An Interpretation of the Akkadian Stative as a Nominal Sentence. *Journal of Near Eastern Studies* 27:1–14.

———. 1988. The State of the [Akkadian] "Stative." Pp. 153–89 in *Fucus: A Semitic/Afrasian Gathering in Remembrance of Albert Ehrman*, ed. Y. L. Arbeitman. Amsterdam: John Benjamins.

V. Christian. 1935. Die kausative Bedeutung des semitischen Steigerungsstammes. Pp. 41–45 in *Miscellanea Orientalia dedicata Antonio Deimel*. Analecta Orientalia 12. Rome: Pontifical Biblical Institute.

M. Cohen. 1924. *Le Système verbal sémitique et l'expression du temps*. Paris: Imprimerie Nationale.

Igor Diakonoff. 1965. *Semito-Hamitic Languages*. Moscow: Nauka.

August Dillmann. 1857. *Grammatik der äthiopischen Sprache*. Leipzig: Tauchitz (2d ed. in 1899).

W. Fisher. 1972. *Grammatik des klassischen Arabisch*. Wiesbaden: Harrassowitz.

Henri Fleisch. 1947. *Introduction à l'étude des langues sémitiques*. Paris: Adrien-Maisonneuve.

Z. Frajzyngier. 1979. Notes on the $R^1R^2R^3$ Stems in Semitic. *Journal of Semitic Studies* 24:1–12.

P. Fronzaroli. 1973–74. Classe et genre hamito-sémitiques. *Melangés de l'Université Saint-Joseph* 48:1–20.

Cyrus H. Gordon. 1987. Eblaitica. Vol. 1, pp. 19–28 in *Eblaitica: Essays on the Ebla Archives and Eblaite Language*, ed. C. H. Gordon, G. A. Rendsburg, and N. H. Winter. Winona Lake, Indiana: Eisenbrauns.

———. 1987. *WM-* "and" in Eblaite and Hebrew. Vol. 1, pp. 29–30 in *Eblaitica: Essays on the Ebla Archives and Eblaite Language*, ed. C. H. Gordon, G. A. Rendsburg, and N. H. Winter. Winona Lake, Indiana: Eisenbrauns.

Cyrus H. Gordon, G. A. Rendsburg, and N. H. Winter, eds. 1987. *Eblaitica: Essays on the Ebla Archives and Eblaite Language*, vol. 1. Winona Lake, Indiana: Eisenbrauns.

M. H. Goshen-Gottstein. 1969. The System of Verbal Stems in the Classical Semitic Languages. Pp. 70–91 in *Proceedings of the International Conference on Semitic Studies Held in Jerusalem, 19–23 July 1965*. Jerusalem: Israel Academy of Sciences and Humanities.

———. 1985. Problems of Semitic Verbal Stems. *Bibliotheca Orientalis* 42:278–83.

J. H. Greenberg. 1950. The Patterning of Root Morphemes in Semitic. *Word* 6:162–81.

Paul Haupt. 1878. The Oldest Semitic Verb-Form. *Journal of the Royal Asiatic Society* 10:244–52.

———. 1894. Transitive and Intransitive Verbs in Semitic. *Journal of the American Oriental Society*. 16:ci–cii.

Robert Hetzron. 1967. Agaw Numerals and Incongruence in Semitic. *Journal of Semitic Studies* 12:169–97.

———. 1969. The Evidence for Perfect **y'aqtul* and Jussive **yaqt'ul* in Proto-Semitic. *Journal of Semitic Studies* 14:1–21.

———. 1969. Third Person Singular Pronoun Suffixes in Proto-Semitic (with a theory on the connective vowels in Tiberian Hebrew). *Orientalia Suecana* 18:101–27.

Carleton T. Hodge. 1970. Afroasiatic: An Overview. Pp. 237–54 in *Current Trends in Linguistics. 6. Linguistics in South West Asia and North Africa*, ed. T. A. Sebeok et al. The Hague: Mouton.

_____. 1975. The Nominal Sentence in Semitic. *Afroasiatic Linguistics* 2:69–75.

_____. 1976. Lisramic (Afroasiatic): An Overview. Pp. 43–65 in *The Non-Semitic Languages of Ethiopia*, ed. M. Lionel Bender. East Lansing: African Studies Center, Michigan State University.

_____. 1981. Lislakh [= Nostratic = Indo-European + Afroasiatic] Labials. *Anthropological Linguistics* 23:368–82.

_____. 1983. Relating Afroasiatic to Indo-European. Pp. 33–50 in *Studies in Chadic and Afroasiatic Linguistics*, ed. E. Wolff and H. Meyer-Bahlburg. Hamburg: Buske.

_____. 1983–84. Afroasiatic: The Horizon and Beyond. *Jewish Quarterly Review* 74:137–58.

J. H. Hospers, ed. 1973–74. *A Basic Bibliography for the Study of the Semitic Languages*. 2 vols. Leiden: Brill.

John Huehnergard. 1983. Asseverative *la* and Hypothetical *lu/law* in Semitic. *Journal of the American Oriental Society* 103:569–93.

_____. 1987. Three Notes on Akkadian Morphology. Pp. 181–93 in *"Working with No Data": Semitic and Egyptian Studies Presented to Thomas O. Lambdin*, ed. D. M. Golomb. Winona Lake, Indiana: Eisenbrauns.

_____. 1987. "Stative," Predicative Form, Pseudo-Verb [Akkadian verbless clauses]. *Journal of Near Eastern Studies* 46:215–32.

G. Janssens. 1975–76. The Feminine Ending -(a)t in Semitic. *Orientalia Lovaniensia Periodica* 6–7:277–84.

G. A. Khan. 1984. Object Markers and Agreement Pronouns in Semitic Languages. *Bulletin of the School of Oriental and African Studies* 47:468–500.

_____. 1988. *Studies in Semitic Syntax*. London Oriental Series 38. Oxford: Oxford University, 1988.

J. Kuryłowicz. 1972. *Studies in Semitic Grammar and Metrics*. Wrocław: Polska Akademia Nauk Komitet Językoznawstwa.

_____. 1973. Verbal Aspect in Semitic. *Orientalia* 42:114–20.

E. Y. Kutscher. 1966. Review of Moscati et al., *Introduction to the Comparative Grammar of the Semitic Languages* (1964). *Asian and African Studies* 2:192–201. Rpt. as pp. 174–83 in *Hebrew and Aramaic Studies*, ed. Z. Ben Ḥayyim, A. Dotan, and G. Sarfatti. Jerusalem: Magnes, 1977.

F. Leemhuis. 1977. *The D and H Stems in Koranic Arabic*. Leiden: Brill.

A. Loprieno. 1986. *Das Verbalsystem im Ägyptischen und im Semitischen: Zur Grundlegung einer Aspekttheorie*. Wiesbaden: Harrassowitz.

John J. McCarthy. 1985. *Formal Problems in Semitic Phonology and Morphology*. New York: Garland.

Ernest N. McCarus. 1976. A Semantic Analysis of Arabic Verbs. Pp. 3–28 in *Michigan Oriental Studies in Honor of George G. Cameron*, ed. L. L. Orlin et al.. Ann Arbor: Department of Near Eastern Studies, University of Michigan.

W. J. Martin. 1957. Some Notes on the Imperative in the Semitic Languages. *Rivista degli Studi Orientali* 32:315–19.

P. Matthiae. 1981. *Ebla: An Empire Rediscovered*. Garden City, New York: Doubleday.

Sabatino Moscati et al. 1964. *An Introduction to the Comparative Grammar of the Semitic Languages*. Porta Linguarum Orientalium N.S. 6. Wiesbaden: Harrassowitz.

M. Palmaitis. 1981. On the Origin of the Semitic Marker of the Feminine. *Archiv Orientální* 49:263–69.

G. Pettinato. 1981. *The Archives of Ebla*. Garden City, New York: Doubleday.

M. A. Powell. 1979. Notes on Akkadian Numbers and Number Syntax. *Journal of Semitic Studies* 24:13–18.

H. Y. Priebatsch. 1978. Der Weg des semitischen Perfekts. *Ugarit-Forschungen* 10:337–47.

C. Rabin. 1963. The Origins of the Subdivisions of Semitic. Pp. 103–15 in *Hebrew and Semitic Studies Presented to Godfrey Rolles Driver*, ed. D. W. Thomas and W. D. McHardy. Oxford: Clarendon.

_____. 1969. The Structure of the Semitic System of Case Endings. Pp. 190–204 in *Proceedings of the International Conference on Semitic Studies Held in Jerusalem, 19–23 July 1965*. Jerusalem: Israel Academy of Sciences and Humanities.

K. K. Riemschneider. 1969. *Lehrbuch des Akkadischen*. Leipzig: Verlag Enzyklopädie.

Frithiof Rundgren. 1955. *Über Bildungen mit š- und n-t- Demonstrativen im Semitischen*. Uppsala: Almqvist & Wiksells.

Wolfram von Soden. 1965. Zur Methode der semitisch-hamitischen Sprachvergleichung. *Journal of Semitic Studies* 10:159–77.

_____. 1969. *Grundriss der akkadischen Grammatik*. Analecta Orientalia 33/47. Rome: Pontifical Biblical Institute.

_____. 1987. Ableitungen von Zahlwörtern im Semitischen. Pp. 403–14 in *Language, Literature, and History: Philological and Historical Studies Presented to Erica Reiner*, ed. F. Rochberg-Halton. New Haven: American Oriental Society.

J. M. Solá-Solé. 1961. *L'Infinitif sémitique* [Inf. A = infinitive construct; Inf. B = infinitive absolute]. Bibliothèque de l'Ecole pratiques des hautes études 315. Paris: Honoré Champion.

E. A. Speiser. 1936. Studies in Semitic Formatives. *Journal of the American Oriental Society* 56:22–46. Rpt. as pp. 403–32 in *Oriental and Biblical Studies*, ed. J. J. Finkelstein and Moshe Greenberg. Philadelphia: University of Pennsylvania, 1967.

_____. 1938. The Pitfalls of Polarity. *Language* 14:187–202. Rpt. as pp. 433–54 in *Oriental and Biblical Studies*, ed. J. J. Finkelstein and Moshe Greenberg. Philadelphia: University of Pennsylvania, 1967.

_____. 1952. The Elative in West Semitic and Akkadian. *Journal of Cuneiform Studies* 6:81–92. Rpt. as pp. 465–93 in *Oriental and Biblical Studies*, ed. J. J. Finkelstein and Moshe Greenberg. Philadelphia: University of Pennsylvania, 1967.

_____. 1967. *Oriental and Biblical Studies*. Edited by J. J. Finkelstein and Moshe Greenberg. Philadelphia: University of Pennsylvania.

Richard C. Steiner. 1977. *The Case for Fricative-Laterals in Semitic.* American Oriental Series 59. New Haven: American Oriental Society.

————. 1982. *Affricated Ṣade in the Semitic Languages.* New York: American Academy for Jewish Research.

[A. Ungnad–]L. Matouš. 1964. *Grammatik des Akkadischen.* Munich: Beck.

Rainer M. Voigt. 1983. Review of Bergsträsser-Daniels, *Introduction to the Semitic Languages* (1983). *Welt des Orients* 14:262–67.

William Wright. 1890. *Lectures on the Comparative Grammar of the Semitic Languages.* Cambridge: Cambridge University.

————. 1896–98. *A Grammar of the Arabic Language.* 3d ed. 2 vols. Cambridge: Cambridge University.

Andrzej Zaborski. 1976. The Semitic External Plural in an Afroasiatic Perspective. *Afroasiatic Linguistics* 3:111–19.

4. General Linguistic and Literary Studies; Studies of Non-Semitic Languages

Emile Benveniste. 1971. *Essays on General Linguistics.* Coral Gables, Florida: University of Miami.

F. Blass and A. Debrunner. 1961. *A Greek Grammar of the New Testament.* Translated by R. W. Funk. Chicago: University of Chicago.

Leonard Bloomfield. 1933. *Language.* New York: Holt.

Raymond E. Brown. 1966. *The Gospel according to John (i–xii).* Anchor Bible 29. Garden City, New York: Doubleday.

Karl Brugmann. 1897. *The Nature and Origin of the Noun Genders in the Indo-European Languages.* Translated by E. Y. Robbins. New York: Scribner.

Christopher Butler. 1984. *Interpretation, Deconstruction, and Ideology.* Oxford: Clarendon.

Bernard Comrie. 1976. *Aspect: An Introduction to the Study of Verbal Aspect and Related Problems.* Cambridge: Cambridge University.

————. 1981. *Language Universals and Language Typology.* Chicago: University of Chicago.

————. 1985. *Tense.* Cambridge: Cambridge University.

David Crystal. 1985. *A Dictionary of Linguistics and Phonetics.* Oxford: Basil Blackwell.

————. 1987. *The Cambridge Encyclopedia of Language.* Cambridge: Cambridge University.

Suzette Haden Elgin. 1979. *What Is Linguistics?* Englewood Cliffs, New Jersey: Prentice-Hall.

B. Elson and V. B. Pickett. 1964. *An Introduction to Morphology and Syntax.* Santa Ana, California: Summer Institute of Linguistics.

Frederic W. Farrar. 1865. *Chapters on Language.* London: Longmans, Green.

Burton Feldman and R. D. Richardson, eds. 1972. *The Rise of Modern Mythology.* Bloomington: Indiana University.

E. D. Floyd. 1981. Levels of Phonological Restriction in Greek Affixes. Vol. 1, pp. 87–106 in *Bono Homini Donum: Essays in Historical Linguistics in Memory of J. Alexander Kerns,* ed. Y. L. Arbeitman and A. R. Bomhard. Amsterdam: John Benjamins.

D. G. Frantz. 1968. Translation and Underlying Structure. 1. Relations. Pp. 22–23 in *Notes on Translation.* Santa Ana, California: Summer Institute of Linguistics.

Paul Friedrich. 1975. *Proto-Indo-European Syntax: The Order of Meaningful Elements.* Journal of Indo-European Studies Monograph 1. Butte: Montana College of Mineral Science and Technology.

————.1986. *The Language Parallax.* Austin: University of Texas.

I. J. Gelb. 1963 *A Study of Writing: The Foundations of Grammatology.* 2d ed. Chicago: University of Chicago.

Robert Godel, ed. 1969. *A Geneva School Reader in Linguistics.* Bloomington: Indiana University.

J. H. Greenberg. 1977. *A New Invitation to Linguistics.* Garden City, New York: Doubleday.

————, ed. 1966. *Universals of Language.* Cambridge: MIT.

E. A. Gregersen. 1967. *Prefix and Pronoun in Bantu.* International Journal of American Linguistics, Memoir 21. Baltimore: Indiana University.

M. A. K. Halliday. 1973. *Explorations of the Functions of Language.* London: Edward Arnold.

————. 1975. *Language as Social Semiotic.* London: Edward Arnold.

————. 1985. *Introduction to Functional Grammar.* London: Edward Arnold.

E. Haugen and M. Bloomfield, eds. 1974. *Language as a Human Problem.* New York: Norton.

Louis Hjelmslev. 1970. *Language: An Introduction.* Translated by F. J. Whitfield. Madison: University of Wisconsin.

C. F. Hockett. 1958. *A Course in Modern Linguistics.* New York: Macmillan.

Fred W. Householder. 1986. Review of Rosén, *Studies in the Syntax of the Verbal Noun in Early Latin* (1981). *Mediterranean Language Review* 2:150–52.

S. F. D. Hughes. 1986. Salutory Lessons from the History of Linguistics. Pp. 306–22 in *The Real-World Linguist,* ed. P. C. Bjarkman and V. Raskin. Norwood, New Jersey: Ablex.

Muhammad Hassan Ibrahim. 1973. *Grammatical Gender: Its Origin and Development.* Janua Linguarum, Series Minor 166. The Hague: Mouton.

Roman Jakobson. 1959. On Linguistic Aspects of Translation. Pp. 232–39 in *On Translation,* ed. R. A. Brower. Cambridge: Harvard University. Rpt. as pp. 428–35 in *Language in Literature,* ed. K. Pomorska and S. Rudy. Cambridge: Harvard University, 1987.

————. 1984. *Russian and Slavic Grammar: Studies, 1931–1981.* Edited by L. R. Waugh and M. Halle. Berlin: Mouton.

Roman Jakobson and Linda Waugh. 1979. *The Sound Shape of Language.* Bloomington: Indiana University.

Paul Kiparsky. 1968. Tense and Mood in Indo-European Syntax. *Foundations of Language* 4:30–55.

G. R. Kress, ed. 1976. *Halliday: System and Function in Language*. London: Oxford University.

D. T. Langendoen. 1969. *The Study of Syntax*. New York: Holt, Rinehart & Winston.

Claude Lévi-Strauss. 1966. *The Savage Mind*. Chicago: University of Chicago.

R. E. Longacre, ed. 1984. *Theory and Application in Processing Texts in Non-Indoeuropean Languages*. Papiere zur Textlinguistik 43. Hamburg: Buske.

Marie Lusted. 1976. Anywa. Pp. 495–512 in *The Non-Semitic Languages of Ethiopia*, ed. M. Lionel Bender. East Lansing: African Studies Center, Michigan State University.

Jean Lydall. 1976. Hamer. Pp. 393–438 in *The Non-Semitic Languages of Ethiopia*, ed. M. Lionel Bender. East Lansing: African Studies Center, Michigan State University.

John Lyons. 1968. *Introduction to Theoretical Linguistics*. Cambridge: Cambridge University.

C. F. D. Moule. 1959. *An Idiom Book of New Testament Greek*. 2d ed. Cambridge: Cambridge University.

E. A. Nida. 1976. *Componential Analysis of Meaning: An Introduction to Semantic Structures*. Paris: Mouton.

F. R. Palmer. 1971. *Grammar*. Harmondsworth: Penguin.

———. 1976. *Semantics: A New Outline*. London: Cambridge University.

H. H. Paper, ed. 1975. *Language and Texts: The Nature of Linguistic Evidence*. Ann Arbor: Center for Coördination of Ancient and Modern Studies, University of Michigan.

Mario A. Pei. 1966. *Glossary of Linguistic Terminology*. New York: Columbia University.

Mario A. Pei and Frank Gaynor. 1969. *A Dictionary of Linguistics*. Totowa, New Jersey: Littlefield, Adams.

Wilbur Pickering. 1980. *A Framework for Discourse Analysis*. Summer Institute of Linguistics Publications in Linguistics 64. Dallas: Summer Institute of Linguistics and the University of Texas at Arlington.

Paul M. Postal. 1971. *Cross-Over Phenomena*. New York: Harcourt, Brace.

R. Quirk and S. Greenbaum. 1973. *A Concise Grammar of Contemporary English*. New York: Harcourt Brace Jovanovich.

R. Quirk, S. Greenbaum, G. Leech, and J. Svartvik. 1972. *A Grammar of Contemporary English*. Harlow, Essex: Longman.

C. E. Reagan and David Stewart, eds. 1978. *The Philosophy of Paul Ricoeur: An Anthology of His Works*. Boston: Beacon.

R. H. Robins. 1951. *Ancient and Mediaeval Grammatical Theory in Europe*. London: Bell.

———. 1967. *A Short History of Linguistics*. Bloomington: Indiana University.

Hannah Rosén. 1981. *Studies in the Syntax of the Verbal Noun in Early Latin*. Munich: Wilhelm Fink.

M. Ruhlen. 1987. *A Guide to the World's Languages. 1. Classification*. Stanford: Stanford University.

John Ruskin. 1971. *The Literary Criticism of John Ruskin*. Edited by H. Bloom. New York: Norton.

F. de Saussure. 1966. *Course in General Linguistics*. New York: McGraw-Hill.

———. 1967. *Cours de linguistique générale*. Edited by R. Engler. Wiesbaden: Harrassowitz. Originally Paris: Payot, 1915.

P. Swiggers. 1986. La Conception du changement linguistique chez Antoine Meillet. *Folia Linguistica Historica* 7:21–30.

———. 1986. Le Mot comme unité linguistique dans la théorie grammaticale au dix-huitième siècle. *Indogermanische Forschungen* 91:1–26.

———. 1987. Le Mot: Unité d'intégration. Pp. 57–66 in *Etudes de linguistique générale et de linguistique Latine . . . Guy Serbat*. Paris: Société pour l'Information Grammaticale.

———. 1987. Comparaison des langues et grammaire comparée. *Linguistica* 27:3–10.

———. 1987. L'Encyclopédie et la grammaire: à la recherche des fondements de la linguistique générale. *Acta Linguistica Hafniensa* 20:119–56.

———. 1987. Subjectivité dans le langage. *Cahiers de l'Institut de Linguistique de Louvain* 13:107–16.

P. Swiggers and W. Van Hoecke, eds. 1986. *Mot et Parties du Discours/Word and Word Classes/Wort und Wortarten*. La Pensée linguistique 1. Peeters: Leuven.

Egon Werlich. 1975. *Typologie der Texte*. Heidelberg: Puelle und Meyer.

Indexes

The four indexes, used in connection with the chapter tables of contents, should guide the reader in using this book. The indexes of *topics* and of *Hebrew words* are arranged by *section and paragraph number* (e.g., 17.4.2a), by *chapter and note number* (e.g., 17n13), or, infrequently, by chapter number (e.g., 17). In the *Index of Topics*, the entries *nouns, semantics of* and *verbs, semantics of* gather in a wide variety of material. Broad remarks about books of the Bible are given in the *Index of Topics*.

The indexes of *authorities* and of *scripture references* are arranged by *page number* (e.g., 310) or by *page and note number* (e.g., 310n13). For major authorities cited, subheadings are sometimes used (e.g., separating references to Bergsträsser's Hebrew grammar [GB] from those to his *Introduction to the Semitic Languages* [*Introduction*]). Ancient and medieval persons are listed in the *Index of Topics*, as are some major post-Renaissance figures; exceptions involve late medieval (and early modern) grammarians whose writings survive: these are listed in the *Index of Authorities*. Some overlap is to be allowed for.

The *Index of Hebrew Words*, including words cited in both square characters and transliteration, gives the root only of verbal forms where this suffices. The various uses of ה and ו are listed in the *Index of Topics* (under *he* and *waw*), as are standard (especially Latinate) grammatical terms that include a word or letter name (e.g., *beth essentiae*). A dagger following an entry in the word index indicates that not only is the indexed form discussed but so also are closely related forms (e.g., of a different gender or of multiple stems). Glosses are used sparingly; the form אֵת (־אֹת) is marked (*part.*) and אֵת (־אֶת) is glossed *with*. Minor variations in spellings are ignored for the sake of saving space: a form cited plene may be indexed in a defective spelling or vice versa.

Index of Topics

Index of Authorities

Index of Hebrew Words

Index of Scripture References

The book
was produced in Winona
Lake, Indiana. The manuscript was
prepared in the first instance by Kevin D.
Zuber, who inserted the Hebrew examples.
The book was designed by David C. Baker, Cynthia
Miller, and James E. Eisenbraun. The case was designed
by David French and Jennifer S. Ortega. The type was
set and proofed by Mark J. Highman, Barbara Manahan,
Pamela Nichols, and James E. Eisenbraun, who also produced
the pagination. Marjory Hailstone managed the traffic.
David P. Aiken styled the manuscript, proofed the Hebrew,
and found many of the mistakes.

EISENBRAUNS

The body type is Times Roman English and Frank Ruehl
Hebrew. The display faces are Helvetica Medium
and Friz Quadrata. The book is printed on 50-
pound natural pH-neutral paper by Thomson-
Shore, Dexter, Michigan, and case-bound
in Kivar 6 cloth by John H. Dekker
and Sons, Grand Rapids,
Michigan.